Clarence E. Wilbur

THE WORKS

OF

JOSEPH ADDISON.

COMPLETE

IN THREE VOLUMES

EMBRACING

THE WHOLE OF THE "SPECTATOR," &c

VOL. II.

NEW YORK:
HARPER & BROTHERS, PUBLISHERS,
FRANKLIN SQUARE.
1864.

THE SPECTATOR

No. 315.] *Saturday, March* 1, 1711-12.

Nec deus intersit nisi dignus vindice nodus
Inciderit——— *Hor. Ars Poet.* v. 191.

Never presume to make a god appear
But for a business worthy of a god.—*Roscommon.*

HORACE advises a poet to consider thoroughly the nature and force of his genius. Milton seems to have known perfectly well wherein his strength lay, and has therefore chosen a subject entirely conformable to those talents of which he was master. As his genius was wonderfully turned to the sublime, his subject is the noblest that could have entered into the thoughts of man. Every thing that is truly great and astonishing has a place in it. The whole system of the intellectual world; the chaos, and the creation: heaven, earth, and hell; enter into the constitution of his poem.

Having in the first and second books represented the infernal world with all its horrors, the thread of his fable naturally leads him into the opposite regions of bliss and glory.

If Milton's majesty forsakes him any where, it is in those parts of his poem where the divine persons are introduced as speakers. One may, I think, observe, that the author proceeds with a kind of fear and trembling, whilst he describes the sentiments of the Almighty. He dares not give his imagination its full play, but chooses to confine himself to such thoughts as are drawn from the books of the most orthodox divines, and to such expressions as may be met with in scripture. The beauties, therefore, which we are apt to look for in these speeches, are not of a poetical nature, nor so proper to fill the mind with sentiments of grandeur, as with thoughts of devotion. The passions which they are designed to raise, are a divine love and religious fear. The particular beauty of the speeches in the third book, consists in that shortness and perspicuity of style, in which the poet has couched the greatest mysteries of Christianity, and drawn together, in a regular scheme, the whole dispensation of Providence with respect to man. He has represented all the abstruse doctrines of predestination, free-will and grace, as also the great points of incarnation and redemption, (which naturally grow up in a poem that treats of the fall of man) with great energy of expression, and in a clearer and stronger light than I ever met with in any other writer. As these points are dry in themselves to the generality of readers, the concise and clear manner in which he has treated them is very much to be admired, as is likewise that particular art which he has made use of in the interspersing of all those graces of poetry which the subject was capable of receiving.

The survey of the whole creation, and of every thing that is transacted in it, is a prospect worthy of Omniscience, and as much above that in which Virgil has drawn his Jupiter, as the Christian idea of the Supreme Being is more rational and sublime than that of the Heathens. The particular objects on which he is described to have cast his eye, are represented in the most beautiful and lively manner:

Now had th' Almighty Father from above
(From the pure empyrean where he sits
High thron'd above all height) bent down his eye,
His own works and their works at once to view
About him all the sanctities of heaven
Stood thick as stars, and from his sight receiv'd
Beatitude past utterance. On his right
The radiant image of his glory sat,
His only Son. On earth he first beheld
Our two first parents, yet the only two
Of mankind, in the happy garden plac'd,
Reaping immortal fruits of joy and love.
Uninterrupted joy, unrivall'd love,
In blissful solitude. He then survey'd
Hell and the gulf between, and Satan there
Coasting the wall of heav'n on this side night,
In the dun air sublime; and ready now
To stoop with wearied wings and willing feet
On the bare outside of this world, that seem'd
Firm land imbosom'd without firmament;
Uncertain which, in ocean or in air.
Him God beholding from his prospect high,
Wherein past, present, future he beholds,
Thus to his only Son foreseeing spake.

Satan's approach to the confines of the creation is finely imaged in the beginning of the speech which immediately follows. The effects of this speech in the blessed spirits, and in the divine person to whom it was addressed, cannot but fill the mind of the reader with a secret pleasure and complacency:

Thus while God spake, ambrosial fragrance fill'd
All heav'n, and in the blessed spirits elect
Sense of new joy ineffable diffus'd.
Beyond compare the Son of God was seen
Most glorious; in him all his Father shone,
Substantially express'd; and in his face
Divine compassion visibly appear'd,
Love without end, and without measure grace.

I need not point out the beauty of that circumstance, wherein the whole host of angels are represented as standing mute; nor show how proper the occasion was to produce such a silence in heaven. The close of this divine colloquy, with the hymn of angels that follows upon it, are so wonderfully beautiful and poetical, that I should not forbear inserting the whole passage, if the bounds of my paper would give me leave:

> No sooner had th' Almighty ceas'd, but all
> The multitude of angels with a shout
> (Loud as from numbers without number, sweet
> As from blest voices) utt'ring joy, heav'n rung
> With jubilee, and loud Hosannas fill'd
> Th' eternal regions, &c. &c.——

Satan's walk upon the outside of the universe, which at a distance appeared to him of a globular form, but upon his nearer approach looked like an unbounded plain, is natural and noble; as his roaming upon the frontiers of the creation, between that mass of matter which was wrought into a world, and that shapeless unformed heap of materials which still lay in chaos and confusion, strikes the imagination with something astonishingly great and wild. I have before spoken of the Limbo of Vanity, which the poet places upon this outermost surface of the universe, and shall here explain myself more at large on that, and other parts of the poem, which are of the same shadowy nature.

Aristotle observes, that the fable of an epic poem should abound in circumstances that are both credible and astonishing; or, as the French critics choose to phrase it, the fable should be filled with the probable and the marvellous. This rule is as fine and just as any in Aristotle's whole Art of Poetry.

If the fable is only probable, it differs nothing from a true history; if it is only marvellous, it is no better than a romance. The great secret, therefore, of heroic poetry is to relate such circumstances as may produce in the reader at the same time both belief and astonishment. This is brought to pass in a well-chosen fable, by the account of such things as have really happened, or at least of such things as have happened according to the received opinions of mankind. Milton's fable is a master-piece of this nature; as the war in heaven, the condition of the fallen angels, the state of innocence, the temptation of the serpent, and the fall of man, though they are very astonishing in themselves, are not only credible, but actual points of faith.

The next method of reconciling miracles with credibility, is by a happy invention of the poet: as in particular, when he introduces agents of a superior nature, who are capable of effecting what is wonderful, and what is not to be met with in the ordinary course of things. Ulysses's ship being turned into a rock, and Æneas's fleet into a shoal of water-nymphs, though they are very surprising accidents, are nevertheless probable when we are told, that they were the gods who thus transformed them. It is this kind of machinery which fills the poems both of Homer and Virgil with such circumstances as are wonderful but not impossible, and so frequently produce in the reader the most pleasing passion that can rise in the mind of man, which is admiration. If there be any instance in the Æneid liable to exception upon this account, it is in the beginning of the third book, where Æneas is represented as tearing up the myrtle that dropped blood. To qualify this wonderful circumstance, Polydorus tells a story from the root of the myrtle, that the barbarous inhabitants of the country having pierced him with spears and arrows, the blood which was left in his body took root in his wounds, and gave birth to that bleeding tree. This circumstance seems to have the marvellous without the probable, because it is represented as proceeding from natural causes, without the interposition of any god, or other supernatural power capable of producing it. The spears and arrows grow of themselves without so much as the modern help of enchantment. If we look into the fiction of Milton's fable, though we find it full of surprising incidents, they are generally suited to our notions of the things and persons described, and tempered with a due measure of probability. I must only make an exception to the Limbo of Vanity, with his episode of Sin and Death, and some of the imaginary persons in his chaos.—These passages are astonishing, but not credible: the reader cannot so far impose upon himself as to see a possibility in them; they are the description of dreams and shadows, not of things or persons. I know that many critics look upon the stories of Circe, Polypheme, the Sirens, nay the whole Odyssey and Iliad, to be allegories; but allowing this to be true, they are fables, which, considering the opinions of mankind that prevailed in the age of the poet, might possibly have been according to the letter. The persons are such as might have acted what is ascribed to them, as the circumstances in which they are represented might possibly have been truths and realities. This appearance of probability is so absolutely requisite in the greater kinds of poetry, that Aristotle observes the ancient tragic writers made use of the names of such great men as had actually lived in the world, though the tragedy proceeded upon adventures they were never engaged in, on purpose to make the subject more credible. In a word, besides the hidden meaning of an epic allegory, the plain literal sense ought to appear probable. The story should be such as an ordinary reader may acquiesce in, whatever natural, moral, or political truth may be discovered in it by men of greater penetration.

Satan, after having long wandered upon the surface or outermost wall of the universe, discovers at last a wide gap in it, which led into the creation, and is described as the opening through which the angels pass to and fro into the lower world, upon their errands to mankind. His sitting upon the brink of this passage, and taking a survey of the whole face of nature, that appeared to him new and fresh in all its beauties, with the simile illustrating this circumstance, fills the mind of the reader with as surprising and glorious an idea as any that arises in the whole poem. He looks down into that vast hollow of the universe with the eye, or (as Milton calls it in his first book) with the ken of an angel. He surveys all the wonders in this immense amphitheatre that lie between both the poles of heaven, and takes in at one view the whole round of the creation.

His flight between the several worlds that shined on every side of him, with the particular description of the sun, are set forth in all the wantonness of a luxuriant imagination. His shape, speech, and behaviour, upon his transforming himself into an angel of light, are touched with exquisite beauty. The poet's thought of directing Satan to the sun, which, in the vulgar opinion of mankind, is the most conspicuous part of the creation, and the placing in it an angel, is a circumstance very finely contrived, and the more adjusted to a poetical probability, as it was a received doctrine among the most famous philosophers, that every orb had its intelligence; and as an apostle in sacred writ is said to have seen such an angel in the sun. In the answer which the angel returns to the disguised evil spirit, there is such a becoming majesty as is altogether suitable to a superior being. The part of it in which he represents himself as present at the creation, is very noble in itself, and not only proper where it is introduced, but requisite to prepare the reader for what follows in the seventh book:

> I saw when at his word the formless mass,
> This world's material mould, came to a heap:
> Confusion heard his voice, and wild Uproar
> Stood rul'd, stood vast infinitude confin'd;
> Till at his second bidding Darkness fled,
> Light shone, &c.

In the following part of the speech he points out the earth with such circumstances, that the reader can scarce forbear fancying himself employed on the same distant view of it.

> Look downward on that globe, whose hither side
> With light from hence, though but reflected, shines;
> That place is earth, the seat of man, that light
> His day, &c.

I must not conclude my reflections upon this third book of Paradise Lost, without taking notice of that celebrated complaint of Milton with which it opens, and which certainly deserves all the praises that have been given it; though, as I have before hinted, it may rather be looked upon as an excrescence than as an essential part of the poem. The same observation might be applied to that beautiful digression upon hypocrisy in the same book. L.

No. 316.] *Monday, March* 3, 1711-12.

> Libertas; quæ sera, tamen respexit inertem.
> *Virg.* Ecl. i. 28.

> Freedom, which came at length, though slow to come
> *Dryden.*

'Mr. Spectator,—If you ever read a letter which is sent with the more pleasure for the reality of its complaints, this may have reason to hope for a favourable acceptance; and if time be the most irretrievable loss, the regrets which follow will be thought, I hope, the most justifiable. The regaining of my liberty from a long state of indolence and inactivity, and the desire of resisting the farther encroachments of idleness, make me apply to you; and the uneasiness with which I recollect the past years, and the apprehensions with which I expect the future, soon determined me to it. Idleness is so general a distemper, that I cannot but imagine a speculation on this subject will be of universal use. There is hardly any one person without some allay of it; and thousands besides myself spend more time in an idle uncertainty which to begin first of two affairs, than would have been sufficient to have ended them both. The occasion of this seems to be the want of some necessary employment, to put the spirits in motion, and awaken them out of their lethargy. If I had less leisure, I should have more; for I should then find my time distinguished into portions, some for business, and others for the indulging of pleasures; but now one face of indolence overspreads the whole, and I have no landmark to direct myself by. Were one's time a little straitened by business, like water enclosed in its banks, it would have some determined course; but unless it be put into some channel it has no current, but becomes a deluge without either use or motion.

'When Scanderbeg, Prince of Epirus, was dead, the Turks, who had but too often felt the force of his arm in the battles he had won from them, imagined that by wearing a piece of his bones near their heart, they should be animated with a vigour and force like to that which inspired him when living. As I am like to be but of little use whilst I live, I am resolved to do what good I can after my decease; and have accordingly ordered my bones to be disposed of in this manner for the good of my countrymen, who are troubled with too exorbitant a degree of fire. All fox-hunters, upon wearing me, would in a short time be brought to endure their beds in a morning, and perhaps even quit them with regret at ten. Instead of hurrying away to tease a poor animal, and run away from their own thoughts, a chair or a chariot would be thought the most desirable means of performing a remove from one place to another. I should be a cure for the unnatural desire of John Trot for dancing, and a specific to lessen the inclination Mrs. Fidget has to motion, and cause her always to give her approbation to the present place she is in. In fine, no Egyptian mummy was ever half so useful in physic, as I should be to these feverish constitutions, to repress the violent sallies of youth, and give each action its proper weight and repose.

'I can stifle any violent inclination, and oppose a torrent of anger, or the solicitations of revenge, with success. Indolence is a stream which flows slowly on, but yet undermines the foundation of every virtue. A vice of a more lively nature were a more desirable tyrant than this rust of the mind, which gives a tincture of its nature to every action of one's life. It were as little hazard to be lost in a storm, as to lie thus perpetually becalmed: and it is to no purpose to have within one the seeds of a thousand good qualities, if we want the vigour and resolution necessary for the exerting them. Death brings all persons back to an equality; and this image of it, this slumber of the mind, leaves no difference between the greatest genius, and the meanest understanding. A faculty of doing things remarkably praiseworthy, thus concealed, is of no more use to the owner than a heap of gold to the man who dares not use it.

'To-morrow is still the fatal time when all is to be rectified. To-morrow comes, it goes, and still I please myself with the shadow, whilst I lose the reality: unmindful that the present time alone is ours, the future is yet unborn, and the past is dead, and can only live (as parents in their children,) in the actions it has produced.

'The time we live ought not to be computed by the number of years, but by the use that has been made of it; thus, it is not the extent of ground, but the yearly rent, which gives the value to the estate. Wretched and thoughtless creatures, in the only place where covetousness were a virtue, we turn prodigals! Nothing lies upon our hands with such uneasiness, nor have there been so many devices for any one thing, as to make it slide away imperceptibly and to no purpose. A shilling shall be hoarded up with care, whilst that which is above the price of an estate is flung away with disregard and contempt. There is nothing now-a-days, so much avoided, as a solicitous improvement of every part of time; it is a report must be shunned as one tenders the name of a wit and a fine genius, and as one fears the dreadful character of a laborious plodder: but notwithstanding this, the greatest wits any age has produced thought far otherwise; for who can think either Socrates or Demosthenes lost any reputation by their continual pains both in overcoming the defects and improving the gifts of nature? All are acquainted with the labour and assiduity with which Tully acquired his eloquence. Seneca in his letters to Lucilius assures him there was not a day in which he did not either write something, or read and epitomize some good author; and I remember Pliny in one of his letters, where he gives an account of the various methods he used to fill up every vacancy of time, after several employments which he enumerates; "Sometimes," says he, "I hunt: but even then I carry with me a pocket-book, that whilst my servants are busied in disposing of the nets and other matters, I may be employed in something that may be useful to me in my studies; and that if I miss of my game, I may at the least bring home some of my own thoughts with me, and not have the mortification of having caught nothing all day."

'Thus, sir, you see how many examples I recall to mind, and what arguments I use with myself to regain my liberty: but as I am afraid it is no ordinary persuasion that will be of service, I shall expect your thoughts on this subject with the greatest impatience, especially since the good will not be confined to me alone, but will be of universal use. For there is no hope of amendment where men are pleased with their ruin, and whilst they think laziness is a desirable character; whether it be that they like the state itself, or that they think it gives them a new lustre when they do exert themselves, seemingly to be able to do that without labour and application, which others attain to but with the greatest diligence. I am, sir, your most obliged humble servant, SAMUEL SLACK.'

Clytander to Cleone.

'MADAM,—Permission to love you is all that I desire, to conquer all the difficulties those about you place in my way, to surmount and acquire all those qualifications you expect in him who pretends to the honour of being, madam, your most devoted humble servant,

Z. 'CLYTANDER.'

No. 317.] *Tuesday, March 4*, 1711-12.

——**Fruges consumere nati.** *Hor.* Ep. ii. Lib. 1. 27.

——**Born to drink and eat.** *Creech.*

AUGUSTUS, a few minutes before his death, asked his friends who stood about him, if they thought he had acted his part well; and upon receiving such an answer as was due to his extraordinary merit, 'Let me, then,' says he, 'go off the stage with your applause;' using the expression with which the Roman actors made their exit at the conclusion of a dramatic piece.* I could wish that men, while they are in health, would consider well the nature of the part they are engaged in, and what figure it will make in the minds of those they leave behind them, whether it was

* Vos valete et plaudite

worth coming into the world for; whether it be suitable to a reasonable being; in short, whether it appears graceful in this life, or will turn to an advantage in the next. Let the sycophant, or the buffoon, the satirist, or the good companion, consider with himself, when his body shall be laid in the grave, and his soul pass into another state of existence, how much it will redound to his praise to have it said of him that no man in England ate better, that he had an admirable talent at turning his friends into ridicule, that nobody out-did him at an ill-natured jest, or that he never went to bed before he had despatched his third bottle. These are, however, very common funeral orations and eulogiums on deceased persons who have acted among mankind with some figure and reputation.

But if we look into the bulk of our species, they are such as are not likely to be remembered a moment after their disappearance. They leave behind them no traces of their existence, but are forgotten as though they had never been. They are neither wanted by the poor, regretted by the rich, nor celebrated by the learned. They are neither missed in the commonwealth, nor lamented by private persons. Their actions are of no significancy to mankind, and might have been performed by creatures of much less dignity than those who are distinguished by the faculty of reason. An eminent French author speaks somewhere to the following purpose: I have often seen from my chamber window two noble creatures, both of them of an erect countenance and endowed with reason. These two intellectual beings are employed from morning to night in rubbing two smooth stones one upon another; that is, as the vulgar phrase is, in polishing marble.

My friend, Sir Andrew Freeport, as we were sitting in the club last night, gave us an account of a sober citizen, who died a few days since. This honest man being of greater consequence in his own thoughts than in the eye of the world, had for some years past kept a journal of his life. Sir Andrew showed us one week of it. Since the occurrences set down in it mark out such a road of action as that I have been speaking of, I shall present my reader with a faithful copy of it; after having first informed him, that the deceased person had in his youth been bred to trade, but finding himself not so well turned for business, he had for several years last past lived altogether upon a moderate annuity.*

MONDAY, eight o'clock. I put on my clothes and walked into the parlour.

Nine o'clock ditto. Tied my knee-strings, and washed my hands.

Hours ten, eleven, and twelve. Smoked three pipes of Virginia. Read the Supplement and Daily Courant. Things go ill in the north. Mr. Nisby's opinion thereupon.

One o'clock in the afternoon. Chid Ralph for mislaying my tobacco-box.

Two o'clock. Sat down to dinner. Mem. Too many plumbs, and no suet.

From three to four. Took my afternoon's nap.

From four to six. Walked in the fields. Wind S. S. E.

From six to ten. At the Club. Mr. Nisby's opinion about the peace.

Ten o'clock. Went to bed, slept sound.

TUESDAY, being holiday, eight o'clock, rose as usual.

Nine o'clock. Washed hands and face, shaved, put on my double-soled shoes.

Ten, eleven, twelve. Took a walk to Islington.

One. Took a pot of Mother Cob's mild.

Between two and three. Returned, dined on a knuckle of veal and bacon. Mem. Sprouts wanting.

Three. Nap as usual.

From four to six. Coffee-house. Read the news. A dish of twist. Grand vizier strangled.

From six to ten. At the club. Mr. Nisby's account of the Great Turk.

Ten. Dream of the grand vizier. Broken sleep.

WEDNESDAY, eight o'clock. Tongue of my shoe-buckle broke. Hands but not face.

Nine. Paid off the butcher's bill. Mem. To be allowed for the last leg of mutton.

Ten, eleven. At the Coffee-house. More work in the north. Stranger in a black wig asked me how stocks went.

From twelve to one. Walked in the fields. Wind to the south.

From one to two. Smoked a pipe and a half.

Two. Dined as usual. Stomach good.

Three. Nap broke by the falling of a pewter dish. Mem. Cook-maid in love, and grown careless.

From four to six. At the coffee-house. Advice from Smyrna that the grand vizier was first of all strangled, and afterwards beheaded.

Six o'clock in the evening. Was half an hour in the club before any body else came. Mr. Nisby of opinion that the grand vizier was not strangled the sixth instant.

Ten at night. Went to bed. Slept without waking until nine the next morning.

THURSDAY, nine o'clock. Staid within until two o'clock for Sir Timothy; who did not bring me my annuity according to his promise.

Two in the afternoon. Sat down to dinner. Loss of appetite. Small-beer sour Beef over-corned

* It has been conjectured that this journal was intended to ridicule a gentleman who was a member of the congregation named Independents, where a Mr. Nesbit officiated as minister. See John Dunton's account of his Life, Errors and Opinions.

Three. Could not take my nap.

Four and five. Gave Ralph a box on the ear. Turned off my cook-maid. Sent a messenger to Sir Timothy. Mem. I did not go to the club to night. Went to bed at nine o'clock.

FRIDAY. Passed the morning in meditation upon Sir Timothy, who was with me a quarter before twelve.

Twelve o'clock. Bought a new head to my cane, and a tongue to my buckle. Drank a glass of purl to recover appetite.

Two and three. Dined and slept well.

From four to six. Went to the coffee-house. Met Mr. Nisby there. Smoked several pipes. Mr. Nisby of opinion that laced coffee is bad for the head.

Six o'clock. At the club as steward. Sat late.

Twelve o'clock. Went to bed, dreamt that I drank small beer with the grand vizier.

SATURDAY. Waked at eleven, walked in the fields, wind N. E.

Twelve. Caught in a shower.

One in the afternoon. Returned home and dried myself.

Two. Mr. Nisby dined with me. First course, marrow-bones; second, ox-cheek, with a bottle of Brooks and Hellier.

Three. Overslept myself.

Six. Went to the club. Like to have fallen into a gutter. Grand vizier certainly dead, &c.

I question not but the reader will be surprised to find the above-mentioned journalist taking so much care of a life that was filled with such inconsiderable actions, and received so very small improvements; and yet, if we look into the behaviour of many whom we daily converse with, we shall find that most of their hours are taken up in those three important articles of eating, drinking, and sleeping. I do not suppose that a man loses his time, who is not engaged in public affairs, or in an illustrious course of action. On the contrary, I believe our hours may very often be more profitably laid out in such transactions as make no figure in the world, than in such as are apt to draw upon them the attention of mankind. One may become wiser and better by several methods of employing one's self in secrecy and silence, and do what is laudable without noise or ostentation. I would, however, recommend to every one of my readers, the keeping a journal of their lives for one week, and setting down punctually their whole series of employments during that space of time. This kind of self-examination would give them a true state of themselves, and incline them to consider seriously what they are about. One day would rectify the omissions of another, and make a man weigh all those indifferent actions, which though they are easily forgotten, must certainly be accounted for. L.

No. 318.] *Wednesday, March* 5, 1711-12.

——non omnia possumus omnes.

Virg. Ecl. viii. 63.

With different talents form'd, we variously excel.*

'MR. SPECTATOR,—A certain vice, which you have lately attacked, has not yet been considered by you as growing so deep in the heart of man, that the affectation outlives the practice of it. You must have observed, that men who have been bred in arms preserve to the most extreme and feeble old age, a certain daring in their aspect. In like manner, they who have passed their time in gallantry and adventure, keep up, as well as they can, the appearance of it, and carry a petulant inclination to their last moments. Let this serve for a preface to a relation I am going to give you of an old beau in town, that has not only been amorous, and a follower of women in general, but also, in spite of the admonition of grey hairs, been from his sixty-third year to his present seventieth, in an actual pursuit of a young lady, the wife of his friend, and a man of merit. The gay old Escalus has wit, good health, and is perfectly well-bred; but from the fashion and manners of the court when he was in his bloom, has such a natural tendency to amorous adventure, that he thought it would be an endless reproach to him to make no use of a familiarity he was allowed at a gentleman's house, whose good humour and confidence exposed his wife to the addresses of any who should take it in their head to do him the good office. It is not impossible that Escalus might also resent that the husband was particularly negligent of him; and though he gave many intimations of a passion towards the wife, the husband either did not see them, or put him to the contempt of overlooking them. In the mean time Isabella, for so we shall call our heroine, saw his passion, and rejoiced in it, as a foundation for much diversion, and an opportunity of indulging herself in the dear delight of being admired, addressed to, and flattered, with no ill consequence to her reputation. This lady is of a free and disengaged behaviour, ever in good-humour, such as is the image of innocence with those who are innocent, and an encouragement to vice with those who are abandoned. From this kind of carriage, and an apparent approbation of his gallantry, Escalus had frequent opportunities of laying amorous epistles in her way, of fixing his eyes attentively upon her actions, of performing a thousand little offices which are neglected by the unconcerned, but are so many approaches towards happiness with the enamoured. It was now, as is above hinted, almost the end of the seventh year of his passion, when Escalus, from general terms, and the ambigu

* The motto to this paper in folio was,
'Rideat, et pulset lasciva decentius ætas.'—*Hor*

ous respect which criminal lovers retain in their addresses, began to bewail that his passion grew too violent for him to answer any longer for his behaviour towards her, and that he hoped she would have consideration for his long and patient respect, to excuse the emotions of a heart now no longer under the direction of the unhappy owner of it. Such, for some months, had been the language of Escalus, both in his talk and his letters to Isabella, who returned all the profusion of kind things which had been the collection of fifty years, with "I must not hear you; you will make me forget that you are a gentleman; I would not willingly lose you as a friend;" and the like expressions, which the skilful interpret to their own advantage, as well knowing that a feeble denial is a modest assent. I should have told you, that Isabella, during the whole progress of this amour, communicated it to her husband; and that an account of Escalus's love was their usual entertainment after half a day's absence. Isabella therefore, upon her lover's late more open assaults, with a smile told her husband she could hold out no longer, but that his fate was now come to a crisis. After she had explained herself a little farther, with her husband's approbation, she proceeded in the following manner. The next time that Escalus was alone with her, and repeated his importunity, the crafty Isabella looked on her fan with an air of great attention, as considering of what importance such a secret was to her; and upon the repetition of a warm expression, she looked at him with an eye of fondness, and told him he was past that time of life which could make her fear he would boast of a lady's favour; then turned away her head, with a very well acted confusion, which favoured the escape of the aged Escalus. This adventure was matter of great pleasantry to Isabella and her spouse; and they had enjoyed it two days before Escalus could recollect himself enough to form the following letter:

"Madam,—What happened the other day gives me a lively image of the inconsistency of human passions and inclinations. We pursue what we are denied, and place our affections on what is absent, though we neglected it when present. As long as you refused my love, your refusal did so strongly excite my passion, that I had not once the leisure to think of recalling my reason to aid me against the design upon your virtue. But when that virtue began to comply in my favour, my reason made an effort over my love, and let me see the baseness of my behaviour in attempting a woman of honour. I own to you, it was not without the most violent struggle that I gained this victory over myself; nay, I will confess my shame, and acknowledge, I could not have prevailed but by flight. However, madam, I beg that you will believe a moment's weakness has not destroyed the esteem I had for you, which was confirmed by so many years of obstinate virtue. You have reason to rejoice that this did not happen within the observation of one of the young fellows, who would have exposed your weakness, and gloried in his own brutish inclinations.

"I am, Madam, your most devoted humble servant."

'Isabella, with the help of her husband, returned the following answer:

"Sir,—I cannot but account myself a very happy woman, in having a man for a lover that can write so well, and give so good a turn to a disappointment. Another excellence you have above all other pretenders I ever heard of; on occasions where the most reasonable men lose all their reason, you have yours most powerful. We have each of us to thank our genius that the passion of one abated in proportion as that of the other grew violent. Does it not yet come into your head to imagine, that I knew my compliance was the greatest cruelty I could be guilty of towards you? In return for your long and faithful passion, I must let you know that you are old enough to become a little more gravity; but if you will leave me, and coquet it any where else, may your mistress yield.

T. "ISABELLA."

No. 319.] *Thursday, March* 6, 1711-12.

Quo teneam vultus mutantem Protea nodo?
Hor. Ep. i. Lib. 1. 90.

Say while they change on thus, what chains can bind
These varying forms, this Proteus of the mind?
Francis.

I have endeavoured in the course of my papers to do justice to the age, and have taken care, as much as possible, to keep myself a neuter between both sexes. I have neither spared the ladies out of complaisance, nor the men out of partiality, but notwithstanding the great integrity with which I have acted in this particular, I find myself taxed with an inclination to favour my own half of the species. Whether it be that the women afford a more fruitful field for speculation, or whether they run more in my head than the men, I cannot tell; but I shall set down the charge as it is laid against me in the following letter.

'Mr. Spectator,—I always make one among a company of young females, who peruse your speculations every morning. I am at present commissioned by our whole assembly to let you know, that we fear you are a little inclined to be partial towards your own sex. We must, however, acknowledge, with all due gratitude, that in some cases you have given us our revenge on the men, and done us justice. We could not easily have forgiven you several strokes in the dissection of the coquette's heart, if you had not, much about the same time, made a sacrifice to us of a beau's skull.

'You may further, sir, please to remember, that not long since you attacked our hoods and commodes in such a manner, as, to use your own expression, made very many of us ashamed to show our heads. We must therefore beg leave to represent to you that we are in hopes, if you will please to make a due inquiry, the men in all ages would be found to have been little less whimsical in adorning that part than ourselves. The different forms of their wigs, together with the various cocks of their hats, all flatter us in this opinion.

'I had an humble servant last summer, who the first time he declared himself, was in a full-bottomed wig; but the day after, to my no small surprise, he accosted me in a thin natural one. I received him at this our second interview as a perfect stranger, but was extremely confounded when his speech discovered who he was. I resolved, therefore to fix his face in my memory for the future; but as I was walking in the Park the same evening, he appeared to me in one of those wigs that I think you call a night-cap, which had altered him more effectually than before. He afterwards played a couple of black riding-wigs upon me with the same success, and, in short, assumed a new face almost every day in the first month of his courtship.

'I observed afterwards, that the variety of cocks into which he moulded his hat, had not a little contributed to his impositions upon me.

'Yet, as if all these ways were not sufficient to distinguish their heads, you must doubtless, sir, have observed, that great numbers of young fellows have, for several months last past, taken upon them to wear feathers.

'We hope, therefore, that these may, with as much justice, be called Indian princes, as you have styled a woman in a coloured hood an Indian queen; and that you will in due time take these airy gentlemen into consideration.

'We the more earnestly beg that you would put a stop to this practice, since it has already lost us one of the most agreeable members of our society, who after having refused several good estates, and two titles, was lured from us last week by a mixed feather.

'I am ordered to present you with the respects of our whole company, and am,

'Sir, your very humble servant,

'DORINDA.'

'Note. The person wearing the feather, though our friend took him for an officer in the guards, has proved to be an errant linen-draper.'*

I am not now at leisure to give my opinion upon the hat and feather; however, to wipe off the present imputation, and gratify my female correspondent, I shall here print a letter which I lately received from a man of mode, who seems to have a very extraordinary genius in his way.

'Sir,—I presume I need not inform you, that among men of dress it is a common phrase to say, "Mr. Such-a-one has struck a bold stroke;" by which we understand, that he is the first man who has had courage enough to lead up a fashion. Accordingly, when our tailors take measure of us, they always demand "whether we will have a plain suit, or strike a bold stroke?" I think I may without vanity say, that I have struck some of the boldest and most successful strokes of any man in Great Britain. I was the first that struck the long pocket about two years since; I was likewise the author of the frosted button, which when I saw the town come readily into, being resolved to strike while the iron was hot, I produced much about the same time the scallop flap, the knotted cravat, and made a fair push for the silver-clocked stocking.

'A few months after I brought up the modish jacket, or the coat with close sleeves. I struck this at first in a plain Doily; but that failing, I struck it a second time in a blue camlet, and repeated the stroke in several kinds of cloth, until at last it took effect. There are two or three young fellows at the other end of the town who have always their eye upon me, and answer me stroke for stroke. I was once so unwary as to mention my fancy in relation to a new-fashioned surtout before one of these gentlemen, who was disingenuous enough to steal my thought, and by that means prevented my intended stroke.

'I have a design this spring to make very considerable innovations in the waistcoat; and have already begun with a *coup d'essai* upon the sleeves, which has succeeded very well.

'I must further inform you, if you will promise to encourage, or at least to connive at me, that it is my design to strike such a stroke the beginning of the next month as shall surprise the whole town.

'I do not think it prudent to acquaint you with all the particulars of my intended dress; but will only tell you, as a sample of it, that I shall very speedily appear at White's in a cherry-coloured hat. I took this hint from the ladies' hoods, which I look upon as the boldest stroke that sex has struck for these hundred years last past. I am, sir, your most obedient, most humble servant, WILL SPRIGHTLY.'

I have not time at present to make any reflections on this letter; but must not however omit that having shown it to Will Honeycomb, he desires to be acquainted with the gentleman who writ it. X.

* Only an ensign in the train-bands. *Spect. in folio.*

No. 320.] *Friday, March 7, 1711-12.*

——————non pronuba Juno,
Non Hymenæus adest, non illi gratia lecto:
Eumenides stravere torum————
Ovid. Met. Lib. 6. 428.

Nor Hymen, nor the Graces here preside,
Nor Juno to befriend the blooming bride;
But fiends with fun'ral brands the process led,
And furies waited at the genial bed.—*Croxal.*

'Mr. Spectator,—You have given many hints in your papers to the disadvantage of persons of your own sex, who lay plots upon women. Among other hard words you have published the term "Male Coquettes," and have been very severe upon such as give themselves the liberty of a little dalliance of heart, and playing fast and loose between love and indifference, until perhaps an easy young girl is reduced to sighs, dreams, and tears, and languishes away her life for a careless coxcomb, who looks astonished, and wonders at such an effect from what in him was all but common civility. Thus you have treated the men who are irresolute in marriage; but if you design to be impartial, pray be so honest as to print the information I now give you of a certain set of women who never coquet for the matter, but, with a high hand, marry whom they please to whom they please. As for my part, I should not have concerned myself with them, but that I understand that I am pitched upon by them to be married, against my will, to one I never saw in my life. It has been my misfortune, sir, very innocently, to rejoice in a plentiful fortune, of which I am master, to bespeak a fine chariot, to give directions for two or three handsome snuff-boxes, and as many suits of fine clothes; but before any of these were ready I heard reports of my being to be married to two or three different young women. Upon my taking notice of it to a young gentleman who is often in my company, he told me smiling, I was in the inquisition. You may believe I was not a little startled at what he meant, and more so, when he asked me if I had bespoke any thing of late that was fine. I told him several; upon which he produced a description of my person, from the tradesmen whom I had employed, and told me that they had certainly informed against me. Mr. Spectator, whatever the world may think of me, I am more coxcomb than fool, and I grew very inquisitive upon this head, not a little pleased with the novelty. My friend told me, there were a certain set of women of fashion, whereof the number of six made a committee, who sat thrice a week, under the title of "The Inquisition on Maids and Bachelors." It seems, whenever there comes such an unthinking gay thing as myself to town, he must want all manner of necessaries, or be put into the inquisition by the first tradesman he employs. They have constant intelligence with cane-shops, perfumers, toy-men, coach-makers, and china-houses. From these several places these undertakers for marriages have as constant and regular a correspondence as the funeral-men have with vintners and apothecaries. All bachelors are under their immediate inspection: and my friend produced to me a report given in to their board, wherein an old uncle of mine, who came to town with me, and myself, were inserted, and we stood thus: the uncle smoky, rotten, poor; the nephew raw, but no fool; sound at present, very rich. My information did not end here; but my friend's advices are so good, that he could show me a copy of the letter sent to the young lady who is to have me; which I enclose to you:

"Madam—This is to let you know that you are to be married to a beau that comes out on Thursday, six in the evening. Be at the Park. You cannot but know a virgin fop; they have a mind to look saucy, but are out of countenance. The board has denied him to several good families. I wish you joy.

"CORINNA."

What makes my correspondent's case the more deplorable is, that, as I find by the report from my censor of marriages, the friend he speaks of is employed by the inquisition to take him in, as the phrase is. After all that is told him, he has information only of one woman that is laid for him, and that the wrong one; for the lady commissioners have devoted him to another than the person against whom they have employed their agent his friend to alarm him. The plot is laid so well about this young gentleman, that he has no friend to retire to, no place to appear in, or part of the kingdom to fly into, but he must fall into the notice, and be subject to the power of the inquisition. They have their emissaries and substitutes in all parts of this united kingdom. The first step they usually take, is to find from a correspondence, by their messengers and whisperers, with some domestic of the bachelor, (who is to be hunted into the toils they have laid for him,) what are his manners, his familiarities, his good qualities, or vices; not as the good in him is a recommendation, or the ill a diminution, but as they affect to contribute to the main inquiry, what estate he has in him. When this point is well reported to the board, they can take in a wild roaring fox-hunter, as easily as a soft, gentle young fop of the town. The way is to make all places uneasy to him, but the scenes in which they have allotted him to act. His brother huntsmen, bottle companions, his fraternity of fops, shall be brought into the conspiracy against him. Then this matter is not laid in so barefaced a manner before him as to have it intimated, Mrs. Such-a-one would make him a very proper wife; but by the force of their correspondence, they shall make it (as Mr. Waller said of the marriage of the dwarfs,) as impracticable to have any woman besides her they design him, as it would have been in Adam to have refused Eve. The man named by the commission for Mrs. Such-a-one shall neither be in fashion, nor dare ever appear in company, should he attempt to evade their determination.

The female sex wholly govern domestic life; and by this means, when they think fit, they can sow dissensions between the nearest friends, nay, make father and son irreconcilable enemies, in spite of all the ties of gratitude on one part, and the duty of protection to be paid on the other. The ladies of the inquisition understand this perfectly well; and where love is not a motive to a man's choosing one whom they allot, they can with very much art insinuate stories to the disadvantage of his honesty or courage, until the creature is too much dispirited to bear up against a general ill reception, which he every where meets with, and in due time falls into their appointed wedlock for shelter. I have a long letter bearing date the fourth instant, which gives me a large account of the policies of this court; and find there is now before them a very refractory person who has escaped all their machinations for two years last past; but they have prevented two successive matches which were of his own inclination; the one by a report that his mistress was to be married, and the very day appointed, wedding-clothes bought, and all things ready for her being given to another; the second time by insinuating to all his mistress's friends and acquaintance, that he had been false to several other women, and the like. The poor man is now reduced to profess he designs to lead a single life; but the inquisition give out to all his acquaintance, that nothing is intended but the gentleman's own welfare and happiness. When this is urged, he talks still more humbly, and protests he aims only at a life without pain or reproach; pleasure, honour, and riches, are things for which he has no taste. But notwithstanding all this, and what else he may defend himself with, as that the lady is too old or too young, of a suitable humour, or the quite contrary, and that it is impossible they can ever do other than wrangle from June to January, every body tells him all this is spleen, and he must have a wife; while all the members of the inquisition are unanimous in a certain woman for him, and they think they altogether are better able to judge than he, or any other private person whatsoever.

'Temple, March 3, 1711.

'SIR,—Your speculation this day on the subject of idleness has employed me ever since I read it, in sorrowful reflections on my having loitered away the term (or rather the vacation) of ten years in this place, and unhappily suffered a good chamber and study to lie idle as long. My books (except those I have taken to sleep upon,) have been totally neglected, and my Lord Coke and other venerable authors were never so slighted in their lives. I spend most of the day at a neighbouring coffee-house, where we have what I may call a lazy club. We generally come in night-gowns, with our stockings about our heels, and sometimes but one on. Our salutation at entrance is a yawn and a stretch, and then without more ceremony we take our place at the lolling-table, where our discourse is, what I fear you would not read out, therefore shall not insert. But I assure you, sir, I heartily lament this loss of time, and am now resolved, (if possible, with double diligence,) to retrieve it, being effectually awakened by the arguments of Mr. Slack, out of the senseless stupidity that has so long possessed me. And to demonstrate that penitence accompanies my confessions, and constancy my resolutions, I have locked my door for a year, and desire you would let my companions know I am not within. I am with great respect, sir, your most obedient servant,

T. 'N. B.'

No. 321.] *Saturday, March* 8, 1711-12.

Nec satis est pulchra esse poemata, dulcia sunto.
Hor. Ars Poet. v. 99.

'Tis not enough a poem's finely writ;
It must affect and captivate the soul.—*Roscommon.*

THOSE who know how many volumes have been written on the poems of Homer and Virgil will easily pardon the length of my discourse upon Milton. The Paradise Lost is looked upon by the best judges, as the greatest production, or at least the noblest work of genius in our language, and therefore deserves to be set before an English reader in its full beauty. For this reason, though I have endeavoured to give a general idea of its graces and imperfections in my first six papers, I thought myself obliged to bestow one upon every book in particular. The first three books I have already despatched, and am now entering upon the fourth. I need not acquaint my reader that there are multitudes of beauties in this great author, especially in the descriptive parts of this poem, which I have not touched upon; it being my intention to point out those only which appear to me the most exquisite, or those which are not so obvious to ordinary readers. Every one that has read the critics who have written upon the Odyssey, the Iliad, and the Æneid, knows very well, that though they agree in their opinions of the great beauties in those poems, they have nevertheless each of them discovered several master-strokes, which have escaped the observation of the rest. In the same manner, I question not but any writer, who shall treat of this subject after me may find several beauties in Milton, which I have not taken notice of. I must likewise observe, that as the greatest masters of critical learning differ among one another, as to some particular points in an epic poem, I have not bound myself scrupulously to the rules which any one of them has laid down upon that art, but have taken the liberty sometimes to join with one, and sometimes with another, and sometimes to differ from all of them, when I have thought that the reason of the thing was on my side.

We may conclude the beauties of the fourth book under three heads. In the first are those pictures of still-life, which we meet with in the description of Eden, Paradise, Adam's bower, &c. In the next are the machines, which comprehend the speeches and behaviour of the good and bad angels. In the last is the conduct of Adam and Eve, who are the principal actors in the poem.

In the description of Paradise, the poet has observed Aristotle's rule of lavishing all the ornaments of diction on the weak unactive parts of the fable, which are not supported by the beauty of sentiments and characters. Accordingly the reader may observe, that the expressions are more florid and elaborate in these descriptions, than in most other parts of the poem. I must further add, that though the drawings of gardens, rivers, rainbows, and the like dead pieces of nature, are justly censured in an heroic poem, when they run out into an unnecessary length—the description of Paradise would have been faulty, had not the poet been very particular in it, not only as it is the scene of the principal action, but as it is requisite to give us an idea of that happiness from which our first parents fell. The plan of it is wonderfully beautiful, and formed upon the short sketch which we have of it in holy writ. Milton's exuberance of imagination has poured forth such a redundancy of ornaments on this seat of happiness and innocence, that it would be endless to point out each particular.

I must not quit this head without further observing, that there is scarce a speech of Adam or Eve in the whole poem, wherein the sentiments and allusions are not taken from this their delightful habitation. The reader, during their whole course of action always finds himself in the walks of Paradise. In short, as the critics have remarked, that in those poems wherein shepherds are the actors, the thoughts ought always to take a tincture from the woods, fields, and rivers; so we may observe, that our first parents seldom lose sight of their happy station in any thing they speak or do; and, if the reader will give me leave to use the expression, that their thoughts are always 'paradisaical.'

We are in the next place to consider the machines of the fourth book. Satan being now within the prospect of Eden, and looking round upon the glories of the creation, is filled with sentiments different from those which he discovered whilst he was in hell. The place inspires him with thoughts more adapted to it. He reflects upon the happy condition from whence he fell, and breaks forth into a speech that is softened with several transient touches of remorse and self-accusation: but at length he confirms himself in impenitence, and in his design of drawing man into his own state of guilt and misery. This conflict of passions is raised with a great deal of art, as the opening of his speech to the sun is very bold and noble:

'O thou, that with surpassing glory crown'd,
Look'st from thy sole dominion like the god
Of this new world; at whose sight all the stars
Hide their diminish'd heads; to thee I call,
But with no friendly voice; and add thy name,
O sun! to tell thee how I hate thy beams,
That bring to my remembrance from what state
I fell, how glorious once above thy sphere.'

This speech is, I think, the finest that is ascribed to Satan in the whole poem. The evil spirit afterwards proceeds to make his discoveries concerning our first parents, and to learn after what manner they may be best attacked. His bounding over the walls of Paradise: his sitting in the shape of a cormorant upon the tree of life, which stood in the centre of it, and overtopped all the other trees of the garden; his alighting among the herd of animals, which are so beautifully represented as playing about Adam and Eve; together with his transforming himself into different shapes, in order to hear their conversation; are circumstances that give an agreeable surprise to the reader, and are devised with great art, to connect that series of adventures in which the poet has engaged this artificer of fraud.

The thought of Satan's transformation into a cormorant, and placing himself on the tree of life, seems raised upon that passage in the Iliad, where two deities are described as perching on the top of an oak in the shape of vultures.

His planting himself at the ear of Eve under the form of a toad, in order to produce vain dreams and imaginations, is a circumstance of the same nature; as his starting up in his own form is wonderfully fine, both in the literal description, and in the moral which is concealed under it. His answer upon his being discovered, and demanded to give an account of himself, is conformable to the pride and intrepidity of of his character:

'Know ye not, then,' said Satan, fill'd with scorn,
'Know ye not me!' Ye knew me once no mate
For you, there sitting where you durst not soar:
Not to know me argues yourselves unknown,
The lowest of your throng———.'

Zephon's rebuke, with the influence it had on Satan, is exquisitely graceful and moral. Satan is afterwards led away to Gabriel, the chief of the guardian angels, who kept watch in Paradise. His disdainful behaviour on this occasion is so remarkable a beauty, that the most ordinary reader cannot but take notice of it. Gabriel's discovering his approach at a distance is drawn with great strength and liveliness of imagination:

'O friends, I hear the tread of nimble feet
Hasting this way, and now by glimpse discern
Ithuriel and Zephon through the shade,
And with them comes a third of regal port,
But faded splendour wan; who by his gait
And fierce demeanour seems the prince of Hell:
Not likely to part hence without contest;
Stand firm, for in his look defiance low'rs.'

The conference between Gabriel and Satan abounds with sentiments proper for the occasion, and suitable to the persons of the two speakers. Satan clothing himself with terror when he prepares for the combat is truly sublime, and at least equal to Homer's description of Discord, celebrated by Longinus, or to that of Fame in Virgil, who are both represented with their feet standing upon the earth, and their heads reaching above the clouds:

While thus he spake, th' angelic squadron bright
Turn'd fiery red, sharp'ning in mooned horns
Their phalanx, and began to hem him round
With ported spears, &c.
——On th' other side Satan alarm'd,
Collecting all his might, dilated stood
Like Teneriffe, or Atlas, unremoved:
His stature reach'd the sky, and on his crest
Sat Horror plum'd.——

I must here take notice, that Milton is every where full of hints, and sometimes literal translations, taken from the greatest of the Greek and Latin poets. But this I may reserve for a discourse by itself, because I would not break the thread of these speculations, that are designed for English readers, with such reflections as would be of no use but to the learned.

I must, however, observe in this place, that the breaking off the combat between Gabriel and Satan, by the hanging out of the golden scales in heaven, is a refinement upon Homer's thought, who tells us, that before the battle between Hector and Achilles, Jupiter weighed the event of it in a pair of scales. The reader may see the whole passage in the 22d Iliad.

Virgil, before the last decisive combat describes Jupiter in the same manner, as weighing the fates of Turnus and Æneas. Milton, though he fetched this beautiful circumstance from the Iliad and Æneid, does not only insert it as a poetical embellishment, like the author's above-mentioned, but makes an artful use of it for the proper carrying on of his fable, and for the breaking off the combat between the two warriors, who were upon the point of engaging. To this we may further add, that Milton is the more justified in this passage, as we find the same noble allegory in holy writ, where a wicked prince, some few hours before he was assaulted and slain, is said to have been 'weighed in the scales, and to have been found wanting.'

I must here take notice, under the head of the machines, that Uriel's gliding down to the earth upon a sun-beam, with the poet's device to make him descend, as well in his return to the sun as in his coming from it, is a prettiness that might have been admired in a little fanciful poet, but seems below the genius of Milton. The description of the host of armed angels walking their nightly round in Paradise is of another spirit:

So saying on he led his radiant files,
Dazzling the moon;

as that account of the hymns which our first parents used to hear them sing in these their midnight walks is altogether divine, and inexpressibly amusing to the imagination.

We are in the last place, to consider the parts which Adam and Eve act in the fourth book. The description of them, as they first appeared to Satan, is exquisitely drawn, and sufficient to make the fallen angel gaze upon them with all that astonishment, and those emotions of envy in which he is represented:

Two of far nobler shape, erect and tall,
God-like erect, with native honour clad
In naked majesty, seem'd lords of all;
And worthy seem'd; for in their looks divine
The image of their glorious maker shone,
Truth, wisdom, sanctitude severe and pure;
Severe, but in true filial freedom plac'd:
For contemplation he and valour form'd,
For softness she and sweet attractive grace;
He for God only, she for God in him.
His fair large front, and eye sublime declar'd
Absolute rule; and hyacinthine locks
Round from his parted forelock manly hung
Clust'ring, but not beneath his shoulders broad.
She, as a veil, down to her slender waist
Her unadorned golden tresses wore
Dishevell'd, but in wanton ringlets wav'd.
So pass'd they naked on, nor shunn'd the sight
Of God or angels, for they thought no ill:
So hand in hand they pass'd, the loveliest pair
That ever since in love's embraces met.

There is a fine spirit of poetry in the lines which follow, wherein they are described as sitting on a bed of flowers by the side of a fountain, amidst a mixed assembly of animals.

The speeches of these two first lovers flow equally from passion and sincerity. The professions they make to one another are full of warmth; but at the same time founded on truth. In a word they are the gallantries of Paradise:

——When Adam first of men——
'Sole partner and sole part of all these joys,
Dearer thyself than all:——
But let us ever praise Him, and extol
His bounty, following our delightful task,
To prune these growing plants, and tend these flow'rs:
Which were it toilsome, yet with thee were sweet.'
To whom thus Eve reply'd. 'O thou, for whom
And from whom I was form'd, flesh of thy flesh,
And without whom am to no end, my guide
And head, what thou hast said is just and right.
For we to him indeed all praises owe
And daily thanks; I chiefly, who enjoy
So far the happier lot, enjoying thee,
Pre-eminent by so much odds, while thou
Like consort to thyself canst no where find.' &c.

The remaining part of Eve's speech, in which she gives an account of herself upon her first creation, and the manner in which she was brought to Adam, is, I think, as beautiful a passage as any in Milton, or perhaps in any other poet whatsoever. These passages are all worked off with so much art, that they are capable of pleasing the most delicate reader, without offending the most severe.

'That day I oft remember, when from sleep,' &c.

A poet of less judgment and invention than this great author, would have found it very difficult to have filled these tender parts of the poem with sentiments proper for a state of innocence; to have described the warmth of love, and the professions of it, without artifice or hyperbole; to have made the man speak the most endearing things without descending from his natural dignity, and the woman receiving them without departing from the modesty of her character: in a word, to adjust the prerogatives of wisdom and beauty, and make each appear to the other in its proper force and loveliness. This mutual subordination of the two sexes is wonderfully kept up in the whole poem, as particularly in the speech of Eve I have before mentioned, and upon the conclusion of it in the following lines:

So spake our general mother, and with eyes
Of conjugal attraction unreprov'd,
And meek surrender, half embracing lean'd
On our first father; half her swelling breast
Naked met his, under the flowing gold
Of her loose tresses hid; he in delight
Both of her beauty and submissive charms
Smil'd with superior love.———

The poet adds, that the devil turned away with envy at the sight of so much happiness.

We have another view of our first parents in their evening discourses, which is full of pleasing images and sentiments suitable to their condition and characters. The speech of Eve in particular, is dressed up in such a soft and natural turn of words and sentiments, as cannot be sufficiently admired.

I shall close my reflections upon this book with observing the masterly transition which the poet makes to their evening worship in the following lines:

Thus at their shady lodge arriv'd, both stood,
Both turn'd, and under open sky ador'd
The God that made both sky, air, earth, and heav'n,
Which they beheld, the moon's resplendent globe,
And starry pole: 'Thou also mad'st the night,
Maker omnipotent, and thou the day,' &c.

Most of the modern heroic poets have imitated the ancients, in beginning a speech without premising that the person said thus or thus; but as it is easy to imitate the ancients in the omission of two or three words, it requires judgment to do it in such a manner as they shall not be missed, and that the speech may begin naturally without them. There is a fine instance of this kind out of Homer, in the twenty-third chapter of Longinus. L.

No. 322.] *Monday, March* 10, 1711-12.

——Ad humum mœrore gravi deducit et angit.
Hor. Ars Poet. v. 110.

——Grief wrings her soul, and bends it down to earth.
Francis.

It is often said, after a man has heard a story with extraordinary circumstances, 'It is a very good one, if it be true:' but as for the following relation, I should be glad were I sure it were false. It is told with such simplicity, and there are so many artless touches of distress in it, that I fear it comes too much from the heart.

'Mr. Spectator,—Some years ago it happened that I lived in the same house with a young gentleman of merit, with whose good qualities I was so much taken, as to make it my endeavour to show as many as I was able in myself. Familiar converse improved general civilities into an unfeigned passion on both sides. He watched an opportunity to declare himself to me; and I, who could not expect a man of so great an estate as his, received his addresses in such terms, as gave him no reason to believe I was displeased with them, though I did nothing to make him think me more easy than was decent. His father was a very hard worldly man, and proud; so that there was no reason to believe he would easily be brought to think there was any thing in any woman's person, or character, that could balance the disadvantage of an unequal fortune. In the mean time the son continued his application to me, and omitted no occasion of demonstrating the most disinterested passion imaginable to me; and in plain direct terms offered to marry me privately, and keep it so till he should be so happy as to gain his father's approbation, or become possessed of his estate. I passionately loved him, and you will believe I did not deny such a one what was my interest also to grant. However, I was not so young as not to take the precaution of carrying with me a faithful servant, who had been also my mother's maid, to be present at the ceremony. When that was over, I demanded a certificate to be signed by the minister, my husband, and the servant I just now spoke of. After our nuptials, we conversed together very familiarly in the same house; but the restraints we were generally under, and the interviews we had being stolen and interrupted, made our behaviour to each other have rather the impatient fondness which is visible in lovers, than the regular and gratified affection, which is to be observed in man and wife. This observation made the father very anxious for his son, and press him to a match he had in his eye for him. To relieve my husband from this importunity, and conceal the secret of our marriage, which I had reason to know would not be long in my power in town, it was resolved that I should retire into a remote place in the country, and converse under feigned names by letter. We long continued this way of commerce; and I with my needle, a few books, and reading over and over my husband's letters, passed my time in a resigned expectation of better days. Be pleased to take notice, that within four months after I left my husband I was delivered of a daughter, who died within a few hours after her birth. This accident, and the retired manner of life I led, gave criminal hopes to a neighbouring brute of a country gentleman, whose folly was the source of all my affliction. This rustic is one of those rich clowns who supply the want of all manner of breeding by the neglect of it, and with noisy mirth, half understanding and ample fortune, force themselves upon persons and things, without any sense of time or place. The poor ignorant people where I lay concealed, and now passed for a widow, wondered I could be so shy and strange, as they called it, to the 'squire; and were bribed by him to admit him whenever he thought fit: I happened to be sitting in a little parlour which belonged to my own part of the house, and musing over one of the fondest of my husband's letters, in which I always kept the certificate of my marriage, when this rude fellow came in, and with the nauseous familiarity of such unbred brutes snatched the papers out of my hand. I was immediately under so great a concern, that I threw myself at his feet, and begged of him to return them. He, with the same odious pretence to freedom and gaiety, swore he would read them. I grew more importunate, he more curious, till at last, with an indignation arising from a passion I then first discovered in him, he threw the papers into the fire, swearing that since he was not to read them, the man who writ them should never be so happy as to have me read them over again. It is insignificant to tell you my tears and reproaches made the boisterous calf leave the room ashamed and out of countenance, when I had leisure to ruminate on this accident with more than ordinary sorrow. However, such was then my confidence in my husband, that I writ to him the misfortune, and desired another paper of the same kind. He deferred writing two or three posts, and at last answered me in general, that he could not then send me what I asked for; but when he could find a proper conveyance, I should be sure to have it. From this time his letters were more cold every day than other, and, as he grew indifferent I grew jealous. This has at last brought me to town, where I find both the witnesses of my marriage dead, and that my husband, after three month's cohabitation, has buried a young lady whom he married in obedience to his father. In a word he shuns and disowns me. Should I come to the house and confront him, the father would join in supporting him against me, though he believed my story; should I talk it to the world, what reparation can I expect for an injury I cannot make out? I believe he means to bring me, through necessity, to resign my pretensions to him for some provision for my life; but I will die first. Pray bid him remember what he said, and how he was charmed when he laughed at the heedless discovery I often made of myself; let him remember how awkward I was in my dissembled indifference towards him before company; ask him how I, who could never conceal my love for him, at his own request can part with him for ever? Oh, Mr. Spectator, sensible spirits know no indifference in marriage: what then do you think is my piercing affliction?——I leave you to represent my distress your own way in which I desire you to be speedy, if you have compassion for innocence exposed to infamy. OCTAVIA.'

No. 323.] *Tuesday, March* 11, 1711-12.

——Modo vir, modo fœmina. *Virg.*

Sometimes a man, sometimes a woman.

The journal with which I presented my reader on Tuesday last has brought me in several letters, with accounts of many private lives cast into that form. I have the 'Rake's Journal,' the 'Sot's Journal,' the 'Whoremaster's Journal,' and, among several others, a very curious piece, entitled, 'The Journal of a Mohock.' By these instances, I find that the intention of my last Tuesday's paper has been mistaken by many of my readers. I did not design so much to expose vice as idleness, and aimed at those persons who passed away their time rather in trifles and impertinence, than in crimes and immoralities. Offences of this latter kind are not to be dallied with, or treated in so ludicrous a manner. In short, my journal only holds up folly to the light, and shows the disagreeableness of such actions as are indifferent in themselves, and blameable only as they proceed from creatures endowed with reason.

My following correspondent, who calls herself Clarinda, is such a journalist as I require. She seems by her letter to be placed in a modish state of indifference between vice and virtue, and to be susceptible of either, were there proper pains taken with her. Had her journal been filled with gallantries, or such occurrences as had shown her wholly divested of her natural innocence, notwithstanding it might have been more pleasing to the generality of readers, I should not have published it: but as it is only the picture of a life filled with a fashionable kind of gaiety and laziness, I shall set down five days of it, as I have received it from the hand of my fair correspondent.

'Dear Mr. Spectator,—You having set your readers an exercise in one of your last week's papers, I have performed mine according to your orders, and herewith send it you enclosed. You must know, Mr. Spectator, that I am a maiden lady of a good fortune, who have had several matches offered me for these ten years last past, and have at present warm applications made to me by 'a very pretty fellow.' As I am at my own disposal, I come up to town every winter, and pass my time in it after the manner you will find in the following journal, which I began to write the very day after your Spectator upon that subject.'

TUESDAY night. Could not go to sleep till one in the morning for thinking of my journal.

WEDNESDAY. From eight till ten. Drank two dishes of chocolate in bed, and fell asleep after them.

From ten to eleven. Eat a slice of bread and butter, drank a dish of bohea, and read the Spectator.

From eleven to one. At my toilette; tried a new hood. Gave orders for Veny to be combed and washed. Mem. I look best in blue.

From one till half an hour after two. Drove to the 'Change. Cheapened a couple of fans.

Till four. At dinner. Mem. Mr. Froth passed by in his new liveries.

From four to six. Dressed: paid a visit to old lady Blithe and her sister, having before heard they were gone out of town that day.

From six to eleven. At basset. Mem. Never set again upon the ace of diamonds.

THURSDAY. From eleven at night to eight in the morning. Dreamed that I punted* to Mr. Froth.

From eight to ten. Chocolate. Read two acts in Aurengzebe a-bed.

From ten to eleven. Tea-table. Sent to borrow lady Faddle's Cupid for Veny. Read the play-bills. Received a letter from Mr. Froth. Mem. Locked it up in my strong box.

Rest of the morning. Fontange, the tire-woman, her account of my lady Blithe's wash. Broke a tooth in my little tortoise-shell comb.

Sent Frank to know how my lady Hectic rested after her monkey's leaping out at window. Looked pale. Fontange tells me my glass is not true. Dressed by three.

From three to four. Dinner cold before I sat down.

From four to eleven. Saw company. Mr. Froth's opinion of Milton. His account of the Mohocks. His fancy of a pin-cushion. Picture in the lid of his snuff-box. Old lady Faddle promises me her woman to cut my hair. Lost five guineas at crimp.

Twelve o'clock at night. Went to bed.

FRIDAY. Eight in the morning. A-bed. Read over all Mr. Froth's letters. Cupid and Veny.

Ten o'clock. Stayed within all day, not at home.

From ten to twelve. In conference with my mantua-maker. Sorted a suit of ribands. Broke my blue china cup.

From twelve to one. Shut myself up in my chamber, practised lady Betty Modely's skuttle.†

One in the afternoon. Called for my flowered handkerchief. Worked half a violet leaf in it. Eyes ached and head out of order. Threw by my work, and read over the remaining part of Aurengzebe.

From three to four. Dined.

From four to twelve. Changed my mind, dressed, went abroad, and played at crimp till midnight. Found Mrs. Spitely at home. Conversation: Mrs. Brilliant's necklace false stones. Old lady Love-day going to be married to a young fellow that is not worth a groat. Miss Prue gone into the country. Tom Townly has red hair. Mem. Mrs. Spitely whispered in my ear, that she had something to tell me about Mr. Froth; I am sure it is not true.

Between twelve and one. Dreamed that Mr. Froth lay at my feet, and called me Indamora.

SATURDAY. Rose at eight o'clock in the morning. Sat down to my toilette.

From eight to nine. Shifted a patch for half an hour before I could determine it. Fixed it above my left eyebrow.

From nine to twelve. Drank my tea, and dressed.

From twelve to two. At chapel. A great deal of good company. Mem. The third air in the new opera. Lady Blithe dressed frightfully.

From three to four. Dined. Miss Kitty called upon me to go to the opera before I was risen from table.

From dinner to six. Drank tea. Turned off a footman for being rude to Veny.

Six o'clock. Went to the opera. I did not see Mr. Froth till the beginning of the second act. Mr. Froth talked to a gentleman in a black wig; bowed to a lady in the front box. Mr. Froth and his friend clapped Nicolini in the third act. Mr. Froth cried out 'Ancora.' Mr. Froth led me to my chair. I think he squeezed my hand.

Eleven at night. Went to bed. Melancholy dreams. Methought Nicolini said he was Mr. Froth.

SUNDAY. Indisposed.

MONDAY. Eight o'clock. Waked by Miss Kitty. Aurengzebe lay upon the chair by me. Kitty repeated without book the eight best lines in the play. Went in our mobs‡ to the dumb man, according to appointment. Told me that my lover's name began with a G. Mem. The conjuror§ was within a letter of Mr. Froth's name, &c.

'Upon looking back into this my journal, I find that I am at a loss to know whether I pass my time well or ill; and indeed never thought of considering how I did it before I perused your speculation upon that subject. I scarce find a single action in these five days that I can thoroughly approve of, excepting the working upon the violet-leaf, which I am resolved to finish the first day

* A term in the game of basset.
† A pace of affected precipitation
‡ A sort of dress so named.
§ Duncan Campbell.

I am at leisure. As for Mr. Froth and Veny, I did not think they took up so much of my time and thoughts as I find they do upon my journal. The latter of them I will turn off, if you insist upon it; and if Mr. Froth does not bring matters to a conclusion very suddenly, I will not let my life run away in a dream. Your humble servant, CLARINDA.'

To resume one of the morals of my first paper, and to confirm Clarinda in her good inclinations, I would have her consider what a pretty figure she would make among posterity, were the history of her whole life published like these five days of it. I shall conclude my paper with an epitaph written by an uncertain author on Sir Philip Sydney's sister, a lady who seems to have been of a temper very much different from that of Clarinda. The last thought of it is so very noble, that I dare say my reader will pardon me the quotation.

ON THE COUNTESS DOWAGER OF PEMBROKE.

Underneath this marble hearse
Lies the subject of all verse,
Sidney's sister, Pembroke's mother:
Death, ere thou hast kill'd another,
Fair and learn'd and good as she,
Time shall throw a dart at thee.

L.

No. 324.] *Wednesday, March* 12, 1711-12.

O curvæ in terris animæ, et cœlestium inanes!
Pers. Sat. ii. 61.

O souls, in whom no heavenly fire is found,
Flat minds, and ever grovelling on the ground!*
Dryden.

'MR. SPECTATOR,—The materials you have collected together towards a general history of clubs, make so bright a part of your speculations, that I think it is but justice we all owe the learned world, to furnish you with such assistance as may promote that useful work. For this reason I could not forbear communicating to you some imperfect informations of a set of men (if you will allow them a place in that species of being) who have lately erected themselves into a nocturnal fraternity, under the title of the Mohock-club, a name borrowed it seems from a sort of cannibals in India, who subsist by plundering and devouring all the nations about them. The president is styled, 'Emperor of the Mohocks;' and his arms are a Turkish crescent, which his imperial majesty bears at present in a very extraordinary manner engraven upon his forehead. Agreeable to their name, the avowed design of their institution is mischief; and upon this foundation all their rules and orders are framed. An outrageous ambition of doing all possible hurt to their fellow-creatures, is the great cement of their assembly, and the only qualification required in the members. In order to exert this principle in its full strength and perfection, they take care to drink themselves to a pitch, that is, beyond the possibility of attending to any motions of reason or humanity; then make a general sally, and attack all that are so unfortunate as to walk the streets through which they patrole. Some are knocked down, others stabbed, others cut and carbonadoed. To put the watch to a total rout, and mortify some of those inoffensive militia, is reckoned a *coup d'eclat.* The particular talents by which these misanthropes are distinguished from one another, consist in the various kinds of barbarities which they execute upon the prisoners. Some are celebrated for a happy dexterity in tipping the lion upon them; which is performed by squeezing the nose flat to the face, and boring out the eyes with their fingers. Others are called the dancing-masters, and teach their scholars to cut capers by running swords through their legs; a new invention, whether originally French I cannot tell. A third sort are the tumblers, whose office is to set women on their heads, and commit certain indecencies, or rather barbarities, on the limbs which they expose. But these I forbear to mention, because they cannot but be very shocking to the reader as well as the Spectator. In this manner they carry on a war against mankind; and by the standing maxims of their policy, are to enter into no alliances but one, and that is offensive and defensive with all bawdy-houses in general, of which they have declared themselves protectors and guarantees.

'I must own, sir, these are only broken, incoherent memoirs of this wonderful society; but they are the best I have been yet able to procure: for, being but of late established, it is not ripe for a just history; and, to be serious, the chief design of this trouble is to hinder it from ever being so. You have been pleased, out of a concern for the good of your countrymen, to act, under the character of a Spectator, not only the part of a looker-on, but an overseer of their actions; and whenever such enormities as this infest the town, we immediately fly to you for redress. I have reason to believe, that some thoughtless youngsters, out of a false notion of bravery, and an immoderate fondness to be distinguished for fellows of fire, are insensibly hurried into this senseless, scandalous project. Such will probably stand corrected by your reproofs, especially if you inform them, that it is not courage for half a score fellows, mad with wine and lust, to set upon two or three soberer than themselves; and that the manners of Indian savages are not becoming accomplishments to an English fine gentleman. Such of them as have been bullies and scowerers of a long standing, and are grown veterans in this kind of service, are, I fear, too hardened to receive any impres

---

* The motto prefixed to this paper *in folio*, is from Juvenal:

Savis inter se convenit ursis.
Even bears with bears agree.

sions from your admonitions. But I beg you would recommend to their perusal your ninth speculation. They may there be taught to take warning from the club of duellists; and be put in mind, that the common fate of those men of honour was, to be hanged. I am, sir, your most humble servant, PHILANTHROPOS.

'March 10, 1711-12.'

The following letter is of a quite contrary nature; but I add it here, that the reader may observe, at the same view, how amiable ignorance may be, when it is shown in its simplicities; and how detestable in barbarities. It is written by an honest countryman to his mistress, and came to the hands of a lady of good sense, wrapped about a thread-paper, who has long kept it by her as an image of artless love.

'*To her I very much respect, Mrs. Margaret Clark.*

'Lovely, and oh that I could write loving, Mrs. Margaret Clark, I pray you let affection excuse presumption. Having been so happy as to enjoy the sight of your sweet countenance and comely body, sometimes when I had occasion to buy treacle or liquorish powder at the apothecary's shop, I am so enamoured with you, that I can no more keep close my flaming desires to become your servant.* And I am the more bold now to write to your sweet self, because I am now my own man, and may match where I please; for my father is taken away, and now I am come to my living, which is ten yard land, and a house; and there is never a yard land,† in our field, but it is as well worth ten pounds a year as a thief is worth a halter, and all my brothers and sisters are provided for: besides, I have good household stuff, though I say it, both brass and pewter, linens and woollens; and though my house be thatched, yet, if you and I match, it shall go hard but I will have one half of it slated. If you think well of this motion, I will wait upon you as soon as my new clothes are made, and hay harvest is in. I could, though I say it, have good ——.' The rest is torn off; and posterity must be contented to know, that Mrs. Margaret Clark was very pretty; but are left in the dark as to the name of her lover.

T.

* A note in Mr. Chalmers's edition of the Spectator informs us, that this letter was really conveyed in the manner here mentioned to a Mrs. Cole, of Northampton: the writer was a gentleman of the name of Bullock:—the part torn off is given in the note alluded to as follows: '——good matches amongst my neighbours. My mother, peace be with her soul! the good old gentlewoman, has left me good store of household linen of her own spinning, a chest full. If you and I lay our means together, it shall go hard but I will pave the way to do well. Your loving servant till death, Mister Gabriel Bullock, now my father is dead.' See No. 328.*

† A yard land [*virgata terra*] in some counties, contains 20 acres, in some 24, and in others 30 acres of land.—*Les Termes de la Ley*. Ed. 1667.

No. 325.] *Thursday, March* 13, 1711-12.

——Quid frustra simulacra fugacia captas?
Quod petis, est nusquam: quod amas avertere, perdes.
Ista repercussæ, quam cernis, imaginis umbra est,
Nil habet ista sui: tecum venitque, manetque;
Tecum discedet; si tu discedere possis.
Ovid. Met. Lib. iii. 432.

[*From the fable of Narcissus.*]

What could, fond youth, this helpless passion move?
What kindled in thee this unpitied love?
Thy own warm blush within the water glows;
With thee the colour'd shadow comes and goes;
Its empty being on thyself relies:
Step thou aside, and the frail charmer dies.—*Addison.*

Will Honeycomb diverted us last night with an account of a young fellow's first discovering his passion to his mistress. The young lady was one, it seems, who had long before conceived a favourable opinion of him, and was still in hopes that he would some time or other make his advances. As he was one day talking with her in company of her two sisters, the conversation happening to turn upon love, each of the young ladies was, by way of raillery, recommending a wife to him; when, to the no small surprise of her who languished for him in secret, he told them, with a more than ordinary seriousness, that his heart had been long engaged to one whose name he thought himself obliged in honour to conceal; but that he could show her picture in the lid of his snuff-box. The young lady, who found herself most sensibly touched by this confession, took the first opportunity that offered of snatching his box out of his hand. He seemed desirous of recovering it; but finding her resolved to look into the lid, begged her, that, if she should happen to know the person, she would not reveal her name. Upon carrying it to the window, she was very agreeably surprised to find there was nothing within the lid but a little looking-glass; on which, after she had viewed her own face with more pleasure than she had ever done before, she returned the box with a smile, telling him she could not but admire his choice.

Will, fancying that this story took, immediately fell into a dissertation on the usefulness of looking-glasses; and, applying himself to me, asked if there were any looking-glasses in the times of the Greeks and Romans; for that he had often observed, in the translations of poems out of those languages, that people generally talked of seeing themselves in wells, fountains, lakes, and rivers. Nay, says he, I remember Mr. Dryden, in his Ovid, tells us of a swinging fellow, called Polypheme, that made use of the sea for his looking-glass, and could never dress himself to advantage but in a calm.

My friend Will, to show us the whole compass of his learning upon this subject, further informed us, that there were still several nations in the world so very barbarous as not to have any looking-glasses among them; and that he had lately read a voyage to the South Sea, in which it is said that the ladies of Chili always dressed their heads over a basin of water.

I am the more particular in my account of Will's last night's lecture on these natural mirrors, as it seems to bear some relation to the following letter, which I received the day before.

'SIR,—I have read your last Saturday's observations on the fourth book of Milton with great satisfaction, and am particularly pleased with the hidden moral which you have taken notice of in several parts of the poem. The design of this letter is to desire your thoughts, whether there may not also be some moral couched under that place in the same book, where the poet lets us know, that the first woman immediately after her creation ran to a looking-glass, and became so enamoured of her own face, that she had never removed to view any of the other works of nature, had she not been led off to a man? If you think fit to set down the whole passage from Milton, your readers will be able to judge for themselves, and the quotation will not a little contribute to the filling up of your paper. Your humble servant, R. T.'

The last consideration urged by my querist is so strong, that I cannct forbear closing with it. The passage he alludes to is part of Eve's speech to Adam, and one of the most beautiful passages in the whole poem:

'That day I oft remember, when from sleep
I first awak'd, and found myself repos'd
Under a shade of flowers, much wond'ring where
And what I was, whence hither brought, and how.
Not distant far from thence a murmuring sound
Of waters issued from a cave, and spread
Into a liquid plain, and stood unmov'd
Pure as th' expanse of heaven: I thither went
With unexperienc'd thought, and laid me down
On the green bank, to look into the clear
Smooth lake, that to me seem'd another sky.
As I bent down to look, just opposite,
A shape within the watery gleam appear'd,
Bending to look on me; I started back,
It started back; but pleas'd I soon return'd,
Pleas'd it return'd as soon with answering looks
Of sympathy and love: there I had fix'd
Mine eyes till now, and pin'd with vain desire,
Had not a voice thus warn'd me: "What thou seest,
What there thou seest, fair creature, is thyself;
With thee it came and goes; but follow me,
And I will bring thee where no shadow stays
Thy coming and thy soft embraces; he
Whose image thou art, him thou shalt enjoy,
Inseparably thine; to him shalt bear
Multitudes like thyself, and thence be call'd
Mother of human race." What could I do,
But follow straight, invisibly thus led?
Till I espy'd thee, fair indeed and tall,
Under a plantain; yet, methought, less fair,
Less winning soft, less amiably mild,
Than that smooth watery image: back I turn'd;
Thou following cry'dst aloud, "Return, fair Eve!
Whom fly'st thou? Whom thou fly'st, of him thou art,
His flesh, his bone; to give thee being, I lent
Out of my side to thee, nearest my heart,
Substantial life, to have thee by my side,
Henceforth an individual solace dear:
Part of my soul, I seek thee, and thee claim,
My other half!"—With that thy gentle hand
Seiz'd mine; I yielded, and from that time see
How beauty is excell'd by manly grace
And wisdom, which alone is truly fair.'
So spake our general mother——

X.

No. 326.] *Friday, March* 14, 1711-1[illegible]

Inclusam Danaen turris ahenea,
Robustæque fores, et vigilum canum
Tristes excubiæ munierant satis
Nocturnis ab adulteris:
Si non—— *Hor.* Lib. iii. Od. xvi [illegible]

Of watchful dogs an odious ward
Right well one hapless virgin guard,
When in a tower of brass immur'd,
By mighty bars of steel secur'd,
Although by mortal rake-hells lewd
With all their midnight arts pursu'd,
Had not—— *Francis*, vol. ii. p. 7[illegible]

ADAPTED.

Be to her faults a little blind,
Be to her virtues very kind,
And clap your padlock on her mind.—*Padlock.*

'MR. SPECTATOR,—Your correspondent's letter relating to fortune-hunters, and your subsequent discourse upon it, have given me encouragement to send you a state of my case, by which you will see, that the matter complained of is a common grievance both to city and country.

'I am a country-gentleman of between five and six thousand a year. It is my misfortune to have a very fine park and an only daughter; upon which account I have been so plagued with deer-stealers and fops, that for these four years past I have scarce enjoyed a moment's rest. I look upon myself to be in a state of war; and am forced to keep as constant watch in my seat, as a governor would do that commanded a town on the frontier of an enemy's country. I have indeed pretty well secured my park, having for this purpose provided myself of four keepers, who are left-handed, and handle a quarter-staff beyond any other fellows in the country. And for the guard of my house, besides a band of pensioner matrons and an old maiden relation whom I keep on constant duty, I have blunderbusses always charged, and fox-gins planted in private places about my garden, of which I have given frequent notice in the neighbourhood; yet so it is, that in spite of all my care, I shall every now and then have a saucy rascal ride by, reconnoitering (as I think you call it) under my windows, as sprucely dressed as if he were going to a ball. I am aware of this way of attacking a mistress on horseback, having heard that it is a common practice in Spain; and have therefore taken care to remove my daughter from the road-side of the house, and to lodge her next the garden. But to cut short my story: What can a man do after all? I durst not stand for member of parliament last election, for fear of some ill consequence from my being off my post. What I would therefore desire of you is, to promote a project I have set on foot, and upon which I have written to some of my friends: and that is, that care may be taken to secure our daughters by law, as well as our deer; and that some honest gentleman, of a public spirit, would move for leave to bring in a bill for the better preserving of the female game. I am, sir, your humble servant.'

'Mile-End-Green, March 6, 1711-12.

'MR. SPECTATOR,—Here is a young man walks by our door every day about the dusk of the evening. He looks up at my window, as if to see me; and if I steal towards it to peep at him, he turns another way, and looks frightened at finding what he was looking for. The air is very cold; and pray let him know, that if he knocks at the door he will be carried to the parlour fire, and I will come down soon after, and give him an opportunity to break his mind.

'I am, sir, your most humble servant,

'MARY COMFIT.

'If I observe he cannot speak, I'll give him time to recover himself, and ask him how he does.'

'DEAR SIR,—I beg you to print this without delay, and by the first opportunity give us the natural causes of longing in women; or put me out of fear that my wife will one time or other be delivered of something as monstrous as any thing that has yet appeared to the world; for they say the child is to bear a resemblance of what was desired by the mother. I have been married upwards of six years, have had four children, and my wife is now big with the fifth. The expenses she has put me to, in procuring what she has longed for during her pregnancy with them, would not only have handsomely defrayed the charges of the month, but of their education too: her fancy being so exorbitant for the first year or two, as not to confine itself to the usual objects of eatables and drinkables, but running out after equipages and furniture, and the like extravagances. To trouble you only with a few of them: when she was with child of Tom, my eldest son, she came home one day just fainting, and told me she had been visiting a relation, whose husband had made her a present of a chariot and a stately pair of horses; and that she was positive she could not breathe a week longer, unless she took the air in the fellow to it of her own within that time. This, rather than lose an heir, I readily complied with. Then the furniture of her best room must be instantly changed, or she should mark the child with some of the frightful figures in the old fashioned tapestry. Well, the upholsterer was called, and her longing saved that bout. When she went with Molly she had fixed her mind upon a new set of plate, and as much china as would have furnished an Indian shop: these also I cheerfully granted, for fear of being father to an Indian pagod. Hitherto I found her demands rose upon every concession; and had she gone on, I had been ruined: but by good fortune, with her third, which was Peggy, the height of her imagination came down to the corner of a venison pasty, and brought her once even upon her knees to gnaw off the ears of a pig from the spit. The gratifications of her palate were easily preferred to those of her vanity; and sometimes a partridge, or a quail, or a wheatear, or the pestle of a lark, were cheerfully purchased; nay, I could be contented though I were to feed her with green peas in April, or cherries in May. But with the babe she now goes, she is turned girl again, and fallen to eating of chalk, pretending it will make the child's skin white; and nothing will serve her but I must bear her company, to prevent its having a shade of my brown. In this, however, I have ventured to deny her. No longer ago than yesterday, as we were coming to town, she saw a parcel of crows so heartily at breakfast upon a piece of horse-flesh, that she had an invincible desire to partake with them, and (to my infinite surprise) begged the coachman to cut her off a slice, as if it were for himself, which the fellow did; and as soon as she came home, she fell to it with such an appetite, that she seemed rather to devour than eat it. What her next sally will be I cannot guess, but, in the mean time, my request to you is, that if there be any way to come at these wild unaccountable rovings of imagination by reason and argument, you would speedily afford us your assistance. This exceeds the grievance of pin-money; and I think in every settlement there ought to be a clause inserted, that the father should be answerable for the longings of his daughter. But I shall impatiently expect your thoughts in this matter; and am, sir, your most obliged and most faithful humble servant, T. B.

'Let me know whether you think the next child will love horses as much as Molly does china-ware.' T.

No. 327.] *Saturday, March* 15, 1711-12.

——Major rerum mihi nascitur ordo.
Virg. Æn. vii. 43.

A larger scene of action is display'd.—*Dryden.*

WE were told in the foregoing book, how the evil spirit practised upon Eve as she lay asleep, in order to inspire her with thoughts of vanity, pride, and ambition. The author, who shows a wonderful art throughout his whole poem, in preparing the reader for the several occurrences that arise in it, founds, upon the above-mentioned circumstance, the first part of the fifth book. Adam, upon his awaking, finds Eve still asleep, with an unusual discomposure in her looks. The posture in which he regards her is described with a tenderness not to be expressed, as the whisper with which he awakens her is the softest that ever was conveyed to a lover's ear.

His wonder was, to find unwaken'd Eve
With tresses discompos'd, and glowing cheek,
As through unquiet rest: he on his side
Leaning half-rais'd, with looks of cordial love
Hung over her enamour'd, and beheld
Beauty, which, whether waking or asleep,
Shot forth peculiar graces: then, with voice
Mild as when Zephyrus on Flora breathes,

Her hand soft touching, whisper'd thus: 'Awake,
My fairest, my espous'd, my latest found,
Heaven's last best gift, my ever new delight!
Awake: the morning shines, and the fresh field
Calls us; we lose the prime, to mark how spring
Our tender plants, how blows the citron grove,
What drops the myrrh, and what the balmy reed,
How nature paints her colours, how the bee
Sits on the bloom, extracting liquid sweet.'
Such whispering wak'd her, but with startled eye
On Adam, whom embracing, thus she spake:
'O soul, in whom my thoughts find all repose,
My glory, my perfection! glad I see
Thy face, and morn return'd———.'

I cannot but take notice, that Milton, in the conferences between Adam and Eve, had his eye very frequently upon the book of Canticles, in which there is a noble spirit of eastern poetry, and very often not unlike what we meet with in Homer, who is generally placed near the age of Solomon. I think there is no question but the poet in the preceding speech remembered those two passages which are spoken on the like occasion, and filled with the same pleasing images of nature.

'My beloved spake, and said unto me, Rise up, my love, my fair one, and come away! for, lo! the winter is past, the rain is over and gone, the flowers appear on the earth, the time of the singing of birds is come, and the voice of the turtle is heard in our land. The fig-tree putteth forth her green figs, and the vines with the tender grapes give a good smell. Arise, my love, my fair one, and come away!

'Come, my beloved! let us go forth into the field, let us get up early to the vineyards, let us see if the vine flourish, whether the tender grapes appear, and the pomegranates bud forth.'

His preferring the garden of Eden to that

———Where the sapient king
Held dalliance with his fair Egyptian spouse,

shows that the poet had this delightful scene in his mind.

Eve's dream is full of those high conceits engendering pride, which, we are told, the devil endeavoured to instil into her. Of this kind is that part of it where she fancies herself awakened by Adam in the following beautiful lines:

'Why sleep'st thou, Eve? Now is the pleasant time,
The cool, the silent, save where silence yields
To the night-warbling bird, that now awake
Tunes sweetest his love-labour'd song: now reigns
Full-orb'd the moon, and with more pleasing light
Shadowy sets off the face of things. In vain,
If none regard. Heav'n wakes with all his eyes,
Whom to behold but thee, nature's desire;
In whose sight all things joy, with ravishment,
Attracted by thy beauty still to gaze.'

An injudicious poet would have made Adam talk through the whole work in such sentiments as these: but flattery and falsehood are not the courtship of Milton's Adam, and could not be heard by Eve in her state of innocence, excepting only in a dream produced on purpose to taint her imagination. Other vain sentiments of the same kind, in this relation of her dream, will be obvious to every reader. Though the catastrophe of the poem is finely presaged on this occasion, the particulars of it are so artfully shadowed, that they do not anticipate the story which follows in the ninth book. I shall only add, that though the vision itself is founded upon truth, the circumstances of it are full of that wildness and inconsistency which are natural to a dream. Adam, conformable to his superior character for wisdom, instructs and comforts Eve upon this occasion:

So cheer'd he his fair spouse, and she was cheer'd,
But silently a gentle tear let fall
From either eye, and wiped them with her hair;
Two other precious drops, that ready stood
Each in their crystal sluice, he, ere they fell,
Kiss'd, as the gracious signs of sweet remorse
And pious awe, that fear'd to have offended.

The morning hymn is written in imitation of one of those psalms where, in the overflowings of gratitude and praise, the psalmist calls not only upon the angels, but upon the most conspicuous parts of the inanimate creation, to join with him in extolling their common Maker. Invocations of this nature fill the mind with glorious ideas of God's works, and awaken that divine enthusiasm which is so natural to devotion. But if this calling upon the dead parts of nature is at all times a proper kind of worship, it was in a peculiar manner suitable to our first parents, who had the creation fresh upon their minds, and had not seen the various dispensations of Providence, nor consequently could be acquainted with those many topics of praise which might afford matter to the devotions of their posterity. I need not remark the beautiful spirit of poetry which runs through this whole hymn, nor the holiness of that resolution with which it concludes.

Having already mentioned those speeches which are assigned to the persons in this poem, I proceed to the description which the poet gives of Raphael. His departure from before the throne, and his flight through the choirs of angels, is finely imagined. As Milton every where fills his poem with circumstances that are marvellous and astonishing, he describes the gate of heaven as framed after such a manner that it opened of itself upon the approach of the angel who was to pass through it.

———Till at the gate
Of heav'n arriv'd, the gate self-open'd wide,
On golden hinges turning, as, by work
Divine, the sovereign Architect had fram'd.

The poet here seems to have regarded two or three passages in the 18th Iliad, as that in particular where, speaking of Vulcan, Homer says that he had made twenty tripods running on golden wheels; which, upon occasion, might go of themselves to the assembly of the gods, and, when there was no more use for them, return again after the same manner. Scaliger has rallied Homer very severely upon this point, as M. Dacier has endeavoured to defend it. I will not pretend to determine whether, in this particular of Homer, the marvellous does not lose sight of the probable. As the miraculous workmanship of Milton's gates is not so extraordinary as this of the tripods, so I am persuaded he would not have mentioned it, had he not been supported in it by a passage in the Scripture which speaks of wheels in heaven that had life in them, and moved of themselves, or stood still, in conformity with the cherubims, whom they accompanied.

There is no question but Milton had this circumstance in his thoughts; because in the following book he describes the chariot of the Messiah with living wheels, according to the plan in Ezekiel's vision:

——Forth rush'd with whirlwind sound
The chariot of paternal Deity,
Flashing thick flames, wheel within wheel undrawn,
Itself instinct with spirit.——

I question not but Bossu, and the two Daciers, who are for vindicating every thing that is censured in Homer, by something parallel in holy writ, would have been very well pleased had they thought of confronting Vulcan's tripods with Ezekiel's wheels.

Raphael's descent to the earth, with the figure of his person, is represented in very lively colours. Several of the French, Italian, and English poets, have given a loose to their imaginations in the description of angels; but I do not remember to have met with any so finely drawn, and so conformable to the notions which are given of them in Scripture, as this in Milton. After having set him forth in all his heavenly plumage, and represented him as alighted upon the earth, the poet concludes his description with a circumstance which is altogether new, and imagined with the greatest strength of fancy.

——Like Maia's son he stood,
And shook his plumes, that heavenly fragrance fill'd
The circuit wide——

Raphael's reception of the guardian angels, his passing through the wilderness of sweets, his distant appearance to Adam, have all the graces that poetry is capable of bestowing. The author afterwards gives us a particular description of Eve in her domestic employments:

So saying, with despatchful looks in haste
She turns, on hospitable thoughts intent,
What choice to choose for delicacy best,
What order, so contriv'd, as not to mix
Tastes, not well join'd, inelegant, but bring
Taste after taste, upheld with kindliest change;
Bestirs her then, &c.

Though in this, and other parts of the same book, the subject is only the housewifery of our first parent, it is set off with so many pleasing images and strong expressions, as make it none of the least agreeable parts in this divine work.

The natural majesty of Adam, and, at the same time, his submissive behaviour to the superior being who had vouchsafed to be his guest; the solemn 'hail' which the angel bestows upon the mother of mankind, with the figure of Eve ministering at the table; are circumstances which deserve to be admired.

Raphael's behaviour is every way suitable to the dignity of his nature, and to that character of a sociable spirit with which the author has so judiciously introduced him. He had received instructions to converse with Adam, as one friend converses with another, and to warn him of the enemy, who was contriving his destruction: accordingly, he is represented as sitting down at table with Adam, and eating of the fruits of Paradise. The occasion naturally leads him to his discourse on the food of angels. After having thus entered into conversation with man upon more indifferent subjects, he warns him of his obedience, and makes a natural transition to the history of that angel who was employed in the circumvention of our first parents.

Had I followed Monsieur Bossu's method in my first paper on Milton, I should have dated the action of Paradise Lost from the beginning of Raphael's speech in this book, as he supposes the action of the Æneid to begin in the second book of that poem. I could allege many reasons for my drawing the action of the Æneid rather from its immediate beginning in the first book, than from its remote beginning in the second; and show why I have considered the sacking of Troy as an episode, according to the common acceptation of that word. But as this would be a dry unentertaining piece of criticism, and perhaps unnecessary to those who have read my first paper, I shall not enlarge upon it. Whichsoever of the notions be true, the unity of Milton's action is preserved according to either of them; whether we consider the fall of man in its immediate beginning, as proceeding from the resolutions taken in the infernal council, or, in its more remote beginning, as proceeding from the first revolt of the angels in heaven. The occasion which Milton assigns for this revolt, as it is founded on hints in holy writ, and on the opinion of some great writers, so it was the most proper that the poet could have made use of.

The revolt in heaven is described with great force of imagination, and a fine variety of circumstances. The learned reader cannot but be pleased with the poet's imitation of Homer in the last of the following lines:

At length into the limits of the north
They came, and Satan took his royal seat
High on a hill, far blazing, as a mount
Rais'd on a mount, with pyramids and tow'rs
From diamond quarries hewn, and rocks of gold
The palace of great Lucifer, (so call
That structure in the dialect of men
Interpreted.)——

Homer mentions persons and things, which, he tells us, in the language of the gods are called by different names from those they go by in the language of men. Milton has imitated him with his usual judgment in this particular place, wherein he has likewise the authority of scripture to justify him. The part of Abdiel, who was the only spirit that in this infinite host of angels preserved his allegiance to his Maker, exhibits to us a noble moral of religious singularity. The zeal of the seraphim breaks forth in a becoming warmth of sentiments and expressions, as the character which is given us of him denotes that generous scorn and intrepidity which attends heroic virtue. The author doubtless designed it as a pattern to those who live among mankind in their present state of degeneracy and corruption:

So spake the seraph Abdiel, faithful found
Among the faithless, faithful only he;
Among innumerable false, unmov'd,
Unshaken, unseduc'd unterrify'd;
His loyalty he kept, his love, his zeal:
Nor number nor example with him wrought
To swerve from truth, or change his constant mind,
Though single. From amidst them forth he pass'd,
Long way thro' hostile scorn, which he sustain'd
Superior, nor of violence fear'd aught;
And with retorted scorn his back he turn'd
On those proud tow'rs to swift destruction doom'd.

L.

No. 328.] *Monday, March* 17, 1711-12.

Nullum me a labore reclinat otium.
Hor. Epod. xvii. 24.

Day chases night, and night the day,
But no relief to me convey. *Duncombe.*

'Mr. Spectator,—As I believe that this is the first complaint that ever was made to you of this nature, so you are the first person I ever could prevail upon myself to lay it before. When I tell you I have a healthy, vigorous constitution, a plentiful estate, no inordinate desires, and am married to a virtuous lovely woman, who neither wants wit nor good-nature, and by whom I have a numerous offspring to perpetuate my family, you will naturally conclude me a happy man. But notwithstanding these promising appearances, I am so far from it, that the prospect of being ruined and undone by a sort of extravagance, which of late years is in a less degree crept into every fashionable family, deprives me of all the comforts of my life, and renders me the most anxious, miserable man on earth. My wife, who was the only child and darling care of an indulgent mother, employed her early years in learning all those accomplishments we generally understand by good breeding and polite education. She sings, dances, plays on the lute, and harpsichord, paints prettily, is a perfect mistress of the French tongue, and has made a considerable progress in Italian. She is besides excellently skilled in all domestic sciences, as preserving, pickling, pastry, making wines of fruits of our own growth, embroidering, and needleworks of every kind. Hitherto, you will be apt to think, there is very little cause of complaint; but suspend your opinion till I have further explained myself, and then I make no question, you will come over to mine. You are not to imagine I find fault that she either possesses or takes delight in the exercises of those qualifications I just now mentioned; it is the immoderate fondness she has to them that I lament, and that what is only designed for the innocent amusement and recreation of life is become the whole business and study of hers. The six months we are in town, (for the year is equally divided between that and the country,) from almost break of day till noon, the whole morning is laid out in practising with her several masters; and to make up the losses occasioned by her absence in summer, every day in the week their attendance is required; and, as they are all people eminent in their professions, their skill and time must be recompensed accordingly. So, how far these articles extend, I leave you to judge. Limning, one would think, is no expensive diversion; but, as she manages the matter, it is a very considerable addition to her disbursements; which you will easily believe, when you know she paints fans for all her female acquaintance, and draws all her relations' pictures, in miniature: the first must be mounted by nobody but Colmar, and the other set by nobody but Charles Mather.* What follows is still much worse than the former; for, as I told you, she is a great artist at her needle, it is incredible what sums she expends in embroidery; for, besides what is appropriated to her personal use as mantuas, petticoats, stomachers, handkerchiefs, purses, pin-cushions, and working aprons, she keeps four French protestants continually employed in making divers pieces of superfluous furniture, as quilts, toilets, hangings for closets, beds, window-curtains, easy chairs, and tabourets: nor have I any hopes of ever reclaiming her from this extravagance, while she obstinately persists in thinking it a notable piece of good housewifery, because they are made at home, and she has had some share in the performance. There would be no end of relating to you the particulars of the annual charge, in furnishing her storeroom with a profusion of pickles and preserves; for she is not contented with having every thing, unless it be done every way, in which she consults an hereditary book of receipts: for her female ancestors have been always famed for good house-wifery, one of whom is made immortal by giving her name to an eye-water, and two sorts of puddings. I cannot undertake to recites all her medicinal preparations, as salves, sere cloths, powders, confects, cordials, ratafia, persico, orange-flower, and cherry-brandy, together with innumerable sorts of simple waters. But there is nothing I lay so much to my heart as that detestable catalogue of counterfeit wines, which derive their names from the fruits, herbs, or trees, of whose

* A well-known toyman in Fleet-street at the time

juices they are chiefly compounded. They are loathsome to the taste, and pernicious to the health; and as they seldom survive the year, and then are thrown away, under a false pretence of frugality, I may affirm they stand me in more than if I entertained all our visitors with the best burgundy and champaign. Coffee, chocolate, and green imperial, peco, and bohea teas, seem to be trifles; but when the proper appurtenances of the tea-table are added, they swell the account higher than one would imagine. I cannot conclude without doing her justice in one article; where her frugality is so remarkable, I must not deny her the merit of it; and that is in relation to her children, who are all confined, both boys and girls, to one large room in the remotest part of the house, with bolts on the doors and bars to the windows, under the care and tuition of an old woman, who had been dry nurse to her grandmother. This is their residence all the year round; and as they are never allowed to appear, she prudently thinks it needless to be at any expense in apparel or learning. Her eldest daughter to this day would have neither read nor wrote, if it had not been for the butler, who, being the son of a country attorney, has taught her such a hand as is generally used for engrossing bills in Chancery. By this time I have sufficiently tired your patience with my domestic grievances; which I hope you will agree could not well be contained in a narrower compass, when you consider what a paradox I undertook to maintain in the beginning of my epistle, and which manifestly appears to be but too melancholy a truth. And now I heartily wish the relation I have given of my misfortunes may be of use and benefit to the public. By the example I have set before them, the truly virtuous wives may learn to avoid those errors which have so unhappily misled mine, and which are visibly these three; First, in mistaking the proper objects of her esteem, and fixing her affections upon such things as are only the trappings and decorations of her sex: Secondly, in not distinguishing what becomes the different stages of life. And, lastly, the abuse and corruption of some excellent qualities, which, if circumscribed within just bounds, would have been the blessing and prosperity of her family; but by a vicious extreme, are like to be the bane and destruction of it.'

T.†

No. 328.*] *Monday, March* 17, 1711-12.

Delectata illa urbanitate tam stulta.

Petron. Arb.

Delighted with unaffected plainness.

THAT useful part of learning which consists in emendations, knowledge of different readings, and the like, is what in all ages persons extremely wise and learned have had in great veneration. For this reason I cannot but rejoice at the following epistle, which lets us into the true author of the letter to Mrs. Margaret Clark, part of which I did myself the honour to publish in a former paper. I must confess I do not naturally affect critical learning; but finding myself not so much regarded as I am apt to flatter myself I may deserve from some professed patrons of learning, I could not but do myself the justice to show I am not a stranger to such erudition as they smile upon, if I were duly encouraged. However, this is only to let the world see what I could do: and shall not give my reader any more of this kind, if he will forgive the ostentation I show at present.

'March 13, 1711-12.

'SIR,—Upon reading your paper of yesterday, I took the pains to look out a copy I had formerly taken, and remembered to be very like your last letter: comparing them, I found they were the very same; and have, underwritten, sent you that part of it which you say was torn off. I hope you will insert it, that posterity may know it was Gabriel Bullock that made love in that natural style of which you seem to be fond. But to let you see I have other manuscripts in the same way, I have sent you inclosed three copies, faithfully taken by my own hand from the originals, which were wrote by a Yorkshire gentleman of a good estate, to madam Mary, and an uncle of hers, a knight very well known by the most ancient gentry in that and several other counties of Great Britain. I have exactly followed the form and spelling. I have been credibly informed that Mr. William Bullock, the famous comedian, is the descendant of this Gabriel, who begot Mr. William Bullock's great-grandfather, on the body of the above-mentioned Mrs. Margaret Clark. As neither Speed, nor Baker, nor Selden, take notice of it, I will not pretend to be positive; but desire that the letter may be reprinted, and what is here recovered may be in Italics. I am, sir, your daily reader.'

'*To her I very much respect, Mrs. Margaret Clark.*

'Lovely, and oh that I could write loving, Mrs. Margaret Clark, I pray you let affection excuse presumption. Having been so happy as to enjoy the sight of your sweet countenance and comely body sometimes when I had occasion to buy treacle or liquorish powder at the apothecary's shop, I am so enamoured with you, that I can no more keep close my flaming desire to become your servant. And I am the more bold now to write to your sweet self, because I am now my own man, and may match where I please; for my father is taken away; and now I am come to my

† The above Paper was very early substituted for the one now immediately following, which latter is here reprinted from the original folio, numbered, as at first, 328.*

living, which is ten yard land, and a house; and there is never a yard land* in our field but is as well worth ten pounds a year as a thief's worth a halter; and all my brothers and sisters are provided for: besides, I have good household stuff, though I say it, both brass and pewter, linens and woollens; and though my house be thatched, yet if you and I match, it shall go hard but I will have one half of it slated. If you shall think well of this motion, I will wait upon you as soon as my new clothes are made, and hay-harvest is in. I could, though I say it, have good *matches in our town; but my mother (God's peace be with her,) charged me upon her death-bed to marry a gentlewoman, one who had been well trained up in the sowing and cookery. I do not think but that if you and I can agree to marry, and lay our means together, I shall be made grand jury-man ere two or three years come about, and that will be a great credit to us. If I could have got a messenger for sixpence, I would have sent one on purpose, and some trifle or other for a token of my love: but I hope there is nothing lost for that neither. So, hoping you will take this letter in good part, and answer it with what care and speed you can, I rest and remain,* yours, if my own,

'Mr. GABRIEL BULLOCK,
'now my father is dead.

'Swepston, Leicestershire.

'When the coal carts come, I shall send oftener; and may come in one of them myself.'†

'For sir William to go to london at westminster remember a parlement.

'Sir,—William, i hope that you are well. i write to let you know that i am in troubel about a lady your nease; and i do desire that you will be my friend: for when i did com to see her at your hall, i was mighty Abuesed. i would fain a see you at topecliff, and thay would not let me go to you; but i desire that you will be our friends, for it is no dishonour neither for you nor she, for God did make us all. i wish that i might see you, for thay say that you are a good man; and many doth wounder at it, but madam norton is abuesed and ceated two i believe. i might a had many a lady, but i con have none but her with a good consons, for there is a God that know our hearts. if you and madam norton will come to York, there i shill meet you if God be willing and if you be pleased. so be not angterie till you know the trutes of things.

'George Nelson. 'I give my to me lady and to Mr. Aysenby, and to madam norton, March the 19th, 1706.'

* "In some counties 20, in some 24, and in others 30 acres of land. *Virgata Terra.*"

† See No. 324, and note.

'This is for madam mary norton disforth Lady she went to York.

'Madam Mary. Deare loving sweet lady, i hope you are well. Do not go to london, for they will put you in the nunnery; and heed not Mrs. Lucy what she saith to you, for she will ly and ceat you. go from to another place, and we will gate wed so with speed. mind what i write to you, for if they gate you to london they will keep you there; and so let us gate wed, and we will both go. so if you go to london, you rueing yourself. so heed not what none of them saith to you let us gate wed, and we shall lie to gader any time. i will do any thing for you to my poore. i hope the devil will faile them all, for a hellish company there be. from there cursed trick and mischiefus ways good lord bless and deliver both you and me.

'I think to be at York the 24 day.'

'This is for madam mary norton to go to london for a lady that belongs to dishforth.

'Madam Mary, i hope you are well. i am soary that you went away from York. deare loving sweet lady, i writ to let you know that i do remain faithfull; and if can let me know where i can meet you, i will wed you, and i will do any thing to my poor; for you are a good woman, and will be a loving misteris. i am in trouble for you, so if you will come to york i will wed you. so with speed come, and i will have none but you. so, sweet love, heed not what to say to me, and with speed come; heed not what none of them say to you; your Maid makes you believe ought.

'So deare love think of Mr. george Nillson with speed; i sent 2 or 3 letters before.

'I gave misteris elcock some nots, and thay put me in pruson all the night for me pains, and non new whear I was, and i did gat cold.

'But it is for mrs. Lucy to go a good way from home, for in york and round about she is known; to writ any more her deeds, the same will tell her soul is black within, her corkis stinks of hell. March 19th, 1706.'‡

No. 329.] *Tuesday, March* 18, 1711-12.

Ire tamen restat, Numo qua devenit et Ancus.
Hor. Ep. vi. Lib. 1. 27.

With Ancus, and with Numa, kings of Rome,
We must descend into the silent tomb.

My friend Sir Roger de Coverley told me t'other night, that he had been reading my paper upon Westminster-abbey, in which, says he, there are a great many ingenious fancies. He told me at the same

‡ In the original folio edition of the Spectator, the following letter is added to No. 330; it is given here as evidently relating to this paper, which, as already observed, was suppressed soon after its first publication. See 328.*

'March 18, 1711-12.

'Mr. Spectator,—The ostentation you showed yesterday [March 17] would have been pardonable, had time, that he observed I had promised another paper upon the tombs, and that he should be glad to go and see them with me, not having visited them since he had read history. I could not imagine how this came into the knight's head, till I recollected that he had been very busy all last summer upon Baker's Chronicle, which he has quoted several times in his disputes with Sir Andrew Freeport since his last coming to town. Accordingly I promised to call upon him the next morning, that we might go together to the abbey.

I found the knight under his butler's hands, who always shaves him. He was no sooner dressed, than he called for a glass of the widow Truby's water, which he told me he always drank before he went abroad. He recommended to me a dram of it at the same time, with so much heartiness, that I could not forbear drinking it. As soon as I had got it down, I found it very unpalatable; upon which the knight, observing that I had made several wry faces, told me that he knew I should not like it at first, but that it was the best thing in the world against the stone or gravel.

I could have wished indeed that he had acquainted me with the virtues of it sooner; but it was too late to complain, and I knew what he had done was out of good will. Sir Roger told me further, that he looked upon it to be very good for a man whilst he staid in town, to keep off infection, and that he got together a quantity of it upon the first news of the sickness being at Dantzick: when of a sudden turning short to one of his servants, who stood behind him, he bid him call a hackney-coach, and take care it was an elderly man that drove it.

He then resumed the discourse upon Mrs. Truby's water, telling me that the widow Truby was one who did more good than all the doctors and apothecaries in the country; that she distilled every poppy that grew within five miles of her; that she distributed her water gratis among all sorts of people: to which the knight added that she had a very great jointure, and that the whole country would fain have it a match between him and her; 'and truly,' says Sir Roger, 'if I had not been engaged, perhaps I could not have done better.'

His discourse was broken off by his man's telling him he had called a coach. Upon our going to it, after having cast his eye upon the wheels, he asked the coachman if his axle-tree was good: upon the fellow's telling him he would warrant it, the knight turned to me, told me he looked like an honest man, and went in without further ceremony.

We had not gone far, when Sir Roger popping out his head, called the coachman down from his box, and, upon presenting himself at the window, asked him if he smoked. As I was considering what this would end in, he bid him stop by the way at any good tobacconist's, and take in a roll of their best Virginia. Nothing material happened in the remaining part of our journey, till we were set down at the west end of the abbey.

As we went up the body of the church, the knight pointed at the trophies upon one of the new monuments, and cried out, 'A brave man, I warrant him!' Passing afterwards by Sir Cloudesly Shovel, he flung his hand that way, and cried, "Sir Cloudesly Shovel! a very gallant man.' As we stood before Busby's tomb, the knight uttered himself again after the same manner: 'Dr. Busby: a great man: he whipped my grandfather; a very great man, I should have gone to him myself, if I had not been a blockhead: a very great man!'

We were immediately conducted into the little chapel on the right hand. Sir Roger, planting himself at our historian's elbow, was very attentive to every thing he said, particularly to the account he gave us of the lord who had cut off the king of Morocco's head. Among several other figures, he was very well pleased to see the statesman Cecil upon his knees; and concluding them all to be great men, was conducted to the figure which represents that martyr to good housewifery who died by the prick of a needle. Upon our interpreter's telling us that she was a maid of honour to queen Elizabeth, the knight was very inquisitive into her name and family; and, after having regarded her finger for some time, 'I wonder,' says he, 'that Sir Richard Baker has said nothing of her in his Chronicle.'

We were then conveyed to the two coronation chairs, where my old friend, after having heard that the stone underneath the most ancient of them, which was brought from Scotland, was called Jacob's pillar, sat himself down in the chair, and, looking like the figure of an old Gothic king, asked our interpreter, what authority they had to say that Jacob had ever been in Scotland? The fellow instead of returning him an answer, told him, that he hoped his honour would pay his forfeit. I could observe Sir Roger a little ruffled upon being thus trepanned; but our guide not insisting upon his demand, the knight soon recovered his good humour, and whispered in my ear, that if Will Wimble were with us and saw those two chairs, it would go hard but he would get a tobacco stopper out of one or t'other of them.

Sir Roger, in the next place, laid his hand upon Edward the Third's sword, and, leaning upon the pummel of it, gave

---

you provided better for the two extremities of your paper, and placed in the one the letter R. in the other,

Nescio quid meditans nugarum et totus in illis.

A word to the wise. I am your most humble servant.
T. TRASH.

According to the emendation of the above correspondent, the reader is desired, in the paper of the 17th, to read R for T.'

us the whole history of the Black Prince; concluding, that, in Sir Richard Baker's opinion, Edward the Third was one of the greatest princes that ever sat upon the English throne.

We were then shown Edward the Confessor's tomb: upon which Sir Roger acquainted us, that he was the first who touched for the evil: and afterwards Henry the Fourth's; upon which he shook his head, and told us there was fine reading in the casualties of that reign.

Our conductor then pointed to that monument where there is the figure of one of our English kings without a head; and upon giving us to know, that the head, which was of beaten silver, had been stolen away several years since: 'Some Whig, I'll warrant you,' says Sir Roger; 'you ought to lock up your kings better; they will carry off the body too, if you don't take care.'

The glorious names of Henry the Fifth and queen Elizabeth gave the knight great opportunities of shining, and of doing justice to Sir Richard Baker, who, as our knight observed with some surprise, had a great many kings in him, whose monuments he had not seen in the abbey.

For my own part, I could not but be pleased to see the knight show such an honest passion for the glory of his country, and such a respectful gratitude to the memory of its princes.

I must not omit, that the benevolence of my good old friend, which flows out towards every one he converses with, made him very kind to our interpreter, whom he looked upon as an extraordinary man: for which reason he shook him by the hand at parting, telling him, that he should be very glad to see him at his lodgings in Norfolk-buildings, and talk over these matters with him more at leisure. L.

No. 330.] *Wednesday, March* 19, 1711-12.

Maxima debetur pueris reverentia——

Juv. Sat. xiv. 47.

To youth the greatest reverence is due.

The following letters, written by two very considerate correspondents, both under twenty years of age, are very good arguments of the necessity of taking into consideration the many incidents which affect the education of youth.

'Sir—I have long expected that, in the course of your observations upon the several parts of human life, you would one time or other fall upon a subject, which, since you have not, I take the liberty to recommend to you. What I mean is, the patronage of young modest men to such as are able to countenance and introduce them into the world. For want of such assistances, a youth of merit languishes in obscurity or poverty when his circumstances are low, and runs into riot and excess when his fortunes are plentiful. I cannot make myself better understood, than by sending you a history of myself, which I shall desire you to insert in your paper, it being the only way I have of expressing my gratitude for the highest obligations imaginable.

'I am the son of a merchant of the city of London, who, by many losses, was reduced from a very luxuriant trade and credit to very narrow circumstances, in comparison to that of his former abundance. This took away the vigour of his mind, and all manner of attention to a fortune which he now thought desperate; insomuch that he died without a will, having before buried my mother, in the midst of his other misfortunes. I was sixteen years of age when I lost my father; and an estate of 200*l.* a year came into my possession, without friend or guardian to instruct me in the management or enjoyment of it. The natural consequence of this was (though I wanted no director, and soon had fellows who found me out for a smart young gentleman, and led me into all the debaucheries of which I was capable,) that my companions and I could not well be supplied without running in debt, which I did very frankly, till I was arrested, and conveyed, with a guard strong enough for the most desperate assassin, to a bailiff's house, where I lay four days, surrounded with very merry, but not very agreeable company. As soon as I had extricated myself from that shameful confinement, I reflected upon it with so much horror, that I deserted all my old acquaintance, and took chambers in an inn of court, with a resolution to study the law with all possible application. I trifled away a whole year in looking over a thousand intricacies, without a friend to apply to in any case of doubt; so that I only lived there among men, as little children are sent to school before they are capable of improvement, only to be out of harm's way. In the midst of this state of suspense, not knowing how to dispose of myself, I was sought for by a relation of mine, who, upon observing a good inclination in me, used me with great familiarity, and carried me to his seat in the country. When I came there, he introduced me to all the good company in the county; and the great obligation I have to him for this kind notice, and residence with him ever since, has made so strong an impression upon me, that he has an authority of a father over me, founded upon the love of a brother. I have a good study of books, a good stable of horses, always at my command; and though I am not now quite eighteen years of age, familiar converse on his part, and a strong inclination to exert myself on mine, have had an effect upon me that makes me acceptable wherever I go. Thus, Mr. Spectator, by this gentleman's favour and patronage, it is my own fault if I am not wiser and richer every day I live. I speak this, as well by subscribing the initial letters of my name to thank him, as to incite others to an imitation of his virtue. It would be a worthy work to show what great charities are to be done without expense, and how many noble actions are lost, out of inadvertency, in persons capable of performing them, if they were put in mind of it. If a gentleman of figure in a county would make his family a pattern of sobriety, good sense, and breeding, and would kindly endeavour to influence the education and growing prospect of the younger gentry about him, I am apt to believe it would save him a great deal of stale beer on a public occasion, and render him the leader of his county from their gratitude to him, instead of being a slave to their riots and tumults in order to be made their representative. The same thing might be recommended to all who have made any progress in any parts of knowledge, or arrived at any degree in a profession Others may gain preferments and fortunes from their patrons; but I have, I hope, received from mine good habits and virtues. I repeat to you, sir, my request to print this, in return for all the evil a helpless orphan shall ever escape, and all the good he shall receive in this life; both which are wholly owing to this gentleman's favour to, sir, your most obedient servant, S. P.'

'Mr. Spectator—I am a lad of about fourteen. I find a mighty pleasure in learning. I have been at the Latin school four years. I don't know I ever played truant, or neglected any task my master set me in my life. I think on what I read in the school as I go home at noon and night, and so intently, that I have often gone half a mile out of my way, not minding whither I went. Our maid tells me she often hears me talk Latin in my sleep, and I dream two or three nights in a week I am reading Juvenal and Homer. My master seems as well pleased with my performances as any boy's in the same class. I think, if I know my own mind, I would choose rather to be a scholar than a prince without learning. I have a very good, affectionate father; but though very rich, yet so mighty near, that he thinks much of the charges of my education. He often tells me he believes my schooling will ruin him; that I cost him God knows what, in books. I tremble to tell him I want one. I am forced to keep my pocket-money, and lay it out for a book now and then, that he don't know of. He has ordered my master to buy no more books for me, but says he will buy them himself. I asked him for Horace t'other day, and he told me in a passion he did not believe I was fit for it, but only my master had a mind to make him think I had got a great way in my learning. I am sometimes a month behind other boys in getting the books my master gives orders for. All the boys in the school, but I, have the classic authors *in usum Delphini*, gilt and lettered on the back. My father is often reckoning up how long I have been at school, and tells me he fears I do little good. My father's carriage so discourages me, that he makes me grow dull and melancholy. My master wonders what is the matter with with me; I am afraid to tell him; for he is a man that loves to encourage learning, and would be apt to chide my father, and, not knowing his temper, may make him worse. Sir, if you have any love for learning, I beg you would give me some instructions in this case, and persuade parents to encourage their children when they find them diligent and desirous of learning. I have heard some parents say, they would do any thing for their children, if they would but mind their learning: I would be glad to be in their place. Dear sir, pardon my boldness. If you will but consider and pity my case, I will pray for your prosperity as long as I live. Your humble servant,

'JAMES DISCIPULUS.

'London, March 2, 1711.' T.

No. 331.] *Thursday, March* 20, 1711-12.

——— Stolidam præbet tibi vellere barbam.
Pers. Sat. ii. 28.

Holds out his foolish beard for thee to pluck.

When I was last with my friend Sir Roger in Westminster-abbey, I observed that he stood longer than ordinary before the bust of a venerable old man. I was at a loss to guess the reason of it; when, after some time, he pointed to the figure, and asked me if I did not think that our forefathers looked much wiser in their beards than we do without them? 'For my part,' says he, 'when I am walking in my gallery in the country, and see my ancestors, who many of them died before they were of my age, I cannot forbear regarding them as so many old patriarchs, and at the same time, looking upon myself as an idle smock-faced young fellow. I love to see your Abrahams, your Isaacs, and your Jacobs, as we have them in old pieces of tapestry, with beards below their girdles, that cover half the hangings.' The knight added, 'if I would recommend beards in one of my papers, and endeavour to restore human faces to their ancient dignity, that, upon a month's warning he would undertake to lead up the fashion himself in a pair of whiskers.'

I smiled at my friend's fancy; but, after we parted, could not forbear reflecting on the metamorphosis our faces have undergone in this particular.

The beard, conformable to the notion of my friend Sir Roger, was for many ages looked upon as the type of wisdom. Lucian more than once rallies the philosophers of his time, who endeavoured to rival one an other in beards; and represents a learned man who stood for a professorship in philosophy, as unqualified for it by the shortness of his beard.

Ælian, in his account of Zoilus, the pretended critic, who wrote against Homer and Plato, and thought himself wiser than all who had gone before him, tells us that this Zoilus had a very long beard that hung down upon his breast, but no hair upon his head, which he always kept close shaved, regarding, it seems, the hairs of his head as so many suckers, which if they had been suffered to grow, might have drawn away the nourishment from his chin, and by that means have starved his beard.

I have read somewhere, that one of the popes refused to accept an edition of a saint's works, which were presented to him, because the saint, in his effigies before the book, was drawn without a beard.

We see by these instances what homage the world has formerly paid to beards; and that a barber was not then allowed to make those depredations on the faces of the learned, which have been permitted him of late years.

Accordingly several wise nations have been so extremely jealous of the least ruffle offered to their beards, that they seem to have fixed the point of honour principally in that part. The Spaniards were wonderfully tender in this particular. Don Quevedo, in his third vision on the last judgment, has carried the humour very far, when he tells us that one of his vainglorious countrymen, after having received sentence, was taken into custody by a couple of evil spirits; but that his guides happening to disorder his mustaches, they were forced to recompose them with a pair of curling-irons, before they could get him to file off.

If we look into the history of our own nation, we shall find that the beard flourished in the Saxon heptarchy, but was very much discouraged under the Norman line. It shot out, however, from time to time, in several reigns under different shapes. The last effort it made seems to have been in queen Mary's days, as the curious reader may find if he pleases to peruse the figures of Cardinal Pole and Bishop Gardiner: though, at the same time, I think it may be questioned, if zeal against popery has not induced our protestant painters to extend the beards of these two persecutors beyond their natural dimensions, in order to make them appear the more terrible.

I find but few beards worth taking notice of in the reign of King James the first.

During the civil wars there appeared one, which makes too great a figure in story to be passed over in silence: I mean that of the redoubted Hudibras, an account of which Butler has transmitted to posterity in the following lines:

'His tawny beard was th' equal grace
Both of his wisdom and his face;
In cut and dye so like a tile,
A sudden view it would beguile;
The upper part thereof was whey,
The nether orange mixt with grey.'

The whisker continued for some time among us after the expiration of beards; but this is a subject which I shall not here enter upon, having discussed it at large in a distinct treatise, which I keep by me in manuscript, upon the mustache.

If my friend Sir Roger's project of introducing beards should take effect, I fear the luxury of the present age would make it a very expensive fashion. There is no question but the beaux would soon provide themselves with false ones of the lightest colours and the most immoderate lengths. A fair beard of the tapestry size, which Sir Roger seems to approve, could not come under twenty guineas. The famous golden beard of Æsculapius would hardly be more valuable than one made in the extravagance of the fashion.

Besides, we are not certain that the ladies would not come into the mode, when they take the air on horseback. They already appear in hats and feathers, coats and periwigs; and I see no reason why we may not suppose that they would have their riding-beards on the same occasion.

N. B. I may give the moral of this discourse in another paper. X.

No. 332.] *Friday, March* 21, 1712.

————Minus aptus acutis
Naribus horum hominum——*Hor.* Sat. iii. Lib. 1. 29.

He cannot bear the raillery of the age. *Creech.*

'Dear Short Face,—In your speculation of Wednesday last, you have given us some account of that worthy society of brutes the Mohocks, wherein you have particularly specified the ingenious performances of the lion-tippers, the dancing-masters, and the tumblers; but as you acknowledged you had not then a perfect history of the whole club, you might very easily omit one of the most notable species of it, the sweaters, which may be reckoned a sort of dancing-masters too. It is, it seems, the custom for half a dozen, or more, of these well-disposed savages, as soon as they have enclosed the person upon whom they design the favour of a sweat, to whip out their swords, and holding them parallel to the horizon, they describe a sort of magic circle round about him with the points. As soon as this piece of conjuration is performed, and the patient without doubt already beginning to wax warm, to forward the operation, that member of the circle towards whom he is so rude as to turn his back first, runs his sword directly into that part of the patient whereon school-boys are punished; and as it is very natural to imagine this will soon make him tack about to some other point, every gentleman does himself the same justice as often as he receives the affront. After this jig has gone two or three times round, and the patient is thought to have sweat sufficiently, he is very handsomely rubbed down by some attendants, who carry with them instruments for that purpose, and so discharged. This relation I had from a friend of mine, who has lately been under this discipline. He tells me he had the honour to dance before the emperor himself, not without the applause and acclamations both of his imperial majesty and the whole ring; though I dare say, neither I, nor any of his acquaintance, ever dreamt he would have merited any reputation by his activity.

'I can assure you, Mr. Spectator, I was very near being qualified to have given you a faithful and painful account of this walking bagnio, if I may so call it, myself. Going the other night along Fleet-street, and having, out of curiosity, just entered into discourse with a wandering female who was travelling the same way, a couple of fellows advanced towards us, drew their swords, and cried out to each other, "A sweat! a sweat!" Whereon, suspecting they were some of the ring-leaders of the bagnio, I also drew my sword, and demanded a parley; but finding none would be granted me, and perceiving others behind them filing off with great diligence to take me in flank, I began to sweat for fear of being forced to it: but very luckily betaking myself to a pair of heels, which I had good reason to believe would do me justice, I instantly got possession of a very snug corner in a neighbouring alley that lay in my rear; which post I maintained for above half an hour with great firmness and resolution, though not letting this success so far overcome me as to make me unmindful of the circumspection that was necessary to be observed upon my advancing again towards the street; by which prudence and good management I made a handsome and orderly retreat, having suffered no other damage in this action than the loss of my baggage, and the dislocation of one of my shoe heels, which last I am just now informed is in a fair way of recovery. These sweaters, by what I can learn from my friend, and by as near a view as I was able to take of them myself, seem to me to have at present but a rude kind of discipline among them. It is probable, if you would take a little pains with them, they might be brought into better order. But I'll leave this to your own discretion; and will only add, that if you think it worth while to insert this by way of caution to those who have a mind to preserve their skins whole from this sort of cupping, and tell them at the same time the hazard of treating with night-walkers, you will perhaps oblige others, as well as your very humble servant,

'JACK LIGHTFOOT.

'P. S. My friend will have me acquaint you, that though he would not willingly detract from the merit of that extraordinary strokesman Mr. Sprightly, yet it is his real opinion, that some of those fellows who are employed as rubbers to this new-fashioned bagnio, have struck as bold strokes as ever he did in his life.

'I had sent this four-and-twenty hours sooner, if I had not had the misfortune of being in a great doubt about the orthography of the word bagnio. I consulted several dictionaries, but found no relief: at last having recourse both to the bagnio in Newgate street, and to that in Chancery-lane, and finding the original manuscripts upon the sign-posts of each to agree literally with my own spelling, I returned home full of satisfaction in order to despatch this epistle.'

'MR. SPECTATOR—As you have taken most of the circumstances of human life into your consideration, we the underwritten thought it not improper for us also to represent to you our condition. We are three ladies who live in the country, and the greatest improvement we make is by reading. We have taken a small journal of our lives, and find it extremely opposite to your last Tuesday's speculation. We rise by seven, and pass the beginning of each day in devotion, and looking into those affairs that fall within the occurrences of a retired life; in the afternoon we sometimes enjoy the good company of some friend or neighbour, or else work or read: at night we retire to our chambers, and take leave of each other for the whole night at ten o'clock. We take particular care never to be sick of a Sunday. Mr. Spectator, we are all very good maids, but ambitious of characters which we think more laudable, that of being very good wives. If any of your correspondents inquire for a spouse for an honest country gentleman, whose estate is not dipped, and wants a wife that can save half his revenue, and yet make a better figure than any of his neighbours of the same estate, with finer bred women, you shall have further notice from, sir, your courteous readers,

'MARTHA BUSIE,
'DEBORAH THRIFTY,
T. 'ALICE EARLY.'

No. 333.] *Saturday, March* 22, 1711-12.

——vocat in certamina divos.—*Virg.*

He calls embattled deities to arms.

WE are now entering upon the sixth book of Paradise Lost, in which the poet describes the battle of the angels; having raised his reader's expectation, and prepared him for it by several passages in the preceding books. I omitted quoting these passages in my observations on the former books, having purposely reserved them for the opening of this, the subject of which gave occasion to them. The author's imagination was so inflamed with this great scene of action, that wherever he speaks of it, he rises, if possible, above himself. Thus, where he mentions Satan in the beginning of his poem,

——Him the almighty Power
Hurl'd headlong flaming from th' ethereal sky,
With hideous ruin and combustion, down
To bottomless perdition, there to dwell
In adamantine chains and penal fire,
Who durst defy th' Omnipotent to arms.

We have likewise several noble hints of it n the infernal conference:

'O prince! O chief of many throned powers,
That led the embattled seraphim to war,
Too well I see and rue the dire event,
That with sad overthrow and foul defeat
Hath lost us heav'n; and all this mighty host
In horrible destruction laid thus low.
But see! the angry victor has recall'd
His ministers of vengeance and pursuit
Back to the gates of heav'n. The sulphurous hai
Shot after us in storm, o'erblown, hath laid
The fiery surge, that from the precipice
Of heav'n received us falling; and the thunder,
Wing'd with red lightning and impetuous rage,
Perhaps has spent his shafts, and ceases now
To bellow through the vast and boundless deep.

There are several other very sublime images on the same subject in the first book, as also in the second:

'What when we fled amain, pursued and struck
With heav'n's afflicting thunder, and besought
The deep to shelter us; this hell then seem'd
A refuge from those wounds——————'

In short, the poet never mentions any thing of this battle, but in such images of greatness and terror as are suitable to the subject. Among several others I cannot forbear quoting that passage where the Power, who is described as presiding over the chaos, speaks in the second book:

Thus Satan; and him thus the Anarch old,
With fault'ring speech and visage incompos'd,
Answer'd: "I know thee, stranger, who thou art,
That mighty leading angel, who of late
Made head against heav'n's King, though overthrown
I saw and heard; for such a numerous host
Fled not in silence through the frighted deep
With ruin upon ruin, rout on rout,
Confusion worse confounded; and heaven's gates
Pour'd out by millions her victorious bands
Pursuing——————

It required great pregnancy of invention, and strength of imagination, to fill this battle with such circumstances as should raise and astonish the mind of the reader; and at the same time an exactness of judgment, to avoid every thing that might appear light or trivial. Those who look into Homer are surprised to find his battles still rising one above another, and improving in horror to the conclusion of the Iliad. Milton's fight of angels is wrought up with the same beauty. It is ushered in with such signs of wrath as are suitable to Omnipotence incensed. The first engagement is carried on under a cope of fire, occasioned by the flights of innumerable burning darts and arrows which are discharged from either host. The second onset is still more terrible, as it is filled with those artificial thunders, which seem to make the victory doubtful, and produce a kind of consternation even in the good angels. This is followed by the tearing up of mountains and promontories; till in the last place Messiah comes forth in the fulness of majesty and terror. The pomp of his appearance, amidst the roarings of his thunders, the flashes of his lightnings, and the noise of his chariot wheels, is described with the utmost flights of human imagination.

There is nothing in the firs and last days' engagement, which does not appear natural, and agreeable enough to the ideas most readers would conceive of a fight between two armies of angels.

The second day's engagement is apt to startle an imagination which has not been raised and qualified for such a description by the reading of the ancient poets, and of Homer in particular. It was certainly a very bold thought in our author, to ascribe the first use of artillery to the rebel angels. But as such a pernicious invention may be well supposed to have proceeded from such authors, so it enters very properly into the thoughts of that being, who is all along described as aspiring to the majesty of his Maker. Such engines were the only instruments he could have made use of to imitate those thunders, that in all poetry, both sacred and profane, are represented as the arms of the Almighty. The tearing up the hills was not altogether so daring a thought as the former. We are, in some measure, prepared for such an incident by the description of the giants' war, which we meet with among the ancient poets. What still made this circumstance the more proper for the poet's use, is the opinion of many learned men, that the fable of the giants' war, which makes as great a noise in antiquity, and gave birth to the sublimest description in Hesiod's works, was an allegory founded upon this very tradition of a fight between the good and bad angels.

It may, perhaps, be worth while to consider with what judgment Milton, in this narration, has avoided every thing that is mean and trivial in the description of the Latin and Greek poets; and at the same time improved every great hint which he met with in their works upon this subject. Homer, in that passage which Longinus has celebrated for its sublimeness, and which Virgil and Ovid have copied after him, tells us, that the giants threw Ossa upon Olympus, and Pelion upon Ossa. He adds an epithet to Pelion (εἰνοσίφυλλον) which very much swells the idea, by bringing up to the reader's imagination all the woods that grew upon it. There is further a greater beauty in his singling out by names these three remarkable mountains so well known to the Greeks. This last is such a beauty, as the scene of Milton's war could not possibly furnish him with. Claudian, in his fragment upon the giants' war, has given full scope to that wildness of imagination which was natural to him. He tells us that the giants tore up whole islands by the roots, and threw them at the gods. He describes one of them in particular taking up Lemnos in his arms, and whirling it to the skies, with all Vulcan's shop in the midst of it. Another tears up mount Ida, with the river Enipeus, which ran down the sides of it; but the poet, not content to describe him with this mountain upon his shoulders, tells us that the river flowed down his back as he held it up in that posture. It is visible to every judicious reader, that such ideas savour more of the burlesque than of the sublime. They proceed from a wantonness of imagination, and rather divert the mind than astonish it. Milton has taken every thing that is sublime in these several passages, and composes out of them the following great image:

From their foundations loos'ning to and fro,
They pluck'd the seated hills, with all their load,
Rocks, waters, woods, and by the shaggy tops
Uplifting bore them in their hands.

We have the full majesty of Homer in this short description, improved by the imagination of Claudian, without its puerilities.

I need not point out the description of the fallen angels seeing the promontories hanging over their heads in such a dreadful manner, with the other numberless beauties in this book, which are so conspicuous, that they cannot escape the notice of the most ordinary reader.

There are indeed so many wonderful strokes of poetry in this book, and such a variety of sublime ideas, that it would have been impossible to have given them a place within the bounds of this paper. Besides that I find it in a great measure done to my hand at the end of my lord Roscommon's Essay on Translated Poetry. I shall refer my reader thither for some of the master-strokes of the sixth book of Paradise Lost, though at the same time there are many others which that noble author has not taken notice of.

Milton, notwithstanding the sublime genius he was master of, has in this book drawn to his assistance all the helps he could meet with among the ancient poets. The sword of Michael, which makes so great a havoc among the bad angels, was given him, we are told, out of the armoury of God:

———But the sword
Of Michael from the armoury of God
Was giv'n him, temper'd so, that neither keen
Nor solid might resist that edge: it met
The sword of Satan, with steep force to smite
Descending, and in half cut sheer———

This passage is a copy of that in Virgil, wherein the poet tells us, that the sword of Æneas, which was given him by a deity, broke into pieces the sword of Turnus, which came from a mortal forge. As the moral in this place is divine, so by the way we may observe, that the bestowing on a man who is favoured by heaven such an allegorical weapon is very conformable to the old eastern way of thinking. Not only Homer has made use of it, but we find the Jewish hero in the book of Maccabees, who had fought the battles of the chosen people with so much glory and success, receiving in his dream a sword from the hand of the prophet Jeremiah. The following passage, wherein Satan is described as wounded by the sword of Michael, is in imitation of Homer:

The griding sword with discontinuous wound
Pass'd through him; but th' ethereal substance clos'd
Not long divisible; and from the gash
A stream of nectarous humour issuing flow'd
Sanguine, (such as celestial spirits may bleed)
And all his armour stain'd———

Homer tells us in the same manner, that upon Diomede's wounding the gods, there flowed from the wound an ichor, or pure kind of blood, which was not bred from mortal viands; and that though the pain was exquisitely great, the wound soon closed up and healed in those beings who are vested with immortality.

I question not but Milton, in his description of his furious Moloch flying from the battle, and bellowing with the wound he had received, had his eye on Mars in the Iliad; who, upon his being wounded, is represented as retiring out of the fight, and making an outcry louder than that of a whole army when it begins the charge. Homer adds, that the Greeks and Trojans who were engaged in a general battle, were terrified on each side with the bellowing of this wounded deity. The reader will easily observe how Milton has kept all the horror of this image without running into the ridicule of it:

———Where the might of Gabriel fought,
And with fierce ensigns pierc'd the deep array
Of Moloch, furious king! who him defy'd,
And at his chariot-wheels to drag him bound
Threaten'd, nor from the Holy One of heav'n
Refrain'd his tongue blasphemous: but anon
Down cloven to the waist, with shatter'd arms
And uncouth pain, fled bellowing———

Milton has likewise raised his description in this book with many images taken out of the poetical parts of scripture. The Messiah's chariot, as I have before taken notice, is formed upon a vision of Ezekiel, who, as Grotius observes, has very much in him of Homer's spirit in the poetical parts of his prophecy.

The following lines, in that glorious commission which is given the Messiah to extirpate the host of rebel angels, is drawn from a sublime passage in the psalms:

Go then, thou mightiest, in thy Father's might!
Ascend my chariot, guide the rapid wheels
That take heav'n's basis; bring forth all my war,
My bow, my thunder, my almighty arms
Gird on, and sword on thy puissant thigh.

The reader will easily discover many other strokes of the same nature.

There is no question but Milton had heated his imagination with the fight of the gods in Homer, before he entered into this engagement of the angels. Homer there gives us a scene of men, heroes, and gods, mixed together in battle. Mars animates the contending armies, and lifts up his voice in such a manner, that it is heard distinctly amidst all the shouts and confusion of the fight. Jupiter at the same time thunders over their heads; while Neptune raises such a tempest, that the whole field of battle, and all the tops of the mountains, shake about them. The poet tells, that Pluto himself, whose habitation was in the very centre of the earth, was so affrighted at the shock, that he leapt from his throne.

Homer afterwards describes Vulcan as pouring down a storm of fire upon the river Xanthus, and Minerva as throwing a rock at Mars; who, he tells us, covered seven acres in his fall.

As Homer has introduced into his battle of the gods every thing that is great and terrible in nature, Milton has filled his fight of good and bad angels with all the like circumstances of horror. The shout of armies, the rattling of brazen chariots, the hurling of rocks and mountains, the earthquake, the fire, the thunder, are all of them employed to lift up the reader's imagination, and give him a suitable idea of so great an action. With what art has the poet represented the whole body of the earth trembling, even before it was created!

All heav'n resounded; and had earth been then,
All earth had to its centre shook——

In how sublime and just a manner does he afterwards describe the whole heaven shaking under the wheels of the Messiah's chariot, with that exception to the throne of God!

——Under his burning wheels
The steadfast empyrean shook throughout,
All but the throne itself of God——

Notwithstanding the Messiah appears clothed with so much terror and majesty, the poet has still found means to make his readers conceive an idea of him beyond what he himself is able to describe:

Yet half his strength he put not forth, but check'd
His thunder in mid volley; for he meant
Not to destroy, but root them out of heaven.

In a word, Milton's genius, which was so great in itself, and so strengthened by all the helps of learning, appears in this book every way equal to his subject, which was the most sublime that could enter into the thoughts of a poet. As he knew all the arts of affecting the mind, he has given it certain resting-places and opportunities of recovering itself from time to time; several speeches, reflections, similitudes, and the like reliefs, being interspersed to diversify his narration, and ease the attention of the reader. L.

No. 334.] *Monday, March* 24, 1711-12.

——Voluisti, in suo genere, unumquemque nostrum quasi quendam esse Roscium, dixistique non tam ea quæ recta essent probari, quam quæ prava sunt fastidiis adhærescere. *Cic. de Gestu.*

You would have each of us be a kind of Roscius in his way; and you have said, that fastidious men are not so much pleased with what is right, as disgusted at what is wrong.

It is very natural to take for our whole lives a light impression of a thing, which at first fell into contempt with us for want of consideration. The real use of a certain qualification (which the wiser part of mankind look upon as at the best an indifferent thing, and generally a frivolous circumstance) shows the ill consequence of such prepossessions. What I mean is the art, skill, accomplishment, or whatever you will call it, of dancing. I knew a gentleman of great abilities, who bewailed the want of this part of his education to the end of a very honourable life. He observed that there was not occasion for the common use of great talents; that they are but seldom in demand; and that these very great talents were often rendered useless to a man for want of small attainments. A good mien (a becoming motion, gesture, and aspect) is natural to some men; but even these would be highly more graceful in their carriage, if what they do from the force of nature were confirmed and heightened from the force of reason. To one who has not at all considered it, to mention the force of reason on such a subject will appear fantastical; but when you have a little attended to it, an assembly of men will have quite another view; and they will tell you, it is evident from plain and infallible rules, why this man, with those beautiful features, and a well-fashioned person, is not so agreeable as he who sits by him without any of those advantages. When we read, we do it without any exerted act of memory that presents the shape of the letters; but habit makes us do it mechanically, without staying, like children, to recollect and join those letters. A man who has not had the regard of his gesture in any part of his education, will find himself unable to act with freedom before new company, as a child that is but now learning would be to read without hesitation. It is for the advancement of the pleasure we receive in being agreeable to each other in ordinary life, that one would wish dancing were generally understood, as conducive, as it really is, to a proper deportment in matters that appear the most remote from it. A man of learning and sense is distinguished from others as he is such, though he never runs upon points too difficult for the rest of the world; in like manner the reaching out of the arm, and the most ordinary motion, discovers whether a man ever learnt to know what is the true harmony and composure of his limbs and countenance. Whoever has seen Booth in the character of Pyrrhus, march to his throne to receive Orestes, is convinced that majestic and great conceptions are expressed in the very step; but, perhaps, though no other man could perform that incident as well as he does, he himself would do it with a yet greater elevation were he a dancer. This is so dangerous a subject to treat with gravity, that I shall not at present enter into it any further: but the author of the following letter has treated it in the essay he speaks of in such a manner, that I am beholden to him for a resolution, that I will never hereafter think meanly of any thing, till I have heard what they who have another opinion of it have to say in its defence.

'MR. SPECTATOR—Since there are scarce any of the arts and sciences that have not been recommended to the world by the pens of some of the professors, masters, or lovers of them, whereby the usefulness, excellence, and benefit arising from them, both as to the speculative and practical part, have been made public, to the great advantage and improvement of such arts and sciences; why should dancing, an art celebrated by the ancients in so extraordinary a manner, be totally neglected by the moderns, and left destitute of any pen to recommend its various excellencies and substantial merit to mankind?

'The low ebb to which dancing is now fallen, is altogether owing to this silence. The art is esteemed only as an amusing trifle; it lies altogether uncultivated, and is unhappily fallen under the imputation of illiterate and mechanic. As Terence, in one of his prologues, complains of the rope-dancers drawing all the spectators from his play, so we may well say, that capering and tumbling is now preferred to, and supplies the place of, just and regular dancing on our theatres. It is, therefore, in my opinion, high time that some one should come to its assistance, and relieve it from the many gross and growing errors that have crept into it, and overcast its real beauties; and to set dancing in its true light, would show the usefulness and elegance of it, with the pleasure and instruction produced from it; and also lay down some fundamental rules, that might so tend to the improvement of its professors, and information of the spectators, that the first might be the better enabled to perform, and the latter rendered more capable of judging what is (if there be any thing) valuable in this art.

'To encourage, therefore, some ingenious pen capable of so generous an undertaking, and in some measure to relieve dancing from the disadvantages it at present lies under, I, who teach to dance,* have attempted a small treatise as an Essay towards a History of Dancing: in which I have inquired into its antiquity, origin, and use, and shown what esteem the ancients had for it. I have likewise considered the nature and perfection of all its several parts, and how beneficial and delightful it is, both as a qualification and an exercise; and endeavoured to answer all objections that have been maliciously raised against it. I have proceeded to give an account of the particular dances of the Greeks and Romans, whether religious, warlike, or civil: and taken particular notice of that part of dancing relating to the ancient stage, in which the pantomimes had so great a share. Nor have I been wanting in giving an historical account of some particular masters excellent in that surprising art; after which I have advanced some observations on modern dancing, both as to the stage, and that part of it so absolutely necessary for the qualification of gentlemen and ladies; and have concluded with some short remarks on the origin and progress of the character by which dances are writ down, and communicated to one master from another. If some great genius after this would arise, and advance this art to that perfection it seems capable of receiving, what might not be expected from it? For, if we consider the origin of arts and sciences, we shall find that some of them took rise from beginnings so mean and unpromising, that it is very wonderful to think that ever such surprising structures should have been raised upon such ordinary foundations. But what cannot a great genius effect? Who would have thought that the clangorous noise of smiths' hammers should have given the first rise to music? Yet Macrobius in his second book relates, that Pythagoras, in passing by a smith's shop, found that the sounds proceeding from the hammers were either more grave or acute, according to the different weights of the hammers. The philosopher, to improve this hint, suspends different weights by strings of the same bigness, and found in like manner that the sounds answered to the weights. This being discovered, he finds out those numbers which produced sounds that were consonant: as that two strings of the same substance and tension, the one being double the length of the other, gave that interval which is called diapason, or an eighth; the same was also effected from two strings of the same length and size, the one having four times the tension of the other. By these steps, from so mean a beginning, did this great man reduce, what was only before noise to one of the most delightful sciences, by marrying it to the mathematics; and by that means caused it to be one of the most abstract and demonstrative of sciences. Who knows, therefore, but motion, whether decorous or representative, may not (as it seems highly probable it may,) be taken into consideration by some person capable of reducing it into a regular science, though not so demonstrative as that proceeding from sounds, yet sufficient to entitle it to a place among the magnified arts?

Now, Mr. Spectator, as you have declared yourself visitor of dancing-schools, and this being an undertaking which more immediately respects them, I think myself indispensably obliged, before I proceed to the publication of this my essay, to ask your advice; and hold it absolutely necessary to have your approbation, in order to recommend my treatise to the perusal of the parents of such as learn to dance, as well as to the young ladies, to whom as visitor you ought to be a guardian.

'I am, sir,

'Your most humble servant

'Salop, March 10, 1711-12.'

* An Essay towards the History of Dancing, &c. By John Weaver 12mo. 1712.

No. 335.] *Tuesday, March* 25, 1711-12.

Respicere exemplar vitæ morumque jubebo
Doctum imitatorum et veras hinc ducere voces.
Hor. Ars Poet. v. 327.

Keep nature's great original in view,
And thence the living images pursue.—*Francis.*

My friend, Sir Roger de Coverley, when we last met together at the club, told me that he had a great mind to see the new tragedy* with me, assuring me at the same time, that he had not been at a play these twenty years. 'The last I saw,' said Sir Roger, 'was The Committee, which I should not have gone to neither, had not I been told beforehand that it was a good church of England comedy.' He then proceeded to inquire of me who this distrest mother was; and upon hearing that she was Hector's widow, he told me that her husband was a brave man, and that when he was a schoolboy he had read his life at the end of the dictionary. My friend asked me in the next place, if there would not be some danger in coming home late, in case the Mohocks should be abroad. 'I assure you,' says he, 'I thought I had fallen into their hands last night; for I observed two or three lusty black men that followed me half way up Fleet-street, and mended their pace behind me, in proportion as I put on to get away from them. You must know,' continued the knight with a smile, 'I fancied they had a mind to hunt me; for I remember an honest gentleman in my neighbourhood, who was served such a trick in King Charles the Second's time, for which reason he has not ventured himself in town ever since. I might have shown them very good sport, had this been their design; for, as I am an old fox-hunter, I should have turned and dodged, and have played them a thousand tricks they had never seen in their lives before.' Sir Roger added that 'if these gentlemen had any such intention, they did not succeed very well in it, for I threw them out,' says he, 'at the end of Norfolk-street, where I doubled the corner, and got shelter in my lodgings before they could imagine what was become of me. However,' says the knight, 'if Captain Sentry will make one with us to-morrow night, and you will both of you call upon me about four o'clock, that we may be at the house before it is full, I will have my own coach in readiness to attend you, for John tells me he has got the fore-wheels mended.'

The captain, who did not fail to meet me there at the appointed hour, bid Sir Roger fear nothing, for that he had put on the same sword which he made use of at the battle of Steenkirk. Sir Roger's servants, and among the rest my old friend the butler, had, I found, provided themselves with good oaken plants, to attend their master upon this occasion. When we had placed him in his coach, with myself at his left hand, the captain before him, and his butler at the head of his footmen in the rear, we convoyed him in safety to the playhouse, where after having marched up the entry in good order, the captain and I went in with him, and seated him betwixt us in the pit. As soon as the house was full, and the candles lighted, my old friend stood up, and looked about him with that pleasure which a mind seasoned with humanity naturally feels in itself, at the sight of a multitude of people who seem pleased with one another, and partake of the same common entertainment. I could not but fancy to myself, as the old man stood up in the middle of the pit, that he made a very proper centre to a tragic audience. Upon the entering of Pyrrhus, the knight told me, that he did not believe the king of France himself had a better strut. I was indeed very attentive to my old friend's remarks, because I looked upon them as a piece of natural criticism, and was well pleased to hear him, at the conclusion of almost every scene telling me that he could not imagine how the play would end. One while he appeared much concerned for Andromache; and a little while after as much for Hermione; and was extremely puzzled to think what would become of Pyrrhus.

When Sir Roger saw Andromache's obstinate refusal to her lover's importunities, he whispered me in the ear, that he was sure she would never have him; to which he added, with a more than ordinary vehemence, 'You can't imagine, sir, what it is to have to do with a widow.' Upon Pyrrhus's threatening afterwards to leave her, the knight shook his head, and muttered to himself, 'Ay, do if you can.' This part dwelt so much upon my friend's imagination, that at the close of the third act, as I was thinking of something else, he whispered me in my ear, 'These widows, sir, are the most perverse creatures in the world. But pray,' says he, 'you that are a critic, is the play according to your dramatic rules, as you call them? Should your people in tragedy always talk to be understood? Why, there is not a single sentence in this play that I do not know the meaning of.'

The fourth act very luckily began before I had time to give the old gentleman an answer. 'Well,' says the knight, sitting down with great satisfaction, 'I suppose we are now to see Hector's ghost.' He then renewed his attention, and, from time to time fell a-praising the widow. He made, indeed, a little mistake as to one of her pages, whom at his first entering he took for Astyanax; but quickly set himself right in that particular, though, at the same time, he owned he should have been very glad to have seen the little boy, who, says he, must needs be a very fine child by the account that is given of him. Upon Hermione's going off with a menace to Pyrrhus, the audience gave a loud clap, to which Sir Roger added, 'On my word, a notable young baggage!'

* The Distrest Mother.

As there was a very remarkable silence and stillness in the audience during the whole action, it was natural for them to take the opportunity of the intervals between the acts to express their opinion of the players, and of their respective parts. Sir Roger, hearing a cluster of them praise Orestes, struck in with them, and told them, that he thought his friend Pylades was a very sensible man. As they were afterwards applauding Pyrrhus, Sir Roger put in a second time. 'And let me tell you,' says he, 'though he speaks but little, I like the old fellow in whiskers as well as any of them.' Captain Sentry, seeing two or three wags who sat near us, lean with an attentive ear towards Sir Roger, and fearing lest they should smoke the knight, plucked him by the elbow, and whispered something in his ear, that lasted till the opening of the fifth act. The knight was wonderfully attentive to the account which Orestes gives of Pyrrhus's death, and at the conclusion of it, told me it was such a bloody piece of work that he was glad it was not done upon the stage. Seeing afterwards Orestes in his raving fit, he grew more than ordinarily serious, and took occasion to moralize (in his way,) upon an evil conscience, adding, that Orestes, in his madness, looked as if he saw something.

As we were the first that came into the house, so we were the last that went out of it; being resolved to have a clear passage for our old friend, whom we did not care to venture among the jostling of the crowd. Sir Roger went out fully satisfied with his entertainment, and we guarded him to his lodging in the same manner that we brought him to the playhouse; being highly pleased for my own part, not only with the performance of the excellent piece which had been presented, but with the satisfaction which it had given to the old man. L.

No. 336.] *Wednesday, March* 26, 1711-12.

——Clament periisse pudorem
Cuncti pene patres: ea cum reprehendere coner,
Quæ gravis Æsopus, quæ doctus Roscius egit;
Vel quia nil rectum, nisi quod placuit sibi, ducunt
Vel quia turpe putant parere minoribus, et quæ
Imberbes didicere, senes perpenda fateri.

Hor. Ep. i. Lib. 2. 80.

IMITATED.

One tragic sentence if I dare deride,
With Betterton's grave action dignified,
Or well-mouth'd Booth with emphasis proclaims,
(Though but, perhaps, a muster-roll of names,)
How will our fathers rise up in a rage,
And swear all shame is lost in George's age?
You'd think no fools disgrac'd the former reign,
Did not some grave examples yet remain,
Who scorn a lad should teach his father skill,
And, having once been wrong, will be so still.

Pope.

'Mr. Spectator,—As you are the daily endeavourer to promote learning and good sense, I think myself obliged to suggest to your consideration whatever may promote or prejudice them. There is an evil which has prevailed from generation to generation, which gray hairs and tyrannical custom continue to support: I hope your spectatorial authority will give a seasonable check to the spread of the infection; I mean old men's overbearing the strongest sense of their juniors by the mere force of seniority; so that, for a young man in the bloom of life, and vigour of age, to give a reasonable contradiction to his elders, is esteemed an unpardonable insolence, and regarded as reversing the decrees of nature. I am a young man, I confess; yet I honour the gray head as much as any one; however, when, in company with old men, I hear them speak obscurely, or reason preposterously, (into which absurdities, prejudice, pride, or interest, will sometimes throw the wisest,) I count it no crime to rectify their reasonings, unless conscience must truckle to ceremony, and truth fall a sacrifice to complaisance. The strongest arguments are enervated, and the brightest evidence disappears, before those tremendous reasonings and dazzling discoveries of venerable old age. "You are young, giddy-headed fellows; you have not yet had experience of the world." Thus we young folks find our ambition cramped, and our laziness indulged; since while young we have little room to display ourselves; and, when old, the weakness of nature must pass for strength of sense, and we hope that hoary heads will raise us above the attacks of contradic tion. Now, sir, as you would enliven our activity in the pursuit of learning, take our case into consideration; and, with a gloss on brave Elihu's sentiments, assert the rights of youth, and prevent the pernicious encroachments of age. The generous reasonings of that gallant youth would adorn your paper; and I beg you would insert them, not doubting but that they will give good entertainment to the most intelligent of your readers.'

"So these three men ceased to answer Job, because he was righteous in his own eyes. Then was kindled the wrath of Elihu, the son of Barachel the Buzite, of the kin dred of Ram: against Job was his wrath kindled, because he justified himself rather than God. Also against his three friends was his wrath kindled, because they had found no answer, and yet had condemned Job. Now Elihu had waited till Job had spoken, because they were elder than he. When Elihu saw there was no answer in the mouth of these three men, then his wrath was kindled. And Elihu, the son of Barachel the Buzite, answered and said, I am young, and ye are very old; wherefore I was afraid and durst not show you mine opinion. I said, days should speak, and multitude of years should teach wisdom. But there is a spirit in man, and the inspiration of the Almighty giveth them understanding. Great men are not always wise: neither do the aged understand judgment. Therefore I said, Hearken to me, I also will show mine opinion. Behold, I waited for your words; I gave ear to your reasons, whilst you searched out what to say. Yea, I attended unto you: and behold there was none of you that convinced Job, or that answered his words: lest you should say, We have found out wisdom: God thrusteth him down, not man. Now he hath not directed his words against me: neither will I answer him with your speeches. They were amazed: they answered no more; they left off speaking. When I had waited (for they spake not, but stood still and answered no more,) I said, I will answer also my part, I also will show mine opinion. For I am full of matter, the spirit within me constraineth me. Behold, my belly is as wine which hath no vent, it is ready to burst like new bottles. I will speak that I may be refreshed: I will open my lips and answer. Let me not, I pray you, accept any man's person, neither let me give flattering titles unto man. For I know not to give flattering titles: in so doing my Maker would soon take me away."

'MR. SPECTATOR,—I have formerly read with great satisfaction your paper about idols, and the behaviour of gentlemen in those coffee-houses where women officiate; and impatiently waited to see you take India and China shops into consideration: but since you have passed us over in silence, either that you have not as yet thought us worth your notice, or that the grievances we lie under have escaped your discerning eye, I must make my complaints to you, and am encouraged to do it because you seem a little at leisure at this present writing. I am, dear sir, one of the top China-women about town; and though I say it, keep as good things and receive as fine company as any over this end of the town, let the other be who she will. In short, I am in a fair way to be easy, were it not for a club of female rakes, who, under pretence of taking their innocent rambles, forsooth, and diverting the spleen, seldom fail to plague me twice or thrice a day, to cheapen tea, or buy a skreen. What else should they mean? as they often repeat it. These rakes are your idle ladies of fashion, who, having nothing to do, employ themselves in tumbling over my ware. One of these no-customers (for by the way they seldom or never buy any thing,) calls for a set of tea-dishes, another for a bason, a third for my best green tea, and even to the punch-bowl, there's scarce a piece in my shop but must be displaced, and the whole agreeable architecture disordered, so that I can compare them to nothing but to the night-goblins that take a pleasure to overturn the disposition of plates and dishes in the kitchens of your housewifery maids. Well, after all this racket and clatter, this is too dear, that is their aversion; another thing is charming, but not wanted; the ladies are cured of the spleen, but I am not a shilling the better for it. Lord, what signifies one poor pot of tea, considering the trouble they put me to? Vapours, Mr. Spectator, are terrible things; for, though I am not possessed by them myself, I suffer more from them than if I were. Now I must beg of you to admonish all such day-goblins to make fewer visits, or to be less troublesome when they come to one's shop; and to convince them that we honest shop-keepers have something better to do than to cure folks of the vapours gratis. A young son of mine, a school-boy, is my secretary, so I hope you will make allowances. I am, sir, your constant reader, and very humble servant,

'REBECCA *the distressed*.

'March the 22d.' T.

No. 337.] *Thursday, March 27, 1712.*

Fingit equum tenera docilem cervice magister,
Ire viam quam monstrat eques——
Hor. Ep. 2. Lib. 1. 64.

The jockey trains the young and tender horse
While yet soft-mouth'd, and breeds him to the course.
Creech.

I HAVE lately received a third letter from the gentleman who has already given the public two essays upon education. As his thoughts seem to be very just and new upon this subject, I shall communicate them to the reader.

'SIR,—If I had not been hindered by some extraordinary business, I should have sent you sooner my further thoughts upon education. You may please to remember, that in my last letter, I endeavoured to give the best reasons that could be urged in favour of a private or public education. Upon the whole, it may perhaps be thought that I seemed rather inclined to the latter, though at the same time I confessed that virtue, which ought to be our first and principal care, was more usually acquired in the former.

'I intended, therefore, in this letter, to offer at methods, by which I conceive boys might be made to improve in virtue as they advance in letters.

'I know that in most of our public schools vice is punished and discouraged, whenever it is found out: but this is far from being sufficient, unless our youth are at the same time taught to form a right judgment of things, and to know what is properly virtue.

'To this end, whenever they read the lives and actions of such men as have been famous in their generation, it should not be thought enough to make them barely understand so many Greek or Latin sentences; but they should be asked their opinion of such an action or saying, and obliged to give their reasons why they take it to be good or bad. By this means they would insensibly arrive at proper notions of courage, temperance, honour, and justice.

'There must be great care taken how

the example of any particular person is recommended to them in gross; instead of which they ought to be taught wherein such a man, though great in some respects, was weak and faulty in others. For want of this caution, a boy is often so dazzled with the lustre of a great character, that he confounds its beauties with its blemishes, and looks even upon the faulty part of it with an eye of admiration.

'I have often wondered how Alexander, who was naturally of a generous and merciful disposition, came to be guilty of so barbarous an action as that of dragging the governor of a town after his chariot. I know this is generally ascribed to his passion for Homer, but I lately met with a passage in Plutarch, which, if I am not very much mistaken, still gives us a clearer light into the motives of this action. Plutarch tells us, that Alexander in his youth had a master named Lysimachus, who, though he was a man destitute of all politeness, ingratiated himself both with Philip and his pupil, and became the second man at court, by calling the king Peleus, the Prince Achilles, and himself Phœnix. It is no wonder if Alexander, having been thus used not only to admire but to personate Achilles, should think it glorious to imitate him in this piece of cruelty and extravagance.

'To carry this thought yet further, I shall submit it to your consideration, whether, instead of a theme or copy of verses, which are the usual exercises, as they are called in the school phrase, it would not be more proper that a boy should be tasked, once or twice a week, to write down his opinion of such persons and things as occur to him by his reading; that he should descant upon the actions of Turnus, or Æneas; show wherein they excelled, or were defective; censure or approve any particular action; observe how it might have been carried to a greater degree of perfection, and how it exceeded or fell short of another. He might at the same time mark what was moral in any speech, and how far it agreed with the character of the person speaking. This exercise would soon strengthen his judgment in what is blameable or praiseworthy, and give him an early seasoning of morality.

'Next to those examples which may be met with in books, I very much approve Horace's way of setting before youth the infamous or honourable characters of their contemporaries. That poet tells us, this was the method his father made use of to incline him to any particular virtue, or give him an aversion to any particular vice. "If," says Horace, "my father advised me to live within bounds, and be contented with the fortune he should leave me; 'Do you not see,' says he, 'the miserable condition of Burrus, and the son of Albus? Let the misfortunes of those two wretches teach you to avoid luxury and extravagance If he would inspire me with an abhorrence of debauchery, 'Do not,' says he, 'make yourself like Sectanus, when you may be happy in the enjoyment of lawful pleasures. How scandalous,' says he, 'is the character of Trebonius, who was lately caught in bed with another man's wife!'" To illustrate the force of this method, the poet adds, that as a headstrong patient who will not follow at first his physician's prescriptions, grows orderly when he hears that the neighbours die all about him; so youth is often frightened from vice, by hearing the ill report it brings upon others.

'Xenophon's schools of equity, in his Life of Cyrus the Great, are sufficiently famous He tells us, that the Persian children went to school, and employed their time as diligently in learning the principles of justice and sobriety, as the youth in other countries did to acquire the most difficult arts and sciences; their governors spent most part of the day in hearing their mutual accusations one against the other, whether for violence, cheating, slander, or ingratitude; and taught them how to give judgment against those who were found to be any ways guilty of these crimes. I omit the story of the long and short coat, for which Cyrus himself was punished, as a case equally known with any in Littleton.

'The method which Apuleius tells us the Indian Gymnosophists took to educate their disciples, is still more curious and remarkable. His words are as follow: "When their dinner is ready, before it is served up, the masters inquire of every particular scholar how he has employed his time since sun-rising: some of them answer, that, having been chosen as arbiters between two persons, they have composed their differences, and made them friends; some that they have been executing the orders of their parents; and others, that they have either found out something new by their own application, or learnt it from the instructions of their fellows. But if there happens to be any one among them who cannot make it appear that he has employed the morning to advantage, he is immediately excluded from the company, and obliged to work while the rest are at dinner."

'It is not impossible, that from these several ways of producing virtue in the minds of boys, some general method might be invented. What I would endeavour to inculcate is, that our youth cannot be too soon taught the principles of virtue, seeing the first impressions which are made on the mind, are always the strongest.

'The archbishop of Cambray makes Telemachus say, that, though he was young in years, he was old in the art of knowing how to keep both his own and his friends' secrets. "When my father," says the prince, "went to the siege of Troy, he took me on his knees, and, after having embraced and blessed me, as he was surrounded by the nobles of Ithaca, 'O my friends,' says he, 'into your hands I commit the education of my son: if ever you loved his father, show it in your care towards him; but, above all, do not omit to form him just, sincere, and faithful in keeping a secret.' These words of my father," says Telemachus, "were continually repeated to me by his friends in his absence; who made no scruple of communicating to me their uneasiness to see my mother surrounded with lovers, and the measures they designed to take on that occasion." He adds, that he was so ravished at being thus treated like a man, and at the confidence reposed in him, that he never once abused it; nor could all the insinuations of his father's rivals ever get him to betray what was committed to him under the seal of secrecy.

'There is hardly any virtue which a lad might not thus learn by practice and example.

'I have heard of a good man, who used at certain times to give his scholars sixpence a-piece, that they might tell him the next day how they had employed it. The third part was always to be laid out in charity, and every boy was blamed, or commended, as he could make it appear he had chosen a fit object.

'In short, nothing is more wanting to our public schools, than that the masters of them should use the same care in fashioning the manners of their scholars, as in forming their tongues to the learned languages. Wherever the former is omitted, I cannot help agreeing with Mr. Locke, that a man must have a very strange value for words, when, preferring the languages of the Greeks and Romans to that which made them such brave men, he can think it worth while to hazard the innocence and virtue of his son for a little Greek and Latin.

'As the subject of this essay is of the highest importance, and what I do not remember to have yet seen treated by any author, I have sent you what occurred to me on it from my own observation, or reading, and which you may either suppress or publish, as you think fit. I am, sir, yours, &c.' X.

No. 338.] *Friday, March* 28, 1712.

———Nil fuit unquam
Tam dispar sibi.——— *Hor.* Sat. iii. Lib. 1. 18.

Made up of nought but inconsistencies.

I FIND the tragedy of the Distrest Mother* is published to-day. The author of the prologue,† I suppose, pleads an old excuse I have read somewhere, of 'being dull with design;' and the gentleman who writ the epilogue‡ has, to my knowledge, so much of greater moment to value himself upon, that he will easily forgive me for publishing the exceptions made against gaiety at the end of serious entertainments in the following letter: I should be more unwilling to pardon him, than any body, a practice which cannot have any ill consequence but from the abilities of the person who is guilty of it.

'MR. SPECTATOR,—I had the happiness the other night of sitting very near you, and your worthy friend Sir Roger, at the acting of the new tragedy, which you have, in a late paper or two, so justly recommended. I was highly pleased with the advantageous situation fortune had given me in placing me so near two gentlemen, from one of which I was sure to hear such reflections on the several incidents of the play as pure nature suggested, and from the other, such as flowed from the exactest art and judgment: though I must confess that my curiosity led me so much to observe the knight's reflections, that I was not well at leisure to improve myself by yours. Nature, I found, played her part in the knight pretty well, till at the last concluding lines she entirely forsook him. You must know, sir, that it is always my custom, when I have been well entertained at a new tragedy, to make my retreat before the facetious epilogue enters; not but that those pieces are often very well written, but having paid down my half-crown, and made a fair purchase of as much of the pleasing melancholy as the poet's art can afford me, or my own nature admit of, I am willing to carry some of it home with me: and cannot endure to be at once tricked out of all, though by the wittiest dexterity in the world. However, I kept my seat the other night in hopes of finding my own sentiments of the matter favoured by your friends; when, to my great surprise, I found the knight entering with equal pleasure into both parts, and as much satisfied with Mrs. Oldfield's gaiety as he had been before with Andromache's greatness. Whether this were no more than an effect of the knight's peculiar humanity, pleased to find at last, that, after all the tragical doings, every thing was safe and well, I do not know; but for my own part, I must confess, I was so dissatisfied, that I was sorry the poet had saved Andromache, and could heartily have wished that he had left her stone-dead upon the stage. For you cannot imagine, Mr. Spectator, the mischief she was reserved to do me. I found my soul, during the action, gradually worked up to the highest pitch, and felt the exalted passion which all generous minds conceive at the sight of virtue in distress. The impression, believe me, sir, was so strong upon me, that I am persuaded, if I had been let alone in it, I could, at an extremity, have ventured to defend yourself and Sir Roger against half a score of the fiercest Mohocks; but the ludicrous epilogue in the close extinguished all my ardour, and made

---

* By A. Phillips, first published in 1712

† Steele; See Tat. No. 38.

‡ Eustace Budgell.

me look upon all such noble achievements as downright silly and romantic. What the rest of the audience felt, I cannot so well tell. For myself I must declare, that at the end of the play I found my soul uniform, and all of a piece; but at the end of the epilogue it was so jumbled together, and divided between jest and earnest, that, if you will forgive me an extravagant fancy, I will here set it down. I could not but fancy, if my soul had at that moment quitted my body, and descended to the poetical shades in the posture it was then in, what a strange figure it would have made among them. They would not have known what to have made of my motley spectre, half comic and half tragic, all over resembling a ridiculous face that at the same time laughs on one side and cries on the other. The only defence, I think, I have ever heard made for this, as it seems to me the most unnatural tack of the comic tail to the tragic head, is this, that the minds of the audience must be refreshed, and gentlemen and ladies not sent away to their own homes with too dismal and melancholy thoughts about them: for who knows the consequence of this? We are much obliged, indeed, to the poets, for the great tenderness they express for the safety of our persons, and heartily thank them for it. But if that be all, pray, good sir, assure them, that we are none of us like to come to any great harm; and that, let them do their best, we shall in all probability live out the length of our days, and frequent the theatres more than ever. What makes me more desirous to have some information of this matter is, because of an ill consequence or two attending it: for a great many of our church musicians being related to the theatre, they have, in imitation of these epilogues, introduced, in their farewell voluntaries, a sort of music quite foreign to the design of church-services, to the great prejudice of well-disposed people. Those fingering gentlemen should be informed, that they ought to suit their airs to the place and business, and that the musician is obliged to keep to the text as much as the preacher. For want of this, I have found by experience a great deal of mischief. When the preacher has often, with great piety, and art enough, handled his subject, and the judicious clerk has with the utmost diligence culled out two staves proper to the discourse, and I have found in myself and the rest of the pew, good thoughts and dispositions, they have been, all in a moment, dissipated by a merry jig from the organ-loft. One knows not what further ill effects the epilogues I have been speaking of may in time produce: but this I am credibly informed of, that Paul Lorrain* has resolved upon a very sudden reformation in his tragical dramas; and that, at the next monthly performance, he designs, instead of a penitential psalm, to dismiss his audience with an excellent new ballad of his own composing. Pray, sir, do what you can to put a stop to these growing evils, and you will very much oblige your humble servant,

'PHYSIBULUS.'

* The ordinary of Newgate at this time. See the Tatler, No. 63.

No. 339.] *Saturday, March* 29, 1712.

——Ut his exordia primis
Omnia, et ipse tener mundi concreverit orbis,
Tum durare solum et discludere Nerea ponto
Cœperit, et rerum paullatim sumere formas.
Virg. Ecl. v. 33

He sung the secret seeds of nature's frame:
How seas, and earth, and air, and active flame,
Fell through the mighty void, and in their fall
Were blindly gather'd in this goodly ball.
The tender soil then stiff'ning by degrees,
Shut from the bounded earth the bounding seas,
The earth and ocean various forms disclose,
And a new sun to the new world arose.—*Dryden.*

LONGINUS has observed that there may be a loftiness in sentiments where there is no passion, and brings instances out of ancient authors to support this his opinion. The pathetic, as that great critic observes, may animate and inflame the sublime, but is not essential to it. Accordingly, as he further remarks, we very often find that those who excel most in stirring up the passions very often want the talent of writing in the great and sublime manner, and so on the contrary. Milton has shown himself a master in both these ways of writing. The seventh book, which we are now entering upon, is an instance of that sublime which is not mixed and worked up with passion. The author appears in a kind of composed and sedate majesty; and though the sentiments do not give so great an emotion as those in the former book, they abound with as magnificent ideas. The sixth book, like a troubled ocean, represents greatness in confusion; the seventh affects the imagination like the ocean in a calm, and fills the mind of the reader, without producing in it any thing like tumult or agitation.

The critic above-mentioned, among the rules which he lays down for succeeding in the sublime way of writing, proposes to his reader, that he should imitate the most celebrated authors who have gone before him, and have been engaged in works of the same nature; as in particular that, if he writes on poetical subjects, he should consider how Homer would have spoken on such an occasion. By this means one great genius often catches the flame from another, and writes in his spirit, without copying servilely after him. There are a thousand shining passages in Virgil, which have been lighted up by Homer.

Milton, though his own natural strength of genius was capable of furnishing out a perfect work, has doubtless very much raised and ennobled his conceptions by such an imitation as that which Longinus has recommended.

In this book which gives us an account of the six days' works, the poet received but very few assistances from heathen writers, who are strangers to the wonders of creation. But as there are many glorious strokes of poetry upon this subject in holy writ, the author has numberless allusions to them through the whole course of this book. The great critic I have before mentioned, though a heathen, has taken notice of the sublime manner in which the lawgiver of the Jews has described the creation in the first chapter of Genesis; and there are many other passages in scripture which rise up to the same majesty, where the subject is touched upon. Milton has shown his judgment very remarkably, in making use of such of these as were proper for his poem, and in duly qualifying those strains of eastern poetry which were suited to readers whose imaginations were set to a higher pitch than those of colder climates.

Adam's speech to the angel, wherein he desires an account of what had passed within the regions of nature before the creation, is very great and solemn. The following lines, in which he tells him, that the day is not too far spent for him to enter upon such a subject, are exquisite in their kind:

And the great light of day yet wants to run
Much of his race, though steep; suspense in heav'n
Held by thy voice, thy potent voice he hears,
And longer will delay to hear thee tell
His generation, &c.

The angel's encouraging our first parents in a modest pursuit after knowledge, with the causes which he assigns for the creation of the world, are very just and beautiful. The Messiah, by whom, as we are told in scripture, the heavens were made, goes forth in the power of his Father, surrounded with a host of angels, and clothed with such a majesty as becomes his entering upon a work which, according to our conceptions, appears the utmost exertion of Omnipotence. What a beautiful description has our author raised upon that hint in one of the prophets! 'And behold there came four chariots out from between two mountains, and the mountains were mountains of brass:'

About his chariot numberless were pour'd
Cherub and seraph, potentates and thrones,
And virtues, winged spirits, and chariots wing'd
From the armoury of God, where stand of old
Myriads between two brazen mountains lodg'd
Against a solemn day, harness'd at hand,
Celestial equipage! and now came forth
Spontaneous, for within them spirit liv'd,
Attendant on their Lord: heav'n open'd wide
Her ever-during gates, harmonious sound!
On golden hinges moving———

I have before taken notice of these chariots of God, and of these gates of heaven; and shall here only add, that Homer gives us the same idea of the latter as opening of themselves; though he afterwards takes off from it, by telling us, that the Hours first of all removed those prodigious heaps of clouds which lay as a barrier before them.

I do not know any thing in the whole poem more sublime than the description which follows, where the Messiah is represented at the head of his angels, as looking down into the chaos, calming its confusion, riding into the midst of it, and drawing the first outline of the creation:

On heav'nly ground they stood, and from the shore
They view'd the vast immeasurable abyss
Outrageous as a sea, dark, wasteful, wild,
Up from the bottom turn'd by furious winds
And surging waves, as mountains to assault
Heav'n's height, and with the centre mix the pole.
"Silence, ye troubled waves; and thou, deep, peace!"
Said then th' omnific Word, "Your discord end!"
Nor staid, but, on the wings of cherubim
Uplifted, in paternal glory rode
Far into Chaos, and the world unborn;
For Chaos heard his voice. Him all his train
Follow'd in bright procession, to behold
Creation, and the wonders of his might.
Then stay'd the fervid wheels; and in his hand
He took the golden compasses, prepar'd
In God's eternal store to circumscribe
The universe, and all created things:
One foot he centred, and the other turn'd
Round through the vast profundity obscure,
And said, "Thus far extend, thus far thy bounds,
This be thy just circumference, O world!"

The thought of the golden compasses is conceived altogether in Homer's spirit, and is a very noble incident in this wonderful description. Homer, when he speaks of the gods, ascribes to them several arms and instruments with the same greatness of imagination. Let the reader only peruse the description of Minerva's ægis or buckler, in the fifth book, with her spear which would overturn whole squadrons, and her helmet that was sufficient to cover an army drawn out of a hundred cities. The golden compasses, in the above-mentioned passage, appear a very natural instrument in the hand of him whom Plato somewhere calls the Divine Geometrician. As poetry delights in clothing abstracted ideas in allegories and sensible images, we find a magnificent description of the creation, formed after the same manner, in one of the prophets, wherein he describes the Almighty Architect as measuring the waters in the hollow of his hand, meting out the heavens with his span, comprehending the dust of the earth in a measure, weighing the mountains in scales, and the hills in a balance. Another of them describing the Supreme Being in this great work of creation, represents him as laying the foundations of the earth, and stretching a line upon it; and, in another place, as garnishing the heavens, stretching out the north over the empty place, and hanging the earth upon nothing. This last noble thought Milton has expressed in the following verse:

And earth self-balanced on her centre hung.

The beauties of description in this book lie so very thick, that it is impossible to enumerate them in this paper. The poet has employed on them the whole energy of our tongue. The several great scenes of the creation rise up to view one after another, in such a manner, that the reader seems present at this wonderful work, and to assist among the choirs of angels who are the spectators of it. How glorious is the conclusion of the first day!

——Thus was the first day even and morn,
Nor past uncelebrated, nor unsung
By the celestial choirs, when orient light
Exhaling first from darkness they beheld;
Birth-day of heav'n and earth! with joy and shout
The hollow universal orb they fill'd.

We have the same elevation of thought in the third day, when the mountains were brought forth, and the deep was made:

Immediately the mountains huge appear
Emergent, and their broad bare backs upheave
Into the clouds, their tops ascend the sky:
So high as heav'n the tumid hills, so low
Down sunk a hollow bottom broad and deep,
Capacious bed of waters——

We have also the rising of the whole vegetable world, described in this day's work, which is filled with all the graces that other poets have lavished on their description of the spring, and leads the reader's imagination into a theatre equally surprising and beautiful.

The several glories of the heavens make their appearance on the fourth day:

First in his east the glorious lamp was seen,
Regent of day, and all the horizon round
Invested with bright rays, jocund to run
His longitude through heavn's high road; the gray
Dawn, and the Pleiades before him danc'd,
Shedding sweet influence. Less bright the moon,
But opposite in levell'd west was set,
His mirror, with full face borrowing her light
From him, for other lights she needed none
In that aspect, and still the distance keeps
Till night; then in the east her turn she shines,
Revolv'd on heav'n's great axle, and her reign
With thousand lesser lights dividual holds,
With thousand thousand stars, that then appear'd
Spangling the hemisphere——

One would wonder how the poet could be so concise in his description of the six days' works, as to comprehend them within the bounds of an episode, and, at the same time, so particular, as to give us a lively idea of them. This is still more remarkable in his account of the fifth and sixth days, in which he has drawn out to our view the whole animal creation, from the reptile to the behemoth. As the lion and the leviathan are two of the noblest productions in the world of living creatures, the reader will find a most exquisite spirit of poetry in the account which our author gives us of them. The sixth day concludes with the formation of man, upon which the angel takes occasion, as he did after the battle in heaven, to remind Adam of his obedience, which was the principal design of this visit.

The poet afterwards represents the Messiah returning into heaven, and taking a survey of his great work. There is something inexpressibly sublime in this part of the poem, where the author describes the great period of time, filled with so many glorious circumstances; when the heavens and earth were finished; when the Messiah ascended up in triumph through the everlasting gates; when he looked down with pleasure upon his new creation; when every part of nature seemed to rejoice in its existence, when the morning-stars sang together, and all the sons of God shouted for joy.

So even and morn accomplish'd the sixth day:
Yet not till the Creator from his work
Desisting, though unwearied, up return'd,
Up to the heaven of heavens, his high abode,
Thence to behold his new created world
The addition of his empire, how it show'd
In prospect from his throne, how good, how fair,
Answering his great idea. Up he rode,
Follow'd with acclamation and the sound
Symphonious of ten thousand harps, that tun'd
Angelic harmonies, the earth, the air,
Resounded, (thou rememberest, for thou heard'st)
The heavens and all the constellations rung,
The planets in their station list'ning stood,
While the bright pomp ascended jubilant.
"Open, ye everlasting gates!" they sung,
"Open, ye heavens, your living doors! let in
The great Creator from his work return'd
Magnificent, his six days' work—a world!"

I cannot conclude this book upon the creation without mentioning a poem which has lately appeared under that title.* The work was undertaken with so good an intention, and is executed with so great a mastery, that it deserves to be looked upon as one of the most useful and noble productions in our English verse. The reader cannot but be pleased to find the depths of philosophy enlivened with all the charms of poetry, and to see so great a strength of reason, amidst so beautiful a redundancy of the imagination. The author has shown us that design in all the works of nature which necessarily leads us to the knowledge of its first cause. In short, he has illustrated, by numberless and incontestable instances, that divine wisdom which the son of Sirach has so nobly ascribed to the Supreme Being in his formation of the world, when he tells us, that 'He created her, and saw her, and numbered her, and poured her out upon all his works.'

No. 340.] *Monday, March* 31, 1712.

Quis novus hic nostris successit sedibus hospes?
Quem sese ore ferens! quam forti pectore et armis
Virg. Æn. iv. 10.

What chief is this that visits us from far,
Whose gallant mien bespeaks him train'd to war!

I TAKE it to be the highest instance of a noble mind, to bear great qualities without discovering in a man's behaviour any consciousness that he is superior to the rest of the world. Or, to say it otherwise, it is the duty of a great person so to demean himself, as that, whatever endowments he may have, he may appear to value himself upon no qualities but such as any man may arrive at. He ought to think no man valuable but for his public spirit, justice, and integrity; and all other endowments to be esteemed

* By Sir Richard Blackmore

only as they contribute to the exerting those virtues. Such a man, if he is wise or valiant, knows it is of no consideration to other men that he is so, but as he employs those high talents for their use and service. He who affects the applauses and addresses of a multitude, or assumes to himself a preeminence upon any other consideration, must soon turn admiration into contempt. It is certain that there can be no merit in any man who is not conscious of it; but the sense that it is valuable only according to the application of it, makes that superiority amiable, which would otherwise be invidious. In this light it is considered as a thing in which every man bears a share. It annexes the ideas of dignity, power, and fame, in an agreeable and familiar manner, to him who is possessor of it; and all men who are strangers to him are naturally incited to indulge a curiosity in beholding the person, behaviour, feature, and shape of him in whose character, perhaps, each man had formed something in common with himself.

Whether such, or any other, are the causes, all men have a yearning curiosity to behold a man of heroic worth. I have had many letters from all parts of this kingdom, that request I would give them an exact account of the stature, the mien, the aspect of the prince who lately visited England, and has done such wonders for the liberty of Europe. It would puzzle the most curious to form to himself the sort of man my several correspondents expect to hear of by the action mentioned, when they desire a description of him. There is always something that concerns themselves, and growing out of their own circumstances, in all their inquiries. A friend of mine in Wales beseeches me to be very exact in my account of that wonderful man who had marched an army and all its baggage over the Alps; and if possible, to learn whether the peasant who showed him the way, and is drawn in the map, be yet living. A gentleman from the university, who is deeply intent on the study of humanity, desires me to be as particular, if I had an opportunity, in observing the whole interview between his highness and our late general. Thus do men's fancies work according to their several educations and circumstances; but all pay a respect, mixed with admiration, to this illustrious character. I have waited for his arrival in Holland, before I would let my correspondents know that I have not been so uncurious a Spectator as not to have seen prince Eugene.* It would be very difficult, as I said just now, to answer every expectation of those who have written to me on that head; nor is it possible for me to find words to let one know what an artful glance there is in his countenance who surprised Cremona; how daring he appears who forced the trenches at Turin: but in general I can say, that he who beholds him will easily expect from him any thing that is to be imagined, or executed, by the wit or force of man. The prince is of that stature which makes a man most easily become all parts of exercise; has height to be graceful on occasions of state and ceremony, and no less adapted for agility and despatch: his aspect is erect and composed: his eye lively and thoughtful, yet rather vigilant than sparkling; his action and address the most easy imaginable, and his behaviour in an assembly peculiarly graceful in a certain art of mixing insensibly with the rest, and becoming one of the company, instead of receiving the courtship of it. The shape of his person, and composure of his limbs, are remarkably exact and beautiful. There is in his looks something sublime, which does not seem to arise from his quality or character, but the innate disposition of his mind. It is apparent that he suffers the presence of much company, instead of taking delight in it: and he appeared in public, while with us, rather to return good-will, or satisfy curiosity, than to gratify any taste he himself had of being popular. As his thoughts are never tumultuous in danger, they are as little discomposed on occasions of pomp and magnificence. A great soul is affected, in either case, no further than in considering the properest methods to extricate itself from them. If this hero has the strong incentives to uncommon enterprises that were remarkable in Alexander, he prosecutes and enjoys the fame of them with the justness, propriety, and good sense of Cæsar. It is easy to observe in him a mind as capable of being entertained with contemplation as enterprise; a mind ready for great exploits, but not impatient for occasions to exert itself. The prince has wisdom and valour in as high perfection as man can enjoy it; which noble faculties, in conjunction, banish all vain-glory, ostentation, ambition, and all other vices which might intrude upon his mind, to make it unequal. These habits and qualities of soul and body render his personage so extraordinary, that he appears to have nothing in him but what every man should have in him, the exertion of his very self, abstracted from the circumstances in which fortune has placed him. Thus, were you to see prince Eugene, and were told he was a private gentleman, you would say he is a man of modesty and merit. Should you be told that was prince Eugene, he would be diminished no otherwise, than that part of your distant admiration would turn into a familiar good-will.

This I thought fit to entertain my reader with, concerning a hero who never was equalled but by one man:† over whom also

* He stood godfather to Steele's second son, who was named Eugene after this prince.

† The duke of Marlborough, who was disgraced abou this time.

he has this advantage, that he has had an opportunity to manifest an esteem for him in his adversity. T.

No. 341.] *Tuesday, April* 1, 1712.

——Revocate animos, mœstumque timorem
Mittite—— *Virg. Æn.* i. 206.

Resume your courage, and dismiss your fear.
Dryden.

Having, to oblige my correspondent Physibulus, printed his letter last Friday, in relation to the new epilogue, he cannot take it amiss if I now publish another, which I have just received from a gentleman who does not agree with him in his sentiments upon that matter.

'Sir,—I am amazed to find an epilogue attacked in your last Friday's paper, which has been so generally applauded by the town, and received such honours as were never before given to any in an English theatre.

'The audience would not permit Mrs. Oldfield to go off the stage the first night till she had repeated it twice; the second night the noise of *ancora* was as loud as before, and she was obliged again to speak it twice: the third night it was still called for a second time; and, in short, contrary to all other epilogues, which are dropped after the third representation of the play, this has already been repeated nine times.

'I must own, I am the more surprised to find this censure in opposition to the whole town, in a paper which has hitherto been famous for the candour of its criticisms.

'I can by no means allow your melancholy correspondent, that the new epilogue is unnatural because it is gay. If I had a mind to be learned, I could tell him that the prologue and epilogue were real parts of the ancient tragedy; but every one knows, that, on the British stage, they are distinct performances by themselves, pieces entirely detached from the play, and no way essential to it.

'The moment the play ends, Mrs. Oldfield is no more Andromache but Mrs. Oldfield; and though the poet had left Andromache stone-dead upon the stage, as your ingenious correspondent phrases it, Mrs. Oldfield might still have spoken a merry epilogue. We have an instance of this in a tragedy where there is not only a death, but a martyrdom. St. Catherine was there personated by Nell Gwin; she lies stone-dead upon the stage, but upon those gentlemen's offering to remove her body, whose business it is to carry off the slain in our English tragedies, she breaks out into that abrupt beginning of what was a very ludicrous, but at the same time thought a very good epilogue:

'Hold! are you mad? you damn'd confounded dog,
I am to rise and speak the epilogue.'

'This diverting manner was always practised by Mr. Dryden, who, if he was not the best writer of tragedies in his time, was allowed by every one to have the happiest turn for a prologue, or an epilogue. The epilogues to Cleomenes, Don Sebastian, The duke of Guise, Aurengzebe, and Love Triumphant, are all precedents of this nature.

'I might further justify this practice by that excellent epilogue which was spoken, a few years since, after the tragedy of Phædra and Hippolytus;* with a great many others, in which the authors have endeavoured to make the audience merry. If they have not all succeeded so well as the writer of this, they have however shown that it was not for the want of good-will.

'I must further observe, that the gaiety of it may be still the more proper, as it is at the end of a French play; since every one knows that nation, who are generally esteemed to have as polite a taste as any in Europe, always close their tragic entertainment with what they call a *petite piece*, which is purposely designed to raise mirth, and send away the audience well pleased. The same person who has supported the chief character in the tragedy very often plays the principal part in the *petite piece*; so that I have myself seen, at Paris, Orestes and Lubin acted the same night by the same man.

'Tragi-comedy, indeed, you have yourself in a former speculation, found fault with very justly, because it breaks the tide of the passions while they are yet flowing; but this is nothing at all to the present case, where they have already had their full course.

'As the new epilogue is written conformably to the practice of our best poets, so it is not such a one, which, as the duke of Buckingham says in his Rehearsal, might serve for any other play; but wholly rises out of the occurrences of the piece it was composed for.

'The only reason your mournful correspondent gives against this facetious epilogue, as he calls it, is, that he has a mind to go home melancholy. I wish the gentleman may not be more grave than wise. For my own part, I must confess, I think it very sufficient to have the anguish of a fictitious piece remain upon me while it is representing; but I love to be sent home to bed in a good humour. If Physibulus is, however, resolved to be inconsolable, and not to have his tears dried up, he need only continue his old custom, and when he has had his half-crown's worth of sorrow, slink out before the epilogue begins.

'It is pleasant enough to hear this tragical genius complaining of the great mischief Andromache had done him. What was that? Why she made him laugh. The poor gentleman's sufferings put me in mind of Harlequin's case, who was tickled to

* Mr. Edmund Neal, alias Smith, 8vo. 1707. Addison wrote a prologue to this play to ridicule the Italian operas. The epilogue was written by Prior.

death. He tells us soon after, through a small mistake of sorrow for rage, that during the whole action he was so very sorry, that he thinks he could have attacked half a score of the fiercest Mohocks in the excess of his grief. I cannot but look upon it as an unhappy accident, that a man who is so bloody-minded in his affliction was diverted from this fit of outrageous melancholy. The valour of this gentleman in his distress brings to one's memory the Knight of the sorrowful Countenance, who lays about him at such an unmerciful rate in an old romance. I shall readily grant him that his soul, as he himself says, would have made a very ridiculous figure, had it quitted the body, and descended to the poetical shades, in such an encounter.

'As to his conceit of tacking a tragic head with a comic tail, in order to refresh the audience, it is such a piece of jargon, that I do not know what to make of it.

'The elegant writer makes a very sudden transition from the playhouse to the church, and from thence to the gallows.

'As for what relates to the church, he is of opinion that these epilogues have given occasion to those merry jigs from the organ-loft, which have dissipated those good thoughts and dispositions he has found in himself, and the rest of the pew, upon the singing of two staves culled out by the judicious and diligent clerk.

'He fetches his next thought from Tyburn: and seems very apprehensive lest there should happen any innovations in the tragedies of his friend Paul Lorrain.

'In the mean time, sir, this gloomy writer, who is so mightily scandalized at a gay epilogue after a serious play, speaking of the fate of those unhappy wretches who are condemned to suffer an ignominious death by the justice of our laws, endeavours to make the reader merry on so improper an occasion, by those poor burlesque expressions of tragical dramas and monthly performances. I am, sir, with great respect, your most obedient, most humble servant, PHILOMEDES.'

X.

No. 342.] *Wednesday, April* 2, 1712.

Justitiæ partes sunt non violare homines: verecundiæ, non offendere. *Tull.*

Justice consists in doing no injury to men: decency, in giving them no offence.

As regard to decency is a great rule of life in general, but more especially to be consulted by the female world, I cannot overlook the following letter, which describes an egregious offender.

'MR. SPECTATOR,—I was this day looking over your papers, and reading, in that of December the 6th, with great delight, the amiable grief of Asteria for the absence of her husband; it threw me into a great deal of reflection. I cannot say but this arose very much from the circumstances of my own life, who am a soldier, and expect every day to receive orders, which will oblige me to leave behind me a wife that is very dear to me, and that very deservedly. She is at present, I am sure, no way below your Asteria for conjugal affection: but I see the behaviour of some women so little suited to the circumstances wherein my wife and I shall soon be, that it is with a reluctance, I never knew before, I am going to my duty. What puts me to present pain is the example of a young lady, whose story you shall have as well as I can give it you. 'Hortensius, an officer of good rank in his majesty's service, happened, in a certain part of England, to be brought to a country gentleman's house, where he was received with that more than ordinary welcome with which men of domestic lives entertain such few soldiers whom a military life, from the variety of adventures, has not rendered overbearing, but humane, easy, and agreeable. Hortensius staid here some time, and had easy access at all hours, as well as unavoidable conversation, at some parts of the day, with the beautiful Sylvana, the gentleman's daughter. People who live in cities are wonderfully struck with every little country abode they see when they take the air; and it is natural to fancy they could live in every neat cottage (by which they pass) much happier than in their present circumstances. The turbulent way of life which Hortensius was used to, made him reflect with much satisfaction on all the advantages of a sweet retreat one day; and, among the rest, you will think it not improbable it might enter into his thought, that such a woman as Sylvana would consummate the happiness. The world is so debauched with mean considerations, that Hortensius knew it would be received as an act of generosity, if he asked for a woman of the highest merit, without further questions, of a parent who had nothing to add to her personal qualifications. The wedding was celebrated at her father's house. When that was over, the generous husband did not proportion his provision for her to the circumstances of her fortune, but considered his wife as his darling, his pride, and his vanity; or, rather, that it was in the woman he had chosen that a man of sense could show pride or vanity with an excuse, and therefore adorned her with rich habits and valuable jewels. He did not, however, omit to admonish her, that he did his very utmost in this; that it was an ostentation he could not be guilty of but to a woman he had so much pleasure in, desiring her to consider it as such; and begged of her also to take these matters rightly, and believe the gems, the gowns, the laces, would still become her better, if her air and behaviour was such, that it might appear she dressed thus rather in compliance to his humour that way, than out of any value she herself had for the trifles. To this lesson, too hard for a woman, Hortensius added, that she must be sure to stay with her friends in the country till his return. As soon as Hortensius departed, Sylvana saw in her looking-glass, that the love he conceived for her was wholly owing to the accident of seeing her; and she was convinced it was only her misfortune the rest of mankind had not beheld her, or men of much greater quality and merit had contended for one so genteel, though bred in obscurity; so very witty, though never acquainted with court or town. She therefore resolved not to hide so much excellence from the world; but, without any regard to the absence of the most generous man alive, she is now the gayest lady about this town, and has shut out the thoughts of her husband, by a constant retinue of the vainest young fellows this age has produced; to entertain whom, she squanders away all Hortensius is able to supply her with, though that supply is purchased with no less difficulty than the hazard of his life."

'Now, Mr. Spectator, would it not be a work becoming your office, to treat this criminal as she deserves? You should give it the severest reflections you can. You should tell women, that they are more accountable for behaviour in absence, than after death. The dead are not dishonoured by their levities; the living may return, and be laughed at by empty fops, who will not fail to turn into ridicule the good man, who is so unseasonable as to be still alive, and come and spoil good company. I am, sir, your most obedient humble servant.'

All strictness of behaviour is so unmercifully laughed at in our age, that the other much worse extreme is the more common folly. But let any woman consider, which of the two offences a husband would the more easily forgive, that of being less entertaining than she could to please company, or raising the desires of the whole room to his disadvantage; and she will easily be able to form her conduct. We have indeed carried women's characters too much into public life, and you shall see them now-a-days affect a sort of fame: but I cannot help venturing to disoblige them for their service, by telling them, that the utmost of a woman's character is contained in domestic life; she is blameable or praiseworthy according as her carriage affects the house of her father or her husband. All she has to do in this world, is contained within the duties of a daughter, a sister, a wife, and a mother. All these may be well performed, though a lady should not be the very finest woman at an opera or an assembly. They are likewise consistent with a moderate share of wit, a plain dress, and a modest air. But when the very brains of the sex are turned, and they place their ambition on circumstances, wherein to excel is no addition to what is truly commendable where can this end, but as it frequently does, in their placing all their industry, pleasure, and ambition, on things which will naturally make the gratifications of life last, at best, no longer than youth and good fortune? When we consider the least ill consequence, it can be no less than looking on their own condition, as years advance, with a disrelish of life, and falling into contempt of their own persons, or being the derision of others: But when they consider themselves as they ought, no other than an additional part of the species (for their own happiness and comfort, as well as that of those for whom they were born,) their ambition to excel will be directed accordingly; and they will in no part of their lives want opportunities of being shining ornaments to their fathers, husbands, brothers, or children. T.

No. 343.] *Thursday, April* 3, 1712.

——Errat, et illinc
Huc venit, hinc illuc, et quoslibet occupat artus
Spiritus; eque feris humana in corpora transit,
Inque feras noster——

Ovid. Met. Lib. xv. 165.

——All things are but alter'd; nothing dies;
And here and there the unbody'd spirit flies,
By time, or force, or sickness, dispossess'd,
And lodges. where it lights, in man or beast.

Dryden.

WILL HONEYCOMB, who loves to show upon occasion all the little learning he has picked up, told us yesterday at the club, that he thought there might be a great deal said for the transmigration of souls; and that the eastern parts of the world believed in that doctrine to this day. 'Sir Paul Rycaut,' says he, 'gives us an account of several well-disposed Mahometans that purchase the freedom of any little bird they see confined to a cage, and think they merit as much by it as we should do here by ransoming any of our countrymen from their captivity at Algiers. You must know,' says Will, 'the reason is, because they consider every animal as a brother or sister in disguise; and therefore think themselves obliged to extend their charity to them, though under such mean circumstances. They'll tell you,' says Will, 'that the soul of a man, when he dies, immediately passes into the body of another man, or of some brute, which he resembled in his humour, or his fortune, when he was one of us.'

As I was wondering what this profusion of learning would end in, Will told us, that 'Jack Freelove, who was a fellow of whim, made love to one of those ladies who throw away all their fondness on parrots, monkeys, and lap-dogs. Upon going to pay her a visit one morning, he writ a very pretty epistle upon this hint. Jack,' says he, 'was conducted into the parlour, where he diverted himself for some time with her favourite monkey, which was chained in one of the windows; till at length observing a pen and ink lie by him, he writ the following letter to his mistress in the person of the monkey, and upon her not coming down so soon as he expected, left it in the window, and went about his business.

'The lady soon after coming into the parlour and seeing her monkey look upon a paper with great earnestness, took it up, and to this day is in some doubt,' says Will, 'whether it was written by Jack or the monkey.'

'MADAM,—Not having the gift of speech, I have a long time waited in vain for an opportunity of making myself known to you; and having at present the convenience of pen, ink, and paper, by me, I gladly take the occasion of giving you my history in writing, which I could not do by word of mouth. You must know, madam, that about a thousand years ago I was an Indian brachman, and versed in all those mysterious secrets which your European philosopher, called Pythagoras, is said to have learned from our fraternity. I had so ingratiated myself, by my great skill in the occult sciences, with a demon whom I used to converse with, that he promised to grant me whatever I should ask of him. I desired that my soul might never pass into the body of a brute creature; but this, he told me, was not in his power to grant me. I then begged, that, into whatever creature I should chance to transmigrate, I should still retain my memory, and be conscious that I was the same person who lived in different animals. This, he told me, was in his power, and accordingly promised, on the word of a demon, that he would grant me what I desired. From that time forth, I lived so unblameably, that I was made president of a college of brachmans, an office which I discharged with great integrity until the day of my death.

'I was then shuffled into another human body, and acted my part so well in it, that I became first minister to a prince who reigned upon the banks of the Ganges. I here lived in great honour for several years, but by degrees lost all the innocence of the brachman, being obliged to rifle and oppress the people to enrich my sovereign; till at length I became so odious, that my master, to recover his credit with his subjects, shot me through the heart with an arrow, as I was one day addressing myself to him at the head of his army.

'Upon my next remove, I found myself in the woods under the shape of a jackal, and soon listed myself in the service of a lion. I used to yelp near his den about midnight, which was his time of rousing and seeking after prey. He always followed me in the rear, and when I had run down a fat buck, a wild goat, or a hare, after he had feasted very plentifully upon it himself, would now and then throw me a bone that was but half-picked, for my encouragement; but, upon my being unsuccessful in two or three chases, he gave me such a confounded gripe in his anger that I died of it.

'In my next transmigration, I was again set upon two legs, and became an Indian tax-gatherer; but having been guilty of great extravagances, and being married to an expensive jade of a wife, I ran so cursedly in debt, that I durst not show my head. I could no sooner step out of my house but I was arrested by somebody or other that lay in wait for me. As I ventured abroad one night in the dusk of the evening, I was taken up and hurried into a dungeon, where I died a few months after.

'My soul then entered into a flying-fish, and in that state led a most melancholy life for the space of six years. Several fishes of prey pursued me when I was in the water; and if I betook myself to my wings, it was ten to one but I had a flock of birds aiming at me. As I was one day flying amidst a fleet of English ships, I observed a huge sea-gull whetting his bill, and hovering just over my head; upon my dipping into the water to avoid him, I fell into the mouth of a monstrous shark, that swallowed me down in an instant.

'I was some years afterwards, to my great surprise, an eminent banker in Lombard street; and, remembering how I had formerly suffered for want of money, became so very sordid and avaricious, that the whole town cried shame of me. I was a miserable little old fellow to look upon; for I had in a manner starved myself, and was nothing but skin and bone when I died.

'I was afterwards very much troubled and amazed to find myself dwindled into an emmet. I was heartily concerned to make so insignificant a figure, and did not know but some time or other I might be reduced to a mite, if I did not mend my manners. I therefore applied myself with great diligence to the offices that were allotted to me, and was generally looked upon as the notablest ant in the whole mole-hill. I was at last picked up as I was groaning under a burden, by an unlucky cock-sparrow, that lived in the neighbourhood, and had before made great depredations upon our commonwealth.

'I then bettered my condition a little, and lived a whole summer in the shape of a bee; but being tired with the painful and penurious life I had undergone in my two last transmigrations, I fell into the other extreme, and turned drone. As I one day headed a party to plunder a hive, we were received so warmly by the swarm which defended it, that we were most of us left dead upon the spot.

'I might tell you of many other transmigrations which I went through: how I was a town-rake, and afterwards did penance in a bay gelding for ten years; as also how I was a tailor, a shrimp, and a tom-tit. In the last of these my shapes, I was shot in the Christmas holidays by a young jacka napes, who would needs try his new gun upon me.

'But I shall pass over these and several other stages of life, to remind you of the young beau who made love to you about six years since. You may remember, madam, how he masked, and danced, and sung, and played a thousand tricks to gain you; and how he was at last carried off by a cold that he got under your window one night in a serenade. I was that unfortunate young fellow to whom you were then so cruel. Not long after my shifting that unlucky body, I found myself upon a hill in Ethiopia, where I lived in my present grotesque shape, till I was caught by a servant of the English factory, and sent over into Great Britain. I need not inform you how I came into your hands. You see, madam, this is not the first time that you have had me in a chain: I am, however, very happy in this my captivity, as you often bestow on me those kisses and caresses which I would have given the world for when I was a man. I hope this discovery of my person will not tend to my disadvantage, but that you will still continue your accustomed favours to your most devoted humble servant,

'PUGG.'

'P. S. I would advise your little shock-dog to keep out of my way; for as I look upon him to be the most formidable of my rivals, I may chance one time or other to give him such a snap as he won't like.'

No. 344.] *Friday, April* 4, 1712.

——In solo vivendi causa palato est.
Juv. Sat. xi. 11.

Such whose sole bliss is eating: who can give
But that one brutal reason why they live.
Congreve.

Mr. Spectator,—I think it has not yet fallen into your way to discourse on little ambition, or the many whimsical ways men fall into to distinguish themselves among their acquaintance. Such observations, well pursued, would make a pretty history of low life. I myself am got into a great reputation, which arose (as most extraordinary occurrences in a man's life seem to do,) from a mere accident. I was some days ago unfortunately engaged among a set of gentlemen, who esteem a man according to the quantity of food he throws down at a meal. Now I, who am ever for distinguishing myself according to the notions of superiority which the rest of the company entertain, ate so immoderately, for their applause, as had like to have cost me my life. What added to my misfortune was, that having naturally a good stomach, and having lived soberly for some time, my body was as well prepared for this contention as if it had been by appointment. I had quickly vanquished every glutton in company but one who was such a prodigy in his way, and withal so very merry during the whole entertainment, that he insensibly betrayed me to continue his competitor, which in a little time concluded in a complete victory over my rival; after which, by way of insult, I ate a considerable proportion beyond what the spectators thought me obliged in honour to do. The effect, however, of this engagement, has made me resolve never to eat more for renown; and I have, pursuant to this resolution, compounded three wagers I had depending on the strength of my stomach, which happened very luckily, because it had been stipulated in our articles either to play or pay. How a man of common sense could be thus engaged is hard to determine; but the occasion of this is, to desire you to inform several gluttons of my acquaintance, who look on me with envy, that they had best moderate their ambition in time, lest infamy or death attend their success. I forgot to tell you, sir, with what unspeakable pleasure I received the acclamations and applause of the whole board, when I had almost eat my antagonist into convulsions. It was then that I returned his mirth upon him with such success, as he was hardly able to swallow, though prompted by a desire of fame, and a passionate fondness for distinction. I had not endeavoured to excel so far, had not the company been so loud in their approbation of my victory. I don't question but the same thirst after glory has often caused a man to drink quarts without taking breath, and prompted men to many other as difficult enterprises: which, if otherwise pursued, might turn very much to a man's advantage. This ambition of mine was indeed extravagantly pursued; however, I cannot help observing, that you hardly ever see a man commended for a good stomach, but he immediately falls to eating more, (though he had before dined,) as well to confirm the person that commended him in his good opinion of him, as to convince any other at the table, who may have been unattentive enough not to have done justice to his character. I am, sir, your humble servant,

'EPICURE MAMMON.'

'Mr. Spectator,—I have wrote to you three or four times, to desire you would take notice of an impertinent custom the women, the fine women, have lately fallen into, of taking snuff. This silly trick is attended with such a coquette air in some ladies, and such a sedate masculine one in others, that I cannot tell which most to complain of: but they are to me equally disagreeable. Mrs. Santer is so impatient of being without it, that she takes it as often as she does salt at meals: and as she affects a wonderful ease and negligence in all her manner, an upper lip mixed with snuff and the sauce, is what is presented to the observation of all who have the honour to eat with her. The pretty creature, her niece, does all she can to be as disagreeable as her aunt; and if she is not as offensive to the eye, she is quite as much to the ear, and makes up all she wants in a confident air, by a nauseous rattle of the nose, when the snuff is delivered, and the fingers make the stops and closes on the nostrils. This, perhaps, is not a very courtly image in speaking of ladies; that is very true: but where arises the offence? Is it in those who commit, or those who observe it? As for my part, I have been so extremely disgusted with this filthy physic hanging on the lip, that the most agreeable conversation, or person, has not been able to make up for it. As to those who take it for no other end but to give themselves occasion for pretty action, or to fill up little intervals of discourse, I can bear with them; but then they must not use it when another is speaking, who ought to be heard with too much respect, to admit of offering at that time from hand to hand the snuff-box. But Flavilla is so far taken with her behaviour in this kind, that she pulls out her box (which is indeed full of good Brazil,) in the middle of the sermon; and, to show she has the audacity of a well-bred woman, she offers it to the men as well as to the women who sit near her: but since by this time all the world knows she has a fine hand, I am in hopes she may give herself no further trouble in this matter. On Sunday was sevennight, when they came about for the offering, she gave her charity with a very good air, but at the same time asked the church-warden if he would take a pinch. Pray, sir, think of these things in time, and you will oblige, your humble servant.'

T.

No. 345.] *Saturday, April 5, 1712.*

Sanctius his animal, mentisque capacius altæ
Deerat adhuc, et quod dominari in cætera posset,
Natus homo est.——— *Ovid. Met.* Lib. i. 76.

A creature of a more exalted kind
Was wanting yet, and then was man design'd:
Conscious of thought, of more capacious breast,
For empire form'd, and fit to rule the rest.—*Dryden.*

THE accounts which Raphael gives of the battle of angels, and the creation of the world, have in them those qualifications which the critics judge requisite to an episode. They are nearly related to the principal action, and have a just connexion with the fable.

The eighth book opens with a beautiful description of the impression which this discourse of the archangel made on our first parents. Adam afterwards, by a very natural curiosity, inquires concerning the motions of those celestial bodies which make the most glorious appearance among the six days' work. The poet here, with a great deal of art, represents Eve as withdrawing from this part of their conversation, to amusements more suitable to her sex. He well knew that the episode in this book, which is filled with Adam's account of his passion and esteem for Eve, would have been improper for her hearing, and has therefore devised very just and beautiful reasons for her retiring:

So spake our sire, and by his countenance seem'd
Ent'ring on studious thoughts abtruse; which Eve
Perceiving, where she sat retir'd in sight,
With lowliness majestic from her seat,
And grace that won who saw to wish her stay,
Rose; and went forth among her fruits and flowers,
To visit how they prosper'd, bud and bloom,
Her nursery: they at her coming sprung,
And, touch'd by her fair tendance, gladlier grew.
Yet went she not, as not with such discourse,
Delighted, or not capable her ear
Of what was high: such pleasure she reserv'd,
Adam relating, she sole auditress;
Her husband the relator she prefer'd
Before the angel, and of him to ask
Chose rather: he, she knew, would intermix
Grateful digressions, and solve high dispute
With conjugal caresses; from his lip
Not words alone pleas'd her. O, when meet now
Such pairs, in love and mutual honour join'd!

The angel's returning a doubtful answer to Adam's inquiries, was not only proper for the moral reason which the poet assigns, but because it would have been highly absurd to have given the sanction of an archangel to any particular system of philosophy. The chief points in the Ptolemaic and Copernican hypotheses are described with great conciseness and perspicuity, and at the same time dressed in very pleasing and poetical images.

Adam, to detain the angel, enters afterwards upon his own history, and relates to him the circumstances in which he found himself upon his creation; as also his conversation with his Maker, and his first meeting with Eve. There is no part of the poem more apt to raise the attention of the reader than this discourse of our great ancestor; as nothing can be more surprising and delightful to us, than to hear the sentiments that arose in the first man, while he was yet new and fresh from the hands of his Creator. The poet has interwoven every thing which is delivered upon this subject in holy writ with so many beautiful imaginations of his own, that nothing can be conceived more just and more natural than this whole episode. As our author knew this subject could not but be agreeable to his reader he would not throw it into the relation of the six days' work, but reserved it for a distinct episode, that he might have an opportunity of expatiating upon it more at large. Before I enter upon this part of the poem, I cannot but take notice of two shining passages in the dialogue between Adam and the angel. The first is that wherein our ancestor gives an account of the pleasure he took in conversing with him, which contains a very noble moral.

For while I sit with thee, I seem in heaven,
And sweeter thy discourse is to my ear
Than fruits of palm-trees (pleasantest to thirst
And hunger both, from labour) at the hour
Of sweet repast; they satiate and soon fill,
Though pleasant; but thy words, with grace divine
Imbued, bring to their sweetness no satiety

The other I shall mention, is that in which the angel gives a reason why he should be glad to hear the story Adam was about to relate.

'For I that day was absent as befel,
Bound on a voyage uncouth and obscure,
Far on excursion towards the gates of hell,
Squar'd in full legion (such command we had,)
To see that none thence issued forth a spy,
Or enemy, while God was in his work,
Lest he, incens'd at such eruption bold,
Destruction with creation might be mix'd.'

There is no question but our poet drew the image in what follows from that in Virgil's sixth book, where Æneas and the Sybil stand before the adamantine gates, which are there described as shut upon the place of torments, and listen to the groans, the clank of chains, and the noise of iron whips, that were heard in those regions of pain and sorrow.

——'Fast we found, fast shut
The dismal gates, and barricado'd strong;
But long ere our approaching heard within
Noise, other than the sound of dance or song,
Torment, and loud lament, and furious rage.'

Adam then proceeds to give an account of his condition and sentiments immediately after his creation. How agreeably does he represent the posture in which he found himself, the delightful landscape that surrounded him, and the gladness of heart which grew up in him on that occasion!

——'As new wak'd from soundest sleep,
Soft on the flow'ry herb I found me laid
In balmy sweat, which with his beams the sun
Soon dry'd, and on the reeking moisture fed,
Straight towards heaven my wond'ring eyes I turn'd
And gaz'd awhile the ample sky; till rais'd
By quick instinctive motion, up I sprung,
As thitherward endeavouring, and upright
Stood on my feet. About me round I saw
Hill, dale, and shady woods, and sunny plains,
And liquid lapse of murmuring streams: by these,
Creatures that liv'd and mov'd, and walk'd, or flew,
Birds on the branches warbling; all things smil'd
With fragrance, and with joy my heart o'erflow'd.'

Adam is afterwards described as surprised at his own existence, and taking a survey of himself and of all the works of nature. He likewise is represented as discovering, by the light of reason, that he, and every thing about him, must have been the effect of some Being infinitely good and powerful, and that this Being had a right to his worship and adoration. His first address to the Sun, and to those parts of the creation which made the most distinguished figure, is very natural and amusing to the imagination:

——'Thou Sun,' said I, 'Fair light,
And thou enlighten'd earth, so fresh and gay,
Ye hills, and dales, ye rivers, woods, and plains,
And ye that live and move, fair creatures, tell,
Tell, if ye saw, how came I thus? how here?'

His next sentiment, when, upon his first going to sleep, he fancies himself losing his existence, and falling away into nothing, can never be sufficiently admired. His dream, in which he still preserves the consciousness of his existence, together with his removal into the garden which was prepared for his reception, are also circumstances finely imagined, and grounded upon what is delivered in sacred story.

These and the like wonderful incidents in this part of the work, have in them all the beauties of novelty, at the same time that they have all the graces of nature.

They are such as none but a great genius could have thought of; though, upon the perusal of them, they seem to rise of themselves from the subject of which he treats. In a word, though they are natural, they are not obvious; which is the true character of all fine writing.

The impression which the interdiction of the tree of life left in the mind of our first parent is described with great strength and judgment; as the image of the several beasts and birds passing in review before him is very beautiful and lively:

——'Each bird and beast behold
Approaching two and two, these cow'ring low
With blandishment; each bird stoop'd on his wing.
I nam'd them as they pass'd.'——

Adam in the next place, describes a conference which he held with his Maker upon the subject of solitude. The poet here represents the Supreme Being as making an essay of his own work, and putting to the trial that reasoning faculty with which he had endued his creature. Adam urges, in this divine colloquy, the impossibility of his being happy, though he was the inhabitant of Paradise, and lord of the whole creation, without the conversation and society of some rational creature who should partake those blessings with him. This dialogue, which is supported chiefly by the beauty of the thoughts, without other poetical ornament, is as fine a part as any in the whole poem. The more the reader examines the justness and delicacy of its sentiments, the more he will find himself pleased with it. The poet has wonderfully preserved the character of majesty and condescension in the Creator, and, at the same time, that of humility and adoration in the creature, as particularly in the following lines:

'Thus I presumptuous; and the vision bright,
As with a smile more brighten'd, thus reply'd, &c.
——I with leave of speech implor'd,
And humble deprecation, thus reply'd:
"Let not my words offend thee, Heavenly Power,
My Maker, be propitious while I speak." &c.

Adam then proceeds to give an account of his second sleep, and of the dream in which he beheld the formation of Eve. The new passion that was awakened in him at the sight of her is touched very finely.

'Under his forming hands a creature grew,
Manlike, but diff'rent sex: so lovely fair,
That what seem'd fair in all the world, seem'd now
Mean, or in her summ'd up, in her contain'd,
And in her looks, which from that time infus'd
Sweetness into my heart, unfelt before;
And into all things from her air inspir'd
The spirit of love and amorous delight.'

Adam's distress upon losing sight of this beautiful phantom, with his exclamations of joy and gratitude at the discovery of a real creature who resembled the apparition which had been presented to him in his dream; the approaches he makes to her, and his manner of courtship, are all laid together in a most exquisite propriety of sentiments.

Though this part of the poem is worked up with great warmth and spirit, the love which is described in it is every way suitable to a state of innocence. If the reader compares the description which Adam here gives of his leading Eve to the nuptial bower, with that which Mr. Dryden has made on the same occasion in a scene of his Fall of Man, he will be sensible of the great care which Milton took to avoid all thoughts on so delicate a subject that might be offensive to religion or good manners. The sentiments are chaste, but not cold; and convey to the mind ideas of the most transporting passion, and of the greatest purity. What a noble mixture of rapture and innocence has the author joined together, in the reflection which Adam makes on the pleasures of love, compared to those of sense!

Thus have I told thee, all my state, and brought
My story to the sum of earthly bliss
Which I enjoy; and must confess to find
In all things else delight indeed, but such
As us'd or not, works in the mind no change
Nor vehement desire; these delicacies,
I mean of taste, sight, smell, herbs, fruits, and flowers,
Walks, and the melody of birds: but here
Far otherwise, transported I behold,
Transported touch; here passion first I felt,
Commotion strange! in all enjoyments else
Superior and unmov'd, here only weak
Against the charm of beauty's pow'rful glance.
Or nature fail'd in me, and left some part
Not proof enough such object to sustain;
Or from my side subducting, took perhaps
More than enough; at least on her bestow'd
Too much of ornament, in outward show
Elaborate, of inward less exact.
——————When I approach
Her loveliness, so absolute she seems,
And in herself complete, so well to know
Her own, that what she wills to do or say,
Seems wisest, virtuousest, discreetest, best;
All higher knowledge in her presence falls
Degraded: wisdom in discourse with her
Loses, discountenanc'd, and like folly shows:
Authority and reason on her wait,
As one intended first, not after made
Occasionally; and to consummate all,
Greatness of mind and nobleness their seat
Build in her loveliest, and create an awe
About her, as a guard angelic plac'd.'

These sentiments of love in our first parent, gave the angel such an insight into human nature, that he seems apprehensive of the evils which might befall the species in general, as well as Adam in particular, from the excess of his passion. He therefore fortifies him against it by timely admonitions; which very artfully prepare the mind of the reader for the occurrences of the next book, where the weakness, of which Adam here gives such distant discoveries, brings about that fatal event which is the subject of the poem. His discourse, which follows the gentle rebuke he received from the angel, shows that his love, however violent it might appear, was still founded in reason, and consequently not improper for Paradise:

'Neither her outside form'd so fair, nor aught
In procreation common to all kinds,
(Though higher of the genial bed by far,
And with mysterious reverence I deem)
So much delights me, as those graceful acts,
Those thousand decencies that daily flow
From all her words and actions, mix'd with love
And sweet compliance, which declare unfeign'd
Union of mind, or in us both one soul:
Harmony to behold in wedded pair!'

Adam's speech at parting with the angel, has in it a deference and gratitude agreeable to an inferior nature, and at the same time a certain dignity and greatness suitable to the father of mankind in his state of innocence. L.

No. 346.] *Monday, April* 7, 1712.

Consuetudinem benignitatis largitioni munerum longe antepono. Hæc est gravium hominum atque magnorum; illa quasi assentatorum populi, multitudinis levitatem voluptate quasi titillantium. *Tull.*

I esteem a habit of benignity greatly preferable to munificence. The former is peculiar to great and distinguished persons; the latter belongs to flatterers of the people, who tickle the levity of the multitude with a kind of pleasure.

When we consider the offices of human life, there is, methinks, something in what we ordinarily call generosity, which, when carefully examined, seems to flow rather from a loose and unguarded temper than an honest and liberal mind. For this reason it is absolutely necessary that all liberality should have for its basis and support frugality. By this means the beneficent spirit works in a man from convictions of reason, not from the impulse of passion. The generous man in the ordinary acceptation, without respect of the demands of his family, will soon find upon the foot of his account, that he has sacrificed to fools, knaves, flatterers, or the deservedly unhappy, all the opportunities of affording any future assistance where it ought to be. Let him therefore reflect, that if to bestow be in itself laudable, should not a man take care to secure an ability to do things praiseworthy as long as he lives? Or could there be a more cruel piece of raillery upon a man who should have reduced his fortune below the capacity of acting according to his natural temper, than to say of him, 'That gentleman was generous?' My beloved author therefore has, in the sentence on the top of my paper, turned his eye with a certain satiety from beholding the addresses to the people by largesses and public entertainments, which he asserts to be in general vicious, and are always to be regulated according to the circumstances of time and a man's own fortune. A constant benignity in commerce with the rest of the world, which ought to run through all a man's actions, has effects more useful to those whom you oblige and is less ostentatious in yourself. He turns his recommendation of this virtue on commercial life: and, according to him, a citizen who is frank in his kindnesses, and abhors severity in his demands: he who, in buying, selling, lending, doing acts of good neighbourhood, is just and easy; he who appears naturally averse to disputes, and above the sense of little sufferings; bears a noble character, and does much more good to mankind than any other man's fortune, without commerce, can possibly support. For the citizen above all other men, has opportunities of arriving at 'the highest fruit of wealth,' to be liberal without the least expense of a man's own fortune. It is not to be denied but such a practice is liable to hazard; but this therefore adds to the obligation, that, among traders, he who obliges is as much concerned to keep the favour a secret as he who receives it. The unhappy distinctions among us in England are so great, that to celebrate the intercourse of commercial friendship (with which I am daily made acquainted) would be to raise the virtuous man so many enemies of the contrary party. I am obliged to conceal all I know of 'Tom the Bounteous,' who lends at the ordinary interest, to give men of less fortune opportunities of making greater advantages. He conceals, under a rough air and distant behaviour, a bleeding compassion and womanish tenderness. This is governed by the most exact circumspection, that there is no industry wanting in the person whom he is to serve, and that he is guilty of no improper expenses. This I know of Tom; but who dare say it of so known a Tory? The same care I was forced to use some time ago, in the report of another's virtue, and said fifty instead of a hundred, because the man I pointed at was a Whig. Actions of this kind are popular, without being invidious: for every man of ordinary circumstances looks upon a man who has this known benignity in his nature as a person ready to be his friend upon such terms as he ought to expect it; and the wealthy who may envy such a character, can do no injury to its interests, but by the imitation of it, in which the good citizen will rejoice to be rivalled. I know not how to form to myself a greater idea of human life, than in what is the practice of some wealthy men whom I could name, that make no step to the improvement of their own fortunes, wherein they do not also advance those of other men who would languish in poverty without that munificence. In a nation where there are so many public funds to be supported, I know not whether he can be called a good subject, who does not embark some part of his fortune with the state, to whose vigilance he owes the security of the whole. This certainly is an immediate way of laying an obligation upon many, and extending your benignity the farthest a man can possibly, who is not engaged in commerce. But he who trades, besides giving the state some part of this sort of credit he gives his banker, may, in all the occurrences of his life, have his eye upon removing want from the door of the industrious, and defending the unhappy upright man from bankruptcy. Without this benignity, pride or vengeance will precipitate a man to choose the receipt of half his demands from one whom he has undone, rather than the whole from one to whom he has shown mercy. This benignity is essential to the character of a fair trader, and any man who designs to enjoy his wealth with honour and self-satisfaction; nay, it would not be hard to maintain, that the practice of supporting good and industrious men would carry a man farther even to his profit, than indulging the propensity of serving and obliging the fortunate. My author argues on this subject, in order to incline men's minds to those who want them most, after this manner. 'We must always consider the nature of things, and govern ourselves accordingly. The wealthy man, when he has repaid you, is upon a balance, with you; but the person whom you favoured with a loan, if he be a good man, will think himself in your debt after he has paid you. The wealthy and the conspicuous are not obliged by the benefits you do them; they think they conferred a benefit when they received one. Your good offices are always suspected, and it is with them the same thing to expect their favour as to receive it. But the man below you, who knows, in the good you have done him, you respected himself more than his circumstances, does not act like an obliged man only to him from whom he has received a benefit, but also to all who are capable of doing him one. And whatever little offices he can do for you, he is so far from magnifying it, that he will labour to extenuate it in all his actions and expressions. Moreover, the regard to what you do to a great man at best is taken notice of no further than by himself or his family; but what you do to a man of an humble fortune (provided always that he is a good and a modest man) raises the affections towards you of all men of that character (of which there are many) in the whole city.

There is nothing gains a reputation to a preacher so much as his own practice; I am therefore casting about what act of benignity is in the power of a Spectator. Alas! that lies but in a very narrow compass; and I think the most immediately under my patronage are either players, or such whose circumstances bear an affinity with theirs. All, therefore, I am able to do at this time of this kind, is to tell the town, that on Friday the 11th of this instant, April, there will be performed in York-Buildings, a concert of vocal and instrumental music, for the benefit of Mr. Edward Keen, the father of twenty children; and that this day the haughty George Powell hopes all the good-natured part of the town will favour him, whom they applauded in Alexander, Timon, Lear, and Orestes, with their company this night, when he hazards all his heroic glory for their approbation in the humble condition of honest Jack Falstaff. T

No. 347.] *Tuesday, April 8, 1712.*

Quis furor, o cives! quæ tanta licentia ferri!
Lucan, Lib. i. 8.

What blind, detested fury, could afford
Such horrid license to the barb'rous sword!

I do not question but my country readers have been very much surprised at the several accounts they have met with in our public papers, of that species of men among us, lately known by the name of Mohocks. I find the opinions of the learned, as to their origin and designs, are altogether various, insomuch that very many begin to doubt whether indeed there were ever any such society of men. The terror which spread itself over the whole nation some years since on account of the Irish, is still fresh in most people's memories, though it afterwards appeared there was not the least ground for that general consternation.

The late panic fear was in the opinion of many deep and penetrating persons of the same nature. These will have it that the Mohocks are like those spectres and apparitions which frighten several towns and villages in her majesty's dominions, though they were never seen by any of the inhabitants. Others are apt to think that these Mohocks are a kind of bull-beggars, first invented by prudent married men, and masters of families, in order to deter their wives and daughters from taking the air at unseasonable hours; and that when they tell them 'the Mohocks will catch them,' it is a caution of the same nature with that of our forefathers, when they bid their children have a care of Raw-head and Bloody-bones.

For my own part, I am afraid there was too much reason for the great alarm the whole city has been in upon this occasion; though at the same time I must own, that I am in some doubt whether the following pieces are genuine and authentic; the more so, because I am not fully satisfied that the name by which the emperor subscribes himself, is altogether conformable to the Indian orthography.

I shall only farther inform my readers, that it was some time since I received the following letter and manifesto, though, for particular reasons, I did not think fit to publish them till now.

' *To the Spectator.*

'Sir,—Finding that our earnest endeavours for the good of mankind have been basely and maliciously represented to the world, we send you enclosed our imperial manifesto, which it is our will and pleasure that you forthwith communicate to the public, by inserting it in your next daily paper. We do not doubt of your ready compliance in this particular, and therefore bid you heartily farewell.

(Signed)
'TAW WAW EBEN ZAN KALADAR,
'*Emperor of the Mohocks.*'

' *The Manifesto of Taw Waw Eben Zan Kaladar, Emperor of the Mohocks.*

'Whereas we have received information, from sundry quarters of this great and populous city, of several outrages committed on the legs, arms, noses, and other parts, of the good people of England, by such as have styled themselves our subjects; in order to vindicate our imperial dignity from those false aspersions which have been cast on it, as if we ourselves might have encouraged or abetted any such practices, we have, by these presents, thought fit to signify our utmost abhorrence and detestation of all such tumultuous and irregular proceedings; and do hereby farther give notice, that if any person or persons has or have suffered any wound, hurt, damage, or detriment, in his or their limb or limbs otherwise than shall be hereafter specified, the said person or persons, upon applying themselves to such as we shall appoint for the inspection and redress of the grievances aforesaid, shall be forthwith committed to the care of our principal surgeon, and be cured at our own expense, in some one or other of those hospitals which we are now erecting for that purpose.

'And to the end that no one may, either through ignorance or inadvertency, incur those penalties which we have thought fit to inflict on persons of loose and dissolute lives, we do hereby notify to the public, that if any man be knocked down or assaulted while he is employed in his lawful business, at proper hours, that it is not done by our order; and we do hereby permit and allow any such person, so knocked down or assaulted, to rise again, and defend himself in the best manner that he is able.

'We do also command all and every our good subjects, that they do not presume, upon any pretext whatsoever, to issue and sally forth from their respective quarters till between the hours of eleven and twelve. That they never tip the lion upon man, woman, or child, till the clock at St. Dunstan's shall have struck one.

'That the sweat be never given but between the hours of one and two; always provided, that our hunters may begin to hunt a little after the close of the evening, any thing to the contrary herein notwithstanding. Provided also, that if ever they are reduced to the necessity of pinking, it shall always be in the most fleshy parts, and such as are least exposed to view.

'It is also our imperial will and pleasure, that our good subjects the sweaters do establish their hummums in such close places, alleys, nooks, and corners, that the patient or patients may not be in danger of catching cold.

'That the tumblers, to whose care we chiefly commit the female sex, confine themselves to Drury-lane, and the purlieus of the Temple; and that every other party and division of our subjects do each of them keep within the respective quarters we have allotted to them. Provided, nevertheless, that nothing herein contained shall in any wise be construed to extend to the hunters, who have our full license and permission to enter into any part of the town wherever their game shall lead them.

'And whereas we have nothing more at our imperial heart than the reformation of the cities of London and Westminster, which to our unspeakable satisfaction we have in some measure already effected, we do hereby earnestly pray and exhort all husbands, fathers, house-keepers, and masters of families, in either of the aforesaid cities, not only to repair themselves to their respective habitations at early and seasonable hours, but also to keep their wives and daughters, sons, servants, and apprentices, from appearing in the streets at those times and seasons which may expose them to a military discipline, as it is practised by our good subjects the Mohocks; and we do further promise on our imperial word, that as soon as the reformation aforesaid shall be brought about, we will forthwith cause all hostilities to cease.

'Given from our court, at the Devil-tavern,
'March 15, 1712.' X.

No. 348.] *Wednesday, April* 9, 1712.

Invidiam placare paras virtute relicta.
Hor. Sat. iii. Lib. 2. 13

To shun detraction, wouldst thou virtue fly?

'MR. SPECTATOR,—I have not seen you lately at any of the places where I visit, so that I am afraid you are wholly unacquainted with what passes among my part of the world, who are, though I say it, without controversy, the most accomplished and best bred of the town. Give me leave to tell you, that I am extremely discomposed when I hear scandal, and am an utter enemy to all manner of detraction, and think it the greatest meanness that people of distinction can be guilty of. However, it is hardly possible to come into company, where you do not find them pulling one another to pieces, and that from no other provocation but that of hearing any one commended. Merit, both as to wit and beauty, is become no other than the possession of a few trifling people's favour, which you cannot possibly arrive at, if you have really any thing in you that is deserving. What they would bring to pass is, to make all good and evil consist in report, and with whispers, calumnies, and impertinences, to have the conduct of those reports. By this means, innocents are blasted upon their first appearance in town, and there is nothing more required to make a young woman the object of envy and hatred, than to deserve love and admiration. This abominable endeavour to suppress or lessen every thing that is praiseworthy, is as frequent among the men as the women. If I can remember what passed at a visit last night, it will serve as an instance that the sexes are equally inclined to defamation, with equal malice and impotence. Jack Triplett came into my lady Airy's about eight of the clock. You know the manner we sit at a visit, and I need not describe the circle; but Mr. Triplett came in, introduced by two tapers supported by a spruce servant, whose hair is under a cap till my lady's candles are all lighted up, and the hour of ceremony begins: I say Jack Triplett came in, and singing (for he is really good company) "Every feature, charming creature,"——he went on, "It is a most unreasonable thing, that people cannot go peaceably to see their friends, but these murderers are let loose. Such a shape! such an air! what a glance was that as her chariot passed by mine!"—My lady herself interrupted him; "Pray, who is this fine thing?"—"I warrant," says another, "'tis the creature I was telling your ladyship of, just now."—"You were telling of?" says Jack; "I wish I had been so happy as to have come in and heard you; for I have not words to say what she is: but if an agreeable height, a modest air, a virgin shame, and impatience of being beheld amidst a blaze of ten thousand charms——" The whole room flew out—"Oh Mr. Triplett!"——When Mrs. Lofty, a known prude, said she believed she knew whom the gentleman meant; but she was indeed, as he civilly represented her, impatient of being beheld.—Then turning to the lady next to her,—"The most unbred creature you ever saw!" Another pursued the discourse; "As unbred, madam, as you may think her, she is extremely belied if she is the novice she appears; she was last week at a ball till two in the morning: Mr. Triplett knows whether he was the happy man that took care of her home; but—" This was followed by some particular exception that each woman in the room made to some peculiar grace or advantage; so that Mr. Triplett was beaten from one limb and feature to another, till he was forced to resign the whole woman. In the end, I took notice Triplett recorded all this malice in his heart; and saw in his countenance, and a certain waggish shrug, that he designed to repeat the conversation: I therefore let the discourse die, and soon after took an occasion to recommend a certain gentleman of my acquaintance for a person of singular modesty, courage, integrity, and withal as a man of an entertaining conversation, to which advantages he had a shape and manner peculiarly graceful. Mr. Triplett, who is a woman's man seemed to hear me with patience enough commend the qualities of his mind.—He never heard indeed but that he was a very honest man, and no fool; but for a fine gentleman, he must ask pardon. Upon no other foundation than this, Mr. Triplett took occasion to give the gentleman's pedigree, by what methods some part of the estate was acquired, now much it was beholden to a marriage for the present circumstances of it: after all he could see nothing but a common man in his person, his breeding, or understanding.

'Thus, Mr. Spectator, this impertinent humour of diminishing every one who is produced in conversation to their advantage, runs through the world; and I am, I confess, so fearful of the force of ill tongues, that I have begged of all those who are my well-wishers never to commend me, for it will but bring my frailties into examination; and I had rather be unobserved, than conspicuous for disputed perfections. I am confident a thousand young people, who would have been ornaments to society, have, from fear of scandal, never dared to exert themselves in the polite arts of life. Their lives have passed away in an odious rusticity in spite of great advantages of person, genius, and fortune. There is a vicious terror of being blamed in some well-inclined people, and a wicked pleasure in suppressing them in others; both which I recommend to your spectatorial wisdom to animadvert upon; and if you can be successful in it, I need not say how much you will deserve of the town; but new toasts will owe to you their beauty, and new wits their fame. I am, sir, your most obedient humble servant, 'MARY.'

T.

No. 349.] *Thursday, April* 10, 1712.

——————Quos ille timorum
Maximus haud urget lethi metus: inde ruendi
In ferrum mens prona viris, animæque capaces
Mortis—————   *Lucan.* Lib. i. 454.

Thrice happy they beneath their northern skies,
Who that worst fear, the fear of death, despise!
Hence they no cares for this frail being feel,
But rush undaunted on the pointed steel.
Provoke approaching fate, and bravely scorn
To spare that life which must so soon return.—*Rowe.*

I AM very much pleased with a consolatory letter of Phalaris, to one who had lost a son that was a young man of great merit. The thought with which he comforts the afflicted father is, to the best of my memory as follows:—That he should consider death had set a kind seal upon his son's character, and placed him out of the reach of vice and infamy: that, while he lived, he was still within the possibility of falling away from virtue, and losing the fame of which he was possessed. Death only closes a man's reputation, and determines it as good or bad.

This, among other motives, may be one reason why we are naturally averse to the launching out into a man's praise till his head is laid in the dust. Whilst he is capable of changing, we may be forced to retract our opinion. He may forfeit the esteem we have conceived of him, and some time or other appear to us under a different light from what he does at present. In short, as the life of any man cannot be called happy, or unhappy, so neither can it be pronounced vicious or virtuous before the conclusion of it.

It was upon this consideration that Epaminondas, being asked whether Chabrias Iphicrates, or he himself, deserved most to be esteemed? 'You must first see us die,' saith he, 'before that question can be answered.'

As there is not a more melancholy consideration to a good man than his being obnoxious to such a change, so there is nothing more glorious than to keep up an uniformity in his actions, and preserve the beauty of his character to the last.

The end of a man's life is often compared to the winding up of a well-written play, where the principal persons still act in character, whatever the fate is which they undergo. There is scarce a great person in the Grecian or Roman history, whose death has not been remarked upon by some writer or other, and censured or applauded according to the genius or principles of the person who has descanted on it. Monsieur de St. Evremond is very particular in setting forth the constancy and courage of Petronius Arbiter during his last moments, and thinks he discovers in them a greater firmness of mind and resolution than in the death of Seneca, Cato, or Socrates. There is no question but this polite author's affectation of appearing singular in his remarks, and making discoveries which had escaped the observations of others, threw him into this course of reflection. It was Petronius's merit that he died in the same gaiety of temper, in which he lived; but as his life was altogether loose and dissolute, the indifference which he showed at the close of it is to be looked upon as a piece of natural carelessness and levity, rather than fortitude. The resolution of Socrates proceeded from very different motives, the consciousness of a well-spent life, and the prospect of a happy eternity. If the ingenious author above-mentioned was so pleased with gaiety of humour in a dying man, he might have found a much nobler instance of it in our countryman Sir Thomas More.

This great and learned man was famous for enlivening his ordinary discourses with wit and pleasantry; and as Erasmus tells him in an epistle dedicatory, acted in all parts of life like a second Democritus.

He died upon a point of religion, and is respected as a martyr by that side for which he suffered. That innocent mirth, which had been so conspicuous in his life, did not forsake him to the last. He maintained the same cheerfulness of heart upon the scaffold which he used to show at his table; and upon laying his head on the block, gave instances of that good humour with which he had always entertained his friends in the most ordinary occurrences. His death was of a piece with his life. There was nothing in it new, forced, or affected. He did not look upon the severing his head from his body as a circumstance that ought to produce any change in the disposition of his mind; and as he died under a fixed and settled hope of immortality, he thought any unusual degree of sorrow and concern improper on such an occasion, as had nothing in it which could deject or terrify him.

There is no great danger of imitation from this example. Men's natural fears will be a sufficient guard against it. I shall only observe, that what was philosophy in this extraordinary man, would be phrensy in one who does not resemble him as well in the cheerfulness of his temper as in the sanctity of his life and manners.

I shall conclude this paper with the instance of a person who seems to me to have shown more intrepidity and greatness of soul in his dying moments than what we meet with among any of the most celebrated Greeks and Romans. I met with this instance in the History of the Revolutions in Portugal, written by the abbot de Vortot.

When Don Sebastian, king of Portugal, had invaded the territories of Muli Moluc, emperor of Morocco, in order to dethrone him, and set the crown upon the head of his nephew, Moluc was wearing away with a distemper which he himself knew was incurable. However, he prepared for the reception of so formidable an enemy. He was, indeed, so far spent with his sickness, that he did not expect to live out the whole day when the last decisive battle was given; but knowing the fatal consequences that would happen to his children and people, in case he should die before he put an end to that war, he commanded his principal officers, that if he died during the engagement, they should conceal his death from the army, and that they should ride up to the litter in which his corpse was carried, under pretence of receiving orders from him as usual. Before the battle began, he was carried, through all the ranks of his army in an open litter, as they stood drawn up in array, encouraging them to fight valiantly in defence of their religion and country. Finding afterwards the battle to go against him, though he was very near his last agonies, he threw himself out of his litter, rallied his army, and led them on to the charge: which afterwards ended in a complete victory on the side of the Moors. He had no sooner brought his men to the engagement, but, finding himself utterly spent, he was again replaced in his litter, where, laying his finger on his mouth, to enjoin secrecy to his officers who stood about him, he died in a few moments after in that posture. L.

No. 350.] *Friday, April* 11, 1712.

Ea animi elatio quæ cernitur in periculis, si justitia vacat, pugnatque pro suis commodis, in vitio est. *Tull.*

That elevation of mind which is displayed in dangers, if it wants justice, and fights for its own conveniency, is vicious.

Captain Sentry was last night at a club, and produced a letter from Ipswich, which his correspondent desired him to communicate to his friend the Spectator. It contained an account of an engagement between a French privateer, commanded by one Dominic Pottiere, and a little vessel of that place laden with corn, the master whereof, as I remember, was one Goodwin. The Englishman defended himself with incredible bravery, and beat off the French, after having been boarded three or four times. The enemy still came on with great fury, and hoped by his number of men to carry the prize; till at last the Englishman, finding himself sink apace, and ready to perish, struck: but the effect which this singular gallantry had upon the captain of the privateer was no other than an unmanly desire of vengeance for the loss he had sustained in his several attacks. He told the Ipswich man in a speaking trumpet, that he would not take him aboard, and that he stayed to see him sink. The Englishman at the same time observed a disorder in the vessel, which he rightly judged to proceed from the disdain which the ship's crew had of their captain's inhumanity. With this hope he went into his boat, and approached the enemy. He was taken in by the sailors in spite of their commander: but though they received him against his command, they treated him, when he was in the ship, in the manner he directed. Pottiere caused his men to hold Goodwin, while he beat him with a stick, till he fainted with loss of blood and rage of heart; after which he ordered him into irons, without allowing him any food, but such as one or two of the men stole to him under peril of the like usage: and having kept him several days overwhelmed with the misery of stench, hunger, and soreness, he brought him into Calais. The governor of the place was soon acquainted with all that had passed, dismissed Pottiere from his charge with ignominy, and gave Goodwin all the relief which a man of honour would bestow upon an enemy barbarously treated, to recover the imputation of cruelty upon his prince and country.

When Mr. Sentry had read his letter, full of many other circumstances which aggravate the barbarity, he fell into a sort of criticism upon magnanimity and courage, and argued that they were inseparable; and that courage, without regard to justice and humanity, was no other than the fierceness of a wild beast. 'A good and truly bold spirit,' continued he, 'is ever actuated by reason, and a sense of honour and duty. The affectation of such a spirit exerts itself in an impudent aspect, an overbearing confidence, and a certain negligence of giving offence. This is visible in all the cocking youths you see about this town, who are noisy in assemblies, unawed by the presence of wise and virtuous men; in a word, insensible of all the honours and decencies of human life. A shameless fellow takes advantage of merit clothed with modesty and magnanimity, and, in the eyes of little people, appears sprightly and agreeable: while the man of resolution and true gallantry is overlooked and disregarded, if not despised. There is a propriety in all things; and I believe what you scholars call just and sublime, in opposition to turgid and bombast expression, may give you an idea of what I mean, when I say modesty is the certain indication of a great spirit, and impudence the affectation of it. He that writes with judgment, and never rises into improper warmths, manifests the true force of genius; in like manner, he who is quiet and equal in his behaviour is supported in that deportment by what we may call true courage. Alas! it is not so easy a thing to be a brave man as the unthinking part of mankind imagine. To dare is not all there is in it. The privateer we were just now talking of had boldness enough to attack his enemy, but not greatness of mind enough to admire the same quality exerted by that enemy in defending himself. Thus his base and little mind was wholly taken up in the sordid regard to the prize of which he failed, and the damage done to his own vessel; and therefore he used an honest man, who defended his own from him, in the manner as he would a thief that should rob him.

'He was equally disappointed, and had not spirit enough to consider, that one case would be laudable, and the other criminal. Malice, rancour, hatred, vengeance, are what tear the breasts of mean men in fight; but fame, glory, conquests, desire of opportunities to pardon and oblige their opposers, are what glow in the minds of the gallant.' The captain ended his discourse with a specimen of his book-learning; and gave us to understand that he had read a French author on the subject of justness in point of gallantry. 'I love,' said Mr. Sentry 'a critic who mixes the rules of life with annotations upon writers. My author,' added he, 'in his discourse upon epic poems, takes occasion to speak of the same quality of courage drawn in the two different characters of Turnus and Æneas. He makes courage the chief and greatest ornament of Turnus; but in Æneas there are many others which outshine it; among the rest that of piety. Turnus is, therefore, all along painted by the poet full of ostentation, his language haughty and vain-glorious, as placing his honour in the manifestation of his valour; Æneas speaks little, is slow to action, and shows only a sort of defensive courage. If equipage and address make Turnus appear more courageous than Æneas, conduct and success prove Æneas more valiant than Turnus. T.

No. 351.] *Saturday, April* 12, 1712.

In te omnis domus inclinata recumbit.
Virg. Æn. xii. 59.

On thee the fortunes of our house depend.

If we look into the three great heroic poems which have appeared in the world, we may observe that they are built upon very slight foundations. Homer lived near 300 years after the Trojan war; and, as the writing of history was not then in use among the Greeks, we may very well suppose that the tradition of Achilles and Ulysses had brought down but very few particulars to his knowledge; though there is no question but he has wrought into his two poems such of their remarkable adventures as were still talked of among his contemporaries.

The story of Æneas, on which Virgil founded his poem, was likewise very bare of circumstances, and by that means afforded him an opportunity of embellishing it with fiction, and giving a full range to his own invention. We find, however, that he has interwoven, in the course of his fable, the principal particulars, which were generally believed among the Romans, of Eneas's voyage and settlement in Italy.

The reader may find an abridgment of the whole story, as collected out of the ancient historians, and as it was received among the Romans, in Dionysius Halicarnassus.

Since none of the critics have considered Virgil's fable with relation to this history of Æneas, it may not perhaps be amiss to examine it in this light, so far as regards my present purpose. Whoever looks into the abridgment above-mentioned, will find that the character of Æneas is filled with piety to the gods, and a superstitious observation of prodigies, oracles, and predictions. Virgil has not only preserved his character in the person of Æneas, but has given a place in his poem to those particular prophecies which he found recorded of him in history and tradition. The poet took the matters of fact as they came down to him, and circumstanced them after his own manner, to make them appear the more natural, agreeable, or surprising. I believe very many readers have been shocked at that ludicrous prophecy which one of the harpies pronounces to the Trojans in the third book; namely, that before they had built their intended city they should be reduced by hunger to eat their very tables. But, when they hear that this was one of the circumstances that had been transmitted to the Romans in the history of Æneas, they will think the poet did very well in taking notice of it. The historian above-mentioned acquaints us, that a prophetess had foretold Æneas, that he should take his voyage westward, till his companions should eat their tables; and that accordingly, upon his landing in Italy, as they were eating their flesh upon cakes of bread for want of other conveniences, they afterwards fed on the cakes themselves: upon which one of the company said merrily, 'We are eating our tables.' They immediately took the hint, says the historian, and concluded the prophecy to be fulfilled. As Virgil did not think it proper to omit so material a particular in the history of Æneas, it may be worth while to consider with how much judgment he has qualified it, and taken off every thing that might have appeared improper for a passage in a heroic poem. The prophetess who foretells it is a hungry harpy, as the person who discovers it is young Ascanius:

> 'Heus etiam mensas consumimus, inquit Iulus!'
> *Æn.* vii. 116.
>
> 'See we devour the plates on which we fed!'
> *Dryden.*

Such an observation, which is beautiful in the mouth of a boy, would have been ridiculous from any other of the company. I am apt to think that the changing of the Trojan fleet into water-nymphs, which is the most violent machine in the whole Æneid, and has given offence to several critics, may be accounted for the same way. Virgil himself, before he begins that relation, premises, that what he was going to tell appeared incredible, but that it was justified by tradition. What further confirms me that this change of the fleet was a celebrated circumstance in the history of Æneas, is, that Ovid has given a place to the same metamorphosis in his account of the heathen mythology.

None of the critics I have met with have considered the fable of the Æneid in this light, and taken notice how the tradition on which it was founded authorizes those parts in it which appear most exceptionable. I hope the length of this reflection will not make it unacceptable to the curious part of my readers.

The history which was the basis of Milton's poem is still shorter than either that of the Iliad or Æneid. The poet has likewise taken care to insert every circumstance of it in the body of his fable. The ninth book, which we are here to consider, is raised upon that brief account in scripture, wherein we are told that the serpent was more subtle than any beast of the field; that he tempted the woman to eat of the forbidden fruit; that she was overcome by this temptation, and that Adam followed her example. From these few particulars Milton has formed one of the most entertaining fables that invention ever produced. He has disposed of these several circumstances among so many agreeable and natural fictions of his own, that his whole story looks only like a comment upon sacred writ, or rather seems to be a full and complete relation of what the other is only an epitome. I have insisted the longer on this consideration, as I look upon the disposition and contrivance of the fable to be the principal beauty of the ninth book, which has more story in it, and is fuller of incidents, than any other in the whole poem. Satan's traversing the globe, and still keeping within the shadow of the night, as fearing to be discovered by the angel of the sun, who had before detected him, is one of those beautiful imaginations with which he introduces this his second series of adventures. Having examined the nature of every creature, and found out one which was the most proper for his purpose, he again returns to Paradise; and to avoid discovery, sinks by night with a river that ran under the garden, and rises up again through a fountain that issued from it by the tree of life. The poet, who, as we have before taken notice, speaks as little as possible in his own person, and, after the example of Homer, fills every part of his work with manners and characters, introduces a soliloquy of this infernal agent, who was thus restless in the destruction of man. He is then described as gliding through the garden, under the resemblance of a mist, in order to find out the creature in which he designed to tempt our first parents. This description has something in it very poetical and surprising:

> So saying, through each thicket dank or dry,
> Like a black mist low creeping, he held on
> His midnight search, where soonest he might find
> The serpent: him fast sleeping soon he found,
> In labyrinth of many a round self-roll'd
> His head the midst, well stor'd with subtil wiles.

The author afterwards gives us a description of the morning which is wonderfully suitable to a divine poem, and peculiar to that first season of nature. He represents the earth before it was cursed, as a great altar, breathing out its incense from all parts, and sending up a pleasant savour to the nostrils of its Creator; to which he adds a noble idea of Adam and Eve, as offering their morning worship, and filling up the universal concert of praise and adoration:

> Now when a sacred light began to dawn
> In Eden on the humid flowers, that breath'd
> Their morning incense; when all things that breathe
> From th' earth's great altar send up silent praise
> To the Creator, and his nostrils fill
> With grateful smell; forth came the human pair
> And join'd their vocal worship to the choir
> Of creatures wanting voice.———

The dispute which follows between our two first parents is represented with great art. It proceeds from a difference of judgment, not of passion, and is managed with reason, not with heat. It is such a dispute as we may suppose might have happened in Paradise, had man continued happy and innocent. There is a great delicacy in the moralities which are interspersed in Adam's discourse, and which the most ordinary reader cannot but take notice of. That force of love which the father of mankind so finely describes in the eighth book, and which is inserted in my last Saturday's paper, shows itself here in many fine instances: as in those fond regards he casts towards Eve at her parting from him:

Her long with ardent look his eye pursu'd
Delighted, but desiring more her stay,
Oft he to her his charge of quick return
Repeated; she to him as oft engaged
To be return'd by noon amid the bow'r.

In his impatience and amusement during her absence:

——————Adam the while,
Waiting desirous her return, had wove
Of choicest flow'rs a garland to adorn
Her tresses, and her rural labours crown,
As reapers oft are wont their harvest queen.
Great joy he promis'd to his thoughts, and new
Solace in her return, so long delay'd.

But particularly in that passionate speech, where, seeing her irrecoverably lost, he resolves to perish with her, rather than to live without her:

——————Some cursed fraud
Of enemy hath beguil'd thee, yet unknown,
And me with thee hath ruin'd; for with thee
Certain my resolution is to die:
How can I live without thee? how forego
Thy sweet converse and love so dearly join'd
To live again in these wild woods forlorn?
Should God create another Eve, and I
Another rib afford, yet loss of thee
Would never from my heart; no, no! I feel
The link of nature draw me: flesh of flesh,
Bone of my bone thou art, and from thy state
Mine never shall be parted, bliss or woe.

The beginning of this speech, and the preparation to it, are animated with the same spirit as the conclusion, which I have here quoted.

The several wiles which are put in practice by the tempter, when he found Eve separated from her husband, the many pleasing images of nature which are intermixed in this part of the story, with its gradual and regular progress to the fatal catastrophe, are so very remarkable, that it would be superfluous to point out their respective beauties.

I have avoided mentioning any particular similitudes in my remarks on this great work, because I have given a general account of them in my paper on the first book. There is one, however, in this part of the poem which I shall here quote, as it is not only very beautiful, but the closest of any in the whole poem; I mean that where the serpent is described as rolling forward in all his pride, animated by the evil spirit, and conducting Eve to her destruction, while Adam was at too great a distance from her to give her his assistance. These several particulars are all of them wrought into the following similitude:

——————Hope elevates, and joy
Brightens his crest; as when a wandering fire
Compact of unctious vapour, which the night
Condenses, and the cold environs round,
Kindled through agitation to a flame,
(Which oft, they say, some evil spirit attends)
Hovering and blazing with delusive light,
Misleads th' amaz'd night-wanderer from his way
To bogs and mires, and oft through pond or pool,
There swallow'd up and lost from succour far.

The secret intoxication of pleasure, with all those transient flushings of guilt and joy, which the poet represents in our first parents upon their eating the forbidden fruit, to those flaggings of spirit, damps of sorrow, and mutual accusations which succeed it, are conceived with a wonderful imagination, and described in very natural sentiments.

When Dido, in the fourth Æneid, yielded to that fatal temptation which ruined her, Virgil tells us the earth trembled, the heavens were filled with flashes of lightning, and the nymphs howled upon the mountain tops. Milton, in the same poetical spirit, has described all nature as disturbed upon Eve's eating the forbidden fruit.

So saying, her rash hand in evil hour,
Forth reaching to the fruit, she pluck'd, she eat,
Earth felt the wound, and Nature, from her seat
Sighing, through all her works gave signs of woe
That all was lost.————

Upon Adam's falling into the same guilt, the whole creation appears a second time in convulsions.

——————He scrupled not to eat
Against his better knowledge; not deceiv'd
But fondly overcome with female charm,
Earth trembled from her entrails, as again
In pangs, and Nature gave a second groan;
Sky lower'd, and, muttering thunder, some sad drops
Wept at completing of the mortal sin.

As all nature suffered by the guilt of our first parents, these symptoms of trouble and consternation are wonderfully imagined, not only as prodigies, but as marks of her sympathizing in the fall of man.

Adam's converse with Eve, after having eaten the forbidden fruit, is an exact copy of that between Jupiter and Juno in the fourteenth Iliad. Juno there approaches Jupiter with the girdle which she had received from Venus: upon which he tells her, that she appeared more charming and desirable than she had ever done before, even when their loves were at the highest. The poet afterwards describes them as reposing on a summit of Mount Ida, which produced under them a bed of flowers, the lotus, the crocus, and the hyacinth; and concludes his description with their falling asleep.

Let the reader compare this with the following passage in Milton, which begins with Adam's speech to Eve:

'For never did thy beauty since the day
I saw thee first and wedded thee, adorn'd,
With all perfections, so inflame my sense
With ardour to enjoy thee, fairer now
Than ever, bounty of this virtuous tree.'
So said he, and forbore not glance or toy
Of amorous intent, well understood
Of Eve, whose eye darted contagious fire.
Her hand he seiz'd, and to a shady bank,
Thick overhead with verdant roof embower'd,
He led her nothing loth; flowers were the couch,
Pansies, and violets, and asphodel,
And hyacinth, Earth's freshest softest lap.
There they their fill of love and love's disport
Took largely, of their mutual guilt the seal,
The solace of their sin, till dewy sleep
Oppress'd them.————

As no poet seems ever to have studied Homer more, or to have more resembled him in the greatness of genius, than Milton, I think I should have given but a very imperfect account of its beauties, if I had not observed the most remarkable passages which look like parallels in these two great authors. I might, in the course of these criticisms, have taken notice of many particular lines and expressions which are translated from the Greek poet; but as I thought this would have appeared too minute and over-curious, I have purposely omitted them. The greater incidents, however, are not only set off by being shown in the same light with several of the same nature in Homer, but by that means may be also guarded against the cavils of the tasteless or ignorant. L.

No. 352.] *Monday, April* 14, 1712.

————Si ad honestatem nati sumus, ea aut sola expetenda est, aut certe omni pondere gravior est habenda quam reliqua omnia. *Tull.*

If we be made for honesty, either it is solely to be sought, or certainly to be estimated much more highly than all other things.

Will Honeycomb was complaining to me yesterday, that the conversation of the town is so altered of late years, that a fine gentleman is at a loss for matter to start discourse, as well as unable to fall in with the talk he generally meets with. Will takes notice, that there is now an evil under the sun which he supposes to be entirely new, because not mentioned by any satirist, or moralist, in any age. 'Men,' said he, 'grow knaves sooner than they ever did since the creation of the world before.' If you read the tragedies of the last age, you find the artful men, and persons of intrigue, are advanced very far in years, and beyond the pleasures and sallies of youth; but now Will observes, that the young have taken in the vices of the aged, and you shall have a man of five-and-twenty, crafty, false, and intriguing, not ashamed to over-reach, cozen, and beguile. My friend adds, that till about the latter end of king Charles's reign there was not a rascal of any eminence under forty. In the places of resort for conversation, you now hear nothing but what relates to improving men's fortunes, without regard to the methods towards it. This is so fashionable, that young men form themselves upon a certain neglect of every thing that is candid, simple, and worthy of true esteem; and affect being yet worse than they are, by acknowledging, in their general turn of mind and discourse, that they have not any remaining value for true honour and honesty; preferring the capacity of being artful to gain their ends, to the merit of despising those ends when they come in competition with their honesty. All this is due to the very silly pride that generally prevails of being valued for the ability of carrying their point; in a word, from the opinion that shallow and inexperienced people entertain of the short lived force of cunning. But I shall, before I enter upon the various faces which folly covered with artifice, puts on to impose upon the unthinking, produce a great authority for asserting that nothing but truth and ingenuity has any lasting good effect, even upon a man's fortune and interest.

'Truth and reality have all the advantages of appearance, and many more. If the show of any thing be good for any thing, I am sure sincerity is better, for why does any man dissemble, or seem to be that which he is not, but because he thinks it good to have such a quality as he pretends to? for to counterfeit and dissemble is to put on the appearance of some real excellency. Now the best way in the world for a man to seem to be any thing, is really to be what he would seem to be. Besides, that it is many times as troublesome to make good the pretence of a good quality, as to have it; and if a man have it not, it is ten to one but he is discovered to want it, and then all his pains and labour to seem to have it is lost. There is something unnatural in painting, which a skilful eye will easily discern from native beauty and complexion.

'It is hard to personate and act a part long; for where truth is not at the bottom, nature will always be endeavouring to return, and will peep out and betray herself one time or other. Therefore, if any man think it convenient to seem good, let him be so indeed, and then his goodness will appear to every body's satisfaction; so that upon all accounts sincerity is true wisdom. Particularly as to the affairs of this world, integrity has many advantages over all the fine and artificial ways of dissimulation and deceit; it is much the plainer and easier, much the safer and more secure way of dealing in the world: it has less of trouble and difficulty, of entanglement and perplexity, of danger and hazard in it: it is the shortest and nearest way to our end, carrying us thither in a straight line, and will hold out and last longest. The arts of deceit and cunning do continually grow weaker and less effectual and serviceable to them that use them; whereas integrity gains strength by use, and the more and longer any man practiseth it, the greater service it does him, by confirming his reputation, and encouraging those with whom he hath to do to repose the greatest trust and confidence in him, which is an unspeakable advantage in the business and affairs of life.

'Truth is always consistent with itself, and needs nothing to help it out; it is always near at hand, and sits upon our lips, and is ready to drop out before we are aware; whereas a lie is troublesome, and sets a man's invention upon the rack, and one trick needs a great many more to make it good. It is like building upon a false foundation, which constantly stands in need of props to shore it up, and proves at last more chargeable than to have raised a substantial building at first upon a true and solid foundation; for sincerity is firm and substantial, and there is nothing hollow and unsound in it; and, because it is plain and open, fears no discovery; of which the crafty man is always in danger: and when he thinks he walks in the dark, all his pretences are so transparent, that he that runs may read them: he is the last man that finds himself to be found out; and whilst he takes it for granted that he makes fools of others, he renders himself ridiculous.

'Add to all this, that sincerity is the most compendious wisdom, and an excellent instrument for the speedy despatch of business; it creates confidence in those we have to deal with, saves the labour of many inquiries, and brings things to an issue in a few words. It is like travelling in a plain beaten road, which commonly brings a man sooner to his journey's end than by-ways, in which men often lose themselves. In a word, whatsoever convenience may be thought to be in falsehood and dissimulation, it is soon over; but the inconvenience of it is perpetual, because it brings a man under an everlasting jealousy and suspicion, so that he is not believed when he speaks the truth, nor trusted perhaps when he means honestly. When a man has once forfeited the reputation of his integrity, he is set fast; and nothing will then serve his turn, neither truth nor falsehood.

'And I have often thought, that God hath in his great wisdom, hid from men of false and dishonest minds the wonderful advantages of truth and integrity to the prosperity even of our worldly affairs: these men are so blinded by their covetousness and ambition. that they cannot look beyond a present advantage, nor forbear to seize upon it, though by ways never so indirect; they cannot see so far as to the remote consequence of a steady integrity, and the vast benefit and advantages which it will bring a man at last. Were but this sort of men wise and clear-sighted enough to discern this, they would be honest out of very knavery, not out of any love to honesty and virtue, but with a crafty design to promote and advance more effectually their own interests; and therefore the justice of the Divine Providence hath hid this truest point of wisdom from their eyes, that bad men might not be upon equal terms with the just and upright, and serve their own wicked designs by honest and lawful means.

'Indeed, if a man were only to deal in the world for a day, and should never have occasion to converse more with mankind, never more need their good opinion or good word, it were then no great matter (speaking as to the concernments of this world,) if a man spent his reputation all at once, and ventured it at one throw; but if he be to continue in the world, and would have the advantage of conversation whilst he is in it, let him make use of truth and sincerity in all his words and actions; for nothing but this will last and hold out to the end: all other arts will fail, but truth and integrity will carry a man through, and bear him out to the last.' T.

No. 353.] *Tuesday, April* 15, 1712.

In tenui labor———— *Virg.* Georg. v. 6.

Though low the subject, it deserves our pains.

The gentleman who obliges the world in general, and me in particular, with his thoughts upon education, has just sent me the following letter:

'Sir,—I take the liberty to send you a fourth letter upon the education of youth. In my last I gave you my thoughts upon some particular tasks, which I conceived it might not be amiss to mix with their usual exercises, in order to give them an early seasoning of virtue: I shall in this propose some others, which I fancy might contribute to give them a right turn for the world, and enable them to make their way in it.

'The design of learning is, as I take it, either to render a man an agreeable companion to himself, and teach him to support solitude with pleasure; or, if he is not born to an estate, to supply that defect, and furnish him with the means of acquiring one. A person who applies himself to learning with the first of these views may be said to study for ornament; as he who proposes to himself the second, properly studies for use. The one does it to raise himself a fortune; the other to set off that which he is already possessed of. But as far the greater part of mankind are included in the latter class, I shall only propose some methods at present for the service of such who expect to advance themselves in the world by their learning. In order to which, I shall premise, that many more estates have been acquired by little accomplishments than by extraordinary ones; those qualities which make the greatest figure in the eye of the world not being always the most useful in themselves, or the most advantageous to their owners.

'The posts which require men of shining and uncommon parts to discharge them are so very few, that many a great genius goes out of the world without ever having an opportunity to exert itself; whereas, persons of ordinary endowments meet with occasions fitted to their parts and capacities every day in the common occurrences of life.

'I am acquainted with two persons who were formerly school-fellows,* and have been good friends ever since. One of them was not only thought an impenetrable blockhead at school, but still maintained his reputation at the university; the other was the pride of his master, and the most celebrated person in the college of which he was a member. The man of genius is at

* "Swift, and Mr. Stratford, a merchant. 'Stratford is worth a plumb, and is now lending the government 40,000*l.* yet we were educated together at the same school and university.' Swift's Works, vol. xxii. p. 10, cr. 8vo.—Stratford was afterwards a bankrupt." *Chalmers*

present buried in a country parsonage of eight-score pounds a year; while the other, with the bare abilities of a common scrivener, has got an estate of above a hundred thousand pounds.

'I fancy from what I have said, it will almost appear a doubtful case to many a wealthy citizen, whether or no he ought to wish his son should be a great genius: but this I am sure of, that nothing is more absurd than to give a lad the education of one, whom nature has not favoured with any particular marks of distinction.

'The fault, therefore, of our grammar schools is, that every boy is pushed on to works of genius: whereas, it would be far more advantageous for the greatest part of them to be taught such little practical arts and sciences as do not require any great share of parts to be master of them, and yet may come often into play during the course of a man's life.

'Such are all the parts of practical geometry. I have known a man contract a friendship with a minister of state, upon cutting a dial in his window; and remember a clergyman who got one of the best benefices in the west of England, by setting a country gentleman's affairs in some method, and giving him an exact survey of his estate.

'While I am upon this subject, I cannot forbear mentioning a particular which is of use in every station of life, and which, methinks, every master should teach scholars; I mean the writing of English letters. To this end, instead of perplexing them with Latin epistles, themes, and verses, there might be a punctual correspondence established between two boys, who might act in any imaginary parts of business, or be allowed sometimes to give a range to their own fancies, and communicate to each other whatever trifles they thought fit, provided neither of them ever failed at the appointed time to answer his correspondent's letter.

'I believe I may venture to affirm, that the generality of boys would find themselves more advantaged by this custom, when they come to be men, than by all the Greek and Latin their masters can teach them in seven or eight years.

'The want of it is very visible in many learned persons, who, while they are admiring the styles of Demosthenes or Cicero, want phrases to express themselves on the most common occasions. I have seen a letter from one of these Latin orators which would have been deservedly laughed at by a common attorney.

'Under this head of writing, I cannot omit accounts and short-hand, which are learned with little pains, and very properly come into the number of such arts as I have been here recommending.

'You must doubtless, sir, observe that I have hitherto chiefly insisted upon these things for such boys as do not appear to have any thing extraordinary in their natural talents, and consequently are not qualified for the finer parts of learning; yet I believe I might carry this matter still further, and venture to assert, that a lad of genius has sometimes occasion for these little acquirements, to be as it were the forerunners of his parts, and to introduce him into the world.

'History is full of examples of persons who, though they have had the largest abilities, have been obliged to insinuate themselves into the favour of great men, by these trivial accomplishments; as the complete gentleman in some of our modern comedies, makes his first advances to his mistress under the disguise of a painter or a dancing-master.

'The difference is, that in a lad of genius these are only so many accomplishments, which in another are essentials; the one diverts himself with them, the other works at them. In short, I look upon a great genius, with these little additions, in the same light as I regard the Grand Seignior, who is obliged, by an express command in the Alcoran, to learn and practise some handicraft trade; though I need not to have gone for my instance farther than Germany, where several emperors have voluntarily done the same thing. Leopold the last, worked in wood: and I have heard there are several handicraft works of his making to be seen at Vienna, so neatly turned that the best joiner in Europe might safely own them without any disgrace to his profession.*

'I would not be thought, by any thing I have said, to be against improving a boy's genius to the utmost pitch it can be carried. What I would endeavour to show in this essay is, that there may be methods taken to make learning advantageous even to the meanest capacities. I am, sir, yours, &c.

X.

No. 354.] *Wednesday, April* 16, 1712.

——Cum magnis virtutibus affers
Grande supercilium.—— *Juv.* Sat. vi. 168

Their signal virtues hardly can be borne,
Dash'd as they are with supercilious scorn.

'MR. SPECTATOR,—You have in some of your discourses described most sort of women in their distinct and proper classes, as the ape, the coquette, and many others; but I think you have never yet said any thing of a devotee. A devotee is one of those who disparage religion by their indiscreet and unseasonable introduction of the mention of virtue on all occasions. She professes she is what nobody ought to doubt she is; and betrays the labour she is put to, to be what she ought to be with cheerfulness and alacrity. She lives in the world, and denies herself none of the diversions of it, with a constant declaration how insipid all things in it are to her. She is never

* The well-known labours of the Czar Peter may be added to those enumerated above.

herself but at church; there she displays her virtue, and is so fervent in all her devotions, that I have frequently seen her pray herself out of breath. While other young ladies in the house are dancing, or playing at questions and commands, she reads aloud in her closet. She says, all love is ridiculous, except it be celestial; but she speaks of the passion of one mortal to another with too much bitterness for one that had no jealousy mixed with her contempt of it. If at any time she sees a man warm in his addresses to his mistress, she will lift up her eyes to heaven, and cry, "What nonsense is that fool talking! Will the bell never ring for prayers?" We have an eminent lady of this stamp in our country, who pretends to amusements very much above the rest of her sex. She never carries a white shock-dog with bells under her arm, nor a squirrel or dormouse in her pocket, but always an abridged piece of morality, to steal out when she is sure of being observed. When she went to the famous ass-race, (which I must confess was but an odd diversion to be encouraged by people of rank and figure,) it was not, like other ladies, to hear those poor animals bray, nor to see fellows run naked, or to hear country 'squires in bob wigs and white girdles make love at the side of a coach, and cry, "Madam this is dainty weather." Thus she described the diversion; for she went only to pray heartily that nobody might be hurt in the crowd, and to see if the poor fellow's face, which was distorted with grinning, might any way be brought to itself again. She never chats over her tea, but covers her face, and is supposed in an ejaculation before she tastes a sup. This ostentatious behaviour is such an offence to true sanctity, that it disparages it, and makes virtue not only unamiable, but also ridiculous. The sacred writings are full of reflections which abhor this kind of conduct; and a devotee is so far from promoting goodness, that she deters others by her example. Folly and vanity in one of these ladies is like vice in a clergyman; it does not only debase him, but makes the inconsiderate part of the world think the worse of religion. I am, sir, your humble servant,

'HOTSPUR.'

'Mr. Spectator,—Xenophon in his short account of the Spartan commonwealth speaking of the behaviour of their young men in the streets, says, "There was so much modesty in their looks, that you might as soon have turned the eyes of a marble statue upon you as theirs; and that in all their behaviour they were more modest than a bride when put to bed upon her wedding-night." This virtue, which is always subjoined to magnanimity, had such an influence upon their courage, that in battle an enemy could not look them in the face, and they durst not but die for their country.

'Whenever I walk into the streets of London and Westminster, the countenances of all the young fellows that pass by me make me wish myself in Sparta: I meet with such blustering airs, big looks, and bold fronts, that, to a superficial observer, would bespeak a courage above those Grecians. I am arrived to that perfection in speculation, that I understand the language of the eyes, which would be a great misfortune to me had I not corrected the testiness of old age by philosophy. There is scarce a man in a red coat who does not tell me, with a full stare, he is a bold man: I see several swear inwardly at me, without any offence of mine, but the oddness of my person; I meet contempt in every street; expressed in different manners by the scornful look, the elevated eye-brow, and the swelling nostrils of the proud and prosperous. The 'prentice speaks his disrespect by an extended finger, and the porter by stealing out his tongue. If a country gentleman appears a little curious in observing the edifices, clocks, signs, coaches, and dials, it is not to be imagined how the polite rabble of this town, who are acquainted with these objects, ridicule his rusticity. I have known a fellow with a burden on his head steal a hand down from his load, and slily twirl the cock of a 'squire's hat behind him; while the offended person is swearing, or out of countenance, all the wag-wits in the highway are grinning in applause of the ingenious rogue that gave him the tip, and the folly of him who had not eyes all round his head to prevent receiving it. These things arise from a general affectation of smartness, wit, and courage. Wycherly somewhere rallies the pretensions this way, by making a fellow say, "Red breeches are a certain sign of valour;" and Otway makes a man, to boast his agility, trip up a beggar on crutches. From such hints I beg a speculation on this subject: in the mean time I shall do all in the power of a weak old fellow in my own defence; for as Diogenes, being in quest of an honest man, sought for him when it was broad daylight with a lantern and candle, so I intend for the future to walk the streets with a dark lantern, which has a convex crystal in it; and if any man stares at me, I give fair warning that I will direct the light full into his eyes. Thus despairing to find men modest, I hope by this means to evade their impudence. I am, sir, your humble servant,

T. 'SOPHROSUNIUS.'

No. 355.] *Thursday, April* 17, 1712.

Non ego mordaci distrinxi carmine quenquam.
Ovid. Trist. Lib. ii. 563.

I ne'er in gall dipp'd my envenom'd pen,
Nor branded the bold front of shameless men.

I have been very often tempted to write invectives upon those who have detracted from my works, or spoken in derogation of my person; but I look upon it as a particular happiness, that I have always hindered my resentments from proceeding to this extremity. I once had gone through half a satire, but found so many motions of humanity rising in me towards the persons whom I had severely treated, that I threw it into the fire without ever finishing it. I have been angry enough to make several little epigrams and lampoons; and, after having admired them a day or two, have likewise committed them to the flames. These I look upon as so many sacrifices to humanity, and have received much greater satisfaction from suppressing such performances, than I could have done from any reputation they might have procured me, or from any mortification they might have given my enemies in case I had made them public. If a man has any talent in writing, it shows a good mind to forbear answering calumnies and reproaches in the same spirit of bitterness with which they are offered. But when a man has been at some pains in making suitable returns to an enemy, and has the instruments of revenge in his hands, to let drop his wrath, and stifle his resentments, seems to have something in it great and heroical. There is a particular merit in such a way of forgiving an enemy; and the more violent and unprovoked the offence has been, the greater still is the merit of him who thus forgives it.

I never met with a consideration that is more finely spun, and what has better pleased me, than one in Epictetus, which places an enemy in a new light, and gives us a view of him altogether different from that in which we are used to regard him. The sense of it is as follows: 'Does a man reproach thee for being proud or ill-natured, envious or conceited, ignorant or detracting? Consider with thyself whether his reproaches are true. If they are not, consider that thou art not the person whom he reproaches, but that he reviles an imaginary being, and perhaps loves what thou really art, though he hates what thou appearest to be. If his reproaches are true, if thou art the envious, ill-natured man he takes thee for, give thyself another turn, become mild, affable, and obliging, and his reproaches of thee naturally cease. His reproaches may indeed continue, but thou art no longer the person whom he reproaches.'*

I often apply this rule to myself; and when I hear of a satirical speech or writing that is aimed at me, I examine my own heart, whether I deserve it or not. If I bring in a verdict against myself, I endeavour to rectify my conduct for the future in those particulars which have drawn the censure upon me; but if the whole invective be grounded upon a falsehood, I trouble myself no further about it, and look upon my name at the head of it to signify no more than one of those fictitious names made use of by an author to introduce an imaginary character. Why should a man be sensible of the sting of a reproach, who is a stranger to the guilt that is implied in it; or subject himself to the penalty, when he knows he has never committed the crime? This is a piece of fortitude, which every one owes to his own innocence, and without which it is impossible for a man of any merit or figure to live at peace with himself, in a country that abounds with wit and liberty.

The famous Monsieur Balzac, in a letter to the chancellor of France, who had prevented the publication of a book against him, has the following words, which are a lively picture of the greatness of mind so visible in the works of that author: 'If it was a new thing, it may be I should not be displeased with the suppression of the first libel that should abuse me; but since there are enough of them to make a small library, I am secretly pleased to see the number increased, and take delight in raising a heap of stones that envy has cast at me without doing me any harm.'

The author here alludes to those monuments of the eastern nations which were mountains of stones raised upon the dead bodies by travellers, that used to cast every one his stone upon it as they passed by. It is certain that no monument is so glorious as one which is thus raised by the hands of envy. For my part, I admire an author for such a temper of mind as enables him to bear an undeserved reproach without resentment, more than for all the wit of any the finest satirical reply.

Thus far I thought necessary to explain myself in relation to those who have animadverted on this paper, and to show the reasons why I have not thought fit to return them any formal answer. I must further add, that the work would have been of very little use to the public, had it been filled with personal reflections and debates; for which reason I have never once turned out of my way to observe those little cavils which have been made against it by envy or ignorance. The common fry of scribblers, who have no other way of being taken notice of but by attacking what has gained some reputation in the world, would have furnished me with business enough had they found me disposed to enter the lists with them.

I shall conclude with the fable of Boccalini's traveller, who was so pestered with the noise of grasshoppers in his ears that he alighted from his horse in great wrath to kill them all. 'This,' says the author, 'was troubling himself to no manner of purpose. Had he pursued his journey without taking notice of them, the troublesome insects would have died of themselves in a very few weeks, and he would have suffered nothing from them.'

L

* Epict. Ench. cap. 48 and 64.

No. 356.] *Friday, April* 18, 1712.

———Aptissima quæque dabunt dii,
Charior est illis homo quam sibi ———
Juv. Sat. x. 349.

———The gods will grant
What their unerring wisdom sees they want:
In goodness as in greatness, they excel;
Ah! that we lov'd ourselves but half as well!
Dryden.

It is owing to pride, and a secret affectation of a certain self-existence, that the noblest motive for action that ever was proposed to man is not acknowledged the glory and happiness of their being. The heart is treacherous to itself, and we do not let our reflections go deep enough to receive religion as the most honourable incentive to good and worthy actions. It is our natural weakness to flatter ourselves into a belief, that if we search into our inmost thoughts, we find ourselves wholly disinterested, and divested of any views arising from self-love and vain-glory. But however spirits of superficial greatness may disdain at first sight to do any thing, but from a noble impulse in themselves, without any future regards in this, or any other being; upon stricter inquiry they will find, to act worthily, and expect to be rewarded only in another world, is as heroic a pitch of virtue as human nature can arrive at. If the tenor of our actions have any other motive than the desire to be pleasing in the eye of the Deity, it will necessarily follow that we must be more than men, if we are not too much exalted in prosperity and depressed in adversity. But the Christian world has a Leader, the contemplation of whose life and sufferings, must administer comfort in affliction, while the sense of his power and omnipotence must give them humiliation in prosperity.

It is owing to the forbidding and unlovely constraint with which men of low conceptions act when they think they conform themselves to religion, as well as to the more odious conduct of hypocrites, that the word Christian does not carry with it, at first view, all that is great, worthy, friendly, generous, and heroic. The man who suspends his hopes of the reward of worthy actions till after death, who can bestow unseen, who can overlook hatred, do good to his slanderer, who can never be angry at his friend, never revengeful to his enemy, is certainly formed for the benefit of society. Yet these are so far from heroic virtues, that they are but the ordinary duties of a Christian.

When a man with a steady faith looks back on the great catastrophe of this day,* with what bleeding emotions of heart must he contemplate the life and sufferings of his deliverer! When his agonies occur to him, how will he weep to reflect that he has often forgot them for the glance of a wanton, for the applause of a vain world, for a heap of fleeting past pleasures, which are at present aching sorrows!

How pleasing is the contemplation of the lowly steps our Almighty Leader took in conducting us to his heavenly mansions! In plain and apt parable, similitude and allegory, our great Master enforced the doctrine of our salvation, but they of his acquaintance, instead of receiving what they could not oppose, were offended at the presumption of being wiser than they. They could not raise their little ideas above the consideration of him, in those circumstances familiar to them, or conceive that he, who appeared not more terrible or pompous, should have any thing more exalted than themselves; he in that place therefore would no longer ineffectually exert a power which was incapable of conquering the prepossession of their narrow and mean conceptions.

Multitudes followed him, and brought him the dumb, the blind, the sick, and maimed; whom when their Creator had touched, with a second life they saw, spoke, leaped, and ran. In affection to him, and admiration of his actions, the crowd could not leave him, but waited near him till they were almost as faint and helpless as others they brought for succour. He had compassion on them, and by a miracle supplied their necessities. Oh, the ecstatic entertainment, when they could behold their food immediately increase to the distributor's hand, and see their God in person feeding and refreshing his creatures! Oh envied happiness! But why do I say envied? as if our God did not still preside over our temperate meals, cheerful hours, and innocent conversations.

But though the sacred story is every where full of miracles, not inferior to this, and though in the midst of those acts of divinity he never gave the least hint of a design to become a secular prince, yet had not hitherto the apostles themselves any other than hopes of worldly power, preferment, riches, and pomp; for Peter, upon an accident of ambition among the apostles, hearing his Master explain that his kingdom was not of this world, was so scandalized that he whom he had so long followed should suffer the ignominy, shame, and death, which he foretold, that he took him aside and said, 'Be it far from thee, Lord, this shall not be unto thee:' for which he suffered a severe reprehension from his Master, as having in his view the glory of man rather than that of God.

The great change of things began to draw near, when the Lord of nature thought fit, as a saviour and deliverer, to make his public entry into Jerusalem with more than the power and joy, but none of the ostentation and pomp of a triumph; he came humble, meek, and lowly; with an unfelt new ecstasy, multitudes strewed his way with garments and olive-branches, crying, with loud gladness and acclama

* Good Friday, 1712, the day of publication of this paper.

tion, 'Hosannah to the Son of David! Blessed is he that cometh in the name of the Lord!' At this great King's accession to his throne, men were not ennobled, but saved; crimes were not remitted, but sins forgiven. He did not bestow medals, honours, favours; but health, joy, sight, speech. The first object the blind ever saw was the Author of sight; while the lame ran before, and the dumb repeated the hosannah. Thus attended, he entered into his own house, the sacred temple, and by his divine authority expelled traders and worldlings that profaned it; and thus did he for a time use a great and despotic power, to let unbelievers understand that it was not want of, but superiority to, all worldly dominion, that made him not exert it. But is this then the Saviour? Is this the Deliverer? Shall this obscure Nazarene command Israel, and sit on the throne of David? Their proud and disdainful hearts, which were petrified with the love and pride of this world, were impregnable to the reception of so mean a benefactor; and were now enough exasperated with benefits to conspire his death. Our Lord was sensible of their design, and prepared his disciples for it, by recounting to them now more distinctly what should befal him; but Peter, with an ungrounded resolution, and in a flush of temper, made a sanguine protestation, that though all men were offended in him, yet would not he be offended. It was a great article of our Saviour's business in the world to bring us to a sense of our inability, without God's assistance, to do any thing great or good; he therefore told Peter, who thought so well of his courage and fidelity, that they would both fail him, and even he should deny him thrice that very night.

'But what heart can conceive, what tongue utter the sequel? Who is that yonder, buffetted, mocked, and spurned? Whom do they drag like a felon? Whither do they carry my Lord, my King, my Saviour, and my God? And will he die to expiate those very injuries? See where they have nailed the Lord and giver of life! How his wounds blacken, his body writhes, and heart heaves with pity and with agony! Oh Almighty sufferer, look down, look down from thy triumphant infamy! Lo, he inclines his head to his sacred bosom! Hark, he groans! See, he expires! The earth trembles, the temple rends, the rocks burst, the dead arise. Which are the quick? Which are the dead? Sure nature, all nature is departing with her Creator.'

T.

No. 357.] *Saturday, April* 19, 1712.

——————Quis talia fando
Temperet a lachrymis?———— *Virg. Æn.* ii. 6.

Who can relate such woes without a tear?

THE tenth book of Paradise Lost has a greater variety of persons in it than any other in the whole poem. The author, upon the winding up of his action, introduces all those who had any concern in it, and shows with great beauty the influence which it had upon each of them. It is like the last act of a well-written tragedy, in which all who had a part in it are generally drawn up before the audience, and represented under those circumstances in which the determination of the action places them.

I shall therefore consider this book under four heads, in relation to the celestial, the infernal, the human, and the imaginary persons, who have their respective parts allotted in it.

To begin with the celestial persons: the guardian angels of Paradise are described as returning to heaven upon the fall of man, in order to approve their vigilance; their arrival, their manner of reception, with the sorrow which appeared in themselves, and in those spirits who are said to rejoice at the conversion of a sinner, are very finely laid together in the following lines:

Up into heav'n from Paradise in haste
Th' angelic guards ascended, mute and sad
For man; for of his state by this they knew;
Much wond'ring how the subtle fiend had stol'n
Entrance unseen. Soon as th' unwelcome news
From earth arriv'd at heaven gate, displeas'd
All were who heard; dim sadness did not spare
That time celestial visages; yet mixt
With pity, violated not their bliss.
About the new arriv'd, in multitudes
Th' ethereal people ran to hear and know
How all befel. They tow'rds the throne supreme
Accountable made haste, to make appear
With righteous plea, their utmost vigilance,
And easily approv'd; when the Most High
Eternal Father, from his secret cloud
Amidst, in thunder utter'd thus his voice.

The same Divine Person, who in the foregoing parts of this poem interceded for our first parents before their fall, overthrew the rebel angels, and created the world, is now represented as descending to Paradise, and pronouncing sentence upon the three offenders. The cool of the evening being a circumstance with which holy writ introduces this great scene, it is poetically described by our author, who has also kept religiously to the form of words in which the three several sentences were passed upon Adam, Eve, and the serpent. He has rather chosen to neglect the numerousness of his verse, than to deviate from those speeches which are recorded on this great occasion. The guilt and confusion of our first parents, standing naked before their judge, is touched with great beauty. Upon the arrival of Sin and Death into the works of creation, the Almighty is again introduced as speaking to his angels that surrounded him.

'See! with what heat these dogs of hell advance,
To waste and havoc yonder world, which I
So fair and good created,' &c.

The following passage is formed upon that glorious image in holy writ, which compares the voice of an innumerable host of angels uttering hallelujahs, to the voice of mighty thunderings, or of many waters.

He ended, and the heav'nly audience loud
Sung hallelujah, as the sound of seas,
Through multitude that sung: 'Just are thy ways,
Righteous are thy decrees in all thy works,
Who can extenuate thee?'———

Though the author, in the whole course of his poem, and particularly in the book we are now examining, has infinite allusions to places of Scripture, I have only taken notice in my remarks of such as are of a poetical nature, and which are woven with great beauty into the body of his fable. Of this kind is that passage in the present book, where, describing Sin as marching through the works of nature, he adds,

———Behind her Death
Close following pace for pace, not mounted yet
On his pale horse———

Which alludes to that passage in Scripture so wonderfully poetical, and terrifying to the imagination: 'And I looked, and behold, a pale horse, and his name that sat on him was Death, and Hell followed with him: and power was given unto them over the fourth part of the earth, to kill with sword, and with hunger, and with sickness, and with the beasts of the earth.' Under this first head of celestial persons we must likewise take notice of the command which the angels received, to produce the several changes in nature, and sully the beauty of creation. Accordingly they are represented as infecting the stars and planets with malignant influences, weakening the light of the sun, bringing down the winter into the milder regions of nature, planting winds and storms in several quarters of the sky, storing the clouds with thunder, and, in short, perverting the whole frame of the universe to the condition of its criminal inhabitants. As this is a noble incident in the poem, the following lines, in which we see the angels heaving up the earth, and placing it in a different posture to the sun from what it had before the fall of man, is conceived with that sublime imagination which was so peculiar to this great author:

'Some say he bid his angels turn askance
The poles of earth twice ten degrees and more
From the sun's axle; they with labour push'd
Oblique the centric globe,———

We are in the second place to consider the infernal agents under the view which Milton has given us of them in this book. It is observed, by those who would set forth the greatness of Virgil's plan, that he conducts his reader through all the parts of the earth which were discovered in his time. Asia, Africa, and Europe, are the several scenes of his fable. The plan of Milton's poem is of an infinitely greater extent, and fills the mind with many more astonishing circumstances. Satan, having surrounded the earth seven times, departs at length from Paradise. We then see him steering his course among the constellations; and, after having traversed the whole creation, pursuing his voyage through the chaos, and entering into his own infernal dominions.

His first appearance in the assembly of fallen angels is worked up with circumstances which give a delightful surprise to the reader: but there is no incident in the whole poem which does this more than the transformation of the whole audience, that follows the account their leader gives them of his expedition. The gradual change of Satan himself is described after Ovid's manner, and may vie with any of those celebrated transformations which are looked upon as the most beautiful parts in that poet's works. Milton never fails of improving his own hints, and bestowing the last finishing touches in every incident which is admitted into his poem. The unexpected hiss which arises in this episode, the dimensions and bulk of Satan so much superior to those of the infernal spirits who lay under the same transformation, with the annual change which they are supposed to suffer, are instances of this kind. The beauty of the diction is very remarkable in this whole episode, as I have observed in the sixth paper of these remarks the great judgment with which it was contrived.

The parts of Adam and Eve, or the human persons, come next under our consideration. Milton's art is no where more shown, than in his conducting the parts of these our first parents. The representation he gives of them, without falsifying the story, is wonderfully contrived to influence the reader with pity and compassion towards them. Though Adam involves the whole species in misery, his crime proceeds from a weakness which every man is inclined to pardon and commiserate, as it seems rather the frailty of human nature, than of the person who offended. Every one is apt to excuse a fault which he himself might have fallen into. It was the excess of love for Eve that ruined Adam and his posterity. I need not add, that the author is justified in this particular by many of the fathers, and the most orthodox writers. Milton has by this means filled a great part of his poem with that kind of writing which the French critics call the *tendre*, and which is in a particular manner engaging to all sorts of readers.

Adam and Eve, in the book we are now considering, are likewise drawn with such sentiments as do not only interest the reader in their afflictions, but raise in him the most melting passions of humanity and commiseration. When Adam sees the several changes of nature produced about him, he appears in a disorder of mind suitable to one who had forfeited both his innocence and his happiness: he is filled with horror, remorse, despair; in the anguish of his heart he expostulates with his Creator for having given him an unasked existence:

'Did I request thee, Maker, from my clay
To mould me man? Did I solicit thee
From darkness to promote me? or here place
In this delicious garden? As my will
Concurr'd not to my being, 'twere but right

And equal to reduce me to my dust,
Desirous to resign, and render back
All I receiv'd.'————

He immediately after recovers from his presumption, owns his doom to be just, and begs that the death which is threatened him may be inflicted on him:

'————Why delays
His hand to execute what his decree
Fix'd on this day? Why do I over-live?
Why am I mock'd with death, and lengthen'd out
To deathless pain? How gladly would I meet
Mortality my sentence, and be earth
Insensible! how glad would lay me down,
As in my mother's lap! There should I rest
And sleep secure; his dreadful voice no more
Would thunder in my ears: no fear of worse
To me, and to my offspring, would torment me
With cruel expectation.'————

This whole speech is full of the like emotion, and varied with all those sentiments which we may suppose natural to a mind so broken and disturbed. I must not omit that generous concern which our first father shows in it for his posterity, and which is so proper to affect the reader:

'————Hide me from the face
Of God, whom to behold was then my height
Of happiness! yet well, if here would end
The misery: I deserved it, and would bear
My own deservings: but this will not serve;
All that I eat, or drink, or shall beget,
Is propagated curse. O voice once heard
Delightfully, "Increase and multiply:"
Now death to hear!————
————In me all
Posterity stands curst! Fair patrimony,
That I must leave ye, sons! O were I able
To waste it all myself, and leave you none!
So disinherited, how would you bless
Me, now your curse! Ah, why should all mankind,
For one man's fault, thus guiltless be condemn'd
If guiltless? But from me what can proceed
But all corrupt?'————

Who can afterwards behold the father of mankind, extended upon the earth, uttering his midnight complaints, bewailing his existence, and wishing for death, without sympathizing with him in his distress?

Thus Adam to himself lamented loud
Through the still night; not now (as ere man fell)
Wholesome, and cool, and mild, but with black air,
Accompanied with damps and dreadful gloom;
Which to his evil conscience represented
All things with double terror. On the ground
Outstretch'd he lay; on the cold ground! and oft
Curs'd his creation; death as oft accus'd
Of tardy execution.'————

The part of Eve in this book is no less passionate, and apt to sway the reader in her favour. She is represented with great tenderness as approaching Adam, but is spurned from him with a spirit of upbraiding and indignation, conformable to the nature of man, whose passions had now gained the dominion over him. The following passage, wherein she is described as renewing her addresses to him, with the whole speech that follows it, have something in them exquisitely moving and pathetic:

He added not, and from her turn'd: but Eve,
Not so repuls'd, with tears that ceas'd not flowing,
And tresses all disorder'd, at his feet
Fell humble; and embracing them besought
His peace, and thus proceeded in her plaint:
'Forsake me not thus, Adam! Witness Heav'n
What love sincere, and rev'rence in my breast
I bear thee and unweeting have offended,
Unhappily deceiv'd Thy suppliant
I beg, and clasp thy knees. Bereave me not
(Whereon I live;) thy gentle looks, thy aid,
Thy counsel in this uttermost distress,
My only strength, and stay! Forlorn of thee,
Whither shall I betake me! where subsist?
While yet we live (scarce one short hour perhaps)
Between us two let there be peace.' &c.

Adam's reconcilement to her is worked up in the same spirit of tenderness. Eve afterwards proposes to her husband, in the blindness of her despair, that to prevent their guilt from descending upon posterity, they should resolve to live childless; or, if that could not be done, they should seek their own deaths by violent methods. As these sentiments naturally engage the reader to regard the mother of mankind with more than ordinary commiseration, they likewise contain a very fine moral. The resolution of dying to end our miseries does not show such a degree of magnanimity as a resolution to bear them, and submit to the dispensations of Providence. Our author has, therefore, with great delicacy, represented Eve as entertaining this thought, and Adam as disapproving it.

We are, in the last place, to consider the imaginary persons, or Death and Sin, who act a large part in this book. Such beautiful extended allegories are certainly some of the finest compositions of genius; but, as I have before observed, are not agreeable to the nature of a heroic poem. This of Sin and Death is very exquisite in its kind, if not considered as a part of such a work. The truths contained in it are so clear and open, that I shall not lose time in explaining them; but shall only observe, that a reader, who knows the strength of the English tongue, will be amazed to think how the poet could find such apt words and phrases to describe the actions of those two imaginary persons, and particularly in that part where Death is exhibited as forming a bridge over the chaos; a work suitable to the genius of Milton.

Since the subject I am upon gives me an opportunity of speaking more at large of such shadowy and imaginary persons as may be introduced into heroic poems, I shall beg leave to explain myself in a matter which is curious in its kind, and which none of the critics have treated of. It is certain Homer and Virgil are full of imaginary persons, who are very beautiful in poetry, when they are just shown without being engaged in any series of action. Homer, indeed, represents sleep as a person, and ascribes a short part to him in his Iliad; but we must consider, that though we now regard such a person as entirely shadowy and unsubstantial, the heathens made statues of him, placed him in their temples, and looked upon him, as a real deity. When Homer makes use of other such allegorical persons, it is only in short expressions, which convey an ordinary thought to the mind in the most pleasing manner, and may rather be looked upon as poetical phrases, than allegorical descriptions. Instead of telling us that men naturally fly when they are terrified, he introduces the persons of Flight and Fear, who he tells us, are inseparable companions. Instead of saying that the time was come when Apollo ought to have received his recompence, he tells us that the Hours brought him his reward. Instead of describing the effects which Minerva's ægis produced in battle, he tells us that the brims of it were encompassed by Terror, Rout, Discord, Fury, Pursuit, Massacre, and Death. In the same figure of speaking, he represents Victory as following Diomedes; Discord as the mother of funerals and mourning; Venus as dressed by the Graces; Bellona as wearing Terror and Consternation like a garment. I might give several other instances out of Homer, as well as a great many out of Virgil. Milton has likewise very often made use of the same way of speaking, as where he tells us that Victory sat on the right hand of the Messiah, when he marched forth against the rebel angels; that, at the rising of the sun, the Hours unbarred the gates of light; that Discord was the daughter of Sin. Of the same nature are those expressions, where, describing the singing of the nightingale, he adds, 'Silence was pleased;' and upon the Messiah's bidding peace to the chaos, 'Confusion heard his voice.' I might add innumerable instances of our poet's writing in this beautiful figure. It is plain that these I have mentioned, in which persons of an imaginary nature are introduced, are such short allegories as are not designed to be taken in the literal sense, but only to convey particular circumstances to the reader, after an unusual and entertaining manner. But when such persons are introduced as principal actors, and engaged in a series of adventures, they take too much upon them, and are by no means proper for an heroic poem, which ought to appear credible in its principal parts. I cannot forbear therefore thinking, that Sin and Death are as improper agents in a work of this nature, as Strength and Necessity in one of the tragedies of Æschylus, who represented those two persons nailing down Prometheus to a rock; for which he has been justly censured by the greatest critics. I do not know any imaginary person made use of in a more sublime manner of thinking than that in one of the prophets, who, describing God as descending from heaven, and visiting the sins of mankind, adds that dreadful circumstance, 'Before him went the Pestilence.' It is certain this imaginary person might have been described in all her purple spots. The Fever might have marched before her, Pain might have stood at her right hand, Phrensy on her left, and Death in her rear. She might have been introduced as gliding down from the tail of a comet, or darted upon the earth in a flash of lightning. She might have tainted the atmosphere with her breath. The very glaring of her eyes might have scattered infection. But I believe every reader will think, that in such sublime writings the mentioning of her, as it is done in Scripture, has something in it more just, as well as great, than all that the most fanciful poet could have bestowed upon her in the richness of his imagination. L.*

No. 358.] *Monday, April* 21, 1712.

———Desipere in loco. *Hor.* Od. xii. Lib. 4. ult.

'Tis joyous folly that unbends the mind.—*Francis.*

CHARLES LILLY attended me the other day, and made me a present of a large sheet of paper, on which is delineated a pavement in Mosaic work, lately discovered at Stunsfield near Woodstock.† A person who has so much the gift of speech as Mr. Lilly, and can carry on a discourse without a reply, had great opportunity on that occasion to expatiate upon so fine a piece of antiquity. Among other things, I remember he gave me his opinion, which he drew from the ornaments of the work, that this was the floor of a room dedicated to Mirth and Concord. Viewing this work, made my fancy run over the many gay expressions I have read in ancient authors, which contained invitations to lay aside care and anxiety, and give a loose to that pleasing forgetfulness wherein men put off their characters of business, and enjoy their very selves. These hours were usually passed in rooms adorned for that purpose, and set out in such a manner, as the objects all around the company gladdened their hearts; which, joined to the cheerful looks of well-chosen and agreeable friends, gave new vigour to the airy, produced the latent fire of the modest, and gave grace to the slow humour of the reserved. A judicious mixture of such company, crowned with chaplets of flowers, and the whole apartment glittering with gay lights, cheered with a profusion of roses, artificial falls of water, and intervals of soft notes to songs of love and wine, suspended the cares of human life, and made a festival of mutual kindness. Such parties of pleasure as these, and the reports of the agreeable passages in their jollities, have in all ages awakened the dull part of mankind to pretend to mirth and good humour, without capacity for such entertainments; for if I may be allowed to say so, there are a hundred men fit for any employment, to one who is capable of passing a night in company of the first taste, without shocking any member of the society, over-rating his own part of the conversation, but equally receiving

* The original motto to this paper was the same as that now prefixed to No. 279.

Reddere personæ scit convenientia cuique.
Hor. Ars Poet. v. 316.

To each character he gives what best befits.

† See Gough's British Topography, vol. ii. p. 88.

and contributing to the pleasure of the whole company. When one considers such collections of companions in past times, and such as one might name in the present age, with how much spleen must a man needs reflect upon the awkward gaiety of those who affect the frolic with an ill grace! I have a letter from a correspondent of mine, who desires me to admonish all loud, mischievous, airy, dull companions, that they are mistaken in what they call a frolic. Irregularity in itself is not what creates pleasure and mirth; but to see a man, who knows what rule and decency are, descend from them agreeably in our company, is what denominates him a pleasant companion. Instead of that, you find many whose mirth consists only in doing things which do not become them, with a secret consciousness that all the world knows they know better: to this is always added something mischievous to themselves or others. I have heard of some very merry fellows among whom the frolic was started, and passed by a great majority, that every man should immediately draw a tooth: after which they have gone in a body and smoked a cobler. The same company, at another night, has each man burned his cravat; and one perhaps, whose estate would bear it, has thrown a long wig and hat into the same fire. Thus they have jested themselves stark-naked, and run into the streets and frighted women very successfully. There is no inhabitant of any standing in Covent Garden, but can tell you a hundred good humours, where people have come off with a little bloodshed, and yet scoured all the witty hours of the night. I know a gentleman that has several wounds in the head by watch-poles, and has been thrice run through the body, to carry on a good jest. He is very old for a man of so much good humour; but to this day he is seldom merry but he has occasion to be valiant at the same time. But, by the favour of these gentlemen, I am humbly of opinion, that a man may be a very witty man, and never offend one statute of this kingdom, not excepting that of stabbing.

The writers of plays have what they call unity of time and place, to give a justness to their representation; and it would not be amiss if all who pretend to be companions would confine their actions to the place of meeting; for a frolic carried farther may be better performed by other animals than men. It is not to rid much ground, or do much mischief, that should denominate a pleasant fellow; but that is truly frolic which is the play of the mind, and consists of various and unforced sallies of imagination. Festivity of spirit is a very uncommon talent, and must proceed from an assemblage of agreeable qualities in the same person. There are some few whom I think peculiarly happy in it, but it is a talent one cannot name in a man, especially when one considers, that it is never very grateful but where it is regarded by him who possesses it in the second place. The best man that I know of, for heightening the revel gaiety of a company, is Estcourt, whose jovial humour diffuses itself from the highest person at an entertainment to the meanest waiter. Merry tales, accompanied with apt gestures and lively representations of circumstances and persons, beguile the gravest mind into a consent to be as humourous as himself. Add to this, that when a man is in his good graces, he has a mimickry that does not debase the person he represents; but which, taking from the gravity of the character, adds to the agreeableness of it. This pleasant fellow gives one some idea of the ancient pantomime, who is said to have given the audience, in dumb-show, an exact idea of any character or passion, or an intelligible relation of any public occurrence, with no other expression than that of his looks and gestures. If all who have been obliged to these talents in Estcourt will be at Love for Love to-morrow night, they will but pay him what they owe him, at so easy a rate as being present at a play which nobody would omit seeing, that had, or had not, ever seen it before. T.

No. 359.] *Tuesday, April* 22, 1712.

Torva leæna lupum sequitur, lupus ipse capellam;
Florentem cytisum sequitur lasciva capella.
Virg. Ecl. vi. 63

Lions the wolves, and wolves the kids pursue,
The kids sweet thyme,—and still I follow you.
Warton.

As we were at the club last night, I observed that my old friend Sir Roger, contrary to his usual custom, sat very silent, and, instead of minding what was said by the company, was whistling to himself in a very thoughtful mood, and playing with a cork. I jogged Sir Andrew Freeport, who sat between us; and, as we were both observing him we saw the knight shake his head, and heard him say to himself, 'A foolish woman! I can't believe it.' Sir Andrew gave him a gentle pat upon the shoulder, and offered to lay him a bottle of wine that he was thinking of the widow. My old friend started, and, recovering out of his brown study, told Sir Andrew, that once in his life he had been in the right. In short, after some little hesitation, Sir Roger told us in the fulness of his heart, that he had just received a letter from his steward, which acquainted him that his old rival and antagonist in the country, Sir David Dundrum, had been making a visit to the widow. 'However,' says Sir Roger, 'I can never think that she will have a man that's half a year older than I am, and a noted republican into the bargain.'

Will Honeycomb, who looks upon love as his particular province, interrupting our friend with a jaunty laugh, 'I thought, knight,' said he, 'thou hadst lived long enough in the world not to pin thy happiness upon one that is a woman and a widow. I think that, without vanity, I may pretend to know as much of the female world as any man in Great Britain; though the chief of my knowledge consists in this, that they are not to be known.' Will immediately, with his usual fluency, rambled into an account of his own amours. 'I am now,' says he, 'upon the verge of fifty.' (though by the way we all knew he was turned of three-score.) 'You may easily guess,' continued Will, 'that I have not lived so long in the world without having had some thoughts of settling in it, as the phrase is. To tell you truly, I have several times tried my fortune that way, though I cannot much boast of my success.

'I made my first addresses to a young lady in the country; but, when I thought things were pretty well drawing to a conclusion, her father happening to hear that I had formerly boarded with a surgeon, the old put forbade me his house, and within a fortnight after married his daughter to a fox-hunter in the neighbourhood.

'I made my next application to a widow, and attacked her so briskly, that I thought myself within a fortnight of her. As I waited upon her one morning, she told me, that she intended to keep her ready-money and jointure in her own hand, and desired me to call upon her attorney in Lyon's-Inn, who would adjust with me what it was proper for me to add to it. I was so rebuffed by this overture, that I never inquired either for her or her attorney afterwards.

'A few months after, I addressed myself to a young lady who was an only daughter, and of a good family. I danced with her at several balls, squeezed her by the hand, said soft things to her, and, in short, made no doubt of her heart; and, though my fortune was not equal to hers, I was in hopes that her fond father would not deny her the man she had fixed her affections upon. But as I went one day to the house, in order to break the matter to him, I found the whole family in confusion, and heard to my unspeakable surprise, that Miss Jenny was that very morning run away with the butler.

'I then courted a second widow, and am at a loss to this day how I came to miss her, for she had often commended my person and behaviour. Her maid indeed told me one day, that her mistress said she never saw a gentleman with such a spindle pair of legs as Mr. Honeycomb.

'After this I laid siege to four heiresses successively, and, being a handsome young dog in those days, quickly made a breach in their hearts, but I don't know how it came to pass, though I seldom failed of getting the daughter's consent, I could never in my life get the old people on my side.

'I could give you an account of a thousand other unsuccessful attempts, particularly of one which I made some years since upon an old woman, whom I had certainly borne away with flying colours, if her relations had not come pouring in to her assistance from all parts of England; nay, I believe I should have got her at last, had not she been carried off by a hard frost.'

As Will's transitions are extremely quick, he turned from Sir Roger, and, applying himself to me, told me there was a passage in the book I had considered last Saturday, which deserves to be writ in letters of gold. and taking out a pocket Milton, read the following lines, which are part of one of Adam's speeches to Eve after the fall.

'——————Oh! why did our
Creator wise! that peopled highest heaven
With spirits masculine, create at last
This novelty on earth, this fair defect
Of nature, and not fill the world at once
With men, as angels, without feminine?
Or find some other way to generate
Mankind? This mischief had not then befall'n,
And more that shall befall, innumerable
Disturbances on earth, through female snares,
And straight conjunction with this sex: for either
He shall never find out fit mate; but such
As some misfortune brings him, or mistake;
Or whom he wishes most shall seldom gain,
Through her perverseness; but shall see her gain'd
By a far worse: or, if she love, withheld
By parents; or his happiest choice too late
Shall meet, already link'd and wedlock bound
To a fell adversary, his hate or shame:
Which infinite calamity shall cause
To human life, and household peace confound.'

Sir Roger listened to this passage with great attention; and, desiring Mr. Honeycomb to fold down a leaf at the place, and lend him his book, the knight put it up in his pocket, and told us that he would read over these verses again before he went to bed.

X.

No. 360.] *Wednesday, April* 23, 1712.

——————De paupertate tacentes,
Plus poscente ferent. *Hor.* Ep. xvii. Lib. 1. 43

The man who all his wants conceals,
Gains more than he who all his wants reveals.
Duncombe.

I HAVE nothing to do with the business of this day, any further than affixing the piece of Latin on the head of my paper; which I think a motto not unsuitable; since, if silence of our poverty is a recommendation, still more commendable is his modesty who conceals it by a decent dress.

'MR. SPECTATOR,—There is an evil under the sun, which has not yet come within your speculation, and is the censure, disesteem, and contempt, which some young fellows meet with from particular persons, for the reasonable methods they take to avoid them in general. This is by appearing in a better dress than may seem to a relation regularly consistent with a small fortune; and therefore may occasion a judgment of a suitable extravagance in other particulars; but the disadvantage with which the man of narrow circumstances acts and speaks, is so feelingly set forth in a little book called the Christian Hero, that the appearing to be otherwise is not only pardonable, but necessary. Every one knows the hurry of conclusions that are made in contempt of a person that appears to be calamitous; which makes it very excusable to prepare one's self for the company of those that are of a superior quality and fortune, by appearing to be in a better condi tion than one is, so far as such appearance shall not make us really of worse.

'It is a justice due to the character of one who suffers hard reflections from any particular person upon this account, that such persons would inquire into his manner of spending his time; of which, though no further information can be had than that he remains so many hours in his chamber, yet if this is cleared, to imagine that a reasonable creature, wrung with a narrow for tune, does not make the best use of this retirement, would be a conclusion extremely uncharitable. From what has, or will be said, I hope no consequence can be extorted, implying, that I would have any young fellow spend more time than the common leisure which his studies require, or more money than his fortune or allowance may admit of, in the pursuit of an acquaintance with his betters: for as to his time, the gross of that ought to be sacred to more substantial acquisitions; for each irrecoverable moment of which he ought to believe he stands religiously accountable. As to his dress, I shall engage myself no further than in the modest defence of two plain suits a year: for being perfectly satisfied in Eutrapelus's contrivance of making a Mohock of a man, by presenting him with laced and embroidered suits, I would by no means be thought to controvert the conceit, by insi nuating the advantages of foppery. It is an assertion which admits of much proof, that a stranger of tolerable sense, dressed like a gentleman, will be better received by those of quality above him, than one of much better parts, whose dress is regulated by the rigid notions of frugality. A man's appearance falls within the censure of every one that sees him; his parts and learning very few are judges of; and even upon these few they cannot at first be well intruded; for policy and good-breeding will counsel him to be reserved among strangers, and to support himself only by the common spirit of conversation. Indeed among the injudicious, the words, "delicacy, idiom, fine images, structure of periods, genius, fire," and the rest, made use of with a frugal and comely gravity, will maintain the figure of immense reading, and the depth of criti cism.

'All gentlemen of fortune, at least the young and middle-aged, are apt to pride themselves a little too much upon their dress, and consequently to value others in some measure upon the same consideration. With what confusion is a man of figure obliged to return the civilities of the hat to a person whose air and attire hardly entitle him to it! for whom nevertheless the other has a particular esteem, though he is ashamed to have it challenged in so public a manner. It must be allowed, that any young fellow that affects to dress and appear genteelly, might with artificial management, save ten pounds a-year; as instead of fine holland he might mourn in sack-cloth, and in other particulars be proportionably shabby: but of what service would this sum be to avert any misfortune, whilst it would leave him deserted by the little good acquaintance he has, and prevent his gaining any other? As the appearance of an easy fortune is necessary towards making one, I don't know but it might be of advantage sometimes to throw into one's discourse certain exclamations about bank stock, and to show a marvellous surprise upon its fall, as well as the most affected triumph upon its rise. The veneration and respect which the practice of all ages has preserved to appearances, without doubt suggested to our tradesmen that wise and politic custom, to apply and recommend themselves to the public by all those decorations upon their sign-posts and houses which the most eminent hands in the neighbourhood can furnish them with. What can be more attractive to a man of letters, than that immense erudition of all ages and languages, which a skilful bookseller, in conjunction with a painter, shall image upon his column, and the extremities of his shop? The same spirit of maintaining a handsome appearance reigns among the grave and solid apprentices of the law (here I could be particularly dull in proving the word apprentice to be significant of a barrister,) and you may easily distinguish who has most lately made his pretensions to business, by the whitest and most ornamental frame of his window; if indeed the chamber is a ground-room, and has rails before it, the finery is of necessity more extended and the pomp of business better maintained. And what can be a greater indication of the dignity of dress, than that burdensome finery which is the regular habit of our judges, nobles, and bishops, with which upon certain days we see them incumbered? And though it may be said, this is lawful, and necessary for the dignity of the state, yet the wisest of them have been remarkable, before they arrived at their present stations, for being very well dressed persons. As to my own part, I am near thirty; and since I left school have not been idle, which is a modern phrase for having studied hard. I brought off a clean system of moral philosophy, and a tolerable jargon of metaphysics, from the university· since that I have been engaged in the clear ing part of the perplexed style and matte · of the law, which so hereditarily descend to all its professors. To all which severe studies I have thrown in, at proper interims, the pretty learning of the classics. Notwithstanding which, I am ·vhat Shak speare calls a fellow of no mark or likelihood, which makes me understand the more fully that since the regular methods of making friends and a fortune by the mere force of a profession is so very slow and uncertain, a man should take all reasonable opportunities, by enlarging a good acquaintance, to court that time and chance which is said to happen to every man.

T.

No. 361.] *Thursday, April* 24, 1712.

Tartaream intendit vocem, qua protinus omnis
Contremuit domus—— *Virg. Æn.* vii. 514.

The blast Tartarean spreads its notes around;
The house astonish'd trembles at the sound.

I HAVE lately received the following letter from a country gentleman:

'MR. SPECTATOR,—The night before I left London I went to see a play called The Humourous Lieutenant. Upon the rising of the curtain I was very much surprised with the great concert of cat-calls which was exhibited that evening, and began to think with myself that I had made a mistake, and gone to a music-meeting instead of the play-house. It appeared indeed a little odd to me, to see so many persons of quality, of both sexes, assembled together at a kind of caterwauling, for I cannot look upon that performance to have been any thing better, whatever the musicians themselves might think of it. As I had no acquaintance in the house to ask questions of, and was forced to go out of town early the next morning, I could not learn the secret of this matter. What I would therefore desire of you, is, to give me some account of this strange instrument, which I found the company called a cat-call; and particularly to let me know whether it be a piece of music lately come from Italy. For my own part to be free with you, I would rather hear an English fiddle; though I durst not show my dislike whilst I was in the play-house, it being my chance to sit the very next man to one of the performers. I am, sir, your most affectionate friend and servant, JOHN SHALLOW, ESQ.'

In compliance with Squire Shallow's request, I design this paper as a dissertation upon the cat-call. In order to make myself a master of the subject, I purchased one the beginning of last week, though not without great difficulty, being informed at two or three toy-shops that the players had lately bought them all up. I have since consulted many learned antiquaries in relation to its original, and find them very much divided among themselves upon that particular. A fellow of the Royal Society who is my good friend, and a great proficient in the mathematical part of music, concludes, from the simplicity of its make, and the uniformity of its sound, that the cat-call is older than any of the inventions of Jubal. He observes very well, that musical instruments took their first rise from the notes of birds, and other melodious animals; 'and what,' says he, 'was more natural than for the first ages of mankind to imitate the voice of a cat, that lived under the same roof with them?' He added, that the cat had contributed more to harmony than any other animal; as we are not only beholden to her for this wind instrument, but for our string-music in general.

Another virtuoso of my acquaintance will not allow the cat-call to be older than Thespis, and is apt to think it appeared in the world soon after the ancient comedy; for which reason it has still a place in our dramatic entertainments. Nor must I here omit what a very curious gentleman, who is lately returned from his travels, has more than once assured me; namely, that there was lately dug up at Rome the statue of a Momus, who holds an instrument in his right hand, very much resembling our modern cat-call.

There are others who ascribe this invention to Orpheus, and look upon the cat-call to be one of those instruments which that famous musician made use of to draw the beasts about him. It is certain that the roasting of a cat does not call together a greater audience of that species than this instrument, if dexterously played upon in proper time and place.

But, notwithstanding these various and learned conjectures, I cannot forbear thinking that the cat-call is originally a piece of English music. Its resemblance to the voice of some of our British songsters, as well as the use of it, which is peculiar to our nation, confirms me in this opinion. It has at least received great improvements among us, whether we consider the instrument itself, or those several quavers and graces which are thrown into the playing of it. Every one might be sensible of this who heard that remarkable overgrown cat-call which was placed in the centre of the pit, and presided over all the rest at the celebrated performance lately exhibited at Drury-lane.

Having said thus much concerning the origin of the cat-call, we are in the next place to consider the use of it. The cat-call exerts itself to most advantage in the British theatre. It very much improves the sound of nonsense, and often goes along with the voice of the actor who pronounces it, as the violin or harpsichord accompanies the Italian recitativo.

It has often supplied the place of the ancient chorus, in the words of Mr. ***. In short, a bad poet has as great an antipathy to a cat-call as many people have to a real cat.

Mr. Collier in his ingenious essay upon music, has the following passage:

'I believe it is possible to invent an instrument that shall have a quite contrary effect to those martial ones now in use; an instrument that shall sink the spirits and shake the nerves, and curdle the blood, and inspire despair, and cowardice, and consternation, at a surprising rate. 'Tis probable the roaring of lions, the warbling of cats and screech-owls, together with a mixture of the howling of dogs, judiciously imitated and compounded, might go a great way in this invention. Whether such anti-music as this might not be of service in a camp, I shall leave to the military men to consider.'

What this learned gentleman supposes in speculation, I have known actually verified in practice. The cat-call has struck a damp into generals, and frighted heroes off the stage. At the first sound of it I have seen a crowned head tremble, and a princess fall into fits. The humourous lieutenant himself could not stand it; nay, I am told that even Almanzor looked like a mouse, and trembled at the voice of this terrifying instrument.

As it is of a dramatic nature, and peculiarly appropriated to the stage, I can by no means approve the thought of that angry lover, who, after an unsuccessful pursuit of some years, took leave of his mistress in a serenade of cat-calls.

I must conclude this paper with the account I have lately received of an ingenious artist, who has long studied this instrument, and is very well versed in all the rules of the drama. He teaches to play on it by book, and to express by it the whole art of criticism. He has his bass and his treble cat-call; the former for tragedy, the latter for comedy; only in tragi-comedies they may both play together in concert. He has a particular squeak, to denote the violation of each of the unities, and has different sounds to show whether he aims at the poet or the player. In short, he teaches the smut-note, the fustian-note, the stupid-note, and has composed a kind of air that may serve as an act-tune to an incorrigible play, and which takes in the whole compass of the cat-call. L.

No. 362.] *Friday, April 25, 1712.*

Laudibus arguitur vini vinosus——
Hor. Ep. xix. Lib. 1. 6.

He praises wine; and we conclude from thence,
He lik'd his glass, on his own evidence.

'Temple, April 24.

'MR. SPECTATOR,—Several of my friends were this morning got over a dish of tea in very good health, though we had celebrated yesterday with more glasses that we could have dispensed with, had we not been beholden to Brooke and Hellier. In gratitude, therefore, to those citizens, I am, in the name of the company, to accuse you of great negligence in overlooking their merit, who have imported true and generous wine, and taken care that it should not be adulterated by the retailers before it comes to the tables of private families, or the clubs of honest fellows. I cannot imagine how a Spectator can be supposed to do his duty, without frequent resumption of such subjects as concern our health, the first thing to be regarded, if we have a mind to relish any thing else. It would, therefore, very well become your spectatorial vigilance, to give it in orders to your officer for inspecting signs, that in his march he would look into the itinerants who deal in provisions, and inquire where they buy their several wares. Ever since the decease of Colly-Molly-Puff, of agreeable and noisy memory, I cannot say I have observed any thing sold in carts, or carried by horse, or ass, or, in fine, in any moving market, which is not perished or putrefied; witness the wheel-barrows of rotten raisins, almonds, figs, and currants, which you see vended by a merchant dressed in a second-hand suit of a foot soldier. You should consider that a child may be poisoned for the worth of a farthing; but except his poor parents send him to one certain doctor in town, they can have no advice for him under a guinea. When poisons are thus cheap, and medicines thus dear, how can you be negligent in inspecting what we eat and drink, or take no notice of such as the above-mentioned citizens, who have been so serviceable to us of late in that particular? It was a custom among the old Romans, to do him particular honours who had saved the life of a citizen. How much more does the world owe to those who prevent the death of multitudes! As these men deserve well of your office, so such as act to the detriment of our health, you ought to represent to themselves and their fellow-subjects in the colours which they deserve to wear. I think it would be for the public good, that all who vend wines should be under oath in that behalf. The chairman at the quarter-sessions should inform the country, that the vintner who mixes wine to his customers, shall (upon proof that the drinker thereof died within a year and a day after taking it,) be deemed guilty of wilful murder, and the jury shall be instructed to inquire and present such delinquents accordingly. It is no mitigation of the crime, nor will it be conceived that it can be brought in chance-medley, or man-slaughter, upon proof that it shall appear wine joined to wine, or right Herefordshire poured into Port O Port: but his selling it for one thing, knowing it to be another, must justly bear the foresaid guilt of wilful murder: for that he, the said vintner, did an unlawful act willingly in the false mixture, and is therefore with equity liable to all the pains to which a man would be, if it were proved that he designed only to run a man through the arm whom he whipped through the lungs. This is my third year at the Temple, and this is, or should be, law. An ill intention, well proved, should meet with no alleviation, because it outran itself. There cannot be too great severity used against the injustice as well as cruelty of those who play with men's lives, by preparing liquors whose nature, for aught they know, may be noxious when mixed, though innocent when apart: and Brooke and Hellier, who have insured our safety at our meals, and driven jealousy from our cups in conversation, deserve the custom and thanks of the whole town; and it is your duty to remind them of the obligation. I am, sir, your humble servant,

'TOM POTTLE.'

'MR. SPECTATOR,—I am a person who was long immured in a college, read much, saw little; so that I knew no more of the world than what a lecture or view of the map taught me. By this means I improved in my study, but became unpleasant in conversation. By conversing generally with the dead, I grew almost unfit for the society of the living; so by a long confinement I contracted an ungainly aversion to conversation, and ever discoursed with pain to myself, and little entertainment to others. At last I was in some measure made sensible of my failing, and the mortification of never being spoken to, or speaking, unless the discourse ran upon books, put me upon forcing myself among men. I immediately affected the politest company, by the frequent use of which, I hoped to wear off the rust I had contracted: but, by an uncouth imitation of men, used to act in public, I got no further than to discover I had a mind to appear a finer thing than I really was.

'Such I was, and such was my condition, when I became an ardent lover, and passionate admirer of the beauteous Belinda. Then it was that I really began to improve. This passion changed all my fears and diffidences in my general behaviour to the sole concern of pleasing her. I had not now to study the action of a gentleman; but love possessing all my thoughts, made me truly be the thing I had a mind to appear. My thoughts grew free and generous; and the ambition to be agreeable to her I admired, produced in my carriage a faint similitude of that disengaged manner of my Belinda. The way we are in at present is, that she sees my passion, and sees I at present forbear speaking of it through prudential regards. This respect to her she returns with much civility, and makes my value for her as little misfortune to me as is consistent with discretion. She sings very charmingly, and is readier to do so at my request, because she knows I love her. She will dance with me rather than another for the same reason. My fortune must alter from what it is, before I can speak my heart to her: and her circumstances are not considerable enough to make up for the narrowness of mine. But I write to you now, only to give you the character of Belinda, as a woman that has address enough to demonstrate a gratitude to her lover, without giving him hopes of success in his passion. Belinda has from a great wit, governed by as great prudence, and both adorned with innocence, the happiness of always being ready to discover her real thoughts. She has many of us, who now are her admirers; but her treatment of us is so just and proportioned to our merit towards her, and what we are in ourselves, that I protest to you I have neither jealousy nor hatred towards my rivals. Such is her goodness, and the acknowledgment of every man who admires her, that he thinks he ought to believe she will take him who best deserves her. I will not say that this peace among us is not owing to self-love, which prompts each to think himself the best deserver. I think there is something uncommon and worthy of imitation in this lady's character. If you will please to print my letter, you will oblige the little fraternity of happy rivals, and in a more particular manner, sir, your most humble servant,

'WILL CYMON.'

No. 363.] *Saturday, April* 26, 1712.

——————Crudelis ubique
Luctus, ubique pavor, et plurima mortis imago.
Virg. Æn. ii. 368.

All parts resound with tumults, plaints, and fears,
And grisly Death in sundry shapes appears.—*Dryden.*

MILTON has shown a wonderful art in describing that variety of passions which arise in our first parents upon the breach of the commandment that had been given them. We see them gradually passing from the triumph of their guilt, through remorse, shame, despair, contrition, prayer and hope, to a perfect and complete repentance. At the end of the tenth book they are represented as prostrating themselves upon the ground, and watering the earth with their tears: to which the poet joins this beautiful circumstance, that they offered up their penitential prayers on the very place where their judge appeared to them when he pronounced their sentence:

——They forthwith to the place
Repairing where he judg'd them, prostrate fell
Before him reverent, and both confess'd
Humbly their faults, and pardon begg'd, with tears
Watering the ground.——

There is a beauty of the same kind in a tragedy of Sophocles, where Œdipus, after having put out his own eyes, instead of breaking his neck from the palace battlements, (which furnishes so elegant an entertainment for our English audience) desires that he may be conducted to Mount Cithæron, in order to end his life in that very place where he was exposed in his infancy, and where he should then have died, had the will of his parents been executed.*

As the author never fails to give a poetical

* This paragraph was not in the original paper in folio, but added on the republication of the papers in volumes.

turn to his sentiments, he describes in the beginning of this book the acceptance which these their prayers met with, in a short allegory formed upon that beautiful passage in holy writ, 'And another angel came and stood at the altar, having a golden censer; and there was given unto him much incense, that he should offer it with the prayers of all saints upon the golden altar, which was before the throne: and the smoke of the incense, which came with the prayers of the saints, ascended up before God.'*

———To heaven their prayer
Flew up, nor miss'd the way, by envious winds
Blown vagabond or frustrate; in they pass'd
Dimensionless through heav'nly doors, then clad
With incense, where the golden altar fum'd
By their great Intercessor, came in sight
Before the Father's throne.———

We have the same thought expressed a second time in the intercession of the Messiah, which is conceived in very emphatical sentiments and expressions.

Among the poetical parts of Scripture, which Milton has so finely wrought into this part of his narration, I must not omit that wherein Ezekiel, speaking of the angels who appeared to him in a vision adds, that every one had four faces, and that their whole bodies, and their backs, and their hands, and their wings, were full of eyes round about:

———The cohort bright
Of watchful cherubim, four faces each
Had, like a double Janus, all their shape
Spangled with eyes.———

The assembling of all the angels of heaven, to hear the solemn decree passed upon man, is represented in very lively ideas. The Almighty is here described as remembering mercy in the midst of judgment, and commanding Michael to deliver his message in the mildest terms, lest the spirit of man, which was already broken with the sense of his guilt and misery, should fail before him:

'———Yet lest they fain
At the sad sentence rigorously urg'd,
For I behold them soften'd, and with tears
Bewailing their excess, all terror hide.'

The conference of Adam and Eve is full of moving sentiments. Upon their going abroad, after the melancholy night which they had passed together, they discover the lion and the eagle, each of them pursuing their prey towards the eastern gates of Paradise. There is a double beauty in this incident, not only as it presents great and just omens, which are always agreeable in poetry, but as it expresses that enmity which was now produced in the animal creation. The poet, to show the like changes in nature, as well as to grace his fable with a noble prodigy, represents the sun in an eclipse. This particular incident has likewise a fine effect upon the imagination of the reader, in regard to what follows; for at the same time that the sun is under an eclipse, a bright cloud descends in the western quarter of the heavens, filled with a host of angels, and more luminous than the sun itself. The whole theatre of nature is darkened, that this glorious machine may appear with all its lustre and magnificence.

'———Why in the east
Darkness ere day's mid-course? and morning light
More orient in that western cloud that draws
O'er the blue firmament a radiant white,
And slow descends with something heavenly fraught?'
He err'd not, for by this the heavenly bands
Down from a sky of jasper lighted now
In Paradise, and on a hill made halt;
A glorious apparition.———

I need not observe how properly this author, who always suits his parts to the actors whom he introduces, has employed Michael in the expulsion of our first parents from Paradise. The archangel on this occasion neither appears in his proper shape, nor in the familiar manner with which Raphael, the sociable spirit, entertained the father of mankind before the fall. His person, his port, and behaviour, are suitable to a spirit of the highest rank, and exquisitely described in the following passage.

———Th' archangel soon drew nigh,
Not in his shape celestial; but as man
Clad to meet man: over his lucid arms
A military vest of purple flow'd,
Livelier than Melibœan, or the grain
Of Sarra, worn by kings and heroes old,
In time of truce: Iris had dipt the woof:
His starry helm, unbuckled, show'd him prime
In manhood where youth ended; by his side,
As in a glist'ring zodiac, hung the sword,
Satan's dire dread, and in his hand the spear.
Adam bow'd low; he kingly from his state
Inclin'd not, but his coming thus declared.

Eve's complaint, upon hearing that she was to be removed from the garden of Paradise, is wonderfully beautiful. The sentiments are not only proper to the subject, but have something in them particularly soft and womanish:

'Must I then leave thee, Paradise? Thus leave
Thee, native soil, these happy walks and shades
Fit haunt of gods, where I had hope to spend
Quiet, though sad, the respite of that day
That must be mortal to us both? O flowers,
That never will in other climate grow,
My early visitation, and my last
At even, which I bred up with tender hand
From the first opening bud, and gave you names!
Who now shall rear you to the sun, or rank
Your tribes, and water from th' ambrosial fount?
Thee, lastly, nuptial bower, by me adorn'd
With what to sight or smell was sweet: from thee
How shall I part? and whither wander down
Into a lower world, to this, obscure
And wild? How shall we breathe in other air
Less pure, accustomed to immortal fruits?'

Adam's speech abounds with thoughts which are equally moving, but of a more masculine and elevated turn. Nothing can be conceived more sublime and poetical than the following passage in it:

This most afflicts me, that departing hence
As from his face I shall be hid, deprived
His blessed count'nance; here I could frequent,
With worship, place by place, where he vouchsaf'd
Presence divine; and to my sons relate,
On this mount he appear'd, under this tree
Stood visible, among these pines his voice
I heard; here with him at this fountain talk'd,
So many grateful altars I would rear
Of grassy turf, and pile up every stone

* Rev. viii. 3, 4.

Of lustre from the brook, in memory
Or monuments to ages, and thereon
Offer sweet-smelling gums and flow'rs.
In yonder nether world, where shall I seek
His bright appearances, or footsteps trace?
For though I fled him angry, yet recall'd
To life prolong'd and promis'd race, I now
Gladly behold though but his utmost skirts
Of glory, and far off his steps adore.'

The angel afterwards leads Adam to the highest mount of Paradise, and lays before him a whole hemisphere, as a proper stage for those visions which were to be represented on it. I have before observed how the plan of Milton's poem is in many particulars greater than that of the Iliad or Æneid. Virgil's hero, in the last of these poems, is entertained with a sight of all those who are to descend from him; but though that episode is justly admired as one of the noblest designs in the whole Æneid, every one must allow that this of Milton is of a much higher nature. Adam's vision is not confined to any particular tribe of mankind, but extends to the whole species.

In this great review which Adam takes of all his sons and daughters, the first objects he is presented with exhibit to him the story of Cain and Abel, which is drawn together with much closeness and propriety of expression. The curiosity and natural horror which arises in Adam at the sight of the first dying man is touched with great beauty.

'But have I now seen death? Is this the way
I must return to native dust? O sight
Of terror foul, and ugly to behold!
Horrid to think, how horrible to feel!'

The second vision sets before him the image of death in a great variety of appearances. The angel, to give him a general idea of those effects which his guilt had brought upon his posterity, places before him a large hospital, or lazar-house, filled with persons lying under all kinds of mortal diseases. How finely has the poet told us that the sick persons languished under lingering and incurable distempers, by an apt and judicious use of such imaginary beings as those I mentioned in my last Saturday's paper:

Dire was the tossing, deep the groans; Despair
Tended the sick, busy from couch to couch;
And over them triumphant Death his dart
Shook, but delay'd to strike, tho' oft invok'd
With vows, as their chief good and final hope.

The passion which likewise rises in Adam on this occasion is very natural:

Sight so deform what heart of rock could long
Dry-ey'd behold? Adam could not, but wept,
Though not of woman born; compassion quell'd
His best of man, and gave him up to tears.

The discourse between the angel and Adam which follows, abounds with noble morals.

As there is nothing more delightful in poetry than a contrast and opposition of incidents, the author, after this melancholy prospect of death and sickness, raises up a scene of mirth, love, and jollity. The secret pleasure that steals into Adam's heart, as he is intent upon this vision, is imagined with great delicacy. I must not omit the description of the loose female troop, who seduced the sons of God, as they are called in Scripture.

'For that fair female troop thou saw'st, that seem'd
Of goddesses, so blythe, so smooth, so gay,
Yet empty of all good, wherein consists
Woman's domestic honour, and chief praise:
Bred only and completed to the taste
Of lustful appetence, to sing, to dance,
To dress, and troule the tongue, and roll the eye;
To these that sober race of men, whose lives
Religious titled them the sons of God,
Shall yield up all their virtue, all their fame,
Ignobly, to the trains and to the smiles
Of those fair atheists.'———

The next vision is of a quite contrary nature, and filled with the horrors of war. Adam at the sight of it melts into tears, and breaks out into that passionate speech,

———O what are these!
Death's ministers, not men, who thus deal death
Inhumanly to men, and multiply
Ten thousandfold the sin of him who slew
His brother: for of whom such massacre
Make they, but of their brethren, men of men?

Milton to keep up an agreeable variety in his visions, after having raised in the mind of his reader the several ideas of terror which are conformable to the description of war, passes on to those softer images of triumphs and festivals, in that vision of lewdness and luxury which ushers in the flood.

As it is visible that the poet had his eye upon Ovid's account of the universal deluge, the reader may observe with how much judgment he has avoided every thing that is redundant or puerile in the Latin poet. We do not here see the wolf swimming among the sheep, nor any of those wanton imaginations which Seneca found fault with, as unbecoming this great catastrophe of nature. If our poet has imitated that verse in which Ovid tells us that there was nothing but sea, and that this sea had no shore to it, he has not set the thought in such a light as to incur the censure which critics have passed upon it. The latter part of that verse in Ovid is idle and superfluous, but just and beautiful in Milton,

Jamque mare et tellus nullum discrimen habebant;
Nil nisi pontus erat; deerant quoque littora ponto.
Ovid. Met. i. 291.

Now seas and earth were in confusion lost;
A world of waters, and without a coast.—*Dryden.*

———Sea cover'd sea,
Sea without shore.——— *Milton.*

In Milton the former part of the description does not forestall the latter. How much more great and solemn on this occasion is that which follows in our English poet.

———And in their palaces,
Where luxury late reign'd, sea-monsters whelp'd
And stabled———

than that in Ovid, where we are told that the sea-calf lay in those places where the goats were used to browse! The reader may find several other parallel passages in the Latin and English description of the deluge; wherein our poet has visibly the advantage. The sky's being overcharged with clouds, the descending of the rains, the rising of the seas, and the appearance of the rainbow, are such descriptions as every one must take notice of. The circumstance relating to Paradise is so finely imagined, and suitable to the opinions of many learned authors, that I cannot forbear giving it a place in this paper.

———Then shall this mount
Of Paradise, by might of waves be mov'd
Out of his place, push'd by the horned flood;
With all his verdure spoil'd, and trees adrift
Down the great river to th' op'ning gulf,
And there take root; an island salt and bare,
The haunt of seals and orcs and sea-mews' clang.

The transition which the poet makes from the vision of the deluge, to the concern it occasioned in Adam, is exquisitely graceful, and copied after Virgil, though the first thought it introduces is rather in the spirit of Ovid:

How didst thou grieve then, Adam, to behold
The end of all thy offspring, end so sad,
Depopulation! Thee another flood,
Of tears and sorrow, a flood, thee also drown'd,
And sunk thee as thy sons; till gently rear'd
By th' angel, on thy feet thou stood'st at last,
Though comfortless, as when a father mourns
His children all in view destroy'd at once.

I have been the more particular in my quotations out of the eleventh book of Paradise Lost, because it is not generally reckoned among the most shining books of this poem: for which reason the reader might be apt to overlook those many passages in it which deserve our admiration. The eleventh and twelfth are indeed built upon that single circumstance of the removal of our first parents from Paradise: but though this is not in itself so great a subject as that in most of the foregoing books, it is extended and diversified with so many surprising incidents and pleasing episodes, that these two last books can by no means be looked upon as unequal parts of this divine poem.

I must further add, that, had not Milton represented our first parents as driven out of Paradise, his fall of man would not have been complete, and consequently his action would have been imperfect. L.

No. 364.] *Monday, April* 28, 1712.

———Navibus atque
Quadrigis petimus bene vivere.
Hor. Ep. xi. Lib. 1. 29.

Anxious through seas and land to search for rest,
Is but laborious idleness at best.—*Francis.*

'Mr. Spectator,—A lady of my acquaintance, for whom I have too much respect to be easy while she is doing an indiscreet action, has given occasion to this trouble. She is a widow, to whom the indulgence of a tender husband has entrusted the management of a very great fortune, and a son about sixteen, both of which she is extremely fond of. The boy has parts of the middle size, neither shining nor despicable, and has passed the common exercises of his years with tolerable advantage, but is withal what you would call a forward youth: by the help of this last qualification, which serves as a varnish to all the rest, he is enabled to make the best use of his learning, and display it at full length upon all occasions. Last summer he distinguished himself two or three times very remarkably, by puzzling the vicar, before an assembly of most of the ladies in the neighbourhood; and from such weighty considerations as these, as it too often unfortunately falls out, the mother is become invincibly persuaded that her son is a great scholar; and that to chain him down to the ordinary methods of education, with others of his age, would be to cramp his faculties, and do an irreparable injury to his wonderful capacity.

'I happened to visit at the house last week, and missing the young gentleman at the tea-table, where he seldom fails to officiate, could not upon so extraordinary a circumstance avoid inquiring after him. My lady told me he was gone out with her woman, in order to make some preparation for their equipage; for that she intended very speedily to carry him to "travel." The oddness of the expression shocked me a little; however, I soon recovered myself enough to let her know, that all I was willing to understand by it was, that she designed this summer to show her son his estate in a distant county, in which he had never yet been. But she soon took care to rob me of that agreeable mistake, and let me into the whole affair. She enlarged upon young master's prodigious improvements, and his comprehensive knowledge of all book-learning; concluding, that, it was now high time he should be made acquainted with men and things; that she had resolved he should make the tour of France and Italy, but could not bear to have him out of her sight, and therefore intended to go along with him.

I was going to rally her for so extravagant a resolution, but found myself not in a fit humour to meddle with a subject that demanded the most soft and delicate touch imaginable. I was afraid of dropping something that might seem to bear hard either upon the son's abilities, or the mother's discretion, being sensible that in both these cases, though supported with all the powers of reason, I should, instead of gaining her ladyship over to my opinion, only expose myself to her disesteem: I therefore immediately determined to refer the whole matter to the Spectator.

'When I came to reflect at night, as my custom is, upon the occurrences of the day, I could not but believe that this humour of carrying a boy to travel in his mother's lap, and that upon pretence of learning men and things, is a case of an extraordinary nature, and carries on it a peculiar stamp of folly. I did not remember to have met with its parallel within the compass of my observation, though I could call to mind some not extremely unlike it. From hence my thoughts took occasion to ramble into the general notion of travelling, as it is now made a part of education. Nothing is more frequent than to take a lad from grammar and taw, and, under the tuition of some poor scholar, who is willing to be banished for thirty pounds a year, and a little victuals, send him crying and snivelling into foreign countries. Thus he spends his time as children do at puppet-shows, and with much the same advantage, in staring and gaping at an amazing variety of strange things; strange indeed to one who is not prepared to comprehend the reasons and meaning of them, whilst he should be laying the solid foundations of knowledge in his mind, and furnishing it with just rules to direct his future progress in life under some skilful master of the art of instruction.

'Can there be a more astonishing thought in nature, than to consider how men should fall into so palpable a mistake? It is a large field, and may very well exercise a sprightly genius; but I do not remember you have yet taken a turn in it. I wish, sir, you would make people understand that "travel" is really the last step to be taken in the institution of youth, and that to set out with it, is to begin where they should end.

'Certainly the true end of visiting foreign parts, is to look into their customs and policies, and observe in what particulars they excel or come short of our own; to unlearn some odd peculiarities in our manners, and wear off such awkward stiffnesses and affectations in our behaviour, as possibly may have been contracted from constantly associating with one nation of men, by a more free, general, and mixed conversation. But how can any of these advantages be attained by one who is a mere stranger to the customs and policies of his native country, and has not yet fixed in his mind the first principles of manners and behaviour? To endeavour it, is to build a gaudy structure without any foundation; or, if I may be allowed the expression, to work a rich embroidery upon a cob web.

'Another end of travelling, which deserves to be considered, is the improving our taste of the best authors of antiquity, by seeing the places where they lived, and of which they wrote; to compare the natural face of the country with the descriptions they have given us, and observe how well the picture agrees with the original. This must certainly be a most charming exercise to the mind that is rightly turned for it; besides that, it may in a good measure be made subservient to morality, if the person is capable of drawing just conclusions concerning the uncertainty of human things, from the ruinous alterations time and barbarity have brought upon so many palaces, cities, and whole countries, which make the most illustrious figures in history. And this hint may be not a little improved by examining every little spot of ground that we find celebrated as the scene of some famous action, or retaining any footsteps of a Cato, Cicero, or Brutus, or some such great virtuous man. A nearer view of any such particular, though really little and trifling in itself, may serve the more powerfully to warm a generous mind to an emulation of their virtues, and a greater ardency of ambition to imitate their bright examples, if it comes duly tempered and prepared for the impression. But this I believe you will hardly think those to be, who are so far from entering into the sense and spirit of the ancients, that they do not yet understand their language with any exactness.*

'But I have wandered from my purpose, which was only to desire you to save, if possible, a fond English mother, and mother's own son, from being shown a ridiculous spectacle through the most polite parts of Europe. Pray tell them, that though to be sea-sick, or jumbled in an outlandish stage-coach, may perhaps be healthful for the constitution of the body, yet it is apt to cause such dizziness in young empty heads as too often lasts their life-time. I am, sir, your most humble servant.

'PHILIP HOMEBRED.'

'Birchin-lane.

'SIR,—I was married on Sunday last, and went peaceably to bed; but, to my surprise, was awakened the next morning by the thunder of a set of drums. These warlike sounds (methinks) are very improper in a marriage-concert, and give great offence; they seem to insinuate, that the joys of this state are short, and that jars and discords soon ensue. I fear they have been ominous to many matches, and sometimes proved a prelude to a battle in the honey-moon. A nod from you may hush them; therefore, pray, sir, let them be silenced, that for the future none but soft airs may usher in the morning of a bridal night; which will be a favour not only to those who come after, but to me, who can still subscribe myself, your most humble and most obedient servant,

'ROBIN BRIDEGROOM.'

'MR. SPECTATOR,—I am one of that sort of women whom the gayer part of our sex are apt to call a prude. But to show them

* The following paragraph, in the first edition of this paper in folio, was afterwards suppressed. It is here reprinted from the Spect. in folio, No. 364.

'I cannot quit this head without paying my acknowledgments to one of the most entertaining pieces this age has produced, for the pleasure it gave me. You will easily guess that the book I have in my head is Mr. Addison's Remarks upon Italy. That ingenious gentleman has with so much art and judgment applied his exact knowledge of all the parts of classical learning, to illustrate the several occurrences of his travels, that his work alone is a pregnant proof of what I have said Nobody that has a taste this way, can read him going from Rome to Naples, and making Horace and Silius Italicus his chart, but he must feel some uneasiness in himself to reflect that he was not in his retinue. I am sure I wished it ten times in every page, and that not without a secret vanity to think in what state I should have travelled the Appian road, with Horace for a guide, and in company with a countryman of my own, who, of all men living, knows best how to follow his steps' that I have very little regard to their raillery, I shall be glad to see them all at The Amorous Widow, or The Wanton Wife, which is to be acted for the benefit of Mrs. Porter, on Monday the 28th instant. I assure you I can laugh at an amorous widow, or wanton wife, with as little temptation to imitate them, as I could at any other vicious character. Mrs. Porter obliged me so very much in the exquisite sense she seemed to have of the honourable sentiments and noble passions in the character of Hermione, that I shall appear in her behalf at a comedy, though I have no great relish for any entertainments where the mirth is not seasoned with a certain severity, which ought to recommend it to people who pretend to keep reason and authority over all their actions. I am, sir, your frequent reader,

T. 'ALTAMIRA.'

No. 365.] *Tuesday, April* 29, 1712.

Vere magis, quia vere calor redit ossibus—— .
Virg. Georg. iii. 272.

But most in spring; the kindly spring inspires
Reviving heat, and kindles genial fires.

ADAPTED.

Flush'd by the spirit of the genial year,
Be greatly cautious of your sliding hearts.
Thomson's Spring, 160, &c.

THE author of the Menagiana acquaints us, that discoursing one day with several ladies of quality about the effects of the month of May, which infuses a kindly warmth into the earth, and all its inhabitants, the marchioness of S——, who was one of the company, told him, that though she would promise to be chaste in every month besides, she could not engage for herself in May. As the beginning therefore of this month is now very near, I design this paper for a caveat to the fair sex, and publish it before April is quite out, that if any of them should be caught tripping, they may not pretend they had not timely notice.

I am induced to this, being persuaded the above-mentioned observation is as well calculated for our climate as that of France, and that some of our British ladies are of the same constitution with the French marchioness.

I shall leave it among physicians to determine what may be the cause of such an anniversary inclination; whether or no it is that the spirits, after having been as it were frozen and congealed by winter, are now turned loose and set a rambling; or, that the gay prospects of fields and meadows, with the courtship of the birds in every bush, naturally unbend the mind, and soften it to pleasure; or that, as some have imagined, a woman is prompted by a kind of instinct to throw herself on a bed of flowers, and not to let those beautiful couches which nature has provided lie useless. However it be, the effects of this month on the lower part of the sex, who act without disguise, are very visible. It is at this time that we see the young wenches in a country-parish dancing round a May-pole, which one of our learned antiquaries supposes to be a relick of a certain pagan worship that I do not think fit to mention.

It is likewise on the first day of this month that we see the ruddy milk-maid exerting herself in a most sprightly manner under a pyramid of silver tankards, and, like the virgin Tarpeia,* oppressed by the costly ornaments which her benefactors lay upon her.

I need not mention the ceremony of the green gown, which is also peculiar to this gay season.

The same periodical love-fit spreads through the whole sex, as Mr. Dryden well observes in his description of this merry month.

'For thee, sweet month, the groves green liv'ries wear,
If not the first, the fairest of the year;
For thee the graces lead the dancing hours,
And nature's ready pencil paints the flowers.
The sprightly May commands our youth to keep
The vigils of her night, and breaks their sleep;
Each gentle breast with kindly warmth she moves,
Inspires new flames, revives extinguish'd loves.'

Accordingly, among the works of the great masters in painting, who have drawn this genial season of the year, we often observe Cupids confused with Zephyrs, flying up and down promiscuously in several parts of the picture. I cannot but add from my own experience, that about this time of the year love-letters come up to me in great numbers, from all quarters of the nation.

I received an epistle in particular by the last post from a Yorkshire gentleman, who makes heavy complaints of one Zelinda, whom it seems he has courted unsuccessfully these three years past. He tells me that he designs to try her this May; and if he does not carry his point, he will never think of her more.

Having thus fairly admonished the female sex, and laid before them the dangers they are exposed to in this critical month, I shall in the next place lay down some rules and directions for the better avoiding those calentures which are so very frequent in this season.

In the first place, I would advise them never to venture abroad in the fields, but in the company of a parent, a guardian, or some other sober discreet person. I have before shown how apt they are to trip in the flowery meadow; and shall further observe to them, that Proserpine was out a-maying when she met with that fatal adventure to which Milton alludes when he mentions—

——That fair field
Of Enna, where Proserpine gath'ring flowers,
Herself a fairer flower, by gloomy Dis
Was gather'd.——

---

* T. Livii Hist. Dec. 1. lib. 1. cap. xi.

Since I am going into quotations, I shall conclude this head with Virgil's advice to young people while they are gathering wild strawberries and nosegays, that they should have a care of the 'snake in the grass.'

In the second place, I cannot but approve those prescriptions which our astrological physicians give in their almanacks for this month: such as are 'a spare and simple diet, with a moderate use of phlebotomy.'

Under this head of abstinence I shall also advise my fair readers to be in a particular manner careful how they meddle with romances, chocolate, novels, and the like inflamers, which I look upon as very dangerous to be made use of during this great carnival of nature.

As I have often declared that I have nothing more at heart than the honour of my dear country-women, I would beg them to consider, whenever their resolutions begin to fail them, that there are but one-and-thirty days of this soft season, and if they can but weather out this one month, the rest of the year will be easy to them. As for that part of the fair sex who stay in town, I would advise them to be particularly cautious how they give themselves up to their most innocent entertainments. If they cannot forbear the playhouse, I would recommend tragedy to them rather than comedy; and should think the puppet-show much safer for them than the opera, all the while the sun is in Gemini.

The reader will observe, that this paper is written for the use of those ladies who think it worth while to war against nature in the cause of honour. As for that abandoned crew, who do not think virtue worth contending for, but give up their reputation at the first summons, such warnings and premonitions are thrown away upon them. A prostitute is the same easy creature in all months of the year, and makes no difference between May and December.

X.

No. 366.] *Wednesday, April* 30, 1712.

Pone me pigris ubi nulla campis
Arbor æstiva recreatur aura;
Dulce ridentem Lalagen amabo,
Dulce loquentem. *Hor.* Od. xxii. Lib. 1. 17.

Set me where on some pathless plain
The swarthy Africans complain,
To see the chariot of the sun
So near the scorching country run;
The burning zone, the frozen isles,
Shall hear me sing of Celia's smiles;
All cold, but in her breast, I will despise,
And dare all heat but that of Celia's eyes.
Roscommon.

THERE are such wild inconsistencies in the thoughts of a man in love, that I have often reflected there can be no reason for allowing him more liberty than others possessed with phrenzy, but that his distemper has no malevolence in it to any mortal. That devotion to his mistress kindles in his mind a general tenderness, which exerts itself towards every object as well as his fair one. When this passion is represented by writers, it is common with them to endeavour at certain quaintnesses and turns of imagination, which are apparently the work of a mind at ease; but the men of true taste can easily distinguish the exertion of a mind which overflows with tender sentiments, and the labour of one which is only describing distress. In performances of this kind, the most absurd of all things is to be witty; every sentiment must grow out of the occasion, and be suitable to the circumstances of the character. Where this rule is transgressed, the humble servant in all the fine things he says, is but showing his mistress how well he can dress, instead of saying how well he loves. Lace and drapery is as much a man, as wit and turn is passion.

'MR. SPECTATOR,—The following verses are a translation of a Lapland love-song, which I met with in Scheffer's history of that country.* I was agreeably surprised to find a spirit of tenderness and poetry in a region which I never suspected for delicacy. In hotter climates, though altogether uncivilized, I had not wondered if I had found some sweet wild notes among the natives, where they live in groves of oranges, and hear the melody of the birds about them. But a Lapland lyric, breathing sentiments of love and poetry, not unworthy old Greece or Rome; a regular ode from a climate pinched with frost, and cursed with darkness so great a part of the year; where it is amazing that the poor natives should get food, or be tempted to propagate their species—this, I confess, seemed a greater miracle to me than the famous stories of their drums, their winds, and enchantments.

'I am the bolder in commending this northern song, because I have faithfully kept to the sentiments, without adding or diminishing; and pretend to no greater praise from my translation, than they who smooth and clean the furs of that country which have suffered by carriage. The numbers in the original are as loose and unequal as those in which the British ladies sport their Pindarics; and perhaps the fairest of them might not think it a disagreeable present from a lover. But I have ventured to bind it in stricter measures, as being more proper for our tongue, though perhaps wilder graces may better suit the genius of the Laponian language.

'It will be necessary to imagine that the author of this song, not having the liberty of visiting his mistress at her father's house, was in hopes of spying her at a distance in her fields.

---

* Mr. Ambrose Phillips was the supposed author of this love-song.

'Thou rising sun, whose gladsome ray
Invites my fair to rural play,
Dispel the mist, and clear the skies,
And bring my Orra to my eyes.

Oh! were I sure my dear to view,
I'd climb that pine-tree's topmost bough,
Aloft in air that quiv'ring plays,
And round and round for ever gaze.

My Orra Moor, where art thou laid?
What wood conceals my sleeping maid?
Fast by the roots enrag'd I'd tear
The trees that hide my promis'd fair.

Oh! could I ride the clouds and skies,
Or on the raven's pinions rise!
Ye storks, ye swans, a moment stay,
And waft a lover on his way!

My bliss too long my bride denies,
Apace the wasting summer flies:
Nor yet the wintry blasts I fear,
Not storms, or night shall keep me here.

What may for strength with steel compare?
Oh! love has fetters stronger far!
By bolts of steel are limbs confin'd,
But cruel love enchains the mind.

No longer then perplex thy breast;
When thoughts torment, the first are best;
'Tis mad to go, 'tis death to stay;
Away to Orra! haste away!"

'April the 10th.

'Mr. Spectator,—I am one of those despicable creatures called a chambermaid, and have lived with a mistress for some time, whom I love as my life, which has made my duty and pleasure inseparable. My greatest delight has been in being employed about her person; and indeed she is very seldom out of humour for a woman of her quality. But here lies my complaint, sir. To bear with me is all the encouragement she is pleased to bestow upon me; for she gives her cast-off clothes from me to others; some she is pleased to bestow in the house to those that neither want nor wear them, and some to hangers-on, that frequent the house daily, who come dressed out in them. This, sir, is a very mortifying sight to me, who am a little necessitous for clothes, and love to appear what I am; and causes an uneasiness, so that I cannot serve with that cheerfulness as formerly; which my mistress takes notice of, and calls envy and ill-temper, at seeing others preferred before me. My mistress has a younger sister lives in the house with her, that is some thousands below her in estate, who is continually heaping her favours on her maid; so that she can appear every Sunday, for the first quarter, in a fresh suit of clothes of her mistress's giving, with all other things suitable. All this I see without envying, but not without wishing my mistress would a little consider what a discouragement it is to me to have my perquisites divided between fawners and jobbers, which others enjoy entire to themselves. I have spoken to my mistress, but to little purpose; I have desired to be discharged (for indeed I fret myself to nothing,) but that she answers with silence. I beg, sir, your direction what to do, for I am fully resolved to follow your counsel; who am your admirer and humble servant,

'CONSTANTIA COMB-BRUSH.

'I beg that you will put it in a better dress, and let it come abroad, that my mistress, who is an admirer of your specula tions, may see it.' T.

No. 367.] *Thursday, May* 1, 1712.

————Periturae parcite chartae.—*Juv.* Sat. i. 18

In mercy spare us when we do our best
To make as much waste paper as the rest.

I have often pleased myself with con sidering the two kinds of benefits which accrue to the public from these my speculations, and which, were I to speak after the manner of logicians, I would distinguish into the material and the formal. By the latter I understand those advantages which my readers receive, as their minds are either improved or delighted by these my daily labours; but having already several times descanted on my endeavours in this light, I shall at present wholly confine myself to the consideration of the former. By the word material, I mean those benefits which arise to the public from these my speculations, as they consume a considerable quantity of our paper-manufacture, employ our artisans in printing, and find business for great numbers of indigent persons.

Our paper-manufacture takes into it several mean materials which could be put to no other use, and affords work for several hands in the collection of them which are incapable of any other employment. Those poor retailers, whom we see so busy in every street, deliver in their respective gleanings to the merchant. The merchant carries them in loads to the paper-mill, where they pass through a fresh set of hands, and give life to another trade. Those who have mills on their estate, by this means considerably raise their rents, and the whole nation is in a great measure supplied with a manufacture for which formerly she was obliged to her neighbours.

The materials are no sooner wrought into paper, but they are distributed among the presses, when they again set innumerable artists at work, and furnish business to another mystery. From hence, accordingly as they are stained with news and politics, they fly through the town in Postmen, Post-boys, Daily Courants, Reviews, Medleys, and Examiners. Men, women, and children contend who shall be the first bearers of them, and get their daily sustenance by spreading them. In short, when I trace in my mind a bundle of rags to a quire of Spectators, I find so many hands em ployed in every step they take through their whole progress, that while I am writing a Spectator, I fancy myself providing bread for a multitude.

If I do not take care to obviate some of my witty readers, they will be apt to tell me, that my paper, after it is thus printed and published, is still beneficial to the public on several occasions. I must confess I have lighted my pipe with my own works for this twelvemonth past. My landlady often sends up her little daughter to desire some of my old Spectators, and has frequently told me, that the paper they are printed on is the best in the world to wrap spices in. They likewise made a good foundation for a mutton pie, as I have more than once experienced, and were very much sought for last Christmas by the whole neighbourhood.

It is pleasant enough to consider the changes that a linen fragment undergoes by passing through the several hands above mentioned. The finest pieces of Holland, when worn to tatters, assume a new whiteness more beautiful than the first, and often return in the shape of letters to their native country. A lady's shift may be metamorphosed into billets-doux, and come into her possession a second time. A beau may peruse his cravat after it is worn out, with greater pleasure and advantage than ever he did in a glass. In a word, a piece of cloth, after having officiated for some years as a towel or a napkin, may by this means be raised from a dunghill, and become the most valuable piece of furniture in a prince's cabinet.

The politest nations of Europe have endeavoured to vie with one another for the reputation of the finest printing. Absolute governments, as well as republics, have encouraged an art which seems to be the noblest and most beneficial that ever was invented among the sons of men. The present king of France, in his pursuits after glory, has particularly distinguished himself by the promoting of this useful art, insomuch that several books have been printed in the Louvre at his own expense, upon which he sets so great a value that he considers them as the noblest presents he can make to foreign princes and ambassadors. If we look into the commonwealths of Holland and Venice, we shall find that in this particular they have made themselves the envy of the greatest monarchies. Elzevir and Aldus are more frequently mentioned than any pensioner of the one or doge of the other.

The several presses which are now in England, and the great encouragement which has been given to learning for some years last past, has made our own nation as glorious upon this account as for its late triumphs and conquests. The new edition which is given us of Cæsar's Commentaries* has already been taken notice of in foreign gazettes, and is a work that does honour to the English press. It is no wonder that an edition should be very correct which has passed through the hands of one of the most accurate, learned, and judicious writers this age has produced. The beauty of the paper, of the character, and of the several cuts with which this noble work is illustrated, makes it the finest book that I have ever seen; and is a true instance of the English genius, which, though it does not come the first into any art, generally carries it to greater heights than any other country in the world. I am particularly glad that this author comes from a British printing-house in so great a magnificence, as he is the first who has given us any tolerable account of our country.

My illiterate readers, if any such there are, will be surprised to hear me talk of learning as the glory of a nation, and of printing as an art that gains a reputation to a people among whom it flourishes. When men's thoughts are taken up with avarice and ambition, they cannot look upon any thing as great or valuable which does not bring with it an extraordinary power or interest to the person who is concerned in it. But as I shall never sink this paper so far as to engage with Goths and Vandals, I shall only regard such kind of reasoners with that pity which is due to so deplorable a degree of stupidity and ignorance. L.

* A most magnificent edition of Cæsar's Commentaries published about this time, by Dr. Samuel Clarke.

No. 368.] *Friday, May 2, 1712.*

———————Nos decebat
Lugere ubi esset aliquis in lucem editus,
Humanæ vitæ varia reputantes mala:
At qui labores morte finisset graves,
Omnes amicos laude et lætitia exequi.
Eurip. apud *Tull.*

When first an infant draws the vital air,
Officious grief should welcome him to care:
But joy should life's concluding scene attend,
And mirth be kept to grace a dying friend.

As the Spectator is, in a kind, a paper of news from the natural world, as others are from the busy and politic part of mankind, I shall translate the following letter, written to an eminent French gentleman in this town from Paris, which gives us the exit of a heroine who is a pattern of patience and generosity.

'Paris, April 18, 1712.

'Sir,—It is so many years since you left your native country, that I am to tell you the characters of your nearest relations as much as if you were an utter stranger to them. The occasion of this is to give you an account of the death of Madam de Villacerfe, whose departure out of this life I know not whether a man of your philosophy will call unfortunate or not, since it was attended with some circumstances as much to be desired as to be lamented. She was her whole life happy in an uninterrupted health, and was always honoured for an evenness of temper and greatness of mind. On the 10th instant that lady was taken with an indisposition which confined her to her chamber, but was such as was too slight to make her take a sick bed, and yet too grievous to admit of any satisfaction in being out of it. It is notoriously known, that some years ago Monsieur Festeau, one of the most considerable surgeons in Paris, was desperately in love with this lady. Her quality placed her above any application to her on the account of his passion: but as a woman always has some regard to the person whom she believes to be her real admirer, she now took it into her head (upon advice of her physicians to lose some of her blood) to send for Monsieur Festeau on that occasion. I happened to be there at that time, and my near relation gave me the privilege to be present. As soon as her arm was stripped bare, and he began to press it, in order to raise the vein, his colour changed, and I observed him seized with a sudden tremor, which made me take the liberty to speak of it to my cousin with some apprehension. She smiled, and said, she knew M. Festeau had no inclination to do her injury. He seemed to recover himself, and, smiling also, proceeded in his work. Immediately after the operation, he cried out, that he was the most unfortunate of all men, for that he had opened an artery instead of a vein. It is as impossible to express the artist's distraction as the patient's composure. I will not dwell on little circumstances, but go on to inform you, that within three days' time it was thought necessary to take off her arm. She was so far from using Festeau as it would be natural for one of a lower spirit to treat him, that she would not let him be absent from any consultation about her present condition; and, after having been about a quarter of an hour alone, she bid the surgeons, of whom poor Festeau was one, go on in their work. I know not how to give you the terms of art, but there appeared such symptoms after the amputation of her arm, that it was visible she could not live four-and-twenty hours. Her behaviour was so magnanimous throughout the whole affair, that I was particularly curious in taking notice of what past as her fate approached nearer and nearer, and took notes of what she said to all about her, particularly word for word what she spoke to M. Festeau, which was as follows:

"Sir, you give me inexpressible sorrow for the anguish with which I see you overwhelmed. I am removed to all intents and purposes from the interests of human life, therefore I am to begin to think like one wholly unconcerned in it. I do not consider you as one by whose error I have lost my life; no, you are my benefactor, as you have hastened my entrance into a happy immortality. This is my sense of this accident: but the world in which you live may have thoughts of it to your disadvantage: I have therefore taken care to provide for you in my will, and have placed you above what you have to fear from their ill-nature."

'While this excellent woman spoke these words, Festeau looked as if he received a condemnation to die, instead of a pension for his life. Madame de Villacerfe lived till eight of the clock the next night; and though she must have laboured under the most exquisite torments, she possessed her mind with so wonderful a patience, that one may rather say she ceased to breathe, than she died at that hour. You, who had not the happiness to be personally known to this lady, have nothing but to rejoice in the honour you had of being related to so great merit; but we, who have lost her conversation, cannot so easily resign our own happiness by reflection upon hers. I am, sir, your affectionate kinsman, and most obedient humble servant,

'PAUL REGNAUD.'

There hardly can be a greater instance of a heroic mind than the unprejudiced manner in which this lady weighed this misfortune. The regard of life could not make her overlook the contrition of the unhappy man, whose more than ordinary concern for her was all his guilt. It would certainly be of singular use to human society to have an exact account of this lady's ordinary conduct, which was crowned by so uncommon magnanimity. Such greatness was not to be acquired in the last article; nor is it to be doubted but it was a constant practice of all that is praiseworthy, which made her capable of beholding death, not as the dissolution, but consummation of her life.

T.

No. 369.] *Saturday, May* 3, 1712.

Segnius irritant animos demissa per aures,
Quam quæ sunt oculis subjecta fidelibus.——

Hor. Ars Poet. v. 180

What we hear moves less than what we see.

Roscommon.

MILTON, after having represented in vision the history of mankind to the first great period of nature, despatches the remaining part of it in narration. He has devised a very handsome reason for the angel's proceeding with Adam after this manner; though doubtless the true reason was the difficulty which the poet would have found to have shadowed out so mixed and complicated a story in visible objects. I could wish, however, that the author had done it, whatever pains it might have cost him. To give my opinion freely, I think that the exhibiting part of the history of mankind in vision, and part in narrative, is as if a history-painter should put in colours one half of his subject, and write down the remaining part of it. If Milton's poem flags any where, it is in this narration, where in some places the author has been so attentive to his divinity that he has neglected his poetry. The narration, however, rises very happily on several occa sions, where the subject is capable of poetical ornaments, as particularly in the confusion which he describes among the builders of Babel, and in his short sketch of the plagues of Egypt. The storm of hail and fire, with the darkness that overspread the land for three days, are described with great strength. The beautiful passage which follows is raised upon noble hints in Scripture:

'——————Thus with ten wounds
The river dragon tam'd, at length submits
To let his sojourners depart; and oft
Humbles his stubborn heart; but still, as ice,
More harden'd after thaw: till in his rage
Pursuing whom he late dismiss'd, the sea
Swallows him with his host; but then lets man
As on dry land between two crystal walls,
Aw'd by the rod of Moses so to stand
Divided————'

The river dragon is an allusion to the crocodile, which inhabits the Nile, from whence Egypt derives her plenty. This allusion is taken from that sublime passage in Ezekiel: 'Thus saith the Lord God, Behold I am against thee, Pharaoh, king of Egypt, the great dragon that lieth in the midst of his rivers, which hath said, My river is mine own, and I have made it for myself.' Milton has given us another very noble and poetical image in the same description, which is copied almost word for word out of the history of Moses!

'All night he will pursue, but his approach
Darkness defends between till morning watch
Then through the fiery pillar and the cloud
God looking forth will trouble all his host,
And craze their chariot wheels: when by command
Moses once more his potent rod extends
Over the sea: the sea his rod obeys:
On their embattled ranks the waves return
And overwhelm their war————'

As the principal design of this episode was to give Adam an idea of the holy person who was to reinstate human nature in that happiness and perfection from which it had fallen, the poet confines himself to the line of Abraham, from whence the Messiah was to descend. The angel is described as seeing the patriarch actually travelling towards the land of promise, which gives a particular liveliness to this part of the narration:

'I see him, but thou canst not, with what faith
He leaves his gods, his friends, his native soil,
Ur of Chaldea, passing now the ford
To Haran; after him a cumbrous train
Of herds, and flocks, and num'rous servitude;
Not wand'ring poor, but trusting all his wealth
With God, who call'd him in a land unknown.
Canaan he now attains: I see his tents
Pitch'd about Sechem, and the neighbouring plain
Of Moreh; there by promise he receives
Gift to his progeny of all that land;
From Hamath northward to the desert south:
(Things by their names I call, though yet unnam'd.)'

As Virgil's vision in the sixth Æneid probably gave Milton the hint of this whole episode, the last line is a translation of that verse where Anchises mentions the names of places, which they were to bear hereafter:

Hæc tum nomina erunt, nunc sunt sine nomine terræ.

The poet has very finely represented the joy and gladness of heart which arises in Adam upon his discovery of the Messiah. As he sees his day at a distance through types and shadows, he rejoices in it; but when he finds the redemption of man completed, and Paradise again renewed, he breaks forth in rapture and transport:

'O goodness infinite! goodness immense!
That all this good of evil shall produce,' &c.

I have hinted in my sixth paper on Milton, that a heroic poem, according to the opinion of the best critics, ought to end happily, and leave the mind of the reader, after having conducted it through many doubts and fears, sorrows and disquietudes, in a state of tranquillity and satisfaction. Milton's fable, which had so many other qualifications to recommend it, was deficient in this particular. It is here therefore that the poet has shown a most exquisite judgment, as well as the finest invention, by finding out a method to supply this natural defect in his subject. Accordingly he leaves the adversary of mankind, in the last view which he gives of him, under the lowest state of mortification and disappointment. We see him chewing ashes, grovelling in the dust, and loaden with supernumerary pains and torments. On the contrary, our two first parents are comforted by dreams and visions, cheered with promises of salvation, and in a manner raised to a greater happiness than that which they had forfeited. In short, Satan is represented miserable in the height of his triumphs, and Adam triumphant in the height of misery.

Milton's poem ends very nobly. The last speeches of Adam and the archangel are full of moral and instructive sentiments. The sleep that fell upon Eve, and the effects it had in quieting the disorders of her mind, produces the same kind of consolation in the reader, who cannot peruse the last beautiful speech, which is ascribed to the mother of mankind, without a secret pleasure and satisfaction:

'Whence thou return'st, and whither went'st, I know:
For God is also in sleep, and dreams advise,
Which he hath sent propitious, some great good
Presaging, since with sorrow and heart's distress
Wearied I fell asleep: but now lead on;
In me is no delay: with thee to go,
Is to stay here, without thee here to stay,
Is to go hence unwilling: thou to me
Art all things under heav'n, all places thou,
Who for my wilful crime art banish'd hence
This farther consolation yet secure
I carry hence; though all by me is lost,
Such favour I unworthy am vouchsaf'd,
By me the promis'd seed shall all restore.'

The following lines, which conclude the poem, rise in a most glorious blaze of poetical images and expressions.

Heliodorus in the Æthiopics acquaints us, that the motion of the gods differs from that of mortals, as the former do not stir their feet, nor proceed step by step, but slide over the surface of the earth by an uniform swimming of the whole body. The reader may observe with how poetical a description Milton has attributed the same kind of motion to the angels who were to take possession of Paradise:

So spake our mother Eve; and Adam heard
Well pleas'd, but answer'd not; for now too nigh
Th' archangel stood; and from the other hill
To their fix'd station, all in bright array
The cherubim descended; on the ground
Gliding meteorous, as evening mist
Ris'n from a river, o'er the marish glides,
And gathers ground fast at the lab'rer's heel
Homeward returning. High in front advanc'd
The brandish'd sword of God before them blaz'd
Fierce as a comet——————

The author helped his invention in the following passage, by reflecting on the behaviour of the angel, who in holy writ has the conduct of Lot and his family. The circumstances drawn from that relation are very gracefully made use of on this occasion:

In either hand the hast'ning angel caught
Our ling'ring parents, and to th' eastern gate
Led them direct; and down the cliff as fast
To the subjected plain; then disappear'd,
They looking back, &c.

The scene which our first parents are surprised with, upon their looking back on Paradise, wonderfully strikes the reader's imagination, as nothing can be more natural than the tears they shed on that occasion:

They looking back, all th' eastern side beheld
Of Paradise, so late their happy seat,
Wav'd over by that flaming brand, the gate
With dreadful faces throng'd and fiery arms:
Some natural tears they dropp'd but wip'd them soon;
The world was all before them, where to choose
Their place of rest, and Providence their guide.

If I might presume to offer at the smallest alteration in this divine work, I should think the poem would end better with the passage here quoted, than with the two verses which follow:

They hand in hand, with wand'ring steps and slow
Through Eden took their solitary way.

These two verses, though they have their beauty, fall very much below the foregoing passage, and renew in the mind of the reader that anguish which was pretty well laid by that consideration:

The world was all before them, where to choose
Their place of rest, and Providence their guide.

The number of books in Paradise Lost is equal to those of the Æneid. Our author, in his first edition, had divided his poem into ten books, but afterwards broke the seventh and the eleventh each of them into two different books, by the help of some small additions. This second division was made with great judgment, as any one may see who will be at the pains of examining it. It was not done for the sake of such a chimerical beauty as that of resembling Virgil in this particular, but for the more just and regular disposition of this great work.

Those who have read Bossu, and many of the critics who have written since his time, will not pardon me if I do not find out the particular moral which is inculcated in Paradise Lost. Though I can by no means think, with the last-mentioned French author, that an epic writer first of all pitches upon a certain moral, as the ground-work and foundation of his poem, and afterwards finds out a story to it; I am however of opinion, that no just heroic poem ever was or can be made, from whence one great moral may not be deduced. That which reigns in Milton is the most universal and most useful that can be imagined. It is, in short, this, that obedience to the will of God makes men happy and that disobedience makes them miserable. This is visibly the moral of the principal fable, which turns upon Adam and Eve, who continued in Paradise while they kept the command that was given them, and were driven out of it as soon as they had transgressed. This is likewise the moral of the principal episode, which shows us how an innumerable multitude of angels fell from their disobedience. Besides this great moral, which may be looked upon as the soul of the fable, there are an infinity of under-morals which are to be drawn from the several parts of the poem, and which make this work more useful and instructive than any other poem in any language.

Those who have criticised on the Odyssey, the Iliad, and Æneid, have taken a great deal of pains to fix the number of months and days contained in the action of each of these poems. If any one thinks it worth his while to examine this particular in Milton, he will find, that from Adam's first appearance in the fourth book, to his expulsion from Paradise in the twelfth, the author reckons ten days. As for that part of the action which is described in the three first books, as it does not pass within the regions of nature, I have before observed that it is not subject to any calculations of time.

I have now finished my observations on a work which does an honour to the English nation. I have taken a general view of it under these four heads—the fable, the characters, the sentiments, and the language, and made each of them the subject of a particular paper. I have in the next place spoke of the censures which our author may incur under each of these heads, which I have confined to two papers, though I might have enlarged the number if I had been disposed to dwell on so ungrateful a subject. I believe, however, that the severest reader will not find any little fault in heroic poetry, which this author has fallen into, that does not come under one of those heads among which I have distributed his several blemishes. After having thus treated at large of Paradise Lost, I could not think it sufficient to have celebrated this poem in the whole without descending to particulars. I have therefore bestowed a paper upon each book, and endeavoured not only to prove that the poem is beautiful in general, but to point out its particular beauties; and to deter mine wherein they consist, I have endeavoured to show how some passages are beautiful by being sublime, others by being soft, others by being natural; which of them are recommended by the passion, which by the moral, which by the sentiment, and which by the expression. I have likewise endeavoured to show how the genius of the poet shines by a happy invention, a distant allusion, or a judicious imitation; how he has copied or improved Homer or Virgil, and raises his own imaginations by the use which he has made of several poetical passages in Scripture. I might have inserted also several passages in Tasso, which our author has imitated: but, as I do not look upon Tasso to be a sufficient voucher, I would not perplex my reader with such quotations as might do more honour to the Italian than to the English poet. In short, I have endeavoured to particularize those innumerable kinds of beauty which it would be tedious to recapitulate, but which are essential to poetry, and which may be met with in the works of this great author. Had I thought, at my first engaging in this design, that it would have led me to so great a length, I believe I should never have entered upon it; but the kind reception which it has met with among those whose judgment I have a value for, as well as the uncommon demands which my bookseller tells me have been made for these particular discourses, give me no reason to repent of the pains I have been at in composing them. L.

No. 370.] *Monday, May 5, 1712.*

Totus mundus agit histrionem.

————All the world's a stage,
And all the men and women merely players.
Shakspeare.

Many of my fair readers, as well as very gay and well-received persons of the other sex, are extremely perplexed at the Latin sentences at the head of my speculations. I do not know whether I ought not to indulge them with translations of each of them: however, I have to-day taken down from the top of the stage in Drury-lane, a bit of Latin, which often stands in their view, and signifies, that 'The whole world acts the player.' It is certain that if we look all around us, and behold the different employments of mankind, you hardly see one who is not, as the player is, in an assumed character. The lawyer, who is vehement and loud in a cause wherein he knows he has not the truth of the question on his side, is a player as to the personated part, but incomparably meaner than he as to the prostitution of himself for hire; because the pleader's falsehood introduces injustice: the player feigns for no other end but to divert or instruct you. The divine, whose passions transport him to say any thing with any view but promoting the interests of true piety and religion, is a player with a still greater imputation of guilt, in proportion to his depreciating a character more sacred. Consider all the different pursuits and employments of men, and you will find half their actions tend to nothing else but disguise and imposture; and all that is done which proceeds not from a man's very self, is the action of a player. For this reason it is that I make so frequent mention of the stage. It is with me a matter of the highest consideration, what parts are well or ill performed, what passions or sentiments are indulged or cultivated, and consequently what manners and customs are transfused from the stage to the world, which reciprocally imitate each other. As the writers of epic poems introduce shadowy persons, and represent vices and virtues under the character of men and women; so I, who am a Spectator in the world, may perhaps sometimes make use of the names of the actors of the stage, to represent or admonish those who transact affairs in the world. When I am commending Wilks for representing the tenderness of a husband and a father in Macbeth, the contrition of a reformed prodigal in Harry the Fourth, the winning emptiness of a young man of good-nature and wealth in The Trip to the Jubilee, the officiousness of an artful servant in the Fox; when thus I celebrate Wilks, I talk to all the world who are engaged in any of those circumstances. If I were to speak of merit neglected, misapplied, or misunderstood, might I not say Estcourt has a great capacity? But it is not the interest of others who bear a figure on the stage, that his talents were understood; it is their business to impose upon him what cannot become him, or keep out of his hands any thing in which he would shine. Were one to raise a suspicion of himself in a man who passes upon the world for a fine thing, in order to alarm him, one might say, If Lord Foppington was not on the stage (Cibber acts the false pretensions to a genteel behaviour so very justly,) he would have in the generality of mankind more that would admire than deride him. When we come to characters directly comical, it is not to be imagined what effect a well-regulated stage would have upon men's manners. The craft of an usurer, the absurdity of a rich fool, the awkward roughness of a fellow of half courage, the ungraceful mirth of a creature of half wit, might for ever be put out of countenance by proper parts for Dogget. Johnson, by acting Corbacchio the other night, must have given all who saw him a thorough detestation of aged avarice. The petulancy of a peevish old fellow, who loves and hates he knows not why, is very excellently performed by the ingenious Mr. William Penkethman, in the Fop's Fortune; where, in the character of Don Choleric Snap Shorto de Testy, he answers no questions but to those whom he likes, and wants no account of any thing from those he approves. Mr. Penkethman is also master of as many faces in the dumb scene as can be expected from a man in the circumstances of being ready to perish out of fear and hunger. He wanders through the whole scene very masterly, without neglecting his victuals. If it be, as I have heard it sometimes mentioned, a great qualification of the world to follow business and pleasure too, what is it in the ingenious Mr. Penkethman to represent a sense of pleasure and pain at the same time, as you may see him do this evening?

As it is certain that a stage ought to be wholly suppressed or judiciously encouraged, while there is one in the nation, men turned for regular pleasure cannot employ their thoughts more usefully, for the diversion of mankind, than by convincing them that it is in themselves to raise this entertainment to the greatest height. It would be a great improvement, as well as embellishment to the theatre, if dancing were more regarded, and taught to all the actors. One who has the advantage of such an agreeable girlish person as Mrs. Bicknell, joined with her capacity of imitation, could in proper gesture and motion represent all the decent characters of female life. An amiable modesty in one aspect of a dancer, and assumed confidence in another, a sudden joy in another, a falling off with an impatience of being beheld, a return towards the audience with an unsteady resolution to approach them, and well-acted solicitude to please, would revive in the company all the fine touches of mind raised in observing all the objects of affection and passion they had before beheld. Such elegant entertainments as these would polish the town into judgment in their gratifications; and delicacy in pleasure is the first step people of condition take in reformation from vice. Mrs. Bicknell has the only capacity for this sort of dancing of any on the stage; and I dare say all who see her performance to-morrow night, when sure the romp will do her best for her own benefit, will be of my mind. T.

No. 371.] *Tuesday, May* 6, 1712.

Jamne igitur laudas quod de sapientibus unus
Ridebat?——— *Juv.* Sat. x. 28.

And shall the sage your approbation win,
Whose laughing features wore a constant grin?

I SHALL communicate to my readers the following letter for the entertainment of this day.

'SIR,—You know very well that our nation is more famous for that sort of men who are called "whims" and "humourists," than any other country in the world; for which reason it is observed, that our English comedy excels that of all other nations in the novelty and variety of its characters.

'Among those innumerable sets of whims which our country produces, there are none whom I have regarded with more curiosity than those who have invented any particular kind of diversion for the entertainment of themselves and their friends. My letter shall single out those who take delight in sorting a company that has something of burlesque and ridicule in its appearance. I shall make myself understood by the following example: One of the wits of the last age, who was a man of a good estate,* thought he never laid out his money better than in a jest. As he was one year at the Bath, observing that, in the great confluence of fine people, there were several among them with long chins, a part of the visage by which he himself was very much distinguished, he invited to dinner half a score of these remarkable persons who had their mouths in the middle of their faces. They had no sooner placed themselves about the table but they began to stare upon one another, not being able to imagine what had brought them together. Our English proverb says,

'’Tis merry in the hall,
When beards wag all.'

It proved so in the assembly I am now speaking of, who seeing so many peaks of faces agitated with eating, drinking, and discourse, and observing all the chins that were present meeting together very often over the centre of the table, every one grew sensible of the jest, and gave into it with so much good humour, that they lived in strict friendship and alliance from that day forward.

'The same gentleman some time after packed together a set of oglers, as he called them, consisting of such as had an unlucky cast in their eyes. His diversion on this occasion was to see the cross bows, mistaken signs, and wrong connivances, that passed amidst so many broken and refracted rays of sight.

'The third feast which this merry gentleman exhibited was to the stammerers, whom he got together in a sufficient body to fill his table. He had ordered one of his servants, who was placed behind a screen, to write down their table-talk, which was very easy to be done without the help of short-hand. It appears by the notes which were taken, that though their conversation never fell, there were not above twenty words spoken during the first course; that upon serving up the second, one of the company was a quarter of an hour in telling them that the ducklings and asparagus were very good; and that another took up the same time in declaring himself of the same opinion. This jest did not, however, go off so well as the former; for one of the guests being a brave man, and fuller of resentment than he knew how to express, went out of the room, and sent the facetious

* Villars, Duke of Buckingham.

inviter a challenge in writing, which, though it was afterwards dropped by the interposition of friends, put a stop to these ludicrous entertainments.

'Now, sir, I dare say you will agree with me, that as there is no moral in these jests, they ought to be discouraged, and looked upon rather as pieces of unluckiness than wit. However, as it is natural for one man to refine upon the thought of another; and impossible for any single person, how great soever his parts may be, to invent an art, and bring it to its utmost perfection; I shall here give you an account of an honest gentleman of my acquaintance, who upon hearing the character of the wit above-mentioned, has himself assumed it, and endeavoured to convert it to the benefit of mankind. He invited half a dozen of his friends one day to dinner, who were each of them famous for inserting several redundant phrases in their discourse, as "D'ye hear me?—D'ye see?—That is,—And so, sir." Each of his guests making use of his particular elegance, appeared so ridiculous to his neighbour, that he could not but reflect upon himself as appearing equally ridiculous to the rest of the company. By this means, before they had sat long together, every one, talking with the greatest circumspection, and carefully avoiding his favourite expletive, the conversation was cleared of its redundancies, and had a greater quantity of sense, though less of sound in it.

'The same well-meaning gentleman took occasion, at another time, to bring together such of his friends as were addicted to a foolish habitual custom of swearing. In order to show them the absurdity of the practice, he had recourse to the invention above-mentioned, having placed an amanuensis in a private part of the room. After the second bottle, when men open their minds without reserve, my honest friend began to take notice of the many sonorous but unnecessary words that had passed in his house since their sitting down at table, and how much good conversation they had lost by giving way to such superfluous phrases. "What a tax," says he, "would they have raised for the poor, had we put the laws in execution upon one another!" Every one of them took this gentle reproof in good part; upon which he told them, that, knowing their conversation would have no secrets in it, he ordered it to be taken down in writing, and, for the humour-sake, would read it to them, if they pleased. There were ten sheets of it, which might have been reduced to two, had there not been those abominable interpolations I have before mentioned. Upon the reading of it in cold blood, it looked rather like a conference of fiends than of men. In short, every one trembled at himself upon hearing calmly what he had pronounced amidst the heat and inadvertency of discourse.

'I shall only mention another occasion wherein he made use of the same invention to cure a different kind of men, who are the pests of all polite conversation, and murder time as much as either of the two former, though they do it more innocently—I mean, that dull generation of story-tellers. My friend got together about half a dozen of his acquaintance, who were infected with this strange malady. The first day one of them sitting down, entered upon the siege of Namur, which lasted till four o'clock, their time of parting. The second day a North Briton took possession of the discourse, which it was impossible to get out of his hands so long as the company stayed together. The third day was engrossed after the same manner by a story of the same length. They at last began to reflect upon this barbarous way of treating one another, and by this means awakened out of that lethargy with which each of them had been seized for several years.

'As you have somewhere declared, that extraordinary and uncommon characters of mankind are the game which you delight in, and as I look upon you to be the greatest sportsman, or, if you please, the Nimrod among this species of writers, I thought this discovery would not be unacceptable to you. I am, sir, &c.' I.

No. 372.] *Wednesday, May 7, 1712.*

> ———Pudet hæc opprobria nobis
> Et dici potuisse, et non potuisse refelli.
> *Ovid. Met.* i. 759.

> To hear an open slander, is a curse;
> But not to find an answer is a worse *Dryden.*

'May 6, 1712.

'MR. SPECTATOR,—I am sexton of the parish of Covent-garden, and complained to you some time ago, that as I was tolling in to prayers at eleven in the morning, crowds of people of quality hastened to assemble at a puppet-show on the other side of the garden. I had at the same time a very great disesteem for Mr. Powell and his little thoughtless commonwealth, as if they had enticed the gentry into those wanderings: but let that be as it will, I am convinced of the honest intentions of the said Mr. Powell and company, and send this to acquaint you, that he has given all the profits which shall arise to-morrow night by his play to the use of the poor charity-children of this parish. I have been informed, sir, that in Holland all persons who set up any show, or act any stage-play, be the actors either of wood and wire, or flesh and blood, are obliged to pay out of their gains such a proportion to the honest and industrious poor in the neighbourhood: by this means they make diversion and pleasure pay a tax to labour and industry. I have been told also, that all the time of Lent, in Roman-Catholic countries, the persons of condition administer to the necessities of the poor, and attend the beds of lazars and diseased persons. Our Protestant

. adies and gentlemen are so much to seek for proper ways of passing time, that they are obliged to punchinello for knowing what to do with themselves. Since the case is so, I desire only you would entreat our people of quality, who are not to be interrupted in their pleasure, to think of the practice of any moral duty, that they would at least fine for their sins, and give something to these poor children: a little out of their luxury and superfluity would atone, in some measure, for the wanton use of the rest of their fortunes. It would not, methinks, be amiss, if the ladies who haunt the cloisters and passages of the play-house were upon every offence obliged to pay to this excellent institution of schools of charity. This method would make offenders themselves do service to the public. But in the mean time I desire you would publish this voluntary reparation which Mr. Powell does our parish, for the noise he has made in it by the constant rattling of coaches, drums, trumpets, triumphs, and battles. The destruction of Troy, adorned with Highland dances, are to make up the entertainment of all who are so well disposed as not to forbear a light entertainment, for no other reason but that it is to do a good action. I am, sir, your most humble servant, RALPH BELFRY.

'I am credibly informed, that all the insinuations which a certain writer made against Mr. Powell at the Bath, are false and groundless.'

'Mr. Spectator,—My employment, which is that of a broker, leading me often into taverns about the Exchange, has given me occasion to observe a certain enormity, which I shall here submit to your animadversion. In three or four of these taverns, I have at different times, taken notice of a precise set of people, with grave countenances, short wigs, black clothes, or dark camlet trimmed with black, and mourning gloves and hat-bands, who meet on certain days at each tavern successively, and keep a sort of moving club. Having often met with their faces, and observed a certain slinking way in their dropping in one after another, I had the curiosity to inquire into their characters, being the rather moved to it by their agreeing in the singularity of their dress; and I find, upon due examination, they are a knot of parish clerks, who have taken a fancy to one another, and perhaps settle the bills of mortality over their half-pints. I have so great a value and veneration for any who have but even an assenting Amen in the service of religion, that I am afraid lest these persons should incur some scandal by this practice; and would therefore have them, without raillery, advised to send the Florence and pullets home to their own houses, and not pretend to live as well as the overseers of the poor. I am, sir, your most humble servant, HUMPHRY TRANSFER.'

'May 6.

'Mr. Spectator,—I was last Wednesday night at a tavern in the city, among a set of men who call themselves "the lawyers' club." You must know, sir, this club consists only of attorneys; and at this meeting every one proposes the cause he has then in hand to the board, upon which each member gives his judgment according to the experience he has met with. If it happens that any one puts a case of which they have had no precedent, it is noted down by their clerk, Will Goosequill (who registers all their proceedings,) that one of them may go the next day with it to a counsel. This indeed is commendable, and ought to be the principal end of their meeting; but had you been there to have heard them relate their methods of managing a cause, their manner of drawing out their bills, and, in short, their arguments upon the several ways of abusing their clients, with the applause that is given to him who has done it most artfully, you would before now have given your remarks on them. They are so conscious that their discourses ought to be kept a secret, that they are very cautious of admitting any person who is not of their profession. When any who are not of the law are let in, the person who introduces him says he is a very honest gentleman, and he is taken in, as their cant is, to pay costs. I am admitted upon the recommendation of one of their principals, as a very honest good-natured fellow, that will never be in a plot, and only desires to drink his bottle and smoke his pipe. You have formerly remarked upon several sorts of clubs; and as the tendency of this is only to increase fraud and deceit, I hope you will please to take notice of it. I am, with respect, your humble servant, H. R.'

T.

No. 373.] *Thursday, May* 8, 1712.

Fallit enim vitium specie virtutis et umbra.
Juv. Sat. xiv. 109

Vice oft is hid in Virtue's fair disguise,
And in her borrow'd form escapes inquiring eyes

Mr. Locke, in his treatise of Human Understanding, has spent two chapters upon the abuse of words. The first and most palpable abuse of words, he says, is when they are used without clear and distinct ideas; the second, when we are so unconstant and unsteady in the application of them, that we sometimes use them to signify one idea, sometimes another. He adds, that the result of our contemplations and reasonings, while we have no precise ideas fixed to our words, must needs be very confused and absurd. To avoid this inconvenience, more especially in moral discourses, where the same word should be constantly used in the same sense, he earnestly recommends the use of definitions. 'A definition,' says he, 'is the only way whereby the precise meaning of moral words can be known.' He therefore accuses those of great negligence who discourse of moral things with the least obscurity in the terms they make use of; since, upon the 'forementioned ground, he does not scruple to say that he thinks 'morality is capable of demonstration as well as the mathematics.'

I know no two words that have been more abused by the different and wrong interpretations which are put upon them, than those two, modesty and assurance. To say such a one is a modest man, sometimes indeed passes for a good character; but at present is very often used to signify a sheepish, awkward fellow, who has neither good breeding, politeness, nor any knowledge of the world.

Again, a man of assurance, though at first it only denoted a person of a free and open carriage, is now very usually applied to a profligate wretch, who can break through all the rules of decency and morality without a blush.

I shall endeavour therefore in this essay to restore these words to their true meaning, to prevent the idea of modesty from being confounded with that of sheepishness, and to hinder impudence from passing for assurance.

If I was put to define modesty, I would call it 'the reflection of an ingenious mind, either when a man has committed an action for which he censures himself, or fancies that he is exposed to the censure of others.'

For this reason a man truly modest is as much so when he is alone as in company, and as subject to a blush in his closet as when the eyes of multitudes are upon him. I do not remember to have met with any instance of modesty with which I am so well pleased as that celebrated one of the young prince, whose father being a tributary king to the Romans, had several complaints laid against him before the senate, as a tyrant and oppressor of his subjects. The prince went to Rome to defend his father; but coming into the senate, and hearing a multitude of crimes proved upon him, was so oppressed when it came to his turn to speak, that he was unable to utter a word. The story tells us, that the fathers were more moved at this instance of modesty and ingenuity than they could have been by the most pathetic oration, and, in short, pardoned the guilty father, for this early promise of virtue in the son.

I take 'assurance to be the faculty of possessing a man's self, or of saying and doing indifferent things without any uneasiness or emotion in the mind.' That which generally gives a man assurance is a moderate knowledge of the world, but above all, a mind fixed and determined in itself to do nothing against the rules of honour and decency. An open and assured behaviour is the natural consequence of such a resolution. A man thus armed, if his words or actions are at any time misrepresented, retires within himself, and from a consciousness of his own integrity, assumes force enough to despise the little censures of ignorance and malice.

Every one ought to cherish and encourage in himself the modesty and assurance I have here mentioned.

A man without assurance is liable to be made uneasy by the folly or ill-nature of every one he converses with. A man without modesty is lost to all sense of honour and virtue.

It is more than probable that the prince above-mentioned possessed both these qualifications in a very eminent degree. Without assurance he would never have undertaken to speak before the most august assembly in the world: without modesty he would have pleaded the cause he had taken upon him, though it had appeared ever so scandalous.

From what has been said, it is plain that modesty and assurance are both amiable, and may very well meet in the same person. When they are thus mixed and blended together, they compose what we endeavour to express when we say 'a modest assurance;' by which we understand the just mean between bashfulness and impudence.

I shall conclude with observing, that as the same man may be both modest and assured, so it is also possible for the same to be both impudent and bashful.

We have frequent instances of this odd kind of mixture in people of depraved minds, and mean education, who, though they are not able to meet a man's eyes, or pronounce a sentence without confusion, can voluntarily commit the greatest villanies or most indecent actions.

Such a person seems to have made a resolution to do ill even in spite of himself, and in defiance of all those checks and restraints his temper and complexion seem to have laid in his way.

Upon the whole I would endeavour to establish this maxim, that the practice of virtue is the most proper method to give a man a becoming assurance in his words and actions. Guilt always seeks to shelter itself in one of the extremes, and is sometimes attended with both. X.

No. 374.] *Friday, May* 9, 1712.

Nil actum reputans si quid superesset agendum.
Lucan, Lib. ii. 57

He reckon'd not the past, while aught remain'd
Great to be done, or mighty to be gain'd. *Rowe*

There is a fault, which, though common, wants a name. It is the very contrary to procrastination. As we lose the present hour by delaying from day to day to execute what we ought to do immediately, so most of us take occasion to sit still and throw away the time in our possession, by retrospect on what is passed, imagining we have already acquitted ourselves, and established our characters in the sight of mankind. But when we thus put a value upon ourselves for what we have already done, any farther than to explain ourselves in order to assist our future conduct, that will give us an over-weening opinion of our merit, to the prejudice of our present industry. The great rule, methinks, should be, to manage the instant in which we stand, with fortitude, equanimity and moderation, according to men's respective circumstances. If our past actions reproach us, they cannot be atoned for by our own severe reflections so effectually as by a contrary behaviour. If they are praise-worthy, the memory of them is of no use but to act suitably to them. Thus a good present behaviour is an implicit repentance for any miscarriage in what is past; but present slackness will not make up for past activity. Time has swallowed up all that we contemporaries did yesterday, as irrevocably as it has the actions of the antediluvians. But we are again awake, and what shall we do to-day—to-day, which passes while we are yet speaking? Shall we remember the folly of last night, or resolve upon the exercise of virtue to-morrow? Last night is certainly gone, and to-morrow may never arrive. This instant make use of. Can you oblige any man of honour and virtue? Do it immediately. Can you visit a sick friend? Will it revive him to see you enter, and suspend your own ease and pleasure to comfort his weakness, and hear the impertinences of a wretch in pain? Do not stay to take coach, but be gone; your mistress will bring sorrow, and your bottle madness. Go to neither. Such virtues and diversions as these are mentioned because they occur to all men. But every man is sufficiently convinced that to suspend the use of the present moment, and resolve better for the future only, is an unpardonable folly. What I attempted to consider, was the mischief of setting such a value upon what is past, as to think we have done enough. Let a man have filled all the offices of life with the highest dignity till yesterday, and begin to live only to himself to-day, he must expect he will, in the effects upon his reputation, be considered as the man who died yesterday. The man who distinguishes himself from the rest, stands in a press of people: those before him intercept his progress; and those behind him, if he does not urge on, will tread him down. Cæsar, of whom it was said that he thought nothing done while there was left any thing for him to do, went on in performing the greatest exploits, without assuming to himself a privilege of taking rest upon the foundation of the merit of his former actions. It was the manner of that glorious captain to write down what scenes he had passed through, but it was rather to keep his affairs in method, and capable of a clear review, in case they should be examined by others, than that he built a renown upon any thing that was past. I shall produce two fragments of his, to demonstrate that it was his rule of life to support himself rather by what he should perform, than what he had done already. In the tablet which he wore about him, the same year in which he obtained the battle of Pharsalia, there were found these loose notes of his own conduct. It is supposed by the circumstances they alluded to, that they might be set down the evening of the same night.

'My part is now but begun, and my glory must be sustained by the use I make of this victory; otherwise my loss will be greater than that of Pompey. Our personal reputation will rise or fall as we bear our respective fortunes. All my private enemies among the prisoners shall be spared. I will forget this, in order to obtain such another day. Trebutius is ashamed to see me: I will go to his tent, and be reconciled in private. Give all the men of honour, who take part with me, the terms I offered before the battle. Let them owe this to their friends who have been long in my interests. Power is weakened by the full use of it, but extended by moderation. Galbinius is proud, and will be servile in his present fortune: let him wait. Send for Stertinius: he is modest, and his virtue is worth gaining. I have cooled my heart with reflection, and am fit to rejoice with the army to-morrow. He is a popular general, who can expose himself like a private man during a battle; but he is more popular who can rejoice but like a private man after a victory.'

What is particularly proper for the example of all who pretend to industry in the pursuit of honour and virtue, is, that this hero was more than ordinarily solicitous about his reputation, when a common mind would have thought itself in security, and given itself a loose to joy and triumph. But though this is a very great instance of his temper, I must confess I am more taken with his reflections when he retired to his closet in some disturbance upon the repeated ill omens of Calphurnia's dream, the night before his death. The literal translation of that fragment shall conclude this paper.

'Be it so, then. If I am to die to-morrow, that is what I am to do to-morrow. It will not be then, because I am willing it should be then; nor shall I escape it because I am unwilling. It is in the gods when, but in myself how, I shall die. If Calphurnia's dreams are fumes of indigestion, how shall I behold the day after to-morrow? If they are from the gods, their admonition is not to prepare me to escape from their decree, but to meet it. I have lived to a fulness of days and of glory: what is there that Cæsar has not done with as much honour as ancient heroes? Cæsar has not yet died! Cæsar is prepared to die.'

T

No. 375.] *Saturday, May* 10, 1712.

Non possidentem multa vocaveris
Recte beatum: rectius occupat
Nomen beati, qui deorum
Muneribus sapienter uti,
Duramque callet pauperiem pati,
Pejusque letho flagitium timet.
Hor. Od. ix. Lib. 4. 45.

We barbarously call them blest,
Who are of largest tenements possest,
While swelling coffers break their owner's rest.
More truly happy those who can
Govern that little empire man;
Who spend their treasure freely, as 'twas giv'n
By the large bounty of indulgent heav'n;
Who in a fix'd unalterable state,
Smile at the doubtful tide of Fate,
And scorn alike her friendship and her hate;
Who poison less than falsehood fear,
Loth to purchase life so dear. *Stepney.*

I HAVE more than once had occasion to mention a noble saying of Seneca the philosopher, that a virtuous person struggling with misfortunes, and rising above them, is an object on which the gods themselves may look down with delight. I shall therefore set before my reader a scene of this kind of distress in private life, for the speculation of this day.

An eminent citizen, who had lived in good fashion and credit, was, by a train of accidents, and by an unavoidable perplexity in his affairs, reduced to a low condition. There is a modesty usually attending faultless poverty, which made him rather choose to reduce his manner of living to his present circumstances, than solicit his friends in order to support the show of an estate when the substance was gone. His wife, who was a woman of sense and virtue, behaved herself on this occasion with uncommon decency, and never appeared so amiable in his eyes as now. Instead of upbraiding him with the ample fortune she had brought, or the many great offers she had refused for his sake, she redoubled all the instances of her affection, while her husband was continually pouring out his heart to her in complaints that he had ruined the best woman in the world. He sometimes came home at a time when she did not expect him, and surprised her in tears, which she endeavoured to conceal, and always put on an air of cheerfulness to receive him. To lessen their expense, their eldest daughter, (whom I shall call Amanda) was sent into the country, to the house of an honest farmer, who had married a servant of the family. This young woman was apprehensive of the ruin which was approaching, and had privately engaged a friend in the neighbourhood to give her an account of what passed from time to time in her father's affairs. Amanda was in the bloom of her youth and beauty, when the Lord of the manor, who often called in at the farmer's house as he followed his country sports, fell passionately in love with her. He was a man of great generosity, but from a loose education, had contracted a hearty aversion to marriage. He therefore entertained a design upon Amanda's virtue, which at present he thought fit to keep private. The innocent creature, who never suspected his intentions, was pleased with his person; and, having observed his growing passion for her, hoped by so advantageous a match she might quickly be in a capacity of supporting her impoverished relations. One day, as he called to see her, he found her in tears over a letter she had just received from a friend, which gave an account that her father had lately been stripped of every thing by an execution. The lover, who with some difficulty found out the cause of her grief, took this occasion to make her a proposal. It is impossible to express Amanda's confusion when she found his pretensions were not honourable. She was now deserted of all her hopes, and had no power to speak, but, rushing from him in the utmost disturbance, locked herself up in her chamber. He immediately despatched a messenger to her father with the following letter:

'SIR,—I have heard of your misfortunes, and have offered your daughter, if she will live with me, to settle on her four hundred pounds a year, and to lay down the sum for which you are now distressed. I will be so ingenuous as to tell you that I do not intend marriage; but if you are wise, you will use your authority with her not to be too nice, when she has an opportunity of saving you and your family, and of making herself happy. I am, &c.'

This letter came to the hands of Amanda's mother. She opened and read it with great surprise and concern. She did not think it proper to explain herself to the messenger, but, desiring him to call again the next morning, she wrote to her daughter as follows:

'DEAREST CHILD,—Your father and I have just received a letter from a gentleman who pretends love to you, with a proposal that insults our misfortunes, and would throw us to a lower degree of misery than any thing which is come upon us. How could this barbarous man think that the tenderest of parents would be tempted to supply their wants by giving up the best of children to infamy and ruin? It is a mean and cruel artifice to make this proposal at a time when he thinks our necessities must compel us to any thing; but we will not eat the bread of shame; and therefore we charge thee not to think of us, but to avoid the snare which is laid for thy virtue. Beware of pitying us: it is not so bad as you perhaps have been told. All things will yet be well, and I shall write my child better news.

'I have been interrupted: I know not how I was moved to say things would mend. As I was going on, I was startled by the noise of one that knocked at the door, and hath brought us an unexpected supply of a debt which has long been owing. Oh! I will now tell thee all. It is some days I have lived almost without support, having conveyed what little money I could raise to your poor father. Thou wilt weep to think where he is, yet be assured he will soon be at liberty. That cruel letter would have broke his heart, but I have concealed it from him. I have no companion at present besides little Fanny, who stands watching my looks as I write, and is crying for her sister. She says she is sure you are not well, having discovered that my present trouble is about you. But do not think I would thus repeat my sorrows to grieve thee. No; it is to entreat thee not to make them insupportable, by adding what would be worse than all. Let us bear cheerfully an affliction which we have not brought on ourselves, and remember there is a power who can better deliver us out of it than by the loss of thy innocence. Heaven preserve my dear child! thy affectionate mother,

'——.'

The messenger, notwithstanding he promised to deliver this letter to Amanda, carried it first to his master, who he imagined would be glad to have an opportunity of giving it into her hands himself. His master was impatient to know the success of his proposal, and therefore broke open the letter privately to see the contents. He was not a little moved at so true a picture of virtue in distress; but at the same time was infinitely surprised to find his offers rejected. However, he resolved not to suppress the letter, but carefully sealed it up again, and carried it to Amanda. All his endeavours to see her were in vain till she was assured he brought a letter from her mother. He would not part with it but upon condition that she would read it without leaving the room. While she was perusing it, he fixed his eyes on her face with the deepest attention. Her concern gave a new softness to her beauty, and, when she burst into tears, he could no longer refrain from bearing a part in her sorrow, and telling her, that he too had read the letter, and was resolved to make reparation for having been the occasion of it. My reader will not be displeased to see the second epistle which he now wrote to Amanda's mother.

'Madam,—I am full of shame, and will never forgive myself if I have not your pardon for what I lately wrote. It was far from my intention to add trouble to the afflicted; nor could any thing but my being a stranger to you have betrayed me into a fault, for which, if I live, I shall endeavour to make you amends, as a son. You cannot be unhappy while Amanda is your daughter; nor shall be, if any thing can prevent it which is in the power of, madam, your most obedient humble servant,

'——.'

This letter he sent by his steward, and soon after went up to town himself to complete the generous act he had now resolved on. By his friendship and assistance Amanda's father was quickly in a condition of retrieving his perplexed affairs. To conclude, he married Amanda, and enjoyed the double satisfaction of having restored a worthy family to their former prosperity, and of making himself happy by an alliance to their virtues.

No. 376.] *Monday, May* 12, 1712.

Pavone ex Pythagoreo. *Pers.* Sat. vi. 11

From the Pythagorean peacock.

'Mr. Spectator,—I have observed that the officer you some time ago appointed, as inspector of signs, has not done his duty so well as to give you an account of very many strange occurrences in the public streets, which are worthy of, but have escaped, your notice. Among all the oddnesses which I have ever met with, that which I am now telling you gave me most delight. You must have observed that all the criers in the street attract the attention of the passengers, and of the inhabitants in the several parts, by something very particular in their tone itself, in the dwelling upon a note, or else making themselves wholly unintelligible by a scream. The person I am so delighted with has nothing to sell, but very gravely receives the bounty of the people, for no other merit but the homage they pay to his manner of signifying to them that he wants a subsidy. You must sure have heard speak of an old man who walks about the city, and that part of the suburbs which lies beyond the Tower, performing the office of a day-watchman, followed by a goose, which bears the bob of his ditty, and confirms what he says with a Quack, quack. I gave little heed to the mention of this known circumstance, till, being the other day in those quarters, I passed by a decrepit old fellow with a pole in his hand, who just then was bawling out, 'Half an hour after one o'clock!' and immediately a dirty goose behind made her response, 'Quack, quack.' I could not forbear attending this grave procession for the length of half a street, with no small amazement to find the whole place so familiarly acquainted with a melancholy mid-night voice at noon-day, giving them the hour, and exhorting them of the departure of time, with a bounce at their doors. While I was full of this novelty, I went into a friend's house, and told him how I was diverted with their whimsical monitor and his equipage. My friend gave me the history; and interrupted my commendation of the man, by telling me the livelihood of these two animals is purchased rather by the good parts of the goose than of the leader; for it seems the peripatetic who walked before her was a watchman in that neighbourhood; and the goose, of herself, by frequent hearing his tone, out of her natural vigilance, not only observed, but answered it very regularly from time to time. The watchman was so affected with it, that he bought her, and has taken her in partner, only altering their hours of duty from night to day. The town has come into it, and they live very comfortably. This is the matter of fact. Now I desire you, who are a profound philosopher, to consider this alliance of instinct and reason. Your speculation may turn very naturally upon the force the superior part of mankind may have upon the spirits of such as, like this watchman, may be very near the standard of geese. And you may add to this practical observation, how in all ages and times, the world has been carried away by odd unaccountable things, which one would think would pass upon no creature which had reason; and, under the symbol of this goose you may enter into the manner and method of leading creatures with their eyes open through thick and thin, for they know not what, they know not why.

'All which is humbly submitted to your spectatorial wisdom, by sir, your most humble servant, MICHAEL GANDER.'

'Mr. Spectator,—I have for several years had under my care the government and education of young ladies, which trust I have endeavoured to discharge with due regard to their several capacities and fortunes. I have left nothing undone to imprint in every one of them an humble, courteous mind, accompanied with a graceful becoming mien, and have made them pretty much acquainted with the household part of family affairs; but still I find there is something very much wanting in the air of my ladies, different from what I have observed in those who are esteemed your fine-bred women. Now, sir, I must own to you, I never suffered my girls to learn to dance; but since I have read your discourse of dancing, where you have described the beauty and spirit there is in regular motion, I own myself your convert, and resolve for the future, to give my young ladies that accomplishment. But, upon imparting my design to their parents, I have been made very uneasy for some time, because several of them have declared, that if I did not make use of the master they recommended, they would take away their children. There was colonel Jumper's lady, a colonel of the train-bands, that has a great interest in her parish, she recommends Mr. Trott for the prettiest master in town; that no man teaches a jig like him; that she has seen him rise six or seven capers together with the greatest ease imaginable; and that his scholars twist themselves more ways than the scholars of any master in town: besides, there is Madam Prim, an alderman's lady, recommends a master of their own name, but she declares he is not of their family; yet a very extraordinary man in his way; for, besides a very soft air he has in dancing, he gives them a particular behaviour at a tea-table, and in presenting their snuff box; teaches to twirl, slip, or flirt a fan, and how to place patches to the best advantage, either for fat or lean, long or oval faces; for my lady says there is more in these things than the world imagines. But I must confess, the major part of those I am concerned with leave it to me. I desire, therefore, according to the enclosed direction, you would send your correspondent, who has writ to you on that subject, to my house. If proper application this way can give innocence new charms, and make virtue legible in the countenance, I shall spare no charge to make my scholars, in their very features and limbs, bear witness how careful I have been in the other parts of their education. I am, sir, your most humble servant,

'RACHEL WATCHFUL.'

No. 377.] *Tuesday, May* 13, 1712.

Quid quisque vitei, nunquam homini satis
Cautum est in horas. *Hor.* Lib. 2. Od. xiii. 13.

What each should fly, is seldom known;
We, unprovided, are undone. *Creech.*

Love was the mother of poetry, and still produces, among the most ignorant and barbarous, a thousand imaginary distresses and poetical complaints. It makes a footman talk like Oroondates, and converts a brutal rustic into a gentle swain. The most ordinary plebeian or mechanic in love, bleeds and pines away with a certain elegance and tenderness of sentiments which this passion naturally inspires.

These inward languishings of a mind infected with this softness have given birth to a phrase which is made use of by all the melting tribe, from the highest to the lowest —I mean that of 'dying for love.'

Romances, which owe their very being to this passion, are full of these metaphorical deaths. Heroes and heroines, knights, squires, and damsels, are all of them in a dying condition. There is the same kind of mortality in our modern tragedies, where every one gasps, faints, bleeds, and dies. Many of the poets, to describe the execution which is done by this passion, represent the fair-sex as basilisks, that destroy with their eyes; but I think Mr. Cowley has, with great justness of thought, compared a beautiful woman to a porcupine, that sends an arrow from every part.

I have often thought that there is no way so effectual for the cure of this general infirmity, as a man's reflecting upon the motives that produce it. When the passion proceeds from the sense of any virtue or perfection in the person beloved, I would by no means discourage it; but if a man considers that all his heavy complaints of wounds and death arise from some little affectations of coquetry, which are improved into charms by his own fond imagination, the very laying before himself the cause of his distemper may be sufficient to effect the cure of it.

It is in this view that I have looked over the several bundles of letters which I have received from dying people, and composed out of them the following bill of mortality, which I shall lay before my reader without any farther preface, as hoping that it may be useful to him in discovering those several places where there is most danger, and those fatal arts which are made use of to destroy the heedless and unwary.

Lysander, slain at a puppet-show on the third of September.

Thyrsis, shot from a casement in Piccadilly.

T. S. wounded by Zelinda's scarlet stocking, as she was stepping out of a coach.

Will Simple, smitten at the opera by the glance of an eye that was aimed at one who stood by him.

Tho. Vainlove, lost his life at a ball.

Tim. Tattle, killed by the tap of a fan on his left shoulder, by Coquetilla, as he was talking carelessly with her in a bow-window.

Sir Simon Softly, murdered at the playhouse in Drury-lane by a frown.

Philander, mortally wounded by Cleora, as she was adjusting her tucker.

Ralph Gapley, esq. hit by a random-shot at the ring.

F. R. caught his death upon the water, April the 1st.

W. W. killed by an unknown hand, that was playing with the glove off upon the side of the front-box in Drury-lane.

Sir Christopher Crazy, bart. hurt by the brush of a whale-bone petticoat.

Sylvius, shot through the sticks of a fan at St. James's church.

Damon, struck through the heart by a diamond necklace.

Thomas Trusty, Francis Goosequill, William Meanwell, Edward Callow, esqrs. standing in a row, fell all four at the same time, by an ogle of the widow Trapland.

Tom Rattle, chancing to tread upon a lady's tail as he came out of the play-house, she turned full upon him, and laid him dead upon the spot.

Dick Tastewell, slain by a blush from the queen's box in the third act of the Trip to the Jubilee.

Samuel Felt, haberdasher, wounded in his walks to Islington, by Mrs. Susanna Cross-stitch, as she was clambering over a stile.

R. F., T. W., S. I., M. P. &c. put to death in the last birth-day massacre.

Roger Blinko, cut off in the twenty-first year of his age by a white-wash.

Musidorus, slain by an arrow that flew out of a dimple in Belinda's left cheek.

Ned Courtly, presenting Flavia with her glove (which she had dropped on purpose) she received it, and took away his life with a courtesy.

John Gosselin, having received a slight hurt from a pair of blue eyes, as he was making his escape, was despatched by a smile.

Strephon, killed by Clarinda as she looked down into the pit.

Charles Careless, shot flying by a girl of fifteen, who unexpectedly popped her head upon him out of a coach.

Josiah Wither, aged three score and three, sent to his long home by Elizabeth Jetwell, spinster.

Jack Freelove murdered by Melissa in her hair.

William Wiseacre, gent. drowned in a flood of tears by Moll Common.

John Pleadwell, esq. of the Middle Temple, barrister at law, assassinated in his chambers the 6th instant, by Kitty Sly, who pretended to come to him for his advice.

No. 378.] *Wednesday, May* 14, 1712.

Aggredere, O magnos! aderit jam tempus honores.
Virg. Ecl. iv. 48.

Mature in years, to ready honours move.—*Dryden.*

I WILL make no apology for entertaining the reader with the following poem, which is written by a great genius, a friend of mine* in the country, who is not ashamed to employ his wit in the praise of his Maker.

MESSIAH:

A SACRED ECLOGUE.

Composed of several passages of Isaiah the Prophet.

Written in Imitation of Virgil's Pollio.

Ye nymphs of Solyma! begin the song:
To heav'nly themes sublimer strains belong.
The mossy fountains, and the sylvan shades,
The dreams of Pindus, and th' Aonian maids,
Delight no more.—O Thou my voice inspire,
Who touch'd Isaiah's hallow'd lips with fire!
Rapt into future times, the bard begun,
A virgin shall conceive, a virgin bear a son!
From Jesse's root behold a branch arise, Isa. xi. 1.
Whose sacred flower with fragrance fills the skies:
Th' æthereal Spirit o'er its leaves shall move,
And on its top descends the mystic dove.
Ye heavens! from high the dewy nectar pour, xlv. 8
And in soft silence shed the kindly shower!
The sick and weak the healing plant shall aid, xxv. 4
From storms a shelter, and from heat a shade.
All crimes shall cease, and ancient fraud shall fail;
Returning justice lift aloft her scale: ix. 7
Peace o'er the world her olive wand extend,
And white-rob'd Innocence from heav'n descend.
Swift fly the years, and rise the expected morn!
Oh spring to light, auspicious Babe, be born! xxxv. 2
See Nature hastes her earliest wreaths to bring,
With all the incense of the breathing spring:
See lofty Lebanon his head advance,
See nodding forests on the mountains dance,
See spicy clouds from lowly Sharon rise,
And Carmel's flowery top perfumes the skies!
Hark! a glad voice the lonely desert cheers: xi. 3, 4.
Prepare the way! a God, a God appears;
A God! a God! the vocal hills reply,
The rocks proclaim th' approaching Deity.
Lo earth receives him from the bending skies!
Sink down, ye mountains; and ye valleys rise!

* Pope. See No. 534.

With heads declin'd, ye cedars, homage pay;
Be smooth, ye rocks; ye rapid floods, give way!
The Saviour comes! by ancient bards foretold!
Hear him, ye deaf; and all ye blind, behold! Isa. xlii. 18.
He from thick films shall purge the visual ray, xxxv. 5. 6.
And on the sightless eye-ball pour the day.
'Tis He th' obstructed paths of sound shall clear,
And bid new music charm th' unfolding ear;
The dumb shall sing, the lame his crutch forego,
And leap exulting like the bounding roe:
No sigh, no murmur, the wide world shall hear,
From every face he wipes off every tear. xxv. 8.
In adamantine chains shall death be bound,
And hell's grim tyrant feel th' eternal wound. xl. 11.
As the good shepherd tends his fleecy care,
Seeks freshest pastures and the purest air,
Explores the lost, the wandering sheep directs,
By day o'ersees them, and by night protects,
The tender lamb he raises in his arms,
Feeds from his hand, and in his bosom warms;
Mankind shall thus his guardian care engage,
The promis'd father of the future age. ix. 6.
No more shall nation against nation rise, ii. 4.
Nor ardent warriors meet with hateful eyes,
Nor fields with gleaming steel be cover'd o'er,
The brazen trumpets kindle rage no more;
But useless lances into scythes shall bend,
And the broad falchion in a ploughshare end.
Then palaces shall rise; the joyful son lxv. 21, 22.
Shall finish what the short-liv'd sire begun;
Their vines a shadow to their race shall yield,
And the same hand that sow'd shall reap the field.
The swain in barren deserts with surprise xxxv. 1. 7.
Sees lilies spring, and sudden verdure rise,
And starts amidst the thirsty wilds to hear
New falls of water murmuring in his ear;
On rifted rocks, the dragon's late abodes,
The green reed trembles, and the bulrush nods.
Waste sandy valleys, once perplex'd with thorn, xli. 19,
The spiry fir and shapely box adorn: [& lv. 13.
The leafless shrubs the flowering palms succeed,
And od'rous myrtle to the noisome weed.
The lambs with wolves shall grace the verdant mead, xl.
And boys in flowery bands the tiger lead; [6, 7, 8.
The steer and lion at one crib shall meet,
And harmless serpents lick the pilgrim's feet:
The smiling infant in his hand shall take
The crested basilisk and speckled snake—
Pleas'd the green lustre of the scales survey, [play.
And with their forked tongue, and pointless sting shall
Rise, crown'd with light, imperial Salem, rise! lx. 1.
Exalt thy towery head, and lift thy eyes!
See a long race thy spacious courts adorn! lx. 4.
See future sons and daughters yet unborn
In crowding ranks on every side arise,
Demanding life, impatient for the skies!
See barb'rous nations at thy gate attend, lx. 3.
Walk in thy light, and in thy temple bend!
See thy bright altars throng'd with prostrate kings,
And heap'd with products of Sabæan springs! lx. 6.
For thee Idume's spicy forests blow, lx.
And seeds of gold in Ophir's mountains glow.
See heaven its sparkling portals wide display,
And break upon thee with a flood of day!
No more the rising sun shall gild the morn, lx. 19, 20.
Nor evening Cynthia fill her silver horn, li. 6.
But lost, dissolv'd in thy superior rays,
One tide of glory, one unclouded blaze,
O'erflow thy courts: the Light Himself shall shine
Reveal'd, and God's eternal day be thine!
The seas shall waste, the skies in smoke decay, li. 6, &
Rocks fall to dust, and mountains melt away; [lvi. 10.
But fix'd His word, His saving power remains;
Thy realm for ever lasts, thy own Messiah reigns.

T.

No. 379.] *Thursday, May* 15, 1712.

Scire tuum nihil est, nisi te scire hoc sciat alter.
Pers. Sat. i. 27.

——Science is not science till reveal'd.—*Dryden.*

I HAVE often wondered at that ill-natured position which has been sometimes maintained in the schools, and is comprised in an old Latin verse, namely, that 'A man's knowledge is worth nothing if he communicates what he knows to any one besides.' There is certainly no more sensible pleasure to a good-natured man, than if he can by any means gratify or inform the mind of another. I might add that this virtue naturally carries its own reward along with it, since it is almost impossible it should be exercised without the improvement of the person who practises it. The reading of books and the daily occurrences of life, are continually furnishing us with matter for thought and reflection. It is extremely natural for us to desire to see such our thoughts put in the dress of words, without which, indeed, we can scarce have a clear and distinct idea of them ourselves. When they are thus clothed in expressions, nothing so truly shows us whether they are just or false, as those effects which they produce in the minds of others.

I am apt to flatter myself, that, in the course of these my speculations, I have treated of several subjects, and laid down many such rules for the conduct of a man's life, which my readers were either wholly ignorant of before, or which at least those few who were acquainted with them looked upon as so many secrets they have found out for the conduct of themselves, but were resolved never to have made public.

I am the more confirmed in this opinion from my having received several letters, wherein I am censured for having prostituted learning to the embraces of the vulgar, and made her, as one of my correspondents phrases it, a common strumpet. I am charged by another with laying open the arcana or secrets of prudence to the eyes of every reader.

The narrow spirit which appears in the letters of these my correspondents, is the less surprising, as it has shown itself in all ages; there is still extant an epistle written by Alexander the Great, to his tutor Aristotle, upon that philosopher's publishing some part of his writings; in which the prince complains of his having made known to all the world those secrets in learning which he had before communicated to him in private lectures; concluding that he had rather excel the rest of mankind in knowledge than in power.

Louisa de Padilla, a lady of great learning, and countess of Aranda, was in like manner angry with the famous Gratian, upon his publishing his treatise of the Discreto, wherein she fancied that he had laid open those maxims to common readers, which ought only to have been reserved for the knowledge of the great.

These objections are thought by many of so much weight, that they often defend the above-mentioned authors by affirming they have affected such an obscurity in their style and manner of writing, that, though every one may read their works, there will be but very few who can comprehend their meaning.

Persius, the Latin satirist, affected obscurity for another reason; with which, however, Mr. Cowley is so offended, that, writing to one of his friends, 'You,' says he, 'tell me that you do not know whether Persius be a good poet or no, because you cannot understand him; for which very reason I affirm that he is not so.'

However, this art of writing unintelligibly has been very much improved, and followed by several of the moderns, who, observing the general inclination of mankind to dive into a secret, and the reputation many have acquired by concealing their meaning under obscure terms and phrases, resolve, that they may be still more abstruse, to write without any meaning at all. This art, as it is at present practised by many eminent authors, consists in throwing so many words at a venture into different periods, and leaving the curious reader to find the meaning of them.

The Egyptians, who made use of hieroglyphics to signify several things, expressed a man who confined his knowledge and discoveries altogether within himself by the figure of a dark lantern closed on all sides; which, though it was illuminated within, afforded no manner of light or advantage to such as stood by it. For my own part, as I shall from time to time communicate to the public whatever discoveries I happen to make, I should much rather be compared to an ordinary lamp, which consumes and wastes itself for the benefit of every passenger.

I shall conclude this paper with the story of Rosicrusius's sepulchre. I suppose I need not inform my readers that this man was the author of the Rosicrusian sect, and that his disciples still pretend to new discoveries, which they are never to communicate to the rest of mankind.*

'A certain person having occasion to dig somewhat deep in the ground, where this philosopher lay interred, met with a small door, having a wall on each side of it. His curiosity, and the hopes of finding some hidden treasure, soon prompted him to force open the door. He was immediately surprised by a sudden blaze of light, and discovered a very fair vault. At the upper end of it was a statue of a man in armour, sitting by a table, and leaning on his left arm. He held a truncheon in his right hand, and had a lamp burning before him. The man had no sooner set one foot within the vault, than the statue erected itself from its leaning posture, stood bolt upright, and, upon the fellow's advancing another step, lifted up the truncheon in his right hand. The man still ventured a third step, when the statue, with a furious blow, broke the lamp into a thousand pieces, and left his guest in a sudden darkness.

'Upon the report of this adventure, the country people soon came with lights to the sepulchre, and discovered that the statue, which was made of brass, was nothing more than a piece of clock-work; that the floor of the vault was all loose, and underlaid with several springs, which upon any man's entering, naturally produced that which had happened.'

Rosicrusius, say his disciples, made use of this method to show the world that he had reinvented the ever-burning lamps of the ancients, though he was resolved no one should reap any advantage from the discovery. X.

* See Comte de Gaba.is, par l'Abbe Villars. Warburton's Pope. vol. i. p. 109, 12mo.

No. 380.] *Friday, May* 16, 1712.

Rivalem patienter habe.——————
Ovid. Ars Am. ii. 538.

With patience bear a rival in thy love.

'Thursday, May 8, 1712.

'Sir,—The character you have in the world of being the ladies' philosopher, and the pretty advice I have seen you give to others in your papers, make me address myself to you in this abrupt manner, and to desire your opinion of what in this age a woman may call a lover. I have lately had a gentleman that I thought made pretensions to me, insomuch that most of my friends took notice of it, and thought we were really married. I did not take much pains to undeceive them, and especially a young gentlewoman of my particular acquaintance, who was then in the country. She coming to town, and seeing our intimacy so great, she gave herself the liberty of taking me to task concerning it. I ingenuously told her we were not married, but I did not know what might be the event. She soon got acquainted with the gentleman, and was pleased to take upon her to examine him about it. Now, whether a new face had made a greater conquest than the old I will leave you to judge. I am informed that he utterly denied all pretensions to courtship, but withal professed a sincere friendship for me; but, whether marriages are proposed by way of friendship or not, is what I desire to know, and what I may really call a lover? There are so many who talk in a language fit only for that character, and yet guard themselves against speaking in direct terms to the point, that it is impossible to distinguish between courtship and conversation. I hope you will do me justice both upon my lover and my friend, if they provoke me further. In the mean time I carry it with so equal a behaviour, that the nymph and the swain too are mightily at a loss: each believes I, who know them both well, think myself revenged in their love to one another which creates an irreconcilable jealousy If all comes right again, you shall hear fur her from, sir, your most obedient servant,

'MYRTILLA.'

'April 28, 1712.

'MR. SPECTATOR,—Your observations on persons that have behaved themselves irreverently at church, I doubt not have had a good effect on some that have read them; but there is another fault which has hitherto escaped your notice; I mean of such persons as are there very zealous and punctual to perform an ejaculation that is only preparatory to the service of the church, and yet neglect to join in the service itself. There is an instance of this in a friend of Will Honeycomb's, who sits opposite to me. He seldom comes in till the prayers are about half over: and when he has entered his seat, (instead of joining with the congregation,) he devoutly holds his hat before his face for three or four moments, then bows to all his acquaintance, sits down, takes a pinch of snuff, (if it be the evening service, perhaps takes a nap,) and spends the remaining time in surveying the congregation. Now, sir, what I would desire is, that you would animadvert a little on this gentleman's practice. In my opinion, this gentleman's devotion, cap in hand, is only a compliance to the custom of the place, and goes no farther than a little ecclesiastical good-breeding. If you will not pretend to tell us the motives that bring such trifles to solemn assemblies, yet let me desire that you will give this letter a place in your paper, and I shall remain, sir, your obliged humble servant, J. S.'

'May the 5th.

'MR. SPECTATOR,—The conversation at a club of which I am a member, last night, falling upon vanity and the desire of being admired, put me in mind of relating how agreeably I was entertained at my own door last Thursday, by a clean fresh-coloured girl, under the most elegant and the best furnished milk-pail I had ever observed. I was glad of such an opportunity of seeing the behaviour of a coquette in low life, and how she received the extraordinary notice that was taken of her; which I found had affected every muscle of her face, in the same manner as it does the features of a first-rate toast at a play or in an assembly. This hint of mine made the discourse turn upon the sense of pleasure; which ended in a general resolution, that the milk-maid enjoys her vanity as exquisitely as the woman of quality. I think it would not be an improper subject for you to examine this frailty, and trace it to all conditions of life; which is recommended to you as an occasion of obliging many of your readers, among the rest, your most humble servant, T. B.'

'May 12, 1712.

'SIR,—Coming last week into a coffee-house, not far from the Exchange, with my basket under my arm, a Jew, of considerable note, as I am informed, takes half a dozen oranges of me, and at the same time slides a guinea into my hand; I made him a courtesy, and went my way. He followed me, and, finding I was going about my business, he came up with me, and told me plainly that he gave me the guinea with no other intent but to purchase my person for an hour. "Did you so, sir?" says I; "you gave it me then to make me wicked; I will keep it to make me honest; however, not to be in the least ungrateful, I promise you I will lay it out in a couple of rings, and wear them for your sake." I am so just sir, besides, as to give every body that asks how I came by my rings, this account of my benefactor; but to save me the trouble of telling my tale over and over again, I humbly beg the favour of you to tell it once for all, and you will extremely oblige your humble servant,

'BETTY LEMON.'

'St. Bride's, May 15, 1712.

'SIR,—'Tis a great deal of pleasure to me, and I dare say will be no less satisfactory to you, that I have an opportunity of informing you, that the gentlemen and others of the parish of St. Bride's, have raised a charity-school of fifty girls, as before of fifty boys. You were so kind to recommend the boys to the charitable world; and the other sex hope you will do them the same favour in Friday's Spectator for Sunday next, when they are to appear with their humble airs at the parish church of Saint Bride's. Sir, the mention of this may possibly be serviceable to the children; and sure no one will omit a good action attended with no expense. I am, sir, your very humble servant,

T. 'THE SEXTON.'

No. 381.] *Saturday, May* 17, 1712.

Æquam memento rebus in arduis
Servare mentem, non secus in bonis
Ab insolenti temperatam
Lætitia, moriture Deli. *Hor.* Od. 3. l. 2. v. 1.

Be calm, my Delius, and serene,
However fortune change the scene:
In thy most dejected state,
Sink not underneath the weight;
Nor yet, when happy days begin,
And the full tide comes rolling in
Let a fierce, unruly joy,
The settled quiet of thy mind destroy. *Anon*

I HAVE always preferred cheerfulness to mirth. The latter I consider as an act, the former as a habit of the mind. Mirth is short and transient, cheerfulness fixed and permanent. Those are often raised into the greatest transports of mirth, who are subject to the greatest depressions of melancholy. On the contrary, cheerfulness though it does not give the mind such an exquisite gladness, prevents us from falling into any depths of sorrow. Mirth is like a flash of lightning, that breaks through a gloom of clouds, and glitters for a moment; cheerfulness keeps up a kind of day-light in the mind, and fills it with a steady and perpetual serenity.

Men of austere principles look upon mirth as too wanton and dissolute for a state of probation, and as filled with a certain triumph and insolence of heart that is inconsistent with a life which is every moment obnoxious to the greatest dangers. Writers of this complexion have observed, that the Sacred Person who was the great pattern of perfection, was never seen to laugh.

Cheerfulness of mind is not liable to any of these exceptions; it is of a serious and composed nature; it does not throw the mind into a condition improper for the present state of humanity, and is very conspicuous in the characters of those who are looked upon as the greatest philosophers among the heathens, as well as among those who have been deservedly esteemed as saints and holy men among Christians.

If we consider cheerfulness in three lights, with regard to ourselves, to those we converse with, and to the great Author of our being, it will not a little recommend itself on each of these accounts. The man who is possessed of this excellent frame of mind, is not only easy in his thoughts, but a perfect master of all the powers and faculties of his soul. His imagination is always clear, and his judgment undisturbed; his temper is even and unruffled, whether in action or in solitude. He comes with relish to all those goods which nature has provided for him, tastes all the pleasures of the creation, which are poured about him, and does not feel the full weight of those accidental evils which may befall him.

If we consider him in relation to the persons whom he converses with, it naturally produces love and good-will towards him. A cheerful mind is not only disposed to be affable and obliging; but raises the same good-humour in those who come within its influence. A man finds himself pleased, he does not know why, with the cheerfulness of his companion. It is like a sudden sunshine that awakens a secret delight in the mind, without her attending to it. The heart rejoices of its own accord, and naturally flows out into friendship and benevolence towards the person who has so kindly an effect upon it.

When I consider this cheerful state of mind in its third relation, I cannot but look upon it as a constant habitual gratitude to the great Author of nature. An inward cheerfulness is an implicit praise and thanksgiving to Providence under all its dispensations. It is a kind of acquiescence in the state wherein we are placed, and a secret approbation of the divine will in his conduct towards man.

There are but two things which, in my opinion, can reasonably deprive us of this cheerfulness of heart. The first of these is the sense of guilt. A man who lives in a state of vice and impenitence can have no title to that evenness and tranquillity of mind which is the health of the soul, and the natural effect of virtue and innocence. Cheerfulness in an ill man deserves a harder name than language can furnish us with, and is many degrees beyond what we commonly call folly or madness.

Atheism, by which I mean a disbelief of a Supreme Being, and consequently of a future state, under whatsoever titles it shelters itself, may likewise very reasonably deprive a man of this cheerfulness of temper. There is something so particularly gloomy and offensive to human nature in the prospect of non-existence, that I cannot but wonder, with many excellent writers, how it is possible for a man to outlive the expectation of it. For my own part, I think the being of a God is so little to be doubted, that it is almost the only truth we are sure of; and such a truth as we meet with in every object, in every occurrence, and in every thought. If we look into the characters of this tribe of infidels, we generally find they are made up of pride, spleen, and cavil. It is indeed no wonder, that men who are uneasy to themselves should be so to the rest of the world; and how is it possible for a man to be otherwise than uneasy in himself, who is in danger every moment of losing his entire existence, and dropping into nothing?

The vicious man and atheist have therefore no pretence to cheerfulness, and would act very unreasonably should they endeavour after it. It is impossible for any one to live in good humour, and enjoy his present existence, who is apprehensive either of torment or of annihilation; of being miserable, or of not being at all.

After having mentioned these two great principles, which are destructive of cheerfulness, in their own nature, as well as in right reason, I cannot think of any other that ought to banish this happy temper from a virtuous mind. Pain and sickness, shame and reproach, poverty and old age, nay, death itself, considering the shortness of their duration, and the advantage we may reap from them, do not deserve the name of evils. A good mind may bear up under them with fortitude, with indolence, and with cheerfulness of heart. The tossing of a tempest does not discompose him, which he is sure will bring him to a joyful harbour.

A man who uses his best endeavours to live according to the dictates of virtue and right reason has two perpetual sources of cheerfulness, in the consideration of his own nature, and of that Being on whom he has a dependance. If he looks into himself, he cannot but rejoice in that existence which is so lately bestowed upon him, and which, after millions of ages, will be still new, and still in its beginning. How many self-congratulations naturally rise in the mind, when it reflects on this its entrance into eternity, when it takes a view of those improvable faculties which in a few years, and even at its first setting out, have made so considerable a progress, and which will still be receiving an increase of perfection, and consequently an increase of happiness! The consciousness of such a being spreads a perpetual diffusion of joy through the soul of a virtuous man, and makes him look upon himself every moment as more happy than he knows how to conceive.

The second source of cheerfulness, to a good mind, is the consideration of that Being on whom we have our dependence, and in whom, though we behold him as yet but in the first faint discoveries of his perfections, we see every thing that we can imagine as great, glorious, or amiable. We find ourselves every where upheld by his goodness, and surrounded with an immensity of love and mercy. In short, we depend upon a Being, whose power qualifies him to make us happy by an infinity of means, whose goodness and truth engage him to make those happy who desire it of him, and whose unchangeableness will secure us in this happiness to all eternity.

Such considerations, which every one should perpetually cherish in his thoughts, will banish from us all that secret heaviness of heart which unthinking men are subject to when they lie under no real affliction: all that anguish which we may feel from any evil that actually oppresses us, to which I may likewise add those little cracklings of mirth and folly that are apter to betray virtue than support it; and establish in us such an even and cheerful temper, as makes us pleasing to ourselves, to those with whom we converse, and to Him whom we were made to please. L.

No. 382.] *Monday, May* 19, 1712.

Habes confitentem reum. *Tull.*

The accused confesses his guilt.

I OUGHT not to have neglected a request of one of my correspondents so long as I have; but I dare say I have given him time to add practice to profession. He sent me some time ago a bottle or two of excellent wine, to drink the health of a gentleman who had by the penny-post advertised him of an egregious error in his conduct. My correspondent received the obligation from an unknown hand with the candour which is natural to an ingenuous mind; and promises a contrary behaviour in that point for the future. He will offend his monitor with no more errors of that kind, but thanks him for his benevolence. This frank carriage makes me reflect upon the amiable atonement a man makes in an ingenuous acknowledgment of a fault. All such miscarriages as flow from inadvertency are more than repaid by it; for reason, though not concerned in the injury, employs all its force in the atonement. He that says, he did not design to disoblige you in such an action, does as much as if he should tell you, that though the circumstance which displeased was never in his thoughts, he has that respect for you, that he is unsatisfied till it is wholly out of yours. It must be confessed, that when an acknowledgment of an offence is made out of poorness of spirit, and not conviction of heart, the circumstance is quite different. But in the case of my correspondent, where both the notice is taken, and the return made in private, the affair begins and ends with the highest grace on each side. To make the acknowledgment of a fault in the highest manner graceful, it is lucky when the circumstances of the offender place him above any ill consequences from the resentment of the person offended. A dauphin of France, upon a review of the army, and a command of the king to alter the posture of it by a march of one of the wings, gave an improper order to an officer at the head of a brigade, who told his highness, he presumed he had not received the last orders, which were to move a contrary way. The prince, instead of taking the admonition, which was delivered in a manner that accounted for his error with safety to his understanding, shaked a cane at the officer, and, with the return of opprobrious language, persisted in his own orders. The whole matter came necessarily before the king, who commanded his son, on foot, to lay his right hand on the gentleman's stirrup as he sat on horseback in sight of the whole army, and ask his pardon. When the prince touched his stirrup, and was going to speak, the officer with an incredible agility, threw himself on the earth and kissed his feet.

The body is very little concerned in the pleasure or sufferings of souls truly great; and the reparation, when an honour was designed this soldier, appeared as much too great to be borne by his gratitude, as the injury was intolerable to his resentment.

When we turn our thoughts from these extraordinary occurrences into common life, we see an ingenuous kind of behaviour not only make up for faults committed, but in a manner expiate them in the very commission. Thus many things wherein a man has pressed too far, he implicitly excuses, by owning, 'This is a trespass: you'll pardon my confidence; I am sensible I have no pretensions to this favour;' and the like. But commend me to those gay fellows about town who are directly impudent, and make up for it no otherwise than by calling themselves such and exulting in it. But this sort of carriage, which prompts a man against rules to urge what he has a mind to, is pardonable only when you sue for another. When you are confident in preference of yourself to others of equal merit, every man that loves virtue and modesty ought, in defence of those qualities, to oppose you. But, without considering the morality of the thing, let us at this time behold any natural consequence of candour when we speak of ourselves.

The Spectator writes often in an elegant, often in an argumentative, and often in a sublime style, with equal success; but how would it hurt the reputed author of that paper to own, that of the most beautiful pieces under his title he is barely the publisher? There is nothing but what a man really performs can be an honour to him; what he takes more than he ought in the eye of the world, he loses in the conviction of his own heart; and a man must lose his consciousness, that is, his very self, before he can rejoice in any falsehood without inward mortification.

Who has not seen a very criminal at the bar, when his counsel and friends have done all that they could for him in vain, prevail on the whole assembly to pity him, and his judge to recommend his case to the mercy of the throne, without offering any thing new in his defence, but that he whom before we wished convicted, became so out of his own mouth, and took upon himself all the shame and sorrow we were just before preparing for him? The great opposition to this kind of candour arises from the unjust idea people ordinarily have of what we call a high spirit. It is far from greatness of spirit to persist in the wrong in any thing; nor is it a diminution of greatness of spirit to have been in the wrong. Perfection is not the attribute of man, therefore he is not degraded by the acknowledgment of an imperfection; but it is the work of little minds to imitate the fortitude of great spirits on worthy occasions, by obstinacy in the wrong. This obstinacy prevails so far upon them, that they make it extend to the defence of faults in their very servants. It would swell this paper to too great a length should I insert all the quarrels and debates which are now on foot in this town; where one party, and in some cases both, *is* sensible of being on the faulty side, and *have* not spirit enough to acknowledge it. Among the ladies the case is very common; for there are very few of them who know that it is to maintain a true and high spirit, to throw away from it all which itself disapproves, and to scorn so pitiful a shame, as that which disables the heart from acquiring a liberality of affections and sentiments. The candid mind, by acknowledging and discharging its faults, has reason and truth for the foundations of all its passions and desires, and consequently is happy and simple; the disingenuous spirit, by indulgence of one unacknowledged error, is entangled with an after-life of guilt, sorrow, and perplexity. T.

No. 383.] *Tuesday, May* 20, 1712.

Criminibus debent hortos.——— *Juv.* Sat. i. 75.
A beauteous garden, but by vice maintain'd.

As I was sitting in my chamber, and thinking on a subject for my next Spectator, I heard two or three irregular bounces at my landlady's door, and upon the opening of it, a loud cheerful voice inquiring whether the philosopher was at home. The child who went to the door answered very innocently, that he did not lodge there. I immediately recollected that it was my good friend sir Roger's voice; and that I had promised to go with him on the water to Spring-garden,* in case it proved a good evening. The knight put me in mind of my promise from the bottom of the staircase, but told me, that if I was speculating, he would stay below till I had done. Upon my coming down, I found all the children of the family got about my old friend; and my landlady herself, who is a notable prating gossip engaged in a conference with him; being mightily pleased with his stroking her little boy on the head, and bidding him to be a good child and mind his book.

We were no sooner come to the Temple-stairs, but we were surrounded with a crowd of watermen, offering us their respective services. Sir Roger, after having looked about him very attentively, spied one with a wooden leg, and immediately gave him orders to get his boat ready. As we were walking towards it, 'You must know,' says Sir Roger, 'I never make use of any body to row me, that has not lost either a leg or an arm. I would rather bate him a few strokes of his oar than not employ an honest man that has been wounded in the queen's service. If I was a lord or a bishop, and kept a barge, I would not put a fellow in my livery that had not a wooden leg.'

My old friend, after having seated himself, and trimmed the boat with his coachman, who, being a very sober man, always serves for ballast on these occasions, we made the best of our way for Vauxhall. Sir Roger obliged the waterman to give us the history of his right leg; and, hearing that he had left it at La Hogue, with many particulars which passed in that glorious action, the knight, in the triumph of his heart, made several reflections on the greatness of the British nation; as that one Englishman could beat three Frenchmen; that we could never be in danger of popery so long as we took care of our fleet; that the Thames was the noblest river in Europe; that London bridge was a greater piece of work than any of the seven wonders of the world; with many other honest prejudices which naturally cleave to the heart of a true Englishman.

After some short pause, the old knight turning about his head twice or thrice, to take a survey of this great metropolis, bid me observe how thick the city was set with churches, and that there was scarce a single steeple on this side Temple-bar. 'A most heathenish sight!' says sir Roger:

* Or Vauxhall.

'there is no religion at this end of the town. The fifty new churches will very much mend the prospect; but church-work is slow, church-work is slow.'

I do not remember I have any where mentioned in Sir Roger's character, his custom of saluting every body that passes by him with a good-morrow, or a good-night. This the old man does out of the overflowings of his humanity; though, at the same time, it renders him so popular among all his country neighbours, that it is thought to have gone a good way in making him once or twice knight of the shire. He cannot forbear this exercise of benevolence even in town, when he meets with any one in his morning or evening walk. It broke from him to several boats that passed by us on the water; but, to the knight's great surprise, as he gave the good-night to two or three young fellows a little before our landing, one of them, instead of returning the civility, asked us, what queer old put we had in the boat, and whether he was not ashamed to go a wenching at his years? with a great deal of the like Thames-ribaldry. Sir Roger seemed a little shocked at first, but at length assuming a face of magistracy, told us, that if he were a Middlesex justice, he would make such vagrants know that her majesty's subjects were no more to be abused by water than by land.

We were now arrived at Spring-garden, which is exquisitely pleasant at this time of the year. When I considered the fragrancy of the walks and bowers, with the choirs of birds, that sung upon the trees, and the loose tribe of people that walked under their shades, I could not but look upon the place as a kind of Mahometan Paradise. Sir Roger told me it put him in mind of a little coppice by his house in the country, which his chaplain used to call an aviary of nightingales. 'You must understand,' says the knight, 'that there is nothing in the world that pleases a man in love so much as your nightingale. Ah, Mr. Spectator, the many moonlight nights that I have walked by myself, and thought on the widow by the music of the nightingale!' Here he fetched a deep sigh, and was falling into a fit of musing, when a mask, who came behind him, gave him a gentle tap upon the shoulder, and asked him if he would drink a bottle of mead with her? But the knight being startled at so unexpected a familiarity, and displeased to be interrupted in his thoughts of the widow, told her she was a wanton baggage; and bid her go about her business.

We concluded our walk with a glass of Burton ale, and a slice of hung beef. When we had done eating ourselves, the knight called a waiter to him, and bid him carry the remainder to the waterman that had but one leg. I perceived the fellow stared upon him at the oddness of the message, and was going to be saucy; upon which I ratified the knight's commands with a peremptory look.

As we were going out of the garden, my old friend thinking himself obliged, as a member of the quorum, to animadvert upon the morals of the place, told the mistress of the house, who sat at the bar, that he should be a better customer to her garden, if there were more nightingales and fewer strumpets. I.

No. 384.] *Wednesday, May* 21, 1712.

'Hague, May 24, N. S. The same republican hands, who have so often since the chevalier de St. George's recovery killed him in our public prints, have now reduced the young dauphin of France to that desperate condition of weakness, and death itself, that it is hard to conjecture what method they will take to bring him to life again. Meantime we are assured, by a very good hand from Paris, that on the 20th instant this young prince was as well as ever he was known to be since the day of his birth. As for the other, they are now sending his ghost, we suppose (for they never had the modesty to contradict their assertion of his death,) to Commerci in Lorrain, attended only by four gentlemen, and a few domestics of little consideration. The Baron de Bothmar* having delivered in his credentials to qualify him as an ambassador to this state (an office to which his greatest enemies will acknowledge him to be equal,) is gone to Utrecht, whence he will proceed to Hanover, but not stay long at that court, for fear the peace should be made during his lamentable absence.'—*Post-Boy*, May 20.

I SHOULD be thought not able to read should I overlook some excellent pieces lately come out. My lord bishop of St. Asaph† has just now published some sermons, the preface to which seems to me to determine a great point. He has, like a good man, and a good Christian, in opposition to all the flattery and base submission of false friends to princes, asserted, that Christianity left us where it found us as to our civil rights. The present entertainment shall consist only of a sentence out of the Post-Boy, and the said preface of the lord of St. Asaph. I should think it a little odd if the author of the Post-Boy should with impunity call men republicans for a gladness on the report of the death of the pretender; and treat baron Bothmar, the minister of Hanover, in such a manner as you see in my motto. I must own, I think every man in England concerned to support the succession of that family.

'The publishing a few sermons, whilst I live, the latest of which was preached about eight years since, and the first above seventeen, will make it very natural for people to inquire into the occasion of doing so; and to such I do very willingly assign these following reasons:

'First, from the observations I have been able to make for these many years last past upon our public affairs, and from the natural tendency of several principles and practices, that have of late been studiously revived, and from what has followed there

* Ambassador from Hanover, and afterwards agen here for the Hanoverian family.

† Dr. William Fleetwood.

upon, I could not help both fearing and presaging, that these nations should some time or other, if ever we should have an enterprising prince upon the throne, of more ambition than virtue, justice, and true honour, fall into the way of all other nations, and lose their liberty.

'Nor could I help foreseeing to whose charge a great deal of this dreadful mischief, whenever it should happen, would be laid; whether justly or unjustly, was not my business to determine; but I resolved, for my own particular part, to deliver myself, as well as I could, from the reproaches and the curses of posterity, by publicly declaring to all the world, that, although in the constant course of my ministry I have never failed, on proper occasions, to recommend, urge, and insist upon the loving, honouring, and reverencing the prince's person, and holding it, according to the laws, inviolable and sacred; and paying all obedience and submission to the laws, though never so hard and inconvenient to private people: yet did I never think myself at liberty, or authorized to tell the people, that either Christ, St. Peter, or St. Paul, or any other holy writer, had, by any doctrine delivered by them, subverted the laws and constitutions of the country in which they lived, or put them in a worse condition, with respect to their civil liberties, than they would have been had they not been Christians. I ever thought it a most impious blasphemy against that holy religion, to father any thing upon it that might encourage tyranny, oppression, or injustice in a prince, or that easily tended to make a free and happy people slaves and miserable. No: people may make themselves as wretched as they will, but let not God be called into that wicked party. When force and violence, and hard necessity, have brought the yoke of servitude upon a people's neck, religion will supply them with a patient and submissive spirit under it till they can innocently shake it off: but certainly religion never puts it on. This always was, and this at present is, my judgment of these matters: and I would be transmitted to posterity (for the little share of time such names as mine can live) under the character of one who loved his country, and would be thought a good Englishman, as well as a good clergyman.

'This character I thought would be transmitted by the following sermons, which were made for and preached in a private audience, when I could think of nothing else but doing my duty on the occasions that were then offered by God's providence, without any manner of design of making them public; and for that reason I give them now as they were then delivered; by which I hope to satisfy those people who have objected a change of principles to me, as if I were not now the same man I formerly was. I never had but one opinion of these matters; and that I think is so reasonable and well-grounded, that I believe I can never have any other.

'Another reason of my publishing these sermons at this time is, that I have a mind to do myself some honour by doing what honour I could to the memory of two most excellent princes, and who have very highly deserved at the hands of all the people of these dominions, who have any true value for the Protestant religion, and the constitution of the English government of which they were the great deliverers and defenders. I have lived to see their illustrious names very rudely handled, and the great benefits they did this nation treated slightly and contemptuously. I have lived to see our deliverance from arbitrary power and popery traduced and vilified by some who formerly thought it was their greatest merit, and made it part of their boast and glory to have had a little hand and share in bringing it about; and others who, without it, must have lived in exile, poverty, and misery, meanly disclaiming it, and using ill the glorious instruments thereof. Who could expect such a requital of such merit? I have, I own it, an ambition of exempting myself from the number of unthankful people: and as I loved and honoured those great princes living, and lamented over them when dead, so I would gladly raise them up a monument of praise as lasting as any thing of mine can be; and I choose to do it at this time, when it is so unfashionable a thing to speak honourably of them.

'The sermon that was preached upon the duke of Gloucester's death was printed quickly after, and is now, because the subject was so suitable, joined to the others. The loss of that most promising and hopeful prince was at that time, I saw, unspeakably great; and many accidents since have convinced us that it could not have been overvalued. That precious life, had it pleased God to have prolonged it the usual space, had saved us many fears and jealousies, and dark distrusts, and prevented many alarms, that have long kept us, and will keep us still, waking and uneasy. Nothing remained to comfort and support us under this heavy stroke, but the necessity it brought the king and nation under of settling the succession in the house of Hanover, and giving it a hereditary right by act of parliament, as long as it continues Protestant. So much good did God, in his merciful providence, produce from a misfortune, which we could never otherwise have sufficiently deplored!

'The fourth sermon was preached upon the queen's accession to the throne, and the first year in which that day was solemnly observed (for by some accident or other it had been overlooked the year before;) and every one will see, without the date of it, that it was preached very early in this reign, since I was able only to promise and presage its future glories and successes, from the good appearances of things, and the happy turn our affairs began to take; and could not then count up the victories and triumphs that, for seven years after, made it, in the prophet's language, a name and a praise among all the people of the earth. Never did seven such years together pass over the head of any English monarch, nor cover it with so much honour. The crown and sceptre seemed to be the queen's least ornaments; those, other princes wore in common with her, and her great personal virtues were the same before and since; but such was the fame of her administration of affairs at home, such was the reputation of her wisdom and felicity in choosing ministers, and such was then esteemed their faithfulness and zeal, their diligence and great abilities in executing her commands; to such a height of military glory did her great general and her armies carry the British name abroad; such was the harmony and concord betwixt her and her allies; and such was the blessing of God upon all her councils and undertakings, that I am as sure as history can make me, no prince of ours ever was so prosperous and successful, so beloved, esteemed, and honoured by their subjects and their friends, nor near so formidable to their enemies. We were, as all the world imagined then, just entering on the ways that promised to lead to such a peace as would have answered all the prayers of our religious queen, the care and vigilance of a most able ministry, the payments of a willing and most obedient people, as well as all the glorious toils and hazards of the soldiery; when God, for our sins, permitted the spirit of discord to go forth, and by troubling sore the camp, the city and the country, (and oh that it had altogether spared the places sacred to his worship!) to spoil, for a time, this beautiful and pleasing prospect, and give us in its stead, I know not what———Our enemies will tell the rest with pleasure. It will become me better to pray to God to restore us to the power of obtaining such a peace as will be to his glory, the safety, honour, and welfare of the queen and her dominions, and the general satisfaction of all her high and mighty allies.*

'May 2, 1712.'

No. 385.] *Thursday, May 22, 1712.*

———Thesea pectora juncta fide.
Ovid. Trist. iii. Lib. 1. 66.

Breasts that with sympathizing ardour glow'd,
And holy friendship, such as Theseus vow'd.

I INTEND the paper for this day as a loose essay upon friendship, in which I shall throw my observations together without any set form, that I may avoid repeating what has been often said on this subject.

Friendship is a strong and habitual inclination in two persons to promote the good and happiness of one another. Though the pleasures and advantages of friendship have been largely celebrated by the best moral writers, and are considered by all as great ingredients of human happiness, we very rarely meet with the practice of this virtue in the world.

Every man is ready to give in a long catalogue of those virtues and good qualities he expects to find in the person of a friend, but very few of us are careful to cultivate them in ourselves.

Love and esteem are the first principles of friendship, which always is imperfect where either of these two is wanting.

As, on the one hand, we are soon ashamed of loving a man whom we cannot esteem; so, on the other, though we are truly sensible of a man's abilities, we can never raise ourselves to the warmth of friendship, without an affectionate good-will towards his person.

Friendship immediately banishes envy under all its disguises. A man who can once doubt whether he should rejoice in his friend's being happier than himself, may depend upon it that he is an utter stranger to this virtue.

There is something in friendship so very great and noble, that in those fictitious stories which are invented to the honour of any particular person, the authors have thought it as necessary to make their hero a friend as a lover. Achilles has his Patroclus, and Æneas his Achates. In the first of these instances we may observe, for the reputation of the subject I am treating of, that Greece was almost ruined by the hero's love, but was preserved by his friendship.

The character of Achates suggests to us an observation we may often make on the intimacies of great men, who frequently choose their companions rather for the qualities of the heart than those of the head, and prefer fidelity in an easy, inoffensive, complying temper, to those endowments which make a much greater figure among mankind. I do not remember that Achates, who is represented as the first favourite, either gives his advice, or strikes a blow, through the whole Æneid.

A friendship which makes the least noise is very often most useful: for which reason I should prefer a prudent friend to a zealous one.

Atticus, one of the best men of ancient Rome, was a very remarkable instance of what I am here speaking. This extraordinary person, amidst the civil wars of his country, when he saw the designs of all parties equally tended to the subversion of liberty, by constantly preserving the esteem and affection of both the competitors, found means to serve his friends on either side: and, while he sent money to young Marius, whose father was declared an enemy to the commonwealth, he was himself one of

---

* This Preface was seized on by the Tory ministry, and condemned, by a motion of the House of Commons, to be burned by the common hangman.—See *Biographia Britannica*, vol. iii. p. 1974.

Sylla's chief favourites, and always near that general.

During the war between Cæsar and Pompey, he still maintained the same conduct. After the death of Cæsar, he sent money to Brutus in his troubles, and did a thousand good offices to Antony's wife and friends when that party seemed ruined. Lastly, even in that bloody war between Antony and Augustus, Atticus still kept his place in both their friendships: insomuch that the first, says Cornelius Nepos, whenever he was absent from Rome in any part of the empire, writ punctually to him what he was doing, what he read, and whither he intended to go; and the latter gave him constantly an exact account of all his affairs.

A likeness of inclinations in every particular is so far from being requisite to form a benevolence in two minds towards each other, as it is generally imagined, that I believe we shall find some of the firmest friendships to have been contracted between persons of different humours; the mind being often pleased with those perfections which are new to it, and which it does not find among its own accomplishments. Besides that a man in some measure supplies his own defects, and fancies himself at second-hand possessed of those good qualities and endowments, which are in the possession of him who in the eye of the world is looked upon as his other self.

The most difficult province in friendship is the letting a man see his faults and errors, which should, if possible, be so contrived, that he may perceive our advice is given him not so much to please ourselves as for his own advantage. The reproaches therefore of a friend should always be strictly just, and not too frequent.

The violent desire of pleasing in the person reproved may otherwise change into a despair of doing it, while he finds himself censured for faults he is not conscious of. A mind that is softened and humanized by friendship cannot bear frequent reproaches; either it must quite sink under the oppression, or abate considerably of the value and esteem it had for him who bestows them.

The proper business of friendship is to inspire life and courage: and a soul thus supported outdoes itself: whereas, if it be unexpectedly deprived of these succours, it droops and languishes.

We are in some measure more inexcusable if we violate our duties to a friend than to a relation; since the former arise from a voluntary choice, the latter from a necessity to which we could not give our own consent.

As it has been said on one side, that a man ought not to break with a faulty friend, that he may not expose the weakness of his choice; it will doubtless hold much stronger with respect to a worthy one, that he may never be upbraided for having lost so valuable a treasure which was once in his possession. X.

No. 386.] *Friday, May 23, 1712.*

Cum tristibus severe, cum remissis jucunde, cum senibus graviter, cum juventute comiter vivere.

Tully.

The piece of Latin on the head of this paper is part of a character extremely vicious, but I have set down no more than may fall in with the rules of justice and honour. Cicero spoke it of Catiline, who, he said, 'lived with the sad severely, with the cheerful agreeably, with the old gravely, with the young pleasantly;' he added, 'with the wicked boldly, with the wanton lasciviously.' The two last instances of his complaisance I forbear to consider, having it in my thoughts at present only to speak of obsequious behaviour as it sits upon a companion in pleasure, not a man of design and intrigue. To vary with every humour in this manner cannot be agreeable, except it comes from a man's own temper and natural complexion; to do it out of an ambition to excel that way, is the most fruitless and unbecoming prostitution imaginable. To put on an artful part to obtain no other end but an unjust praise from the undiscerning, is of all endeavours the most despicable. A man must be sincerely pleased to become pleasure, or not to interrupt that of others; for this reason it is a most calamitous circumstance, that many people who want to be alone, or should be so, will come into conversation. It is certain that all men, who are the least given to reflection, are seized with an inclination that way, when, perhaps, they had rather be inclined to company; but indeed they had better go home and be tired with themselves, than force themselves upon others to recover their good humour. In all this, the case of communicating to a friend a sad thought or difficulty, in order to relieve a heavy heart, stands excepted; but what is here meant is, that a man should always go with inclination to the turn of the company he is going into, or not pretend to be of the party. It is certainly a very happy temper to be able to live with all kinds of dispositions, because it argues a mind that lies open to receive what is pleasing to others, and not obstinately bent on any particularity of his own.

This is it which makes me pleased with the character of my good acquaintance Acasto. You meet him at the tables and conversations of the wise, the impertinent, the grave, the frolic, and the witty; and yet his own character has nothing in it that can make him particularly agreeable to any one sect of men; but Acasto has natural good sense, good-nature, and discretion, so that every man enjoys himself in his company; and though Acasto contributes nothing to the entertainment, he never was at a place where he was not welcome a second time. Without the subordinate good qualities of Acasto, a man of wit and learning would be painful to the generality of man kind, instead of being pleasing. Witty men are apt to imagine they are agreeable as such, and by that means grow the worst companions imaginable; they deride the absent or rally the present in a wrong manner, not knowing that if you pinch or tickle a man till he is uneasy in his seat, or ungracefully distinguished from the rest of the company, you equally hurt him.

I was going to say, the true art of being agreeable in company (but there can be no such thing as art in it) is to appear well pleased with those you are engaged with, and rather to seem well entertained, than to bring entertainment to others. A man thus disposed is not indeed what we ordinarily call a good companion, but essentially is such, and in all the parts of his conversation has something friendly in his behaviour, which conciliate men's minds more than the highest sallies of wit or starts of humour can possibly do. The feebleness of age in a man of this turn has something which should be treated with respect even in a man no otherwise venerable. The forwardness of youth, when it proceeds from alacrity and not insolence, has also its allowances. The companion who is formed for such by nature, gives to every character of life its due regards, and is ready to account for their imperfections, and receive their accomplishments as if they were his own. It must appear that you receive law from, and not give it to, your company, to make you agreeable.

I remember Tully, speaking, I think, of Antony, says, that, *In eo facetiæ erant, quæ nulla arte tradi possunt:* 'He had a witty mirth, which could be acquired by no art.' This quality must be of the kind of which I am now speaking; for all sorts of behaviour which depend upon observation and knowledge of life are to be acquired; but that which no one can describe, and is apparently the act of nature, must be every where prevalent, because every thing it meets is a fit occasion to exert it; for he who follows nature can never be improper or unseasonable.

How unaccountable then must their behaviour be, who, without any manner of consideration of what the company they have now entered are upon, give themselves the air of a messenger, and make as distinct relations of the occurrences they last met with, as if they had been despatched from those they talk to, to be punctually exact in a report of those circumstances! It is unpardonable to those who are met to enjoy one another, that a fresh man shall pop in, and give us only the last part of his own life, and put a stop to ours during the history. If such a man comes from 'Change, whether you will or not, you must hear how the stocks go; and, though you are never so intently employed on a graver subject, a young fellow of the other end of the town will take his place, and tell you, Mrs. Such-a-one is charmingly handsome, because he just now saw her. But I think I need not dwell on this subject, since I have acknowledged there can be no rules made for excelling this way; and precepts of this kind fare like rules for writing poetry, which, it is said, may have prevented ill poets, but never made good ones. T.

No. 387.] *Saturday, May* 24, 1712.

Quid pure tranquillet——

Hor. Ep. xviii. Lib. 102.

What calms the breast and makes the mind serene.

In my last Saturday's paper, I spoke of cheerfulness as it is a moral habit of the mind, and accordingly mentioned such moral motives as are apt to cherish and keep alive this happy temper in the soul of man. I shall now consider cheerfulness in its natural state, and reflect on those motives to it which are indifferent either as to virtue or vice.

Cheerfulness is, in the first place, the best promoter of health. Repinings, and secret murmurs of heart, give imperceptible strokes to those delicate fibres of which the vital parts are composed, and wear out the machine insensibly; not to mention those violent ferments which they stir up in the blood, and those irregular disturbed motions which they raise in the animal spirits. I scarce remember, in my own observation, to have met with many old men, or with such, who (to use our English phrase,) wear well, that had not at least a certain indolence in their humour, if not a more than ordinary gayety and cheerfulness of heart. The truth of it is, health and cheerfulness mutually beget each other, with this difference, that we seldom meet with a great degree of health which is not attended with a certain cheerfulness, but very often see cheerfulness where there is no great degree of health.

Cheerfulness bears the same friendly regard to the mind as to the body. It banishes all anxious care and discontent, soothes and composes the passions, and keeps the soul in a perpetual calm. But having already touched on this last consideration, I shall here take notice, that the world in which we are placed is filled with innumerable objects that are proper to raise and keep alive this happy temper of mind.

If we consider this world in its subserviency to man, one would think it was made for our use; but if we consider it in its natural beauty and harmony, one would be apt to conclude it was made for our pleasure. The sun, which is as the great soul of the universe, and produces all the necessaries of life, has a particular influence in cheering the mind of man, and making the heart glad.

Those several living creatures which are made for our service or sustenance; at the same time either fill the woods with their music, furnish us with game, or raise pleas ing ideas in us by the delightfulness of their appearance. Fountains, lakes, and rivers, are as refreshing to the imagination, as to the soil through which they pass.

There are writers of great distinction, who have made it an argument for Providence, that the whole earth is covered with green rather than with any other colour, as being such a right mixture of light and shade, that it comforts and strengthens the eye, instead of weakening or grieving it. For this reason several painters have a green cloth hanging near them to ease the eye upon, after too great an application to their colouring. A famous modern philosopher* accounts for it in the following manner. All colours that are more luminous, overpower and dissipate the animal spirits which are employed in sight; on the contrary, those that are more obscure do not give the animal spirits a sufficient exercise; whereas, the rays that produce in us the idea of green, fall upon the eye in such a due proportion, that they give the animal spirits their proper play, and, by keeping up the struggle in a just balance, excite a very pleasing and agreeable sensation. Let the cause be what it will, the effect is certain; for which reason, the poets ascribe to this particular colour the epithet of cheerful.

To consider further this double end in the works of nature, and how they are at the same time both useful and entertaining, we find that the most important parts in the vegetable world are those which are the most beautiful. These are the seeds by which the several races of plants are propagated and continued, and which are always lodged in the flowers or blossoms. Nature seems to hide her principal design, and to be industrious in making the earth gay and delightful, while she is carrying on her great work, and intent upon her own preservation. The husbandman, after the same manner, is employed in laying out the whole country into a kind of garden or landscape, and making every thing smile about him, whilst in reality he thinks of nothing but of the harvest, and the increase which is to arise from it.

We may further observe how Providence has taken care to keep up this cheerfulness in the mind of man, by having formed it after such a manner as to make it capable of conceiving delight from several objects which seem to have very little use in them; as from the wildness of rocks and deserts, and the like grotesque parts of nature. Those who are versed in philosophy may still carry this consideration higher, by observing, that if matter had appeared to us endowed only with those real qualities which it actually possesses, it would have made but a very joyless and uncomfortable figure; and why has Providence given it a power of producing in us such imaginary qualities, and tastes and colours, sounds and smells, heat and cold, but that man, while he is conversant in the lower stations of nature, might have his mind cheered and delighted with agreeable sensations? In short, the whole universe is a kind of theatre filled with objects that either raise in us pleasure, amusement, or admiration.

* Sir Isaac Newton.

The reader's own thoughts will suggest to him the vicissitude of day and night, the change of seasons, with all that variety of scenes which diversify the face of nature, and fill the mind with a perpetual succession of beautiful and pleasing images.

I shall not here mention the several entertainments of art, with the pleasures of friendship, books, conversation, and other accidental diversions of life, because I would only take notice of such incitements to a cheerful temper as offer themselves to persons of all ranks and conditions, and which may sufficiently show us that Providence did not design this world should be filled with murmurs and repinings, or that the heart of man should be involved in gloom and melancholy.

I the more inculcate this cheerfulness of temper, as it is a virtue in which our countrymen are observed to be more deficient than any other nation. Melancholy is a kind of demon that haunts our island, and often conveys herself to us in an easterly wind. A celebrated French novelist, in opposition to those who begin their romances with the flowery season of the year, enters on his story thus, 'In the gloomy month of November, when the people of England hang and drown themselves, a disconsolate lover walked out into the fields,' &c.

Every one ought to fence against the temper of his climate or constitution, and frequently to indulge in himself those considerations which may give him a serenity of mind, and enable him to bear up cheerfully against those little evils and misfortunes which are common to human nature, and which, by a right improvement of them, will produce a satiety of joy, and an uninterrupted happiness.

At the same time that I would engage my reader to consider the world in its most agreeable lights, I must own there are many evils which naturally spring up amidst the entertainments that are provided for us; but these, if rightly considered, should be far from overcasting the mind with sorrow, or destroying that cheerfulness of temper which I have been recommending. This interspersion of evil with good, and pain with pleasure, in the works of nature, is very truly ascribed by Mr. Locke, in his Essay on Human Understanding, to a moral reason, in the following words.

'Beyond all this, we may find another reason why God hath scattered up and down several degrees of pleasure and pain, in all the things that environ and affect us, and blended them together, in almost all that our thoughts and senses have to do with; that we, finding imperfection, dissatisfaction, and want of complete happiness, in all the enjoyments which the creatures can afford us, might be led to seek it in the enjoyment of Him with whom "there is fulness of joy, and at whose right hand are pleasures for evermore."' L.

No. 288.] *Monday, May* 26, 1712.

——Tibi res antiquæ laudis et artis
Ingredior; sanctos ausus recludere fontes.
Virg. Georg. ii. 174.

For thee, I dare unlock the sacred spring,
And arts disclos'd by ancient sages sing.

'Mr. Spectator,—It is my custom, when I read your papers, to read over the quotations in the authors from whence you take them. As you mentioned a passage lately out of the second chapter of Solomon's Song, it occasioned my looking into it; and, upon reading it, I thought the ideas so exquisitely soft and tender, that I could not help making this paraphrase of it: which, now it is done, I can as little forbear sending to you. Some marks of your approbation, which I have already received, have given me so sensible a taste of them, that I cannot forbear endeavouring after them as often as I can with any appearance of success. I am, sir, your most obedient humble servant.'

THE SECOND CHAPTER OF SOLOMON'S SONG.

I.

"As when in Sharon's field the blushing rose
Does its chaste bosom to the morn disclose,
Whilst all around the Zephyrs bear
The fragrant odours through the air,
Or as the lily in the shady vale
Does o'er each flow'r with beauteous pride prevail,
And stands with dews and kindest sunshine blest,
In fair pre-eminence, superior to the rest:
So if my Love, with happy influence, shed
His eyes' bright sunshine on his lover's head,
Then shall the rose of Sharon's field,
And whitest lilies, to my beauties yield,
Then fairest flow'rs with studious art combine,
The roses with the lilies join,
And their united charms are less than mine.

II.

" As much as fairest lilies can surpass
A thorn in beauty, or in height the grass;
So does my Love, among the virgins shine,
Adorn'd with graces more than half divine:
Or as a tree, that, glorious to behold,
Is hung with apples all of ruddy gold,
Hesperian fruit, and, beautifully high,
Extends its branches to the sky;
So does my Love the virgins' eyes invite;
'Tis he alone can fix their wand'ring sight,
Among ten thousand eminently bright.

III.

" Beneath his pleasing shade
My wearied limbs at ease I laid,
And on his fragrant boughs reclin'd my head,
I pull'd the golden fruit with eager haste;
Sweet was the fruit, and pleasing to the taste!
With sparkling wine he crown'd the bowl,
With gentle ecstacies he fill'd my soul;
Joyous we sat beneath the shady grove,
And o'er my head he hung the banners of his love.

IV.

" I faint! I die! my lab'ring breast
Is with the mighty weight of love opprest!
I feel the fire possess my heart,
And pain convey'd to every part.
Through all my veins the passion flies,
My feeble soul forsakes its place,
A trembling faintness seals my eyes,
And paleness dwells upon my face:
O! let my love with pow'rful odours stay
My fainting love-sick soul, that dies away
One hand beneath me let him place,
With t'other press me in a chaste embrace.

V.

" I charge you, nymphs of Sion, as you go
Arm'd with the sounding quiver and the bow,
Whilst thro' the lonesome woods you rove,
You ne'er disturb my sleeping love.
Be only gentle Zephyrs there
With downy wings to fan the air;
Let sacred silence dwell around,
To keep off each intruding sound.
And when the balmy slumber leaves his eyes,
May he to joys, unknown till then, arise!

VI.

"But see! he comes! with what majestic gait
He onward bears his lovely state!
Now through the lattice he appears,
With softest words dispels my fears.
Arise, my fair one, and receive
All the pleasures love can give!
For now the sullen winter's past,
No more we fear the northern blast;
No storms nor threat'ning clouds appear,
No falling rains deform the year;
My love admits of no delay,
Arise, my fair, and come away!

VII.

" Already, see! the teeming earth
Brings forth the flow'rs, her beauteous birth,
The dews, and soft-descending show'rs,
Nurse the new-born tender flow'rs.
Hark! the birds melodious sing,
And sweetly usher in the spring.
Close by his fellow sits the dove,
And billing whispers her his love.
The spreading vines with blossoms swell,
Diffusing round a grateful smell.
Arise, my fair one, and receive
All the blessings love can give:
For love admits of no delay,
Arise, my fair, and come away!

VIII.

" As to its mate the constant dove
Flies through the covert of the spicy grove,
So let us hasten to some lonely shade,
There let me safe in thy lov'd arms be laid,
Where no intruding hateful noise
Shall damp the sound of thy melodious voice;
Where I may gaze, and mark each beauteous grace:
For sweet thy voice, and lovely is thy face.

IX.

" As all of me, my Love, is thine,
Let all of thee be ever mine,
Among the lilies we will play,
Fairer, my Love, thou art, than they;
Till the purple morn arise,
And balmy sleep forsake thine eyes;
Till the gladsome beams of day
Remove the shades of night away;
Then when soft sleep shall from thy eyes depart,
Rise like the bounding roe, or lusty hart,
Glad to behold the light again
From Bether's mountains darting o'er the plain."

T.

No. 389.] *Tuesday, May* 27, 1712.

——Meliora pii docuere parentes. *Hor.*

Their pious sires a better lesson taught.

Nothing has more surprised the learned in England, than the price which a small book, entitled Spaccio della Bestia triomfante, bore in a late auction.* This book

---

* The book here mentioned, was bought by Walter Clavel, esq. at the auction of the library of Charles Barnard, esq. in 1711, for 28 pounds. The same copy became successively the property of Mr. John Nicholas, of

was sold for thirty pounds. As it was written by one Jordanus Brunus, a professed atheist, with a design to depreciate religion, every one was apt to fancy, from the extravagant price it bore, that there must be something in it very formidable.

I must confess that, happening to get a sight of one of them myself, I could not forbear perusing it with this apprehension; but found there was so very little danger in it, that I shall venture to give my reader a fair account of the whole plan upon which this wonderful treatise is built.

The author pretends that Jupiter once upon a time, resolved upon a reformation of the constellations: for which purpose, having summoned the stars together, he complains to them of the great decay of the worship of the gods, which he thought so much the harder, having called several of those celestial bodies by the names of the heathen deities, and by that means made the heavens as it were a book of the pagan theology. Momus tells him that this is not to be wondered at, since there were so many scandalous stories of the deities. Upon which the author takes occasion to cast reflections upon all other religions, concluding that Jupiter, after a full hearing, discarded the deities out of heaven, and called the stars by the names of the moral virtues.

The short fable, which has no pretence in it to reason or argument, and but a very small share of wit, has however recommended itself, wholly by its impiety, to those weak men who would distinguish themselves by the singularity of their opinions.

There are two considerations which have been often urged against atheists, and which they never yet could get over. The first is, that the greatest and most eminent persons of all ages have been against them, and always complied with the public forms of worship established in their respective countries, when there was nothing in them either derogatory to the honour of the Supreme Being, or prejudicial to the good of mankind.

The Platos and Ciceros among the ancients; the Bacons, the Boyles, and the Lockes, among our own countrymen; are all instances of what I have been saying; not to mention any of the divines, however celebrated, since our adversaries challenge all those, as men who have too much interest in this case to be impartial evidences.

But what has been often urged as a consideration of much more weight, is not only the opinion of the better sort, but the general consent of mankind to this great truth; which I think could not possibly have come to pass, but from one of the three following reasons: either that the idea of a God is innate and co-existent with the mind itself; or that this truth is so very obvious, that it is discovered by the first exertion of reason in persons of the most ordinary capacities; or lastly, that it has been delivered down to us through all ages by a tradition from the first man.

The atheists are equally confounded, to whichever of these three causes we assign it; they have been so pressed by this last argument from the general consent of mankind, that after great search and pains they pretend to have found out a nation of atheists, I mean that polite people the Hottentots.

I dare not shock my readers with the description of the customs and manners of these barbarians, who are in every respect scarce one degree above brutes, having no language among them but a confused gabble, which is neither well understood by themselves nor others.

It is not, however, to be imagined how much the atheists have gloried in these their good friends and allies.

If we boast of a Socrates or a Seneca, they may now confront them with these great philosophers the Hottentots.

Though even this point has, not without reason, been several times controverted, I see no manner of harm it could do to religion, if we should entirely give them up this elegant part of mankind.

Methinks nothing more shows the weakness of their cause, than that no division of their fellow-creatures join with them but those among whom they themselves own reason is almost defaced, and who have but little else but their shape which can entitle them to any place in the species.

Besides these poor creatures, there have now and then been instances of a few crazy people in several nations who have denied the existence of a deity.

The catalogue of these is, however, very short; even Vanina, the most celebrated champion for the cause, professed before his judges that he believed the existence of a God: and, taking up a straw which lay before him on the ground, assured them that alone was sufficient to convince him of it: alleging several arguments to prove that it was impossible nature alone could create any thing.

I was the other day reading an account of Casimir Lyszynski, a gentleman of Poland, who was convicted and executed for this crime. The manner of his punishment was very particular. As soon as his body was

---

Mr. Joseph Ames, of Sir Peter Thompson, and of M. C. Tutet, esq. among whose books it was lately sold by auction, at Mr. Gerrard's in Litchfield-street. The author of this book, Giordano Bruno, was a native of Nola, in the kingdom of Naples, and burnt at Rome by order of the inquisition in 1600. Morhoff, speaking of atheists, says, '*Jordanum tamen Brunum huic classi non annumerarem,—manifesto in illo atheismi vestigia non deprehendo.*' Polyhist. i. 1. 8. 22. Bruno published many other writings said to be atheistical. The book spoken of here was printed, not at Paris, as is said in the title-page, nor in 1544, but at London, and in 1584, 12mo. dedicated to sir Philip Sidney. It was for some time so little regarded, that it was sold with five other books of the same author, for 25 pence French, at the sale of Mr. Bigor's library in 1706; but it is now very scarce, and has been sold at the exorbitant price of 50*l*. Niceron. Hommes I'lust. tom. xvii. p. 211. There was an edition of it in English in 1713.

burnt, his ashes were put into a cannon, and shot into the air towards Tartary.

I am apt to believe, that if something like this method of punishment should prevail in England (such is the natural good sense of the British nation,) that whether we rammed an atheist whole into a great gun, or pulverized our infidels, as they do in Poland, we should not have many charges.

I should, however, premise, while our ammunition lasted, that, instead of Tartary, we should always keep two or three cannons ready pointed towards the Cape of Good Hope, in order to shoot our unbelievers into the country of the Hottentots.

In my opinion, a solemn judicial death is too great an honour for an atheist; though I must allow the method of exploding him, as it is practised in this ludicrous kind of martyrdom, has something in it proper enough to the nature of his offence.

There is indeed a great objection against this manner of treating them. Zeal for religion is of so effective a nature that it seldom knows where to rest: for which reason I am afraid, after having discharged our atheists, we might possibly think of shooting off our sectaries; and as one does not foresee the vicissitudes of human affairs, it might one time or other come to a man's own turn to fly out of the mouth of a demi-culverin.

If any of my readers imagine that I have treated these gentlemen in too ludicrous a manner, I must confess, for my own part, I think reasoning against such unbelievers, upon a point that shocks the common sense of mankind, is doing them too great an honour, giving them a figure in the eye of the world, and making people fancy that they have more in them than they really have.

As for those persons who have any scheme of religious worship, I am for treating such with the utmost tenderness, and should endeavour to show them their errors with the greatest temper and humanity; but as these miscreants are for throwing down religion in general, for stripping mankind of what themselves own is of excellent use in all great societies, without once offering to establish any thing in the room of it, I think the best way of dealing with them, is to retort their own weapons upon them, which are those of scorn and mockery. X.

No. 390.] *Wednesday, May* 28, 1712.

Non pudendo, sed non fasciendo id quod non decet, impudentiæ nomen effugere debemus. *Tull.*

It is not by blushing, but by not doing what is unbecoming, that we ought to guard against the imputation of impudence.

MANY are the epistles I receive from ladies extremely afflicted that they lie under the observation of scandalous people, who love to defame their neighbours, and make the unjustest interpretation of innocent and indifferent actions. They describe their own behaviour so unhappily, that there indeed lies some cause of suspicion upon them. It is certain, that there is no authority for persons who have nothing else to do, to pass away hours of conversation upon the miscarriages of other people; but since they will do so, they who value their reputation should be cautious of appearances to their disadvantage: but very often our young women, as well as the middle-aged, and the gay part of those growing old, without entering into a formal league for that purpose, to a woman, agree upon a short way to preserve their characters, and go on in a way that at best is only not vicious. The method is, when an ill-natured or talkative girl has said any thing that bears hard upon some part of another's carriage, this creature, if not in any of their little cabals, is run down for the most censorious, dangerous body in the world. Thus they guard their reputation rather than their modesty; as if guilt lay in being under the imputation of a fault, and not in a commission of it. Orbicilla is the kindest poor thing in town, but the most blushing creature living. It is true, she has not lost the sense of shame, but she has lost the sense of innocence. If she had more confidence, and never did any thing which ought to stain her cheeks, would she not be much more modest, without that ambiguous suffusion which is the livery both of guilt and innocence? Modesty consists in being conscious of no ill, and not in being ashamed of having done it. When people go upon any other foundation than the truth of their own hearts for the conduct of their actions, it lies in the power of scandalous tongues to carry the world before them, and make the rest of mankind fall in with the ill for fear of reproach. On the other hand, to do what you ought, is the ready way to make calumny either silent, or ineffectually malicious. Spenser, in his Fairy Queen, says admirably to young ladies under the distress of being defamed:

'The best,' said he, 'that I can you advise,
Is to avoid th' occasion of the ill:
For when the cause, whence evil doth arise,
Removed is, th' effect surceaseth still.
Abstain from pleasure, and restrain your will,
Subdue desire, and bridle loose delight:
Use scanty diet, and forbear your fill;
Shun secresy, and talk in open sight;
So shall you soon repair your present evil plight.'

Instead of this care over their words and actions, recommended by a poet in old queen Bess's days, the modern way is to say and do what you please, and yet be the prettiest sort of woman in the world. If fathers and brothers will defend a lady's honour, she is quite as safe as in her own innocence. Many of the distressed, who suffer under the malice of evil tongues, are so harmless, that they are every day they live asleep till twelve at noon; concern themselves with nothing but their own persons till two; take their necessary food between that time and four; visit, go to the play, and sit up at cards till towards the ensuing morn; and the malicious world shall draw conclusions from innocent glances, short whispers, or pretty familiar railleries with fashionable men, that these fair ones are not as rigid as vestals. It is certain, say these 'goodest' creatures, very well, that virtue does not consist in constrained behaviour and wry faces; that must be allowed: but there is a decency in the aspect and manner of ladies, contracted from a habit of virtue, and from general reflections that regard a modest conduct, all which may be understood, though they cannot be described. A young woman of this sort claims an esteem mixed with affection and honour, and meets with no defamation; or, if she does, the wild malice is overcome with an undisturbed perseverance in her innocence. To speak freely, there are such coveys of coquettes about this town, that if the peace were not kept by some impertinent tongues of their own sex, which keep them under some restraint, we should have no manner of engagement upon them to keep them in any tolerable order.

As I am a Spectator, and behold how plainly one part of woman-kind balance the behaviour of the other, whatever I may think of tale-bearers or slanderers, I cannot wholly suppress them, no more than a general would discourage spies. The enemy would easily surprise him whom they knew had no intelligence of their motions. It is so far otherwise with me, that I acknowledge I permit a she-slanderer or two in every quarter of the town, to live in the characters of coquettes, and take all the innocent freedoms of the rest, in order to send me information of the behaviour of the respective sisterhoods.

But as the matter of respect to the world which looks on, is carried on, methinks it is so very easy to be what is in general called virtuous, that it need not cost one hour's reflection in a month to deserve that appellation. It is pleasant to hear the pretty rogues talk of virtue and vice among each other. 'She is the laziest creature in the world, but I must confess, strictly virtuous; the peevishest hussy breathing, but as to her virtue, she is without blemish. She has not the least charity for any of her acquaintance, but I must allow her rigidly virtuous.' As the unthinking part of the male world call every man a man of honour who is not a coward; so the crowd of the other sex terms every woman who will not be a wench, virtuous.

T.

No. 391.] *Thursday, May 29, 1712.*

———Non tu prece poscis emaci,
Quæ nisi seductis nequeas committere divis:
At bona pars procerum tacita libabit acerra. [susurros
Haud cuivis promptum est, murmurque humilesque
Tollere de templis; et aperto vivere voto.
Mens bona, fama, fides; hæc clare, et ut audiat hospes,
Illa sibi introrsum et sub lingua immurmurat: O si
Ebullit patrui præclarum funus! Et O si
Sub rastro crepet argenti mihi seria dextro
Hercule! pupillumve utinam, quem proximus hæres
Impello, expungam! *Pers.* Sat. ii. v. 3.

————Thou know'st to join
No bribe unhallow'd to a prayer of thine;
Thine, which can ev'ry ear's full test abide,
Nor need be mutter'd to the gods aside!
No, thou aloud may'st thy petitions trust;
Thou need'st not whisper, other great ones must.
For few, my friend, few dare like thee be plain,
And prayer's low artifice at shrines disdain.
Few from their pious mumblings dare depart,
And make profession of their inmost heart.
Keep me, indulgent Heaven, through life sincere,
Keep my mind sound, my reputation clear,
These wishes they can speak, and we can hear.
Thus far their wants are audibly express'd;
Then sinks the voice, and muttering groans the rest
Hear, hear at length, good Hercules, my vow!
O chink some pot of gold beneath my plow!
Could I, O could I to my ravish'd eyes
See my rich uncle's pompous funeral rise;
Or could I once my ward's cold corpse attend;
Then all were mine!'

Where Homer represents Phœnix, the tutor of Achilles, as persuading his pupil to lay aside his resentment, and give himself up to the entreaties of his countrymen, the poet, in order to make him speak in character, ascribes to him a speech full of those fables and allegories which old men take delight in relating, and which are very proper for instruction. 'The gods,' says he, 'suffer themselves to be prevailed upon by entreaties. When mortals have offended them by their transgressions, they appease them by vows and sacrifices. You must know, Achilles, that prayers are the daughters of Jupiter. They are crippled by frequently kneeling, have their faces full of scars and wrinkles, and their eyes always cast towards heaven. They are constant attendants on the goddess Ate, and march behind her. This goddess walks forward with a bold and haughty air; and, being very light of foot, runs through the whole earth, grieving and afflicting the sons of men. She gets the start of Prayers, who always follow her, in order to heal those persons whom she wounds. He who honours these daughters of Jupiter, when they draw near to him, receives great benefit from them; but as for him who rejects them, they entreat their father to give his orders to the goddess Ate, to punish him for his hardness of heart.' This noble allegory needs but little explanation; for, whether the goddess Ate signifies injury, as some have explained it; or guilt in general, as others; or divine justice, as I am more apt to think; the interpretation is obvious enough.

I shall produce another heathen fable relating to prayers, which is of a more diverting kind. One would think by some passages in it, that it was composed by Lucian, or at least by some author who has endeavoured to imitate his way of writing; but as dissertations of this nature are more curious than useful, I shall give my reader the fable, without any further inquiries after the author.

'Menippus the philosopher was a second time taken up into heaven by Jupiter, when for his entertainment, he lifted up a trap-door that was placed by his footstool. At its rising, there issued through it such a din of cries as astonished the philosopher. Upon his asking what they meant, Jupiter told him they were the prayers that were sent up to him from the earth. Menippus, amidst the confusion of voices, which was so great that nothing less than the ear of Jove could distinguish them, heard the words "riches, honour," and "long life," repeated in several different tones and languages. When the first hubbub of sounds was over, the trap-door being left open, the voices came up more separate and distinct. The first prayer was a very odd one; it came from Athens, and desired Jupiter to increase the wisdom and beard of his humble supplicant. Menippus knew it by the voice to be the prayer of his friend Licander the philosopher. This was succeeded by the petition of one who had just laden a ship, and promised Jupiter, if he took care of it, and returned it home again full of riches, he would make him an offering of a silver cup. Jupiter thanked him for nothing; and bending down his ear more attentively than ordinary, heard a voice complaining to him of the cruelty of an Ephesian widow, and begged him to breed compassion in her heart. "This," says Jupiter, "is a very honest fellow. I have received a great deal of incense from him; I will not be so cruel to him as not to hear his prayers." He was then interrupted with a whole volley of vows which were made for the health of a tyrannical prince by his subjects, who prayed for him in his presence. Menippus was surprised after having listened to prayers offered up with so much ardour and devotion, to hear low whispers from the same assembly, expostulating with Jove for suffering such a tyrant to live, and asking him how his thunder could lie idle? Jupiter was so offended with these prevaricating rascals, that he took down the first vows, and puffed away the last. The philosopher, seeing a great cloud mounting upwards, and making its way directly to the trap-door, inquired of Jupiter what it meant. "This," says Jupiter, "is the smoke of a whole hecatomb that is offered me by the general of an army, who is very importunate with me to let him cut off a hundred thousand men that are drawn up in array against him. What does the impudent wretch think I see in him, to believe that I will make a sacrifice of so many mortals as good as himself, and all this to his glory forsooth? But hark!" says Jupiter, "there is a voice I never heard but in time of danger: 'tis a rogue that is shipwrecked in the Ionian sea. I saved him on a plank but three days ago upon his promise to mend his manners; the scoundrel is not worth a groat, and yet has the impudence to offer me a temple, if I will keep him from sinking.—But yonder," says he, "is a special youth for you; he desires me to take his father, who keeps a great estate from him, out of the miseries of human life. The old fellow shall live till he makes his heart ache, I can tell him that for his pains." This was followed up by the soft voice of a pious lady, desiring Jupiter that she might appear amiable and charming in the sight of her emperor. As the philosopher was reflecting on this extraordinary petition, there blew a gentle wind through the trap-door which he at first took for a gentle gale of zephyrs, but afterwards found it to be a breeze of sighs. They smelt strong of flowers and incense, and were succeeded by most passionate complaints of wounds and torments, fire and arrows, cruelty, despair and death. Menippus fancied that such lamentable cries arose from some general execution, or from wretches lying under the torture; but Jupiter told him that they came up to him from the isle of Paphos, and that he every day received complaints of the same nature from that whimsical tribe of mortals who are called lovers. "I am so trifled with," says he, "by this generation of both sexes, and find it so impossible to please them, whether I grant or refuse their petitions, that I shall order a western wind for the future to intercept them in their passage, and blow them at random upon the earth." The last petition I heard was from a very aged man of near a hundred years old, begging but for one year more of life, and then promising to be contented. "This is the rarest old fellow!" says Jupiter; "he has made this prayer to me for above twenty years together. When he was but fifty years old, he desired only that he might live to see his son settled in the world: I granted it. He then begged the same favour for his daughter, and afterwards that he might see the education of a grandson. When all this was brought about, he puts up a petition that he might live to finish a house he was building. In short, he is an unreasonable old cur, and never wants an excuse; I will hear no more of him." Upon which he flung down the trap-door in a passion, and was resolved to give no more audiences that day.'

Notwithstanding the levity of this fable, the moral of it very well deserves our attention, and is the same with that which has been inculcated by Socrates and Plato, not to mention Juvenal and Persius, who have each of them made the finest satire in their whole works upon this subject. The vanity of men's wishes which are the natural prayers of the mind, as well as many of those secret devotions which they offer to the Supreme Being, are sufficiently exposed by it. Among other reasons for set forms of prayer, I have often thought it a very good one, that by this means the folly and extravagance of men's desires may be kept within due bounds, and not break out in absurd and ridiculous petitions on so great and solemn an occasion

I

No. 392.] *Friday, May* 30, 1712.

Per ambages et ministeria deorum
ræcipitandus est liber spiritus. *Petron.*

By fable's aid ungovern'd fancy soars,
And claims the ministry of heav'nly powers.

The transformation of Fidelio into a looking-glass.

'Mr. Spectator,—I was lately at a tea-table, where some young ladies entertained the company with a relation of a coquette in the neighbourhood, who had been discovered practising before her glass. To turn the discourse, which from being witty grew to be malicious, the matron of the family took occasion from the subject to wish that there were to be found amongst men such faithful monitors to dress the mind by, as we consult to adorn the body. She added, that if a sincere friend were miraculously changed into a looking-glass, she should not be ashamed to ask its advice very often. This whimsical thought worked so much upon my fancy the whole evening, that it produced a very odd dream.

'Methought that, as I stood before my glass, the image of a youth of an open ingenuous aspect appeared in it, who with a shrill voice spoke in the following manner:

"The looking-glass you see was heretofore a man, even I, the unfortunate Fidelio. I had two brothers, whose deformity in shape was made up by the clearness of their understanding. It must be owned, however, that (as it generally happens) they had each a perverseness of humour suitable to their distortion of body. The eldest, whose belly sunk in monstrously, was a great coward, and, though his splenetic contracted temper made him take fire immediately, he made objects that beset him appear greater than they were. The second, whose breast swelled into a bold relievo, on the contrary, took great pleasure in lessening every thing, and was perfectly the reverse of his brother. These oddnesses pleased company once or twice, but disgusted when often seen; for which reason, the young gentlemen were sent from court to study mathematics at the university.

"I need not acquaint you, that I was very well made, and reckoned a bright polite gentleman. I was the confidant and darling of all the fair; and if the old and ugly spoke ill of me, all the world knew it was because I scorned to flatter them. No ball, no assembly, was attended till I had been consulted. Flavia coloured her hair before me, Celia showed me her teeth, Panthea heaved her bosom, Cleora brandished her diamond; I have seen Cloe's foot, and tied artificially the garters of Rhodope.

"It is a general maxim, that those who dote upon themselves can have no violent affection for another; but on the contrary, I found that the women's passion rose for me in proportion to the love they bore to themselves. This was verified in my amour with Narcissa, who was so constant to me, that is was pleasantly said, had I been little enough, she would have hung me at her girdle. The most dangerous rival I had, was a gay empty fellow, who by the strength of a long intercourse with Narcissa, joined to his natural endowments, had formed himself into a perfect resemblance with her. I had been discarded, had she not observed that he frequently asked my opinion about matters of the last consequence. This made me still more considerable in her eye.

"Though I was eternally caressed by the ladies, such was their opinion of my honour, that I was never envied by the men. A jealous lover of Narcissa one day thought he had caught her in an amorous conversation: for, though he was at such a distance that he could hear nothing, he imagined strange things from her airs and gestures. Sometimes with a serene look she stepped back in a listening posture, and brightened into an innocent smile. Quickly after she swelled into an air of majesty and disdain, then kept her eyes half shut after a languishing manner, then covered her blushes with her hand, breathed a sigh, and seemed ready to sink down. In rushed the furious lover; but how great was his surprise to see no one there but the innocent Fidelio with his back against the wall betwixt two windows!

"It were endless to recount all my adventures. Let me hasten to that which cost me my life, and Narcissa her happiness.

"She had the misfortune to have the small-pox, upon which I was expressly forbid her sight, it being apprehended that it would increase her distemper, and that I should infallibly catch it at the first look. As soon as she was suffered to leave her bed, she stole out of her chamber, and found me all alone in an adjoining apartment. She ran with transport to her darling, and without mixture of fear lest I should dislike her. But, oh me! what was her fury when she heard me say, I was afraid and shocked at so loathsome a spectacle! She stepped back, swollen with rage, to see if I had the insolence to repeat it. I did, with this addition, that her ill-timed passion had increased her ugliness. Enraged, inflamed, distracted, she snatched a bodkin, and with all her force stabbed me to the heart. Dying, I preserved my sincerity, and expressed the truth though in broken words; and by reproachful grimaces to the last I mimicked the deformity of my murderess.

"Cupid, who always attends the fair, and pitied the fate of so useful a servant as I was, obtained of the destinies, that my body should remain incorruptible, and retain the qualities my mind had possessed. I immediately lost the figure of a man, and became smooth, polished, and bright, and to this day am the first favourite of the ladies." T.

No. 393.] *Saturday, May* 31, 1712.

Nescio qua præter solitum dulcedine læti.
Virg. Georg. i. 412.

Unusual sweetness purer joys inspires.

LOOKING over the letters that have been sent me, I chanced to find the following one, which I received about two years ago from an ingenious friend who was then in Denmark.

'Copenhagen, May 1, 1710.

'DEAR SIR,—The spring with you has already taken possession of the fields and woods. Now is the season of solitude, and of moving complaints upon trivial sufferings. Now the griefs of lovers begin to flow, and the wounds to bleed afresh. I, too, at this distance from the softer climates, am not without my discontents at present. You may perhaps laugh at me for a most romantic wretch, when I have disclosed to you the occasion of my uneasiness: and yet I cannot help thinking my unhappiness real, in being confined to a region which is the very reverse of Paradise. The seasons here are all of them unpleasant, and the country quite destitute of rural charms. I have not heard a bird sing, nor a brook murmur, nor a breeze whisper, neither have I been blest with the sight of a flowery meadow, these two years. Every wind here is a tempest, and every water a turbulent ocean. I hope, when you reflect a little, you will not think the grounds of my complaint in the least frivolous and unbecoming a man of serious thought; since the love of woods, of fields and flowers, of rivers and fountains, seems to be a passion implanted in our natures the most early of any, even before the fair sex had a being. I am, sir, &c.

Could I transport myself with a wish, from one country to another, I should choose to pass my winter in Spain, my spring in Italy, my summer in England, and my autumn in France. Of all these seasons there is none that can vie with the spring for beauty and delightfulness. It bears the same figure among the seasons of the year, that the morning does among the divisions of the day, or youth among the stages of life. The English summer is pleasanter than that of any other country in Europe, on no other account but because it has a greater mixture of spring in it. The mildness of our climate, with those frequent refreshments of dews and rains that fall among us, keep up a perpetual cheerfulness in our fields, and fill the hottest months of the year with a lively verdure.

In the opening of the spring, when all nature begins to recover herself, the same animal pleasure which makes the birds sing, and the whole brute creation rejoice, rises very sensibly in the heart of man. I know none of the poets who have observed so well as Milton those secret overflowings of gladness which diffuse themselves through the mind of the beholder, upon surveying the gay scenes of nature: he has touched upon it twice or thrice in his Paradise Lost, and describes it very beautifully under the name of 'vernal delight,' in that passage where he represents the devil himself as almost sensible of it:

Blossoms and fruits at once a golden hue
Appear'd, with gay enamell'd colours mixt:
On which the sun more glad impress'd his beams
Than in fair evening cloud, or humid bow,
When God hath shower'd the earth; so lovely seem'd
That landskip, and of pure now purer air
Meets his approach, and to the heart inspires
Vernal delight, and joy able to drive
All sadness, but despair, &c.

Many authors have written on the vanity of the creature, and represented the barrenness of every thing in this world, and its incapacity of producing any solid or substantial happiness. As discourses of this nature are very useful to the sensual and voluptuous, those speculations which show the bright side of things, and lay forth those innocent entertainments which are to be met with among the several objects that encompass us, are no less beneficial to men of dark and melancholy tempers. It was for this reason that I endeavoured to recommend a cheerfulness of mind in my two last Saturday's papers, and which I would still inculcate, not only from the consideration of ourselves, and of that Being on whom we depend, nor from the general survey of that universe in which we are placed at present, but from reflections on the particular season in which this paper is written. The creation is a perpetual feast to the mind of a good man; every thing he sees cheers and delights him. Providence has imprinted so many smiles on nature, that it is impossible for a mind which is not sunk in more gross and sensual delights, to take a survey of them without several secret sensations of pleasure. The psalmist has, in several of his divine poems, celebrated those beautiful and agreeable scenes which make the heart glad, and produce in it that vernal delight which I have before taken notice of.

Natural philosophy quickens this taste of the creation, and renders it not only pleasing to the imagination, but to the understanding. It does not rest in the murmur of brooks and the melody of birds, in the shade of groves and woods, or in the embroidery of fields and meadows; but considers the several ends of Providence which are served by them, and the wonders of divine wisdom which appear in them. It heightens the pleasures of the eye, and raises such a rational admiration in the soul as is little inferior to devotion.

It is not in the power of every one to offer up this kind of worship to the great Author of nature, and to indulge these more refined meditations of heart, which are doubtless highly acceptable in his sight, I shall therefore conclude this short essay on that pleasure which the mind naturally conceives from the present season of the year, by the recommending of a practice for which every one has sufficient abilities.

I would have my readers endeavour to moralize this natural pleasure of the soul, and to improve this vernal delight, as Milton calls it, into a Christian virtue. When we find ourselves inspired with this pleasing instinct, this secret satisfaction and complacency arising from the beauties of the creation, let us consider to whom we stand indebted for all these entertainments of sense, and who it is that thus opens his hand and fills the world with good. The apostle instructs us to take advantage of our present temper of mind, to graft upon it such a religious exercise as is particularly conformable to it, by that precept which advises those who are sad to pray, and those who are merry to sing psalms. The cheerfulness of heart which springs up in us from the survey of nature's works, is an admirable preparation for gratitude. The mind has gone a great way towards praise and thanksgiving, that is filled with such secret gladness—a grateful reflection on the supreme cause who produces it, sanctifies it in the soul, and gives it its proper value. Such an habitual disposition of mind consecrates every field and wood, turns an ordinary walk into a morning or evening sacrifice, and will improve those transient gleams of joy which naturally brighten up and refresh the soul on such occasions, into an inviolable and perpetual state of bliss and happiness. I.

No. 394.] *Monday, June* 2, 1712.

Bene colligitur hæc pueris et mulierculis et servis et servorum similimis liberis esse grata: gravi vero homini et ea quæ fiunt judicio certo ponderanti, probari posse nullo modo.—*Tull.*

It is obvious to see, that these things are very acceptable to children, young women, and servants, and to such as most resemble servants; but that they can by no means meet with the approbation of people of thought and consideration.

I HAVE been considering the little and frivolous things which give men accesses to one another, and power with each other, not only in the common and indifferent accidents of life, but also in matters of greater importance. You see in elections for members to sit in parliament, how far saluting rows of old women, drinking with clowns, and being upon a level with the lowest part of mankind in that wherein they themselves are lowest, their diversions, will carry a candidate. A capacity for prostituting a man's self in his behaviour, and descending to the present humour of the vulgar, is perhaps as good an ingredient as any other for making a considerable figure in the world; and if a man has nothing else or better to think of, he could not make his way to wealth and distinction by properer methods, than studying the particular bent or inclination of people with whom he converses, and working from the observation of such their bias in all matters wherein he has any intercourse with them: for his ease and comfort he may assure himself, he need not be at the expense of any great talent or virtue to please even those who are possessed of the highest qualifications. Pride, in some particular disguise or other, (often a secret to the proud man himself) is the most ordinary spring of action among men. You need no more than to discover what a man values himself for; then of all things admire that quality, but be sure to be failing in it yourself in comparison of the man whom you court. I have heard, or read, of a secretary of state in Spain, who served a prince who was happy in an elegant use of the Latin tongue, and often writ despatches in it with his own hand. The king showed his secretary a letter he had written to a foreign prince, and, under the colour of asking his advice, laid a trap for his applause. The honest man read it as a faithful counsellor, and not only excepted against his tying himself down too much by some expressions, but mended the phrase in others. You may guess the despatches that evening did not take much longer time. Mr. Secretary as soon as he came to his own house, sent for his eldest son, and communicated to him that the family must retire out of Spain as soon as possible: 'for,' said he, 'the king knows I understand Latin better than he does.'

This egregious fault in a man of the world should be a lesson to all who would make their fortunes; but regard must be carefully had to the person with whom you have to do; for it is not to be doubted but a great man of common sense must look with secret indignation, or bridled laughter, on all the slaves who stand around him with ready faces to approve and smile at all he says in the gross. It is good comedy enough to observe a superior talking half sentences, and playing an humble admirer's countenance from one thing to another, with such perplexity, that he knows not what to sneer in approbation of. But this kind of complaisance is peculiarly the manner of courts; in all other places you must constantly go further in compliance with the persons you have to do with, than a mere conformity of looks and gestures. If you are in a country life, and would be a leading man, a good stomach, a loud voice, and rustic cheerfulness, will go a great way, provided you are able to drink, and drink any thing. But I was just now going to draw the manner of behaviour I would advise people to practise under some maxim; and intimated, that every one almost was governed by his pride. There was an old fellow about forty years ago so peevish and fretful, though a man of business, that no one could come at him; but he frequented a particular little coffee-house, where he triumphed over every body at trick-track and backgammon. The way to pass his office well, was first to be insulted by him at one of those games in his leisure hours; for his vanity was to show that he was a man of pleasure as well as business. Next to this sort of insinuation, which is called in all places (from its taking its birth in the household of princes) making one's court, the most prevailing way is, by what better-bred people call a present, the vulgar a bribe. I humbly conceive that such a thing is conveyed with more gallantry in a billet-doux that should be understood at the Bank, than in gross money: but as to stubborn people, who are so surly as to accept of neither note nor cash, having formerly dabbled in chemistry, I can only say, that one part of matter asks one thing, and another another, to make it fluent: but there is nothing but may be dissolved by a proper mean. Thus, the virtue which is too obdurate for gold or paper, shall melt away very kindly in a liquid. The island of Barbadoes (a shrewd people) manage all their appeals to Great Britain by a skilful distribution of citron water* among the whisperers about men in power. Generous wines do every day prevail, and that in great points, where ten thousand times their value would have been rejected with indignation.

But, to wave the enumeration of the sundry ways of applying by presents, bribes, management of people's passions and affections, in such a manner as it shall appear that the virtue of the best man is by one method or other corruptible, let us look out for some expedient to turn those passions and affections on the side of truth and honour. When a man has laid it down for a position, that parting with his integrity, in the minuter circumstance, is losing so much of his very self, self-love will become a virtue. By this means good and evil will be the only objects of dislike and approbation; and he that injures any man, has effectually wounded the man of this turn as much as if the harm had been to himself. This seems to be the only expedient to arrive at an impartiality; and a man who follows the dictates of truth and right reason, may by artifice be led into error, but never can into guilt. T.

No. 395.] *Tuesday, June 3*, 1712.

Quod nunc ratio est, impetus ante fuit.
Ovid. Rem. Amor. 10.

'Tis reason now, 'twas appetite before.

BEWARE of the ides of March,' said the Roman augur to Julius Cæsar: 'Beware of the month of May,' says the British Spectator to his fair country-women. The caution of the first was unhappily neglected, and Cæsar's confidence cost him his life. I am apt to flatter myself that my pretty readers had much more regard to the advice I gave them, since I have yet received very few accounts of any notorious trips made in the last month.

But, though I hope for the best, I shall not pronounce too positively on this point, till I have seen forty weeks well over; at which period of time, as my good friend Sir Roger has often told me, he has more business as justice of peace, among the dissolute young people in the country, than at any other season of the year.

Neither must I forget a letter which I received near a fortnight since from a lady, who, it seems, could hold out no longer, telling me she looked upon the month as then out, for that she had all along reckoned by the new style.

On the other hand, I have great reason to believe, from several angry letters which have been sent to me by disappointed lovers, that my advice has been of very signal service to the fair sex, who, according to the old proverb, were 'forewarned, forearmed.'

One of these gentlemen tells me, that he would have given me a hundred pounds, rather than I should have published that paper; for that his mistress, who had promised to explain herself to him about the beginning of May, upon reading that discourse told him, that she would give him her answer in June.

Thyrsis acquaints me, that when he desired Sylvia to take a walk in the fields, she told him, the Spectator had forbidden her.

Another of my correspondents, who writes himself Mat Meager, complains that, whereas he constantly used to breakfast with his mistress upon chocolate; going to wait upon her the first of May, he found his usual treat very much changed for the worse, and has been forced to feed ever since upon green tea.

As I begun this critical season with a caveat to the ladies, I shall conclude it with a congratulation, and do most heartily wish them joy of their happy deliverance.

They may now reflect with pleasure on the dangers they have escaped, and look back with as much satisfaction on the perils that threatened them, as their great grandmothers did formerly on the burning ploughshares, after having passed through the ordeal trial. The instigations of the spring are now abated. The nightingale gives over her 'love-labour'd song,' as Milton phrases it; the blossoms are fallen, and the beds of flowers swept away by the scythe of the mower.

I shall now allow my fair readers to return to their romances and chocolate, provided they make use of them with moderation, till about the middle of the month, when the sun shall have made some progress in the Crab. Nothing is more dangerous than too much confidence and security. The Trojans, who stood upon their guard all the while the Grecians lay before their city, when they fancied the siege was raised, and the danger past, were the very next night burnt in their beds. I must also observe, that as in some climates there is perpetual spring, so in some female consti

---

* Then commonly called Barbadoes water.

tutions there is a perpetual May. These are a kind of valetudinarians in chastity, whom I would continue in a constant diet. I cannot think these wholly out of danger, till they have looked upon the other sex at least five years through a pair of spectacles. Will Honeycomb has often assured me, that it is much easier to steal one of this species, when she has passed her grand climacteric, than to carry off an icy girl on this side five-and-twenty; and that a rake of his acquaintance, who had in vain endeavoured to gain the affections of a young lady of fifteen, had at last made his fortune by running away with her grandmother.

But as I do not design this speculation for the evergreens of the sex, I shall again apply myself to those who would willingly listen to the dictates of reason and virtue, and can now hear me in cold blood. If there are any who have forfeited their innocence, they must now consider themselves under that melancholy view in which Chamont regards his sister, in those beautiful lines:

'——— Long she flourish'd,
Grew sweet to sense, and lovely to the eye.
Till at the last a cruel spoiler came,
Cropt this fair rose, and rifled all its sweetness,
Then cast it like a loathsome weed away.'

On the contrary, she who has observed the timely cautions I gave her, and lived up to the rules of modesty, will now flourish like 'a rose in June,' with all her virgin blushes and sweetness about her. I must, however, desire these last to consider, how shameful it would be for a general who has made a successful campaign, to be surprised in his winter quarters. It would be no less dishonourable for a lady to lose, in any other month in the year, what she has been at the pains to preserve in May.

There is no charm in the female sex that can supply the place of virtue. Without innocence, beauty is unlovely, and quality contemptible; good-breeding degenerates into wantonness, and wit into impudence. It is observed, that all the virtues are represented by both painters and statuaries under female shapes; but if any of them has a more particular title to that sex, it is modesty. I shall leave it to the divines to guard them against the opposite vice, as they may be overpowered by temptations. It is sufficient for me to have warned them against it, as they may be led astray by instinct.

I desire this paper may be read with more than ordinary attention, at all tea-tables within the cities of London and Westminster. X.

No. 396.] *Wednesday, June 4, 1712.*

Barbara, Celarent, Darii, Ferio, Baralipton.

HAVING a great deal of business upon my hands at present, I shall beg the reader's leave to present him with a letter that I received about half a year ago from a gentleman at Cambridge, who styles himself Peter de Quir. I have kept it by me some months; and, though I did not know at first what to make of it, upon my reading it over very frequently I have at last discovered several conceits in it: I would not therefore have my reader discouraged if he does not take them at the first perusal.

'*To the Spectator.*

'From St. John's College, Cambridge, Feb. 3, 1712.

'SIR,—The monopoly of puns in this university has been an immemorial privilege of the Johnians:* and we can't help resenting the late invasion of our ancient rights as to that particular, by a little pretender to clenching in a neighbouring college, who in application to you by way of letter, a while ago, styled himself Philobrune. Dear sir, as you are by character a professed well-wisher to speculation, you will excuse a remark which this gentleman's passion for the brunette has suggested to a brother theorist; it is an offer towards a mechanical account of his lapse to punning, for he belongs to a set of mortals who value themselves upon an uncommon mastery in the more humane and polite parts of letters.

'A conquest by one of this species of females gives a very odd turn to the intellectuals of the captivated person, and very different from that way of thinking which a triumph from the eyes of another, more emphatically of the fair sex, does generally occasion. It fills the imagination with an assemblage of such ideas and pictures as are hardly any thing but shade, such as night, the devil, &c. These portraitures very near overpower the light of the understanding, almost benight the faculties, and give that melancholy tincture to the most sanguine complexion, which this gentleman calls an inclination to be in a brown-study, and is usually attended with worse consequences in case of a repulse. During this twilight of intellects the patient is extremely apt, as love is the most witty passion in nature, to offer at some pert sallies now and then, by way of flourish, upon the amiable enchantress, and unfortunately stumbles upon that mongrel miscreated (to speak in Miltonic) kind of wit, vulgarly termed the pun. It would not be much amiss to consult Dr. T—— W—— (who is certainly a very able projector, and whose system of divinity and spiritual mechanics obtains very much among the better part of our under-graduates) whether a general intermarriage, enjoined by parliament, between this sisterhood of the olive-beauties and the fraternity of the people called quakers, would not be a very serviceable expedient, and abate that overflow of light which shines within them so powerfully, that it dazzles their eyes, and dances them into a thousand vagaries of error and enthu-

* The students of St. John's College.

siasm. These reflections may impart some light towards a discovery of the origin of punning among us, and the foundation of its prevailing so long in this famous body. It is notorious from the instance under consideration, that it must be owing chiefly to the use of brown jugs, muddy belch, and the fumes of a certain memorable place of rendezvous with us at meals, known by the name of Staincoat Hole: for the atmosphere of the kitchen, like the tail of a comet, predominates least about the fire, but resides behind, and fills the fragrant receptacle above mentioned. Besides, it is further observable, that the delicate spirits among us, who declare against these nauseous proceedings, sip tea, and put up for critic and amour, profess likewise an equal abhorrence for punning, the ancient innocent diversion of this society. After all, sir, though it may appear something absurd that I seem to approach you with the air of an advocate for punning, (you who have justified your censures of the practice in a set dissertation upon that subject*) yet I am confident you will think it abundantly atoned for by observing, that this humbler exercise may be as instrumental in diverting us from any innovating schemes and hypotheses in wit, as dwelling upon honest orthodox logic would be in securing us from heresy in religion. Had Mr. W——n's† researches been confined within the bounds of Ramus or Crackenthorp, that learned news-monger might have acquiesced in what the holy oracles pronounced upon the deluge like other Christians; and had the surprising Mr. L——y been content with the employment of refining upon Shakspeare's points and quibbles (for which he must be allowed to have a superlative genius,) and now and then penning a catch or a ditty, instead of inditing odes and sonnets, the gentlemen of the *bon gout* in the pit would never have been put to all that grimace in damning the frippery of state, the poverty and languor of thought, the unnatural wit, and inartificial structure of his dramas. I am, sir, your very humble servant,

'PETER DE QUIR.'

No. 397.] *Thursday, June 5, 1712.*

——Dolor ipse disertam
Fecerat—— *Ovid.* Met. xiii. 225.

Her grief inspired her then with eloquence.

As the stoic philosophers discard all passions in general, they will not allow a wise man so much as to pity the afflictions of another, 'If thou seest thy friend in trouble,' says Epictetus, 'thou mayest put on a look of sorrow, and condole with him, but take care that thy sorrow be not real.' The more rigid of this sect would not comply so far as to show even such an outward appearance of grief; but when one told them of any calamity that had befallen even the nearest of their acquaintance, would immediately reply, 'What is that to me?' If you aggravated the circumstance of the affliction, and showed how one misfortune was followed by another, the answer was still, 'All this may be true, and what is it to me?'

For my own part, I am of opinion, compassion does not only refine and civilize human nature, but has something in it more pleasing and agreeable than what can be met with in such an indolent happiness, such an indifference to mankind, as that in which the Stoics placed their wisdom. As love is the most delightful passion, pity is nothing else but love softened by a degree of sorrow In short, it is a kind of pleasing anguish, as well as generous sympathy, that knits mankind together, and blends them in the same common lot.

Those who have laid down rules for rhetoric or poetry, advise the writer to work himself up, if possible, to the pitch of sorrow which he endeavours to produce in others. There are none therefore who stir up pity so much as those who indite their own sufferings. Grief has a natural eloquence belonging to it, and breaks out in more moving sentiments than can be supplied by the finest imagination. Nature on this occasion dictates a thousand passionate things which cannot be supplied by art.

It is for this reason that the short speeches or sentences which we often meet with in history make a deeper impression on the mind of the reader than the most laboured strokes in a well-written tragedy. Truth and matter of fact sets the person actually before us in the one, whom fiction places at a greater distance from us in the other. I do not remember to have seen any ancient or modern story more affecting than a letter of Ann of Bologne, wife to king Henry the Eighth, and mother to Queen Elizabeth, which is still extant in the Cotton library, as written by her own hand.

Shakspeare himself could not have made her talk in a strain so suitable to her condition and character. One sees in it the expostulation of a slighted lover, the resentment of an injured woman, and the sorrows of an imprisoned queen. I need not acquaint my readers that this princess was then under prosecution for disloyalty to the king's bed, and that she was afterwards publicly beheaded upon the same account; though this prosecution was believed by many to proceed, as she herself intimates, rather from the king's love to Jane Seymour, than from any actual crime of Ann of Bologne.

Queen Anne Boleyn's last letter to King Henry.

'SIR,

Cotton Lib. Otho C. 10. } Your grace's displeasure, and my imprisonment, are things so strange unto me, as what to write, or

---

* See Spect. No. 61.

† Mr. Whiston.

what to excuse, I am altogether ignorant. Whereas you send unto me, (willing me to confess a truth, and to obtain your favour) by such an one, whom you know to be mine ancient professed enemy, I no sooner received this message by him, than I rightly conceived your meaning; and if, as you say, confessing a truth indeed may procure my safety, I shall with all willingness and duty perform your command.

'But let not your grace ever imagine, that your poor wife will ever be brought to acknowledge a fault, where not so much as a thought thereof proceeded. And to speak a truth, never prince had wife more loyal in all duty, and in all true affection, than you have ever found in Ann Boleyn: with which name and place I could willingly have contented myself, if God and your grace's pleasure had been so pleased. Neither did I at any time so far forget myself in my exaltation, or received queenship, but that I always looked for such an alteration as I now find; for the ground of my preferment being on no surer foundation than your grace's fancy, the least alteration I knew was fit and sufficient to draw that fancy to some other object. You have chosen me from a low estate to be your queen and companion, far beyond my desert or desire. If then you found me worthy of such honour, good your grace, let not any light fancy, or bad counsel of mine enemies, withdraw your princely favour from me; neither let that stain, that unworthy stain of a disloyal heart towards your good grace, ever cast so foul a blot on your most dutiful wife, and the infant princess your daughter. Try me, good king, but let me have a lawful trial, and let not my sworn enemies sit as my accusers and judges; yea, let me receive an open trial, for my truth shall fear no open shame; then shall you see either mine innocence cleared, your suspicion and conscience satisfied, the ignominy and slander of the world stopped, or my guilt openly declared. So that, whatever God or you may determine of me, your grace may be freed from an open censure; and mine offence being so lawfully proved, your grace is at liberty, both before God and man, not only to execute worthy punishment on me as an unlawful wife, but to follow your affection, already settled on that party, for whose sake I am now as I am, whose name I could some good while since have pointed unto your grace, not being ignorant of my suspicion therein.

'But if you have already determined of me, and that not only my death, but an infamous slander must bring you the enjoying of your desired happiness; then I desire of God, that he will pardon your great sin therein, and likewise mine enemies, the instruments thereof; and that he will not call you to a strict account for your unprincely and cruel usage of me, at his general judgment seat, where both you and myself must shortly appear, and in whose judgment I doubt not (whatever the world may think of me,) mine innocence shall be openly known, and sufficiently cleared.

'My last and only request shall be, that myself may only bear the burden of your grace's displeasure, and that it may not touch the innocent souls of those poor gentlemen who (as I understand,) are likewise in straight imprisonment for my sake. If ever I have found favour in your sight, if ever the name of Ann Boleyn hath been pleasing in your ears, then let me obtain this request, and I will so leave to trouble your grace any further, with mine earnest prayers to the Trinity, to have your grace in his good keeping, and to direct you in all your actions. From my doleful prison in the Tower, this sixth of May; your most loyal and ever faithful wife,

L. 'ANN BOLEYN.'

No. 398.] *Friday, June* 6, 1712.

Insanire pares certa ratione modoque.
Hor. Sat. iii. Lib. 2. 272

——You'd be a fool,
With art and wisdom, and be mad by rule.
Creech.

CYNTHIO and Flavia are persons of distinction in this town, who have been lovers these ten months last past, and writ to each other for gallantry sake under those feigned names; Mr. Such-a-one and Mrs. Such-a-one not being capable of raising the soul out of the ordinary tracts and passages of life, up to that elevation which makes the life of the enamoured so much superior to that of the rest of the world. But ever since the beauteous Cecilia has made such a figure as she now does in the circle of charming women, Cynthio has been secretly one of her adorers. Cecilia has been the finest woman in the town these three months, and so long Cynthio has acted the part of a lover very awkwardly in the presence of Flavia. Flavia has been too blind towards him, and has too sincere a heart of her own to observe a thousand things which would have discovered this change of mind to any one less engaged than she was. Cynthio was musing yesterday in the piazza in Covent-garden, and was saying to himself that he was a very ill man to go on in visiting and professing love to Flavia, when his heart was enthralled to another. It is an infirmity that I am not constant to Flavia; but it would be a still greater crime, since I cannot continue to love her, to profess that I do. To marry a woman with the coldness that usually indeed comes on after marriage, is ruining one's self with one's eyes open; besides, it is really doing her an injury. This last consideration, forsooth, of injuring her in persisting, made him resolve to break off upon the first favourable opportunity of making her angry. When he was in this thought, he saw Robin the porter, who waits at Will's coffee-house, passing by. Robin, you must know, is the best man in the town for carrying a billet; the fellow has a thin body, swift step, demure looks, sufficient sense, and knows the town. This man carried Cynthio's first letter to Flavia, and, by frequent errands ever since, is well known to her. The fellow covers his knowledge of the nature of his messages with the most exquisite low humour imaginable. The first he obliged Flavia to take, was by complaining to her that he had a wife and three children, and if she did not take that letter, which he was sure there was no harm in, but rather love, his family must go supperless to bed, for the gentleman would pay him according as he did his business. Robin, therefore, Cynthio now thought fit to make use of, and gave him orders to wait before Flavia's door, and if she called him to her, and asked whether it was Cynthio who passed by, he should at first be loth to own it was, but upon importunity confess it. There needed not much search into that part of the town to find a well-dressed hussey fit for the purpose Cynthio designed her. As soon as he believed Robin was posted, he drove by Flavia's lodgings in a hackney-coach, and a woman in it. Robin was at the door, talking with Flavia's maid, and Cynthio pulled up the glass as surprised, and hid his associate. The report of this circumstance soon flew up stairs, and Robin could not deny but the gentleman favoured* his master; yet, if it was he, he was sure the lady was but his cousin, whom he had seen ask for him: adding, that he believed she was a poor relation; because they made her wait one morning till he was awake. Flavia immediately writ the following epistle, which Robin brought to Will's.

'June 4, 1712.

'SIR,—It is in vain to deny it, basest, falsest of mankind; my maid, as well as the bearer, saw you. The injured

'FLAVIA.'

After Cynthio had read the letter, he asked Robin how she looked, and what she said at the delivery of it. Robin said she spoke short to him, and called him back again, and had nothing to say to him, and bid him and all the men in the world go out of her sight; but the maid followed, and bid him bring an answer.

Cynthio returned as follows:

'June 4, Three afternoon, 1712.

'MADAM,—That your maid and the bearer have seen me very often is very certain; but I desire to know, being engaged at piquet, what your letter means by "'tis in vain to deny it." I shall stay here all the evening. Your amazed

'CYNTHIO.'

As soon as Robin arrived with this, Flavia answered:

* Resembled.

'DEAR CYNTHIO,—I have walked a turn or two in my ante-chamber since I writ to you, and have recovered myself from an impertinent fit which you ought to forgive me, and desire you would come to me immediately to laugh off a jealousy that you and a creature of the town went by in a hackney-coach an hour ago. I am your your humble servant, FLAVIA.

'I will not open the letter which my Cynthio writ upon the misapprehension you must have been under, when you writ, for want of hearing the whole circumstance.'

Robin came back in an instant, and Cynthio answered:

'Half an hour six minutes after three, June 4, Will's coffee-house.

'MADAM,—It is certain I went by your lodgings with a gentlewoman to whom I have the honour to be known; she is indeed my relation, and a pretty sort of a woman. But your starting manner of writing, and owning you have not done me the honour so much as to open my letter, has in it something very unaccountable, and alarms one that has had thoughts of passing his days with you. But I am born to admire you with all your little imperfections.

'CYNTHIO'

Robin ran back and brought for answer·

'Exact sir, that are at Will's coffee-house, six minutes after three, June 4; one that has had thoughts, and all my little imperfections. Sir, come to me immediately, or I shall determine what may perhaps not be very pleasing to you. FLAVIA.'

Robin gave an account that she looked excessive angry when she gave him the letter; and that he told her, for she asked, that Cynthio only looked at the clock, taking snuff, and writ two or three words on the top of the letter when he gave him his.

Now the plot thickened so well, as that Cynthio saw he had not much more to accomplish, being irreconcilably banished: he writ,

'MADAM,—I have that prejudice in favour of all you do, that it is not possible for you to determine upon what will not be very pleasing to your obedient servant,

'CYNTHIO.'

This was delivered, and the answer returned, in a little more than two seconds.

'SIR,—Is it come to this? You never loved me, and the creature you were with is the properest person for your associate. I despise you, and hope I shall soon hate you as a villain to the credulous

'FLAVIA.'

Robin ran back with:

'MADAM,—Your credulity when you are to gain your point, and suspicion when you fear to lose it, make it a very hard part to behave as becomes your humble slave,

'CYNTHIO.'

Robin whipt away and returned with,

'MR. WELLFORD,—Flavia and Cynthio are no more. I relieve you from the hard part of which you complain, and banish you from my sight for ever.

'ANN HEART.'

Robin had a crown for his afternoon's work; and this is published to admonish Cecilia to avenge the injury done to Flavia.

T.

No. 399.] *Saturday, June 7, 1712.*

Ut nemo in sese tentat descendere!—*Per.* Sat. iv. 23.

None, none descends into himself to find
The secret imperfections of his mind. *Dryden.*

HYPOCRISY at the fashionable end of the town is very different from hypocrisy in the city. The modish hypocrite endeavours to appear more vicious than he really is, the other kind of hypocrite more virtuous. The former is afraid of every thing that has the show of religion in it, and would be thought engaged in many criminal gallantries and amours which he is not guilty of. The latter assumes a face of sanctity, and covers a multitude of vices under a seeming religious deportment.

But there is another kind of hypocrisy, which differs from both these, and which I intend to make the subject of this paper: I mean that hypocrisy, by which a man does not only deceive the world, but very often imposes on himself: that hypocrisy which conceals his own heart from him, and makes him believe he is more virtuous than he really is, and either not attend to his vices, or mistake even his vices for virtues. It is this fatal hypocrisy, and self-deceit, which is taken notice of in those words. 'Who can understand his errors? cleanse thou me from secret faults.'

If the open professors of impiety deserve the utmost application and endeavours of moral writers to recover them from vice and folly, how much more may those lay a claim to their care and compassion, who are walking in the paths of death, while they fancy themselves engaged in a course of virtue! I shall endeavour therefore to lay down some rules for the discovery of those vices that lurk in the secret corners of the soul, and to show my reader those methods by which he may arrive at a true and impartial knowledge of himself. The usual means prescribed for this purpose are to examine ourselves by the rules which are laid down for our direction in sacred writ, and to compare our lives with the life of that person who acted up to the perfection of human nature, and is the standing example, as well as the great guide and instructor, of those who receive his doctrines. Though these two heads cannot be too much insisted upon, I shall but just mention them, since they have been handled by many great and eminent writers.

I would therefore propose the following methods to the consideration of such as would find out their secret faults, and make a true estimate of themselves.

In the first place, let them consider well what are the characters which they bear among their enemies. Our friends very often flatter us, as much as our own hearts. They either do not see our faults, or conceal them from us, or soften them by their representations, after such a manner that we think them too trivial to be taken notice of. An adversary, on the contrary, makes a stricter search into us, discovers every flaw and imperfection in our tempers; and though his malice may set them in too strong a light, it has generally some ground for what it advances. A friend exaggerates a man's virtues, an enemy inflames his crimes. A wise man should give a just attention to both of them, so far as they may tend to the improvement of one, and the diminution of the other. Plutarch has written an essay on the benefits which a man may receive from his enemies, and, among the good fruits of enmity, mentions this in particular, that by the reproaches which it casts upon us we see the worst side of ourselves, and open our eyes to several blemishes and defects in our lives and conversations, which we should not have observed without the help of such ill-natured monitors.

In order likewise to come at a true knowledge of ourselves, we should consider on the other hand how far we may deserve the praises and approbations which the world bestow upon us; whether the actions they celebrate proceed from laudable and worthy motives; and how far we are really possessed of the virtues which gain us applause among those with whom we converse. Such a reflection is absolutely necessary, if we consider how apt we are either to value or condemn ourselves by the opinions of others, and to sacrifice the report of our own hearts to the judgment of the world.

In the next place, that we may not deceive ourselves in a point of so much importance, we should not lay too great a stress on any supposed virtues we possess that are of a doubtful nature: and such we may esteem all those in which multitudes of men dissent from us, who are as good and wise as ourselves. We should always act with great cautiousness and circumspection in points where it is not impossible that we may be deceived. Intemperate zeal, bigotry, and persecution for any party or opinion, how praise-worthy soever they may appear to weak men of our own principles, produce infinite calamities among mankind, and are highly criminal in their own nature: and yet how many persons eminent for piety suffer such monstrous and absurd principles of action to take root in their minds under the colour of virtues!

For my own part, I must own I never yet knew any party so just and reasonable, that a man could follow it in its height and violence, and at the same time be innocent.

We should likewise be very apprehensive of those actions which proceed from natural constitutions, favourite passions, particular education, or whatever promotes our worldly interest or advantage. In these and the like cases, a man's judgment is easily perverted, and a wrong bias hung upon his mind. These are the inlets of prejudice, the unguarded avenues of the mind, by which a thousand errors and secret faults find admission, without being observed or taken notice of. A wise man will suspect those actions to which he is directed by something besides reason, and always apprehend some concealed evil in every resolution that is of a disputable nature, when it is conformable to his particular temper, his age, or way of life, or when it favours his pleasure or his profit.

There is nothing of greater importance to us than thus diligently to sift our thoughts, and examine all these dark recesses of the mind, if we would establish our souls in such a solid and substantial virtue, as will turn to account in that great day when it must stand the test of infinite wisdom and justice.

I shall conclude this essay with observing that the two kinds of hypocrisy I have here spoken of, namely, that of deceiving the world, and that of imposing on ourselves, are touched with wonderful beauty in the hundred and thirty-ninth psalm. The folly of the first kind of hypocrisy is there set forth by reflections on God's omniscience and omnipresence, which are celebrated in as noble strains of poetry as any other I ever met with, either sacred or profane. The other kind of hypocrisy, whereby a man deceives himself, is intimated in the two last verses, where the psalmist addresses himself to the great Searcher of hearts in that emphatical petition: 'Try me, O God! and seek the ground of my heart; prove me, and examine my thoughts. Look well if there be any way of wickedness in me, and lead me in the way everlasting.' L.

No. 400.] *Monday, June* 9, 1712.

——Latet anguis in herba.—*Virg*. Ecl. iii. 93.

There's a snake in the grass.—*English Proverb.*

It should, methinks, preserve modesty and its interests in the world, that the transgression of it always creates offence; and the very purposes of wantonness are defeated by a carriage which has in it so much boldness, as to intimate that fear and reluctance are quite extinguished in an object which would be otherwise desirable. It was said of a wit of the last age,

'Sedley has that prevailing gentle art,
Which can with a resistless charm impar
The loosest wishes to the chastest heart;
Raise such a conflict, kindle such a fire,
Between declining virtue and desire,
That the poor vanquish'd maid dissolves away
In dreams all night, in sighs and tears all day.'

This prevailing gentle art was made up of complaisance, courtship, and artful conformity to the modesty of a woman's manners. Rusticity, broad expression and forward obtrusion, offend those of education, and make the transgressors odious to all who have merit enough to attract regard. It is in this taste that the scenery is so beautifully ordered in the description which Antony makes in the dialogue between him and Dolabella, of Cleopatra in her barge.

'Her galley down the silver Cidnos row'd:
The tackling silk, the streamers wav'd with gold:
The gentle winds were lodg'd in purple sails;
Her nymphs, like Nereids, round her couch were plac'd
Where she, another sea-born Venus, lay;
She lay, and lean'd her cheek upon her hand,
And cast a look so languishingly sweet,
As if, secure of all beholders' hearts,
Neglecting she could take them. Boys, like Cupids,
Stood fanning with their painted wings the winds
That play'd about her face; but if she smil'd,
A darting glory seem'd to blaze abroad,
That men's desiring eyes were never weary'd,
But hung upon the object. To soft flutes
The silver oars kept time; and while they play'd
The hearing gave new pleasure to the sight;
And both to thought————'*

Here the imagination is warmed with all the objects presented, and yet there is no thing that is luscious, or what raises any idea more loose than that of a beautiful woman set off to advantage. The like, or a more delicate and careful spirit of modesty, appears in the following passage in one of Mr. Phillips's pastorals.

Breathe soft, ye winds! ye waters, gently flow!
Shield her, ye trees! ye flowers, around her grow!
Ye swains, I beg you pass in silence by!
My love in yonder vale asleep does lie.

Desire is corrected when there is a ten derness or admiration expressed which partakes the passion. Licentious language has something brutal in it, which disgraces humanity, and leaves us in the condition of the savages in the field. But it may be asked, To what good use can tend a discourse of this kind at all? It is to alarm chaste ears against such as have, what is above called, the 'prevailing gentle art.' Masters of that talent are capable of clothing their thoughts in so soft a dress, and something so distant from the secret purpose of their heart, that the imagination of the unguarded is touched with a fondness, which grows too insensibly to be resisted. Much care and concern for the lady's wel fare, to seem afraid lest she should be annoyed by the very air which surrounds her, and this uttered rather with kind looks, and expressed by an interjection, an 'ah,' or an 'oh,' at some little hazard in moving or making a step, than in any direct profession of love, are the methods of skilful admirers. They are honest arts when their purpose is such, but infamous when misap-

---

* Dryden's Al fo Love, act iii. sc. 1

plied. It is certain that many a young woman in this town has had her heart irrecoverably won, by men who have not made one advance which ties their admirers, though the females languish with the utmost anxiety. I have often, by way of admonition to my female readers, given them warning against agreeable company of the other sex, except they are well acquainted with their characters. Women may disguise it if they think fit; and the more to do it, they may be angry at me for saying it; but I say it is natural to them, that they have no manner of approbation of men, without some degree of love. For this reason he is dangerous to be entertained as a friend or visitant, who is capable of gaining any eminent esteem or observation, though it be never so remote from pretensions as a lover. If a man's heart has not the abhorrence of any treacherous design, he may easily improve approbation into kindness, and kindness into passion. There may possibly be no manner of love between them in the eyes of all their acquaintance; no, it is all friendship; and yet they may be as fond as shepherd and shepherdess, in a pastoral, but still the nymph and the swain may be to each other, no other, I warrant you, than Pylades and Orestes.

'When Lucy decks with flowers her swelling breast,
And on her elbow leans, dissembling rest;
Unable to refrain my madding mind,
Nor sheep nor pasture worth my care I find.

Once Delia slept, on easy moss reclin'd,
Her lovely limbs half bare, and rude the wind:
I smooth'd her coats, and stole a silent kiss:
Condemn me, shepherds, if I did amiss.'

Such good offices as these, and such friendly thoughts and concerns for another, are what make up the amity, as they call it, between man and woman.

It is the permission of such intercourse that makes a young woman come to the arms of her husband, after the disappointment of four or five passions which she has successively had for different men, before she is prudentially given to him for whom she has neither love nor friendship. For what should a poor creature do that has lost all her friends? There's Marinet the agreeable has, to my knowledge, had a friendship for lord Welford, which had like to break her heart: then she had so great a friendship for colonel Hardy, that she could not endure any woman else should do any thing but rail at him. Many and fatal have been disasters between friends who have fallen out, and these resentments are more keen than ever those of other men can possibly be; but in this it happens unfortunately, that as there ought to be nothing concealed from one friend to another, the friends of different sexes very often find fatal effects from their unanimity.

For my part, who study to pass life in as much innocence and tranquillity as I can, I shun the company of agreeable women as much as possible; and must confess that I have, though a tolerable good philosopher, but a low opinion of Platonic love: for which reason I thought it necessary to give my fair readers a caution against it, having, to my great concern, observed the waist of a Platonist lately swell to a roundness which is inconsistent with that philosophy.

T

No. 401.] *Tuesday, June* 10, 1712.

In amore hæc omnia insunt vitia. Injuriæ,
Suspiciones inimitiæ, induciæ,
Bellum, pax rursum. *Ter. Eun.* Act i. Sc. 1

It is the capricious state of love, to be attended with injuries, suspicions, enmities, truces, quarrelling, and reconcilement.

I SHALL publish for the entertainment of this day, an odd sort of a packet, which I have just received from one of my female correspondents.

'MR. SPECTATOR,—Since you have often confessed that you are not displeased your papers should sometimes convey the complaints of distressed lovers to each other, I am in hopes you will favour one who gives you an undoubted instance of her reformation, and at the same time a convincing proof of the happy influence your labours have had over the most incorrigible part of the most incorrigible sex. Yor must know, sir, I am one of that species of women, whom you have often characterized under the name of "jilts," and that I send you these lines as well to do public penance for having so long continued in a known error, as to beg pardon of the party offended. I the rather choose this way, because it in some measure answers the terms on which he intimated the breach between us might possibly be made up, as you will see by the letter he sent me the next day after I had discarded him; which I thought fit to send you a copy of, that you might the better know the whole case.

'I must further acquaint you, that before I jilted him, there had been the greatest intimacy between us for a year and a half together, during all which time I cherished his hopes, and indulged his flame. I leave you to guess, after this, what must be his surprise, when upon his pressing for my full consent one day, I told him I wondered what could make him fancy he had ever any place in my affections. His own sex allow him sense, and all ours good-breeding. His person is such as might, without vanity, make him believe himself not incapable of being beloved. Our fortunes, indeed, weighed in the nice scale of interest, are not exactly equal, which by the way was the true cause of my jilting him; and I had the assurance to acquaint him with the following maxim, that I should always believe that man's passion to be the most violent, who could offer me the largest settlement. I have since changed my opinion, and have endeavoured to let him know so much by several letters, but the barbarous man has refused them all; so that I have no way left of writing to him but by your assistance. If you can bring him about once more, I promise to send you all gloves and favours, and shall desire the favour of Sir Roger and yourself to stand as godfathers to my first boy. I am, sir, your most obedient humble servant,

'AMORET.'

Philander to Amoret.

'MADAM,—I am so surprised at the question you were pleased to ask me yesterday, that I am still at a loss what to say to it. At least my answer would be too long to trouble you with, as it would come from a person, who, it seems, is so very indifferent to you. Instead of it, I shall only recommend to your consideration the opinion of one whose sentiments on these matters I have often heard you say are extremely just. "A generous and constant passion," says your favourite author, "in an agreeable lover, where there is not too great a disparity in their circumstances, is the greatest blessing that can befal a person beloved; and if overlooked in one, may perhaps never be found in another."

'I do not, however, at all despair of being very shortly much better beloved by you than Antenor is at present; since, whenever my fortune shall exceed his, you were pleased to intimate, your passion would increase accordingly.

'The world has seen me shamefully lose that time to please a fickle woman, which might have been employed much more to my credit and advantage in other pursuits. I shall therefore take the liberty to acquaint you, however harsh it may sound in a lady's ears, that though your love-fit should happen to return, unless you could contrive a way to make your recantation as well known to the public as they are already apprized of the manner with which you have treated me, you shall never more see

'PHILANDER.'

Amoret to Philander.

'SIR,—Upon reflection, I find the injury I have done both to you and myself to be so great, that, though the part I now act may appear contrary to that decorum usually observed by our sex, yet I purposely break through all rules, that my repentance may in some measure equal my crime. I assure you, that in my present hopes of recovering you, I look upon Antenor's estate with contempt. The fop was here yesterday in a gilt chariot and new liveries, but I refused to see him.—Though I dread to meet your eyes, after what has passed, I flatter myself, that, amidst all their confusion, you will discover such a tenderness in mine, as none can imitate but those who love. I shall be all this month at lady D——'s in the country; but the woods, the fields, and gardens, without Philander, afford no pleasure to the unhappy

'AMORET.'

'I must desire you, dear Mr. Spectator, to publish this my letter to Philander as soon as possible, and to assure him that I know nothing at all of the death of his rich uncle in Gloucestershire.' X.

No. 402.] *Wednesday, June* 11, 1712.

——————et quæ
Ipse sibi tradit Spectator.——
Hor Ars Poet. 1. 181.

Sent by the Spectator to himself.

WERE I to publish all the advertisements I receive from different hands, and persons of different circumstances and quality, the very mention of them, without reflections on the several subjects, would raise all the passions which can be felt by human minds. As instances of this, I shall give you two or three letters; the writers of which can have no recourse to any legal power for redress, and seem to have written rather to vent their sorrow than to receive consolation.

'MR SPECTATOR,—I am a young woman of beauty and quality, and suitably married to a gentleman who doats on me. But this person of mine is the object of an unjust passion in a nobleman who is very intimate with my husband. This friendship gives him very easy access and frequent opportunities of entertaining me apart. My heart is in the utmost anguish, and my face is covered over with confusion, when I impart to you another circumstance, which is, that my mother, the most mercenary of all women, is gained by this false friend of my husband's to solicit me for him. I am frequently chid by the poor believing man, my husband, for showing an impatience of his friend's company; and I am never alone with my mother, but she tells me stories of the discretionary part of the world, and such-a-one, and such-a-one, who are guilty of as much as she advises me to. She laughs at my astonishment; and seems to hint to me, that, as virtuous as she has always appeared, I am not the daughter of her husband. It is possible that printing this letter may relieve me from the unnatural importunity of my mother, and the perfidious courtship of my husband's friend. I have an unfeigned love of virtue, and am resolved to preserve my innocence. The only way I can think of to avoid the fatal consequences of the discovery of this matter, is to fly away for ever, which I must do to avoid my husband's fatal resentment against the man who attempts to abuse him, and the shame of exposing a parent to infamy. The persons concerned will know these circumstances relate to them; and though the regard to virtue is dead in them, I have some hopes from their fear of shame upon reading this in your paper; which I conjure you to publish, if you have any compassion for injured virtue.

'SYLVIA.'

'MR. SPECTATOR,—I am the husband of a woman of merit, but am fallen in love, as they call it, with a lady of her acquaintance, who is going to be married to a gentleman who deserves her. I am in a trust relating to this lady's fortune, which makes my concurrence in this matter necessary; but I have so irresistible a rage and envy rise in me when I consider his future happiness, that against all reason, equity, and common justice, I am ever playing mean tricks to suspend the nuptials. I have no manner of hopes for myself; Emilia, for so I'll call her, is a woman of the most strict virtue; her lover is a gentleman whom of all others I could wish my friend; but envy and jealousy, though placed so unjustly, waste my very being; and, with the torment and sense of a demon, I am ever cursing what I cannot but approve. I wish it were the beginning of repentance, that I sit down and describe my present disposition with so hellish an aspect: but at present the destruction of these two excellent persons would be more welcome to me than their happiness. Mr. Spectator, pray let me have a paper on these terrible groundless sufferings, and do all you can to exorcise crowds who are in some degree possessed as I am. CANIBAL.'

'MR. SPECTATOR,—I have no other means but this to express my thanks to one man, and my resentment against another. My circumstances are as follow: I have been for five years last past courted by a gentleman of greater fortune than I ought to expect, as the market for women goes. You must, to be sure, have observed people who live in that sort of way, as all their friends reckon it will be a match, and are marked out by all the world for each other. In this view we have been regarded for some time, and I have above these three years loved him tenderly. As he is very careful of his fortune, I always thought he lived in a near manner, to lay up what he thought was wanting in my fortune to make up what he might expect in another. Within these few months I have observed his carriage very much altered, and he has affected a certain air of getting me alone, and talking with a mighty profusion of passionate words, how I am not to be resisted longer, how irresistible his wishes are, and the like. As long as I have been acquainted with him, I could not on such occasions say downright to him, "You know you may make me yours when you please." But the other night he with great frankness and impudence explained to me, that he thought of me only as a mistress. I answered this declaration as it deserved; upon which he only doubled the terms on which he proposed my yielding. When my anger heightened upon him, he told me he was sorry he had made so little use of the unguarded hours we had been together so remote from company; "as, indeed," continued he, "so we are at present." I flew from him to a neighbouring gentlewoman's house, and though her husband was in the room, threw myself on a couch, and burst into a passion of tears. My friend desired her husband to leave the room. "But," said he, "there is something so extraordinary in this, that I will partake in the affliction; and be it what it will, she is so much your friend, she knows she may command what services I can do her." The man sat down by me, and spoke so like a brother, that I told him my whole affliction. He spoke of the injury done me with so much indignation, and animated me against the love he said he saw I had for the wretch who would have betrayed me, with so much reason and humanity to my weakness, that I doubt not of my perseverance. His wife and he are my comforters, and I am under no more restraint in their company than if I were alone; and I doubt not but in a small time contempt and hatred will take place of the remains of affection to a rascal. I am, sir, your affectionate reader, DORINDA.'

'MR. SPECTATOR,—I had the misfortune to be an uncle before I knew my nephews from my nieces: and now we are grown up to better acquaintance, they deny me the respect they owe. One upbraids me with being their familiar, another will hardly be persuaded that I am an uncle, a third calls me little uncle, and a fourth tells me there is no duty at all due to an uncle. I have a brother-in-law whose son will win all my affection, unless you shall think this worthy of your cognizance, and will be pleased to prescribe some rules for our future reciprocal behaviour. It will be worthy the particularity of your genius to lay down some rules for his conduct who was, as it were, born an old man; in which you will much oblige, sir, your most obedient servant,

T. 'CORNELIUS NEPOS.'

No. 403.] *Thursday, June* 12, 1712.

Qui mores hominum multorum vidit——
Hor. Ars Poet. v. 142.

Of many men he saw the manners.

WHEN I consider this great city in its several quarters and divisions, I look upon it as an aggregate of various nations distinguished from each other by their respective customs, manners, and interests. The courts of two countries do not so much differ from one another, as the court and city, in their peculiar ways of life and conversation. In short, the inhabitants of St. James's, notwithstanding they live under the same laws, and speak the same language, are a distinct people from those of Cheapside, who are likewise removed from those of the Temple on one side, and those of Smithfield on the other, by several climates and degrees in their way of thinking and conversing together.

For this reason, when any public affair is upon the anvil, I love to hear the reflections that arise upon it in the several districts and parishes of London and Westminster, and to ramble up and down a whole day together, in order to make myself acquainted with the opinions of my ingenious countrymen. By this means I know the faces of all the principal politicians within the bills of mortality; and as every coffee-house has some particular statesman belonging to it, who is the mouth of the street where he lives, I always take care to place myself near him, in order to know his judgment on the present posture of affairs. The last progress that I made with this intention was about three months ago, when we had a current report of the king of France's death. As I foresaw this would produce a new face of things in Europe, and many curious speculations in our British coffee-houses, I was very desirous to learn the thoughts of our most eminent politicians on that occasion.

That I might begin as near the fountain-head as possible, I first of all called in at St. James's, where I found the whole outward room in a buzz of politics. The speculations were but very indifferent towards the door, but grew finer as you advanced to the upper end of the room, and were so very much improved by a knot of theorists, who sat in the inner room, within the steams of the coffee-pot, that I there heard the whole Spanish monarchy disposed of, and all the line of Bourbon provided for in less than a quarter of an hour.

I afterwards called in at St. Giles's, where I saw a board of French gentlemen sitting upon the life and death of their grand monarque. Those among them who had espoused the whig interest, very positively affirmed, that he departed this life about a week since, and therefore proceeded without any further delay to the release of their friends in the galleys, and to their own re-establishment; but, finding they could not agree among themselves, I proceeded on my intended progress.

Upon my arrival at Jenny Man's I saw an *alerte* young fellow that cocked his hat upon a friend of his who entered just at the same time with myself, and accosted him after the following manner: 'Well, Jack, the old prig is dead at last. Sharp's the word. Now or never, boy. Up to the walls of Paris directly.' With several other deep reflections of the same nature.

I met with very little variation in the politics between Charing-cross and Covent-garden. And upon my going into Will's, I found their discourse was gone off from the death of the French king to that of monsieur Boileau, Racine, Corneille and several other poets, whom they regretted on this occasion, as persons who would have obliged the world with very noble elegies on the death of so great a prince, and so eminent a patron of learning.

At a coffee-house near the Temple, I found a couple of young gentlemen engaged very smartly in a dispute on the succession to the Spanish monarchy. One of them seemed to have been retained as an advocate for the duke of Anjou, the other for his imperial majesty. They were both for regulating the title to that kingdom by the statute laws of England; but finding them going out of my depth, I passed forward to St. Paul's church-yard, where I listened with great attention to a learned man, who gave the company an account of the deplorable state of France during the minority of the deceased king.

I then turned on my right hand into Fish-street, where the chief politician of that quarter, upon hearing the news, (after having taken a pipe of tobacco, and ruminated for some time,) 'If,' says he, 'the king of France is certainly dead, we shall have plenty of mackerel this season: our fishery will not be disturbed by privateers, as it has been for these ten years past.' He afterwards considered how the death of this great man would affect our pilchards, and by several other remarks infused a general joy into his whole audience.

I afterwards entered a by-coffee-house, that stood at the upper end of a narrow lane, where I met with a nonjuror, engaged very warmly with a lace-man who was the great support of a neighbouring conventicle. The matter in debate was, whether the late French king was most like Augustus Cæsar or Nero. The controversy was carried on with great heat on both sides; and as each of them looked upon me very frequently during the course of their debate, I was under some apprehension that they would appeal to me, and therefore laid down my penny at the bar, and made the best of my way to Cheapside.

I here gazed upon the signs for some time before I found one to my purpose. The first object I met in the coffee-room was a person who expressed a great grief for the death of the French king: but upon explaining himself, I found his sorrow did not arise from the loss of the monarch, but from his having sold out of the bank about three days before he heard the news of it. Upon which a haberdasher, who was the oracle of the coffee-house, and had his circle of admirers about him, called several to witness that he had declared his opinion above a week before, that the French king was certainly dead; to which he added, that, considering the late advices we had received from France, it was impossible that it could be otherwise. As he was laying these together, and dictating to his hearers with great authority, there came in a gentleman from Garraway's, who told us that there were several letters from France just come in, with advice that the king was in good health, and was gone out a-hunting the very morning the post came away: upon which the haberdasher stole off his hat that hung upon a wooden peg by him, and retired to his shop with great confusion. This intelligence put a stop to my travels, which I had prosecuted with so much satisfaction; not being a little pleased to hear so many different opinions upon so great an event, and to observe how naturally upon such a piece of news every one is apt to consider it with regard to his particular interest and advantage. L.

No. 404.] *Friday, June* 13, 1712.

——Non omnia possumus omnes.—*Virg.* Ecl. viii. 63.

With different talents form'd, we variously excel.

NATURE does nothing in vain: the Creator of the universe has appointed every thing to a certain use and purpose, and determined it to a settled course and sphere of action, from which if it in the least deviates, it becomes unfit to answer those ends for which it was designed. In like manner it is in the dispositions of society, the civil economy is formed in a chain as well as the natural: and in either case the breach but of one link puts the whole in some disorder. It is, I think, pretty plain, that most of the absurdity and ridicule we meet with in the world, is generally owing to the impertinent affectation of excelling in characters men are not fit for, and for which nature never designed them.

Every man has one or more qualities which may make him useful both to himself and others. Nature never fails of pointing them out; and while the infant continues under her guardianship, she brings him on in his way, and then offers herself as a guide in what remains of the journey; if he proceeds in that course he can hardly miscarry. Nature makes good her engagements: for, as she never promises what she is not able to perform, so she never fails of performing what she promises. But the misfortune is, men despise what they may be masters of, and affect what they are not fit for; they reckon themselves already possessed of what their genius inclined them to, and so bend all their ambition to excel in what is out of their reach. Thus they destroy the use of their natural talents, in the same manner as covetous men do their quiet and repose: they can enjoy no satisfaction in what they have, because of the absurd inclination they are possessed with for what they have not.

Cleanthes has good sense, a great memory, and a constitution capable of the closest application. In a word, there was no profession in which Cleanthes might not have made a very good figure; but this won't satisfy him; he takes up an unaccountable fondness for the character of a fine gentleman; all his thoughts are bent upon this; instead of attending a dissection, frequenting the courts of justice, or studying the fathers, Cleanthes reads plays, dances, dresses, and spends his time in drawing-rooms; instead of being a good lawyer, divine, or physician, Cleanthes is a downright coxcomb, and will remain to all that know him a contemptible example of talents misapplied. It is to this affectation the world owes its whole race of coxcombs. Nature in her whole drama never drew such a part; she has sometimes made a fool, but a coxcomb is always of a man's own making, by applying his talents otherwise than Nature designed, who ever bears a high resentment for being put out of her course, and never fails of taking her revenge on those that do so. Opposing her tendency in the application of a man's parts has the same success as declining from her course in the production of vegetables, by the assistance of art and a hot-bed. We may possibly extort an unwilling plant, or an untimely salad; but how weak, how tasteless and insipid. Just as insipid as the poetry of Valerio. Valerio had an universal character, was genteel, had learning, thought justly, spoke correctly; it was believed there was nothing in which Valerio did not excel; and it was so far true, that there was but one; Valerio had no genius for poetry, yet he is resolved to be a poet; he writes verses, and takes great pains to convince the town that Valerio is not that extraordinary person he was taken for.

If men would be content to graft upon Nature, and assist her operations, what mighty effects might we expect! Tully would not stand so much alone in oratory, Virgil in poetry, or Cæsar in war. To build upon Nature, is laying a foundation upon a rock; every thing disposes itself into order as it were of course, and the whole work is half done as soon as undertaken. Cicero's genius inclined him to oratory, Virgil's to follow the train of the Muses; they piously obeyed the admonition, and were rewarded. Had Virgil attended the bar, his modest and ingenuous virtue would surely have made but a very indifferent figure; and Tully's declamatory inclination would have been as useless in poetry. Nature, if left to herself, leads us on in the best course, but will do nothing by compulsion and constraint; and if we are not always satisfied to go her way, we are always the greatest sufferers by it.

Wherever nature designs a production, she always disposes seeds proper for it, which are as absolutely necessary to the formation of any moral or intellectual excellence, as they are to the being and growth of plants, and I know not by what fate and folly it is, that men are taught not to reckon him equally absurd that will write verses in spite of Nature, with that gardener that should undertake to raise a jonquil or tulip without the help of their respective seeds.

As there is no good or bad quality that does not affect both sexes, so it is not to be imagined but the fair sex must have suffered by an affectation of this nature, at least as much as the other. The ill effect of it is in none so conspicuous as in the two opposite characters of Cælia and Iras; Cælia has all the charms of person, together with an abundant sweetness of nature, but wants wit, and has a very ill voice; Iras is ugly and ungenteel, but has wit and good sense. If Cælia would be silent, her beholders would adore her; if Iras would talk, her hearers would admire her; but Cælia's tongue runs incessantly, while Iras gives herself silent airs and soft languors, so that it is difficult to persuade oneself that Cælia has beauty, and Iras wit: each neglects her own excellence, and is ambitious of the other's character; Iras would be thought to have as much beauty as Cælia, and Cælia as much wit as Iras.

The great misfortune of this affectation is, that men not only lose a good quality, but also contract a bad one. They not only are unfit for what they were designed, but they assign themselves to what they are not fit for; and, instead of making a very good figure one way, make a very ridiculous one another. If Semanthe would have been satisfied with her natural complexion, she might still have been celebrated by the name of the olive beauty; but Semanthe has taken up an affectation to white and red, and is now distinguished by the character of the lady that paints so well. In a word, could the world be reformed to the obedience of that famed dictate, 'Follow Nature,' which the oracle of Delphos pronounced to Cicero, when he consulted what course of studies he should pursue, we should see almost every man as eminent in his proper sphere as Tully was in his, and should in a very short time find impertinence and affectation banished from among the women, and coxcombs and false characters from among the men. For my part I could never consider this preposterous repugnancy to Nature any otherwise, than not only as the greatest folly, but also one of the most heinous crimes, since it is a direct opposition to the disposition of Providence, and (as Tully expresses it) like the sin of the giants, an actual rebellion against heaven. Z.

No. 405.] *Saturday, June* 14, 1712

Οι δε πανημεριοι μολπη Θεον ιλασκοντο
Καλον αειδοντες Παιηονα κουροι Αχαιων,
Μελποντες Εκαεργον· ο δε φρενα τερπετ' ακουων.
Hom. Iliad. i. 472.

With hymns divine the joyous banquet ends;
The pæans lengthen'd till the sun descends;
The Greeks restor'd the grateful notes prolong;
Apollo listens and approves the song.—*Pope*

I AM very sorry to find, by the opera bills for this day, that we are likely to lose the greatest performer in dramatic music that is now living, or that perhaps ever appeared upon a stage. I need not acquaint my readers that I am speaking of signior Nicolini. The town is highly obliged to that excellent artist, for having shown us the Italian music in its perfection, as well as for that generous approbation he lately gave to an opera of our own country, in which the composer endeavoured to do justice to the beauty of the words, by following that noble example, which has been set him by the greatest foreign masters in that art.

I could heartily wish there was the same application and endeavours to cultivate and improve our church-music as have been lately bestowed on that of the stage. Our composers have one very great incitement to it. They are sure to meet with excellent words, and at the same time a wonderful variety of them. There is no passion that is not finely expressed in those parts of the inspired writings, which are proper for divine songs and anthems.

There is a certain coldness and indifference in the phrases of our European languages, when they are compared with the oriental forms of speech; and it happens very luckily, that the Hebrew idioms run into the English tongue with a particular grace and beauty. Our language has received innumerable elegances and improvements, from that infusion of Hebraisms, which are derived to it out of the poetical passages in holy writ. They give a force and energy to our expression, warm and animate our language, and convey our thoughts in more ardent and intense phrases, than any that are to be met with in our own tongue. There is something so pathetic in this kind of diction, that it often sets the mind in a flame, and makes our hearts burn within us. How cold and dead does a prayer appear, that is composed in the most elegant and polite forms of speech, which are natural to our tongue, when it is not heightened by that solemnity of phrase which may be drawn from the sacred writings! It has been said by some of the ancients, that if the gods were to talk with men, they would certainly speak in Plato's style; but I think we may say with justice, that when mortals converse with their Creator, they cannot do it in so proper a style as in that of the holy scriptures.

If any one would judge of the beauties of poetry that are to be met with in the divine writings, and examine how kindly the Hebrew manners of speech mix and incorporate with the English language; after having perused the book of Psalms; let him read a literal translation of Horace or Pindar. He will find in these two last such an absurdity and confusion of style, with such a comparative poverty of imagination, as will make him very sensible of what I have been here advancing.

Since we have therefore such a treasury of words, so beautiful in themselves, and so proper for the airs of music, I cannot but wonder that persons of distinction should give so little attention and encouragement to that kind of music, which would have its foundation in reason, and which would improve our virtue in proportion as it raises our delight. The passions that are excited by ordinary compositions generally flow from such silly and absurd occasions, that a man is ashamed to reflect upon them seriously; but the fear, the love, the sorrow, the indignation, that are awakened in the mind by hymns and anthems, make the heart better, and proceed from such causes as are altogether reasonable and praiseworthy. Pleasure and duty go hand in hand, and the greater our satisfaction is, the greater is our religion.

Music among those who are styled the chosen people was a religious art. The songs of Sion, which we have reason to believe were in high repute among the courts of the eastern monarchs, were nothing else but psalms and pieces of poetry that adored or celebrated the Supreme Being. The greatest conqueror in the holy nation, after the manner of the old Grecian lyrics, did not only compose the words of his divine odes, but generally set them to music himself: after which, his works, though they were consecrated to the tabernacle, became the national entertainment, as well as the devotion of the people.

The first original of the drama was a religious worship, consisting only of a chorus, which was nothing else but a hymn to a deity. As luxury and voluptuousness prevailed over innocence and religion, this form of worship degenerated into tragedies; in which however the chorus so far remembered its first office, as to brand every thing that was vicious, and recommend every thing that was laudable, to intercede with heaven for the innocent, and to implore its vengeance on the people.

Homer and Hesiod intimate to us how this art should be applied, when they represent the Muses as surrounding Jupiter, and warbling their hymns about his throne. I might show, from innumerable passages in ancient writers, not only that vocal and instrumental music were made use of in their religious worship, but that their most favourite diversions were filled with songs and hymns to their respective deities. Had we frequent entertainments of this nature among us, they would not a little purify and exalt our passions, give our thoughts a proper turn, and cherish those divine impulses in the soul, which every one feels that has not stifled them by sensual and immoral pleasures.

Music, when thus applied, raises noble hints in the mind of the hearer, and fills it with great conceptions. It strengthens devotion, and advances praise into rapture, lengthens out every act of worship, and produces more lasting and permanent impressions in the mind, than those which accompany any transient form of words that are uttered in the ordinary method of religious worship. O.

No. 406.] *Monday, June* 16, 1712.

Hæc studia adolescentiam alunt, senectutem, oblectant, secundas res ornant, adversis solatium et perfugium præbent; delectant domi, non impediunt foris; pernoctant nobiscum, peregrinatur, rusticantur.—*Tull.*

These studies nourish youth; delight old age; are the ornament of prosperity; the solacement and the refuge of adversity; they are delectable at home, and not burdensome abroad; they gladden us at nights, and on our journeys, and in the country.

The following letters bear a pleasing image of the joys and satisfactions of a private life. The first is from a gentleman to a friend, for whom he has a very great respect, and to whom he communicates the satisfaction he takes in retirement; the other is a letter to me, occasioned by an ode written by my Lapland lover: this correspondent is so kind as to translate another of Scheffer's songs in a very agreeable manner. I publish them together, that the young and old may find something in the same paper which may be suitable to their respective tastes in solitude; for I know no fault in the description of ardent desires, provided they are honourable.

'Dear Sir,—You have obliged me with a very kind letter; by which I find you shift the scene of your life from the town to the country, and enjoy that mixed state, which wise men both delight in and are qualified for. Methinks most of the philosophers and moralists have run too much into extremes in praising entirely either solitude or public life; in the former, men generally grow useless by too much rest; and, in the latter, are destroyed by too much precipitation; as waters lying still putrify and are good for nothing; and running violently on, do but the more mischief in their passage to others, and are swallowed up and lost the sooner themselves. Those who, like you, can make themselves useful to all states, should be like gentle streams, that not only glide through lonely vales and forests, amidst the flocks and shepherds, but visit populous towns in their course, and are at once of ornament and service to them. But there is another sort of people who seem designed for solitude, those I mean who have more to hide than to show. As for my own part, I am one of those whom Seneca says, '*Tam umbratiles sunt, ut putent in turbido esse quicquid in luce est.* Some men like pictures, are fitter for a corner than a full light; and I believe such as have a natural bent to solitude are like waters, which may be forced into fountains, and, exalted to a great height, may make a much nobler figure, and a much louder noise, but after all run more smoothly, equally, and plentifully in their own natural course upon the ground. The consideration of this would make me very well contented with the possession only of that quiet which Cowley calls the companion of obscurity; but whoever has the muses too for his companions can never be idle enough to be uneasy. Thus, sir, you see I would flatter myself into a good opinion of my own way of living: Plutarch just now told me, that it is in human life as in a game at tables: one may wish he had the highest cast; but, if his chance be otherwise, he is even to play it as well as he can, and make the best of it. I am, sir, your most obliged and most humble servant.'

'Mr. Spectator,—The town being so well pleased with the fine picture of artless love, which nature inspired the Laplander to paint in the ode you lately printed, we were in hopes that the ingenious translator would have obliged it with the other also which Scheffer has given us: but since he has not, a much inferior hand has ventured to send you this.

'It is a custom with the northern lovers to divert themselves with a song, whilst they journey through the fenny moors to pay a visit to their mistresses. This is addressed by the lover to his rein-deer, which is the creature that in that country supplies the want of horses. The circumstances which successively present themselves to him in his way, are, I believe you will think, naturally interwoven. The anxiety of absence, the gloominess of the roads, and his resolution of frequenting only those, since those only can carry him to the object of his desires; the dissatisfaction he expresses even at the greatest swiftness with which he is carried, and his joyful surprise at an unexpected sight of his mistress as she is bathing, seem beautifully described in the original.

'If those pretty images of rural nature are lost in the imitation, yet possibly you may think fit to let this supply the place of a long letter, when want of leisure, or indisposition for writing, will not permit our being entertained by your own hand. I propose such a time, because, though it is natural to have a fondness for what one does oneself, yet, I assure you, I would not have any thing of mine displace a single line of yours.

I.

"Haste, my rein-deer, and let us nimbly go
Our am'rous journey through this dreary waste;
Haste, my rein-deer! still, still thou art too slow,
Impetuous love demands the lightning's haste.

II.

'Around us far the rushy moors are spread:
Soon will the sun withdraw his cheerful ray:
Darkling and tir'd we shall the marshes tread,
No lay unsung to cheat the tedious way.

III.

'The wat'ry length of these unjoyous moors
Does all the flow'ry meadows' pride excel;
Through these I fly to her my soul adores;
Ye flow'ry meadows, empty pride, farewell.

IV.

"Each moment from the charmer I'm confin'd,
My breast is tortur'd with impatient fires;
Fly, my rein-deer, fly swifter than the wind,
Thy tardy feet wing with my fierce desires.

V

"Our pleasing toil will then be soon o'erpaid,
And thou, in wonder lost, shalt view my fair;
Admire each feature of the lovely maid,
Her artless charms, her bloom, her sprightly air.

VI.

"But lo! with graceful motion there she swims,
Gently removing each ambitious wave;
The crowding waves transported clasp her limbs;
When, when, oh! when shall I such freedoms have

VII.

"In vain, ye envious streams, so fast ye flow.
To hide her from her lover's ardent gaze:
From every touch you more transparent grow,
And all reveal'd the beauteous wanton plays."

No. 407.] *Tuesday, June 17, 1712.*

————— abest facundis gratia dictis.
Ovid. Met. Lib. xiii. 127.

Eloquent words a graceful manner want. T.

Most foreign writers, who have given any character of the English nation, whatever vices they ascribe to it, allow, in general, that the people are naturally modest. It proceeds, perhaps, from this our national virtue, that our orators are observed to make use of less gesture or action than those of other countries. Our preachers stand stock still in the pulpit, and will not so much as move a finger to set off the best sermon in the world. We meet with the same speaking statues at our bars, and in all public places of debate. Our words flow from us in a smooth continued stream, without those strainings of the voice, motions of the body, and majesty of the hand, which are so much celebrated in the orators of Greece and Rome. We can talk of life and death in cold blood, and keep our temper in a discourse which turns upon every thing that is dear to us. Though our zeal breaks out in the finest tropes and figures, it is not able to stir a limb about us. I have heard it observed more than once, by those who have seen Italy, that an untravelled Englishman cannot relish all the beauties of Italian pictures, because the postures which are expressed in them are often such as are peculiar to that country. One who has not seen an Italian in the pulpit, will not know what to make of that noble gesture in Raphael's picture of St. Paul's preaching at Athens, where the apostle is represented as lifting up both his arms, and pouring out the thunder of his rhetoric amidst an audience of pagan philosophers

It is certain that proper gestures and vehement exertions of the voice cannot be too much studied by a public orator. They are a kind of comment to what he utters, and enforce every thing he says, with weak hearers, better than the strongest argument he can make use of. They keep the audience awake, and fix their attention to what s delivered to them, at the same time that they show the speaker is in earnest, and affected himself with what he so passionately recommends to others. Violent gesture and vociferation naturally shake the hearts of the ignorant, and fill them with a kind of religious horror. Nothing is more frequent than to see women weep and tremble at the sight of a moving preacher, though he is placed quite out of their hearing; as in England we very frequently see people lulled to sleep, with solid and elaborate discourses of piety, who would be warmed and transported out of themselves by the bellowing and distortions of enthusiasm.

If nonsense, when accompanied with such an emotion of voice and body, has such an influence on men's minds, what might we not expect from many of those admirable discourses which are printed in our tongue, were they delivered with a becoming fervour, and with the most agreeable graces of voice and gesture!

We are told that the great Latin orator very much impaired his health by the *laterum contentio,* the vehemence of action, with which he used to deliver himself. The Greek orator was likewise so very famous for this particular in rhetoric, that one of his antagonists, whom he had banished from Athens, reading over the oration which had procured his banishment, and seeing his friends admire it, could not forbear asking them, if they were so much affected by the bare reading of it, how much more they would have been alarmed, had they heard him actually throwing out such a storm of eloquence?

How cold and dead a figure, in comparison of these two great men, does an orator often make at the British bar, holding up his head with the most insipid serenity, and stroking the sides of a long wig that reaches down to his middle! The truth of it is, there is often nothing more ridiculous than the gestures of an English speaker: you see some of them running their hands into their pockets as far as ever they can thrust them, and others looking with great attention on a piece of paper that has nothing written on it; you may see many a smart rhetorician turning his hat in his hands, moulding it into several different cocks, examining sometimes the lining of it, and sometimes the button, during the whole course of his harangue. A deaf man would think he was cheapening a beaver, when perhaps he is talking of the fate of the British nation. I remember, when I was a young man, and used to frequent Westminster-hall, there was a counsellor who never pleaded without a piece of pack-thread in his hand, which he used to twist about a thumb or a finger all the while he was speaking: the wags of those days used to call it 'the thread of his discourse,' for he was unable to utter a word without it. One of his clients, who was more merry than wise, stole it from him one day in the midst of his pleading; but he had better have let it alone, for he lost his cause by his jest.

I have all along acknowledged myself to be a dumb man, and therefore may be thought a very improper person to give rules for oratory; but I believe every one will agree with me in this, that we ought either to lay aside all kinds of gesture (which seems to be very suitable to the genius of our nation,) or at least to make use of such only as are graceful and expressive.

O.

No. 408.] *Wednesday, June* 18, 1712.

Decet affectus animi neque se nimium erigere, nec subjacere, serviliter.—*Tull. de Finibus.*

The affections of the heart ought not to be too much indulged, nor servilely depressed.

'Mr. Spectator,—I have always been a very great lover of your speculations, as well in regard to the subject as to your manner of treating it. Human nature I always thought the most useful object of human reason; and to make the consideration of it pleasant and entertaining, I always thought the best employment of human wit: other parts of philosophy may perhaps make us wiser, but this not only answers that end, but makes us better too. Hence it was that the oracle pronounced Socrates the wisest of all men living, because he judiciously made choice of human nature for the object of his thoughts; an inquiry into which, as much exceeds all other learning, as it is of more consequence to adjust the true nature and measures of right and wrong, than to settle the distances of the planets, and compute the time of their circumvolutions.

'One good effect that will immediately arise from a near observation of human nature, is, that we shall cease to wonder at those actions which men are used to reckon wholly unaccountable; for, as nothing is produced without a cause, so by observing the nature and course of the passions, we shall be able to trace every action from its first conception to its death. We shall no more admire at the proceedings of Catiline or Tiberius, when we know the one was actuated by a cruel jealousy, the other by a furious ambition: for the actions of men follow their passions as naturally as light does heat, or as any other effect flows from its cause; reason must be employed in adjusting the passions, but they must ever remain the principles of action.

'The strange and absurd variety that is so apparent in men's actions, shows plainly they can never proceed immediately from reason; so pure a fountain emits no such troubled waters: they must necessarily arise from the passions, which are to the mind as the winds to a ship; they can only move it, and they too often destroy it: if fair and gentle, they guide it into the harbour; if contrary and furious, they overset it in the waves. In the same manner is the mind assisted or endangered by the passions; reason must then take the place of pilot, and can never fail of securing her charge if she be not wanting to herself. The strength of the passions will never be accepted as an excuse for complying with them: they were designed for subjection; and if a man suffers them to get the upper hand, he then betrays the liberty of his own soul.

'As nature has framed the several species of being as it were in a chain, so man seems to be placed as the middle link between angels and brutes. Hence he participates both of flesh and spirit by an admirable tie, which in him occasions perpetual war of passions; and as man inclines to the angelic or brute part of his constitution, he is then denominated good or bad, virtuous or wicked; if love, mercy, and good-nature prevail, they speak him of the angel: if hatred, cruelty, and envy predominate, they declare his kindred to the brute. Hence it was that some of the ancients imagined, that as men in this life inclined more to the angel or the brute, so, after their death, they should transmigrate into the one or the other; and it would be no unpleasant notion to consider the several species of brutes, into which we may imagine that tyrants, misers, the proud, malicious, and ill-natured, might be changed.

'As a consequence of this original, all passions are in all men, but appear not in all; constitution, education, custom of the country, reason, and the like causes, may improve or abate the strength of them; but still the seeds remain, which are ever ready to sprout forth upon the least encouragement. I have heard a story of a good religious man, who having been bred with the milk of a goat, was very modest in public, by a careful reflection he made on his actions; but he frequently had an hour in secret, wherein he had his frisks and capers; and if we had an opportunity of examining the retirement of the strictest philosophers, no doubt but we should find perpetual returns of those passions they so artfully conceal from the public. I remember Machiavel observes, that every state should entertain a perpetual jealousy of its neighbours, that so it should never be unprovided when an emergency happens; in like manner should reason be perpetually on its guard against the passions, and never suffer them to carry on any design that may be destructive of its security: yet, at the same time, it must be careful that it do not so far break their strength as to render them contemptible, and consequently itself unguarded.

'The understanding, being of itself too slow and lazy to exert itself into action, it is necessary it should be put in motion by the gentle gales of the passions, which may preserve it from stagnating and corruption; for they are necessary to the health of the mind, as the circulation of the animal spirits is to the health of the body: they keep it in life, and strength, and vigour; nor is it possible for the mind to perform its offices without their assistance. These motions are given us with our being; they are little spirits that are born and die with us; to some they are mild, easy, and gentle; to others, wayward and unruly, yet never too strong for the reins of reason and the guidance of judgment.

'We may generally observe a pretty nice proportion between the strength of reason and passion; the greatest geniuses have commonly the strongest affections, as, on the other hand, the weaker understandings have generally the weaker passions; and it is fit the fury of the coursers should not be too great for the strength of the charioteer. Young men, whose passions are not a little unruly, give small hopes of their ever being considerable: the fire of youth will of course abate, and is a fault, if it be a fault, that mends every day; but, surely, unless a man has fire in his youth, he can hardly have warmth in old age. We must therefore be very cautious, lest, while we think to regulate the passions, we should quite extinguish them, which is putting out the light of the soul; for to be without passion, or to be hurried away with it, makes a man equally blind. The extraordinary severity used in most of our schools has this fatal effect, it breaks the spring of the mind, and most certainly destroys more good geniuses than it can possibly improve. And surely it is a mighty mistake that the passions should be so entirely subdued: for little irregularities are sometimes not only to be borne with, but to be cultivated too, since they are frequently attended with the greatest perfections. All great geniuses have faults mixed with their virtues, and resemble the flaming bush which has thorns amongst lights.

'Since, therefore, the passions are the principles of human actions, we must endeavour to manage them so as to retain their vigour, yet keep them under strict command; we must govern them rather like free subjects than slaves, lest, while we intend to make them obedient, they become abject, and unfit for those great purposes to which they were designed. For my part, I must confess I could never have any regard to that sect of philosophers who so much insisted upon an absolute indifference and vacancy from all passion; for it seems to me a thing very inconsistent, for a man to divest himself of humanity in order to acquire tranquillity of mind; and to eradicate the very principles of action, because it is possible they may produce ill effects.
I am, sir, your affectionate admirer,

Z. 'T. B.'

No. 409.] *Thursday, June* 19, 1712.

——Musæo contingere cuncta lepore.
Lucr. Lib. i. 933.

To grace each subject with enliv'ning wit.

Gratian very often recommends fine taste as the utmost perfection of an accomplished man.

As this word arises very often in conversation, I shall endeavour to give some account of it, and to lay down rules how we may know whether we are possessed of it, and how we may acquire that fine taste of writing, which is so much talked of among the polite world.

Most languages make use of this metaphor, to express that faculty of the mind which distinguishes all the most concealed faults and nicest perfections in writing. We may be sure this metaphor would not have been so general in all tongues, had there not been a very great conformity between that mental taste, which is the subject of this paper, and that sensitive taste which gives us a relish of every different flavour that affects the palate. Accordingly we find there are as many degrees of refinement in the intellectual faculty as in the sense, which is marked out by this common denomination.

I knew a person who possessed the one in so great a perfection, that, after having tasted ten different kinds of tea, he would distinguish, without seeing the colour of it, the particular sort which was offered him; and not only so, but any two sorts of them that were mixed together in an equal proportion; nay, he has carried the experiment so far, as, upon tasting the composition of three different sorts, to name the parcels from whence the three several ingredients were taken. A man of fine taste in writing will discern, after the same manner, not only the general beauties and imperfections of an author, but discover the several ways of thinking and expressing himself, which diversify him from all other authors, with the several foreign infusions of thought and language, and the particular authors from whom they were borrowed.

After having thus far explained what is generally meant by a fine taste in writing, and shown the propriety of the metaphor which is used on this occasion, I think I may define it to be 'that faculty of the soul which discerns the beauties of an author with pleasure, and the imperfections with dislike.' If a man would know whether he is possessed of this faculty, I would have him read over the celebrated works of antiquity, which have stood the test of so many different ages and countries, or those works among the moderns which have the sanction of the politer part of our contemporaries. If, upon the perusal of such writings, he does not find himself delighted in an extraordinary manner, or if, upon reading the admired passages in such authors, he finds a coldness and indifference in his thoughts, he ought to conclude, not (as is too usual among tasteless readers,) that the author wants those perfections which have been admired in him, but that he himself wants the faculty of discovering them.

He should, in the second place, be very careful to observe, whether he tastes the distinguishing perfections, or, if I may be allowed to call them so, the specific qualities of the author whom he peruses; whether he is particularly pleased with Livy, for his manner of telling a story, with Sallust, for entering into those internal principles of action which arise from the characters and manners of the person he describes, or, with Tacitus, for displaying those outward motives of safety and interest which gave birth to the whole series of transactions which he relates.

He may likewise consider how differently he is affected by the same thought which presents itself in a great writer, from what he is when he finds it delivered by a person of an ordinary genius; for there is as much difference in apprehending a thought clothed in Cicero's language, and that of a common author, as in seeing an object by the light of a taper, or by the light of the sun.

It is very difficult to lay down rules for the acquirement of such a taste as that I am here speaking of. The faculty must in some degree be born with us; and it very often happens, that those who have other qualities in perfection are wholly void of this. One of the most eminent mathematicians of the age has assured me, that the greatest pleasure he took in reading Virgil was in examining Æneas's voyage by the map; as I question not but many a modern compiler of history would be delighted with little more in that divine author than the bare matters of fact.

But, notwithstanding this faculty must in some measure be born with us, there are several methods for cultivating and improving it, and without which it will be very uncertain, and of little use to the person that possesses it. The most natural method for this purpose is to be conversant among the writings of the most polite authors. A man who has any relish for fine writing, either discovers new beauties, or receives stronger impressions, from the masterly strokes of a great author every time he peruses him; besides that he naturally wears himself into the same manner of speaking and thinking.

Conversation with men of a polite genius is another method for improving our natural taste. It is impossible for a man of the greatest parts to consider any thing in its whole extent, and in all its variety of lights. Every man besides those general observations which are to be made upon an author, forms several reflections that are peculiar to his own manner of thinking; so that conversation will naturally furnish us with hints which we did not attend to, and make us enjoy other men's parts and reflections as well as our own. This is the best reason I can give for the observation which several have made, that men of great genius in the same way of writing seldom rise up singly, but at certain periods of time appear together, and in a body; as they did at Rome in the reign of Augustus, and in Greece about the age of Socrates. I cannot think that Corneille, Racine, Moliere, Boileau, La Fontaine, Bruyere, Bossu, or the Daciers, would have written so well as they have done, had they not been friends and contemporaries.

It is likewise necessary for a man who would form to himself a finished taste of good writing, to be well versed in the works of the best critics, both ancient and modern. I must confess that I could wish there were authors of this kind, who, beside the mechanical rules, which a man of very little taste may discourse upon, would enter into the very spirit and soul of fine writing, and show us the several sources of that pleasure which rises in the mind upon the perusal of a noble work. Thus, although in poetry it be absolutely necessary that the unities of time, place, and action, with other points of the same nature, should be thoroughly explained and understood, there is still something more essential to the art, something that elevates and astonishes the fancy, and gives a greatness of mind to the reader, which few of the critics besides Longinus have considered.

Our general taste in England is for epigram, turns of wit, and forced conceits, which have no manner of influence either for the bettering or enlarging the mind of him who reads them, and have been carefully avoided by the greatest writers, both among the ancients and moderns. I have endeavoured in several of my speculations, to banish this gothic taste, which has taken possession among us. I entertained the town for a week together with an essay upon wit, in which I endeavoured to detect several of those false kinds which have been admired in the different ages of the world, and at the same time to show wherein the nature of true wit consists. I afterwards gave an instance of the great force which lies in a natural simplicity of thought to affect the mind of the reader, from such vulgar pieces as have little else besides this single qualification to recommend them. I have likewise examined the works of the greatest poet which our nation, or perhaps any other, has produced, and particularized most of those rational and manly beauties which give a value to that divine work. I shall next Saturday enter upon an essay on 'The Pleasures of the Imagination,' which, though it shall consider the subject at large, will perhaps suggest to the reader what it is that gives a beauty to many passages of the finest writers both in prose and verse. As an undertaking of this nature is entirely new, I question not but it will be received with candour. O.

No. 410.] *Friday, June 20, 1712.*

————Dum foris sunt, nihil videtur mundius,
Nec magis compositum quidquam, nec magis elegans
Quæ, cum amatore suo cum cænant, liguriunt.
Harum videre ingluviem, sordes, inopiam:
Quam inhonestæ solæ sint domi, atque avidæ cibi,
Quo pacto ex jure hesterno panem atrum vorent;
Nosse omnia hæc, salus est adolescentulis.

Ter. Eun. Act v. Sc. 4.

'When they are abroad, nothing so clean and nicely dressed; and when at supper with a gallant, they do but piddle, and pick the choicest bits; but to see their nastiness and poverty at home, their gluttony, and how they devour black crusts dipped in yesterday's broth, is a perfect antidote against wenching.'

Will Honeycomb, who disguises his present decay by visiting the wenches of the town only by way of humour, told us, that the last rainy night he, with Sir Roger de Coverley, was driven into the Temple cloister, whither had escaped also a lady most exactly dressed from head to foot. Will made no scruple to acquaint us, that she saluted him very familiarly by his name, and turning immediately to the knight, she said, she supposed that was his good friend Sir Roger de Coverley: upon which nothing less could follow than Sir Roger's approach to salutation, with 'Madam, the same, at your service.' She was dressed in a black tabby mantua and petticoat, without ribands; her linen striped muslin, and in the whole an agreeable second mourning; decent dresses being often affected by the creatures of the town, at once consulting cheapness and the pretension to modesty. She went on with a familiar easy air, 'Your friend, Mr. Honeycomb, is a little surprised to see a woman here alone and unattended; but I dismissed my coach at the gate, and tripped it down to my counsel's chambers; for lawyers' fees take up too much of a small disputed jointure to admit any other expenses but mere necessaries.' Mr. Honeycomb begged they might have the honour of setting her down, for Sir Roger's servant was gone to call a coach. In the interim the footman returned with 'no coach to be had;' and there appeared nothing to be done but trusting herself with Mr. Honeycomb and his friend, to wait at the tavern at the gate for a coach, or to be subjected to all the impertinence she must meet with in that public place. Mr. Honeycomb being a man of honour, determined the choice of the first, and Sir Roger as the better man, took the lady by the hand, leading her through all the shower, covering her with his hat, and gallanting a familiar acquaintance through rows of young fellows, who winked at Sukey in the state she marched off, Will Honeycomb bringing up the rear.

Much importunity prevailed upon the fair one to admit of a collation, where, after declaring she had no stomach, and having eaten a couple of chickens, devoured a truss of sallet, and drank a full bottle to her share, she sung the Old Man's Wish to Sir Roger. The knight left the room for some time after supper, and writ the following billet, which he conveyed to Sukey and Sukey to her friend Will Honeycomb. Will has given it to Sir Andrew Freeport, who read it last night to the club.

'I am not so mere a country gentleman, but I can guess at the law business you had at the Temple. If you would go down to the country, and leave off all your vanities but your singing, let me know at my lodgings in Bow-street, Covent-garden, and you shall be encouraged by your humble servant, ROGER DE COVERLEY.'

My good friend could not well stand the raillery which was rising upon him; but to put a stop to it, I delivered Will Honeycomb the following letter, and desired him to read it to the board.

'MR. SPECTATOR,—Having seen a translation of one of the chapters in the Canticles into English verse inserted among your late papers, I have ventured to send you the seventh chapter of the Proverbs in a poetical dress. If you think it worthy appearing among your speculations, it will be a sufficient reward for the trouble of your constant reader, A. B.

"My son, th' instruction that my words impart,
Grave on the living tablet of thy heart;
And all the wholesome precepts that I give
Observe with strictest reverence, and live.
"Let all thy homage be to Wisdom paid,
Seek her protection, and implore her aid;
That she may keep thy soul from harm secure,
And turn thy footsteps from the harlot's door,
Who with curs'd charms lures the unwary in,
And soothes with flattery their souls to sin.
"Once from my window, as I cast mine eye
On those that pass'd in giddy numbers by,
A youth among the foolish youths I spy'd,
Who took not sacred wisdom for his guide.
"Just as the sun withdrew his cooler light,
And evening soft led on the shades of night,
He stole in covert twilight to his fate,
And pass'd the corner near the harlot's gate;
When lo, a woman comes!——
Loose her attire, and such her glaring dress,
As aptly did the harlot's mind express;
Subtle she is, and practis'd in the arts
By which the wanton conquer heedless hearts:
Stubborn and loud she is; she hates her home;
Varying her place and form, she loves to roam:
Now she's within, now in the street doth stray,
Now at each corner stands, and waits her prey.
The youth she seiz'd; and laying now aside
All modesty, the female's justest pride,
She said with an embrace, 'Here at my house
Peace-offerings are, this day I paid my vows.
I therefore came abroad to meet my dear,
And lo, in happy hour, I find thee here.
My chamber I've adorn'd, and o'er my bed
Are coverings of the richest tap'stry spread,
With linen it is deck'd from Egypt brought,
And carvings by the curious artist wrought:
It wants no glad perfume Arabia yields
In all her citron groves, and spicy fields;
Here all her store of richest odour meets,
I'll lay thee in a wilderness of sweets;
Whatever to the sense can grateful be
I have collected there——I want but thee.
My husband's gone a journey far away,
Much gold he took abroad, and long will stay:
He nam'd for his return a distant day.'
"Upon her tongue did such smooth mischief dwell,
And from her lips such welcome flatt'ry fell,
Th' unguarded youth, in silken fetters ty'd,
Resign'd his reason, and with ease comply'd.
Thus does the ox to his own slaughter go,
And thus is senseless of the impending blow,
Thus flies the simple bird into the snare,
That skilful fowlers for his life prepare.
But let my sons attend. Attend may they
Whom youthful vigour may to sin betray;
Let them false charmers fly, and guard their hearts
Against the wily wanton's pleasing arts;
With care direct their steps, nor turn astray
To tread the paths of her deceitful way;
Lest they too late of her fell pow'r complain,
And fall, where many mightier have been slain."

T.

No. 411.] *Saturday, June* 21, 1712.

PAPER I.

ON THE PLEASURES OF THE IMAGINATION.

Contents—The perfection of our sight above our other senses. The pleasures of the imagination arise originally from sight. The pleasures of the imagination divided under two heads. The pleasures of the imagination in some respects equal to those of the understanding. The extent of the pleasures of the imagination. The advantages a man receives from a relish of these pleasures. In what respect they are preferable to those of the understanding.

Avia Pieridum peragro loca nullius ante
Trita solo: juvat integros accedere fonteis,
Atque haurire—— *Lucr.* Lib. i. 925.

In wild unclear'd, to Muses a retreat,
O'er ground untrod before I devious roam,
And deep-enamour'd, into latent springs
Presume to peep at coy virgin Naiads.

OUR sight is the most perfect and most delightful of all our senses. It fills the mind with the largest variety of ideas, converses with its objects at the greatest distance, and continues the longest in action without being tired or satiated with its proper enjoyments. The sense of feeling can indeed give us a notion of extension, shape, and all other ideas that enter at the eye, except colours; but at the same time it is very much strained, and confined in its operations, to the number, bulk, and distance of its particular objects. Our sight seems designed to supply all these defects, and may be considered as a more delicate and diffusive kind of touch, that spreads itself over an infinite multitude of bodies, comprehends the largest figures, and brings into our reach some of the most remote parts of the universe.

It is this sense which furnishes the imagination with its ideas; so that by 'the pleasures of the imagination,' or 'fancy,' (which I shall use promiscuously) I here mean such as arise from visible objects, either when we have them actually in our view, or when we call up their ideas into our minds by paintings, statues, descriptions, or any the like occasion. We cannot indeed have a single image in the fancy that did not make its first appearance through the sight; but we have the power of retaining, altering, and compounding those images, which we have once received, into all the varieties of picture and vision that are most agreeable to the imagination; for by this faculty a man in a dungeon is capable of entertaining himself with scenes and landscapes more beautiful than any that can be found in the whole compass of nature.

There are few words in the English language which are employed in a more loose and uncircumscribed sense than those of the fancy and the imagination I therefore thought it necessary to fix and determine the notion of these two words, as I intend to make use of them in the thread of my following speculations, that the reader may conceive rightly what is the subject which I proceed upon. I must therefore desire him to remember, that by 'the pleasures of the imagination,' I mean only such pleasures as arise originally from sight, and that I divide these pleasures into two kinds: my design being first of all to discourse of those primary pleasures of the imagination, which entirely proceed from such objects as are before our eyes; and in the next place to speak of those secondary pleasures of the imagination which flow from the ideas of visible objects, when the objects are not actually before the eye, but are called up into our memories or formed into agreeable visions of things that are either absent or fictitious.

The pleasures of the imagination, taken in the full extent, are not so gross as those of sense, nor so refined as those of the understanding. The last are indeed more preferable, because they are founded on some new knowledge or improvement in the mind of man; yet it must be confessed, that those of the imagination are as great and as transporting as the other. A beautiful prospect delights the soul as much as a demonstration; and a description in Homer has charmed more readers than a chapter in Aristotle. Besides, the pleasures of the imagination have this advantage above those of the understanding, that they are more obvious, and more easy to be acquired. It is but opening the eye, and the scene enters. The colours paint themselves on the fancy, with very little attention of thought or application of the mind in the beholder. We are struck, we know not how, with the symmetry of any thing we see, and immediately assent to the beauty of an object, without inquiring into the particular causes and occasions of it.

A man of a polite imagination is let into a great many pleasures that the vulgar are not capable of receiving. He can converse with a picture and find an agreeable companion in a statue. He meets with a secret refreshment in a description, and often feels a greater satisfaction in the prospect of fields and meadows, than another does in the possession. It gives him, indeed, a kind of property in every thing he sees, and makes the most rude uncultivated parts of nature administer to his pleasures: so that he looks upon the world as it were in another light, and discovers in it a multitude of charms, that conceal themselves from the generality of mankind.

There are indeed but very few who know how to be idle and innocent, or have a relish of any pleasures that are not criminal; every diversion they take is at the expense of some one virtue or another, and their very first step out of business is into vice or folly. A man should endeavour, therefore, to make the sphere of his innocent pleasures as wide as possible, that he may retire into them with safety, and find in them such a satisfaction as a wise man would not blush to take. Of this nature are those of the imagination, which do not require such a bent of thought as is necessary to our more serious employments, nor at the same time, suffer the mind to sink into that negligence and remissness, which are apt to accompany our more sensual delights, but, like a gentle exercise to the faculties, awaken them from sloth and idleness, without putting them upon any labour or difficulty.

We might here add, that the pleasures of the fancy are more conducive to health than those of the understanding, which are worked out by dint of thinking, and attended with too violent a labour of the brain. Delightful scenes, whether in nature, painting, or poetry, have a kindly influence on the body, as well as the mind; and not only serve to clear and brighten the imagination, but are able to disperse grief and melancholy, and to set the animal spirits in pleasing and agreeable motions. For this reason Sir Francis Bacon, in his Essay upon Health, has not thought it improper to prescribe to his reader a poem or a prospect, where he particularly dissuades him from knotty and subtle disquisitions, and advises him to pursue studies that fill the mind with splendid and illustrious objects, as histories, fables, and contemplations of nature.

I have in this paper, by way of introduction, settled the notion of those pleasures of the imagination which are the subject of my present undertaking, and endeavoured, by several considerations, to recommend to my reader the pursuit of those pleasures. I shall in my next paper examine the several sources from whence these pleasures are derived. O.

No. 412.] *Monday, June* 23, 1712.

PAPER II.

ON THE PLEASURES OF THE IMAGINATION.

Contents.—Three sources of all the pleasures of the imagination, in our survey of outward objects. How what is great pleases the imagination. How what is new pleases the imagination. How what is beautiful in our own species pleases the imagination. How what is beautiful in general pleases the imagination What other accidental causes may contribute to the heightening of those pleasures.

——Divisum, sic breve fiet opus.—*Mart.* Ep. iv. 83.

The work, divided aptly, shorter grows.

I SHALL first consider those pleasures of the imagination which arise from the actual view and survey of outward objects; and these, I think, all proceed from the sight of what is great, uncommon, or beautiful. There may, indeed, be something so terrible or offensive, that the horror or loathsomeness of an object may overbear the pleasure which results from its greatness, novelty, or beauty; but still there will be such a mixture of delight in the very disgust it gives us, as any of these three qualifications are most conspicuous and prevailing.

By greatness, I do not only mean the bulk of any single object, but the largeness of a whole view, considered as one entire piece. Such are the prospects of an open champaign country, a vast uncultivated desert, of huge heaps of mountains, high rocks and precipices, or a wide expanse of water, where we are not struck with the novelty or beauty of the sight, but with that rude kind of magnificence which appears in many of these stupendous works of Nature. Our imagination loves to be filled with an object, or to grasp at any thing that is too big for its capacity. We are flung into a pleasing astonishment at such unbounded views, and feel a delightful stillness and amazement in the soul at the apprehensions of them. The mind of man naturally hates every thing that looks like a restraint upon t, and is apt to fancy itself under a sort of confinement, when the sight is pent up in a narrow compass, and shortened on every side by the neighbourhood of walls or mountains. On the contrary, a spacious horizon is an image of liberty, where the eye has room to range abroad, to expatiate at large on the immensity of its views, and to lose itself amidst the variety of objects that offer themselves to its observation. Such wide and undetermined prospects are as pleasing to the fancy as the speculations of eternity or infinitude are to the understanding. But if there be a beauty of uncommonness joined with this grandeur, as in a troubled ocean, a heaven adorned with stars and meteors, or a spacious landscape cut out into rivers, woods, rocks and meadows, the pleasure still grows upon us, as it arises from more than a single principle.

Every thing that is new or uncommon, raises a pleasure in the imagination because it fills the soul with an agreeable surprise, gratifies its curiosity, and gives it an idea of which it was not before possessed. We are indeed so often conversant with one set of objects, and tired out with so many repeated shows of the same things, that whatever is new or uncommon contributes a little to vary human life, and to divert our minds, for a while, with the strangeness of its appearance. It serves us for a kind of refreshment, and takes off from that satiety we are apt to complain of, in our usual and ordinary entertainments. It is this that bestows charms on a monster, and makes even the imperfections of nature please us. It is this that recommends variety, where the mind is every instant called off to something new, and the attention not suffered to dwell too long, and waste itself on any particular object. It is this, likewise, that improves what is great or beautiful and makes it afford the mind a double entertainment. Groves, fields, and meadows, are at any season of the year pleasant to look upon, but never so much as in the opening of the spring, when they are all new and fresh, with their first gloss upon them, and not yet too much accustomed and familiar to the eye. For this reason there is nothing more enlivens a prospect than rivers, jetteaus, or falls of water, where the scene is perpetually shifting, and entertaining the sight every moment with something that is new. We are quickly tired with looking upon hills and valleys, where every thing continues fixed and settled in the same place and posture, but find our thoughts a little agitated and relieved at the sight of such objects as are ever in motion, and sliding away from beneath the eye of the beholder.

But there is nothing that makes its way more directly to the soul than beauty, which immediately diffuses a secret satisfaction and complacency through the imagination, and gives a finishing to any thing that is great or uncommon. The very first discovery of it strikes the mind with an inward joy, and spreads a cheerfulness and delight through all its faculties. There is not perhaps any real beauty or deformity more in one piece of matter than another, because we might have been so made, that whatsoever now appears loathsome to us might have shown itself agreeable; but we find by experience that there are several modifications of matter, which the mind, without any previous consideration, pronounces at first sight beautiful or deformed. Thus we see that every different species of sensible creatures has its different notions of beauty, and that each of them is most affected with the beauties of its own kind. This is no where more remarkable than in birds of the same shape and proportion, where we often see the mate determined in his courtship by the single grain or tincture of a feather, and never discovering any charms but in the colour of its species.

'Scit thalamo servare fidem, sanctasque veretur
Connubii leges; non illum in pectore candor
Solicitat niveus; neque pravum accendit amorem
Splendida lanugo, vel honesta in vertice crista,
Purpureusve nitor pennarum; ast agmina late
Fœminea explorat cautus, maculasque requirit
Cognatas, paribusque interlita corpora guttis:
Ni faceret, pictis sylvam circum undique monstris
Confusam aspiceres vulgo partusque biformes,
Et genus ambiguum, et veneris monumenta nefandæ
'Hinc Merula in nigro se oblectat nigra marito,
Hinc socium lasciva petit Philomela canorum,
Agnoscitque pares sonitus, hinc Noctua tetram
Canitiem alarum, et glaucos miratur ocellos.
Nempe sibi semper constat, crescitque quotannis
Lucida progenies, castos confessa parentes;
Dum virides inter saltus lucosque sonoros
Vere novo exultat, plumasque decora juventus
Explicat ad solem patriisque coloribus ardet.'*

'The feather'd husband, to his partner true
Preserves connubial rites inviolate,
With cold indifference every charm he sees,
The milky whiteness of the stately neck,

* It would seem from his manner of introducing them, that Mr. Addison was himself the author of these fine verses.

The raining down, proud crest, and purple wings:
But cautious with a searching eye explores
The female tribes his proper mate to find,
With kindred colours mark'd; did he not so,
The grove with painted monsters would abound,
Th' ambiguous product of unnatural love.
The blackbird hence selects her sooty spouse;
The nightingale, her musical compeer,
Lur'd by the well-known voice: the bird of night,
Smit with his dusky wings and greenish eyes,
Woos his dun paramour. The beauteous race
Speak the chaste loves of their progenitors
When, by the spring invited, they exult
In woods and fields, and to the sun unfold
Their plumes, that with paternal colours glow.'

There is a second kind of beauty that we find in the several products of art and nature, which does not work in the imagination with that warmth and violence as the beauty that appears in our proper species, but is apt however to raise in us a secret delight, and a kind of fondness for the places or objects in which we discover it. This consists either in the gaiety or variety of colours, in the symmetry and proportion of parts, in the arrangement and disposition of bodies, or in a just mixture and concurrence of all together. Among these several kinds of beauty the eye takes most delight in colours. We no where meet with a more glorious or pleasing show in nature than what appears in the heavens at the rising and setting of the sun, which is wholly made up of those different stains of light that show themselves in clouds of a different situation. For this reason we find the poets, who are always addressing themselves to the imagination, borrowing more of their epithets from colours than from any other topic.

As the fancy delights in every thing that is great, strange, or beautiful, and is still more pleased the more it finds of these perfections in the same object, so it is capable of receiving a new satisfaction by the assistance of another sense. Thus, any continued sound, as the music of birds, or a fall of water, awakens every moment the mind of the beholder, and makes him more attentive to the several beauties of the place that lie before him. Thus, if there arises a fragrancy of smells or perfumes, they heighten the pleasures of the imagination, and make even the colours and verdure of the landscape appear more agreeable; for the ideas of both senses recommend each other, and are pleasanter together than when they enter the mind separately; as the different colours of a picture, when they are well disposed, set off one another and receive an additional beauty from the advantages of their situation. O.

No 413.] *Tuesday, June* 24, 1712.

PAPER III.

ON THE PLEASURES OF THE IMAGINATION.

Contents.—Why the necessary cause of our being pleased with what is great, new, or beautiful, unknown. Why the final cause more known and more useful. The final cause of our being pleased with what is great. The final cause of our being pleased with what is new. The final cause of our being pleased with what is beautiful in our own species. The final cause of our being pleased with what is beautiful in general.

——Causa latet, vis est notissima——
Ovid. Met. ix. 207.

The cause is secret, but th' effect is known.—*Addison.*

Though in yesterday's paper we considered how every thing that is great, new, or beautiful, is apt to affect the imagination with pleasure, we must own that it is impossible for us to assign the necessary cause of this pleasure, because we know neither the nature of an idea, nor the substance of a human soul, which might help us to discover the conformity or disagreeableness of the one to the other; and therefore, for want of such a light, all that we can do in speculations of this kind, is to reflect on those operations of the soul that are most agreeable, and to range, under their proper heads, what is pleasing or displeasing to the mind, without being able to trace out the several necessary and efficient causes from whence the pleasure or displeasure arises.

Final causes lie more bare and open to our observation, as there are often a greater variety that belong to the same effect; and these, though they are not altogether so satisfactory, are generally more useful than the other, as they give us greater occasion of admiring the goodness and wisdom of the first Contriver.

One of the final causes of our delight in any thing that is great may be this. The Supreme Author of our being has so formed the soul of man, that nothing but himself can be its last, adequate, and proper happiness. Because, therefore, a great part of our happiness must arise from the contemplation of his being, that he might give our souls a just relish of such a contemplation, he has made them naturally delight in the apprehension of what is great or unlimited. Our admiration, which is a very pleasing motion of the mind, immediately rises at the consideration of any object that takes up a great deal of room in the fancy, and, by consequence, will improve into the highest pitch of astonishment and devotion when we contemplate his nature, that is neither circumscribed by time nor place, nor to be comprehended by the largest capacity of a created being.

He has annexed a secret pleasure to the idea of any thing that is new or uncommon, that he might encourage us in the pursuit after knowledge, and engage us to search into the wonders of his creation; for every new idea brings such a pleasure along with it as rewards any pains we have taken in its acquisition, and consequently serves as a motive to put us upon fresh discoveries.

He has made every thing that is beautiful in our own species pleasant, that all creatures might be tempted to multiply their kind, and fill the world with inhabitants; for it is very remarkable, that wherever nature is crossed in the production of a monster (the result of any unnatural mixture) the breed is incapable of propagating its likeness, and of founding a new order of creatures: so that, unless all animals were allured by the beauty of their own species, generation would be at an end, and the earth unpeopled.

In the last place, he has made every thing that is beautiful in all other objects pleasant, or rather has made so many objects appear beautiful, that he might render the whole creation more gay and delightful. He has given almost every thing about us the power of raising an agreeable idea in the imagination: so that it is impossible for us to behold his works with coldness or indifference, and to survey so many beauties without a secret satisfaction and complacency. Things would make but a poor appearance to the eye, if we saw them only in their proper figures and motions: and what reason can we assign for their exciting in us many of those ideas which are different from any thing that exists in the objects themselves (for such are light and colours,) were it not to add supernumerary ornaments to the universe, and make it more agreeable to the imagination? we are every where entertained with pleasing shows and apparitions; we discover imaginary glories in the heavens, and in the earth, and see some of this visionary beauty poured out upon the whole creation: but what a rough unsightly sketch of nature should we be entertained with, did all her colouring disappear, and the several distinctions of light and shade vanish? In short, our souls are at present delightfully lost and bewildered in a pleasing delusion, and we walk about like the enchanted hero in a romance, who sees beautiful castles, woods, and meadows; and, at the same time, hears the warbling of birds, and the purling of streams; but, upon the finishing of some secret spell, the fantastic scene breaks up, and the disconsolate knight finds himself on a barren heath, or in a solitary desert. It is not improbable that something like this may be the state of the soul after its first separation, in respect of the images it will receive from matter; though indeed the ideas of colours are so pleasing and beautiful in the imagination, that it is possible the soul will not be deprived of them, but perhaps find them excited by some other occasional cause, as they are at present by the different impressions of the subtle matter on the organ of sight.

I have here supposed that my reader is acquainted with that great modern discovery, which is at present universally acknowledged by all the inquirers into natural philosophy: namely, that light and colours, as apprehended by the imagination, are only ideas in the mind, and not qualities that have any existence in matter. As this is a truth which has been proved incontestibly by many modern philosophers, and is indeed one of the finest speculations in that science, if the English reader would see the notion explained at large, he may find it in the eighth chapter of the second book of Mr. Locke's Essay on Human Understanding.

The following letter of Steele to Addison is reprinted here from the original edition of the Spectator in folio.

'June 24, 1712.

'Mr. Spectator,—I would not divert the course of your discourses, when you seem bent upon obliging the world with a train of thinking, which, rightly attended to, may render the life of every man who reads it more easy and happy for the future. The pleasures of the imagination are what bewilder life, when reason and judgment do not interpose; it is therefore a worthy action in you to look carefully into the powers of fancy, that other men, from the knowledge of them, may improve their joys, and allay their griefs, by a just use of that faculty. I say, sir, I would not interrupt you in the progress of this discourse; but if you will do me the favour of inserting this letter in your next paper, you will do some service to the public, though not in so noble a way of obliging, as that of improving their minds. Allow me, sir, to acquaint you with a design (of which I am partly author,) though it tends to no greater good than that of getting money. I should not hope for the favour of a philosopher in this matter, if it were not attempted under all the restrictions which you sages put upon private acquisitions. The first purpose which every good man is to propose to himself, is the service of his prince and country; after that is done, he cannot add to himself, but he must also be beneficial to them. This scheme of gain is not only consistent with that end, but has its very being in subordination to it; for no man can be a gainer here but at the same time he himself, or some other, must succeed in their dealings with the government. It is called 'The Multiplication Table,' and is so far calculated for the immediate service of her majesty, that the same person who is fortunate in the lottery of the state may receive yet further advantage in this table. And I am sure nothing can be more pleasing to her gracious temper than to find out additional methods of increasing their good fortune who adventure any thing in her service, or laying occasions for others to become capable of serving their country who are at present in too low circumstances to exert themselves. The manner of executing the design is by giving out receipts for half guineas received, which shall entitle the fortunate bearer to certain sums in the table, as it is set forth at large in the proposals printed the twenty-third instant. There is another circumstance in this design which gives me hopes of your favour to it, and that is what Tully advises, to wit, that the benefit is made as diffusive as possible. Every one that has half a guinea is put into the possibility, from that small sum to raise himself an easy fortune: when these little parcels of wealth are, as it were, thus thrown back again into the redonation of providence, we are to expect that some who live under hardships or obscurity may be produced to the world in the figure they deserve by this means. I doubt not but this last argument will have force with you; and I cannot add another to it, but what your severity will, I fear, very little regard; which is, that I am, sir, your greatest admirer,

'RICHARD STEELE.'

No. 414.] *Wednesday, June* 25, 1712.

PAPER IV.

ON THE PLEASURES OF THE IMAGINATION.

Contents.—The works of nature more pleasant to the imagination than those of art. The works of nature still more pleasant, the more they resemble those of art. The works of art more pleasant, the more they resemble those of nature. Our English plantations and gardens considered in the foregoing light.

——————Alterius sic
Altera poscit opem res, et conjurat amice.
Hor. Ars Poet. v. 414.

But mutually they need each other's help.
Roscommon.

If we consider the works of nature and art as they are qualified to entertain the imagination, we shall find the last very defective in comparison of the former; for though they may sometimes appear as beautiful or strange, they can have nothing in them of that vastness and immensity, which afford so great an entertainment to the mind of the beholder. The one may be as polite and delicate as the other, but can never show herself so august and magnificent in the design. There is something more bold and masterly in the rough careless strokes of nature, than in the nice touches and embellishments of art. The beauties of the most stately garden or palace lie in a narrow compass, the imagination immediately runs them over, and requires something else to gratify her; but in the wide fields of nature, the sight wanders up and down without confinement, and is fed with an infinite variety of images, without any certain stint or number. For this reason we always find the poet in love with the country life, where nature appears in the greatest perfection, and furnishes out all those scenes that are most apt to delight the imagination.

Scriptorum chorus omnis amat nemus, et fugit urbes.
Hor. Lib. 2. Ep. ii. 77.

——To grottos and to groves we run,
To ease and silence, ev'ry muse's son.
Pope.

Hic secura quies, et nescia fallere vita,
Dives opum variarum, hic latis otia fundis,
Speluncæ, vivique lacus; hic frigida Tempe,
Mugitusque boum, mollesque sub abore somni.
Virg. Georg. ii. 470.

Here easy quiet, a secure retreat,
A harmless life that knows not how to cheat,
With home-bred plenty the rich owner bless,
And rural pleasures crown his happiness.
Unvex'd with quarrels, undisturb'd with noise,
The country king his peaceful realm enjoys:
Cool grots, and living lakes, the flow'ry pride
Of meads and streams that through the valley glide;
And shady groves that easy sleep invite,
And, after toilsome days, a sweet repose at night.
Dryden.

But though there are several of those wild scenes, that are more delightful than any artificial shows, yet we find the works of nature still more pleasant, the more they resemble those of art: for in this case our pleasure rises from a double principle; from the agreeableness of the objects to the eye, and from their similitude to other objects. We are pleased as well with comparing their beauties, as with surveying them, and can represent them to our minds, either as copies or originals. Hence it is that we take delight in a prospect which is well laid out, and diversified with fields and meadows, woods and rivers; in those accidental landscapes of trees, clouds, and cities, that are sometimes found in the veins of marble; in the curious fret-work of rocks and grottos; and, in a word, in any thing that hath such a variety or regularity as may seem the effect of design in what we call the works of chance.

If the products of nature rise in value according as they more or less resemble those of art, we may be sure that artificial works receive a greater advantage from their resemblance of such as are natural; because here the similitude is not only pleasant, but the pattern more perfect. The prettiest landscape I ever saw, was one drawn on the walls of a dark room, which stood opposite on one side to a navigable river, and on the other to a park. The experiment is very common in optics. Here you might discover the waves and fluctuations of the water in strong and proper colours, with a picture of a ship entering at one end, and sailing by degrees through the whole piece. On another there appeared the green shadows of trees, waving to and fro with the wind, and herds of deer among them in miniature, leaping about upon the wall. I must confess the novelty of such a sight may be one occasion of its pleasantness to the imagination; but certainly its chief reason is its nearest resemblance to nature, as it does not only, like other pictures, give the colour and figure, but the motions of the things it represents.

We have before observed, that there is generally in nature something more grand and august than what we meet with in the curiosities of art. When, therefore, we see this imitated in any measure, it gives us a nobler and more exalted kind of pleasure than what we receive from the nicer and more accurate productions of art. On this account our English gardens are not so entertaining to the fancy as those in France and Italy, where we see a large extent of ground covered over with an agreeable mixture of garden and forest, which represent every where an artificial rudeness, much more charming than that neatness and elegancy which we meet with in those of our own country. It might indeed be of ill consequence to the public, as well as unprofitable to private persons, to alienate so much ground from pasturage and the plough, in many parts of a country that is so well peopled, and cultivated to a far greater advantage. But why may not a whole estate be thrown into a kind of garden by frequent plantations, that may turn as much to the profit as the pleasure of the owner? A marsh overgrown with willows, or a mountain shaded with oaks, are not only more beautiful but more beneficial, than when they lie bare and unadorned. Fields of corn make a pleasant prospect; and if the walks were a little taken care of that lie between them, if the natural embroidery of the meadows were helped and improved by some small additions of art, and the several rows of hedges set off by trees and flowers that the soil was capable of receiving, a man might make a pretty landscape of his own possessions.

Writers, who have given us an account of China, tell us the inhabitants of that country laugh at the plantations of our Europeans, which are laid out by the rule and line; because they say, any one may place trees in equal rows and uniform figures. They chose rather to show a genius in works of this nature, and therefore always conceal the art by which they direct themselves. They have a word, it seems, in their language, by which they express the particular beauty of a plantation that thus strikes the imagination at first sight, without discovering what it is that has so agreeable an effect. Our British gardeners, on the contrary, instead of humouring nature, love to deviate from it as much as possible. Our trees rise in cones, globes, and pyramids. We see the marks of the scissars upon every plant and bush. I do not know whether I am singular in my opinion, but, for my own part, I would rather look upon a tree in all its luxuriancy and diffusion of boughs and branches, than when it is thus cut and trimmed into a mathematical figure; and cannot but fancy that an orchard in flower looks infinitely more delightful than all the little labyrinths of the most finished parterre. But, as our great modellers of gardens have their magazines of plants to dispose of, it is very natural for them to tear up all the beautiful plantations of fruit-trees, and contrive a plan that may most turn to their own profit, in taking off their ever-greens, and the like moveable plants, with which their shops are plentifully stocked.

O.

No. 415.] *Thursday, June 26, 1712.*

PAPER V.

ON THE PLEASURES OF THE IMAGINATION.

Contents.—Of architecture, as it affects the imagination. Greatness in architecture relates either to the bulk or to the manner. Greatness of bulk in the ancient oriental buildings. The ancient accounts of these buildings confirmed. 1. From the advantages for raising such works, in the first ages of the world, and in eastern climates. 2. From several of them which are still extant. Instances how greatness of manner affects the imagination. A French author's observations on this subject. Why convex and concave figures give a greatness of manner to works of architecture. Every thing that pleases the imagination in architecture, is either great, beautiful, or new.

Adde tot egregias urbes, operumque laborem.
Virg. Georg. ii. 155.

Witness our cities of illustrious name,
Their costly labour and stupendous frame.
Dryden

HAVING already shown how the fancy is affected by the works of nature, and afterwards considered in general both the works of nature and of art, how they mutually assist and complete each other in forming such scenes and prospects as are most apt to delight the mind of the beholder, I shall in this paper throw together some reflections on that particular art, which has a more immediate tendency, than any other, to produce those primary pleasures of the imagination which have hitherto been the subject of this discourse. The art I mean is that of architecture, which I shall consider only with regard to the light in which the foregoing speculations have placed it, without entering into those rules and maxims which the great masters of architecture have laid down, and explained at large in numberless treatises upon that subject.

Greatness, in the works of architecture, may be considered as relating to the bulk and body of the structure, or to the manner in which it is built. As for the first, we find the ancients, especially among the eastern nations of the world, infinitely superior to the moderns.

Not to mention the tower of Babel, of which an old author says, there were the foundations to be seen in his time, which looked like a spacious mountain; what could be more noble than the walls of Babylon, its hanging gardens, and its temple to Jupiter Belus, that rose a mile high by eight several stories, each story a furlong in height, and on the top of which was the Babylonian observatory? I might here, likewise, take notice of the huge rock that was cut into the figure of Semiramis, with the smaller rocks that lay by it in the shape of tributary kings; the prodigious basin, or artificial lake, which took in the whole Euphrates, till such time as a new canal was formed for its reception, with the several trenches through which that river was conveyed. I know there are persons who look upon some of these wonders of art as fabulous: but I cannot find any ground for such a suspicion; unless it be that we have no such works among us at present. There were indeed many greater advantages for building in those times, and in that part of the world, than have been met with ever since. The earth was extremely fruitful; men lived generally on pasturage, which requires a much smaller number of hands than agriculture. There were few trades to employ the busy part of mankind, and fewer arts and sciences to give work to men of speculative tempers; and what is more than all the rest, the prince was absolute; so that when he went to war, he put himself at the head of the whole people, as we find Semiramis leading her three millions to the field, and yet overpowered by the number of her enemies. It is no wonder, therefore, when she was at peace, and turning her thoughts on building, that she could accomplish such great works, with such a prodigious multitude of labourers; besides that, in her climate there was small interruption of frosts and winters, which make the northern workmen lie half the year idle. I might mention, too, among the benefits of the climate, what historians say of the earth, that it sweated out a bitumen, or natural kind of mortar, which is doubtless the same with that mentioned in holy writ, as contributing to the structure of Babel: 'Slime they used instead of mortar.'

In Egypt we stiil see their pyramids, which answer to the descriptions that have been made of them; and I question not but a traveller might find out some remains of the labyrinth that covered a whole province, and had a hundred temples disposed among its several quarters and divisions.

The wall of China is one of these eastern pieces of magnificence, which makes a figure even in the map of the world, although an account of it would have been thought fabulous, were not the wall itself still extant.

We are obliged to devotion for the noblest buildings that have adorned the several countries of the world. It is this which has set men at work on temples and public places of worship, not only that they might, by the magnificence of the building, invite the Deity to reside within it, but that such stupendous works might, at the same time, open the mind to vast conceptions, and fit it to converse with the divinity of the place. For every thing that is majestic imprints an awfulness and reverence on the mind of the beholder, and strikes in with the natural greatness of the soul.

In the second place we are to consider greatness of manner in architecture, which has such force upon the imagination, that a small building, where it appears, shall give the mind nobler ideas than any one of twenty times the bulk, where the manner is ordinary or little. Thus, perhaps, a man would have been more astonished with the majestic air that appeared in one of Lysippus's statues of Alexander, though no bigger than the life, than he might have been with mount Athos, had it been cut into the figure of the hero, according to the proposal of Phidias,* with a river in one hand, and a city in the other.

Let any one reflect on the disposition of mind he finds in himself at his first entrance into the Pantheon at Rome, and how the imagination is filled with something great and amazing; and, at the same time, consider how little, in proportion, he is affected with the inside of a Gothic cathedral, though it be five times larger than the other; which can arise from nothing else but the greatness of the manner in the one, and the meanness in the other.

I have seen an observation upon this subject in a French author, which very much pleased me. It is Monsieur Freart's Parallel of the ancient and modern Architecture. I shall give it the reader with the same terms of art which he has made use of. 'I am observing,' says he, 'a thing which, in my opinion, is very curious, whence it proceeds, that in the same quantity of superfices, the one manner seems great and magnificent, and the other poor and trifling; the reason is fine and uncommon. I say, then, that to introduce into architecture this grandeur of manner, we ought so to proceed, that the division of the principal members of the order may consist but of few parts, that they be all great, and of a bold and ample relievo, and swelling; and that the eye, beholding nothing little and mean, the imagination may be more vigorously touched and affected with the work that stands before it. For example, in a cornice, if the gola or cymatium of the corona, the coping, the modillions, or dentelli, make a noble show by their graceful productions, if we see none of that ordinary confusion, which is the result of those little cavities, quarter rounds of the astragal, and I know not how many other intermingled particulars, which produce no effect in great and massy works, and which very unprofitably take up place to the prejudice of the principal member, it is most certain that this manner will appear solemn and great; as, on the contrary, that it will have but a poor and mean effect, where there is a redundancy of those smaller ornaments, which divide and scatter the angles of the sight into such a multitude of rays, so pressed together that the whole will appear but a confusion.'

Among all the figures of architecture, there are none that have a greater air than the concave and the convex; and we find in all the ancient and modern architecture, as well as in the remote parts of China, as in countries nearer home, that round pillars and vaulted roofs make a great part of those buildings which are designed for pomp and magnificence. The reason I take to be, because in these figures we generally see more of the body than in those of other

* Dinocrates.

kinds. There are, indeed, figures of bodies, where the eye may take in two-thirds of the surface; but, as in such bodies the sight must split upon several angles, it does not take in one uniform idea, but several ideas of the same kind. Look upon the outside of a dome, your eye half surrounds it; look upon the inside, and at one glance you have all the prospect of it; the entire concavity falls into your eye at once, the sight being as the centre that collects and gathers into it the lines of the whole circumference; in a square pillar, the sight often takes in but a fourth part of the surface; and in a square concave, must move up and down to the different sides, before it is master of all the inward surface. For this reason, the fancy is infinitely more struck with the view of the open air and skies, that passes through an arch, than what comes through a square, or any other figure. The figure of the rainbow does not contribute less to its magnificence than the colours to its beauty, as it is very poetically described by the son of Sirach: 'Look upon the rainbow, and praise him that made it; very beautiful it is in its brightness; it encompasses the heavens with a glorious circle; and the hands of the Most High have bended it.'

Having thus spoken of that greatness which affects the mind in architecture, I might next show the pleasure that rises in the imagination from what appears new and beautiful in this art! but as every beholder has naturally greater taste of these two perfections in every building which offers itself to his view, than of that which I have hitherto considered, I shall not trouble my readers with any reflections upon it. It is sufficient for my present purpose to observe, that there is nothing in this whole art which pleases the imagination, but as it is great, uncommon, or beautiful. O.

No. 416.] *Friday, June 27, 1712.*

PAPER VI.

ON THE PLEASURES OF THE IMAGINATION.

Contents.—The secondary pleasures of the imagination. The several sources of these pleasures (statuary, painting, description, and music) compared together. The final cause of our receiving pleasure from these several sources. Of descriptions in particular. The power of words over the imagination. Why one reader is more pleased with descriptions than another.

Quatenus hoc simile est oculis, quod mente videmus.
Lucr. ix. 754.

So far as what we see with our minds bears similitude to what we see with our eyes.

I AT first divided the pleasures of the imagination into such as arise from objects that are actually before our eyes, or that once entered in at our eyes, and are afterwards called up into the mind either barely by its own operations, or on occasion of something without us, as statues, or descriptions. We have already considered the first division, and shall therefore enter on the other, which, for distinction sake, I have called 'The Secondary Pleasures of the Imagination.' When I say the ideas we receive from statues, descriptions, or such-like occasions, are the same that were once actually in our view, it must not be understood that we had once seen the very place, action, or person, that are carved or described. It is sufficient that we have seen places, persons, or actions in general, which bear a resemblance, or at least some remote analogy, with what we find represented; since it is in the power of the imagination, when it is once stocked with particular ideas, to enlarge, compound, and vary them at her own pleasure.

Among the different kinds of representation, statuary is the most natural, and shows us something *likest* the object that is represented. To make use of a common instance: let one who is born blind take an image in his hands, and trace out with his fingers the different furrows and impressions of the chisel, and he will easily conceive how the shape of a man, or beast, may be represented by it; but should he draw his hand over a picture, where all is smooth and uniform, he would never be able to imagine how the several prominences and depressions of a human body could be shown on a plain piece of canvass, that has in it no unevenness or irregularity. Description runs yet farther from the things it represents than painting; for a picture bears a real resemblance to its original, which letters and syllables are wholly void of. Colours speak all languages, but words are understood only by such a people or nation. For this reason, though men's necessities quickly put them on finding out speech, writing is probably of a later invention than painting; particularly, we are told that in America, when the Spaniards first arrived there, expresses were sent to the emperor of Mexico in paint, and the news of his country delineated by the strokes of a pencil, which was a more natural way than that of writing, though at the same time much more imperfect, because it is impossible to draw the little connections of speech, or to give the picture of a conjunction or an adverb. It would be yet more strange to represent visible objects by sounds that have no ideas annexed to them, and to make something like description in music. Yet it is certain, there may be confused imperfect notions of this nature raised in the imagination by an artificial composition of notes, and we find that great masters in the art are able, sometimes, to set their hearers in the heat and hurry of a battle, to overcast their minds with melancholy scenes and apprehensions of deaths and funerals, or to lull them into pleasing dreams of groves and elysiums.

In all these instances, this secondary pleasure of the imagination proceeds from that action of the mind which compares the ideas arising from the original objects with the ideas we receive from the statue, picture, description, or sound, that represents them. It is impossible for us to give the necessary reason why this operation of the mind is attended with so much pleasure, as I have before observed on the same occasion; but we find a great variety of entertainments derived from this single principle; for it is this that not only gives us a relish of statuary, painting, and description, but makes us delight in all the actions and arts of mimickry. It is this that makes the several kinds of wit pleasant, which consists, as I have formerly shown, in the affinity of ideas: and we may add, it is this also that raises the little satisfaction we sometimes find in the different sorts of false wit; whether it consists in the affinity of letters, as an anagram, acrostic; or of syllables, as in doggrel rhymes, echoes; or of words, as in puns, quibbles; or of a whole sentence or poem, as wings and altars. The final cause, probably, of annexing pleasure to this operation of the mind, was to quicken and encourage us in our searches after truth, since the distinguishing one thing from another, and the right discerning betwixt our ideas, depend wholly upon our comparing them together, and observing the congruity or disagreement that appears among the several works of nature.

But I shall here confine myself to those pleasures of the imagination which proceed from ideas raised by words, because most of the observations that agree with descriptions are equally applicable to painting and statuary.

Words, when well chosen, have so great a force in them, that a description often gives us more lively ideas than the sight of things themselves. The reader finds a scene drawn in stronger colours, and painted more to the life in his imagination by the help of words, than by an actual survey of the scene which they describe. In this case, the poet seems to get the better of nature: he takes, indeed, the landscape after her, but gives it more vigorous touches, heightens its beauty, and so enlivens the whole piece, that the images which flow from the object themselves appear weak and faint, in comparison of those that come from the expressions. The reason, probably, may be, because in the survey of any object, we have only so much of it painted on the imagination as comes in at the eye: but in its description, the poet gives us as free a view of it as he pleases, and discovers to us several parts, that either we did not attend to, or that lay out of our sight when we first beheld it. As we look on any object, our idea of it is, perhaps, made up of two or three simple ideas; but when the poet represents it, he may either give us a more complex idea of it, or only raise in us such ideas as are most apt to affect the imagination.

It may here be worth our while to examine how it comes to pass that several readers, who are all acquainted with the same language, and know the meaning of the words they read, should nevertheless have a different relish of the same descriptions. We find one transported with a passage, which another runs over with coldness and indifference; or finding the representation extremely natural, where another can perceive nothing of likeness and conformity. This different taste must proceed either from the perfection of imagination in one more than in another, or from the different ideas that several readers affix to the same words. For to have a true relish and form a right judgment of a description, a man should be born with a good imagination, and must have well weighed the force and energy that lie in the several words of a language, so as to be able to distinguish which are most significant and expressive of their proper ideas, and what additional strength and beauty they are capable of receiving from conjunction with others. The fancy must be warm, to retain the print of those images it hath received from outward objects, and the judgment discerning, to know what expressions are most proper to clothe and adorn them to the best advantage. A man who is deficient in either of these respects, though he may receive the general notion of a description, can never see distinctly all its particular beauties; as a person with a weak sight may have the confused prospect of a place that lies before him, without entering into its several parts, or discerning the variety of its colours in their full glory and perfection. O.

No. 417.] *Saturday, June* 28, 1712.

PAPER VII.

ON THE PLEASURES OF THE IMAGINATION.

Contents.—How a whole set of ideas hang together, &c. A natural cause assigned for it. How to perfect the imagination of a writer. Who among the ancient poets had this faculty in its greatest perfection. Homer excelled in imagining what is great; Virgil in imagining what is beautiful; Ovid in imagining what is new. Our own countryman, Milton, very perfect in all these three respects.

Quem tu, Melpomene, semel
Nascentem placido lumine videris,
Illum non labor Isthmius
Clarabit pugilem, non equus impiger, &c.

Sed quæ Tibur aquæ fertile perfluent,
Et spissæ nemorum comæ
Fingent Æolio carmine nobilem.
Hor. Od. iii. Lib. 4. 1

He on whose birth the lyric queen
Of numbers smil'd, shall never grace
The Isthmian gauntlet, or be seen
First in the fame'd Olympic race.

But him the streams that warbling flow
Rich Tiber's fertile meads along,
And shady groves, his haunts, shall know
The master of th' Æolian song. *Atterbury.*

We may observe, that any single circumstance of what we have formerly seen often raises up a whole scene of imagery, and awakens numberless ideas that before slept in the imagination; such a particular smell or colour is able to fill the mind, on a sudden, with the picture of the fields or gardens where we first met with it, and to bring up into view all the variety of images that once attended it. Our imagination takes the hint, and leads us unexpectedly into cities or theatres, plains or meadows. We may further observe, when the fancy thus reflects on the scenes that have passed in it formerly, those which were at first pleasant to behold appear more so upon reflection, and that the memory heightens the delightfulness of the original. A Cartesian would account for both these instances in the following manner:

The set of ideas which we received from such a prospect or garden, having entered the mind at the same time, have a set of traces belonging to them in the brain, bordering very near upon one another: when, therefore, any one of these ideas arises in the imagination, and consequently despatches a flow of animal spirits to its proper trace, these spirits, in the violence of their motion, run not only into the trace to which they were more particularly directed, but into several of those that lie about it. By this means they awaken other ideas of the same set, which immediately determine a new despatch of spirits, that in the same manner open other neighbouring traces, till at last the whole set of them is blown up, and the whole prospect or garden flourishes in the imagination. But because the pleasure we receive from these places far surmounted, and overcame the little disagreeableness we found in them, for this reason there was at first a wider passage worn in the pleasure traces, and, on the contrary, so narrow a one in those which belonged to the disagreeable ideas, that they were quickly stopt up, and rendered incapable of receiving any animal spirits, and consequently of exciting any unpleasant ideas in the memory.

It would be in vain to inquire whether the power of imagining things strongly proceeds from any greater perfection in the soul, or from any nicer texture in the brain of one man than another. But this is certain, that a noble writer should be born with this faculty in its full strength and vigour, so as to be able to receive lively ideas from outward objects, to retain them long, and to range them together, upon occasion, in such figures and representations, as are most likely to hit the fancy of the reader. A poet should take as much pains in forming his imagination, as a philosopher in cultivating his understanding. He must gain a due relish of the works of nature, and be thoroughly conversant in the various scenery of a country life.

When he is stored with country images, if he would go beyond pastoral, and the lower kinds of poetry, he ought to acquaint himself with the pomp and magnificence of courts. He should be very well versed in every thing that is noble and stately in the productions of art, whether it appear in painting or statuary, in the great works of architecture, which are in their present glory; or in the ruins of those which flourished in former ages.

Such advantages as these help to open man's thoughts, and to enlarge his imagination, and will therefore have their influence on all kinds of writing, if the author know how to make right use of them. And among those of the learned languages who excel in this talent, the most perfect in their several kinds are, perhaps, Homer, Virgil, and Ovid. The first strikes the imagination wonderfully with what is great, the second with what is beautiful, and the last with what is strange. Reading the Iliad, is like travelling through a country uninhabited, where the fancy is entertained with a thousand savage prospects of vast deserts, wide uncultivated marshes, huge forests, misshapen rocks and precipices. On the contrary, the Æneid is like a well-ordered garden, where it is impossible to find out any part unadorned, or to cast our eyes upon a single spot that does not produce some beautiful plant or flower. But when we are in the Metamorphoses, we are walking on enchanted ground, and see nothing but scenes of magic lying round us.

Homer is in his province, when he is describing a battle or a multitude, a hero or a god. Virgil is never better pleased than when he is in his elysium, or copying out an entertaining picture. Homer's epithets generally mark out what is great; Virgil's what is agreeable. Nothing can be more magnificent than the figure Jupiter makes in the first Iliad, nor more charming than that of Venus in the first Æneid.

'Η και κυανεησιν επ' οφρυσ' νευσε Κρονιων,
'Αμβροσιαι δ' αρα χαιται επερρωσαντο ανακτος
Κρατος απ' 'αθανατοιο· μεγαν δ' ελελιξεν Ολυμπον.
Iliad, i. 528.

He spoke, and awful bends his sable brows;
Shakes his ambrosial curls, and gives the nod,
The stamp of fate, and sanction of the god:
High heav'n with trembling the dread signal took,
And all Olympus to the centre shook. *Pope*

Dixit: et avertens rosea cervice refulsit,
Ambrosiæque comæ divinum vertice odorem
Spiravere: pedes vestis defluxit ad imos,
Et vera incessu patuit dea.——— *Virg. Æn.* i. 406

Thus having said, she turn'd, and made appear
Her neck refulgent, and dishevell'd hair;
Which, flowing from her shoulders reach'd the ground
And widely spread ambrosial scents around:
In length of train descends her sweeping gown,
And by her graceful walk the queen of love is known
Dryden.

Homer's persons are most of them godlike and terrible: Virgil has scarce admitted any into his poem who are not beautiful, and has taken particular care to make his hero so.

————————Lumenque juventæ
Purpureum, et lætos oculis afflarat honores.
Virg. Æn. i. 594.

And gave his rolling eyes a sparkling grace,
And breath'd a youthful vigour on his face.—*Dryden.*

In a word, Homer fills his readers with sublime ideas, and, I believe, has raised th imagination of all the good poets that have come after him. I shall only instance Horace, who immediately takes fire at the first hint of any passage in the Iliad or Odyssey, and always rises above himself when he has Homer in his view. Virgil has drawn together, into his Æneid, all the pleasing scenes his subject is capable of admitting, and in his Georgics has given us a collection of the most delightful landscapes that can be made out of fields and woods, herds of cattle, and swarms of bees.

Ovid, in his Metamorphoses, has shown us how the imagination may be affected by what is strange. He describes a miracle in every story, and always gives us the sight of some new creature at the end of it. His art consists chiefly in well-timing his description, before the first shape is quite worn off, and the new one perfectly finished; so that he every where entertains us with something we never saw before, and shows us monster after monster to the end of the Metamorphoses.

If I were to name a poet that is a perfect master in all these arts of working on the imagination, I think Milton may pass for one: and if his Paradise Lost falls short of the Æneid or Iliad in this respect, it proceeds rather from the fault of the language in which it is written, than from any defect of genius in the author. So divine a poem in English, is like a stately palace built of brick, where one may see architecture in as great a perfection as one of marble, though the materials are of a coarser nature. But to consider it only as it regards our present subject: What can be conceived greater than the battle of angels, the majesty of Messiah, the stature and behaviour of Satan and his peers? What more beautiful than Pandæmonium, Paradise, Heaven, Angels, Adam and Eve? What more strange than the creation of the world, the several metamorphoses of the fallen angels, and the surprising adventures their leader meets with in his search after Paradise? No other subject could have furnished a poet with scenes so proper to strike the imagination, as no other poet could have painted those scenes in more strong and lively colours. O.

No. 418.] *Monday, June* 30, 1712.

PAPER VIII.

ON THE PLEASURES OF THE IMAGINATION.

Contents.—Why any thing that is unpleasant to behold pleases the imagination when well described. Why the imagination receives a more exquisite pleasure from the description of what is great, new, or beautiful. The pleasure still heightened, if what is described raises passion in the mind. Disagreeable passions pleasing when raised by apt descriptions. Why terror and grief are pleasing to the mind when excited by description. A particular advantage the writers in poetry and fiction have to please the imagination. What liberties are allowed them.

——ferat et rubus asper amomum. *Virg.* Ecl. iii. 89.

The rugged thorn shall bear the fragrant rose.

THE pleasures of these secondary views of the imagination are of a wider and more universal nature than those it has when joined with sight; for not only what is great, strange, or beautiful, but any thing that is disagreeable when looked upon, pleases us in an apt description. Here, therefore, we must inquire after a new principle of pleasure, which is nothing else but the action of the mind, which compares the ideas that arise from words with the ideas that arise from objects themselves; and why this operation of the mind is attended with so much pleasure, we have before considered. For this reason, therefore, the description of a dunghill is pleasing to the imagination, if the image be represented to our minds by suitable expressions; though, perhaps, this may be more properly called the pleasure of the understanding than of the fancy, because we are not so much delighted with the image that is contained in the description, as with the aptness of the description to excite the image.

But if the description of what is little, common, or deformed, be acceptable to the imagination, the description of what is great, surprising, or beautiful is much more so; because here we are not only delighted with comparing the representation with the original, but are highly pleased with the original itself. Most readers, I believe, are more charmed with Milton's description of Paradise, than of hell; they are both, perhaps, equally perfect in their kind; but in the one the brimstone and sulphur are not so refreshing to the imagination, as the beds of flowers and the wilderness of sweets in the other.

There is yet another circumstance which recommends a description more than all the rest; and that is, if it represents to us such objects as are apt to raise a secret ferment in the mind of the reader, and to work with violence upon his passions. For, in this case, we are at once warmed and enlightened, so that the pleasure becomes more universal, and is several ways qualified to entertain us. Thus in painting, it is pleasant to look on the picture of any face where the resemblance is hit; but the pleasure increases if it be the picture of a face that is beautiful; and is still greater, if the beauty be softened with an air of melancholy or sorrow. The two leading passions which the more serious parts of poetry endeavour to stir up in us, are terror and pity. And here, by the way, one would wonder how it comes to pass that such passions as are very unpleasant at all other times, are very agreeable when excited by proper descriptions. It is not strange, that we should take delight in such passages as are apt to produce hope, joy, admiration, love, or the like emotions in us, because they never rise in the mind without an inward pleasure which attends them. But how comes it to pass, that we should take delight in being terrified or dejected by a description, when we find so much uneasiness in the fear or grief which we receive from any other occasion?

If we consider, therefore, the nature of this pleasure, we shall find that it does not arise so properly from the description of what is terrible, as from the reflection we make on ourselves at the time of reading it. When we look on such hideous objects, we are not a little pleased to think we are in no danger of them.* We consider them at the same time, as dreadful and harmless; so that the more frightful appearance they make, the greater is the pleasure we receive from the sense of our own safety. In short, we look upon the terrors of a description with the same curiosity and satisfaction that we survey a dead monster.

——————Informe cadaver
Protrahitur: nequeunt expleri corda tuendo
Terribiles oculos, vultum villosaque setis
Pectora semiferi atque extinctos faucibus ignes.
Virg. Æn. viii. 264.

—————They drag him from his den.
The wond'ring neighbourhood, with glad surprise,
Behold his shagged breast, his giant size,
His mouth that flames no more, and his extinguish'd eyes.
Dryden.

It is for the same reason that we are delighted with the reflecting upon dangers that are past, or in looking on a precipice at a distance, which would fill us with a different kind of horror, if we saw it hanging over our heads.

In the like manner, when we read of torments, wounds, deaths, and the like dismal accidents, our pleasure does not flow so properly from the grief which such melancholy descriptions give us, as from the secret comparison which we make between ourselves and the person who suffers. Such representations teach us to set a just value upon our own condition, and make us prize our good fortune, which exempts us from the like calamities. This is, however, such a kind of pleasure as we are not capable of receiving, when we see a person actually lying under the tortures that we meet with in a description; because, in this case, the object presses too close upon our senses, and bears so hard upon us, that it does not give us time or leisure to reflect on ourselves. Our thoughts are so intent upon the miseries of the sufferer, that we cannot turn them upon our own happiness. Whereas, on the contrary, we consider the misfortunes we read in history or poetry, either as past or as fictitious; so that the reflection upon ourselves rises in us insensibly, and overbears the sorrow we conceive for the sufferings of the afflicted.

But because the mind of man requires something more perfect in matter than what it finds there, and can never meet with any sight in nature which sufficiently answers its highest ideas of pleasantness; or, in other words, because the imagination can fancy to itself things more great, strange, or beautiful than the eye ever saw, and is stil sensible of some defect in what it has seen; on this account it is the part of a poet to humour the imagination in our own notions, by mending and perfecting nature where he describes a reality, and by adding greater beauties than are put together in nature, where he describes a fiction.

He is not obliged to attend her in the slow advances which she makes from one season to another, or to observe her conduct in the successive production of plants and flowers. He may draw into his description all the beauties of the spring and autumn, and make the whole year contribute something to render it the more agreeable. His rose trees, woodbines, and jasmines, may flower together, and his beds be covered at the same time with lilies, violets, and amaranths. His soil is not restrained to any particular set of plants, but is proper either for oaks or myrtles, and adapts itself to the products of every climate. Oranges may grow wild in it; myrrh may be met with in every hedge; and if he thinks it proper to have a grove of spices, he can quickly command sun enough to raise it. If all this will not furnish out an agreeable scene, he can make several new species of flowers, with richer scents and higher colours than any that grow in the gardens of nature. His concerts of birds may be as full and harmonious, and his woods as thick and gloomy as he pleases. He is at no more expense in a long vista than a short one, and can as easily throw his cascades from a precipice of half a mile high, as from one of twenty yards. He has the choice of the winds, and can turn the course of his rivers in all the variety of meanders that are most delightful to the reader's imagination. In a word, he has the modelling of nature in his own hands, and may give her what charms he pleases, provided he does not reform her too much, and run into absurdities by endeavouring to excel. O.

* 'Suave mare dulci turbantibus æquora ventis,' &c. *Lucr.*

No. 419.] *Tuesday, July* 1, 1712.

PAPER IX.

ON THE PLEASURES OF THE IMAGINATION.

Contents.—Of that kind of poetry which Mr. Dryden calls 'the fairy way of writing.' How a poet should be qualified for it. The pleasures of the imagination that arise from it. In this respect why the moderns excel the ancients. Why the English excel the moderns. Who the best among the English. Of emblematical persons.

————Mentis gratissimus error.
Hor. 2. Ep. ii. Lib. 2. 140.

The sweet delusion of a raptur'd mind.

There is a kind of writing wherein the poet quite loses sight of nature, and entertains his reader's imagination with the characters and actions of such persons as have many of them no existence but what he bestows on them. Such are fairies, witches, magicians, demons, and departed spirits.

This Mr. Dryden calls 'the fairy way of writing,' which is indeed more difficult than any other that depends on the poet's fancy, because he has no pattern to follow in it, and must work altogether out of his own invention.

There is a very odd turn of thought required for this sort of writing; and it is impossible for a poet to succeed in it, who has not a particular cast of fancy, and an imagination naturally fruitful and superstitious. Besides this, he ought to be very well versed in legends and fables, antiquated romances, and the traditions of nurses and old women, that he may fall in with our natural prejudices, and humour those notions which we have imbibed in our infancy. For otherwise he will be apt to make his fairies talk like people of his own species, and not like other sets of beings, who converse with different objects, and think in a different manner from that of mankind.

> Sylvis deducti caveant, me judice, fauni,
> Ne velut innati triviis, ac pene forenses,
> Aut nimium teneris juvenentur versibus.
>
> *Hor. Ars Poet.* v. 244.

> Let not the wood-born satyr fondly sport
> With am'rous verses, as if bred at court.—*Francis.*

I do not say, with Mr. Bays in the Rehearsal, that spirits must not be confined to speak sense: but it is certain their sense ought to be a little discoloured, that it may seem particular, and proper to the person and condition of the speaker.

These descriptions raise a pleasing kind of horror in the mind of the reader, and amuse his imagination with the strangeness and novelty of the persons who are represented to them. They bring up into our memory the stories we have heard in our childhood, and favour those secret terrors and apprehensions to which the mind of man is naturally subject. We are pleased with surveying the different habits and behaviours of foreign countries: how much more must we be delighted and surprised when we are led, as it were, into a new creation, and see the person and manners of another species! Men of cold fancies and philosophical dispositions, object to this kind of poetry, that it has not probability enough to affect the imagination. But to this it may be answered, that we are sure, in general, there are many intellectual beings in the world besides ourselves, and several species of spirits, who are subject to different laws and economies from those of mankind: when we see, therefore, any of these represented naturally, we cannot look upon the representation as altogether impossible; nay, many are prepossessed with such false opinions, as dispose them to believe these particular delusions; at least we have all heard so many pleasing relations in favour of them, that we do not care for seeing through the falsehood, and willingly give ourselves up to so agreeable an imposture.

The ancients have not much of this poetry among them; for, indeed, almost the whole substance of it owes its original to the darkness and superstition of later ages, when pious frauds were made use of to amuse mankind, and frighten them into a sense of their duty. Our forefathers looked upon nature with more reverence and horror, before the world was enlightened by learning and philosophy; and loved to astonish themselves with the apprehensions of witchcraft, prodigies, charms, and enchantments. There was not a village in England that had not a ghost in it, the church-yards were all haunted; every large common had a circle of fairies belonging to it; and there was scarce a shepherd to be met with who had not seen a spirit.

Among all the poets of this kind our English are much the best, by what I have yet seen; whether it be that we abound with more stories of this nature, or that the genius of our country is fitter for this sort of poetry. For the English are naturally fanciful, and very often disposed, by that gloominess and melancholy of temper which is so frequent in our nation, to many wild notions and visions, to which others are not so liable.

Among the English, Shakspeare has incomparably excelled all others. That noble extravagance of fancy, which he had in so great perfection, thoroughly qualified him to touch this weak superstitious part of his reader's imagination; and made him capable of succeeding, where he had nothing to support him besides the strength of his own genius. There is something so wild, and yet so solemn, in the speeches of his ghosts, fairies, witches, and the like imaginary persons, that we cannot forbear thinking them natural, though we have no rule by which to judge of them, and must confess if there are such beings in the world, it looks highly probable they should talk and act as he has represented them.

There is another sort of imaginary beings, that we sometimes meet with among the poets, when the author represents any passion, appetite, virtue or vice, under a visible shape, and makes it a person or an actor in his poem. Of this nature are the descriptions of Hunger and Envy in Ovid, of Fame in Virgil, and of Sin and Death in Milton. We find a whole creation of the like shadowy persons in Spencer, who had an admirable talent in representations of this kind. I have discoursed of these emblematical persons in former papers, and shall therefore only mention them in this place. Thus we see how many ways poetry addresses itself to the imagination, as it has not only the whole circle of nature for its province, but makes new worlds of its own, shows us persons who are not to be found in being, and represents even the faculties of the soul, with the several virtues and vices, in a sensible shape and character.

I shall in my two following papers, consider, in general, how other kinds of writing are qualified to please the imagination; with which I intend to conclude this essay. O.

No. 420.] *Wednesday, July 2, 1712.*

PAPER X.

ON THE PLEASURES OF THE IMAGINATION.

Contents.—What authors please the imagination. Who have nothing to do with fiction. How history pleases the imagination. How the authors of the new philosophy please the imagination. The bounds and defects of the imagination. Whether these defects are essential to the imagination.

——Quocunque volunt mentem auditoris agunto.
Hor. Ars Poet. v. 100.

And raise men's passions to what height they will.
Roscommon.

As the writers in poetry and fiction borrow their several materials from outward objects, and join them together at their own pleasure, there are others who are obliged to follow nature more closely, and to take entire scenes out of her. Such are historians, natural philosophers, travellers, geographers, and, in a word, all who describe visible objects of a real existence.

It is the most agreeable talent of an historian to be able to draw up his armies and fight his battles in proper expressions, to set before our eyes the divisions, cabals, an jealousies of great men, to lead us step by step into the several actions and events of his history. We love to see the subject unfolding itself by just degrees, and breaking upon us insensibly, so that we may be kept in a pleasing suspense, and have time given us to raise our expectations, and to side with one of the parties concerned in the relation. I confess this shows more the art than the veracity of the historian; but I am only to speak of him as he is qualified to please the imagination; and in this respect Livy has, perhaps, excelled all who went before him, or have written since his time. He describes every thing in so lively a manner that his whole history is an admirable picture, and touches on such proper circumstances in every story, that his reader becomes a kind of spectator, and feels in himself all the variety of passions which are correspondent to the several parts of the relations.

But among this set of writers there are none who more gratify and enlarge the imagination than the authors of the new philosophy, whether we consider their theories of the earth or heavens, the discoveries they have made by glasses, or any other of their contemplations on nature. We are not a little pleased to find every green leaf swarm with millions of animals, that at their largest growth are not visible to the naked eye. There is something very engaging to the fancy, as well as to our reason, in the treatises of metals, minerals, plants, and meteors. But when we survey the whole earth at once, and the several planets that lie within its neighbourhood, we are filled with a pleasing astonishment, to see so many worlds hanging one above another, and sliding round their axles in such an amazing pomp and solemnity. If, after this, we contemplate those wild* fields of æther that reach in height as far as from Saturn to the fixed stars, and run abroad almost to an infinitude, our imagination finds its capacity filled with so immense a prospect; and puts itself upon the stretch to comprehend it. But if we yet rise higher, and consider the fixed stars as so many vast oceans of flame, that are each of them attended with a different set of planets, and still discover new firmaments and new lights that are sunk farther in those unfathomable depths of æther, so as not to be seen by the strongest of our telescopes, we are lost in such a labyrinth of suns and worlds, and confounded with the immensity and magnificence of nature.

Nothing is more pleasant to the fancy, than to enlarge itself by degrees, in its contemplation of the various proportions which its several objects bear to each other, when it compares the body of man to the bulk of the whole earth, the earth to the circle it describes round the sun, that circle to the sphere of the fixed stars, the sphere of the fixed stars to the circuit of the whole creation, the whole creation itself to the infinite space that is every where diffused about it; or when the imagination works downward, and considers the bulk of a human body in respect of an animal a hundred times less than a mite, the particular limbs of such an animal, the different springs that actuate the limbs, the spirits which set the springs a-going, and the proportionable minuteness of these several parts, before they have arrived at their full growth and perfection; but if, after all this, we take the least particle of these animal spirits, and consider its capacity of being wrought into a world that shall contain within those narrow dimensions a heaven and earth, stars and planets, and every different species of living creatures, in the same analogy and proportion they bear to each other in our own universe; such a speculation, by reason of its nicety, appears ridiculous to those who have not turned their thoughts that way, though at the same time it is founded on no less than the evidence of a demonstration. Nay, we may yet carry it farther, and discover in the smallest particle of this little world a new inexhausted fund of matter, capable of being spun out into another universe.

I have dwelt the longer on this subject, because I think it may show us the proper limits, as well as the defectiveness of our imagination; how it is confined to a very small quantity of space, and immediately stopt in its operation, when it endeavours to take in any thing that is very great or

* Vid. ed. in folio.

very little. Let a man try to conceive the different bulk of an animal, which is twenty, from another which is an hundred times less than a mite, or to compare in his thoughts a length of a thousand diameters of the earth, with that of a million, and he will quickly find that he has no different measures in his mind adjusted to such extraordinary degrees of grandeur or minuteness. The understanding, indeed, opens an infinite space on every side of us; but the imagination, after a few faint efforts, is immediately at a stand, and finds herself swallowed up in the immensity of the void that surrounds it. Our reason can pursue a particle of matter through an infinite variety of divisions; but the fancy soon loses sight of it, and feels in itself a kind of chasm, that wants to be filled with matter of a more sensible bulk. We can neither widen nor contract the faculty to the dimension of either extreme. The object is too big for our capacity, when we would comprehend the circumference of a world; and dwindles into nothing when we endeavour after the idea of an atom.

It is possible this defect of imagination may not be in the soul itself, but as it acts in conjunction with the body. Perhaps there may not be room in the brain for such a variety of impressions, or the animal spirits may be incapable of figuring them in such a manner as is necessary to excite so very large or very minute ideas. However it be, we may well suppose that beings of a higher nature very much excel us in this respect, as it is probable the soul of man will be infinitely more perfect hereafter in this faculty, as well as in all the rest; insomuch that, perhaps, the imagination will be able to keep pace with the understanding, and to form in itself distinct ideas of all the different modes and quantities of space.

O.

No. 421.] *Thursday, July* 3, 1712.

PAPER XI.

ON THE PLEASURES OF THE IMAGINATION.

Contents.—How those please the imagination who treat of subjects abstract from matter, by allusions taken from it. What allusions are most pleasing to the imagination. Great writers, how faulty in this respect. Of the art of imagining in general. The imagination capable of pain as well as pleasure. In what degree the imagination is capable either of pain or pleasure.

Ignotis errare locis, ignota videre,
Flumina gaudebat; studio minuente laborem.
Ovid. Met. vi. 294.

He sought fresh fountains in a foreign soil:
The pleasure lessen'd the attending toil.—*Addison.*

The pleasures of the imagination are not wholly confined to such particular authors as are conversant in material objects, but are often to be met with among the polite masters of morality, criticism, and other speculations abstracted from matter, who, though they do not directly treat of the visible parts of nature, often draw from them their similitudes, metaphors, and allegories. By these allusions, a truth in the understanding is, as it were, reflected by the imagination; we are able to see something like colour and shape in a notion, and to discover a scheme of thoughts traced out upon matter. And here the mind receives a great deal of satisfaction, and has two of its faculties gratified at the same time, while the fancy is busy in copying after the understanding, and transcribing ideas out of the intellectual world into the material.

The great art of a writer shows itself in the choice of pleasing allusions, which are generally to be taken from the great or beautiful works of art or nature; for, though whatever is new or uncommon is apt to delight the imagination, the chief design of an allusion being to illustrate and explain the passages of an author, it should be always borrowed from what is more known and common than the passages which are to be explained.

Allegories, when well chosen, are like so many tracks of light in a discourse, that make every thing about them clear and beautiful. A noble metaphor, when it is placed to an advantage, casts a kind of glory round it, and darts a lustre through a whole sentence. These different kinds of allusion are but so many different manners of similitude; and that they may please the imagination, the likeness ought to be very exact or very agreeable, as we love to see a picture where the resemblance is just, or the posture and air graceful. But we often find eminent writers very faulty in this respect; great scholars are apt to fetch their comparisons and allusions from the sciences in which they are most conversant, so that a man may see the compass of their learning in a treatise on the most indifferent subject. I have read a discourse upon love, which none but a profound chymist could understand, and have heard many a sermon that should only have been preached before a congregation of Cartesians. On the contrary, your men of business usually have recourse to such instances as are too mean and familiar. They are for drawing the reader into a game of chess or tennis, or for leading him from shop to shop, in the cant of particular trades and employments. It is certain, there may be found an infinite variety of very agreeable allusions in both these kinds; but, for the generality, the most entertaining ones lie in the works of nature, which are obvious to all capacities, and more delightful than what is to be found in arts and sciences.

It is this talent of affecting the imagination that gives an embellishment to good sense, and makes one man's composition more agreeable than another's. It sets off all writings in general, but is the very life and highest perfection of poetry, where it shines in an eminent degree: it has preserved several poems for many ages, that have nothing else to recommend them; and where all the other beauties are present, the work appears dry and insipid, if this single one be wanting. It has something in it like creation. It bestows a kind of existence, and draws up to the reader's view several objects which are not to be found in being. It makes additions to nature, and gives greater variety to God's works. In a word, it is able to beautify and adorn the most illustrious scenes in the universe, or to fill the mind with more glorious shows and apparitions than can be found in any part of it.

We have now discovered the several originals of those pleasures that gratify the fancy; and here, perhaps, it would not be very difficult to cast under their proper heads those contrary objects, which are apt to fill it with distaste and terror; for the imagination is as liable to pain as pleasure. When the brain is hurt by any accident, or the mind disordered by dreams or sickness, the fancy is overrun with wild dismal ideas, and terrified with a thousand hideous monsters of its own framing.

Eumenidum veluti demens videt agmina Pentheus,
Et solem geminum, et duplices se ostendere Thebas:
Aut Agamemnonius scenis agitatus Orestes,
Armatam facibus matrem et serpentibus atris
Cum fugit, ultricesque sedent in limine diræ.
Virg. Æn. 469.

Like Pentheus, when distracted with his fear,
He saw two suns, and double Thebes appear;
Or mad Orestes, when his mother's ghost
Full in his face infernal torches tost,
And shook her snaky locks: he shuns the sight,
Flies o'er the stage, surpris'd with mortal fright;
The furies guard the door, and intercept his flight.
Dryden.

There is not a sight in nature so mortifying as that of a distracted person, when his imagination is troubled, and his whole soul disordered and confused. Babylon in ruins is not so melancholy a spectacle. But to quit so disagreeable a subject, I shall only consider, by way of conclusion, what an infinite advantage this faculty gives an almighty Being over the soul of man, and how great a measure of happiness or misery we are capable of receiving from the imagination only.

We have already seen the influence that one man has over the fancy of another, and with what ease he conveys into it a variety of imagery: how great a power then may we suppose lodged in Him who knows all the ways of affecting the imagination, who can infuse what ideas he pleases, and fill those ideas with terror and delight to what degree he thinks fit! He can excite images in the mind without the help of words, and make scenes rise up before us, and seem present to the eye, without the assistance of bodies or exterior objects. He can transport the imagination with such beautiful and glorious visions as cannot possibly enter into our present conceptions, or haunt it with such ghastly spectres and apparitions as would make us hope for annihilation, and think existence no better than a curse. In short, he can so exquisitely ravish or torture the soul through this single faculty, as might suffice to make the whole heaven or hell of any finite being.

[This essay on the Pleasures of the Imagination having been published in separate papers, I shall conclude it with a table of the principal contents of each paper.*]
O.

No. 422.] *Friday, July* 4, 1712.

Hæc scripsi non otii abundantia, sed amoris ergate.
Tull. Epist

I have written this not out of the abundance of leisure, but of my affection towards you.

I do not know any thing which gives greater disturbance to conversation, than the false notion which people have of raillery. It ought certainly to be the first point to be aimed at in society, to gain the goodwill of those with whom you converse; the way to that is, to show you are well inclined towards them. What then can be more absurd, than to set up for being extremely sharp and biting, as the term is, in your expressions to your familiars? A man who has no good quality but courage, is in a very ill way towards making an agreeable figure in the world, because that which he has superior to other people cannot be exerted without raising himself an enemy. Your gentleman of a satirical vein is in the like condition. To say a thing which perplexes the heart of him you speak to, or brings blushes into his face, is a degree of murder; and it is, I think, an unpardonable offence to show a man you do not care whether he is pleased or displeased. But won't you then take a jest?—Yes: but pray let it be a jest. It is no jest to put me, who am so unhappy as to have an utter aversion to speaking to more than one man at a time, under a necessity to explain myself in much company, and reducing me to shame and derision, except I perform what my infirmity of silence disables me to do.

Callisthenes had great wit accompanied with that quality without which a man can have no wit at all—a sound judgment. This gentleman rallies the best of any man I know: for he forms his ridicule upon a circumstance which you are in your heart not unwilling to grant him; to wit, that you are guilty of an excess in something which is in itself laudable. He very well understands what you would be, and needs not fear your anger for declaring you are a little too much that thing. The generous will bear being reproached as lavish, and the valiant as rash, without being provoked to resentment against their monitor. What has been said to be a mark of a good writer will fall in with the character of a good companion. The good writer makes his reader better

* These contents are printed all together in the original folio, at the end of No. 421; but are in this edition arranged in their proper places, and placed at the beginnings of the several papers.

pleased with himself, and the agreeable man makes his friends enjoy themselves, rather than him, while he is in their company. Callisthenes does this with inimitable pleasantry. He whispered a friend the other day, so as to be overheard by a young officer, who gave symptoms of cocking upon the company, 'That gentleman has very much the air of a general officer.' The youth immediately put on a composed behaviour, and behaved himself suitably to the conceptions he believed the company had of him. It is to be allowed that Callisthenes will make a man run into impertinent relations to his own advantage, and express the satisfaction he has in his own dear self, till he is very ridiculous: but in this case the man is made a fool by his own consent, and not exposed as such whether he will or no. I take it, therefore, that to make raillery agreeable, a man must either not know he is rallied, or think never the worse of himself if he sees he is.

Acetus is of a quite contrary genius, and is more generally admired than Callisthenes, but not with justice. Acetus has no regard to the modesty or weakness of the person he rallies; but if his quality or humility gives him any superiority to the man he would fall upon, he has no mercy in making the onset. He can be pleased to see his best friends out of countenance, while the laugh is loud in his own applause. His raillery always puts the company into little divisions and separate interests, while that of Callisthenes cements it, and makes every man not only better pleased with himself, but also with all the rest in the conversation.

To rally well, it is absolutely necessary that kindness must run through all you say; and you must ever preserve the character of a friend to support your pretensions to be free with a man. Acetus ought to be banished human society, because he raises his mirth upon giving pain to the person upon whom he is pleasant. Nothing but the malevolence which is too general towards those who excel could make his company tolerated; but they with whom he converses are sure to see some man sacrificed wherever he is admitted; and all the credit he has for wit is owing to the gratification it gives to other men's ill-nature.

Minutius has a wit that conciliates a man's love, at the same time that it is exerted against his faults. He has an art of keeping the person he rallies in countenance, by insinuating that he himself is guilty of the same imperfection. This he does with so much address, that he seems rather to bewail himself, than fall upon his friend.

It is really monstrous to see how unaccountably it prevails among men, to take the liberty of displeasing each other. One would think sometimes that the contention is, who shall be most disagreeable. Allusions to past follies, hints which revive what a man has a mind to forget for ever, and desires that all the rest of the world should, are commonly brought forth even in company of men of distinction. They do not thrust with the skill of fencers, but cut up with the barbarity of butchers. It is, methinks, below the character of men of humanity and good manners to be capable of mirth while there is any of the company in pain and disorder. They who have the true taste of conversation, enjoy themselves in communication of each other's excellencies, and not in a triumph over their imperfections. Fortius would have been reckoned a wit, if there had never been a fool in the world: he wants not foils to be a beauty, but has that natural pleasure in observing perfection in others, that his own faults are overlooked out of gratitude by all his acquaintance.

After these several characters of men who succeed or fail in raillery, it may not be amiss to reflect a little farther what one takes to be the most agreeable kind of it; and that to me appears when the satire is directed against vice, with an air of contempt of the fault, but no ill-will to the criminal. Mr. Congreve's Doris is a masterpiece of this kind. It is the character of a woman utterly abandoned; but her impudence, by the finest piece of raillery, is made only generosity.

> 'Peculiar therefore is her way,
> Whether by nature taught
> I shall not undertake to say,
> Or by experience bought;
>
> 'For who o'ernight obtain'd her grace,
> She can next day disown,
> And stare upon the strange man's face,
> As one she ne'er had known.
>
> 'So well she can the truth disguise,
> Such artful wonder frame,
> The lover or distrusts his eyes,
> Or thinks 'twas all a dream.
>
> 'Some censure this as lewd or low,
> Who are to bounty blind;
> But to forget what we bestow,
> Bespeaks a noble mind.'

T.

No. 423.] *Saturday, July 5, 1712.*

> ——Nuper idoneus.
>
> *Hor.* Od. xxvi. Lib. 3. 1.
>
> Once fit myself.

I LOOK upon myself as a kind of guardian to the fair, and am always watchful to observe any thing which concerns their interest. The present paper shall be employed in the service of a very fine young woman and the admonitions I give her may not be unuseful to the rest of her sex. Gloriana shall be the name of the heroine in to-day's entertainment; and when I have told you that she is rich, witty, young, and beautiful, you will believe she does not want admirers. She has had, since she came to town, about twenty-five of those lovers who made their addresses by way of jointure and settlement: these come and go with great indifference on both sides; and as beautiful as she is, a line in a deed has had exception enough against it to outweigh the lustre of her eyes, the readiness of her understanding, and the merit of her general character. But among the crowd of such cool adorers, she has two who are very assiduous in their attendance. There is something so extraordinary and artful in their manner of application, that I think it but common justice to alarm her in it. I have done it in the following letter:

'MADAM,—I have for some time taken notice of two young gentlemen who attend you in all public places, both of whom have also easy access to you at your own house. The matter is adjusted between them; and Damon, who so passionately addresses you, has no design upon you; but Strephon, who seems to be indifferent to you, is the man who is, as they have settled it, to have you. The plot was laid over a bottle of wine; and Strephon, when he first thought of you, proposed to Damon to be his rival. The manner of his breaking of it to him, I was so placed at a tavern, that I could not avoid hearing. "Damon," said he, with a deep sigh, "I have long languished for that miracle of beauty, Gloriana; and if you will be very steadfastly my rival, I shall certainly obtain her. Do not," continued he, "be offended at this overture; for I go upon the knowledge of the temper of the woman, rather than any vanity that I should profit by any opposition of your pretensions to those of your humble servant. Gloriana has very good sense, a quick relish of the satisfactions of life, and will not give herself, as the crowd of women do, to the arms of a man to whom she is indifferent. As she is a sensible woman, expressions of rapture and adoration will not move her neither; but he that has her must be the object of her desire, not her pity. The way to this end I take to be, that a man's general conduct should be agreeable, without addressing in particular to the woman he loves. Now, sir, if you will be so kind as to sigh and die for Gloriana, I will carry it with great respect towards her, but seem void of any thoughts as a lover. By this means I shall be in the most amiable light of which I am capable; I shall be received with freedom, you with reserve." Damon who has himself no designs of marriage at all, easily fell into the scheme; and you may observe, that wherever you are, Damon appears also. You see he carries on an unaffected exactness in his dress and manner, and strives always to be the very contrary of Strephon. They have already succeeded so far, that your eyes are ever in search of Strephon, and turn themselves of course from Damon. They meet and compare notes upon your carriage; and the letter which was brought to you the other day was a contrivance to remark your resentment. When you saw the billet subscribed Damon, and turned away with a scornful air, and cried "impertinence!" you gave hopes to him that shuns you, without mortifying him that languishes for you.

'What I am concerned for, madam, is, that in the disposal of your heart, you should know what you are doing, and examine it before it is lost. Strephon contradicts you in discourse with the civility of one who has a value for you, but gives up nothing like one that loves you. This seeming unconcern gives his behaviour the advantage of sincerity, and insensibly obtains your good opinion by appearing disinterested in the purchase of it. If you watch these correspondents hereafter, you will find that Strephon makes his visit of civility immediately after Damon has tired you with one of love. Though you are very discreet, you will find it no easy matter to escape the toils so well laid; as, when one studies to be disagreeable in passion, the other to be pleasing without it. All the turns of your temper are carefully watched, and their quick and faithful intelligence gives your lovers irresistible advantage. You will please, madam, to be upon your guard, and take all the necessary precautions against one who is amiable to you before you know he is enamoured. I am, madam, your most obedient servant.'

Strephon makes great progress in this lady's good graces; for most women being actuated by some little spirit of pride and contradiction, he has the good effects of both those motives by this covert way of courtship. He received a message yesterday from Damon in the following words, superscribed 'With speed.'

'All goes well; she is very angry at me, and I dare say hates me in earnest. It is a good time to visit. Yours.'

The comparison of Strephon's gaiety to Damon's languishment strikes her imagination with a prospect of very agreeable hours with such a man as the former, and abhorrence of the insipid prospect with one like the latter. To know when a lady is displeased with another, is to know the best time of advancing yourself. This method of two persons playing into each other's hand is so dangerous, that I cannot tell how a woman could be able to withstand such a siege. The condition of Gloriana I am afraid is irretrievable; for Strephon has had so many opportunities of pleasing without suspicion, that all which is left for her to do is to bring him, now she is advised, to an explanation of his passion, and beginning again, if she can conquer the kind sentiments she has conceived for him. When one shows himself a creature to be avoided, the other proper to be fled to for succour, they have the whole woman between them, and can occasionally rebound her love and hatred from one to the other, in such a manner as to keep her at a distance from all the rest of the world, and cast lots for the conquest.

N. B. I have many other secrets which concern the empire of love; but I consider, that, while I alarm my women, I instruct my men. T.

No. 424.] *Monday, July* 7, 1712.

Est Ulubris, animus si te non deficit æquus.
Hor. Ep. xi. Lib. 1. 30.

'Tis not the place disgust or pleasure brings:
From our own mind our satisfaction springs.

'London, June 24.

'MR. SPECTATOR,—A man who has it in his power to choose his own company, would certainly be much to blame, should he not, to the best of his judgment, take such as are of a temper most suitable to his own; and where that choice is wanting, or where a man is mistaken in his choice, and yet under a necessity of continuing in the same company, it will certainly be his interest to carry himself as easily as possible.

'In this I am sensible I do but repeat what has been said a thousand times, at which however I think nobody has any title to take exception, but they who never failed to put this in practice.—Not to use any longer preface, this being the season of the year in which great numbers of all sorts of people retire from this place of business and pleasure to country solitude, I think it not improper to advise them to take with them as great a stock of good-humour as they can; for though a country life is described as the most pleasant of all others, and though it may in truth be so, yet it is so only to those who know how to enjoy leisure and retirement.

'As for those who cannot live without the constant helps of business or company, let them consider, that in the country there is no Exchange, there are no playhouses, no variety of coffee-houses, nor many of those other amusements which serve here as so many reliefs from the repeated occurrences in their own families; but that there the greatest part of their time must be spent within themselves, and consequently it behoves them to consider how agreeable it will be to them before they leave this dear town.

'I remember, Mr. Spectator, we were very well entertained last year with the advices you gave us from Sir Roger's country-seat; which I the rather mention, because it is almost impossible not to live pleasantly, where the master of the family is such a one as you there describe your friend, who cannot therefore (I mean as to his domestic character,) be too often recommended to the imitation of others. How amiable is that affability and benevolence with which he treats his neighbours, and every one, even the meanest of his own family! and yet how seldom imitated! Instead of which we commonly meet with ill-natured expostulations, noise, and chidings.—And this I hinted, because the humour and disposition of the head is what chiefly influences all the other parts of a family.

'An agreement and kind correspondence between friends and acquaintance is the greatest pleasure of life. This is an undoubted truth; and yet any man who judges from the practice of the world will be almost persuaded to believe the contrary; for how can we suppose people should be so industrious to make themselves uneasy? What can engage them to entertain and foment jealousies of one another upon every or the least occasion? Yet so it is, there are people who (as it should seem) delight in being troublesome and vexatious, who (as Tully speaks) *Mira sunt alacritate ad litigandum*, 'have a certain cheerfulness in wrangling.' And thus it happens, that there are very few families in which there are not feuds and animosities; though it is every one's interest, there more particularly, to avoid them, because there (as I would willingly hope) no one gives another uneasiness without feeling some share of it. But I am gone beyond what I designed, and had almost forgot what I chiefly proposed: which was, barely to tell you how hardly we, who pass most of our time in town, dispense with a long vacation in the country, how uneasy we grow to ourselves, and to one another, when our conversation is confined; insomuch that, by Michaelmas, it is odds but we come to downright squabbling, and make as free with one another to our faces as we do with the rest of the world behind their backs. After I have told you this, I am to desire that you would now and then give us a lesson of good-humour, a family-piece, which, since we are all very fond of you, I hope may have some influence upon us.

'After these plain observations, give me leave to give you a hint of what a set of company of my acquaintance, who are now gone into the country, and have the use of an absent nobleman's seat, have settled among themselves, to avoid the inconveniences above mentioned. They are a collection of ten or twelve of the same good inclination towards each other, but of very different talents and inclinations: from hence they hope that the variety of their tempers will only create variety of pleasures. But as there always will arise, among the same people, either for want of diversity of objects, or the like causes, a certain satiety, which may grow into ill-humour or discontent, there is a large wing of the house which they design to employ in the nature of an infirmary. Whoever says a peevish thing, or acts any thing which betrays a sourness or indisposition to company, is im mediately to be conveyed to his chambers in the infirmary; from whence he is not to be relieved, till by his manner of submission, and the sentiments expressed in his petition for that purpose, he appears to the majority of the company to be again fit for society. You are to understand, that all ill-natured words or uneasy gestures are sufficient cause for banishment; speaking impatiently to servants, making a man repeat what he says, or any thing that betrays inattention or dishumour, are also criminal without reprieve. But it is provided, that whoever observes the ill-natured fit coming upon himself, and voluntarily retires, shall be received at his return from the infirmary with the highest marks of esteem. By these and other wholesome methods, it is expected that if they cannot cure one another, yet at least they have taken care that the ill-humour of one shall not be troublesome to the rest of the company. There are many other rules which the society have established for the preservation of their ease and tranquillity, the effects of which, with the incidents that arise among them, shall be communicated to you from time to time, for the public good, by, sir, your most humble servant, R. O.'

T.

No. 425.] *Tuesday, July* 8, 1712.

Frigora mitescunt zephyris; ver proterit æstas
  Interitura, simul
Pomifer autumnus fruges effuderit; et mox
  Bruma recurrit iners. *Hor.* Od. vii. Lib. 4. 9.

The cold grows soft with western gales,
The summer over spring prevails,
  But yields to autumn's fruitful rain,
As this to winter storms and hails;
  Each loss the hasting moon repairs again.
Sir W. Temple.

'Mr. Spectator,—There is hardly any thing gives me a more sensible delight than the enjoyment of a cool still evening after the uneasiness of a hot sultry day. Such a one I passed not long ago, which made me rejoice when the hour was come for the sun to set, that I might enjoy the freshness of the evening in my garden, which then affords me the pleasantest hours I pass in the whole four and twenty. I immediately rose from my couch, and went down into it. You descend at first by twelve stone steps into a large square divided into four grass-plots, in each of which is a statue of white marble. This is separated from a large parterre by a low wall; and from thence, through a pair of iron gates, you are led into a long broad walk of the finest turf, set on each side with tall yews, and on either hand bordered by a canal, which on the right divides the walk from a wilderness parted into variety of alleys and arbours, and on the left from a kind of amphitheatre, which is the receptacle of a great number of oranges and myrtles. The moon shone bright, and seemed then most agreeably to supply the place of the sun, obliging me with as much light as was necessary to discover a thousand pleasing objects, and a the same time divested of all power of heat. The reflection of it in the water, the fanning of the wind rustling on the leaves, the singing of the thrush and nightingale, and the coolness of the walks, all conspired to make me lay aside all displeasing thoughts, and brought me into such a tranquillity of mind, as is, I believe, the next happiness to that of hereafter. In this sweet retirement I naturally fell into the repetition of some lines out of a poem of Milton's, which he entitles Il Penseroso, the ideas of which were exquisitely suited to my present wanderings of thought.

"Sweet bird! that shunn'st the noise of folly
Most musical! most melancholy!
Thee, chantress, oft, the woods among,
I woo to hear thy ev'ning song:
And missing thee I walk unseen
On the dry smooth-shaven green,
To behold the wand'ring moon,
Riding near her highest noon,
Like one that hath been led astray,
Through the heaven's wide pathless way,
And oft, as if her head she bow'd,
Stooping through a fleecy cloud.

"Then let some strange mysterious dream
Wave with its wings in airy stream
Of lively portraiture display'd
Softly on my eyelids laid:
And as I wake, sweet music breathe
Above, about, or underneath,
Sent by spirits to mortals' good,
Or the unseen genius of the wood."

'I reflected then upon the sweet vicissitudes of night and day, on the charming disposition of the seasons, and their return again in a perpetual circle: and oh! said I, that I could from these my declining years return again to my first spring of youth and vigour; but that, alas! is impossible; all that remains within my power is to soften the inconveniences I feel; with an easy contented mind, and the enjoyment of such delights as this solitude affords me. In this thought I sat me down on a bank of flowers, and dropt into a slumber, which, whether it were the effect of fumes and vapours, or my present thoughts, I know not; but methought the genius of the garden stood before me, and introduced into the walk where I lay this drama and different scenes of the revolution of the year, which, whilst I then saw, even in my dream, I resolved to write down, and send to the Spectator.

'The first person whom I saw advancing towards me was a youth of a most beautiful air and shape, though he seemed not yet arrived at that exact proportion and symmetry of parts which a little more time would have given him; but, however, there was such a bloom in his countenance, such satisfaction and joy, that I thought it the most desirable form that I had ever seen. He was clothed in a flowing mantle of green silk, interwoven with flowers; he had a chaplet of roses on his head, and a narcissus in his hand; primroses and violets sprang up under his feet, and all nature was cheered at his approach. Flora was on one hand,

and Vertumnus on the other, in a robe of changeable silk. After this I was surprised to see the moon-beams reflected with a sudden glare from armour, and to see a man completely armed, advancing with his sword drawn. I was soon informed by the genius it was Mars, who had long usurped a place among the attendants of the Spring. He made way for a softer appearance. It was Venus, without any ornament but her own beauties, not so much as her own cestus, with which she had encompassed a globe, which she held in her right hand, and in her left hand she had a sceptre of gold. After her followed the Graces, with arms entwined within one another; their girdles were loosed, and they moved to the sound of soft music, striking the ground alternately with their feet. Then came up the three Months which belong to this season. As March advanced towards me, there was, methought in his look a lowering roughness, which ill-befitted a month which was ranked in so soft a season; but as he came forwards, his features became insensibly more mild and gentle; he smoothed his brow, and looked with so sweet a countenance, that I could not but lament his departure, though he made way for April. He appeared in the greatest gaiety imaginable, and had a thousand pleasures to attend him: his look was frequently clouded, but immediately returned to its first composure, and remained fixed in a smile. Then came May, attended by Cupid, with his bow strung, and in a posture to let fly an arrow: as he passed by, methought I heard a confused noise of soft complaints, gentle ecstacies, and tender sighs of lovers; vows of constancy, and as many complainings of perfidiousness; all which the winds wafted away as soon as they had reached my hearing. After these I saw a man advance in the full prime and vigour of his age; his complexion was sanguine and ruddy, his hair black, and fell down in beautiful ringlets beneath his shoulders; a mantle of hair-coloured silk hung loosely upon him: he advanced with a hasty step after the Spring, and sought out the shade and cool fountains which played in the garden. He was particularly well pleased when a troop of Zephyrs fanned him with their wings. He had two companions, who walked on each side, that made him appear the most agreeable; the one was Aurora with figures of roses, and her feet dewy, attired in gray; the other was Vesper, in a robe of azure beset with drops of gold, whose breath he caught while it passed over a bundle of honeysuckles and tuberoses which he held in his hand. Pan and Ceres followed them with four reapers, who danced a morrice to the sound of oaten-pipes and cymbals. Then came the attendant Months. June retained still some small likeness of the Spring; but the other two seemed to step with a less vigorous tread, especially August, who seemed almost to faint, whilst for half the steps he took, the dog-star levelled his rays full at his head. They passed on, and made way for a person that seemed to bend a little under the weight of years; his beard and hair, which were full grown, were composed of an equal number of black and gray; he wore a robe which he had girt round him, of a yellowish cast, not unlike the colour of fallen leaves, which he walked upon. I thought he hardly made amends for expelling the foregoing scene by the large quantity of fruits which he bore in his hands. Plenty walked by his side with a healthy fresh countenance, pouring out from a horn all the various products of the year. Pomona followed with a glass of cider in her hand, with Bacchus in a chariot drawn by tigers, accompanied by a whole troop of satyrs, fauns, and sylvans. September, who came next, seemed in his looks to promise a new Spring, and wore the livery of those months. The succeeding month was all soiled with the juice of grapes, as he had just come from the wine-press. November, though he was in this division, yet, by the many stops he made, seemed rather inclined to the Winter which followed close at his heels. He advanced in the shape of an old man in the extremity of age; the hair he had was so very white, it seemed a real snow; his eyes were red and piercing, and his beard hung with great quantity of icicles; he was wrapt up in furs, but yet so pinched with excess of cold, that his limbs were all contracted, and his body bent to the ground, so that he could not have supported himself had it not been for Comus, the god of revels, and Necessity, the mother of Fate, who sustained him on each side. The shape and mantle of Comus was one of the things that most surprised me: as he advanced towards me, his countenance seemed the most desirable I had ever seen. On the fore part of his mantle was pictured joy, delight, and satisfaction, with a thousand emblems of merriment, and jests with faces looking two ways at once; but as he passed from me I was amazed at a shape so little correspondent to his face: his head was bald, and all the rest of his limbs appeared old and deformed. On the hinder part of his mantle was represented Murder* with dishevelled hair and a dagger all bloody, Anger in a robe of scarlet, and Suspicion squinting with both eyes; but above all, the most conspicuous was the battle of Lapithæ and the Centaurs. I detested so hideous a shape, and turned my eyes upon Saturn, who was stealing away behind him, with a scythe in one hand and an hour-glass in the other, unobserved. Behind Necessity was Vesta, the goddess of fire, with a lamp that was perpetually supplied with oil, and whose flame was eternal. She cheered the rugged brow of Necessity, and warmed her so far as al-

* The English are branded, perhaps unjustly, with being addicted to suicide about this time of the year.

most to make her assume the features and likeness of Choice. December, January, and February, passed on after the rest, all in furs: there was little distinction to be made amongst them; and they were only more or less displeasing as they discovered more or less haste towards the grateful return of Spring. Z.

No. 426.] *Wednesday, July* 9, 1712.

——Quid non mortalia pectora cogis,
Auri sacra fames? *Virg. Æn.* iii. 56.

O cursed hunger of pernicious gold?
What bands of faith can impious lucre hold!
Dryden.

A VERY agreeable friend of mine the other day, carrying me in his coach into the country to dinner, fell into a discourse concerning the 'care of parents due to their children,' and the 'piety of children towards their parents.' He was reflecting upon the succession of particular virtues and qualities there might be preserved from one generation to another, if these regards were reciprocally held in veneration: but as he never fails to mix an air of mirth and good-humour with his good sense and reasoning, he entered into the following relation.

'I will not be confident in what century, or under what reign it happened, that this want of mutual confidence and right understanding between father and son was fatal to the family of the Valentines in Germany. Basilius Valentinus was a person who had arrived at the utmost perfection in the hermetic art, and initiated his son Alexandrinus in the same mysteries: but, as you know they are not to be attained but by the painful, the pious, the chaste, and pure of heart, Basilius did not open to him, because of his youth, and the deviations too natural to it, the greatest secrets of which he was master, as well knowing that the operation would fail in the hands of a man so liable to errors in life as Alexandrinus. But believing, from a certain indisposition of mind as well as body, his dissolution was drawing nigh, he called Alexandrinus to him, and as he lay on a couch, over against which his son was seated, and prepared by sending out servants one after another, and admonition to examine that no one overheard them, he revealed the most important of his secrets with the solemnity and language of an adept. "My son," said he, "many have been the watchings, long the lucubrations, constant the labours of thy father, not only to gain a great and plentiful estate to his posterity, but also to take care that he should have no posterity. Be not amazed my child: I do not mean that thou shalt be taken from me, but that I will never leave thee, and consequently cannot be said to have posterity. Behold, my dearest Alexandrinus, the effect of what was propagated in nine months. We are not to contradict nature, but to follow and to help her; just as long as an infant is in the womb of its parent, so long are these medicines of revivification in preparing. Observe this small phial and this little gallipot—in this an ungent, in the other a liquor. In these, my child, are collected such powers, as shall revive the springs of life when they are yet but just ceased, and give new strength, new spirits, and, in a word, wholly restore all the organs and senses of the human body to as great a duration as it had before enjoyed from its birth to the day of the application of these my medicines. But, my beloved son, care must be taken to apply them within ten hours after the breath is out of the body, while yet the clay is warm with its late life, and yet capable of resuscitation. I find my frame grown crazy with perpetual toil and meditation; and I conjure you, as soon as I am dead, anoint me with this ungent; and when you see me begin to move, pour into my lips this inestimable liquor, else the force of the ointment will be ineffectual. By this means you will give me life as I gave you, and we will from that hour mutually lay aside the authority of having bestowed life on each other, live as brethren, and prepare new medicines against such another period of time as will demand another application of the same restoratives." In a few days, after these wonderful ingredients were delivered to Alexandrinus, Basilius departed this life. But such was the pious sorrow of the son at the loss of so excellent a father, and the first transports of grief had so wholly disabled him from all manner of business, that he never thought of the medicines till the time to which his father had limited their efficacy was expired. To tell the truth, Alexandrinus was a man of wit and pleasure, and considered his father had lived out his natural time; his life was long and uniform, suitable to the regularity of it; but that he himself, poor sinner, wanted a new life to repent of a very bad one hitherto; and, in the examination of his heart, resolved to go on as he did with this natural being of his, but repent very faithfully, and spend very piously the life to which he should be restored by application of these rarities, when time should come to his own person.

'It has been observed, that Providence frequently punishes the self-love of men, who would do immoderately for their own offspring, with children very much below their characters and qualifications; insomuch that they only transmit their names to be borne by those who give daily proofs of the vanity of the labour and ambition of their progenitors.

'It happened thus in the family of Basilius; for Alexandrinus began to enjoy his ample fortune in all the extremities of household expense, furniture, and insolent equipage; and this he pursued till the day of his own departure began, as he grew sensible, to approach. As Basilius was punished with a son very unlike him, Alexandrinus was visited by one of his own disposition. It is natural that ill men should be suspicious; and Alexandrinus, besides that jealousy, had proofs of the vicious disposition of his son Renatus, for that was his name.

'Alexandrinus, as I have observed, having very good reason for thinking it unsafe to trust the real secret of his phial and gallipot to any man living, projected to make sure work, and hope for his success depending from the avarice, not the bounty of his benefactor.

'With this thought he called Renatus to his bed-side, and bespoke him in the most pathetic gesture and accent. "As much, my son, as you have been addicted to vanity and pleasure, as I also have been before you,* you nor I could escape the fame or the good effects of the profound knowledge of our progenitor, the renowned Basilius. His symbol is very well known in the philosophic world; and I shall never forget the venerable air of his countenance, when he let me into the profound mysteries of the smaragdine tables of Hermes. "It is true," said he, "and far removed from all colour of deceit; that which is inferior is like that which is superior, by which are acquired and perfected all the miracles of a certain work. The father is the sun, the mother the moon, the wind is the womb, the earth is the nurse of it, and mother of all perfection. All this must be received with modesty and wisdom." The chymical people carry, in all their jargon, a whimsical sort of piety which is ordinary with great lovers of money, and is no more but deceiving themselves, that their regularity and strictness of manners, for the ends of this world, has some affinity to the innocence of heart which must recommend them to the next. Renatus wondered to hear his father talk so like an adept, and with such a mixture of piety; while Alexandrinus, observing his attention fixed, proceeded. "This phial, child, and this little earthen pot, will add to thy estate so much as to make thee the richest man in the German empire. I am going to my long home, but shall not return to common dust." Then he resumed a countenance of alacrity, and told him, that if within an hour after his death he anointed his whole body, and poured down his throat that liquor which he had from old Basilius, the corpse would be converted into pure gold. I will not pretend to express to you the unfeigned tenderness that passed between these two extraordinary persons; but if the father recommended the care of his remains with vehemence and affection, the son was not behind hand in professing that he would not cut the least bit off him, but upon the utmost extremity, or to provide for his younger brothers and sisters.

* The word 'neither' seems omitted here, though it is not in the original publication in folio, or in the edition in 8vo. of 1712.

'Well, Alexandrinus died, and the heir of his body (as our term is) could not forbear, in the wantonness of his heart, to measure the length and breadth of his beloved father, and cast up the ensuing value of him before he proceeded to the operation. When he knew the immense reward of his pains, he began the work: but, lo! when he had anointed the corpse all over, and began to apply the liquor, the body stirred, and Renatus, in a fright, broke the phial.'

T.

No. 427.] *Thursday, July* 10, 1712.

Quantum a rerum turpitudine abes, tantum te a verborum libertate sejungas. *Tull.*

We should be as careful of our words, as our actions; and as far from speaking, as from doing ill.

It is a certain sign of an ill heart to be inclined to defamation. They who are harmless and innocent can have no gratification that way; but it ever arises from a neglect of what is laudable in a man's self, and an impatience in seeing it in another. Else why should virtue provoke? Why should beauty displease in such a degree, that a man given to scandal never lets the mention of either pass by him, without offering something to the diminution of it? A lady the other day at a visit, being attacked somewhat rudely by one whose own character has been very rudely treated, answered a great deal of heat and intemperance very calmly, "Good madam, spare me, who am none of your match; I speak ill of nobody, and it is a new thing to me to be spoken ill of." Little minds think fame consists in the number of votes they have on their side among the multitude, whereas it is really the inseparable follower of good and worthy actions. Fame is as natural a follower of merit, as a shadow is of a body. It is true, when crowds press upon you, this shadow cannot be seen; but when they separate from around you, it will again appear. The lazy, the idle, and the froward, are the persons who are most pleased with the little tales which pass about the town to the disadvantage of the rest of the world. Were it not for the pleasure of speaking ill, there are numbers of people who are too lazy to go out of their own houses, and too ill-natured to open their lips in conversation. It was not a little diverting the other day to observe a lady reading a post-letter, and at these words, 'After all her airs, he has heard some story or other, and the match is broken off,' gives orders in the midst of her reading, 'Put to the horses.' That a young woman of merit had missed an advantageous settlement was news not to be delayed, lest somebody else should have given her malicious acquaintance that satisfaction before her. The unwillingness to receive good tidings is a quality as inseparable from a scandal-bearer, as the readiness to divulge bad. But, alas! how wretchedly low and contemptible is that state of mind, that cannot be pleased but by what is the subject of lamentation. This temper has ever been, in the highest degree, odious to gallant spirits. The Persian soldier, who was heard reviling Alexander the Great, was well admonished by his officer, 'Sir, you are paid to fight against Alexander, and not to rail at him.'

Cicero, in one of his pleadings, defending his client from general scandal, says very handsomely, and with much reason, 'There are many who have particular engagements to the prosecutor; there are many who are known to have ill-will to him for whom I appear; there are many who are naturally addicted to defamation, and envious of any good to any man, who may have contributed to spread reports of this kind; for nothing is so swift as scandal, nothing is more easily set abroad, nothing received with more welcome, nothing diffuses itself so universally. I shall not desire, that if any report to our disadvantage has any ground for it, you would overlook or extenuate it: but if there be any thing advanced, without a person who can say whence he had it, or which is attested by one who forgot who told him it, or who had it from one of so little consideration that he did not think it worth his notice, all such testimonies as these, I know, you will think too slight to have any credit against the innocence and honour of your fellow citizens.' When an ill report is traced, it very often vanishes among such as the orator has here recited. And how despicable a creature must that be, who is in pain for what passes among so frivolous a people! There is a town in Warwickshire, of good note, and formerly pretty famous for much animosity and dissention, the chief families of which have now turned all their whispers, backbitings, envies, and private malices, into mirth and entertainment, by means of a peevish old gentlewoman, known by the title of the lady Bluemantle. This heroine had, for many years together outdone the whole sisterhood of gossips in invention, quick utterance, and unprovoked malice. This good body is of a lasting constitution, though extremely decayed in her eyes, and decrepid in her feet. The two circumstances of being always at home, from her lameness, and very attentive from her blindness, make her lodgings the receptacle of all that passes in town, good or bad; but for the latter she seems to have the better memory. There is another thing to be noted of her, which is, that, as it is usual with old people, she has a livelier memory of things which passed when she was very young than of late years. Add to all this, that she does not only not love any body, but she hates every body. The statue in Rome* does not serve to vent malice half so well as this old lady does to disperse it. She does not know the author of any thing that is told her, but can readily repeat the matter itself; therefore, though she exposes all the whole town, she offends no one body in it. She is so exquisitely restless and peevish, that she quarrels with all about her, and sometimes in a freak will instantly change her habitation. To indulge this humour, she is led about the grounds belonging to the same house she is in; and the persons to whom she is to remove being in the plot, are ready to receive her at her own chamber again. At stated times the gentlewoman at whose house she supposes she is at the time, is sent for to quarrel with, according to her common custom. When they have a mind to drive the jest, she is immediately urged to that degree, that she will board in a family with which she has never yet been; and away she will go this instant, and tell them all that the rest have been saying of them. By this means she has been an inhabitant of every house in the place, without stirring from the same habitation: and the many stories which every body furnishes her with, to favour the deceit, make her the general intelligencer of the town of all that can be said by one woman against another. Thus groundless stories die away, and sometimes truths are smothered under the general word, when they have a mind to discountenance a thing, 'Oh! that is in my lady Bluemantle's Memoirs.'

Whoever receives impressions to the disadvantage of others, without examination, is to be had in no other credit for intelligence than this good lady Bluemantle, who is subjected to have her ears imposed upon for want of other helps to better information. Add to this, that other scandal-bearers suspend the use of these faculties which she has lost, rather than apply them to do justice to their neighbours: and I think, for the service of my fair readers, to acquaint them, that there is a voluntary lady Blue mantle at every visit in town. T.

* A statue of Pasquin in that city, on which sarcastic remarks were pasted, and thence called Pasquinades.

No. 428.] *Friday, July* 11, 1712.

Occupet extremum scabies.——

Hor Ars Poet. ver. 417

The devil take the hindmost!——*English Proverbs.*

It is an impertinent and unreasonable fault in conversation, for one man to take up all the discourse. It may possibly be objected to me myself, that I am guilty in this kind, in entertaining the town every day, and not giving so many able persons, who have it more in their power, and as much in their inclination, an opportunity to oblige mankind with their thoughts. 'Besides,' said one whom I overheard the other day, 'why must this paper turn altogether upon topics of learning and morality? Why should it pretend only to wit, humour, or the like—things which are useful only to men of literature, and superior education? I would have it consist also of all things which may be necessary or useful to any part of society; and the mechanic arts should have their place as well as the liberal. The ways of gain, husbandry, and thrift, will serve a greater number of people than discourses upon what was well said or done by such a philosopher, hero, general, or poet.'—I no sooner heard this critic talk of my works, but I minuted what he had said; and from that instant resolved to enlarge the plan of my speculations, by giving notice to all persons of all orders, and each sex, that if they are pleased to send me discourses, with their names and places of abode to them, so that I can be satisfied the writings are authentic, such their labours shall be faithfully inserted in this paper. It will be of much more consequence to a youth, in his apprenticeship, to know by what rules and arts such-a-one became sheriff of the city of London, than to see the sign of one of his own quality with a lion's heart in each hand. The world, indeed, is enchanted with romantic and improbable achievements, when the plain path to respective greatness and success, in the way of life a man is in, is wholly overlooked. Is it possible that a young man at present could pass his time better than in reading the history of stocks, and knowing by what secret springs they have had such sudden ascents and falls in the same day! Could he be better conducted in his way to wealth, which is the great article of life, than in a treaties dated from 'Change-alley by an able proficient there? Nothing certainly could be more useful, than to be well instructed in his hopes and fears; to be diffident when others exult; and with a secret joy buy when others think it their interest to sell. I invite all persons who have any thing to say for the profitable information of the public, to take their turns in my paper: they are welcome from the late noble inventor of the longitude, to the humble author of straps for razors. If to carry ships in safety, to give help to a people tossed in a troubled sea, without knowing to what shores they bear, what rocks to avoid, or what coast to pray for in their extremity, be a worthy labour, and an invention that deserves a statue; at the same time, he who has found a means to let the instrument which is to make your visage less horrible, and your person more snug, easy in the operation, is worthy of some kind of good reception. If things of high moment meet with renown, those of little consideration, since of any consideration, are not to be despised. In order that no merit may lie hid, and no art unimproved, I repeat it, that I call artificers, as well as philosophers, to my assistance in the public service. It would be of great use if we had an exact history of the successes of every great shop within the city walls, what tracts of land have been purchased by a constant attendance within a walk of thirty foot. If it could also be noted in the equipage of those who are ascended from the successful trade of their ancestors into figure and equipage, such accounts would quicken industry in the pursuit of such acquisitions, and discountenance luxury in the enjoyment of them.

To diversify these kinds of information, the industry of the female world is not to be unobserved. She to whose household virtues it is owing, that men do honour to her husband, should be recorded with veneration; she who has wasted his labours, with infamy. When we are come into domestic life in this manner, to awaken caution and attendance to the main point, it would not be amiss to give now and then a touch of tragedy, and describe that most dreadful of all human conditions, the case of bank ruptcy: how plenty, credit, cheerfulness, full hopes, and easy possessions, are in an instant turned into penury, feint aspects, diffidence, sorrow, and misery; how the man, who with an open hand the day before could administer to the extremities of others is shunned to-day by the friend of his bosom. It would be useful to show how just this is on the negligent, how lamentable on the industrious. A paper written by a merchant might give this island a true sense of the worth and importance of his character, it might be visible from what he could say, that no soldier entering a breach adventures more for honour, than the trader does for wealth to his country. In both cases, the adventurers have their own advantage; but I know no cases wherein every body else is a sharer in the success.

It is objected by readers of history, that the battles in those narrations are scarce ever to be understood. This misfortune is to be ascribed to the ignorance of historians in the methods of drawing up, changing the forms of a battalia, and the enemy retreating from, as well as approaching to, the charge. But in the discourses from the correspondents, whom I now invite, the danger will be of another kind; and it is necessary to caution them only against using terms of art, and describing things that are familiar to them in words unknown to the reader. I promise myself a great harvest of new circumstances, persons, and things, from this proposal; and a world, which many think they are well acquainted with, discovered as wholly new. This sort of intelligence will give a lively image of the chain and mutual dependance of human society, take off impertinent prejudices, enlarge the minds of those whose views are confined to their own circumstances; and, in short, if the knowing in several arts, professions, and trades, will exert themselves, it cannot but produce a new field of diversion and instruction, more agreeable than has yet appeared. T

No. 429.] *Saturday, July* 12, 1712.

——Populumque falsis ded)cet uti
Vocibus—— *Hor.* Od. ii. Lib. 2. 19.

From cheats of words the :rowd she brings
To real estimate of things —*Creech.*

'Mr. Spectator,—Since I gave an account of an agreeable set of company which were gone down into the country, I have received advices from thence, that the institution of an infirmary for those who should be out of humour has had very good effects. My letters mention particular circumstances of two or three persons, who had the good sense to retire of their own accord, and notified that they were withdrawn, with the reasons of it to the company in their respective memorials.'

" *The humble Memorial of Mrs. Mary Dainty, Spinster,*

"Showeth,

"That conscious of her own want of merit, accompanied with a vanity of being admired, she had gone into exile of her own accord.

"She is sensible, that a vain person is the most insufferable creature living in a well-bred assembly.

"That she desired, before she appeared in public again, she might have assurances, that though she might be thought handsome, there might not more address of compliment be paid to her than to the rest of the company.

"That she conceived it a kind of superiority, that one person should take upon him to commend another.

"Lastly, that she went into the infirmary, to avoid a particular person, who took upon him to profess an admiration of her.

"She therefore prayed, that to applaud out of due place might be declared an offence, and punished in the same manner with detraction, in that the latter did but report persons defective, and the former made them so.

"All which is submitted, &c."

'There appeared a delicacy and sincerity in this memorial very uncommon; but my friend informs me, that the allegations of it were groundless, insomuch that this declaration of an aversion to being praised was understood to be no other than a secret trap to purchase it, for which reason it lies still on the table unanswered.'

" *The humble Memorial of the Lady Lydia Loller,*

"Showeth,

"That the lady Lydia is a woman of quality; married to a private gentleman.

"That she finds herself neither well nor ill.

"That her husband is a clown.

"That the lady Lydia cannot see company.

"That she desires the infirmary may be her apartment dui ng her stay in the countı y.

"That they would please to make merry with their equals.

"That Mr. Loller might stay with them if he thought fit."

'It was immediately resolved, that lady Lydia was still at London.'

" *The humble Memorial of Thomas Sudden, Esq. of the Inner Temple,*

"Showeth,

"That Mr. Sudden is conscious that he is too much given to argumentation.

"That he talks loud.

"That he is apt to think all things matter of debate.

"That he stayed behind in Westminster-hall, when the late shake of the roof happened, only because a counsel of the other side asserted it was coming down.

"That he cannot for his life consent to any thing.

"That he stays in the infirmary to forget himself.

"That as soon as he has forgot himself, he will wait on the company."

'His indisposition was allowed to be sufficient to require a cessation from company.'

" *The Memorial of Frank Jolly,*

"Showeth,

"That he hath put himself into the infirmary, in regard he is sensible of a certain rustic mirth, which renders him unfit for polite conversation.

"That he intends to prepare himself, by abstinence and thin diet, to be one of the company.

"That at present he comes into a room as if he were an express from abroad.

"That he has chosen an apartment with a matted antechamber, to practise motion without being heard.

"That he bows, talks, drinks, eats, and helps himself before a glass, to learn to act with moderation.

"That by reason of his luxuriant health he is oppressive to persons of composed behaviour.

"That he is endeavouring to forget the word 'pshaw, pshaw.'

"That he is also weaning himself from his cane.

"That when he has learnt to live without his said cane, he will wait on the company, &c."

" *The Memorial of John Rhubarb, Esq.*

"Showeth,

"That your petitioner has retired to the infirmary, but that he is in perfect good health, except that he has by long use, and for want of discourse, contracted an habit of complaint that he is sick.

"That he wants for nothing under the sun, but what to say, and therefore has fallen into this unhappy malady of complaining that he is sick.

"That this custom of his makes him, by his own confession, fit only for the infirmary, and therefore he has not waited for being sentenced to it.

"That he is conscious there is nothing more improper than such a complaint in good company, in that they must pity, whether they think the lamenter ill or not; and that the complainant must make a silly figure, whether he is pitied or not.

"Your petitioner humbly prays that he may have people to know how he does, and he will make his appearance."

'The valetudinarian was likewise easily excused: and the society, being resolved not only to make it their business to pass their time agreeably for the present season, but also to commence such habits in themselves as may be of use in their future conduct in general, are very ready to give into a fancied or real incapacity to join with their measures, in order to have no humourist, proud man, impertinent or sufficient fellow, break in upon their happiness. Great evils seldom happen to disturb company; but indulgence in particularities of humour is the seed of making half our time hang in suspense, or waste away under real discomposures.

'Among other things, it is carefully provided that there may not be disagreeable familiarities. No one is to appear in the public rooms undressed, or enter abruptly into each other's apartment without intimation. Every one has hitherto been so careful in his behaviour, that there has but one offender, in ten days' time, been sent into the infirmary, and that was for throwing away his cards at whist.

'He has offered his submission in the following terms:

"*The humble Petition of Jeoffry Hotspur, Esq.*

"Showeth,

"Though the petitioner swore, stamped, and threw down his cards, he has all imaginable respect for the ladies, and the whole company.

"That he humbly desires it may be considered, in the case of gaming, there are many motives which provoke the disorder.

"That the desire of gain, and the desire of victory, are both thwarted in losing.

"That all conversations in the world have indulged human infirmity in this case.

"Your petitioner therefore most humbly prays, that he may be restored to the company: and he hopes to bear ill-fortune with a good grace for the future, and to demean himself so as to be no more than cheerful when he wins, than grave when he loses."

T.

No. 430.] *Monday, July* 14, 1712.

Quære peregrinum, vicinia rauca reclamat.
Hor. Ep. xvii. Lib. 1. 62.

———The crowd replies,
Go seek a stranger to believe thy lies.—*Creech.*

'SIR,—As you are a Spectator-general, you may with authority censure whatever looks ill, and is offensive to the sight; the worst nuisance of which kind, methinks, is the scandalous appearance of poor in all parts of this wealthy city. Such miserable objects affect the compassionate beholder with dismal ideas, discompose the cheerfulness of his mind, and deprive him of the pleasure he might otherwise take in surveying the grandeur of our metropolis. Who can without remorse see a disabled sailor, the purveyor of our luxury, destitute of necessaries? Who can behold the honest soldier that bravely withstood the enemy, prostrate and in want among friends? It were endless to mention all the variety of wretchedness, and the numberless poor that not only singly, but in companies, implore your charity. Spectacles of this nature every where occur; and it is unaccountable that amongst the many lamentable cries that infest this town, your comptroller-general should not take notice of the most shocking, viz. those of the needy and afflicted. I cannot but think he waived it merely out of good breeding, choosing rather to waive his resentment than upbraid his countrymen with inhumanity: however, let not charity be sacrificed to popularity; and if his ears were deaf to their complaint, let not your eyes overlook their persons. There are, I know, many impostors among them. Lameness and blindness are certainly very often acted; but can those who have their sight and limbs employ them better than in knowing whether they are counterfeited or not? I know not which of the two misapplies his senses most, he who pretends himself blind to move compassion, or he who beholds a miserable object without pitying it. But in order to remove such impediments, I wish, Mr. Spectator, you would give us a discourse upon beggars, that we may not pass by true objects of charity, or give to impostors. I looked out of my window the other morning earlier than ordinary, and saw a blind beggar, an hour before the passage he stands in is frequented, with a needle and a thread thriftily mending his stockings. My astonishment was still greater, when I beheld a lame fellow, whose legs were too big to walk within an hour after, bring him a pot of ale. I will not mention the shakings distortions, and convulsions, which many of them practise to gain an alms; but sure I am they ought to be taken care of in this condition, either by the beadle or the magistrate. They, it seems, relieve their posts according to their talents. There is the voice of an old woman never begins to beg till nine in the evening; and then she is destitute of lodging, turned out for want of rent, and has the same ill fortune every night in the year. You should employ an officer to hear the distress of each beggar that is constant at a particular place, who is ever in the same tone, and succeeds because his audience is continually changing, though he does not alter his lamentation. If we have nothing else for our money, let us have more invention to be cheated with. All which is submitted to your spectatorial vigilance; and I am, sir, your most humble servant.'

'SIR,—I was last Sunday highly transported at our parish-church; the gentleman in the pulpit pleaded movingly in behalf of the poor children, and they for themselves much more forcibly by singing a hymn; and I had the happiness of being a contributor to this little religious institution of innocents, and am sure I never disposed of money more to my satisfaction and advantage. The inward joy I find in myself, and the good-will I bear to mankind, make me heartily wish those pious works may be encouraged, that the present promoters may reap delight, and posterity the benefit of them. But whilst we are building this beautiful edifice, let not the old ruins remain in view to sully the prospect. Whilst we are cultivating and improving this young hopeful offspring, let not the ancient and helpless creatures be shamefully neglected. The crowds of poor, or pretended poor, in every place, are a great reproach to us, and eclipse the glory of all other charity. It is the utmost reproach to society, that there should be a poor man unrelieved, or a poor rogue unpunished. I hope you will think no part of human life out of your consideration, but will, at your leisure, give us the history of plenty and want, and the natural gradations towards them, calculated for the cities of London and Westminster. I am, sir, your most humble servant,

'T. D.'

'MR. SPECTATOR,—I beg you would be pleased to take notice of a very great indecency, which is extremely common, though, I think, never yet under your censure. It is, sir, the strange freedoms some ill-bred married people take in company; the unseasonable fondness of some husbands, and the ill-timed tenderness of some wives. They talk and act as if modesty was only fit for maids and bachelors, and that too before both. I was once, Mr. Spectator, where the fault I speak of was so very flagrant, that (being, you must know, a very bashful fellow, and several young ladies in the room,) I protest I was quite out of countenance. Lucina, it seems, was breeding; and she did nothing but entertain the company with a discourse upon the difficulty of reckoning to a day; and said she knew those who were certain to an hour; then fell a laughing at a silly inexperienced creature, who was a month above her time. Upon her husband's coming in, she put several questions to him; which he, not caring to resolve, "Well," cries Lucina, "I shall have 'em all at night."—But lest I should seem guilty of the very fault I write against, I shall only entreat Mr. Spectator to correct such misdemeanors.

"For higher of the genial bed by far,
And with mysterious reverence, I deem."

I am, sir, your humble servant,

'THOMAS MEANWELL.'

No. 431.] *Tuesday, July* 15, 1712.

Quid dulcius hominum generi a natura datum est, quam sui quique liberi? *Tull.*

What is there in nature so dear to a man as his own children?

I HAVE lately been casting in my thoughts the several unhappinesses of life, and comparing the infelicities of old age to those of infancy. The calamities of children are due to the negligence and misconduct of parents; those of age to the past life which led to it. I have here the history of a boy and girl to their wedding-day, and I think I cannot give the reader a livelier image of the insipid way in which time uncultivated passes, than by entertaining him with their authentic epistles, expressing all that was remarkable in their lives, till the period of their life above-mentioned. The sentence at the head of this paper, which is only a warm interrogation, 'What is there in nature so dear as a man's own children to him?' is all the reflection I shall at present make on those who are negligent or cruel in the education of them.

'MR. SPECTATOR,—I am now entering into my one and twentieth year, and do not know that I had one day's thorough satisfaction since I came to years of any reflection, till the time they say others lose their liberty—the day of my marriage. I am son to a gentleman of a very great estate, who resolved to keep me out of the vices of the age; and, in order to it, never let me see any thing that he thought could give me any pleasure. At ten years old I was put to a grammar-school, where my master received orders every post to use me very severely, and have no regard to my having a great estate. At fifteen I was removed to the university, where I lived, out of my father's great discretion, in scandalous poverty and want, till I was big enough to be married, and I was sent for to see the lady who sends you the underwritten. When we were put together, we both considered that we could not be worse than we were in taking one another, and, out of a desire of liberty, entered into wedlock. My father says I am now a man, and may speak to him like another gentleman. I am, sir, your most humble servant,

'RICHARD RENTFREE.'

'MR. SPEC,—I grew tall and wild at my mother's, who is a gay widow, and did not care for showing me, till about two years and a half ago; at which time my guardian-uncle sent me to a boarding-school, with orders to contradict me in nothing, for I had been misused enough already. I had not been there above a month when, being in the kitchen, I saw some oatmeal on the dresser; I put two or three corns in my mouth, liked it, stole a handful, went into my chamber, chewed it, and for two months after never failed taking toll of every pennyworth of oatmeal that came into the house; but one day playing with a tobacco-pipe between my teeth, it happened to break in my mouth, and the spitting out the pieces left such a delicious roughness on my tongue, that I could not be satisfied till I had champed up the remaining part of the pipe. I forsook the oatmeal and stuck to the pipes three months, in which time I had dispensed with thirty-seven foul pipes, all to the bowls: they belonged to an old gentleman, father to my governess. He locked up the clean ones. I left off eating of pipes, and fell to licking of chalk. I was soon tired of this. I then nibbled all the red wax of our last ball-tickets, and, three weeks after, the black wax from the burying-tickets of the old gentleman. Two months after this, I lived upon thunder-bolts, a certain long round blueish stone which I found among the gravel in our garden. I was wonderfully delighted with this; but thunder-bolts growing scarce, I fastened tooth and nail upon our garden-wall, which I stuck to almost a twelvemonth, and had in that time peeled and devoured half a foot towards our neighbour's yard. I now thought myself the happiest creature in the world; and I believe, in my conscience, I had eaten quite through, had I had it in my chamber; but now I became lazy and unwilling to stir, and was obliged to seek food nearer home. I then took a strange hankering to coals; I fell to scranching 'em, and had already consumed, I am certain, as much as would have dressed my wedding dinner, when my uncle came for me home. He was in the parlour with my governess, when I was called down. I went in, fell on my knees, for he made me call him father; and when I expected the blessing I asked, the good gentleman, in a surprise, turns himself to my governess, and asks, "whether this (pointing to me) was his daughter? This," added he, "is the very picture of death. My child was a plump-faced, hale, fresh-coloured girl; but this looks as if she was half-starved, a mere skeleton." My governess, who is really a good woman, assured my father I had wanted for nothing; and withal told him I was continually eating some trash or other, and that I was almost eaten up with the green-sickness, her orders being never to cross me. But this magnified but little with my father, who presently, in a kind of pet, paying for my board, took me home with him. I had not been long at home, but one Sunday at church (I shall never forget it) I saw a young neighbouring gentleman that pleased me hugely; I liked him of all men I ever saw in my life, and began to wish I could be as pleasing to him. The very next day he came with his father a visiting to our house: we were left alone together, with directions on both sides to be in love with one another; and in three weeks time we were married. I regained my former health and complexion, and am now as happy as the day is long. Now, Mr. Spec, I desire you would find out some name for these craving damsels, whether dignified or distinguished under some or all of the following denominations, to wit, "Trash eaters, Oatmeal-chewers, Pipe-champers, Chalk-lickers, Wax-nibblers, Coal-scranchers, Wall-peelers, or Gravel-diggers;" and, good sir, do your utmost endeavour to prevent (by exposing) this unaccountable folly, so prevailing among the young ones of our sex, who may not meet with such sudden good luck as, sir, your constant reader, and very humble servant,

'SABINA GREEN,

T. 'Now SABINA RENTFREE.'

No. 432.] *Wednesday, July* 16, 1712.

——Inter strepit anser olores. *Virg.* Ecl. ix. 30.

He gabbles like a goose amidst the swan-like quire. *Dryden.*

'Oxford, July 14.

'MR. SPECTATOR,—According to a late invitation in one of your papers to every man who pleases to write, I have sent you the following short dissertation against the vice of being prejudiced. Your most humble servant.'

"Man is a sociable creature, and a lover of glory; whence it is, that when several persons are united in the same society, they are studious to lessen the reputation of others, in order to raise their own. The wise are content to guide the springs in silence, and rejoice in secret at their regular progress. To prate and triumph is the part allotted to the trifling and superficial. The geese were providentially ordained to save the Capitol. Hence it is, that the invention of marks and devices to distinguish parties is owing to the beaus and belles of this island. Hats moulded into different cocks and pinches, have long bid mutual defiance; patches have been set against patches in battle array: stocks have risen and fallen in proportion to head-dresses; and peace and war been expected, as the white or the red hood hath prevailed. These are the standard-bearers in our contending armies, the dwarfs and 'squires who carry the impresses of the giants or knights, not born to fight themselves, but to prepare the way for the ensuing combat.

"It is a matter of wonder to reflect how far men of weak understanding, and strong fancy, are hurried by their prejudices, even to the believing that the whole body of the adverse party are a band of villains and dæmons. Foreigners complain that the English are the proudest nation under heaven. Perhaps they too have their share, but be that as it will, general charges against bodies of men is the fault I am writing against. It must be owned, to our shame, that our common people, and most who have not travelled, have an irrational contempt for the language, dress, customs, and even the shape and minds of other nations. Some men, otherwise of sense, have wondered that a great genius should spring out of Ireland; and think you mad in affirming that fine odes have been written in Lapland.

"This spirit of rivalship, which heretofore reigned in the two universities, is extinct, and almost over betwixt college and college. In parishes and schools the thirst for glory still obtains. At the seasons of foot-ball and cock-fighting, these little republics reassume their national hatred to each other. My tenant in the country is verily persuaded, that the parish of the enemy hath not one honest man in it.

"I always hated satires against women, and satires against men: I am apt to suspect a stranger who laughs at the religion of the faculty: my spleen rises at a dull rogue who is severe upon mayors and aldermen; and I was never better pleased than with a piece of justice executed upon the body of a Templar who was very arch upon parsons.

"The necessities of mankind require various employments; and whoever excels in his province is worthy of praise. All men are not educated after the same manner, nor have all the same talents. Those who are deficient deserve our compassion, and have a title to our assistance. All cannot be bred in the same place; but in all places there arise, at different times, such persons as do honour to their society, which may raise envy in little souls, but are admired and cherished by generous spirits.

"It is certainly a great happiness to be educated in societies of great and eminent men. Their instructions and examples are of extraordinary advantage. It is highly proper to instil such a reverence of the governing persons, and concern for the honour of the place, as may spur the growing members to worthy pursuits and honest emulation; but to swell young minds with vain thoughts of the dignity of their own brotherhood, by debasing and vilifying all others, doth them a real injury. By this means I have found that their efforts have become languid, and their prattle irksome, as thinking it sufficient praise that they are children of so illustrious and ample a family. I should think it a surer as well as more generous method, to set before the eyes of youth such persons as have made a noble progress in fraternities less talked of; which seems tacitly to reproach their sloth, who loll so heavily in the seats of mighty improvement. Active spirits hereby would enlarge their notions; whereas, by a servile imitation of one, or perhaps two, admired men in their own body, they can only gain a secondary and derivative kind of fame. These copiers of men, like those of authors or painters, run into affectations of some oddness, which perhaps was not disagreeable in the original, but sits ungracefully on the narrow-souled transcriber.

"By such early corrections of vanity, while boys are growing into men, they will gradually learn not to censure superficially; but imbibe those principles of general kindness and humanity, which alone can make them easy to themselves, and beloved by others.

"Reflections of this nature have expunged all prejudice out of my heart; insomuch, that though I am a firm protestant, I hope to see the pope and cardinals without violent emotions; and though I am naturally grave, I expect to meet good company at Paris. I am, sir, your humble servant."

'Mr. Spectator,—I find you are a general undertaker, and have, by your correspondents or self, an insight into most things; which makes me apply myself to you at present, in the sorest calamity that ever befel man. My wife has taken something ill of me, and has not spoke one word, good or bad, to me, or any body in the family, since Friday was seven-night. What must a man do in that case? Your advice would be a great obligation to, sir, your most humble servant,

'RALPH THIMBLETON.'

'July 15, 1712.

'Mr. Spectator,—When you want a trifle to fill up a paper, in inserting this you will lay an obligation on your humble servant, OLIVIA.'

"Dear Olivia,—It is but this moment I have had the happiness of knowing to whom I am obliged for the present I received the second of April. I am heartily sorry it did not come to hand the day before; for I cannot but think it very hard upon people to lose their jest, that offer at one but once a-year. I congratulate myself however upon the earnest given me of something farther intended in my favour, for I am told that the man who is thought worthy by a lady to make a fool of stands fair enough in her opinion to become one day her husband. Till such time as I have the honour of being sworn, I take leave to subscribe myself, dear Olivia, your fool elect, NICODEMUNCIO."

T.

No. 433.] *Thursday, July 17, 1712.*

Perlege Mæonio cantatas carmine ranas,
Et frontem nugis solvere disce meis.
Mart. Epig. clxxxiii. 14.

To banish anxious thought, and quiet pain,
Read Homer's frogs, or my more trifling strain.

The moral world, as consisting of males and females, is of a mixed nature, and filled with several customs, fashions, and ceremonies, which would have no place in it were there but one sex. Had our species no females in it, men would be quite different creatures from what they are at present: their endeavours to please the opposite sex polishes and refines them out of those manners which are most natural to them, and often sets them upon modelling themselves, not according to the plans which they approve in their own opinions, but according to those plans which they think are most agreeable to the female world. In a word, man would not only be an unhappy, but a rude unfinished creature, were he conversant with none but those of his own make.

Women, on the other side, are apt to form themselves in every thing with regard to that other half of reasonable creatures with whom they are here blended and confused: their thoughts are ever turned upon appearing amiable to the other sex; they talk, and move, and smile, with a design upon us; every feature of their faces, every part of their dress, is filled with snares and allurements. There would be no such animals as prudes or coquettes in the world, were there not such an animal as man. In short, it is the male that gives charms to woman-kind, that produces an air in their faces, a grace in their motions, a softness in their voices, and a delicacy in their complexions.

As this mutual regard between the two sexes tends to the improvement of each of them, we may observe that men are apt to degenerate into rough and brutal natures who live as if there were no such things as women in the world; as, on the contrary, women who have an indifference or aversion for their counterparts in human nature are generally sour and unamiable, sluttish and censorious.

I am led into this train of thoughts by a little manuscript which is lately fallen into my hands, and which I shall communicate to the reader, as I have done some other curious pieces of the same nature without troubling him with any inquiries about the author of it. It contains a summary account of two different states which bordered upon one another. The one was a commonwealth of Amazons, or women without men; the other was a republic of males, that had not a woman in the whole community. As these two states bordered upon one another, it was their way, it seems, to meet upon their frontiers at a certain season of the year, where those among the men who had not made their choice in any former meeting, associated themselves with particular women, whom they were afterwards obliged to look upon as their wives in every one of these yearly rencounters. The children that sprung up from this alliance, if males, were sent to their respective fathers; if females, continued with their mothers. By means of this anniversary carnival, which lasted about a week, the commonwealths were recruited from time to time, and supplied with their respective subjects.

These two states were engaged together in a perpetual league, offensive and defensive; so that if any foreign potentate offered to attack either of them, both of the sexes fell upon him at once, and quickly brought him to reason. It was remarkable that for many ages this agreement continued inviolable between the two states, notwithstanding, as was said before, they were husbands and wives; but this will not appear so wonderful, if we consider that they did not live together above a week in a year.

In the account which my author gives of the male republic, there were several customs very remarkable. The men never shaved their beards, or paired their nails, above once in a twelvemonth, which was probably about the time of the great annual meeting upon their frontiers. I find the name of a minister of state in one part of their history, who was fined for appearing too frequently in clean linen; and of a certain great general, who was turned out of his post for effeminacy, it having been proved upon him by several credible witnesses that he washed his face every morning. If any member of the commonwealth had a soft voice, a smooth face, or a supple behaviour, he was banished into the commonwealth of females, where he was treated as a slave, dressed in petticoats, and set a spinning. They had no titles of honour among them, but such as denoted some bodily strength or perfection, as such-a-one 'the tall,' such-a-one 'the stocky,' such-a-one 'the gruff.' Their public debates were generally managed with kicks and cuffs, insomuch that they often came from the council-table with broken shins, black eyes, and bloody noses. When they would reproach a man in the most bitter terms, they would tell him his teeth were white, or that he had a fair skin and a soft hand. The greatest man I meet with in their history, who was one who could lift five hundred weight, and wore such a prodigious pair of whiskers as had never been seen in the commonwealth before his time. These accomplishments, it seems, had rendered him so popular, that if he had not died very seasonably, it is thought he might have enslaved the republic. Having made this short extract out of the history of the male commonwealth, I shall look into the history of the neighbouring state, which consisted of females; and if I find any thing in it, will not fail to communicate it to the public.

C.

No. 434.] *Friday, July* 18, 1712.

Quales Threiciæ, cum flumina Thermodoontis
Pulsant, et pictis bellantur Amazones armis:
Seu circum Hyppolyten, seu cum se Martia curru
Penthesilea refert, magnoque ululante tumultu,
Fœminea exultant lunatis agmina peltis:

Virg. Æn. viii. 660

So march'd the Thracian Amazons of old,
When Thermodon with bloody billows roll'd:
Such troops as these in shining arms were seen,
When Theseus met in fight their maiden queen.
Such to the field Penthesilea led,
From the fierce virgin when the Grecians fled.
With such return'd triumphant from the war,
Her maids with cries attend the lofty car:
They clash with manly force their moony shields;
With female shouts resound the Phrygian fields.
Dryden.

HAVING carefully perused the manuscript I mentioned in my yesterday's paper, so far as it relates to the republic of women, I find in it several particulars which may very well deserve the reader's attention.

The girls of quality, from six to twelve years old, were put to public schools, where they learned to box and play at cudgles, with several other accomplishments of the same nature: so that nothing was more usual than to see a little miss returning home at night with a broken pate, or two or three teeth knocked out of her head. They were afterwards taught to ride the great horse, to shoot, dart or sling, and listed into several companies, in order to perfect themselves in military exercises. No woman was to be married till she had killed her man. The ladies of fashion used to play with young lions instead of lap-dogs; and when they made any parties of diversion, instead of entertaining themselves at ombre and piquet, they would wrestle and pitch the bar for a whole afternoon together. There was never any such thing as a blush seen, or a sigh heard, in the whole commonwealth. The women never dressed but to look terrible; to which end they would sometimes, after a battle, paint their cheeks with the blood of their enemies. For this reason, likewise, the face which had the most scars was looked upon as the most beautiful. If they found lace, jewels, ribands, or any ornaments in silver or gold, among the booty which they had taken, they used to dress their horses with it, but never entertained a thought of wearing it themselves. There were particular rights and privileges allowed to any member of the commonwealth who was a mother of three daughters. The senate was made up of old women, for by the laws of the country, none was to be a counsellor of state that was not past child-bearing. They used to boast that their republic had continued four thousand years, which is altogether improbable, unless we may suppose, what I am very apt to think, that they measured their time by lunar years.

There was a great revolution brought about in this female republic by means of a neighbouring king, who had made war upon them several years with various success, and at length overthrew them in a very great battle. This defeat they ascribe to several causes: some say that the secretary of state, having been troubled with the vapours, had committed some fatal mistakes in several despatches about that time. Others pretend that the first minister being big with child, could not attend the public affairs as so great an exigency of state required; but this I can give no manner of credit to, since it seems to contradict a fundamental maxim in their government, which I have before mentioned. My author gives the most probable reason of this great disaster; for he affirms that the general was brought to bed, or (as others say) miscarried, the very night before the battle: however it was, this single overthrow obliged them to call in the male republic to their assistance; but, notwithstanding their common efforts to repulse the victorious enemy, the war continued for many years before they could entirely bring it to a happy conclusion.

The campaigns which both sexes passed together made them so well acquainted with one another, that at the end of the war they did not care for parting. In the beginning of it they lodged in separate camps, but afterwards, as they grew more familiar, they pitched their tents promiscuously.

From this time, the armies being checkered with both sexes, they polished apace. The men used to invite their fellow soldiers into their quarters, and would dress their tents with flowers and boughs for their reception. If they chanced to like one more than another, they would be cutting her name in the table, or chalking out her figure upon a wall, or talking of her in a kind of rapturous language, which by degrees improved into verse and sonnet. These were as the first rudiments of architecture, painting, and poetry, among this savage people. After any advantage over the enemy, both sexes used to jump together, and make a clattering with their swords and shields, for joy, which in a few years produced several regular tunes and set dances.

As the two armies romped together upon these occasions, the women complained of the thick bushy beards and long nails of their confederates, who thereupon took care to prune themselves into such figures as were most pleasing to their friends and allies.

When they had taken any spoils from the enemy, the men would make a present of every thing that was rich and showy to the women whom they most admired, and would frequently dress the necks, or heads, or arms, of their mistresses, with any thing which they thought appeared gay or pretty. The women observing that the men took delight in looking upon them when they were adorned with such trappings and gewgaws, set their heads at work to find out new inventions and to outshine one another in all councils of war, or the like solemn meetings. On the other hand, the men observing how the women's hearts were set upon finery, begun to embellish themselves, and look as agreeably as they could in the eyes of their associates. In short, after a few years' conversing toge ther, the women had learned to smile, and the men to ogle; the women grew soft, and the men lively.

When they had thus insensibly formed one another, upon finishing of the war, which concluded with an entire conquest of their common enemy, the colonels in one army married the colonels in the other; the captains in the same manner took the captains to their wives: the whole body of common soldiers were matched after the example of their leaders. By this means the two republics incorporated with one another, and became the most flourishing and polite government in the part of the world which they inhabited. C.

No. 435.] *Saturday, July* 19, 1712.

Nec duo sunt, et forma duplex, nec fœmina dici,
Nec puer ut possint, neutrumque et utrumque videntur.
Ovid. Met. iv. 378.

Both bodies in a single body mix,
A single body with a double sex.—*Addison*

MOST of the papers I give the public are written on subjects that never vary, but are for ever fixed and immutable. Of this kind are all my more serious essays and discourses; but there is another sort of speculations, which I consider as occasional papers, that take their rise from the folly, extravagance, and caprice of the present age. For I look upon myself as one set to watch the manners and behaviour of my countrymen and contemporaries, and to mark down every absurd fashion, ridiculous custom, or affected form of speech, that makes its appearance in the world during the course of my speculations. The petticoat no sooner begun to swell, but I observed its motions. The party-patches had not time to muster themselves before I detected them. I had intelligence of the coloured hood the very first time it appeared in a public assembly. I might here mention several other the like contingent subjects, upon which I have bestowed distinct papers. By this means I have so effectually quashed those irregularities which gave occasion to them, that I am afraid posterity will scarce have a sufficient idea of them to relish those discourses which were in no little vogue at the time they were written. They will be apt to think that the fashions and customs I attacked were some fantastic conceits of my own, and that their great grandmothers could not be so whimsical as I have represented them. For this reason, when I think on the figure my several volumes of speculations will make about a hundred years hence, I consider them as so many pieces of old plate, where the weight will be regarded, but the fashion lost.

Among the several female extravagances I have already taken notice of, there is one which still keeps its ground. I mean that of the ladies who dress themselves in a hat and feather, a riding-coat, and a periwig, or at least tie up their hair in a bag or riband, in imitation of the smart part of the opposite sex. As in my yesterday's paper I gave an account of the mixture of two sexes in one commonwealth, I shall here take notice of this mixture of two sexes in one person. I have already shown my dislike of this immodest custom more than once; but in contempt of every thing I have hitherto said, I am informed that the highways about this great city are still very much infested with these female cavaliers.

I remember when I was at my friend Sir Roger de Coverley's, about this time twelvemonth, an equestrian lady of this order appeared upon the plains which lay at a distance from his house. I was at that time walking in the fields with my old friend; and as his tenants ran out on every side to see so strange a sight, Sir Roger asked one of them, who came by us, what it was? To which the country fellow replied, ''Tis a gentlewoman, saving your worship's presence, in a coat and hat.' This produced a great deal of mirth at the knight's house, where we had a story at the same time of another of his tenants, who meeting this gentleman-like lady on the highway, was asked by her whether that was Coverley-hall? The honest man seeing only the male part of the querist, replied, 'Yes, sir;' but upon the second question, whether Sir Roger de Coverley was a married man? having dropped his eye upon the petticoat, he changed his note into 'No, madam.'

Had one of these hermaphrodites appeared in Juvenal's days, with what an indignation should we have seen her described by that excellent satirist! he would have represented her in a riding habit as a greater monster than the centaur. He would have called for sacrifices of purifying waters, to expiate the appearance of such a prodigy. He would have invoked the shades of Portia and Lucretia, to see into what the Roman ladies had transformed themselves.

For my own part, I am for treating the sex with greater tenderness, and have all along made use of the most gentle methods to bring them off from any little extravagance into which they have sometimes unwarily fallen. I think it however absolutely necessary to keep up the partition between the two sexes, and to take notice of the smallest encroachments which the one makes upon the other. I hope therefore I shall not hear any more complaints on this subject. I am sure my she-disciples, who peruse these my daily lectures, have profited but little by them, if they are capable of giving into such an amphibious dress. This I should not have mentioned, had I not lately met one of these my female readers in Hyde-park, who looked upon me with a masculine assurance, and cocked her hat full in my face.

For my part, I have one general key to the behaviour of the fair sex. When I see them singular in any part of their dress, I conclude it is not without some evil intention: and therefore question not but the design of this strange fashion is to smite more effectually their male beholders. Now to set them right in this particular, I would fain have them consider with themselves, whether we are not more likely to be struck by a figure entirely female, than with such a one as we may see every day in our glasses. Or, if they please, let them reflect upon their own hearts, and think how they would be affected should they meet a man on horseback, in his breeches and jack-boots, and at the same time dressed up in a commode and a nightraile.

I must observe that this fashion was first of all brought to us from France, a country which has infected all the nations of Europe with its levity. I speak not this in derogation of a whole people, having more than once found fault with those general reflections which strike at kingdoms or commonwealths in the gross—a piece of cruelty, which an ingenious writer of our own compares to that of Caligula, who wished that the Roman people had all but one neck, that he might behead them at a blow. I shall therefore only remark, that as liveliness and assurance are in a peculiar manner the qualifications of the French nation, the same habits and customs will not give the same offence to that people which they produce amongst those of our own country. Modesty is our distinguishing character, as vivacity is theirs: and when this our national virtue appears in that female beauty for which our British ladies are celebrated above all others in the universe, it makes up the most amiable object that the eye of man can possibly behold. C.

No. 436.] *Monday, July* 21, 1712.

——————Verso pollice vulgi
Quemlibet occidunt populariter. *Juv.* Sat. iii. 30.

With thumbs bent back, they popularly kill.
Dryden.

Being a person of insatiable curiosity, I could not forbear going on Wednesday last to a place of no small renown for the gallantry of the lower order of Britons, to the Bear-garden, at Hockley in the Hole; where (as a whitish brown paper, put into my hand in the street, informed me) there was to be a trial of skill exhibited between two masters of the noble science of defence, at two of the clock precisely. I was not a little charmed with the solemnity of the challenge which ran thus:

'I James Miller, sergeant, (lately come from the frontier of Portugal) master of the noble science of defence, hearing in most places where I have been of the great fame of Timothy Buck, of London, master of the said science, do invite him to meet me and exercise at the several weapons following, viz:

'Back sword,	Single falchion,
'Sword and dagger,	Case of falchions,
'Sword and buckler,	Quarter staff.'

If the generous ardour in James Miller to dispute the reputation of Timothy Buck had something resembling the old heroes of romance, Timothy Buck returned answer in the same paper with the like spirit, adding a little indignation at being challenged, and seeming to condescend to fight James Miller, not in regard to Miller himself, but in that as the fame went about, he had fought Parkes of Coventry. The acceptance of the combat ran in these words:

'I Timothy Buck, of Clare-market, master of the noble science of defence, hearing he did fight Mr. Parkes* of Coventry, will not fail (God willing) to meet this fair inviter at the time and place appointed, desiring a clear stage and no favour.

'Vivat Regina.'

I shall not here look back on the spectacles of the Greeks and Romans of this kind, but must believe this custom took its rise from the ages of knight-errantry; from those who loved one woman so well, that they hated all men and women else; from those who would fight you, whether you were or not of their mind; from those who demanded the combat of their contemporaries, both for admiring their mistress or discommending her. I cannot therefore but lament, that the terrible part of the ancient fight is preserved, when the amorous side of it is forgotten. We have retained the barbarity, but lost the gallantry of the old combatants. I could wish, methinks, these gentlemen had consulted me in the promulgation of the conflict. I was obliged by a fair young maid, whom I understood to be called Elizabeth Preston, daughter of the keeper of the garden, with a glass of water; who I imagined might have been, for form's sake, the general representative of the lady fought for, and from her beauty the proper Amaryllis on these occasions. It would have run better in the challenge, 'I James Miller, sergeant, who have travelled parts abroad, and came last from the frontier of Portugal, for the love of Elizabeth Preston, do assert that the said Elizabeth is the fairest of women.' Then the

---

* On a large tomb, in the great church-yard of Coventry, is the following inscription:

'To the memory of Mr. John Sparkes, a native of this city: he was a man of a mild disposition, a gladiator by profession: who, after having fought 350 battles in the principal parts of Europe with honour and applause, at length quitted the stage, sheathed his sword, and, with Christian resignation, submitted to the grand victor in the 52d year of his age. *Anno salutis humanæ* 1733.'

His friend, sergeant Miller, here mentioned, a man of vast athletic accomplishments, was advanced afterwards to the rank of a captain in the British army, and did notable service in Scotland under the duke of Cumberland, in 1745.

answer; 'I Timothy Buck, who have staid in Great Britain during all the war in foreign parts, for the sake of Susannah Page, do deny that Elizabeth Preston is so fair as the said Susannah Page. Let Susannah Page look on, and I desire of James Miller no favour.'

This would give the battle quite another turn; and a proper station for the ladies, whose complexion was disputed by the sword, would animate the disputants with a more gallant incentive than the expectation of money from the spectators; though I would not have that neglected, but thrown to that fair one whose lover was approved by the donor.

Yet, considering the thing wants such amendments, it was carried with great order. James Miller came on first, preceded by two disabled drummers, to show, I suppose, that the prospect of maimed bodies did not in the least deter him. There ascended with the daring Miller a gentleman, whose name I could not learn, with a dogged air, as unsatisfied that he was not principal. This son of anger lowered at the whole assembly, and, weighing himself as he marched round from side to side, with a stiff knee and shoulder, he gave intimations of the purpose he smothered till he saw the issue of the encounter. Miller had a blue ribbon tied round the sword arm; which ornament I conceive to be the remains of that custom of wearing a mistress's favour on such occasions of old.

Miller is a man of six foot eight inches height, of a kind but bold aspect, well fashioned, and ready of his limbs; and such readiness as spoke his ease in them was obtained from a habit of motion in military exercise.

The expectation of the spectators was now almost at its height; and the crowd pressing in, several active persons thought they were placed rather according to their fortune than their merit, and took it in their heads to prefer themselves from the open area or pit to the galleries. The dispute between desert and property brought many to the ground, and raised others in proportion to the highest seats by turns, for the space of ten minutes, till Timothy Buck came on, and the whole assembly, giving up their disputes, turned their eyes upon the champions. Then it was that every man's affection turned to one or the other irresistibly. A judicious gentleman near me said, 'I could, methinks, be Miller's second, but I had rather have Buck for mine.' Miller had an audacious look, that took the eye; Buck, a perfect composure, that engaged the judgment. Buck came on in a plain coat, and kept all his air till the instant of engaging; at which time he undressed to his shirt, his arm adorned with a bandage of red riband. No one can describe the sudden concern in the whole assembly; the most tumultuous crowd in nature was as still and as much engaged as if all their lives depended on the first blow. The combatants met in the middle of the stage, and shaking hands, as removing all malice, they retired with much grace to the extremities of it; from whence they immediately faced about, and approached each other, Miller with a heart full of resolution, Buck with a watchful untroubled countenance; Buck regarding principally his own defence, Miller chiefly thoughtful of annoying his opponent. It is not easy to describe the many escapes and imperceptible defences between two men of quick eyes and ready limbs; but Miller's heat laid him open to the rebuke of the calm Buck, by a large cut on the forehead. Much effusion of blood covered his eyes in a moment, and the huzzas of the crowd undoubtedly quickened the anguish. The Assembly was divided into parties upon their different ways of fighting; while a poor nymph in one of the galleries apparently suffered for Miller, and burst into a flood of tears. As soon as his wound was wrapped up, he came on again with a little rage, which still disabled him farther. But what brave man can be wounded into more patience and caution? The next was a warm eager onset, which ended in a decisive stroke on the left leg of Miller. The lady in the gallery, during this second strife, covered her face, and for my part I could not keep my thoughts from being mostly employed on the consideration of her unhappy circumstance that moment, hearing the clashing of swords, and apprehending life or victory concerning her lover in every blow, but not daring to satisfy herself on whom they fell. The wound was exposed to the view of all who could delight in it, and sewed up on the stage. The surly second of Miller declared at this time, that he would that day fortnight fight Mr. Buck at the same weapons, declaring himself the master of the renowned Gorman; but Buck denied him the honour of that courageous disciple, and asserting that he himself had taught that champion, accepted the challenge.

There is something in nature very unaccountable on such occasions, when we see the people take a certain painful gratification in beholding these encounters. Is it cruelty that administers this sort of delight? or is it a pleasure which is taken in the exercise of pity? It was, methought, pretty remarkable that the business of the day being a trial of skill, the popularity did not run so high as one would have expected on the side of Buck. Is it that people's passions have their rise in self-love, and thought themselves (in spite of all the courage they had) liable to the fate of Miller, but could not so easily think themselves qualified like Buck?

Tully speaks of this custom with less horror than one would expect, though he confesses it was much abused in his time, and seems directly to approve of it under its first regulations, when criminals only fought before the people. '*Crudele gladiatorum spectaculum et inhumanum nonnullis videri solet, et haud scio annon ita sit ut nunc fit; cum vero sontes ferro depugnabant, auribus fortasse multa, oculis quidem nulla, poterat esse fortior contra dolorem et mortem disciplina.*' 'The shows of gladiators may be thought barbarous and inhuman, and I know not but it is so as now practised; but in those times when only criminals were combatants, the ear perhaps might receive many better instructions, but it is impossible that any thing which affects our eyes should fortify us so well against pain and death.' T.

No. 437.] *Tuesday, July* 22, 1712.

Tune impune hæc facias? Tune hic homines adolescentulos,
Imperitos rerum, eductos libere, in fraudem illicis?
Sollicitando et pollicitando eorum animos lactas?
Ac meretricios amores nuptiis conglutinas?
Ter. And. Act v. Sc. 4.

Shall you escape with impunity: you who lay snares for young men of a liberal education, but unacquainted with the world, and by force of importunity and promises, draw them in to marry harlots?

THE other day passed by me in her chariot a lady with that pale and wan complexion which we sometimes see in young people who are fallen into sorrow, and private anxiety of mind, which antedate age and sickness. It is not three years ago since she was gay, airy, and a little towards libertine in her carriage; but, methought, I easily forgave her that little insolence, which she so severely pays for in her present condition. Flavilla, of whom I am speaking, is married to a sullen fool with wealth. Her beauty and merit are lost upon the dolt, who is insensible of perfection in any thing. Their hours together are either painful or insipid. The minutes she has to herself in his absence are not sufficient to give vent at her eyes, to the grief and torment of his last conversation. This poor creature was sacrificed (with a temper which, under the cultivation of a man of sense, would have made the most agreeable companion) into the arms of this loathsome yoke-fellow by Sempronia. Sempronia is a good lady, who supports herself in an affluent condition, by contracting friendship with rich young widows, and maids of plentiful fortunes at their own disposal, and bestowing her friends upon worthless indigent fellows; on the other side, she ensnares inconsiderate and rash youths of great estates into the arms of vicious women. For this purpose, she is accomplished in all the arts which can make her acceptable at impertinent visits; she knows all that passes in every quarter, and is well acquainted with all the favourite servants, busy-bodies, dependents, and poor relations, of all persons of condition in the whole town. At the price of a good sum of money, Sempronia, by the instigation of Flavilla's mother, brought about the match for the daughter; and the reputation of this, which is apparently, in point of fortune, more than Flavilla could expect, has gained her the visits and frequent attendance of the crowd of mothers, who had rather see their children miserable in great wealth, than the happiest of the race of mankind in a less conspicuous state of life. When Sempronia is so well acquainted with a woman's temper and circumstances, that she believes marriage would be acceptable to her, and advantageous to the man who shall get her, her next step is to look out for some one, whose condition has some secret wound in it, and wants a sum, yet, in the eye of the world, not unsuitable to her. If such is not easily had, she immediately adorns a worthless fellow with what estate she thinks convenient, and adds as great a share of good humour and sobriety as is requisite. After this is settled, no importunities, arts, and devices, are omitted, to hasten the lady to her happiness. In the general, indeed, she is a person of so strict justice that she marries a poor gallant to a rich wench, and a moneyless girl to a man of fortune. But then she has no manner of conscience in the disparity, when she has a mind to impose a poor rogue for one of an estate: she has no remorse in adding to it, that he is illiterate, ignorant, and unfashioned; but makes these imperfections arguments of the truth of his wealth; and will on such an occasion, with a very grave face, charge the people of condition with negligence in the education of their children. Exception being made the other day against an ignorant booby of her own clothing, whom she was putting off for a rich heir: 'Madam,' said she, 'you know there is no making of children, who know they have estates, attend their books.'

Sempronia, by these arts, is loaded with presents, importuned for her acquaintance, and admired by those who do not know the first taste of life, as a woman of exemplary good breeding. But sure to murder and rob are less iniquities, than to raise profit by abuses as irreparable as taking away life; but more grievous as making it lastingly unhappy. To rob a lady at play of half her fortune, is not so ill as giving the whole and herself to an unworthy husband. But Sempronia can administer consolation to an unhappy fair at home, by leading her to an agreeable gallant elsewhere. She then can preach the general condition of all the married world, and tell an unexperienced young woman the methods of softening her affliction, and laugh at her simplicity and want of knowledge, with an 'Oh! my dear, you will know better.'

The wickedness of Sempronia, one would think, should be superlative: but I cannot but esteem that of some parents equal to it: I mean such as sacrifice the greatest endowments and qualifications to base bargains.

A parent who forces a child of a liberal and ingenious* spirit into the arms of a clown or a blockhead, obliges her to a crime too odious for a name. It is in a degree the unnatural conjunction of rational and brutal beings. Yet what is there so common, as the bestowing an accomplished woman with such a disparity? And I could name crowds who lead miserable lives for want of knowledge in their parents of this maxim, That good sense and good-nature always go together. That which is attributed to fools, and called good-nature, is only an inability of observing what is faulty, which turns, in marriage, into a suspicion of every thing as such, from a consciousness of that inability.

'Mr. Spectator,—I am entirely of your opinion with relation to the equestrian females, who affect both the masculine and feminine air at the same time; and cannot forbear making a presentment against another order of them, who grow very numerous and powerful; and since our language is not very capable of good compound words, I must be contented to call them only "the naked-shouldered." These beauties are not contented to make lovers wherever they appear, but they must make rivals at the same time. Were you to see Gatty walk the Park at high mall, you would expect those who followed her and those who met her would immediately draw their swords for her. I hope, sir, you will provide for the future, that women may stick to their faces for doing any farther mischief, and not allow any but direct traders in beauty to expose more than the fore-part of the neck, unless you please to allow this after-game to those who are very defective in the charms of the countenance. I can say, to my sorrow, the present practice is very unfair, when to look back is death; and it may be said of our beauties, as a great poet did of bullets,

"They kill and wound, like Parthians, as they fly."

'I submit this to your animadversion; and am, for the little while I have left, your humble servant, the languishing

'PHILANTHUS.

'P. S. Suppose you mended my letter, and made a simile about the "porcupine;" but I submit that also.'

* Ingenuous.

No. 438.] *Wednesday, July* 23, 1712.

——Animum rege, qui, nisi paret,
Imperat—— *Hor.* Ep. ii. Lib. 1. 62.

——Curb thy soul,
And check thy rage, which must be rul'd or rule.
Creech.

It is a very common expression, that such a one is very good-natured, but very passionate. The expression, indeed, is very good-natured, to allow passionate people so much quarter; but I think a passionate man deserves the least indulgence imaginable. It is said, it is soon over; that is, all the mischief he does is quickly despatched, which, I think, is no great recommendation to favour. I have known one of those good-natured passionate men say in a mixed company, even to his own wife or child, such things as the most inveterate enemy of his family would not have spoken, even in imagination. It is certain that quick sensibility is inseparable from a ready understanding; but why should not that good understanding call to itself all its force on such occasions, to master that sudden inclination to anger? One of the greatest souls now in the world* is the most subject by nature to anger, and yet so famous for a conquest of himself this way, that he is the known example when you talk of temper and command of a man's self. To contain the spirit of anger, is the worthiest discipline we can put ourselves to. When a man has made any progress this way, a frivolous fellow in a passion is to him as contemptible as a froward child. It ought to be the study of every man, for his own quiet and peace. When he stands combustible and ready to flame upon every thing that touches him, life is as uneasy to himself as it is to all about him. Syncropius leads, of all men living, the most ridiculous life; he is ever offending and begging pardon. If his man enters the room without what he was sent for—'That blockhead,' begins he—'Gentlemen, I ask your pardon, but servants now-a-days'—The wrong plates are laid, they are thrown into the middle of the room: his wife stands by in pain for him, which he sees in her face, and answers as if he had heard all she was thinking:—'Why? what the devil! Why don't you take care to give orders in these things?' His friends sit down to a tasteless plenty of every thing, every minute expecting new insults from his impertinent passions. In a word, to eat with, or visit Syncropius, is no other than going to see him exercise his family, exercise their patience, and his own anger.

It is monstrous that the shame and confusion in which this good-natured angry man must needs behold his friends, while he thus lays about him, does not give him so much reflection as to create an amendment. This is the most scandalous disuse of reason imaginable; all the harmless part of him is no more than that of a bull-dog, they are tame no longer than they are not offended. One of these good-natured angry men shall, in an instant, assemble together so many allusions to secret circumstances, as are enough to dissolve the peace of all the families and friends he is acquainted with, in a quarter of an hour, and yet the next moment be the best natured man in the world. If you would see passion in its purity, without mixture of reason, behold

* Lord Somers.

it represented in a mad hero, drawn by a mad poet. Nat. Lee makes his Alexander say thus:

'Away! begone! and give a whirlwind room,
Or I will blow you up like dust! Avaunt!
Madness but meanly represents my toil,
Eternal discord!
Fury! revenge! disdain and indignation!
Tear my swol'n breast, make way for fire and tempest.
My brain is burst, debate and reason quench'd;
The storm is up, and my hot bleeding heart
Splits with the rack; while passions, like the wind,
Rise up to heav'n, and put out all the stars.'

Every passionate fellow in town talks half the day with as little consistency, and threatens things as much out of his power.

The next disagreeable person to the outrageous gentleman, is one of a much lower order of anger, and he is what we commonly call a peevish fellow. A peevish fellow is one who has some reason in himself for being out of humour, or has a natural incapacity for delight, and therefore disturbs all who are happier than himself with pishes and pshaws, or other well-bred interjections, at every thing that is said or done in his presence. There should be physic mixed in the food of all which these fellows eat in good company. This degree of anger passes, forsooth, for a delicacy of judgment, that won't admit of being easily pleased; but none above the character of wearing a peevish man's livery ought to bear with his ill manners. All things among men of sense and condition should pass the censure, and have the protection of the eye of reason.

No man ought to be tolerated in an habitual humour, whim, or particularity of behaviour, by any who do not wait upon him for bread. Next to the peevish fellow is the snarler. This gentleman deals mightily in what we call the irony; and as those sort of people exert themselves most against those below them, you see their humour best in their talk to their servants. 'That is so like you; You are a fine fellow; Thou art the quickest head-piece;' and the like. One would think the hectoring, the storming, the sullen, and all the different species and subordinations of the angry should be cured, by knowing they live only as pardoned men; and how pitiful is the condition of being only suffered! But I am interrupted by the pleasantest scene of anger, and the disappointment of it, that I have ever known, which happened while I was yet writing, and I overheard as I sat in the back-room at a French bookseller's. There came into the shop a very learned man with an erect solemn air; and, though a person of great parts otherwise, slow in understanding any thing which makes against himself. The composure of the faulty man, and the whimsical perplexity of him that was justly angry, is perfectly new. After turning over many volumes, said the seller to the buyer, 'Sir, you know I have long asked you to send me back the first volume of French sermons I formerly lent you.' 'Sir,' said the chapman, 'I have often looked for it, but cannot find it; it is certainly lost, and I know not to whom I lent it, it is so many years ago.' 'Then, sir, here is the other volume; I'll send you home that, and please to pay for both.' 'My friend,' replied he, 'canst thou be so senseless as not to know that one volume is as imperfect in my library as in your shop?' 'Yes, sir, but it is you have lost the first volume; and, to be short, I will be paid.' 'Sir,' answered the chapman, 'you are a young man, your book is lost; and learn by this little loss to bear much greater adversities, which you must expect to meet with.' 'Yes, I'll bear when I must, but I have not lost now, for I say you have it, and shall pay me.' 'Friend, you grow warm; I tell you the book is lost; and foresee, in the course even of a prosperous life, that you will meet afflictions to make you mad, if you cannot bear this trifle.' 'Sir, there is, in this case, no need of bearing, for you have the book.' 'I say, sir, I have not the book; but your passion will not let you hear enough to be informed that I have it not. Learn resignation of yourself to the distresses of this life: nay, do not fret and fume; it is my duty to tell you that you are of an impatient spirit, and an impatient spirit is never without woe.' 'Was ever any thing like this?' 'Yes, sir, there have been many things like this: the loss is but a trifle; but your temper is wanton, and incapable of the least pain; therefore let me advise you, be patient, the book is lost, but do not for that reason lose yourself.' T.*

No. 439.] *Thursday, July* 24, 1712.

Hi narrata ferunt alio: mensuraque ficti
Crescit; et auditis aliquid novus adjicit auctor.
Ovid, Met. xii. 57.

Some tell what they have heard, or tales devise;
Each fiction still improv'd with added lies.

Ovid describes the palace of Fame as situated in the very centre of the universe, and perforated with so many windows as gave her the sight of every thing that was done in the heavens, in the earth, and in the sea. The structure of it was contrived in so admirable a manner, that it echoed every word which was spoken in the whole compass of nature; so that the palace, says the poet, was always filled with a confused hubbub of low, dying sounds, the voices being almost spent and worn out before they arrived at this general rendezvous of speeches and whispers.

I consider courts with the same regard to the governments which they superintend, as Ovid's palace of Fame with regard to the universe. The eyes of a watchful minister run through the whole people. There is scarce a murmur or complaint that does

* By Steele. See No. 324, ad finem.

This scene passed in the shop of Mr. Vaillant, now of Mr. James Payne, in the Strand; and the subject of it was (for it is still in remembrance) a volume of Massillon's Sermons.

not reach his ears. They have news-gatherers and intelligencers distributed into their several walks and quarters, who bring in their respective quotas, and make them acquainted with the discourse and conversation of the whole kingdom or commonwealth where they are employed. The wisest of kings, alluding to these invisible and unsuspected spies, who are planted by kings and rulers over their fellow-citizens, as well as to those voluntary informers that are buzzing about the ears of a great man, and making their court by such secret methods of intelligence, has given us a very prudent caution:* 'Curse not the king, no not in thy thought, and curse not the rich in thy bed-chamber; for a bird of the air shall carry the voice, and that which hath wings shall tell the matter.'

As it is absolutely necessary for rulers to make use of other people's eyes, they should take particular care to do it in such a manner that it may not bear too hard on the person whose life and conversation are inquired into. A man who is capable of so infamous a calling as that of a spy, is not very much to be relied upon. He can have no great ties of honour or checks of conscience, to restrain him in those covert evidences, where the person accused has no opportunity of vindicating himself. He will be more industrious to carry that which is grateful than that which is true. There will be no occasion for him if he does not hear and see things worth discovery; so that he naturally inflames every word and circumstance, aggravates what is faulty, perverts what is good, and misrepresents what is indifferent. Nor is it to be doubted but that such ignominious wretches let their private passions into these their clandestine informations, and often wreak their particular spite and malice against the person whom they are set to watch. It is a pleasant scene enough, which an Italian author describes between a spy and a cardinal who employed him. The cardinal is represented as minuting down every thing that is told him. The spy begins with a low voice, 'Such a one, the advocate, whispered to one of his friends, within my hearing, that your eminence was a very great poltroon;' and after having given his patron time enough to take it down, adds, that another called him a mercenary rascal in a public conversation. The cardinal replies, 'Very well,' and bids him go on. The spy proceeds and loads him with reports of the same nature, till the cardinal rises in great wrath, calls him an impudent scoundrel, and kicks him out of the room.

It is observed of great and heroic minds, that they have not only shown a particular disregard to those unmerited reproaches which have been cast upon them, but have been altogether free from that impertinent curiosity of inquiring after them, or the poor revenge of resenting them. The histories of Alexander and Cæsar are full of this kind of instances. Vulgar souls are of a quite contrary character. Dionysius, the tyrant of Sicily, had a dungeon which was a very curious piece of architecture; and of which, as I am informed, there are still to be seen some remains in that island. It was called Dionysius's Ear, and built with several little windings and labyrinths in the form of a real ear. The structure of it made it a kind of whispering place, but such a one as gathered the voice of him who spoke into a funnel, which was placed at the very top of it. The tyrant used to lodge all his state criminals, or those whom he supposed to be engaged together in any evil design upon him, in this dungeon. He had at the same time an apartment over it, where he used to apply himself to the funnel, and by that means overheard every thing that was whispered in the dungeon. I believe one may venture to affirm, that a Cæsar or an Alexander would have rather died by the treason than have used such disingenuous means for the detecting of it.

A man who in ordinary life is very inquisitive after every thing which is spoken ill of him, passes his time but very indifferently. He is wounded by every arrow that is shot at him, and puts it in the power of every insignificant enemy to disquiet him. Nay, he will suffer from what has been said of him, when it is forgotten by those who said or heard it. For this reason I could never bear one of those officious friends, that would be telling every malicious report, every idle censure, that passed upon me. The tongue of man is so petulant, and his thoughts so variable, that one should not lay too great a stress upon any present speeches and opinions. Praise and obloquy proceed very frequently out of the same mouth upon the same person; and upon the same occasion. A generous enemy will sometimes bestow commendations, as the dearest friend cannot sometimes refrain from speaking ill. The man who is indifferent in either of these respects, gives his opinion at random, and praises or disapproves as he finds himself in humour.

I shall conclude this essay with part of a character, which is finely drawn by the earl of Clarendon, in the first book of his History, which gives us the lively picture of a great man teasing himself with an absurd curiosity.

'He had not that application and submission, and reverence for the queen, as might have been expected from his wisdom and breeding; and often crossed her pretences and desires with more rudeness than was natural to him. Yet he was impertinently solicitous to know what her majesty said of him in private, and what resentments she had towards him. And when by some confidants, who had their ends upon him from those offices, he was informed of some bitter expressions falling

* Eccl. x 20.

from her majesty, he was so exceedingly afflicted and tormented with the sense of it, that sometimes by passionate complaints and representations to the king, sometimes by more dutiful addresses and expostulations with the queen in bewailing his misfortune, he frequently exposed himself, and left his condition worse than it was before, and the éclaircissement commonly ended in the discovery of the persons from whom he had received his most secret intelligence.'

O.

No. 440.] *Friday, July* 25, 1712.

Vivere si recte nescis, discede peritis.
Hor. Ep. ii. Lib. 2. 213.

Learn to live well, or fairly make your will.
Pope.

I HAVE already given my reader an account of a set of merry fellows who are passing their summer together in the country, being provided with a great house, where there is not only a convenient apartment for every particular person, but a large infirmary for the reception of such of them as are any way indisposed or out of humour. Having lately received a letter from the secretary of the society, by order of the whole fraternity, which acquaints me with their behaviour during the last week, I shall here make a present of it to the public.

'MR. SPECTATOR,—We are glad to find that you approve the establishment which we have here made for the retrieving of good manners and agreeable conversation, and shall use our best endeavours so to improve ourselves in this our summer retirement, that we may next winter serve as patterns to the town. But to the end that this our institution may be no less advantageous to the public than to ourselves, we shall communicate to you one week of our proceedings, desiring you at the same time, if you see any thing faulty in them, to favour us with your admonitions: for you must know, sir, that it has been proposed amongst us to choose you for our visitor; to which I must farther add, that one of the college having declared last week he did not like the Spectator of the day, and not being able to assign any just reasons for such dislike, he was sent to the infirmary *nemine contradicente.*

'On Monday the assembly was in very good humour, having received some recruits of French claret that morning; when, unluckily, towards the middle of the dinner, one of the company swore at his servant in a very rough manner for having put too much water in his wine. Upon which, the president of the day, who is always the mouth of the company, after having convinced him of the impertinence of his passion, and the insult he had made upon the company, ordered his man to take him from the table, and convey him to the infirmary. There was but one more sent away that day; this was a gentleman who is reckoned by some persons one of the greatest wits, and by others one of the greatest boobies about town. This you will say is a strange character; but what makes it stranger yet, is a very true one, for he is perpetually the reverse of himself, being always merry or dull to excess. We brought him hither to divert us, which he did very well upon the road, having lavished away as much wit and laughter upon the hackney coachman as might have served during his whole stay here, had it been duly managed. He had been lumpish for two or three days, but was so far connived at, in hopes of recovery, that we despatched one of the briskest fellows among the brotherhood into the infirmary for having told him at table he was not merry. But our president observing that he indulged himself in this long fit of stupidity, and construing it as a contempt of the college, ordered him to retire into the place prepared for such companions. He was no sooner got into it, but his wit and mirth returned upon him in so violent a manner, that he shook the whole infirmary with the noise of it, and had so good an effect upon the rest of the patients, that he brought them all out to dinner with him the next day.

'On Tuesday we were no sooner sat down, but one of the company complained that his head ached; upon which, another asked him in an insolent manner, what he did there then? This insensibly grew into some warm words; so that the president, in order to keep the peace, gave directions to take them both from the table, and lodge them in the infirmary. Not long after, another of the company telling us he knew, by a pain in his shoulder, that we should have some rain, the president ordered him to be removed, and placed at a weather-glass in the apartment above-mentioned.

'On Wednesday a gentleman having received a letter written in a woman's hand, and changing colour twice or thrice as he read it, desired leave to retire into the infirmary. The president consented, but denied him the use of pen, ink, and paper, till such time as he had slept upon it. One of the company being seated at the lower end of the table, and discovering his secret discontent, by finding fault with every dish that was served up, and refusing to laugh at any thing that was said, the president told him, that he found he was in an uneasy seat, and desired him to accommodate himself better in the infirmary. After dinner, a very honest fellow chanced to let a pun fall from him; his neighbour cried out, "To the infirmary;" at the same time pretending to be sick at it, as having the same natural antipathy to a pun which some have to a cat. This produced a long debate. Upon the whole, the punster was acquitted, and his neighbour sent off.

'On Thursday there was but one delinquent. This was a gentleman of strong voice, but weak understanding. He had unluckily engaged himself in a dispute with a man of excellent sense, but of a modest elocution. The man of heat replied to every answer of his antagonist with a louder note than ordinary, and only raised his voice when he should have enforced his argument. Finding himself at length driven to an absurdity, he still reasoned in a more clamorous and confused manner; and to make the greater impression upon his hearers, concluded with a loud thump upon the table. The president immediately ordered him to be carried off, and dieted with water-gruel, till such time as he should be sufficiently weakened for conversation.

'On Friday there passed very little remarkable, saving only, that several petitions were read of the persons in custody, desiring to be released from their confinement, and vouching for one another's good behaviour for the future.

'On Saturday we received many excuses from persons who had found themselves in an unsociable temper, and had voluntarily shut themselves up. The infirmary was, indeed, never so full as on this day, which I was at some loss to account for, till, upon my going abroad, I observed that it was an easterly wind. The retirement of most of my friends has given me opportunity and leisure of writing you this letter, which I must not conclude without assuring you, that all the members of our college, as well those who are under confinement as those who are at liberty, are your very humble servants, though none more than,

C. &c.'

No. 441.] *Saturday, July* 26, 1712.

Si fractus illabatur orbis,
Impavidum ferient ruinæ. *Hor.* Od. iii. Lib. 3. 7.

Should the whole frame of nature round him break
In ruin and confusion hurl'd,
He, unconcern'd, would hear the mighty crack,
And stand secure amidst a falling world.—*Anon.*

Man, considered in himself, is a very helpless and a very wretched being. He is subject every moment to the greatest calamities and misfortunes. He is beset with dangers on all sides; and may become unhappy by numberless casualties, which he could not foresee, nor have prevented had he foreseen them.

It is our comfort while we are obnoxious to so many accidents, that we are under the care of One who directs contingencies, and has in his hands the management of every thing that is capable of annoying or offending us; who knows the assistance we stand in need of, and is always ready to bestow it on those who ask it of him.

The natural homage which such a creature bears to so infinitely wise and good a Being, is a firm reliance on him for the blessings and conveniences of life, and an habitual trust in him for deliverance out of all such dangers and difficulties as may befall us.

The man who always lives in this disposition of mind, has not the same dark and melancholy views of human nature, as he who considers himself abstractedly from this relation to the Supreme Being. At the same time that he reflects upon his own weakness and imperfection, he comforts himself with the contemplation of those divine attributes which are employed for his safety and his welfare. He finds his want of foresight made up by the Omniscience of Him who is his support. He is not sensible of his own want of strength, when he knows that his helper is almighty. In short, the person who has a firm trust on the Supreme Being is powerful in His power, wise by His wisdom, happy by His happiness. He reaps the benefit of every divine attribute, and loses his own insufficiency in the fulness of infinite perfection.

To make our lives more easy to us, we are commanded to put our trust in Him, who is thus able to relieve and succour us; the divine goodness having made such reliance a duty, notwithstanding we should have been miserable had it been forbidden us.

Among several motives which might be made use of to recommend this duty to us, I shall only take notice of those that follow.

The first and strongest is, that we are promised, He will not fail those who put their trust in Him.

But, without considering the supernatural blessing which accompanies this duty, we may observe, that it has a natural tendency to its own reward, or, in other words, that this firm trust and confidence in the great Disposer of all things, contributes very much to the getting clear of any affliction, or to the bearing it manfully. A person who believes he has his succour at hand, and that he acts in the sight of his friend, often exerts himself beyond his abilities, and does wonders that are not to be matched by one who is not animated with such a confidence of success. I could produce instances from history, of generals, who, out of a belief that they were under the protection of some invisible assistant, did not only encourage their soldiers to do their utmost, but have acted themselves beyond what they would have done had they not been inspired by such a belief. I might in the same manner show how such a trust in the assistance of an Almighty Being naturally produces patience, hope, cheerfulness, and all other dispositions of mind that alleviate those calamities which we are not able to remove.

The practice of this virtue administers great comfort to the mind of man in times of poverty and affliction, but most of all in the hour of death. When the soul is hovering in the last moments of its separation, when it is just entering on another state of existence, to converse with scenes, and objects and companions that are altogether new,—what can support her under such tremblings of thought, such fear, such anxiety, such apprehensions, but the casting of all her cares upon Him who first gave her being, who has conducted her through one stage of it, and will be always with her to guide and comfort her in her progress through eternity?

David has very beautifully represented this steady reliance on God Almighty in his twenty-third psalm, which is a kind of pastoral hymn, and filled with those allusions which are usual in that kind of writing. As the poetry is very exquisite, I shall present my reader with the following translation of it:

I.

'The Lord my pasture shall prepare,
And feed me with a shepherd's care:
His presence shall my wants supply,
And guard me with a watchful eye;
My noon-day walks he shall attend,
And all my midnight hours defend.

II.

'When in the sultry glebe I faint,
Or on the thirsty mountain pant,
To fertile vales and dewy meads
My weary, wand'ring steps he leads,
Where peaceful rivers, soft, and slow,
Amid the verdant landscape flow.

III.

'Though in the paths of death I tread,
With gloomy horrors overspread,
My steadfast heart shall fear no ill,
For thou, O Lord, art with me still;
Thy friendly crook shall give me aid,
And guide me through the dreadful shade.

IV.

'Though in a bare and rugged way,
Through devious, lonely wilds I stray,
Thy bounty shall my pains beguile:
The barren wilderness shall smile
With sudden greens and herbage crown'd,
And streams shall murmur all around.'

C.

No. 442.] *Monday, July* 28, 1712.

Scribimus indocti doctique——

Hor. Ep. i. Lib. 2. 117.

——Those who cannot write, and those who can,
All rhyme and scrawl, and scribble to a man.

Pope.

I do not know whether I enough explained myself to the world, when I invited all men to be assistant to me in this my work of speculation; for I have not yet acquainted my readers, that besides the letters and valuable hints I have from time to time received from my correspondents, I have by me several curious and extraordinary papers sent with a design (as no one will doubt when they are published) that they may be printed entire, and without any alteration, by way of Spectator. I must acknowledge also, that I myself being the first projector of the paper, thought I had a right to make them my own, by dressing them in my own style, by leaving out what would not appear like mine, and by adding whatever might be proper to adapt them to the character and genius of my paper, with which it was almost impossible these could exactly correspond, it being certain that hardly two men think alike; and, therefore, so many men so many Spectators. Besides, I must own my weakness for glory is such, that, if I consulted that only, I might be so far swayed by it, as almost to wish that no one could write a Spectator besides myself; nor can I deny but, upon the first perusal of those papers, I felt some secret inclinations of ill-will towards the persons who wrote them. This was the impression I had upon the first reading them; but upon a late review (more for the sake of entertainment than use,) regarding them with another eye than I had done at first (for by converting them as well as I could to my own use, I thought I had utterly disabled them from ever offending me again as Spectators,) I found myself moved by a passion very different from that of envy; sensibly touched with pity, the softest and most generous of all passions, when I reflected what a cruel disappointment the neglect of those papers must needs have been to the writers who impatiently longed to see them appear in print, and who, no doubt, triumphed to themselves in the hopes of having a share with me in the applause of the public; a pleasure so great, that none but those who have experienced it can have a sense of it. In this manner of viewing those papers, I really found I had not done them justice, there being something so extremely natural and peculiarly good in some of them, that I will appeal to the world whether it was possible to alter a word in them without doing them a manifest hurt and violence; and whether they can ever appear rightly, and as they ought, but in their own native dress and colours. And therefore I think I should not only wrong them, but deprive the world of a considerable satisfaction, should I any longer delay the making them public.

After I have published a few of these Spectators, I doubt not but I shall find the success of them to equal, if not surpass, that of the best of my own. An author should take all methods to humble himself in the opinion he has of his own performances. When these papers appear to the world, I doubt not but they will be followed by many others; and I shall not repine, though I myself shall have left me but a very few days to appear in public: but preferring the general weal and advantage to any consideration of myself, I am resolved for the future to publish any Spectator that deserves it entire, and without any alteration; assuring the world (if there can be need of it) that it is none of mine, and if the authors think fit to subscribe their names, I will add them.

I think the best way of promoting this generous and useful design, will be by giving out subjects or themes of all kinds whatsoever, on which (with a preamble of the extraordinary benefit and advantages that may accrue thereby to the public) I will invite all manner of persons, whether scholars, citizens, courtiers, gentlemen of the town or country, and all beaus, rakes, smarts, prudes, coquettes, housewives, and all sorts of wits, whether male or female, and however distinguished, whether they be true wits, whole or half wits, or whether arch, dry, natural, acquired, genuine, or depraved wits; and persons of all sorts of tempers and complexions, whether the severe, the delightful, the impertinent, the agreeable, the thoughtful, the busy or careless, the serene or cloudy, jovial or melancholy, untowardly or easy, the cold, temperate, or sanguine; and of what manners or dispositions soever, whether the ambitious or humble-minded, the proud or pitiful, ingenuous or base-minded, good or ill-natured, public-spirited or selfish; and under what fortune or circumstance soever, whether the contented or miserable, happy or unfortunate, high or low, rich or poor (whether so through want of money, or desire of more,) healthy or sickly, married or single: nay, whether tall or short, fat or lean; and of what trade, occupation, profession, station, country, faction, party, persuasion, quality, age, or condition soever; who have ever made thinking a part of their business or diversion, and have any thing worthy to impart on these subjects to the world, according to their several and respective talents or geniuses; and, as the subjects given out hit their tempers, humours, or circumstances, or may be made profitable to the public by their particular knowledge or experience in the matter proposed, to do their utmost on them by such a time, to the end they may receive the inexpressible and irresistible pleasure of seeing their essays allowed of and relished by the rest of mankind.

I will not prepossess the reader with too great expectation of the extraordinary advantages which must redound to the public by these essays, when the different thoughts and observations of all sorts of persons, according to their quality, age, sex, education, professions, humours, manners, and conditions, &c. shall be set out by themselves in the clearest and most genuine light, and as they themselves would wish to have them appear to the world.

The thesis proposed for the present exercise of the adventurers to write Spectators, is Money; on which subject all persons are desired to send in their thoughts within ten days after the date hereof. T.

No. 443.] *Tuesday, July 29, 1712.*

Sublatum ex oculis quærimus invidi.
Hor. Od. xxiv. Lib. 3. 33.

Snatch'd from our sight, we eagerly pursue,
And fondly would recall her to our view.

Camilla to the Spectator.*

'Venice, July 10, N. S.

'MR. SPECTATOR,—I take it extremely ill, that you do not reckon conspicuous persons of your nation are within your cognizance, though out of the dominions of Great Britain. I little thought, in the green years of my life, that I should ever call it a happiness to be out of dear England; but as I grew to woman, I found myself less acceptable in proportion to the increase of my merit. Their ears in Italy are so differently formed from the make of yours in England, that I never come upon the stage, but a general satisfaction appears in every countenance of the whole people. When I dwell upon a note, I behold all the men accompanying me with heads inclining, and falling of their persons on one side, as dying away with me. The women too do justice to my merit, and no ill-natured, worthless creature cries, "The vain thing," when I am rapt in the performance of my part, and sensibly touched with the effect my voice has upon all who hear me. I live here distinguished as one whom nature has been liberal to in a graceful person, and exalted mien, and heavenly voice. These particularities in this strange country are arguments for respect and generosity to her who is possessed of them. The Italians see a thousand beauties I am sensible I have no pretence to, and abundantly make up to me the injustice I received in my own country, of disallowing me what I really had. The humour of hissing which you have among you, I do not know any thing of; and their applauses are uttered in sighs, and bearing a part at the cadences of voice with the persons who are performing. I am often put in mind of those complaisant lines of my own countryman,† when he is calling all his faculties together to hear Arabella.

"Let all be hush'd, each softest motion cease,
Be ev'ry loud tumultuous thought at peace;
And ev'ry ruder gasp of breath
Be calm, as in the arms of death:
And thou, most fickle, most uneasy part,
Thou restless wanderer, my heart,
Be still; gently, ah! gently leave,
Thou busy, idle thing, to heave:
Stir not a pulse; and let my blood,
That turbulent, unruly flood,
Be softly staid:
Let me be all, but my attention dead."

The whole city of Venice is as still when I am singing as this polite hearer was to Mrs. Hunt. But when they break that silence, did you know the pleasure I am in, when every man utters his applauses, by calling me aloud, "The dear Creature! The Angel! The Venus! What attitudes she moves with! Hush, she sings again!" We have no boisterous wits who dare disturb an audience, and break the public peace merely to show they dare. Mr.

* Mrs. Tofts, who played the part of Camilla in the opera of that name.
† Mr. Congreve

Spectator, I write this to you thus in haste, to tell you I am so very much at ease here that I know nothing but joy; and I will not return, but leave you in England to hiss all merit of your own growth off the stage. I know, sir, you were always my admirer, and therefore I am yours, CAMILLA.

'P. S. I am ten times better dressed than ever I was in England.'

'MR. SPECTATOR,—The project in yours of the 11th instant, of furthering the correspondence and knowledge of that considerable part of mankind, the trading world, cannot but be highly commendable. Good lectures to young traders may have very good effects on their conduct; but beware you propagate no false notions of trade: let none of your correspondents impose on the world by putting forth base methods in a good light, and glazing them over with improper terms. I would have no means of profit set for copies to others, but such as are laudable in themselves. Let not noise be called industry, nor impudence courage. Let not good fortune be imposed on the world for good management, nor poverty be called folly: impute not always bankruptcy to extravagance, nor an estate to foresight. Niggardliness is not good husbandry, nor generosity profusion.

'Honestus is a well-meaning and judicious trader, hath substantial goods, and trades with his own stock, husbands his money to the best advantage, without taking all the advantages of the necessities of his workmen, or grinding the face of the poor. Fortunatus is stocked with ignorance, and consequently with self-opinion; the quality of his goods cannot but be suitable to that of his judgment. Honestus pleases discerning people, and keeps their custom by good usage; makes modest profit by modest means, to the decent support of his family; while Fortunatus, blustering always, pushes on, promising much and performing little; with obsequiousness offensive to people of sense, strikes at all, catches much the greater part, and raises a considerable fortune by imposition on others, to the discouragement and ruin of those who trade fair in the same way.

'I give here but loose hints, and beg you to be very circumspect in the province you have now undertaken: if you perform it successfully, it will be a very great good; for nothing is more wanting than that mechanic industry were set forth with the freedom and greatness of mind which ought always to accompany a man of liberal education. Your humble servant,

'From my shop under
the Royal Exchange, July 14. R. C.'

'July 24, 1712.

'MR. SPECTATOR,—Notwithstanding the repeated censures that your spectatorial wisdom has passed upon people more remarkable for impudence than wit, there are yet some remaining, who pass with the giddy part of mankind for sufficient sharers of the latter, who have nothing but the former qualification to recommend them. Another timely animadversion is absolutely necessary: be pleased, therefore, once for all, to let these gentlemen know, that there is neither mirth nor good humour in hooting a young fellow out of countenance; nor that it will ever constitute a wit, to conclude a tart piece of buffoonery with a "What makes you blush?" Pray please to inform them again, that to speak what they know is shocking, proceeds from ill-nature and sterility of brain; especially when the subject will not admit of raillery, and their discourse has no pretension to satire but what is in their design to disoblige. I should be very glad too if you would take notice, that a daily repetition of the same overbearing insolence is yet more insupportable, and a confirmation of very extraordinary dulness. The sudden publication of this may have an effect upon a notorious offender of this kind whose reformation would redound very much to the satisfaction and quiet of your most humble servant, F. B.'

T.

No. 444.] *Wednesday, July* 30, 1712.

Paturiunt montes——
Hor. Ars Poet. v. 139.

The mountain labours.*

IT gives me much despair in the design of reforming the world by my speculations, when I find there always arise, from one generation to another, successive cheats and bubbles, as naturally as beasts of prey, and those which are to be their food. There is hardly a man in the world, one would think, so ignorant, as not to know that the ordinary quack-doctors who publish their great abilities in little brown billets, distributed to all that pass by, are to a man impostors and murderers; yet such is the credulity of the vulgar, and the impudence of those professors, that the affair still goes on, and new promises, of what was never done before, are made every day. What aggravates the jest is, that even this promise has been made as long as the memory of man can trace it, yet nothing performed, and yet still prevails. As I was passing along to-day, a paper given into my hand by a fellow without a nose, tells us as follows what good news is come to town, to wit, that there is now a certain cure for the French disease, by a gentleman just come from his travels.—

'In Russel-court, over-against the Cannon ball, at the Surgeon's-arms, in Drury lane, is lately come from his travels, a

* Former motto:—
Quid dignum tento feret hic promissor hiatu.—*Hor.*
Great cry and little wool.—*English Proverb*

surgeon who hath practised surgery and physic both by sea and land, these twenty-four years. He (by the blessing) cures the yellow jaundice, green-sickness, scurvy, dropsy, surfeits, long sea-voyages, campaigns, and women's miscarriages, lying-in, &c. as some people that *has* been lame these thirty years can testify; in short, he cureth all diseases incident to men, women, or children.'

If a man could be so indolent as to look upon this havoc of the human species, which is made by vice and ignorance, it would be a good ridiculous work to comment upon the declaration of this accomplished traveller. There is something unaccountably taking among the vulgar in those who come from a great way off. Ignorant people of quality, as many there are of such, doat excessively this way; many instances of which every man will suggest to himself, without my enumeration of them. The ignorants of lower order, who cannot, like the upper ones, be profuse of their money to those recommended by coming from a distance, are no less complaisant than the others, for they venture their lives from the same admiration.

'The doctor is lately come from his travels,' and has 'practised both by sea and land,' and therefore cures 'the green-sickness, long sea-voyages, campaigns, and lyings-in.' Both by sea and land!—I will not answer for the distempers called sea-voyages and campaigns; but I dare say those of green-sickness and lying-in might be as well taken care of if the doctor staid ashore. But the art of managing mankind is only to make them stare a little, to keep up their astonishment, to let nothing be familiar to them, but ever have something in their sleeve, in which they must think you are deeper than they are. There is an ingenious fellow, a barber of my acquaintance, who, besides his broken fiddle and a dried sea-monster, has a twined-cord, strained with two nails at each end, over his window, and the words 'rainy, dry, wet,' and so forth, written to denote the weather, according to the rising or falling of the cord. We very great scholars are not apt to wonder at this; but I observed a very honest fellow, a chance customer, who sat in the chair before me to be shaved, fix his eye upon this miraculous performance during the operation upon his chin and face. When those and his head also were cleared of all incumbrances and excrescences, he looked at the fish, then at the fiddle, still grubbing in his pockets, and casting his eye again at the twine, and the words writ on each side; then altered his mind as to farthings, and gave my friend a silver sixpence. The business, as I said, is to keep up the amazement; and if my friend had had only the skeleton and kit, he must have been contented with a ess payment. But the doctor we were talking of adds to his long voyages the testimony of some people 'that *has* been thirty years lame.' When I received my paper, a sagacious fellow took one at the same time and read till he came to the thirty years' confinement of his friends, and went off very well convinced of the doctor's sufficiency. You have many of those prodigious persons, who have had some extraordinary accident at their birth, or a great disaster in some part of their lives. Any thing, however foreign from the business the people want of you, will convince them of your ability in that you profess. There is a doctor in Mouse-Alley, near Wapping, who sets up for curing cataracts, upon the credit of having, as his bill sets forth, lost an eye in the emperor's service. His patients come in upon this, and he shows his muster-roll, which confirms that he was in his imperial majesty's troops; and he puts out their eyes with great success. Who would believe that a man should be a doctor for the cure of bursten children, by declaring that his father and grandfather were both bursten? But Charles Ingolston, next door to the Harp in Barbican, has made a pretty penny by that asservation. The generality go upon their first conception, and think no farther; all the rest is granted. They take it, that there is something uncommon in you, and give you credit for the rest. You may be sure it is upon that I go, when sometimes, let it be to the purpose or not, I keep a Latin sentence in my front; and I was not a little pleased, when I observed one of my readers say, casting his eye upon my twentieth paper, 'More Latin still? What a prodigious scholar is this man!' But as I have taken much liberty with this learned doctor, I must make up all I have said by repeating what he seems to be in earnest in, and honestly promises to those who will not receive him as a great man—to wit, 'That from eight to twelve, and from two to six, he attends, for the good of the public, to bleed for three pence.' T.

No. 445.] *Thursday, July* 31, 1712.

Tanti non es, ais. Sapis, Luperce.
Mart. Epig. 118. l. 1. v. ult.

You say, Lupercus, what I write
I'nt worth so much: you're in the right.

This is the day on which many eminent authors will probably publish their last words. I am afraid that few of our weekly historians, who are men that above all others delight in war, will be able to subsist under the weight of a stamp,* and an approaching peace. A sheet of blank paper that must have this new imprimatur clapt upon

* August 1, 1712, the stamp duty here alluded to, took place, and every single half-sheet paid a half-penny to the queen. 'Have you seen the red stamp? Methinks the stamping is worth a half-penny. The Observator is fallen; the Medleys are jumbled together with the flying Post; the Examiner is deadly sick. The Spectator keeps up and doubles its price.'
Swift's Works, cr. 8vo. vol. xix. p. 173.

it, before it is qualified to communicate any thing to the public, will make its way in the world but very heavily. In short, the necessity of carrying a stamp, and the improbability of notifying a bloody battle, will, I am afraid, both concur to the sinking of those thin folios, which have every other day retailed to us the history of Europe for several years last past. A facetious friend of mine, who loves a pun, calls this present mortality among authors, 'The fall of the leaf.'

I remember, upon Mr. Baxter's death, there was published a sheet of very good sayings, inscribed, 'The last words of Mr. Baxter.' The title sold so great a number of these papers, that about a week after there came out a second sheet, inscribed, 'More last words of Mr. Baxter.' In the same manner I have reason to think that several ingenious writers, who have taken their leave of the public, in farewell papers, will not give over so, but intend to appear again, though perhaps under another form, and with a different title. Be that as it will, it is my business, in this place, to give an account of my own intentions, and to acquaint my reader with the motives by which I act, in this great crisis of the republic of letters.

I have been long debating in my own heart, whether I should throw up my pen as an author that is cashiered by the act of parliament which is to operate within this four-and-twenty hours, or whether I should still persist in laying my speculations, from day to day, before the public. The argument which prevails with me most on the first side of the question is, that I am informed by my bookseller he must raise the price of every single paper to two pence, or that he shall not be able to pay the duty of it. Now, as I am very desirous my readers should have their learning as cheap as possible, it is with great difficulty that I comply with him in this particular.

However, upon laying my reasons together in the balance, I find that those who plead for the continuance of this work, have much the greater weight. For in the first place, in recompence for the expense to which this will put my readers, it is to be hoped they may receive from every paper so much instruction as will be a very good equivalent. And, in order to this, I would not advise any one to take it in, who, after the perusal of it, does not find himself two pence the wiser, or the better man for it, or who, upon examination, does not believe that he has had two-penny worth of mirth or instruction for his money.

But I must confess there is another motive which prevails with me more than the former. I consider that the tax on paper was given for the support of the government; and as I have enemies who are apt to pervert every thing I do or say, I fear they would ascribe the laying down my paper, on such an occasion, to a spirit of malcontentedness, which I am resolved that none shall ever justly upbraid me with. No, I shall glory in contributing my utmost to the public weal; and, if my country receives five or six pounds a day by my labours, I shall be very well pleased to find myself so useful a member. It is a received maxim, that no honest man should enrich himself by methods that are prejudicial to the community in which he lives; and by the same rule I think we may pronounce the person to deserve very well of his countrymen, whose labours bring more into the public coffers than into his own pocket.

Since I have mentioned the word enemies, I must explain myself so far as to acquaint my reader, that I mean only the insignificant party zealots on both sides; men of such poor narrow souls, that they are not capable of thinking on any thing but with an eye to whig or tory. During the course of this paper, I have been accused by these despicable wretches of trimming, time-serving, personal reflection, secret satire, and the like. Now, though in these my compositions it is visible to any reader of common sense that I consider nothing but my subject, which is always of an indifferent nature, how it is possible for me to write so clear of party, as not to lie open to the censures of those who will be applying every sentence, and finding out persons and things in it, which it has no regard to?

Several paltry scribblers and declaimers have done me the honour to be dull upon me in reflections of this nature; but, notwithstanding my name has been sometimes traduced by this contemptible tribe of men, I have hitherto avoided all animadversions upon them. The truth of it is, I am afraid of making them appear considerable by taking notice of them: for they are like those imperceptible insects which are discovered by the microscope, and cannot be made the subject of observation without being magnified.

Having mentioned those few who have shown themselves the enemies of this paper, I should be very ungrateful to the public, did I not at the same time testify my gratitude to those who are its friends, in which number I may reckon many of the most distinguished persons, of all conditions, parties, and professions, in the isle of Great Britain. I am not so vain as to think approbation is so much due to the performance as to the design. There is, and ever will be, justice enough in the world to afford patronage and protection for those who endeavour to advance truth and virtue, without regard to the passions and prejudices of any particular cause or faction. If I have any other merit in me it is that I have new pointed all the batteries of ridicule. They have been generally planted against persons who have appeared serious rather than absurd: or at best, have aimed rather at what is unfashionable than what is vicious. For my own part, I have endeavoured to make nothing ridiculous that is not in some measure criminal. I have set up the immoral man as the object of derision. In short, if I have not formed a new weapon against vice and irreligion, I have at least shown how that weapon may be put to a right use, which has so often fought the battles of impiety and profaneness. C.

No. 446.] *Friday, August* 1, 1712.

Quid deceat, quid non; quo virtus, quo ferat error.
Hor. Ars Poet. v. 303.

What fit, what not: what excellent, or ill.
Roscommon.

SINCE two or three writers of comedy, who are living, have taken their farewell of the stage, those who succeed them, finding themselves incapable of rising up to their wit, humour, and good sense, have only imitated them in some of those loose unguarded strokes, in which they complied with the corrupt taste of the more vicious part of their audience. When persons of a low genius attempt this kind of writing, they know no difference between being merry and being lewd. It is with an eye to some of these degenerate compositions that I have written the following discourse.

Were our English stage but half so virtuous as that of the Greeks and Romans, we should quickly see the influence of it in the behaviour of all the politer part of mankind. It would not be fashionable to ridicule religion; or its professors; the man of pleasure would not be the complete gentleman; vanity would be out of countenance; and every quality which is ornamental to human nature would meet with that esteem which is due to it.

If the English stage were under the same regulations the Athenian was formerly, it would have the same effect that had, in recommending the religion, the government, and public worship of its country. Were our plays subject to proper inspections and imitations, we might not only pass away several of our vacant hours in the highest entertainments, but should always rise from them wiser and better than we sat down to them.

It is one of the most unaccountable things in our age, that the lewdness of our theatre should be so much complained of, so well exposed, and so little redressed. It is to be hoped, that some time or other we may be at leisure to restrain the licentiousness of the theatre, and make it contribute its assistance to the advancement of morality, and to the reformation of the age. As matters stand at present, multitudes are shut out from this noble diversion, by reason of those abuses and corruptions that accompany it. A father is often afraid that his daughter should be ruined by those entertainments, which were invented for the accomplishment and refining of human nature. The Athenian and Roman plays were written with such a regard to morality, that Socrates used to frequent the one, and Cicero the other.

It happened once, indeed, that Cato dropped into the Roman theatre when the Floralia were to be represented; and as, in that performance, which was a kind of religious ceremony, there were several indecent parts to be acted, the people refused to see them whilst Cato was present. Martial, on this hint, made the following epigram, which we must suppose was applied to some grave friend of his, that had been accidentally present at some such entertainment:

'Nosses jocosæ dulce cum sacrum Floræ,
Festosque lusus, et licentium vulgi,
Cur in theatrum, Cato severe, venisti?
An ideo tantum veneras, ut exires?' Epig. 3. 1.

Why dost thou come, great censor of thy age,
To see the loose diversions of the stage?
With awful countenance, and brow severe,
What in the name of goodness dost thou here?
See the mixt crowd! how giddy, lewd, and vain!
Didst thou come in but to go out again?

An accident of this nature might happen once in an age among the Greeks and Romans; but they were too wise and good to let the constant nightly entertainment be of such a nature, that people of the most sense and virtue could not be at it. Whatever vices are represented upon the stage, they ought to be so marked and branded by the poet, as not to appear either laudable or amiable in the person who is tainted with them. But if we look into the English comedies above-mentioned, we would think they were formed upon a quite contrary maxim, and that this rule, though it held good upon the heathen stage, was not to be regarded in christian theatres. There is another rule likewise, which was observed by authors of antiquity; and which these modern geniuses have no regard to, and that was, never to choose an improper subject for ridicule. Now a subject is improper for ridicule, if it is apt to stir up horror and commiseration rather than laughter. For this reason, we do not find any comedy, in so polite an author as Terence, raised upon the violations of the marriage-bed. The falsehood of the wife or husband has given occasion to noble tragedies; but a Scipio and Lelius would have looked upon incest or murder to have been as proper subjects for comedy. On the contrary, cuckoldom is the basis of most of our modern plays. If an alderman appears upon the stage, you may be sure it is in order to be cuckolded. A husband that is a little grave or elderly, generally meets with the same fate. Knights and baronets, country 'squires, and justices of the quorum, come up to town for no other purpose. I have seen poor Dogget cuckolded in all these capacities. In short, our English writers are as frequently severe upon this innocent unhappy creature, commonly known by the name of a cuckold, as the ancient comic writers were upon an eating parasite, or a vain-glorious soldier.

At the same time the poet so contrives

matters, that the two criminals are the favourites of the audience. We sit still, and wish well to them through the whole play, are pleased when they meet with proper opportunities, and out of humour when they are disappointed. The truth of it is, the accomplished gentleman upon the English stage, is the person that is familiar with other men's wives, and indifferent to his own; as the fine woman is generally a composition of sprightliness and falsehood. I do not know whether it proceeds from barrenness of invention, depravation of manners, or ignorance of mankind, but I have often wondered that our ordinary poets cannot frame to themselves the idea of a fine man who is not a whore-master, or a fine woman that is not a jilt.

I have sometimes thought of compiling a system of ethicks out of the writings of those corrupt poets under the title of Stage Morality. But I have been diverted from this thought by a project which has been executed by an ingenious gentleman of my acquaintance. He has composed, it seems, the history of a young fellow who has taken all his notions of the world from the stage, and who has directed himself in every circumstance of his life and conversation, by the maxims and examples of the fine gentleman in English comedies. If I can prevail upon him to give me a copy of this new-fashioned novel, I will bestow on it a place in my works, and question not but it may have as good an effect upon the drama as Don Quixote had upon romance.

C.

No. 447.] *Saturday, August* 2, 1712.

Φημι πολυχρονιην μελετην εμεναι, φιλε· και δη
Ταυτην ανθρωποισι τελευτωσαν φυσιν ειναι.

Long exercise, my friend, inures the mind;
And what we once dislik'd we pleasing find.

THERE is not a common saying which has a better turn of sense in it, than what we often hear in the mouths of the vulgar, that 'custom is a second nature.' It is indeed able to form the man anew, and to give him inclinations and capacities altogether different from those he was born with. Dr. Plot, in his History of Staffordshire, tells us of an idiot that, chancing to live within the sound of a clock, and always amusing himself with counting the hour of the day whenever the clock struck, the clock being spoiled by accident, the idiot continued to strike and count the hour without the help of it, in the same manner as he had done when it was entire. Though I dare not vouch for the truth of this story, it is very certain that custom has a mechanical effect upon the body at the same time that it has a very extraordinary influence upon the mind.

I shall in this paper consider one very remarkable effect which custom has upon human nature, and which, if rightly observed, may lead us into very useful rules of life. What I shall here take notice of in custom, is its wonderful efficacy in making every thing pleasant to us. A person who is addicted to play or gaming, though he took but little delight in it at first, by degrees contracts so strong an inclination towards it, and gives himself up so entirely to it, that it seems the only end of his being. The love of a retired or busy life will grow upon a man insensibly, as he is conversant in the one or the other, till he is utterly unqualified for relishing that to which he has been for some time disused. Nay, a man may smoke, or drink, or take snuff, till he is unable to pass away his time without it; not to mention how our delight in any particular study, art, or science, rises and improves, in proportion to the application which we bestow upon it. Thus, what was at first an exercise becomes at length an entertainment. Our employments are changed into our diversions. The mind grows fond of those actions she is accustomed to, and is drawn with reluctancy from those paths in which she has been used to walk.

Not only such actions as were at first indifferent to us, but even such as are painful, will by custom and practice become pleasant. Sir Francis Bacon observes, in his Natural Philosophy, that our taste is never pleased better than with those things which at first created disgust in it. He gives particular instances, of claret, coffee, and other liquors, which the palate seldom approves upon the first taste; but, when it has once got a relish of them, generally retains it for life. The mind is constituted after the same manner, and after having habituated herself to any particular exercise or employment, not only loses her first aversion towards it, but conceives a certain fondness and affection for it. I have heard one of the greatest geniuses this age has produced,* who had been trained up in all the polite studies of antiquity, assure me, upon his being obliged to search into several rolls and records, that notwithstanding such an employment was at first very dry and irksome to him, he at last took an incredible pleasure in it, and preferred it even to the reading of Virgil or Cicero. The reader will observe, that I have not here considered custom as it makes things easy, but as it renders them delightful; and though others have often made the same reflections, it is possible they may not have drawn those uses from it, with which I intend to fill the remaining part of this paper.

If we consider attentively this property of human nature, it may instruct us in very fine moralities. In the first place, I would have no man discouraged with that kind of life, or series of action, in which the choice of others or his own necessities may have engaged him. It may, perhaps, be very

* Dr. A terbury.

disagreeable to him at first; but use and application will certainly render it not only less painful, but pleasing and satisfactory.

In the second place, I would recommend to every one that admirable precept which Pythagoras is said to have given to his disciples, and which that philosopher must have drawn from the observation I have enlarged upon, *Optimum vitæ genus eligito, nam consuetudo faciet jucondissimum:* 'Pitch upon that course of life which is the most excellent, and custom will render it the most delightful.' Men, whose circumstances will permit them to choose their own way of life, are inexcusable if they do not pursue that which their judgment tells them is the most laudable. The voice of reason is more to be regarded than the bent of any present inclination, since, by the rule above-mentioned, inclination will at length come over to reason, though we can never force reason to comply with inclination.

In the third place, this observation may teach the most sensual and irreligious man to overlook those hardships and difficulties which are apt to discourage him from the prosecution of a virtuous life. 'The gods,' said Hesiod, 'have placed labour before virtue: the way to her is at first rough and difficult, but grows more smooth and easy the farther you advance in it.' The man who proceeds in it with steadiness and resolution, will in a little time find that 'her ways are ways of pleasantness, and that all her paths are peace.'

To enforce this consideration, we may farther observe, that the practice of religion will not only be attended with that pleasure which naturally accompanies those actions to which we are habituated, but with those supernumerary joys of heart that rise from the consciousness of such a pleasure, from the satisfaction of acting up to the dictates of reason, and from the prospect of a happy immortality.

In the fourth place, we may learn from this observation, which we have made on the mind of man, to take particular care, when we are once settled in a regular course of life, how we too frequently indulge ourselves in any the most innocent diversions and entertainments; since the mind may insensibly fall off from the relish of virtuous actions, and, by degrees, exchange that pleasure which it takes in the performance of its duty, for delights of a much more inferior and unprofitable nature.

The last use which I shall make of this remarkable property in human nature, of being delighted with those actions to which it is accustomed, is to show how absolutely necessary it is for us to gain habits of virtue in this life, if we would enjoy the pleasures of the next. The state of bliss we call heaven will not be capable of affecting those minds which are not thus qualified for it; we must, in this world, gain a relish of truth and virtue, if we would be able to taste that knowledge and perfection, which are to make us happy in the next. The seeds of those spiritual joys and raptures, which are to rise up and flourish in the soul to all eternity, must be planted in her during this her present state of probation. In short, heaven is not to be looked upon only as the reward, but as the natural effect of a religious life.

On the other hand, those evil spirits, who, by long custom, have contracted in the body habits of lust and sensuality, malice and revenge, and aversion to every thing that is good, just, or laudable, are naturally seasoned and prepared for pain and misery. Their torments have already taken root in them; they cannot be happy when divested of the body, unless we may suppose, that Providence will in a manner create them anew, and work a miracle in the rectification of their faculties. They may, indeed, taste a kind of malignant pleasure in those actions to which they are accustomed, whilst in this life; but when they are removed from all those objects which are here apt to gratify them, they will naturally become their own tormentors, and cherish in themselves those painful habits of mind which are called, in scripture phrase, 'the worm which never dies.' This notion of heaven and hell is so very conformable to the light of nature, that it was discovered by several of the most exalted heathens. It has been finely improved by many eminent divines of the last age, as in particular by archbishop Tillotson and Dr. Sherlock: but there is none who has raised such noble speculations upon it as Dr. Scot, in the first book of his Christian Life, which is one of the finest and most rational schemes of divinity that is written in our tongue, or in any other. That excellent author has shown how every particular custom and habit of virtue will, in its own nature, produce the heaven, or a state of happiness, in him who shall hereafter practise it: as on the contrary, how every custom or habit of vice will be the natural hell of him in whom it subsists. C.

No. 448.] *Monday, August 4, 1712.*

Fœdius hoc aliquid quandoque audebis.
Juv. Sat. ii. 82.

In time to greater baseness you'll proceed.

THE first steps towards ill are very carefully to be avoided, for men insensibly go on when they are once entered, and do not keep up a lively abhorrence of the least unworthiness. There is a certain frivolous falsehood that people indulge themselves in, which ought to be had in greater detestation than it commonly meets with. What I mean is a neglect of promises made on small and indifferent occasions, such as parties of pleasure, entertainments, and sometimes meetings out of curiosity, in men of like faculties, to be in each other's company. There are many causes to which one may assign this light infidelity. Jack Sippet never keeps the hour he has appointed to come to a friend's to dinner; but he is an insignificant fellow, who does it out of vanity. He could never, he knows, make any figure in company, but by giving a little disturbance at his entry, and therefore takes care to drop in when he thinks you are just seated. He takes his place after having discomposed every body, and desires there may be no ceremony; then does he begin to call himself the saddest fellow, in disappointing so many places as he was invited to elsewhere. It is the fop's vanity to name houses of better cheer, and to acquaint you that he chose yours out of ten dinners which he was obliged to be at that day. The last time I had the fortune to eat with him, he was imagining how very fat he should have been had he eaten all he had ever been invited to. But it is impertinent to dwell upon the manners of such a wretch as obliges all whom he disappoints, though his circumstances constrain them to be civil to him. But there are those that every one would be glad to see, who fall into the same detestable habit. It is a merciless thing that any one can be at ease, and suppose a set of people who have a kindness for him, at that moment waiting out of respect to him, and refusing to taste their food or conversation, with the utmost impatience. One of these promisers sometimes shall make his excuses for not coming at all, so late that half the company have only to lament, that they have neglected matters of moment to meet him whom they find a trifler. They immediately repent of the value they had for him; and such treatment repeated, makes company never depend upon his promises any more; so that he often comes at the middle of a meal, where he is secretly slighted by the persons with whom he eats, and cursed by the servants, whose dinner is delayed by his prolonging their master's entertainment. It is wonderful that men guilty this way could never have observed, that the whiling time, and gathering together, and waiting a little before dinner, is the most awkwardly passed away of any part in the four-and-twenty hours. If they did think at all, they would reflect upon their guilt, in lengthening such a suspension of agreeable life. The constant offending this way has, in a degree, an effect upon the honesty of his mind who is guilty of it, as common swearing is a kind of habitual perjury: it makes the soul unattentive to what an oath is, even while it utters it at the lips. Phocion beholding a wordy orator, while he was making a magnificent speech to the people, full of vain promises; 'Methinks,' said he, 'I am now fixing my eyes upon a cypress tree; it has all the pomp and beauty imaginable in its branches, leaves, and height: but alas! it bears no fruit.'

Though the expectation which is raised by impertinent promises is thus barren, their confidence, even after failures, is so great, that they subsist by still promising on. I have heretofore discoursed of the insignificant liar, the boaster, and the castle builder, and treated them as no ill-designing men (though they are to be placed among the frivolous false ones,) but persons who fall into that way purely to recommend themselves by their vivacities; but indeed I cannot let heedless promisers, though in the most minute circumstances, pass with so slight a censure. If a man should take a resolution to pay only sums above a hundred pounds, and yet contract with different people debts of five and ten, how long can we suppose he will keep his credit? This man will as long support his good name in business, as he will in conversation, who without difficulty makes assignations which he is indifferent whether he keeps or not.

I am the more severe upon this vice, because I have been so unfortunate as to be a very great criminal myself. Sir Andrew Freeport, and all my other friends who are scrupulous to promises of the meanest consideration imaginable, from a habit of virtue that way, have often upbraided me with it. I take shame upon myself for this crime, and more particularly for the greatest I ever committed of the sort, that when as agreeable a company of gentlemen and ladies as ever were got together, and I forsooth, Mr. Spectator, to be of the party with women of merit, like a booby as I was, mistook the time of meeting, and came the night following. I wish every fool who is negligent in this kind, may have as great a loss as I had in this; for the same company will never meet more, but are dispersed into various parts of the world, and I am left under the compunction that I deserve, in so many different places to be called a trifler.

This fault is sometimes to be accounted for, when desirable people are fearful of appearing precise and reserved by denials; but they will find the apprehension of that imputation will betray them into a childish impotence of mind, and make them promise all who are so kind to ask it of them. This leads such soft creatures into the misfortune of seeming to return overtures of good-will with ingratitude. The first steps in the breach of a man's integrity are much more important than men are aware of. The man who scruples not breaking his word in little things, would not suffer in his own conscience so great pain for failures of consequence, as he who thinks every little offence against truth and justice a disparagement. We should not make any thing we ourselves disapprove habitual to us, if we would be sure of our integrity.

I remember a falsehood of the trivial sort, though not in relation to assignations, that exposed a man to a very uneasy adventure. Will Trap and Jack Stint were chamber-fellows in the Inner-Temple about twenty-five years ago. They one night sat in the pit together at a comedy, where they both observed and liked the same young woman in the boxes. Their kindness for her entered both hearts deeper than they imagined. Stint had a good faculty in writing letters of love, and made his address privately that way; while Trap proceeded in the ordinary course, by money and her waiting-maid. The lady gave them both encouragement, received Trap into the utmost favour, answering at the same time Stint's letters, and giving him appointments at third places. Trap began to suspect the epistolary correspondence of his friend, and discovered also that Stint opened all his letters which came to their common lodgings, in order to form his own assignations. After much anxiety and restlessness, Trap came to a resolution, which he thought would break off their commerce with one another without any hazardous explanation. He therefore writ a letter in a feigned hand to Mr. Trap at his chambers in the Temple. Stint, according to custom, seized and opened it, and was not a little surprised to find the inside directed to himself, when, with great perturbation of spirit, he read as follows:

'Mr. Stint,—You have gained a slight satisfaction at the expense of doing a very heinous crime. At the price of a faithful friend you have obtained an inconstant mistress. I rejoice in this expedient I have thought of to break my mind to you, and tell you, you are a base fellow, by a means which does not expose you to the affront except you deserve it. I know, sir, as criminal as you are, you have still shame enough to avenge yourself against the hardiness of any one that should publicly tell you of it. I therefore, who have received so many secret hurts from you, shall take satisfaction with safety to myself. I call you base, and you must bear it, or acknowledge it; I triumph over you that you cannot come at me; nor do I think it dishonourable to come in armour to assault him, who was in ambuscade when he wounded me.

'What need more be said to convince you of being guilty of the basest practice imaginable, than that it is such as has made you liable to be treated after this manner, while you yourself cannot in your own conscience but allow the justice of the upbraidings of your injured friend,

T. 'RALPH TRAP.'

No. 449.] *Tuesday, August 5, 1712.*

——Tibi scriptus, matrona, libellus.

Mart. iii. 68.

A book the chastest matron may peruse.

When I reflect upon my labours for the public, I cannot but observe, that part of the species, of which I profess myself a friend and guardian, is sometimes treated with severity; that is, there are in my writings many descriptions given of ill persons, and not any direct encomium made of those who are good. When I was convinced of this error, I could not but immediately call to mind several of the fair sex of my acquaintance, whose characters deserve to be transmitted to posterity in writings which will long outlive mine. But I do not think that a reason why I should not give them their place in my diurnal as long as it will last. For the service thereof of my female readers, I shall single out some characters of maids, wives, and widows which deserve the imitation of the sex. She who shall lead this small illustrious number of heroines shall be the amiable Fidelia.

Before I enter upon the particular parts of her character, it is necessary to preface, that she is the only child of a decrepid father, whose life is bound up in hers. This gentleman has used Fidelia from her cradle with all the tenderness imaginable, and has viewed her growing perfections with the partiality of a parent, that soon thought her accomplished above the children of all other men, but never thought she was come to the utmost improvement of which she herself was capable. This fondness has had very happy effects upon his own happiness; for she reads, she dances, she sings, uses her spinet and lute to the utmost perfection; and the lady's use of all these excellences is to divert the old man in his easy chair, when he is out of the pangs of a chronical distemper. Fidelia is now in the twenty-third year of her age; but the application of many lovers, her vigorous time of life, her quick sense of all that is truly gallant and elegant in the enjoyment of a plentiful fortune, are not able to draw her from the side of her good old father. Certain it is, that there is no kind of affection so pure and angelic as that of a father to a daughter. He beholds her both with and without regard to her sex. In love to our wives there is desire, to our sons there is ambition; but in that to our daughters, there is something which there are no words to express. Her life is designed wholly domestic, and she is so ready a friend and companion, that every thing that passes about a man is accompanied with the idea of her presence. Her sex also is naturally so much exposed to hazard, both as to fortune and innocence, that there is perhaps a new cause of fondness arising from that consideration also. None but fathers can have a true sense of these sort of pleasures and sensations; but my familiarity with the father of Fidelia, makes me let drop the words which I have heard him speak, and observe upon his tenderness towards her.

Fidelia, on her part, as I was going to say, as accomplished as she is, with her beauty, wit, air, and mien, employs her whole time in care and attendance upon her father. How have I been charmed to see one of the most beautiful women the age has produced, on her knees, helping on an old man's slipper! Her filial regard to him is what she makes her diversion, her business, and her glory. When she was asked by a friend of her deceased mother to admit of the courtship of her son, she answered that she had a great respect and gratitude to her for the overture in behalf of one so dear to her, but that during her father's life she would admit into her heart no value for any thing that should interfere with her endeavour to make his remains of life as happy and easy as could be expected in his circumstances. The lady admonished her of the prime of life with a smile; which Fidelia answered with a frankness that always attends unfeigned virtue: 'It is true, madam, there are to be sure very great satisfactions to be expected in the commerce of a man of honour whom one tenderly loves; but I find so much satisfaction, in the reflection, how much I mitigate a good man's pains, whose welfare depends upon my assiduity about him, that I willingly exclude the loose gratifications of passion for the solid reflections of duty. I know not whether any man's wife would be allowed, and (what I still more fear) I know not whether I, a wife, should be willing to be so officious as I am at present about my parent.' The happy father has her declaration that she will not marry during his life, and the pleasure of seeing that resolution not uneasy to her. Were one to paint filial affection in its utmost beauty, he could not have a more lively idea of it than in beholding Fidelia serving her father at his hours of rising, meals, and rest.

When the general crowd of female youth are consulting their glasses, preparing for balls, assemblies, or plays; for a young lady, who could be regarded among the foremost in those places, either for her person, wit, fortune, or conversation, and yet contemn all these entertainments, to sweeten the heavy hours of a decrepid parent, is a resignation truly heroic. Fidelia performs the duty of a nurse with all the beauty of a bride; nor does she neglect her person, because of her attendance on him, when he is too ill to receive company, to whom she may make an appearance.

Fidelia, who gives him up her youth, does not think it any great sacrifice to add to it the spoiling of her dress. Her care and exactness in her habit convince her father of the alacrity of her mind; and she has of all women the best foundation for affecting the praise of a seeming negligence. What adds to the entertainment of the good old man is, that Fidelia, where merit and fortune cannot be overlooked by epistolary lovers, reads over the accounts of her conquests, plays on her spinet the gayest airs (and while she is doing so you would think her formed only for gallantry) to intimate to him the pleasures she despises for his sake.

Those who think themselves the pattern of good-breeding and gallantry would be astonished to hear that, in those intervals when the old gentleman is at ease, and can bear company, there are at his house, in the most regular order, assemblies of people of the highest merit; where there is conversation without mention of the faults of the absent, benevolence between men and women without passion, and the highest subjects of morality treated of as natural and accidental discourse; all which is owing to the genius of Fidelia; who at once makes her father's way to another world easy, and herself capable of being an honour to his name in this.

'Mr. Spectator,—I was the other day at the Bear-garden, in hopes to have seen your short face: but not being so fortunate, I must tell you, by way of letter, that there is a mystery among the gladiators which has escaped your spectatorial penetration. For, being in a box at an ale-house near that renowned seat of honour above-mentioned, I overheard two masters of the science agreeing to quarrel on the next opportunity. This was to happen in a company of a set of the fraternity of basket hilts, who were to meet that evening. When this was settled, one asked the other, "Will you give cuts or receive?" The other answered, "Receive." It was replied, "Are you a passionate man?" "No, provided you cut no more nor no deeper than we agree." I thought it my duty to acquaint you with this, that the people may not pay their money for fighting, and be cheated. Your humble servant, SCABBARD RUSTY.'

T.

No. 450.] *Wednesday, August* 6, 1712.

——Quærenda pecunia primum,
Virtus post nummos. *Hor. Ep.* i. Lib. 1. 53.

——Get money, money still;
And then let virtue follow, if she will.—*Pope.*

'Mr. Spectator,—All men through different paths, make at the same common thing, money: and it is to her we owe the politician, the merchant, and the lawyer; nay, to be free with you, I believe to that also we are beholden for our Spectator. I am apt to think, that could we look into our own hearts, we should see money engraved in them in more lively and moving characters than self-preservation; for who can reflect upon the merchant hoisting sail in a doubtful pursuit of her, and all mankind sacrificing their quiet to her, but must perceive that the characters of self-preservation (which were doubtless originally the brightest) are sullied, if not wholly defaced; and that those of money (which at first was only valuable as a mean to security) are of late so brightened, that the characters of self-preservation, like a less light set by a greater, are become almost imperceptible? Thus has money got the upper hand of what all mankind formerly thought most dear, viz. security: and I wish I could say she had here put a stop to her victories; but, alas! common honesty fell a sacrifice to her. This is the way scholastic men talk of the greatest good in the world: but I, a tradesman, shall give you another account of this matter in the plain narrative of my own life. I think it proper, in the first place, to acquaint my readers, that since my setting out in the world, which was in the year 1660, I never wanted money, having begun with an indifferent good stock in the tobacco-trade, to which I was bred; and by the continual successes it has pleased Providence to bless my endeavours with, I am at last arrived at what they call a plum. To uphold my discourse in the manner of your wits or philosophers, by speaking fine things, or drawing inferences, as they pretend, from the nature of the subject, I account it vain; having never found any thing in the writings of such men, that did not savour more of the invention of the brain, or what is styled speculation, than of sound judgment or profitable observation. I will readily grant indeed, that there is what the wits call natural in their talk; which is the utmost those curious authors can assume to themselves, and is indeed all they endeavour at, for they are but lamentable teachers. And what, I pray, is natural? That which is pleasing and easy. —And what are pleasing and easy? Forsooth, a new thought, or conceit dressed up in smooth quaint language, to make you smile and wag your head, as being what you never imagined before, and yet wonder why you had not; mere frothy amusements, fit only for boys or silly women to be caught with.

'It is not my present intention to instruct my readers in the method of acquiring riches; that may be the work of another essay; but to exhibit the real and solid advantages I have found by them in my long and manifold experience; nor yet all the advantages of so worthy and valuable a blessing, (for who does not know or imagine the comforts of being warm or living at ease, and that power and pre-eminence are their inseparable attendants?) but only to instance the great supports they afford us under the severest calamities and misfortune; to show that the love of them is a special antidote against immorality and vice; and that the same does likewise naturally dispose men to actions of piety and devotion. All which I can make out by my own experience, who think myself no ways particular from the rest of mankind, nor better nor worse by nature than generally other men are.

'In the year 1665, when the sickness was, I lost by it my wife and two children, which were all my stock. Probably I might have had more, considering I was married between four and five years; but finding her to be a teeming woman, I was careful, as having then little above a brace of thousand pounds to carry on my trade and maintain a family with. I loved them as usually men do their wives and children, and therefore could not resist the first impulses of nature on so wounding a loss; but I quickly roused myself, and found means to alleviate, and at last conquer, my affliction, by reflecting how that she and her children having been no great expense to me, the best part of her fortune was still left; that my charge being reduced to myself, a journeyman, and a maid, I might live far cheaper than before; and that being now a childless widower, I might perhaps marry a no less deserving woman, and with a much better fortune than she brought, which was but 800*l.* And, to convince my readers that such considerations as these were proper and apt to produce such an affect, I remember it was the constant observation at that deplorable time, when so many hundreds were swept away daily, that the rich ever bore the loss of their families and relations far better than the poor; the latter having little or nothing beforehand, and living from hand to mouth, placed the whole comfort and satisfaction of their lives in their wives and children, and were therefore inconsolable.

'The following year happened the fire. at which time, by good providence, it was my fortune to have converted the greatest part of my effects into ready money, on the prospect of an extraordinary advantage which I was preparing to lay hold on. This calamity was very terrible and astonishing, the fury of the flames being such, that whole streets, at several distant places, were destroyed at one and the same time, so that (as it is well known) almost all our citizens were burnt out of what they had. But what did I then do? I did not stand gazing on the ruins of our noble metropolis; I did not shake my head, wring my hands, sigh and shed tears; I considered with myself what could this avail; I fell a plodding what advantages might be made of the ready cash I had; and immediately bethought myself that wonderful pennyworths might be bought of the goods that were saved out of the fire. In short, with about 2000*l.* and a little credit, I bought as much tobacco as raised my estate to the value of 10,000*l.* I then "looked on the ashes of our city, and the misery of its late inhabitants, as an effect of the just wrath and indignation of heaven towards a sinful and perverse people."

'After this I married again; and that wife dying, I took another; but both proved to be idle baggages: the first gave me a great deal of plague and vexation by her extravagances, and I became one of the by-words of the city. I knew it would be to no manner of purpose to go about to curb the fancies and inclinations of women, which fly out the more for being restrained; but what I could I did; I watched her narrowly, and by good luck found her in the embraces (for which I had two witnesses with me) of a wealthy spark of the court-end of the town; of whom I recovered 15,000*l.* which made me amends for what she had idly squandered, and put a silence to all my neighbours, taking off my reproach by the gain they saw I had by it. The last died about two years after I married her, in labour of three children. I conjecture they were begot by a country kinsman of hers, whom, at her recommendation, I took into my family, and gave wages to as a journeyman. What this creature expended in delicacies and high diet with her kinsman (as well as I could compute by the poulterer's, fishmonger's, and grocer's bills,) amounted in the said two years to one hundred eighty-six pounds four shillings and five-pence half-penny. The fine apparel, bracelets, lockets, and treats, &c. of the other, according to the best calculation, came, in three years and about three quarters, to seven hundred-forty four pounds seven shillings and nine pence. After this I resolved never to marry more, and found I had been a gainer by my marriages, and the damages granted me for the abuses of my bed (all charges deducted) eight thousand three hundred pounds, within a trifle.

'I come now to show the good effects of the love of money on the lives of men, towards rendering them honest, sober, and religious. When I was a young man, I had a mind to make the best of my wits, and over-reached a country chap in a parcel of unsound goods; to whom, upon his upbraiding, and threatening to expose me for it, I returned the equivalent of his loss; and upon his good advice, wherein he clearly demonstrated the folly of such artifices, which can never end but in shame, and the ruin of all correspondence, I never after transgressed. Can your courtiers, who take bribes, or your lawyers or physicians in their practice, or even the divines who intermeddle in worldly affairs, boast of making but one slip in their lives, and of such a thorough and lasting reformation? Since my coming into the world I do not remember I was ever overtaken in drink, save nine times, once at the christening of my first child, thrice at our city feasts, and five times at driving of bargains. My reformation I can attribute to nothing so much as the love and esteem of money, for I found myself to be extravagant in my drink, and apt to turn projector, and make rash bargains. As for women, I never knew any except my wives: for my reader must know, and it is what he may confide in as an excellent recipe, that the love of business and money is the greatest mortifier of inordinate desires imaginable, as employing the mind continually in the careful oversight of what one has in the eager quest after more, in looking after the negligences and deceits of servants, in the due entering and stating of accounts, in hunting after chaps, and in the exact knowledge of the state of markets; which things whoever thoroughly attends to, will find enough and enough to employ his thoughts on every moment of the day; so that I cannot call to mind, that in all the time I was a husband, which, off and on, was above twelve years, I ever once thought of my wives but in bed. And, lastly, for religion, I have ever been a constant churchman, both forenoons and afternoons on Sundays, never forgetting to be thankful for any gain or advantage I had had that day; and on Saturday nights, upon casting up my accounts, I always was grateful for the sum of my week's profits, and at Christmas for that of the whole year. It is true, perhaps, that my devotion has not been the most fervent; which, I think, ought to be imputed to the evenness and sedateness of my temper, which never would admit of any impetuosities of any sort: and I can remember, that in my youth and prime of manhood, when my blood ran brisker, I took greater pleasure in religious exercises than at present, or many years past, and that my devotion sensibly declined as age, which is dull and unwieldy, came upon me.

'I have, I hope, here proved, that the love of money prevents all immorality and vice; which if you will not allow, you must, that the pursuit of it obliges men to the same kind of life as they would follow if they were really virtuous; which is all I have to say at present, only recommending to you, that you would think of it, and turn ready wit into ready money as fast as you can. I conclude, your servant,

T. 'EPHRAIM WEED.'

No. 451.] *Thursday, August* 7, 1712.

———Jam sævus apertam
In rabiam cæpit verti jocus, et per honestas
Ire minax impune domos————

Hor. Ep. i. Lib. 2. 148.

————Times corrupt, and nature ill inclin'd,
Produc'd the point that left the sting behind;
Till, friend with friend, and families at strife,
Triumphant malice rag'd through private life.—*Pope*

THERE is nothing so scandalous to a government, and detestable in the eyes of all good men, as defamatory papers and pamphlets; but at the same time there is no thing so difficult to tame as a satirical author. An angry writer who cannot appear in print, naturally vents his spleen in libels and lampoons. A gay old woman, says the fable, seeing all her wrinkles represented in a large looking-glass, threw it upon the ground in a passion, and broke it in a thousand pieces; but as she was afterwards surveying the fragments with a spiteful kind of pleasure, she could not forbear uttering herself in the following soliloquy: 'What have I got by this revengeful blow of mine? I have only multiplied my deformity, and see a hundred ugly faces, where before I saw but one.'

It has been proposed, to oblige every person that writes a book, or a paper, to swear himself the author of it, and enter down in a public register his name and place of abode.

This indeed would have effectually suppressed all printed scandal, which generally appears under borrowed names, or under none at all. But it is to be feared that such an expedient would not only destroy scandal, but learning. It would operate promiscuously, and root up the corn and tares together. Not to mention some of the most celebrated works of piety, which have proceeded from anonymous authors, who have made it their merit to convey to us so great a charity in secret; there are few works of genius that come out at first with the author's name. The writer generally makes a trial of them in the world before he owns them; and, I believe, very few, who are capable of writing, would set pen to paper, if they knew beforehand that they must not publish their productions but on such conditions. For my own part, I must declare, the papers I present the public are like fairy favours, which shall last no longer than while the author is concealed.

That which makes it particularly difficult to restrain these sons of calumny and defamation is, that all sides are equally guilty of it, and that every dirty scribbler is countenanced by great names, whose interests he propagates by such vile and infamous methods. I have never yet heard of a ministry who have inflicted an exemplary punishment on an author that has supported their cause with falsehood and scandal, and treated, in a most cruel manner, the names of those who have been looked upon as their rivals and antagonists. Would a government set an everlasting mark of their displeasure upon one of those infamous writers, who makes his court to them by tearing to pieces the reputation of a competitor, we should quickly see an end put to this race of vermin, that are a scandal to government, and a reproach to human nature. Such a proceeding would make a minister of state shine in history, and would fill all mankind with a just abhorrence of persons who should treat him unworthily, and employ against him those arms which he scorned to make use of against his enemies.

I cannot think that any one will be so unjust as to imagine, what I have here said is spoken with respect to any party or faction. Every one who has in him the sentiments either of a Christian or a gentleman, cannot but be highly offended at this wicked and ungenerous practice, which is so much in use among us at present, that it is become a kind of national crime, and distinguishes us from all the governments that lie about us. I cannot but look upon the finest strokes of satire which are aimed at particular persons, and which are supported even with the appearances of truth, to be the marks of an evil mind, and highly criminal in themselves. Infamy, like other punishments, is under the direction and distribution of the magistrate, and not of any private person. Accordingly we learn, from a fragment of Cicero, that though there were very few capital punishments in the twelve tables, a libel or lampoon, which took away the good name of another, was to be punished by death. But this is far from being our case. Our satire is nothing but ribaldry and billingsgate. Scurrility passes for wit; and he who can call names in the greatest variety of phrases, is looked upon to have the shrewdest pen. By this means the honour of families is ruined; the highest posts and the greatest titles are rendered cheap and vile in the sight of the people; the noblest virtues and most exalted parts exposed to the contempt of the vicious and the ignorant. Should a foreigner, who knows nothing of our private factions, or one who is to act his part in the world when our present heats and animosities are forgot—should, I say, such a one form to himself a notion of the greatest men of all sides in the British nation, who are now living, from the characters which are given them in some or other of those abominable writings which are daily published among us, what a nation of monsters must we appear!

As this cruel practice tends to the utter subversion of all truth and humanity among us, it deserves the utmost detestation and discouragement of all who have either the love of their country, or the honour of their religion at heart. I would therefore earnestly recommend it to the consideration of those who deal in these pernicious arts of writing, and of those who take pleasure in the reading of them. As for the first, I have spoken of them in former papers, and have not stuck to rank them with the murderer and assassin. Every honest man sets as high a value upon a good name, as upon life itself: and I cannot but think that those who privily assault the one, would destroy the other, might they do it with the same security and impunity.

As for persons who take pleasure in the reading and dispersing such detestable libels, I am afraid they fall very little short of the guilt of the first composers. By a law of the emperors Valentinian and Valens, it was made death for any person not only to write a libel, but, if he met with one by chance, not to tear or burn it. But because I would not be thought singular in my opinion of this matter, I shall conclude my paper with the words of Monsieur Bayle, who was a man of great freedom of thought, as well as of exquisite learning and judgment.

'I cannot imagine that a man who disperses a libel, is less desirous of doing mischief than the author himself. But what shall we say of the pleasure which a man takes in the reading of a defamatory libel? Is it not a heinous sin in the sight of God? We must distinguish in this point

This pleasure is either an agreeable sensation we are affected with, when we meet with a witty thought which is well expressed, or it is a joy which we conceive from the dishonour of the person who is defamed. I will say nothing to the first of these cases; for perhaps some would think that my morality is not severe enough, if I should affirm that a man is not master of those agreeable sensations, any more than of those occasioned by sugar or honey, when they touch his tongue; but as to the second, every one will own that pleasure to be a heinous sin. The pleasure in the first case is of no continuance; it prevents our reason and reflection, and may be immediately followed by a secret grief, to see our neighbour's honour blasted. If it does not cease immediately, it is a sign that we are not displeased with the ill nature of the satirist, but are glad to see him defame his enemy by all kinds of stories; and then we deserve the punishment to which the writer of the libel is subject. I shall here add the words of a modern author. St. Gregory, upon excommunicating those writers who had dishonoured Castorius, does not except those who read their works; because, says he, if calumnies have always been the delight of their hearers, and a gratification of those persons who have no other advantage over honest men, is not he who takes pleasure in reading them as guilty as he who composed them? It is an uncontested maxim, that they who approve an action, would certainly do it if they could; that is, if some reason of self-love did not hinder them. There is no difference, says Cicero, between advising a crime, and approving it when committed. The Roman law confirmed this maxim, having subjected the approvers and authors of this evil to the same penalty. We may therefore conclude, that those who are pleased with reading defamatory libels, so far as to approve the authors and dispersers of them, are as guilty as if they had composed them; for, if they do not write such libels themselves, it is because they have not the talent of writing, or because they will run no hazard.'

The author produces other authorities to confirm his judgment in this particular.

C.

No. 452.] *Friday, August* 8, 1712.

Est natura hominum novitatis avida.

Plin. apud Lilium.

Human nature is fond of novelty.

THERE is no humour in my countrymen, which I am more inclined to wonder at, than their general thirst after news. There are about half a dozen ingenious men, who live very plentifully upon this curiosity of their fellow-subjects. They all of them receive the same advices from abroad, and very often in the same words; but their way of cooking it is so very different, that there is no citizen, who has an eye to the public good, that can leave the coffee-house with a peace of mind, before he has given every one of them a reading. These several dishes of news are so very agreeable to the palate of my countrymen, that they are not only pleased with them when they are served up hot, but when they are again set cold before them, by those penetrating politicians who oblige the public with their reflections and observations upon every piece of intelligence that is sent us from abroad. This text is given us by one set of writers, and the comment by another.

But notwithstanding we have the same tale told us in so many different papers, and if occasion requires, in so many articles of the same paper; notwithstanding, in a scarcity of foreign posts, we hear the same story repeated by different advices from Paris, Brussels, the Hague, and from every great town in Europe; notwithstanding the multitude of annotations, explanations, reflections, and various readings which it passes through, our time lies heavy on our hands till the arrival of a fresh mail: we long to receive farther particulars, to hear what will be the next step, or what will be the consequences of that which we have already taken. A westerly wind keeps the whole town in suspense, and puts a stop to conversation.

This general curiosity has been raised and inflamed by our late wars, and if rightly directed, might be of good use to a person who has such a thirst awakened in him. Why should not a man, who takes delight in reading every thing that is new, apply himself to history, travels, and other writings of the same kind, where he will find perpetual fuel for his curiosity, and meet with much more pleasure and improvement than in these papers of the week? An honest tradesman, who languishes a whole summer in expectation of a battle, and perhaps is baulked at last, may here meet with half a dozen in a day. He may read the news of a whole campaign in less time than he now bestows upon the products of a single post. Fights, conquests, and revolutions, lie thick together. The reader's curiosity is raised and satisfied every moment, and his passions disappointed or gratified, without being detained in a state of uncertainty from day to day, or lying at the mercy of the sea and wind; in short, the mind is not here kept in a perpetual gape after knowledge, nor punished with that eternal thirst, which is the portion of all our modern newsmongers and coffee-house politicians.

All matters of fact, which a man did not know before, are news to him; and I do not see how any haberdasher in Cheapside is more concerned in the present quarrel of the Cantons, than he was in that of the League. At least, I believe, every one will allow me, it is of more importance to an

Englishman to know the history of his ancestors, than that of his contemporaries who live upon the banks of the Danube or the Borysthenes. As for those who are of another mind, I shall recommend to them the following letter from a projector, who is willing to turn a penny by this remarkable curiosity of his countrymen.

'MR. SPECTATOR,—You must have observed that men who frequent coffee-houses, and delight in news, are pleased with every thing that is matter of fact, so it be what they have not heard before. A victory or a defeat are equally agreeable to them. The shutting of a cardinal's mouth pleases them one post, and the opening of it another. They are glad to hear the French court is removed to Marli, and are afterwards as much delighted with its return to Versailles. They read the advertisements with the same curiosity as the articles of public news; and are as pleased to hear of a pie-bald horse that is strayed out of a field near Islington, as of a whole troop that have been engaged in any foreign adventure. In short, they have a relish for every thing that is news, let the matter of it be what it will; or, to speak more properly, they are men of a voracious appetite, but no taste. Now, sir, since the great fountain of news, I mean the war, is very near being dried up; and since these gentlemen have contracted such an inextinguishable thirst after it, I have taken their case and my own into consideration, and have thought of a project which may turn to the advantage of us both. I have thoughts of publishing a daily paper, which shall comprehend in it all the most remarkable occurrences in every little town, village, and hamlet, that lie within ten miles of London, or, in other words, within the verge of the penny-post. I have pitched upon this scene of intelligence for two reasons; first, because the carriage of letters will be very cheap; and, secondly, because I may receive them every day. By this means my readers will have their news fresh and fresh, and many worthy citizens, who cannot sleep with any satisfaction at present, for want of being informed how the world goes, may go to bed contentedly, it being my design to put out my paper every night at nine o'clock precisely. I have already established correspondences in these several places, and received very good intelligence.

'By my last advices from Knightsbridge, I hear that a horse was clapped into the pound on the third instant, and that he was not released when the letters came away.

'We are informed from Pankridge,* that a dozen weddings were lately celebrated in the mother-church of that place, but are referred to their next letters for the names of the parties concerned.

* St. Pancras, then a fashionable place for weddings.

'Letters from Brumpton advise, that the widow Blight had received several visits from John Mildew; which affords great matter of speculation in those parts.

'By a fisherman who lately touched at Hammersmith, there is advice from Putney, that a certain person well known in that place, is like to lose his election for churchwarden; but this being boat-news, we cannot give entire credit to it.

'Letters from Paddington bring little more than that William Squeak, the sow-gelder, passed through that place the fifth instant.

'They advise from Fulham that things remained there in the same state they were. They had intelligence, just as the letters came away, of a tub of excellent ale just set abroach at Parson's Green; but this wanted confirmation.

'I have here, sir, given you a specimen of the news with which I intend to entertain the town, and which, when drawn up regularly in the form of a newspaper, will, I doubt not, be very acceptable to many of those public-spirited readers who take more delight in acquainting themselves with other people's business than their own. I hope a paper of this kind, which lets us know what is done near home, may be more useful to us than those which are filled with advices from Zug and Bender, and make some amends for that dearth of intelligence which we may justly apprehend from times of peace. If I find that you receive this project favourably, I will shortly trouble you with one or two more; and in the mean time am, most worthy sir, with all due respect, your most obedient and humble servant.' C.

No. 453.] *Saturday, August* 9, 1712.

Non usitata nec tenui ferar
Penna——— *Hor.* Od. xx. Lib. 2. 1.

No weak, no common wing shall bear
My rising body through the air.—*Creech.*

THERE is not a more pleasing exercise of the mind than gratitude. It is accompanied with such an inward satisfaction, that the duty is sufficiently rewarded by the performance. It is not like the practice of many other virtues, difficult and painful, but attended with so much pleasure, that were there no positive command which enjoined it, nor any recompence laid up for it hereafter, a generous mind would indulge in it, for the natural gratification that accompanies it.

If gratitude is due from man to man, how much more from man to his Maker! The Supreme Being does not only confer upon us those bounties, which proceed more immediately from his hand, but even those benefits which are conveyed to us by others. Every blessing we enjoy, by what means soever it may be derived upon us, is the gift of Him who is the great Author of good, and Father of mercies.

If gratitude, when exerted towards one another, naturally produces a very pleasing sensation in the mind of a grateful man, it exalts the soul into rapture, when it is employed on this great object of gratitude, on this beneficent Being, who has given us every thing we already possess, and from whom we expect every thing we yet hope for.

Most of the works of the pagan poets were either direct hymns to their deities, or tended indirectly to the celebration of their respective attributes and perfections. Those who are acquainted with the works of the Greek and Latin poets which are still extant, will, upon reflection, find this observation so true that I shall not enlarge upon it. One would wonder that more of our Christian poets have not turned their thoughts this way, especially if we consider that our idea of the Supreme Being is not only infinitely more great and noble than what could possibly enter into the heart of a heathen, but filled with every thing that can raise the imagination, and give an opportunity for the sublimest thoughts and conceptions.

Plutarch tells us of a heathen who was singing a hymn to Diana, in which he celebrated her for her delight in human sacrifices, and other instances of cruelty and revenge; upon which, a poet who was present at this piece of devotion, and seems to have had a truer idea of the divine nature, told the votary, by way of reproof, that, in recompense for his hymn, he heartily wished he might have a daughter of the same temper with the goddess he celebrated. It was impossible to write the praises of one of those false deities, according to the pagan creed, without a mixture of impertinence and absurdity.

The Jews, who before the time of Christianity were the only people who had the knowledge of the true God, have set the Christian world an example how they ought to employ this divine talent of which I am speaking. As that nation produced men of great genius, without considering them as inspired writers, they have transmitted to us many hymns and divine odes, which excel those that are delivered down to us by the ancient Greeks and Romans, in the poetry, as much as in the subject to which it was consecrated. This I think might easily be shown if there were occasion for it.

I have already communicated to the public some pieces of divine poetry; and, as they have met with a very favourable reception, I shall from time to time publish any work of the same nature, which has not yet appeared in print, and may be acceptable to my readers.

I.

'When all thy mercies, O my God,
My rising soul surveys;
Transported with the view, I'm lost
In wonder, love, and praise:

II.

'O how shall words with equal warmth
The gratitude declare,
That glows within my ravish'd heart?
But thou canst read it there.

III.

'Thy providence my life sustain'd,
And all my wants redrest,
When in the silent womb I lay,
And hung upon the breast.

IV.

'To all my weak complaints and cries
Thy mercy lent an ear,
Ere yet my feeble thoughts had learn'd
To form themselves in pray'r.

V.

'Unnumber'd comforts to my soul
Thy tender care bestow'd,
Before my infant heart conceiv'd
From whom those comforts flow'd.

VI.

'When in the slipp'ry paths of youth,
With heedless steps I ran,
Thine arm unseen convey'd me safe,
And led me up to man.

VII.

'Through hidden dangers, toils, and deaths
It gently clear'd my way,
And through the pleasing snares of vice,
More to be fear'd than they.

VIII.

'When worn with sickness oft hast Thou
With health renew'd my face,
And when in sins and sorrows sunk,
Reviv'd my soul with grace.

IX.

'Thy bounteous hand with worldly bliss
Has made my cup run o'er,
And in a kind and faithful friend
Has doubled all my store

X.

'Ten thousand thousand precious gifts
My daily thanks employ;
Nor is the least a cheerful heart,
That tastes those gifts with joy.

XI.

'Through every period of my life
Thy goodness I'll pursue;
And after death, in distant worlds
The glorious theme renew.

XII.

'When nature fails and day and night
Divide thy works no more,
My ever grateful heart, O Lord,
Thy mercy shall adore.

XIII.

'Through all eternity to Thee
A joyful song I'll raise;
For oh! eternity's too short
To utter all thy praise.' C.

No. 454.] *Monday, August,* 11, 1712.

Sine me, vacivum tempus ne quod dem mihi
Laboris. *Ter. Heaut.* Act. i. Sc. 1.

Give me leave to allow myself no respite from labour.

It is an inexpressible pleasure to know a little of the world, and be of no character or significancy in it.

To be ever unconcerned, and ever looking on new objects with an endless curiosity, is a delight known only to those who are turned for speculation: nay, they who enjoy it, must value things only as they are the objects of speculation, without drawing any worldly advantage to themselves from them, but just as they are what contribute to their amusement, or the improvement of the mind. I lay one night last week at Richmond; and being restless, not out of dissatisfaction, but a certain busy inclination one sometimes has, I rose at four in the morning, and took boat for London, with a resolution to rove by boat and coach for the next four-and-twenty hours, till the many different objects I must needs meet with should tire my imagination, and give me an inclination to a repose more profound than I was at that time capable of. I beg people's pardon for an odd humour I am guilty of, and was often that day, which is saluting any person whom I like, whether I know him or not. This is a particularity would be tolerated in me, if they considered that the greatest pleasure I know I receive at my eyes, and that I am obliged to an agreeable person for coming a broad into my view, as another is for a visit of conversation at their own houses.

The hours of the day and night are taken up in the cities of London and Westminster, by people as different from each other as those who are born in different centuries. Men of six o'clock give way to those of nine, they of nine, to the generation of twelve; and they of twelve disappear, and make room for the fashionable world, who have made two o'clock the noon of the day.

When we first put off from shore, we soon fell in with a fleet of gardeners, bound for the several market-ports of London; and it was the most pleasing scene imaginable to see the cheerfulness with which those industrious people plyed their way to a certain sale of their goods. The banks on each side are as well peopled, and beautified with as agreeable plantations as any spot on tne earth; but the Thames itself, loaded with the product of each shore, added very much to the landscape. It was very easy to observe by their sailing, and the countenances of the ruddy virgins, who were supercargoes, the part of the town to which they were bound. Their was an air in the purveyors for Covent-garden, who frequently converse with morning rakes, very unlike the seeming sobriety of those bound for Stocks-market.

Nothing remarkable happened in our voyage; but I landed with ten sail of apricot boats, at Strand-bridge, after having put in at Nine-Elms, and taken in melons, consigned by Mr. Cuffee, of that place, to Sarah Sewell and company, at their stall in Covent-garden. We arrived at Strand-bridge at six of the clock, and were unloading, when the hackney-coachmen of the foregoing night took their leave of each other at the Dark-House, to go to bed before the day was too far spent. Chimney-sweepers passed by us as we made up to the market, and some raillery happened between one of the fruit-wenches and those black men, about the Devil and Eve, with allusion to their several professions. I could not believe any place more entertaining than Covent-garden; where I strolled from one fruit-shop to another, with crowds of agreeable young women around me, who were purchasing fruit for their respective families. It was almost eight of the clock before I could leave that variety of objects. I took coach and followed a young lady, who tripped into another just before me, attended by her maid. I saw immediately she was of the family of the Vain-loves. There are a set of these, who of all things, effect the play of Blindman's-buff, and leading men into love for they know not whom, who are fled they know not where. This sort of woman is usually a janty slattern; she hangs on her clothes, plays her head, varies her posture, and changes place incessantly, and all with an appearance of striving at the same time to hide herself, and yet give you to understand she is in humour to laugh at you. You must have often seen the coachmen make signs with their fingers, as they drive by each other, to intimate how much they have got that day. They can carry on that language to give intelligence where they are driving. In an instant my coachman took the wink to pursue; and the lady's driver gave the hint that he was going through Long-acre towards St. James's: while he whipped up James-street, we drove for King-street, to save the pass at St. Martin's-lane. The coachman took care to meet, jostle, and threaten each other for way, and be entangled at the end of Newport-street and Long-acre. The fright, you must believe, brought down the lady's coach door, and obliged her, with her mask off, to inquire into the bustle,—when she sees the man she would avoid. The tackle of the coach window is so bad she cannot draw it up again, and she drives on sometimes wholly discovered and sometimes half escaped, according to the accident of carriages in her way. One of these ladies keeps her seat in a hackney-coach, as well as the best rider does on a managed horse. The laced shoe on her left foot, with a careless gesture just appearing on the opposite cushion, held her both firm, and in proper attitude to receive the next jolt.

As she was an excellent coach-woman, many were the glances at each other which we had for an hour and a half, in all parts of the town, by the skill of our drivers; till at last my lady was conveniently lost, with notice from her coachman to ours to make off, and he should hear where she went. This chase was now at an end; and the fellow who drove her came to us, and discovered that he was ordered to come again in an hour, for that she was a Silk-worm. I was surprised with this phrase, but found it was a cant among the hackney fraternity for their best customers, women who ramble twice or thrice a week from shop to shop, to turn over all the goods in town without buying any thing. The silk-worms are, it seems, indulged by the tradesmen; for, though they never buy, they are ever talking of new silks, laces and ribands, and serve the owners in getting them customers as their common dunners do in making them pay.

The day of people of fashion began now to break, and carts and hacks were mingled with equipages of show and vanity; when I resolved to walk it, out of cheapness; but my unhappy curiosity is such, that I find it always my interest to take coach; for some odd adventure among beggars, ballad singers, or the like, detains and throws me into expense. It happened so immediately; for at the corner of Warwick-street, as I was listening to a new ballad, a ragged rascal, a beggar who knew me, came up to me, and began to turn the eyes of the good company upon me, by telling me he was extremely poor, and should die in the street for want of drink, except I immediately would have the charity to give him sixpence go into the next ale-house and save his life. He urged with a melancholy face, that all his family had died of thirst. All the mob have humour, and two or three began to take the jest; by which Mr. Sturdy carried his point, and let me sneak off to a coach. As I drove along, it was a pleasing reflection to see the world so prettily checkered since I left Richmond, and the scene still filling with children of a new hour. This satisfaction increased as I moved towards the city; and gay signs, well-disposed streets, magnificent public structures, and wealthy shops, adorned with contented faces, made the joy still rising till we came into the centre of the city, and centre of the world of trade, the Exchange of London. As other men in the crowds about me were pleased with their hopes and bargains, I found my account in observing them, in attention to their several interests. I indeed, looked upon myself as the richest man that walked the Exchange that day; for my benevolence made me share the gains of every bargain that was made. It was not the least of my satisfaction in my survey, to go up stairs, and pass the shops of agreeable females; to observe so many pretty hands busy in the folding of ribands, and the utmost eagerness of agreeable faces in the sale of patches, pins, and wires, on each side of the counters, was an amusement in which I could longer have indulged myself, had not the dear creatures called to me, to ask what I wanted, when I could not answer, only 'To look at you.' I went to one of the windows which opened to the area below, where all the several voices lost their distinction, and rose up in a confused humming; which created in me a reflection that could not come into the mind of any but one a little too studious; for I said to myself with a kind of pun in thought, 'What nonsense is all the hurry of this world to those who are above it?' In these, or not much wiser thoughts, I had liked to have lost my place at the chop-house, where every man, according to the natural bashfulness or sullenness of our nation, eats in a public room a mess of broth, or chop of meat, in dumb silence, as if they had no pretence to speak to each other on the foot of being men, except they were of each other's acquaintance.

I went afterwards to Robin's, and saw people who had dined with me at the five-penny ordinary just before, give bills for the value of large estates; and could not but behold with great pleasure, property lodged in, and transferred in a moment from, such as would never be masters of half as much as is seemingly in them, and given from them, every day they live. But before five in the afternoon I left the city, came to my common scene of Covent-garden, and passed the evening at Will's, in attending the discourses of several sets of people, who relieved each other, within my hearing, on the subjects of cards, dice, love, learning, and politics. The last subject kept me till I heard the streets in the possession of the bell-man, who had now the world to himself, and cried 'Past two o'clock.' This roused me from my seat; and I went to my lodgings, led by a light, whom I put into the discourse of his private economy, and made him give me an account of the charge, hazard, profit, and loss of a family that depended upon a link, with a design to end my trivial day with the generosity of sixpence, instead of a third part of that sum. When I came to my chambers, I writ down these minutes: but was at a loss what instruction I should propose to my reader from the enumeration of so many insignificant matters and occurrences: and I thought it of great use, if they could learn with me to keep their minds open to gratification, and ready to receive it from any thing it meets with. This one circumstance will make every face you see give you the satisfaction you now take in beholding that of a friend; will make every object a pleasing one; will make all the good which arrives to any man, an increase of happiness to yourself. T.

No. 455.] *Tuesday, August* 12, 1712.

————Ego apis matinæ
More modoque,
Grata carpentis thyma per laborem
Plurimum————

Hor. Od. ii Lib. 4 27

————My timorous muse
Unambitious tracts pursues:
Does with weak unballast wings,
About the mossy brooks and springs,
Like the laborious bee,
For little drops of honey fly,
And there with humble sweets contents her industry.
Cowley.

THE following letters have in them reflections which will seem of importance both to the learned world and to domestic life. There is in the first, an allegory so well carried on, that it cannot but be very pleasing to those who have a taste of good writing; and the other billets may have their use in common life.

'MR. SPECTATOR,—As I walked the other day in a fine garden, and observed the great variety of improvements in plants and flowers, beyond what they otherwise would have been, I was naturally led into a reflection upon the advantages of education, or modern culture: how many good qualities in the mind are lost for want of the like due care in nursing and skilfully managing them; how many virtues are choked by the multitude of weeds which are suffered to grow among them; how excellent parts are often starved and useless, by being planted in a wrong soil; and how very seldom do these moral seeds produce the noble fruits which might be expected from them, by a neglect of proper manuring, necessary pruning, and an artful management of our tender inclinations and first spring of life. These obvious speculations made me at length conclude, that there is a sort of vegetable principle in the mind of every man when he comes into the world. In infants, the seeds lie buried and undiscovered, till after a while they sprout forth in a kind of rational leaves, which are words; and in due season the flowers begin to appear in a variety of beautiful colours, and all the gay pictures of youthful fancy and imagination; at last the fruit knits and is formed, which is green perhaps at first, sour and unpleasant to the taste, and not fit to be gathered: till, ripened by due care and application, it discovers itself in all the noble productions of philosophy, mathematics, close reasoning, and handsome argumentation. These fruits, when they arrive at just maturity, and are of a good kind, afford the most vigorous nourishment to the minds of men. I reflected farther on the intellectual leaves before mentioned, and found almost as great a variety among them as in the vegetable world. I could easily observe the smooth shining Italian leaves, the nimble French aspen, always in motion, the Greek and Latin ever-greens, the Spanish myrtle, the English oak, the Scotch thistle, the Irish shambrogue, the prickly German and Dutch holly, the Polish and Russian nettle, besides a vast number of exotics imported from Asia, Africa, and America. I saw several barren plants, which bore only leaves, without any hopes of flower or fruit. The leaves of some were fragrant and well-shaped, and others ill-scented and irregular. I wondered at a set of old whimsical botanists, who spent their whole lives in the contemplation of some withered Egyptian, Coptic, Armenian, or Chinese leaves; while others made it their business to collect, in voluminous herbals, all the several leaves of some one tree. The flowers afford a most diverting entertainment, in a wonderful variety of figures, colours, and scents; however, most of them withered soon, or at best are but annuals. Some professed florists make them their constant study and employment, and despise all fruit; and now and then a few fanciful people spend all their time in the cultivation of a single tulip, or a carnation. But the most agreeable amusement seems to be the well-choosing, mixing, and binding together these flowers in pleasing nosegays, to present to ladies. The scent of Italian flowers is observed, like their other perfumes, to be too strong, and to hurt the brain; that of the French with glaring gaudy colours, yet faint and languid: German and northern flowers have little or no smell, or sometimes an unpleasant one. The ancients had a secret to give a lasting beauty, colour, and sweetness, to some of their choice flowers, which flourish to this day, and which few of the moderns can effect. These are becoming enough and agreeable in their seasons, and do often handsomely adorn an entertainment: but an over-fondness of them seems to be a disease. It rarely happens, to find a plant vigorous enough to have (like an orange-tree,) at once beautiful and shining leaves, fragrant flowers, and delicious, nourishing fruit. Sir, yours, &c.'

'August 6, 1712.

'DEAR SPEC,—You have given us, in your Spectator of Saturday last, a very excellent discourse upon the force of custom, and its wonderful efficacy in making every thing pleasant to us. I cannot deny but that I received above two-pennyworth of instruction from your paper, and in the general was very well pleased with it; but I am, without a compliment, sincerely troubled that I cannot exactly be of your opinion, that it makes every thing pleasing to us. In short, I have the honour to be yoked to a young lady, who is, in plain English, for her standing, a very eminent scold. She began to break her mind very freely, both to me and to her servants, about two months after our nuptials; and, though I have been accustomed to this humour of hers these three years, yet I do not know what 's the matter with me, but I am no more delighted with it than I was at the very first. I have advised with her relations about her, and they all tell me that her mother and her grandmother before her were both taken much after the same manner; so that, since it runs in the blood, I have but small hopes of her recovery. I should be glad to have a little of your advice in this matter. I would not willingly trouble you to contrive how it may be a pleasure to me; if you will but put me in a way that I may bear it with indifference, I shall rest satisfied,

'Dear Spec, your very humble servant.

'P. S. I must do the poor girl the justice to let you know, that this match was none of her own choosing, (or indeed of mine either;) in consideration of which I avoid giving her the least provocation; and, indeed, we live better together than usually folks do who hated one another when they were first joined. To evade the sin against parents, or at least to extenuate it, my dear rails at my father and mother, and I curse hers for making the match.'

'August 8, 1712.

'Mr. Spectator,—I like the theme you lately gave out extremely, and should be as glad to handle it as any man living: but I find myself no better qualified to write about money than about my wife; for, to tell you a secret, which I desire may go no further, I am master of neither of those subjects. Yours, PILL GARLICK.'

'Mr. Spectator,—I desire you will print this in italic, so as it may be generally taken notice of. It is designed only to admonish all persons, who speak either at the bar, pulpit, or any public assembly whatsoever, how they discover their ignorance in the use of similies. There are, in the pulpit itself, as well as in other places, such gross abuses in this kind, that I give this warning to all I know. I shall bring them for the future before your spectatorial authority. On Sunday last, one, who shall be nameless, reproving several of his congregation for standing at prayers, was pleased to say, "One would think, like the elephant, you had no knees." Now I myself saw an elephant, in Bartholomew fair, kneel down to take on his back the ingenious Mr. William Penkethman. Your most humble servant.' T.

No. 456.] *Wednesday, August* 13, 1712.

De quo libelli in celeberrimis locis proponuntur, huic ne perire quidem tacite conceditur.—*Tull.*

The man whose conduct is publicly arraigned, is not suffered even to be undone quietly.

Otway, in his tragedy of Venice Preserved, has described the misery of a man whose effects are in the hands of the law, with great spirit. The bitterness of being the scorn and laughter of base minds, the anguish of being insulted by men hardened beyond the sense of shame or pity, and the injury of a man's fortune being wasted, under pretence of justice, are excellently aggravated in the following speech of Pierre to Jaffier:

'I pass'd this very moment by thy doors,
And found them guarded by a troop of villains:
The sons of public rapine were destroying.
They told me by the sentence of the law,
They had commission to seize all thy fortune;
Nay, more, Priuli's cruel hand had sign'd it.
Here stood a ruffian with a horrid face,
Lording it o'er a pile of massy plate,
Tumbled into a heap for public sale.
There was another making villanous jests
At thy undoing. He had ta'en possession
Of all thy ancient most domestic ornaments,
Rich hangings intermix'd and wrought with gold;
The very bed, which on thy wedding-night
Receiv'd thee to the arms of Belvidera.
The scene of all thy joys, was violated
By the coarse hands of fi thy dungeon villains,
And thrown amongst the common lumber.'

Nothing indeed can be more unhappy than the condition of bankruptcy. The calamity which happens to us by ill-fortune, or by the injury of others, has in it some consolation; but what arises from our own misbehaviour, or error, is the state of the most exquisite sorrow. When a man considers not only an ample fortune, but even the very necessaries of life, his pretence to food itself, at the mercy of his creditors, he cannot but look upon himself in the state of the dead, with his case thus much worse, that the last office is performed by his adversaries instead of his friends. From this hour the cruel world does not only take possession of his whole fortune, but even of every thing else which had no relation to it. All his indifferent actions have new interpretations put upon them; and those whom he has favoured in his former life, discharge themselves of their obligations to him, by joining in the reproaches of his enemies. It is almost incredible that it should be so; but it is too often seen that there is a pride mixed with the impatience of the creditor; and there are who would rather recover their own by the downfal of a prosperous man, than be discharged to the common satisfaction of themselves and their creditors. The wretched man, who was lately master of abundance, is now under the direction of others; and the wisdom, economy, good sense, and skill in human life before, by reason of his present misfortune, are of no use to him in the disposition of any thing. The incapacity of an infant or a lunatic is designed for his provision and accommodation; but that of a bankrupt, without any mitigation in respect of the accidents by which it arrived, is calculated for his utter ruin, except there be a remainder ample enough, after the discharge of his creditors, to bear also the expense of rewarding those by whose means the effect of all this labour was transferred from him. This man is to look on and see others giving directions upon what terms and conditions his goods are to be purchased; and all this usually done, not with an air of trustees to dispose of his effects, but destroyers to divide and tear them to pieces.

There is something sacred in misery to great and good minds; for this reason all wise lawgivers have been extremely tender how they let loose even the man who has right on his side, to act with any mixture of resentment against the defendant. Virtuous and modest men, though they be used with some artifice, and have it in their power to avenge themselves, are slow in the application of that power, and are ever constrained to go into rigorous measures. They are careful to demonstrate themselves not only persons injured, but also that to bear it longer would be a means to make the offender injure others, before they proceed. Such men clap their hands upon their hearts, and consider what it is to have at their mercy the life of a citizen. Such would have it to say to their own souls, if possible, that they were merciful when they could have destroyed, rather than when it was in their power to have spared a man, they destroyed. This is a due to the common calamity of human life, due in some measure to our very enemies. They who scruple in doing the least injury are cautious of exacting the utmost justice.

Let any one who is conversant in the variety of human life reflect upon it, and he will find the man who wants mercy has a taste of no enjoyment of any kind. There is a natural disrelish of every thing which is good in his very nature, and he is born an enemy to the world. He is ever extremely partial to himself in all his actions, and has no sense of iniquity but from the punishment which shall attend it. The law of the land is his gospel, and all his cases of conscience are determined by his attorney. Such men know not what it is to gladden the heart of a miserable man; that riches are the instruments of serving the purposes of heaven or hell, according to the disposition of the possessor. The wealthy can torment or gratify all who are in their power, and choose to do one or other, as they are affected with love or hatred to mankind. As for such who are insensible of the concerns of others, but merely as they affect themselves, these men are to be valued only for their mortality, and as we hope better things from their heirs. I could not but read with great delight, a letter from an eminent citizen, who has failed, to one who was intimate with him in his better fortune, and able by his countenance to retrieve his lost condition.

'SIR,—It is in vain to multiply words and make apologies for what is never to be defended by the best advocate in the world, the guilt of being unfortunate. All that a man in my condition can do or say, will be received with prejudice by the generality of mankind, but I hope not with you: you have been a great instrument in helping me to get what I have lost; and I know (for that reason, as well as kindness to me) you cannot but be in pain to see me undone. To show you I am not a man incapable of bearing calamity, I will, though a poor man, lay aside the distinction between us, and talk with the frankness we did when we were nearer to an equality: as all I do will be received with prejudice, all you do will be looked upon with partiality. What I desire of you is, that you, who are courted by all, would smile upon me, who am shunned by all. Let that grace and favour which your fortune throws upon you, be turned to make up the coldness and indifference that is used towards me. All good and generous men will have an eye of kindness for me for my own sake, and the rest of the world will regard me for yours. There is a happy contagion in riches, as well as a destructive one in poverty: the rich can make rich without parting with any of their store; and the conversation of the poor makes men poor, though they borrow nothing of them. How this is to be accounted for I know not; but men's estimation follows us according to the company we keep. If you are what you were to me, you can go a great way towards my recovery; if you are not, my good fortune, if ever it returns, will return by slower approaches. I am, sir, your affectionate friend, and humble servant.'

This was answered by a condescension that did not, by long impertinent professions of kindness, insult his distress, but was as follows:

'DEAR TOM,—I am very glad to hear that you have heart enough to begin the world a second time. I assure you, I do not think your numerous family at all diminished (in the gifts of nature, for which I have ever so much admired them,) by what has so lately happened to you. I shall not only countenance your affairs with my appearance for you, but shall accommodate you with a considerable sum at common interest for three years. You know I could make more of it; but I have so great a love for you, that I can waive opportunities of gain to help you; for I do not care whether they say of me after I am dead, that I had a hundred or fifty thousand pounds more than I wanted when I was living. Your obliged humble servant.'

T.

No. 457.] *Thursday, August* 14, 1712.

——Multa et præclara minantis.

Hor. Sat. iii. Lib. 2. 9

Seeming to promise something wondrous great.

I SHALL this day lay before my readers a letter, written by the same hand with that of last Friday, which contained proposals for a printed newspaper that should take in the whole circle of the penny-post.

'SIR,—The kind reception you gave my last Friday's letter, in which I broached my project of a newspaper, encourages me to lay before you two or three more; for, you must know, sir, that we look upon you to be the Lowndes* of the learned world, and cannot think any scheme practicable or rational before you have approved of it, though all the money we raise by it is in our own funds, and for our private use.

'I have often thought that a news-letter of whispers, written every post, and sent about the kingdom, after the same manner as that of Mr. Dyer, Mr. Dawkes, or any other epistolary historian, might be highly gratifying to the public, as well as bene-

* Secretary at this time of the treasury, and director of the mint.

ficial to the author By whispers I mean those pieces of news which are communicated as secrets, and which bring a double pleasure to the hearer: first, as they are private history; and, in the next place, as they have always in them a dash of scandal. These are the two chief qualifications in an article of news, which recommend it in a more than ordinary manner, to the ears of the curious. Sickness of persons in high posts, twilight visits paid and received by ministers of state, clandestine courtships and marriages, secret amours, losses at play, applications for places, with their respective successes and repulses, are the materials in which I chiefly intend to deal. I have two persons, that are each of them the representative of a species, who are to furnish me with those whispers which I intend to convey to my correspondents. The first of these is Peter Hush, descended from the ancient family of the Hushes. The other is the old lady Blast, who has a very numerous tribe of daughters in the two great cities of London and Westminster. Peter Hush has a whispering-hole in most of the great coffee-houses about town. If you are alone with him in a wide room, he carries you up into a corner of it, and speaks in your ear. I have seen Peter seat himself in a company of seven or eight persons whom he never saw before in his life; and, after having looked about to see there was no one that overheard him, has communicated to them in a low voice, and under the seal of secresy, the death of a great man in the country, who was, perhaps, a fox-hunting the very moment this account was given of him. If upon your entering into a coffee-house you see a circle of heads bending over the table, and lying close to one another, it is ten to one but my friend Peter is among them. I have known Peter publishing the whisper of the day by eight o'clock in the morning at Garraway's, by twelve at Will's, and before two at the Smyrna. When Peter has thus effectually launched a secret, I have been very well pleased to hear people whispering it to one another at second-hand, and spreading it about as their own; for you must know, sir, the great incentive to whispering is the ambition which every one has of being thought in the secret, and being looked upon as a man who has access to greater people than one would imagine. After having given you this account of Peter Hush, I proceed to that virtuous lady, the old lady Blast, who is to communicate to me the private transactions of the crimp-table, with all the arcana of the fair-sex. The lady Blast, you must understand, has such a particular malignity in her whisper, that it blights like an easterly wind, and withers every reputation that it breathes upon. She has a particular knack at making private weddings, and last winter married above five women of quality to their footmen. Her whisper can make an innocent young woman big with child, or fill a healthy young fellow with distempers that are not to be named. She can turn a visit into an intrigue, and a distant salute into an assignation. She can beggar the wealthy, and degrade the noble. In short, she can whisper men base or foolish, jealous or ill-natured: or, if occasion requires, can tell you the slips of their great grandmothers, and traduce the memory of honest coachmen, that have been in their graves above these hundred years. By these and the like helps, I question not but I shall furnish out a very handsome news-letter. If you approve my project, I shall begin to whisper by the very next post, and question not but every one of my customers will be very well pleased with me, when he considers that every piece of news I send him is a word in his ear, and lets him into a secret.

'Having given you a sketch of this project, I shall, in the next place, suggest to you another for a monthly pamphlet, which I shall likewise submit to your spectatorial wisdom. I need not tell you, sir, that there are several authors in France, Germany, and Holland, as well as in our own country,* who publish every month what they call An Account of the Works of the Learned, in which they give us an abstract of all such books as are printed in any part of Europe. Now, sir, it is my design to publish every month, An Account of the Works of the Unlearned. Several late productions of my own countrymen, who, many of them make a very eminent figure in the illiterate world, encourage me in this undertaking. I may, in this work, possibly make a review of several pieces which have appeared in the foreign accounts above mentioned, though they ought not to have been taken notice of in works which bear such a title. I may likewise take into consideration such pieces as appear, from time to time, under the names of those gentlemen who compliment one another in public assemblies, by the title of "The Learned Gentlemen." Our party-authors will also afford me a great variety of subjects, not to mention the editors, commentators, and others, who are often men of no learning, or, what is as bad, of no knowledge. I shall not enlarge upon this hint; but if you think any thing can be made of it, I shall set about it with all the pains and application that so useful a work deserves. I am ever, most worthy sir, &c.' C.

No. 458.] *Friday, August 15, 1712.*

Αἰδὼς οὐκ ἀγαθή—— *Hes.*

——Pudor malus—— *Hor.*

False modesty.

I COULD not but smile at the account tha was yesterday given me of a modest young

* Mr. Michael de la Roche, 38 vols. 8vo. in Engl. under different titles; and in Fr. 8 tomes, 24mo.

gentleman, who, being invited to an entertainment, though he was not used to drink, had not the confidence to refuse his glass in his turn, when on a sudden he grew so flustered, that he took all the talk of the table into his own hands, abused every one of the company, and flung a bottle at the gentleman's head who treated him. This has given me occasion to reflect upon the ill effects of a vicious modesty, and to remember the saying of Brutus, as it is quoted by Plutarch, that 'the person has had but an ill education, who has not been taught to deny any thing.' This false kind of modesty has, perhaps, betrayed both sexes into as many vices as the most abandoned impudence; and is the more inexcusable to reason, because it acts to gratify others rather than itself, and is punished with a kind of remorse, not only like other vicious habits when the crime is over, but even at the very time that it is committed.

Nothing is more amiable than true modesty, and nothing is more contemptible than the false. The one guards virtue, the other betrays it. True modesty is ashamed to do any thing that is repugnant to the rules of right reason; false modesty is ashamed to do any thing that is opposite to the humour of the company. True modesty avoids every thing that is criminal, false modesty every thing that is unfashionable. The latter is only a general undetermined instinct; the former is that instinct, limited and circumscribed by the rules of prudence and religion.

We may conclude that modesty to be false and vicious which engages a man to do any thing that is ill or indiscreet, or which restrains him from doing any thing that is of a contrary nature. How many men, in the common concerns of life, lend sums of money which they are not able to spare, are bound for persons whom they have but little friendship for, give recommendatory characters of men whom they are not acquainted with, bestow places on those whom they do not esteem, live in such a manner as they themselves do not approve, and all this merely because they have not the confidence to resist solicitation, importunity, or example!

Nor does this false modesty expose us only to such actions as are indiscreet, but very often to such as are highly criminal. When Xenophanes was called timorous, because he would not venture his money in a game of dice: 'I confess,' said he, 'that I am exceeding timorous, for I dare not do an ill thing.' On the contrary, a man of vicious modesty complies with every thing, and is only fearful of doing what may look singular in the company where he is engaged. He falls in with the torrent, and lets himself go to every action or discourse, however unjustifiable in itself, so it be in vogue among the present party. This, though one of the most common, is one of the most ridiculous dispositions in human nature, that men should not be ashamed of speaking or acting in a dissolute or irrational manner, but that one who is in their company should be ashamed of governing himself by the principles of reason and virtue.

In the second place, we are to consider false modesty as it restrains a man from doing what is good and laudable. My reader's own thoughts will suggest to him many instances and examples under this head. I shall only dwell upon one reflection, which I cannot make without a secret concern. We have in England a particular bashfulness in every thing that regards religion. A well-bred man is obliged to conceal any serious sentiment of this nature, and very often to appear a greater libertine than he is, that he may keep himself in countenance among the men of mode. Our excess of modesty makes us shamefaced in all the exercises of piety and devotion. This humour prevails upon us daily; insomuch that, at many well-bred tables, the master of the house is so very modest a man, that he has not the confidence to say grace at his own table: a custom which is not only practised by all the nations about us, but was never omitted by the heathens themselves. English gentlemen, who travel into Roman-catholic countries, are not a little surprised to meet with people of the best quality kneeling in their churches, and engaged in their private devotions, though it be not at the hours of public worship. An officer of the army, or a man of wit and pleasure, in those countries, would be afraid of passing not only for an irreligious, but an ill-bred man, should he be seen to go to bed, or sit down at table, without offering up his devotions on such occasions. The same show of religion appears in all the foreign reformed churches, and enters so much in their ordinary conversation, that an Englishman is apt to term them hypocritical and precise.

This little appearance of a religious deportment in our nation, may proceed in some measure from that modesty which is natural to us; but the great occasion of it is certainly this. Those swarms of sectaries that overran the nation in the time of the great rebellion, carried their hypocrisy so high, that they had converted our whole language into a jargon of enthusiasm: insomuch, that upon the restoration, men thought they could not recede too far from the behaviour and practice of those persons who had made religion a cloak to so many villanies. This led them into the other extreme; every appearance of devotion was looked upon as puritanical, and falling into the hands of the 'ridiculers' who flourished in that reign, and attacked every thing that was serious, it has ever since been out of countenance among us. By this means we are gradually fallen into that vicious modesty, which has in some measure worn out from among us the ap pearance of Christianity in ordinary life and conversation, and which distinguishes us from all our neighbours.

Hypocrisy cannot indeed be too much detested, but at the same time it is to be preferred to open impiety. They are both equally destructive to the person who is possessed with them; but, in regard to others, hypocrisy is not so pernicious as bare-faced irreligion. The due mean to be observed is, 'to be sincerely virtuous, and at the same time to let the world see we are so.' I do not know a more dreadful menace in the holy writings, than that which is pronounced against those who have this perverted modesty to be ashamed before men in a particular of such unspeakable importance.

No. 459.] *Saturday, August 16, 1712.*

——Quicquid dignum sapiente bonoque est.
Hor. Ep. iv. Lib. 1. 5.

——Whate'er befits the wise and good.—*Creech.*

RELIGION may be considered under two general heads. The first comprehends what we are to believe, the other what we are to practise. By those things which we are to believe, I mean whatever is revealed to us in the holy writings, and which we could not have obtained the knowledge of by the light of nature; by the things which we are to practise, I mean all those duties to which we are directed by reason or natural religion. The first of these I shall distinguish by the name of faith, the second by that of morality.

If we look into the more serious part of mankind, we find many who lay so great a stress upon faith, that they neglect morality; and many who build so much upon morality, that they do not pay a due regard to faith. The perfect man should be defective in neither of these particulars, as will be very evident to those who consider the benefits which arise from each of them, and which I shall make the subject of this day's paper.

Notwithstanding this general division of Christian duty into morality and faith, and that they have both their peculiar excellencies, the first has the pre-eminence in several respects.

First, Because the greatest part of morality (as I have stated the notion of it,) is of a fixed eternal nature, and will endure when faith shall fail, and be lost in conviction.

Secondly, Because a person may be qualified to do greater good to mankind, and become more beneficial to the world, by morality without faith, than by faith without morality.

Thirdly, Because morality gives a greater perfection to human nature, by quieting the mind, moderating the passions, and advancing the happiness of every man in his private capacity.

Fourthly, Because the rule of morality is much more certain than that of faith, all the civilized nations of the world agreeing in the great points of morality, as much as they differ in those of faith.

Fifthly, Because infidelity is not of so malignant a nature as immorality; or, to put the same reason in another light, because it is generally owned, there may be salvation for a virtuous infidel, (particularly in the case of invincible ignorance,) but none for a vicious believer.

Sixthly, Because faith seems to draw its principal, if not all its excellency, from the influence it has upon morality; as we shall see more at large, if we consider wherein consists the excellency of faith, or the belief of revealed religion; and this I think is,

First, In explaining, and carrying to greater height, several points of morality.

Secondly, In furnishing new and stronger motives to enforce the practice of morality.

Thirdly, In giving us more amiable ideas of the Supreme Being, more endearing notions of one another, and a truer state of ourselves, both in regard to the grandeur and vileness of our natures.

Fourthly, By showing us the blackness and deformity of vice, which in the Christian system is so very great, that he who is possessed of all perfection, and the sovereign judge of it, is represented by several of our divines as hating sin to the same degree that he loves the sacred person who was made the propitiation of it.

Fifthly, In being the ordinary and prescribed method of making morality effectual to salvation.

I have only touched on these several heads, which every one who is conversant in discourses of this nature will easily enlarge upon in his own thoughts, and draw conclusions from them which may be useful to him in the conduct of his life. One I am sure is so obvious that he cannot miss it, namely, that a man cannot be perfect in his scheme of morality, who does not strengthen and support it with that of the Christian faith.

Besides this, I shall lay down two or three other maxims, which I think we may deduce from what has been said.

First, That we should be particularly cautious of making any thing an article of faith, which does not contribute to the confirmation or improvement of morality.

Secondly, That no article of faith can be true and authentic, which weakens or subverts the practical part of religion, or what I have hitherto called morality.

Thirdly, That the greatest friend of morality and natural religion cannot possibly apprehend any danger from embracing Christianity, as it is preserved pure and uncorrupt in the doctrines of our national church.*

There is likewise another maxim which

---

* The Gospel.

I think may be drawn from the foregoing considerations, which is this, that we should, in all dubious points, consider any ill consequences that may arise from them, supposing they should be erroneous, before we give up our assent to them.

For example, In that disputable point of persecuting men for conscience sake, besides the embittering their minds with hatred, indignation, and all the vehemence of resentment, and ensnaring them to profess what they do not believe, we cut them off from the pleasures and advantages of society, afflict their bodies, distress their fortunes, hurt their reputations, ruin their families, make their lives painful, or put an end to them. Sure when I see such dreadful consequences rising from a principle, I would be as fully convinced of the truth of it, as of a mathematical demonstration, before I would venture to act upon it, or make it a part of my religion.

In this case the injury done our neighbour is plain and evident; the principle that puts us upon doing it, of a dubious and disputable nature. Morality seems highly violated by the one; and whether or no a zeal for what a man thinks the true system of faith may justify it, is very uncertain. I cannot but think, if our religion produces charity as well as zeal, it will not be for showing itself by such cruel instances. But to conclude with the words of an excellent author, 'We have just enough of religion to make us hate, but not enough to make us love one another.'

No. 460.] *Monday, August* 18, 1712.

Decipimur specie recti— *Hor. Ars Poet.* v. 25.

Deluded by a seeming excellence.—*Roscommon.*

Our defects and follies are too often unknown to us; nay, they are so far from being known to us, that they pass for demonstrations of our worth. This makes us easy in the midst of them, fond to show them, fond to improve them, and to be esteemed for them. Then it is that a thousand unaccountable conceits, gay inventions, and extravagant actions, must afford us pleasures, and display us to others in the colours which we ourselves take a fancy to glory in. Indeed there is something so amusing for the time in this state of vanity and ill-grounded satisfaction, that even the wiser world has chosen an exalted word to describe its enchantments and called it, 'The Paradise of Fools.'

Perhaps the latter part of this reflection may seem a false thought to some, and bear another turn than what I have given; but it is at present none of my business to look after it, who am going to confess that I have been lately amongst them in a vision.

Methought I was transported to a hill, green, flowery, and of an easy ascent. Upon the broad top of it resided squint-eyed Error, and Popular Opinion with many heads; two that dwelt in sorcery, and were famous for bewitching people with the love of themselves. To these repaired a multitude from every side, by two different paths which lead towards each of them. Some who had the most assuming air went directly of themselves to Error, without expecting a conductor; others of a softer nature went first to Popular Opinion, from whence, as she influenced and engaged them with their own praises, she delivered them over to his government.

When we had ascended to an open part of the summit where Opinion abode, we found her entertaining several who had arrived before us. Her voice was pleasing; she breathed odours as she spoke. She seemed to have a tongue for every one; every one thought he heard of something that was valuable in himself, and expected a paradise which she promised as the reward of his merit. Thus were we drawn to follow her, till she should bring us where it was to be bestowed; and it was observable that, all the way we went, the company was either praising themselves in their qualifications, or one another for those qualifications which they took to be conspicuous in their own characters, or dispraising others for wanting theirs, or vying in the degrees of them.

At last we approached a bower, at the entrance of which Error was seated. The trees were thick woven, and the place where he sat artfully contrived to darken him a little. He was disguised in a whitish robe, which he had put on, that he might appear to us with a nearer resemblance to Truth; and as she has a light whereby she manifests the beauties of nature to the eyes of her adorers, so he had provided himself with a magical wand, that he might do something in imitation of it, and please with delusions. This he lifted solemnly, and, muttering to himself, bid the glories which he kept under enchantment to appear before us. Immediately we cast our eyes on that part of the sky to which he pointed, and observed a thin blue prospect, which cleared as mountains in a summer morning when the mist goes off, and the palace of Vanity appeared to sight.

The foundation seemed hardly a foundation, but a set of curling clouds, which it stood upon by magical contrivance. The way by which we ascended was painted like a rainbow; and as we went, the breeze that played about us bewitched the senses. The walls were gilded all for show; the lowest set of pillars were of the slight fine Corinthian order, and the top of the building being rounded, bore so far the resemblance of a bubble.

At the gate the travellers neither met with a porter, nor waited till one should appear; every one thought his merits a sufficient passport, and pressed forward. In the hall we met with several phantoms, that roved amongst us, and ranged the company according to their sentiments. There was decreasing Honour, that had nothing to show but an old coat of his ancestor's achievements. There was Ostentation, that made himself his own constant subject; and Gallantry strutting upon his tiptoes. At the upper end of the hall stood a throne, whose canopy glittered with all the riches that gayety could contrive to lavish on it; and between the gilded arms sat Vanity, decked in the peacock's feathers, and acknowledged for another Venus by her votaries. The boy who stood beside her for a Cupid, and who made the world to bow before her, was called Self-Conceit. His eyes had every now and then a cast inwards, to the neglect of all objects about him; and the arms which he made use of for conquest, were borrowed from those against whom he had a design. The arrow which he shot at the soldier, was fledged from his own plume of feathers; the dart he directed against the man of wit, was winged from the quills he writ with; and that which he sent against those who presumed upon their riches, was headed with gold out of their treasuries. He made nets for statesmen from their own contrivances; he took fire from the eyes of the ladies, with which he melted their hearts; and lightning from the tongues of the eloquent, to inflame them with their own glories. At the foot of the throne sat three false Graces; Flattery with a shell of paint, Affectation with a mirror to practise at, and Fashion ever changing the posture of her clothes. These applied themselves to secure the conquests which Self-Conceit had gotten, and had each of them their particular polities. Flattery gave new colours and complexions to all things; Affectation new airs and appearances, which, as she said, were not vulgar; and Fashion both concealed some home defects, and added some foreign external beauties.

As I was reflecting upon what I saw, I heard a voice in the crowd bemoaning the condition of mankind, which is thus managed by the breath of Opinion, deluded by Error, fired by Self-Conceit, and given up to be trained in all the courses of Vanity, till Scorn or Poverty come upon us. These expressions were no sooner handed about, but I immediately saw a general disorder, till at last there was a parting in one place, and a grave old man, decent and resolute, was led forward to be punished for the words he had uttered. He appeared inclined to have spoken in his own defence, but I could not observe that any one was willing to hear him. Vanity cast a scornful smile at him; Self-Conceit was angry; Flattery, who knew him for Plain-Dealing, put on a vizard, and turned away; Affectation tossed her fan, made mouths, and called him Envy or Slander: and Fashion would have it, that at least he must be Ill-manners. Thus slighted and despised by all, he was driven out for abusing people of merit and figure; and I heard it firmly resolved, that he should be used no better wherever they met with him hereafter.

I had already seen the meaning of most part of that warning which he had given, and was considering how the latter words should be fulfilled, when a mighty noise was heard without, and the door was blackened by a numerous train of harpies crowding in upon us. Folly and Broken-Credit were seen in the house before they entered. Trouble, Shame, Infamy, Scorn, and Poverty, brought up the rear. Vanity, with her Cupid and Graces, disappeared; her subjects ran into holes and corners; but many of them were found and carried off (as I was told by one who stood near me) either to prisons or cellars, solitude, or little company, the mean arts or the viler crafts of life. 'But these,' added he, with a disdainful air, 'are such who would fondly live here, when their merits neither matched the lustre of the place, nor their riches its expenses. We have seen such scenes as these before now; the glory you saw will all return when the hurry is over.' I thanked him for his information; and believing him so incorrigible as that he would stay till it was his turn to be taken, I made off to the door, and overtook some few, who, though they would not hearken to Plain-Dealing, were now terrified to good purpose by the example of others. But when they had touched the threshold, it was a strange shock to them to find that the delusion of Error was gone, and they plainly discerned the building to hang a little up in the air without any real foundation. At first we saw nothing but a desperate leap remained for us, and I a thousand times blamed my unmeaning curiosity that had brought me into so much danger. But as they began to sink lower in their own minds, methought the palace sunk along with us, till they were arrived at the due point of esteem which they ought to have for themselves, then the part of the building in which they stood touched the earth, and we departing out, it retired from our eyes. Now, whether they who stayed in the palace were sensible of this descent, I cannot tell: it was then my opinion that they were not. However it be, my dream broke up at it, and has given me occasion all my life to reflect upon the fatal consequences of following the suggestions of Vanity.

'MR. SPECTATOR,—I write to you to desire that you would again touch upon a certain enormity, which is chiefly in use among the politer and better-bred part of mankind; I mean the ceremonies, bows, courtesies, whisperings, smiles, winks, nods, with other familiar arts of salutation, which take up in our churches so much time that might be better employed, and which seem so utterly inconsistent with the duty and true intent of our entering into those religious assemblies. The resemblance which this bears to our indeed proper behaviour in theatres, may be some instance of its incongruity in the above-mentioned places. In Roman-catholic churches and chapels abroad, I myself have observed, more than once, persons of the first quality, of the nearest relation, and intimatest acquaintance, passing by one another unknowing as it were, and unknown, and with so little notice of each other, that it looked like having their minds more suitably and more solemnly engaged; at least it was an acknowledgment that they ought to have been so. I have been told the same even of Mahometans, with relation to the propriety of their demeanour in the conventions of their erroneous worship; and I cannot but think either of them sufficient laudable patterns for our imitation in this particular.

'I cannot help, upon this occasion, remarking on the excellent memories of those devotionists, who upon returning from church shall give a particular account how two or three hundred people were dressed: a thing, by reason of its variety, so difficult to be digested and fixed in the head, that it is a miracle to me how two poor hours of divine service can be time sufficient for so elaborate an undertaking, the duty of the place too being jointly, and no doubt oft pathetically, performed along with it. Where it is said in sacred writ, that "the woman ought to have a covering on her head because of the angels," the last word is by some thought to be metaphorically used, and to signify young men. Allowing this interpretation to be right, the text may not appear to be wholly foreign to our present purpose.

'When you are in a disposition proper for writing on such a subject, I earnestly recommend this to you; and am, sir, your humble servant.' T.

No. 461.] *Tuesday, August* 19, 1712.

—Sed non ego credulis illus. *Virg.* Ecl. ix. 34.

But I discern their flatt'ry from their praise.
Dryden.

For want of time to substitute something else in the room of them, I am at present obliged to publish compliments above my desert in the following letters. It is no small satisfaction to have given occasion to ingenious men to employ their thoughts upon sacred subjects from the approbation of such pieces of poetry as they have seen in my Saturday's papers. I shall never publish verse on that day but what is written by the same hand:* yet I shall not accompany those writings with eulogiums, but leave them to speak for themselves.

For the Spectator.

'Mr. Spectator,—You very much promote the interests of virtue, while you reform the taste of a profane age; and persuade us to be entertained with divine poems, whilst we are distinguished by so many thousand humours, and split into so many different sects and parties; yet persons of every party, sect, and humour, are fond of conforming their taste to yours. You can transfuse your own relish of a poem into all your readers, according to their capacity to receive; and when you recommend the pious passion that reigns in the verse, we seem to feel the devotion, and grow proud and pleased inwardly, that we have souls capable of relishing what the Spectator approves.

'Upon reading the hymns that you have published in some late papers, I had a mind to try yesterday whether I could write one. The cxivth psalm appears to me an admirable ode, and I began to turn it into our language. As I was describing the journey of Israel from Egypt, and added the Divine Presence amongst them, I perceived a beauty in this psalm which was entirely new to me, and which I was going to lose; and that is that the poet utterly conceals the presence of God in the beginning of it, and rather lets a possessive pronoun go without a substantive, than he will so much as mention any thing of divinity there. "Judah was his sanctuary, and Israel his dominion or kingdom." The reason now seems evident, and this conduct necessary: for, if God had appeared before, there could be no wonder why the mountains should leap and the sea retire: therefore, that this convulsion of nature may be brought in with due surprise, his name is not mentioned till afterward; and then, with a very agreeable turn of thought, God is introduced at once in all his majesty. This is what I have attempted to imitate in a translation without paraphrase, and to preserve what I could of the spirit of the sacred author.

'If the following essay be not too incorrigible, bestow upon it a few brightenings from your genius, that I may learn how to write better, or to write no more. Your daily admirer and humble servant,* &c.'

PSALM CXIV.

I.

"When Israel, freed from Pharaoh's hand
Left the proud tyrant and his land,
The tribes with cheerful homage own
Their king, and Judah was his throne.

II.

"Across the deep their journey lay,
The deep divides to make them way:
The streams of Jordan saw, and fled†
With backward current to their head.

III.

"The mountains shook like frighted sheep,
Like lambs the little hillocks leap;
Not Sinai on her base could stand,
Conscious of sov'reign power at hand.

IV.

"What power could make the deep divide?
Make Jordan backward roll his tide?

---

* Addison

* Dr. Isaac Watts.

† Jordan beheld their march, and fled
With backward current to his head.—*Watts's Ps.*

Why did ye leap, ye little hills?
And whence the fright that Sinai feels?

V.

'Let every mountain, every flood,
Retire, and know th' approaching God,
The King of Israel. See him here;
Tremble, thou earth, adore and fear.

VI.

'He thunders—and all nature mourns;
The rock to standing pools he turns.
Flints spring with fountains at his word,
And fires and seas confess their Lord."

'MR. SPECTATOR,—There are those who take the advantage of your putting a halfpenny value upon yourself, above the rest of our daily writers, to defame you in public conversation, and strive to make you unpopular upon the account of this said halfpenny. But, if I were you, I would insist upon that small acknowledgment for the superior merit of yours, as being a work of invention. Give me leave, therefore, to do you justice, and say in your behalf, what you cannot yourself, which is, that your writings have made learning a more necessary part of good-breeding than it was before you appeared; that modesty is become fashionable, and impudence stands in need of some wit, since you have put them both in their proper lights. Profaneness, lewdness, and debauchery, are not now qualifications; and a man may be a very fine gentleman, though he is neither a keeper nor an infidel.

'I would have you tell the town the story of the Sibyls, if they deny giving you two pence. Let them know, that those sacred papers were valued at the same rate after two thirds of them were destroyed, as when there was the whole set. There are so many of us who will give you your own price, that you may acquaint your non-conformist readers, that they shall not have it, except they come in within such a day, under three pence. I do not know but you might bring in the Date Obolum Belisario with a good grace. The witlings come in clusters to two or three coffee-houses which have left you off; and I hope you will make us, who fine to your wit, merry with their characters who stand out against it. I am your most humble servant.

'P. S. I have lately got the ingenious authors of blacking for shoes, powder for colouring the hair, pomatum for the hands, cosmetic for the face, to be your constant customers; so that your advertisements will as much adorn the outward man, as your paper does the inward.' T.

No. 462.] *Wednesday, August* 20, 1712.

Nil ego prætulerim jocundo sanus amico.
Hor. Sat. v. Lib. 1. 44.

Nothing so grateful as a pleasant friend.

PEOPLE are not aware of the very great force which pleasantry in company has upon all those with whom a man of that talent converses. His faults are generally overlooked by all his acquaintance; and a certain carelessness, that constantly attends all his actions, carries him on with greater success than diligence and assiduity does others who have no share in this endowment. Dacinthus breaks his word upon all occasions, both trivial and important; and, when he is sufficiently railed at for that abominable quality, they who talk of him end with, 'After all, he is a very pleasant fellow.' Dacinthus is an ill-natured husband, and yet the very women end their freedom of discourse upon this subject, 'But, after all, he is very pleasant company.' Dacinthus is neither, in point of honour, civility, good breeding, or good-nature, unexceptionable; and yet all is answered, 'For he is a very pleasant fellow.' When this quality is conspicuous in a man who has, to accompany it, manly and virtuous sentiments, there cannot certainly be any thing which can give so pleasing a gratification as the gayety of such a person; but when it is alone, and serves only to gild a crowd of ill qualities, there is no man so much to be avoided as your pleasant fellow. A very pleasant fellow shall turn your good name to a jest, make your character contemptible, debauch your wife or daughter, and yet be received by the rest of the world with welcome wherever he appears. It is very ordinary with those of this character to be attentive only to their own satisfactions, and have very little bowels for the concerns or sorrows of other men; nay, they are capable of purchasing their own pleasures at the expense of giving pain to others. But they who do not consider this sort of men thus carefully, are irresistibly exposed to their insinuations. The author of the following letter carries the matter so high, as to intimate that the liberties of England have been at the mercy of a prince, merely as he was of this pleasant character.

'MR. SPECTATOR,—There is no one passion which all mankind so naturally give into as pride, or any other passion which appears in such different disguises it is to be found in all habits and complexions. It is not a question, whether it does more harm or good in the world; and if there be not such a thing as what we may call a virtuous and laudable pride?

'It is this passion alone, when misapplied, that lays us so open to flatterers; and he who can agreeably condescend to soothe our humour or temper, finds always an open avenue to our soul; especially if the flatterer happen to be our superior.

'One might give many instances of this in a late English monarch, under the title of "The gayeties of king Charles II." This prince was by nature extremely familiar, of very easy access, and much delighted to see and be seen; and this happy temper, which in the highest degree gratified his people's vanity, did him more service with his loving subjects than all his other virtues, though it must be confessed he had many. He delighted, though a mighty king, to give and take a jest, as they say: and a prince of this fortunate disposition, who were inclined to make an ill use of his power, may have any thing of his people, be it never so much to their prejudice. But this good king made generally a very innocent use, as to the public of this ensnaring temper; for, it is well known he pursued pleasure more than ambition. He seemed to glory in being the first man at cock-matches, horse-races, balls, and plays; he appeared highly delighted on those occasions, and never failed to warm and gladden the heart of every spectator. He more than once dined with his good citizens of London on their lord-mayor's day, and did so the year that Sir Robert Viner was mayor. Sir Robert was a very loyal man, and, if you will allow the expression, very fond of his sovereign; but, what with the joy he felt at heart for the honour done him by his prince, and through the warmth he was in with continual toasting healths to the royal family, his lordship grew a little fond of his majesty, and entered into a familiarity not altogether so graceful in so public a place. The king understood very well how to extricate himself in all kinds of difficulties, and, with a hint to the company to avoid ceremony, stole off and made towards his coach, which stood ready for him in Guildhall-yard. But the mayor liked his company so well, and was grown so intimate, that he pursued him hastily, and catching him fast by the hand, cried out with a vehement oath and accent, "Sir, you shall stay and take t'other bottle." The airy monarch looked kindly at him over his shoulder, and with a smile and graceful air (for I saw him at the time, and do now) repeated this line of the old song:

"He that is drunk is as great as a king;"

and immediately turned back and complied with his landlord.

'I give you this story, Mr. Spectator, because, as I said, I saw the passage; and I assure you it is very true, and yet no common one; and when I tell you the sequel, you will say I have a better reason for it. This very mayor, afterwards erected a statue of his merry monarch in Stocks-market,* and did the crown many and great services; and it was owing to this humour of the king that his family had so great a fortune shut up in the exchequer of their pleasant sovereign. The many good-natured condescensions of this prince are vulgarly known; and it is excellently said of him, by a great hand† which writ his character, "That he was not a king a quarter of an hour together in his whole reign." He would receive visits even from fools and half madmen, and at times I have met with people who have boxed, fought at back-sword, and taken poison before king Charles II. In a word, he was so pleasant a man, that no one could be sorrowful under his government. This made him capable of baffling, with the greatest ease imaginable, all suggestions of jealousy; and the people could not entertain notions of any thing terrible in him, whom they saw every way agreeable. This scrap of the familiar part of that prince's history I thought fit to send you, in compliance to the request you lately made to your correspondents. I am, sir, your most humble servant.'

T.

No. 463.] *Thursday, August 21, 1712.*

Omnia quæ sensu volvuntur vota diurno,
  Pectore sopito reddit amica quies.
Venator defessa toro cum membra reponit,
  Mens tamen ad sylvas et sua lustra redit:
Judicibus lites, aurigæ somnia currus.
  Vanaque nocturnis meta cavetur equis.
Me quoque Musarum studium sub nocte silenti
  Artibus assuetis solicitare solet. *Claud.*

In sleep when fancy is let loose to play,
Our dreams repeat the wishes of the day.
Though farther toils his tired limbs refuse,
The dreaming hunter still the chase pursues.
The judge a-bed dispenses still the laws
And sleeps again o'er the unfinish'd cause.
The dozing racer hears his chariot roll,
Smacks the vain whip, and shuns the fancy'd goal.
Me too the Muses, in the silent night,
With wonted chimes of jingling verse delight.

I WAS lately entertaining myself with comparing Homer's balance, in which Jupiter is represented as weighing the fates of Hector and Achilles, with a passage of Virgil, wherein that deity is introduced as weighing the fates of Turnus and Æneas. I then considered how the same way of thinking prevailed in the eastern parts of the world, as in those noble passages of Scripture, wherein we are told, that the great king of Babylon, the day before his death, had been 'weighed in the balance, and been found wanting.' In other places of the holy writings, the Almighty is described as weighing the mountains in scales, making the weight for the winds, knowing the balancings of the clouds; and in others, as weighing the actions of men, and laying their calamities together in a balance.

---

* "The Mansion-house and many adjacent buildings, stand on the site of Stocks-market; which took its name from a pair of stocks for the punishment of offenders, erected in an open place near this spot, as early as the year 1281. This was the great market of the city during many centuries. In it stood the famous equestrian statue erected in honour of Charles II. by his most loyal subject sir Robert Viner, lord-mayor. Fortunately his lordship discovered one (made at Leghorn) of John Sobieski, King of Poland, trampling on a Turk. The good knight caused some alterations to be made, and christened the Polish Monarch by the name of Charles, and bestowed on the turbaned Turk that of Oliver Cromwell; and thus, new-named, it arose on this spot in honour of his convivial monarch. The statue was removed in 1738, to make room for the Mansion-house. It remained many years afterward in an inn-yard; and in 1779 it was bestowed, by the common-council, on Robert Viner, Esq. who removed it to grace his country-seat.—*Pennant's London*, p. 368.

† Sheffield duke of Buckingham, who said, that, on a premeditation, Charles II. could not act the part of a king for a moment.

Milton, as I have observed in a former paper, had an eye to several of these foregoing instances in that beautiful description, wherein he represents the archangel and the evil spirit as addressing themselves for the combat, but parted by the balance which appeared in the heavens, and weighed the consequences of such a battle.

'Th' Eternal to prevent such horrid fray,
Hung forth in heav'n his golden scales, yet seen
Betwixt Astrea and the Scorpion sign:
Wherein all things created first he weigh'd,
The pendulous round earth, with balanc'd air,
In counterpoise, now ponders all events,
Battles and realms; in these he put two weights,
The sequel each of parting and of fight,
The latter quick upflew and kick'd the beam;
Which Gabriel spying, thus bespake the fiend:
"Satan, I know thy strength, and thou know'st mine,
Neither our own, but giv'n. What folly then
To boast what arms can do, since thine no more
Than heav'n permits; nor mine, though doubled now
To trample thee as mire! For proof look up,
And read thy lot in yon celestial sign,
Where thou art weigh'd and shown how light, how weak,
If thou resist." The fiend look'd up, and knew
His mounted scale aloft; nor more but fled
Murm'ring, and with him fled the shades of night.'

These several amusing thoughts having taken possession of my mind some time before I went to sleep, and mingling themselves with my ordinary ideas, raised in my imagination a very odd kind of vision. I was, methought, replaced in my study, and seated in my elbow-chair, where I had indulged the foregoing speculations with my lamp burning by me as usual. Whilst I was here meditating on several subjects of morality, and considering the nature of many virtues and vices, as materials for those discourses with which I daily entertain the public, I saw, methought a pair of golden scales hanging by a chain of the same metal, over the table that stood before me; when, on a sudden, there were great heaps of weights thrown down on each side of them. I found, upon examining these weights, they showed the value of every thing that is in esteem among men. I made an essay of them, by putting the weight of wisdom in one scale, and that of riches in another; upon which the latter, to show its comparative lightness, immediately flew up and kicked the beam.

But, before I proceed, I must inform my reader, that these weights did not exert their natural gravity till they were laid in the golden balance, insomuch that I could not guess which was light or heavy whilst I held them in my hand. This I found by several instances; for upon my laying a weight in one of the scales, which was inscribed by the word 'Eternity,' though I threw in that of Time, Prosperity, Affliction, Wealth, Poverty, Interest, Success, with many other weights, which in my hand seemed very ponderous, they were not able to stir the opposite balance; nor could they have prevailed, though assisted with the weight of the Sun, the Stars, and the Earth.

Upon emptying the scales, I laid several titles and honours, with Pomp, Triumphs, and many weights of the like nature, in one of them; and seeing a little glittering weight lie by me, I threw it accidentally into the other scale, when, to my great surprise, it proved so exact a counterpoise, that it kept the balance in an equilibrium. This little glittering weight was inscribed upon the edges of it with the word 'Vanity.' I found there were several other weights which were equally heavy, and exact counterpoises to one another; a few of them I tried, as Avarice and Poverty, Riches and Content, with some others.

There were likewise several weights that were of the same figure, and seemed to correspond with each other, but were entirely different when thrown into the scales; as Religion and Hypocrisy, Pedantry and Learning, Wit and Vivacity, Superstition and Devotion, Gravity and Wisdom, with many others.

I observed one particular weight lettered on both sides; and upon applying myself to the reading of it, I found on one side written, 'In the dialect of men,' and underneath it, 'Calamities:' on the other side was written, 'In the language of the gods,' and underneath 'Blessings.' I found the intrinsic value of this weight to be much greater than I imagined, for it overpowered Health, Wealth, Good-fortune, and many other weights, which were much more ponderous in my hand than the other.

There is a saying among the Scotch, that an ounce of mother-wit is worth a pound of clergy: I was sensible of the truth of this saying, when I saw the difference between the weight of Natural Parts and that of Learning. The observations which I made upon these two weights opened to me a new field of discoveries; for notwithstanding the weight of Natural Parts was much heavier than that of Learning, I observed that it weighed a hundred times heavier than it did before, when I put Learning into the same scale with it. I made the same observation upon Faith and Morality; for, notwithstanding the latter outweighed the former separately, it received a thousand times more additional weight from its conjunction with the former, than what it had by itself. This odd phenomenon showed itself in other particulars, as in Wit and Judgment, Philosophy and Religion, Justice and Humanity, Zeal and Charity, depth of Sense and perspicuity of Style, with innumerable other particulars too long to be mentioned in this paper.

As a dream seldom fails of dashing seriousness with impertinence, mirth with gravity, methought I made several other experiments of a more ludicrous nature, by one of which I found that an English octavo was very often heavier than a French folio; and, by another, that an old Greek or Latin author weighed down a whole library of moderns. Seeing one of my Spectators lying by me, I laid it into one of the scales, and flung a two-penny piece into the other. The reader will not inquire into the event, if he remembers the first trial which I have recorded in this paper. I afterwards threw both the sexes into the balance; but as it is not for my interest to disoblige either of them, I shall desire to be excused from telling the result of this experiment. Having an opportunity of this nature in my hands, I could not forbear throwing into one scale the principles of a Tory, and into the other those of a Whig; but, as I have all along declared this to be a neutral paper, I shall likewise desire to be silent under this head also, though upon examining one of the weights, I saw the word 'TEKEL' engraven on it in capital letters.

I made many other experiments; and though I have not room for them all in this day's speculation, I may perhaps reserve them for another. I shall only add, that upon my awaking, I was sorry to find my golden scales vanished; but resolved for the future to learn this lesson from them, not to despise or value any thing for their appearances, but to regulate my esteem and passions towards them according to their real and intrinsic value. C.

No. 464.] *Friday, August* 22, 1712.

Auream quisquis mediocritatem
Diligit, tutus caret obsoleti
Sordibus tecti, caret invidenda
Sobrius aula. *Hor.* Od. x. Lib. 2. 5.

The golden mean, as she's too nice to dwell
Among the ruins of a filthy cell,
So is her modesty withal as great,
To balk the envy of a princely seat.—*Norris.*

I AM wonderfully pleased when I meet with any passage in an old Greek or Latin author that is not blown upon, and which I have never met with in a quotation. Of this kind is a beautiful saying in Theognis: 'Vice is covered by wealth, and virtue by poverty;' or to give it in the verbal translation, 'Among men there are some who have their vices concealed by wealth, and others who have their virtues concealed by poverty.' Every man's observation will supply him with instances of rich men, who have several faults and defects that are overlooked, if not entirely hidden, by means of their riches; and I think, we cannot find a more natural description of a poor man, whose merits are lost in his poverty, than that in the words of the wise man: 'There was a little city, and few men within it; and there came a great king against it, and besieged it, and built great bulwarks against it. Now there was found in it a poor wise man, and he, by his wisdom, delivered the city; yet no man remembered that same poor man. Then, said I, wisdom is better than strength; nevertheless, the poor man's wisdom is despised, and his words are not heard.'

The middle condition seems to be the most advantageously situated for the gaining of wisdom. Poverty turns our thoughts too much upon the supplying of our wants, and riches, upon enjoying our superfluities and, as Cowley has said in another case, 'It is hard for a man to keep a steady eye upon truth, who is always in a battle or a triumph.'

If we regard poverty and wealth, as they are apt to produce virtues or vices in the mind of man, one may observe that there is a set of each of these growing out of poverty, quite different from that which rises out of wealth. Humility and patience, industry and temperance, are very often the good qualities of a poor man. Humanity, and good-nature, magnanimity and a sense of honour, are as often the qualifications of the rich. On the contrary, poverty is apt to betray a man into envy, riches into arrogance; poverty is too often attended with fraud, vicious compliance, repining, murmur and discontent. Riches expose a man to pride and luxury, a foolish elation of heart, and too great a fondness for the present world. In short, the middle condition is most eligible to the man who would improve himself in virtue; as I have before shown it is the most advantageous for the gaining of knowledge. It was upon this consideration that Agur founded his prayer, which, for the wisdom of it, is recorded in holy writ. 'Two things have I required of thee; deny me them not before I die. Remove far from me vanity and lies, give me neither poverty nor riches; feed me with food convenient for me; lest I be full and deny thee, and say, Who is the Lord? or lest I be poor and steal, and take the name of my God in vain.'

I shall fill the remaining part of my paper with a very pretty allegory, which is wrought into a play by Aristophanes the Greek comedian. It seems originally designed as a satire upon the rich, though, in some parts of it, it is like the foregoing discourse, a kind of comparison between wealth and poverty.

Chremylus, who was an old and a good man, and withal exceeding poor, being desirous to leave some riches to his son, consults the oracle of Apollo upon the subject. The oracle bids him follow the first man he should see upon his going out of the temple. The person he chanced to see was to appearance an old sordid blind man, but, upon his following him from place to place, he at last found, by his own confession, that he was Plutus the god of riches, and that he was just come out of the house of a miser. Plutus farther told him, that when he was a boy, he used to declare, that as soon as he came to age he would distribute wealth to none but virtuous and just men; upon which Jupiter considering the pernicious consequences of such a resolution, took his sight away from him, and left him to stroll about the world in the blind condition wherein Chremylus beheld him. With much ado Chremylus prevailed upon him to go to his house, where he met an old woman in a tattered raiment, who had been his guest for many years, and whose name was Poverty. The old woman refusing to turn out so easily as he would have her, he threatened to banish her, not only from his own house, but out of all Greece, if she made any more words upon the matter. Poverty on this occasion pleads her cause very notably, and represents to her old landlord, that should she be driven out of the country, all their trades, arts, and sciences, would be driven out with her; and that, if every one was rich, they would never be supplied with those pomps, ornaments, and conveniences of life which made riches desirable. She likewise represented to him the several advantages which she bestowed upon her votaries in regard to their shape, their health, and their activity, by preserving them from gouts, dropsies, unwieldiness, and intemperance. But whatever she had to say for herself, she was at last forced to troop off. Chremylus immediately considered how he might restore Plutus to his sight; and, in order to it, conveyed him to the temple of Æsculapius, who was famous for cures and miracles of this nature. By this means the deity recovered his eyes, and began to make a right use of them, by enriching every one that was distinguished by piety towards the gods and justice towards men: and at the same time by taking away his gifts from the impious and undeserving. This produces several merry incidents, till in the last act Mercury descends with great complaints from the gods, that since the good men were grown rich, they had received no sacrifices; which is confirmed by a priest of Jupiter, who enters with a remonstrance, that since the late innovation he was reduced to a starving condition, and could not live upon his office. Chremylus, who in the beginning of the play was religious in his poverty, concludes it with a proposal, which was relished by all the good men who had now grown rich as well as himself, that they should carry Plutus in a solemn procession to the temple, and install him in the place of Jupiter. This allegory instructed the Athenians in two points: first as it vindicted the conduct of Providence in its ordinary distributions of wealth; and, in the next place, as it showed the great tendency of riches to corrupt the morals of those who possessed them. C.

No. 465.] *Saturday, August* 23, 1712.

Qua ratione queas traducere leniter ævum;
Ne te semper inops agitet vexetque cupido;
Ne pavor et rerum mediocriter utilium spes.
Hor. Ep. xviii. Lib. 1. 97.

How you may glide with gentle ease
Adown the current of your days;
Nor vex'd by mean and low desires,
Nor warm'd by wild ambitious fires;
By hope alarm'd, depress'd by fear,
For things but little worth your care.—*Francis.*

Having endeavoured in my last Saturday's paper to show the great excellency of faith, I shall here consider what are the proper means of strengthening and confirming it in the mind of man. Those who delight in reading books of controversy which are written on both sides of the question on points of faith, do very seldom arrive at a fixed and settled habit of it. They are one day entirely convinced of its important truths, and the next meet with something that shakes and disturbs them. The doubt which was laid revives again, and shows itself in new difficulties, and that generally for this reason, because the mind, which is perpetually tost in controversies and disputes, is apt to forget the reasons which had once set it at rest, and to be disquieted with any former perplexity, when it appears in a new shape, or is started by a different hand. As nothing is more laudable than an inquiry after truth, so nothing is more irrational than to pass away our whole lives, without determining ourselves, one way or other, in those points which are of the last importance to us. There are indeed many things from which we may withhold our assent; but in cases by which we are to regulate our lives, it is the greatest absurdity to be wavering and unsettled, without closing with that side which appears the most safe and the most probable. The first rule, therefore, which I shall lay down is this; that when by reading or discourse we find ourselves thoroughly convinced of the truth of any article, and of the reasonableness of our belief in it, we should never after suffer ourselves to call it in question. We may perhaps forget the arguments which occasioned our conviction, but we ought to remember the strength they had with us, and therefore still to retain the conviction which they once produced. This is no more than what we do in every common art or science; nor is it possible to act otherwise, considering the weakness and limitation of our intellectual faculties. It was thus that Latimer, one of the glorious army of martyrs, who introduced the reformation in England, behaved himself in that great conference which was managed between the most learned among the protestants and papists in the reign of Queen Mary. This venerable old man, knowing his abilities were impaired by age, and that it was impossible for him to recollect all those reasons which had directed him in the choice of his religion, left his companions, who were in the full possession of their parts and learning, to baffle and confound their antagonists by the force of reason. As for himself, he only repeated to his adversaries the articles in which he firmly believed, and in the profession of which he was determined to die. It is in this manner that the mathematician proceeds upon propositions which he has once demonstrated: and though the demonstration may have slipped out of his memory, he builds upon the truth, because he knows it was demonstrated. This rule is absolutely necessary for weaker minds, and in some measure for men of the greatest abilities; but to these last I would propose, in the second place, that they should lay up in their memories, and always keep by them in readiness, those arguments which appear to them of the greatest strength, and which cannot be got over by all the doubts and cavils of infidelity.

But, in the third place, there is nothing which strengthens faith more than morality. Faith and morality naturally produce each other. A man is quickly convinced of the truth of religion, who finds it is not against his interest that it should be true. The pleasure he receives at present, and the happiness which he promises himself from it hereafter, will both dispose him very powerfully to give credit to it, according to the ordinary observation, that 'we are easy to believe what we wish.' It is very certain, that a man of sound reason cannot forbear closing with religion upon an impartial examination of it; but at the same time it is certain, that faith is kept alive in us, and gathers strength from practice more than from speculation.

There is still another method, which is more persuasive than any of the former; and that is an habitual adoration of the Supreme Being, as well in constant acts of mental worship, as in outward forms. The devout man does not only believe, but feels there is a deity. He has actual sensations of him; his experience concurs with his reason; he sees him more and more in all his intercourses with him, and even in this life almost loses his faith in conviction.

The last method which I shall mention for the giving life to a man's faith, is frequent retirement from the world, accompanied with religious meditation. When a man thinks of any thing in the darkness of the night, whatever deep impressions it may make in his mind, they are apt to vanish as soon as the day breaks upon him. The light and noise of the day, which are perpetually soliciting his senses, and calling off his attention, wear out of his mind the thoughts that imprinted themselves in it, with so much strength, during the silence and darkness of the night. A man finds the same difference as to himself in a crowd and in a solitude: the mind is stunned and dazzled amidst that variety of objects which press upon her in a great city. She cannot apply herself to the consideration of those things which are of the utmost concern to her. The cares or pleasures of the world strike in with every thought, and a multitude of vicious examples give a kind of justification to our folly. In our retirements, every thing disposes us to be serious. In courts and cities we are entertained with the works of men; in the country with those of God. One is the province of art, the other of nature. Faith and devotion naturally grow in the mind of every reasonable man, who sees the impressions of divine power and wisdom in every object on which he casts his eye. The Supreme Being has made the best arguments for his own existence, in the formation of the heavens and the earth; and these are arguments which a man of sense cannot forbear attending to, who is out of the noise and hurry of human affairs. Aristotle says, that should a man live under ground, and there converse with the works of art and mechanism, and should afterward be brought up into the open day, and see the several glories of the heaven and earth, he would immediately pronounce them the works of such a being as we define God to be. The psalmist has very beautiful strokes of poetry to this purpose, in that exalted strain: 'The heavens declare the glory of God; and the firmament showeth his handy work. One day telleth another; and one night certifieth another. There is neither speech nor language; but their voices are heard among them. Their sound is gone out into all lands; and their words into the ends of the world.' As such a bold and sublime manner of thinking furnishes very noble matter for an ode, the reader may see it wrought into the following one.

I.

"The spacious firmament on high,
With all the blue ethereal sky,
And spangled heavens, a shining frame,
Their great Original proclaim:
Th' unwearied sun, from day to day,
Does his Creator's power display,
And publishes to every land
The work of an almighty hand.

II.

"Soon as the evening shades prevail,
The moon takes up the wondrous tale,
And nightly to the list'ning earth
Repeats the story of her birth:
Whilst all the stars that round her burn,
And all the planets in their turn,
Confirm the tidings as they roll,
And spread the truth from pole to pole.

III.

"What though, in solemn silence, all
Move round the dark terrestrial ball?
What though no real voice nor sound
Amid their radiant orbs be found?
In reason's ear they all rejoice,
And utter forth a glorious voice,
For ever singing, as they shine,
The hand that made us is divine."

No. 466.] *Monday, August 25, 1712.*

——Vera incessu patuit dea.—*Virg. Æn.* i. 409.

And by her graceful walk the queen of love is known
Dryden.

When Æneas, the hero of Virgil, is lost in the wood, and a perfect stranger in the place on which he is landed, he is accosted by a lady in a habit for the chase. She inquires of him, whether he has seen pass by that way any young woman dressed as she was? whether she were following the sport in the wood, or any other way employed, according to the custom of huntresses? The hero answers with the respect due to the beautiful appearance she made; tells her, he saw no such person as she inquired for; but intimates that he knows her to be one of the deities, and desires she would conduct a stranger. Her form, from her first appearance, manifested she was more than mortal; but, though she was certainly a goddess, the poet does not make her known to be the goddess of beauty till she moved. All the charms of an agreeable person are then in their highest exertion, every limb and feature appears with its respective grace. It is from this observation that I cannot help being so passionate an admirer as I am of good dancing. As all art is an imitation of nature, this is an imitation of nature in its highest excellence, and at a time when she is most agreeable. The business of dancing is to display beauty; and for that reason all distortions and mimickries, as such, are what raise aversion instead of pleasure; but things that are in themselves excellent, are ever attended with imposture and false imitation. Thus, as in poetry there are labouring fools who write anagrams and acrosticks, there are pretenders in dancing, who think merely to do what others cannot, is to excel. Such creatures should be rewarded like him who has acquired a knack of throwing a grain of corn through the eye of a needle, with a bushel to keep his hand in use. The dancers on our stage are very faulty in this kind; and what they mean by writhing themselves into such postures, as it would be a pain for any of the spectators to stand in, and yet hope to please those spectators, is unintelligible. Mr. Prince has a genius, if he were encouraged, would prompt him to better things. In all the dances he invents, you see he keeps close to the characters he represents. He does not hope to please by making his performers move in a manner in which no one else ever did but by motions proper to the characters he represents. He gives to clowns and lubbards clumsy graces: that is, he makes them practise what they would think graces; and I have seen dances of his, which might give hints that would be useful to a comic writer. These performances have pleased the taste of such as have not reflection enough to know their excellence, because they are in nature; and the distorted motions of others have offended those who could not form reasons to themselves for their displeasure, from their being a contradiction to nature.

When one considers the inexpressible advantage there is in arriving at some excellence in this art, it is monstrous to behold it so much neglected. The following letter has in it something very natural on this subject

'MR. SPECTATOR,—I am a widower with but one daughter: she was by nature much inclined to be a romp; and I had no way of educating her, but commanding a young woman, whom I entertained to take care of her, to be very watchful in her care and attendance about her. I am a man of business, and obliged to be much abroad. The neighbours have told me, that in my absence our maid has let in the spruce servants in the neighbourhood to junketings, while my girl played and romped even in the street. To tell you the plain truth, I catched her once, at eleven years old, at chuck-farthing among the boys. This put me upon new thoughts about my child, and I determined to place her at a boarding-school; and at the same time gave a very discreet young gentlewoman her maintenance at the same place and rate, to be her companion. I took little notice of my girl from time to time, but saw her now and then in good health, out of harm's way, and was satisfied. But, by much importunity, I was lately prevailed with to go to one of their balls. I cannot express to you the anxiety my silly heart was in, when I saw my romp, now fifteen, taken out: I never felt the pangs of a father upon me so strongly in my whole life before; and I could not have suffered more had my whole fortune been at stake. My girl came on with the most becoming modesty I had ever seen, and casting a respectful eye, as if she feared me more than all the audience, I gave a nod, which I think gave her all the spirit she assumed upon it: but she rose properly to that dignity of aspect. My romp, now the most graceful person of her sex, assumed a majesty which commanded the highest respect; and when she turned to me, and saw my face in rapture, she fell into the prettiest smile, and I saw in all her motions that she exulted in her father's satisfaction. You, Mr. Spectator, will, better than I can tell you, imagine to yourself all the different beauties and changes of aspect in an accomplished young woman setting forth all her beauties with a design to please no one so much as her father. My girl's lover can never know half the satisfaction that I did in her that day. I could not possibly have imagined that so great improvement could have been wrought by an art that I always held in itself ridiculous and contemptible. There is, I am convinced, no method like this, to give young women a sense of their own value and dignity: and I am sure there can be none so expeditious to communicate that value to others. As for the flippant insipidly gay, and wantonly forward, whom you behold among dancers, that carriage is more to be attributed to the perverse genius of the performers, than imputed to the art itself. For my part, my child has danced herself into my esteem; and I have as great an honour for her as ever I had for her mother, from whom she derived those latent good qualities which appeared in her countenance when she was dancing; for my girl, though I say it myself, showed in one quarter of an hour the innate principles of a modest virgin, a tender wife, a generous friend, a kind mother, and an indulgent mistress. I'll strain hard but I will purchase for her a husband suitable to her merit. I am your convert in the admiration of what I thought you jested when you recommended; and if you please to be at my house on Thursday next, I make a ball for my daughter, and you shall see her dance, or, if you will do her that honour dance with her. I am, sir, your humble servant,

'PHILIPATER.'

I have some time ago spoken of a treatise written by Mr. Weaver on this subject, which is now, I understand, ready to be published. This work sets this matter in a very plain and advantageous light; and I am convinced from it, that if the art was under proper regulations, it would be a mechanic way of implanting insensibly, in minds not capable of receiving it so well by any other rules, a sense of good-breeding and virtue.

Were any one to see Mariamne* dance, let him be never so sensual a brute, I defy him to entertain any thoughts but of the highest respect and esteem towards her. I was showed last week a picture in a lady's closet, for which she had a hundred different dresses, that she could clap on round the face on purpose to demonstrate the force of habits in the diversity of the same countenance. Motion, and change of posture and aspect, has an effect no less surprising on the person of Mariamne when she dances.

Chloe is extremely pretty, and as silly as she is pretty. This idiot has a very good ear, and a most agreeable shape; but the folly of the thing is such, that it smiles so impertinently, and affects to please so sillily, that while she dances you see the simpleton from head to foot. For you must know (as trivial as this art is thought to be,) no one was ever a good dancer that had not a good understanding. If this be a truth, I shall leave the reader to judge, from that maxim, what esteem they ought to have for such impertinents as fly, hop, caper, tumble, twirl, turn round, and jump over their heads; and, in a word, play a thousand pranks which many animals can do better than a man, instead of performing to perfection what the human figure only is capable of performing.

It may perhaps appear odd, that I, who set up for a mighty lover, at least of virtue, should take so much pains to recommend what the soberer part of mankind look upon to be a trifle; but, under favour of the soberer part of mankind, I think they have not enough considered this matter, and for that reason only disesteem it. I must also, in my own justification, say, that I attempt to bring into the service of honour and virtue every thing in nature that can pretend to give elegant delight. It may possibly be proved, that vice is in itself destructive of pleasure, and virtue in itself conducive to it. If the delights of a free fortune were under proper regulations, this truth would not want much argument to support it; but it would be obvious to every man, that there is a strict affinity between all things that are truly laudable and beautiful, from the highest sentiment of the soul to the most indifferent gesture of the body. T.

* Probably Mrs. Bicknell.

No. 467.] *Tuesday, August* 26, 1712.

—Quodcunque meæ poterunt audere Camœnæ,
Seu tibi par poterunt; seu, quod spes abnuit, ultra;
Sive minus; certeque canent minus: omne vovemus
Hoc tibi: ne tanto careat mihi nomine charta.
Tibull. ad Messalem, Eleg. iv. Lib. 1. 24.

Whate'er my muse adventurous dares indite,
Whether the niceness of thy piercing sight
Applaud my lays, or censure what I write:
To thee I sing, and hope to borrow fame,
By adding to my page Messala's name.

THE love of praise is a passion deeply fixed in the mind of every extraordinary person; and those who are most affected with it, seem most to partake of that particle of the divinity which distinguishes mankind from the inferior creation. The Supreme Being himself is most pleased with praise and thanksgiving: the other part of our duty is but an acknowledgment of our faults, whilst this is the immediate adoration of his perfections. 'Twas an excellent observation, that we then only despise commendation when we cease to deserve it; and we have still extant two orations of Tully and Pliny, spoken to the greatest and best princes of all the Roman emperors, who, no doubt, heard with the greatest satisfaction, what even the most disinterested persons, and at so large a distance of time, cannot read without admiration. Cæsar thought his life consisted in the breath of praise, when he professed he had lived long enough for himself, when he had for his glory. Others have sacrificed themselves for a name which was not to begin till they were dead, giving away themselves to purchase a sound which was not to commence till they were out of hearing. But by merit and superior excellencies, not only to gain, but, whilst living, to enjoy a great and universal reputation, is the last degree of happiness which we can hope for here Bad characters are dispersed abroad with profusion; I hope for example's sake, and (as punishments are designed by the civil power) more for the deterring the innocent than the chastising the guilty. The good are less frequent, whether it be that there are indeed fewer originals of this kind to copy after, or that, through the malignity of our nature, we rather delight in the ridicule than the virtues we find in others. However, it is but just, as well as pleasing, even for variety, sometimes to give the world a representation of the bright side of human nature, as well as the dark and gloomy The desire of imitation may, perhaps, be a greater incentive to the practice of what is good, than the aversion we may conceive at what is blameable: the one immediately directs you what you should do, whilst the other only shows what you should avoid; and I cannot at present do this with more satisfaction than by endeavouring to do some justice to the character of Manilius.

It would far exceed my present design, to give a particular description of Manilius through all the parts of his excellent life. I shall now only draw him in his retirement, and pass over in silence the various arts, the courtly manners, and the undesigning honesty by which he attained the honours he has enjoyed, and which now give a dignity and veneration to the ease he does enjoy. 'Tis here that he looks back with pleasure on the waves and billows through which he has steered to so fair a haven: he is now intent upon the practice of every virtue, which a great knowledge and use of mankind has discovered to be the most useful to them. Thus in his private domestic employments he is no less glorious than in his public; for it is in reality a more difficult task to be conspicuous in a sedentary inactive life, than in one that is spent in hurry and business: persons engaged in the latter, like bodies violently agitated, from the swiftness of their motion, have a brightness added to them, which often vanishes when they are at rest; but if it then still remain, it must be the seeds of intrinsic worth that thus shine out without any foreign aid or assistance.

His liberality in another might almost bear the name of profusion: he seems to think it laudable even in the excess, like that river which most enriches when it overflows. But Manilius has too perfect a taste of the pleasure of doing good, ever to let it be out of his power; and for that reason he will have a just economy and a splendid frugality at home, the fountain from whence those streams should flow which he disperses abroad. He looks with disdain on those who propose their death as the time when they are to begin their munificence: he will both see and enjoy (which he then does in the highest degree,) what he bestows himself; he will be the living executor of his own bounty, whilst they who have the happiness to be within his care and patronage, at once pray for the continuation of his life and their own good fortune. No one is out of the reach of his obligations; he knows how, by proper and becoming methods, to raise himself to a level with those of the highest rank; and his good-nature is a sufficient warrant against the want of those who are so unhappy as to be in the very lowest. One may say of him, as Pindar bids his muse say of Theron,

'Swear, that Theron sure has sworn,
No one near him should be poor.
Swear, that none e'er had such a graceful art,
Fortune's free gifts as freely to impart,
With an unenvious hand, and an unbounded heart.'

Never did Atticus succeed better in gaining the universal love and esteem of all men; nor steer with more success between the extremes of two contending parties. 'Tis his peculiar happiness that, while he espouses neither with an intemperate zeal, he is not only admired, but, what is a more rare and unusual felicity, he is beloved and caressed by both; and I never yet saw any person, of whatever age or sex, but was immediately struck with the merit of Manilius. There are many who are acceptable to some particular persons, whilst the rest of mankind look upon them with coldness and indifference; but he is the first whose entire good fortune it is ever to please and to be pleased, wherever he comes to be admired, and wherever he is absent to be lamented. His merit fares like the pictures of Raphael, which are either seen with admiration by all, or at least no one dare own he has no taste for a composition which has received so universal an applause. Envy and malice find it against their interest to indulge slander and obloquy. 'Tis as hard for an enemy to detract from, as for a friend to add to, his praise. An attempt upon his reputation is a sure lessening of one's own; and there is but one way to injure him, which is to refuse him his just commendations, and be obstinately silent.

It is below him to catch the sight with any care of dress; his outward garb is but the emblem of his mind. It is genteel, plain and unaffected; he knows that gold and embroidery can add nothing to the opinion which all have of his merit, and that he gives a lustre to the plainest dress, whilst 'tis impossible the richest should communicate any to him. He is still the principal figure in the room. He first engages your eye, as if there were some point of light which shone stronger upon him than on any other person.

He puts me in mind of a story of the famous Bussy d'Amboise, who, at an assembly at court, where every one appeared with the utmost magnificence, relying upon his own superior behaviour, instead of adorning himself like the rest, put on that day a plain suit of clothes, and dressed all his servants in the most costly gay habits he could procure. The event was, that the eyes of the whole court were fixed upon him; all the rest looked like his attendants, while he alone had the air of a person of quality and distinction.

Like Aristippus, whatever shape or condition he appears in, it still sits free and easy upon him; but in some part of his character, 'tis true, he differs from him; for as he is altogether equal to the largeness of his present circumstances, the rectitude of his judgment has so far corrected the inclinations of his ambition, that he will not trouble himself with either the desires or pursuits of any thing beyond his present enjoyments.

A thousand obliging things flow from him upon every occasion; and they are always so just and natural, that it is impossible to think he was at the least pains to look for them. One would think it was the dæmon of good thoughts that discovered to him those treasures, which he must have blinded others from seeing, they lay so directly in their way. Nothing can equal the pleasure that is taken in hearing him speak, but the satisfaction one receives in the civility and attention he pays to the discourse of others. His looks are a silent commendation of what is good and praiseworthy, and a secret reproof of what is licentious and extravagant. He knows how to appear free and open without danger of intrusion, and to be cautious without seeming reserved. The gravity of his conversation is always enlivened with his wit and humour, and the gayety of it is tempered with something that is instructive, as well as barely agreeable. Thus, with him you are sure not to be merry at the expense of your reason, nor serious with the loss of your good-humour; but by a happy mixture of his temper, they either go together, or perpetually succeed each other. In fine, his whole behaviour is equally distant from constraint and negligence, and he commands your respect while he gains your heart.

There is in his whole carriage such an engaging softness, that one cannot persuade one's self he is ever actuated by those rougher passions, which, wherever they find place, seldom fail of showing themselves in the outward demeanour of the persons they belong to; but his constitution is a just temperature between indolence on one hand, and violence on the other. He is mild and gentle, wherever his affairs will give him leave to follow his own inclinations; but yet never failing to exert himself with vigour and resolution in the service of his prince, his country, or his friend.

Z.

No. 468.] *Wednesday, August* 27, 1712.

Erat homo ingeniosus, acutus, acer, et qui plurimum et salis, haberet et fellis, nec candoris minus.

Plin. Epist.

He was an ingenious, pleasant fellow, and one who had a great deal of wit and satire, with an equal share of good-humour.

My paper is, in a kind, a letter of news, but it regards rather what passes in the world of conversation than that of business. I am very sorry that I have at present a circumstance before me, which is of very great importance to all who have a relish for gayety, wit, mirth, or humour; I mean the death of poor Dick Eastcourt. I have been obliged to him for so many hours of jollity, that it is but a small recompence though all I can give him, to pass a moment or two in sadness for the loss of so agreeable a man. Poor Eastcourt! the last time I saw him, we were plotting to show the town his great capacity for acting in its full light, by introducing him as dictating to a set of young players, in what manner to speak this sentence and utter t'other passion. He had so exquisite a discerning of what was defective in any object before him, that in an instant he could show you the ridiculous side of what would pass for beautiful and just, even to men of no ill judgment, before he had pointed at the failure. He was no less skilful in the knowledge of beauty; and I dare say, there is no one who knew him well, but can repeat more well-turned compliments, as well as smart repartees of Mr. Eastcourt's, than of any other man in England. This was easily to be observed in his inimitable faculty of telling a story, in which he would throw in natural and unexpected incidents to make his court to one part, and rally the other part of the company. Then he would vary the usage he gave them, according as he saw them bear kind or sharp language. He had the knack to raise up a pensive temper, and mortify an impertinently gay one, with the most agreeable skill imaginable. There are a thousand things which crowd into my memory, which make me too much concerned to tell on about him. Hamlet, holding up the skull which the grave-digger threw at him, with an account that it was the head of the king's jester, falls into very pleasing reflection, and cries out to his companion,

'Alas, poor Yorick! I knew him, Horatio: a fellow of infinite jest, of most excellent fancy; he hath borne me on his back a thousand times: and now how abhorred in my imagination it is! my gorge rises at it. Here hung those lips that I have kissed I know not how oft. Where be your gibes now, your gambols, your songs, your flashes of merriment, that were wont to set the table on a roar? Not one now to mock your own grinning? quite chap-fallen? Now get you to my lady's chamber, and tell her, let her paint an inch thick, to this favour she must come. Make her laugh at that.'

It is an insolence natural to the wealthy, to affix, as much as in them lies, the character of a man to his circumstances. Thus it is ordinary with them to praise faintly the good qualities of those below them, and say it is very extraordinary in such a man as he is, or the like, when they are forced to acknowledge the value of him whose lowness upbraids their exaltation. It is to this humour only, that it is to be ascribed, that a quick wit in conversation, a nice judgment upon any emergency that could arise, and a most blameless inoffensive behaviour, could not raise this man above being received only upon the foot of contributing to mirth and diversion. But he was as easy under that condition, as a man of so excellent talents was capable; and since they would have it, that to divert was his business, he did it with all the seeming alacrity imaginable, though it stung him to the heart that it was his business. Men of sense, who could taste his excellencies, were well satisfied to let him lead the way in conversation, and play after his own manner; but fools, who provoked him to mimickry, found he had the indignation to let it be at their expense who called for it, and he would show the form of conceited heavy fellows as jests to the company at their own request, in revenge for interrupting him from being a companion to put on the character of a jester.

What was peculiarly excellent in this memorable companion, was, that in the accounts he gave of persons and sentiments, he did not only hit the figure of their faces, and manner of their gestures, but he would in his narration fall into their very way of thinking, and this, when he recounted passages wherein men of the best wits were concerned, as well as such wherein were represented men of the lowest rank of understanding. It is certainly as great an instance of self-love to a weakness, to be impatient of being mimicked, as any can be imagined. There were none but the vain, the formal, the proud, or those who were incapable of amending their faults, that dreaded him; to others he was in the highest degree pleasing: and I do not know any satisfaction of any indifferent kind I ever tasted so much, as having got over an impatience of my seeing myself in the air he could put me in when I have displeased him. It is indeed to his exquisite talent this way, more than any philosophy I could read on the subject, that my person is very little of my care, and it is indifferent to me what is said of my shape, my air, my manner, my speech, or my address. It is to poor Eastcourt I chiefly owe that I am arrived at the happiness of thinking nothing a diminution to me, but what argues a depravity of my will.

It has as much surprised me as any thing in nature, to have it frequently said, that he was not a good player: but that must be owing to a partiality for former actors in the parts in which he succeeded them, and judging by comparison of what was liked before, rather than by the nature of the thing. When a man of his wit and smartness could put on an utter absence of common sense in his face, as he did in the character of Bullfinch, in the Northern Lass, and an air of insipid cunning and vivacity in the character of Pounce in The Tender Husband, it is folly to dispute his capacity and success, as he was an actor.

Poor Eastcourt! let the vain and proud be at rest, thou wilt no more disturb their admiration of their dear selves; and thou art no longer to drudge in raising the mirth of stupids, who know nothing of thy merit, for thy maintenance.

It is natural for the generality of mankind to run into reflections upon our mortality, when disturbers of the world are laid at rest, but to take no notice when they who can please and divert are pulled from us. But for my part, I cannot but think the loss of such talents as the man of whom I am speaking was master of, a more melancholy instance of mortality than the dissolution of persons of never so high characters in the world, whose pretensions were that they were noisy and mischievous.

But I must grow more succinct, and as a Spectator, give an account of this extraordinary man, who, in his way, never had an equal in any age before him, or in that wherein he lived. I speak of him as a companion, and a man qualified for conversation. His fortune exposed him to an obsequiousness towards the worst sort of company, but his excellent qualities rendered him capable of making the best figure in the most refined. I have been present with him among men of the most delicate taste a whole night, and have known him (for he saw it was desired) keep the discourse to himself the most part of it, and maintain his good-humour with a countenance, in a language so delightful, without offence to any person or thing upon earth, still preserving the distance his circumstances obliged him to; I say, I have seen him do all this in such a charming manner, that I am sure none of those I hint at will read this without giving him some sorrow for their abundant mirth, and one gush of tears for so many bursts of laughter. I wish it were any honour to the pleasant creature's memory, that my eyes are too much suffused to let me go on—T.

*** The following severe passage in this number of the Spectator in folio, apparently levelled at Dr. Radcliffe, was suppressed in all the subsequent editions:

'It is a felicity his friends may rejoice in, that he had his senses, and used them as he ought to do, in his last moments. It is remarkable that his judgment was in its calm perfection to the utmost article; for when his wife out of her fondness, desired she might send for a certain illiterate humourist (whom he had accompanied in a thousand mirthful moments, and whose insolence makes fools think he assumes from conscious merit,) he answered, "Do what you please, but he won't come near me." Let poor Eastcourt's negligence about this message convince the unwary of a triumphant empiric's ignorance and inhumanity.'

No. 469.] *Thursday, August 28, 1712.*

Detrahere aliquid alteri, et hominem hominis incommodo suum augere commodum, magis est contra naturam, quam mors, quam paupertas, quam dolor, quam cætera quæ possunt aut corpori accidere, aut rebus externis. *Tull.*

To detract any thing from another, and for one man to multiply his own conveniencies by the inconveniencies of another, is more against nature than death than poverty, than pain, and the other things which can befall the body or external circumstances.

I AM persuaded there are few men, of generous principles, who would seek after great places were it not rather to have an opportunity in their hands of obliging their particular friends, or those whom they look upon as men of worth, than to procure wealth and honour for themselves. To an honest mind, the best perquisites of a place are the advantages it gives a man of doing good.

Those who are under the great officers of state, and are the instruments by which they act, have more frequent opportunities for the exercise of compassion and benevolence, than their superiors themselves. These men know every little case that is to come before the great man, and, if they are possessed with honest minds, will consider poverty as a recommendation in the person who applies himself to them, and make the justice of his cause the most powerful solicitor in his behalf. A man of this temper, when he is in a post of business, becomes a blessing to the public. He patronises the orphan and the widow, assists the friendless, and guides the ignorant. He does not reject the person's pretensions, who does not know how to explain them, or refuse doing a good office for a man because he cannot pay the fee of it. In short, though he regulates himself in all his proceedings by justice and equity, he finds a thousand occasions for all the good-natured offices of generosity and compassion.

A man is unfit for such a place of trust, who is of a sour untractable nature, or has any other passion that makes him uneasy to those who approach him. Roughness of temper is apt to discountenance the timorous or modest. The proud man discourages those from approaching him, who are of a mean condition, and who most want his assistance. The impatient man will not give himself time to be informed of the matter that lies before him. An officer, with one or more of these unbecoming qualities, is sometimes looked upon as a proper person to keep off impertinence and solicitation from his superior; but this is a kind of merit that can never atone for the injustice which may very often arise from it.

There are two other vicious qualities, which render a man very unfit for such a place of trust. The first of these is a dilatory temper, which commits innumerable cruelties without design. The maxim which several have laid down for a man's conduct in ordinary life, should be inviolable with a man in office, never to think of doing that to-morrow which may be done to-day. A man who defers doing what ought to be done, is guilty of injustice so long as he defers it. The despatch of a good office is very often as beneficial to the solicitor as the good office itself. In short, if a man compared the inconveniencies which another suffers by his delays, with the trifling motives and advantages which he himself may reap by them, he would never be guilty of a fault which very often does an irreparable prejudice to the person who depends upon him, and which might be remedied with little trouble to himself.

But in the last place, there is no man so improper to be employed in business, as he who is in any degree capable of corruption, and such a one is the man who, upon any pretence whatsoever, receives more than what is the stated and unquestioned fee of his office. Gratifications, tokens of thankfulness, despatch money, and the like specious terms, are the pretences under which corruption very frequently shelters itself. An honest man will however look on all these methods as unjustifiable, and will enjoy himself better in a moderate fortune, that is gained with honour and reputation, than in an overgrown estate that is cankered with the acquisitions of rapine and exaction. Were all our offices discharged with such an inflexible integrity, we should not see men in all ages, who grow up to exorbitant wealth, with the abilities which are to be met with in an ordinary mechanic. I cannot but think that such a corruption proceeds chiefly from men's employing the first that offer themselves, or those who have the character of shrewd worldly men, instead of searching out such as have had a liberal education, and have been trained up in the studies of knowledge and virtue.

It has been observed, that men of learning who take to business, discharge it generally with greater honesty than men of the world. The chief reason for it I take to be as follows. A man that has spent his youth in reading, has been used to find virtue extolled, and vice stigmatized. A man that has passed his time in the world, has often seen vice triumphant, and virtue discountenanced. Extortion, rapine, and injustice, which are branded with infamy in books, often give a man a figure in the world; while several qualities, which are celebrated in authors, as generosity, ingenuity, and good-nature, impoverish and ruin him. This cannot but have a proportionable effect on men whose tempers and principles are equally good and vicious.

There would be at least this advantage in employing men of learning and parts in business; that their prosperity would sit more gracefully on them, and that we should not see many worthless persons shot up into the greatest figures of life. O.

No. 470.] *Friday, August* 29, 1712.

> Turpe est difficiles habere nugas,
> Et stultus labor est ineptiarum.
> *Mart.* Epig. lxxxvi. Lib. 2. 9.
>
> 'Tis folly only, and defect of sense,
> Turns trifles into things of consequence.

I HAVE been very often disappointed of late years, when, upon examining the new edition of a classic author, I have found above half the volume taken up with various readings. When I have expected to meet with a learned note upon a doubtful passage in a Latin poet, I have only been informed, that such or such ancient manuscripts for an *et* write an *ac*, or of some other notable discovery of the like importance. Indeed, when a different reading gives us a different sense or a new elegance in an author, the editor does very well in taking notice of it; but when he only entertains us with the several ways of spelling the same word, and gathers together the various blunders and mistakes of twenty or thirty different transcribers, they only take up the time of the learned readers, and puzzle the minds of the ignorant. I have often fancied with myself how enraged an old Latin author would be, should he see the several absurdities, in sense and grammar, which are imputed to him by some or other of these various readings. In one he speaks nonsense; in another makes use of a word that was never heard of; and indeed there is scarce a solecism in writing which the best author is not guilty of, if we may be at liberty to read him in the words of some manuscript which the laborious editor has thought fit to examine in the prosecution of his work.

I question not but the ladies and pretty fellows will be very curious to understand what it is that I have been hitherto talking of. I shall therefore give them a notion of this practice, by endeavouring to write after the manner of several persons who make an eminent figure in the republic of letters. To this end we will suppose that the following song is an old ode, which I present to the public in a new edition, with the several various readings which I find of it in former editions, and in ancient manuscripts. Those who cannot relish the various readings, will perhaps find their account in the song, which never before appeared in print.

'My love was fickle once and changing,
Nor e'er would settle in my heart;
From beauty still to beauty ranging,
In every face I found a dart.

''Twas first a charming shape enslav'd me;
An eye then gave the fatal stroke:
Till by her wit Corinna sav'd me,
And all my former fetters broke.

'But now a long and lasting anguish
For Belvidera I endure;
Hourly I sigh, and hourly languish,
Nor hope to find the wonted cure.

'For here the false unconstant lover,
After a thousand beauties shown,
Does new surprising charms discover,
And finds variety in one.'

Various Readings.

Stanza the first, verse the first. *And changing.*] The *and* in some manuscripts is written thus, &; but that in the Cotton library writes it in three distinct letters.

Verse the second. *Nor e'er would.*] Aldus reads it *ever would;* but as this would hurt the metre, we have restored it to the genuine reading, by observing that synæresis which had been neglected by ignorant transcribers.

Ibid. *In my heart.*] Scaliger and others, *on my heart.*

Verse the fourth. *I found a dart.*] The Vatican manuscript for *I reads it;* but this must have been the hallucination of the transcriber, who probably mistook the dash of the *I* for a *T*.

Stanza the second, verse the second. *The fatal stroke.*] Scioppius, Salmasius, and many others, for *the* read *a;* but I have stuck to the usual reading.

Verse the third. *Till by her wit.*] Some manuscripts have it *his wit*, others *your*, others *their wit*. But as I find Corinna to be the name of a woman in other authors, I cannot doubt but it should be *her*.

Stanza the third, verse the first. *A long and lasting anguish.*] The German manuscript reads *a lasting passion*, but the rhyme will not admit it.

Verse the second. *For Belvidera I endure.*] Did not all the manuscripts reclaim, I should change *Belvidera* into *Pelvidera; Pelvis* being used by several of the ancient comic writers for a looking-glass, by which means the etymology of the word is very visible, and *Pelvidera* will signify a lady who often looks in her glass; as indeed she had very good reason, if she had all those beauties which our poet here ascribes to her.

Verse the third. *Hourly I sigh and hourly languish.*] Some for the word *hourly* read *daily*, and others *nightly;* the last has great authorities of its side.

Verse the fourth. *The wonted cure.*] The elder Stevens reads *wanted cure.*

Stanza the fourth, verse the second. *After a thousand beauties.*] In several copies we meet with a *hundred beauties*, by the usual error of the transcribers, who probably omitted a cypher, and had not taste enough to know that the word *thousand* was ten times a greater compliment to the poet's mistress than a *hundred.*

Verse the fourth. *And finds variety in one.*] Most of the ancient manuscripts have it *in two.* Indeed so many of them concur in this last reading, that I am very much in doubt whether it ought not to take place. There are but two reasons which incline me to the reading as I have published it: first, because the rhyme; and, secondly, because the sense is preserved by it. It might likewise proceed from the oscitancy of transcribers, who, to despatch their work the sooner, used to write all numbers in cypher, and seeing the figure 1 followed by a little dash of the pen, as is customary in old manuscripts, they perhaps mistook the dash for a second figure, and, by casting up both together, composed out of them the figure 2. But this I shall leave to the learned, without determining any thing in a matter of so great uncertainty. C.

No. 471.] *Saturday, August* 30, 1712.

'Εν ελπισιν χρη τους σοφυς' εχειν βιοου. ***Euripid.***

The wise with hope support the pains of life.

The time present seldom affords sufficient employment in the mind of man.

Objects of pain or pleasure, love or admiration, do not lie thick enough together in life to keep the soul in constant action, and supply an immediate exercise to its faculties. In order, therefore, to remedy this defect, that the mind may not want business, but always have materials for thinking, she is endowed with certain powers, that can recall what is passed, and anticipate what is to come.

That wonderful faculty, which we call the memory, is perpetually looking back, when we have nothing present to entertain us. It is like those repositories in several animals that are filled with stores of their former food, on which they may ruminate when their present pasture fails.

As the memory relieves the mind in her vacant moments, and prevents any chasms of thought by ideas of what is passed, we have other faculties that agitate and employ her for what is to come. These are the passions of hope and fear.

By these two passions we reach forward into futurity, and bring up to our present thoughts objects that lie hid in the remotest depths of time. We suffer misery and enjoy happiness, before they are in being; we can set the sun and stars forward, or lose sight of them by wandering into those retired parts of eternity, when the heavens and earth shall be no more. By the way, who can imagine that the existence of a creature is to be circumscribed by time, whose thoughts are not? But I shall, in this paper, confine myself to that particular passion which goes by the name of hope.

Our actual enjoyments are so few and transient, that man would be a very miserable being, were he not endowed with this passion, which gives him a taste of those good things that may possibly come into his possession. 'We should hope for every thing that is good,' says the old poet Linus, 'because there is nothing which may not be hoped for, and nothing but what the gods are able to give us.' Hope quickens all the still parts of life, and keeps the mind awake in her most remiss and indolent hours. It gives habitual serenity and good humour. It is a kind of vital heat in the soul, that cheers and gladdens her, when she does not attend to it. It makes pain easy, and labour pleasant.

Besides these several advantages which rise from hope, there is another which is none of the least, and that is, its great efficacy in preserving us from setting too high a value on present enjoyments. The saying of Cæsar is very well known. When he had given away all his estate in gratuities among his friends, one of them asked what he had left for himself; to which that great man replied, 'Hope.' His natural magnanimity hindered him from prizing what he was certainly possessed of, and turned all his thoughts upon something more valuable that he had in view. I question not but every reader will draw a moral from this story, and apply it to himself without my direction.

The old story of Pandora's box (which many of the learned believe was formed among the heathens upon the tradition of the fall of man) shows us how deplorable a state they thought the present life, without hope. To set forth the utmost condition of misery, they tell us, that our forefather, according to the pagan theology, had a great vessel presented him by Pandora. Upon his lifting up the lid of it, says the fable, there flew out all the calamities and distempers incident to men, from which, till that time, they had been altogether exempt. Hope, who had been enclosed in the cup with so much bad company, instead of flying off with the rest, stuck so close to the lid of it, that it was shut down upon her.

I shall make but two reflections upon what I have hitherto said. First, that no kind of life is so happy as that which is full of hope, especially when the hope is well grounded, and when the object of it is of an exalted kind, and in its nature proper to make the person happy who enjoys it. This proposition must be very evident to those who consider how few are the present enjoyments of the most happy man, and how insufficient to give him an entire satisfaction and acquiescence in them.

My next observation is this, that a religious life is that which most abounds in a well-grounded hope, and such a one as is fixed on objects that are capable of making us entirely happy. This hope in a religious man is much more sure and certain than the hope of any temporal blessing, as it is strengthened not only by reason, but by faith. It has at the same time its eye perpetually fixed on that state, which implies in the very notion of it the most full and complete happiness.

I have before shown how the influence of hope in general sweetens life, and makes our present condition supportable, if not pleasing; but a religious hope has still greater advantages. It does not only bear up the mind under her sufferings, but makes her rejoice in them, as they may be the instruments of procuring her the great and ultimate end of all her hope.

Religious hope has likewise this advantage above any other kind of hope, that it is able to revive the dying man, and to fill his mind not only with secret comfort and refreshment, but sometimes with rapture and transport. He triumphs in his agonies, whilst the soul springs forward with delight to the great object which she has always had in view, and leaves the body with an expectation of being reunited to her in a glorious and joyful resurrection.

I shall conclude this essay with those emphatical exprussions of a lively hope, which the psalmist made use of in the midst of those dangers and adversities which surrounded him; for the following passage had its present and personal, as well as its future and prophetic sense. 'I have set the Lord always before me. Because he is at my right hand I shall not be moved. Therefore my heart is glad, and my glory rejoiceth. My flesh also shall rest in hope. For thou wilt not leave my soul in hell, neither wilt thou suffer thine holy one to see corruption. Thou wilt show me the path of life. In thy presence is fulness of joy, at thy right hand there are pleasures for evermore.' C.

No. 472.] *Monday, September* 1, 1712.

——Voluptas
Solamenque malio—— *Virg. Æn.* iii. 660.
This only solace his hard fortune sends.—*Dryden.*

I RECEIVED some time ago a proposal, which had a preface to it, wherein the author discoursed at large of the innumerable objects of charity in a nation, and admonished the rich, who were afflicted with any distemper of body, particularly to regard the poor in the same species of affliction, and confine their tenderness to them, since it is impossible to assist all who are presented to them. The proposer had been relieved from a malady in his eyes by an operation performed by Sir William Read, and, being a man of condition, had taken a resolution to maintain three poor blind men during their lives, in gratitude for that great blessing. This misfortune is so very great and unfrequent, that one would think an establishment for all the poor under it, might be easily accomplished, with the addition of a very few others to those wealthy who are in the same calamity. However, the thought of the proposer arose from a very good motive; and the parcelling of ourselves out, as called to particular acts of beneficence, would be a pretty cement of society and virtue. It is the ordinary foundation for men's holding a commerce with each other, and becoming familiar, that they agree in the same sort of pleasure; and sure it may also be some reason for amity, that they are under one common distress. If all the rich who are lame with the gout, from a life of ease, pleasure, and luxury, would help those few who have it without a previous life of pleasure, and add a few of such laborious men, who are become lame from unhappy blows, falls, or other accidents of age or sickness; I say, would such gouty persons administer to the necessities of men disabled like themselves, the consciousness of such a behaviour would be the best julep, cordial, and anodyne, in the feverish, faint, and tormenting vicissitudes of that miserable distemper. The same may be said of all other, both bodily and intellectual evils. These classes of charity would certainly bring down blessings upon an age and people; and if men were not petrified with the love of this world, against all sense of the commerce which ought to be among them, it would not be an unreasonable bill for a poor man in the agony of pain, aggravated by want and poverty, to draw upon a sick alderman after this form:

'MR. BASIL PLENTY,—Sir, you have the gout and stone, with sixty thousand pounds sterling; I have the gout and stone, not worth one farthing; I shall pray for you, and desire you would pay the bearer twenty shillings, for value received from, sir, your humble servant,

'LAZARUS HOPEFUL.

'Cripplegate, August 29, 1712.'

The reader's own imagination will suggest to him the reasonableness of such correspondences, and diversify them into a thousand forms; but I shall close this as I began upon the subject of blindness. The following letter seems to be written by a man of learning, who is returned to his study, after a suspense of ability to do so. The benefit he reports himself to have received, may well claim the handsomest encomium he can give the operator.

'MR. SPECTATOR,—Ruminating lately on your admirable discourses on the Pleasures of the Imagination, I began to consider to which of our senses we are obliged for the greatest and most important share of those pleasures; and I soon concluded that it was to the sight. That is the sovereign of the senses, and mother of all the arts and sciences, that have refined the rudeness of the uncultivated mind to a politeness that distinguishes the fine spirits from the barbarous *gout* of the great vulgar and the small. The sight is the obliging benefactress that bestows on us the most transporting sensations that we have from the various and wonderful products of nature. To the sight we owe the amazing discoveries of the height, magnitude, and motion of the planets, their several revolutions about their common centre of light, heat and motion, the sun. The sight travels yet farther to the fixed stars, and furnishes the understanding with solid reasons to prove, that each of them is a sun, moving on its own axis, in the centre of its own vortex, or turbillion, and performing the same offices to its dependant planets that our glorious sun does to this. But the inquiries of the sight will not be stopped here, but make their progress through the immense expanse to the Milky Way, and there divide the blended fires of the galaxy into infinite and different worlds, made up of distinct suns, and their peculiar equipage of planets, till, unable to pursue this track any farther, it deputes the imagination to go on to new discoveries, till it fill the unboundless space with endless worlds.

'The sight informs the statuary's chisel

with power to give breath to lifeless brass and marble, and the painter's pencil to swell the flat canvass with moving figures actuated by imaginary souls. Music indeed may plead another original, since Jubal, by the different falls of his hammer on the anvil, discovered by the ear the first rude music that pleased the antediluvian fathers; but then the sight has not only reduced those wilder sounds into artful order and harmony, but conveys that harmony to the most distant parts of the world without the help of sound. To the sight we owe not only all the discoveries of philosophy, but all the divine imagery of poetry that transports the intelligent reader of Homer, Milton, and Virgil.

'As the sight has polished the world, so does it supply us with the most grateful and lasting pleasure. Let love, let friendship, paternal affection, filial piety, and conjugal duty, declare the joys the sight bestows on a meeting after absence. But it would be endless to enumerate all the pleasures and advantages of sight; every one that has it, every hour he makes use of it, finds them, feels them, enjoys them.

'Thus, as our greatest pleasures and knowledge are derived from the sight, so has Providence been more curious in the formation of its seat, the eye, than of the organs of the other senses. That stupendous machine is composed, in a wonderful manner, of muscles, membranes, and humours. Its motions are admirably directed by the muscles; the perspicuity of the humours transmits the rays of light; the rays are regularly refracted by their figure; the black lining of the sclerotes effectually prevents their being confounded by reflection. It is wonderful indeed to consider how many objects the eye is fitted to take in at once, and successively in an instant, and at the same time to make a judgment of their position, figure, or colour. It watches against our dangers, guides our steps, and lets in all the visible objects, whose beauty and variety instruct and delight.

'The pleasures and advantages of sight being so great, the loss must be very grievous; of which Milton, from experience, gives the most sensible idea, both in the third book of his Paradise Lost, and in his Samson Agonistes.

'To light, in the former:

"——————Thee I revisit safe,
And feel thy sov'reign vital lamp; but thou
Revisit'st not these eyes, that roll in vain
To find thy piercing ray, but find no dawn."

'And a little after:

'Seasons return, but not to me returns
Day, or the sweet approach of ev'n or morn,
Or sight of vernal bloom, or summer's rose,
Or flocks of herds, or human face divine;
But cloud instead, and ever-during dark
Surround me: from the cheerful ways of men
Cut off, and for the book of knowledge fair,
Presented with an universal blank
Of nature's works, to me expung'd and raz'd,
And wisdom at one entrance quite shut out.'

'Again, in Samson Agonistes:

"——————But chief of all,
O loss of sight! of thee I must complain:
Blind among enemies! O worse than chains,
Dungeon, or beggary, or decrepit age!
Light, the prime work of God, to me's extinct,
And all her various objects of delight
Annull'd——————"

"——————Still as a fool,
In pow'r of others, never in my own,
Scarce half I seem to live, dead more than half:
O dark! dark! dark! amid the blaze of noon:
Irrecoverably dark, total eclipse,
Without all hopes of day."

'The enjoyment of sight then being so great a blessing, and the loss of it so terrible an evil, how excellent and valuable is the skill of that artist which can restore the former, and redress the latter! My frequent perusal of the advertisements in the public newspapers (generally the most agreeable entertainment they afford,) has presented me with many and various benefits of this kind done to my countrymen by that skilful artist, Dr. Grant, her majesty's oculist extraordinary, whose happy hand has brought and restored to sight several hundreds in less than four years. Many have received sight by his means who came blind from their mother's womb, as in the famous instance of Jones of Newington. I myself have been cured by him of a weakness in my eyes next to blindness, and am ready to believe any thing that is reported of his ability this way; and know that many who could not purchase his assistance with money, have enjoyed it from his charity. But a list of particulars would swell my letter beyond its bounds: what I have said being sufficient to comfort those who are in the like distress, since they may conceive hopes of being no longer miserable in this kind, while there is yet alive so able an oculist as Dr. Grant. I am the Spectator's humble servant,

T. 'PHILANTHROPUS.'

No. 473.] *Tuesday, September 2, 1712.*

Quid? si quis vultu torvo ferus et pede nudo,
Exiguæque togæ simulet textore Catonam;
Virtutemne repræsentet, moresque Catonis?
Hor. Ep. xix. Lib. 1. 12.

Suppose a man the coarsest gown should wear,
No shoes, his forehead rough, his look severe,
And ape great Cato in his form and dress;
Must he his virtues and his mind express?
Creech.

'To the Spectator.

'SIR,—I am now in the country, and employ most of my time in reading, or thinking upon what I have read. Your paper comes constantly down to me, and it affects me so much, that I find my thoughts run into your way: and I recommend to you a subject upon which you have not yet touched, and that is, the satisfaction some men seem to take in their imperfections: I think one may call it glorying in their insufficiency. A certain great author is of opinion it is the contrary to envy, though perhaps it may proceed from it. Nothing is so common as to hear men of this sort, speaking of themselves, add to their own merit (as they think,) by impairing it, in praising themselves for their defects, freely allowing they commit some few frivolous errors, in order to be esteemed persons of uncommon talents and great qualifications. They are generally professing an injudicious neglect of dancing, fencing, and riding, as also an unjust contempt for travelling, and the modern languages; as for their part, they say, they never valued or troubled their heads about them. This panegyrical satire on themselves certainly is worthy of your animadversion. I have known one of these gentlemen think himself obliged to forget the day of an appointment, and sometimes even that you spoke to him; and when you see 'em, they hope you'll pardon 'em, for they have the worst memory in the world. One of 'em started up t'other day in some confusion, and said, "Now I think on 't, I am to meet Mr. Mortmain, the attorney, about some business, but whether it is today or to-morrow, faith I can 't tell." Now, to my certain knowledge, he knew his time to a moment, and was there accordingly. These forgetful persons have, to heighten their crime, generally the best memories of any people, as I have found out by their remembering sometimes through inadvertency. Two or three of 'em that I know, can say most of our modern tragedies by heart. I asked a gentleman the other day, that is famous for a good carver, (at which acquisition he is out of countenance, imagining it may detract from some of his more essential qualifications,) to help me to something that was near him; but he excused himself, and blushing told me, "Of all things he could never carve in his life;" though it can be proved upon him that he cuts up, disjoints, and uncases with incomparable dexterity. I would not be understood as if I thought it laudable for a man of quality and fortune to rival the acquisitions of artificers, and endeavour to excel in little handy qualities; no, I argue only against being ashamed of what is really praise-worthy. As these pretences to ingenuity show themselves several ways, you will often see a man of this temper ashamed to be clean, and setting up for wit, only from negligence in his habit. Now I am upon this head, I cannot help observing also upon a very different folly proceeding from the same cause. As these above-mentioned arise from affecting an equality with men of greater talents, from having the same faults, there are others that would come at a parallel with those above them, by possessing little advantages which they want. I heard a young man not long ago, who has sense, comfort himself in his ignorance of Greek, Hebrew, and the Orientals: at the same time that he published his aversion to those languages, he said that the knowledge of them was rather a diminution than an advancement of a man's character; though, at the same time, I know he languishes and repines he is not master of them himself. Whenever I take any of these fine persons thus detracting from what they do not understand, I tell them I will complain to you; and say I am sure you will not allow it an exception against a thing, that he who contemns it is an ignorant in it. I am, sir, your most humble servant,

'S. T.'

'Mr. Spectator,—I am a man of a very good estate, and am honourably in love. I hope you will allow, when the ultimate purpose is honest, there may be, without trespass against innocence, some toying by the way. People of condition are perhaps too distant and formal on those occasions; but however that is, I am to confess to you that I have writ some verses to atone for my offence. You professed authors are a little severe upon us, who write like gentlemen: but if you are a friend to love, you will insert my poem. You cannot imagine how much service it would do me with my fair one, as well as reputation with all my friends, to have something of mine in the Spectator. My crime was, that I snatched a kiss, and my poetical excuse as follows'

I.

"Belinda, see from yonder flowers
 The bee flies loaded to its cell:
Can you perceive what it devours?
 Are they impaired in show or smell?

II.

"So, though I robb'd you of a kiss,
 Sweeter than their ambrosial dew;
Why are you angry at my bliss?
 Has it at all impoverish'd you?

III.

"'Tis by this cunning I contrive,
 In spite of your unkind reserve,
To keep my famish'd love alive,
 Which you inhumanly would starve."

'I am, sir, your humble servant,

'TIMOTHY STANZA.'

'Aug. 23, 1712.

'Sir,—Having a little time upon my hands, I could not think of bestowing it better, than in writing an epistle to the Spectator, which I now do, and am, sir, your humble servant, BOB SHORT.

'P. S. If you approve of my style, I am likely enough to become your correspondent. I desire your opinion of it. I design it for that way of writing called by the judicious "the familiar."' T.

No. 474.] *Wednesday, September* 3, 1712.

Asperitas agrestis et inconcinna——
Hor. Ep. 18. Lib. 1. 6.

Rude, rustic, and inelegant.

'Mr. Spectator,—Being of the number of those that have lately retired from the centre of business and pleasure, my uneasiness in the country where I am, arises rather from the society than the solitude of it. To be obliged to receive and return visits from and to a circle of neighbours, who, through diversity of age or inclinations, can neither be entertaining nor serviceable to us, is a vile loss of time, and a slavery from which a man should deliver himself, if possible: for why must I lose the remaining part of my life, because they have thrown away the former part of theirs? It is to me an insupportable affliction, to be tormented with the narrations of a set of people, who are warm in their expressions of the quick relish of that pleasure which their dogs and horses have a more delicate taste of. I do also in my heart detest and abhor that damnable doctrine and position of the necessity of a bumper, though to one's own toast; for though it be pretended that these deep potations are used only to inspire gayety, they certainly drown that cheerfulness which would survive a moderate circulation. If at these meetings it were left to every stranger either to fill his glass according to his own inclination, or to make his retreat when he finds he has been sufficiently obedient to that of others, these entertainments would be governed with more good sense, and consequently with more good-breeding, than at present they are. Indeed, where any of the guests are known to measure their fame or pleasure by their glass, proper exhortations might be used to these to push their fortunes in this sort of reputation; 'but, where it is unseasonably insisted on to a modest stranger, this drench may be said to be swallowed with the same necessity, as if it had been tendered in the horn for that purpose, with this aggravating circumstance, that distresses the entertainer's guest in the same degree as it relieves his horses.

'To attend without impatience an account of five-barred gates, double ditches, and precipices, and to survey the orator with desiring eyes, is to me extremely difficult, but absolutely necessary, to be upon tolerable terms with him: but then the occasional bursting out into laughter, is of all other accomplishments the most requisite. I confess at present I have not that command of these convulsions as is necessary to be good company; therefore I beg you would publish this letter, and let me be known all at once for a queer fellow and avoided. It is monstrous to me, that we who are given to reading and calm conversation should ever be visited by these roarers: but they think they themselves, as neighbours, may come into our rooms with the same right that they and their dogs hunt in our grounds.

'Your institution of clubs I have always admired, in which you constantly endeavoured the union of the metaphorically defunct, that is, such as are neither serviceable to the busy and enterprising part of mankind, nor entertaining to the retired and speculative. There should certainly, therefore, in each country, be established a club of the persons whose conversations I have described, who for their own private, as also public emolument, should exclude, and be excluded, all other society. Their attire, should be the same with their huntsmen's, and none should be admitted into this green conversation piece, except he had broke his collar-bone thrice. A broken rib or two might also admit a man without the least opposition. The president must necessarily have broken his neck, and have been taken up dead once or twice: for the more maims this brotherhood shall have met with, the easier will their conversation flow and keep up; and when any one of these vigorous invalids had finished his narration of the collar-bone, this naturally would introduce the history of the ribs. Besides, the different circumstances of their falls and fractures would help to prolong and diversify their relations. There should also be another club of such men who have not succeeded so well in maiming themselves, but are however in the constant pursuit of these accomplishments. I would by no means be suspected, by what I have said, to traduce in general the body of fox-hunters; for whilst I look upon a reasonable creature full speed after a pack of dogs by way of pleasure, and not of business, I shall always make honourable mention of it.

'But the most irksome conversation of all others I have met with in the neighbourhood, has been among two or three of your travellers, who have overlooked men and manners, and have passed through France and Italy with the same observation that the carriers and the stage-coachmen do through Great Britain; that is, their stops and stages have been regulated according to the liquor they have met with in their passage. They indeed remember the names of abundance of places, with the particular fineries of certain churches; but their distinguishing mark is certain prettinesses of foreign languages, the meaning of which they could have better expressed in their own. The entertainment of these fine observers Shakspeare has described to consist

"In taking of the Alps and Appennines
The Pyrenean, and the river Po:"

'and then concludes with a sigh:

"Now this is worshipful society!"

'I would not be thought in all this to hate such honest creatures as dogs; I am only unhappy that I cannot partake in their diversions. But I love them so well, as dogs, that I often go with my pockets stuffed with bread to dispense my favours, or make my way through them at neighbours' houses. There is in particular a young hound of great expectation, vivacity, and enterprise, that attends my flights wherever he spies me. This creature observes my countenance and behaves himself accordingly. His mirth, his frolic, and joy, upon the sight of me has been observed, and I have been gravely desired not to encourage him so much, for it spoils his parts; but I think he shows them sufficiently in the several boundings, friskings, and scourings, when he makes his court to me: but I foresee in a little time he and I must keep company with one another only, for we are fit for no other in these parts. Having informed you how I do pass my time in the country where I am, I must proceed to tell you how I would pass it, had I such a fortune as would put me above the observance of ceremony and custom.

'My scheme of a country life then should be as follows. As I am happy in three or four very agreeable friends, these I would constantly have with me; and the freedom we took with one another at school and the university, we would maintain and exert upon all occasions with great courage. There should be certain hours of the day to be employed in reading, during which time it should be impossible for any one of us to enter the other's chamber, unless by storm. After this we would communicate the trash or treasure we had met with, with our own reflections upon the matter; the justness of which we would controvert with good-humoured warmth, and never spare one another out of that complaisant spirit of conversation, which makes others affirm and deny the same matter in a quarter of an hour. If any of the neighbouring gentlemen, not of our turn, should take it in their heads to visit me, I should look upon these persons in the same degree enemies to my particular state of happiness, as ever the French were to that of the public, and I would be at an annual expense in spies to observe their motions. Whenever I should be surprised with a visit, as I hate drinking, I would be brisk in swilling bumpers, upon this maxim, that it is better to trouble others with my impertinence, than to be troubled myself with theirs. The necessity of an infirmary makes me resolve to fall into that project; and as we should be but five, the terrors of an involuntary separation, which our number cannot so well admit of, would make us exert ourselves in opposition to all the particulars mentioned in your institution of that equitable confinement. This my way of life I know would subject me to the imputation of a morose, covetous, and singular fellow. These and all other hard words, with all manner of insipid jests, and all other reproach, would be matter of mirth to me and my friends: besides, I would destroy the application of the epithets morose and covetous, by a yearly relief of my undeservedly necessitous neighbours, and by treating my friends and domestics with a humanity that should express the obligation to lie rather on my side; and as for the word singular I was always of opinion every man must be so, to be what one would desire him. Your very humble servant, J. R.'

'MR. SPECTATOR,—About two years ago I was called upon by the younger part of a country family, by my mother's side related to me, to visit Mr. Campbell,* the dumb man; for they told me that that was chiefly what brought them to town, having heard wonders of him in Essex. I who always wanted faith in matters of that kind, was not easily prevailed on to go; but, lest they should take it ill, I went with them; when, to my surprise, Mr. Campbell related all their past life; in short, had he not been prevented, such a discovery would have come out as would have ruined the next design of their coming to town, *viz.* buying wedding clothes. Our names—though he never heard of us before—and we endeavoured to conceal—were as familiar to him as to ourselves. To be sure, Mr. Spectator, he is a very learned and wise man. Being impatient to know my fortune, having paid my respects in a family Jacobus, he told me, after his manner, among several other things, that in a year and nine months I should fall ill of a fever, be given over by my physicians, but should with much difficulty recover; that, the first time I took the air afterwards, I should be addressed to by a young gentleman of a plentiful fortune, good sense, and a generous spirit. Mr. Spectator, he is the purest man in the world, for all he said is come to pass, and I am the happiest she in Kent. I have been in quest of Mr. Campbell these three months, and cannot find him out. Now, hearing you are a dumb man too, I thought you might correspond, and be able to tell me something; for I think myself highly obliged to make his fortune, as he has mine. It is very possible your worship, who has spies all over this town, can inform me how to send to him. If you can, I beseech you be as speedy as possible, and you will highly oblige your constant reader and admirer,

'DULCIBELLA THANKLEY.'

Ordered, That the inspector I employ about wonders, inquire at the Golden-Lion, opposite to the Half-Moon tavern in Drury-lane, into the merits of this silent sage, and report accordingly. T.

No. 475.] *Thursday, September 4, 1712.*

—Quæ res in se neque consilium, neque modum
Habet ullum, eam consilio regere non potes.

Ter. Eun. Act i. Sc. 1

The thing that in itself has neither measure nor consideration, counsel cannot rule.

It is an old observation, which has been made of politicians who would rather ingratiate themselves with their sovereign, than promote his real service, that they

* Duncan Campbell announced himself to the public as a Scotch highlander, gifted with the second sight.

accommodate their counsels to his inclinations, and advise him to such actions only as his heart is naturally set upon. The privy counsellor of one in love must observe the same conduct, unless he would forfeit the friendship of the person who desires his advice. I have known several odd cases of this nature. Hipparchus was going to marry a common woman, but being resolved to do nothing without the advice of his friend Philander, he consulted him upon the occasion. Philander told him his mind freely, and represented his mistress to him in such strong colours, that the next morning he received a challenge for his pains, and before twelve o'clock was run through the body by the man who had asked his advice. Celia was more prudent on the like occasion. She desired Leonilla to give her opinion freely upon the young fellow who made his addresses to her. Leonilla, to oblige her, told her, with great frankness, that she looked upon him as one of the most worthless—Celia, foreseeing what a character she was to expect, begged her not to go on, for that she had been privately married to him above a fortnight. The truth of it is, a woman seldom asks advice before she has bought her wedding clothes. When she has made her own choice, for form's sake, she sends a *conge d' elire* to her friends.

If we look into the secret springs and motives that set people at work on these occasions, and put them upon asking advice which they never intend to take; I look upon it to be none of the least, that they are incapable of keeping a secret which is so very pleasing to them. A girl longs to tell her confidant that she hopes to be married in a little time; and, in order to talk of the pretty fellow that dwells so much in her thoughts, asks her very gravely, what she would advise her to do in a case of so much difficulty. Why else should Melissa, who had not a thousand pounds in the world, go into every quarter of the town to ask her acquaintance, whether they would advise her to take Tom Townly, that made his addresses to her with an estate of five thousand a year. It is very pleasant, on this occasion, to hear the lady propose her doubts, and to see the pains she is at to get over them.

I must not here omit a practice which is in use among the vainer part of our sex, who will often ask a friend's advice in relation to a fortune whom they are never like to come at. Will Honeycomb, who is now on the verge of threescore, took me aside not long since, and asked me in his most serious look, whether I would advise him to marry my lady Betty Single, who, by the way, is one of the greatest fortunes about town. I stared him full in the face upon so strange a question; upon which he immediately gave me an inventory of her jewels and estate, adding, that he was resolved to do nothing in a matter of such consequence without my approbation. Finding he would have an answer, I told him if he could get the lady's consent, he had mine. This is about the tenth match, which, to my knowledge, Will has consulted his friends upon, without ever opening his mind to the party herself.

I have been engaged in this subject by the following letter, which comes to me from some notable young female scribe, who, by the contents of it, seems to have carried matters so far, that she is ripe for asking advice: but as I would not lose her good will, nor forfeit the reputation which I have with her for wisdom, I shall only communicate the letter to the public, without returning any answer to it.

'MR. SPECTATOR,—Now, sir, the thing is this; Mr. Shapely is the prettiest gentleman about town. He is very tall, but not too tall neither. He dances like an angel. His mouth is made I do not know how, but it is the prettiest that I ever saw in my life. He is always laughing, for he has an infinite deal of wit. If you did but see how he rolls his stockings! He has a thousand pretty fancies, and I am sure, if you saw him, you would like him. He is a very good scholar, and can talk Latin as fast as English. I wish you could but see him dance. Now you must understand, poor Mr. Shapely has no estate; but how can he help that, you know? And yet my friends are so unreasonable as to be always teasing me about him, because he has no estate; but I am sure he has what is better than an estate; for he is a good-natured, ingenious, modest, civil, tall, well-bred, handsome man; and I am obliged to him for his civilities ever since I saw him. I forgot to tell you that he has black eyes, and looks upon me now and then as if he had tears in them. And yet my friends are so unreasonable; that they would have me be uncivil to him. I have a good portion which they cannot hinder me of, and I shall be fourteen on the 29th day of August next, and am therefore willing to settle in the world as soon as I can, and so is Mr. Shapely. But every body I advise with here is poor Mr. Shapely's enemy. I desire therefore you will give me your advice, for I know you are a wise man; and if you advise me well, I am resolved to follow it. I heartily wish you could see him dance; and am, sir, your most humble servant, B. D.

'He loves your Spectators mightily.' C.

he was, or pretended to be, deaf and dumb, and succeeded in making a fortune to himself by practising for some years on the credulity of the vulgar in the ignominious character of a fortune-teller.

No. 476.] *Friday, September 5, 1712.*

——Lucidus ordo. *Hor. Ars Poet.* 41.

Method gives light.

AMONG my daily papers which I bestow on the public, there are some which are written with regularity and method, and others that run out into the wildness of those compositions which go by the name of essays. As for the first, I have the whole scheme of the discourse in my mind before I set pen to paper. In the other kind of writing it is sufficient that I have several thoughts on a subject, without troubling myself to range them in such order, that they may seem to grow out of one another, and be disposed under the proper heads. Seneca and Montaigne, are patterns for writing in this last kind, as Tully and Aristotle excel in the other. When I read an author of genius who writes without method, I fancy myself in a wood that abounds with a great many noble objects, rising one among another in the greatest confusion and disorder. When I read a methodical discourse, I am in a regular plantation, and can place myself in its several centres, so as to take a view of all the lines and walks that are struck from them. You may ramble in the one a whole day together, and every moment discover something or other that is new to you; but when you have done, you will have but a confused, imperfect notion of the place: in the other your eye commands the whole prospect, and gives you such an idea of it as is not easily worn out of the memory.

Irregularity and want of method are only supportable in men of great learning or genius, who are often too full to be exact, and therefore choose to throw down their pearls in heaps before the reader, rather than be at the pains of stringing them.

Method is of advantage to a work, both in respect to the writer and the reader. In regard to the first, it is a great help to his invention. When a man has planned his discourse, he finds a great many thoughts rising out of every head, that do not offer themselves upon the general survey of a subject. His thoughts are at the same time more intelligible, and better discover their drift and meaning, when they are placed in their proper lights, and follow one another in a regular series, than when they are thrown together without order and connexion. There is always an obscurity in confusion; and the same sentence that would have enlightened the reader in one part of a discourse, perplexes him in another. For the same reason, likewise, every thought in a methodical discourse shows itself in its greatest beauty, as the several figures in a piece of painting receive new grace from their disposition in the picture. The advantages of a reader from a methodical discourse are correspondent with those of the writer. He comprehends every thing easily, takes it in with pleasure, and retains it long.

Method is not less requisite in ordinary conversation than in writing, provided a man would talk to make himself understood. I, who hear a thousand coffee-house debates every day, am very sensible of this want of method in the thoughts of my honest countrymen. There is not one dispute in ten which is managed in those schools of politics, where, after the three first sentences, the question is not entirely lost. Our disputants put me in mind of the scuttle-fish, that when he is unable to extricate himself, blackens all the water about him until he becomes invisible. The man who does not know how to methodise his thoughts, has always to borrow a phrase from the Dispensary, 'a barren superfluity of words;' the fruit is lost amidst the exuberance of leaves.

Tom Puzzle is one of the most eminent immethodical disputants of any that has fallen under my observation. Tom has read enough to make him very impertinent: his knowledge is sufficient to raise doubts, but not to clear them. It is a pity that he has so much learning, or that he has not a great deal more. With these qualifications Tom sets up for a freethinker, finds a great many things to blame in the constitution of his country, and gives shrewd intimations that he does not believe another world. In short, Puzzle is an atheist as much as his parts will give him leave. He has got about half a dozen common-place topics, into which he never fails to turn the conversation, whatever was the occasion of it. Though the matter in debate be about Douay or Denain, it is ten to one but half his discourse runs upon the unreasonableness of bigotry and priest-craft. This makes Mr. Puzzle the admiration of all those who have less sense than himself, and the contempt of all those who have more. There is none in town whom Tom dreads so much as my friend Will Dry. Will, who is acquainted with Tom's logic, when he finds him running off the question, cuts him short with a "What then? We allow all this to be true; but what is it to our present purpose?" I have known Tom eloquent half an hour together, and triumphing, as he thought, in the superiority of the argument, when he has been nonplussed on a sudden by Mr. Dry's desiring him to tell the company what it was that he endeavoured to prove. In short, Dry is a man of a clear methodical head, but few words, and gains the same advantage over Puzzle that a small body of regular troops would gain over a numberless undisciplined militia.

C.

No. 477.] *Saturday, September* 6, 1712

——An me ludit amabilis
Insania? audire et videor pios
Errare per lucos, amœnæ
Quos et aquæ subeunt et auræ.

Hor. Od. iv. Lib 3. 5.

——Does airy fancy cheat
My mind, well pleas'd with the deceit?
I seem to hear, I seem to move,
And wander through the happy groves,
Where smooth springs flow, and murm'ring breeze
Wantons through the waving trees.—*Creech*

'Sir,—Having lately read your essay on the Pleasures of the Imagination, I was so taken with your thoughts upon some of our English gardens, that I cannot forbear troubling you with a letter upon that subject. I am one, you must know, who am looked upon as a humourist in gardening. I have several acres about my house which I call my garden, and which a skilful gardener would not know what to call. It is a confusion of kitchen and parterre, orchard and flower-garden, which lie so mixed and interwoven with one another, that if a foreigner, who had seen nothing of our country, should be conveyed into my garden at his first landing, he would look upon it as a natural wilderness, and one of the uncultivated parts of our country. My flowers grow up in several parts of the garden in the greatest luxuriancy and profusion. I am so far from being fond of any particular one, by reason of its rarity, that if I meet with any one in a field which pleases me, I give it a place in my garden. By this means, when a stranger walks with me, he is surprised to see several large spots of ground covered with ten thousand different colours, and has often singled out flowers that he might have met with under a common hedge, in a field, or in a meadow, as some of the greatest beauties of the place. The only method I observe in this particular, is to range in the same quarter the products of the same season, that they may make their appearance together, and compose a picture of the greatest variety. There is the same irregularity in my plantations, which run into as great a wilderness as their natures will permit. I take in none that do not naturally rejoice in the soil; and am pleased, when I am walking in a labyrinth of my own raising, not to know whether the next tree I shall meet with is an apple or an oak, an elm or a pear-tree. My kitchen has likewise its particular quarters assigned it; for, besides the wholesome luxury which that place abounds with, I have always thought a kitchen-garden a more pleasant sight than the finest orangery or artificial green-house. I love to see every thing in its perfection; and am more pleased to survey my rows of coleworts and cabbages, with a thousand nameless pot-herbs, springing up in their full fragrancy and verdure, than to see the tender plants of foreign countries kept alive by artificial heats, or withering in an air and soil that are not adapted to them. I must not omit, that there is a fountain rising in the upper part of my garden, which forms a little wandering rill, and administers to the pleasure as well as to the plenty of the place. I have so conducted it, that it visits most of my plantations; and have taken particular care to let it run in the same manner as it would do in an open field, so that it generally passes through banks of violets and primroses, plats of willow or other plants, that seem to be of its own producing. There is another circumstance in which I am very particular, or, as my neighbours call me, very whimsical: as my garden invites into it all the birds of the country, by offering them the conveniency of springs and shades, solitude and shelter, I do not suffer any one to destroy their nests in the spring, or drive them from their usual haunts in fruit-time; I value my garden more for being full of blackbirds than cherries, and very frankly give them fruit for their songs. By this means I have always the music of the season in its perfection, and am highly delighted to see the jay or the thrush hopping about my walks, and shooting before my eyes across the several little glades and alleys that I pass through, I think there are as many kinds of gardening as of poetry. your makers of parterres and flower-gardens are epigrammatists and sonnetteers in this art; contrivers of bowers and grottos, treillages and cascades, are romance writers. Wise and London are our heroic poets; and if, as a critic, I may single out any passage of their works to commend, I shall take notice of that part in the upper garden at Kensington, which was at first nothing but a gravel-pit. It must have been a fine genius for gardening that could have thought of forming such an unsightly hollow into so beautiful an area, and to have hit the eye with so uncommon and agreeable a scene as that which it is now wrought into. To give this particular spot of ground the greatest effect, they have made a very pleasing contrast; for as on one side of the walk you see this hollow basin, with its several little plantations, lying so conveniently under the eye of the beholder, on the other side of it there appears a seeming mount, made up of trees rising one higher than another, in proportion as they approach the centre. A spectator, who has not heard this account of it, would think this circular mount was not only a real one, but that it had been actually scooped out of that hollow space which I have before mentioned. I never yet met with any one, who has walked in this garden, who was not struck with that part of it which I have here mentioned. As for myself, you will find, by the account which I have already given you, that my compositions in gardening are altogether after the Pindaric manner, and run into the beautiful wildness of nature, without affecting the nicer elegancies of art. What I am now going to mention will, perhaps, deserve your attention more than any thing I have yet said. I find that, in the discourse which I spoke of at the beginning of my letter, you are against filling an English garden with evergreens: and indeed I am so far of your opinion, that I can by no means think the verdure of an evergreen comparable to that which shoots out annually, and clothes our trees in the summer season. But I have often wondered that those who are like myself, and love to live in gardens, have never thought of contriving a winter garden, which would consist of such trees only as never cast their leaves. We have very often little snatches of sunshine and fair weather in the most uncomfortable parts of the year, and have frequently several days in November and January that are as agreeable as any in the finest months. At such times, therefore, I think there could not be a greater pleasure than to walk in such a winter garden as I have proposed. In the summer season the whole country blooms, and is a kind of garden; for which reason we are not so sensible of those beauties that at this time may be every where met with; but when nature is in her desolation, and presents us with nothing but bleak and barren prospects, there is something unspeakably cheerful in a spot of ground which is covered with trees that smile amidst all the rigour of winter, and give us a view of the most gay season in the midst of that which is the most dead and melancholy. I have so far indulged myself in this thought, that I have set apart a whole acre of ground for the executing of it. The walls are covered with ivy instead of vines. The laurel, the horn-beam, and the holly, with many other trees and plants of the same nature, grow so thick in it, that you cannot imagine a more lively scene. The glowing redness of the berries, with which they are hung at this time, vies with the verdure of their leaves, and is apt to inspire the heart of the beholder with that vernal delight which you have somewhere taken notice of in your former papers. It is very pleasant, at the same time, to see the several kinds of birds retiring into this little green spot, and enjoying themselves among the branches and foliage, when my great garden, which I have before mentioned to you, does not afford a single leaf for their shelter.

'You must know, sir, that I look upon the pleasure which we take in a garden as one of the most innocent delights in human life. A garden was the habitation of our first parents before the fall. It is naturally apt to fill the mind with calmness and tranquillity, and to lay all its turbulent passions at rest. It gives us a great insight into the contrivance and wisdom of Providence, and suggests innumerable subjects for meditation. I cannot but think the very complacency and satisfaction which a man takes in these works of nature to be a laudable, if not a virtuous, habit of mind. For all which reasons I hope you will pardon the length of my present letter. I am, sir, &c.' C.

No. 478.] *Monday, September* 8, 1712.

——————Usus,
Quem penes arbitrium est, et jus et norma——
Hor. Ars Poet. v. 72.

Fashion, sole arbitress of dress.

'Mr. Spectator,—I happened lately that a friend of mine, who had many things to buy for his family, would oblige me to walk with him to the shops. He was very nice in his way, and fond of having every thing shown; which at first made me very uneasy; but, as his humour still continued, the things which I had been staring at along with him began to fill my head, and led me into a set of amusing thoughts concerning them.

'I fancied it must be very surprising to any one who enters into a detail of fashions to consider how far the vanity of mankind has laid itself out in dress, what a prodigious number of people it maintains, and what a circulation of money it occasions. Providence in this case makes use of the folly which we will not give up, and it becomes instrumental to the support of those who are willing to labour. Hence it is that fringe-makers, lace-men, tire-women, and a number of other trades, which would be useless in a simple state of nature, draw their subsistence; though it is seldom seen that such as these are extremely rich, because their original fault of being founded upon vanity keeps them poor by the light inconstancy of its nature. The variableness of fashion turns the stream of business, which flows from it, now into one channel, and anon into another; so that the different sets of people sink or flourish in their turns by it.

'From the shops we retired to the tavern, where I found my friend express so much satisfaction for the bargains he had made, that my moral reflections (if I had told them) might have passed for a reproof; so I chose rather to fall in with him, and let the discourse run upon the use of fashions.

'Here we remembered how much man is governed by his senses, how lively he is struck by the objects which appear to him in an agreeable manner, how much clothes contribute to make us agreeable objects, and how much we owe it to ourselves that we should appear so.

'We considered man as belonging to societies; societies as formed of different ranks; and different ranks distinguished by habits, that all proper duty or respect might attend their appearance.

'We took notice of several advantages which are met with in the occurrences of conversation; how the bashful man has been sometimes so raised, as to express himself with an air of freedom when he imagines that his habit introduces him to company with a becoming manner; and again, how a fool in fine clothes shall be suddenly heard with attention, till he has betrayed himself; whereas a man of sense appearing with a dress of negligence, shall be but coldly received till he be proved by time, and established in a character. Such things as these we could recollect to have happened to our own knowledge so very often, that we concluded the author had his rea sons, who advises his son to go in dress rather above his fortune than under it.

'At last the subject seemed so considerable, that it was proposed to have a repository built for fashions, as there are chambers for medals and other rarities. The building may be shaped as that which stands among the pyramids, in the form of a woman's head. This may be raised upon pillars, whose ornaments shall bear a just relation to the design. Thus there may be an imitation of fringe carved in the base, a sort of appearance of lace in the frieze, and a representation of curling locks, with bows of ribband sloping over them, may fill up the work of the cornice. The inside may be divided into two apartments appropriated to each sex. The apartments may be filled with shelves, on which boxes are to stand as regularly as books in a library. These are to have folding doors, which, being opened, you are to behold a baby dressed out in some fashion which has flourished, and standing upon a pedestal, where the time of its reign is marked down. For its farther regulation, let it be ordered, that every one who invents a fashion shall bring in his box, whose front he may at pleasure have either worked or painted with some amorous or gay device, that, like books with gilded leaves and covers, it may the sooner draw the eyes of the beholders. And to the end that these may be preserved with all due care, let there be a keeper appointed, who shall be a gentleman qualified with a competent knowledge in clothes; so that by this means the place will be a comfortable support for some beau who has spent his estate in dressing.

'The reasons offered, by which we expected to gain the approbation of the public, were as follows:—

'First, That every one who is considerable enough to be a mode, and has any imperfection of nature or chance, which it is possible to hide by the advantage of clothes, may, by coming to this repository, be furnished herself, and furnish all who are under the same misfortune, with the most agreeable manner of concealing it; and that, on the other side, every one, who has any beauty in face or shape, may also be furnished with the most agreeable manner of showing it.

'Secondly, That whereas some of our young gentlemen who travel, give us great reason to suspect that they only go abroad to make or improve a fancy for dress, a project of this nature may be a means to keep them at home; which is in effect the keeping of so much money in the kingdom. And perhaps the balance of fashion in Europe, which now leans upon the side of France, may be so altered for the future, that it may become as common with Frenchmen to come to England for their finishing stroke of breeding, as it has been for Englishmen to go to France for it.

'Thirdly, Whereas several great scholars, who might have been otherwise useful to the world, have spent their time in studying to describe the dresses of the ancients from dark hints, which they are fain to interpret and support with much learning; it will from henceforth happen that they shall be freed from the trouble, and the world from useless volumes. This project will be a registry, to which posterity may have recourse, for the clearing such obscure passages as tend that way in authors; and therefore we shall not for the future submit ourselves to the learning of etymology, which might persuade the age to come that the farthingale was worn for cheapness, or the furbelow for warmth.

'Fourthly, Whereas they, who are old themselves, have often a way of railing at the extravagance of youth, and the whole age in which their children live; it is hoped that this ill-humour will be much suppressed, when we can have recourse to the fashions of their times, produce them in our vindication, and be able to show, that it might have been as expensive in queen Elizabeth's time only to wash and quill a ruff, as it is now to buy cravats or neck handkerchiefs.

'We desire also to have it taken notice of, that because we would show a particular respect to foreigners, which may induce them to perfect their breeding here in a knowledge which is very proper for pretty gentlemen, we have conceived the motto for the house in the learned language. There is to be a picture over the door, with a looking-glass and a dressing chair in the middle of it; then on one side are to be seen, above one another, patch-boxes, pincushions, and little bottles; on the other, powder-bags, puffs, combs, and brushes; beyond these, swords with fine knots, whose points are hidden, and fans almost closed, with the handles downward, are to stand out interchangeably from the sides, until they meet at the top, and form a semicircle over the rest of the figures: beneath all, the writing is to run in this pretty sounding manner:

"Adeste, O quotquot sunt, Veneres, Gratiæ, Cupidines,
En vobis adsunt in promptu
Faces, vincula, spicula;
Hinc eligite, sumite, regite."

"All ye Venusses, Graces, and Cupids, attend:
See, prepared to your hands,
Darts, torches, and bands:
Your weapons here choose, and your empire extend"

'I am, sir,
'Your most humble servant,
'A. B.'

The proposal of my correspondent I cannot but look upon as an ingenious method of placing persons (whose parts make them ambitious to exert themselves in frivolous things) in a rank by themselves. In order to this, I would propose that there be a board of directors of the fashionable society; and, because it is a matter of too much weight for a private man to determine alone, I should be highly obliged to my correspondents if they would give in lists of persons qualified for this trust. If the chief coffee-houses, the conversations of which places are carried on by persons, each of whom has his little number of followers and admirers, would name from among themselves two or three to be inserted, they should be put up with great faithfulness. Old beaus are to be represented in the first place; but as that sect, with relation to dress, is almost extinct, it will, I fear, be absolutely necessary to take in all time-servers, properly so deemed; that is, such as, without any conviction of conscience, or view of interest, change with the world, and that merely from a terror of being out of fashion. Such also, who from facility of temper, and too much obsequiousness, are vicious against their will, and follow leaders whom they do not approve, for want of courage to go their own way, are capable persons for this superintendency. Those who are loth to grow old, or would do any thing contrary to the course and order of things, out of fondness to be in fashion, are proper candidates. To conclude, those who are in fashion without apparent merit, must be supposed to have latent qualities, which would appear in a post of direction; and therefore are to be regarded in forming these lists. Any who shall be pleased according to these, or what farther qualifications may occur to himself, to send a list, is desired to do it within fourteen days from this date.

N. B. The place of the physician to this society, according to the last mentioned qualification, is already engaged. T.

No. 479.] *Tuesday, September* 9, 1712.

——Dare jura maritis. *Hor. Ars Poet.* 398.

To regulate the matrimonial life.

Many are the epistles I every day receive from husbands who complain of vanity, pride, but, above all, ill-nature in their wives. I cannot tell how it is, but I think I see in all their letters that the cause of their uneasiness is in themselves; and indeed I have hardly ever observed the married condition unhappy, but for want of judgment or temper in the man. The truth is, we generally make love in a style and with sentiments very unfit for ordinary life: they are half theatrical and half romantic. By this means we raise our imaginations to what is not to be expected in human life; and, because we did not beforehand think of the creature we are enamoured of, as subject to dishonour, age, sickness, impatience, or sullenness, but altogether considered her as the object of joy; human nature itself is often imputed to her as her particular imperfection, or defect.

I take it to be a rule, proper to be observed in all occurrences of life, but more especially in the domestic, or matrimonial part of it, to preserve always a disposition to be pleased. This cannot be supported but by considering things in their right light, and as Nature has formed them, and not as our own fancies or appetites would have them. He then who took a young lady to his bed, with no other consideration than the expectation of scenes of dalliance, and thought of her (as I said before) only as she was to administer to the gratification of desire; as that desire flags, will, without her fault, think her charms and her merit abated: from hence must follow indifference, dislike, peevishness, and rage. But the man who brings his reason to support his passion, and beholds what he loves as liable to all the calamities of human life, both in body and mind, and even at the best what must bring upon him new cares, and new relations; such a lover, I say, will form himself accordingly, and adapt his mind to the nature of his circumstances. This latter person will be prepared to be a father, a friend, an advocate, a steward for people yet unborn, and has proper affections ready for every incident in the marriage state. Such a man can hear the cries of children with pity instead of anger; and, when they run over his head, he is not disturbed at their noise, but is glad of their mirth and health. Tom Trusty has told me, that he thinks it doubles his attention to the most intricate affair he is about, to hear his children, for whom all his cares are applied, make a noise in the next room: on the other side, Will Sparkish cannot put on his periwig, or adjust his cravat at the glass, for the noise of those damned nurses and squalling brats; and then ends with a gallant reflection upon the comforts of matrimony, runs out of the hearing, and drives to the chocolate-house.

According as the husband is disposed in himself, every circumstance of his life is to give him torment or pleasure. When the affection is well placed, and supported by the considerations of duty, honour, and friendship, which are in the highest degree engaged in this alliance, there can nothing rise in the common course of life, or from the blows or favours of fortune, in which a man will not find matters of some delight unknown to a single condition.

He who sincerely loves his wife and family, and studies to improve that affection in himself, conceives pleasure from the most indifferent things; while the married man, who has not bid adieu to the fashions and false gallantries of the town, is perplexed with every thing around him. In both these cases men cannot, indeed, make a sillier figure than in repeating such pleasures and pains to the rest of the world; but I speak of them only as they sit upon those who are involved in them. As I visit all sorts of people, I cannot indeed but smile, when the good lady tells her husband what extraordinary things the child spoke since he went out. No longer than yesterday I was prevailed with to go home with a fond husband: and his wife told him, that his son, of his own head, when the clock in the parlour struck two, said papa would come home to dinner presently. While the father has him in a rapture in his arms, and is drowning him with kisses, the wife tells me he is but just four years old. Then they both struggle for him, and bring him up to me, and repeat his observation of two o'clock. I was called upon, by looks upon the child, and then at me, to say something; and I told the father that this remark of the infant of his coming home, and joining the time with it, was a certain indication that he would be a great historian and chronologer. They are neither of them fools, yet received my compliment with great acknowledgment of my prescience. I fared very well at dinner, and heard many other notable sayings of their heir, which would have given very little entertainment to one less turned to reflection than I was: but it was a pleasing speculation to remark on the happiness of a life, in which things of no moment give occasion of hope, self-satisfaction, and triumph. On the other hand, I have known an ill-natured coxcomb, who has hardly improved in any thing but bulk, for want of this disposition, silence the whole family as a set of silly women and children, for recounting things which were really above his own capacity.

When I say all this, I cannot deny but there are perverse jades that fall to men's lots, with whom it requires more than common proficiency in philosophy to be able to live. When these are joined to men of warm spirits, without temper or learning, they are frequently corrected with stripes; but one of our famous lawyers* is of opinion, 'that this ought to be used sparingly;' as I remember, those are his very words: but as it is proper to draw some spiritual use out of all afflictions, I should rather recommend to those who are visited with women of spirit, to form themselves for the world by patience at home. Socrates, who is by all accounts the undoubted head of the sect of the hen-pecked, owned and acknowledged that he owed great part of his virtue to the exercise which his useful wife constantly gave it. There are several good instructions may be drawn from his wise answers to the people of less fortitude than himself on her subject. A friend, with indignation, asked how so good a man could live with so violent a creature? He observed to him, that they who learn to keep a good seat on horse-back, mount the least manageable they can get; and, when they have mastered them, they are sure never to be discomposed on the backs of steeds less restive. At several times, to different persons, on the same subject he has said, 'My dear friend, you are beholden to Xantippe, that I bear so well your flying out in a dispute.' To another, 'My hen clacks very much, but she brings me chickens. They that live in a trading street are not disturbed at the passage of carts.' I would have, if possible, a wise man be contented with his lot, even with a shrew; for, though he cannot make her better, he may, you see, make himself better by her means.

But, instead of pursuing my design of displaying conjugal love in its natural beauties and attractions, I am got into tales to the disadvantage of that state of life. I must say, therefore, that I am verily persuaded, that whatever is delightful in human life is to be enjoyed in greater perfection in the married than in the single condition. He that has this passion in perfection, in occasions of joy, can say to himself, besides his own satisfaction, 'How happy will this make my wife and children!' Upon occurrences of distress or danger, can comfort himself: 'But all this while my wife and children are safe.' There is something in it that doubles satisfactions, because others participate them; and dispels afflictions, because others are exempt from them. All who are married without this relish of their circumstances, are in either a tasteless indolence and negligence, which is hardly to be attained, or else live in the hourly repetition of sharp answers, eager upbraidings, and distracting reproaches. In a word, the married state, with and without the affection suitable to it, is the completest image of heaven and hell we are capable of receiving in this life. T.

* Bracton.

No. 480.] *Wednesday, September 10, 1712.*

Responsare cupidinibus, contemnere honores,
Fortis, et in seipso totus teres, atque rotundus.
Hor. Sat. vii. Lib. 2. 85.

He, sir, is proof to grandeur, pride, or pelf,
And, greater still, he's master of himself:
Not to and fro by fears and factions hurl'd,
But loose to all the interests of the world;
And while the world turns round, entire and whole,
He keeps the sacred tenor of his soul.—*Pitt.*

The other day, looking over those old manuscripts of which I have formerly given some account, and which relate to the character of the mighty Pharamond of France, and the close friendship between him and his friend Eucrate, I found among the letters which had been in the custody of the latter, an epistle from a country gentleman to Pharamond, wherein he excuses himself from coming to court. The gentleman, it seems, was contented with his condition, had formerly been in the king's service; but at the writing the following letter, had, from leisure and reflection, quite another sense of things than that which he had in the more active part of his life.

'*Monsieur Chezluy to Pharamond.*

'Dread sir,—I have from your own hand (enclosed under the cover of Mr.

Eucrate, of your majesty's bed-chamber) a letter which invites me to court. I understand this great honour to be done me out of respect and inclination to me, rather than regard to our own service; for which reason I beg leave to lay before your majesty my reasons for declining to depart from home; and will not doubt but, as your motive in desiring my attendance was to make me a happier man, when you think that will not be effected by my remove, you will permit me to stay where I am. Those who have an ambition to appear in courts, have either an opinion that their persons or their talents are particularly formed for the service or ornament of that place! or else are hurried by downright desire of gain, or what they call honour, to take upon themselves whatever the generosity of their master can give them opportunities to grasp at. But your goodness shall not be thus imposed upon by me: I will therefore confess to you, that frequent solitude, and long conversation with such who know no arts which polish life, have made me the plainest creature in your dominions. Those less capacities of moving with a good grace, bearing a ready affability to all around me, and acting with ease before many, have quite left me. I am come to that, with regard to my person, that I consider it only as a machine I am obliged to take care of, in order to enjoy my soul in its faculties with alacrity; well remembering that this habitation of clay will in a few years be a meaner piece of earth than any utensil about my house. When this is, as it really is, the most frequent reflection I have, you will easily imagine how well I should become a drawing-room: add to this, what shall a man without desires do about the generous Pharamond? Monsieur Eucrate has hinted to me, that you have thoughts of distinguishing me with titles. As for myself, in the temper of my present mind, appellations of honour would but embarrass discourse, and new behaviour towards me perplex me in every habitude of life. I am also to acknowledge to you, that my children of whom your majesty condescended to inquire, are all of them mean, both in their persons and genius. The estate my eldest son is heir to, is more than he can enjoy with a good grace. My self-love will not carry me so far as to impose upon mankind the advancement of persons (merely for their being related to me) into high distinctions, who ought for their own sakes, as well as that of the public, to affect obscurity. I wish, my generous prince, as it is in your power to give honours and offices, it were also to give talents suitable to them: were it so, the noble Pharamond would reward the zeal of my youth with abilities to do him service in my age.

'Those who accept of favour without merit, support themselves in it at the expense of your majesty. Give me leave to tell you, sir, this is the reason that we in the country hear so often repeated the word prerogative. That part of your law which is reserved in yourself, for the readier service and good of the public, slight men are eternally buzzing in our ears, to cover their own follies and miscarriages. It would be an addition to the high favour you have done me, if you would let Eucrate send me word how often, and in what cases, you allow a constable to insist upon the prerogative. From the highest to the lowest officer in your dominions, something of their own carriage they would exempt from examination, under the shelter of the word prerogative. I would fain, most noble Pharamond, see one of your officers assert your prerogative by good and gracious actions. When is it used to help the afflicted, to rescue the innocent, to comfort the stranger? Uncommon methods, apparently undertaken to attain worthy ends, would never make power invidious. You see, sir, I talk to you with the freedom your noble nature approves in all whom you admit to your conversation.

'But, to return to your majesty's letter, I humbly conceive that all distinctions are useful to men, only as they are to act in public; and it would be a romantic madness for a man to be lord in his closet. Nothing can be honourable to a man apart from the world, but reflection upon worthy actions; and he that places honour in a consciousness of well doing will have but little relish for any outward homage that is paid him, since what gives him distinction to himself, cannot come within the observation of his beholders. Thus all the words of lordship, honour, and grace, are only repetitions to a man that the king has ordered him to be called so; but no evidences that there is any thing in himself, that would give the man, who applies to him, those ideas, without the creation of his master.

'I have, most noble Pharamond, all honours and all titles in your approbation: I triumph in them as they are in your gift, I refuse them as they are to give me the observation of others. Indulge me, my noble master, in this chastity of renown; let me know myself in the favour of Pharamond; and look down upon the applause of the people. I am, in all duty and loyalty, your majesty's most obedient subject and servant,

JEAN CHEZLUY.'

'Sir,—I need not tell with what disadvantages men of low fortunes and great modesty come into the world; what wrong measures their diffidence of themselves, and fear of offending, often oblige them to take; and what a pity it is that their greatest virtues and qualities, that should soonest recommend them, are the main obstacles in the way of their preferment.

'This, sir, is my case; I was bred at a country-school, where I learned Latin and Greek. The misfortunes of my family forced me up to town, where a profession of the politer sort has protected me against infamy and want. I am now clerk to a lawyer, and, in times of vacancy and recess from business, have made myself master of Italian and French; and though the progress I have made in my business has gained me reputation enough for one of my standing, yet my mind suggests to me every day, that it is not upon that foundation I am to build my fortune.

'The person I have my present dependence upon has in his nature, as well as in his power, to advance me, by recommending me to a gentleman that is going beyond sea, in a public employment. I know the printing this letter would point me out to those I want confidence to speak to, and I hope it is not in your power to refuse making any body happy. Yours, &c.

'September 9, 1712. M. D.'

T.

No. 481.] *Thursday, September* 11, 1712.

——————Uti non
Compositus melius cum Bitho Bacchius: in jus
Acres procurrunt——————
Hor. Sat. vii. Lib. 1. 19.

Who shall decide when doctors disagree,
And soundest casuists doubt like you and me?
Pope.

It is sometimes pleasant enough to consider the different notions which different persons have of the same thing. If men of low condition very often set a value on things which are not prized by those who are in a higher station of life, there are many things these esteem which are in no value among persons of an inferior rank. Common people are, in particular, very much astonished when they hear of those solemn contests and debates, which are made among the great upon the punctilios of a public ceremony; and wonder to hear that any business of consequence should be retarded by those little circumstances, which they represent to themselves as trifling and insignificant. I am mightily pleased with a porter's decision in one of Mr. Southern's plays, which is founded upon that fine distress of a virtuous woman's marrying a second husband, while her first was yet living. The first husband, who was supposed to have been dead, returning to his house, after a long absence, raises a noble perplexity for the tragic part of the play. In the meanwhile the nurse and the porter conferring upon the difficulties that would ensue in such a case, honest Samson thinks the matter may be easily decided, and solves it very judiciously by the old proverb, that if his first master be still living, 'the man must have his mare again.' There is nothing in my time which has so much surprised and confounded the greatest part of my honest countrymen, as the present controversy between Count Rechteren and Monsieur Mesnager, which employs the wise heads of so many nations, and holds all the affairs of Europe in suspense.

Upon my going into a coffee-house yesterday, and lending an ear to the next table, which was encompassed with a circle of inferior politicians, one of them, after having read over the news very attentively, broke out into the following remarks: 'I am afraid,' says he, 'this unhappy rupture between the footmen at Utrecht will retard the peace of Christendom. I wish the pope may not be at the bottom of it. His holiness has a very good hand in fomenting a division, as the poor Swiss cantons have lately experienced to their cost. If Monsieur What-d'ye-call-him's domestics will not come to an accommodation, I do not know how the quarrel can be ended but by a religious war.'

'Why, truly,' says a wiseacre that sat by him, 'were I as the king of France, I would scorn to take part with the footmen of either side; here's all the business of Europe stands still, because Monsieur Mesnager's man has had his head broke. If Count Rectrum* had given them a pot of ale after it, all would have been well, without any of this bustle; but they say he's a warm man, and does not care to be made mouths at.'

Upon this, one that had held his tongue hitherto began to exert himself; declaring, that he was very well pleased the plenipotentiaries of our Christian princes took this matter into their serious consideration; for that lackeys were never so saucy and pragmatical as they are now-a-days, and that he should be glad to see them taken down in the treaty of peace, if it might be done without prejudice to the public affairs.

One who sat at the other end of the table, and seemed to be in the interests of the French king, told them, that they did not take the matter right, for that his most Christian majesty did not resent this matter because it was an injury done to Monsieur Mesnager's footmen; 'for,' says he, 'what are Monsieur Mesnager's footmen to him? but because it was done to his subjects. Now,' says he, 'let me tell you, it would look very odd for a subject of France to have a bloody nose, and his sovereign not to take notice of it. He is obliged in honour to defend his people against hostilities; and if the Dutch will be so insolent to a crowned head, as in any wise to cuff or kick those who are under his protection, I think he is in the right to call them to an account for it.'

This distinction set the controversy upon a new foot, and seemed to be very well approved by most that heard it, until a little warm fellow, who had declared himself a friend to the house of Austria, fell most unmercifully upon his Gallic majesty,

* Count Rechteren.

as encouraging his subjects to make mouths at their betters, and afterwards screening them from the punishment that was due to their insolence. To which he added, that the French nation was so addicted to grimace, that, if there was not a stop put to it at the general congress, there would be no walking the streets for them in a time of peace, especially if they continued masters of the West Indies. The little man proceeded with a great deal of warmth, declaring that, if the allies were of his mind, he would oblige the French king to burn his galleys, and tolerate the protestant religion in his dominions, before he would sheath his sword. He concluded with calling Monsieur Mesnager an insignificant prig.

The dispute was now growing very warm, and one does not know where it would have ended, had not a young man of about one-and-twenty, who seems to have been brought up with an eye to the law, taken the debate into his hand, and given it as his opinion, that neither Count Rechteren nor Monsieur Mesnager had behaved themselves right in this affair. 'Count Rechteren,' says he, 'should have made affidavit that his servant had been affronted, and then Monsieur Mesnager would have done him justice, by taking away their liveries from them, or some other way that he might have thought the most proper; for, let me tell you, if a man makes a mouth at me, I am not to knock the teeth out of it for his pains. Then again, as for Monsieur Mesnager, upon his servant's being beaten, why he might have had his action of assault and battery. But as the case now stands, if you will have my opinion, I think they ought to bring it to referees.'

I heard a great deal more of this conference, but I must confess with little edification, for all I could learn at last from these honest gentlemen was, that the matter in debate was of too high a nature for such heads as theirs, or mine, to comprehend.

O.

No. 482.] *Friday, September* 12, 1712.

Floriferis ut apes in saltibus omnia libant.
Lucr. Lib. iii. 11.

As from the sweetest flowers the lab'ring bee
Extracts her precious sweets.—*Creech.*

When I have published any single paper that falls in with the popular taste, and pleases more than ordinary, it always brings me in a great return of letters. My Tuesday's discourse, wherein I gave several admonitions to the fraternity of the hen-pecked, has already produced me very many correspondents; the reason I cannot guess, unless it be, that such a discourse is of general use, and every married man's money. An honest tradesman, who dates his letter from Cheapside, sends me thanks in the name of a club, who, he tells me, meet as often as their wives will give them leave, and stay together till they are sent for home. He informs me that my paper has administered great consolation to their whole club, and desires me to give some farther account of Socrates, and to acquaint them in whose reign he lived, whether he was a citizen or a courtier, whether he buried Xantippe, with many other particulars: for that by his sayings, he appears to have been a very wise man, and a good Christian. Another who writes himself Benjamin Bamboo, tells me that, being coupled with a shrew, he had endeavoured to tame her by such lawful means as those which I mentioned in my last Tuesday's paper, and that in his wrath he had often gone farther than Bracton always allows in those cases: but that for the future he was resolved to bear it like a man of temper and learning, and consider her only as one who lives in his house to teach him philosophy. Tom Dapperwit says that he agrees with me in that whole discourse, excepting only the last sentence, where I affirm the married state to be either a heaven or a hell. Tom has been at the charge of a penny upon this occasion to tell me, that by his experience it is neither one nor the other, but rather that middle kind of state, commonly known by the name of purgatory.

The fair-sex have likewise obliged me with their reflections upon the same discourse. A lady, who calls herself Euterpe, and seems a woman of letters, asks me whether I am for establishing the Salic law in every family, and why it is not fit that a woman who has discretion and learning should sit at the helm, when the husband is weak and illiterate? Another, of a quite contrary character, subscribes herself Xantippe, and tells me that she follows the example of her namesake; for being married to a bookish man, who has no knowledge of the world, she is forced to take their affairs into her own hands, and to spirit him up now and then, that he may not grow musty, and unfit for conversation.

After this abridgment of some letters which are come to my hands upon this occasion, I shall publish one of them at large.

'Mr. Spectator,—You have given us a lively picture of that kind of husband who comes under the denomination of the hen-pecked; but I do not remember that you have ever touched upon one that is quite of the different character, and who, in several places of England, goes by the name of 'a cot-queen.' I have the misfortune to be joined for life with one of this character, who in reality is more a woman than I am. He was bred up under the tuition of a tender mother, till she had made him as good a housewife as herself. He could preserve apricots, and make jellies, before he had been two years out of the nursery. He was never suffered to go abroad, for fear of catching cold; when he should have been hunting down a buck, he was by his mother's side learning how to season it, or put it in crust; and making paper boats with his sisters, at an age when other young gentlemen are crossing the seas, or travelling into foreign countries. He has the whitest hand you ever saw in your life, and raises paste better than any woman in England. These qualifications make him a sad husband. He is perpetually in the kitchen, and has a thousand squabbles with the cook-maid. He is better acquainted with the milk-score than his steward's accounts. I fret to death when I hear him find fault with a dish that is not dressed to his liking, and instructing his friends that dine with him in the best pickle for a walnut, or sauce for a haunch of venison. With all this he is a very good-natured husband, and never fell out with me in his life but once, upon the over-roasting of a dish of wild fowl. At the same time I must own, I would rather he was a man of a rough temper, and would treat me harshly sometimes, than of such an effeminate busy nature, in a province that does not belong to him. Since you have given us the character of a wife who wears the breeches, pray say somewhat of a husband that wears the petticoat. Why should not a female character be as ridiculous in a man, as a male character in one of our sex? I am, &c. O.

No. 483.] *Saturday, September* 13, 1712.

Nec deus intersit, nisi dignus vindice nodus
Inciderit—— *Hor. Ars Poet.* ver. 191.

Never presume to make a god appear,
But for a business worthy of a god.—Roscommon.

We cannot be guilty of a greater act of uncharitableness than to interpret the afflictions which befall our neighbours as punishments and judgments. It aggravates the evil to him who suffers, when he looks upon himself as the mark of divine vengeance, and abates the compassion of those towards him who regard him in so dreadful a light. This humour, of turning every misfortune into a judgment, proceeds from wrong notions of religion, which in its own nature produces good-will towards men, and puts the mildest construction upon every accident that befalls them. In this case, therefore, it is not religion that sours a man's temper, but it is his temper that sours his religion. People of gloomy, uncheerful imaginations, or of envious malignant tempers, whatever kind of life they are engaged in, will discover their natural tincture of mind in all their thoughts, words, and actions. As the finest vines have often the taste of the soil, so even the most religious thoughts often draw something that is particular from the constitution of the mind in which they arise. When folly or superstition strike in with this natural depravity of temper it is not in the power, even of religion itself, to preserve the character of the person who is possessed with it from appearing highly absurd and ridiculous.

An old maiden gentlewoman, whom I shall conceal under the name of Nemesis, is the greatest discoverer of judgments that I have met with. She can tell you what sin it was that set such a man's house on fire, or blew down his barns. Talk to her of an unfortunate young lady that lost her beauty by the small-pox, she fetches a deep sigh, and tells you, that when she had a fine face she was always looking on it in her glass. Tell her of a piece of good fortune that has befallen one of her acquaintance, and she wishes it may prosper with her, but her mother used one of her nieces very barbarously. Her usual remarks turn upon people who had great estates, but never enjoyed them by reason of some flaw in their own or their father's behaviour. She can give you the reason why such a one died childless; why such a one was cut off in the flower of his youth; why such a one was unhappy in her marriage; why one broke his leg on such a particular spot of ground; and why another was killed with a back-sword, rather than with any other kind of weapon. She has a crime for every misfortune that can befall any of her acquaintance; and when she hears of a robbery that has been made, or a murder that has been committed, enlarges more on the guilt of the suffering person, than on that of the thief, or assassin. In short, she is so good a Christian, that whatever happens to herself is a trial, and whatever happens to her neighbours is a judgment.

The very description of this folly, in ordinary life, is sufficient to expose it: but, when it appears in a pomp and dignity of style, it is very apt to amuse and terrify the mind of the reader. Herodotus and Plutarch very often apply their judgments as impertinently as the old woman I have before mentioned, though their manner of relating them makes the folly itself appear venerable. Indeed most historians, as well Christian as pagan, have fallen into this idle superstition, and spoken of ill success, unforeseen disasters, and terrible events, as if they had been let into the secrets of Providence, and made acquainted with that private conduct by which the world is governed. One would think several of our own historians in particular had many revelations of this kind made to them. Our old English monks seldom let any of their kings depart in peace, who had endeavoured to diminish the power of wealth of which the ecclesiastics were in those times possessed. William the Conqueror's race generally found their judgments in the New Forest where their father had pulled down churches and monasteries. In short, read one of the chronicles written by an author of this frame of mind, and you would think you were reading a history of the kings of Israel and Judah, where the historians were actually inspired, and where, by a particular scheme of Providence, the kings were distinguished by judgments, or blessings, according as they promoted idolatry or the worship of the true God.

I cannot but look upon this manner of judging upon misfortunes, not only to be very uncharitable in regard to the person on whom they fall, but very presumptuous in regard to him who is supposed to inflict them. It is a strong argument for a state of retribution hereafter, that in this world virtuous persons are very often unfortunate, and vicious persons prosperous; which is wholly repugnant to the nature of a Being who appears infinitely wise and good in all his works, unless we may suppose that such a promiscuous and undistinguished distribution of good and evil, which was necessary for carrying on the designs of Providence in this life, will be rectified, and made amends for, in another. We are not therefore to expect that fire should fall from heaven in the ordinary course of Providence; nor, when we see triumphant guilt or depressed virtue in particular persons, that Omnipotence will make bare his holy arm in the defence of one, or punishment of the other. It is sufficient that there is a day set apart for the hearing and requiting of both, according to their respective merits.

The folly of ascribing temporal judgments to any particular crimes, may appear from several considerations. I shall only mention two: First, that, generally speaking, there is no calamity or affliction, which is supposed to have happened as a judgment to a vicious man, which does not sometimes happen to men of approved religion and virtue. When Diagoras the atheist was on board one of the Athenian ships, there arose a very violent tempest: upon which the mariners told him, that it was a just judgment upon them for having taken so impious a man on board. Diagoras begged them to look upon the rest of the ships that were in the same distress, and asked them whether or no Diagoras was on board every vessel in the fleet. We are all involved in the same calamities, and subject to the same accidents: and when we see any one of the species under any particular oppression, we should look upon it as arising from the common lot of human nature, rather than from the guilt of the person who suffers.

Another consideration, that may check our presumption in putting such a construction upon a misfortune, is this, that it is impossible for us to know what are calamities and what are blessings. How many accidents have passed for misfortunes, which have turned to the welfare and prosperity of the persons to whose lot they have fallen! How many disappointments have, in their consequences, saved a man from ruin! If we could look into the effects of every thing, we might be allowed to pronounce boldly upon blessings and judgments; but for a man to give his opinion of what he sees but in part, and in its beginnings, is an unjustifiable piece of rashness and folly. The story of Biton and Clitobus, which was in great reputation among the heathens, (for we see it quoted by all the ancient authors, both Greek and Latin, who have written upon the immortality of the soul,) may teach us a caution in this matter. These two brothers, being the sons of a lady who was priestess to Juno, drew their mother's chariot to temple at the time of a great solemnity, the persons being absent who, by their office, were to have drawn her chariot on that occasion. The mother was so transported with this instance of filial duty, that she petitioned her goddess to bestow upon them the greatest gift that could be given to men; upon which they were both cast into a deep sleep, and the next morning found dead in the temple. This was such an event, as would have been construed into a judgment, had it happened to the two brothers after an act of disobedience, and would doubtless have been represented as such by any ancient historian who had given us an account of it. O.

No. 484.] *Monday, September* 15, 1712.

Neque cuiquam tam statim clarum ingenium est, ut possit emergere; nisi illi materia, occasio, fautor etiam, commendatorque contingat. *Plin. Epist.*

Nor has any one so bright a genius as to become illustrious instantaneously, unless it fortunately meets with occasion and employment, with patronage too, and commendation.

'MR SPECTATOR,—OF all the young fellows who are in their progress through any profession, none seem to have so good a title to the protection of the men of eminence in it as the modest man, not so much because his modesty is a certain indication of his merit, as because it is a certain obstacle to the producing of it. Now, as of all professions, this virtue is thought to be more particularly unnecessary in that of the law than in any other, I shall only apply myself to the relief of such who follow this profession with this disadvantage. What aggravates the matter is, that those persons who, the better to prepare themselves for this study, have made some progress in others, have, by addicting themselves to letters, increased their natural modesty, and consequently heightened the obstruction to this sort of preferment; so that every one of these may emphatically be said to be such a one as "laboureth and taketh pains, and is still the more behind." It may be a matter worth discussing, then, why that which made a youth so amiable to the ancients, should make him appear so ridiculous to the moderns? and why, in our days, there should be neglect, and even oppression of young beginners, instead of that protection which was the pride of theirs? In the profession spoken of, it is obvious to every one whose attendance is required at Westminster-hall, with what difficulty a youth of any modesty has been permitted to make an observation, that could in no wise detract from the merit of his elders, and is absolutely necessary for the advancing of his own. I have often seen one of these not only molested in his utterance of something very pertinent, but even plundered of his question, and by a strong sergeant shouldered out of his rank, which he has recovered with much difficulty and confusion. Now, as great part of the business of this profession might be despatched by one that perhaps

> ———Abest virtute diserti,
> Messalæ, nec scit quantum Causellius Aulus;
> *Hor. Ars Poet.* v. 370.

> ———wants Messala's powerful eloquence,
> And is less read than deep Causellius:
> *Roscommon.*

so I cannot conceive the injustice done to the public, if the men of reputation in this calling would introduce such of the young ones into business, whose application in this study will let them into the secrets of it, as much as their modesty will hinder them from the practice: I say, it would be laying an everlasting obligation upon a young man, to be introduced at first only as a mute, till by this countenance, and a resolution to support the good opinion conceived of him in his betters, his complexion shall be so well settled, that the litigious of this island may be secure of this obstreperous aid. If I might be indulged to speak in the style of a lawyer, I would say, that any one about thirty years of age might make a common motion to the court with as much elegance and propriety as the most aged advocates in the hall.

'I cannot advance the merit of modesty by any argument of my own so powerfully as by inquiring into the sentiments the greatest among the ancients of different ages entertained upon this virtue. If we go back to the days of Solomon, we shall find favour a necessary consequence to a shame-faced man. Pliny the greatest lawyer and most elegant writer of the age he lived in, in several of his epistles is very solicitous in recommending to the public some young men, of his own profession, and very often undertakes to become an advocate, upon condition that some one of these his favourites might be joined with him, in order to produce the merit of such, whose modesty otherwise would have suppressed it. It may seem very marvellous to a saucy modern, that *multum sanguinis, multum verecundiæ, multum sollicitudinis in ore,* "to have the face first full of blood, then the countenance dashed with modesty, and then the whole aspect as of one dying with fear, when a man begins to speak," should be esteemed by Pliny the necessary qualifications of a fine speaker. Shakspeare also has expressed himself in the same favourable strain of modesty, when he says,

> ———In the modesty of fearful duty
> I read as much as from the rattling tongue
> Of saucy and audacious eloquence———

'Now, since these authors have professed themselves for the modest man, even in the utmost confusions of speech and countenance, why should an intrepid utterance and a resolute vociferation thunder so successfully in our courts of justice? And why should that confidence of speech and behaviour, which seems to acknowledge no superior, and to defy all contradiction, prevail over that deference and resignation with which the modest man implores that favourable opinion which the other seems to command?

'As the case at present stands, the best consolation that I can administer to those who cannot get into that stroke of business (as the phrase is) which they deserve, is to reckon every particular acquisition of knowledge in this study as a real increase of their fortune; and fully to believe, that one day this imaginary gain will certainly be made out by one more substantial. I wish you would talk to us a little on this head; you would oblige, sir, your humble servant.'

The author of this letter is certainly a man of good sense; but I am perhaps particular in my opinion on this occasion: for I have observed that, under the notion of modesty, men have indulged themselves in spiritless sheepishness, and been for ever lost to themselves, their families, their friends, and their country. When a man has taken care to pretend to nothing but what he may justly aim at, and can execute as well as any other, without injustice to any other, it is ever want of breeding or courage to be brow-beaten or elbowed out of his honest ambition. I have said often, modesty must be an act of the will, and yet it always implies self-denial; for, if a man has an ardent desire to do what is laudable for him to perform, and, from an unmanly bashfulness, shrinks away, and lets his merit languish in silence, he ought not to be angry at the world that a more unskilful actor succeeds in his part, because he has not confidence to come upon the stage himself. The generosity my correspondent mentions of Pliny cannot be enough applauded. To cherish the dawn of merit, and hasten its maturity, was a work worthy a noble Roman and a liberal scholar. That concern which is described in the letter, is to all the world the greatest charm imaginable; but then the modest man must proceed, and show a latent resolution in himself; for the admiration of modesty arises from the manifestation of his merit. I must confess we live in an age wherein a few empty blusterers carry away the praise of speaking, while a crowd of fellows over-stocked with knowledge are run down by them: I say, over-stocked, because they certainly are so, as to their service of mankind, if from their very store they raise to themselves ideas of respect, and greatness of the occasion, and I know not what, to disable themselves from explaining their thoughts. I must confess, when I have seen Charles Frankair rise up with a commanding mien, and torrent of handsome words, talk a mile off the purpose, and drive down twenty bashful boobies of ten times his sense, who at the same time were envying his impudence, and despising his understanding, it has been matter of great mirth to me; but it soon ended in a secret lamentation, that the fountains of every thing praiseworthy in these realms, the universities, should be so muddled with a false sense of this virtue, as to produce men capable of being so abused. I will be bold to say, that it is a ridiculous education which does not qualify a man to make his best appearance before the greatest man, and the finest woman, to whom he can address himself. Were this judiciously corrected in the nurseries of learning, pert coxcombs would know their distance: but we must bear with this false modesty in our young nobility and gentry, till they cease at Oxford and Cambridge to grow dumb in the study of eloquence. T.

No. 485.] *Tuesday, September* 16, 1712.

Nihil tam firmum est, cui periculum non sit, etiam ab invalido. *Quint. Curt.* l. vii. c. 8.

The strongest things are not so well established as to be out of danger from the weakest.

'Mr. Spectator,—My Lord Clarendon has observed, that few men have done more harm than those who have been thought to be able to do least; and there cannot be a greater error, than to believe a man, whom we see qualified with too mean parts to do good, to be therefore incapable of doing hurt. There is a supply of malice, of pride, of industry, and even of folly, in the weakest, when he sets his heart upon it, that makes a strange progress in mischief. What may seem to the reader the greatest paradox in the reflection of the historian is, I suppose, that folly which is generally thought incapable of contriving or executing any design, should be so formidable to those whom it exerts itself to molest. But this will appear very plain, if we remember that Solomon says, "It is a sport to a fool to do mischief;" and that he might the more emphatically express the calamitous circumstances of him who falls under the displeasure of this wanton person, the same author adds farther, that "A stone is heavy, and the sand weighty, but a fool's wrath is heavier than them both." It is impossible to suppress my own illustration upon this matter, which is that as the man of sagacity bestirs himself to distress his enemy by methods probable and reducible to reason, so the same reason will fortify his enemy to elude these his regular efforts; but your fool projects, acts, and concludes, with such notable inconsistency, that no regular course of thought can evade or counterplot his prodigious machinations. My frontispiece, I believe, may be extended to imply, that several of our misfortunes arise from things, as well as persons, that seem of very little consequence. Into what tragical extravagances does Shakspeare hurry Othello, upon the loss of a handkerchief only! And what barbarities does Desdemona suffer, from a slight inadvertency in regard to this fatal trifle! If the schemes of all enterprising spirits were to be carefully examined, some intervening accident, not considerable enough to occasion any debate upon, or give them any apprehension of ill consequence from it, will be found to be the occasion of their ill success, rather than any error in points of moment and difficulty, which naturally engaged their maturest deliberations. If you go to the levee of any great man, you will observe him exceeding gracious to several very insignificant fellows; and upon this maxim, that the neglect of any person must arise from the mean opinion you have of his capacity to do you any service or prejudice; and that this calling his sufficiency in question must give him inclination, and where this is there never wants strength, or opportunity to annoy you. There is nobody so weak of invention that cannot aggravate, or make some little stories to vilify his enemy; there are very few but have good inclinations to hear them; and it is infinite pleasure to the majority of mankind to level a person superior to his neighbours. Besides, in all matter of controversy, that party which has the greatest abilities labours under this prejudice, that he will certainly be supposed, upon account of his abilities, to have done an injury, when perhaps he has received one. It would be tedious to enumerate the strokes that nations and particular friends have suffered from persons very contemptible.

'I think Henry IV. of France, so formidable to his neighbours, could no more be secured against the resolute villany of Ravillac, than Villiers duke of Buckingham could be against that of Felton. And there is no incensed person so destitute, but can provide himself with a knife or a pistol, if he finds stomach to apply them. That things and persons of no moment should give such powerful revolutions to the progress of those of the greatest, seems a providential disposition to baffle and abate the pride of human sufficiency; as also to engage the humanity and benevolence of superiors to all below them, by letting them into this secret, that the stronger depends upon the weaker. I am, sir, your very humble servant.'

'Temple, Paper-buildings.

'DEAR SIR,—I received a letter from you some time ago, which I should have answered sooner, had you informed me in yours to what part of this island I might have directed my impertinence; but having been let into the knowledge of that matter, this handsome excuse is no longer serviceable. My neighbour Prettyman shall be the subject of this letter; who, falling in with the Spectator's doctrine concerning the month of May, began from that season to dedicate himself to the service of the fair, in the following manner. I observed at the beginning of the month he bought him a new night-gown, either side to be worn outwards, both equally gorgeous and attractive; but till the end of the month I did not enter so fully into the knowledge of his contrivance as the use of that garment has since suggested to me. Now you must know, that all new clothes raise and warm the wearer's imagination into a conceit of his being a much finer gentleman than he was before, banishing all sobriety and reflection, and giving him up to gallantry and amour. Inflamed, therefore, with this way of thinking, and full of the spirit of the month of May, did this merciless youth resolve upon the business of captivating. At first he confined himself to his room, only now and then appearing at his window, in his night-gown, and practising that easy posture which expresses the very top and dignity of languishment. It was pleasant to see him diversify his loveliness, sometimes obliging the passengers only with a side-face, with a book in his hand; sometimes being so generous as to expose the whole in the fulness of its beauty; at other times, by a judicious throwing back his periwig, he would throw in his ears. You know he is that sort of person which the mob call a handsome jolly man; which appearance cannot miss of captives in this part of the town. Being emboldened by daily success, he leaves his room with a resolution to extend his conquests; and I have apprehended him in his night-gown smiting in all parts of this neighbourhood.

'This I, being of an amorous complexion, saw with indignation, and had thoughts of purchasing a wig in these parts; into which, being at a greater distance from the earth, I might have thrown a very liberal mixture of white horse-hair, which would make a fairer, and consequently a handsomer, appearance, while my situation would secure me against any discoveries. But the passion of the handsome gentleman seems to be so fixed to that part of the building, that it must be extremely difficult to divert it to mine; so that I am resolved to stand boldly to the complexion of my own eyebrow, and prepare me an immense black wig of the same sort of structure with that of my rival. Now, though by this I shall not, perhaps, lessen the number of the admirers of his complexion, I shall have a fair chance to divide the passengers by the irresistible force of mine.

'I expect sudden despatches from you, with advice of the family you are in now, how to deport myself upon this so delicate a conjuncture; with some comfortable resolutions in favour of the handsome black man against the handsome fair one. I am, sir, your most humble servant.' C.

N. B. He who writ this is a black man, two pair of stairs; the gentleman of whom he writes is fair, and one pair of stairs.

'MR. SPECTATOR,—I only say, that it is impossible for me to say how much I am yours, ROBIN SHORTER.

'P. S. I shall think it is a little hard, if you do not take as much notice of this epistle as you have of the ingenious Mr. Short's. I am not afraid of letting the world see which is the deeper man of the two.'

ADVERTISEMENT.

London, September 15.

Whereas a young woman on horseback, in an equestrian habit, on the 13th instant in the evening, met the Spectator within a mile and a half of this town, and flying in the face of justice, pulled off her hat, in which there was a feather, with the mien and air of a young officer, saying at the same time, 'Your servant, Mr. Spec,' or words to that purpose: this is to give notice, that if any person can discover the name and place of abode of the said offender, so as she can be brought to justice, the informant shall have all fitting encouragement.

T.

No. 486.] *Wednesday, September* 17, 1712.

Audire est operæ pretium, procedere recte
Qui mœchis non vultis——
Hor. Sat. ii. Lib. 1. 38

IMITATED.

All you who think the city ne'er can thrive
Till ev'ry cuckold-maker's flead alive,
Attend———— *Pope.*

'MR. SPECTATOR,—There are very many of my acquaintance followers of Socrates, with more particular regard to that part of his philosophy which we among ourselves call his domestics; under which denomination, or title, we include all the conjugal joys and sufferings. We have indeed, with very great pleasure, observed the honour you do the whole fraternity of the hen-pecked in placing that illustrious man at our head, and it does in a very great measure baffle the raillery of pert rogues, who have no advantage above us, but in that they are single. But, when you look about into the crowd of mankind, you will find the fair-sex reigns with greater tyranny over lovers than husbands. You shall hardly meet one in a thousand who is wholly exempt from their dominion, and those that are so are capable of no taste of life, and breathe and walk about the earth as insignificants. But I am going to desire your farther favour of our harmless brotherhood, and hope you will show in a true light the unmarried hen-pecked, as well as you have done justice to us, who submit to the conduct of our wives. I am very particularly acquainted with one who is under entire submission to a kind girl, as he calls her; and though he knows I have been witness both to the ill usage he has received from her, and his inability to resist her tyranny, he still pretends to make a jest of me for a little more than ordinary obsequiousness to my spouse. No longer than Tuesday last he took me with him to visit his mistress; and having, it seems, been a little in disgrace before, thought by bringing me with him she would constrain herself, and insensibly fall into general discourse with him; and so he might break the ice, and save himself all the ordinary compunctions and mortifications she used to make him suffer before she would be reconciled, after any act of rebellion on his part. When we came into the room, we were received with the utmost coldness; and when he presented me as Mr. Such-a-one, his very good friend, she just had patience to suffer my salutation; but when he himself, with a very gay air, offered to follow me, she gave him a thundering box on the ear, called him a pitiful poor-spirited wretch—how durst he see her face? His wig and hat fell on different parts of the floor. She seized the wig too soon for him to recover it, and, kicking it down stairs, threw herself into an opposite room, pulling the door after her by force, that you would have thought the hinges would have given way. We went down you must think, with no very good countenances; and, as we were driving home together, he confessed to me, that her anger was thus highly raised, because he did not think fit to fight a gentleman who had said she was what she was: "but," says he, "a kind letter or two, or fifty pieces, will put her in humour again." I asked him why he did not part with her: he answered, he loved her with all the tenderness imaginable, and she had too many charms to be abandoned for a little quickness of spirit. Thus does this illegitimate hen-pecked overlook the hussy's having no regard to his very life and fame, in putting him upon an infamous dispute about her reputation: yet has he the confidence to laugh at me, because I obey my poor dear in keeping out of harm's way, and not staying too late from my own family, to pass through the hazards of a town full of ranters and debauchees. You that are a philosopher, should urge in our behalf, that, when we bear with a froward woman, our patience is preserved, in consideration that a breach with her might be a dishonour to children who are descended from us, and whose concern makes us tolerate a thousand frailties, for fear they should redound dishonour upon the innocent. This and the like circumstances, which carry with them the most valuable regards of human life, may be mentioned for our long-suffering; but in the case of gallants, they swallow ill usage from one to whom they have no obligation, but from a base passion, which it is mean to indulge, and which it would be glorious to overcome.

'These sort of fellows are very numerous, and some have been conspicuously such, without shame; nay, they have carried on the jest in the very article of death, and, to the diminution of the wealth and happiness of their families, in bar of those honourably near to them, have left immense wealth to their paramours. What is this but being a cully in the grave! Sure this is being hen-pecked with a vengeance! But, without dwelling upon these less frequent instances of eminent cullyism, what is there so common as to hear a fellow curse his fate that he cannot get rid of a passion to a jilt, and quote a half line out of a miscellany poem to prove his weakness is natural? If they will go on thus, I have nothing to say to it; but then let them not pretend to be free all this while, and laugh at us poor married patients.

'I have known one wench in this town carry a haughty dominion over her lovers so well, that she has at the same time been kept by a sea-captain in the Straits, a merchant in the city, a country gentleman in Hampshire, and had all her correspondences managed by one whom she kept for her own uses. This happy man (as the phrase is) used to write very punctually, every post, letters for the mistress to transcribe. He would sit in his night-gown and slippers, and be as grave giving an account, only changing names, that there was nothing in those idle reports they had heard of such a scoundrel as one of the other lovers was; and how could he think she could condescend so low, after such a fine gentleman as each of them? For the same epistle said the same thing to, and of, every one of them. And so Mr. Secretary and his lady went to bed with great order.

'To be short, Mr. Spectator, we husbands shall never make the figure we ought in the imaginations of young men growing up in the world, except you can bring it about that a man of the town shall be as infamous a character as a woman of the town. But, of all that I have met with in my time, commend me to Betty Duall: she is the wife of a sailor, and the kept mistress of a man of quality; she dwells with the latter during the seafaring of the former. The husband asks no questions, sees his apartments furnished with riches not his, when he comes into port, and the lover is as joyful as a man arrived at his haven, when the other puts to sea. Betty is the most eminently victorious of any of her sex, and ought to stand recorded the only woman of the age in which she lives, who has possessed at the same time two abused, and two contented—' T.

No. 487.] *Thursday, September* 18, 1712.

——Cum prostrata sopore
Urget membra quies, et mens sine pondere ludit.
Petr.

While sleep oppresses the tir'd limbs, the mind
Plays without weight, and wantons unconfin'd.

Though there are many authors who have written on dreams, they have generally considered them only as revelations of what has already happened in distant parts of the world, or as presages of what is to happen in future periods of time.

I shall consider this subject in another light, as dreams may give us some idea of the great excellency of a human soul, and some intimations of its independency on matter.

In the first place, our dreams are great instances of that activity which is natural to the human soul, and which is not in the power of sleep to deaden or abate. When the man appears to be tired and worn out with the labours of the day, this active part in his composition is still busied and unwearied. When the organs of sense want their due repose and necessary reparations, and the body is no longer able to keep pace with that spiritual substance to which it is united, the soul exerts herself in her several faculties, and continues in action until her partner is again qualified to bear her company. In this case dreams look like the relaxations and amusements of the soul, when she is disencumbered of her machine, her sports, and recreations, when she has laid her charge asleep.

In the second place, dreams are an instance of that agility and perfection which is natural to the faculties of the mind, when they are disengaged from the body. The soul is clogged and retarded in her operations, when she acts in conjunction with a companion that is so heavy and unwieldy in its motion. But in dreams it is wonderful to observe with what a sprightliness and alacrity she exerts herself. The slow of speech make unpremeditated harangues, or converse readily in languages that they are but little acquainted with. The grave abound in pleasantries, the dull in repartees and points of wit. There is not a more painful action of the mind than invention; yet in dreams it works with that ease and activity that we are not sensible of, when the faculty is employed. For instance, I believe every one some time or other, dreams that he is reading papers, books, or letters; in which case the invention prompts so readily, that the mind is imposed upon, and mistakes its own suggestions for the compositions of another.

I shall, under this head, quote a passage out of the Religio Medici,* in which the ingenious author gives an account of himself in his dreaming and his waking thoughts. 'We are somewhat more than ourselves in our sleeps, and the slumber of the body seems to be but the waking of the soul. It is the ligation of sense, but the liberty of reason; and our waking conceptions do not match the fancies of our sleeps. At my nativity my ascendant was the watery sign of Scorpius: I was born in the planetary hour of Saturn, and I think I have a piece of that leaden planet in me. I am no way facetious, nor disposed for the mirth and galliardise of company; yet in one dream I can compose a whole comedy, behold the action, apprehend the jests, and laugh myself awake at the conceits thereof. Were my memory as faithful as my reason is then fruitful, I would never study but in my dreams; and this time also would I choose for my devotions; but our grosser memories have then so little hold of our abstracted understandings, that they forget the story, and can only relate to our awaked souls a confused and broken tale of that that has passed. Thus it is observed that men sometimes, upon the hour of their departure, do speak and reason above themselves; for then the soul, beginning to be freed from the ligaments of the body, begins to reason like herself, and to discourse in a strain above mortality.'

We may likewise observe, in the third place, that the passions affect the mind with greater strength when we are asleep than when we are awake. Joy and sorrow give us more vigorous sensations of pain or pleasure at this time than any other. Devotion likewise, as the excellent author above mentioned has hinted, is in a very particular manner heightened and inflamed, when it rises in the soul at a time that the body is thus laid at rest. Every man's experience will inform him in this matter, though it is very probable that this may happen differently in different constitutions. I shall conclude this head with the two following problems, which I shall leave to the solution of my reader. Supposing a man always happy in his dreams, and miserable in his waking thoughts, and that his life was equally divided between them; whether would he be more happy or miserable? Were a man a king in his dreams, and a beggar awake, and dreamt as consequentially, and in as continued unbroken schemes, as he thinks when awake; whether would he be in reality a king or a beggar; or, rather, whether he would not be both?

There is another circumstance, which methinks gives us a very high idea of the nature of the soul, in regard to what passes in dreams. I mean that innumerable multitude and variety of ideas which then arise in her. Were that active and watchful being only conscious of her own existence at such a time, what a painful solitude would our hours of sleep be! Were the soul

* By Sir T. Brown, M. D. author of the curious book on "Vulgar Errors," which appeared in folio, in 1646.

sensible of her being alone in her sleeping moments, after the same manner that she is sensible of it while awake, the time would hang very heavy on her, as it often actually does when she dreams that she is in such a solitude.

> ——————Semperque relinqui
> Sola sibi, semper longam incomitata videtur
> Ire viam——————
>
> *Virg*. En. iv. 466.
>
> ——————She seems alone
> To wander in her sleep through ways unknown,
> Guideless and dark.—*Dryden*.

But this observation I only make by the way. What I would here remark, is that wonderful power in the soul, of producing her own company on these occasions. She converses with numberless beings of her own creation, and is transported into ten thousand scenes of her own raising. She is herself the theatre, the actor, and the beholder. This puts me in mind of a saying which I am infinitely pleased with, and which Plutarch ascribes to Heraclitus, that all men whilst they are awake are in one common world; but that each of them, when he is asleep, is in a world of his own. The waking man is conversant in the world of nature: when he sleeps he retires to a private world that is particular to himself. There seems something in this consideration that intimates to us natural grandeur and perfection in the soul, which is rather to be admired than explained.

I must not omit that argument for the excellency of the soul which I have seen quoted out of Tertullian, namely, its power of divining in dreams. That several such divinations have been made, none can question, who believes the holy writings, or who has but the least degree of a common historical faith; there being innumerable instances of this nature in several authors both ancient and modern, sacred and profane. Whether such dark presages, such visions of the night, proceed from any latent power in the soul, during this her state of abstraction, or from any communication with the Supreme Being, or from any operation of subordinate spirits, has been a great dispute among the learned; the matter of fact is, I think, incontestible, and has been looked upon as such by the greatest writers, who have been never suspected either of superstition or enthusiasm.

I do not suppose that the soul in these instances is entirely loose and unfettered from the body; it is sufficient if she is not so far sunk and immersed in matter, nor entangled and perplexed in her operations with such motions of blood and spirits, as when she actuates the machine in its waking hours. The corporeal union is slackened enough to give the mind more play. The soul seems gathered within herself, and recovers that spring which is broke and weakened, when she operates more in concert with the body.

The speculations I have here made, if they are not arguments, they are at least strong intimations, not only of the excellency of the human soul, but of its independence on the body; and, if they do not prove, do at least confirm these two great points, which are established by many other reasons that are altogether unanswerable. O.

No. 488.] *Friday, September* 19, 1712.

> Quanti emptæ? parvo. Quanti ergo? octo assibus.
> Eheu! *Hor*. Sat. iii. Lib. 2. 156.
>
> What doth it cost? Not much upon my word,
> How much pray? Why, Two pence. Two pence! O
> Lord!—*Creech*.

I FIND, by several letters which I receive daily, that many of my readers would be better pleased to pay three half-pence for my paper than two pence. The ingenious T. W. tells me that I have deprived him of the best part of his breakfast; for that, since the rise of my paper, he is forced every morning to drink his dish of coffee by itself, without the addition of the Spectator, that used to be better than lace to it. Eugenius informs me, very obligingly, that he never thought he should have disliked any passage in my paper, but that of late there have been two words in every one of them which he could heartily wish left out, *viz.* 'Price Two Pence.' I have a letter from a soap-boiler, who condoles with me very affectionately upon the necessity we both lie under of setting a high price on our commodities since the late tax has been laid upon them, and desiring me, when I write next on that subject, to speak a word or two upon the present duties on Castile soap. But there is none of these my correspondents, who writes with a greater turn of good sense, and elegance of expression, than the generous Philomedes, who advises me to value every Spectator at sixpence, and promises that he himself will engage for above a hundred of his acquaintance, who shall take it in at that price.

Letters from the female world are likewise come to me, in great quantities, upon the same occasion; and, as I naturally bear a great deference to this part of our species, I am very glad to find that those who approve my conduct in this particular are much more numerous than those who condemn it. A large family of daughters have drawn me up a very handsome remonstrance, in which they set forth that their father having refused to take in the Spectator, since the additional price was set upon it, they offered him unanimously to bate him the article of bread and butter in the tea-table account, provided the Spectator might be served up to them every morning as usual. Upon this the old gentleman, being pleased, it seems, with their desire of improving themselves, has granted them the continuance both of the Spectator and their bread and butter, having given particular orders that the tea-table shall be set forth every morning with its customary bill of fare, and without any manner of defalcation. I thought myself obliged to mention this particular, as it does honour to this worthy gentleman; and if the young lady Lætitia, who sent me this account, will acquaint me with his name, I will insert it at length in one of my papers, if he desires it.

I should be very glad to find out any expedient that might alleviate the expense which this my paper brings to any of my readers; and in order to it, must propose two points to their consideration. First, that if they retrench any of the smallest particular in their ordinary expense, it will easily make up the half-penny a day which we have now under consideration. Let a lady sacrifice but a single riband to her morning studies, and it will be sufficient: let a family burn but a candle a night less than their usual number, and they may take in the Spectator without detriment to their private affairs.

In the next place, if my readers will not go to the price of buying my papers by retail, let them have patience, and they may buy them in the lump without the burden of a tax upon them. My speculations, when they are sold single, like cherries upon the stick, are delights for the rich and wealthy: after some time they come to market in greater quantities, and are every ordinary man's money. The truth of it is, they have a certain flavour at their first appearance, from several accidental circumstances of time, place, and person, which they may lose if they are not taken early; but, in this case, every reader is to consider, whether it is not better for him to be half a year behind-hand with the fashionable and polite part of the world, than to strain himself beyond his circumstances. My bookseller has now about ten thousand of the third and fourth volumes, which he is ready to publish, having already disposed of as large an edition both of the first and second volumes. As he is a person whose head is very well turned to his business, he thinks they would be a very proper present to be made to persons at christenings, marriages, visiting days, and the like joyful solemnities, as several other books are frequently given at funerals. He has printed them in such a little portable volume, that many of them may be ranged together upon a single plate; and is of opinion, that a salver of Spectators would be as acceptable an entertainment to the ladies as a salver of sweet-meats.

I shall conclude this paper with an epigram lately sent to the writer of the Spectator, after having returned my thanks to the ingenious author of it.

'SIR,—Having heard the following epigram very much commended, I wonder that it has not yet had a place in any of your papers; I think the suffrage of our poet laureat should not be over-looked, which shows the opinion he entertains of your paper, whether the notion he proceeds upon be true or false. I make bold to convey it to you, not knowing if it has yet come to your hands.'

ON THE SPECTATOR

BY MR. TATE.

———Aliusque et idem
Nasceris——— *Hor.* Carm. Sæc. 10.

You rise another and the same.

When first the Tatler to a mute was turn'd,
Great Britain for her censor's silence mourn'd;
Robb'd of his sprightly beams, she wept the night,
Till the Spectator rose and blaz'd as bright.
So the first man the sun's first setting view'd,
And sigh'd till circling day his joys renew'd.
Yet, doubtful how that second sun to name,
Whether a bright successor, or the same.
So we; but now from this suspense are freed,
Since all agree, who both with judgment read,
'Tis the same sun, and does himself succeed. O.

No. 489.] *Saturday, September 20, 1712.*

Βαθυρρειταο μεγα σθενος Ὠκεανοιο. *Homer.*

The mighty force of ocean's troubled flood.

'SIR,—Upon reading your essay concerning the Pleasures of the Imagination, I find among the three sources of those pleasures which you have discovered, that greatness is one. This has suggested to me the reason why, of all objects that I have ever seen, there is none which affects my imagination so much as the sea, or ocean. I cannot see the heavings of this prodigious bulk of waters, even in a calm, without a very pleasing astonishment; but when it is worked up in a tempest, so that the horizon on every side is nothing but foaming billows and floating mountains, it is impossible to describe the agreeable horror that rises from such a prospect. A troubled ocean, to a man who sails upon it, is, I think, the biggest object that he can see in motion, and consequently gives his imagination one of the highest kinds of pleasure that can arise from greatness. I must confess it is impossible for me to survey this world of fluid matter without thinking on the hand that first poured it out, and made a proper channel for its reception. Such an object naturally raises in my thoughts the idea of an Almighty Being, and convinces me of his existence as much as a metaphysical demonstration. The imagination prompts the understanding, and, by the greatness of the sensible object, produces in it the idea of a being who is neither circumscribed by time nor space.

'As I have made several voyages upon the sea, I have often been tossed in storms and on that occasion have frequently reflected on the descriptions of them in ancient poets. I remember Longinus highly recommends one in Homer, because the poet has not amused himself with little fancies upon the occasion, as authors of an inferior genius, whom he mentions, had done, but because he has gathered together those circumstances which are the most apt to terrify the imagination, and which really happen in the raging of a tempest. It is for the same reason that I prefer the following description of a ship in a storm, which the psalmist has made, before any other I have ever met with. "They that go down to the sea in ships, that do business in great waters; these see the works of the Lord, and his wonders in the deep. For he commandeth and raiseth the stormy wind, which lifteth up the waters thereof. They mount up to the heaven, they go down again to the depths, their soul is melted because of trouble. They reel to and fro, and stagger like a drunken man, and are at their wit's end. Then they cry unto the Lord in their trouble, and he bringeth them out of their distresses. He maketh the storm a calm, so that the waves thereof are still. Then they are glad, because they be quiet, so he bringeth them unto their desired haven."*

'By the way; how much more comfortable, as well as rational, is this system of the psalmist, than the pagan scheme in Virgil and other poets, where one deity is represented as raising a storm, and another as laying it! Were we only to consider the sublime in this piece of poetry, what can be nobler than the idea it gives us of the Supreme Being thus raising a tumult among the elements, and recovering them out of their confusion; thus troubling and becalming nature?

'Great painters do not only give us landscapes of gardens, groves, and meadows, but very often employ their pencils upon sea-pieces. I could wish you would follow their example. If this small sketch may deserve a place among your works, I shall accompany it with a divine ode made by a gentleman upon the conclusion of his travels.

I.

" How are thy servants blest, O Lord!
How sure is their defence!
Eternal wisdom is their guide,
Their help Omnipotence.

II.

" In foreign realms and lands remote,
Supported by thy care,
Through burning climes I pass'd unhurt,
And breath'd in tainted air.

III.

" Thy mercy sweeten'd every soil,
Made ev'ry region please:
The hoary Alpine hills it warm'd,
And smooth'd the Tyrrhene seas.

IV.

" Think, O my soul, devoutly think,
How, with affrighted eyes,
Thou saw'st the wide extended deep
In all its horrors rise!

V.

"Confusion dwelt in ev'ry face,
And fear in ev'ry heart;
When waves on waves, and gulfs in gulfs
O'ercame the pilot's art.

VI.

'Yet then from all my griefs, O Lord,
Thy mercy set me free,
Whilst, in the confidence of prayer
My soul took hold on thee.

VII.

For though in dreadful whirls we hung
High on the broken wave,
I knew thou wert not slow to hear,
Nor impotent to save.

VIII.

" The storm was laid, the winds retir'd,
Obedient to thy will;
The sea that roar'd at thy command,
At thy command was still.

IX.

" In midst of dangers, fears, and death,
Thy goodness I'll adore,
And praise thee for thy mercies past,
And humbly hope for more.

X.

" My life, if thou preserv'st my life,
Thy sacrifice shall be;
And death, if death must be my doom,
Shall join my soul to thee."

* Ps. cvii 23, *et seq.*

No. 490.] *Monday, September* 22, 1712.

Domus et placens uxor.—*Hor.* Od. xiv. Lib. 2. 21.

Thy house and pleasing wife.—*Creech.*

I HAVE very long entertained an ambition to make the word wife the most agreeable and delightful name in nature. If it be not so in itself all the wiser part of mankind, from the beginning of the world to this day, has consented in an error. But our unhappiness in England has been, that a few loose men of genius for pleasure, have turned it all to the gratification of ungoverned desires, in despite of good sense, form, and order; when in truth, any satisfaction beyond the boundaries of reason is but a step towards madness and folly. But is the sense of joy and accomplishment of desire no way to be indulged or attained? And have we appetites given us not to be at all gratified? Yes, certainly. Marriage is an institution calculated for a constant scene of delight, as much as our being is capable of. Two persons, who have chosen each other out of all the species, with design to be each other's mutual comfort and entertainment, have in that action bound themselves to be good-humoured, affable, discreet, forgiving, patient, and joyful, with respect to each other's frailties and perfections, to the end of their lives. The wiser of the two (and it always happens one of them is such) will, for her or his own sake, keep things from outrage with the utmost sanctity. When this union is thus preserved, (as I have often said) the most indifferent circumstance administers delight: their condition is an endless source of new gratifications. The married man can say, 'If I am unacceptable to all the world beside, there is one whom I entirely love, that will receive me with joy and transport, and think herself obliged to double her kindness and caresses of me from the gloom with which she sees me overcast. I need not dissemble the sorrow of my heart to be agreeable there; that very sorrow quickens her affection.'

This passion towards each other, when once well fixed, enters into the very constitution, and the kindness flows as easily and silently as the blood in the veins. When this affection is enjoyed in the sublime degree, unskilful eyes see nothing of it; but when it is subject to be changed, and has an allay in it that may make it end in distaste, it is apt to break into rage, or overflow into fondness, before the rest of the world.

Uxander and Viramira are amorous and young, have been married these two years; yet do they so much distinguish each other in company, that in your conversation with the dear things, you are still put to a sort of cross-purposes. Whenever you address yourself in ordinary discourse to Viramira, she turns her head another way, and the answer is made to the dear Uxander. If you tell a merry tale, the application is still directed to her dear; and when she should commend you, she says to him, as if he had spoke it, 'That is, my dear, so pretty.'—This puts me in mind of what I have somewhere read in the admired memoirs of the famous Cervantes; where, while honest Sancho Panca is putting some necessary humble question concerning Rozinante, his supper, or his lodging, the knight of the sorrowful countenance is ever improving the harmless lowly hints of his 'squire to the poetical conceit, rapture, and flight, in contemplation of the dear dulcinea of his affections.

On the other side, Dictamnus and Moria are ever squabbling; and you may observe them, all the time they are in company, in a state of impatience. As Uxander and Viramira wish you all gone, that they may be at freedom for dalliance; Dictamnus and Moria wait your absence, that they may speak their harsh interpretations on each other's words and actions, during the time you were with them.

It is certain that the greater part of the evils, attending this condition of life, arises from fashion. Prejudice in this case is turned the wrong way; and, instead of expecting more happiness than we shall meet with in it, we are laughed into a prepossession, that we shall be disappointed if we hope for lasting satisfactions.

With all persons who have made good sense the rule of action, marriage is described as the state capable of the highest human felicity. Tully has epistles full of affectionate pleasure, when he writes to his wife, or speaks of his children. But, above all the hints of this kind I have met with in writers of ancient date, I am pleased with an epigram of Martial, in honour of the beauty of his wife Cleopatra. Commentators say it was written the day after his wedding-night. When his spouse was retired to the bathing-room in the heat of the day, he, it seems, came in upon her when she was just going into the water. To her beauty and carriage on this occasion we owe the following epigram, which I showed my friend Will Honeycomb in French, who has translated it as follows, without understanding the original. I expect it will please the English better than the Latin reader.

'When my bright consort, now nor wife nor maid,
Asham'd and wanton, of embrace afraid,
Fled to the streams, the streams my fair betray'd;
To my fond eyes she all transparent stood;
She blush'd; I smil'd at the slight covering flood.
Thus through the glass the lovely lily glows;
Thus through the ambient gem shines forth the rose.
I saw new charms, and plung'd to seize my store,
Kisses I snatch'd—the waves prevented more.'

My friend would not allow that this luscious account could be given of a wife, and therefore used the word consort; which, he learnedly said, would serve for a mistress as well, and give a more gentlemanly turn to the epigram. But, under favour of him and all other such fine gentlemen, I cannot be persuaded but that the passion a bridegroom has for a virtuous young woman will, by little and little, grow into friendship, and then it has ascended to a higher pleasure than it was in its first fervour. Without this happens, he is a very unfortunate man who has entered into this state, and left the habitudes of life he might have enjoyed with a faithful friend. But when the wife proves capable of filling serious as well as joyous hours, she brings happiness unknown to friendship itself. Spenser speaks of each kind of love with great justice, and attributes the highest praise to friendship; and indeed there is no disputing that point, but by making that friendship take its place between two married persons.

'Hard is the doubt, and difficult to deem,
When all three kinds of love together meet,
And do dispart the heart with power extreme,
Whether shall weigh the balance down; to wit,
The dear affection unto kindred sweet,
Or raging fire of love to womankind,
Or zeal of friends combin'd by virtues meet;
But, of them all, the band of virtues mind
Methinks the gentle heart should most assured bind.

'For natural affection soon doth cease,
And quenched is with Cupid's greater flame:
But faithful friendship doth them both suppress,
And them with mastering discipline doth tame,
Through thoughts aspiring to eternal fame.
For as the soul doth rule the earthly mass,
And all the service of the body frame;
So love of soul doth love of body pass,
No less than perfect gold surmounts the meanest brass.

T.

No. 491.] *Tuesday, September* 23, 1712.

——Digna satis fortuna revisit.

Virg. Æn. iii. 318.

A just reverse of fortune on him waits.

It is common with me to run from book to book to exercise my mind with many objects, and qualify myself for my daily labours. After an hour spent in this loitering way of reading, something will remain to be food to the imagination. The writings that please me most on such occasions are stories, for the truth of which there is good authority. The mind of man is naturally a lover of justice. And when we read a story wherein a criminal is overtaken, in whom there is no quality which is the object of pity, the soul enjoys a certain revenge for the offence done to its nature, in the wicked actions committed in the preceding part of the history. This will be better understood by the reader from the following narration itself, than from any thing which I can say to introduce it.

When Charles duke of Burgundy, surnamed The Bold, reigned over spacious dominions now swallowed up by the power of France, he heaped many favours and honours upon Claudius Rhynsault, a German, who had served him in his wars against the insults of his neighbours. A great part of Zealand was at that time in subjection to that dukedom. The prince himself was a person of singular humanity and justice. Rhynsault, with no other real quality than courage, had dissimulation enough to pass upon his generous and unsuspicious master for a person of blunt honesty and fidelity, without any vice that could bias him from the execution of justice. His highness, prepossessed to his advantage, upon the decease of the governor of his chief town of Zealand, gave Rhynsault that command. He was not long seated in that government before he cast his eyes upon Sapphira, a woman of exquisite beauty, the wife of Paul Danvelt, a wealthy merchant of the city under his protection and government. Rhynsault was a man of a warm constitution, and violent inclination to women, and not unskilled in the soft arts which win their favour. He knew what it was to enjoy the satisfactions which are reaped from the possession of beauty, but was an utter stranger to the decencies, honours, and delicacies, that attend the passion towards them in elegant minds. However, he had so much of the world, that he had a great share of the language which usually prevails upon the weaker part of that sex; and he could with his tongue utter a passion with which his heart was wholly untouched. He was one of those brutal minds which can be gratified with the violation of innocence and beauty, without the least pity, passion, or love, to that with which they are so much delighted. Ingratitude is a vice inseparable to a lustful man; and the possession of a woman by him, who has no thought but allaying a passion painful to himself, is necessarily followed by distaste and aversion. Rhynsault, being resolved to accomplish his will on the wife of Danvelt, left no arts untried to get into a familiarity at her house; but she knew his character and disposition too well, not to shun all occasions that might ensnare her into his conversation. The governor, despairing of success by ordinary means, apprehended and imprisoned her husband, under pretence of an information, that he was guilty of a correspondence with the enemies of the duke to betray the town into their possession. This design had its desired effect; and the wife of the unfortunate Danvelt, the day before that which was appointed for his execution, presented herself in the hall of the governor's house; and, as he passed through the apartment, threw herself at his feet, and, holding his knees, beseeched his mercy. Rhynsault beheld her with a dissembled satisfaction; and, assuming an air of thought and authority, he bid her arise, and told her she must follow him to his closet; and, asking her whether she knew the hand of the letter he pulled out of his pocket, went from her, leaving this admonition aloud: 'If you will save your husband, you must give me an account of all you know without prevarication: for every body is satisfied he was too fond of you to be able to hide from you the names of the rest of the conspirators, or any other particulars whatsoever.' He went to his closet, and soon after the lady was sent for to an audience. The servant knew his distance when matters of state were to be debated; and the governor, laying aside the air with which he had appeared in public, began to be the supplicant, to rally an affliction, which it was in her power easily to remove, and relieve an innocent man from his imprisonment. She easily perceived his intention; and bathed in tears, began to deprecate so wicked a design. Lust, like ambition, takes all the faculties of the mind and body into its service and subjection. Her becoming tears, her honest anguish, the wringing of her hands, and the many changes of her posture and figure in the vehemence of speaking, were but so many attitudes in which he beheld her beauty, and farther incentives of his desires. All humanity was lost in that one appetite, and he signified to her in so many plain terms, that he was unhappy till he had possessed her, and nothing less should be the price of her husband's life, and she must, before the following noon, pronounce the death, or enlargement, of Danvelt. After this notification, when he saw Sapphira enough again distracted, to make the subject of their discourse to common eyes appear different from what it was, he called servants to conduct her to the gate. Loaded with insupportable affliction, she immediately repairs to her husband; and, having signified to his gaolers that she had a proposal to make to her husband from the governor, she was left alone with him, revealed to him all that had passed, and represented the endless conflict she was in between love to his person, and fidelity to his bed. It is easy to imagine the sharp affliction this honest pair was in upon such an incident, in lives not used to any but ordinary occurrences. The man was bridled by shame from speaking what his fear prompted, upon so near an approach of death; but let fall words that signified to her, he should not think her polluted, though she had not yet confessed to him that the governor had violated her person, since he knew her will had no part in the action. She parted from him with this oblique permission to save a life he had not resolution enough to resign for the safety of his honour.

The next morning the unhappy Sapphira attended the governor, and being led into a remote apartment, submitted to his desires. Rhynsault commended her charms, claimed a familiarity after what had passed between them, and with an air of gayety, in the language of a gallant, bid her return, and take her husband out of prison: 'but,' continued he, 'my fair one must not be offended that I have taken care he should not be an interruption to our future assignations.' These last words foreboded what she found when she came to the gaol—her husband executed by the order of Rhynsault!

It was remarkable that the woman, who was full of tears and lamentations during the whole course of her afflictions, uttered neither sigh nor complaint, but stood fixed with grief at this consummation of her misfortunes. She betook herself to her abode; and, after having in solitude paid her devotions to him who is the avenger of innocence, she repaired privately to court. Her person, and a certain grandeur of sorrow, negligent of forms, gained her passage into the presence of the duke her sovereign. As soon as she came into the presence, she broke forth into the following words: 'Behold, O mighty Charles, a wretch weary of life, though it has always been spent with innocence and virtue. It is not in your power to redress my injuries, but it is to avenge them. And if the protection of the distressed, and the punishment of oppressors, is a task worthy of a prince, I bring the duke of Burgundy ample matter for doing honour to his own great name, and wiping infamy off from mine.'

When she had spoke this, she delivered the duke a paper reciting her story. He read it with all the emotions that indignation and pity could raise in a prince jealous of his honour in the behaviour of his officers, and prosperity of his subjects.

Upon an appointed day, Rhynsault was sent for to court, and, in the presence of a few of the council, confronted by Sapphira. The prince asking, 'Do you know that lady?' Rhynsault, as soon as he could recover his surprise, told the duke he would marry her, if his highness would please to think that a reparation. The duke seemed contented with this answer, and stood by during the immediate solemnization of the ceremony. At the conclusion of it he told Rhynsault, 'Thus far you have done as constrained by my authority: I shall not be satisfied of your kind usage to her, without you sign a gift of your whole estate to her after your decease.' To the performance of this also the duke was a witness. When these two acts were executed, the duke turned to the lady, and told her, 'It now remains for me to put you in quiet possession of what your husband has so bountifully bestowed on you;' and ordered the immediate execution of Rhynsault. T

No. 492.] *Wednesday, September* 24, 1712.

Quicquid est boni moris levitate extinguitur. *Seneca*

Levity of behaviour is the bane of all that is good and virtuous.

'Tunbridge, Sept. 18.

'DEAR MR. SPECTATOR,—I am a young woman of eighteen years of age, and I do assure you a maid of unspotted reputation, founded upon a very careful carriage in all my looks, words, and actions. At the same time I must own to you, that it is with much constraint to flesh and blood that my behaviour is so strictly irreproachable; for I am naturally addicted to mirth, to gayety, to a free air, to motion, and gadding. Now, what gives me a great deal of anxiety, and is some discouragement in the pursuit of virtue, is, that the young women who run into greater freedoms with the men are more taken notice of than I am. The men are such unthinking sots, that they do not prefer her who restrains all her passions and affections, and keeps much within the bounds of what is lawful, to her who goes to the utmost verge of innocence and parleys at the very brink of vice, whether she shall be a wife or a mistress. But I must appeal to your spectatorial wisdom, who, I find, have passed very much of your time in the study of woman, whether this is not a most unreasonable proceeding. I have read somewhere that Hobbes of Malmesbury asserts that continent persons have more of what they contain than those who give a loose to their desires. According to this rule, let there be equal age, equal wit, and equal good-humour, in the woman of prudence, and her of liberty; what stores has he to expect who takes the former? What refuse must he be contented with who chooses the latter? Well, but I sat down to write to you to vent my indignation against several pert creatures who are addressed to and courted in this place, while poor I, and two or three like me, are wholly unregarded.

'Every one of these affect gaining the hearts of your sex. This is generally attempted by a particular manner of carrying themselves with familiarity. Glycera has a dancing walk, and keeps time in her ordinary gait. Chloe, her sister, who is unwilling to interrupt her conquests, comes into the room before her with a familiar run. Dulcissa takes advantage of the approach of the winter, and has introduced a very pretty shiver; closing up her shoulders, and shrinking as she moves. All that are in this mode carry their fans between both hands before them. Dulcissa herself, who is author of this air, adds the pretty run to it: and has also, when she is in very good humour, a taking familiarity in throwing herself into the lowest seat in the room, and etting her hooped petticoats fall with a lucky decency about her. I know she practises this way of sitting down in her chamber; and indeed she does it as well as you may have seen an actress fall down dead in a tragedy. Not the least indecency in her posture. If you have observed what pretty carcasses are carried off at the end of a verse at the theatre, it will give you a notion how Dulcissa plumps into a chair. Here is a little country girl that is very cunning, that makes her use of being young and unbred, and outdoes the ensnarers, who are almost twice her age. The air that she takes is to come into company after a walk, and is very successfully out of breath upon occasion. Her mother is in the secret, and calls her romp, and then looks round to see what young men stare at her.

'It would take up more than can come into one of your papers, to enumerate all the particular airs of the younger company in this place. But I cannot omit Dulceorella, whose manner is the most indolent imaginable, but still as watchful of conquest as the busiest virgin among us. She has a peculiar art of staring at a young fellow, till she sees she has got him, and inflamed him by so much observation. When she sees she has him, and he begins to toss his head upon it, she is immediately short-sighted, and labours to observe what he is at a distance, with her eyes half shut. Thus the captive that thought her first struck, is to make very near approaches, or be wholly disregarded. This artifice has done more execution than all the ogling of the rest of the women here, with the utmost variety of half glances, attentive heedlessnesses, childish inadvertencies, haughty contempts, or artificial oversights. After I have said thus much of ladies among us who fight thus regularly, I am to complain to you of a set of familiar romps, who have broken through all common rules, and have thought of a very effectual way of showing more charms than all of us. These, Mr. Spectator, are the swingers. You are to know these careless pretty creatures are very innocents again; and it is to be no matter what they do for it is all harmless freedom. They get on ropes, as you must have seen the children, and are swung by their men visitants. The jest is, that Mr. Such-a-one can name the colour of Mrs. Such-a-one's stockings; and she tells him he is a lying thief, so he is, and full of roguery; and she will lay a wager, and her sister shall tell the truth if he says right, and he cannot tell what colour her garters are of. In this diversion there are very many pretty shrieks, not so much for fear of falling, as that their petticoats should untie; for there is a great care had to avoid improprieties; and the lover who swings the lady is to tie her clothes very close together with his hatband, before she admits him to throw up her heels.

'Now, Mr. Spectator, except you can note these wantonnesses in their beginnings, and bring us sober girls into observation, there is no help for it; we must swim with the tide; the coquettes are too powerful a party for us. To look into the merit of a regular and well behaved woman is a slow thing. A loose trivial song gains the affections, when a wise homily is not attended to. There is no other way but to make war upon them, or we must go over to them. As for my part, I will show all the world it is not for want of charms that I stand so long unasked; and if you do not take measures for the immediate redress of us rigids, as the fellows call us, I can move with a speaking mien, can look significantly, can lisp, can trip, can loll, can start, can blush, can rage, can weep, if I must do it, and can be frighted as agreeably as any she in England. All which is humbly submitted to your spectatorial consideration, with all humility, by your most humble servant,

T. 'MATILDA MOHAIR.'

No. 493.] *Thursday, September 25, 1712.*

Qualem commendes etiam atque etiam adspice, ne mox
Incutiant aliena tibi peccata pudorem.

Hor. Lib. 1. Ep. xviii. 76.

Commend not, till a man is thoroughly known:
A rascal prais'd, you make his faults your own.

Anon

It is no unpleasant matter of speculation to consider the recommendatory epistles that pass round this town from hand to hand, and the abuse people put upon one another in that kind. It is indeed come to that pass, that, instead of being the testimony of merit in the person recommended, the true reading of a letter of this sort is, 'The bearer hereof is so uneasy to me, that it will be an act of charity in you to take him off my hands; whether you prefer him or not, it is all one; for I have no manner of kindness for him, or obligation to him or his; and do what you please as to that.' As negligent as men are in this respect, a point of honour is concerned in it; and there is nothing a man should be more ashamed of, than passing a worthless creature into the service or interests of a man who has never injured you. The women indeed are a little too keen in their resentments to trespass often this way: but you shall sometimes know, that the mistress and the maid shall quarrel, and give each other very free language, and at last the lady shall be pacified to turn her out of doors, and give her a very good word to any body else. Hence it is that you see, in a year and a half's time, the same face a domestic in all parts of the town. Good-breeding and good-nature lead people in a great measure to this injustice: when suitors of no consideration will have confidence enough to press upon their superiors those in power are tender of speaking the exceptions they have against them, and are mortgaged into promises out of their impatience of importunity. In this latter case, it would be a very useful inquiry to know the history of recommendations. There are, you must know, certain abettors of this way of torment, who make it a profession to manage the affairs of candidates. These gentlemen let out their impudence to their clients, and supply any defective recommendation, by informing how such and such a man is to be attacked. They will tell you, get the least scrap from Mr. Such-a-one, and leave the rest to them. When one of these undertakers has your business in hand, you may be sick, absent in town or country, and the patron shall be worried, or you prevail. I remember to have been shown a gentleman some years ago, who punished a whole people for their facility in giving their credentials. This person had belonged to a regiment which did duty in the West Indies, and, by the mortality of the place, happened to be commanding officer in the colony. He oppressed his subjects with great frankness, till he became sensible that he was heartily hated by every man under his command. When he had carried his point to be thus detestable, in a pretended fit of dishumour, and feigned uneasiness of living where he found he was so universally unacceptable, he communicated to the chief inhabitants a design he had to return for England, provided they would give him ample testimonials of their approbation. The planters came into it to a man, and in proportion to his deserving the quite contrary, the words justice, generosity, and courage, were inserted in his commission, not omitting the general good liking of people of all conditions in the colony. The gentleman returns for England, and within a few months after came back to them their governor, on the strength of their own testimonials.

Such a rebuke as this cannot indeed happen to easy recommenders, in the ordinary course of things from one hand to another; but how would a man bear to have it said to him, 'The person I took into confidence on the credit you gave him, has proved false, unjust, and has not answered any way the character you gave me of him?'

I cannot but conceive very good hopes of that rake Jack Toper of the Temple, for an honest scrupulousness in this point. A friend of his meeting with a servant that had formerly lived with Jack, and having a mind to take him, sent to him to know what faults the fellow had, since he could not please such a careless fellow as he was. His answer was as follows:

'SIR,—Thomas, that lived with me, was turned away because he was too good for me. You know I live in taverns: he is an orderly sober rascal, and thinks much to sleep in an entry until two in the morning. He told me one day, when he was dressing me, that he wondered I was not dead before now, since I went to dinner in the evening, and went to supper at two in the morning. We were coming down Essex-street one night a little flustered, and I was giving him the word to alarm the watch; he had the impudence to tell me it was against the law. You that are married, and live one day after another the same way, and so on the whole week, I dare say will like him, and he will be glad to have his meat in due season. The fellow is certainly very honest. My service to your lady. Yours, J. T.'

Now this was very fair dealing. Jack knew very well, that though the love of order made a man very awkward in his equipage, it was a valuable quality among the queer people who live by rule; and had too much good-sense and good-nature to let the fellow starve, because he was not fit to attend his vivacities.

I shall end this discourse with a letter of recommendation from Horace to Claudius Nero. You will see in that letter a slowness to ask a favour, a strong reason for being unable to deny his good word any longer, and that it is a service to the person to whom he recommends, to comply with what is asked: all which are necessary circumstances, both in justice and good-breeding, if a man would ask so as to have reason to complain of a denial; and indeed a man should not in strictness ask otherwise. In hopes the authority of Horace, who perfectly understood how to live with great men, may have a good effect towards amending this facility in people of condition, and the confidence of those who apply to them without merit, I have translated the epistle.

'To Claudius Nero.

'SIR,—Septimus, who waits upon you with this, is very well acquainted with the place you are pleased to allow me in your friendship. For when he beseeches me to recommend him to your notice in such a manner as to be received by you, who are delicate in the choice of your friends and domestics, he knows our intimacy, and understands my ability to serve him better than I do myself. I have defended myself against his ambition to be yours, as long as I possibly could; but fearing the imputation of hiding my power in you out of mean and selfish considerations, I am at last prevailed upon to give you this trouble. Thus, to avoid the appearance of a greater fault, I have put on this confidence. If you can forgive this transgression of modesty in behalf of a friend, receive this gentleman into your interests and friendship, and take it from me that he is an honest and a brave man.' T.

No. 494.] *Friday, September* 26, 1712.

Ægritudinem laudare, unan rem maxime detestabilem, quorum est tandem philosophorum? *Cicero.*

What kind of philosophy is it to extol melancholy, the most detestable thing in nature?

ABOUT an age ago it was the fashion in England for every one that would be thought religious to throw as much sanctity as possible into his face, and in particular to abstain from all appearances of mirth and pleasantry, which were looked upon as the marks of a carnal mind. The saint was of a sorrowful countenance, and generally eaten up with spleen and melancholy. A gentleman, who was lately a great ornament* to the learned world, has diverted me more than once with an account of the reception which he met with from a very famous independent minister, who was head of a college† in those times. This gentleman was then a young adventurer in the republic of letters, and just fitted out for the university with a good cargo of Latin and Greek. His friends were resolved that he should try his fortune at an election which was drawing near in the college, of which the independent minister whom I have before mentioned was governor. The youth, according to custom, waited on him in order to be examined. He was received at the door by a servant who was one of that gloomy generation that were then in fashion. He conducted him with great silence and seriousness, to a long gallery, which was darkened at noon-day, and had only a single candle burning in it. After a short stay in this melancholy apartment, he was led into a chamber hung with black, where he entertained himself for some time by the glimmering of a taper, until at length the head of the college came out to him from an inner room, with half a dozen night-caps upon his head, and religious horror in his countenance. The young man trembled: but his fears increased, when instead of being asked what progress he had made in learning, he was examined how he abounded in grace. His Latin and Greek stood him in little stead; he was to give an account only of the state of his soul; whether he was of the number of the elect; what was the occasion of the conversion, upon what day of the month, and hour of the day it happened; how it was carried on, and when completed. The whole examination was summed up with one short question, namely, whether he was prepared for death? The boy, who had been bred up by honest parents, was frighted out of his wits at the solemnity of the proceeding, and by the last dreadful interrogatory; so that, upon making his escape out of this house of mourning, he could never be brought a second time, to the examination, as not being able to go through the terrors of it.

Notwithstanding this general form and outside of religion is pretty well worn out among us, there are many persons who, by a natural uncheerfulness of heart, mistaken notions of piety, or weakness of understanding, love to indulge this uncomfortable way of life, and give up themselves a prey to grief and melancholy. Superstitious fears and groundless scruples cut them off from the pleasures of conversation, and all those social entertainments, which are not only innocent, but laudable: as if mirth was made for reprobates, and cheerfulness of heart denied those who are the only persons that have a proper title to it.

Sombrius is one of these sons of sorrow. He thinks himself obliged in duty to be sad and disconsolate. He looks on a sudden fit of laughter as a breach of his baptismal vow. An innocent jest startles him like blasphemy. Tell him of one who is advanced to a title of honour, he lifts up his hands and eyes: describe a public ceremony, he shakes his head; show him a gay equipage, he blesses himself. All the little ornaments of life are pomps and vanities. Mirth is wanton, and wit profane. He is scandalized at youth for being lively, and at childhood for being playful. He sits at a christening, or marriage-feast, as at a funeral; sighs at the convulsion of a merry story, and grows devout when the rest of the company grow pleasant. After all, Sombrius is a religious man, and would have behaved himself very properly, had he lived when christianity was under a general persecution.

I would by no means presume to tax such characters with hypocrisy, as is done too frequently; that being a vice which I think none but He who knows the secrets of men's hearts should pretend to discover in another, where the proofs of it do not amount to a demonstration. On the contrary, as there are many excellent persons who are weighed down by this habitual sorrow of heart, they rather deserve our compassion than our reproaches. I think, however, they would do well to consider whether such a behaviour does not deter men from a religious life, by representing it as an unsociable state, that extinguishes all joy and gladness, darkens the face of nature, and destroys the relish of being itself.

I have, in former papers, shown how great a tendency there is to cheerfulness in religion, and how such a frame of mind is

* The gentleman alluded to was Anthony Henley, Esq. son of Sir Robert Henley, of the Grange, in Hampshire. He was the intimate friend of the most considerable wits of the time, and is believed to have been an ample contributor to the *Tatler*. Dr. Garth entertained so high an opinion of him, that he dedicated his *Dispensary* to him " in terms which must lead the reader to form a very exalted idea of his virtues and accomplishments." Mr. Henley died in August, 1711.

† This was Dr. Thomas Goodwin, S. T. P. President of Magdalen College, Oxford, and one of the assembly of divines that sat at Westminster. Wood styles him and Dr. Owen " the two Atlasses and Patriarchs of independency." In the character prefixed to his works, he is described as a man " much addicted to retirement and deep contemplation ; that he had been much exercised in the controversies agitated in the age in which he lived, and had a deep insight into the grace of God, and the covenant of grace." He attended Cromwell, his friend and patron, upon his death-bed, and was very confident he would not die, from a supposed revelation communicated to him in prayer, but a few minutes before his death. When he found himself mistaken, in a subsequent address to God, he exclaimed, " Thou hast deceived us, and we were deceived." He died in Feb. 1679, in the eightieth year of his age.—See Granger vol. ii.

not only the most lovely, but the most commendable in a virtuous person. In short, those who represent religion in so unamiable a light, are like the spies sent by Moses to make a discovery of the Land of Promise, when by their reports they discouraged the people from entering upon it. Those who show us the joy, the cheerfulness, the good humour, that naturally spring up in this happy state, are like the spies bringing along with them the clusters of grapes, and delicious fruits, that might invite their companions into the pleasant country which produced them.

An eminent pagan writer* has made a discourse to show that the atheist, who denies a God, does him less dishonour than the man who owns his being; but at the same time believes him to be cruel, hard to please, and terrible to human nature. 'For my own part,' says he, 'I would rather it should be said of me, that there was never any such man as Plutarch, than that Plutarch was ill-natured, capricious, or inhuman.'

If we may believe our logicians, man is distinguished from all other creatures by the faculty of laughter. He has a heart capable of mirth, and naturally disposed to it. It is not the business of virtue to extirpate the affections of the mind, but to regulate them. It may moderate and restrain, but was not designed to banish gladness from the heart of man. Religion contracts the circle of our pleasures, but leaves it wide enough for her votaries to expatiate in. The contemplation of the divine Being, and the exercise of virtue, are in their own nature, so far from excluding all gladness of heart, that they are perpetually sources of it. In a word, the true spirit of religion cheers, as well as composes, the soul; it banishes indeed all levity of behaviour, all vicious and dissolute mirth; but in exchange fills the mind with a perpetual serenity, uninterrupted cheerfulness, and an habitual inclination to please others, as well as to be pleased in itself. O.

No. 495.] *Saturday, September* 27, 1712.

> Duris ut ilex tonsa bipennibus
> Nigræ feraci frondis in Algido,
> Per damna, per cædes, ab ipso
> Ducit opes animumque ferro.
> *Hor.* Od. iv. Lib. 4. 57.

> ——Like an oak on some cold mountain's brow,
> At ev'ry wound they sprout and grow:
> The axe and sword new vigour give,
> And by their ruins they revive.—*Anon.*

As I am one who, by my profession, am obliged to look into all kinds of men, there are none whom I consider with so much pleasure, as those who have any thing new or extraordinary in their characters or ways of living. For this reason I have often amused myself with speculations on the race of people called Jews, many of whom I have met with in most of the considerable towns which I have passed through in the course of my travels. They are, indeed, so disseminated through all the trading parts of the world, that they are become the instruments by which the most distant nations converse with one another, and by which mankind are knit together in a general correspondence. They are like the pegs and nails in a great building, which, though they are but little valued in themselves, are absolutely necessary to keep the whole frame together.

That I may not fall into any common beaten tracks of observation, I shall consider this people in three views: First, with regard to their number; secondly, their dispersion; and thirdly their adherence to their religion: and afterwards endeavour to show first, what natural reasons, and secondly, what providential reasons, may be assigned for these three remarkable particulars.

The Jews are looked upon by many to be as numerous at present, as they were formerly in the land of Canaan.

This is wonderful, considering the dreadful slaughter made of them under some of the Roman emperors, which historians describe by the death of many hundred thousands in a war; and the innumerable massacres and persecutions they have undergone in Turkey, as well as in all Christian nations of the world. The rabbins, to express the great havoc which has been sometimes made of them, tell us, after their usual manner of hyperbole, that there were such torrents of holy blood shed, as carried rocks of a hundred yards in circumference above three miles into the sea.

Their dispersion is the second remarkable particular in this people. They swarm over all the East, and are settled in the remotest parts of China. They are spread through most of the nations in Europe and Africa, and many families of them are established in the West Indies: not to mention whole nations bordering on Prester-John's country, and some discovered in the inner parts of America, if we may give any credit to their own writers.

Their firm adherence to their religion is no less remarkable than their numbers and dispersion, especially considering it as persecuted or contemned over the face of the whole earth. This is likewise the more remarkable, if we consider the frequent apostacies of this people, when they lived under their kings in the land of promise, and within sight of the temple.

If in the next place we examine what may be the natural reasons of these three particulars which we find in the Jews, and which are not to be found in any other religion or people, I can, in the first place, attribute their numbers to nothing but their constant employment, their abstinence, their exemption from wars, and, above all,

---

* Plut. Περὶ Δεισιδαιμονίας. Plut. Opera, tom. i. p. 286. H. Steph. 1572, 12mo.

their frequent marriages; for they look on celibacy as an accursed state, and generally are married before twenty, as hoping the Messiah may descend from them.

The dispersion of the Jews into all the nations of the earth, is the second remarkable particular of that people, though not so hard to be accounted for. They were always in rebellions and tumults while they had the temple and holy city in view, for which reason they have often been driven out of their old habitations in the land of promise. They have as often been banished out of most other places where they have settled, which must very much disperse and scatter a people, and oblige them to seek a livelihood where they can find it. Besides, the whole people is now a race of such merchants as are wanderers by profession, and, at the same time, are in most, if not all places, incapable of either lands or offices, that might engage them to make any part of the world their home.

This dispersion would probably have lost their religion, had it not been secured by the strength of its constitution: for they are to live all in a body, and generally within the same enclosure; to marry among themselves, and to eat no meats that are not killed or prepared their own way. This shuts them out from all table conversation, and the most agreeable intercourses of life; and, by consequence, excludes them from the most probable means of conversion.

If, in the last place, we consider what providential reasons may be assigned for these three particulars, we shall find that their numbers, dispersion, and adherence to their religion, have furnished every age, and every nation of the world, with the strongest arguments for the Christian faith, not only as these very particulars are foretold of them, but as they themselves are the depositaries of these, and all the other prophecies, which tend to their own confusion. Their number furnishes us with a sufficient cloud of witnesses that attest the truth of the old Bible. Their dispersion spreads these witnesses through all parts of the world. The adherence to their religion makes their testimony unquestionable. Had the whole body of the Jews been converted to Christianity, we should certainly have thought all the prophecies of the Old Testament, that relate to the coming and history of our blessed Saviour, forged by Christians, and have looked upon them with the prophecies of the Sybils, as made many years after the events they pretended to foretell. O.

No. 496.] *Monday, September* 29, 1712.

Gnatum pariter uti his decuit aut etiam amplius,
Quod illa ætas magis ad hæc utenda idonea est.
Terent. Heaut. Act. i. Sc. 1.

Your son ought to have shared in these things, because youth is best suited to the enjoyment of them.

'Mr. Spectator,—Those ancients who were the most accurate in their remarks on the genius and temper of mankind, by considering the various bent and scope of our actions throughout the progress of life, have with great exactness allotted inclinations and objects of desire particular to every stage, according to the different circumstances of our conversation and fortune, through the several periods of it. Hence they were disposed easily to excuse those excesses which might possibly arise from a too eager pursuit of the affections more immediately proper to each state. They indulged the levity of childhood with tenderness, overlooked the gayety of youth with good-nature, tempered the forward ambition and impatience of ripened manhood with discretion, and kindly imputed the tenacious avarice of old men to their want of relish for any other enjoyment. Such allowances as these were no less advantageous to common society than obliging to particular persons; for, by maintaining a decency and regularity in the course of life, they supported the dignity of human nature, which then suffers the greatest violence when the order of things is inverted; and in nothing is it more remarkably vilified and ridiculous, than when feebleness preposterously attempts to adorn itself with that outward pomp and lustre, which serve only to set off the bloom of youth with better advantage. I was insensibly carried into reflections of this nature, by just now meeting Paulino (who is in his climacteric) bedecked with the utmost splendour of dress and equipage, and giving an unbounded loose to all manner of pleasure, whilst his only son is debarred all innocent diversion, and may be seen frequently solacing himself in the Mall with no other attendance than one antiquated servant of his father's for a companion and director.

'It is a monstrous want of reflection, that a man cannot consider, that when he cannot resign the pleasures of life in his decay of appetite and inclination to them, his son must have a much uneasier task to resist the impetuosity of growing desires. The skill therefore should methinks be, to let a son want no lawful diversion, in proportion to his future fortune, and the figure he is to make in the world. The first step towards virtue that I have observed, in young men of condition that have run into excesses, has been that they had a regard to their quality and reputation in the management of their vices. Narrowness in their circumstances has made many youths, to supply themselves as debauchees, commence cheats and rascals. The father who allows his son to the utmost ability avoids this latter evil, which as to the world is much greater than the former. But the contrary practice has prevailed so much among some men, that I have known them deny them what was merely necessary for education suitable to their quality. Poor young Antonio is a lamentable instance of ill conduct in this kind. The young man did not want natural talents; but the father of him was a coxcomb, who affected being a fine gentleman so unmercifully, that he could not endure in his sight, or the frequent mention of one, who was his son, growing into manhood, and thrusting him out of the gay world. I have often thought the father took a secret pleasure in reflecting that, when that fine house and seat came into the next hands, it would revive his memory, as a person who knew how to enjoy them, from observation of the rusticity and ignorance of his successor. Certain it is, that a man may, if he will, let his heart close to the having no regard to any thing but his dear self, even with exclusion of his very children. I recommend this subject to your consideration, and am, sir, your most humble servant, T. B.'

'London, Sept. 26, 1712.

'Mr. Spectator,—I am just come from Tunbridge, and have since my return read Mrs. Matilda Mohair's letter to you. She pretends to make a mighty story about the diversions of swinging in that place. What was done was only among relations; and no man swung any woman who was not second cousin at farthest. She is pleased to say, care was taken that the gallants tied the ladies' legs before they were wafted into the air. Since she is so spiteful, I will tell you the plain truth.—There was no such nicety observed, since we were all, as I just now told you, near relations; but Mrs. Mohair herself has been swung there, and she invents all this malice, because it was observed she had crooked legs, of which I was an eye witness. Your humble servant,

'RACHEL SHOESTRING.'

'Tunbridge, Sept. 26, 1712.

'Mr. Spectator,—We have just now read your paper, containing Mrs. Mohair's letter. It is an invention of her own from one end to the other; and I desire you would print the enclosed letter by itself, and shorten it so as to come within the compass of your half sheet. She is the most malicious minx in the world, for all she looks so innocent. Do not leave out that part about her being in love with her father's butler, which makes her shun men; for that is the truest of it all. Your humble servant, SARAH TRICE.

'P. S. She has crooked legs.'

'Tunbridge, Sept. 26, 1712.

'Mr. Spectator,—All that Mrs. Mohair is so vexed at against the good company of this place is, that we all know she has crooked legs. This is certainly true. I do not care for putting my name, because one would not be in the power of the creature. Your humble servant, unknown.'

'Tunbridge, Sept. 26, 1712.

'Mr. Spectator,—That insufferable prude, Mrs. Mohair, who has told such stories of the company here, is with child, for all her nice airs and her crooked legs. Pray be sure to put her in for both those two things, and you will oblige every body here, especially, your humble servant,

'ALICE BLUEGARTER.'

No. 497.] *Tuesday, September* 30, 1712.

Ουτος εστι γωλεωτης γερων. *Menander.*

A cunning old fox this!

A favour well bestowed is almost as great an honour to him who confers it as to him who receives it. What indeed makes for the superior reputation of the patron in this case is, that he is always surrounded with specious pretences of unworthy candidates, and is often alone in the kind inclination he has towards the well deserving. Justice is the first quality in the man who is in a post of direction; and I remember to have heard an old gentleman talk of the civil wars, and in his relation give an account of a general officer, who with this one quality, without any shining endowments, became so popularly beloved and honoured, that all decisions between man and man were laid before him by the parties concerned, in a private way; and they would lay by their animosities implicitly, if he bid them be friends, or submit themselves in the wrong without reluctance, if he said it, without waiting the judgment of courts-martial. His manner was to keep the dates of all commissions in his closet, and wholly dismiss from the service such who were deficient in their duty; and after that took care to prefer according to the order of battle. His familiars were his entire friends, and could have no interested views in courting his acquaintance; for his affection was no step to their preferment, though it was to their reputation. By this means a kind aspect, a salutation, a smile, and giving out his hand, had the weight of what is esteemed by vulgar minds more substantial. His business was very short, and he who had nothing to do but justice was never affronted with a request of a familiar daily visitant for what was due to a brave man at a distance. Extraordinary merit he used to recommend to the king for some distinction at home; till the order of battle made way for his rising in the troops. Add to this, that he had an excellent way of getting rid of such who he observed were good at a halt, as his phrase was. Under this description he comprehended all those who were contented to live without reproach, and had no promptitude in their minds towards glory. These fellows were also recommended to the king, and taken off the general's hands into posts wherein diligence and common honesty were all that were necessary. This general had no weak part in his line, but every man had as much care upon him, and as much honour to lose as himself. Every officer could answer for what passed where he was; and the general's presence was never necessary any where, but where he had placed himself at the first disposition, except that accident happened from extraordinary efforts of the enemy which he could not foresee; but it was remarkable that it never fell out from failure in his own troops. It must be confessed the world is just so much out of order, as an unworthy person possesses what should be in the direction of him who has better pretensions to it.

Instead of such a conduct as this old fellow used to describe in his general, all the evils which have ever happened among mankind have arose from the wanton disposition of the favours of the powerful. It is generally all that men of modesty and virtue can do, to fall in with some whimsical turn in a great man, to make way for things of real and absolute service. In the time of Don Sebastian of Portugal, or some time since, the first minister would let nothing come near him but what bore the most profound face of wisdom and gravity. They carried it so far, that, for the greater show of their profound knowledge, a pair of spectacles tied on their noses with a black riband round their heads, was what completed the dress of those who made their court at his levee, and none with naked noses were admitted to his presence. A blunt honest fellow, who had a command in the train of artillery, had attempted to make an impression upon the porter, day after day in vain, until at length he made his appearance in a very thoughtful dark suit of clothes, and two pair of spectacles on at once. He was conducted from room to room, with great deference, to the minister; and, carrying on the farce of the place, he told his excellency that he had pretended in this manner to be wiser than he really was, but with no ill intention: but he was honest Such-a-one of the train, and he came to tell him that they wanted wheel-barrows and pick-axes. The thing happened not to displease, the great man was seen to smile, and the successful officer was re-conducted with the same profound ceremony out of the house.

When Leo X. reigned pope of Rome, his holiness, though a man of sense, and of an excellent taste of letters, of all things affected fools, buffoons, humourists, and coxcombs. Whether it were from vanity, and that he enjoyed no talents in other men but what were inferior to him, or whatever it was, he carried it so far, that his whole delight was in finding out new fools, and as our phrase is, playing them off, and making them show themselves to advantage. A priest of his former acquaintance, suffered a great many disappointments in attempting to find access to him in a regular character, until at last in despair he retired from Rome, and returned in an equipage so very fantastical, both as to the dress of himself and servants, that the whole court were in an emulation who should first introduce him to his holiness. What added to the expectation his holiness had of the pleasure he should have in his follies, was, that this fellow, in a dress the most exquisitely ridiculous, desired he might speak to him alone, for he had matters of the highest importance, upon which he wanted a conference. Nothing could be denied to a coxcomb of so great hope; but when they were apart, the impostor revealed himself, and spoke as follows:

'Do not be surprised, most holy father, at seeing, instead of a coxcomb to laugh at, your old friend, who has taken this way of access to admonish you of your own folly. Can any thing show your holiness how unworthy you treat mankind, more than my being put upon this difficulty to speak with you? It is a degree of folly to delight to see it in others, and it is the greatest insolence imaginable to rejoice in the disgrace of human nature. It is a criminal humility in a person of your holiness's understanding, to believe you cannot excel but in the conversation of half-wits, humourists, coxcombs, and buffoons. If your holiness has a mind to be diverted like a rational man, you have a great opportunity for it, in disrobing all the impertinents you have favoured, of all their riches and trappings at once, and bestowing them on the humble, the virtuous, and the meek. If your holiness is not concerned for the sake of virtue and religion, be pleased to reflect, that for the sake of your own safety it is not proper to be so very much in jest. When the pope is thus merry, the people will in time begin to think many things, which they have hitherto beheld with great veneration, are in themselves objects of scorn and derision. If they once get a trick of knowing how to laugh, your holiness's saying this sentence in one night cap, and the other with the other, the change of your slippers, bringing you your staff in the midst of a prayer, then stripping you of one vest, and clapping on a second during divine service, will be found out to have nothing in it. Consider, sir, that at this rate a head will be reckoned never the wiser for being bald, and the ignorant will be apt to say, that going bare-foot does not at all help on the way to heaven. The red cap and the cowl will fall under the same contempt; and the vulgar will tell us to our faces, that we shall have no authority over them but from the force of our arguments and the sanctity of our lives.' T.

No. 498.] *Wednesday, October* 1, 1712.

——Frustra retinacula tendens,
Fertur equis auriga, neque audit currus habenas.
Virg. Georg. i. 514

Nor reins, nor curbs, nor cries the horses fear,
But force along the trembling charioteer.—*Dryden.*

To the Spectator-General of Great Britain.

From the farther end of the Widow's Coffee-house in Devereux-court. Monday evening, twenty-eight minutes and a half past six.

'DEAR DUMB,—In short, to use no farther preface, if I should tell you that I have seen a hackney-coachman, when he has come to set down his fare, which has consisted of two or three very fine ladies, hand them out, and salute every one of them with an air of familiarity, without giving the least offence, you would perhaps think me guilty of a gasconade. But to clear myself from that imputation, and to explain this matter to you, I assure you that there are many illustrious youths within this city, who frequently recreate themselves by driving of a hackney-coach: but those whom, above all others, I would recommend to you, are the young gentlemen belonging to the inns of court. We have, I think, about a dozen coachmen, who have chambers here in the Temple; and, as it is reasonable to believe others will follow their example, we may perhaps in time (if it shall be thought convenient) be drove to Westminster by our own fraternity, allowing every fifth person to apply his meditations this way, which is but a modest computation, as the humour is now likely to take. It is to be hoped, likewise, that there are in the other nurseries of the law to be found a proportionable number of these hopeful plants, springing up to the everlasting renown of their native country. Of how long standing this humour has been, I know not. The first time I had any particular reason to take notice of it was about this time twelvemonth, when, being upon Hampstead-heath with some of these studious young men, who went thither purely for the sake of contemplation, nothing would serve them but I must go through a course of this philosophy too; and, being ever willing to embellish myself with any commendable qualification, it was not long ere they persuaded me into the coachbox; nor indeed much longer, before I underwent the fate of my brother Phaeton; for, having drove about fifty paces with pretty good success, through my own natural sagacity, together with the good instructions of my tutors, who to give them their due, were on all hands encouraging and assisting me in this laudable undertaking: I say, sir, having drove above fifty paces with pretty good success, I must needs be exercising the lash; which the horses resented so ill from my hands, that they gave a sudden start, and thereby pitched me directly upon my head, as I very well remembered about half an hour afterwards; which not only deprived me of all the knowledge I had gained for fifty yards before, but had like to have broke my neck into the bargain. After such a severe reprimand, you may imagine I was not very easily prevailed with to make a second attempt; and indeed, upon mature deliberation, the whole science seemed, at least to me, to be surrounded with so many difficulties, that, notwithstanding the unknown advantages which might have accrued to me thereby, I gave over all hopes of attaining it; and I believe had never thought of it more, but that my memory has been lately refreshed by seeing some of these ingenious gentlemen ply in the open streets, one of which I saw receive so suitable a reward to his labours, that though I know you are no friend of story-telling, yet I must beg leave to trouble you with this at large.

'About a fortnight since, as I was diverting myself with a pennyworth of walnuts at the Temple gate, a lively young fellow in a fustian jacket shot by me, beckoned a coach, and told the coachman he wanted to go as far as Chelsea. They agreed upon the price, and this young gentleman mounts the coach-box: the fellow, staring at him, desired to know if he should not drive until they were out of town. No, no, replied he. He was then going to climb up to him, but received another check, and was then ordered to get into the coach, or behind it, for that he wanted no instructors; "But be sure, you dog you," says he, "do not bilk me." The fellow thereupon surrendered his whip, scratched his head, and crept into the coach. Having myself occasion to go into the Strand about the same time, we started both together; but the street being very full of coaches, and he not so able a coachman as perhaps he imagined himself, I had soon got a little way before him; often, however, having the curiosity to cast my eye back upon him, to observe how he behaved himself in this high station; which he did with great composure, until he came to the pass, which is a military term the brothers of the whip have given to the strait at St. Clement's church. When he was arrived near this place, where are always coaches in waiting, the coachmen began to suck up the muscles of their cheeks, and to tip the wink upon each other, as if they had some roguery in their heads, which I was immediately convinced of; for he no sooner came within reach, but the first of them with his whip took the exact dimension of his shoulders, which he very ingeniously called endorsing: and indeed, I must say, that every one of them took due care to endorse him as he came through their hands. He seemed at first a little uneasy under the operation, and was going in all haste to take the numbers of their coaches; but at length, by the mediation of the worthy gentleman in the coach, his wrath was assuaged, and he prevailed upon to pursue his journey; though indeed I thought they had clapped such a spoke in his wheel, as had disabled him from being a coachman for that day at least: for I am only mistaken, Mr. Spec, if some of these endorsements were not wrote with so strong a hand that they are still legible. Upon my inquiring the reason of this unusual salutation, they told me, that it was a custom among them, whenever they saw a brother tottering or unstable in his post, to lend him a hand, in order to settle him again therein. For my part, I thought their allegations but reasonable, and so marched off. Besides our coachmen, we abound in divers other sorts of ingenious robust youth, who, I hope, will not take it ill if I defer giving you an account of their several recreations to another opportunity. In the mean time, if you would but bestow a little of your wholesome advice upon our coachmen, it might perhaps be a reprieve to some of their necks. As I understand you have several inspectors under you, if you would but send one amongst us here in the Temple, I am persuaded he would not want employment. But I leave this to your own consideration, and am, sir, your humble servant,

'MOSES GREENBAG.

'P. S. I have heard our critics in the coffee-house hereabout talk mightily of the unity of time and place. According to my notion of the matter, I have endeavoured at something like it in the beginning of my epistle. I desire to be informed a little as to that particular. In my next I design to give you some account of excellent watermen, who are bred to the law, and far outdo the land students above-mentioned.'

T.

No. 499.] *Thursday, October 2, 1712.*

——————Nimis uncis
Naribus indulges—— *Pers.* Sat. i. 40.

————You drive the jest too far.—*Dryden.*

My friend Will Honeycomb has told me, for about this half year, that he had a great mind to try his hand at a Spectator, and that he would fain have one of his writing in my works. This morning I received the following letter, which, after having rectified some little orthographical mistakes, I shall make a present of to the public.

'Dear Spec,—I was about two nights ago in company with very agreeable young people of both sexes, where, talking of some of your papers which are written on conjugal love, there arose a dispute among us, whether there were not more bad husbands in the world than bad wives. A gentleman, who was advocate for the ladies, took this occasion to tell us the story of a famous siege in Germany, which I have since found related in my historical dictionary, after the following manner. When the emperor Conrade the Third had besieged Guelphus, duke of Bavaria, in the city of Hensburg, the women, finding that the town could not possibly hold out long, petitioned the emperor that they might depart out of it, with so much as each of them could carry. The emperor, knowing they could not convey away many of their effects, granted them their petition: when the women, to his great surprise, came out of the place with every one her husband upon her back. The emperor was so moved at the sight, that he burst into tears; and, after having very much extolled the women for their conjugal affection, gave the men to their wives, and received the duke into his favour.

'The ladies did not a little triumph at this story, asking us at the same time, whether in our consciences we believed that the men in any town in Great Britain would, upon the same offer, and at the same conjuncture, have loaden themselves with their wives; or rather, whether they would not have been glad of such an opportunity to get rid of them? To this my very good friend, Tom Dapperwit, who took upon him to be the mouth of our sex, replied, that they would be very much to blame if they would not do the same good office for the women, considering that their strength would be greater, and their burdens lighter. As we were amusing ourselves with discourses of this nature, in order to pass away the evening, which now begins to grow tedious, we fell into that laudable and primitive diversion of questions and commands. I was no sooner vested with the regal authority, but I enjoined all the ladies, under pain of my displeasure, to tell the company ingeniously, in case they had been at the siege above-mentioned, and had the same offers made them as the good women of that place, what every one of them would have brought off with her, and have thought most worth the saving? There were several merry answers made to my question, which entertained us until bed-time. This filled my mind with such a huddle of ideas, that, upon my going to sleep, I fell into the following dream:

'I saw a town of this island, which shall be nameless, invested on every side, and the inhabitants of it so strained as to cry for quarter. The general refused any other terms than those granted to the above-mentioned town of Hensburg, namely, that the married women might come out with what they could bring along with them. Immediately the city gates flew open, and a female procession appeared, multitudes of the sex followed one another in a row, and staggering under their respective burdens. I took my stand upon an eminence in the enemy's camp, which was appointed for the general rendezvous of these female carriers, being very desirous to look into their several ladings. The first of them had a huge sack upon her shoulders, which she set down with great care. Upon the opening of it, when I expected to have seen her husband shot out of it, I found it was filled with china-ware. The next appeared in a more decent figure, carrying a handsome young fellow upon her back: I could not forbear commending the young woman for her conjugal affection, when, to my great surprise, I found that she had left the good man at home, and brought away her gallant. I saw the third, at some distance, with a little withered face peeping over her shoulder, whom I could not suspect for any but her spouse, until upon her setting him down I heard her call him dear pug, and found him to be her favourite monkey. A fourth brought a huge bale of cards along with her, and the fifth a Bologna lap-dog; for her husband, it seems, being a very burly man, she thought it would be less trouble for her to bring away little Cupid. The next was the wife of a rich usurer, loaden with a bag of gold; she told us that her spouse was very old, and by the course of nature could not expect to live long; and that to show her tender regards for him, she had saved that which the poor man loved better than his life. The next came towards us with her son upon her back, who, we were told, was the greatest rake in the place, but so much the mother's darling, that she left her husband behind with a large family of hopeful sons and daughters, for the sake of this graceless youth.

'It would be endless to mention the several persons, with their several loads, that appeared to me in this strange vision. All the place about me was covered with packs of ribands, brocades, embroidery, and ten thousand other materials, sufficient to have furnished a whole street of toy-shops. One of the women, having a husband, who was none of the heaviest, was bringing him off upon her shoulders, at the same time that she carried a great bundle of Flanders lace under her arm; but finding herself so overloaden, that she could not save both of them, she dropped the good man, and brought away the bundle. In short, I found but one husband among this great mountain of baggage, who was a lively cobbler, that kicked and spurred all the while his wife was carrying him on, and, as it was said, he had scarce passed a day in his life without giving her the discipline of the strap.

'I cannot conclude my letter, dear Spec, without telling thee one very odd whim in this my dream. I saw, methought, a dozen women employed in bringing off one man; I could not guess who it should be, until upon his nearer approach I discovered thy short phiz. The women all declared that it was for the sake of thy works, and not thy person, that they brought thee off, and that it was on condition that thou shouldst continue the Spectator. If thou thinkest this dream will make a tolerable one, it is at thy service, from, dear Spec, thine, sleeping and waking,

'WILL HONEYCOMB.'

The ladies will see by this letter what I have often told them, that Will is one of those old-fashioned men of wit and pleasure of the town, that shows his parts by raillery on marriage, and one who has often tried his fortune that way without success. I cannot however dismiss this letter, without observing, that the true story on which it is built does honour to the sex, and that, in order to abuse them, the writer is obliged to have recourse to dream and fiction.

O.

No. 500.] *Friday, October* 3, 1712.

——————Huc natas adjice septem,
Et todidem juvenes; et mox generosque nurusque:
Quærite nunc, habeat quam nostra superbia causam
Ovid Met. Lib. vi. 182.

Seven are my daughters, of a form divine,
With seven fair sons, an indefective line.
Go, fools, consider this, and ask the cause
From which my pride its strong presumption draws
Croxal.

'SIR,—You, who are so well acquainted with the story of Socrates, must have read how, upon his making a discourse concerning love, he pressed his point with so much success, that all the bachelors in his audience took a resolution to marry by the first opportunity, and that all the married men immediately took horse and galloped home to their wives. I am apt to think your discourses, in which you have drawn so many agreeable pictures of marriage, have had a very good effect this way in England. We are obliged to you, at least, for having taken off that senseless ridicule, which for many years the witlings of the town have turned upon their fathers and mothers. For my own part, I was born in wedlock, and I do not care who knows it; for which reason, among many others, I should look upon myself as a most insufferable coxcomb, did I endeavour to maintain that cuckoldom was inseparable from marriage, or to make use of husband and wife as terms of reproach. Nay, sir, I will go one step farther, and declare to you, before the whole world, that I am a married man, and at the same time I have so much assurance as not to be ashamed of what I have done.

'Among the several pleasures that accompany this state of life, in which you have described in your former papers, there are two you have not taken notice of, and which are seldom cast into the account by those who write on this subject. You must have observed, in your speculations on human nature, that nothing is more gratifying to the mind of man than power or dominion; and this I think myself amply possessed of, as I am the father of a family. I am perpetually taken up in giving out orders, in prescribing duties, in hearing parties, in administering justice, and in distributing rewards and punishments. To speak in the language of the centurion, I say unto one, Go, and he goeth; and to another, Come, and he cometh; and to my servant, Do this, and he doeth it. In short, sir, I look upon my family as a patriarchal sovereignty, in which I am myself both king and priest. All great governments are nothing else but clusters of these little private royalties, and therefore I consider the masters of families as small deputy-governors, presiding over the several little parcels and divisions of their fellow-subjects. As I take great pleasure in the administration of my government in particular, so I look upon myself not only as a more useful, but as a much greater and happier man than any bachelor in England of my rank and condition.

'There is another accidental advantage in marriage, which has likewise fallen to my share; I mean the having a multitude of children. These I cannot but regard as very great blessings. When I see my little troop before me, I rejoice in the additions which I have made to my species, to my country, and to my religion, in having produced such a number of reasonable creatures, citizens, and Christians. I am pleased to see myself thus perpetuated; and as there is no production comparable to that of a human creature, I am more proud of having been the occasion of ten such glorious productions, than if I had built a hundred pyramids at my own expense, or published as many volumes of the finest wit and learning. In what a beautiful light has the holy scripture represented Abdon, one of the judges of Israel, who had forty sons and thirty grandsons, that rode on threescore and ten ass colts, according to the magnificence of the eastern countries! How must the heart of the old man rejoice, when he saw such a beautiful procession of his own descendants, such a numerous cavalcade of his own raising! For my own part, I can sit in my own parlour with great content when I take a review of half a dozen of my little boys mounting upon hobby horses, and of as many little girls tutoring their babies, each of them endeavouring to excel the rest, and to do something that may gain my favour and approbation. I cannot question but he who has blessed me with so many children, will assist my endeavours in providing for them. There is one thing I am able to give each of them, which is a virtuous education. I think it is Sir Francis Bacon's observation, that in a numerous family of children, the eldest is often spoiled by the prospect of an estate, and the youngest by being the darling of the parents; but that some one or other in the middle, who has not perhaps been regarded, has made his way in the world, and overtopped the rest. It is my business to implant in every one of my children the same seeds of industry, and the same honest principles. By this means I think I have a fair chance, that one or other of them may grow considerable in some way or other of life, whether it be in the army, or in the fleet, in trade or any of the three learned professions; for you must know, sir, that, from long experience and observation, I am persuaded of what seems a paradox to most of those with whom I converse, namely, that a man who has many children, and gives them a good education, is more likely to raise a family, than he who has but one, notwithstanding he leaves him his whole estate. For this reason I cannot forbear amusing myself with finding out a general, an admiral, or an alderman of London, a divine, a physician, or a lawyer, among my little people who are now perhaps in petticoats; and when I see the motherly airs of my little daughters when they are playing with their puppets, I cannot but flatter myself that their husbands and children will be happy in the possession of such wives and mothers.

'If you are a father, you will not perhaps think this letter impertinent; but if you are a single man, you will not know the meaning of it, and probably throw it into the fire. Whatever you determine of it, you may assure yourself that it comes from one who is your most humble servant, and well-wisher,

PHILOGAMUS.'

O.

No. 501.] *Saturday, October* 4, 1712.

Durum: sed levius fit patientia
Quicquid corrigere est nefas.
Hor. Od. xxiv. Lib. 1. 19.

'Tis hard: but when we needs must bear,
Enduring patience makes the burden light.—*Creech*

As some of the finest compositions among the ancients are in allegory, I have endeavoured, in several of my papers, to revive that way of writing, and hope I have not been altogether unsuccessful in it; for I find there is always a great demand for those particular papers, and cannot but observe that several authors have endeavoured of late to excel in works of this nature. Among those, I do not know any one who has succeeded better than a very ingenious gentleman, to whom I am obliged for the following piece, and who was the author of the vision in the 460th paper.

How are we tortured with the absence of what we covet to possess, when it appears to be lost to us! What excursions does the soul make in imagination after it! and how does it turn into itself again, more foolishly fond and dejected at the disappointment! Our grief, instead of having recourse to reason, which might restrain it, searches to find a farther nourishment. It calls upon memory to relate the several passages and circumstances of satisfaction which we formerly enjoyed; the pleasures we purchased by those riches that are taken from us; or the power and splendour of our departed honours; or the voice, the words, the looks, the temper and affections of our friends that are deceased. It needs must happen from hence that the passion should often swell to such a size as to burst the heart which contains it, if time did not make these circumstances less strong and lively, so that reason should become a more equal match for the passion, or if another desire which becomes more present did not overpower them with a livelier representation. These are thoughts which I had when I fell into a kind of vision upon this subject, and may therefore stand for a proper introduction to a relation of it.

I found myself upon a naked shore, with company whose afflicted countenances witnessed their conditions. Before us flowed a water, deep, silent, and called the river of Tears, which, issuing from two fountains on an upper ground, encompassed an island that lay before us. The boat which plied in it was old and shattered, having been sometimes overset by the impatience and haste of single passengers to arrive at the other side. This immediately was brought to us by Misfortune who steers it, and we were all preparing to take our places, when there appeared a woman of a mild and composed behaviour, who began to deter us from it, by representing the dangers which would attend our voyage. Hereupon some who knew her for Patience, and some of those too who until then cried the loudest, were persuaded by her, and returned back. The rest of us went in, and she (whose good-nature would not suffer her to forsake persons in trouble) desired leave to accompany us, that she might at least administer some small comfort or advice while we sailed. We were no sooner embarked but the boat was pushed off, the sheet was spread; and being filled with sighs, which are the winds of that country, we made a passage to the farther bank, through several difficulties of which the most of us seemed utterly regardless.

When we landed, we perceived the island to be strangely overcast with fogs, which no brightness could pierce, so that a kind of gloomy horror sat always brooding over it. This had something in it very shocking to easy tempers, insomuch that some others, whom Patience had by this time gained over, left us here, and privily conveyed themselves round the verge of the island to find a ford by which she told them they might escape.

For my part, I still went along with those who were for piercing into the centre of the place; and joining ourselves to others whom we found upon the same journey, we marched solemnly as at a funeral, through bordering hedges of rosemary, and through a grove of yew-trees, which love to overshadow tombs and flourish in the church-yards. Here we heard on every side the wailings and complaints of several of the inhabitants, who had cast themselves disconsolately at the feet of trees; and as we chanced to approach any of these we might perceive them wringing their hands, beating their breasts, tearing their hair, or after some other manner, visibly agitated with vexation. Our sorrows were heightened by the influence of what we heard and saw, and one of our number was wrought up to such a pitch of wildness, as to talk of hanging himself upon a bough which shot temptingly across the path we travelled in; but he was restrained from it by the kind endeavours of our above-mentioned companion.

We had now gotten into the most dusky silent part of the island, and by the redoubled sounds of sighs, which made a doleful whistling in the branches, the thickness of air, which occasioned faintish respiration, and the violent throbbings of heart which more and more affected us, we found that we approached the Grotto of Grief. It was a wide, hollow, and melancholy cave, sunk deep in a dale, and watered by rivulets that had a colour between red and black. These crept slow and half congealed amongst its windings, and mixed their heavy murmurs with the echo of groans that rolled through all the passages. In the most retired parts of it sat the doleful being herself; the path to her was strewed with goads, stings, and thorns; and her throne on which she sat was broken into a rock, with ragged pieces pointing upwards for her to lean upon. A heavy mist hung above her; her head oppressed with it reclined upon her arm. Thus did she reign over her disconsolate subjects, full of herself to stupidity, in eternal pensiveness, and the profoundest silence. On one side of her stood Dejection, just dropping into a swoon, and Paleness, wasting to a skeleton; on the other side were Care inwardly tormented with imaginations, and Anguish suffering outward troubles to suck the blood from her heart in the shape of vultures. The whole vault had a genuine dismalness in it, which a few scattered lamps, whose blueish flames arose and sunk in their urns, discovered to our eyes with increase. Some of us fell down, overcome and spent with what they suffered in the way, and were given over to those tormenters that stood on either hand of the presence; others galled and mortified with pain, recovered the entrance, where Patience, whom we had left behind, was still waiting to receive us.

With her (whose company was now become more grateful to us by the want we had found of her) we winded round the grotto, and ascended at the back of it, out of the mournful dale in whose bottom it lay. On this eminence we halted, by her advice, to pant for breath; and lifting our eyes, which until then were fixed downwards, felt a sullen sort of satisfaction, in observing, through the shades, what numbers had entered the island. This satisfaction, which appears to have ill-nature in it, was excusable, because it happened at a time when we were too much taken up with our own concern, to have respect to that of others; and therefore we did not consider them as suffering, but ourselves as not suf fering in the most forlorn estate. It had also the ground-work of humanity and compassion in it, though the mind was then too dark and too deeply engaged to perceive it: but as we proceeded onward, it began to discover itself, and, from observing that others were unhappy, we came to question one another, when it was that we met, and what were the sad occasions that brought us together. Then we heard our stories, and compared them, we mutually gave and received pity, and so by degrees became tolerable company.

A considerable part of the troublesome road was thus deceived; at length the openings among the trees grew larger, the air seemed thinner, it lay with less oppression upon us, and we could now and then discern tracks in it of a lighter grayness, like the breakings of day, short in duration, much enlivening, and called in that country gleams of amusement. Within a short while these gleams began to appear more frequent, and then brighter and of a longer continuance: the sighs that hitherto filled the air with so much dolefulness, altered to the sound of common breezes, and in general the horrors of the island were abated.

When we had arrived at last at the ford by which we were to pass out, we met with those fashionable mourners who had been ferried over along with us, and who, being unwilling to go as far as we, had coasted by the shore to find the place, where they waited our coming; that by showing themselves to the world only at the time when we did, they might seem also to have been among the troubles of the grotto. Here the waters that rolled on the other side so deep and silent were much dried up, and it was an easier matter for us to wade over.

The river being crossed, we were received upon the farther bank by our friends and acquaintance, whom Comfort had brought out to congratulate our appearance in the world again. Some of these blamed us for staying so long away from them, others advised us against all temptations of going back; every one was cautious not to renew our trouble, by asking any particulars of the journey; and all concluded that, in a case of so much melancholy and affliction, we could not have made choice of a fitter companion than Patience. Here Patience, appearing serene at her praises, delivered us over to Comfort. Comfort smiled at his receiving the charge: immediately the sky purpled on that side to which he turned, and double day at once broke in upon me.

No. 502.] *Monday, October* 6, 1712.

Melius, pejus, prosit, obsit, nil vident nisi quod lubent.
Ter. Heaut. Act iv. Sc. 1.

Better or worse, profitable or disadvantageous, they see nothing but what they list.

When men read, they taste the matter with which they are entertained, according as their own respective studies and inclinations have prepared them, and make their reflections accordingly. Some, perusing Roman writers, would find in them, whatever the subject of the discourses were, parts which implied the grandeur of that people in their warfare, or their politics. As for my part, who am a mere Spectator, I drew this morning conclusions of their eminence in what I think great, to wit, in having worthy sentiments, from the reading a comedy of Terence. The play was the Self-Tormentor. It is from the beginning to the end a perfect picture of human life; but I did not observe in the whole one passage that could raise a laugh. How well-disposed must that people be, who could be entertained with satisfaction by so sober and polite mirth! In the first scene of the comedy, when one of the old men accuses the other of impertinence for interposing in his affairs, he answers, 'I am a man, and cannot help feeling any sorrow that can arrive at man.'* It is said this sentence was received with an universal applause. There cannot be a greater argument of the general good understanding of a people than a sudden consent to give their approbation of a sentiment which has no emotion in it. If it were spoken with ever so great skill in the actor, the manner of uttering that sentence could have nothing in it which could strike any but people of the greatest humanity, nay, people elegant and skilful in observations upon it. It is possible he might have laid his hand on his breast, and, with a winning insinuation in his countenance, expressed to his neighbour that he was a man who made his case his own; yet I will engage a player in Covent-garden might hit such an attitude a thousand times before he would have been regarded. I have heard that a minister of state in the reign of queen Elizabeth had all manner of books and ballads brought to him, of what kind soever, and took great notice how much they took with the people; upon which he would, and certainly might, very well judge of their present dispositions, and the most proper way of applying them according to his own purposes. What passes on the stage, and the reception it meets with from the audience, is a very useful instruction of this kind. According to what you may observe on our stage, you see them often moved so directly against all common sense and humanity, that you would be apt to pronounce us a nation of savages. It cannot be called a mistake of what is pleasant, but the very contrary to it is what most assuredly takes with them. The other night, an old woman carried off with a pain in her side, with all the distortions and anguish of countenance which is natural to one in that condition, was laughed at and clapped off the stage. Terence's comedy,

---

* Homo sum, et nihil humanum e me alienum puto.
I am a man, and all calamities,
That touch humanity, come home to me.—*Colman.*

which I am speaking of, is indeed written as if he hoped to please none but such as had as good a taste as himself. I could not but reflect upon the natural description of the innocent young woman made by the servant to his master. 'When I came to the house,' said he, 'an old woman opened the door, and I followed her in, because I could, by entering upon them unawares, better observe what was your mistress's ordinary manner of spending her time, the only way of judging any one's inclinations and genius. I found her at her needle in a sort of second mourning, which she wore for an aunt she had lately lost. She had nothing on but what showed she dressed only for herself. Her hair hung negligently about her shoulders. She had none of the arts with which others use to set themselves off, but had that negligence of person which is remarkable in those who are careful of their minds. Then she had a maid who was at work near her that was a slattern, because her mistress was careless; which I take to be another argument of your security in her; for the go-betweens of women of intrigue are rewarded too well to be dirty. When you were named, and I told her you desired to see her, she threw down her work for joy, covered her face, and decently hid her tears.' He must be a very good actor, and draw attention rather from his own character than the words of the author, that could gain it among us for this speech, though so full of nature and good sense.

The intolerable folly and confidence of players putting in words of their own, does in a great measure feed the absurd taste of the audience. But however that is, it is ordinary for a cluster of coxcombs to take up the house to themselves, and equally insult both the actors and the company. These savages, who want all manner of regard and deference to the rest of mankind, come only to show themselves to us, without any other purpose than to let us know they despise us.

The gross of an audience is composed of two sorts of people, those who know no pleasure but of the body, and those who improve or command corporeal pleasures, by the addition of fine sentiments of the mind. At present, the intelligent part of the company are wholly subdued by the insurrections of those who know no satisfactions but what they have in common with all other animals.

This is the reason that when a scene tending to procreation is acted, you see the whole pit in such a chuckle, and old letchers, with mouths open, stare at those loose gesticulations on the stage with shameful earnestness: when the justest pictures of human life in its calm dignity, and the properest sentiments for the conduct of it, pass by like mere narration, as conducing only to somewhat much better which is to come after. I have seen the whole house at some times in so proper a disposition, that indeed I have trembled for the boxes, and feared the entertainment would end in a representation of the rape of the Sabines.

I would not be understood in this talk to argue that nothing is tolerable on the stage but what has an immediate tendency to the promotion of virtue. On the contrary, I can allow, provided there is nothing against the interests of virtue, and is not offensive to good manners, that things of an indifferent nature may be represented. For this reason I have no exception to the well-drawn rusticities in the Country Wake; and there is something so miraculously pleasant in Dogget's acting the awkward triumph and comic sorrow of Hob in different circumstances, that I shall not be able to stay away whenever it is acted. All that vexes me is, that the gallantry of taking the cudgels for Gloucestershire, with the pride of heart in tucking himself up, and taking aim at his adversary, as well as the other's protestation in the humanity of low romance, that he could not promise the 'squire to break Hob's head, but he would, if he could do it in love; then flourish and begin: I say what vexes me is, that such excellent touches as these, as well as the 'squire's being out of all patience at Hob's success, and venturing himself into the crowd, are circumstances hardly taken notice of, and the height of the jest is only in the very point that heads are broken. I am confident, were there a scene written, wherein Pinkethman should break his leg by wrestling with Bullock, and Dicky come in to set it, without one word said but what should be according to the exact rules of surgery, in making this extension, and binding up his leg, the whole house should be in a roar of applause at the dissembled anguish of the patient, the help given by him who threw him down, and the handy address and arch looks of the surgeon. To enumerate the entrance of ghosts, the embattling of armies, the noise of heroes in love, with a thousand other enormities, would be to transgress the bounds of this paper, for which reason it is possible they may have hereafter distinct discourses; not forgetting any of the audience who shall set up for actors, and interrupt the play on the stage; and players who shall prefer the applause of fools to that of the reasonable part of the company. T.

Postscript to the Spectator, No. 502.

N. B. There are in the play of the Self Tormentor of Terence, which is allowed a most excellent comedy, several incidents which would draw tears from any man of sense, and not one which would move his laughter.—Spect. in folio, No. 521.

This speculation, No. 502, is controverted in the Guard. No. 59, by a writer under the fictitious name of John Lizard; perhaps Doctor Edw Young.

No. 503.] *Tuesday, October 7, 1712.*

Deleo omnes dehinc ex animo mulieres.
Ter. Eun. Act ii. Sc. 3.

From henceforward I blot out of my thoughts all memory of womankind.

'Mr. Spectator,—You have often mentioned with great vehemence and indignation the misbehaviour of people at church; but I am at present to talk to you on that subject, and complain to you of one, whom at the same time I know not what to accuse of, except it be looking too well there, and diverting the eyes of the congregation to that one object. However, I have this to say, that she might have staid at her own parish, and not come to perplex those who are otherwise intent upon their duty.

'Last Sunday was seven-night I went into a church not far from London-bridge; but I wish I had been contented to go to my own parish, I am sure it had been better for me; I say I went to church thither, and got into a pew very near the pulpit. I had hardly been accommodated with a seat, before there entered into the aisle a young lady in the very bloom of youth and beauty, and dressed in the most elegant manner imaginable. Her form was such that it engaged the eyes of the whole congregation in an instant, and mine among the rest. Though we were all thus fixed upon her, she was not in the least out of countenance, or under the least disorder, though unattended by any one, and not seeming to know particularly where to place herself. However, she had not in the least a confident aspect, but moved on with the most graceful modesty, every one making way until she came to a seat just over-against that in which I was placed. The deputy of the ward sat in that pew, and she stood opposite to him, and at a glance into the seat, though she did not appear the least acquainted with the gentleman, was let in, with a confusion that spoke much admiration at the novelty of the thing. The service immediately began, and she composed herself for it with an air of so much goodness and sweetness, that the confession which she uttered, so as to be heard where we sat, appeared an act of humiliation more than she had occasion for. The truth is, her beauty had something so innocent, and yet so sublime, that we all gazed upon her like a phantom. None of the pictures which we behold of the best Italian painters have any thing like the spirit which appeared in her countenance, at the different sentiments expressed in the several parts of divine service. That gratitude and joy at a thanksgiving, that lowliness and sorrow at the prayers for the sick and distressed, that triumph at the passages which gave instances of the divine mercy, which appeared respectively in her aspect, will be in my memory to my last hour. I protest to you, sir, that she suspended the devotion of every one around her; and the ease she did every thing with, soon dispersed the churlish dislike and hesitation in approving what is excellent, too frequent among us, to a general attention and entertainment in observing her behaviour. All the while that we were gazing at her, she took notice of no object about her, but had an art of seeming awkwardly attentive, whatever else her eyes were accidentally thrown upon. One thing indeed was particular, she stood the whole service, and never kneeled or sat; I do not question but that it was to show herself with the greater advantage, and set forth to better grace her hands and arms, lifted up with the most ardent devotion; and her bosom, the fairest that was ever seen, bare to observation; while she, you must think, knew nothing of the concern she gave others, any other than as an example of devotion, that threw herself out, without regard to dress or garment, all contrition, and loose of all worldly regards in ecstacy of devotion. Well; now the organ was to play a voluntary, and she was so skilful in music, and so touched with it, that she kept time not only with some motion of her head, but also with a different air in her countenance. When the music was strong and bold, she looked exalted, but serious; when lively and airy, she was smiling and gracious; when the notes were more soft and languishing, she was kind and full of pity. When she had now made it visible to the whole congregation, by her motion and ear, that she could dance, and she wanted now only to inform us that she could sing too; when the psalm was given out, her voice was distinguished above all the rest, or rather people did not exert their own in order to hear her. Never was any heard so sweet and so strong. The organist observed it, and he thought fit to play to her only, and she swelled every note, when she found she had thrown us all out, and had the last verse to herself in such a manner as the whole congregation was intent upon her, in the same manner as we see in the cathedrals they are on the person who sings alone the anthem. Well; it came at last to the sermon, and our young lady would not lose her part in that neither: for she fixed her eye upon the preacher, and as he said any thing she approved, with one of Charles Mather's fine tablets she set down the sentence, at once showing her fine hand, the gold pen, her readiness in writing, and her judgment in choosing what to write. To sum up what I intend by this long and particular account, I appeal to you, whether it is reasonable that such a creature as this shall come from a janty part of the town, and give herself such violent airs, to the disturbance of an innocent and inoffensive congregation, with her sublimities. The fact, I assure you, was as I have related: but I had like to have forgot another very considerable particular. As soon as church was done, she immediately stepped out of her pew, and fell into the finest pitty-patty air, forsooth, wonderfully out of countenance, tossing her head up and down, as she swam along the body of the church. I, with several others of the inhabitants, followed her out, and saw her hold up her fan to a hackney-coach at a distance, who immediately came up to her, and she whipping into it with great nimbleness, pulled the door with a bowing mien, as if she had been used to a better glass. She said aloud, "You know where to go," and drove off. By this time the best of the congregation was at the church-door, and I could hear some say, "A very fine lady;" others, "I'll warrant you she is no better than she should be:" and one very wise old lady said she ought to have been taken up. Mr. Spectator, I think this matter lies wholly before you: for the offence does not come under any law, though it is apparent this creature came among us only to give herself airs, and enjoy her full swing in being admired. I desire you may print this, that she may be confined to her own parish; for I can assure you there is no attending any thing else in a place where she is a novelty. She has been talked of among us ever since, under the name of "the phantom:" but I would advise her to come no more: for there is so strong a party made by the women against her, that she must expect they will not be excelled a second time in so outrageous a manner, without doing her some insult. Young women, who assume after this rate, and affect exposing themselves to view in congregations at the other end of the town, are not so mischievous, because they are rivalled by more of the same ambition, who will not let the rest of the company be particular: but in the name of the whole congregation where I was, I desire you to keep these agreeable disturbances out of the city, where sobriety of manners is still preserved, and all glaring and ostentatious behaviour, even in things laudable, discountenanced. I wish you may never see the phantom, and am, sir, your most humble servant,

T. 'RALPH WONDER.'

No. 504.] *Wednesday, October* 8, 1712.

Lepus tute es, et pulpamentum quæris.
Ter. Eun. Act iii. Sc. 1.

You are a hare yourself, and want dainties, forsooth.

It is a great convenience to those who want wit to furnish out a conversation, that there is something or other in all companies where it is wanted substituted in its stead, which, according to their taste, does the business as well. Of this nature is the agreeable pastime in country-halls of cross purposes, questions and commands, and the like. A little superior to these are those who can play at crambo, or cap verses. Then above them are such as can make verses, that is, rhyme; and among those who have the Latin tongue, such as use to make what they call golden verses. Commend me also to those who have not brains enough for any of these exercises, and yet do not give up their pretensions to mirth. These can slap you on the back unawares, laugh oud, ask you how you do with a twang on your shoulders, say you are dull to-day, and laugh a voluntary to put you in humour; not to mention the laborious way among the miner poets, of making things come into such and such a shape, as that of an egg, a hand, an axe, or any thing that nobody had ever thought on before for that purpose, or which would have cost them a great deal of pains to accomplish if they did. But all these methods, though they are mechanical, and may be arrived at with the smallest capacity, do not serve an honest gentleman who wants wit for his ordinary occasions; therefore it is absolutely necessary that the poor in imagination should save something which may be serviceable to them at all hours, upon all common occurrences. That which we call punning is therefore greatly affected by men of small intellects. These men need not be concerned with you for the whole sentence; but if they can say a quaint thing, or bring in a word which sounds like any one word you have spoken to them, they can turn the discourse, or distract you so that you cannot go on, and by consequence, if they cannot be as witty as you are, they can hinder your being any wittier than they are. Thus if you talk of a candle, he 'can deal' with you; and if you ask him to help you to some bread, a punster should think himself very 'ill-bred' if he did not; and if he is not as 'well-bred' as yourself, he hopes for 'grains' of allowance. If you do not understand that last fancy, you must recollect that bread is made of grain; and so they go on for ever, without possibility of being exhausted.

There are another kind of people of small faculties, who supply want of wit with want of breeding; and because women are both by nature and education more offended at any thing which is immodest than we men are, these are ever harping upon things they ought not to allude to, and deal mightily in double meanings. Every one's own observation will suggest instances enough of this kind, without my mentioning any; for your double meaners are dispersed up and down through all parts of the town or city where there are any to offend, in order to set off themselves. These men are mighty loud laughers, and held very pretty gentlemen with the sillier and unbred part of womankind. But above all already mentioned, or any who ever were, or ever can be in the world, the happiest and surest to be pleasant, are a sort of people whom we have not indeed lately heard much of, and those are your 'biters.'

A biter is one who tells you a thing you have no reason to disbelieve in itself, and perhaps has given you, before he bit you, no reason to disbelieve it for his saying it; and, if you give him credit, laughs in your face, and triumphs that he has deceived you. In a word, a biter is one who thinks you a fool, because you do not think him a knave. This description of him one may insist upon to be a just one; for what else but a degree of knavery is it, to depend upon deceit for what you gain of another, be it in point of wit, or interest, or any thing else?

This way of wit is called 'biting,' by a metaphor taken from beasts of prey, which devour harmless and unarmed animals, and look upon them as their food wherever they meet them. The sharpers about town very ingeniously understood themselves to be to the undesigning part of mankind what foxes are to lambs, and therefore used the word biting, to express any exploit wherein they had over-reached any innocent and inadvertent man of his purse. These rascals of late years have been the gallants of the town, and carried it with a fashionable haughty air, to the discouragement of modesty, and all honest arts. Shallow fops, who are governed by the eye, and admire every thing that struts in vogue, took up from the sharpers the phrase of biting, and used it upon all occasions, either to disown any nonsensical stuff they should talk themselves, or evade the force of what was reasonably said by others. Thus, when one of these cunning creatures was entered into a debate with you, whether it was practicable in the present state of affairs to accomplish such a proposition, and you thought he had let fall what destroyed his side of the question, as soon as you looked with an earnestness ready to lay hold of it, he immediately cried, 'Bite,' and you were immediately to acknowledge all that part was in jest. They carry this to all the extravagance imaginable; and if one of these witlings knows any particulars which may give authority to what he says, he is still the more ingenious if he imposes upon your credulity. I remember a remarkable instance of this kind. There came up a shrewd young fellow to a plain young man, his countryman, and taking him aside with a grave-concerned countenance, goes on at this rate: 'I see you here, and have you heard nothing out of Yorkshire?—You look so surprised, you could not have heard of it—and yet the particulars are such that it cannot be false: I am sorry I am got into it so far that I must tell you; but I know not but it may be for your service to know. On Tuesday last, just after dinner—you know his manner is to smoke—opening his box, your father fell down dead in an apoplexy.' The youth showed the filial sorrow which he ought—Upon which the witty man cried, 'Bite, there was nothing in all this.'

To put an end to this silly, pernicious, frivolous way at once, I will give the reader one late instance of a bite, which no biter for the future will ever be able to equal, though I heartily wish him the same occasion. It is a superstition with some surgeons who beg the bodies of condemned malefactors, to go to the gaol, and bargain for the carcase with the criminal himself. A good honest fellow did so last sessions, and was admitted to the condemned men on the morning wherein they died. The surgeon communicated his business, and fell into discourse with a little fellow, who refused twelve shillings, and insisted upon fifteen for his body. The fellow, who killed the officer of Newgate, very forwardly, and like a man who was willing to deal, told him, 'Look you, Mr. Surgeon, that little dry fellow, who has been half starved all his life, and is now half dead with fear, cannot answer your purpose. I have ever lived highly and freely, my veins are full, I have not pined in imprisonment; you see my crest swells to your knife; and after Jack Catch has done, upon my honour you will find me as sound as ever a bullock in any of the markets. Come, for twenty shillings I am your man.' Says the surgeon, 'Done, there is a guinea.' This witty rogue took the money, and as soon as he had it in his fist, cries, 'Bite; I am to be hung in chains.'

T.

No. 505.] *Thursday, October* 9, 1712.

Non habeo denique nauci marsum augurem,
Non vicanos aruspices, non de circo astrologos.
Non Isiacos conjectores, non interpretes somnium,
Non enim sunt ii, aut scientia, aut arte divina,
Sed superstitiosi vates, impudentesque harioli,
Aut inertes, aut insani, aut quibus egestas imperat:
Qui sui questus causa fictas suscitant sententias,
Qui sibi semitam non sapiunt, alteri monstrant viam
Quibus divitias pollicentur, ab iis drachmam petunt:
De divitiis deducant drachmam, reddant cætera.

Ennius.

Augurs and soothsayers, astrologers,
Diviners, and interpreters of dreams,
I ne'er consult, and heartily despise:
Vain their pretence to more than human skill:
For gain, imaginary schemes they draw;
Wand'rers themselves, they guide another's steps;
And for poor sixpence promise countless wealth:
Let them, if they expect to be believed,
Deduct the sixpence, and bestow the rest.

THOSE who have maintained that men would be more miserable than beasts, were their hopes confined to this life only, among other considerations take notice that the latter are only afflicted with the anguish of the present evil, whereas the former are very often pained by the reflection on what is passed, and the fear of what is to come. This fear of any future difficulties or misfortunes is so natural to the mind, that were a man's sorrows and disquietudes summed up at the end of his life, it would generally be found that he had suffered more from the apprehension of such evils as never happened to him, than from those evils which had really befallen him. To this we may add, that among those evils which befall us, there are many which have been more painful to us in the prospect, than by their actual pressure.

This natural impatience to look into futurity, and to know what accidents may happen to us hereafter, has given birth to many ridiculous arts and inventions. Some found their prescience on the lines of a man's hand, others on the features of his face: some on the signatures which nature has impressed on his body, and others on his own hand-writing: some read men's fortunes in the stars, as others have searched after them in the entrails of beasts, or the flight of birds. Men of the best sense have been touched more or less with these groundless horrors and presages of futurity, upon surveying the most indifferent works of nature. Can any thing be more surprising than to consider Cicero,* who made the greatest figure at the bar and in the senate of the Roman Commonwealth, and at the same time outshined all the philosophers of antiquity in his library, and in his retirements, as busying himself in the college of augurs, and observing with a religious attention after what manner the chickens pecked the several grains of corn which were thrown to them.

Notwithstanding these follies are pretty well worn out of the minds of the wise and learned in the present age, multitudes of weak and ignorant persons are still slaves to them. There are numberless arts of prediction among the vulgar, which are too trifling to enumerate, and infinite observation of days, numbers, voices, and figures, which are regarded by them as portents and prodigies. In short, every thing prophesies to the superstitious man; there is scarce a straw, or a rusty piece of iron that lies in his way by accident.

It is not to be conceived how many wizzards, gipsies, and cunning men, are dispersed through all the counties and market-towns of Great Britain, not to mention the fortune-tellers and astrologers, who live very comfortably upon the curiosity of several well-disposed persons in the cities of London and Westminster.

Among the many pretended arts of divination, there is none which so universally amuses as that by dreams. I have indeed observed in a late speculation, that there have been sometimes, upon very extraordinary occasions, supernatural revelations made to certain persons by this means; but as it is the chief business of this paper to root out popular errors, I must endeavour to expose the folly and superstition of those persons, who, in the common and ordinary course of life, lay any stress upon things of so uncertain, shadowy, and chimerical a nature. This I cannot do more effectually than by the following letter, which is dated from a quarter of the town that has always been the habitation of some prophetic Philomath; it having been usual, time out of mind, for all such people as have lost their wits to resort to that place, either for their cure or for their instruction.

'Moorfields, Oct. 4, 1712.

'MR. SPECTATOR,—Having long considered whether there be any trade wanted in this great city, after having surveyed very attentively all kinds of ranks and professions, I do not find in any quarter of the town an oneiro-critic, or, in plain English, an interpreter of dreams. For want of so useful a person, there are several good people who are very much puzzled in this particular, and dream a whole year together, without being ever the wiser for it. I hope I am pretty well qualified for this office, having studied by candle-light all the rules of art which have been laid down upon this subject. My great uncle by my wife's side was a Scotch highlander, and second-sighted. I have four fingers and two thumbs upon one hand, and was born on the longest night of the year. My Christian and surname begin and end with the same letters. I am lodged in Moorfields, in a house that for these fifty years has always been tenanted by a conjurer.

'If you had been in company, so much as myself, with ordinary women of the town, you must know that there are many of them who every day in their lives, upon seeing or hearing of any thing that is unexpected, cry, "My dream is out;" and cannot go to sleep in quiet the next night, until something or other has happened which has expounded the visions of the preceding one. There are others who are in very great pain for not being able to recover the circumstances of a dream, that made strong impressions upon them while it lasted. In short, sir, there are many whose waking thoughts are wholly employed on their sleeping ones. For the benefit therefore of this curious and inquisitive part of my fellow-subjects, I shall in the first place tell those persons what they dreamt of, who fancy they never dream at all. In the next place I shall make out any dream, upon hearing a single circumstance of it; and in the last place, I shall expound to them the good or bad fortune which such dreams portend. If they do not presage good luck, I shall desire nothing for my pains; not questioning at the same time, that those who consult me will be so reasonable as to afford me a moderate share out of any considerable estate, profit, or emolument, which I shall discover to them. I interpret to the poor for nothing, on condition that their names may be inserted in public advertisements, to attest the truth of such my interpretations. As for people of quality, or others who are indisposed, and do not care to come in person, I can interpret their dreams by seeing their water. I set aside one day in the week for lovers; and

* This censure of Cicero seems to be unfounded: for it is said of him, that he wondered how one augur could meet another without laughing in his face.

interpret by the great for any gentlewoman who is turned of sixty, after the rate of half-a-crown per week, with the usual allowances for good luck. I have several rooms and apartments fitted up at reasonable rates, for such as have not conveniences for dreaming at their own houses.

'TITUS TROPHONIUS.

'N. B. I am not dumb.' O.

No. 506.] *Friday, October* 10, 1712.

Candida perpetuo reside, concordia, lecto,
Tamque pari semper sit Venus æqua jugo.
Diligat illa senem quondam; sed et ipsa marito,
Tunc quoque cum fuerit non videatur anus.
Mart. Epig. xiii. Lib. 4. 7.

Perpetual harmony their bed attend,
And Venus still the well-match'd pair befriend.
May she, when time has sunk him into years,
Love her old man, and cherish his white hairs;
Nor he perceive her charms thro' age decay,
But think each happy sun his bridal day.

THE following essay is written by the gentleman to whom the world is obliged for those several excellent discourses which have been marked with the letter X.

I have somewhere met with a fable that made Wealth the father of Love. It is certain that a mind ought at least to be free from the apprehensions of want and poverty, before it can fully attend to all the softnesses and endearments of this passion; notwithstanding, we see multitudes of married people, who are utter strangers to this delightful passion amidst all the affluence of the most plentiful fortunes.

It is not sufficient to make a marriage happy, that the humours of two people should be alike. I could instance a hundred pair, who have not the least sentiment of love remaining for one another, yet are so like in their humours, that if they were not already married, the whole world would design them for man and wife.

The spirit of love has something so extremely fine in it, that it is very often disturbed and lost, by some little accidents, which the careless and unpolite never attend to, until it is gone past recovery.

Nothing has more contributed to banish it from a married state than too great a familiarity, and laying aside the common rules of decency. Though I could give instances of this in several particulars, I shall only mention that of dress. The beaux and belles about town, who dress purely to catch one another, think there is no farther occasion for the bait, when the first design has succeeded. But besides the too common fault, in point of neatness, there are several others which I do not remember to have seen touched upon, but in one of our modern comedies,* where a French woman offering to undress and dress herself before the lover of the play, and assuring her mistress that it was very usual in France, the lady tells her that is a secret in dress she never knew before, and that she was so unpolished an English woman, as to resolve never to learn to dress even before her husband.

There is something so gross in the carriage of some wives, that they lose their husband's hearts for faults which, if a man has either good-nature or good-breeding, he knows not how to tell them of. I am afraid, indeed, the ladies are generally most faulty in this particular; who, at their first giving into love, find the way so smooth and pleasant, that they fancy it is scarce possible to be tired in it.

There is so much nicety and discretion required to keep love alive after marriage, and make conversation still new and agreeable after twenty or thirty years, that I know nothing which seems readily to promise it, but an earnest endeavour to please on both sides, and superior good sense on the part of the man.

By a man of sense I mean one acquainted with business and letters.

A woman very much settles her esteem for a man, according to the figure he makes in the world, and the character he bears among his own sex. As learning is the chief advantage we have over them, it is, methinks, as scandalous and inexcusable for a man of fortune to be illiterate, as for a woman not to know how to behave herself on the most ordinary occasions. It is this which sets the two sexes at the greatest distance; a woman is vexed and surprised, to find nothing more in the conversation of a man, than in the common tattle of her own sex.

Some small engagement at least in business, not only sets a man's talents in the fairest light, and allots him a part to act in which a wife cannot well intermeddle, but gives frequent occasion for those little absences, which, whatever seeming uneasiness they may give, are some of the best preservatives of love and desire.

The fair-sex are so conscious to themselves that they have nothing in them which can deserve entirely to engross the whole man, that they heartily despise one who, to use their own expression, is always hanging at their apron-strings.

Lætitia is pretty, modest, tender, and has sense enough; she married Erastus, who is in a post of some business, and has a general taste in most parts of polite learning. Lætitia, wherever she visits, has the pleasure to hear of something which was handsomely said or done by Erastus. Erastus, since his marriage, is more gay in his dress than ever, and in all companies is as complaisant to Lætitia as to any other lady. I have seen him give her her fan when it has dropped, with all the gallantry of a lover. When they take the air together, Erastus is continually improving her thoughts, and with a turn of wit and spirit which is peculiar to him, giving her an insight into things

* The Funeral, or Grief Alamode, by Steel

she had no notions of before. Lætitia is transported at having a new world thus opened to her, and hangs upon the man that gives her such agreeable informations. Erastus has carried this point still farther, as he makes her daily not only more fond of him, but infinitely more satisfied with herself. Erastus finds a justness or beauty in whatever she says or observes, that Lætitia herself was not aware of; and by his assistance she has discovered a hundred good qualities and accomplishments in herself, which she never before once dreamed of. Erastus, with the most artful complaisance in the world, by several remote hints, finds the means to make her say or propose almost whatever he has a mind to, which he always receives as her own discovery, and gives her all the reputation of it.

Erastus has a perfect taste in painting, and carried Lætitia with him the other day to see a collection of pictures. I sometimes visit this happy couple. As we were last week walking in the long gallery before dinner,—'I have lately laid out some money in paintings,' says Erastus: 'I bought that Venus and Adonis purely upon Lætitia's judgment; it cost me threescore guineas; and I was this morning offered a hundred for it.' I turned towards Lætitia, and saw her cheeks glow with pleasure, while at the same time she cast a look upon Erastus, the most tender and affectionate I ever beheld.

Flavilla married Tom Tawdry, she was taken with his laced-coat and rich sword-knot; she has the mortification to see Tom despised by all the worthy part of his own sex. Tom has nothing to do after dinner, but to determine whether he will pare his nails at St. James's, White's, or his own house. He has said nothing to Flavilla since they were married which she might not have heard as well from her own woman. He however takes great care to keep up the saucy ill-natured authority of a husband. Whatever Flavilla happens to assert, Tom immediately contradicts with an oath by way of preface, and, 'My dear, I must tell you you talk most confoundedly silly.' Flavilla had a heart naturally as well disposed for all the tenderness of love as that of Lætitia; but as love seldom continues long after esteem, it is difficult to determine, at present whether the unhappy Flavilla hates or despises the person most whom she is obliged to lead her whole life with. X.

No. 507.] *Saturday, October 11, 1712.*

Defendit numerus, junctæque umbone phalanges.
Juv. **Sat. ii. 46.**

Preserv'd from shame by numbers on our side.

There is something very sublime, though very fanciful, in Plato's description of the Supreme Being; that 'truth is his body, and light his shadow.' According to this definition, there is nothing so contradictory to his nature as error and falsehood. The Platonists have so just a notion of the Almighty's aversion to every thing which is false and erroneous, that they looked upon truth as no less necessary than virtue to qualify a human soul for the enjoyment of a separate state. For this reason, as they recommended moral duties to qualify and season the will for a future life, so they prescribed several contemplations and sciences to rectify the understanding. Thus Plato has called mathematical demonstrations the cathartics, or purgatives of the soul, as being the most proper means to cleanse it from error, and give it a relish of truth; which is the natural food and nourishment of the understanding, as virtue is the perfection and happiness of the will.

There are many authors who have shown wherein the malignity of a lie consists, and set forth in proper colours the heinousness of the offence. I shall here consider one particular kind of this crime, which has not been so much spoken to; I mean that abominable practice of party-lying. This vice is so very predominant among us at present, that a man is thought of no principle, who does not propagate a certain system of lies. The coffee-houses are supported by them, the press is choked with them, eminent authors live upon them. Our bottle conversation is so infected with them, that a party-lie is grown as fashionable an entertainment as a lively catch, or a merry story. The truth of it is, half the great talkers in the nation would be struck dumb were this fountain of discourse dried up. There is however one advantage resulting from this detestable practice: the very appearances of truth are so little regarded, that lies are at present discharged in the air, and begin to hurt nobody. When we hear a party-story from a stranger, we consider whether he is a whig or a tory that relates it, and immediately conclude they are words of course, in which the honest gentleman designs to recommend his zeal, without any concern for his veracity. A man is looked upon as bereft of common sense, that gives credit to the relations of party writers; nay, his own friends shake their heads at him, and consider him in no other light than an officious tool, or a well-meaning idiot. When it was formerly the fashion to husband a lie, and trump it up in some extraordinary emergency, it generally did execution, and was not a little serviceable to the faction that made use of it; but at present every man is upon his guard: the artifice has been too often repeated to take effect.

I have frequently wondered to see men of probity, who would scorn to utter a falsehood for their own particular advantage, give so readily into a lie, when it is become the voice of their faction, notwithstanding they are thoroughly sensible of it as such.

How is it possible for those who are men of honour in their persons, thus to become notorious liars in their party? If we look into the bottom of this matter, we may find, I think, three reasons for it, and at the same time discover the insufficiency of these reasons to justify so criminal a practice.

In the first place, men are apt to think that the guilt of a lie, and consequently the punishment may be very much diminished, if not wholly worn out, by the multitudes of those who partake in it. Though the weight of a falsehood would be too much for one to bear, it grows light in their imaginations when it is shared among many. But in this case a man very much deceives himself; guilt, when it spreads through numbers, is not so properly divided as multiplied. Every one is criminal in proportion to the offence which he commits, not to the number of those who are his companions in it. Both the crime and the penalty lie as heavy upon every individual of an offending multitude, as they would upon any single person, had none shared with him in the offence. In a word, the division of guilt is like to that of matter: though it may be separated into infinite portions, every portion shall have the whole essence of matter in it, and consist of as many parts as the whole did before it was divided.

But in the second place, though multitudes, who join in a lie, cannot exempt themselves from the guilt, they may from the shame of it. The scandal of a lie is in a manner lost and annihilated, when diffused among several thousands; as a drop of the blackest tincture wears away and vanishes, when mixed and confused in a considerable body of water; the blot is still in it, but is not able to discover itself. This is certainly a very great motive to several party-offenders, who avoid crimes, not as they are prejudicial to their virtue, but to their reputation. It is enough to show the weakness of this reason, which palliates guilt without removing it, that every man who is influenced by it declares himself in effect an infamous hypocrite, prefers the appearance of virtue to its reality, and is determined in his conduct neither by the dictates of his own conscience, the suggestions of true honour, nor the principles of religion.

The third and last great motive for men's joining in a popular falsehood, or, as I have hitherto called it, a party-lie, notwithstanding they are convinced of it as such, is the doing good to a cause which every party may be supposed to look upon as the most meritorious. The unsoundness of this principle has been so often exposed, and is so universally acknowledged, that a man must be an utter stranger to the principles either of natural religion or Christianity, who suffers himself to be guided by it. If a man might promote the supposed good of his country by the blackest calumnies and falsehoods, our nation abounds more in patriots than any other of the Christian world. When Pompey was desired not to set sail in a tempest that would hazard his life, 'It is necessary for me,' says he, 'to sail, but it is not necessary for me to live.' Every man should say to himself, with the same spirit, 'It is my duty to speak truth, though it is not my duty to be in an office.' One of the fathers has carried this point so high as to declare he would not tell a lie, though he were sure to gain heaven by it. However extravagant such a protestation may appear, every one will own that a man may say, very reasonably, he would not tell a lie if he were to gain hell by it; or, if you have a mind to soften the expression, that he would not tell a lie to gain any temporal reward by it, when he should run the hazard of losing much more than it was possible for him to gain. O.

No. 508.] *Monday, October* 13, 1712.

Omnes autem et habentur et dicuntur tyranni, qui potestate sunt perpetua, in ea civitate quæ libertate usa est. *Corn. Nepos* in Milt. c. 8.

For all those are accounted and denominated tyrants who exercise a perpetual power in that state, which was before free.

The following letters complain of what I have frequently observed with very much indignation; therefore I shall give them to the public in the words with which my correspondents, who suffer under the hardships mentioned in them, describe them.

'Mr. Spectator,—In former ages all pretensions to dominion have been supported and submitted to, either upon account of inheritance, conquest, or election; and all such persons, who have taken upon them any sovereignty over their fellow-creatures upon any other account, have been always called tyrants, not so much because they were guilty of any particular barbarities, as because every attempt to such a superiority was in its nature tyrannical. But there is another sort of potentates, who may with greater propriety be called tyrants than those last mentioned, both as they assume a despotic dominion over those as free as themselves, and as they support it by acts of notable oppression and injustice; and these are the rulers in all clubs and meetings. In other governments the punishments of some have been alleviated by the rewards of others: but what makes the reign of these potentates so particularly grievous is, that they are exquisite in punishing their subjects, at the same time that they have it not in their power to reward them. That the reader may the better comprehend the nature of these monarchs, as well as the miserable state of those that are their vassals, I shall give an account of the king of the company I am fallen into, whom, for his particular tyranny, I shall call Dionysius: as also of the seeds that sprung up to this odd sort of empire.

'Upon all meetings at taverns, it is necessary some one of the company should take it upon him to get all things in such order and readiness, as may contribute as much as possible to the felicity of the convention; such as hastening the fire, getting a sufficient number of candles, tasting the wine with a judicious smack, fixing the supper, and being brisk for the despatch of it. Know, then, that Dionysius went through these offices with an air that seemed to express a satisfaction rather in serving the public that in gratifying any particular inclination of his own. We thought him a person of an exquisite palate, and therefore by consent beseeched him to be always our proveditor; which post, after he had handsomely denied, he could do no otherwise than accept. At first he made no other use of his power than in recommending such and such things to the company, ever allowing these points to be disputable; insomuch that I have often carried the debate for partridge, when his majesty has given intimation of the high relish of duck, but at the same time has cheerfully submitted, and devoured his partridge with most gracious resignation. This submission on his side naturally produced the like on ours; of which he in a little time made such barbarous advantage, as in all those matters, which before seemed indifferent to him, to issue out certain edicts as uncontrollable and unalterable as the laws of the Medes and Persians. He is by turns outrageous, peevish, forward, and jovial. He thinks it our duty for the little offices, as proveditor, that in return all conversation is to be interrupted or promoted by his inclination for or against the present humour of the company. We feel, at present, in the utmost extremity, the insolence of office; however, I, being naturally warm, ventured to oppose him in a dispute about a haunch of venison. I was altogether for roasting, but Dionysius declared himself for boiling with so much prowess and resolution, that the cook thought it necessary to consult his own safety, rather than the luxury of my proposition. With the same authority that he orders what we shall eat and drink, he also commands us where to do it: and we change our taverns according as he suspects any treasonable practices in the settling the bill by the master, or sees any bold rebellion in point of attendance by the waiters. Another reason for changing the seat of empire, I conceive to be the pride he takes in the promulgation of our slavery, though we pay our club for our entertainments, even in these palaces of our grand monarch. When he has a mind to take the air, a party of us are commanded out by way of life-guard, and we march under as great restrictions as they do. If we meet a neighbouring king, we give or keep the way, according as we are out-numbered or not; and if the train of each is equal in number, rather than give battle, the superiority is soon adjusted by a desertion from one of them.

'Now, the expulsion of these unjust rulers out of all societies, would gain a man as everlasting a reputation as either of the Brutus's got for their endeavours to extirpate tyranny from among the Romans. I confess myself to be in a conspiracy against the usurper of our club; and to show my reading, as well as my merciful disposition, shall allow him until the ides of March to dethrone himself. If he seems to affect empire until that time, and does not gradually recede from the incursions he has made upon our liberties, he shall find a dinner dressed which he has no hand in, and shall be treated with an order, magnificence, and luxury, as shall break his proud heart; at the same time that he shall be convinced in his stomach he was unfit for his post, and a more mild and skilful prince receive the acclamations of the people, and be set up in his room: but, as Milton says,

"——————These thoughts
Full counsel must mature. Peace is despair'd,
And who can think submission? War then, war,
Open, or understood, must be resolved."

'I am, sir, your most obedient humble servant.'

'MR. SPECTATOR,—I am a young woman at a gentleman's seat in the country, who is a particular friend of my father's, and came hither to pass away a month or two with his daughters. I have been entertained with the utmost civility by the whole family, and nothing has been omitted which can make my stay easy and agreeable on the part of the family; but there is a gentleman here, a visitant as I am, whose behaviour has given me great uneasiness. When I first arrived here, he used me with the utmost complaisance; but, forsooth, that was not with regard to my sex; and since he has no designs upon me, he does not know why he should distinguish me from a man in things indifferent. He is, you must know, one of those familiar coxcombs, who have observed some well-bred men with a good grace converse with women, and say no fine things, but yet treat them with that sort of respect which flows from the heart and the understanding, but is exerted in no professions or compliments. This puppy, to imitate this excellence, or avoid the contrary fault of being troublesome in complaisance, takes upon him to try his talent upon me, insomuch that he contradicts me upon all occasions, and one day told me I lied. If I had struck him with my bodkin, and behaved myself like a man, since he will not treat me as a woman, I had, I think, served him right. I wish, sir, you would please to give him some maxims of behaviour in these points, and resolve me if all maids are not in point of conversation to be treated by all bachelors as their mistresses? If not so, are they not to be used as gently as their sisters? Is it sufferable that the fop of whom I complain should say that he would rather have such-a-one without a groat, than me with the Indies? What right has any man to make suppositions of things not in his power, and then declare his will to the dislike of one that has never offended him? I assure you these are things worthy your consideration, and I hope we shall have your thoughts upon them. I am, though a woman justly offended, ready to forgive all this, because I have no remedy but leaving very agreeable company sooner than I desire. This also is a heinous aggravation of his offence, that he is inflicting banishment upon me. Your printing this letter may perhaps be an admonition to reform him; as soon as it appears I will write my name at the end of it, and lay it in his way; the making which just reprimand, I hope you will put in the power of, sir, your constant reader, and humble servant.'

T.

No. 509.] *Tuesday, October* 14, 1712.

Hominis frugi et temperantis functus officium.
Ter. Heaut. Act iii. Sc. 3.

Discharging the part of a good economist.

THE useful knowledge in the following letter shall have a place in my paper, though there is nothing in it which immediately regards the polite or the learned world; I say immediately, for upon reflection every man will find there is a remote influence upon his own affairs, in the prosperity or decay of the trading part of mankind. My present correspondent, I believe, was never in print before; but what he says well deserves a general attention, though delivered in his own homely maxims, and a kind of proverbial simplicity; which sort of learning has raised more estates, than ever were, or will be, from attention to Virgil, Horace, Tully, Seneca, Plutarch, or any of the rest, whom, I dare say, this worthy citizen would hold to be indeed ingenious, but unprofitable writers. But to the letter.

'*Mr. William Spectator.*

'Broad-street, Oct. 10, 1712.

'SIR,—I accuse you of many discourses on the subject of money, which you have heretofore promised the public, but have not discharged yourself thereof. But, forasmuch as you seemed to depend upon advice from others what to do in that point, have sat down to write you the needful upon that subject. But, before I enter thereupon, I shall take this opportunity to observe to you, that the thriving frugal man shows it in every part of his expense, dress, servants, and house; and I must, in the first place complain to you, as Spectator, that in these particulars there is at this time, throughout the city of London, a lamentable change from that simplicity of manners, which is the true source of wealth and prosperity. I just now said, the man of thrift shows regularity in every thing; but you may, perhaps, laugh that I take notice of such a particular as I am going to do, for an instance that this city is declining if their ancient economy is not restored. The thing which gives me this prospect, and so much offence, is the neglect of the Royal Exchange. I mean the edifice so called, and the walks appertaining thereunto. The Royal Exchange is a fabric that well deserves to be so called, as well to express that our monarch's highest glory and advantage consists in being the patron of trade, as that it is commodious for business, and an instance of the grandeur both of prince and people. But, alas! at present it hardly seems to be set apart for any such use or purpose. Instead of the assembly of honourable merchants, substantial tradesmen, and knowing masters of ships; the mumpers, the halt, the blind, the lame; and your venders of trash, apples, plums; your raggamuffins, rake-shames, and wenches, have justled the greater number of the former out of that place. Thus it is, especially on the evening change: so that what with the din of squallings, oaths, and cries of beggars, men of the greatest consequence in our city absent themselves from the place. This particular, by the way, is of evil consequence; for, if the 'Change be no place for men of the highest credit to frequent, it will not be a disgrace for those of less abilities to be absent. I remember the time when rascally company were kept out, and the unlucky boys with toys and balls were whipped away by a beadle. I have seen this done indeed of late, but then it has been only to chase the lads from chuck, that the beadle might seize their copper.

'I must repeat the abomination, that the walnut-trade is carried on by old women within the walks, which makes the place impassable by reason of shells and trash. The benches around are so filthy, that no one can sit down, yet the beadles and officers have the impudence at Christmas to ask for their box, though they deserve the strappado. I do not think it impertinent to have mentioned this, because it bespeaks a neglect in the domestic care of the city, and the domestic is the truest picture of a man every where else.

'But I designed to speak on the business of money and advancement of gain. The man proper for this, speaking in the general, is of a sedate, plain good understanding, not apt to go out of his way, but so behaving himself at home, that business may come to him. Sir William Turner, that valuable citizen, has left behind him a most excellent rule, and couched it in very few words, suited to the meanest capacity. He would say, "Keep your shop, and your shop will keep you." It must be confessed, that if a man of a great genius could add steadiness to his vivacities, or substitute slower men of fidelity to transact the methodical part of his affairs, such a one would outstrip the rest of the world; but business and trade are not to be managed by the same heads which write poetry, and make plans for the conduct of life in general. So though we are at this day beholden to the late witty and inventive duke of Buckingham for the whole trade and manufacture of glass, yet I suppose there is no one will aver, that, were his grace yet living, they would not rather deal with my diligent friend and neighbour, Mr. Gumley, for any goods to be prepared and delivered on such a day, than he would with that illustrious mechanic above-mentioned.

'No, no, Mr. Spectator, you wits must not pretend to be rich; and it is possible the reason may be, in some measure, because you despise, or at least you do not value it enough to let it take up your chief attention; which a trader must do, or lose his credit, which is to him what honour, reputation, fame, or glory, is to other sort of men.

'I shall not speak to the point of cash itself, until I see how you approve of these my maxims in general: but I think a speculation upon "many a little makes a mickle, a penny saved is a penny got, penny wise and a pound foolish, it is need that makes the old wife trot," would be very useful to the world; and if you treated them with knowledge, would be useful to yourself, for it would make demands for your paper among those who have no notion of it at present. But of these matters more hereafter. If you did this, as you excel many writers of the present age for politeness, so you would outgo the author of the true razor strops for use.

'I shall conclude this discourse with an explanation of a proverb, which by vulgar error is taken and used when a man is reduced to an extremity, whereas the propriety of the maxim is to use it when you would say there is plenty, but you must make such a choice as not to hurt another who is to come after you.

'Mr. Tobias Hobson,* from whom we have the expression, was a very honourable man, for I shall ever call the man so who gets an estate honestly. Mr. Tobias Hobson was a carrier; and, being a man of great abilities and invention, and one that saw where there might good profit arise, though the duller men overlooked it, this ingenious man was the first in this island who let out hackney-horses. He lived in Cambridge; and, observing that the scholars, rid hard, his manner was to keep a large stable of horses, with boots, bridles, and whips, to furnish the gentlemen at once, without going from college to college to borrow, as they have done since the death of this worthy man. I say, Mr. Hobson kept a stable of forty good cattle, always ready and fit for travelling; but, when a man came for a horse, he was led into the stable, where there was great choice; but he obliged him to take the horse which stood next to the stable door; so that every customer was alike well served according to his chance, and every horse ridden with the same justice; from whence it became a proverb, when what ought to be your election was forced upon you, to say, "Hobson's choice." This memorable man stands drawn in fresco at an inn (which he used) in Bishopsgate-street, with a hundred pound bag under his arm, with this inscription upon the said bag:

"The fruitful mother of a hundred more."†

'Whatever tradesman will try the experiment, and begin the day after you publish this my discourse to treat his customers all alike, and all reasonably and honestly, I will ensure him the same success, I am sir, your loving friend,

T. 'HEZEKIAH THRIFT.'

No. 510.] *Wednesday, October 15, 1712.*

——Si sapis,
Neque præterquam quas ipse amor molestias
Habet addas, et illas, quas habet, recte feras.
Ter. Eun. Act i. Sc. 1.

If you are wise, add not to the troubles which attend the passion of love, and bear patiently those which are inseparable from it.

'I WAS the other day driving in a hack through Gerrard-street, when my eye was immediately catched with the prettiest object imaginable—the face of a very fair girl, between thirteen and fourteen, fixed at the chin to a painted sash, and made part of the landscape. It seemed admirably done, and, upon throwing myself eagerly out of the coach to look at it, it laughed, and flung from the window. This amiable figure dwelt upon me; and I was considering the vanity of the girl, and her pleasant coquetry in acting a picture until she was taken notice of, and raised the admiration of the beholders. This little circumstance made me run into reflections upon the force of beauty, and the wonderful influence the female sex has upon the other part of the species. Our hearts are seized with their enchantments, and there are few of us, but brutal men, who by that hardness lose the chief pleasure in them, can resist their insinuations, though never so much against our own interests and opinion. It is common with women to destroy the good effects a man's following his own way and inclina-

* Mr. Hobson was the carrier between London and Cambridge. At the latter place he erected a handsome stone conduit, and left sufficient land for its maintenance for ever. He died in the time of the plague, 1630, in the eighty-sixth year of his age.

† There is a scarce folio print, I believe, from this picture, engraved by Payne, with eight English verses beneath.

tion might have upon his honour and fortune, by interposing their power over him in matters wherein they cannot influence him, but to his loss and disparagement. I do not know therefore a task so difficult in human life, as to be proof against the importunities of a woman a man loves. There is certainly no armour against tears, sullen looks, or at best constrained familiarities, in her whom you usually meet with transport and alacrity. Sir Walter Raleigh was quoted in a letter (of a very ingenious correspondent of mine) upon this subject. That author, who had lived in courts, and camps, travelled through many countries, and seen many men under several climates, and of as various complexions, speaks of our impotence to resist the wiles of women in very severe terms. His words are as follows:

'What means did the devil find out, or what instruments did his own subtility present him as fittest and aptest to work his mischief by? Even the unquiet vanity of the woman; so as by Adam's hearkening to the voice of his wife, contrary to the express commandment of the living God, mankind by that her incantation became the subject of labour, sorrow, and death; the woman being given to man for a comforter and companion, but not for a counsellor. It is also to be noted by whom the woman was tempted. even by the most ugly and unworthy of all beasts, into whom the devil entered and persuaded. Secondly, What was the motive of her disobedience? Even a desire to know what was most unfitting her knowledge; an affection which has ever since remained in all the posterity of her sex. Thirdly, what was it that moved the man to yield to her persuasions? Even to the same cause which hath moved all men since to the like consent, namely, an unwillingness to grieve her, or make her sad, lest she should pine, and be overcome with sorrow. But if Adam, in the state of perfection, and Solomon the Son of David, God's chosen servant, and himself a man endued with the greatest wisdom, did both of them disobey their Creator by the persuasion, and for the love they bear to a woman, it is not so wonderful as lamentable, that other men in succeeding ages have been allured to so many inconvenient and wicked practices by the persuasion of their wives, or other beloved darlings, who cover over and shadow many malicious purposes with a counterfeit passion of dissimulating sorrow and unquietness.'

The motions of the minds of lovers are no where so well described as in the words of skilful writers for the stage. The scene between Fulvia and Curius, in the second act of Johnson's Catiline, is an excellent picture of the power of a lady over her gallant. The wench plays with his affections; and as a man, of all places of the world, wishes to make a good figure with his mistress, upon her upbraiding him with want of spirit, he alludes to enterprises which he cannot reveal but with the hazard of his life. When he is worked thus far, with a little flattery of her opinion of his gallantry, and desire to know more of it out of her overflowing fondness to him, he brags to her until his life is in her disposal.

When a man is thus liable to be vanquished by the charms of her he loves, the safest way is to determine what is proper to be done; but to avoid all expostulation with her before he executes what he has resolved. Women are ever too hard for us upon a treaty; and one must consider how senseless a thing it is to argue with one whose looks and gestures are more prevalent with you, than your reasons and arguments can be with her. It is a most miserable slavery to submit to what you disapprove and give up a truth for no other reason, but that you had not fortitude to support you in asserting it. A man has enough to do to conquer his own unreasonable wishes and desires; but he does that in vain, if he has those of another to gratify. Let his pride be in his wife and family, let him give them all the conveniences of life in such a manner as if he were proud of them; but let it be his own innocent pride, and not their exorbitant desires which are indulged by him. In this case all the little arts imaginable are used to soften a man's heart, and raise his passion above his understanding. But in all concessions of this kind, a man should consider whether the present he makes flows from his own love, or the importunity of his beloved. If from the latter, he is her slave? if from the former, her friend. We laugh it off, and do not weigh this subjection to women with that seriousness which so important a circumstance deserves. Why was courage given to a man, if his wife's fears are to frustrate it? When this is once indulged, you are no longer her guardian and protector, as you were designed by nature; but, in compliance to her weaknesses, you have disabled yourself from avoiding the misfortunes into which they will lead you both, and you are to see the hour in which you are to be reproached by herself for that very compliance to her. It is indeed the most difficult mastery over ourselves we can possibly attain, to resist the grief of her who charms us; but let the heart ake, be the anguish never so quick and painful, it is what must be suffered and passed through, if you think to live like a gentleman, or be conscious to yourself that you are a man of honesty. The old argument, that 'you do not love me if you deny me this,' which first was used to obtain a trifle, by habitual success will oblige the unhappy man who gives way to it to resign the cause even of his country and his honour.

T.

No. 511.] *Thursday, October* 16, 1712.

Quis non invenit turba quod amaret in illa?
Ovid, Ars Am. Lib. i. 175.

————Who could fail to find,
In such a crowd a mistress to his mind?

'DEAR SPEC,—Finding that my last letter took, I do intend to continue my epistolary correspondence with thee, on those dear confounded creatures, women. Thou knowest, all the little learning I am master of is upon that subject: I never looked in a book but for their sakes. I have lately met with two pure stories for a Spectator, which I am sure will please mightily, if they pass through thy hands. The first of them I found by chance in an English book, called Herodotus, that lay in my friend Dapperwit's window, as I visited him one morning. It luckily opened in the place where I met with the following account. He tells us that it was the manner among the Persians to have several fairs in the kingdom, at which all the young unmarried women were annually exposed to sale. The men who wanted wives came hither to provide themselves. Every woman was given to the highest bidder, and the money which she fetched laid aside for the public use, to be employed as thou shalt hear by and by. By this means the richest people had the choice of the market, and culled out all the most extraordinary beauties. As soon as the fair was thus picked, the refuse was to be distributed among the poor, and among those who could not go to the price of a beauty. Several of these married the agreeables, without paying a farthing for them, unless somebody chanced to think it worth his while to bid for them, in which case the best bidder was always the purchaser. But now you must know, Spec, it happened in Persia, as it does in our own country, that there 'was' as many ugly women as beauties or agreeables; so that by consequence, after the magistrates had put off a great many, there were still a great many that stuck upon their hands. In order therefore to clear the market, the money which the beauties had sold for was disposed of among the ugly; so that a poor man, who could not afford to have a beauty for his wife, was forced to take up with a fortune; the greatest portion being always given to the most deformed. To this the author adds, that every poor man was forced to live kindly with his wife, or, in case he repented of his bargain, to return her portion with her to the next public sale.

'What I would recommend to thee on this occasion is, to establish such an imaginary fair in Great Britain: thou couldst make it very pleasant, by matching women of quality with cobblers and carmen, or describing titles and garters leading off in great ceremony shopkeepers' and farmers' daughters. Though, to tell thee the truth, I am confoundedly afraid, that as the love of money prevails in our island more than it did in Persia, we should find that some of our greatest men would choose out the portions, and rival one another for the richest piece of deformity; and that, on the contrary, the toasts and belles would be bought up by extravagant heirs, gamesters, and spendthrifts. Thou couldst make very pretty reflections upon this occasion in honour of the Persian politicians, who took care, by such marriages, to beautify the upper part of the species, and to make the greatest persons in the government the most graceful. But this I shall leave to thy judicious pen.

'I have another story to tell thee, which I likewise met with in a book. It seems the general of the Tartars, after having laid siege to a strong town in China, and taken it by storm, would set to sale all the women that were found in it. Accordingly he put each of them into a sack, and, after having thoroughly considered the value of the woman who was enclosed, marked the price that was demanded for her upon the sack. There was a great confluence of chapmen, that resorted from every part, with a design to purchase, which they were to do 'unsight unseen.' The book mentions a merchant in particular, who observing one of the sacks to be marked pretty high, bargained for it, and carried it off with him to his house. As he was resting with it upon a halfway bridge, he was resolved to take a survey of his purchase: upon opening the sack, a little old woman popped her head out of it; at which the adventurer was in so great a rage, that he was going to shoot her out into the river. The old lady, however, begged him first of all to hear her story, by which he learned that she was sister to a great mandarin, who would infallibly make the fortune of his brother-in-law as soon as he should know to whose lot she fell. Upon which the merchant again tied her up in his sack, and carried her to his house, where she proved an excellent wife; and procured him all the riches from her brother that she had promised him.

'I fancy, if I was disposed to dream a second time, I could make a tolerable vision upon this plan. I would suppose all the unmarried women in London and Westminster brought to market in sacks, with their respective prices on each sack. The first sack that is sold is marked with five thousand pound. Upon the opening of it, I find it filled with an admirable housewife, of an agreeable countenance. The purchaser, upon hearing her good qualities, pays down her price very cheerfully. The second I would open should be a five hundred pound sack. The lady in it, to our surprise, has the face and person of a toast. As we are wondering how she came to be set at so low a price, we hear that she would have been valued at ten thousand pound, but that the public had made those abatements for her being a scold. I would afterwards find some beautiful, modest, and discreet woman, that should be the top of the market; and perhaps discover half a dozen romps tied up together in the same sack, at one hundred pound a head. The prude and the coquette should be valued at the same price, though the first should go off the better of the two. I fancy thou wouldst like such a vision, had I time to finish it; because, to talk in thy own way, there is a moral in it. Whatever thou mayest think of it, pr'ythee do not make any of thy queer apologies for this letter, as thou didst for my last. The women love a gay lively fellow, and are never angry at the railleries of one who is their known admirer. I am always bitter upon them but well with them. Thine,

'HONEYCOMB.'

No. 512.] *Friday, October* 17, 1712.

Lectorem delectando, pariterque monendo.
Hor. Ars Poet. ver. 344.

Mixing together profit and delight.

THERE is nothing which we receive with so much reluctance as advice. We look upon the man who gives it us as offering an affront to our understanding, and treating us like children or idiots. We consider the instruction as an implicit censure, and the zeal which any shows for our good on such an occasion, as a piece of presumption or impertinence. The truth of it is, the person who pretends to advise, does, in that particular, exercise a superiority over us, and can have no other reason for it, but that, in comparing us with himself, he thinks us defective either in our conduct or our understanding. For these reasons, there is nothing so difficult as the art of making advice agreeable; and indeed all the writers, both ancient and modern, have distinguished themselves among one another, according to the perfection at which they have arrived in this art. How many devices have been made use of, to render this bitter portion palatable! Some convey their instructions to us in the best chosen words, others in the most harmonious numbers; some in points of wit, and others in short proverbs.

But, among all the different ways of giving counsel, I think the finest, and that which pleases the most universally, is fable, in whatsoever shape it appears. If we consider this way of instructing or giving advice, it excels all others, because it is the least shocking, and the least subject to those exceptions which I have before mentioned.

This will appear to us if we reflect in the first place, that upon the reading of a fable we are made to believe we advise ourselves. We peruse the author for the sake of the story, and consider the precepts rather as our own conclusions than his instructions. The moral insinuates itself imperceptibly; we are taught by surprise, and become wiser and better unawares. In short, by this method a man is so far over-reached as to think he is directing himself, while he is following the dictates of another, and consequently is not sensible of that which is the most unpleasing circumstance in advice.

In the next place, if we look into human nature, we shall find that the mind is never so much pleased as when she exerts herself in any action that gives her an idea of her own perfections and abilities. This natural pride and ambition of the soul is very much gratified in the reading of a fable; for, in writings of this kind, the reader comes in for half of the performance; every thing appears to him like a discovery of his own; he is busied all the while in applying characters and circumstances, and is in this respect both a reader and a composer. It is no wonder therefore that on such occasions, when the mind is thus pleased with itself, and amused with its own discoveries, that it is highly delighted with the writing which is the occasion of it. For this reason the Absalom and Achitophel was one of the most popular poems that appeared in English. The poetry is indeed very fine; but had it been much finer, it would not have so much pleased, without a plan which gave the reader an opportunity of exerting his own talents.

This oblique manner of giving advice is so inoffensive, that, if we look into ancient histories, we find the wise men of old very often chose to give counsel to their kings in fables. To omit many which will occur to every one's memory, there is a pretty instance of this nature in a Turkish tale, which I do not like the worse for that little oriental extravagance which is mixed with it.

We are told that the Sultan Mahmoud, by his perpetual wars abroad and his tyranny at home, had filled his dominions with ruin and desolation, and half unpeopled the Persian empire. The vizier to this great sultan (whether a humourist or an enthusiast, we are not informed) pretended to have learned of a certain dervise to understand the language of birds, so that there was not a bird that could open his mouth but the vizier knew what it was he said. As he was one evening with the emperor, in their return from hunting, they saw a couple of owls upon a tree that grew near an old wall out of a heap of rubbish. 'I would fain know,' says the sultan, 'what those two owls are saying to one another; listen to their discourse, and give me an account of it.' The vizier approached the tree, pretending to be very attentive to the two owls. Upon his return to the sultan, 'Sir,' says he, 'I have heard part of their conversation, but dare not tell you what it is.' The sultan would not be satisfied with such an answer, but forced him to repeat word for word every thing the owls had said. 'You must know then,' said the vizier, 'that one of these owls has a son, and the other a daughter, between whom they are now upon a treaty of marriage. The father of the son said to the father of the daughter, in my hearing, "Brother, I consent to this marriage, provided you will settle upon your daughter fifty ruined villages for her portion." To which the father of the daughter replied, "Instead of fifty, I will give her five hundred if you please. God grant a long life to sultan Mahmoud! Whilst he reigns over us, we shall never want ruined villages."

The story says, the sultan was so touched with the fable, that he rebuilt the towns and villages which had been destroyed, and from that time forward consulted the good of his people.

To fill up my paper, I shall add a most ridiculous piece of natural magic, which was taught by no less a philosopher than Democritus, namely, that if the blood of certain birds, which he mentioned, were mixed together, it would produce a serpent of such a wonderful virtue, that whoever did eat it should be skilled in the language of birds, and understand every thing they said to one another. Whether the dervise above-mentioned might not have eaten such a serpent, I shall leave to the determination of the learned. O.

No. 513.] *Saturday, October* 18, 1712.

———Afflata est numine quando
Jam propriore Dei.——— *Virg. Æn.* iv. 50.

When all the god came rushing on her soul.
Dryden.

The following letter comes to me from that excellent man in holy orders, whom I have mentioned more than once as one of that society, who assists me in my speculations. It is a thought in sickness, and of a very serious nature, for which reason I give it a place in the paper of this day.

'Sir,—The indisposition which has long hung upon me is at last grown to such a head, that it must quickly make an end of me or of itself. You may imagine, that whilst I am in this bad state of health, there are none of your works which I read with greater pleasure than your Saturday's papers. I should be very glad if I could furnish you with any hints for that day's entertainment. Were I able to dress up several thoughts of a serious nature, which have made great impressions on my mind during a long fit of sickness, they might not be an improper entertainment for that occasion.

'Among all the reflections which usually rise in the mind of a sick man, who has time and inclination to consider his approaching end, there is none more natural than that of his going to appear naked and unbodied before Him who made him. When a man considers that, as soon as the vital union is dissolved, he shall see that Supreme Being whom he now contemplates at a distance, and only in his works; or, to speak more philosophically, when by some faculty in the soul, he shall apprehend the Divine Being, and be more sensible of his presence, than we are now of the presence of any object which the eye beholds, a man must be lost in carelessness and stupidity, who is not alarmed at such a thought. Dr. Sherlock, in his excellent treatise upon Death, has represented, in very strong and lively colours, the state of the soul in its first separation from the body, with regard to that invisible world which every where surrounds us, though we are not able to discover it through this grosser world of matter, which is accommodated to our senses in this life. His words are as follow:

"That death, which is our leaving this world, is nothing else put putting off these bodies, teaches us that it is only our union to these bodies which intercepts the sight of the other world. The other world is not at such a distance from us as we may imagine; the throne of God indeed is at a great remove from this earth, above the third heavens, where he displays his glory to those blessed spirits which encompass his throne; but as soon as we step out of these bodies we step into the other world, which is not so properly another world (for there is the same heaven and earth still) as a new state of life. To live in these bodies is to live in this world; to live out of them is to remove into the next: for while our souls are confined to these bodies, and can look only through these material casements, nothing but what is material can affect us; nay, nothing but what is so gross that it can reflect light, and convey those shapes and colours of things with it to the eye: so that, though within this visible world there be a more glorious scene of things than what appears to us, we perceive nothing at all of it; for this veil of flesh parts the visible and invisible world: but when we put off these bodies, there are new and surprising wonders present themselves to our views; when these material spectacles are taken off, the soul with its own naked eyes sees what was invisible before; and then we are in the other world, when we can see it, and converse with it. Thus St. Paul tells us, that 'when we are at home in the body, we are absent from the Lord; but when we are absent from the body, we are present with the Lord.' 2 Cor. v. 6. 8. And methinks this is enough to cure us of our fondness for these bodies, unless we think it more desirable to be confined to a prison, and to look through a grate all our lives, which gives us but a very narrow prospect, and that none of the best neither, than to be set at liberty to view all the glories of the world. What would we give now for the least glimpse of that invisible world, which the first step we take out of these bodies will present us with? There are such things 'as eye hath not seen nor ear heard, neither hath it entered into the heart of man to conceive.' Death opens our eyes, enlarges our prospect, presents us with a new and more glorious world, which we can never see while we are shut up in flesh; which should make us as willing to part with this veil, as to take the film off of our eyes which hinders our sight?"

'As a thinking man cannot but be very much affected with the idea of his appearing in the presence of that Being "whom none can see and live," he must be much more affected when he considers that this Being whom he appears before will examine all the actions of his past life, and reward or punish him accordingly. I must confess that I think there is no scheme of religion, besides that of Christianity, which can possibly support the most virtuous person under this thought. Let a man's innocence be what it will, let his virtues rise to the highest pitch of perfection attainable in this life, there will be still in him so many secret sins, so many human frailties, so many offences of ignorance, passion, and prejudice, so many unguarded words and thoughts, and, in short, so many defects in his best actions, that, without the advantages of such an expiation and atonement as Christianity has revealed to us, it is impossible that he should be cleared before his Sovereign Judge, or that he should be able to "stand in his sight." Our holy religion suggests to us the only means whereby our guilt may be taken away, and our imperfect obedience accepted.

'It is this series of thought that I have endeavoured to express in the following hymn, which I have composed during this my sickness.

I.
"When, rising from the bed of death,
O'erwhelm'd with guilt and fear,
I see my Maker face to face,
O how shall I appear!

II.
"If yet while pardon may be found,
And mercy may be sought,
My heart with inward horror shrinks,
And trembles at the thought:

III.
"When thou, O Lord, shall stand disclos'd
In majesty severe,
And sit in judgment on my soul,
O how shall I appear!

IV.
"But thou hast told the troubled mind,
Who does her sins lament,
The timely tribute of her tears,
Shall endless woe prevent.

V.
"Then see the sorrows of my heart,
Ere yet it be too late;
And hear my Saviour's dying groans,
To give those sorrows weight.

VI.
"For never shall my soul despair
Her pardon to procure,
Who knows thine only Son has died
To make her pardon sure."

'There is a noble hymn in French, which Monsieur Bayle has celebrated for a very fine one, and which the famous author of the Art of Speaking calls an admirable one, that turns upon a thought of the same nature. If I could have done it justice in English, I would have sent it to you translated; it was written by Monsieur des Barreux, who had been one of the greatest wits and libertines in France, but in his last years was as remarkable a penitent.

"Grand Dieu, tes jugemens sont remplis d'equite;
Toujours tu prends plaisir a nous etre propice,
Mais j'ai tant fait de mal, que jamais ta bonte
Ne me pardonnera, sans choquer ta justice.
Oui, mon Dieu, la grandeur de mon impiete
Ne laisse ton a pouvoir que le choix du supplice.
Ton interet s'oppose a ma felicite:
Et ta clemence meme attend que je perisse
Contente ton desir, puis qui'l t'est glorieux;
Offense toi des pleurs qui coulent de mes yeux:
Tonne, frappe, il est tems, rens moi guerre pour guerre;
J'adore en perissant la raison qui t'aigrit.
Mais dessus quel endroit tombera ton tonnere,
Qui ne soit tout couvert du sang de Jesus Christ."

'If these thoughts may be serviceable to you, I desire you would place them in a proper light, and am ever, with great sincerity, sir, yours, &c.' O.

No. 514.] *Monday, October* 20, 1712.

———Me Parnasi deserta per ardua dulcis
Raptat amor; juvat ire jugis qua nulla priorum,
Castaliam molli divertitur orbita clivo.
Virg. Georg. iii. 291.

But the commanding Muse my chariot guides,
Which o'er the dubious cliff securely rides:
And pleas'd I am no beaten road to take,
But first the way to new discoveries make.—*Dryden.*

'MR. SPECTATOR,—I came home a little later than usual the other night; and, not finding myself inclined to sleep, I took up Virgil to divert me until I should be more disposed to rest. He is the author whom I always choose on such occasions; no one writing in so divine, so harmonious, nor so equal a strain, which leaves the mind composed and softened into an agreeable melancholy; the temper in which, of all others, I choose to close the day. The passages I turned to were those beautiful raptures in his Georgics, where he professes himself entirely given up to the Muses, and smit with the love of poetry, passionately wishing to be transported to the cool shades and retirements of the mountain Hæmus. I closed the book and went to bed. What I had just before been reading made so strong an impression on my mind, that fancy seemed almost to fulfil to me the wish of Virgil, in presenting to me the following vision.

'Methought I was on a sudden placed in the plains of Bœotia, where at the end of the horizon I saw the mountain Parnassus rising before me. The prospect was of so large an extent, that I long wandered about to find a path which should directly lead me to it, had I not seen at some distance a grove of trees, which, in a plain that had nothing else remarkable enough in it to fix my sight, immediately determined me to go thither. When I arrived at it, I found it parted out into a great number of walks and alleys, which often widened into beautiful openings, as circles or ovals, set round with yews and cypresses, with niches, grottos, and caves, placed on the sides, encompassed with ivy. There was no sound to be heard in the whole place, but only that of a gentle breeze passing over the leaves of the forest; every thing beside was buried in a profound silence. I was captivated with the beauty and retirement of the place, and never so much, before that hour, was pleased with the enjoyment of myself. I indulged the humour, and suffered myself to wander without choice or design. At length, at the end of a range of trees, I saw three figures seated on a bank of moss, with a silent brook creeping at their feet. I adored them as the tutelary divinities of the place, and stood still to take a particular view of each of them. The middlemost, whose name was Solitude, sat with her arms across each other, and seemed rather pensive, and wholly taken up with her own thoughts, than any ways grieved or displeased. The only companions which she admitted into that retirement, were the goddess Silence, who sat on her right hand with her finger on her mouth, and on her left Contemplation, with her eyes fixed upon the heavens. Before her lay a celestial globe, with several schemes of mathematical theorems. She prevented my speech with the greatest affability in the world. "Fear not," said she, "I know your request before you speak it; you would be led to the mountain of the Muses: the only way to it lies through this place, and no one is so often employed in conducting persons thither as myself." When she had thus spoken, she rose from her seat, and I immediately placed myself under her direction; but whilst I passed through the grove I could not help inquiring of her who were the persons admitted into that sweet retirement. "Surely," said I, "there can nothing enter here but virtue and virtuous thoughts; the whole wood seems designed for the reception and reward of such persons as have spent their lives according to the dictates of their conscience, and the commands of the gods." "You imagine right," said she: "assure yourself this place was at first designed for no other: such it continued to be in the reign of Saturn, when none entered here but holy priests, deliverers of their country from oppression and tyranny, who reposed themselves here after their labours, and those whom the study and love of wisdom had fitted for divine conversation. But now it is become no less dangerous than it was before desirable: vice has learned so to mimic virtue, that it often creeps in hither under its disguise. See there; just before you, Revenge stalking by, habited in the robe of Honour. Observe not far from him Ambition, standing alone; if you ask him his name, he will tell you it is Emulation, or Glory. But the most frequent intruder we have is Lust, who succeeds now the deity to whom in better days this grove was entirely devoted. Virtuous Love, with Hymen, and the Graces attending him, once reigned over this happy place; a whole train of virtues waited on him, and no dishonourable thought durst presume for admittance. But now, how is the whole prospect changed! and how seldom renewed by some few who dare despise sordid wealth, and imagine themselves fit companions for so charming a divinity."

'The goddess had no sooner said thus, but we were arrived at the utmost boundaries of the wood, which lay contiguous to a plain that ended at the foot of the mountain. Here I kept close to my guide, being solicited by several phantoms, who assured me they would show me a nearer way to the mountain of the Muses. Among the rest Vanity was extremely importunate, having deluded infinite numbers, whom I saw wandering at the foot of the hill. I turned away from this despicable troop with disdain; and addressing myself to my guide, told her that, as I had some hopes I should be able to reach up part of the ascent, so I despaired of having strength enough to attain the plain on the top. But, being informed by her that it was impossible to stand upon the sides, and that if I did not proceed onwards I should irrevocably fall down to the lowest verge, I resolved to hazard any labour and hardship in the attempt: so great a desire had I of enjoying the satisfaction I hoped to meet with at the end of my enterprise.

'There were two paths, which led up by different ways to the summit of the mountain: the one was guarded by the genius which presides over the moment of our births. He had it in charge to examine the several pretensions of those who desired to pass that way, but to admit none excepting those only whom Melpomene had looked with a propitious eye at the hour of their nativity. The other way was guarded by Diligence, to whom many of those persons applied who had met with a denial the other way; but he was so tedious in granting their request, and indeed after admittance the way was so very intricate and laborious, that many, after they had made some progress, chose rather to return back than proceed, and very few persisted so long as to arrive at the end they proposed. Besides these two paths, which at length severally led to the top of the mountain, there was a third made up of these two, which a little after the entrance joined in one. This carried those happy few, whose good fortune it was to find it, directly to the throne of Apollo. I do not know whether I should even now have had the resolution to have demanded entrance at either of these doors, had I not seen a peasant-like man (followed by a numerous and lovely train of youths of both sexes) insist upon entrance for all whom he led up. He put me in mind of the country clown who is painted in the map for leading prince Eugene over the Alps. He had a bundle of papers in his hand; and producing several, that he said were given to him by hands which he knew Apollo would allow as passes: among which, methought I saw some of my own writing; the whole assembly was admitted, and gave by their presence a new beauty and pleasure to these happy mansions. I found the man did not pretend to enter himself, but served as a kind of forester in the lawns, to direct passengers, who by their own merit, or instructions, he procured for them, had virtue enough to travel that way. I looked very attentively upon this kind homely benefactor; and forgive me, Mr. Spectator, if I own to you I took him for yourself. We were no sooner entered, but we were sprinkled three times with the water of the fountain of Aganippe, which had power to deliver us from all harms, but only envy, which reached even to the end of our journey. We had not proceeded far in the middle path, when we arrived at the summit of the hill, where there immediately appeared to us two figures, which extremely engaged my attention: the one was a young nymph in the prime of her youth and beauty; she had wings on her shoulders and feet, and was able to transport herself to the most distant regions in the smallest space of time. She was continually varying her dress, sometimes into the most natural and becoming habits in the world, and at others into the most wild and freakish garb that can be imagined. There stood by her a man full aged and of great gravity, who corrected her inconsistencies by showing them in his mirror, and still flung her affected and unbecoming ornaments down the mountain, which fell in the plain below, and were gathered up and wore with great satisfaction by those that inhabited it. The name of this nymph was Fancy, the daughter of Liberty, the most beautiful of all the mountain nymphs: the other was Judgment, the offspring of Time, and the only child he acknowledged to be his. A youth, who sat upon a throne just between them, was their genuine offspring; his name was Wit, and his seat was composed of the works of the most celebrated authors. I could not but see with a secret joy, that, though the Greeks and Romans made the majority, yet our own countrymen were the next both in number and dignity. I was now at liberty to take a full prospect of that delightful region. I was inspired with new vigour and life, and saw every thing in nobler and more pleasing views than before: I breathed a purer æther in a sky which was a continued azure, gilded with perpetual sunshine. The two summits of the mountain rose on each side, and formed in the midst a most delicious vale, the habitation of the Muses, and of such as had composed works worthy of immortality. Apollo was seated upon a throne of gold, and for a canopy an aged laurel spread its boughs and its shade over his head. His bow and quiver lay at his feet. He held his harp in his hand, whilst the Muses round about him celebrated with hymns his victory over the serpent Python, and sometimes sung in softer notes the loves of Leucothoe and Daphnis. Homer, Virgil, and Milton were seated the next to them. Behind were a great number of others; among whom I was surprised to see some in the habit of Laplanders, who notwithstanding the uncouthness of their dress had lately obtained a place on the mountain. I saw Pindar walking alone, no one daring to accost him, until Cowley joined himself to him; but, growing weary of one who almost walked him out of breath, he left him for Horace and Anacreon, with whom he seemed infinitely delighted.

'A little farther I saw another group of figures: I made up to them, and found it was Socrates dictating to Xenophon, and the spirit of Plato; but most of all, Musæus had the greatest audience about him. I was at too great a distance to hear what he said, or to discover the faces of his hearers; only I thought I now perceived Virgil, who had joined them, and stood in a posture full of admiration at the harmony of his words.

'Lastly, at the very brink of the hill, I saw Boccalini sending despatches to the world below of what happened upon Parnassus; but I perceived he did it without leave of the Muses, and by stealth, and was unwilling to have them revised by Apollo. I could now, from this height and serene sky, behold the infinite cares and anxieties with which mortals below sought out their way through the maze of life. I saw the path of Virtue lie straight before them, whilst Interest, or some malicious demon, still hurried them out of the way. I was at once touched with pleasure at my own happiness, and compassion at the sight of their inextricable errors. Here the two contending passions rose so high, that they were inconsistent with the sweet repose I enjoyed; and, awaking with a sudden start, the only consolation I could admit of for my loss, was the hopes that this relation of my dream will not displease you.' T.

No. 515.] *Tuesday, October* 21, 1712.

Pudet me et miseret, qui harum mores cantabat mihi
Monuisse frustra—— *Ter. Heaut.* Act ii. Sc. 3.

I am ashamed and grieved, that I neglected his advice, who gave me the character of these creatures.

'Mr. Spectator,—I am obliged to you for printing the account I lately sent you of a coquette who disturbed a sober congregation in the city of London. That intelligence ended at her taking a coach, and bidding the driver go where he knew. I could not leave her so, but dogged her, as hard as she drove, to Paul's church-yard, where there was a stop of coaches attending company coming out of the cathedral. This gave me an opportunity to hold up a crown to her coachman, who gave me the signal that he would hurry on and make no haste, as you know the way is when they favour a chase. By his many kind blunders, driving against other coaches, and slipping off some of his tackle, I could keep up with him, and lodged my fine lady in the parish of St. James's. As I guessed, when I first saw her at church, her business is to win hearts, and throw them away, regarding nothing but the triumph. I have had the happiness, by tracing her through all with whom I heard she was acquainted, to find one who was intimate with a friend of mine, and to be introduced to her notice. I have made so good a use of my time, as to procure from that intimate of hers one of her letters, which she writ to her when in the country. This epistle of her own may serve to alarm the world against her in ordinary life, as mine, I hope, did those who shall behold her at church. The letter was written last winter to the lady who gave it me; and I doubt not but you will find it the soul of a happy self-loving dame, that takes all the admiration she can meet with, and returns none of it in love to her admirers.

"Dear Jenny,—I am glad to find you are likely to be disposed of in marriage so much to your approbation as you tell me. You say you are afraid only of me, for I shall laugh at your spouse's airs. I beg of you not to fear it, for I am too nice a discerner to laugh at any, but whom most other people think fine fellows; so that your dear may bring you hither as soon as his horses are in case enough to appear in town, and you will be very safe against any raillery you may apprehend from me; for I am surrounded with coxcombs of my own making, who are all ridiculous in a manner wherein your good man, I presume, cannot exert himself. As men who cannot raise their fortunes, and are uneasy under the incapacity of shining in courts, rail at ambition; so do awkward and insipid women, who cannot warm the hearts, and charm the eyes of men, rail at affectation: but she that has the joy of seeing a man's heart leap into his eyes at beholding her, is in no pain for want of esteem among the crew of that part of her own sex, who have no spirit but that of envy, and no language but that of malice. I do not in this, I hope, express myself insensible of the merit of Leodacia, who lowers her beauty to all but her husband, and never spreads her charms but to gladden him who has a right to them; I say, I do honour to those who can be coquettes, and are not such; but I despise all who would be so, and, in despair of arriving at it themselves, hate and vilify all those who can. But be that as it will, in answer to your desire of knowing my history: one of my chief present pleasures is in country-dances; and in obedience to me, as well as the pleasure of coming up to me, with a good grace, showing themselves in their address to others in my presence, and the like opportunities, they are all proficients that way; and I had the happiness of being the other night where we made six couple, and every woman's partner a professed lover of mine. The wildest imagination cannot form to itself, on any occasion, higher delight than I acknowledge myself to have been in all that evening. I chose out of my admirers a set of men who must love me, and gave them partners of such of my own sex who most envied me.

"My way is, when any man who is my admirer pretends to give himself airs of merit, as at this time a certain gentleman you know did, to mortify him by favouring in his presence the most insignificant creature I can find. At this ball I was led into the company by pretty Mr. Fanfly, who you know, is the most obsequious, well-shaped, well-bred woman's man in the town. I at first entrance declared him my partner if I danced at all; which put the whole assembly into a grin, as forming no terrors from such a rival. But we had not been long in the room before I overheard the meritorious gentleman above-mentioned say, with an oath, 'There is no raillery in the thing, she certainly loves the puppy.' My gentleman, when we were dancing, took an occasion to be very soft in his ogling upon a lady he danced with, and whom he knew of all women I loved most to outshine. The contest began who could plague the other most. I, who do not care a farthing for him, had no hard task to outvex him. I made Fanfly, with a very little encouragement, cut capers *coupee,* and then sink with all the air and tenderness imaginable. When he performed this, I observed the gentleman you know of, fall into the same way, and imitate as well as he could the despised Fanfly. I cannot well give you, who are so grave a country lady, the idea of the joy we have when we see a stubborn heart breaking, or a man of sense turning fool for our sakes; but this happened to our friend, and I expect his attendance whenever I go to church, to court, to the play, or the park. This is a sacrifice due to us women of genius, who have the eloquence of beauty, an easy mien. I mean by an easy mien, one which can be on occasion easily affected: for I must tell you, dear Jenny, I hold one maxim, which is an uncommon one, to wit, That our greatest charms are owing to affectation. It is to that our arms can lodge so quietly just over our hips, and the fan can play without any force or motion but just of the wrist. It is to affectation we owe the pensive attention of Deidamia at a tragedy, the scornful approbation of Dulcimara at a comedy, and the lowly aspect of Lanquicelsa at a sermon.

"To tell you the plain truth, I know no pleasure but in being admired, and have yet never failed of attaining the approbation of the man whose regard I had a mind to. You see all the men who make a figure in the world (as wise a look as they are pleased to put upon the matter) are moved by the same vanity as I am. What is there in ambition, but to make other people's wills depend upon yours? This indeed is not to be aimed at by one who has a genius no higher than to think of being a very good housewife in a country gentleman's family. The care of poultry and pigs are great enemies to the countenance: the vacant look of a fine lady is not to be preserved, if she admits any thing to take up her thoughts but her own dear person. But I interrupt you too long from your cares, and myself from my conquests. I am, madam, your most humble servant."

'Give me leave, Mr. Spectator, to add her friend's answer to this epistle, who is a very discreet ingenious woman.'

"DEAR GATTY,—I take your raillery in very good part, and am obliged to you for the free air with which you speak of your own gayeties. But this is but a barren superficial pleasure; for, indeed, Gatty, we are made for man; and in serious sadness I must tell you, whether you yourself know it or no, all these gallantries tend to no other end but to be a wife and a mother as fast as you can. I am, madam, your most obedient servant." T.

No. 516.] *Wednesday, October* 22, 1712.

Immortale odium, et nunquam sanabile vulnus:
Inde furor vulgo, quod numina vicinorum
Odit uturque locus; quum solos credit habendos
Esse deos, quos ipse colat.——————
Juv. Sat. xv. 34.

——A grudge, time out of mind, begun,
And mutually bequeathed from sire to son:
Religious spite and pious spleen bred first
The quarrel which so long the bigots nurst:
Each calls the other's god a senseless stock;
His own divine. *Tate.*

OF all the monstrous passions and opinions which have crept into the world, there is none so wonderful as that those who profess the common name of Christians, should pursue each other with rancour and hatred for difference in their way of following the example of their Saviour. It seems so natural that all who pursue the steps of any leader should form themselves after his manner, that it is impossible to account for effects so different from what we might expect from those who profess themselves followers of the highest pattern of meekness and charity, but by ascribing such effects to the ambition and corruption of those who are so audacious with souls full of fury, to serve at the altars of the God of Peace.

The massacres to which the church of Rome has animated the ordinary people, are dreadful instances of the truth of this observation; and whoever reads the history of the Irish rebellion, and the cruelties which ensued thereupon, will be sufficiently convinced to what rage poor ignorants may be worked up by those who profess holiness and become incendiaries, and, under the dispensation of grace, promote evils abhorrent to nature.

The subject and catastrophe, which deserve so well to be remarked by the protestant world, will, I doubt not, be considered by the reverend and learned prelate that preaches to-morrow before many of the descendants of those who perished on that lamentable day, in a manner suitable to the occasion, and worthy his own great virtue and eloquence.

I shall not dwell upon it any farther, but only transcribe out of a little tract, called the Christian Hero,* published in 1701, what I find there in honour of the renowned hero, William III. who rescued that nation from the repetition of the same disasters. His late majesty, of glorious memory, and the most Christian king, are considered at the conclusion of that treatise as heads of the protestant and Roman-catholic world in the following manner.

'There were not ever, before the entrance of the Christian name into the world, men who have maintained a more renowned carriage, than the two great rivals who possess the full fame of the present age, and will be the theme and examination of the future. They are exactly formed by nature for those ends to which heaven seems to have sent them amongst us. Both animated with a restless desire of glory, but pursue it by different means, and with different motives. To one it consists in an extensive undisputed empire over his subjects, to the other in their rational and voluntary obedience. Ones happiness is founded in their want of power, the others in their want of desire to oppose him. The one enjoys the summit of fortune with the luxury of a Persian, the other with the moderation of a Spartan. One is made to oppress, the other to relieve the oppressed. The one is satisfied with the pomp and ostentation of power to prefer and debase his inferiors; the other delighted only with the cause and foundation of it to cherish and protect them. To

* Steele, who was never insensible to his own faults and follies, but who never had courage to correct them, is said to have written this little tract, while plunged in all the dissipation of a soldier's life, to serve the purposes of a private manual, and to have published it under the hope that it would compel him to something like an imitation of the character he had drawn; unfortunately for him, it failed of its effect, and serve but to make his errors the more conspicuous

one therefore religion is but a convenient disguise, to the other a vigorous motive of action.

'For, without such ties of real and solid honour, there is no way of forming a monarch, but after the Machiavelian scheme, by which a prince must seem to have all virtues, but really be master of none; he is to be liberal, merciful, and just, only as they serve his interests; while, with the noble art of hypocrisy, empire would be to be extended, and new conquests be made by new devices, by which prompt address his creatures might insensibly give law in the business of life, by leading men in the entertainment of it.

'Thus, when words and show are apt to pass for the substantial things they are only to express, there would need no more to enslave a country but to adorn a court; for while every man's vanity makes him believe himself capable of becoming luxury, enjoyments are a ready bait for sufferings, and the hopes of preferment invitations to servitude; which slavery would be coloured with all the agreements, as they call it, imaginable. The noblest arts and artists, the finest pens and most elegant minds, jointly employed to set it off with the various embellishments of sumptuous entertainments, charming assemblies, and polished discourses, and those apostate abilities of men, the adored monarch might profusely and skilfully encourage, while they flatter his virtue, and gild his vice at so high a rate, that he, without scorn of the one, or love of the other, would alternately and occasionally use both; so that his bounty should support him in his rapines, his mercy in his cruelties.

'Nor is it to give things a more severe look, than is natural, to suppose such must be the consequences of a prince's having no other pursuit than that of his own glory; for if we consider an infant born into the world, and beholding itself the mightiest thing in it, itself the present admiration and future prospect of a fawning people, who profess themselves great or mean, according to the figure he is to make amongst them, what fancy would not be debauched to believe they were but what they professed themselves—his mere creatures; and use them as such by purchasing with their lives a boundless renown, which he, for want of a more just prospect, would place in the number of his slaves, and the extent of his territories? Such undoubtedly would be the tragical effects of a prince's living with no religion, which are not to be surpassed but by his having a false one.

'If ambition were spirited with zeal, what would follow, but that his people should be converted into an army, whose swords can make right in power, and solve controversy in belief? And if men should be stiff-necked to the doctrine of that visible church, let them be contented with an oar and a chain, in the midst of stripes and anguish, to contemplate on Him "whose yoke is easy and whose burden is light."

'With a tyranny begun on his own subjects, and indignation that others draw their breath independent of his frown or smile, why should he not proceed to the seizure of the world? And if nothing but the thirst of sway were the motive of his actions, why should treatises be other than mere words, or solemn national compacts be any thing but a halt in the march of that army, who are never to lay down their arms until all men are reduced to the necessity of hanging their lives on his wayward will; who might supinely, and at leisure, expiate his own sins by other men's sufferings, while he daily meditates new slaughter and conquests?

'For mere man, when giddy with unbridled power, is an insatiate idol, not to be appeased with myriads offered to his pride, which may be puffed up by the adulation of a base and prostrate world into an opinion that he is something more than human, by being something less: and, alas, what is there that mortal man will not believe of himself, when complimented with the attributes of God? He can then conceive thoughts of a power as omnipresent as his. But, should there be such a foe of mankind now upon earth, have our sins so far provoked Heaven, that we are left utterly naked to his fury? Is there no power, no leader, no genius, that can conduct and animate us to our death, or to our defence? Yes; our great God never gave one to reign by his permission, but he gave to another also to reign by his grace.

'All the circumstances of the illustrious life of our prince seem to have conspired to make him the check and bridle of tyranny; for his mind has been strengthened and confirmed by one continued struggle, and Heaven has educated him by adversity to a quick sense of the distresses and miseries of mankind, which he was born to redress. In just scorn of the trivial glories and light ostentations of power, that glorious instrument of Providence moves, like that, in a steady, calm, and silent course, independent either of applause or calumny; which renders him, if not in a political, yet in a moral, a philosophic, an heroic, and a Christian sense, an absolute monarch: who, satisfied with this unchangeable, just, and ample glory, must needs turn all his regards from himself to the service of others; for he begins his enterprise with his own share in the success of them; for integrity bears in itself its reward, nor can that which depends not on event, ever know disappointment.

'With the undoubted character of a glorious captain, and (what he much more values than the most splendid titles,) that of a sincere and honest man, he is the hope and stay of Europe, an universal good; not to be engrossed by us only, for distant potentates implore his friendship, and injured empires court his assistance. He rules the world, not by an invasion of the people of the earth, but the address of its princes; and, if that world should be again roused from the repose which his prevailing arms had given it, why should we not hope that there is an Almighty, by whose influence the terrible enemy that thinks himself prepared for battle may find he is but ripe for destruction?—and that there may be in the womb of time great incidents, which may make the catastrophe of a prosperous life as unfortunate as the particular scenes of it were successful?—for there does not want a skilful eye and resolute arm to observe and grasp the occasion. A prince, who from—

———Fuit Ilium et ingens
Gloria——— *Virg. Æn.* ii. 325.

Troy is no more, and Ilium was a town.
Dryden.

T.

No. 517.] *Thursday, October* 23, 1712.

Heu pietas! heu prisca fides!———
Virg. Æn. vi. 878.

Mirror of ancient faith!
Undaunted worth! Inviolable truth!—*Dryden.*

We last night received a piece of ill news at our club, which very sensibly afflicted every one of us. I question not but my readers themselves will be troubled at the hearing of it. To keep them no longer in suspense, Sir Roger de Coverley is dead. He departed this life at his house in the country, after a few weeks sickness. Sir Andrew Freeport has a letter from one of his correspondents in those parts, that informs him the old man caught a cold at the county-sessions, as he was very warmly promoting an address of his own penning, in which he succeeded according to his wishes. But this particular comes from a whig justice of peace, who was always Sir Roger's enemy and antagonist. I have letters both from the chaplain and captain Sentry, which mention nothing of it, but are filled with many particulars to the honour of the good old man. I have likewise a letter from the butler, who took so much care of me last summer when I was at the knight's house. As my friend the butler mentions, in the simplicity of his heart, several circumstances the others have passed over in silence, I shall give my reader a copy of his letter, without any alteration or diminution.

'Honoured Sir,—Knowing that you was my old master's good friend, I could not forbear sending you the melancholy news of his death, which has afflicted the whole country, as well as his poor servants, who loved him, I may say, better than we did our lives. I am afraid he caught his death the last county-sessions, where he would go to see justice done to a poor widow woman, and her fatherless children, that had been wronged by a neighbouring gentleman; for you know, sir, my good master was always the poor man's friend. Upon his coming home, the first complaint he made was, that he had lost his roast-beef stomach, not being able to touch a sirloin, which was served up according to custom; and you know he used to take great delight in it. From that time forward he grew worse and worse, but still kept a good heart to the last. Indeed we were once in great hope of his recovery, upon a kind message that was sent him from the widow lady whom he had made love to the forty last years of his life; but this only proved a lightning before death. He has bequeathed to this lady, as a token of his love, a great pearl necklace, and a couple of silver bracelets set with jewels, which belonged to my good old lady his mother. He has bequeathed the fine white gelding that he used to ride a hunting upon to his chaplain, because he thought he would be kind to him; and has left you all his books. He has, moreover, bequeathed to the chaplain a very pretty tenement with good lands about it. It being a very cold day when he made his will, he left for mourning to every man in the parish, a great frieze-coat, and to every woman a black riding-hood. It was a moving sight to see him take leave of his poor servants, commending us all for our fidelity, whilst we were not able to speak a word for weeping. As we most of us are grown gray-headed in our dear master's service, he has left us pensions and legacies, which we may live very comfortably upon the remaining part of our days. He has bequeathed a great deal more in charity, which is not yet come to my knowledge, and it is peremptorily said in the parish, that he has left money to build a steeple to the church; for he was heard to say some time ago, that, if he lived two years longer, Coverley church should have a steeple to it. The chaplain tells every body that he made a very good end, and never speaks of him without tears. He was buried, according to his own directions, among the family of the Coverleys, on the left hand of his father Sir Arthur. The coffin was carried by six of his tenants, and the pall held up by six of the quorum. The whole parish followed the corpse with heavy hearts and in their mourning suits; the men in frieze, and the women in riding-hoods. Captain Sentry, my master's nephew, has taken possession of the Hall-house, and the whole estate. When my old master saw him, a little before his death, he shook him by the hand, and wished him joy of the estate which was falling to him, desiring him only to make a good use of it, and to pay the several legacies, and the gifts of charity, which he told him he had left as quit-rents upon the estate. The captain truly seems a courteous man, though he says but little. He makes much of those whom my master loved, and shows great kindness to the old house-dog, that you know my poor master was so fond of. It would have gone to your heart to have heard the moans the dumb creature made on the day of my master's death. He has never joyed himself since; no more has any of us. It was the melancholiest day for the poor people that ever happened in Worcestershire. This being all from, honoured sir, your most sorrowful servant,

'EDWARD BISCUIT.

'P. S. My master desired, some weeks before he died, that a book which comes up to you by the carrier, should be given to Sir Andrew Freeport in his name.'

This letter, notwithstanding the poor butler's manner of writing it, gave us such an idea of our good old friend, that upon
here was not a dry eye in
ndrew, opening the book, found it to be a collection of acts of parliament. There was in particular the Act of Uniformity, with some passages in it marked by Sir Roger's own hand. Sir Andrew found that they related to two or three points which he had disputed with Sir Roger the last time he appeared at the club. Sir Andrew, who would have been merry at such an incident on another occasion, at the sight of the old man's writing burst into tears, and put the book in his pocket. Captain Sentry informs me that the knight has left rings and mourning for every one in the club. O.

No. 518.] *Friday, October* 24, 1712.

——Miserum est alienæ incumbere famæ,
Ne collapsa ruant subductis recta columnis.
Juv. Sat. viii. 76.

'Tis poor relying on another's fame;
For, take the pillars but away, and all
The superstructure must in ruins fall.—*Stepney.*

THIS being a day of business with me, I must make the present entertainment like a treat at a house-warming, out of such presents as have been sent me by my guests. The first dish which I serve up is a letter come fresh to my hand.

'MR. SPECTATOR,—It is with inexpressible sorrow that I hear of the death of good Sir Roger, and do heartily condole with you upon so melancholy an occasion. I think you ought to have blackened the edges of a paper which brought us so ill news, and to have had it stamped likewise in black. It is expected of you that you should write his epitaph, and, if possible, fill his place in the club with as worthy and diverting a member. I question not but you will receive many recommendations from the public of such as will appear candidates for that post.

'Since I am talking of death, and have mentioned an epitaph, I must tell you, sir, that I have made a discovery of a church-yard in which I believe you might spend an afternoon with great pleasure to yourself and to the public. It belongs to the church of Stebon-Heath, commonly called Stepney. Whether or no it be that the people of that parish have a particular genius for an epitaph, or that there be some poet among them who undertakes that work by the great, I cannot tell; but there are more remarkable inscriptions in that place than in any other I have met with; and I may say, without vanity, that there is not a gentleman in England better read in tombstones than myself, my studies having laid very much in church-yards. I shall beg leave to send you a couple of epitaphs, for a sample of those I have just now mentioned. They are written in a different manner; the first being in the diffused and luxuriant, the second in the close contracted style. The first has much of the simple and pathetic; the second is something light, but nervous. The first is thus:

'Here Thomas Sapper lies interr'd. Ah why!
Born in New England, did in London die;
Was the third son of eight, begot upon
His mother Martha, by his father John.
Much favour'd by his prince he 'gan to be
But nipt by death at th' age of twenty-three.
Fatal to him was that we small-pox name,
By which his mother and two brethren came
Also to breathe their last, nine years before,
And now have left their father to deplore
The loss of all his children, with his wife,
Who was the joy and comfort of his life."

'The second is as follows:

"Here lies the body of Daniel Saul,
Spittlefields weaver, and that's all."

'I will not dismiss you whilst I am upon this subject, without sending a short epitaph which I once met with, though I cannot possibly recollect the place. The thought of it is serious, and in my opinion the finest that I ever met with upon this occasion. You know, sir, it is usual, after having told us the name of the person who lies interred, to launch out into his praises. This epitaph takes a quite contrary turn, having been made by the person himself some time before his death.

"*Hic jacet* R. C. *in expectatione diei supremi. Qualis erat dies iste indicabit.*"

"Here lieth R. C. in expectation of the last day. What sort of a man he was, that day will discover."

'I am, sir, &c.'

The following letter is dated from Cambridge.

'SIR,—Having lately read among your speculations an essay upon physiognomy, I cannot but think, that, if you made a visit to this ancient university, you might receive very considerable lights upon that subject, there being scarce a young fellow in it who does not give certain indications of his particular humour and disposition, conformable to the rules of that art. In courts and cities every body lays a constraint upon his countenance, and endeavours to look like the rest of the world;

but the youth of this place, having not yet formed themselves by conversation, and the knowledge of the world, give their limbs and features their full play.

'As you have considered human nature in all its lights, you must be extremely well apprized, that there is a very close correspondence between the outward and the inward man; that scarce the least dawning, the least parturiency towards a thought can be stirring in the mind of man, without producing a suitable revolution in his exteriors, which will easily discover itself to an adept in the theory of the phiz. Hence it is that the intrinsic worth and merit of a son of Alma Mater is ordinarily calculated from the cast of his visage, the contour of his person, the mechanism of his dress, the disposition of his limbs, the manner of his gait and air, with a number of circumstances of equal consequence and information. The practitioners in this art often make use of a gentleman's eyes to give them light into the posture of his brains; take a handle from his nose to judge of the size of his intellects; and interpret the overmuch visibility and pertness of one ear as an infallible mark of reprobation, and a sign the owner of so saucy a member fears neither God nor man. In conformity to this scheme, a contracted brow, a lumpish downcast look, a sober sedate pace, with both hands dangling quiet and steady in lines exactly parallel to each lateral pocket of his galligaskins, is logic, metaphysics, and mathematics, in perfection. So likewise the belles-lettres, are typified by a saunter in the gait, a fall of one wing of the peruke backward, an insertion of one hand in the fob, and a negligent swing of the other, with a pinch of right fine Barcelona between finger and thumb, a due quantity of the same upon the upper lip, and a noddle case loaden with pulvil. Again, a grave solemn stalking pace is heroic poetry and politics; an unequal one, a genius for the ode, and the modern ballad; and an open breast, with an audacious display of the Holland shirt, is construed a fatal tendency to the art military.

'I might be much larger upon these hints, but I know whom I write to. If you can graft any speculation upon them, or turn them to the advantage of the persons concerned in them, you will do a work very becoming the British Spectator, and oblige, your very humble servant,

'TOM TWEER.'

No. 519.] *Saturday, October* 25, 1712.

Inde hominum pecudumque genus, vitæque volantum,
Et quæ marmoreo fert monstra sub æquore pontus.
Virg. Æn. vi. 728.

Hence men and beasts the breath of life obtain,
And birds of air, and monsters of the main.
Dryden.

THOUGH there is a great deal of pleasure in contemplating the material world, by which I mean that system of bodies into which nature has so curiously wrought the mass of dead matter, with the several relations which those bodies bear to one another; there is still, methinks, something more wonderful and surprising in contemplations on the world of life, by which I mean all those animals with which every part of the universe is furnished. The material world is only the shell of the Universe, the world of life are its inhabitants.

If we consider those parts of the material world which lie the nearest to us, and are therefore subject to our observation and inquiries, it is amazing to consider the infinity of animals with which it is stocked. Every part of matter is peopled; every green leaf swarms with inhabitants. There is scarce a single humour in the body of a man, or of any other animal, in which our glasses do not discover myriads of living creatures. The surface of animals is also covered with other animals, which are in the same manner the basis of other animals that live upon it; nay, we find in the most solid bodies, as in marble itself, innumerable cells and cavities that are crowded with such imperceptible inhabitants as are too little for the naked eye to discover. On the other hand, if we look into the more bulky parts of nature, we see the seas, lakes, and rivers, teeming with numberless kinds of living creatures. We find every mountain and marsh, wilderness and wood, plentifully stocked with birds and beasts; and every part of matter affording proper necessaries and conveniencies for the livelihood of multitudes which inhabit it.

The author* of the Plurality of Worlds draws a very good argument from this consideration for the peopling of every planet; as indeed it seems very probable, from the analogy of reason, that if no part of matter, which we are acquainted with, lies waste and useless, those great bodies which are at such a distance from us, should not be desert and unpeopled, but rather that they should be furnished with beings adapted to their respective situations.

Existence is a blessing to those beings only which are endowed with perception; and is in a manner thrown away upon dead matter, any farther than as it is subservient to beings which are conscious of their existence. Accordingly we find, from the bodies which lie under our observation, that matter is only made as the basis and support of animals, and that there is no more of the one than what is necessary for the existence of the other.

Infinite goodness is of so communicative a nature, that it seems to delight in the conferring of existence upon every degree of perceptive being. As this is a speculation which I have often pursued with great pleasure to myself, I shall enlarge farther

* Fontenelle.—This book was published in 1686 and obtained for the author great reputation.

upon it, by considering that part of the scale of beings which comes within our knowledge.

There are some living creatures which are raised just above dead matter. To mention only that species of shell-fish, which are formed in the fashion of a cone, that grow to the surface of several rocks, and immediately die upon their being severed from the place where they grow. There are many other creatures but one remove from these, which have no other sense but that of feeling and taste. Others have still an additional one of hearing; others of smell, and others of sight. It is wonderful to observe by what a gradual progress the world of life advances through a prodigious variety of species, before a creature is formed that is complete in all its senses; and even among these there is such a different degree of perfection in the senses which one animal enjoys beyond what appears in another, that, though the sense in different animals be distinguished by the same common denomination, it seems almost of a different nature. If after this we look into the several inward perfections of cunning and sagacity, or what we generally call instinct, we find them rising after the same manner imperceptibly one above another, and receiving additional improvements, according to the species in which they are implanted. This progress in nature is so very gradual, that the most perfect of an inferior species comes very near to the most imperfect of that which is immediately above it.

The exuberant and overflowing goodness of the Supreme Being, whose mercy extends to all his works, is plainly seen, as I have before hinted, from his having made so very little matter, at least what falls within our knowledge, that does not swarm with life. Nor is his goodness less seen in the diversity than in the multitude of living creatures. Had he only made one species of animals, none of the rest would have enjoyed the happiness of existence: he has, therefore, specified in his creation every degree of life, every capacity of being. The whole chasm in nature, from a plant to a man, is filled up with diverse kinds of creatures, rising one over another, by such a gentle and easy ascent, that the little transitions and deviations from one species to another are almost insensible. This intermediate space is so well husbanded and managed, that there is scarce a degree of perception which does not appear in some one part of the world of life. Is the goodness or the wisdom of the Divine Being more manifested in this his proceeding?

There is a consequence, besides those I have already mentioned, which seems very naturally deducible from the foregoing considerations. If the scale of being rises by such a regular progress so high as man, we may, by a parity of reason, suppose that it still proceeds gradually through those beings which are of a superior nature to him; since there is an infinitely greater space and room for different degrees of perfection between the Supreme Being and man, than between man and the most despicable insect. This consequence of so great a variety of beings which are superior to us, from that variety which is inferior to us, is made by Mr. Locke, in a passage which I shall here set down, after having premised, that, notwithstanding there is such infinite room between man and his Maker for the creative power to exert itself in, it is impossible that it should ever be filled up, since there will be still an infinite gap or distance between the highest created being and the Power which produced him.

'That there should be more species of intelligent creatures above us, than there are of sensible and material below us, is probable to me from hence: that in all the visible corporeal world we see no chasms, or no gaps. All quite down from us the descent is by easy steps, and a continued series of things, that in each remove differ very little one from the other. There are fishes that have wings, and are not strangers to the airy region; and there are some birds that are inhabitants of the water, whose blood is as cold as fishes, and their flesh so like in taste, that the scrupulous are allowed them on fish days. There are animals so near of kin both to birds and beasts, that they are in the middle between both. Amphibious animals link the terrestrial and aquatic together. Seals live at land and at sea, and porpoises have the warm blood and the entrails of a hog; not to mention what is confidently reported of mermaids, or sea-men, there are some brutes that seem to have as much knowledge and reason as some part that are called men; and the animal and vegetable kingdoms are so nearly joined, that if you will take the lowest of one, and the highest of the other, there will scarce be perceived any great difference between them; and so on until we come to the lowest and the most inorganical parts of matter, we shall find every where that the several species are linked together, and differ but in almost insensible degrees. And, when we consider the infinite power and wisdom of the Maker, we have reason to think that it is suitable to the magnificent harmony of the universe, and the great design and infinite goodness of the architect, that the species of creatures should also by gentle degrees ascend upward from us toward his infinite perfection, as we see they gradually descend from us downward: which if it be probable, we have reason then to be persuaded that there are far more species of creatures above us than there are beneath; we being in degrees of perfection much more remote from the infinite being of God, than we are from the lowest state of being, and that which approaches nearest to nothing. And yet of all those distinct species we have no clear distinct ideas.'

In this system of being, there is no creature so wonderful in its nature, and which so much deserves our particular attention, as man, who fills up the middle space between the animal and intellectual nature, the visible and invisible world, and is that link in the chain of beings which has been often termed the *nexus utriusque mundi.* So that he, who in one respect, being associated with angels and archangels, may look upon a Being 'of infinite perfection,' as his father, and the highest order of spirits as his brethren, may in another respect say to corruption, 'Thou art my father; and to the worm, Thou art my mother and my sister.' O.

No. 520.] *Monday, October* 27, 1712.

Quis desiderio sit pudor aut modus
Tam chari capitis? *Hor.* Od. xxiv. Lib. 1. 1.

And who can grieve too much? What time shall end
Our mourning for so dear a friend?—*Creech.*

'Mr. Spectator,—The just value you have expressed for the matrimonial state is the reason that I now venture to write to you, without fear of being ridiculous, and confess to you that though it is three months since I lost a very agreeable woman who was my wife, my sorrow is still fresh; and I am often, in the midst of company, upon any circumstance that revives her memory, with a reflection what she would say or do on such an occasion: I say upon any occurrence of that nature, which I can give you a sense of, though I cannot express it wholly, I am all over softness, and am obliged to retire and give way to a few sighs and tears before I can be easy. I cannot but recommend the subject of male widowhood to you, and beg of you to touch upon it by the first opportunity. To those who had not lived like husbands during the lives of their spouses, this would be a tasteless jumble of words; but to such (of whom there are not a few) who have enjoyed that state with the sentiments proper for it, you will have every line, which hits the sorrow, attended with a tear of pity and consolation; for I know not by what goodness of Providence it is that every gush of passion is a step towards the relief of it; and there is a certain comfort in the very act of sorrowing, which, I suppose, arises from a secret consciousness in the mind, that the affliction it is under flows from a virtuous cause. My concern is not indeed so outrageous as at the first transport; for I think it has subsided rather into a soberer state of mind than any actual perturbation of spirit. There might be rules formed for men's behaviour on this great incident, to bring them from that misfortnne into the condition I am at present; which is, I think, that my sorrow has converted all roughness of temper into meekness, good nature, and complacency. But, indeed, when in a serious and lonely hour I present my departed consort to my imagination, with that air of persuasion in her countenance when I have been in passion, that sweet affability when I have been in good humour, that tender compassion when I have had any thing which gave me uneasiness; I confess to you I am inconsolable, and my eyes gush with grief, as if I had seen her just then expire. In this condition I am broken in upon by a charming young woman, my daughter, who is the picture of what her mother was on her wedding-day. The good girl strives to comfort me; but how shall I let you know that all the comfort she gives me is to make my tears flow more easily? The child knows she quickens my sorrows, and rejoices my heart at the same time. Oh, ye learned! tell me by what word to speak a motion of the soul for which there is no name. When she kneels, and bids me be comforted, she is my child: when I take her in my arms, and bid her say no more, she is my very wife, and is the very comforter I lament the loss of. I banish her the room, and weep aloud that I have lost her mother, and that I have her.

'Mr. Spectator, I wish it were possible for you to have a sense of these pleasing perplexities; you might communicate to the guilty part of mankind that they are incapable of the happiness which is in the very sorrows of the virtuous.

'But pray spare me a little longer; give me leave to tell you the manner of her death. She took leave of all her family, and bore the vain application of medicines with the greatest patience imaginable. When the physician told her she must certainly die, she desired, as well as she could, that all who were present, except myself, might depart the room. She said she had nothing to say, for she was resigned, and I knew all she knew that concerned us in this world; but she desired to be alone, that in the presence of God only she might, without interruption, do her last duty to me, of thanking me for all my kindness to her: adding that she hoped in my last moments I should feel the same comfort for my goodness to her, as she did in that she had acquitted herself with honour, truth, and virtue to me.

'I curb myself, and will not tell you that this kindness cut my heart in twain, when I expected an accusation for some passionate starts of mine, in some parts of our time together, to say nothing but thank me for the good, if there was any good suitable to her own excellence! All that I had ever said to her, all the circumstances of sorrow and joy between us, crowded upon my mind in the same instant: and when, immediately after, I saw the pangs of death come upon that dear body which I had often embraced with transport: when I saw those cherishing eyes begin to be ghastly, and their last struggle to be to fix themselves on me, how did I lose all patience! She expired in my arms, and in my distraction I thought I saw her bosom still heave. There was certainly life yet still left. I cried, she just now spoke to me. But, alas! I grew giddy, and all things moved about me, from the distemper of my own head; for the best of women was breathless, and gone for ever.

'Now the doctrine I would, methinks, have you raise from this account I have given you, is, that there is a certain equanimity in those who are good and just, which runs into their very sorrow, and disappoints the force of it. Though they must pass through afflictions in common with all who are in human nature, yet their conscious integrity shall undermine their affliction; nay, that very affliction shall add force to their integrity, from a reflection of the use of virtue in the hour of affliction. I sat down with a design to put you upon giving us rules how to overcome such griefs as these, but I should rather advise you to teach men to be capable of them.

'You men of letters have what you call the fine taste in your apprehensions of what is properly done or said. There is something like this deeply grafted in the soul of him who is honest and faithful in all his thoughts and actions. Every thing which is false, vicious, or unworthy, is despicable to him, though all the world should approve it. At the same time he has the most lively sensibility in all enjoyments and sufferings which it is proper for him to have where any duty of life is concerned. To want sorrow when you in decency and truth should be afflicted, is, I should think, a greater instance of a man's being a blockhead, than not to know the beauty of any passage in Virgil. You have not yet observed, Mr Spectator, that the fine gentlemen of this age set up for hardness of heart; and humanity has very little share in their pretences. He is a brave fellow who is always ready to kill a man he hates, but he does not stand in the same degree of esteem who laments for the woman he loves. I should fancy you might work up a thousand pretty thoughts, by reflecting upon the persons most susceptible of the sort of sorrow I have spoken of; and I dare say you will find, upon examination, that they are the wisest and the bravest of mankind who are the most capable of it. I am, sir, your humble servant, F. J.

'Norwich, 7th October, 1712.' T.

No. 521.] *Tuesday, October* 28, 1712.

Vera redit facies, dissimulata perit.—*P. Arb.*

The real face returns, the counterfeit is lost.

'Mr. Spectator,—I have been for many years loud in this assertion, that there are very few that can see or hear. I mean, that can report what they have seen or heard: and this through incapacity or prejudice, one of which disables almost every man who talks to you from representing things as he ought. For which reason I am come to a resolution of believing nothing I hear; and I contemn the man given to narrations under the appellation of "a matter-of-fact man:" and, according to me, a matter-of-fact man is one whose life and conversation is spent in the report of what is not matter-of-fact.

'I remember when prince Eugene was here there was no knowing his height or figure, until you, Mr. Spectator, gave the public satisfaction in that matter. In relations, the force of the expression lies very often more in the look, the tone of voice, or the gesture, than the words themselves; which, being repeated in any other manner by the undiscerning, bear a very different interpretation from their original meaning. I must confess I formerly have turned this humour of mine to very good account; for whenever I heard any narration uttered with extraordinary vehemence, and grounded upon considerable authority, I was always ready to lay any wager that it was not so. Indeed, I never pretended to be so rash as to fix the matter any particular way in opposition to theirs; but as there are a hundred ways of any thing happening, besides that it has happened, I only controverted its falling out in that one manner as they settled it, and left it to the ninety-nine other ways, and consequently had more probability of success. I had arrived at a particular skill in warming a man so far in his narrations as to make him throw in a little of the marvellous, and then, if he has much fire, the next degree is the impossible. Now this is always the time for fixing the wager. But this requires the nicest management, otherwise very probably the dispute may arise to the old determination by battle. In these conceits I have been very fortunate, and have won some wages of those who have professedly valued themselves upon intelligence, and have put themselves to great charge and expense to be misinformed considerably sooner than the rest of the world.

'Having got a comfortable sum by this my opposition to public report, I have brought myself now to so great a perfection in attention, more especially to party-relation, that, at the same time I seem with greedy ears to devour up the discourse, I certainly do not know one word of it, but pursue my own course of thought, whether upon business or amusement, with much tranquillity; I say inattention, because a late act of parliament* has secured all party-liars from the penalty of a wager, and consequently made it unprofitable to

* Stat. 7 Anne, cap. 17.—By it all wagers laid upon a contingency relating to the war with France were declared to be void.

attend to them. However, good-breeding obliges a man to maintain the figure of the keenest attention, the true posture of which in a coffee-house, I take to consist in leaning over a table with the edge of it pressing hard upon your stomach: for the more pain the narration is received with, the more gracious is your bending over; besides that the narrator thinks you forget your pain by the pleasure of hearing him.

'Fort Knock has occasioned several very perplexed and inelegant heats and animosities; and there was one the other day, in a coffee-house where I was, that took upon him to clear that business to me, for he said he was there. I knew him to be that sort of man that had not strength of capacity to be informed of any thing that depended merely upon his being an eye-witness, and therefore was fully satisfied he could give me no information, for the very same reason he believed he could, for he was there. However, I heard him with the same greediness as Shakspeare describes in the following lines:

> "I saw a smith stand on his hammer, thus,
> With open mouth, swallowing a taylor's news."

'I confess of late I have not been so much amazed at the declaimers in coffee-houses as I formerly was, being satisfied that they expect to be rewarded for their vociferations. Of these liars there are two sorts: the genius of the first consists in much impudence, and a strong memory; the others have added to these qualifications a good understanding and smooth language. These therefore have only certain heads, which they are as eloquent upon as they can, and may be called "embellishers;" the others repeat only what they hear from others as literally as their parts or zeal will permit, and are called "reciters." Here was a fellow in town some years ago, who used to divert himself by telling a lie at Charing-cross in the morning at eight of the clock, and following it through all parts of the town until eight at night: at which time he came to a club of his friends, and diverted them with an account what censure it had at Will's in Covent-garden, how dangerous it was believed to be at Child's, and what inference they drew from it with relation to stocks at Jonathan's. I have had the honour to travel with this gentleman I speak of, in search of one of his falsehoods; and have been present when they have described the very man they have spoken to, as him who first reported it, tall or short, black or fair, a gentleman or a raggamuffin, according as they liked the intelligence. I have heard one of our ingenious writers of news say, that, when he has had a customer with an advertisement of an apprentice or a wife run away, he has desired the advertiser to compose himself a little before he dictated the description of the offender: for when a person is put in a public paper by a man who is angry with him, the real description of such person is hid in the deformity with which the angry man describes him; therefore this fellow always made his customers describe him as he would the day before he offended, or else he was sure he would never find him out. These and many other hints I could suggest to you for the elucidation of all fictions; but I leave it to your own sagacity to improve or neglect this speculation. I am, sir, your most obedient, humble servant.' T.

No. 522.] *Wednesday, October* 29, 1712.

> ——Adjuro nunquam eam me deserturum;
> Non, si capiundos mihi sciam esse inimicos omnes homines.
> Hanc mihi expetivi, contigit, conveniunt mores: valeant,
> Qui inter nos discidium volunt: hanc nisi mors, mi adimet nemo. *Ter.* Andr. Act iv. Sc. 2.

I swear never to forsake her; no, though I were sure to make all men my enemies. Her I desired; her I have obtained; our humours agree. Perish all those who would separate us! Death alone shall deprive me of her.

I SHOULD esteem myself a very happy man if my speculation could in the least contribute to the rectifying the conduct of my readers in one of the most important affairs of life, to wit, their choice in marriage. This state is the foundation of community, and the chief band of society; and I do not think I can be too frequent on subjects which may give light to my unmarried readers in a particular which is so essential to their following happiness or misery. A virtuous disposition, a good understanding, an agreeable person, and an easy fortune, are the things which should be chiefly regarded on this occasion. Because my present view is to direct a young lady, who I think is now in doubt whom to take of many lovers, I shall talk at this time to my female readers. The advantages, as I was going to say, of sense, beauty, and riches, are what are certainly the chief motives to a prudent young woman of fortune for changing her condition; but, as she is to have her eye upon each of these, she is to ask herself, whether the man who has most of these recommendations in the lump is not the most desirable. He that has excellent talents, with a moderate estate, and an agreeable person, is preferable to him who is only rich, if it were only that good faculties may purchase riches, but riches cannot purchase worthy endowments. I do not mean that wit, and a capacity to entertain, is what should be highly valued, except it is founded on good-nature and humanity. There are many ingenious men, whose abilities do little else but make themselves and those about them uneasy. Such are those who are far gone in the pleasures of the town, who cannot support life without quick sensations and gay reflections, and are strangers to tranquillity, to right reason, and a calm motion of spirits, without transport or dejection. These ingenious men, of all men living, are most to be avoided by her who would be happy in a husband. They are immediately sated with possession, and must necessarily fly to new acquisitions of beauty to pass away the whiling moments and intervals of life; for with them every hour is heavy that is not joyful. But there is a sort of man of wit and sense, that can reflect upon his own make, and that of his partner, with eyes of reason and honour, and who believes he offends against both these, if he does not look upon the woman, who chose him to be under his protection in sickness and health, with the utmost gratitude, whether from that moment she is shining or defective in person or mind: I say, there are those who think themselves bound to supply with good-nature the failings of those who love them, and who always think those the objects of love and pity who came to their arms the objects of joy and admiration.

Of this latter sort is Lysander, a man of wit, learning, sobriety, and good-nature; of birth and estate below no woman to accept; and of whom it might be said, should he succeed in his present wishes, his mistress raised his fortune, but not that she made it. When a woman is deliberating with herself whom she shall choose of many near each other in other pretensions, certainly he of best understanding is to be preferred. Life hangs heavily in the repeated conversation of one who has no imagination to be fired at the several occasions and objects which come before him, or who cannot strike out of his reflections new paths of pleasing discourse. Honest Will Thrush and his wife, though not married above four months, have scarce had a word to say to each other this six weeks, and one cannot form to one's self a sillier picture than these two creatures, in solemn pomp and plenty, unable to enjoy their fortunes, and at a full stop among a crowd of servants, to whose taste of life they are beholden for the little satisfactions by which they can be understood to be so much as barely in being. The hours of the day, the distinctions of noon and night, dinner and supper, are the greatest notices they are capable of. This is perhaps representing the life of a very modest woman, joined to a dull fellow, more insipid than it really deserves; but I am sure it is not to exalt the commerce with an ingenious companion too high, to say that every new accident or object, which comes in such a gentleman's way, gives his wife new pleasures and satisfactions. The approbation of his words and actions is a continual new feast to her; nor can she enough applaud her good fortune in having her life varied every hour, her mind more improved, and her heart more glad, from every circumstance which they meet with. He will lay out his invention in forming new pleasures and amusements, and make the fortune she had brought him subservient to the honour and reputation of her and hers. A man of sense, who is thus obliged, is ever contriving the happiness of her who did him so great a distinction; while the fool is ungrateful without vice, and never returns a favour because he is not sensible of it. I would, methinks, have so much to say for myself, that, if I fell into the hands of him who treated me ill, he should be sensible when he did so. His conscience should be of my side, whatever became of his inclination. I do not know but it is the insipid choice which has been made by those who have the care of young women, that the marriage state itself has been liable to so much ridicule. But a well-chosen love, moved by passion on both sides, and perfected by the generosity of one party, must be adorned with so many handsome incidents on the other side, that every particular couple would be an example, in many circumstances, to all the rest of the species. I shall end the chat upon this subject with a couple of letters; one from a lover, who is very well acquainted with the way of bargaining on these occasions; and the other from his rival, who has a less estate, but great gallantry of temper. As to my man of prudence, he makes love, as he says, as if he were already a father, and, laying aside the passion, comes to the reason of the thing.

'Madam,—My counsel has perused the inventory of your estate, and considered what estate you have, which it seems is only yours, and to the male-heirs of your body; but, in default of such issue, to the right heirs of your uncle Edward for ever. Thus, madam, I am advised you cannot (the remainder not being in you) dock the entail; by which means my estate, which is fee simple, will come by the settlement proposed to your children begotten by me, whether they are males or females: but my children begotten upon you will not inherit your lands, except I beget a son. Now, madam, since things are so, you are a woman of that prudence, and understand the world so well, as not to expect I should give you more than you can give me. I am, madam, (with great respect,) your most obedient servant, T. W.'

The other lover's estate is less than this gentleman's, but he expressed himself as follows:

'Madam,—I have given in my estate to your counsel, and desired my own lawyer to insist upon no terms which your friends can propose for your certain ease and advantage; for indeed I have no notion of making difficulties of presenting you with what cannot make me happy without you. I am, madam, your most devoted humble servant, B. T.'

You must know the relations have met upon this; and the girl, being mightily taken with the latter epistle, she is laughed at, and uncle Edward is to be dealt with to make her a suitable match to the worthy gentleman who has told her he does not care a farthing for her. All I hope for is, that the fair lady will make use of the first light night to show B. T. she understands a marriage is not to be considered as a common bargain. T.

No. 523.] *Thursday, October* 30, 1712.

> ———Nunc augur Apollo,
> Nunc Lyciæ sortes, nunc et Jove missus ab ipso
> Interpres divum fert horrida jussa per auras.
> Scilicet is superis labor———
>
> *Virg. Æn.* iv. 376.
>
> Now Lycian lots, and now the Delian god,
> Now Hermes is employed from Jove's abode,
> To warn him hence; as if the peaceful state
> Of heavenly pow'rs were touch'd with human fate!
>
> *Dryden.*

I AM always highly delighted with the discovery of any rising genius among my countrymen. For this reason I have read over, with great pleasure, the late miscellany published by Mr. Pope, in which there are many excellent compositions of that ingenious gentleman. I have had a pleasure of the same kind in perusing a poem that is just published, On the Prospect of Peace;* and which, I hope, will meet with such a reward from its patrons as so noble a performance deserves. I was particularly well pleased to find that the author had not amused himself with fables out of the pagan theology, and that when he hints at any thing of this nature he alludes to it only as to a fable.

Many of our modern authors, whose learning very often extends no farther than Ovid's Metamorphoses, do not know how to celebrate a great man, without mixing a parcel of school-boy tales with the recital of his actions. If you read a poem on a fine woman among the authors of this class, you shall see that it turns more upon Venus or Helen than on the party concerned. I have known a copy of verses on a great hero highly commended; but, upon asking to hear some of the beautiful passages, the admirer of it has repeated to me a speech of Apollo, or a description of Polypheme. At other times, when I have searched for the actions of a great man, who gave a subject to the writer, I have been entertained with the exploits of a river god, or have been forced to attend a Fury in her mischievous progress, from one end of the poem to the other When we are at school, it is necessary for us to be acquainted with the system of pagan theology; and we may be allowed to enliven a theme, or point an epigram, with a heathen god; but when we could write a manly panegyric that should carry in it all the colours of truth, nothing can be more ridiculous than to have recourse to our Jupiters and Junos.

No thought is beautiful which is not just; and no thought can be just which is not founded in truth, or at least in that which passes for such.

In mock heroic poems the use of the heathen mythology is not only excusable, but graceful, because it is the design of such compositions to divert, by adapting the fabulous machines of the ancients to low subjects, and, at the same time, by ridiculing such kinds of machinery in modern writers. If any are of opinion that there is a necessity of admitting these classical legends into our serious compositions, in order to give them a more poetical turn, I would recommend to their consideration the pastorals of Mr. Phillips. One would have thought it impossible for this kind of poetry to have subsisted without fawns and satyrs, wood-nymphs and water-nymphs, with all the tribe of rural deities. But we see he has given a new life and a more natural beauty to this way of writing, by substituting in the place of these antiquated fables, the superstitious mythology which prevails among the shepherds of our own country.

Virgil and Homer might compliment their heroes by interweaving the actions of deities with their achievements; but for a Christian author to write in the pagan creed, to make prince Eugene a favourite of Mars, or to carry on a correspondence between Bellona and the Marshal de Villars, would be downright puerility, and unpardonable in a poet that is past sixteen. It is want of sufficient elevation in a genius to describe realities, and place them in a shining light, that makes him have recourse to such trifling antiquated fables; as a man may write a fine description of Bacchus or Apollo that does not know how to draw the character of any of his contemporaries.

In order therefore to put a stop to this absurd practice, I shall publish the following edict, by virtue of that spectatorial authority with which I stand invested.

'Whereas the time of a general peace is, in all appearance, drawing near, being informed that there are several ingenious persons who intend to show their talents on so happy an occasion, and being willing, as much as in me lies, to prevent that effusion of nonsense which we have good cause to apprehend; I do hereby strictly require every person who shall write on this subject, to remember that he is a Christian, and not to sacrifice his catechism to his poetry. In order to it, I do expect of him in the first place to make his own poem, without depending upon Phœbus for any part of it, or calling out for aid upon any one of the Muses by name. I do likewise positively forbid the sending of Mercury with any particular message or despatch relating to the peace, and shall by no means suffer Minerva to take upon her the shape of any plenipotentiary concerned in this great work. I do farther declare, that I shall not allow the Destinies to have had a hand in the deaths of the several thousands who have been slain in the late war, being

* By Mr. Thomas Tickle.

of opinion that all such deaths may be very well accounted for by the Christian system of powder and ball. I do therefore strictly forbid the Fates to cut the thread of man's life upon any pretence whatsoever, unless it be for the sake of the rhyme. And whereas I have good reason to fear that Neptune will have a great deal of business on his hands, in several poems which we may now suppose are upon the anvil, I do also prohibit his appearance, unless it be done in metaphor, simile, or any very short allusion; and that even here he be not permitted to enter but with great caution and circumspection. I desire that the same rule may be extended to his whole fraternity of heathen gods; it being my design to condemn every poem to the flames in which Jupiter thunders, or exercises any other act of authority which does not belong to him: in short, I expect that no pagan agent shall be introduced, or any fact related, which a man cannot give credit to with a good conscience. Provided always, that nothing herein contained shall extend, or be construed to extend, to several of the female poets in this nation, who shall be still left in full possession of their gods and goddesses, in the same manner as if this paper had never been written.' O.

No. 524.] *Friday, October* 31, 1712.

Nos populo damus—— *Sen.*

As the world leads, we follow.

When I first of all took it into my head to write dreams and visions, I determined to print nothing of that nature which was not of my own invention. But several laborious dreamers have of late communicated to me works of this nature, which, for their reputations and my own, I have hitherto suppressed. Had I printed every one that came into my hands, my book of speculations would have been little else but a book of visions. Some of my correspondents have indeed been so very modest as to offer as an excuse for their not being in a capacity to dream better. I have by me, for example, the dream of a young gentleman not passed fifteen: I have likewise by me the dream of a person of quality, and another called The Lady's Dream. In these, and other pieces of the same nature, it is supposed the usual allowances will be made to the age, condition, and sex of the dreamer. To prevent this inundation of dreams, which daily flows in upon me, I shall apply to all dreamers of dreams the advice which Epictetus has couched, after his manner, in a very simple and concise precept. 'Never tell thy dream,' says that philosopher; 'for though thou thyself mayest take a pleasure in telling thy dream, another will take no pleasure in hearing it.' After this short preface, I must do justice to two or three visions which I have lately published, and which I have owned to have been written by other hands. I shall add a dream to these which comes to me from Scotland, by one who declares himself of that country; and, for all I know, may be second-sighted. There is, indeed, something in it of the spirit of John Bunyan; but at the same time a certain sublime which that author was never master of. I shall publish it, because I question not but it will fall in with the taste of all my popular readers, and amuse the imaginations of those who are more profound; declaring, at the same time, that this is the last dream which I intend to publish this season.

'Sir,—I was last Sunday in the evening led into a serious reflection on the reasonableness of virtue, and great folly of vice, from an excellent sermon I had heard that afternoon in my parish church. Among other observations, the preacher showed us that the temptations which the tempter proposed are all on a supposition, that we are either madmen or fools, or with an intention to render us such; that in no other affair we would suffer ourselves to be thus imposed upon, in a case so plainly and clearly against our visible interest. His illustrations and arguments carried so much persuasion and conviction with them, that they remained a considerable while fresh, and working in my memory; until at last the mind, fatigued with thought, gave way to the forcible oppressions of slumber and sleep; whilst fancy, unwilling yet to drop the subject, presented me with the following vision.

'Methought I was just awoke out of a sleep that I could never remember the beginning of; the place where I found myself to be was a wide and spacious plain, full of people that wandered up and down through several beaten paths, whereof some few were straight, and in direct lines, but most of them winding and turning like a labyrinth; but yet it appeared to me afterwards that these last all met in one issue, so that many that seemed to steer quite contrary courses, did at length meet and face one another, to the no little amazement of many of them.

'In the midst of the plain there was a great fountain: they called it the spring of Self-love; out of it issued two rivulets to the eastward and westward: The name of the first was Heavenly-Wisdom; its water was wonderfully clear, but of a yet more wonderful effect: the other's name was Worldly-Wisdom; its water was thick, and yet far from being dormant or stagnating, for it was in a continual violent agitation; which kept the travellers, whom I shall mention by and by, from being sensible of the foulness and thickness of the water; which had this effect, that it intoxicated those who drank it, and made them mistake every object that lay before them. Both rivulets were parted near their springs into so many others, as there were straight and crooked paths, which attended all along to their respective issues.

'I observed from the several paths many now and then diverting, to refresh and otherwise qualify themselves for their journey, to the respective rivulets that ran near them: they contracted a very observable courage and steadiness in what they were about, by drinking these waters. At the end of the perspective of every straight path, all which did end in one issue and point, appeared a high pillar, all of diamond, casting rays as bright as those of the sun into the paths; which rays had also certain sympathizing and alluring virtues in them, so that whosoever had made some considerable progress in his journey onwards towards the pillar, by the repeated impression of these rays upon him, was wrought into an habitual inclination and conversion of his sight towards it, so that it grew at last in a manner natural to him to look and gaze upon it, whereby he was kept steady in the straight paths, which alone led to that radiant body, the beholding of which was now grown a gratification to his nature.

'At the issue of the crooked paths there was a great black tower, out of the centre of which streamed a long succession of flames, which did rise even above the clouds; it gave a very great light to the whole plain, which did sometimes outshine the light, and oppressed the beams of the adamantine pillar; though by the observation I made afterwards, it appeared that it was not from any diminution of light, but that this lay in the travellers, who would sometimes step out of straight paths, where they lost the full prospect of the radiant pillar, and saw it but sideways: but the great light from the black tower, which was somewhat particularly scorching to them, would generally light and hasten them to their proper climate again.

'Round about the black tower there were, methought, many thousands of huge mis-shapen ugly monsters; these had great nets which they were perpetually plying and casting towards the crooked paths, and they would now and then catch up those that were nearest to them: these they took up straight, and whirled over the walls into the flaming tower, and they were no more seen nor heard of.

'They would sometimes cast their nets towards the right paths to catch the stragglers, whose eyes, for want of drinking at the brook that run by them, grew dim, whereby they lost their way: these would sometimes very narrowly miss being catched away, but I could not hear whether any of these had ever been so unfortunate, that had been before very hearty in the straight paths.

'I considered all these strange sights with great attention, until at last I was interrupted by a cluster of the travellers in the crooked paths, who came up to me, bid me go along with them, and presently fell to singing and dancing: they took me by the hand, and so carried me away along with them. After I had followed them a considerable while, I perceived I had lost the black tower of light, at which I greatly wondered; but as I looked and gazed round about me and saw nothing, I began to fancy my first vision had been but a dream, and there was no such thing in reality; but then I considered that if I could fancy to see what was not, I might as well have an allusion wrought on me at present, and not see what was really before me. I was very much confirmed in this thought, by the effect I then just observed the water of Worldly-Wisdom had upon me; for as I had drank a little of it again, I felt a very sensible effect in my head; methought it distracted and disordered all there; this made me stop of a sudden, suspecting some charm or enchantment. As I was casting about within myself what I should do, and whom to apply to in this case, I spied at some distance off me a man beckoning, and making signs to me to come over to him. I cried to him, I did not know the way. He then called to me, audibly, to step at least out of the path I was in; for if I stayed there any longer I was in danger to be catched in a great net that was just hanging over me, and ready to catch me up; that he wondered I was so blind, or so distracted, as not to see so imminent and visible a danger; assuring me, that as soon as I was out of that way, he would come to me to lead me into a more secure path. This I did, and he brought me his palmfull of the water of Heavenly-Wisdom, which was of very great use to me, for my eyes were straight cleared, and I saw the great black tower just before me: but the great net which I spied so near me cast me in such a terror, that I ran back as far as I could in one breath without looking behind me. Then my benefactor thus bespoke me: "You have made the wonderfullest escape in the world; the water you used to drink is of a bewitching nature; you would else have been mightily shocked at the deformities and meanness of the place; for besides the set of blind fools, in whose company you was, you may now behold many others who are only bewitched after another no less dangerous manner. Look a little that way, there goes a crowd of passengers; they have indeed so good a head as not to suffer themselves to be blinded by this bewitching water; the black tower is not vanished out of their sight, they see it whenever they look up to it: but see how they go sideways, and with their eyes downwards, as if they were mad, that they thus may rush into the net, without being beforehand troubled at the thought of so miserable a destruction. Their wills are so perverse, and their hearts so fond of the pleasures of the place, that rather than forego them they will run all hazards, and venture upon all the miseries and woes before them.

"See there that other company; though they should drink none of the bewitching water, yet they take a course bewitching and deluding. See how they choose the crookedest paths, whereby they have often the black tower behind them, and sometimes see the radiant column sideways, which gives them some weak glimpse of it! These fools content themselves with that, not knowing whether any other have any more of its influence and light than themselves: this road is called that of Superstition or Human Invention: they grossly overlook that which the rules and laws of the place prescribe to them, and contrive some other scheme, and set off directions and prescriptions for themselves, which they hope will serve their turn." He showed me many other kinds of fools, which put me quite out of humour with the place. At last he carried me to the right paths, where I found true and solid pleasure, which entertained me all the way, until we came in closer sight of the pillar, where the satisfaction increased to that measure that my faculties were not able to contain it: in the straining of them I was violently waked, not a little grieved at the vanishing of so pleasing a dream.

'Glasgow, Sept. 29.'

No. 525.] *Saturday, November* 1, 1712.

'Ο δ' εις το σωφρον επ' αρετην τ' αγων ερως,
Ζηλωτος ανθρωποισιν.—— *Eurip.*

That love alone, which virtue's laws contro ,
Deserves reception in the human soul.

It is my custom to take frequent opportunities of inquiring, from time to time, what success my speculations meet with in the town. I am glad to find, in particular, that my discourses on marriage have been well received. A friend of mine gives me to understand from Doctor's-commons, that more licenses have been taken out there of late than usual. I am likewise informed of several pretty fellows, who have resolved to commence heads of families by the first favourable opportunity. One of them writes me word that he is ready to enter into the bonds of matrimony, provided I will give it him under my hand (as I now do) that a man may show his face in good company after he is married, and that he need not be ashamed to treat a woman with kindness who puts herself in his power for life.

I have other letters on this subject, which say that I am attempting to make a revolution in the world of gallantry, and that the consequence of it will be that a great deal of the sprightliest wit and satire of the last age will be lost; that a bashful fellow, upon changing his condition, will be no longer puzzled how to stand the raillery of his facetious companions; that he need not own he married only to plunder an heiress of her fortune, nor pretend that he uses her ill, to avoid the ridiculous name of a fond husband.

Indeed, if I may speak my opinion of great part of the writings which once prevailed among us under the notion of humour, they are such as would tempt one to think there had been an association among the wits of those times to rally legitimacy out of our island. A state of wedlock was the common mark of all the adventurers in farce and comedy, as well as the essayers in lampoon and satire, to shoot at; and nothing was a more standing jest, in all clubs of fashionable mirth and gay conversation. It was determined among those airy critics, that the appellation of a sober man should signify a spiritless fellow. And I am apt to think it was about the same time that good-nature, a word so peculiarly elegant in our language, that some have affirmed it cannot well be expressed in any other, came first to be rendered suspicious, and in danger of being transferred from its original sense to so distant an idea as that of folly.

I must confess it has been my ambition, in the course of my writings to restore, as well as I was able, the proper ideas of things. And as I have attempted this already on the subject of marriage in several papers, I shall here add some farther observations which occur to me on the same head.

Nothing seems to be thought, by our fine gentlemen, so indispensable an ornament in fashionable life, as love. 'A knight-errant,' says Don Quixote, 'without a mistress, is like a tree without leaves;' and a man of mode among us who has not some fair one to sigh for, might as well pretend to appear dressed without his periwig. We have lovers in prose innumerable. All our pretenders to rhyme are professed inamoratos; and there is scarce a poet good or bad, to be heard of, who has not some real or supposed Saccharissa to improve his vein.

If love be any refinement, conjugal love must be certainly so in a much higher degree. There is no comparison between the frivolous affectations of attracting the eyes of women with whom you are only captivated by way of amusement, and of whom perhaps you know nothing more than their features; and a regular and uniform endeavour to make yourself valuable, both as a friend and lover, to one whom you have chosen to be the companion of your life. The first is the spring of a thousand fopperies, silly artifices, falsehoods, and perhaps barbarities; or at best rises no higher than to a kind of dancing-school breeding, to give the person a more sparkling air. The latter is the parent of substantial virtues and agreeable qualities, and cultivates the mind while it improves the behaviour. The passion of love to a mistress, even where it is most sincere, resembles too much the flame of a fever, that to a wife is like the vital heat.

I have often thought, if the letters written by men of good-nature to their wives were to be compared with those written by men of gallantry to their mistresses, the former, notwithstanding any inequality of style, would appear to have the advantage. Friendship, tenderness, and constancy, dressed in a simplicity of expression, recommend themselves by a more native elegance, than passionate raptures, extravagant encomiums, and slavish adoration. If we were admitted to search the cabinet of the beautiful Narcissa, among heaps of epistles from several admirers, which are there preserved with equal care, how few should we find but would make any one sick in the reading, except her who is flattered by them? But in how different a style must the wise Benevolus, who converses with that good sense and good humour among all his friends, write to a wife who is the worthy object of his utmost affection? Benevolus, both in public and private, and all occasions of life, appears to have every good quality and desirable ornament. Abroad he is reverenced and esteemed; at home beloved and happy. The satisfaction he enjoys there settles into an habitual complacency, which shines in his countenance, enlivens his wit, and seasons his conversation. Even those of his acquaintance, who have never seen him in his retirement, are sharers in the happiness of it; and it is very much owing to his being the best and best beloved of husbands, that he is the most steadfast of friends, and the most agreeable of companions.

There is a sensible pleasure in contemplating such beautiful instances of domestic life. The happiness of the conjugal state appears heightened to the highest degree it is capable of when we see two persons of accomplished minds not only united in the same interests and affections, but in their taste of the same improvements and diversions. Pliny, one of the finest gentlemen and politest writers of the age in which he lived, has left us, in his letter to Hispulla, his wife's aunt, one of the most agreeable family pieces of this kind I have ever met with. I shall end this discourse with a translation of it, and I believe the reader will be of my opinion, that conjugal love is drawn in it with a delicacy which makes it appear to be, as I have represented it, an ornament as well as a virtue.

'*Pliny to Hispulla.*

'As I remember the great affection which was between you and your excellent brother, and know you love his daughter as your own, so as not only to express the tenderness of the best of aunts, but even to supply that of the best of fathers; I am sure it will be a pleasure to you to hear that she proves worthy of her father, worthy of you, and of your and her ancestors. Her ingenuity is admirable; her frugality extraordinary. She loves me; the surest pledge of her virtue; and adds to this a wonderful disposition to learning, which she has acquired from her affection to me. She reads my writings, studies them, and even gets them by heart. You would smile to see the concern she is in when I have a cause to plead, and the joy she shows when it is over. She finds means to have the first news brought her of the success I meet with in court, how I am heard, and what decree is made. If I recite any thing in public, she cannot refrain from placing herself privately in some corner to hear, where, with the utmost delight, she feasts upon my applauses. Sometimes she sings my verses; and accompanies them with the lute, without any master except love, the best of instructors. From these instances I take the most certain omens of our perpetual and increasing happiness; since her affection is not founded on my youth and person, which must gradually decay, but she is in love with the immortal part of me, my glory and reputation. Nor indeed could less be expected from one who had the happiness to receive her education from you, who in your house was accustomed to every thing that was virtuous and decent, and even began to love me, by your recommendation. For, as you had always the greatest respect for my mother, you were pleased from my infancy to form me, to commend me, and kindly to presage I should be one day what my wife fancies I am. Accept therefore our united thanks: mine, that you have bestowed her on me; and hers, that you have given me to her, as a mutual grant of joy and felicity.'

No. 526.] *Monday, November* 3, 1712.

——Fortius utere loris. *Ovid Met.* Lib. ii. 127.

Keep a stiff rein.—*Addison.*

I AM very loath to come to extremities with the young gentlemen mentioned in the following letter, and do not care to chastise them with my own hand, until I am forced by provocation too great to be suffered without the absolute destruction of my spectatorial dignity. The crimes of these offenders are placed under the observation of one of my chief officers, who is posted just at the entrance of the pass between London and Westminster. As I have great confidence in the capacity, resolution, and integrity of the person deputed by me to give an account of enormities, I doubt not but I shall soon have before me all proper notices which are requisite for the amendment of manners in public, and the instruction of each individual of the human species in what is due from him in respect to the whole body of mankind. The present paper shall consist only of the above-men tioned letter, and the copy of a deputation which I have given to my trusty friend, Mr. John Sly; wherein he is charged to notify to me all that is necessary for my animadversion upon the delinquents mentioned by my correspondent, as well as all others described in the said deputation.

'*To the Spectator General of Great Britain.*

'I grant it does look a little familiar, but I must call you

'DEAR DUMB,—Being got again to the farther end of the Widow's coffee-house, I shall from hence give you some account of the behaviour of our hackney-coachmen since my last. These indefatigable gentlemen, without the least design, I dare say, of self-interest or advantage to themselves, do still ply as volunteers day and night for the good of their country. I will not trouble you with enumerating many particulars, but I must by no means omit to inform you of an infant about six feet high, and between twenty and thirty years of age, who was seen in the arms of a hackney-coachman, driving by Will's coffee-house in Covent-garden, between the hours of four and five in the afternoon of that very day wherein you published a memorial against them. This impudent young cur, though he could not sit in a coach-box without holding, yet would venture his neck to bid defiance to your spectatorial authority, or to any thing that you countenanced. Who he was I know not, but I heard this relation this morning from a gentleman who was an eye witness of this his impudence; and I was willing to take the first opportunity to inform you of him, as holding it extremely requisite that you should nip him in the bud. But I am myself most concerned for my fellow-templars, fellow-students, and fellow-labourers in the law, I mean such of them as are dignified and distinguished under the denomination of hackney-coachmen. Such aspiring minds have these ambitious young men, that they cannot enjoy themselves out of a coach-box. It is, however, an unspeakable comfort to me that I can now tell you that some of them are grown so bashful as to study only in the night time, or in the country. The other night I spied one of our young gentlemen very diligent at his lucubrations in Fleet Street; and, by the way, I should be under some concern, lest this hard student should one time or other crack his brain with studying, but that I am in hopes nature has taken care to fortify him in proportion to the great undertakings he was designed for. Another of my fellow-templars on Thursday last was getting up into his study at the bottom of Gray's-Inn-Lane, in order, I suppose, to contemplate in the fresh air. Now, sir, my request is, that the great modesty of these two gentlemen may be recorded as a pattern to the rest; and if you would but give them two or three touches with your own pen, though you might not perhaps prevail with them to desist entirely from their meditations, yet I doubt not but you would at least preserve them from being public spectacles of folly in our streets. I say two or three touches with your own pen; for I have already observed, Mr. Spec, that those Spectators which are so prettily laced down the sides with little c's, how instinctive soever they may be, do not carry with them that authority as the others. I do again therefore desire, that for the sake of their dear necks, you would bestow one penful of your own ink upon them. I know you are loath to expose them; and it is, I must confess, a thousand pities that any young gentleman who is come of honest parents should be brought to public shame. And indeed I should be glad to have them handled a little tenderly at the first, but if fair means will not prevail, there is then no other way to reclaim them but by making use of some wholesome severities; and I think it is better that a dozen or two of such good-for-nothing fellows should be made examples of, than that the reputation of some hundreds of as hopeful young gentlemen as myself should suffer through their folly. It is not, however, for me to direct you what to do; but, in short, if our coachmen will drive on this trade, the very first of them that I do find meditating in the street, I shall make bold to "take the number of his chambers,"* together with a note of his name, and despatch them to you, that you may chastise him at your own discretion. I am, dear Spec, for ever your's, MOSES GREENBAG,

'Esq. if you please.

'P. S. Tom Hammercloth, one of our coachmen, is now pleading at the bar at the other end of the room, but has a little too much vehemence, and throws out his arms too much to take his audience, with a good grace.'

To my loving and well-beloved John Sly, haberdasher of hats, and tobacconist, between the cities of London and Westminster.

Whereas frequent disorders, affronts, indignities, omissions, and trespasses, for which there are no remedies by any form of law, but which apparently disturb and disquiet the minds of men, happen near the place of your residence; and that you are, as well by your commodious situation, as the good parts with which you are endowed, properly qualified for the observation of the said offences; I do hereby authorize and depute you, from the hours of nine in the morning until four in the afternoon, to keep a strict eye upon all persons and things that are conveyed in coaches, carried in carts, or walk on foot, from the city of London to the city of Westminster, or from the city

* An allusion to the number of a hackney-coach.

of Westminster to the city of London, within the said hours. You are therefore not to depart from your observatory at the end of Devereux-court during the said space of each day, but to observe the behaviour of all persons who are suddenly transported from tramping on pebbles to sit at ease in chariots, what notice they take of their foot acquaintance, and send me the speediest advice, when they are guilty of overlooking, turning from, or appearing grave and distant to, their old friends. When man and wife are in the same coach, you are to see whether they appear pleased or tired with each other, and whether they carry the due mean in the eye of the world, between fondness and coolness. You are carefully to behold all such as shall have addition of honour or riches, and report whether they preserve the countenance they had before such addition. As to persons on foot, you are to be attentive whether they are pleased with their condition, and are dressed suitable to it; but especially to distinguish such as appear discreet, by a low-heel shoe, with the decent ornament of a leather garter: to write down the names of such country gentlemen as, upon the approach of peace, have left the hunting for the military cock of the hat; of all who strut, make a noise, and swear at the drivers of coaches to make haste, when they see it is impossible they should pass; of all young gentlemen in coach-boxes, who labour at a perfection in what they are sure to be excelled by the meanest of the people. You are to do all that in you lies that coaches and passengers give way according to the course of business, all the morning in term-time, towards Westminster, the rest of the year towards the Exchange. Upon these directions, together with other secret articles herein enclosed, you are to govern yourself, and give advertisement thereof to me, at all convenient and spectatorial hours, when men of business are to be seen. Hereof you are not to fail. Given under my seal of office.

T. 'THE SPECTATOR.'

No. 527.] *Tuesday, November* 4, 1712.

Facile invenies et pejorem, et pejus moratam;
Meliorem neque tu reperies, neque sol videt.
Plautus in Stichor.

You will easily find a worse woman; a better the sun never shone upon.

I AM so tender of my women-readers, that I cannot defer the publication of any thing which concerns their happiness or quiet. The repose of a married woman is consulted in the first of the following letters, and the felicity of a maiden lady in the second. I call it a felicity to have the addresses of an agreeable man; and I think I have not any where seen a prettier application of a poetical story than that of his, in making the tale of Cephalus and Procris the history picture of a fan in so gallant a manner as he addresses it. But see the letters.

'MR. SPECTATOR,—It is now almost three months since I was in town about some business; and the hurry of it being over, I took a coach one afternoon, and drove to see a relation, who married about six years ago a wealthy citizen. I found her at home, but her husband gone to the Exchange, and expected back within an hour at the farthest. After the usual salutations of kindness, and a hundred questions about friends in the country, we sat down to piquet, played two or three games, and drank tea. I should have told you that this was my second time of seeing her since marriage; but before, she lived at the same town where I went to school; so that the plea of a relation, added to the innocence of my youth, prevailed upon her good-humour to indulge me in a freedom of conversation as often, and oftener, than the strict discipline of the school would allow of. You may easily imagine, after such an acquaintance, we might be exceeding merry without any offence; as in calling to mind how many inventions I have been put to in deluding the master, how many hands forged for excuses, how many times been sick in perfect health; for I was then never sick but at school, and only then because out of her company. We had whiled away three hours after this manner, when I found it past five; and not expecting her husband would return until late, rose up, and told her I should go early next morning for the country. She kindly answered she was afraid it would be long before she saw me again; so, I took my leave, and parted. Now, sir, I had not been got home a fortnight, when I received a letter from a neighbour of theirs, that ever since that fatal afternoon the lady has been most inhumanly treated, and the husband publicly stormed that he was made a member of too numerous a society. He had, it seems, listened most of the time my cousin and I were together. As jealous ears always hear double, so he heard enough to make him mad; and as jealous eyes always see through magnifying glasses, so he was certain it could not be I whom he had seen, a beardless stripling, but fancied he saw a gay gentleman of the temple, ten years older than myself; and for that reason, I presume, durst not come in, nor take any notice when I went out. He is perpetually asking his wife if she does not think the time long (as she said she should) until she see her cousin again. Pray, sir, what can be done in this case? I have writ to him to assure him I was at his house all that afternoon expecting to see him. His answer is, it is only a trick of hers, and that he neither can nor will believe me. The parting kiss I find mightily nettles him, and confirms him in all his errors. Ben Jonson, as I remember, makes a foreigner, in one of his comedies, "admire the desperate valour of the bold English, who let out their wives to all encounters." The general custom of salutation should excuse the favour done me, or you should lay down rules when such distinctions are to be given or omitted. You cannot imagine, sir, how troubled I am for this unhappy lady's misfortune, and beg you would insert this letter, that the husband may reflect upon this accident coolly. It is no small matter, the ease of a virtuous woman for her whole life. I know she will conform to any regularities (though more strict than the common rules of our country require) to which his particular temper shall incline him to oblige her. This accident puts me in mind how generously Pisistratus, the Athenian tyrant, behaved himself on a like occasion, when he was instigated by his wife to put to death a young gentleman, because, being passionately fond of his daughter, he had kissed her in public, as he met her in the street. "What," said he, "shall we do to those who are our enemies, if we do thus to those who are our friends?" I will not trouble you much longer, but am exceedingly concerned lest this accident may cause a virtuous lady to lead a miserable life with a husband who has no grounds for his jealousy but what I have faithfully related, and ought to be reckoned none. It is to be feared too, if at last he sees his mistake, yet people will be as slow and unwilling in disbelieving scandal as they are quick and forward in believing it. I shall endeavour to enliven this plain honest letter with Ovid's relation about Cybele's image. The ship wherein it was aboard was stranded at the mouth of the Tiber, and the men were unable to move it, until Claudia, a virgin, but suspected of unchastity, by a slight pull hauled it in. The story is told in the fourth book of the Fasti.

"Parent of gods, (began the weeping fair,)
Reward or punish, but oh! hear my prayer:
If lewdness e'er defil'd my virgin bloom,
From heav'n with justice I receive my doom:
But if my honour yet has known no stain,
Thou, goddess, thou my innocence maintain;
Thou, whom the nicest rules of goodness sway'd,
Vouchsafe to follow an unblemish'd maid."
She spoke and touch'd the cord with glad surprise,
(The truth was witness'd by ten thousand eyes)
The pitying goddess easily comply'd,
Follow'd in triumph, and adorn'd her guide;
While Claudia, blushing still for past disgrace,
March'd silent on, with a slow solemn pace:
Nor yet from some was all distrust remov'd,
Though heav'n such virtue by such wonders prov'd.

'I am, sir, your very humble servant.
'PHILAGNOTES.'

'MR. SPECTATOR,—You will oblige a languishing lover, if you will please to print the enclosed verses in your next paper. If you remember the Metamorphoses, you know Procris, the fond wife of Cephalus, is said to have made her husband, who delighted in the sports of the wood, a present of an unerring javelin. In process of time he was so much in the forest, that his lady suspected he was pursuing some nymph, under the pretence of following a chase more innocent. Under this suspicion she hid herself among the trees, to observe his motions. While she lay concealed, her husband, tired with the labour of hunting, came within her hearing. As he was fainting with heat, he cried out, "*Aura veni!*" "Oh, charming air, approach!"

'The unfortunate wife, taking the word air to be the name of a woman, began to move among the bushes; and the husband, believing it a deer, threw his javelin, and killed her. This history, painted on a fan, which I presented to a lady, gave occasion to my growing poetical.'

"Come, gentle air!" the Æolian shepherd said,
While Procris panted in the secret shade;
"Come, gentle air," the fairer Delia cries,
While at her feet the swain expiring lies.
Lo! the glad gales o'er all her beauties stray,
Breathe on her lips, and in her bosom play.
In Delia's hand this toy is fatal found,
Nor did that fabled dart more surely wound.
Both gifts destructive to the givers prove,
Alike both lovers fall by those they love:
Yet guiltless too this bright destroyer lives,
At random wounds, nor knows the wound she gives;
She views the story with attentive eyes,
And pities Procris, while her lover dies.

No. 528.] *Wednesday, November 5,* 1712.

Dum potuit, solita gemitum virtute repressit.
Ovid, Met. ix. 165.

With wonted fortitude she bore the smart,
And not a groan confess'd her burning heart.—*Gay.*

'MR. SPECTATOR,—I who now write to you am a woman loaded with injuries; and the aggravation of my misfortune is, that they are such which are overlooked by the generality of mankind; and, though the most afflicting imaginable, not regarded as such in the general sense of the world. I have hid my vexation from all mankind; but having now taken pen, ink, and paper, am resolved to unbosom myself to you, and lay before you what grieves me and all the sex. You have very often mentioned particular hardships done to this or that lady; but methinks you have not, in any one speculation, directly pointed at the partial freedom men take, the unreasonable confinement women are obliged to, in the only circumstance in which we are necessarily to have a commerce with them, that of love. The case of celibacy is the great evil of our nation; and the indulgence of the vicious conduct of men in that state, with the ridicule to which women are exposed, though ever so virtuous, if long unmarried, is the root of the greatest irregularities of this nation. To show you, sir, that (though you never have given us the catalogue of a lady's library, as you promised) we read books of our own choosing, I shall insert on this occasion a paragraph or two out of Echard's Roman History. In the 44th page of the second volume, the author observes that Augustus, upon his return to Rome at the end of a war, received complaints that too great a number of the young men of quality were unmarried. The emperor thereupon assembled the whole equestrian order; and, having separated the married from the single, did particular honours to the former; but he told the latter, that is to say, Mr. Spectator, he told the bachelors, That their lives and actions had been so peculiar, that he knew not by what name to call them; not by that of men, for they performed nothing that was manly; not by that of citizens, for the city might perish notwithstanding their care; nor by that of Romans, for they designed to extirpate the Roman name. Then, proceeding to show his tender care and hearty affection for his people, he farther told them, that their course of life was of such pernicious consequence to the glory and grandeur of the Roman nation, that he could not choose but tell them, that all other crimes put together could not equalize theirs, for they were guilty of murder, in not suffering those to be born which should proceed from them; of impiety, in causing the names and honours of their ancestors to cease; and of sacrilege, in destroying their kind, which proceed from the immortal gods, and human nature, the principal thing consecrated to them: therefore, in this respect, they dissolved the government in disobeying its laws; betrayed their country, by making it barren and waste; nay, and demolished their city, in depriving it of inhabitants. And he was sensible that all this proceeded not from any kind of virtue or abstinence, but from a looseness and wantonness which ought never to be encouraged in any civil government. There are no particulars dwelt upon that let us into the conduct of these young worthies, whom this great emperor treated with so much justice and indignation; but any one who observes what passes in this town may very well frame to himself a notion of their riots and debaucheries all night, and their apparent preparations for them all day. It is not to be doubted but these Romans never passed any of their time innocently but when they were asleep, and never slept but when they were weary and heavy with excesses, and slept only to prepare themselves for the repetition of them. If you did your duty as a Spectator, you would carefully examine into the number of births, marriages, and burials; and when you had deducted out of your deaths all such as went out of the world without marrying, then cast up the number of both sexes born within such a term of years last past; you might, from the single people departed, make some useful inferences or guesses how many there are left unmarried, and raise some useful scheme for the amendment of the age in that particular. I have not patience to proceed gravely on this abominable libertinism; for I cannot but reflect, as I am writing to you, upon a certain lascivious manner which all our young gentlemen use in public, and examine our eyes with a petulancy in their own which is a downright affront to modesty. A disdainful look on such an occasion is returned with a countenance rebuked, but by averting their eyes from the woman of honour and decency to some flippant creature, who will, as the phrase is, be kinder. I must set down things as they come into my head, without standing upon order. Ten thousand to one but the gay gentleman who stared, at the same time, is a housekeeper; for you must know they are got into a humour of late of being very regular in their sins; and a young fellow shall keep his four maids and three footmen with the greatest gravity imaginable. There are no less than six of these venerable housekeepers of my acquaintance. This humour among young men of condition is imitated by all the world below them, and a general dissolution* of manners arises from this one source of libertinism, without shame or reprehension in the male youth. It is from this one fountain that so many beautiful helpless young women are sacrificed and given up to lewdness, shame, poverty, and disease. It is to this also that so many excellent young women, who might be patterns of conjugal affection, and parents of a worthy race, pine under unhappy passions for such as have not attention to observe, or virtue enough to prefer them to their common wenches. Now, Mr. Spectator, I must be free to own to you that I myself suffer a tasteless insipid being, from a consideration I have for a man who would not, as he said in my hearing, resign his liberty, as he calls it, for all the beauty and wealth the whole sex is possessed of. Such calamities as these would not happen, if it could possibly be brought about, that by fining bachelors as papists, convicts, or the like, they were distinguished to their disadvantage from the rest of the world, who fall in with the measures of civil society. Lest you should think I speak this as being, according to the senseless rude phrase, a malicious old maid, I shall acquaint you I am a woman of condition, not now three-and-twenty, and have had proposals from at least ten different men, and the greater number of them have upon the upshot refused me. Something or other is always amiss when the lover takes to some new wench. A settlement is easily excepted against; and there is very little recourse to avoid the vicious part of our youth, but throwing oneself away upon some lifeless blockhead, who, though he is without vice, is also without virtue. Now-a-days we must be contented if we can get creatures which are not bad; good are not to be expected. Mr. Spectator, I sat near you the other day, and think I did not displease your spectatorial eye-sight; which I shall be a better judge of when I see whe

* Dissoluteness.

ther you take notice of these evils your own way, or print this memorial dictated from the disdainful heavy heart of, sir, your most obedient humble servant,

T. 'RACHEL WELLADAY.'

No. 529.] *Thursday, November* 6, 1712.

Singula quæque locum teneant sortita decenter.
Hor. Ars Poet. v. 92.

Let every thing have its due place.—*Roscommon.*

Upon the hearing of several late disputes concerning rank and precedence, I could not forbear amusing myself with some observations, which I have made upon the learned world, as to this great particular. By the learned world, I here mean at large, all those who are in any way concerned in works of literature, whether in the writing, printing, or repeating part. To begin with the writers: I have observed that the author of a folio, in all companies and conversations, sets himself above the author of a quarto; the author of a quarto above the author of an octavo; and so on, by a gradual descent and subordination, to an author in twenty-fours. This distinction is so well observed, that in an assembly of the learned, I have seen a folio writer place himself in an elbow chair, when the author of a duodecimo has, out of a just deference to his superior quality, seated himself upon a squab. In a word, authors are usually ranged in company after the same manner as their works are upon a shelf.

The most minute pocket author hath beneath him the writers of all pamphlets, or works that are only stitched. As for the pamphleteer, he takes place of none but the authors of single sheets, and of that fraternity who publish their labours on certain days, or on every day in the week. I do not find that the precedency among the individuals in this latter class of writers is yet settled.

For my own part, I have had so strict a regard to the ceremonial which prevails in the learned world, that I never presumed to take place of a pamphleteer, until my daily papers were gathered into those two first volumes which have already appeared. After which, I naturally jumped over the heads not only of all pamphleteers, but of every octavo writer in Great Britain that had written but one book. I am also informed by my bookseller, that six octavos have at all times been looked upon as an equivalent to a folio; which I take notice of, the rather because I would not have the learned world surprised, if, after the publication of half a dozen volumes, I take my place accordingly. When my scattered forces are thus rallied, and reduced into regular bodies, I flatter myself that I shall make no despicable figure at the head of them.

Whether these rules, which have been received time out of mind in the common wealth of letters, were not originally established with an eye to our paper manufacture I shall leave to the discussion of others; and shall only remark farther in this place, that all printers and booksellers take the wall of one another according to the above-mentioned merits of the authors to whom they respectively belong.

I come now to that point of precedency which is settled among the three learned professions by the wisdom of our laws. I need not here take notice of the rank which is allotted to every doctor in each of these professions, who are all of them, though not so high as knights, yet a degree above 'squires; this last order of men, being the illiterate body of the nation, are consequently thrown together in a class below the three learned professions. I mention this for the sake of several rural 'squires, whose reading does not rise so high as to The present State of England, and who are often apt to usurp that precedency which, by the laws of their country, is not due to them. Their want of learning, which has planted them in this station, may in some measure extenuate their misdemeanor; and our professors ought to pardon them when they offend in this particular, considering that they are in a state of ignorance, or, as we usually say, do not know their right hand from their left.

There is another tribe of persons who are retainers to the learned world, and who regulate themselves upon all occasions by several laws peculiar to their body; I mean the players or actors of both sexes. Among these it is a standing and uncontroverted principle, that a tragedian always takes place of a comedian; and it is very well known the merry drolls who make us laugh are always placed at the lower end of the table, and in every entertainment give way to the dignity of the buskin. It is a stage maxim, 'Once a king, and always a king.' For this reason it would be thought very absurd in Mr. Bullock, notwithstanding the height and gracefulness of his person, to sit at the right hand of a hero, though he were but five foot high. The same distinction is observed among the ladies of the theatre. Queens and heroines preserve their rank in private conversation, while those who are waiting-women and maids of honour upon the stage keep their distance also behind the scenes.

I shall only add that by a parity of reason, all writers of tragedy look upon it as their due to be seated, served, or saluted, before comic writers: those who deal in tragi-comedy usually taking their seats between the authors of either side. There has been a long dispute for precedency between the tragic and heroic poets. Aristotle would have the latter yield the *pas* to the former; but Mr. Dryden, and many others, would never submit to this decision. Burlesque writers pay the same deference to the heroic, as comic writers to their serious brothers in the drama.

By this short table of laws order is kept up, and distinction preserved, in the whole republic of letters. O.

No. 530.] *Friday, November* 7, 1712.

> Sic visum Veneri; cui placet impares
> Formas atque animos sub juga ahenea
> Sævo mittere cum joco.
> *Hor.* Od. xxxiii. Lib. 1. 10.

> Thus Venus sports; the rich, the base,
> Unlike in fortune and in face,
> To disagreeing love provokes;
> When cruelly jocose,
> She ties the fatal noose,
> And binds unequals to the brazen yokes.—*Creech.*

It is very usual for those who have been severe upon marriage, in some part or other of their lives, to enter into the fraternity which they have ridiculed, and to see their raillery return upon their own heads. I scarce ever knew a woman-hater that did not, sooner or later, pay for it. Marriage, which is a blessing to another man, falls upon such a one as a judgment. Mr. Congreve's Old Bachelor is set forth to us with much wit and humour, as an example of this kind. In short, those who have most distinguished themselves by railing at the sex in general, very often make an honourable amends, by choosing one of the most worthless persons of it for a companion and yoke-fellow. Hymen takes his revenge in kind on those who turn his mysteries into ridicule.

My friend Will Honeycomb, who was so unmercifully witty upon the women, in a couple of letters which I lately communicated to the public, has given the ladies ample satisfaction by marrying a farmer's daughter; a piece of news which came to our club by the last post. The templar is very positive that he has married a dairy-maid: but Will, in his letter to me on this occasion, sets the best face upon the matter that he can, and gives a more tolerable account of his spouse. I must confess I suspected something more than ordinary, when upon opening the letter I found that Will was fallen off from his former gayety, having changed 'Dear Spec,' which was his usual salute at the beginning of the letter, into 'My worthy Friend,' and subscribed himself in the latter end, at full length, William Honeycomb. In short, the gay, the loud, the vain Will Honeycomb, who had made love to every great fortune that has appeared in town for above thirty years together, and boasted of favours from ladies whom he had never seen, is at length wedded to a plain country girl.

His letter gives us the picture of a converted rake. The sober character of the husband is dashed with the man of the town, and enlivened with those little cant phrases which have made my friend Will often thought very pretty company. But let us hear what he says for himself.

'My worthy friend,—I question not but you, and the rest of my acquaintance, wonder that I, who have lived in the smoke and gallantries of the town for thirty years together, should all on a sudden grow fond of a country life. Had not my dog of a steward ran away as he did, without making up his accounts, I had still been immersed in sin and sea-coal. But since my late forced visit to my estate, I am so pleased with it, that I am resolved to live and die upon it. I am every day abroad among my acres, and can scarce forbear filling my letters with breezes, shades, flowers, meadows, and purling streams. The simplicity of manners, which I have heard you so often speak of, and which appears here in perfection, charms me wonderfully. As an instance of it I must acquaint you, and by your means the whole club, that I have lately married one of my tenant's daughters. She is born of honest parents; and though she has no portion, she has a great deal of virtue. The natural sweetness and innocence of her behaviour, the freshness of her complexion, the unaffected turn of her shape and person, shot me through and through every time I saw her, and did more execution upon me in grogram than the greatest beauty in town or court had ever done in brocade. In short, she is such a one as promises me a good heir to my estate; and if by her means I cannot leave to my children what are falsely called the gifts of birth, high titles, and alliances, I hope to convey to them the more real and valuable gifts of birth—strong bodies, and healthy constitutions. As for your fine women, I need not tell thee that I know them. I have had my share in their graces; but no more of that. It shall be my business hereafter to live the life of an honest man, and to act as becomes the master of a family. I question not but I shall draw upon me the raillery of the town, and be treated to the tune of, 'The Marriage-hater Matched;'* but I am prepared for it. I have been as witty upon others, in my time. To tell thee truly, I saw such a tribe of fashionable young fluttering coxcombs shot up, that I did not think my post of an *homme de ruelle* any longer tenable. I felt a certain stiffness in my limbs, which entirely destroyed the jauntiness of air I was once master of. Besides, for I may now confess my age to thee, I have been eight-and-forty above these twelve years. Since my retirement into the country will make a vacancy in the club, I could wish you would fill up my place with my friend Tom Dapperwit. He has an infinite deal of fire, and knows the

* The name of one of Tom Durfey's miserable comedies. It was Dogget's excellent performance of a character in this play, that first drew the eyes of the public upon him, and marked him out as an actor of superior talents.

town. For my own part, as I have said before, I shall endeavour to live hereafter suitable to a man in my station, as a prudent head of a family, a good husband, a careful father, (when it shall so happen,) and as your most sincere friend,

O. 'WILLIAM HONEYCOMB.'

No. 531.] *Saturday, November* 8, 1712.

Qui mare et terras, variisque mundum
Temperat horis:
Unde nil majus generatur ipso;
Nec viget quicquam simile aut secundum.
Hor. Od. xii. Lib. 1 15.

Who guides below and rules above,
The great disposer, and the mighty King;
Than he none greater, like him none,
That can be, is, or was;
Supreme he singly fills the throne.—*Creech.*

Simonides being asked by Dionysius the tyrant what God was, desired a day's time to consider of it before he made his reply. When the day was expired he desired two days; and afterwards, instead of returning his answer, demanded still double the time to consider of it. This great poet and philosopher, the more he contemplated the nature of the Deity, found that he waded but the more out of his depth; and that he lost himself in the thought, instead of finding an end of it.

If we consider the idea which wise men, by the light of reason, have framed of the Divine Being, it amounts to this; that he has in him all the perfection of a spiritual nature. And since we have no notion of any kind of spiritual perfection but what we discover in our own souls, we join infinitude to each kind of these perfections, and what is a faculty in a human soul becomes an attribute in God. We exist in place and time; the Divine Being fills the immensity of space with his presence, and inhabits eternity. We are possessed of a little power and a little knowledge: the Divine Being is almighty and omniscient. In short, by adding infinity to any kind of perfection we enjoy, and by joining all these different kinds of perfection in one being, we form our idea of the great Sovereign of Nature.

Though every one who thinks must have made this observation, I shall produce Mr. Locke's authority to the same purpose, out of his Essay on Human Understanding. 'If we examine the idea we have of the incomprehensible Supreme Being, we shall find that we come by it the same way; and that the complex ideas we have both of God and separate spirits, are made up of the simple ideas we receive from reflection: *v. g.* having, from what we experience in ourselves, got the ideas of existence and duration, of knowledge and power of pleasure and happiness, and of several other qualities and powers, which it is better to have than to be without: when we would frame an idea the most suitable we can to the Supreme Being, we enlarge every one of these with our own idea of infinity: and so putting them together, make our complex idea of God.'

It is not impossible that there may be many kinds of spiritual perfection, besides those which are lodged in a human soul: but it is impossible that we should have the ideas of any kinds of perfection, except those of which we have some small rays and short imperfect strokes in ourselves. It would therefore be very high presumption to determine whether the Supreme Being has not many more attributes than those which enter into our conceptions of him. This is certain, that if there be any kind of spiritual perfection which is not marked out in a human soul, it belongs in its fulness to the divine nature.

Several eminent philosophers have imagined that the soul, in her separate state, may have new faculties springing up in her, which she is not capable of exerting during her present union with the body; and whether these faculties may not correspond with other attributes in the divine nature, and open to us hereafter new matter of wonder and adoration, we are altogether ignorant. This, as I have said before, we ought to acquiesce in, that the Sovereign Being, the great author of nature, has in him all possible perfection, as well in kind as in degree: to speak according to our methods of conceiving, I shall only add under this head, that when we have raised our notion of this Infinite Being as high as it is possible for the mind of man to go, it will fall infinitely short of what he really is. 'There is no end of his greatness.' The most exalted creature he has made is only capable of adoring it, none but himself can comprehend it.

The advice of the son of Sirach is very just and sublime in this light. 'By his word all things consist. We may speak much, and yet come short: wherefore in some he is all. How shall we be able to magnify him? for he is great above all his works. The Lord is terrible and very great; and marvellous in his power. When you glorify the Lord, exalt him as much as you can; for even yet will he far exceed. And when you exalt him, put forth all your strength, and be not weary; for you can never go far enough. Who hath seen him, that he might tell us? and who can magnify him as he is? There are yet hid greater things than these be, for we have seen but a few of his works.'

I have here only considered the Supreme Being by the light of reason and philosophy. If we would see him in all the wonders of his mercy, we must have recourse to revelation, which represents him to us not only as infinitely great and glorious, but as infinitely good and just in his dispensations towards man. But as this is the theory which falls under every one's consideration, though indeed it can never be sufficiently considered, I shall here only take notice of that habitual worship and veneration which we ought to pay to this Almighty Being. We should often refresh our minds with the thought of him, and annihilate ourselves before him, in the contemplation of our own worthlessness, and of his transcendent excellency and perfection. This would imprint in our minds such a constant and uninterrupted awe and veneration as that which I am here recommending, and which is in reality a kind of incessant prayer, and reasonable humiliation of the soul before him who made it.

This would effectually kill in us all the little seeds of pride, vanity, and self-conceit, which are apt to shoot up in the minds of such whose thoughts turn more on those comparative advantages which they enjoy over some of their fellow-creatures, than on that infinite distance which is placed between them and the supreme model of all perfection. It would likewise quicken our desires and endeavours of uniting ourselves to him by all the acts of religion and virtue.

Such an habitual homage to the Supreme Being would, in a particular manner, banish from among us that prevailing impiety of using his name on the most trivial occasions.

I find the following passage in an excellent sermon, preached at the funeral of a gentleman* who was an honour to his country, and a more diligent as well as successful inquirer into the works of nature than any other our nation has ever produced. 'He had the profoundest veneration for the great God of heaven and earth that I have ever observed in any person. The very name of God was never mentioned by him without a pause and a visible stop in his discourse; in which one, that knew him most particularly above twenty years, has told me that he was so exact, that he does not remember to have observed him once to fail in it.'

Every one knows the veneration which was paid by the Jews to a name so great, wonderful, and holy. They would not let it enter even into their religious discourses. What can we then think of those who make use of so tremendous a name in the ordinary expressions of their anger, mirth, and most impertinent passions? of those who admit it into the most familiar questions and assertions, ludicrous phrases, and works of humour? not to mention those who violate it by solemn perjuries! It would be an affront to reason to endeavour to set forth the horror and profaneness of such a practice. The very mention of it exposes it sufficiently to those in whom the light of nature, not to say religion, is not utterly extinguished. O.

* See bishop Burnet's Sermon, preached at the funeral of the honourable Robert Boyle.

No. 532.] *Monday, November* 10, 1712.

——Fungor vice cotis, acutum
Reddere quæ ferrum valet, exsors ipsa secandi.
Hor. Ars Poet. ver. 304.

I play the whetstone: useless and unfit
To cut myself, I sharpen others wit.—*Creech.*

It is a very honest action to be studious to produce other men's merit; and I make no scruple of saying, I have as much of this temper as any man in the world. It would not be a thing to be bragged of, but that is what any man may be master of, who will take pains enough for it. Much observation of the unworthiness in being pained at the excellence of another will bring you to a scorn of yourself for that unwillingness; and when you have got so far, you will find it a greater pleasure than you ever before knew to be zealous in promoting the fame and welfare of the praiseworthy. I do not speak this as pretending to be a mortified self-denying man, but as one who had turned his ambition into a right channel. I claim to myself the merit of having extorted excellent productions from a person of the greatest abilities, who would not have let them appeared by any other means;† to have animated a few young gentlemen into worthy pursuits, who will be a glory to our age; and at all times, and by all possible means in my power, undermined the interest of ignorance, vice, and folly, and attempted to substitute in their stead, learning, piety, and good sense. It is from this honest heart that I find myself honoured as a gentleman-usher to the arts and sciences.—Mr. Tickell and Mr. Pope have, it seems, this idea of me. The former has writ me an excellent paper of verses, in praise, forsooth, of myself; and the other enclosed for my perusal an admirable poem,‡ which I hope will shortly see the light. In the mean time I cannot suppress any thought of his, but insert this sentiment about the dying words of Adrian. I will not determine in the case he mentions; but have thus much to say in favour of his argument, that many of his own works which I have seen, convince me that very pretty and very sublime sentiments may be lodged in the same bosom without diminution of its greatness.

'Mr. Spectator,—I was the other day in company with five or six men of some learning: where, chancing to mention the famous verses which the emperor Adrian spoke on his death-bed, they were all agreed that it was a piece of gayety unworthy that prince in those circumstances. I could not but dissent from this opinion. Methinks it was by no means a gay but a very serious soliloquy to his soul at the point of his departure: in which sense I naturally took these verses at my first reading them, when I was very young, and be

† Addison. ‡ The Temple of Fame

fore I knew what interpretation the world generally put upon them.

"Animula vagula, blandula,
Hospes comesque corporis,
Quæ nunc abibis in loca?
Pallidula, rigida, nudula,
Nec (ut soles) dabis jocos!"

"Alas, my soul! thou pleasing companion of this body, thou fleeting thing that art now deserting it, whither art thou flying? to what unknown region? Thou art all trembling, fearful, and pensive. Now what is become of thy former wit and humour? Thou shalt jest and be gay no more."

'I confess I cannot apprehend where lies the trifling in all this; it is the most natural and obvious reflection imaginable to a dying man: and, if we consider the emperor was a heathen, that doubt concerning the future state of his soul will seem so far from being the effect of want of thought, that it was scarce reasonable he should think otherwise: not to mention that there is a plain confession included of his belief in its immortality. The diminutive epithets of *vagula, blandula,* and the rest, appear not to me as expressions of levity, but rather of endearment and concern; such as we find in Catullus, and the authors of Hendecasyllabi after him, where they are used to express the utmost love and tenderness for their mistresses. If you think me right in my notion of the last words of Adrian, be pleased to insert this in the Spectator; if not, suppress it.

'I am, &c.'

'To the supposed Author of the Spectator.

'In courts licentious, and a shameless stage,
How long the war shall wit with virtue wage?
Enchanted by this prostituted fair,
Our youth run headlong in the fatal snare;
In height of rapture clasp unheeded pains,
And suck pollution through their tingling veins.

'Thy spotless thoughts unshock'd the priest may hear,
And the pure vestal in her bosom wear.
To conscious blushes and diminish'd pride,
Thy glass betrays what treach'rous love would hide:
Nor harsh thy precepts, but infus'd by stealth,
Please while they cure, and cheat us into health.

'Thy works in Chloe's toilet gain a part,
And with his tailor share the fopling's heart:
Lash'd in thy satire, the penurious cit
Laughs at himself, and finds no harm in wit:
From felon gamesters the raw 'squire is free,
And Britain owes her rescu'd oaks to thee.*
His miss the frolic viscount† dreads to toast,
Or his third cure the shallow templar boast;
And the rash fool, who scorn'd the beaten road,
Dares quake at thunder, and confess his God.

'The brainless stripling, who, expell'd to town,
Damn'd the stiff college and pedantic clown,
Aw'd by thy name is dumb, and thrice a week
Spells uncouth Latin, and pretends to Greek.
A saunt'ring tribe! such, born to wide estates,
With "yea" and "no" in senates hold debates;
At length despis'd, each to his field retires,
First with the dogs, and king amidst the 'squires;
From pert to stupid sinks supinely down,
In youth a coxcomb, and in age a clown.

'Such readers scorn'd, thou wing'st thy daring flight
Above the stars, and tread'st the fields of light;
Fame, heaven, and hell, are thy exalted theme,
And visions such as Jove himself might dream;
Man sunk to slav'ry, though to glory born,
Heaven's pride when upright, and deprav'd his scorn

'Such hints alone could British Virgil lend,‡
And thou alone deserve from such a friend;
A debt so borrow'd is illustrious fame,
And fame when shar'd with him is double fame.
So flush'd with sweets, by beauty's queen bestow'd,
With more than mortal charms Æneas glow'd:
Such gen'rous strifes Eugene and Marlbro' try,
And as in glory so in friendship vie.

'Permit these lines by thee to live—nor blame
A muse that pants and languishes for fame;
That fears to sink when humbled themes she sings,
Lost in the mass of mean forgotten things.
Receiv'd by thee, I prophesy my rhymes
The praise of virgins in succeeding times;
Mix'd with thy works, their life no bounds shall see,
But stand protected as inspir'd by thee.

'So some weak shoot, which else would poorly rise,
Jove's tree adopts and lifts him to the skies;
Through the new pupil fost'ring juices flow,
Thrust forth the gems, and give the flowers to blow
Aloft, immortal reigns the plant unknown,
With borrow'd life, and vigour not his own.'

'To the Spectator General.

'Mr. John Sly humbly showeth:—

'That upon reading the deputation given to the said Mr. John Sly, all persons passing by his observatory behaved themselves with the same decorum as if your honour yourself had been present.

'That your said officer is preparing, according to your honour's secret instructions, hats for the several kinds of heads that make figures in the realms of Great Britain, with cocks significant of their powers and faculties.

'That your said officer has taken due notice of your instructions and admonitions concerning the internals of the head from the outward form of the same. His hats for men of the faculties of law and physic do but just turn up, to give a little life to their sagacity; his military hats glare full in the face; and he has prepared a familiar easy cock for all good companions between the above-mentioned extremes. For this end he has consulted the most learned of his acquaintance for the true form and dimensions of the *lepidum caput,* and made a hat fit for it.

'Your said officer does farther represent, that the young divines about town are many of them got into the cock military and desires your instructions therein.

'That the town has been for several days very well behaved, and farther your said officer saith not.' T.

No. 533.] *Tuesday, November* 11, 1712.

Immo duas dabo, inquit ille, una si parum est;
Et si duarum pœnitebit addentur duæ.—*Plaut.*

Nay, says he, if one is too little, I will give you two,
And if two will not satisfy you, I will add two more

'To the Spectator.

'SIR,—You have often given us very excellent discourses against that unnatural

* Mr. Tickell here alludes to Steel's papers against the sharpers, &c. in the Tatler, and particularly to a letter in Tat. No. 73, signed Will Trusty, and written by Mr. John Hughes.

† Viscount Bolingbroke.

‡ A compliment to Addison.

custom of parents in forcing their children to marry contrary to their inclinations. My own case, without farther preface, I will lay before you, and leave you to judge of it. My father and mother, both being in declining years, would fain see me, their eldest son, as they call it, settled. I am as much for that as they can be; but I must be settled, it seems, not according to my own, but their liking. Upon this account I am teased every day, because I have not yet fallen into love, in spite of nature, with one of a neighbouring gentleman's daughters; for out of their abundant generosity, they give me the choice of four. "Jack," begins my father. "Mrs. Catharine is a fine woman."—"Yes, sir, but she is rather too old."—"She will make the more discreet manager, boy." Then my mother plays her part. "Is not Mrs. Betty exceeding fair?"—"Yes, madam, but she is of no conversation; she has no fire, no agreeable vivacity; she neither speaks nor looks with spirit."—"True, son, but for those very reasons she will be an easy, soft, obliging, tractable creature."—"After all," cries an old aunt, (who belongs to the class of those who read plays with spectacles on,) "what think you, nephew, of proper Mrs. Dorothy?"—"What do I think? why, I think she cannot be above six foot two inches high."—"Well, well, you may banter as long as you please, but height of stature is commanding and majestic."—"Come, come," says a cousin of mine in the family, "I will fit him; Fidelia is yet behind—pretty Miss Fiddy must please you."—"Oh! your very humble servant, dear coz, she is as much too young as her eldest sister is too old."—"Is it so, indeed," quoth she, "good Mr. Pert? You that are but turned of twenty-two, and Miss Fiddy in half a year's time will be in her teens, and she is capable of learning any thing. Then she will be so observant; she will cry perhaps now and then, but never be angry." Thus they will think for me in this matter, wherein I am more particularly concerned than any body else. If I name any woman in the world, one of these daughters has certainly the same qualities. You see by these few hints, Mr. Spectator, what a comfortable life I lead. To be still more open and free with you, I have been passionately fond of a young lady (whom give me leave to call Miranda) now for these three years. I have often urged the matter home to my parents with all the submission of a son, but the impatience of a lover. Pray, sir, think of three years: what inexpressible scenes of inquietude, what variety of misery must I have gone through in three whole years! Miranda's fortune is equal to those I have mentioned; but her relations are not intimates with mine! Ah! there's the rub! Miranda's person, wit, and humour, are what the nicest fancy could imagine; and, though we know you to be so elegant a judge of beauty, yet there is none among all your various characters of fine women preferable to Miranda. In a word, she is never guilty of doing any thing but one amiss, (if she can be thought to do amiss by me) in being as blind to my faults, as she is to her own perfections. I am, sir, your very humble, obedient servant,

'DUSTERERASTUS.'

'MR. SPECTATOR,—When you spent so much time as you did lately in censuring the ambitious young gentlemen who ride in triumph through town and country on coach-boxes, I wish you had employed those moments in consideration of what passes sometimes within-side of those vehicles. I am sure I suffered sufficiently by the insolence and ill-breeding of some persons who travelled lately with me in the stage-coach out of Essex to London. I am sure, when you have heard what I have to say, you will think there are persons under the character of gentlemen, that are fit to be no where else but on the coach-box. Sir, I am a young woman of a sober and religious education, and have preserved that character; but on Monday was fortnight, it was my misfortune to come to London. I was no sooner clapped into the coach, but, to my great surprise, two persons in the habit of gentlemen attacked me with such indecent discourse as I cannot repeat to you, so you may conclude not fit for me to hear. I had no relief but the hopes of a speedy end of my short journey. Sir, form to yourself what a persecution this must needs be to a virtuous and chaste mind; and, in order to your proper handling such a subject, fancy your wife or daughter, if you had any, in such circumstances, and what treatment you would then think due to such dragoons. One of them was called a captain, and entertained us with nothing but filthy stupid questions, or lewd songs, all the way. Ready to burst with shame and indignation, I repined that nature had not allowed us as easily to shut our ears as our eyes. But was not this a kind of rape? Why should there be accessaries in ravishment any more than murder? Why should not every contributor to the abuse of chastity suffer death? I am sure these shameless hell-hounds deserved it highly. Can you exert yourself better than on such an occasion? If you do not do it effectually, I will read no more of your papers. Has every impertinent fellow a privilege to torment me, who pay my coach-hire as well as he? Sir, pray consider us in this respect as the weakest sex, who have nothing to defend ourselves; and I think it is as gentleman-like to challenge a woman to fight as to talk obscenely in her company, especially when she has not power to stir. Pray let me tell you a story which you can make fit for public view. I knew a gentleman who, having a very good opinion of the gentlemen of the army, invited ten or twelve of them to sup with him; and at the same time invited two or three friends who were very severe against the manners and morals of gentlemen of that profession. It happened one of them brought two captains of his regiment newly come into the army, who at the first onset engaged the company with very lewd healths and suitable discourse. You may easily imagine the confusion of the entertainer, who finding some of his friends very uneasy, desired to tell them the story of a great man, one Mr. Locke, (whom I find you frequently mention) that being invited to dine with the then lords Halifax, Anglesey, and Shaftesbury, immediately after dinner, instead of conversation, the cards were called for, where the bad or good success produced the usual passions of gaming. Mr. Locke, retiring to a window, and writing, my lord Anglesey desired to know what he was writing: "Why, my lords," answered he, "I could not sleep last night for the pleasure and improvement I expected from the conversation of the greatest men of the age." This so sensibly stung them, that they gladly compounded to throw their cards in the fire, if he would his paper, and so a conversation ensued fit for such persons. This story pressed so hard upon the young captains, together with the concurrence of their superior officers, that the young fellows left the company in confusion. Sir, I know you hate long things; but if you like it you may contract it, or how you will; but I think it has a moral in it.

'But, sir, I am told you are a famous mechanic as well as a looker-on, and therefore humbly propose you would invent some padlock, with full power under your hand and seal, for all modest persons, either men or women, to clap upon the mouths of all such impertinent impudent fellows: and I wish you would publish a proclamation, that no modest person who has value for her countenance, and consequently would not be put out of it, presume to travel after such a day without one of them in their pockets. I fancy a smart Spectator upon this subject would serve for such a padlock; and that public notice may be given in your paper where they may be had, with directions, price two pence; and that part of the directions may be, when any person presumes to be guilty of the above-mentioned crime, the party aggrieved may produce it to his face, with a request to read it to the company. He must be very much hardened that could outface that rebuke; and his farther punishment I leave you to prescribe. Your humble servant,

T. 'PENANCE CRUEL.'

No. 534.] *Wednesday, November* 12, 1712.

Rarus enim ferme sensus communis in illa
Fortuna—— *Juv. Sat.* viii. 73.

——We seldom find
Much sense with an exalted fortune joined.
Stepney.

Mr. Spectator,—I am a young woman of nineteen, the only daughter of very wealthy parents, and have my whole life been used with a tenderness which did me no great service in my education. I have perhaps an uncommon desire for knowledge of what is suitable to my sex and quality; but, as far as I can remember, the whole dispute about me has been, whether such a thing was proper for the child to do, or not? or whether such or such a food was the more wholesome for the young lady to eat? This was ill for my shape, that for my complexion, and the other for my eyes. I am not extravagant when I tell you, I do not know that I have trod upon the very earth ever since I was ten years old. A coach or chair I am obliged to for all my motions from one place to another ever since I can remember. All who had to do to instruct me, have ever been bringing stories of the notable things I have said, and the womanly manner of my behaving myself upon such and such an occasion. This has been my state until I came towards years of womanhood: and ever since I grew towards the age of fifteen I have been abused after another manner. Now, forsooth, I am so killing, no one can safely speak to me. Our house is frequented by men of sense, and I love to ask questions when I fall into such conversation; but I am cut short with something or other about my bright eyes. There is, sir, a language particular for talking to women in; and none but those of the very first good-breeding (who are very few, and who seldom come into my way) can speak to us without regard to our sex. Among the generality of those they call gentlemen, it is impossible for me to speak upon any subject whatsoever, without provoking somebody to say, "Oh! to be sure, fine Mrs. Such-a-one must be very particularly acquainted with all that; all the world would contribute to her entertainment and information." Thus, sir, I am so handsome, that I murder all who approach me; so wise, that I want no new notices; and so well-bred, that I am treated by all that know me like a fool, for no one will answer as if I were their friend or companion. Pray, sir, be pleased to take the part of us beauties and fortunes into your consideration, and do not let us be thus flattered out of our senses. I have got a huzzy of a maid who is most craftily given to this ill quality. I was at first diverted with a certain absurdity the creature was guilty of in every thing she said. She is a country girl; and in the dialect of the shire she was born in, would tell me that every body reckoned her lady had the purest red and white in the world: then she would tell me I was the most like one Sisly Dobson in their town, who made the miller make away with himself, and walk afterwards in the corn-field where they used to meet. With all this, this cunning huzzy can lay letters in my way, and put a billet in my gloves, and then stand in it she knows nothing of it. I do not know, from my birth to this day, that I have been ever treated by any one as I ought; and if it were not for a few books, which I delight in, I should be at this hour a novice to all common sense. Would it not be worth your while to lay down rules for behaviour in this case, and tell people, that we fair ones expect honest plain answers as well as other people? Why must I, good sir, because I have a good air, a fine complexion, and am in the bloom of my years, be misled in all my actions; and have the notions of good and ill confounded in my mind, for no other offence, but because I have the advantages of beauty and fortune? Indeed, sir, what with the silly homage which is paid to us by the sort of people I have above spoken of, and the utter negligence which others have for us, the conversation of us young women of condition is no other than what must expose us to ignorance and vanity, if not vice. All this is humbly submitted to your spectatorial wisdom, by sir, your humble servant,

'SHARLOT WEALTHY.'

'Will's Coffee-house.

'Mr. Spectator,—Pray, sir, it will serve to fill up a paper if you put in this; which is only to ask, whether that copy of verses which is a paraphrase of Isaiah, in one of your speculations, is not written by Mr. Pope? Then you get on another line, by putting in, with proper distances, as at the end of a letter, I am, sir, your humble servant,

'ABRAHAM DAPPERWIT.'

'Mr. Dapperwit,—I am glad to get another line forward, by saying that excellent piece is Mr. Pope's; and so, with proper distances, I am, your humble servant, THE SPECTATOR.'

'Mr. Spectator,—I was a wealthy grocer in the city, and as fortunate as diligent; but I was a single man, and you know there are women. One in particular came to my shop, who I wished might, but was afraid never would, make a grocer's wife. I thought, however, to take an effectual way of courting, and sold her at less price than I bought, that I might buy at less price than I sold. She, you may be sure, often came and helped me to many customers at the same rate, fancying I was obliged to her. You must needs think this was a good living trade, and my riches must be vastly improved. In fine, I was nigh being declared bankrupt, when I declared myself her lover, and she, herself married. I was just in a condition to support myself, and am now in hopes of growing rich by losing my customers. Yours,

'JEREMY COMFIT.'

'Mr. Spectator,—I am in the condition of the idol you was once pleased to mention, and bar-keeper of a coffee-house. I believe it is needless to tell you the opportunities I must give, and the importunities I suffer. But there is one gentleman who besieges me as close as the French did Bouchain. His gravity makes him work cautious, and his regular approaches denote a good engineer. You need not doubt of his oratory, as he is a lawyer; and especially since he has had so little use of it at Westminster, he may spare the more for me.

'What then can weak women do? I am willing to surrender, but he would have it at discretion, and I with discretion. In the mean time, whilst we parley, our several interests are neglected. As his siege grows stronger, my tea grows weaker; and while he pleads at my bar, none come to him for counsel but *in forma pauperis*. Dear Mr. Spectator, advise him not to insist upon hard articles, nor by his irregular desires contradict the well meaning lines of his countenance. If we were agreed, we might settle to something, as soon as we could determine where we should get most by the law—at the coffee-house, or at Westminster. Your humble servant,

'LUCINDA PARLEY.'

A Minute from Mr. John Sly.

'The world is pretty regular for about forty rod east and ten west of the observatory of the said Mr. Sly; but he is credibly informed, that when they are got beyond the pass into the Strand, or those who move city-ward are got within Temple-bar, they are just as they were before. It is therefore humbly proposed, that moving centries may be appointed all the busy hours of the day between the Exchange and Westminster, and report what passes to your honour, or your subordinate officers, from time to time.'

Ordered,

That Mr. Sly name the said officers, provided he will answer for their principles and morals. T.

No. 535.] *Thursday, November* 13, 1712.

Spem longam reseces.——
Hor. Cd. xi. Lib. 1. 7.

Cut short vain hope.

My four hundred and seventy-first speculation turned upon the subject of hope in general. I design this paper as a speculation upon that vain and foolish hope which is misemployed on temporal objects, and produces many sorrows and calamities in human life.

It is a precept several times inculcated by Horace, that we should not entertain a hope of any thing in life, which lies at a great distance from us. The shortness and uncertainty of our time here makes such a kind of hope unreasonable and absurd. The grave lies unseen between us and the object which we reach after. Where one man lives to enjoy the good he has in view, ten thousand are cut off in the pursuit of it.

It happens likewise unluckily, that one hope no sooner dies in us but another rises up in its stead. We are apt to fancy that we shall be happy and satisfied if we possess ourselves of such and such particular enjoyments; but either by reason of their emptiness, or the natural inquietude of the mind, we have no sooner gained one point, but we extend our hopes to another. We still find new inviting scenes and landscapes lying behind those which at a distance terminated our view.

The natural consequences of such reflections are these, that we should take care not to let our hopes run out into too great a length; that we should sufficiently weigh the objects of our hope, whether they be such as we may reasonably expect from them what we propose in their fruition, and whether they are such as we are pretty sure of attaining, in case our life extend itself so far. If we hope for things which are at too great a distance from us, it is possible that we may be intercepted by death in our progress towards them. If we hope for things which we have not thoroughly considered the value of, our disappointment will be greater than our pleasure in the fruition of them. If we hope for what we are not likely to possess, we act and think in vain, and make life a greater dream and shadow than it really is.

Many of the miseries and misfortunes of life proceed from our want of consideration, in one or all of these particulars. They are the rocks on which the sanguine tribe of lovers daily split, and on which the bankrupt, the politician, the alchymist, and projector, are cast away in every age. Men of warm imaginations and towering thoughts are apt to overlook the goods of fortune which are near them, for something that glitters in the sight at a distance; to neglect solid and substantial happiness for what is showy and superficial; and to contemn that good which lies within their reach, for that which they are not capable of attaining. Hope calculates its schemes for a long and durable life; presses forward to imaginary points of bliss; grasps at impossibilities; and consequently very often ensnares men into beggary, ruin, and dishonour.

What I have here said may serve as a moral to an Arabian fable, which I find translated into French by Monsieur Galland. The fable has in it such a wild but natural simplicity, that I question not but my reader will be as much pleased with it as I have been, and that he will consider himself, if he reflects on the several amusements of hope which have sometimes passed in his mind, as a near relation to the Persian glassman.

Alnaschar, says the fable, was a very idle fellow, that would never set his hand to any business during his father's life. When his father died, he left him to the value of a hundred drachmas in Persian money. Alnaschar, in order to make the best of it, laid it out in glasses, bottles, and the finest earthenware. These he piled up in a large open basket, and, having made choice of a very little shop, placed the basket at his feet: and leaned his back upon the wall, in expectation of customers. As he sat in this posture, with his eyes upon the basket, he fell into a most amusing train of thought, and was overheard by one of his neighbours, as he talked to himself in the following manner: 'This basket,' says he, 'cost me at the wholesale merchant's a hundred drachmas, which is all I have in the world. I shall quickly make two hundred of it, by selling it in retail. These two hundred drachmas will in a very little while rise to four hundred, which of course will amount in time to four thousand. Four thousand drachmas cannot fail of making eight thousand. As soon as by these means I am master of ten thousand, I will lay aside my trade of a glassman, and turn jeweller. I shall then deal in diamonds, pearls, and all sorts of rich stones. When I have got together as much wealth as I well can desire, I will make a purchase of the finest house I can find, with lands, slaves, eunuchs, and horses. I shall then begin to enjoy myself and make a noise in the world. I will not however stop there, but still continue my traffic, until I have got together a hundred thousand drachmas. When I have thus made myself master of a hundred thousand drachmas I shall naturally set myself on the foot of a prince, and will demand the grand vizier's daughter in marriage, after having represented to that minister the information which I have received of the beauty, wit, discretion, and other high qualities which his daughter possesses. I will let him know at the same time, that it is my intention to make him a present of a thousand pieces of gold on our marriage night. As soon as I have married the grand vizier's daughter, I will buy her ten black eunuchs, the youngest and the best that can be got for money. I must afterwards make my father-in-law a visit, with a great train and equipage. And when I am placed at his right hand, which he will do of course, if it be only to honour his daughter, I will give him the thousand pieces of gold which I promised him; and afterwards to his great surprise, will present him with another purse of the same value, with some short speech: as, "Sir, you see I am a man of my word: I always give more than I promise."

'When I have brought the princess to my house, I shall take particular care to breed her in a due respect for me before I give the reins to love and dalliance. To this end I shall confine her to her own apartment, make her a short visit, and talk but little to her. Her women will represent to me that she is inconsolable by reason of my unkindness, and beg me with tears to caress her, and let her sit down by me; but I shall still remain inexorable, and will turn my back upon her all the first night. Her mother will then come and bring her daughter to me, as I am seated upon my sofa. The daughter, with tears in her eyes, will fling herself at my feet, and beg of me to receive her into my favour. Then will I, to imprint in her a thorough veneration for my person, draw up my legs and spurn her from me with my foot, in such a manner that she shall fall down several paces from the sofa.'

Alnaschar was entirely swallowed up in this chimerical vision, and could not forbear acting with his foot what he had in his thoughts; so that unluckily striking his basket of brittle ware, which was the foundation of all his grandeur, he kicked his glasses to a great distance from him into the street, and broke them into ten thousand pieces. O.

No. 536.] *Friday, November* 14, 1712.

O Veræ Phrygiæ, neque enim Phryges!
Virg. Æn. ix 617.

O! less than women in the shapes of men!
Dryden.

As I was the other day standing in my bookseller's shop, a pretty young thing, about eighteen years of age, stepped out of her coach, and, brushing by me, beckoned the man of the shop to the farther end of his counter, where she whispered something to him, with an attentive look, and at the same time presented him with a letter: after which, pressing the end of her fan upon his hand, she delivered the remaining part of her message, and withdrew. I observed, in the midst of her discourse, that she flushed and cast an eye upon me over her shoulder, having been informed by my bookseller that I was the man with the short face whom she had so often read of. Upon her passing by me, the pretty blooming creature smiled in my face, and dropped me a courtesy. She scarce gave me time to return her salute, before she quitted the shop with an easy scuttle, and stepped again into her coach, giving the footmen directions to drive where they were bid. Upon her departure, my bookseller gave me a letter superscribed, 'To the ingenious Spectator,' which the young lady had desired him to deliver into my own hands, and to tell me, that the speedy publication of it would not only oblige herself but a whole tea-table of my friends. I opened it therefore with a resolution to publish it, whatever it should contain, and am sure if any of my male readers will be so severely critical as not to like it, they would have been as well pleased with it as myself, had they seen the face of the pretty scribe.

'London, Nov. 1712.

'MR. SPECTATOR,—You are always ready to receive any useful hint or proposal, and such, I believe, you will think one that may put you in a way to employ the most idle part of the kingdom: I mean that part of mankind who are known by the name of the women's men, or beaux, &c. Mr. Spectator, you are sensible these pretty gentlemen are not made for any manly employments, and for want of business are often as much in the vapours as the ladies. Now what I propose is this, that since knotting is again in fashion, which has been found a very pretty amusement, that you will recommend it to these gentlemen as something that may make them useful to the ladies they admire. And since it is not inconsistent with any game, or other diversion, for it may be done in the play-house, in their coaches, at the tea-table, and in short, in all places where they come for the sake of the ladies, (except at church; be pleased to forbid it there to prevent mistakes,) it will be easily complied with. It is besides an employment that allows, as we see by the fair-sex, of many graces, which will make the beaux more readily come into it; it shows a white hand and a diamond ring to great advantage; it leaves the eyes at full liberty to be employed as before, as also the thoughts and the tongue. In short, it seems in every respect so proper, that it is needless to urge it farther, by speaking of the satisfaction these male knotters will find, when they see their work mixed up in a fringe, and worn by the fair lady for whom and with whom it was done. Truly, Mr. Spectator, I cannot but be pleased I have hit upon something that these gentlemen are capable of; for it is sad so considerable a part of the kingdom (I mean for numbers,) should be of no manner of use. I shall not trouble you farther at this time, but only to say, that I am always your reader, and generally your admirer. C. B.

'P. S. The sooner these fine gentlemen are set to work the better; there being at this time several fine fringes, that stay only for more hands.'

I shall in the next place present my reader with the description of a set of men who are common enough in the world, though I do not remember that I have yet taken notice of them, as they are drawn in the following letter.

'MR. SPECTATOR,—Since you have lately, to so good purpose, enlarged upon conjugal love, it is to be hoped you will discourage every practice that rather proceeds from a regard to interest than to happiness. Now you cannot but observe, that most of our fine young ladies readily fall in with the direction of the graver sort, to retain in their service, by some small encouragement, as great a number as they can of supernumerary and insignificant fellows, which they use like whifflers, and commonly call "shoeing-horns."—These are never designed to know the length of the foot, but only, when a good offer comes, to whet and spur him up to the point. Nay, it is the opinion of that grave lady, madam Matchwell, that it is absolutely convenient for every prudent family to have several of these implements about the house to clap on as occasion serves; and that every spark ought to produce a certificate of his being a shoeing-horn before he be admitted as a shoe. A certain lady whom I could name, if it was necessary, has at present more shoeing-horns of all sizes, countries, and colours in her service, than ever she had new shoes in her life. I have known a woman make use of a shoeing-horn for several years, and finding him unsuccessful in that function, convert him at length into a shoe. I am mistaken if your friend, Mr. William Honeycomb, was not a cast shoeing-horn before his late marriage. As for myself, I must frankly declare to you, that I have been an errant shoeing-horn for above these twenty years. I served my first mistress in that capacity above five of the number, before she was shod. I confess, though she had many who made their application to her, I always thought myself the best shoe in her shop; and it was not until a month before her marriage that I discovered what I was.

This had like to have broke my heart, and raised such suspicions in me, that I told the next I made love to, upon receiving some unkind usage from her, that I began to look upon myself as no more than her shoeing-horn. Upon which, my dear, who was a coquette in her nature, told me I was hypochondriacal, and I might as well look upon myself to be an egg, or a pipkin. But in a very short time after she gave me to know that I was not mistaken in myself. It would be tedious to you to recount the life of an unfortunate shoeing-horn, or I might entertain you with a very long and melancholy relation of my sufferings. Upon the whole, I think, sir, it would very well become a man in your post, to determine in what cases a woman may be allowed with honour to make use of a shoeing-horn, as also to declare whether a maid on this side five-and-twenty, or a widow, who has not been three years in that state, may be granted such a privilege, with other difficulties which will naturally occur to you upon that subject. I am, sir, with the most profound veneration, yours, &c.' O.

No. 537.] *Saturday, November* 15, 1712.

Του μεν γαρ γενος εσμεν. *Arat.*

For we are his offspring. Acts xvii. 28.

'*To the Spectator.*

'SIR,—It has been usual to remind persons of rank, on great occasions in life, of their race and quality, and to what expectations they were born: that by considering what is worthy of them, they may be withdrawn from mean pursuits, and encouraged to laudable undertakings. This is turning nobility into a principle of virtue, and making it productive of merit, as it is understood to have been originally a reward of it.

'It is for the like reason, I imagine, that you have in some of your speculations asserted to your readers the dignity of human nature. But you cannot be insensible that this is a controverted doctrine; there are authors who consider human nature in a very different view, and books of maxims have been written to show the falsity of all human virtues.* The reflections which are made on this subject usually take some tincture from the tempers and characters of those that make them. Politicians can resolve the most shining actions among men into artifice and design; others, who are soured by discontent, repulses, or ill-usage, are apt to mistake their spleen for philosophy; men of profligate lives, and such as find themselves incapable of rising to any distinction among their fellow-creatures, are for pulling down all appearances of merit which seem to upbraid them; and satirists describe nothing but deformity. From all these hands we have such draughts of mankind, as are represented in those burlesque pictures which the Italians call caricaturas; where the art consists in preserving, amidst distorted proportions and aggravated features, some likeness of the person, but in such a manner as to transform the most agreeable beauty into the most odious monster.

'It is very disingenuous to level the best of mankind with the worst, and for the faults of particulars to degrade the whole species. Such methods tend not only to remove a man's good opinion of others, but to destroy that reverence for himself, which is a great guard of innocence, and a spring of virtue.

'It is true indeed, that there are surprising mixtures of beauty and deformity, of wisdom and folly, virtue and vice, in the human make: such a disparity is found among numbers of the same kind; and every individual in some instances, or at some times, is so unequal to himself, that man seems to be the most wavering and inconsistent being in the whole creation. So that the question in morality concerning the dignity of our nature may at first sight appear like some difficult questions in natural philosophy, in which the arguments on both sides seem to be of equal strength. But, as I began with considering this point as it relates to action, I shall here borrow an admirable reflection from monsieur Paschal, which I think sets it in its proper light.

---

* This is an allusion to the Reflections et Maxime Morales de M. le Duc de la Rochefoucault.

"It is of dangerous consequence," says he, "to represent to man how near he is to the level of beasts, without showing him at the same time his greatness. It is likewise dangerous to let him see his greatness without his meanness. It is more dangerous yet to leave him ignorant of either; but very beneficial that he should be made sensible of both." Whatever imperfections we may have in our nature, it is the business of religion and virtue to rectify them, as far as is consistent with our present state. In the mean time it is no small encouragement to generous minds to consider, that we shall put them all off with our mortality. That sublime manner of salutation with which the Jews approach their kings,

"O king, live for ever!"

may be addressed to the lowest and most despised mortal among us, under all the infirmities and distresses with which we see him surrounded. And whoever believes in the immortality of the soul, will not need a better argument for the dignity of his nature, nor a stronger incitement to actions suitable to it.

'I am naturally led by this reflection to a subject I have already touched upon in a former letter, and cannot without pleasure call to mind the thought of Cicero to this purpose, in the close of his book concerning old age. Every one who is acquainted with his writings will remember that the elder Cato is introduced in that discourse as the speaker, and Scipio and Lelius as his auditors. This venerable person is represented looking forward as it were from the verge of extreme old age into a future state, and rising into a contemplation on the unperishable part of his nature, and its existence after death. I shall collect part of his discourse. And as you have formerly offered some arguments for the soul's immortality, agreeable both to reason and the Christian doctrine, I believe your readers will not be displeased to see how the same great truth shines in the pomp of Roman eloquence.

"This (says Cato) is my firm persuasion, that since the human soul exerts itself with so great activity; since it has such a remembrance of the past, such a concern for the future; since it is enriched with so many arts, sciences, and discoveries; it is impossible but the being which contains all these must be immortal."

'The elder Cyrus, just before his death, is represented by Xenophon speaking after this manner: "Think not, my dearest children, that when I depart from you I shall be no more: but remember, that my soul, even while I lived among you, was invisible to you: yet by my actions you were sensible it existed in this body. Believe it therefore existing still, though it be still unseen. How quickly would the honours of illustrious men perish after death, if their souls performed nothing to preserve their fame! For my own part, I never could think that the soul while in a mortal body lives, but when departed out of it dies: or that its consciousness is lost when it is discharged out of an unconscious habitation. But when it is freed from all corporeal alliance, then it truly exists. Farther, since the human frame is broken by death, tell us what becomes of its parts? It is visible whether the materials of other beings are translated; namely, to the source from whence they had their birth. The soul alone, neither present nor departed, is the object of our eyes."

'Thus Cyrus. But to proceed:—"No one shall persuade me, Scipio, that your worthy father or your grandfathers Paulus and Africanus, or Africanus his father or uncle, or many other excellent men whom I need not name, performed so many actions to be remembered by posterity, without being sensible that futurity was their right. And, if I may be allowed an old man's privilege so to speak of myself, do you think I would have endured the fatigue of so many wearisome days and nights, both at home and abroad, if I imagined that the same boundary which is set to my life must terminate my glory? Were it not more desirable to have worn out my days in ease and tranquillity, free from labour and without emulation? But, I know not how, my soul has always raised itself, and looked forward on futurity, in this view and expectation, that when it shall depart out of life it shall then live for ever; and if this were not true, that the mind is immortal, the soul of the most worthy would not, above all others, have the strongest impulse to glory.

"What besides this is the cause that the wisest men die with the greatest equanimity, the ignorant with the greatest concern? Does it not seem that those minds which have the most extensive views foresee they are removing to a happier condition, which those of a narrow sight do not perceive? I, for my part, am transported with the hope of seeing your ancestors: whom I have honoured and loved; and am earnestly desirous of meeting not only those excellent persons whom I have known, but those too of whom I have heard and read, and of whom I myself have written; nor would I be detained from so pleasing a journey. O happy day, when I shall escape from this crowd, this heap of pollution, and be admitted to that divine assembly of exalted spirits! when I shall go not only to those great persons I have named, but to my Cato, my son, than whom a better man was never born, and whose funeral rites I myself performed, whereas he ought rather to have attended mine. Yet has not his soul deserted me, but, seeming to cast back a look on me, is gone before to those habitations to which it was sensible I should follow him. And though I might appear to have borne my loss with courage, I was not unaffected with it; but I comforted myself in the assurance, that it would not be long before we should meet again and be divorced no more." I am, sir, &c.'

No. 538.] *Monday, November* 17, 1712.

——————Ultra
Finem tendere opus.——————
Hor. Sat. i. Lib. 2. 1.

To launch beyond all bounds.

SURPRISE is so much the life of stories, that every one aims at it who endeavours to please by telling them. Smooth delivery, an elegant choice of words, and a sweet arrangement, are all beautifying graces, but not the particulars in this point of conversation which either long command the attention, or strike with the violence of a sudden passion, or occasion the burst of laughter which accompanies humour. I have sometimes fancied that the mind is in this case like a traveller who sees a fine seat in haste; he acknowledges the delightfulness of a walk set with regularity, but would be uneasy if he were obliged to pace it over, when the first view had let him into all its beauties from one end to the other.

However, a knowledge of the success which stories will have when they are attended with a turn of surprise, as it has happily made the characters of some, so has it also been the ruin of the characters of others. There is a set of men who outrage truth, instead of affecting us with a manner in telling it; who overleap the line of probability that they may be seen to move out of the common road; and endeavour only to make their hearers stare by imposing upon them with a kind of nonsense against the philosophy of nature, or such a heap of wonders told upon their own knowledge, as it is not likely one man should have ever met with.

I have been led to this observation by a company into which I fell accidentally. The subject of antipathies was a proper field wherein such false surprisers might expatiate, and there were those present who appeared very fond to show it in its full extent of traditional history. Some of them, in a learned manner, offered to our consideration the miraculous powers which the effluviums of cheese have over bodies whose pores are disposed to receive them in a noxious manner; others gave an account of such who could indeed bear the sight of cheese, but not the taste; for which they brought a reason from the milk of their nurses. Others again discoursed, without endeavouring at reasons, concerning an unconquerable aversion which some stomachs have against a joint of meat when it is whole, and the eager inclination they have for it when, by its being cut up, the shape which had affected them is altered. From hence they passed to eels, then to parsnips, and so from one aversion to another, until we had worked up ourselves to such a pitch of complaisance, that when the dinner was to come in we inquired the name of every dish, and hoped it would be no offence to any in company, before it was admitted. When we had sat down, this civility among us turned the discourse from eatables to other sorts of aversions; and the eternal cat, which plagues every conversation of this nature, began then to engross the subject. One had sweated at the sight of it, another had smelled it out as it lay concealed in a very distant cupboard; and he who crowned the whole set of these stories, reckoned up the number of times in which it had occasioned him to swoon away. 'At last,' says he, 'that you may all be satisfied of my invincible aversion to a cat, I shall give an unanswerable instance. As I was going through a street of London, where I never had been until then, I felt a general damp and faintness all over me, which I could not tell how to account for, until I chanced to cast my eyes upwards, and found that I was passing under a sign-post on which the picture of a cat was hung.'

The extravagance of this turn in the way of surprise, gave a stop to the talk we had been carrying on. Some were silent because they doubted, and others because they were conquered in their own way; so that the gentleman had an opportunity to press the belief of it upon us, and let us see that he was rather exposing himself than ridiculing others.

I must freely own that I did not all this while disbelieve every thing that was said; but yet I thought some in the company had been endeavouring who should pitch the bar farthest; that it had for some time been a measuring cast, and at last my friend of the cat and sign-post had thrown beyond them all.

I then considered the manner in which this story had been received, and the possibility that it might have passed for a jest upon others, if he had not laboured against himself. From hence, thought I, there are two ways which the well-bred world generally takes to correct such a practice, when they do not think fit to contradict it flatly.

The first of these is a general silence, which I would not advise any one to interpret in his own behalf. It is often the effect of prudence in avoiding a quarrel, when they see another drive so fast that there is no stopping him without being run against; and but very seldom the effect of weakness in believing suddenly. The generality of mankind are not so grossly ignorant, as some overbearing spirits would persuade themselves; and if the authority of a character or a caution against danger make us suppress our opinions, yet neither of these are of force enough to suppress our thoughts of them. If a man who has endeavoured to amuse his company with improbabilitie could but look into their minds, he would find that they imagine he lightly esteems of their sense when he thinks to impose upon them, and that he is less esteemed by them for his attempt in doing so. His endeavour to glory at their expense becomes a ground of quarrel, and the scorn and indifference with which they entertain it begins the immediate punishment: and indeed (if we should even go no farther) silence, or a negligent indifference, has a deeper way of wounding than opposition, because opposition proceeds from an anger that has a sort of generous sentiment for the adversary mingling along with it, while it shows that there is some esteem in your mind for him: in short, that you think him worth while to contest with. But silence, or a negligent indifference, proceeds from anger, mixed with a scorn that shows another he is thought by you too contemptible to be regarded.

The other method which the world has taken for correcting this practice of false surprise, is to overshoot such talkers in their own bow, or to raise the story with farther degrees of impossibility, and set up for a voucher to them in such a manner as must let them see they stand detected. Thus I have heard a discourse was once managed upon the effects of fear. One of the company had given an account how it had turned his friend's hair gray in a night, while the terrors of a shipwreck encompassed him. Another, taking the hint from hence, began, upon his own knowledge, to enlarge his instances of the like nature to such a number, that it was not probable he could ever have met with them: and as he still grounded these upon different causes for the sake of variety, it might seem at last, from his share of the conversation, almost impossible that any one who can feel the passion of fear, should all his life escape so common an effect of it. By this time some of the company grew negligent, or desirous to contradict him; but one rebuked the rest with an appearance of severity, and with the known old story in his head, assured them he did not scruple to believe that the fear of any thing can make a man's hair gray, since he knew one whose periwig had suffered so by it. Thus he stopped the talk, and made them easy. Thus is the same method taken to bring us to shame, which we fondly take to increase our character. It is indeed a kind of mimickry, by which another puts on our air of conversation to show us to ourselves. He seems to look ridiculous before you, that you may remember how near a resemblance you bear to him; or that you may know that he will not lie under the imputation of believing you. Then it is that you are struck dumb immediately with a conscientious shame for what you have been saying. Then it is that you are inwardly grieved at the sentiments which you cannot but perceive others entertain concerning you. In short, you are against yourself; the laugh of the company runs against you; the censuring world is obliged to you for that triumph which you have allowed them at your own expense; and truth, which you have injured, has a near way of being revenged on you, when by the bare repetition of your story you become a frequent diversion for the public.

'Mr. Spectator,—The other day, walking in Pancras church-yard, I thought of your paper wherein you mention epitaphs, and am of opinion this has a thought in it worth being communicated to your readers.

"Here innocence and beauty lies, whose breath
Was snatch'd by early, not untimely, death.
Hence did she go, just as she did begin
Sorrow to know, before she knew to sin.
Death, that does sin and sorrow thus prevent,
Is the next blessing to a life well spent."

'I am, sir, your servant.'

No. 539.] *Tuesday, November* 18, 1712.

Heteroclita sunto.—*Quæ Genus.*

Be they heteroclites.

Mr. Spectator,—I am a young widow of good fortune and family, and just come to town; where I find I have clusters of pretty fellows come already to visit me, some dying with hopes, others with fears, though they never saw me. Now, what I would beg of you would be to know whether I may venture to use these pert fellows with the same freedom as I did my country acquaintance. I desire your leave to use them as to me shall seem meet, without imputation of a jilt; for since I make declaration that not one of them shall have me, I think I ought to be allowed the liberty of insulting those who have the vanity to believe it is in their power to make me break that resolution. There are schools for learning to use foils, frequented by those who never design to fight; and this useless way of aiming at the heart, without design to wound it on either side, is the play with which I am resolved to divert myself. The man who pretends to win, I shall use him like one who comes into a fencing-school to pick a quarrel. I hope upon this foundation you will give me the free use of the natural and artificial force of my eyes, looks, and gestures. As for verbal promises, I will make none, but shall have no mercy on the conceited interpreters of glances and motions. I am particularly skilled in the downcast eye, and the recovery into a sudden full aspect and away again, as you may have seen sometimes practised by us country beauties beyond all that you have observed in courts and cities. Add to this, sir, that I have a ruddy heedless look, which covers artifice the best of any thing. Though I can dance very well, I affect a tottering untaught way of walking, by which I appear an easy prey; and never exert my instructed charms, until I find I have engaged a pursuer. Be pleased, sir, to print this letter, which will certainly begin the chase of a rich widow. The many foldings, escapes, returns, and doublings, which I make, I shall from time to time communicate to you, for the better instruction of all females, who set up, like me, for reducing the present exorbitant power and insolence of man. I am, sir, your faithful correspondent, RELICTA LOVELY.'

'DEAR MR. SPECTATOR,—I depend upon your professed respect for virtuous love for your immediately answering the design of this letter: which is no other than to lay before the world the severity of certain parents, who desire to suspend the marriage of a discreet young woman of eighteen, three years longer, for no other reason but that of her being too young to enter into that state. As to the consideration of riches, my circumstances are such, that I cannot be suspected to make my addresses to her on such low motives as avarice or ambition. If ever innocence, wit, and beauty, united their utmost charms, they have in her. I wish you would expatiate a little on this subject, and admonish her parents that it may be from the very imperfection of human nature itself, and not any personal frailty of her or me, that our inclinations baffled at present may alter; and while we are arguing with ourselves to put off the enjoyment of our present passions, our affections may change their objects in the operation. It is a very delicate subject to talk upon; but if it were but hinted, I am in hopes it would give the parties concerned some reflection that might expedite our happiness. There is a possibility, and I hope I may say it without imputation of immodesty to her I love with the highest honour; I say there is a possibility this delay may be as painful to her as it is to me; if it be as much, it must be more, by reason of the severe rules the sex are under, in being denied even the relief of complaint. If you oblige me in this, and I succeed, I promise you a place at my wedding, and a treatment suitable to your spectatorial dignity. Your most humble servant, EUSTACE.'

'SIR,—I yesterday heard a young gentleman, that looked as if he had come just to the gown and a scarf, upon evil speaking: which subject you know archbishop Tillotson has so nobly handled in a sermon in his folio. As soon as ever he had named his text, and had opened a little the drift of his discourse, I was in great hopes he had been one of Sir Roger's chaplains. I have conceived so great an idea of the charming discourse above, that I should have thought one part of my sabbath very well spent in hearing a repetition of it. But, alas! Mr. Spectator, this reverend divine gave us his grace's sermon, and yet I do not know how; even I that am sure have read it at least twenty times, could not tell what to make of it, and was at a loss sometimes to guess what the man aimed at. He was so just, indeed, as to give us all the heads and the subdivisions of the sermon, and farther I think there was not one beautiful thought in it but what we had. But then, sir, this gentleman made so many pretty additions; and he could never give us a paragraph of the sermon but he introduced it with something which methought looked more like a design to show his own ingenuity than to instruct the people. In short, he added and curtailed in such a manner, that he vexed me; insomuch that I could not forbear thinking (what I confess I ought not to have thought in so holy a place,) that this young spark was as justly blameable as Bullock or Penkethman, when they mend a noble play of Shakspeare or Jonson. Pray, sir, take this into your consideration; and, if we must be entertained with the works of any of those great men, desire these gentlemen to give them us as they find them, that so when we read them to our families at home they may the better remember they have heard them at church. Sir, your humble servant.'

No. 540.] *Wednesday, November* 19, 1712.

——Non deficit alter.—*Virg. Æn.* vi. 143.

A second is not wanting.

'MR. SPECTATOR,—There is no part of your writings which I have in more esteem than your criticism upon Milton. It is an honourable and candid endeavour to set the works of our noble writers in the graceful light which they deserve. You will lose much of my kind inclination towards you, if you do not attempt the encomium of Spenser also, or at least indulge my passion for that charming author so far as to print the loose hints I now give you on that subject.

'Spenser's general plan is the representation of six virtues—holiness, temperance, chastity, friendship, justice, and courtesy—in six legends by six persons. The six personages are supposed, under proper allegories suitable to their respective characters, to do all that is necessary for the full manifestation of the respective virtues which they are to exert.

'These, one might undertake to show under the several heads, are admirably drawn; no images improper, and most surprisingly beautiful. The Redcross Knight runs through the whole steps of the Christian life; Guyon does all that temperance can possibly require; Britomartis (a woman) observes the true rules of unaffected chastity; Arthegal is in every respect of life strictly and wisely just; Calidore is rightly courteous.

'In short, in Fairly-land, where knights-errant have a full scope to range, and to do even what Ariostos or Orlandos could not do in the world without breaking into credibility, Spenser's knights have, under those six heads, given a full and truly poetical system of Christian, public, and low life.

'His legend of friendship is more diffuse; and yet even there the allegory is finely drawn, only the heads various; one knight could not there support all the parts.

'To do honour to his country, prince Arthur is a universal hero; in holiness, temperance, chastity, and justice, super-excellent. For the same reason, and to compliment queen Elizabeth, Gloriana, queen of fairies, whose court was the asylum of the oppressed, represents that glorious queen. At her commands all these knights set forth, and only at hers the Redcross Knight destroys the dragon, Guyon overturns the Bower of Bliss, Arthegal (*i. e.* Justice) beats down Geryoneo (*i. e.* Philip II. king of Spain) to rescue Belge (*i. e.* Holland,) and he beats the Grantorto (the same Philip in another light) to restore Irena (*i. e.* Peace) to Europe.

'Chastity being the first female virtue, Britomartis is a Briton; her part is fine, though it requires explication. His style is very poetical; no puns, affectations of wit, forced antitheses, or any of that low tribe.

'His old words are all true English, and numbers exquisite; and since of words there is the *multa renascentur*, since they are all proper, such a poem should not (any more than Milton's) consist all of it of common ordinary words. See instances of descriptions.

Causeless jealousy in Britomartis, v. 6, 14, *in its restlessness.*

"Like as a wayward child, whose sounder sleepe
Is broken with some fearful dream's affright,
With froward will doth set himself to weep,
Ne can be still'd for all his nurse's might,
But kicks and squalls, and shrieks for fell despite:
Now scratching her, and her loose locks misusing,
Now seeking darkness, and now seeking light;
Then craving suck, and then the suck refusing:
Such was this lady's loves in her love's fond accusing."

Curiosity occasioned by jealousy, upon occasion of her lover's absence. Ibid. *Stan.* 8, 9.

"Then as she looked long, at last she spied
One coming towards her with hasty speed,
Well ween'd she then, ere him she plain descry'd,
That it was one sent from her love indeed:
Whereat her heart was fill'd with hope and dread,
Ne would she stay till he in place could come,
But ran to meet him forth to know his tidings somme;
Even in the door him meeting, she begun,
'And where is he, thy lord, and how far hence?
Declare at once: and hath he lost or won?"

Care and his house are described thus, v. 6. 33, 34, 35.

"Not far away, nor meet for any guest,
They spied a little cottage, like some poor man's nest,

34.

"There entering in, they found the good man's se.f
Full busily unto his work ybent,
Who was so weel a wretched wearish elf,
With hollow eyes and rawbone cheeks far spent,
As if he had in prison long been pent.
Full black and griesly did his face appear,
Besmear'd with smoke, that nigh his eye-sight blent
With rugged beard, and hoary shagged hair,
The which he never wont to comb, or comely shear.

35.

Rude was his garment, and to rags all rent,
Ne better had he, ne for better cared;
His blister'd hands amongst the cinders brent,
And fingers filthy, with long nails prepared,
Right fit to rend the food on which he fared.
His name was Care: a blacksmith by his trade,
That neither day nor night from working spared,
But to small purpose iron wedges made:
These be unquiet thoughts that careful minds invade."

'Homer's epithets were much admired by antiquity: see what great justness and variety there are in these epithets of the trees in the forest, where the Redcross Knight lost truth, B. i. Cant. i. *Stan.* 8, 9

"The sailing pine, the cedar proud and tall,
The vine-prop elm, the poplar never dry;
The builder oak, sole king of forests all,
The aspine, good for staves, the cypress funeral.

9.

"The laurel, meed of mighty conquerors,
And poets sage; the fir, that weepeth still,
The willow, worn of forlorn paramours,
The yew, obedient to the bender's will,
The birch for shafts, the sallow for the mill:
The myrrhe sweet, bleeding in the bitter wound,
The war-like beech, the ash, for nothing ill,
The fruitful olive, and the plantane round,
The carver holm, the maple, seldom inward sound."

'I shall trouble you no more, but desire you to let me conclude with these verses, though I think they have already been quoted by you. They are addressed to young ladies oppressed with calumny. v 6. 14.

"The best (said he) that I can you advise
Is to avoid the occasion of the ill;
For when the cause whence evil doth arise,
Removed is, the effect surceaseth still.
Abstain from pleasure and restrain your will,
Subdue desire and bridle loose delight,
Use scanted diet, and forbear your fill,
Shun secresy, and talk in open sight,
So shall you soon repair your present evil plight."

T.

No. 541.] *Thursday, November* 20, 1712.

Format enim natura prius nos intus ad omnem,
Fortunarum habitum: juvat, aut impellit ad iram.
Aut ad humum mœrore gravi deducit, et angit:
Post effert animi motus interprete lingua.
Hor. Ars Poet. ver. 108.

For nature forms and softens us within,
And writes our fortune's changes in our face:
Pleasure enchants, impetuous rage transports,
And grief dejects, and wrings the tortur'd soul:
And these are all interpreted by speech.
Roscommon.

My friend the Templar, whom I have so often mentioned in these writings, having determined to lay aside his poetical studies, in order to a closer pursuit of the law, has put together, as a farewell essay, some thoughts concerning pronunciation and action, which he has given me leave to communicate to the public. They are chiefly collected from his favourite author Cicero, who is known to have been an intimate friend of Roscius the actor, and a good judge of dramatic performances, as well as the most eloquent pleader of the time in which he lived.

Cicero concludes his celebrated books De Oratore with some precepts for pronunciation and action, without which part he affirms that the best orator in the world can never succeed; and an indifferent one, who is master of this, shall gain much greater applause. 'What could make a stronger impression,' says he, 'than those exclamations of Gracchus?'—"Whither shall I turn? Wretch that I am! to what place betake myself? Shall I go to the Capitol? Alas! it is overflowed with my brother's blood. Or shall I retire to my house? Yet there I behold my mother plunged in misery, weeping and despairing!" These breaks and turns of passion, it seems, were so enforced by the eyes, voice, and gesture of the speaker, that his very enemies could not refrain from tears. 'I insist,' says Tully, 'upon this the rather, because our orators, who are as it were actors of the truth itself, have quitted this manner of speaking: and the players, who are but the imitators of truth, have taken it up.'

I shall therefore pursue the hint he has here given me, and for the service of the British stage I shall copy some of the rules which this great Roman master has laid down; yet without confining myself wholly to his thoughts or words: and to adapt this essay the more to the purpose for which I intend it, instead of the examples he has inserted in this discourse out of the ancient tragedies, I shall make use of parallel passages out of the most celebrated of our own.

The design of art is to assist action as much as possible in the representation of nature; for the appearance of reality is that which moves us in all representations, and these have always the greater force the nearer they approach to nature, and the less they show of imitation.

Nature herself has assigned to every motion of the soul its peculiar cast of the countenance, tone of voice, and manner of gesture, through the whole person; all the features of the face and tones of the voice answer, like strings upon musical instruments, to the impressions made on them by the mind. Thus the sounds of the voice, according to the various touches which raise them, form themselves into an acute or grave, quick or slow, loud or soft, tone. These two may be subdivided into various kinds of tones, as the gentle, the rough, the contracted, the diffuse, the continued, the intermitted, the broken, abrupt, winding, softened or elevated. Every one of these may be employed with art and judgment; and all supply the actor, as colours do the painter, with an expressive variety.

Anger exerts its peculiar voice in an acute, raised, and hurrying sound. The passionate character of king Lear, as it is admirably drawn by Shakspeare, abounds with the strongest instances of this kind.

'————Death! Confusion!
Fiery! what quality?—why Gloster! Gloster!
I'd speak with the Duke of Cornwall and his wife.
Are they informed of this? my breath and blood!
Fiery! the fiery duke!'——&c.

Sorrow and complaint demand a voice quite different; flexible, slow, interrupted, and modulated in a mournful tone: as in that pathetical soliloquy of cardinal Wolsey on his fall.

'Farewell!—A long farewell to all my greatness!
This is the state of man!—to day he puts forth
The tender leaves of hope; to-morrow blossoms,
And bears his blushing honours thick upon him;
The third day comes a frost, a killing frost,
And when he thinks, good, easy man, full surely
His greatness is a ripening, nips his root;
And then he falls as I do.'

We have likewise a fine example of this in the whole of Andromache in the Distrest Mother, particularly in these lines—

'I'll go, and in the anguish of my heart
Weep o'er my child——If he must die, my life
Is wrapt in his, I shall not long survive:
'Tis for his sake that I have suffered life,
Groan'd in captivity, and out-liv'd Hector.
Yes, my Astyanax, we'll go together!
Together to the realms of night we'll go,
There to thy ravish'd eyes thy sire I'll show,
And point him out among the shades below.'

Fear expresses itself in a low, hesitating, and abject sound. If the reader considers the following speech of lady Macbeth, while her husband is about the murder of Duncan and his grooms, he will imagine her even affrighted with the sound of her own voice while she is speaking it.

'Alas! I am afraid they have awak'd,
And 'tis not done; th' attempt and not the deed,
Confound us—Hark! I laid the daggers ready,
He could not miss them. Had he not resembled
My father as he slept, I had done it.'

Courage assumes a louder tone, as in tha speech of Don Sebastian.

'Here satiate all your fury:
Let fortune empty her whole quiver on me,
I have a soul, that, like an ample shield,
Can take in all, and verge enough for more.'

Pleasure dissolves into a luxurious, mild, tender, and joyous modulation; as in the following lines in Caius Marius.

'Lavinia! O there's music in the name,
That soft'ning me to infant tenderness,
Makes my heart spring like the first leaps of life.'

And perplexity is different from all these grave, but not bemoaning, with an earnest uniform sound of voice; as in that celebrated speech of Hamlet.

'To be, or not to be!——that is the question.
Whether 'tis nobler in the mind to suffer
The stings and arrows of outrageous fortune:
Or to take arms against a sea of troubles,
And by opposing end them. To die, to sleep.
No more; and by a sleep to say we end
The heart ache, and a thousand natural shocks
That flesh is heir to; 'tis a consummation
Devoutly to be wish'd! To die, to sleep!——
To sleep; perchance to dream! Ay, there's the rub;
For, in that sleep of death, what dreams may come,

When we have shuffled off this mortal coil,
Must give us pause——There's the respect
That makes calamity of so long life;
For who would bear the whips and scorns of time,
Th' oppressor's wrongs, the proud man's contumely,
The pangs of despis'd love, the law's delay,
The insolence of office, and the spurns
That patient merit of the unworthy takes,
When he himself might his quietus make,
With a bare bodkin? Who would fardles bear,
To groan and sweat under a weary life?
But that the dread of something after death,
The undiscovered country, from whose bourn
No traveller returns, puzzles the will,
And makes us rather choose those ills we have,
Than fly to others that we know not of.'

As all these varieties of voice are to be directed by the sense, so the action is to be directed by the voice, and with a beautiful propriety, as it were, to enforce it. The arm, which by a strong figure Tully calls the orator's weapon, is to be sometimes raised and extended: and the hand, by its motion, sometimes to lead, and sometimes to follow, the words as they are uttered. The stamping of the foot too has its proper expression in contention, anger, or absolute command. But the face is the epitome of the whole man, and the eyes are, as it were, the epitome of the face; for which reason, he says, the best judges among the Romans were not extremely pleased even with Roscius himself in his mask. No part of the body, besides the face, is capable of as many changes as there are different emotions in the mind, and of expressing them all by those changes. Nor is this to be done without the freedom of the eyes; therefore Theophratus called one, who barely rehearsed his speech with his eyes fixed, an 'absent actor.'

As the countenance admits of so great variety, it requires also great judgment to govern it. Not that the form of the face is to be shifted on every occasion; lest it turn to farce and buffoonery; but it is certain that the eyes have a wonderful power of marking the emotions of the mind; sometimes by a steadfast look, sometimes by a careless one—now by a sudden regard, then by a joyful sparkling, as the sense of the word is diversified: for action is, as it were, the speech of the features and limbs, and must therefore conform itself always to the sentiments of the soul. And it may be observed, that in all which relates to the gesture there is a wonderful force implanted by nature: since the vulgar, the unskilful, and even the most barbarous, are chiefly affected by this. None are moved by the sound of words but those who understand the language; and the sense of many things is lost upon men of a dull apprehension: but action is a kind of universal tongue: all men are subject to the same passions, and consequently know the same marks of them in others, by which they themselves express them.

Perhaps some of my readers may be of opinion that the hints I have here made use of out of Cicero are somewhat too refined for the players on our theatre; in answer to which I venture to lay it down as a maxim, that without good sense no one can be a good player, and that he is very unfit to personate the dignity of a Roman hero who cannot enter into the rules for pronunciation and gesture delivered by a Roman orator.

There is another thing which my author does not think too minute to insist on, though it is purely mechanical; and that is the right pitching of the voice. On this occasion he tells the story of Gracchus, who employed a servant with a little ivory pipe to stand behind him, and give him the right pitch, as often as he wandered too far from the proper modulation. 'Every voice,' says Tully, 'has its particular medium and compass, and the sweetness of speech consists in leading it through all the variety of tones naturally, and without touching any extreme. Therefore,' says he, 'leave the pipe at home, but carry the sense of custom with you.

No. 542.] *Friday, November* 21, 1712.

Et sibi præferri se gaudet——
Ovid, Met. Lib. ii. 430

——————He heard,
Well pleased, himself before himself preferred.
Addison.

When I have been present in assemblies where my paper has been talked of, I have been very well pleased to hear those who would detract from the author of it observe that the letters which are sent to the Spectator are as good, if not better, than any of his works. Upon this occasion many letters of mirth are usually mentioned, which some think the Spectator writ to himself, and which others commend because they fancy he received them from his correspondents. Such are those from the valetudinarian; the inspector of the sign-posts; the master of the fan exercise; with that of the hooped petticoat; that of Nicholas Hart, the annual sleeper; that from Sir John Envil; that upon London cries; with multitudes of the same nature. As I love nothing more than to mortify the ill-natured, that I may do it effectually, I must acquaint them they have very often praised me when they did not design it, and that they have approved my writings when they thought they had derogated from them. I have heard several of these unhappy gentlemen proving, by undeniable arguments, that I was not able to pen a letter which I had written the day before. Nay, I have heard some of them throwing out ambiguous expressions, and giving the company reason to suspect that they themselves did me the honour to send me such and such a particular epistle, which happened to be talked of with the esteem or approbation of those who were present. These rigid critics are so afraid of allowing me any thing which does not belong to me, that they will not be positive whether the lion, the wild boar, and the flower-pots in the play-house, did not actually write those letters which came to me in their names. I must therefore inform these gentlemen, that I often choose this way of casting my thoughts into a letter, for the following reasons. First, out of the policy of those who try their jest upon another, before they own it themselves. Secondly, because I would extort a little praise from such who will never applaud any thing whose author is known and certain. Thirdly, because it gave me an opportunity of introducing a great variety of characters into my works, which could not have been done had I always written in the person of the Spectator. Fourthly, because the dignity spectatorial would have suffered had I published as from myself those severe ludicrous compositions which I have ascribed to fictitious names and characters. And lastly, because they often serve to bring in more naturally such additional reflections as have been placed at the end of them.

There are others who have likewise done me a very particular honour, though undesignedly. These are such who will needs have it that I have translated or borrowed many of my thoughts out of books which are written in other languages. I have heard of a person, who is more famous for his library than his learning, that has asserted this more than once in his private conversation.* Were it true, I am sure he could not speak it from his own knowledge; but, had he read the books which he has collected, he would find this accusation to be wholly groundless. Those who are truly learned will acquit me in this point, in which I have been so far from offending, that I have been scrupulous, perhaps to a fault, in quoting the authors of several passages which I might have made my own. But, as this assertion is in reality an encomium on what I have published, I ought rather to glory in it than endeavour to confute it.

Some are so very willing to alienate from me that small reputation which might accrue to me from any of these my speculations, that they attribute some of the best of them to those imaginary manuscripts with which I have introduced them. There are others I must confess whose objections have given me a greater concern, as they seem to reflect, under this head, rather on my morality than on my invention. These are they who say an author is guilty of falsehood, when he talks to the public of manuscripts which he never saw, or describes scenes of action or discourse in which he was never engaged. But these gentlemen would do well to consider, that there is not a fable or parable, which ever was made use of, that is not liable to this exception; since nothing, according to this notion, can be related innocently, which was not once matter of fact. Besides I think the most ordinary reader may be able to discover, by my way of writing, what I deliver in these occurrences as truth, and what as fiction.

Since I am unawares engaged in answering the several objections which have been made against these my works, I must take notice that there are some who affirm a paper of this nature should always turn upon diverting subjects, and others who find fault with every one of them that hath not an immediate tendency to the advancement of religion or learning. I shall leave these gentlemen to dispute it out among themselves; since I see one half of my conduct patronized by each side. Were I serious on an improper subject, or trifling in a serious one, I should deservedly draw upon me the censure of my readers: or were I conscious of any thing in my writings that is not innocent at least, or that the greatest part of them were not sincerely designed to discountenance vice and ignorance, and support the interest of truth, wisdom, and virtue, I should be more severe upon myself than the public is disposed to be. In the mean while I desire my reader to consider every particular paper, or discourse, as a distinct tract by itself, and independent of every thing that goes before or after it.

I shall end this paper with the following letter, which was really sent me, as some others have been which I have published, and for which I must own myself indebted to their respective writers.

'SIR,—I was this morning in a company of your well-wishers, when we read over, with great satisfaction, Tully's observation on action adapted to the British theatre: though by the way, we were very sorry to find that you have disposed of another member of your club. Poor Sir Roger is dead, and the worthy clergyman dying; captain Sentry has taken possession of a good estate; Will Honeycomb has married a farmer's daughter; and the Templar withdraws himself into the business of his own profession. What will all this end in? We are afraid it portends no good to the public. Unless you very speedily fix the day for the election of new members, we are under apprehensions of losing the British Spectator. I hear of a party of ladies who intended to address you on this subject: and I question not, if you do not give us the slip very suddenly, that you will receive addresses from all parts of the kingdom to continue so useful a work. Pray deliver us out of this perplexity; and, among the multitude of your readers, you will particularly oblige your most sincere friend and servant,

O. 'PHILO-SPEC.'

* This is an allusion to Mr. Thomas Rowlinson, the celebrated book collector. Addison had already ridiculed him in the Tattler, No. 158, under the name of Tom Folio.

No. 543.] *Saturday, November 22, 1712.*

——————Facies non omnibus una,
Nec diversa tamen—————
Ovid, Met. Lib. ii. 12.

Similar, though not the same.———

Those who were skilful in anatomy, among the ancients, concluded, from the outward and inward make of a human body, that it was the work of a Being transcendently wise and powerful. As the world grew more enlightened in this art, their discoveries gave them fresh opportunities of admiring the conduct of Providence in the formation of a human body. Galen was converted by his dissections, and could not but own a Supreme Being upon a survey of this handy-work. There were, indeed, many parts, of which the old anatomists did not know the certain use; but, as they say that most of those which they examined were adapted with admirable art to their several functions, they did not question but those, whose uses they could not determine, were contrived with the same wisdom for respective ends and purposes. Since the circulation of the blood has been found out, and many other great discoveries have been made by our modern anatomists, we see new wonders in the human frame, and discern several important uses for those parts, which uses the ancients knew nothing of. In short, the body of man is such a subject as stands the utmost test of examination. Though it appears formed with the nicest wisdom, upon the most superficial survey of it, it still mends upon the search, and produces our surprise and amazement in proportion as we pry into it. What I have here said of a human body may be applied to the body of every animal which has been the subject of anatomical observations.

The body of an animal is an object adequate to our senses. It is a particular system of Providence that lies in a narrow compass. The eye is able to command it, and by successive inquiries can search into all its parts. Could the body of the whole earth, or indeed the whole universe, be thus submitted to the examination of our senses, were it not too big and disproportioned for our inquiries, too unwieldy for the management of the eye and hand, there is no question but it would appear to us as curious and well contrived a frame as that of the human body. We should see the same concatenation and subserviency, the same necessity and usefulness, the same beauty and harmony, in all and every of its parts, as what we discover in the body of every single animal.

The more extended our reason is, and the more able to grapple with immense objects, the greater still are those discoveries which it makes of wisdom and providence in the works of the creation. A Sir Isaac Newton, who stands up as the miracle of the present age, can look through a whole planetary system; consider it in its weight, number, and measure; and draw from it as many demonstrations of infinite power and wisdom, as a more confined understanding is able to deduce from the system of a human body.

But to return to our speculations on anatomy, I shall here consider the fabric and texture of the bodies of animals in one particular view: which in my opinion shows the hand of a thinking and all-wise Being in their formation, with the evidence of a thousand demonstrations. I think we may lay this down as an incontested principle, that chance never acts in a perpetual uniformity and consistence with itself. If one should always fling the same number with ten thousand dice, or see every throw just five times less, or five times more in number, than the throw which immediately preceded it, who would not imagine there is some invisible power which directs the cast? This is the proceeding which we find in the operations of nature. Every kind of animal is diversified by different magnitudes, each of which gives rise to a different species. Let a man trace the dog or lion kind, and he will observe how many of the works of nature are published, if I may use the expression, in a variety of editions. If we look into the reptile world, or into those different kinds of animals that fill the element of water, we meet with the same repetition among several species, that differ very little from one another, but in size and bulk. You find the same creature that is drawn at large, copied out in several proportions and ending in miniature. It would be tedious to produce instances of this regular conduct in Providence, as it would be superfluous to those who are versed in the natural history of animals. The magnificent harmony of the universe is such, that we may observe innumerable divisions running upon the same ground. I might also extend this speculation to the dead parts of nature, in which we may find matter disposed into many similar systems, as well in our survey of stars and planets as of stones, vegetables, and other sublunary parts of the creation. In a word, Providence has shown the richness of its goodness and wisdom, not only in the production of many original species, but in the multiplicity of descants which it has made on every original species in particular.

But to pursue this thought still farther. Every living creature, considered in itself, has many very complicated parts that are exact copies of some other parts which it possesses, and which are complicated in the same manner. One eye would have been sufficient for the subsistence and preservation of an animal; but, in order to better his condition, we see another placed with a mathematical exactness in the same most advantageous situation, and in every particular of the same size and texture. Is it possible for chance to be thus delicate and uniform in her operation? Should a million of dice turn up together twice the same number, the wonder would be nothing in comparison with this. But when we see this similitude and resemblance in the arm, the hand, the fingers: when we see one half of the body entirely correspond with the other in all those minute strokes, without which a man might have very well subsisted; nay, when we often see a single part repeated a hundred times in the same body, notwithstanding it consists of the most intricate weaving of numberless fibres, and these parts differing still in magnitude, as the convenience of their particular situation requires; sure a man must have a strange cast of understanding, who does not discover the finger of God in so wonderful a work. These duplicates in those parts of the body, without which a man might have very well subsisted, though not so well as with them, are a plain demonstration of an all-wise Contriver, as those more numerous copyings which are found among the vessels of the same body, are evident demonstrations that they could not be the work of chance. This argument receives additional strength, if we apply it to every animal and insect within our knowledge, as well as to those numberless living creatures that are objects too minute for a human eye; and if we consider how the several species in this whole world of life resemble one another in very many particulars, so far as is convenient for their respective states of existence, it is much more probable that a hundred millions of dice should be casually thrown a hundred millions of times in the same number, than that the body of any single animal should be produced by the fortuitous concourse of matter. And that the like chance should arise in innumerable instances requires a degree of credulity that is not under the direction of common sense. We may carry this consideration yet farther, if we reflect on the two sexes in every living species, with their resemblance to each other, and those particular distinctions that were necessary for the keeping up of this great world of life.

There are many more demonstrations of a Supreme Being, and of his transcendent wisdom, power, and goodness, in the formation of the body of a living creature, for which I refer my reader to other writings, particularly to the sixth book of the poem entitled Creation,* where the anatomy of the human body is described with great perspicuity and elegance. I have been particular on the thought which runs through this speculation, because I have not seen it enlarged upon by others. O.

* Creation. A poem by Sir Richard Blackmore.

No. 544.] *Monday, November 24, 1712.*

Nunquam ita quisquam bene subducta ratione a vitam fuit,
Quin res, ætas, usus, semper aliquid apportet novi,
Aliquid moneat: ut illa, quæ te scire credas, nescias;
Et, quæ tibi putaris prima, in experiundo ut repudies
Ter. Adelph. Act. v. Sc. 4.

No man was ever so completely skilled in the conduct of life, as not to receive new information from age and experience: insomuch that we find ourselves really ignorant of what we thought we understood, and see cause to reject what we fancied our truest interest.

There are, I think, sentiments in the following letter from my friend captain Sentry, which discover a rational and equal frame of mind, as well prepared for an advantageous as an unfortunate change of condition.

'Coverley-hall, Nov. 15, Worcestershire.'

'Sir,—I am come to the succession of the estate of my honoured kinsman, Sir Roger de Coverley; and I assure you I find it no easy task to keep up the figure of master of the fortune which was so handsomely enjoyed by that honest plain man. I cannot (with respect to the great obligations I have, be it spoken) reflect upon his character, but I am confirmed in the truth which I have, I think, heard spoken at the club; to wit, that a man of a warm and well-disposed heart, with a very small capacity, is highly superior in human society to him who, with the greatest talents, is cold and languid in his affections. But alas! why do I make a difficulty in speaking of my worthy ancestor's failings? His little absurdities and incapacity for the conversation of the politest men are dead with him, and his greater qualities are ever now useful to him. I know not whether by naming those disabilities I do not enhance his merit, since he has left behind him a reputation in his country which would be worth the pains of the wisest man's whole life to arrive at. By the way, I must observe to you, that many of your readers have mistook that passage in your writings, wherein Sir Roger is reported to have inquired into the private character of the young woman at the tavern. I know you mentioned that circumstance as an instance of the simplicity and innocence of his mind, which made him imagine it a very easy thing to reclaim one of those criminals, and not as an inclination in him to be guilty with her. The less discerning of your readers cannot enter into that delicacy of description in the character: but indeed my chief business at this time is to represent to you my present state of mind, and the satisfaction I promise to myself in the possession of my new fortune. I have continued all Sir Roger's servants, except such as it was a relief to dismiss into little beings within my manor. Those who are in a list of the good knight's own hand to be taken care of by me, I have quartered upon such as have taken new leases of me, and added so many advantages during the lives of the persons so quartered, that it is the interest of those whom they are joined with, to cherish and befriend them upon all occasions. I find a considerable sum of ready money, which I am laying out among my dependants at the common interest, but with a design to lend it according to their merit, rather than according to their ability. I shall lay a tax upon such as I have highly obliged, to become security to me for such of their own poor youth, whether male or female, as want help towards getting into some being in the world. I hope I shall be able to manage my affairs so as to improve my fortune every year by doing acts of kindness. I will lend my money to the use of none but indigent men, secured by such as have ceased to be indigent by the favour of my family or myself. What makes this the more practicable is, that if they will do any good with my money, they are welcome to it upon their own security: and I make no exceptions against it, because the persons who enter into the obligations do it for their own family. I have laid out four thousand pounds this way, and it is not to be imagined what a crowd of people are obliged by it. In cases where Sir Roger has recommended, I have lent money to put out children, with a clause which makes void the obligation in case the infant dies before he is out of his apprenticeship; by which means the kindred and masters are extremely careful of breeding him to industry, that he may re-pay it himself by his labour, in three years journey-work after his time is out, for the use of his securities. Opportunities of this kind are all that have occurred since I came to my estate: but I assure you I will preserve a constant disposition to catch at all the occasions I can to promote the good and happiness of my neighbourhood.

'But give me leave to lay before you a little establishment which has grown out of my past life, that I doubt not will administer great satisfaction to me in that part of it, whatever that is, which is to come.

'There is a prejudice in favour of the way of life to which a man has been educated, which I know not whether it would not be faulty to overcome. It is like a partiality to the interest of one's own country before that of any other nation. It is from a habit of thinking, grown upon me from my youth spent in arms, that I have ever held gentlemen, who have preserved modesty, good-nature, justice, and humanity, in a soldier's life, to be the most valuable and worthy persons of the human race. To pass through imminent dangers, suffer painful watchings, frightful alarms, and laborious marches, for the greater part of a man's time, and pass the rest in sobriety conformable to the rules of the most virtuous civil life, is a merit too great to deserve the treatment it usually meets with among the other parts of the world. But I assure you, sir, were there not very many who have this worth, we could never have seen the glorious events which we have in our days. I need not say more to illustrate the character of a soldier than to tell you he is the very contrary to him you observe loud, saucy, and overbearing, in a red coat about town. But I was going to tell you that, in honour of the profession of arms, I have set apart a certain sum of money for a table for such gentlemen as have served their country in the army, and will please from time to time to sojourn all, or any part of the year, at Coverley. Such of them as will do me that honour shall find horses, servants, and all things necessary for their accommodation and enjoyment of all the conveniences of life in a pleasant various country. If colonel Camperfelt* be in town, and his abilities are not employed another way in the service, there is no man would be more welcome here. That gentleman's thorough knowledge in his profession, together with the simplicity of his manners and goodness of his heart, would induce others like him to honour my abode; and I should be glad my acquaintance would take themselves to be invited, or not, as their characters have an affinity to his.

'I would have all my friends know that they need not fear (though I am become a country gentleman) I will trespass against their temperance and sobriety. No sir, I shall retain so much of the good sentiments for the conduct of life, which we cultivated in each other at our club, as to contemn all inordinate pleasures; but particularly remember, with our beloved Tully, that the delight in food consists in desire, not satiety. They who most passionately pursue pleasure, seldomest arrive at it. Now I am writing to a philosopher, I cannot forbear mentioning the satisfaction I took in the passage I read yesterday in the same Tully. A nobleman of Athens made a compliment to Plato the morning after he had supped at his house. "Your entertainments do not only please when you give them, but also the day after." I am, my worthy friend, your most obedient humble servant,

T. 'WILLIAM SENTRY.'

No. 545.] *Tuesday, November* 25, 1712.

Quin potius pacem æternam pactosque hymenæos
Exercemus———— *Virg. Æn.* iv. 99.

Let us in bonds of lasting peace unite,
And celebrate the hymeneal rite.

I CANNOT but think the following letter from the emperor of China to the pope of Rome, proposing a coalition of the Chinese and Roman churches, will be acceptable to the curious. I must confess, I myself being of opinion that the emperor has as much authority to be interpreter to him he pre-

* A fine compliment to colonel Kempenfelt, father of the admiral, who was drowned in the Royal George at Spithead, August 29, 1782.

tends to expound, as the pope has to be a vicar of the sacred person he takes upon him to represent, I was not a little pleased with their treaty of alliance. What progress the negotiation between his majesty of Rome and his holiness of China makes, (as we daily writers say upon subjects where we are at a loss,) time will let us know. In the mean time, since they agree in the fundamentals of power and authority, and differ only in matters of faith, we may expect the matter will go on without difficulty.

Copia di lettera dal rè della Cina al Papa, interpretata dal padre segretario dell' India della compagna di Giesù.

'*A voi benedetto sopra i benedetti P. P. ed imperadore grande de' pontifici e pastore Xmo, dispensatore del' oglio dei rè d' Europa Clemente XI.*

'Il favorito amico di Dio, Gionata 7°, potentissimo sopra tutti i potentissimi della terra, altissimo sopra tutti gl'altissimi sotto il sole e la luna, che siede nella sede di smeraldo della Cina sopra cento scalini d'oro, ad interpretare la lingua di Dio a tutti i descendenti fedeli d'Abramo, che da la vita e la morte a cento quindici regni, ed a cento settante isole, scrive con la penna dello struzzo vergine, e manda salute ed accrescimento di vecchiezza.

'Essendo arrivato il tempo in cui il fiore della reale nostro gioventù deve maturare i frutti della nostra vecchiezza, e confortare con quell' i desiderj de' popoli nostri divoti, e propagare il seme di quella pianta che deve proteggerli, abbiamo stabilito d'accompagnarci con una vergine eccelsa ed amorosa allattata alla mammella della leonessa forte e dell' agnella mansueta. Perciò essendoci stato figurato sempre il vostro popolo Europeo Romano per paese di donne invitte, e forte, e caste; allongiamo la nostra mano potente, a stringere una di loro, e questa sarà una vostra nipote, o nipote di qualche altro gran sacerdote Latino, che sia guardata dall' occhio dritto di Dio, sarà seminata in lei l'autorità di Sarra, la fedeltà d'Esther, e la sapienza di Abba; la vogliamo con l'occhio che guarda il cielo, e la terra, e con la bocca della conchiglia che si pasce della ruggiada del matino. La sua età non passi ducento corsi della luna, la sua statura sì alta quanto la spicca dritta del grano verde, e la sua grossezza quanto un manipolo di grano secco. Noi la mandaremmo a vestire per li nostri mandatici ambasciadori, e chi la conduranno a noi, e noi la incontraremmo alla riva del fiume grande facendola salire sul nostro cocchio. Ella potrà adorare appresso di noi il suo Dio, con ventiquattro altre a suo elezzione e potrà cantare con loro, come la tottora alla primavera.

'Soddisfando noi, padre e amico nostro, questa nostra brama, sarete caggione di unire in perpetua amicizia cotesti vostri regni d'Europa al nostro dominante imperio, e si abbracciramo le vostri leggi come l'edera abbraccia la pianta; e noi medesemi spargeremo del nostro seme reale in coteste province, riscaldando i letti di vostri principj con il fuoco amoroso delle nostre amazoni, d'alcune delle quali i nostri mandatici ambasciadori vi porteranno le somiglianze dipinte.

'Vi confirmiamo di tenere in pace le due buone religiose famiglie delli missionarji, gli figlioli d'Ignazio, e li bianchi e neri figlioli di Dominico, il cui consiglio degl' uni e degl' altri ci serve di scorta nel nostro regimento e di lume ad interpretare le divine legge, come appunto fa lume l'oglio che si getta in mare.

'In tanto alzandoci dal nostro trono per abbracciarvi, vi dichiariamo, nostro congiunto e confederato, ed ordiniamo che questo foglio sia segnato col nostro segno imperiale della nostra città, capo del mondo, il quinto giorno della terza lunatione, l'anno quarto del nostro imperio.

'Il sigillo è un sole nella cui faccia è anche quella della luna, ed intorno tra i raggi, vi sono traposte alcune spada.

'Dico il traduttore che secondo il ceremonial di questa lettera e recedentissimo specialmente fossero scritta con la penna dello struzzo-vergine con la quella non soglionsi scrivere quei rè che le preghiere a Dio, e scrivendo a qualche altro principe del mondo, la maggior finezza che usino, è scrivergli con la penna del pavone.'

A letter from the emperor of China to the Pope, interpreted by a father Jesuit, secretary of the Indies.

'*To you, blessed above the blessed, great emperor of bishops and pastor of Christians, dispenser of the oil of the kings of Europe, Clement XI.*

'The favourite friend of God, Gionotta the VIIth, most powerful above the most powerful of the earth, highest above the highest under the sun and moon, who sits on a throne of emerald of China, above 100 steps of gold, to interpret the language of God to the faithful, and who gives life and death to 115 kingdoms, and 170 islands; he writes with the quill of a virgin ostrich, and sends health and increase of old age.

'Being arrived at the time of our age, in which the flower of our royal youth ought to ripen into fruit towards old age, to comfort therewith the desires of our devoted people, and to propagate the seed of that plant which must protect them; we have determined to accompany ourselves with a high amorous virgin, suckled at the breast of a wild lioness, and a meek lamb, and, imagining with ourselves that your European Roman people is the father of unconquerable and chaste ladies, we stretch out our powerful arm to embrace one of them, and she shall be one of your nieces, or the niece of some other great Latin priest, the darling of God's right eye. Let the authority of Sarah be sown in her, the fidelity of Esther, and the wisdom of Abba. We would have her eye like that of a dove, which may look upon heaven and earth, with the mouth of a shell-fish, to feed upon the dew of the morning, her age must not exceed 200 courses of the moon; let her stature be equal to that of an ear of green corn, and her girth a handful.

'We will send our mandarines ambassadors to clothe her, and to conduct her to us, and we will meet her on the bank of a great river, making her to leap up into our chariot. She may with us worship her own God, together with twenty-four virgins of her own choosing; and she may sing with them as the turtle in the spring.

'You, O father and friend, complying with this our desire, may be an occasion of uniting in perpetual friendship our high empire with your European kingdoms, and we may embrace your laws as the ivy embraces the tree; and we ourselves may scatter our royal blood into your provinces, warming the chief of your princes with the amorous fire of our amazons, the resembling pictures of some of which our said mandarines ambassadors shall convey to you.

'We exhort you to keep in peace two good religious families of missionaries, the sons of Ignatius, and the black and white sons of Dominicus; that the counsel, both of the one and the other may serve as a guide to us in our government, and a light to interpret the divine law, as the oil cast into the sea produces light.

'To conclude, we rising up in our throne to embrace you, we declare you our ally and confederate; and have ordered this leaf to be sealed with our imperial signet, in our royal city, the head of the world, the eighth day of the third lunation, and the fourth year of our reign.'

Letters from Rome say, the whole conversation both among gentlemen and ladies has turned upon the subject of this epistle, ever since it arrived. The jesuit who translated it says, it loses much of the majesty of the original in the Italian. It seems there was an offer of the same nature made by the predecessor of the present emperor to Lewis XIII. of France; but no lady of that court would take the voyage, that sex not being at that time so much used in public negotiations. The manner of treating the pope is, according to the Chinese ceremonial, very respectful: for the emperor writes to him with the quill of a virgin ostrich, which was never used before but in writing prayers. Instructions are preparing for the lady who shall have so much zeal as to undertake this pilgrimage, and be an empress for the sake of her religion. The principal of the Indian missionaries has given in a list of the reigning sins in China, in order to prepare indulgencies necessary to this lady and her retinue, in advancing the interests of the Roman-catholic religion in those kingdoms.

'*To the Spectator General.*

'MAY IT PLEASE YOUR HONOUR,—I have of late seen French hats of a prodigious magnitude pass by my observatory.

T. 'JOHN SLY.'

No. 546.] *Wednesday, November* 26, 1712.

Omnia patefacienda, ut ne quid omnino quod venditor norit, emptor ignoret. *Tull.*

Every thing should be fairly told, that the buyer may not be ignorant of any thing which the seller knows.

IT gives me very great scandal to observe, wherever I go, how much skill, in buying all manner of goods, there is necessary to defend yourself from being cheated in whatever you see exposed to sale. My reading makes such a strong impression upon me, that I should think myself a cheat in my way, if I should translate any thing from another tongue, and not acknowledge it to my readers. I understood, from common report, that Mr. Cibber was introducing a French play upon our stage, and thought myself concerned to let the town know what was his, and what was foreign.* When I came to the rehearsal, I found the house so partial to one of their own fraternity, that they gave every thing which was said such grace, emphasis, and force in their action, that it was no easy matter to make any judgment of the performance. Mrs. Oldfield, who, it seems, is the heroic daughter, had so just a conception of her part, that her action made what she spoke appear decent, just, and noble. The passions of terror and compassion they made me believe were very artfully raised, and the whole conduct of the play artful and surprising. We authors do not much relish the endeavours of players in this kind, but have the same disdain as physicians and lawyers have when attorneys and apothecaries give advice. Cibber himself took the liberty to tell me, that he expected I would do him justice, and allow the play well prepared for his spectators, whatever it was for his readers. He added very many particulars not uncurious concerning the manner of taking an audience, and laying wait not only for their superficial applause, but also for insinuating into their affections and passions, by the artful management of the look, voice, and gesture of the speaker. I could not but consent that the Heroic Daughter appeared in the rehearsal a mov-

---

* Ximena, or the Heroic Daughter, a tragedy taken from the Cid of Corneille, by C. Cibber.

This play met with so little encouragement, that the author did not venture to publish it till about two years after it had been performed, when it appeared with a highly complimentary dedication to Sir Richard Steele, but unfortunately at the expense of a much better writer.

ing entertainment, wrought out of a great and exemplary virtue.

The advantages of action, show, and dress, on these occasions are allowable, because the merit consists in being capable of imposing upon us to our advantage and entertainment. All that I was going to say about the honesty of an author in the sale of his ware was, that he ought to own all that he had borrowed from others, and lay in a clear light all that he gives his spectators for their money, with an account of the first manufacturers. But I intended to give the lecture of this day upon the common and prostituted behaviour of traders in ordinary commerce. The philosopher made it a rule of trade, that your profit ought to be the common profit; and it is unjust to make any step towards gain, wherein the gain of even those to whom you sell is not also consulted. A man may deceive himself if he thinks fit, but he is no better than a cheat, who sells any thing without telling the exceptions against it, as well as what is to be said to its advantage. The scandalous abuse of language and hardening of conscience, which may be observed every day in going from one place to another, is what makes a whole city, to an unprejudiced eye, a den of thieves. It was no small pleasure to me for this reason to remark, as I passed by Cornhill, that the shop of that worthy, honest, though lately unfortunate citizen, Mr. John Morton, so well known in the linen trade, is setting up anew. Since a man has been in a distressed condition, it ought to be a great satisfaction to have passed through it in such a manner as not to have lost the friendship of those who suffered with him, but to receive an honourable acknowledgment of his honesty from those very persons to whom the law had consigned his estate.

The misfortune of this citizen is like to prove of a very general advantage to those who shall deal with him hereafter; for the stock with which he now sets up being the loan of his friends, he cannot expose that to the hazard of giving credit, but enters into a ready-money trade, by which means he will both buy and sell the best and cheapest. He imposes upon himself a rule of affixing the value of each piece he sells, to the piece itself; so that the most ignorant servant or child will be as good a buyer at his shop as the most skilful in the trade. For all which, you have all his hopes and fortune for your security. To encourage dealing after this way, there is not only the avoiding the most infamous guilt in ordinary bartering; but this observation, that he who buys with ready money saves as much to his family as the state exacts out of his land for the security and service of his country. That is to say, in plain English, sixteen will do as much as twenty shillings.

'Mr. Spectator,—My heart is so swelled with grateful sentiments on account of some favours which I have lately received, that I must beg leave to give them utterance amongst the crowd of other anonymous correspondents; and writing, I hope, will be as great a relief to my forced silence as it is to your natural taciturnity. My generous benefactor will not suffer me to speak to him in any terms of acknowledgment, but ever treats me as if he had the greatest obligations, and uses me with a distinction that is not to be expected from one so much my superior in fortune, years, and understanding. He insinuates, as if I had a certain right to his favours from some merit, which his particular indulgence to me has discovered; but that is only a beautiful artifice to lessen the pain an honest mind feels in receiving obligations when there is no probability of returning them.

'A gift is doubled when accompanied with such a delicacy of address; but what to me gives it an inexpressible value, is its coming from the man I most esteem in the world. It pleases me indeed, as it is an advantage and addition to my fortune; but when I consider it as an instance of that good man's friendship, it overjoys, it transports me: I look on it with a lover's eye, and no longer regard the gift, but the hand that gave it. For my friendship is so entirely void of any gainful views, that it often gives me pain to think it should have been chargeable to him; and I cannot at some melancholy hours help doing his generosity the injury of fearing it should cool on this account, and that the last favour might be a sort of legacy of a departing friendship.

'I confess these fears seem very groundless and unjust, but you must forgive them to the apprehension of one possessed of a great treasure, who is frighted at the most distant shadow of danger.

'Since I have thus far opened my heart to you, I will not conceal the secret satisfaction I feel there, of knowing the goodness of my friend will not be unrewarded. I am pleased with thinking the providence of the Almighty hath sufficient blessings in store for him, and will certainly discharge the debt, though I am not made the happy instrument of doing it.

'However, nothing in my power shall be wanting to show my gratitude; I will make it the business of my life to thank him; and shall esteem (next to him) those my best friends, who give me the greatest assistance in this good work. Printing this letter would be some little instance of my gratitude; and your favour herein will very much oblige your most humble servant, &c. W. C.

'Nov. 24. T.

No. 547.] *Thursday, November 27, 1712.*

Si vulnus tibi, monstrata radice vel herba,
Non fieret levius, fugeres radice vel herba
Proficiente nihil curarier.

Hor. Ep. ii. Lib. 2. 149

Suppose you had a wound, and one that show'd
An herb, which you apply'd, but found no good;
Would you be fond of this, increase your pain,
And use the fruitless remedy again?—*Creech.*

It is very difficult to praise a man without putting him out of countenance. My following correspondent has found out this uncommon art, and, together with his friends, has celebrated some of my speculations after such a concealed but diverting manner, that if any of my readers think I am to blame in publishing my own commendations, they will allow I should have deserved their censure as much had I suppressed the humour in which they are conveyed to me.

'Sir,—I am often in a private assembly of wits of both sexes, where we generally descant upon your speculations, or upon the subjects on which you have treated. We were last Tuesday talking of those two volumes which you have lately published. Some were commending one of your papers, and some another; and there was scarce a single person in the company that had not a favourite speculation. Upon this a man of wit and learning told us, he thought it would not be amiss if we paid the Spectator the same compliment that is often made in our public prints to Sir William Read, Dr. Grant, Mr. Moor, the apothecary, and other eminent physicians, where it is usual for the patients to publish the cures which have been made upon them, and the several distempers under which they laboured. The proposal took; and the lady where we visited having the two last volumes in large paper interleaved for her own private use, ordered them to be brought down, and laid in the window, whither every one in the company retired, and writ down a particular advertisement in the style and phrase of the like ingenious compositions which we frequently meet with at the end of our newspapers. When we had finished our work, we read them with a great deal of mirth at the fireside, and agreed, *nemine contradicente*, to get them transcribed, and sent to the Spectator. The gentleman who made the proposal entered the following advertisement before the title-page, after which the rest succeeded in order.

'*Remedium efficax et universum*; or, an effectual remedy adapted to all capacities; showing how any person may cure himself of ill-nature, pride, party-spleen, or any other distemper incident to the human system, with an easy way to know when the infection is upon him. The panacea is as innocent as bread, agreeable to the taste, and requires no confinement. It has not its equal in the universe, as abundance of the nobility and gentry throughout the kingdom have experienced.

'N. B. No family ought to be without it.'

Over the two Spectators on jealousy, being the two first in the third volume, Nos. 170, 171.

'I, William Crazy, aged threescore and seven, having been for several years afflicted with uneasy doubts, fears, and vapours, occasioned by the youth and beauty of Mary my wife, aged twenty-five, do hereby, for the benefit of the public, give notice, that I have found great relief from the two following doses, having taken them two mornings, together with a dish of chocolate. Witness my hand, &c.'

'*For the benefit of the Poor.*

'In charity to such as are troubled with the disease of levee-hunting, and are forced to seek their bread every morning at the chamber-doors of great men, I, *A. B.* do testify, that for many years past I laboured under this fashionable distemper, but was cured of it by a remedy which I bought of Mrs. Baldwin, contained in a half sheet of paper, marked No. 193, where any one may be provided with the same remedy at the price of a single penny.'

'An infallible cure for hypochondriac melancholy, Nos. 173, 184, 191, 203, 209, 221, 231, 235, 239, 245, 247, 251.

'*Probatum est.* CHARLES EASY.'

'I, Christopher Query, having been troubled with a certain distemper in my tongue, which showed itself in impertinent and superfluous interrogatories, have not asked one unnecessary question since my perusal of the prescription marked No. 228.'

'The Britannic Beautifier, being an essay on modesty, No. 231, which gives such a delightful blushing colour to the cheeks of those that are white or pale, that it is not to be distinguished from a natural fine complexion, nor perceived to be artificial by the nearest friend, is nothing of paint, or in the least hurtful. It renders the face delightfully handsome: is not subject to be rubbed off, and cannot be paralleled by either wash, powder, cosmetic, &c. It is certainly the best beautifier in the world.

'MARTHA GLOWORM.'

'I, Samuel Self, of the parish of St. James's, having a constitution which naturally abounds with acids, made use of a paper of directions marked No. 177, recommending a healthful exercise called good-nature, and have found it a most excellent sweetener of the blood.'

'Whereas I, Elizabeth Rainbow, was troubled with that distemper in my head, which about a year ago was pretty epidemical among the ladies, and discovered itself in the colour of their hoods: having made use of the doctor's cephalic tincture, which he exhibited to the public in one of his last year's papers, I recovered in a very few days.'

'I, George Gloom, having for a long time been troubled with the spleen, and being advised by my friends to put myself into a course of Steele, did for that end make use of the remedies conveyed to me several mornings, in short letters, from the hands of the invisible doctor. They were marked at the bottom Nathaniel Henroost, Alice Threadneedle, Rebecca Nettletoy, Tom Loveless, Mary Meanwell, Thomas Smoky, Anthony Freeman, Tom Meggot, Rustic Sprightly, &c. which have had so good an effect upon me, that I now find myself cheerful, lightsome, and easy; and therefore do recommend them to all such as labour under the same distemper.'

Not having room to insert all the advertisements which were sent me, I have only picked out some few from the third volume, reserving the fourth for another opportunity. O.

No. 548.] *Friday, November* 28, 1712.

—Vitiis nemo sine nascitur, optimus ille
Qui minimis urgetur. *Hor.* Sat. iii. Lib. 1. 68.

There's none but has some fault; and he's the best,
Most virtuous he that's spotted with the least.
Creech.

'Nov. 27, 1712.

'Mr. Spectator,—I have read this day's paper with a great deal of pleasure, and could send you an account of several elixirs and antidotes in your third volume, which your correspondents have not taken notice of in their advertisements; and at the same time must own to you, that I have seldom seen a shop furnished with such a variety of medicaments, and in which there are fewer soporifics. The several vehicles you have invented for conveying your unacceptable truths to us, are what I most particularly admire, as I am afraid they are secrets which will die with you. I do not find that any of our critical essays are taken notice of in this paper, notwithstanding I look upon them to be excellent cleansers of the brain, and could venture to superscribe them with an advertisement which I have lately seen in one of your newspapers, wherein there is an account given of a sovereign remedy for restoring the taste to all such persons whose palates have been vitiated by distempers, unwholesome food, or any the like occasions. But to let fall the allusion, notwithstanding your criticisms, and particularly the candour which you have discovered in them, are not the least taking part of your works, I find your opinion concerning poetical justice, as it is expressed in the first part or your fortieth Spectator, is controverted by some eminent critics; and as you now seem, to our great grief of heart, to be winding up your bottoms, I hoped you would have enlarged a little upon that subject. It is indeed but a single paragraph in your works, and I believe those who have read it with the same attention I have done, will think there is nothing to be objected against it. I have however drawn up some additional arguments to strengthen the opinion which you have there delivered, having endeavoured to go to the bottom of the matter, which you may either publish or suppress as you think fit.

'Horace, in my motto, says, that all men are vicious, and that they differ from one another only as they are more or less so. Boileau has given the same account of our wisdom, as Horace has of our virtue:

" Tous les hommes sont fous, et malgre tous leurs soins
Ne different entre eux, que de plus et du moins."

"All men," says he, "are fools, and, in spite of their endeavours to the contrary, differ from one another only as they are more or less so."

'Two or three of the old Greek poets have given the same turn to a sentence which describes the happiness of man in this life:

"Το ζην αλυπως, ανδρος εστιν ευτυχους."
" That man is most happy who is the least miserable."

'It will not perhaps be unentertaining to the polite reader to observe how these three beautiful sentences are formed upon different subjects, by the same way of thinking; but I shall return to the first of them.

'Our goodness being of a comparative and not an absolute nature, there is none who in strictness can be called a virtuous man. Every one has in him a natural alloy, though one may be fuller of dross than another: for this reason I cannot think it right to introduce a perfect or a faultless man upon the stage; not only because such a character is improper to move compassion, but because there is no such thing in nature. This might probably be one reason why the Spectator in one of his papers took notice of that late invented term called poetical justice, and the wrong notions into which it has led some tragic writers. The most perfect man has vices enough to draw down punishments upon his head, and to justify Providence in regard to any miseries that may befall him. For this reason I cannot think but that the instruction and moral are much finer, where a man who is virtuous in the main of his character falls into distress, and sinks under the blows of fortune at the end of a tragedy, than when he is represented as happy and triumphant. Such an example corrects the insolence of human nature, softens the mind of the beholder with sentiments of pity and compassion, comforts him under his own private affliction, and teaches him not to judge of men's virtues by their success. I cannot think of one real hero in all antiquity so far raised above human infirmities, that he might not be very naturally represented in a tragedy as plunged in misfortunes and calamities. The poet may still find out some prevailing passion or indiscretion in his character, and show it in such a manner as will sufficiently acquit the gods of any injustice in his sufferings. For, as Horace observes in my text, the best man is faulty, though not in so great a degree as those whom we generally call vicious men.

'If such a strict poetical justice as some gentlemen insist upon was to be observed in this art, there is no manner of reason why it should not extend to heroic poetry as well as tragedy. But we find it so little observed in Homer, that his Achilles is placed in the greatest point of glory and success, though his character is morally vicious, and only poetically good, if I may use the phrase of our modern critics. The Æneid is filled with innocent, unhappy persons. Nisus and Euryalus, Lausus and Pallas, come all to unfortunate ends. The poet takes notice in particular, that, in the sacking of Troy, Ripheus fell, who was the most just man among the Trojans.

——Cadit et Ripheus justissimus unus,
Qui fuit in Teucris, et servantissimus æqui:
Diis aliter visum est—— *Æn.* ii. 427.

And that Pantheus could neither be preserved by his transcendent piety, nor by the holy fillets of Apollo, whose priest he was.

——Nec te tua plurima, Pantheu,
Labentem pietas, nec Apollinis infula texit.
Ibid. ver. 429.

I might here mention the practice of ancient tragic poets, both Greek and Latin; but as this particular is touched upon in the paper above-mentioned, I shall pass it over in silence. I could produce passages out of Aristotle in favour of my opinion; and if in one place he says that an absolutely virtuous man, should not be represented as unhappy, this does not justify any one who shall think fit to bring in an absolutely virtuous man upon the stage. Those who are acquainted with that author's way of writing, know very well that, to take the whole extent of his subject into his divisions of it, he often makes use of such cases as are imaginary, and not reducible to practice. He himself declares that such tragedies as ended unhappily, bore away the prize in theatrical contentions, from those which ended happily; and for the fortieth speculation, which I am now considering, as it has given reasons why these are more apt to please an audience, so it only proves that these are generally preferable to the other, though at the same time it affirms that many excellent tragedies have and may be written in both kinds.

'I shall conclude with observing, that though the Spectator above-mentioned is so far against the rule of poetical justice, as to affirm that good men may meet with an unhappy catastrophe in tragedy, it does not say that ill men may go off unpunished. The reasons for this distinction is very plain, namely, because the best of men are vicious enough to justify Providence for any misfortunes and afflictions which may befall them, but there are many men so criminal that they can have no claim or pretence to happiness. The best of men may deserve punishment, but the worst of men cannot deserve happiness.

No. 549.] *Saturday, November* 29, 1712.

Quamvis digressu veteris confusus amici,
Laudo tamen. *Juv.* Sat. iii. 1

Though griev'd at the departure of my friend,
His purpose of retiring I commend.

I BELIEVE most people begin the world with a resolution to withdraw from it into a serious kind of solitude or retirement when they have made themselves easy in it. Our unhappiness is, that we find out some excuse or other for deferring such our good resolutions until our intended retreat is cut off by death. But among all kinds of people, there are none who are so hard to part with the world as those who are grown old in the heaping up of riches. Their minds are so warped with their constant attention to gain, that it is very difficult for them to give their souls another bent, and convert them towards those objects, which though they are proper for every stage of life, are so more especially for the last. Horace describes an old usurer as so charmed with the pleasures of a country life, that in order to make a purchase he called in all his money; but what was the event of it? Why, in a very few days after he put it out again. I am engaged in this series of thought by a discourse which I had last week with my worthy friend Sir Andrew Freeport, a man of so much natural eloquence, good sense, and probity of mind, that I always hear him with a particular pleasure. As we were sitting together, being the sole remaining members of our club, Sir Andrew gave me an account of the many busy scenes of life in which he had been engaged, and at the same time reckoned up to me abundance of those lucky hits, which at another time he would have called pieces of good fortune; but in the temper of mind he was then, he termed them mercies, favours of Providence, and blessings upon an honest industry. 'Now,' says he, 'you must know, my good friend, I am so used to consider myself as creditor and debtor, that I often state my accounts after the same manner with regard to heaven and my own soul. In this case, when I look upon the debtor side, I find such innumerable articles, that I want arithmetic to cast them up; but when I look upon the creditor side, I find little more than blank paper. Now, though I am very well satisfied that it is not in my power to balance accounts with my Maker, I am resolved however to turn all my future endeavours that way. You must not therefore be surprised, my friend, if you hear that I am breaking myself to a more thoughtful kind of life, and if I meet you no more in this place.'

I could not but approve so good a resolution, notwithstanding the loss I shall suffer by it. Sir Andrew has since explained himself to me more at large in the following letter, which is just come to my hands.

'GOOD MR. SPECTATOR,—Notwithstanding my friends at the club have always rallied me, when I have talked of retiring from business, and repeated to me one of my own sayings, that "a merchant has never enough until he has got a little more;" I can now inform you, that there is one in the world who thinks he has enough, and is determined to pass the remainder of his life in the enjoyment of what he has. You know me so well, that I need not tell you I mean, by the enjoyment of my possessions, the making of them useful to the public. As the greatest part of my estate has been hitherto of an unsteady and volatile nature, either tost upon seas or fluctuating in funds, it is now fixed and settled in substantial acres and tenements. I have removed it from the uncertainty of stocks, winds, and waves, and disposed of it in a considerable purchase. This will give me great opportunity of being charitable in my way, that is, in setting my poor neighbours to work, and giving them a comfortable subsistence out of their own industry. My gardens, my fish-ponds, my arable and pasture grounds, shall be my several hospitals, or rather work-houses, in which I propose to maintain a great many indigent persons, who are now starving in my neighbourhood. I have got a fine spread of improvable lands, and in my own thoughts am already plowing up some of them, fencing others; planting woods, and draining marshes. In fine, as I have my share in the surface of this island, I am resolved to make it as beautiful a spot as any in her majesty's dominions; at least there is not an inch of it which shall not be cultivated to the best advantage, and do its utmost for its owner. As in my mercantile employment I so disposed of my affairs, that, from whatever corner of the compass the wind blew, it was bringing home one or other of my ships; I hope as a husbandman to contrive it so, that not a shower of rain or a glimpse of sunshine shall fall upon my estate without bettering some part of it, and contributing to the products of the season. You know it has been hitherto my opinion of life, that it is thrown away when it is not some way useful to others. But when I am riding out by myself, in the fresh air, on the open heath that lies by my house, I find several other thoughts growing up in me. I am now of opinion, that a man of my age may find business enough on himself, by setting his mind in order, preparing it for another world, and reconciling it to the thoughts of death. I must therefore acquaint you, that besides those usual methods of charity, of which I have before spoken, I am at this very instant finding out a convenient place where I may build an almshouse, which I intend to endow very handsomely for a dozen superannuated husbandmen. It will be a great pleasure to me to say my prayers twice a day with men of my own years, who all of them, as well as myself, may have their thoughts taken up how they shall die, rather than how they shall live. I remember an excellent saying that I learned at school, *Finis coronat opus*. You know best whether it be in Virgil or in Horace, it is my business to apply it. If your affairs will permit you to take the country air with me sometimes, you will find an apartment fitted up for you, and shall be every day entertained with beef or mutton of my own feeding; fish out of my own ponds; and fruit out of my own gardens. You shall have free egress and regress about my house, without having any questions asked you; and in a word, such a hearty welcome as you may expect from your most sincere friend and humble servant,

'ANDREW FREEPORT.'

The club of which I am a member being entirely dispersed, I shall consult my reader next week upon a project relating to the institution of a new one. O.

No. 550.] *Monday, December* 1, 1712.

Quid dignum tanto feret hic promissor hiatu?
Hor. Ars Poet. ver. 138.

In what will all this ostentation end?—*Roscommon.*

SINCE the late dissolution of the club, whereof I have often declared myself a member, there are very many persons who by letters, petitions, and recommendations, put up for the next election. At the same time I must complain, that several indirect and underhand practices have been made use of upon this occasion. A certain country gentleman began to *tap* upon the first information he received of Sir Roger's death; when he sent me up word that, if I would get him chosen in the place of the deceased, he would present me with a barrel of the best October I had ever tasted in my life. The ladies are in great pain to know whom I intend to elect in the room of Will Honeycomb. Some of them indeed are of opinion that Mr. Honeycomb did not take sufficient care of their interest in the club, and are therefore desirous of having in it hereafter a representative of their own sex. A citizen who subscribes himself Y. Z. tells me that he has one-and-twenty shares in the African company, and offers to bribe me with the odd one in case he may succeed Sir Andrew Freeport, which he thinks would raise the credit of that fund. I have several letters, dated from Jenny Man's, by gentlemen who are candidates for captain Sentry's place; and as many from a coffee-house in St. Paul's church-yard of such who would fill up the vacancy occasioned by the death of my worthy friend the clergyman, whom I can never mention but with a particular respect.

Having maturely weighed these several particulars, with the many remonstrances that have been made to me on this subject, and considering how invidious an office I shall take upon me if I make the whole election depend upon my single voice, and being unwilling to expose myself to those clamours, which on such an occasion will not fail to be raised against me for partiality, injustice, corruption, and other qualities, which my nature abhors, I have formed to myself the project of a club as follows.

I have thoughts of issuing out writs to all and every of the clubs that are established in the cities of London and Westminster, requiring them to choose out of their respective bodies a person of the greatest merit, and to return his name to me before Lady-day, at which time I intend to sit upon business.

By this means I may have reason to hope, that the club over which I shall preside will be the very flower and quintessence of all other clubs. I have communicated this my project to none but a particular friend of mine, whom I have celebrated twice or thrice for his happiness in that kind of wit which is commonly known by the name of a pun. The only objection he makes to it is, that I shall raise up enemies to myself if I act with so regal an air, and that my detractors, instead of giving me the usual title of Spectator, will be apt to call me the King of Clubs.

But to proceed on my intended project: it is very well known that I at first set forth in this work with the character of a silent man; and I think I have so well preserved my taciturnity, that I do not remember to have violated it with three sentences in the space of almost two years. As a monosyllable is my delight, I have made very few excursions, in conversations which I have related, beyond a Yes or a No. By this means my readers have lost many good things which I have had in my heart, though I did not care for uttering them.

Now in order to diversify my character, and to show the world how well I can talk if I have a mind, I have thoughts of being very loquacious in the club which I have now under consideration. But that I may proceed the more regularly in this affair, I design, upon the first meeting of the said club, to have my mouth opened in form; intending to regulate myself in this particular by a certain ritual which I have by me, that contains all the ceremonies which are practised at the opening of the mouth of a cardinal. I have likewise examined the forms which were used of old by Pythagoras, when any of his scholars, after an apprenticeship of silence, was made free of his speech. In the mean time, as I have of late found my name in foreign gazettes upon less occasions, I question not but in their next articles from Great Britain they will inform the world, 'that the Spectator's mouth is to be opened on the twenty-fifth of March next.' I may perhaps publish a very useful paper at that time of the proceedings in that solemnity, and of the persons who shall assist at it. But of this more hereafter. O.

No. 551.] *Tuesday, December 2, 1712.*

Sic honor et nomen divinis vatibus atque,
Carminibus venit.——
Hor. Ars Poet. ver. 400.

So ancient is the pedigree of verse,
And so divine a poet's function.—*Roscommon*

'Mr. Spectator,—When men of worthy and excelling geniuses have obliged the world with beautiful and instructive writings, it is in the nature of gratitude that praise should be returned them, as one proper consequent reward of their performances. Nor has mankind ever been so degenerately sunk, but they have made this return, and even when they have not been wrought up by the generous endeavours so as to receive the advantages designed by it. This praise, which arises first in the mouth of particular persons, spreads and lasts according to the merit of authors; and, when it thus meets with a full success, changes its denomination, and is called fame. They, who have happily arrived at this, are, even while they live, inflamed by the acknowledgments of others, and spurred on to new undertakings for the benefit of mankind, notwithstanding the detraction which some abject tempers would cast upon them: but when they decease, their characters being free from the shadow which envy laid them under, begin to shine with the greater splendour; their spirits survive in their works; they are admitted into the highest companies, and they continue pleasing and instructing posterity from age to age. Some of the best gain a character, by being able to show that they are no strangers to them; and others obtain a new warmth to labour for the happiness and ease of mankind, from a reflection upon those honours which are paid to their memories.

'The thought of this took me up as I turned over those epigrams which are the remains of several of the wits of Greece, and perceived many dedicated to the fame of those who had excelled in beautiful poetic performances. Wherefore, in pursuance to my thought, I concluded to do something along with them to bring their praises into a new light and language, for the encouragement of those whose modest tempers may be deterred by the fear of envy or detraction from fair attempts, to which their parts might render them equal. You will perceive them as they follow to be conceived in the form of epitaphs, a sort of writing which is wholly set apart for a short-pointed method of praise.

ON ORPHEUS, WRITTEN BY ANTIPATER.

"No longer, Orpheus, shall thy sacred strains
Lead stones, and trees, and beasts along the plains;
No longer sooth the boisterous winds to sleep,
Or still the billows of the raging deep;
For thou art gone. The Muses mourn thy fall
In solemn strains, thy mother most of all.
Ye mortals, idly for your sons ye moan,
If thus a goddess could not save her own."

'Observe here, that if we take the fable for granted, as if it was believed to be in that age when the epigram was written, the turn appears to have piety to the gods, and a resigning spirit in its application. But if we consider the point with respect to our present knowledge, it will be less esteemed; though the author himself, because he believed it, may still be more valued than any one who should now write with a point of the same nature.

ON HOMER, BY ALPHEUS OF MYTILENE.

"Still in our ears Andromache complains,
And still in sight the fate of Troy remains;
Still Ajax fights, still Hector's dragg'd along:
Such strange enchantment dwells in Homer's song;
Whose birth could more than one poor realm adorn,
For all the world is proud that he was born."

'The thought in the first part of this is natural, and depending upon the force of poesy; in the latter part it looks as if it would aim at the history of seven towns contending for the honour of Homer's birthplace; but when you expect to meet with that common story, the poet slides by, and raises the whole world for a kind of arbiter, which is to end the contention amongst its several parts.

ON ANACREON, BY ANTIPATER.

"This tomb be thine, Anacreon! All around
Let ivy wreathe, let flow'rets deck the ground;
And from its earth, enrich'd with such a prize,
Let wells of milk and streams of wine arise:
So will thine ashes yet a pleasure know,
If any pleasure reach the shades below."

'The poet here written upon is an easy gay author, and he who writes upon him has filled his own head with the character of his subject. He seems to love his theme so much, that he thinks of nothing but pleasing him as if he were still alive, by entering into his libertine spirit; so that the humour is easy and gay, resembling Anacreon in its air, raised by such images, and pointed with such a turn as he might have used. I give it a place here, because the author may have designed it for his honour; and I take an opportunity from it to advise others, that when they would praise they cautiously avoid every looser qualification, and fix only where there is a real foundation in merit.

ON EURIPIDES, BY ION.

"Divine Euripides, this tomb we see
So fair, is not a monument for thee,
So much as thou for it; since all will own
Thy name and lasting praise adorn the stone."

'The thought here is fine, but its fault is, that it is general, that it may belong to any great man, because it points out no particular character. It would be better if, when we light upon such a turn, we join it with something that circumscribes and bounds it to the qualities of our subject. He who gives his praise in gross, will often appear either to have been a stranger to those he writes upon, or not to have found any thing in them which is praise-worthy.

ON SOPHOCLES, BY SIMONIDES.

"Winde, gentle ever-green, to form a shade
Around the tomb where Sophocles is laid:
Sweet ivy winde thy boughs, and intertwine
With blushing roses and the clust'ring vine:
Thus will thy lasting leaves, with beauties hung,
Prove grateful emblems of the lays he sung;
Whose soul, exalted like a god of wit,
Among the Muses and the Graces writ."

'This epigram I have opened more than any of the former: the thought towards the latter end seemed closer couched, so as to require an explanation. I fancied the poet aimed at the picture which is generally made of Apollo and the Muses, he sitting with his harp in the middle, and they around him. This looked beautiful to my thought, and because the image arose before me out of the words of the original as I was reading it, I ventured to explain them so.

ON MENANDER, THE AUTHOR UNNAMED.

"The very bees, O sweet Menander hung
To taste the Muses' spring upon thy tongue;
The very Graces made the scenes you writ
Their happy point of fine expression hit.
Thus still you live, you make your Athens shine,
And raise its glory to the skies in thine."

'This epigram has a respect to the character of its subject; for Menander writ remarkably with a justness and purity of language. It has also told the country he was born in, without either a set or a hidden manner, while it twists together the glory of the poet and his nation, so as to make the nation depend upon his for an increase of its own.

'I will offer no more instances at present to show that they who deserve praise have it returned them from different ages: let these which have been laid down show men that envy will not always prevail. And to the end that writers may more successfully enliven the endeavours of one another, let them consider, in some such manner as I have attempted, what may be the justest spirit and art of praise. It is indeed very hard to come up to it. Our praise is trifling when it depends upon fable; it is false when it depends upon wrong qualifications; it means nothing when it is general; it is extremely difficult to hit when we propose to raise characters high, while we keep to them justly. I shall end this with transcribing that excellent epitaph of Mr. Cowley, wherein, with a kind of grave and philosophic humour, he very beautifully speaks of himself (withdrawn from the world, and dead to all the interests of it,) as of a man really deceased. At the same time it is an instruction how to leave the public with a good grace.

EPITAPHIUM VIVI AUTHORIS.

" Hic, O viator, sub lare parvulo
Couleius hic est conditus, hic jacet
  Defunctus humani laboris
  Sorte, supervacuaque vita;
Non indecora pauperie nitens,
Et non inerti nobilis otio,
  Vanoque dilectis popello
  Divitiis animosus hostis.
Possis ut illum dicere mortuum,
En terra jam nunc quantula sufficit!
  Exempta sit curis, viator,
  Terra sit illa levis, precare.
Hic sparge flores, sparge breves rosas,
Nam vita gaudet mortua floribus,
  Herbisque odoratis corona
  Vatis adhuc cinerem calentem."

THE LIVING AUTHOR'S EPITAPH,

" From life's superfluous cares enlarg'd,
His debt of human toil discharg'd
Here Cowley lies, beneath this shed,
To ev'ry worldly interest dead:
With descent poverty content:
His hours of ease not idly spent;
To fortune's goods a foe profess'd,
And hating wealth, by all caress'd.
'Tis sure, he's dead: for lo! how small
A spot of earth is now his all!
O! wish that earth may lightly lay,
And ev'ry care be far away!
Bring flow'rs, the short-liv'd roses bring,
To life deceas'd fit offering!
And sweets around the poet strow,
Whilst yet with life his ashes glow."

The publication of these criticisms having procured me the following letter from a very ingenious gentleman, I cannot forbear inserting it in the volume,* though it did not come soon enough to have a place in any of my single papers.

'MR. SPECTATOR,—Having read over in your paper, No. 551, some of the epigrams made by the Grecian wits, in commendation of their celebrated poets, I could not forbear sending you another, out of the same collection; which I take to be as great a compliment to Homer as any that has yet been paid him.

Τις ποθ' οτον Τροιης πολεμον, &c.

" Who first transcrib'd the famous Trojan war,
  And wise Ulysses' acts, O Jove, make known:
For since, 'tis certain thine these poems are,
  No more let Homer boast they are his own."

'If you think it worthy of a place in your speculations, for aught I know, (by that means) it may in time be printed as often in English as it has already been in Greek. I am, (like the rest of the world,) sir, your great admirer, G. R.

'4th Dec.'

The reader may observe, that the beauty of this epigram is different from that of the foregoing. An irony is looked upon as the finest palliative of praise; and very often conveys the noblest panegyric under the appearance of satire. Homer is here seemingly accused and treated as a plagiary; but what is drawn up in the form of an accusation is certainly, as my correspondent observes, the greatest compliment that could have been paid to that divine poet.

* The translation of Cowley's epitaph, and all that follows except the concluding letter, signed Philonicus, was not printed in the Spectator in folio, but added in the 8vo. edition of 1712.

'DEAR MR. SPECTATOR,—I am a gentleman of a pretty good fortune, and of a temper impatient of any thing which I think an injury. However, I always quarrelled according to law, and instead of attacking my adversary by the dangerous method of sword and pistol, I made my assaults by that more secure one of writ or warrant. I cannot help telling you, that either by the justice of my causes, or the superiority of my counsel, I have been generally successful: and to my great satisfaction I can say it, that by three actions of slander, and half a dozen trespasses, I have for several years enjoyed a perfect tranquillity in my reputation and estate: by these means also I have been made known to the judges; the serjeants of our circuit are my intimate friends; and the ornamental counsel pay a very profound respect to one who has made so great a figure in the law. Affairs of consequence having brought me to town, I had the curiosity the other day to visit Westminster-hall; and having placed myself in one of the courts, expected to be most agreeably entertained. After the court and counsel were with due ceremony seated, up stands a learned gentleman, and began, When this matter was last "stirred" before your lordship; the next humbly moved to "quash" an indictment; another complained that his adversary had "snapped" a judgment; the next informed the court that his client was "stripped," of his possessions; another begged leave to acquaint his lordship they had been "saddled" with costs. At last up got a grave serjeant, and told us his client had been "hung up" a whole term by a writ of error. At this I could bear it no longer, but came hither, and resolved to apply myself to your honour to interpose with these gentlemen, that they would leave off such low and unnatural expressions: for surely though the lawyers subscribe to hideous French and false Latin, yet they should let their clients have a little decent and proper English for their money. What man that has a value for a good name would like to have it said in a public court, that Mr. Such-a-one was stripped, saddled, or hung up? This being what has escaped your spectatorial observation, be pleased to correct such an illiberal cant among professed speakers, and you will infinitely oblige your humble servant,

'PHILONICUS.

'Joe's Coffee-house, Nov. 28.'

No. 552.] *Wednesday, December* 3, 1712.

——————Qui prægravat artes
Infra se positas, extinctus amabitur idem.
Hor. Ep. i. Lib. 2. 13.

For those are hated that excel the rest,
Although, when dead, they are belov'd and blest.
Creech.

As I was tumbling about the town the other day in a hackney-coach, and delighting myself with busy scenes in the shops of each side of me, it came into my head, with no small remorse, that I had not been frequent enough in the mention and recommendation of the industrious part of mankind. It very naturally, upon this occasion, touched my conscience in particular, that I had not acquitted myself to my friend Mr. Peter Motteux. That industrious man of trade, and formerly brother of the quill, has dedicated to me a poem upon tea. It would injure him, as a man of business, if I did not let the world know that the author of so good verses writ them before he was concerned in traffic. In order to expiate my negligence towards him, I immediately resolved to make him a visit. I found his spacious warehouses filled and adorned with tea, China and Indiaware. I could observe a beautiful ordonnance of the whole; and such different and considerable branches of trade carried on in the same house, I exulted in seeing disposed by a poetical head. In one place were exposed to view silks of various shades and colours, rich brocades, and the wealthiest products of foreign looms. Here you might see the finest laces held up by the fairest hands; and there, examined by the beauteous eyes of the buyers, the most delicate cambrics, muslins, and linens. I could not but congratulate my friend on the humble, but I hoped beneficial, use he had made of his talents, and wished I could be a patron to his trade, as he had been pleased to make me of his poetry. The honest man has, I know, the modest desire of gain which is peculiar to those who understand better things than riches; and, I dare say, he would be contented with much less than what is called wealth at that quarter of the town which he inhabits, and will oblige all his customers with demands agreeable to the moderation of his desires.

Among other omissions of which I have been also guilty, with relation to men of industry of a superior order, I must acknowledge my silence towards a proposal frequently enclosed to me by Mr. Renatus Harris, organ-builder. The ambition of this artificer is to erect an organ in St. Paul's cathedral, over the west door, at the entrance into the body of the church, which in art and magnificence shall transcend any work of that kind ever before invented. The proposal in perspicuous language sets forth the honour and advantage such a performance would be to the British name, as well as that it would apply the power of sounds in a manner more amazingly forcible than, perhaps, has yet been known, and I am sure to an end much more worthy. Had the vast sums which have been laid out upon operas, without skill or conduct, and to no other purpose but to suspend or vitiate our understandings, been disposed this way, we should now perhaps have an engine so formed as to strike the minds of half the people at once in a place of worship, with a forgetfulness of present care and calamity, and a hope of endless rapture, joy, and hallelujah hereafter.

When I am doing this justice, I am not to forget the best mechanic of my acquaintance, that useful servant to science and knowledge, Mr. John Rowley; but I think I lay a great obligation on the public, by acquainting them with his proposals for a pair of new globes. After his preamble he promises in the said proposals that,

'IN THE CELESTIAL GLOBE,

'Care shall be taken that the fixed stars be placed according to their true longitude and latitude, from the many and correct observations of Hevelius, Cassini, Mr. Flamstead, reg. astronomer; Dr. Halley, Savilian professor of geometry in Oxon; and from whatever else can be procured to render the globe more exact, instructive, and useful.

'That all the constellations be drawn in a curious, new, and particular manner; each star in so just, distinct, and conspicuous a proportion, that its magnitude may be readily known by bare inspection, according to the different light and sizes of the stars. That the track or way of such comets as have been well observed, but not hitherto expressed in a globe, be carefully delineated in this.

'IN THE TERRESTRIAL GLOBE,

'That by reason the descriptions formerly made, both in the English and Dutch great globe, are erroneous, Asia, Africa, and America, be drawn in a manner wholly new; by which means it is to be noted that the undertakers will be obliged to alter the latitude of some places in ten degrees, the longitude of others in twenty degrees; besides which great and necessary alterations, there be many remarkable countries, cities, towns, rivers, and lakes, omitted in other globes, inserted here according to the best discoveries made by our late navigators. Lastly, that the course of the trade-winds, the monsoons, and other winds periodically shifting between the tropics, be visibly expressed.

'Now, in regard that this undertaking is of so universal use, as the advancement of the most necessary parts of the mathematics, as well as tending to the honour of the British nation, and that the charge of carrying it on is very expensive, it is desired that all gentlemen who are willing to promote so great a work will be pleased to subscribe on the following conditions.

'1. The undertakers engage to furnish each subscriber with a celestial and terrestrial globe, each of thirty inches diameter, in all respects curiously adorned, the stars gilded, the capital cities plainly distinguished, the frames, meridians, horizons, hour circles, and indexes, so exactly finished up, and accurately divided, that a pair of these globes will appear, in the judgment of any disinterested and intelligent person, worth fifteen pounds more than will be demanded for them by the undertakers.

'2 Whosoever will be pleased to subscribe, and pay twenty-five pounds in the manner following, for a pair of these globes, either for their own use, or to present them to any college in the universities, or any public library or schools, shall have his coat of arms, name, title, seat, or place of residence, &c. inserted in some convenient place of the globe.

'3. That every subscriber do at first pay down the sum of ten pounds, and fifteen pounds more upon the delivery of each pair of globes perfectly fitted up. And that the said globes be delivered within twelve months after the number of thirty subscribers be completed; and that the subscribers be served with globes in the order which they subscribed.

'4. That a pair of these globes shall not hereafter be sold to any person but the subscribers under thirty pounds.

'5. That, if there be not thirty subscribers within four months after the first of December, 1712, the money paid shall be returned on demand, by Mr. John Warner, goldsmith, near Temple-bar, who shall receive and pay the same according to the above-mentioned articles.'

No. 553.] *Thursday, December 4, 1712.*

Nec lusisse pudet, sed non incidere ludum.
Hor. Ep. xiv. Lib. 1. 36.

Once to be wild is no such foul disgrace,
But 'tis so still to run the frantic race.—*Creech.*

THE project which I published on Mon day last has brought me in several packets of letters. Among the rest, I have received one from a certain projector, wherein, after having represented, that in all probability the solemnity of opening my mouth will draw together a great confluence of beholders, he proposes to me the hiring of Stationer's-hall for the more convenient exhibiting of that public ceremony. He undertakes to be at the charge of it himself, provided he may have the erecting of galleries on every side, and the letting of them out upon that occasion. I have a letter also from a bookseller, petitioning me in a very humble manner, that he may have the printing of the speech which I shall make to the assembly upon the first opening of my mouth. I am informed from all parts that there are great canvassings in the several clubs about town, upon the choosing of a proper person to sit with me on those arduous affairs to which I have summoned them. Three clubs have already proceeded to election, whereof one has made a double return. If I find that my enemies shall take advantage of my silence to begin hostilities upon me, or if any other exigency of affairs may so require, since I see elections in so great forwardness, we may possibly meet before the day appointed; or, if matters go on to my satisfaction, I may perhaps put off the meeting to a farther day; but of this, public notice shall be given.

In the mean time, I must confess that I am not a little gratified and obliged by that concern which appears in this great city upon my present design of laying down this paper. It is likewise with much satisfaction, that I find some of the most outlying parts of the kingdom alarmed upon this occasion, having received letters to expostulate with me about it from several of my readers of the remotest boroughs of Great Britain.—Among these I am very well pleased with a letter dated from Berwick-upon-Tweed, wherein my correspondent compares the office, which I have for some time executed in these realms, to the weeding of a great garden; 'which,' says he, 'it is not sufficient to weed once for all, and afterwards to give over, but that the work must be continued daily, or the same spots of ground which are cleared for a while will in a little time be overrun as much as ever.' Another gentleman lays before me several enormities that are already sprouting, and which he believes will discover themselves in their growth immediately after my disappearance. 'There is no doubt,' says he, 'but the ladies' heads will shoot up as soon as they know they are no longer under the Spectator's eye; and I have already seen such monstrous broad-brimmed hats under the arms of foreigners, that I question not but they will overshadow the island within a month or two after the dropping of your paper.' But, among all the letters which are come to my hands, there is none so handsomely written as the following one, which I am the more pleased with as it is sent me from gentlemen who belong to a body which I shall always honour, and where (I cannot speak it without a secret pride) my speculations have met with a very kind reception. It is usual for poets, upon the publishing of their works, to print before them such copies of verses as have been made in their praise. Not that you must imagine they are pleased with their own commendation, but because the elegant compositions of their friends should not be lost. I must make the same apology for the publication of the ensuing letter, in which I have suppressed no part of those praises that are given my speculations with too lavish and good-natured a hand; though my correspondents can witness for me, that at other times I have generally blotted out those parts in the letters which I have received from them. O.

'Oxford, Nov. 25.

'MR. SPECTATOR,—In spite of your invincible silence you have found out the method of being the most agreeable companion in the world: that kind of conversation which you hold with the town, has the good fortune of being always pleasing to the men of taste and leisure, and never offensive to those of hurry and business. You are never heard but at what Horace calls *dextro tempore*, and have the happiness to observe the politic rule, which the same discerning author gave his friend when he enjoined him to deliver his book to Augustus:

"Si validus, si lætus erit, si denique poscet."
Ep. xiii. Lib. 1. 3.

"———When vexing cares are fled,
When well, when merry, when he asks to read."
Creech.

You never begin to talk but when people are desirous to hear you; and I defy any one to be out of humour until you leave off. But I am led unawares into reflections foreign to the original design of this epistle; which was to let you know, that some unfeigned admirers of your inimitable papers, who could without any flattery, greet you with the salutation used to the eastern monarchs, *viz.* "O Spec, live for ever," have lately been under the same apprehensions with Mr. Philo-Spec; that the haste you have made to despatch your best friends, portends no long duration to your own short visage. We could not, indeed, find any just grounds for complaint in the method you took to dissolve that venerable body: no, the world was not worthy of your Divine. Will Honeycomb could not, with any reputation, live single any longer. It was high time for the Templar to turn himself to Coke; and Sir Roger's dying was the wisest thing he ever did in his life. It was, however, matter of great grief to us, to think that we were in danger of losing so elegant and valuable an entertainment. And we could not, without sorrow, reflect that we were likely to have nothing to interrupt our sips in the morning, and to suspend our coffee in mid air, between our lips and right ear, but the ordinary trash of newspapers. We resolved, therefore, not to part with you so. But since, to make use of your own allusion, the cherries began now to crowd the market, and their season was almost over, we consulted our future enjoyments, and endeavoured to make the exquisite pleasure that delicious fruit gave our taste as lasting as we could, and by drying them protract their stay beyond its natural date. We own that thus they have not a flavour equal to that of their juicy bloom; but yet, under this disadvantage, they pique the palate, and become a salver better than any other fruit at its first appearance. To speak plain, there are a number of us who have begun your works afresh, and meet two nights in the week in order to give you a re-hearing. We never come together without drinking your health, and as seldom part without general expressions of thanks to you for our night's improvement. This we conceive to be a more useful institution than any other club whatever, not excepting even that of Ugly Faces. We have one manifest advantage over that renowned society, with respect to Mr. Spectator's company. For though they may brag that you sometimes make your personal appearance amongst them, it is impossible they should ever get a word from you, whereas you are with us the reverse of what Phædria would have his mistress be in his rival's company, "present in your absence." We make you talk as much and as long as we please; and, let me tell you, you seldom hold your tongue for the whole evening. I promise myself you will look with an eye of favour upon a meeting which owes its original to a mutual emulation among its members, who shall show the most profound respect for your paper; not but we have a very great value for your person: and I dare say you can no where find four more sincere admirers, and humble servants, than

'T. F. G. S. J. T. E. T.'

No. 554.] *Friday, December 5, 1712.*

——Tentanda via est, qua me quoque possim
Tollere humo, victorque virum volitare per ora.
Virg. Georg. iii. 9.

New ways I must attempt my grovelling name
To raise aloft, and wing my flight to fame.—*Dryden.*

I AM obliged for the following essay, as well as for that which lays down rules out of Tully for pronunciation and action, to the ingenious author of a poem just published, entitled, An Ode to the Creator of the World, occasioned by the Fragments of Orpheus.

'It is a remark made, as I remember, by a celebrated French author, that no man ever pushed his capacity as far as it was able to extend. I shall not inquire whether this assertion be strictly true. It may suffice to say, that men of the greatest application and acquirements can look back upon many vacant spaces, and neglected parts of time, which have slipped away from them unemployed; and there is hardly any one considering person in the world but is apt to fancy with himself, at some time or other, that if his life were to begin again he could fill it up better.

'The mind is most provoked to cast on itself this ingenuous reproach, when the examples of such men are presented to it as have far outshot the generality of their species in learning, arts, or any valuable improvements.

'One of the most extensive and improved geniuses we have had any instance of in our own nation, or in any other, was that of Sir Francis Bacon, lord Verulam. This great man, by an extraordinary force of nature, compass of thought, and indefatigable study, had amassed to himself such stores of knowledge as we cannot look upon without amazement. His capacity seemed to have grasped all that was revealed in books before his time; and, not satisfied with that, he began to strike out new tracts of science, too many to be travelled over by any one man in the compass of the longest life. These, therefore, he could only mark down, like imperfect coastings on maps, or supposed points of land to be farther discovered and ascertained by the industry of after ages, who should proceed upon his notices or conjectures.

'The excellent Mr. Boyle was the person who seems to have been designed by nature to succeed to the labours and inquiries of that extraordinary genius I have just mentioned. By innumerable experiments, he in a great measure filled up those plans and outlines of science which his predecessor had sketched out. His life was spent in the pursuit of nature through a great variety of forms and changes, and in the most rational as well as devout adoration of its divine Author.

It would be impossible to name many persons who have extended their capacities as far as these two, in the studies they pursued; but my learned readers on this occasion will naturally turn their thoughts to a third,* who is yet living, and is likewise the glory of our own nation. The improvements which others had made in natural and mathematical knowledge have so vastly increased in his hands, as to afford at once a wonderful instance how great the capacity is of a human soul, and inexhaustible the subject of its inquiries; so true is that remark in holy writ, that "though a wise man seek to find out the works of God from the beginning to the end, yet shall he not be able to do it."

'I cannot help mentioning here one character more of a different kind indeed from these, yet such a one as may serve to show the wonderful force of nature and of application, and is the most singular instance of an universal genius I have ever met with. The person I mean is Leonardo da Vinci, an Italian painter, descended from a noble family in Tuscany, about the beginning of the sixteenth† century. In his profession of history-painting he was so great a master, that some have affirmed he excelled all who went before him. It is certain that he raised the envy of Michael Angelo, who was his contemporary, and that from the study of his works Raphael himself learned his best manner of designing. He was a master too in sculpture and architecture, and skilful in anatomy, mathematics, and mechanics. The aqueduct from the river Adda to Milan is mentioned as a work of his contrivance. He had learned several languages, and was acquainted with the studies of history, philosophy, poetry, and music. Though it is not necessary to my present purpose, I cannot but take notice, that all who have writ of him mention likewise his perfection of body. The instances of his strength are almost incredible. He is described to have been a well-formed person, and a master of all genteel exercises. And lastly, we are told that his moral qualities were agreeable to his natural and intellectual endowments, and that he was of an honest and generous mind, adorned with great sweetness of manners. I might break off the account of him here, but I imagine it will be an entertainment to the curiosity of my readers, to find so remarkable a character distinguished by as remarkable a circumstance at his death. The fame of his works having gained him an universal esteem, he was invited to the court of France, where, after some time, he fell sick; and Francis the First coming to see him, he raised himself in his bed to acknowledge the honour which was done him by that visit. The king embraced him, and Leonardo, fainting in the same moment, expired in the arms of that great monarch.

'It is impossible to attend to such instances as these without being raised into a contemplation on the wonderful nature of a human mind, which is capable of such progressions in knowledge, and can contain such a variety of ideas without perplexity or confusion. How reasonable is it from hence to infer its divine original! And whilst we find unthinking matter endued with a natural power to last for ever, unless annihilated by Omnipotence, how absurd would it be to imagine that a being so much superior to it should not have the same privilege!

'At the same time it is very surprising, when we remove our thoughts from such instances as I have mentioned, to consider those we so frequently meet with in the accounts of barbarous nations among the Indians; where we find numbers of people who scarce show the first glimmerings of reason, and seem to have few ideas above those of sense and appetite. These, methinks, appear like large wilds, or vast uncultivated tracts of human nature; and, when we compare them with men of the most exalted characters in arts and learning, we find it difficult to believe that they are creatures of the same species.

'Some are of opinion that the souls of men are all naturally equal, and that the great disparity we so often observe, arises from the different organization or structure of the bodies to which they are united. But, whatever constitutes this first disparity, the next great difference which we find between men in their several acquirements is owing to accidental differences in their education, fortunes, or course of life. The soul is a kind of rough diamond, which requires art, labour, and time to polish it. For want of which many a good-natured genius is lost, or lies unfashioned, like a jewel in the mine.

'One of the strongest incitements to excel in such arts and accomplishments as are in

* Sir Isaac Newton.

† He was born in 1445, and died in 1520.

the highest esteem among men, is the natural passion which the mind of man has for glory; which though it may be faulty in the excess of it, ought by no means to be discouraged. Perhaps some moralists are too severe in beating down this principle, which seems to be a spring implanted by nature to give motion to all the latent powers of the soul, and is always observed to exert itself with the greatest force in the most generous dispositions. The men whose characters have shown the brightest among the ancient Romans, appear to have been strongly animated by this passion. Cicero, whose learning and services to his country are so well known, was inflamed by it to an extravagant degree, and warmly presses Lucceius, who was composing a history of those times, to be very particular and zealous in relating the story of his consulship; and to execute it speedily, that he might have the pleasure of enjoying in his lifetime some part of the honour which he foresaw would be paid to his memory. This was the ambition of a great mind; but he is faulty in the degree of it, and cannot refrain from soliciting the historian upon this occasion to neglect the strict laws of history; and, in praising him, even to exceed the bounds of truth. The younger Pliny appears to have had the same passion for fame, but accompanied with greater chasteness and modesty. His ingenious manner of owning it to a friend, who had prompted him to undertake some great work, is exquisitely beautiful, and raises him to a certain grandeur above the imputation of vanity. "I must confess," says he, "that nothing employs my thoughts more than the desire I have of perpetuating my name; which in my opinion is a design worthy of a man, at least of such a one, who, being conscious of no guilt, is not afraid to be remembered by posterity."

'I think I ought not to conclude without interesting all my readers in the subject of this discourse: I shall therefore lay it down as a maxim, that though all are not capable of shining in learning or the politer arts, yet every one is capable of excelling in something. The soul has in this respect a certain vegetative power which cannot lie wholly idle. If it is not laid out and cultivated into a regular and beautiful garden, it will of itself shoot up in weeds or flowers of a wilder growth.'

No. 555.] *Saturday, December 6, 1712.*

Resque quod non es——
Pers. Sat. iv. 51.

Lay the fictitious character aside.

All the members of the imaginary society, which were described in my first papers, having disappeared one after another, it is high time for the Spectator himself to go off the stage. But now I am to take my leave, I am under much greater anxiety than I have known for the work of any day since I undertook this province. It is much more difficult to converse with the world in a real than a personated character. That might pass for humour in the Spectator, which would look like arrogance in a writer who sets his name to his work. The fictitious person might condemn those who disapproved him, and extol his own performances without giving offence. He might assume a mock authority, without being looked upon as vain and conceited. The praises or censures of himself fall only upon the creature of his imagination; and, if any one finds fault with him, the author may reply with the philosopher of old, 'Thou dost but beat the case of Anaxarchus.' When I speak in my own private sentiments, I cannot but address myself to my readers in a more submissive manner, and with a just gratitude for the kind reception which they have given to these daily papers, which have been published for almost the space of two years last past.

I hope the apology I have made, as to the license allowable to a feigned character, may excuse any thing which has been said in these discourses of the Spectator and his works; but the imputation of the grossest vanity would still dwell upon me, if I did not give some account by what means I was enabled to keep up the spirit of so long and approved a performance. All the papers marked with a C, an L, an I, or an O, that is to say, all the papers which I have distinguished by any letter in the name of the muse Clio, were given me by the gentleman of whose assistance I formerly boasted in the preface and concluding leaf of my Tatlers. I am indeed much more proud of his long continued friendship, than I should be of the fame of being thought the author of any writings which he himself is capable of producing. I remember, when I finished The Tender Husband, I told him there was nothing I so ardently wished, as that we might some time or other publish a work, written by us both, which should bear the name of The Monument, in memory of our friendship. I heartily wish what I have done here was as honorary to that sacred name, as learning, wit, and humanity, render those pieces which I have taught the reader how to distinguish for his. When the play above-mentioned was last acted, there were so many applauded strokes in it which I had from the same hand, that I thought very meanly of myself that I have never publicly acknowledged them. After I have put other friends upon importuning him to publish dramatic as well as other writings he has by him, I shall end what I think I am obliged to say on this head by giving my reader this hint for the better judging of my productions—that the best comment upon them would be an account when the patron to The Tender Husband was in England or abroad.

The reader will also find some papers which are marked with the letter X, for which he is obliged to the ingenious gentleman who diverted the town with the epilogue to The Distressed Mother. I might have owned these several papers with the free consent of these gentlemen, who did not write them with a design of being known for the authors. But, as a candid and sincere behaviour ought to be preferred to all other considerations, I would not let my heart reproach me with a consciousness of having acquired a praise which is not my right.

The other assistances which I have had have been conveyed by letter, sometimes by whole papers, and other times by short hints from unknown hands. I have not been able to trace favours of this kind with any certainty, but to the following names, which I place in the order wherein I received the obligation, though the first I am going to name can hardly be mentioned in a list wherein he would not deserve the precedence. The persons to whom I am to make these acknowledgments are, Mr. Henry Martyn, Mr. Pope, Mr. Hughes, Mr. Carey of New-college in Oxford, Mr. Tickell of Queen's in the same university, Mr. Parnelle, and Mr. Eusden, of Trinity in Cambridge. Thus, to speak in the language of my late friend, Sir Andrew Freeport, I have balanced my accounts with all my creditors for wit and learning. But as these excellent performances would not have seen the light without the means of this paper, I may still arrogate to myself the merit of their being communicated to the public.

I have nothing more to add, but, having swelled this work to five hundred and fifty-five papers, they will be disposed into seven volumes, four of which are already published, and the three others in the press. It will not be demanded of me why I now leave off, though I must own myself obliged to give an account to the town of my time hereafter; since I retire when their partiality to me is so great, that an edition of the former volumes of Spectators, of above nine thousand each book, is already sold off, and the tax on each half-sheet has brought into the stamp-office, one week with another, above 20*l.* a week, arising from the single paper, notwithstanding it at first reduced it to less than half the number that was usually printed before the tax was laid.

I humbly beseech the continuance of this inclination to favour what I may hereafter produce, and hope I have in my occurrences of life tasted so deeply of pain and sorrow, that I am proof against much more prosperous circumstances than any advantages to which my own industry can possibly exalt me. I am, my good-natured reader, your most obedient, most obliged humble servant,

RICHARD STEELE.

Vos valete et plaudite. Ter.

The following letter regards an ingenious set of gentlemen, who have done me the honour to make me one of their society.

'Dec. 4, 1712.

'Mr. Spectator,—The academy of painting, lately established in London, having done you and themselves the honour to choose you one of their directors; that noble and lively art, which before was entitled to your regard as a Spectator, has an additional claim to you, and you seem to be under a double obligation to take some care of her interests.

'The honour of our country is also concerned in the matter I am going to lay before you. We (and perhaps other nations as well as we) have a national false humanity as well as a national vain glory; and, though we boast ourselves to excel all the world in things wherein we are outdone abroad, in other things we attribute to others a superiority which we ourselves possess. This is what is done, particularly in the art of portrait or face-painting.

'Painting is an art of a vast extent, too great by much for any mortal man to be in full possession of in all its parts; it is enough if any one succeed in painting faces, history, battles, landscapes, sea-pieces, fruit, flowers, or drolls, &c. Nay, no man ever was excellent in all the branches (though many in number,) of these several arts, for a distinct art I take upon me to call every one of those several kinds of painting.

'And as one man may be a good land scape painter, but unable to paint a face or a history tolerably well, and so of the rest; one nation may excel in some kinds of painting, and other kinds may thrive better in other climates.

'Italy may have the preference of all other nations for history painting; Holland for drolls and a neat finished manner of working; France for gay, jaunty, fluttering pictures; and England for portraits; but to give the honour of every one of these kinds of painting to any one of those nations on account of their excellence in any of these parts of it, is like adjudging the prize of heroic, dramatic, lyric, or burlesque poetry to him who has done well in any one of them.

'Where there are the greatest geniuses, and most helps and encouragements, it is reasonable to suppose an art will arrive to the greatest perfection: by this rule let us consider our own country with respect to face-painting. No nation in the world delights so much in having their own, or friends' or relations' pictures; whether from their national good-nature, or having a love to painting, and not being encouraged in the great article of religious pictures, which the purity of our worship refuses the free use of, or from whatever other cause. Our helps are not inferior to those of any other people, but rather they are greater; for what the antique statues and bas-reliefs which Italy enjoys are to the history-painters, the beautiful and noble faces with which England is confessed to abound, are to face-painters; and, besides, we have the greatest number of the works of the best masters in that kind of any people, not without a competent number of those of the most excellent in every other part of painting. And for encouragement, the wealth and generosity of the English nation affords that in such a degree as artists have no reason to complain.

'And accordingly, in fact, face-painting is no where so well performed as in England: I know not whether it has lain in your way to observe it, but I have, and pretend to be a tolerable judge. I have seen what is done abroad; and can assure you, that the honour of that branch of painting is justly due to us. I appeal to the judicious observers for the truth of what I assert. If foreigners have oftentimes, or even for the most part excelled our natives, it ought to be imputed to the advantages they have met with here, joined to their own ingenuity and industry; nor has any one nation distinguished themselves so as to raise an argument in favour of their country: but it is to be observed that neither French nor Italians, nor any one of either nation, notwithstanding all our prejudices in their favour, have, or ever had, for any considerable time, any character among us as face-painters.

'This honour is due to our own country, and has been so for near an age: so that, instead of going to Italy, or elsewhere, one that designs for portrait-painting ought to study in England. Hither such should come from Holland, France, Italy, Germany, &c. as he that intends to practise any other kinds of painting should go to those parts where it is in the greatest perfection. It is said the blessed Virgin descended from heaven to sit to St. Luke. I dare venture to affirm that, if she should desire another Madonna to be painted by the life, she would come to England; and am of opinion that your present president, Sir Godfrey Kneller, from his improvement since he arrived in this kingdom, would perform that office better than any foreigner living. I am, with all possible respect, sir, your most humble and most obedient servant, &c.'

⁂ The ingenious letter signed the Weather Glass, with several others, were received, but came too late.

POSTSCRIPT.

It had not come to my knowledge, when I left off the Spectator, that I owe several excellent sentiments and agreeable pieces in this work to Mr. Ince, of Gray's-Inn.*

R. STEELE.

---

* This paper concluded the seventh volume of the Spectator, as originally published. The intermediate time was filled up by our authors in the production of the Guardian.

No. 556.] *Friday, June* 18, 1714.

> Qualis ubi in lucem coluber mala gramina pastus
> Frigida, sub terra tumidum quem bruma tegebat;
> Nunc positis novus exuviis, nitidusque juventa,
> Lubrica convolvit sublato pectore terga
> Arduus ad solem, et linguis micat ore trisulcis.
>
> *Virg. Æn.* ii. 471

> So shines, renew'd in youth, the crested snake,
> Who slept the winter in a thorny brake:
> And casting off his slough, when spring returns,
> Now looks aloft, and with new glory burns:
> Restor'd with pois'nous herbs, his ardent sides
> Reflect the sun, and rais'd on spires he rides;
> High o'er the grass hissing he rolls along,
> And brandishes by fits his forky tongue.—*Dryden.*

Upon laying down the office of Spectator, I acquainted the world with my design of electing a new club, and of opening my mouth in it after a most solemn manner. Both the election and the ceremony are now past; but not finding it so easy, as I at first imagined, to break through a fifty years' silence, I would not venture into the world under the character of a man who pretends to talk like other people, until I had arrived at a full freedom of speech.

I shall reserve for another time the history of such club or clubs of which I am now a talkative but unworthy member; and shall here give an account of this surprising change which has been produced in me, and which I look upon to be as remarkable an accident as any recorded in history, since that which happened to the son of Crœsus, after having been many years as much tongue-tied as myself.

Upon the first opening of my mouth, I made a speech, consisting of about half a dozen well-turned periods; but grew so very hoarse upon it, that for three days together, instead of finding the use of my tongue, I was afraid that I had quite lost it. Besides, the unusual extension of my muscles on this occasion made my face ache on both sides to such a degree, that nothing but an invincible resolution and perseverance could have prevented me from falling back to my monosyllables.

I afterwards made several essays towards speaking; and that I might not be startled at my own voice, which has happened to me more than once, I used to read aloud in my chamber, and have often stood in the middle of the street to call a coach, when I knew there was none within hearing.

When I was thus grown pretty well acquainted with my own voice, I laid hold of all opportunities to exert it. Not caring however to speak much by myself, and to draw upon me the whole attention of those I conversed with, I used for some time to walk every morning in the Mall, and talk in chorus with a parcel of Frenchmen. I found my modesty greatly relieved by the communicative temper of this nation, who are so very sociable as to think they are never better company than when they are all opening at the same time.

I then fancied I might receive great benefit from female conversation, and that I should have a convenience of talking with the greater freedom, when I was not under any impediment of thinking: I therefore threw myself into an assembly of ladies, but could not for my life get in a word among them; and found that if I did not change my company, I was in danger of being reduced to my primitive taciturnity.

The coffee-houses have ever since been my chief places of resort, where I have made the greatest improvements; in order to which I have taken a particular care never to be of the same opinion with the man I conversed with. I was a tory at Button's, and a whig at Child's, a friend to the Englishman, or an advocate for the Examiner, as it best served my turn: some fancy me a great enemy to the French king, though in reality I only make use of him for a help to discourse. In short, I wrangle and dispute for exercise; and have carried this point so far, that I was once like to have been run through the body for making a little too free with my betters.

In a word, I am quite another man to what I was.

————Nil fuit unquam
Tam dispar sibi.————
Hor. Sat. iii. Lib. 1. 18.

Nothing was ever so unlike itself.

My old acquaintance scarce know me; nay, I was asked the other day by a Jew at Jonathan's, whether I was not related to a dumb gentleman, who used to come to that coffee-house? But I think I never was better pleased in my life than about a week ago, when, as I was battling it across the table with a young Templar, his companion gave him a pull by the sleeve, begging him to come away, for that the old prig would talk him to death.

Being now a very good proficient in discourse, I shall appear in the world with this addition to my character, that my countrymen may reap the fruits of my new-acquired loquacity.

Those who have been present at public disputes in the university know that it is usual to maintain heresies for argument's sake. I have heard a man a most impudent Socinian for half an hour, who has been an orthodox divine all his life after. I have taken the same method to accomplish myself in the gift of utterance, having talked above a twelvemonth, not so much for the benefit of my hearers, as of myself. But, since I have now gained the faculty I have been so long endeavouring after, I intend to make a right use of it, and shall think myself obliged for the future, to speak always in truth and sincerity of heart. While a man is learning to fence, he practises both on friend and foe; but when he is a master in the art, he never exerts it but on what he thinks the right side.

That this last allusion may not give my reader a wrong idea of my design in this paper, I must here inform him, that the author of it is of no faction; that he is a friend to no interests but those of truth and virtue; nor a foe to any but those of vice and folly. Though I make more noise in the world than I used to do, I am still resolved to act in it as an indifferent spectator. It is not my ambition to increase the number either of whigs or tories, but of wise and good men; and I could heartily wish there were not faults common to both parties, which afford me sufficient matter to work upon, without descending to those which are peculiar to either.

If in a multitude of counsellors there is safety, we ought to think ourselves the securest nation in the world. Most of our garrets are inhabited by statesmen, who watch over the liberties of their country, and make a shift to keep themselves from starving by taking into their care the properties of their fellow-subjects.

As these politicians of both sides have already worked the nation into a most unnatural ferment, I shall be so far from endeavouring to raise it to a greater height, that, on the contrary, it shall be the chief tendency of my papers to inspire my countrymen with a mutual good-will and benevolence. Whatever faults either party may be guilty of, they are rather inflamed than cured by those reproaches which they cast upon one another. The most likely method of rectifying any man's conduct, is by recommending to him the principles of truth and honour, religion and virtue: and so long as he acts with an eye to these principles, whatever party he is of, he cannot fail of being a good Englishman, and a lover of his country.

As for the persons concerned in this work, the names of all of them, or at least of such as desire it, shall be published hereafter: until which time I must entreat the courteous reader to suspend his curiosity, and rather to consider what is written, than who they are that write it.

Having thus adjusted all necessary preliminaries with my reader, I shall not trouble him with any more prefatory discourses, but proceed in my old method, and entertain him with speculations on every useful subject that falls in my way. C.

No. 557.] *Monday, June* 21, 1714.

Quippe domum timet ambiguam Tyriosque bilingues.
Virg. Æn. i. 665.

He fears the ambiguous race, and Tyrians double tongu'd.

'THERE is nothing,' says Plato, 'so delightful as the hearing or the speaking of truth.' For this reason there is no conversation so agreeable as that of the man of integrity, who hears without any intention to betray, and speaks without any intention to deceive.

Among all the accounts which are given of Cato, I do not remember one that more redounds to his honour than the following passage related by Plutarch. As an advocate was pleading the cause of his client before one of the prætors, he could only produce a single witness in a point where the law required the testimony of two persons; upon which the advocate insisted on the integrity of that person whom he had produced; but the prætor told him, that where the law required two witnesses he would not accept of one, though it were Cato himself. Such a speech from a person who sat at the head of a court of justice, while Cato was still living, shows us, more than a thousand examples, the high reputation this great man had gained among his contemporaries upon the account of his sincerity.

When such an inflexible integrity is a little softened and qualified by the rules of conversation and good-breeding, there is not a more shining virtue in the whole catalogue of social duties. A man however ought to take great care not to publish himself out of his veracity, nor to refind his behaviour to the prejudice of his virtue.

This subject is exquisitely treated in the most elegant sermon of the great British preacher.* I shall beg leave to transcribe out of it two or three sentences, as a proper introduction to a very curious letter, which I shall make the chief entertainment of this speculation.

'The old English plainness and sincerity, that generous integrity of nature, and honesty of disposition, which always argues true greatness of mind, and is usually accompanied with undaunted courage and resolution, is in a great measure lost among us.

'The dialect of conversation is now-a-days so swelled with vanity and compliment, and so surfeited (as I may say) of expressions of kindness and respect, that if a man that lived an age or two ago should return into the world again, he would really want a dictionary to help him to understand his own language, and to know the true intrinsic value of the phrase in fashion; and would hardly at first believe at what a low rate the highest strains and expressions of kindness imaginable do commonly pass in current payment; and when he should come to understand it, it would be a great while before he could bring himself, with a good countenance, and a good conscience, to converse with men upon equal terms and in their own way.'

I have by me a letter which I look upon as a great curiosity, and which may serve as an exemplification to the foregoing passage, cited out of this most excellent prelate. It is said to have been written in king Charles the Second's reign by the ambassador of Bantam,† a little after his arrival in England.

'MASTER,—The people where I now am have tongues farther from their hearts than from London to Bantam; and thou knowest the inhabitants of one of these places do not know what is done in the other. They call thee and thy subjects barbarians, because we speak what we mean; and account themselves a civilized people, because they speak one thing and mean another; truth they call barbarity, and falsehood politeness. Upon my first landing, one, who was sent from the king of this place to meet me, told me that he was extremely sorry for the storm I had met with just before my arrival. I was troubled to hear him grieve and afflict himself upon my account; but in less than a quarter of an hour he smiled, and was as merry as if nothing had happened. Another who came with him told me by my interpreter, he should be glad to do me any service that lay in his power. Upon which I desired him to carry one of my portmanteaus for me; but, instead of serving me according to his promise, he laughed, and bid another do it. I lodged, the first week, at the house of one who desired me to think myself at home, and to consider his house as my own. Accordingly, I the next morning began to knock down one of the walls of it, in order to let in the fresh air, and had packed up some of the household goods, of which I intended to have made thee a present; but the false varlet no sooner saw me falling to work, but he sent word to desire me to give over, for that he would have no such doings in his house. I had not been long in this nation before I was told by one, for whom I had asked a certain favour from the chief of the king's servants, whom they here call the lord treasurer, that I had eternally obliged him. I was so surprised at his gratitude, that I could not forbear saying, "What service is there which one man can do for another, that can oblige him to all eternity!" However, I only asked him, for my reward, that he would lend me his eldest daughter during my stay in this country; but I quickly found that he was as treacherous as the rest of his countrymen.

'At my first going to court, one of the great men almost put me out of countenance, by asking ten thousand pardons of me for only treading by accident upon my toe. They call this kind of lie a compliment; for, when they are civil to a great man they tell him untruths, for which thou wouldest order any of thy officers of state to receive a hundred blows upon his foot. I do not know how I shall negotiate any thing with this people, since there is so little credit to be given to them. When I go to see the king's scribe, I am generally told that he is not at home, though perhaps I saw him go into his house almost the very moment before. Thou wouldest fancy that the whole nation are physicians, for the first question they always ask me is, how I do; I have this question put to me above a hundred times a-day. Nay, they are not

* Archbishop Tillotson, vol. ii. sermon i. folio edition
† In 1682.

only thus inquisitive after my health, but wish it in a more solemn manner, with a full glass in their hands, every time I sit with them at table, though at the same time they would persuade me to drink their liquors in such quantities as I have found by experience will make me sick. They often pretend to pray for thy health also in the same manner; but I have more reason to expect it from the goodness of thy constitution than the sincerity of their wishes. May thy slave escape in safety from this double-tongued race of men, and live to lay nimself once more at thy feet in the royal city of Bantam !'

No. 558.] *Wednesday, June* 23, 1714.

Qui fit, Mæcenas, ut nemo, quam sibi sortem
Seu ratio dederi• ·eu fors objecerit, illa
Contentus vivat: laudet diversa sequentes?
O fortunati mercatores, gravis annis
Miles ait, multo jam fractus membra labore!
Contra mercator, navim jactantibus austris,
Militia est potior. Quid enim? concurritur: hora
Momento cita mors venit, aut victoria læta.
Agricolam laudat juris legumque peritus,
Sub galli cantum consultor ubi ostia pulsat.
Ille, datis vadibus, qui rure extractus in urbem est,
Solos felices viventes clamat in urbe.
Cætera de genere hoc (adeo sunt multa) loquacem
Delassare valent Fabium. Ne te morer, audi
Quo rem deducam. Si quis Deus, en ego, dicat,
Jam faciam quod vultis: eris tu, qui modo miles,
Mercator: tu consultus modo, rusticus. Hinc vos,
Vos hinc mutatis discedite partibus. Eja,
Quid statis? Nolint. Atqui licet esse beatis.
Hor. Sat. i. Lib. 1. 1.

Whence is't, Mæcenas, that so few approve •
The state they're plac'd in, and incline to rove;
Whether against their will by fate impos'd,
Or by consent and prudent choice espous'd?
Happy the merchant the old soldier cries,
Broke with fatigues and warlike enterprise
The merchant, when the dreaded hurricane
Tosses his wealthy cargo on the main,
Applauds the wars and toils of a campaign:
There an engagement soon decides your doom,
Bravely to die, or come victorious home.
The lawyer vows the farmer's life is best,
When at the dawn the clients break his rest.
The farmer, having put in bail t'appear,
And forc'd to town, cries they are happiest there:
With thousands more of this inconstant race,
Would tire e'en Fabius to relate each case.
Not to detain you longer, pray attend
The issue of all this: Should Jove descend,
And grant to every man his rash demand,
To run his lengths with a neglectful hand;
First, grant the harass'd warrior a release;
Bid him to trade, and try the faithless seas,
To purchase treasure and declining ease;
Next call the pleader from his learned strife,
To the calm blessings of a country life;
And, with these separate demands dismiss
Each suppliant to enjoy the promis'd bliss:
Don't you believe they'd run? Not one will move,
Though proffer'd to be happy from above.—*Horneck.*

It is a celebrated thought of Socrates, that if all the misfortunes of mankind were cast into a public stock, in order to be equally distributed among the whole species, those who now think themselves the most unhappy, would prefer the share they are already possessed of before that which could fall to them by such a division. Horace has carried this thought a great deal farther in the motto of my paper, which implies, that the hardships or misfortunes we lie under are more easy to us than those of any other person would be, in case we would change conditions with him.

As I was ruminating upon these two remarks, and seated in my elbow chair, I insensibly fell asleep; when on a sudden, methought, there was a proclamation made by Jupiter, that every mortal should bring in his griefs and calamities, and throw them together in a heap. There was a large plain appointed for this purpose. I took my stand in the centre of it, and saw with a great deal of pleasure the whole human species marching one after another, and throwing down their several loads, which immediately grew up into a prodigious mountain, that seemed to rise above the clouds.

There was a certain lady of a thin airy shape, who was very active in this solemnity. She carried a magnifying glass in one of her hands, and was clothed in a loose flowing robe, embroidered with several figures of fiends and spectres, that discovered themselves in a thousand chimerical shapes, as her garment hovered in the wind. There was something wild and distracted in her looks. Her name was Fancy. She led up every mortal to the appointed place, after having very officiously assisted him in making up his pack, and laying it upon his shoulders. My heart melted within me to see my fellow-creatures groaning under their respective burdens, and to consider that prodigious bulk of human calamities which lay before me.

There were however several persons who gave me great diversion upon this occasion. I observed one bringing in a fardel very carefully concealed under an old embroidered cloak, which, upon his throwing it into the heap, I discovered to be Poverty. Another, after a great deal of puffing, threw down his luggage, which, upon examining, I found to be his wife.

There were multitudes of lovers saddled with very whimsical burdens composed of darts and flames; but, what was very odd, though they sighed as if their hearts would break under these bundles of calamities, they could not persuade themselves to cast them into the heap, when they came up to to it; but, after a few faint efforts, shook their heads, and marched away as heavy loaden as they came. I saw multitudes of old women throw down their wrinkles, and several young ones who stripped themselves of a tawny skin. There were very great heaps of red noses, large lips, and rusty teeth. The truth of it is, I was surprised to see the greatest part of the mountain made up of bodily deformities. Observing one advancing towards the heap with a larger cargo than ordinary upon his back, I found upon his near approach that it was only a natural hump, which he disposed of, with great joy of heart, among this collection of human miseries. There were likewise distempers of all sorts; though I could not but observe, that there were many more imaginary than real. One little packet I could not but take notice of, which was a complication of all the diseases incident to human nature, and was in the hand of a great many fine people: this was called the spleen. But what most of all surprised me, was a remark I made, that there was not a single vice or folly thrown into the whole heap; at which I was very much astonished, having concluded within myself, that every one would take this opportunity of getting rid of his passions, prejudices, and frailties.

I took notice in particular of a very profligate fellow, who I did not question came loaded with his crimes: but upon searching into his bundle I found, that instead of throwing his guilt from him, he had only laid down his memory. He was followed by another worthless rogue, who flung away his modesty instead of his ignorance.

When the whole race of mankind had thus cast their burdens, the phantom which had been so busy on this occasion, seeing me an idle Spectator of what had passed, approached towards me. I grew uneasy at her presence, when of a sudden she held her magnifying glass full before my eyes. I no sooner saw my face in it, but was startled at the shortness of it, which now appeared to me in its utmost aggravation. The immoderate breadth of the features made me very much out of humour with my own countenance, upon which I threw it from me like a mask. It happened very luckily that one who stood by me had just before thrown down his visage, which it seems was too long for him. It was indeed extended to a most shameful length; I believe the very chin was, modestly speaking, as long as my whole face. We had both of us an opportunity of mending ourselves; and all the contributions being now brought in, every man was at liberty to exchange his misfortunes for those of another person. But as there arose many new incidents in the sequel of my vision, I shall reserve them for the subject of my next paper.

No. 559.] *Friday, June 25, 1714.*

Quid causæ est, merito quin illis Jupiter ambas
Iratus buccas inflet, neque se fore posthac
Tam facilem dicat, votis ut præbeat aurem?
Hor. Sat. i. Lib. 1. 20.

Were it not just that Jove, provok'd to heat,
Should drive these triflers from the hallow'd seat,
And unrelenting stand when they entreat?
Horneck.

In my last paper, I gave my reader a sight of that mountain of miseries which was made up of those several calamities that afflict the minds of men. I saw with unspeakable pleasure the whole species thus delivered from its sorrows; though at the same time, as we stood round the heap, and surveyed the several materials of which it was composed, there was scarcely a mortal in this vast multitude, who did not discover what he thought pleasures of life, and wondered how the owners of them ever came to look upon them as burdens and grievances.

As we were regarding very attentively this confusion of miseries, this chaos of calamity, Jupiter issued out a second proclamation, that every one was now at liberty to exchange his affliction, and to return to his habitation with any such other bundle as should be delivered to him.

Upon this, Fancy began again to bestir herself, and, parcelling out the whole heap with incredible activity, recommended to every one his particular packet. The hurry and confusion at this time was not to be expressed. Some observations which I made upon this occasion, I shall communicate to the public. A venerable gray-headed man, who had laid down the colick, and who I found wanted an heir to his estate, snatched up an undutiful son that had been thrown into the heap by his angry father. The graceless youth, in less than a quarter of an hour, pulled the old gentleman by the beard, and had like to have knocked his brains out; so that meeting the true father, who came towards him with a fit of the gripes, he begged him to take his son again, and give him back his colick; but they were incapable either of them to recede from the choice they had made. A poor galley-slave, who had thrown down his chains, took up the gout in their stead, but made such wry faces, that one might easily perceive he was no great gainer by the bargain. It was pleasant enough to see the several exchanges that were made, for sickness against poverty, hunger against want of appetite, and care against pain.

The female world were very busy among themselves in bartering for features: one was trucking a lock of gray hairs for a carbuncle, another was making over a short waist for a pair of round shoulders, and a third cheapening a bad face for a lost reputation: but on all these occasions there was not one of them who did not think the new blemish, as soon as she had got it into her possession, much more disagreeable than the old one. I made the same observation on every other misfortune or calamity which every one in the assembly brought upon himself in lieu of what he had parted with: whether it be that all the evils which befal us, are in some measure suited and proportioned to our strength, or that every evil becomes more supportable by our being accustomed to it, I shall not determine.

I could not from my heart forbear pitying the poor hump-backed gentleman mentioned in the former paper, who went off a very well shaped person with a stone in his bladder; nor the fine gentleman who had struck up this bargain with him, that limped through a whole assembly of ladies, who used to admire him, with a pair of shoulders peeping over his head.

I must not omit my own particular adventure. My friend with a long visage had no sooner taken upon him my short face, but he made such a grotesque figure in it, that as I looked upon him I could not forbear laughing at myself, insomuch that I put my own face out of countenance. The poor gentleman was so sensible of the ridicule, that I found he was ashamed of what he had done: on the other side, I found that I myself had no great reason to triumph, for as I went to touch my forehead I missed the place, and clapped my finger upon my upper lip. Besides, as my nose was exceeding prominent, I gave it two or three unlucky knocks as I was playing my hand about my face, and aiming at some other part of it. I saw two other gentlemen by me who were in the same ridiculous circumstances. These had made a foolish swap between a couple of thick bandy legs and two long trap-sticks that had no calves to them. One of these looked like a man walking upon stilts, and was so lifted up into the air, above his ordinary height, that his head turned round with it; while the other made such awkward circles, as he attempted to walk, that he scarcely knew how to move forward upon his new supporters. Observing him to be a pleasant kind of fellow, I stuck my cane on the ground, and told him I would lay him a bottle of wine that he did not march up to it on a line that I drew for him in a quarter of an hour.

The heap was at last distributed among the two sexes, who made a most piteous sight, as they wandered up and down under the pressure of their several burdens. The whole plain was filled with murmurs and complaints, groans and lamentations. Jupiter at length taking compassion on the poor mortals, ordered them a second time to lay down their loads, with a design to give every one his own again. They discharged themselves with a great deal of pleasure: after which, the phantom who had led them into such gross delusion was commanded to disappear. There was sent in her stead a goddess of a quite different figure; her motions were steady and composed, and her aspect serious but cheerful. She every now and then cast her eyes towards heaven, and fixed them upon Jupiter: her name was Patience. She had no sooner placed herself by the Mount of Sorrows, but, what I thought very remarkable, the whole heap sunk to such a degree, that it did not appear a third part so big as it was before. She afterwards returned every man his own proper calamity, and teaching him how to bear it in the most commodious manner, he marched off with it contentedly, being very well pleased that he had not been left to his own choice as to the kind of evil which fell to his lot.

Besides the several pieces of morality to be drawn out of this vision, I learnt from it never to repine at my own misfortunes, or to envy the happiness of another, since it is impossible for any man to form a right judgment of his neighbour's sufferings; for which reason also I have determined never to think too lightly of another's complaints, but to regard the sorrows of my fellow-creatures with sentiments of humanity and compassion. O

No. 560.] *Monday, June* 28, 1714.

——Verba intermissa retentat.
Ovid, Met. Lib. i. 746.

He tries his tongue, his silence softly breaks.
Dryden.

Every one has heard of the famous conjuror, who, according to the opinion of the vulgar, has studied himself dumb: for which reason, as it is believed, he delivers out his oracles in writing. Be that as it will, the blind Tiresias was not more famous in Greece than this dumb artist has been for some years last past in the cities of London and Westminster. Thus much for the profound gentleman who honours me with the following epistle.

'From my cell, June 24, 1714.

'Sir,—Being informed that you have lately got the use of your tongue, I have some thoughts of following your example, that I may be a fortune-teller, properly speaking. I am grown weary of my taciturnity, and having served my country many years under the title of "the dumb doctor," I shall now prophesy by word of mouth, and (as Mr. Lee says of the magpie, who you know was a great fortune-teller among the ancients) chatter futurity. I have hitherto chosen to receive questions and return answers in writing, that I might avoid the tediousness and trouble of debates, my querists being generally of a humour to think that they have never predictions enough for their money. In short, sir, my case has been something like that of those discreet animals the monkeys, who, as the Indians tell us, can speak if they would, but purposely avoid it that they may not be made to work. I have hitherto gained a livelihood by holding my tongue, but shall now open my mouth in order to fill it. If I appear a little word-bound in my first solutions and responses, I hope it will not be imputed to any want of foresight, but to the long disuse of speech. I doubt not by this invention to have all my former customers over again; for, if I have promised any of them lovers or husbands, riches or good luck, it is my design to confirm to them, *viva voce*, what I have already given them under my hand. If you will honour me with a visit, I will compliment you with the first opening of my mouth: and if you please, you may make an entertaining dialogue out of the conversation of two dumb men. Excuse this trouble, worthy sir, from one who has been a long time, your silent admirer,

'CORNELIUS AGRIPPA.'

I have received the following letter, or rather billet-doux, from a pert young baggage, who congratulates with me upon the same occasion.

'June 23, 1714.

'DEAR MR. PRATE-APACE,—I am a member of a female society who call ourselves the Chit-chat club, and am ordered by the whole sisterhood to congratulate you upon the use of your tongue. We have all of us a mighty mind to hear you talk; and if you will take your place among us for an evening, we have unanimously agreed to allow you one minute in ten, without interruption. I am, sir, your humble servant, S. T.

'P. S. You may find us at my lady Betty Clack's, who will leave orders with her porter, that if an elderly gentleman, with a short face, inquires for her, he shall be admitted, and no questions asked.'

As this particular paper shall consist wholly of what I have received from my correspondents, I shall fill up the remaining part of it with other congratulatory letters of the same nature.

'Oxford, June 25, 1714.

'SIR,—We are here wonderfully pleased with the opening of your mouth, and very frequently open ours in approbation of your design; especially since we find you are resolved to preserve your taciturnity as to all party matters. We do not question but you are as great an orator as sir Hudibras, of whom the poet sweetly sings.

"———He could not ope
His mouth, but out there flew a trope."

If you will send us down the half dozen well-turned periods, that produced such dismal effects in your muscles, we will deposit them near an old manuscript of Tully's orations, among the archives of the university; for we all agree with you, that there is not a more remarkable accident recorded in history, since that which happened to the son of Crœsus; nay, I believe you might have gone higher, and have added Balaam's ass. We are impatient to see more of your productions; and expect what words will next fall from you with as much attention as those who were set to watch the speaking head which friar Bacon formerly erected in this place. We are, worthy sir, your most humble servants, 'B. R. T. D. &c.'

'Middle-Temple, June 24.

'HONEST SPEC,—I am very glad to hear that thou beginnest to prate; and find, by thy yesterday's vision, thou art so used to it, that thou canst not forbear talking in thy sleep. Let me only advise thee to speak like other men; for I am afraid thou wilt be very queer, if thou dost not intend to use the phrases in fashion, as thou callest them in thy second paper. Hast thou a mind to pass for a Bantamite, or to make us all Quakers? I do assure thee, dear Spec, I am not polished out of my veracity when I subscribe myself, thy constant admirer, and humble servant,

'FRANK TOWNLY.'

No. 561.] *Wednesday, June 30, 1714.*

———Paulatim abolere Sichæum
Incipit, et vivo tentat prævertere amore
Jampridem resides animos desuetaque corda.
Virg. Æn. i. 724.

But he———
Works in the pliant bosom of the fair,
And moulds her heart anew, and blots her former care.
The dead is to the living love resign'd,
And all Æneas enters in her mind.—*Dryden.*

'SIR,—I am a tall, broad-shouldered, impudent, black fellow, and as I thought, every way qualified for a rich widow: but after having tried my fortune for above three years together, I have not been able to get one single relict in the mind. My first attacks were generally successful, but always broke off as soon as they came to the word settlement. Though I have not improved my fortune this way, I have my experience, and have learnt several secrets which may be of use to these unhappy gentlemen, who are commonly distinguished by the name of widow-hunters, and who do not know that this tribe of women are, generally speaking, as much upon the catch as themselves. I shall here communicate to you the mysteries of a certain female cabal of this order, who call themselves the Widow-club. This club consists of nine experienced dames, who take their places once a week round a large oval table.

'1. Mrs. President is a person who has disposed of six husbands, and is now determined to take a seventh; being of opinion that there is as much virtue in the touch of a seventh husband as of a seventh son. Her comrades are as follow:

'2. Mrs. Snap, who has four jointures, by four different bed-fellows, of four different shires. She is at present upon the point of marriage with a Middlesex man, and is said to have an ambition of extending her possessions through all the counties in England on this side the Trent.

'3. Mrs. Medlar, who, after two husbands and a gallant, is now wedded to an old gentleman of sixty. Upon her making her report to the club after a week's co habitation, she is still allowed to sit as a widow, and accordingly takes her place at the board.

'4. The widow Quick, married within a fortnight after the death of her last husband. Her weeds have served her thrice, and are still as good as new.

'5. Lady Catherine Swallow. She was a widow at eighteen, and has since buried a second husband and two coachmen.

'6. The lady Waddle. She was married in the fifteenth year of her age to Sir Simon Waddle, knight, aged threescore and twelve, by whom she had twins nine months after his decease. In the fifty-fifth year of her age she was married to James Spindle, Esq. a youth of one-and-twenty, who did not outlive the honey-moon.

'7. Deborah Conquest. The case of this lady is something particular. She is the relict of Sir Sampson Conquest, some time justice of the quorum. Sir Sampson was seven foot high, and two foot in breadth from the tip of one shoulder to the other. He had married three wives, who all of them died in child-bed. This terrified the whole sex, who none of them durst venture on Sir Sampson. At length Mrs. Deborah undertook him, and gave so good an account of him, that in three year's time she very fairly laid him out, and measured his length upon the ground. This exploit has gained her so great a reputation in the club, that they have added Sir Sampson's three victories to her's, and give her the merit of a fourth widowhood; and she takes her place accordingly.

'8. The widow Wildfire, relict of Mr. John Wildfire, fox-hunter, who broke his neck over a six-bar gate. She took his death so much to heart, that it was thought it would have put an end to her life, had she not diverted her sorrows by receiving the addresses of a gentleman in the neighbourhood, who made love to her in the second month of her widowhood. The gentleman was discarded in a fortnight for the sake of a young templar, who had the possession of her for six weeks after, till he was beaten out by a broken officer, who likewise gave up his place to a gentleman at court. The courtier was as short-lived a favourite as his predecessors, but had the pleasure to see himself succeeded by a long series of lovers, who followed the widow Wildfire to the thirty-seventh year of her age, at which time there ensued a cessation of ten years, when John Felt, haberdasher, took it in his head to be in love with her, and it is thought will very suddenly carry her off.

'9. The last is pretty Mrs. Runnet, who broke her first husband's heart before she was sixteen, at which time she was entered of the club, but soon after left it upon account of a second, whom she made so quick a despatch of, that she returned to her seat in less than a twelvemonth. This young matron is looked upon as the most rising member of the society, and will probably be in the president's chair before she dies.

'These ladies, upon their first institution, resolved to give the pictures of their deceased husbands to the club-room; but two of them bringing in their dead at full length, they covered all the walls. Upon which they came to a second resolution, that every matron should give her own picture, and set it round with her husband's in miniature.

'As they have most of them the misfortune to be troubled with the colick, they have a noble cellar of cordials and strong waters. When they grow maudlin, they are very apt to commemorate their former partners with a tear. But ask them which of their husbands they condole, they are not able to tell you, and discover plainly that they do not weep so much for the loss of a husband as for the want of one.

'The principal rule by which the whole society are to govern themselves, is this, to cry up the pleasures of a single life upon all occasions, in order to deter the rest of their sex from marriage, and engross the whole male world to themselves.

'They are obliged, when any one makes love to a member of the society, to communicate his name, at which the whole assembly sit upon his reputation, person, fortune, and good humour, and if they find him qualified for a sister of the club, they lay their heads together how to make him sure. By this means they are acquainted with all the widow-hunters about town, who often afford them great diversion. There is an honest Irish gentleman, it seems, who knows nothing of this society, but at different times has made love to the whole club.

'Their conversation often turns upon their former husbands, and it is very diverting to hear them relate their several arts and stratagems with which they amused the jealous, pacified the choleric, or wheedled the good-natured man, till at last, to use the club phrase, "they sent him out of the house with his heels foremost."

'The politics which are most cultivated by this society of she-Machiavels relate chiefly to these two points, how to treat a lover, and how to manage a husband. As for the first set of artifices, they are too numerous to come within the compass of your paper, and shall therefore be reserved for a second letter.

'The management of a husband is built upon the following doctrines, which are universally assented to by the whole club. Not to give him his head at first. Not to allow him too great freedoms and familiarities. Not to be treated by him like a raw girl, but as a woman that knows the world. Not to lessen any thing of her former figure. To celebrate the generosity, or any other virtue, of a deceased husband, which she would recommend to his successor. To turn away all his old friends and servants, that she may have the dear man to herself. To make him disinherit the undutiful children of any former wife. Never to be thoroughly convinced of his affection, until he has made over to her all his goods and chattels.

'After so long a letter, I am, without more ceremony, your humble servant, &c.'

No. 562.] *Friday, July 2, 1714.*

———Præsens, absens ut sies.
Ter. Eun. Act i. Sc. 2.

Be present as if absent.

'It is a hard and nice subject for a man to speak of himself,' says Cowley; 'it grates his own heart to say any thing of disparagement, and the reader's ears to hear any thing of praise from him.' Let the tenour of his discourse be what it will upon this subject, it generally proceeds from vanity. An ostentatious man will rather relate a blunder or an absurdity he has committed, than be debarred of talking of his own dear person.

Some very great writers have been guilty of this fault. It is observed of Tully in particular, that his works run very much in the first person, and that he takes all occasions of doing himself justice. 'Does he think,' says Brutus, 'that his consulship deserves more applause than my putting Cæsar to death, because I am not perpetually talking of the ides of March, as he is of the nones of December?' I need not acquaint my learned reader, that in the ides of March, Brutus destroyed Cæsar, and that Cicero quashed the conspiracy of Catiline in the calends of December. How shocking soever this great man's talking of himself might have been to his contemporaries, I must confess I am never better pleased than when he is on this subject. Such openings of the heart give a man a thorough insight into his personal character, and illustrate several passages in the history of his life; besides that, there is some little pleasure in discovering the infirmity of a great man, and seeing how the opinion he has of himself agrees with what the world entertains of him.

The gentlemen of Port Royal, who were more eminent for their learning and for their humility than any other in France, banished the way of speaking in the first person out of all their works, as rising from vain-glory and self-conceit. To show their particular aversion to it, they branded this form of writing with the name of an egotism; a figure not to be found among the ancient rhetoricians.

The most violent egotism which I have met with in the course of my reading, is that of Cardinal Wolsey, *ego et rex meus*, 'I and my king;' as perhaps the most eminent egotist that ever appeared in the world was Montaigne, the author of the celebrated Essays. This lively old Gascon has woven all his bodily infirmities into his works; and, after having spoken of the faults or virtues of any other men, immediately publishes to the world how it stands with himself in that particular. Had he kept his own counsel, he might have passed for a much better man, though perhaps he would not have been so diverting an author. The title of an Essay promises perhaps a discourse upon Virgil or Julius Cæsar; but, when you look into it, you are sure to meet with more upon Monsieur Montaigne than of either of them. The younger Scaliger, who seems to have been no great friend to this author, after having acquainted the world that his father sold herrings, adds these words: *La grande fadaise de Montaigne, qui a écrit qu'il aimoit mieux le vin blanc.—Que diable a-t-on à faire de sçavoir ce qu'il aime?* 'For my part,' says Montaigne, 'I am a great lover of your white wines.'—'What the devil signifies it to the public,' says Scaliger, 'whether he is a lover of white wines or of red wines?'

I cannot here forbear mentioning a tribe of egotists, for whom I have always had a mortal aversion—I mean the authors of memoirs, who are never mentioned in any works but their own, and who raise all their productions out of this single figure of speech.

Most of our modern prefaces savour very strongly of the egotism. Every insignificant author fancies it of importance to the world to know that he writ his book in the country, that he did it to pass away some of his idle hours, that it was published at the importunity of friends, or that his natural temper, studies, or conversations, directed him to the choice of his subject:

'———Id populus curat scilicet.'

Such informations cannot but be highly improving to the reader.

In works of humour especially, when a man writes under a fictitious personage, the talking of one's self may give some diversion to the public; but I would advise every other writer never to speak of himself, unless there be something very considerable in his character; though I am sensible this rule will be of little use in the world, because there is no man who fancies his thoughts worth publishing that does not look upon himself as a considerable person.

I shall close this paper with a remark upon such as are egotists in conversation: these are generally the vain or shallow part of mankind, people being naturally full of themselves when they have nothing else in them. There is one kind of egotist which is very common in the world, though I do not remember that any writer has taken notice of them; I mean those empty conceited fellows who repeat, as sayings of their own, or some of their particular friends, several jests which were made before they were born, and which every one who has conversed in the world has heard a hundred times over. A forward young fellow of my acquaintance was very guilty of this absurdity: he would be always laying a new scene for some old piece of wit, and telling us, that, as he and Jack Such-a-one were together, one or t'other of them had such a conceit on such an occasion: upon which he would laugh very heartily, and wonder the company did not join with him. When his mirth was over, I have often reprehended him out of Terence, *Tuumne, obsecro te, hoc dictum erat? vetus credidi.* But finding him still incorrigible, and having a kindness for the young coxcomb, who was otherwise a good-natured fellow, I recommended to his perusal the Oxford and Cambridge jests, with several little pieces of pleasantry of the same nature. Upon the reading of them, he was under no small confusion to find that all his jokes had passed through several editions, and that what he thought a new conceit, and had appropriated to his own use, had appeared in print before he or his ingenious friends were ever heard of. This had so good an effect upon him, that he is content at present to pass for a man of plain sense in his ordinary conversation, and is never facetious but when he knows his company.

No. 563.] *Monday, July 5, 1714.*

——Magni nominis umbra. *Lucan.* Lib. i. 135.

The shadow of a mighty name.

I SHALL entertain my reader with two very curious letters. The first of them comes from a chimerical person, who, I believe, never writ to any body before.

'SIR,—I am descended from the ancient family of the Blanks, a name well known among all men of business. It is always read in those little white spaces of writing which want to be filled up, and which for that reason are called blank spaces, as of right appertaining to our family: for I consider myself as the lord of a manor, who lays his claim to all wastes or spots of ground that are unappropriated. I am a near kinsman to a John-a-Styles and John-a-Nokes; and they, I am told, came in with the conquer. I am mentioned oftener in both houses of parliament than any other person in Great Britain. My name is written, or, more properly speaking, not written, thus: [ ]. I am one that can turn my hand to every thing, and appear under any shape whatsoever. I can make myself man, woman, or child. I am sometimes metamorphosed into a year of our Lord, a day of the month, or an hour of the day. I very often represent a sum of money, and am generally the first subsidy that is granted to the crown. I have now and then supplied the place of several thousands of land-soldiers, and have as frequently been employed in the sea-service.

'Now, sir, my complaint is this, that I am only made use of to serve a turn, being always discarded as soon as a proper person is found out to fill up my place.

'If you have ever been in the playhouse before the curtain rises, you see the most of the front boxes filled with men of my family, who forthwith turn out and resign their stations upon the appearance of those for whom they are retained.

'But the most illustrious branch of the Blanks are those who are planted in high posts, till such time as persons of greater consequence can be found out to supply them. One of these Blanks is equally qualified for all offices; he can serve in time of need for a soldier, a politician, a lawyer, or what you please. I have known in my time many a brother Blank, that has been born under a lucky planet, heap up great riches, and swell into a man of figure and importance, before the grandees of his party could agree among themselves which of them should step into his place. Nay, I have known a Blank continue so long in one of these vacant posts, (for such it is to be reckoned all the time a Blank is in it,) that he has grown too formidable and dangerous to be removed.

'But to return to myself. Since I am so very commodious a person, and so very necessary in all well-regulated governments, I desire you will take my case into consideration, that I may be no longer made a tool of, and only employed to stop a gap. Such usage, without a pun, makes me look very blank. For all which reasons I humbly recommend myself to your protection, and am your most obedient servant,

'BLANK.

'P. S. I herewith send you a paper drawn up by a country-attorney, employed by two gentlemen, whose names he was not acquainted with, and who did not think fit to let him into the secret which they are transacting, I heard him call it a "blank instrument," and read it after the following manner. You may see by this single instance of what use I am to the busy world.

"I, T. Blank, esquire, of Blank town, in the county of Blank, do own myself indebted in the sum of Blank, to Goodman Blank, for the service he did me in procuring for me the goods following; Blank: and I do hereby promise the said Blank to pay unto him the said sum of Blank, on the Blank day of the month of Blank next ensuing, under the penalty and forfeiture of Blank."'

I shall take time to consider the case of this my imaginary correspondent, and in the mean while shall present my reader with a letter which seems to come from a person that is made up of flesh and blood.

'GOOD MR. SPECTATOR,—I am married to a very honest gentleman that is exceeding good-natured, and at the same time very choleric. There is no standing before him when he is in a passion; but as soon as it is over he is the best humoured creature in the world. When he is angry he breaks all my china ware that chances to lie in his way, and the next morning sends me in twice as much as he broke the day before. I may positively say, that he has broke me a child's fortune since we were first married together.

'As soon as he begins to fret, down goes

every thing that is within reach of his cane. I once prevailed upon him never to carry a stick in his hand, but this saved me nothing; for upon seeing me do something that did not please him, he kicked down a great jar that cost him above ten pounds but the week before. I then laid the fragments together in a heap, and gave him his cane again, desiring him that, if he chanced to be in anger, he would spend his passion upon the china that was broke to his hand; but the very next day, upon my giving a wrong message to one of the servants, he flew into such a rage, that he swept down a dozen tea-dishes, which to my misfortune stood very convenient for a side blow.

'I then removed all my china into a room which he never frequents; but I got nothing by this neither, for my looking-glasses immediately went to rack.

'In short, sir, whenever he is in a passion he is angry at every thing that is brittle; and if on such occasions he hath nothing to vent his rage upon, I do not know whether my bones would be in safety. Let me beg of you, sir, to let me know whether there be any cure for this unaccountable distemper; or if not, that you will be pleased to publish this letter: for my husband having a great veneration for your writings, will by that means know you do not approve of his conduct. I am, &c.'

No. 564.] *Wednesday, July 7, 1714.*

——————Adsit
Regula, peccatis quæ pænas irroget æquas,
Ne scutica dignum horribili sectere flagello.
Hor. Sat. iii. Lib. 1. 117.

Let rules be fixed that may our rage contain,
And punish faults with a proportion'd pain;
And do not flay him who deserves alone
A whipping for the fault that he hath done.
Creech.

It is the work of a philosopher to be every day subduing his passions, and laying aside his prejudices. I endeavour at least to look upon men and their actions only as an impartial Spectator, without any regard to them as they happen to advance or cross my own private interest. But while I am thus employed myself, I cannot help observing how those about me suffer themselves to be blinded by prejudice and inclination, how readily they pronounce on every man's character, which they can give in two words, and make him either good for nothing, or qualified for every thing. On the contrary, those who search thoroughly into human nature will find it much more difficult to determine the value of their fellow-creatures, and that men's characters are not thus to be given in general words. There is indeed no such thing as a person entirely good or bad; virtue and vice are blended and mixed together, in a great or less proportion, in every one; and if you would search for some particular good quality in its most eminent degree of perfection, you will often find it in a mind where it is darkened and eclipsed by a hundred other irregular passions.

Men have either no character at all, says a celebrated author, or it is that of being inconsistent with themselves. They find it easier to join extremities, than to be uniform and of a piece. This is finely illustrated in Xenophon's life of Cyrus the Great. That author tells us, that Cyrus having taken a most beautiful lady, named Panthea, the wife of Abradatas, committed her to the custody of Araspas, a young Persian nobleman, who had a little before maintained in discourse that a mind truly virtuous was incapable of entertaining an unlawful passion. The young gentleman had not long been in possession of his fair captive, when a complaint was made to Cyrus, that he not only solicited the lady Panthea to receive him in the room of her absent husband, but that, finding his entreaties had no effect, he was preparing to make use of force. Cyrus, who loved the young man, immediately sent for him, and in a gentle manner representing to him his fault, and putting him in mind of his former assertion, the unhappy youth, confounded with a quick sense of his guilt and shame, burst out into a flood of tears, and spoke as follows:

'Oh Cyrus, I am convinced that I have two souls. Love has taught me this piece of philosophy. If I had but one soul, it could not at the same time pant after virtue and vice, wish and abhor the same thing. It is certain therefore we have two souls: when the good soul rules, I undertake noble and virtuous actions; but, when the bad soul predominates, I am forced to do evil. All I can say at present is, that I find my good soul, encouraged by your presence, has got the better of my bad.'

I know not whether my readers will allow of this piece of philosophy; but if they will not, they must confess we meet with as different passions in one and the same soul as can be supposed in two. We can hardly read the life of a great man who lived in former ages, or converse with any who is eminent among our contemporaries, that is not an instance of what I am saying.

But as I have hitherto only argued against the partiality and injustice of giving our judgment upon men in gross, who are such a composition of virtues and vices, of good and evil, I might carry this reflection still farther, and make it extend to most of their actions. If on the one hand we fairly weighed every circumstance, we should frequently find them obliged to do that action we at first sight condemn, in order to avoid another we should have been much more displeased with. If on the other hand we nicely examined such actions as appear most dazzling to the eye, we should find most of them either deficient and lame in several parts, produced by a bad ambition, or directed to an ill end. The very same action may sometimes be so oddly circum stanced, that it is difficult to determine whether it ought to be rewarded or punished. Those who compiled the laws of England were so sensible of this, that they have laid it down as one of their first maxims, 'It is better suffering a mischief than an inconvenience;' which is as much as to say, in other words, that since no law can take in or provide for all cases, it is better private men should have some injustice done them than that a public grievance should not be redressed. This is usually pleaded in defence of all those hardships which fall on particular persons on particular occasions, which could not be foreseen when a law was made. To remedy this however as much as possible, the court of chancery was erected, which frequently mitigates and breaks the teeth of the common law, in cases of men's properties, while in criminal cases there is a power of pardoning still lodged in the crown.

Notwithstanding this, it is perhaps impossible in a large government to distribute rewards and punishments strictly proportioned to the merits of every action. The Spartan commonwealth was indeed wonderfully exact in this particular; and I do not remember in all my reading to have met with so nice an example of justice as that recorded by Plutarch, with which I shall close my paper of this day.

The city of Sparta being unexpectedly attacked by a powerful army of Thebans, was in very great danger of falling into the hands of their enemies. The citizens suddenly gathered themselves into a body, fought with a resolution equal to the necessity of their affairs, yet no one so remarkably distinguished himself on this occasion, to the amazement of both armies, as Isidas the son of Phœbidas, who was at that time in the bloom of his youth, and very remarkable for the comeliness of his person. He was coming out of the bath when the alarm was given, so that he had not time to put on his clothes, much less his armour; however transported with a desire to serve his country in so great an exigency, snatching up a spear in one hand and a sword in the other, he flung himself into the thickest ranks of his enemies. Nothing could withstand his fury: in what part soever he fought he put the enemies to flight without receiving a single wound.—Whether, says Plutarch, he was the particular care of some god, who rewarded his valour that day with an extraordinary protection, or that his enemies, struck with the unusualness of his dress, and beauty of his shape, supposed him something more than man, I shall not determine.

The gallantry of this action was judged so great by the Spartans, that the ephori, or chief magistrates, decreed he should be presented with a garland; but, as soon as they had done so, fined him a thousand drachmas for going out to the battle unarmed.

No. 565.] *Friday, July* 9, 1714.

————Deum namque ire per omnes
Terrasque, tractusque maris, cœlumque profundum
Virg. Georg. iv. 221.

For God the whole created mass inspires:
Thro' heaven and earth, and ocean's depths he throws
His influence round, and kindles as he goes.—*Dryden*

I WAS yesterday, about sun-set, walking in the open fields, until the night insensibly fell upon me. I at first amused myself with all the richness and variety of colours which appeared in the western parts of heaven; in proportion as they faded away and went out, several stars and planets appeared one after another, until the whole firmament was in a glow. The blueness of the ether was exceedingly heightened and enlivened by the season of the year, and by the rays of all those luminaries that passed through it. The galaxy appeared in its most beautiful white. To complete the scene, the full moon rose at length in that clouded majesty which Milton takes notice of, and opened to the eye a new picture of nature, which was more finely shaded, and disposed among softer lights than that which the sun had before discovered to us.

As I was surveying the moon walking in her brightness, and taking her progress among the constellations, a thought rose in me which I believe very often perplexes and disturbs men of serious and contemplative natures. David himself fell into it in that reflection, 'when I consider the heavens the work of thy fingers, the moon and the stars which thou hast ordained; what is man that thou art mindful of him, and the son of man that thou regardest him!' In the same manner, when I considered that infinite host of stars, or, to speak more philosophically, of suns which were then shining upon me, with those innumerable sets of planets or worlds which were moving round their respective suns when I still enlarged the idea, and supposed another heaven of suns and worlds rising still above this which we discovered, and these still enlightened by a superior firmament of luminaries, which are planted at so great a distance, that they may appear to the inhabitants of the former as the stars do to us; in short, while I pursued this thought, I could not but reflect on that little insignificant figure which I myself bore amidst the immensity of God's works.

Were the sun, which enlightens this part of the creation, with all the host of planetary worlds that move about him, utterly extinguished and annihilated, they would not be missed more than a grain of sand upon the sea-shore. The space they possess is so exceedingly little in comparison of the whole, that it would scarce make a blank in the creation. The chasm would be imperceptible to an eye that could take in the whole compass of nature, and pass from one end of the creation to the other; as it is possible there may be such a sense in ourselves hereafter, or in creatures which are at present more exalted than ourselves. We see many stars by the help of glasses, which we do not discover with our naked eyes; and the finer our telescopes are, the more still are our discoveries. Huygenius carries this thought so far, that he does not think it impossible there may be stars whose light is not yet travelled down to us since their first creation. There is no question but the universe has certain bounds set to it; but when we consider that it is the work of infinite power, prompted by infinite goodness, with an infinite space to exert itself in, how can our imagination set any bounds to it?

To return therefore to my first thought: I could not but look upon myself with secret horror, as a being that was not worth the smallest regard of one who had so great a work under his care and superintendency. I was afraid of being overlooked amidst the immensity of nature, and lost among that infinite variety of creatures, which in all probability swarm through all these immeasurable regions of matter.

In order to recover myself from this mortifying thought, I considered that it took its rise from those narrow conceptions which we are apt to entertain of the divine nature. We ourselves cannot attend to many different objects at the same time. If we are careful to inspect some things, we must of course neglect others. This imperfection, which we observe in ourselves, is an imperfection that cleaves in some degree to creatures of the highest capacities, as they are creatures, that is, beings of finite and limited natures. The presence of every created being is confined to a certain measure of space, and consequently his observation is stinted to a certain number of objects. The sphere in which we move, and act, and understand, is of a wider circumference to one creature than another, according as we rise one above another in the scale of existence. But the widest of these our spheres has its circumference. When, therefore, we reflect on the divine nature, we are so used and accustomed to this imperfection in ourselves, that we cannot forbear in some measure ascribing it to him in whom there is no shadow of imperfection. Our reason indeed assures us that his attributes are infinite; but the poorness of our conceptions is such, that it cannot forbear setting bounds to every thing it contemplates, until our reason comes again to our succour, and throws down all those little prejudices which rise in us unawares, and are natural to the mind of man.

We shall therefore utterly extinguish this melancholy thought, of our being overlooked by our Maker in the multiplicity of his works, and the infinity of those objects among which he seems to be incessantly employed, if we consider, in the first place, that he is omnipresent; and, in the second, that he is omniscient.

If we consider him in his omnipresence, his being passes through, actuates, and supports the whole frame of nature. His creation, and every part of it, is full of him. There is nothing he has made that is either so distant, so little, or so inconsiderable which he does not essentially inhabit. His substance is within the substance of every being, whether material or immaterial, and as intimately present to it as that being is to itself. It would be an imperfection in him, were he able to remove out of one place into another, or to withdraw himself from any thing he has created, or from any part of that space which is diffused and spread abroad to infinity. In short, to speak of him in the language of the old philosopher, he is a Being whose centre is every where, and his circumference no where.

In the second place, he is omniscient as well as omnipresent. His omniscience indeed necessarily and naturally flows from his omnipresence; he cannot but be conscious of every motion that arises in the whole material world, which he thus essentially pervades, and of every thought that is stirring in the intellectual world, to every part of which he is thus intimately united. Several moralists have considered the creation as the temple of God, which he has built with his own hands, and which is filled with his presence. Others have considered infinite space as the receptacle, or rather the habitation, of the Almighty. but the noblest and most exalted way of considering this infinite space is that of Sir Isaac Newton, who calls it the sensorium of the Godhead. Brutes and men have their sensoriola, or little sensoriums, by which they apprehend the presence and perceive the actions of a few objects that lie contiguous to them. Their knowledge and observation turn within a very narrow circle. But as God Almighty cannot but perceive and know every thing in which he resides, infinite space gives room to infinite knowledge, and is, as it were, an organ to omniscience.

Were the soul separate from the body, and with one glance of thought should start beyond the bounds of the creation, should it for millions of years continue its progress through infinite space with the same activity, it would still find itself within the embrace of its Creator, and encompassed round with the immensity of the Godhead. Whilst we are in the body he is not less present with us because he is concealed from us. 'O that I knew where I might find him,' says Job. 'Behold I go forward, but he is not there; and backward, but I cannot perceive him; on the left hand, where he does work, but I cannot behold him: he hideth himself on the right hand that I cannot see him.' In short, reason, as well as revelation assures us, that he cannot be absent from us, notwithstanding he is undiscovered by us.

In this consideration of God Almighty's omnipresence and omniscience, every uncomfortable thought vanishes. He cannot but regard every thing that has being, especially such of his creatures who fear they are not regarded by him. He is privy to all their thoughts, and to that anxiety of heart in particular, which is apt to trouble them on this occasion: for, as it is impossible he should overlook any of his creatures, so we may be confident that he regards with an eye of mercy, those who endeavour to recommend themselves to his notice, and in an unfeigned humility of heart think themselves unworthy that he should be mindful of them.

No. 566.] *Monday, July* 12, 1714.

Militiæ species amor est.—*Ovid Ars Am.* ii. 233.

Love is a kind of warfare.

As my correspondents begin to grow pretty numerous, I think myself obliged to take some notice of them, and shall therefore make this paper a miscellany of letters. I have, since my re-assuming the office of Spectator, received abundance of epistles from gentlemen of the blade, who I find have been so used to action that they know not how to lie still. They seem generally to be of opinion that the fair at home ought to reward them for their services abroad, and that until the cause of their country calls them again into the field, they have a sort of right to quarter themselves upon the ladies. In order to favour their approaches, I am desired by some to enlarge upon the accomplishments of their professions, and by others to give them my advice in carrying on their attacks. But let us hear what the gentlemen say for themselves.

'Mr. Spectator,—Though it may look somewhat perverse amidst the arts of peace to talk too much of war, it is but gratitude to pay the last office to its manes, since even peace itself, is, in some measure, obliged to it for its being.

'You have, in your former papers, always recommended the accomplished to the favour of the fair; and I hope you will allow me to represent some part of a military life not altogether unnecessary to the forming a gentleman. I need not tell you that in France, whose fashions we have been formerly so fond of, almost every one derives his pretences to merit from the sword; and that a man has scarce the face to make his court to a lady, without some credentials from the service to recommend him. As the profession is very ancient, we have reason to think some of the greatest men among the old Romans derived many of their virtues from it, the commanders being frequently in other respects some of the most shining characters of the age.

'The army not only gives a man opportunities of exercising those two great virtues, patience and courage, but often produces them in minds where they had scarce any footing before. I must add, that it is one of the best schools in the world to receive a general notion of mankind in, and a certain freedom of behaviour, which is not so easily acquired in any other place. At the same time I must own, that some military airs are pretty extraordinary, and that a man who goes into the army a coxcomb, will come out of it a sort of public nuisance: but a man of sense, or one who before had not been sufficiently used to a mixed conversation, generally takes the true turn. The court has in all ages been allowed to be the standard of good-breeding; and I believe there is not a juster observation in Monsieur Rochefoucault, than that "a man who has been bred up wholly to business, can never get the air of a courtier at court, but will immediately catch it in the camp." The reason of this most certainly is, that the very essence of good-breeding and politeness consists in several niceties, which are so minute that they escape his observation, and he falls short of the original he would copy after; but when he sees the same things charged and aggravated to a fault, he no sooner endeavours to come up to the pattern which is set before him, than, though he stops somewhat short of that, he naturally rests where in reality he ought. I was, two or three days ago, mightily pleased with the observation of a humorous gentleman upon one of his friends, who was in other respects every way an accomplished person, that "he wanted nothing but a dash of the coxcomb in him;" by which he understood a little of that alertness and unconcern in the common actions of life, which is usually so visible among gentlemen of the army, and which a campaign or two would infallibly have given him.

'You will easily guess, sir, by this my panegyric upon a military education, that I am myself a soldier, and indeed I am so. I remember, within three years after I had been in the army, I was ordered into the country a recruiting. I had very particular success in this part of the service, and was over and above assured, at my going away, that I might have taken a young lady, who was the most considerable fortune in the country, along with me. I preferred the pursuit of fame at that time to all other considerations, and though I was not absolutely bent on a wooden leg, resolved at least to get a scar or two for the good of Europe. I have at present as much as I desire of this sort of honour, and if you could recommend me effectually, should be well enough contented to pass the remainder of my days in the arms of some dear kind creature, and upon a pretty estate in the country. This, as I take it, would be following the example of Lucius Cincinna tus, the old Roman dictator, who, at the end of a war left the camp to follow the plough. I am, sir, with all imaginable re spect, your most obedient, humble servant,

'WILL WARLEY.'

'MR. SPECTATOR,—I am a half-pay officer, and am at present with a friend in the country. Here is a rich widow in the neighbourhood, who has made fools of all the fox-hunters within fifty miles of her. She declares she intends to marry, but has not yet been asked by the man she could like. She usually admits her humble admirers to an audience or two; but, after she has once given them denial, will never see them more. I am assured by a female relation that I shall have fair play at her; but as my whole success depends on my first approaches, I desire your advice, whether I had best storm, or proceed by way of sap. I am, sir, yours, &c.

'P. S. I had forgot to tell you, that I have already carried one of her outworks, that is, secured her maid.'

'MR. SPECTATOR,—I have assisted in several sieges in the Low Countries, and being still willing to employ my talents as a soldier and engineer, lay down this morning at seven o'clock before the door of an obstinate female, who had for some time refused me admittance. I made a lodgement in an outer parlour about twelve: the enemy retired to her bed-chamber, yet I still pursued, and about two o'clock this afternoon she thought fit to capitulate. Her demands are indeed somewhat high, in relation to the settlement of her fortune. But, being in possession of the house, I intend to insist upon *carte blanche*, and am in hopes, by keeping off all other pretenders for the space of twenty-four hours, to starve her into a compliance. I beg your speedy advice, and am, sir, yours,

'PETER PUSH.

'From my camp in Red-lion square, Saturday, four in the afternoon.'

No. 567.] *Wednesday, July* 14, 1714.

——Inceptus clamor frustratur hiantes.
Virg. Æn. vi. 493.

——The weak voice deceives their gasping throats.
Dryden.

I HAVE received private advice from some of my correspondents, that if I would give my paper a general run, I should take care to season it with scandal. I have indeed observed of late that few writings sell which are not filled with great names and illustrious titles. The reader generally casts his eye upon a new book, and, if he finds several letters separated from one another by a dash, he buys it up, and pursues it with great satisfaction. An *M* and an *h*, a *T* and an *r*,* with a short line between them, has sold many insipid pamphlets. Nay, I have known a whole edition go off by virtue of two or three well-written *&c—s.*

A sprinkling of the words "faction, Frenchman, papist, plunderer," and the like significant terms, in an italic character, have also a very good effect upon the eye of the purchaser, not to mention "scribbler, liar, rogue, rascal, knave, and villain," without which it is impossible to carry on a modern controversy.

Our party writers are so sensible of the secret virtue of an innuendo to recommend their productions, that of late they never mention the Q——n or P——t at length, though they speak of them with honour, and with the deference which is due to them from every private person. It gives a secret satisfaction to a pursuer of these mysterious works, that he is able to decypher them without help, and by the strength of his own natural parts, to fill up a blank space, or make out a word that has only the first and last letter to it.

Some of our authors indeed, when they would be more satirical than ordinary, omit only the vowels of a great man's name, and fall most unmercifully upon all the consonants. This way of writing was first of all introduced by T—m B—wn,† of facetious memory, who, after having gutted a proper name of all its intermediate vowels, used to plant it in his works, and make as free with it as he pleased, without any danger of the statute.

That I may imitate these celebrated authors, and publish a paper which shall be more taking than ordinary, I have here drawn up a very curious libel, in which a reader of penetration will find a great deal of concealed satire, and, if he be acquainted with the present posture of affairs, will easily discover the meaning of it.

'If there are four persons in the nation who endeavour to bring all things into confusion, and ruin their native country, I think every honest Englishman ought to be upon his guard. That there are such, every one will agree with me who hears me name ***, with his first friend and favourite ***, not to mention *** nor ***. These people may cry ch-rch, ch-rch as long as they please; but, to make use of a homely proverb, "The proof of the p-dd-ng is in the eating." This I am sure of, that if a certain prince should concur with a certain prelate, (and we have Monsieur Z—n's word for it) our posterity would be in a sweet p-ckle. Must the British nation suffer, forsooth, because my lady Q-p-t-s has been disobliged? Or is it reasonable that our English fleet, which used to be the terror of the ocean, should lie wind-bound for the sake of a ——? I love to speak out, and declare my mind clearly, when I am talking for the good of my country. I will not make my court to an ill man, though he were a B——y or a T——t. Nay, I would not stick to call so wretched a politician a traitor, an enemy to his country: and a bl-nd-rd-ss, &c. &c.'

The remaining part of this political trea-

---

* Marlborough. Treasurer

† Tom Brown

tise, which is written after the manner of the most celebrated authors, in Great Britain, I may communicate to the public at a more convenient season. In the mean while I shall leave this with my curious reader, as some ingenious writers do their enigmas; and, if any sagacious person can fairly unriddle it, I will print his explanation, and, if he pleases, acquaint the world with his name.

I hope this short essay will convince my readers it is not for want of abilities that I avoid state tracts, and that, if I would apply my mind to it, I might in a little time be as great a master of the political scratch as any the most eminent writer of the age. I shall only add, that in order to outshine all the modern race of syncopists, and thoroughly content my English reader, I intend shortly to publish a Spectator that shall not have a single vowel in it.

No. 568.] *Friday, July* 16, 1714.

—Dum recitas, incipit esse tuus.
Mart. Epig. xxxix. 1.

Reciting makes it thine.

I WAS yesterday in a coffee-house not far from the Royal Exchange, where I observed three persons in close conference over a pipe of tobacco; upon which, having filled one for my own use, I lighted it at the little wax candle that stood before them: and, after having thrown in two or three whiffs amongst them, sat down and made one of the company. I need not tell my reader that lighting a man's pipe at the same candle is looked upon among brother smokers as an overture to conversation and friendship. As we here laid our heads together in a very amicable manner, being entrenched under a cloud of our own raising, I took up the last Spectator, and casting my eye over it, 'The Spectator,' says I, 'is very witty to-day:' upon which a lusty lethargic old gentleman, who sat at the upper end of the table, having gradually blown out of his mouth a great deal of smoke which he had been collecting for some time before, 'Ay,' says he, 'more witty than wise, I am afraid.' His neighbour, who sat at his right hand, immediately coloured, and, being an angry politician, laid down his pipe with so much wrath that he broke it in the middle, and by that means furnished me with a tobacco stopper. I took it up very sedately, and, looking him full in the face, made use of it from time to time all the while he was speaking: 'This fellow,' says he, 'cannot for his life keep out of politics. Do you see how he abuses four great men here?' I fixed my eye very attentively on the paper, and asked him if he meant those who were represented by asterisks. 'Asterisks,' says he, 'do you call them? they are all of them stars—he might as well have put garters to them. Then pray do but mind the two or three next lines: Ch-rch and p-dd-ng in the same sentence! Our clergy are very much beholden to him!' Upon this the third gentleman, who was of a mild disposition, and, as I found, a whig in his heart, desired him not to be too severe upon the Spectator neither; 'for,' says he, 'you find he is very cautious of giving offence, and has therefore put two dashes into his pudding.' 'A fig for his dash,' says the angry politician, 'in his next sentence he gives a plain innuendo that our posterity will be in a sweet p-ckle. What does the fool mean by his pickle? Why does he not write it at length, if he means honestly?' 'I have read over the whole sentence,' says I; 'but I look upon the parenthesis in the belly of it to be the most dangerous part, and as full of insinuations as it can hold.' 'But who,' says I, 'is my lady Q-p-t-s?' 'Ay, answer that if you can, sir,' says the furious statesman to the poor whig that sat over against him. But, without giving him time to reply, 'I do assure you,' says he, 'were I my lady Q-p-t-s, I would sue him for *scandalum magnatum.* What is the world come to? Must every body be allowed to---!' He had by this time filled a new pipe, and, applying it to his lips, when we expected the last word of his sentence, put us off with a whiff of tobacco; which he redoubled, with so much rage and trepidation, that he almost stifled the whole company. After a short pause, I owned that I thought the Spectator had gone too far in writing so many letters of my lady Q-p-t-s's name: 'but, however,' says I, 'he has made a little amends for it in his next sentence, where he leaves a blank space without so much as a consonant to direct us. I mean,' says I, 'after those words, "the fleet that used to be the terror of the ocean, should be wind-bound for the sake of a —;" after which ensues a chasm, that in my opinion looks modest enough.' 'Sir,' says my antagonist, 'you may easily know his meaning by his gaping; I suppose he designs his chasm, as you call it, for a hole to creep out at, but I believe it will hardly serve his turn. Who can endure to see the great officers of state, the B---y's and T---t's treated after so scurrilous a manner?' 'I can't for my life,' says I, 'imagine who they are the Spectator means.' 'No!' says he:—'Your humble servant, sir!' Upon which he flung himself back in his chair after a contemptuous manner, and smiled upon the old lethargic gentleman on his left hand, who I found was his great admirer. The whig however had begun to conceive a good-will towards me, and, seeing my pipe out, very generously offered me the use of his box; but I declined it with great civility, being obliged to meet a friend about that time in another quarter of the city.

At my leaving the coffee-house, I could not forbear reflecting with myself upon that gross tribe of fools who may be termed the over-wise, and upon the difficulty of writing any thing in this censorious age which a weak head may not construe into private satire and personal reflection.

A man who has a good nose at an innuendo smells treason and sedition in the most innocent words that can be put together, and never sees a vice or folly stigmatized but finds out one or other of his acquaintance pointed at by the writer. I remember an empty pragmatical fellow in the country, who, upon reading over The Whole Duty of Man, had written the names of several persons in the village at the side of every sin which is mentioned by that excellent author; so that he had converted one of the best books in the world into a libel against the 'squire, church wardens, overseers of the poor, and all other the most considerable persons in the parish. This book, with these extraordinary marginal notes, fell accidentally into the hands of one who had never seen it before; upon which there arose a current report that somebody had written a book against the 'squire and the whole parish. The minister of the place, having at that time a controversy with some of his congregation upon the account of his tithes, was under some suspicion of being the author, until the good man sat his people right, by showing them that the satirical passages might be applied to several others of two or three neighbouring villages, and that the book was written against all the sinners in England.

No. 569.] *Monday, July 19, 1714.*

> Regis dicuntur multis urgere culullis
> Et torquere mero, quem perspexisse laborent,
> An sit amicitia dignus.———
>
> *Hor. Ars Poet.* ver. 434.

> Wise were the kings, who never chose a friend
> Till with full cups they had unmask'd his soul,
> And seen the bottom of his deepest thoughts.
>
> *Roscommon.*

No vices are so incurable as those which men are apt to glory in. One would wonder how drunkenness should have the good luck to be of this number. Anacharsis, being invited to a match of drinking at Corinth, demanded the prize very humorously, because he was drunk before any of the rest of the company: 'for,' says he, 'when we run a race, he who arrives at the goal first is entitled to the reward:' on the contrary, in this thirsty generation, the honour falls upon him who carries off the greatest quantity of liquor, and knocks down the rest of the company. I was the other day with honest Will Funnel, the West Saxon, who was reckoning up how much liquor had passed through him in the last twenty years of his life, which, according to his computation, amounted to twenty-three hogsheads of October, four tons of port, half a kilderkin of small beer, nineteen barrels of cider, and three glasses of champaign; besides which he had assisted at four hundred bowls of punch, not to mention sips, drams, and whets without number. I question not but every reader's memory will suggest to him several ambitious young men who are as vain in this particular as Will Funnel, and can boast of as glorious exploits.

Our modern philosophers observe, that there is a general decay of moisture in the globe of the earth. This they chiefly ascribe to the growth of vegetables, which incorporate into their own substance many fluid bodies that never return again to their former nature: but with submission, they ought to throw into their account those innumerable rational beings which fetch their nourishment chiefly out of liquids: especially when we consider that men, compared with their fellow creatures, drink much more than comes to their share.

But, however highly this tribe of people may think of themselves, a drunken man is a greater monster than any that is to be found among all the creatures which God has made; as indeed there is no character which appears more despicable and deformed, in the eyes of all reasonable persons, than that of a drunkard. Bonosus, one of our own countrymen, who was addicted to this vice, having set up for a share in the Roman empire, and being defeated in a great battle, hanged himself. When he was seen by the army in this melancholy situation; notwithstanding he had behaved himself very bravely, the common jest was, that the thing they saw hanging upon the tree before them was not a man, but a bottle.

This vice has very fatal effects on the mind, the body, and fortune, of the person who is devoted to it.

In regard to the mind, it first of all discovers every flaw in it. The sober man, by the strength of reason, may keep under and subdue every vice or folly to which he is most inclined; but wine makes every latent seed sprout up in the soul and show itself; it gives fury to the passions, and force to those objects which are apt to produce them. When a young fellow complained to an old philosopher that his wife was not handsome, 'put less water in your wine,' says the philosopher, 'and you will quickly make her so.' Wine heightens indifference into love, love into jealousy, and jealousy into madness. It often turns the good-natured man into an idiot, and the choleric into an assassin. It gives bitterness to resentment, it makes vanity insupportable, and displays every little spot of the soul in its utmost deformity.

Nor does this vice only betray the hidden faults of a man, and show them in the most odious colours, but often occasions faults to which he is not naturally subject. There is more of turn than of truth in a saying of Seneca, that drunkenness does not produce but discover faults. Common experience teaches the contrary. Wine throws a man out of himself, and infuses qualities into the mind which she is a stranger to in her sober moments. The person you converse with after the third bottle, is not the same man who at first sat down at table with you. Upon this maxim is founded one of the prettiest sayings I ever met with, which is ascribed to Publius Syrus, '*Qui ebrium ludificat, lædit absentem:*' 'He who jests upon a man that is drunk, injures the absent.'

Thus does drunkenness act in a direct contradiction to reason, whose business it is to clear the mind of every vice which is crept into it, and to guard it against all the approaches of any that endeavours to make its entrance. But besides these ill effects, which this vice produces in the person who is actually under its dominion, it has also a bad influence on the mind, even in its sober moments, as it insensibly weakens the understanding, impairs the memory, and makes those faults habitual which are produced by frequent excesses.

I shall now proceed to show the ill effects which this vice has on the bodies and fortunes of men; but these I shall reserve for the subject of some future paper.

No. 570.] *Wednesday, July* 21, 1714.

——Nugæque canoræ.—*Hor. Ars Poet.* ver. 322.

Chiming trifles.—*Roscommon.*

THERE is scarcely a man living who is not actuated by ambition. When this principle meets with an honest mind and great abilities, it does infinite service to the world; on the contrary, when a man only thinks of distinguishing himself, without being thus qualified for it, he becomes a very pernicious or a very ridiculous creature. I shall here confine myself to that petty kind of ambition, by which some men grow eminent for odd accomplishments and trivial performances. How many are there whose whole reputation depends upon a pun or a quibble? You may often see an artist in the streets gain a circle of admirers by carrying a long pole upon his chin or forehead in a perpendicular posture. Ambition has taught some to write with their feet, and others to walk upon their hands. Some tumble into fame, others grow immortal by throwing themselves through a hoop,

Cætera de genere hoc adeo sunt multa, loquacem.
Delassare valent Fabium.——
Hor. Sat. i. Lib. 1. 13.

With thousands more of this ambitious race
Would tire e'en Fabius to relate each case.
Horneck.

I am led into this train of thought by an adventure I lately met with.

I was the other day at a tavern, where the master of the house* accommodated us himself with every thing we wanted, I accidentally fell into discourse with him; and talking of a certain great man, who shall be nameless, he told me that he had sometimes the honour to treat him with a whistle; adding (by way of parenthesis) 'for you must know, gentlemen, that I whistle the best of any man in Europe.' This naturally put me upon desiring him to give us a sample of his art; upon which he called for a case knife, and, applying the edge of it to his mouth, converted it into a musical instrument, and entertained me with an Italian solo. Upon laying down the knife, he took up a pair of clean tobacco pipes; and, after having slid the small end of them over the table in a most melodious trill, he fetched a tune out of them, whistling to them at the same time in concert. In short, the tobacco pipes became musical pipes in the hands of our virtuoso, who confessed to me ingenuously, he had broken such quantities of them, that he had almost broke himself before he had brought this piece of music to any tolerable perfection. I then told him I would bring a company of friends to dine with him next week, as an encouragement to his ingenuity; upon which he thanked me, saying, that he would provide himself with a new frying-pan against that day. I replied, that it was no matter; roast and boiled would serve our turn. He smiled at my simplicity, and told me that it was his design to give us a tune upon it. As I was surprised at such a promise, he sent for an old frying-pan, and grating it upon the board, whistled to it in such a melodious manner, that you could scarcely distinguish it from a bass-viol. He then took his seat with us at the table, and hearing my friend that was with me hum over a tune to himself, he told him if he would sing out, he would accompany his voice with a tobacco pipe. As my friend has an agreeable bass, he chose rather to sing to the frying-pan, and indeed between them they made up a most extraordinary concert. Finding our landlord so great a proficient in kitchen music, I asked him if he was master of the tongs and key. He told me that he had laid it down some years since, as a little unfashionable; but that, if I pleased, he would give me a lesson upon the gridiron.

* This eccentric man kept a public house, the sign of the Queen's arms, near the end of the Little Piazza in Covent-garden. His death is thus noticed in the London Mag. for April, 1738.

"*Death.*—Near Fishmonger's Hall, the celebrated Mr. John Dentry, better known by the appellation of Signior Denterius, which by way of humour, he assumed and put upon his sign. He kept a public house, not only at the time of his death, but when the Spectators were writing; and from the odd talents he was possessed of, and his whimsical ways of entertaining his customers, furnished a subject for one of those excellent papers. Among many other surprising endowments the Signior had that of whistling, by the help of a knife, to so great a perfection, that he became as famous for that, as most of the Italian Signiors have been for singing, who excel likewise in that way, *by the help of a knife.*"

He then informed me, that he had added two bars to the gridiron, in order to give it a greater compass to sound; and I perceived was as well pleased with the invention as Sappho could have been upon adding two strings to the lute. To be short, I found that his whole kitchen was furnished with musical instruments; and could not but look upon this artist as a kind of burlesque musician.

He afterwards, of his own accord, fell into the imitation of several singing birds. My friend and I toasted our mistresses to the nightingale, when all of a sudden we were surprised with the music of the thrush. He next proceeded to the skylark, mounting up by a proper scale of notes, and afterwards falling to the ground with a very easy and regular descent. He then contracted his whistle to the voice of several birds of the smallest size. As he is a man of a larger bulk and higher stature than ordinary, you would fancy him a giant when you looked upon him, and a tom-tit when you shut your eyes. I must not omit acquainting my reader that this accomplished person was formerly the master of a toy-shop near Temple bar; and that the famous Charles Mathers was bred up under him. I am told that the misfortunes which he has met with in the world are chiefly owing to his great application to his music; and therefore cannot but recommend him to my readers as one who deserves their favour, and may afford them great diversion over a bottle of wine, which he sells at the Queen's arms, near the end of the little piazza in Covent-garden.

No. 571.] *Friday, July* 23, 1714.

———Cœlum quid quærimus ultra?—*Luc.*

What seek we beyond heaven?

As the work I have engaged in will not only consist of papers of humour and learning, but of several essays moral and divine, I shall publish the following one, which is founded on a former Spectator, and sent me by a particular friend, not questioning but it will please such of my readers as think it no disparagement to their understandings to give way sometimes to a serious thought.

'Sir,—In your paper of Friday the ninth instant, you had occasion to consider the ubiquity of the Godhead, and at the same time to show, that, as he is present to every thing, he cannot but be attentive to every thing, and privy to all the modes and parts of its existence: or, in other words, that the omniscience and omnipresence are co-existent and run together through the whole infinitude of space. This consideration might furnish us with many incentives to devotion, and motives to morality; but, as this subject has been handled by several excellent writers, I shall consider it in a light wherein I have not seen it placed by others.

'First, How disconsolate is the condition of an intellectual being, who is thus present with his Maker, but at the same time receives no extraordinary benefit or advantage from this his presence!

'Secondly, How deplorable is the condition of an intellectual being, who feels no other effects from this his presence, but such as proceeds from divine wrath and indignation!

'Thirdly, How happy is the condition of that intellectual being, who is sensible of his Maker's presence, from the secret effects of his mercy and loving kindness!

'First, How disconsolate is the condition of an intellectual being, who is thus present with his Maker, but at the same time receives no extraordinary benefit or advantage from this his presence! Every particle of matter is actuated by this Almighty Being which passes through it. The heavens and the earth, the stars and planets, move and gravitate by virtue of this great principle within them. All the dead parts of nature are invigorated by the presence of their Creator, and made capable of exerting their respective qualities. The several instincts, in the brute creation, do likewise operate and work towards the several ends which are agreeable to them, by this divine energy. Man only, who does not co-operate with his Holy Spirit, and is unattentive to his presence, receives none of those advantages from it which are perfective of his nature, and necessary to his well being. The Divinity is with him, and in him, and every where about him, but of no advantage to him. It is the same thing to a man without religion, as if there were no God in the world. It is indeed impossible for an Infinite Being to remove himself from any of his creatures; but though he cannot withdraw his essence from us, which would argue an imperfection in him, he can withdraw from us all the joys and consolations of it. His presence may perhaps be necessary to support us in our existence; but he may leave this our existence to itself, with regard to its happiness or misery. For, in this sense, he may cast us away from his presence, and take his Holy Spirit from us. This single consideration one would think sufficient to make us open our hearts to all those infusions of joy and gladness which are so near at hand, and ready to be poured in upon us; especially when we consider, secondly, the deplorable condition of an intellectual being who feels no other effects from his Maker's presence but such as proceed from divine wrath and indignation.

We may assure ourselves, that the great Author of nature will not always be as one who is indifferent to any of his creatures. Those who will not feel him in his love, will be sure at length to feel him in his displeasure. And how dreadful is the condi tion of that creature, who is only sensible of the being of his Creator by what he suffers from him! He is as essentially present in hell as in heaven; but the inhabitants of the former behold him only in his wrath, and shrink within the flames to conceal themselves from him. It is not in the power of imagination to conceive the fearful effects of Omnipotence incensed.

'But I shall only consider the wretchedness of an intellectual being, who in this life lies under the displeasure of him, that at all times and in all places is intimately united with him. He is able to disquiet the soul, and vex it in all its faculties. He can hinder any of the greatest comforts of life from refreshing us, and give an edge to every one of its slightest calamities. Who then can bear the thought of being an outcast from his presence, that is, from the comforts of it, or of feeling it only in its terrors! How pathetic is that expostulation of Job, when, for the trial of his patience, he was made to look upon himself in this deplorable condition! "Why hast thou set me as a mark against thee, so that I am become a burden to myself?" But, thirdly, how happy is the condition of that intellectual being, who is sensible of his Maker's presence from the secret effects of his mercy and loving kindness!

'The blessed in heaven behold him face to face; that is, are as sensible of his presence as we are of the presence of any person whom we look upon with our eyes. There is, doubtless, a faculty in spirits, by which they apprehend one another as our senses do material objects; and there is no question but our souls, when they are disembodied, or placed in glorified bodies, will, by this faculty, in whatever part or space they reside, be always sensible of the Divine Presence. We, who have this veil of flesh standing between us and the world of spirits, must be content to know that the Spirit of God is present with us, by the effects which he produces in us. Our outward senses are too gross to apprehend him; we may however taste and see how gracious he is, by his influence upon our minds, by those virtuous thoughts which he awakens in us, by those secret comforts and refreshments which he conveys into our souls, and by those ravishing joys and inward satisfactions which are perpetually springing up, and diffusing themselves among all the thoughts of good men. He is lodged in our very essence, and is as a soul within the soul to irradiate its understanding, rectify its will, purify its passions, and enliven all the powers of man. How happy therefore is an intellectual being, who, by prayer and meditation, by virtue and good works, opens this communication between God and his own soul! Though the whole creation frowns upon him, and all nature looks black about him, he has his light and support within him, that are able to cheer his mind, and bear him up in the midst of all those horrors which encompass him. He knows that his helper is at hand, and is always nearer to him than any thing else can be, which is capable of annoying or terrifying him. In the midst of calumny or contempt, he attends to that Being who whispers better things within his soul, and whom he looks upon as his defender, his glory, and the lifter-up of his head. In his deepest solitude and retirement, he knows that he is in company with the greatest of beings; and perceives within himself such real sensations of his presence, as are more delightful than any thing that can be met with in the conversation of his creatures. Even in the hour of death, he considers the pains of his dissolution to be nothing else but the breaking down of that partition, which stands betwixt his soul and the sight of that Being who is always present with him, and is about to manifest itself to him in fulness of joy.

'If we would be thus happy, and thus sensible of our Maker's presence, from the secret effects of his mercy and goodness, we must keep such a watch over all our thoughts, that, in the language of the Scripture, his soul may have pleasure in us. We must take care not to grieve his Holy Spirit, and endeavour to make the meditations of our hearts always acceptable in his sight, that he may delight thus to reside and dwell in us. The light of nature could direct Seneca to this doctrine, in a very remarkable passage among his epistles: "*Sacer inest in nobis spiritus bonorum malorumque custos, et observator, et quemadmodum nos illum tractamus, ita et ille nos.*" "There is a holy spirit residing in us, who watches and observes both good and evil men, and will treat us after the same manner that we treat him." But I shall conclude this discourse with those more emphatical words in divine revelation, "If a man love me, he will keep my words: and my Father will love him, and we will come unto him, and make our abode with him."'

No. 572.] *Monday, July 26, 1714.*

——Quod medicorum est
Promittunt medici——
Hor. Ep. i. Lib. 2. 115.

Physicians only boast the healing art.

I AM the more pleased with these my papers, since I find they have encouraged several men of learning and wit to become my correspondents: I yesterday received the following essay against quacks, which I shall here communicate to my readers for the good of the public, begging the writer's pardon for those additions and retrenchments which I have made in it.

'The desire of life is so natural and strong a passion, that I have long since ceased to wonder at the great encouragement which the practice of physic finds among us. Well-constituted governments have always made the profession of a physician both honourable and advantageous. Homer's Machaon and Virgil's Iapsis were men of renown, heroes in war, and made at least as much havoc among their enemies as among their friends. Those who have little or no faith in the abilities of a quack, will apply themselves to him, either because he is willing to sell health at a reasonable profit, or because the patient, like a drowning man, catches at every twig, and hopes for relief from the most ignorant, when the most able physicians give him none. Though imprudence and many words are as necessary to these itinerary Galens, as a laced hat to a merry-Andrew, yet they would turn very little to the advantage of the owner, if there were not some inward disposition in the sick man to favour the pretensions of the mountebank. Love of life in the one, and of money in the other, creates a good correspondence between them.

'There is scarce a city in Great Britain but has one of this tribe, who takes it into his protection, and on the market-day harangues the good people of the place with aphorisms and receipts. You may depend upon it he comes not there for his own private interest, but out of a particular affection to the town. I remember one of these public-spirited artists at Hammersmith, who told his audience, that he had been born and bred there; and that, having a special regard for the place of his nativity, he was determined to make a present of five shillings to as many as would accept of it. The whole crowd stood agape, and ready to take the doctor at his word; when putting his hand into a long bag, as every one was expecting his crown-piece, he drew out a handful of little packets, each of which he informed the spectators was constantly sold at five shillings and six-pence, but that he would bate the odd five shillings to every inhabitant of that place: the whole assembly immediately closed with this generous offer, and took off all his physic, after the doctor had made them vouch for one another, that there were no foreigners among them, but that they were all Hammersmith men.

'There is another branch of pretenders to this art, who, without either horse or pickle-herring, lie snug in a garret, and send down notice to the world of their extraordinary parts and abilities by printed bills and advertisements. These seem to have derived their custom from an eastern nation which Herodotus speaks of, among whom it was a law, that, whenever any cure was performed, both the method of the cure, and an account of the distemper, should be fixed in some public place; but, as customs will corrupt, these our moderns provide themselves of persons to attest the cure before they publish or make an experiment of the prescription. I have heard of a porter, who serves as a knight of the post under one of these operators, and, though he was never sick in his life, has been cured of all the diseases in the Dispensary. These are the men whose sagacity has invented elixirs of all sorts, pills, and lozenges, and take it as an affront if you come to them before you are given over by every body else. Their medicines are infallible, and never fail of success—that is, of enriching the doctor, and setting the patient effectually at rest.

'I lately dropt into a coffee-house at Westminster, where I found the room hung round with ornaments of this nature. There were elixirs, tinctures, the Anodyne Fotus, English pills, electuaries, and, in short, more remedies than I believe there are diseases. At the sight of so many inventions, I could not but imagine myself in a kind of arsenal or magazine where store of arms was reposited against any sudden invasion. Should you be attacked by the enemy sideways, here was an infallible piece of defensive armour to cure the pleurisy: should a distemper beat up your head-quarters, here you might purchase an impenetrable helmet: or, in the language of the artist, a cephalic tincture; if your main body be assaulted, here are various kinds of armour in case of various onsets. I began to congratulate the present age upon the happiness men might reasonably hope for in life, when death was thus in a manner defeated, and when pain itself would be of so short a duration, that it would but just serve to enhance the value of pleasure. While I was in these thoughts, I unluckily called to mind a story of an ingenious gentleman of the last age, who, lying violently afflicted with the gout, a person came and offered his services to cure him by a method which he assured him was infallible; the servant who received the message carried it up to his master, who, inquiring whether the person came on foot or in a chariot, and being informed that he was on foot: "Go," says he, "send the knave about his business: was his method as infallible as he pretends, he would long before now have been in his coach and six." In like manner I conclude that, had all these advertisers arrived to that skill they pretend to, they would have had no need for so many years successively to publish to the world the place of their abode, and the virtues of their medicines. One of these gentlemen indeed pretends to an effectual cure for leanness: what effects it may have upon those who have tried it I cannot tell; but I am credibly informed, that the call for it has been so great, that it has effectually cured the doctor himself of that distemper. Could each of them produce so good an instance of the success of his medicines, they might soon persuade the world into an opinion of them.

'I observe that most of the bills agree in one expression, viz. that "with God's blessing" they perform such and such cures: this expression is certainly very proper and emphatical, for that is all they have for it. And if ever a cure is performed on a patient where they are concerned, they can claim no greater share in it than Virgil's Iapis in the curing of Æneas; he tried his skill, was very assiduous about the wound, and indeed was the only visible means that relieved the hero; but the poet assures us it was the particular assistance of a deity that speeded the operation. An English reader may see the whole story in Mr. Dryden's translation:

Propp'd on his lance the pensive hero stood,
And heard, and saw, unmov'd, the mourning crowd.
The fam'd physician tucks his robes around,
With ready hands, and hastens to the wound.
With gentle touches he performs his part,
This way and that soliciting the dart,
And exercises all his heavenly art.
All soft'ning simples, known of sov'reign use,
He presses out, and pours their noble juice;
These first infus'd, to lenify the pain,
He tugs with pincers, but he tugs in vain.
Then to the patron of his art he pray'd:
The patron of his art refus'd his aid.
But now the goddess mother, mov'd with grief,
And pierc'd with pity hastens her relief.
A branch of healing dittany she brought,
Which in the Cretan fields with care she sought;
Rough in the stem, which woolly leaves surround;
The leaves with flowers, the flow'rs with purple crown'd;
Well known to wounded goats; a sure relief
To draw the pointed steel, and ease the grief.
This Venus brings, in clouds involv'd; and brews
Th' extracted liquor with Ambrosian dews,
And od'rous penance: unseen she stands,
Temp'ring the mixture with her heavenly hands;
And pours it in a bowl already crown'd
With juice of med'cinal herbs, prepar'd to bathe the wound.
The leech, unknowing of superior art,
Which aids the cure, with this foments the part;
And in a moment ceas'd the raging smart.
Staunch'd in the blood and in the bottom stands
The steel, but scarcely touch'd with tender hands,
Moves up and follows of its own accord;
And health and vigour are at once restor'd.
Iapis first perceiv'd the closing wound;
And first the footsteps of a god he found:
'Arms, arms!' he cries, 'the sword and shield prepare,
And send the willing chief, renew'd, to war.
This is no mortal work, no cure of mine,
Nor art's effect, but done by hands divine.'

Virg. Æn. Lib. xii. 391, &c.

No. 573.] *Wednesday, July* 28, 1714.

——Castigata remordent. *Juv.* Sat. ii. 35.

Chastised, the accusation they retort.

My paper on the club of widows, has brought me in several letters; and, amongst the rest, a long one from Mrs. President, as follows:

'Smart Sir,—You are pleased to be very merry, as you imagine, with us widows: and you seem to ground your satire on our receiving consolation so soon after the death of our dears, and the number we are pleased to admit for our companions; but you never reflect what husbands we have buried, and how short a sorrow the loss of them was capable of occasioning. For my own part, Mrs. President as you call me, my first husband I was married to at fourteen, by my uncle and guardian, (as I afterwards discovered,) by way of sale, for the third part of my fortune. This fellow looked upon me as a mere child he might breed up after his own fancy: if he kissed my chambermaid before my face, I was supposed so ignorant, how could I think there was any hurt in it? When he came home roaring drunk at five in the morning, it was the custom of all men that live in the world. I was not to see a penny of money, for, poor thing, how could I manage it? He took a handsome cousin of his into the house (as he said,) to be my house-keeper, and to govern my servants; for how should I know how to rule a family? While she had what money she pleased, which was but reasonable for the trouble she was at for my good, I was not to be so censorious as to dislike familiarity and kindness between near relations. I was too great a coward to contend, but not so ignorant a child to be thus imposed upon. I resented his contempt as I ought to do, and as most poor passive blinded wives do, until it pleased heaven to take away my tyrant, who left me free possession of my own land, and a large jointure. My youth and money brought me many lovers, and several endeavoured to establish an interest in my heart while my husband was in his last sickness; the honourable Edward Waitfort was one of the first who addressed to me, advised to it by a cousin of his that was my intimate friend, and knew to a penny what I was worth. Mr. Waitfort is a very agreeable man, and every body would like him as well as he does himself, if they did not plainly see that his esteem and love is all taken up, and by such an object as it is impossible to get the better of; I mean himself. He made no doubt of marrying me within four or five months, and began to proceed with such an assured easy air, that piqued my pride not to banish him; quite contrary, out of pure malice, I heard his first declaration with so much innocent surprise, and blushed so prettily, I perceived it touched his very heart, and he thought me the best-natured silly poor thing on earth. When a man has such a notion of a woman, he loves her better than he thinks he does. I was overjoyed to be thus revenged on him for designing on my fortune; and finding it was in my power to make his heart ache, I resolved to complete my conquest, and entertained several other pretenders. The first impression of my undesigning innocence was so strong in his head, he attributed all my followers to the inevitable force of my charms; and, from several blushes and side glances, concluded himself the favourite; and when I used him like a dog for my diversion, he thought it was all prudence and fear; and pitied the violence I did my own inclinations to comply with my friends, when I married Sir Nicholas Fribble, of sixty years of age. You know, sir, the case of Mrs. Medlar

I hope you would not have had me cry out my eyes for such a husband. I shed tears enough for my widowhood a week after my marriage; and when he was put in his grave, reckoning he had been two years dead, and myself a widow of that standing, I married three weeks afterwards John Sturdy, Esq. his next heir. I had indeed some thoughts of taking Mr. Waitfort, but I found he could stay; and besides, he thought it indecent to ask me to marry again until my year was out; so, privately resolving him for my fourth, I took Mr. Sturdy for the present. Would you believe it, sir, Mr. Sturdy was just five-and-twenty, about six foot high, and the stoutest fox-hunter in the country, and I believe I wished ten thousand times for my old Fribble again; he was following his dogs all the day, and all the night keeping them up at table with him and his companions: however, I think myself obliged to them for leading him a chase in which he broke his neck. Mr. Waitfort began his addresses anew; and I verily believe I had married him now, but there was a young officer in the guards that had debauched two or three of my acquaintance, and I could not forbear being a little vain of his courtship. Mr. Waitfort heard of it, and read me such a lecture upon the conduct of women, I married the officer that very day, out of pure spite to him. Half an hour after I was married I received a penitential letter from the honourable Mr. Edward Waitfort, in which he begged pardon for his passion, as proceeding from the violence of his love. I triumphed when I read it, and could not help, out of the pride of my heart, showing it to my new spouse; and we were very merry together upon it. Alas! my mirth lasted a short time; my young husband was very much in debt when I married him, and his first action afterwards was to set up a gilt chariot and six, in fine trappings before and behind. I had married so hastily, I had not the prudence to reserve my estate in my own hands; my ready money was lost in two nights at the Groom-porter's; and my diamond necklace, which was stole I did not know how, I met in the street upon Jenny Wheedle's neck. My plate vanished piece by piece: and I had been reduced to downright pewter, if my officer had not been deliciously killed in a duel, by a fellow that had cheated him of five hundred pounds, and afterwards, at his own request, satisfied him and me too, by running him through the body. Mr. Waitfort was still in love, and told me so again; and, to prevent all fears of ill usage, he desired me to reserve every thing in my own hands: but now my acquaintance began to wish me joy of his constancy, my charms were declining, and I could not resist the delight I took in showing the young flirts about town it was yet in my power to give pain to a man of sense; this, and some private hopes he would hang himself, and what a glory would it be for me, and how I should be envied, made me accept of being third wife to my lord Friday. I proposed from my rank and his estate, to live in all the joys of pride; but how was I mistaken! he was neither extravagant, nor ill-natured, nor debauched. I suffered however more with him than with all my others. He was splenetic. I was forced to sit whole days hearkening to his imaginary ails; it was impossible to tell what would please him, what he liked when the sun shined made him sick when it rained: he had no distemper, but lived in constant fear of them all. My good genius dictated to me to bring him acquainted with Dr. Gruel; from that day he was always contented, because he had names for all his complaints; the good doctor furnished him with reasons for all his pains; and prescriptions for every fancy that troubled him; in hot weather he lived upon juleps, and let blood to prevent fevers; when it grew cloudy, he generally apprehended a consumption. To shorten the history of this wretched part of my life, he ruined a good constitution by endeavouring to mend it; and took several medicines, which ended in taking the grand remedy, which cured both him and me of all our uneasiness. After his death, I did not expect to hear any more of Mr. Waitfort. I knew he had renounced me to all his friends, and been very witty upon my choice, which he affected to talk of with great indifferency. I gave over thinking of him, being told that he was engaged with a pretty woman and a great fortune; it vexed me a little, but not enough to make me neglect the advice of my cousin Wishwell, that came to see me the day my lord went into the country with Russel; she told me experimentally, nothing put an unfaithful lover and a dear husband so soon out one's head as a new one, and at the same time proposed to me a kinsman of her's. "You understand enough of the world," said she, "to know money is the most valuable consideration; he is very rich, and I am sure cannot live long; he has a cough that must carry him off soon." I knew afterwards she had given the self-same character of me to him; but, however, I was so much persuaded by her, I hastened on the match for fear he should die before the time came; he had the same fears, and was so pressing, I married him in a fortnight, resolving to keep it private a fortnight longer. During this fortnight Mr. Waitfort came to make me a visit: he told me he had waited on me sooner, but had that respect for me, he would not interrupt me in the first day of my affliction for my dead lord; that, as soon as he heard I was at liberty to make another choice, he had broke off a match very advantageous for his fortnne, just upon the point of conclusion, and was forty times more in love with me than ever. I never received more pleasure in my life than from this declaration; but I composed my face to a grave air, and said the news of his engagement had touched me to the heart, that in a rash jealous fit I had married a man I could never have thought on, if I had not lost all hopes of him. Good-natured Mr. Waitfort had liked to have dropped down dead at hearing this, but went from me with such an air as plainly showed me he had laid all the blame upon himself, and hated those friends that had advised him to the fatal application; he seemed as much touched by my misfortune as his own, for he had not the least doubt I was still passionately in love with him. The truth of the story is, my new husband gave me reason to repent I had not staid for him; he had married me for my money, and I soon found he loved money to distraction; there was nothing he would not do to get it; nothing he would not suffer to preserve it; the smallest expense kept him awake whole nights; and when he paid a bill, it was with as many sighs, and after as many delays, as a man that endures the loss of a limb. I heard nothing but reproofs for extravagancy whatever I did. I saw very well that he would have starved me, but for losing my jointures; and he suffered agonies between the grief of seeing me have so good a stomach, and the fear that, if he had made me fast, it might prejudice my health. I did not doubt he would have broke my heart, if I did not break his, which was allowable by the law of self-defence. The way was very easy. I resolved to spend as much money as I could; and, before he was aware of the stroke, appeared before him in a two thousand pound diamond necklace: he said nothing, but went quietly to his chamber, and, as it is thought, composed himself with a dose of opium. I behaved myself so well upon the occasion, that to this day I believe he died of an apoplexy. Mr. Waitfort was resolved not to be too late this time, and I heard from him in two days. I am almost out of my weeds at this present writing, and very doubtful whether I will marry him or no. I do not think of a seventh for the ridiculous reason you mention, but out of pure morality that I think so much constancy should be rewarded, though I may not do it after all perhaps. I do not believe all the unreasonable malice of mankind can give a pretence why I should have been constant to the memory of any of the deceased, or have spent much time in grieving for an insolent, insignificant, negligent, extravagant, splenetic, or covetous husband: my first insulted me, my second was nothing to me, my third disgusted me, the fourth would have ruined me, the fifth tormented me, and the sixth would have starved me. If the other ladies you name would thus give in their husbands' pictures at length, you would see they have had as little reason as myself to lose their hours in weeping and wailing.

No. 574.] *Friday, July* 30, 1714.

Non possidentem multa vocaveris
Recte beatum; rectius occupat
Nomen beati, qui Deorum
Muneribus sapienter uti,
Duramque callet pauperiem pati.
Hor. Od. ix. Lib. 4. 45.

Believe not those that lands possess,
And shining heaps of useless ore,
The only lords of happiness:
But rather those that know
For what kind fates bestow,
And have the art to use the store:
That have the generous skill to bear
The hated weight of poverty.—*Creech.*

I WAS once engaged in discourse with a Rosicrucian about 'the great secret.' As this kind of men (I mean those of them who are not professed cheats) are overrun with enthusiasm and philosophy, it was very amusing to hear this religious adept descanting on his pretended discovery. He talked of the secret as of a spirit which lived within an emerald, and converted every thing that was near it to the highest perfection it is capable of. 'It gives a lustre,' says he, 'to the sun, and water to the diamond. It irradiates every metal, and enriches lead with all the properties of gold. It heightens smoke into flame, flame into light, and light into glory.' He farther added, that 'a single ray of it dissipates pain, and care, and melancholy, from the person on whom it falls. In short,' says he, 'its presence naturally changes every place into a kind of heaven.' After he had gone on for some time in this unintelligible cant, I found that he jumbled natural and moral ideas together in the same discourse, and that his great secret was nothing else but content.

This virtue does indeed produce, in some measure, all those effects which the alchymist usually ascribes to what he calls the philosopher's stone; and if it does not bring riches, it does the same thing, by banishing the desire of them. If it cannot remove the disquietudes arising out of man's mind, body, or fortune, it makes him easy under them. It has indeed a kindly influence on the soul of man, in respect of every being to whom he stands related. It extinguishes all murmur, repining, and ingratitude, towards that Being who has allotted him his part to act in this world. It destroys all inordinate ambition, and every tendency to corruption, with regard to the community wherein he is placed. It gives sweetness to his conversation, and a perpetual serenity to all his thoughts.

Among the many methods which might be made use of for the acquiring of this virtue, I shall only mention the two following. First of all, a man should always consider how much he has more than he wants: and, secondly, how much more unhappy he might be than he really is.

First of all, a man should always consider how much he has more than he wants. I am wonderfully pleased with the reply which Aristippus made to one who condoled him upon the loss of a farm; 'Why,' said he, 'I have three farms still, and you have but one; so that I ought rather to be afflicted for you than you for me.' On the contrary, foolish men are more apt to consider what they have lost than what they possess; and to fix their eyes upon those who are richer than themselves, rather than on those who are under greater difficulties. All the real pleasures and conveniencies of life lie in a narrow compass; but it is the humour of mankind to be always looking forward, and straining after one who has got the start of them in wealth and honour. For this reason, as there are none can be properly called rich who have not more than they want, there are few rich men in any of the politer nations, but among the middle sort of people, who keep their wishes within their fortunes, and have more wealth than they know how to enjoy. Persons of a higher rank live in a kind of splendid poverty, and are perpetually wanting, because, instead of acquiescing in the solid pleasures of life, they endeavour to outvie one another in shadows and appearances. Men of sense have at all times beheld, with a great deal of mirth, this silly game that is playing over their heads, and, by contracting their desires, enjoy all that secret satisfaction which others are always in quest of. The truth is, this ridiculous chase after imaginary pleasures cannot be sufficiently exposed, as it is the great source of those evils which generally undo a nation. Let a man's estate be what it will, he is a poor man if he does not live within it, and naturally sets himself to sale to any one that can give him his price. When Pittacus, after the death of his brother, who had left him a good estate, was offered a great sum of money by the king of Lydia, he thanked him for his kindness, but told him he had already more by half than he knew what to do with. In short, content is equivalent to wealth, and luxury to poverty; or, to give the thought a more agreeable turn, 'Content is natural wealth,' says Socrates; to which I shall add, 'Luxury is artificial poverty.' I shall therefore recommend to the consideration of those who are always aiming after superfluous and imaginary enjoyments, and will not be at the trouble of contracting their desires, an excellent saying of Bion the philosopher; namely, that 'no man has so much care as he who endeavours after the most happiness.'

In the second place, every one ought to reflect how much more unhappy he might be than he really is. The former consideration took in all those who are sufficiently provided with the means to make themselves easy; this regards such as actually lie under some pressure or misfortune. These may receive great alleviation from such a comparison as the unhappy person may make between himself and others, or between the misfortunes which he suffers, and greater misfortunes which might have befallen him.

I like the story of the honest Dutchman, who upon breaking his leg by a fall from the mainmast, told the standers by, it was a great mercy that it was not his neck. To which, since I am got into quotations, give me leave to add the saying of an old philosopher, who, after having invited some of his friends to dine with him, was ruffled by his wife, that came into the room in a passion, and threw down the table that stood before them: 'Every one,' says he, 'has his calamity, and he is a happy man that has no greater than this.' We find an instance to the same purpose in the life of doctor Hammond, written by bishop Fell. As this good man was troubled with a complication of distempers, when he had the gout upon him, he used to thank God that it was not the stone; and when he had the stone, that he had not both these distempers on him at the same time.

I cannot conclude this essay without observing that there never was any system besides that of Christianity, which could effectually produce in the mind of man the virtue I have been hitherto speaking of. In order to make us content with our present condition, many of the ancient philosophers tell us that our discontent only hurts ourselves, without being able to make any alteration in our circumstances; others, that whatever evil befalls us is derived to us by a fatal necessity, to which the gods themselves are subject; while others very gravely tell the man who is miserable, that it is necessary he should be so to keep up the harmony of the universe, and that the scheme of Providence would be troubled and perverted were he otherwise. These, and the like considerations, rather silence than satisfy a man. They may show him that his discontent is unreasonable, but are by no means sufficient to relieve it. They rather give despair than consolation. In a word, a man might reply to one of these comforters as Augustus did to his friend, who advised him not to grieve for the death of a person whom he loved, because his grief could not fetch him again; 'It is for that very reason,' said the emperor, 'that I grieve.'

On the contrary, religion bears a more tender regard to human nature. It prescribes to every miserable man the means of bettering his condition; nay, it shows him that the bearing of his afflictions as he ought to do will naturally end in the removal of them: it makes him easy here, because it can make him happy hereafter.

Upon the whole, a contented mind is the greatest blessing a man can enjoy in this world; and if in the present life his happiness arises from the subduing of his desires, it will arise in the next from the gratification of them.

No. 575.] *Monday, August* 2, 1714.

—Nec morti esse locum— *Virg.* Georg. iv. 226.
No room is left for death. *Dryden.*

A LEWD young fellow seeing an aged hermit go by him barefoot, 'Father,' says he, 'you are in a very miserable condition, if there is not another world.' 'True, son,' said the hermit, 'but what is thy condition if there is?' Man is a creature designed for two different states of being, or rather for two different lives. His first life is short and transient; his second permanent and lasting. The question we are all concerned in is this, in which of these two lives it is our chief interest to make ourselves happy? Or, in other words, whether we should endeavour to secure to ourselves the pleasures and gratifications of a life which is uncertain and precarious, and at its utmost length of a very inconsiderable duration? or to secure to ourselves the pleasures of a life which is fixed and settled, and will never end? Every man, upon the first hearing of this question, knows very well which side of it he ought to close with. But however right we are in theory, it is plain that in practice we adhere to the wrong side of the question. We make provisions for this life as though it were never to have an end, and for the other life as though it were never to have a beginning.

Should a spirit of superior rank, who is a stranger to human nature, accidentally alight upon the earth, and take a survey of its inhabitants, what would his notions of us be? Would not he think that we are a species of beings made for quite different ends and purposes than what we really are? Must not he imagine that we are placed in this world to get riches and honours? Would not he think that it was our duty to toil after wealth, and station, and title? Nay, would not he believe we were forbidden poverty by threats of eternal punishment, and enjoined to pursue our pleasures under pain of damnation? He would certainly imagine that we were influenced by a scheme of duties quite opposite to those which are indeed prescribed to us. And truly, according to such an imagination, he must conclude that we are a species of the most obedient creatures in the universe; that we are constant to our duty; and that we keep a steady eye to the end for which me were sent hither.

But how great would be his astonishment, when he learned that we were beings not designed to exist in this world above threescore and ten years; and that the greatest part of this busy species fall short even of that age? How would he be lost in horror and admiration, when he should know that this set of creatures, who lay out all their endeavours for this life, which scarce deserves the name of existence—when, I say, he should know that this set of creatures are to exist to all eternity in another life, for which they make no preparations? Nothing can be a greater disgrace to reason, than that men, who are persuaded of these two different states of being, should be perpetually employed in providing for a life of threescore and ten years, and neglecting to make provision for that which after many myriads of years will be still new, and still beginning; especially when we consider that our endeavours for making ourselves great, or rich, or honourable, or whatever else we place our happiness in, may after all prove unsuccessful; whereas, if we constantly and sincerely endeavour to make ourselves happy in the other life, we are sure that our endeavours will succeed, and that we shall not be disappointed of our hope.

The following question is started by one of the schoolmen.—Supposing the whole body of the earth were a great ball or mass of the finest sand, and that a single grain or particle of this sand should be annihilated every thousand years? Supposing then that you had it in your choice to be happy all the while this prodigious mass of sand was consuming by this slow method until there was not a grain of it left, on condition you were to be miserable for ever after? Or, supposing that you might be happy for ever after, on condition you would be miserable until the whole mass of sand were thus annihilated at the rate of one sand in a thousand years:—which of these two cases would you make your choice?

It must be confessed in this case, so many thousands of years are to the imagination as a kind of eternity, though in reality they do not bear so great a proportion to that duration which is to follow them as a unit does to the greatest number which you can put together in figures, or as one of those sands to the supposed heap. Reason therefore tells us, without any manner of hesitation, which would be the better part in this choice. However, as I have before intimated, our reason might in such case be so overset by the imagination, as to dispose some persons to sink under the consideration of the great length of the first part of this duration, and of the great distance of that second duration, which is to succeed it. The mind, I say, might give itself up to that happiness which is at hand, considering that it is so very near, and that it would last so very long. But when the choice we actually have before us is this, whether we will choose to be happy for the space of only threescore and ten, nay, perhaps of only twenty or ten years, I might say of only a day or an hour, and miserable to all eternity: or, on the contrary, miserable for this short term of years, and happy for a whole eternity: what words are sufficient to express that folly and want of consideration, which in such a case makes a wrong choice?

I here put the case even at the worst, by supposing, what seldom happens, that a course of virtue makes us miserable in this life: but if we suppose, as it generally happens, that virtue would make us more happy even in this life than a contrary course of vice; how can we sufficiently admire the stupidity or madness of those persons who are capable of making so absurd a choice?

Every wise man therefore will consider this life only as it may conduce to the happiness of the other, and cheerfully sacrifice the pleasures of a few years to those of an eternity.

No. 576.] *Wednesday, August* 4, 1714.

Nitor in adversum; nec me, qui cætera, vincit
Impetus; et rapido contrarius evehor orbi.
Ovid, Met. Lib. ii. 72.

I steer against their motions, nor am I
Borne back by all the current of the sky.—*Addison.*

I REMEMBER a young man of very lively parts, and of a sprightly turn in conversation, who had only one fault, which was an inordinate desire of appearing fashionable. This ran him into many amours, and consequently into many distempers. He never went to bed until two o'clock in the morning, because he would not be a queer fellow; and was every now and then knocked down by a constable, to signalize his vivacity. He was initiated into half a dozen clubs before he was one-and-twenty; and so improved in them his natural gayety of temper, that you might frequently trace him to his lodging by a range of broken windows, and other the like monuments of wit and gallantry. To be short, after having fully established his reputation of being a very agreeable rake, he died of old age at five-and-twenty.

There is indeed nothing which betrays a man into so many errors and inconveniences as the desire of not appearing singular; for which reason it is very necessary to form a right idea of singularity, that we may know when it is laudable, and when it is vicious. In the first place, every man of sense will agree with me that singularity is laudable when, in contradiction to a multitude, it adheres to the dictates of conscience, morality, and honour. In these cases we ought to consider that it is not custom, but duty, which is the rule of action; and that we should be only so far sociable, as we are reasonable creatures. Truth is never the less so for not being attended to: and it is the nature of actions, not the number of actors, by which we ought to regulate our behaviour. Singularity in concerns of this kind is to be looked upon as heroic bravery, in which a man leaves the species only as he soars above it. What greater instance can there be of a weak and pusillanimous temper, than for a man to pass his whole life in opposition to his own sentiments? or not to dare to be what he thinks he ought to be?

Singularity, therefore, is only vicious when it makes men act contrary to reason, or when it puts them upon distinguishing themselves by trifles. As for the first of these, who are singular in any thing that is irreligious, immoral, or dishonourable, I believe every one will easily give them up. I shall therefore speak of those only who are remarkable for their singularity in things of no importance; as in dress, behaviour, conversation, and all the little intercourses of life. In these cases there is a certain deference due to custom; and, notwithstanding there may be a colour of reason to deviate from the multitude in some particulars, a man ought to sacrifice his private inclinations and opinions to the practice of the public. It must be confessed that good sense often makes a humourist; but then it unqualifies him for being of any moment in the world, and renders him ridiculous to persons of a much inferior understanding.

I have heard of a gentleman in the north of England who was a remarkable instance of this foolish singularity. He had laid it down as a rule within himself, to act in the most indifferent parts of life according to the most abstracted notions of reason and good sense, without any regard to fashion or example. This humour broke out at first in many little oddnesses: he had never any stated hours for his dinner, supper, or sleep; because, said he, we ought to attend the calls of nature, and not set our appetites to our meals, but bring our meals to our appetites. In his conversation with country gentlemen, he would not make use of a phrase that was not strictly true; he never told any of them that he was his humble servant, but that he was his well-wisher, and would rather be thought a mal-content, than drink the king's health when he was not dry. He would thrust his head out of his chamber window every morning, and after having gaped for fresh air about half an hour, repeat fifty verses as loud as he could bawl them, for the benefit of his lungs; to which end he generally took them out of Homer—the Greek tongue, especially in that author, being more deep and sonorous, and more conducive to expectoration than any other. He had many other particularities, for which he gave sound and philosophical reasons. As this humour still grew upon him, he chose to wear a turban instead of a periwig; concluding, very justly, that a bandage of clean linen about his head was much more wholesome, as well as cleanly, than the caul of a wig, which is soiled with frequent perspirations. He afterwards judiciously observed that the many ligatures in our English dress must naturally check the circulation of the blood; for which reason he made his breeches and his doublet of one continued piece of cloth, after the manner of the hussars. In short, by following the pure dictates of reason, he at length departed so much from the rest of his countrymen, and indeed from his whole species, that his friends would have clapped him into Bedlam, and have begged his estate; but the judge, being informed he did no harm, contented himself with issuing out a commission of lunacy against him, and putting his estate into the hands of proper guardians.

The fate of this philosopher puts me in mind of a remark in Monsieur Fontenelle's Dialogues of the Dead. 'The ambitious and the covetous,' says he, 'are madmen to all intents and purposes as much as those who are shut up in dark rooms; but they have the good luck to have numbers on their side; whereas the phrensy of one who is given up for a lunatic is a phrensy *hors d'œuvre;*' that is, in other words, something which is singular in its kind, and does not fall in with the madness of a multitude.

The subject of this essay was occasioned by a letter which I received not long since, and which, for want of room at present, I shall insert in my next paper.

No. 577.] *Friday, August* 6, 1714.

———Hoc tolerabile, si non
Et furere incipias——— *Juv.* Sat. vi. 613.

This might be borne with, if you did not rave.

The letter mentioned in my last paper is as follows.

'Sir,—You have so lately decried that custom, too much in use amongst most people, of making themselves the subjects of their writings and conversation, that I had some difficulty to persuade myself to give you this trouble until I had considered that though I should speak in the first person, yet I could not be justly charged with vanity, since I shall not add my name: as also, because what I shall write will not, to say the best, redound to my praise, but is only designed to remove a prejudice conceived against me, as I hope, with very little foundation. My short history is this.

'I have lived for some years last past altogether in London, until about a month ago an acquaintance of mine, for whom I have done some small services in town, invited me to pass part of the summer with him at his house in the country. I accepted his invitation, and found a very hearty welcome. My friend, an honest plain man, not being qualified to pass away his time without the reliefs of business, has grafted the farmer upon the gentleman, and brought himself to submit even to the servile parts of that employment, such as inspecting his plough and the like. This necessarily takes up some of his hours every day; and, as I have no relish for such diversion, I used at these times to retire either to my chamber, or a shady walk near the house, and entertain myself with some agreeable author. Now, you must know, Mr. Spectator, that when I read, especially if it be poetry, it is very usual with me, when I meet with any passage or expression which strikes me much, to pronounce it aloud, with that tone of the voice which I think agreeable to the sentiments there expressed; and to this I generally add some motion or action of the body. It was not long before I was observed by some of the family in one of these heroic fits, who thereupon received impressions very much to my disadvantage. This however I did not soon discover, nor should have done probably, had it not been for the following accident. I had one day shut myself up in my chamber, and was very deeply engaged in the second book of Milton's Paradise Lost. I walked to and fro with the book in my hand; and, to speak the truth, I fear I made no little noise; when presently coming to the following lines:

"————On a sudden open fly,
With impetuous recoil and jarring sound,
Th' infernal doors, and on their hinges grate
Harsh thunder," &c.

I in great transport threw open the door of my chamber, and found the greatest part of the family standing on the outside in a very great consternation. I was in no less confusion, and begged pardon for having disturbed them; addressing myself particularly to comfort one of the children who received an unlucky fall in this action, while he was too intently surveying my meditations through the key-hole. To be short, after this adventure, I easily observed that great part of the family, especially the women and children, looked upon me with some apprehensions of fear; and my friend himself, though he still continues his civilities to me, did not seem altogether easy: I took notice that the butler was never after this accident ordered to leave the bottle upon the table after dinner. Add to this, that I frequently overheard the servants mention me by the name of "the crazed gentleman, the gentleman a little touched, the mad Londoner," and the like. This made me think it high time for me to shift my quarters, which I resolved to do the first handsome opportunity; and was confirmed in this resolution by a young lady in the neighbourhood who frequently visited us, and who one day, after having heard all the fine things I was able to say, was pleased with a scornful smile to bid me "go to sleep."

'The first minute I got to my lodgings in town I set pen to paper to desire your opinion, whether upon the evidence before you, I am mad or not. I can bring certificates that I behave myself soberly before company, and I hope there is at least some merit in withdrawing to be mad. Look you, sir, I am contented to be esteemed a little touched, as they phrase it, but should be sorry to be madder than my neighbours; therefore, pray let me be as much in my senses as you can afford. I know I could bring yourself as an instance of a man who has confessed talking to himself; but yours is a particular case, and cannot justify me, who have not kept silence any part of my life. What if I should own myself in love? You know lovers are always allowed the comfort of soliloquy.—But I will say no more upon this subject, because I have long since observed the ready way to be thought mad is to contend that you are not so: as we generally conclude that man drunk who takes pains to be thought sober. I will therefore leave myself to your determination; but am the more desirous to be thought in my senses, that it may be no discredit to you when I assure you that I have always been very much your admirer.

'P. S. If I must be mad, I desire the young lady may believe it is for her.'

' *The humble Petition of John-a-Nokes and John-a-Styles,*

'SHOWETH,—That your petitioners have causes depending in Westminster-hall above five hundred years, and that we despair of ever seeing them brought to an issue: that your petitioners have not been involved in these law-suits out of any litigious temper of their own, but by the instigation of contentious persons; that the young lawyers in our inns of court are continually setting us together by the ears, and think they do us no hurt, because they plead for us without a fee; that many of the gentlemen of the robe have no other clients in the world besides us two; that when they have nothing else to do, they make us plaintiffs and defendants, though they were never retained by any of us: that they traduce, condemn, or acquit us, without any manner of regard to our reputations and good names in the world. Your petitioners therefore, being thereunto encouraged by the favourable reception which you lately gave to our kinsman Blank, do humbly pray, that you will put an end to the controversies which have been so long depending between us your said petitioners, and that our enmity may not endure from generation to generation; it being our resolution to live hereafter as it becometh men of peaceable dispositions.

'And your petitioners, as in duty bound, shall ever pray, &c.'

No. 578.] *Monday, August* 9, 1714.

—Eque feris humana in corpora transit,
Inque feras noster.—
Ovid, Met. Lib. xv. 167.

—Th' unbodied spirit flies—
And lodges where it lights in man or beast.
Dryden.

THERE has been very great reason, on several accounts, for the learned world to endeavour at settling what it was that might be said to compose personal identity.

Mr. Locke, after having premised that the word person properly signifies a thinking intelligent being that has reason and reflection, and can consider itself as itself, concludes, that it is consciousness alone, and not an identity of substance, which makes this personal identity of sameness. 'Had I the same consciousness,' says that author, 'that I saw the ark and Noah's flood, as that I saw an overflowing of the Thames last winter, or as that I now write; I could no more doubt that I who write this now, that saw the Thames overflow last winter, and that viewed the flood at the general deluge, was the same self, place that self in what substance you please, than that I who write this am the same myself now while I write, whether I consist of all the same substance, material or immaterial, or no, that I was yesterday; for as to this point of being the same self, it matters not whether this present self be made up of the same or other substances.'

I was mightily pleased with a story in some measure applicable to this piece of philosophy, which I read the other day in the Persian Tales, as they are lately very well translated by Mr. Philips; and with an abridgement whereof I shall here present my readers.

I shall only premise that these stories are writ after the eastern manner, but somewhat more correct.

'Fadlallah, a prince of great virtues, succeeded his father Bin Ortoc in the kingdom of Mousel. He reigned over his faithful subjects for some time, and lived in great happiness with his beauteous consort queen Zemroude, when there appeared at his court a young dervis of so lively and entertaining a turn of wit, as won upon the affections of every one he conversed with. His reputation grew so fast every day, that it at last raised a curiosity in the prince himself to see and talk with him. He did so; and, far from finding that common fame had flattered him, he was soon convinced that every thing he had heard of him fell short of the truth.

'Fadlallah immediately lost all manner of relish for the conversation of other men; and, as he was every day more and more satisfied of the abilities of this stranger, offered him the first posts in his kingdom. The young dervis, after having thanked him with a very singular modesty, desired to be excused, as having made a vow never to accept of any employment, and preferring a free and independent state of life to all other conditions.

'The king was infinitely charmed with so great an example of moderation; and though he could not get him to engage in a life of business, made him however his chief companion and first favourite.

'As they were one day hunting together, and happened to be separated from the rest of the company, the dervis entertained Fadlallah with an account of his travels and adventures. After having related to him several curiosities which he had seen in the Indies, "It was in this place," says he, "that I contracted an acquaintance with an old brachman, who was skilled in the most hidden powers of nature: he died within my arms, and with his parting breath communicated to me one of the most valuable secrets, on condition I should never reveal it to any man." The king immediately, reflecting on his young favourite's having refused the late offers of greatness he had made him, told him he presumed it was the power of making gold. "No, sir," says the dervis, "it is somewhat more wonderful than that; it is the power of reanimating a dead body, by flinging my own soul into it."

'While he was yet speaking, a doe came bounding by them, and the king who had his bow ready, shot her through the heart; telling the dervis, that a fair opportunity now offered for him to show his art. The young man immediately left his own body breathless on the ground, while at the same instant that of the doe was reanimated. She came to the king, fawned upon him, and, after having played several wanton tricks, fell again upon the grass; at the same instant the body of the dervis recovered its life. The king was infinitely pleased at so uncommon an operation, and conjured his friend by every thing that was sacred to communicate it to him. The dervis at first made some scruple of violating his promise to the dying brachman; but told him at last that he found he could conceal nothing from so excellent a prince; after having obliged him therefore by an oath to secrecy, he taught him to repeat two cabalistic words, in pronouncing of which the whole secret consisted. The king, impatient to try the experiment, immediately repeated them as he had been taught, and in an instant found himself in the body of the doe. He had but a little time to contemplate himself in this new being; for the treacherous dervis, shooting his own soul into the royal corpse, and bending the princes own bow against him, had laid him dead on the spot, had not the king, who perceived his intent, fled swiftly to the woods.

'The dervis, now triumphing in his villany, returned to Mousel, and filled the throne and bed of the unhappy Fadlallah.

'The first thing he took care of, in order to secure himself in the possession of his new acquired kingdom, was to issue out a proclamation, ordering his subjects to destroy all the deer in the realm. The king had perished among the rest had he not avoided his pursuers by reanimating the body of a nightingale which he saw lie dead at the foot of a tree. In this new shape he winged his way in safety to the palace; where, perching on a tree which stood near the queen's apartment, he filled the whole place with so many melodious and melancholy notes as drew her to the window. He had the mortification to see that, instead of being pitied, he only moved the mirth of his princess, and of a young female slave who was with her. He continued however to serenade her every morning, until at last the queen, charmed with his harmony, sent for the bird-catchers, and ordered them to employ their utmost skill to put that little creature in her possession. The king, pleased with an opportunity of being once more near his beloved consort, easily suffered himself to be taken; and when he was presented to her, though he showed a fearfulness to be touched by any of the other ladies, flew of his own accord, and hid himself in the queen's bosom. Zemroude was highly pleased at the unexpected fondness of her new favourite, and ordered him to be kept in an open cage in her own apartment. He had there an opportunity of making his court to her every morning, by a thousand little actions which his shape allowed him. The queen passed away whole hours every day, in hearing and playing with him. Fadlallah could even have thought himself happy in this state of life, had he not frequently endured the inexpressible torment of seeing the dervis enter the apartment and caress his queen even in his presence.

'The usurper, amidst his toying with his princess, would often endeavour to ingratiate himself with her nightingale; and while the enraged Fadlallah pecked at him with his bill, beat his wings, and showed all the marks of an impotent rage, it only afforded his rival and the queen new matter for their diversion.

'Zemroude was likewise fond of a little lap-dog which she kept in her apartment, and which one night happened to die.

'The king immediately found himself inclined to quit the shape of the nightingale, and enliven his new body. He did so, and the next morning Zemroude saw her favourite bird lie dead in the cage. It is impossible to express her grief on this occasion: and when she called to mind all its little actions, which even appeared to have somewhat in them like reason, she was inconsolable for her loss.

'Her women immediately sent for the dervis to come and comfort her, who after having in vain represented to her the weakness of being grieved at such an accident, touched at last by her repeated complaints, "Well, madam," says he, "I will exert the utmost of my art to please you. Your nightingale shall again revive every morning, and serenade you as before." The queen beheld him with a look which easily showed she did not believe him; when, laying himself down on a sofa, he shot his soul into the nightingale, and Zemroude was amazed to see her bird revive.

'The king, who was a spectator of all that passed, lying under the shape of a lap-dog in one corner of the room, immediately recovered his own body, and running to the cage with the utmost indignation, twisted off the neck of the false nightingale.

'Zemroude was more than ever amazed and concerned at this second accident, until the king, entreating her to hear him, related to her his whole adventure.

'The body of the dervis, which was found dead in the wood, and his edict for killing all the deer, left her no room to doubt of the truth of it: but the story adds, that out of an extreme delicacy, peculiar to the oriental ladies, she was so highly afflicted at the innocent adultery in which she had for some time lived with the dervis, that no arguments, even from Fadlallah himself, could compose her mind. She shortly after died with grief, begging his pardon with her last breath for what the most rigid justice could not have interpreted as a crime.

'The king was so afflicted with her death, that he left his kingdom to one of his nearest relations, and passed the rest of his days in solitude and retirement.'

No. 579.] *Wednesday, August* 11, 1714.

——Odora canum vis.—*Virg. Æn.* iv. 132.

Sagacious hounds.

In the reign of king Charles the First, the company of stationers, into whose hands the printing of the bible is committed by patent, made a very remarkable erratum or blunder in one of the editions: for instead of 'Thou shalt not commit adultery,' they printed off several thousands of copies with 'Thou shalt commit adultery.' Archbishop Laud, to punish this their negligence, laid a considerable fine upon that company in the star-chamber.

By the practice of the world, which prevails in this degenerate age, I am afraid that very many young profligates of both sexes are possessed of this spurious edition of the bible, and observe the commandment according to that faulty reading.

Adulterers, in the first ages of the church, were excommunicated for ever, and unqualified all their lives for bearing a part in Christian assemblies, notwithstanding they might seek it with tears, and all the appearances of the most unfeigned repentance.

I might here mention some ancient laws among the heathens, which punished this crime with death: and others of the same kind, which are now in force among several governments that have embraced the reformed religion. But, because a subject of this nature may be too serious for my ordinary readers, who are very apt to throw by my papers when they are not enlivened with something that is diverting or uncommon, I shall here publish the contents of a little manuscript lately fallen into my hands, and which pretends to great antiquity; though by reason of some modern phrases, and other particulars in it, I can by no means allow it to be genuine, but rather the production of a modern sophist.

It is well known by the learned, that there was a temple upon Mount Ætna dedicated to Vulcan, which was guarded by dogs of so exquisite a smell, say the historians, that they could discern whether the persons who came thither were chaste or otherwise. They used to meet and fawn upon such who were chaste, caressing them as the friends of their master Vulcan; but flew at those who were polluted, and never ceased barking at them till they had driven them from the temple.

My manuscript gives the following account of these dogs, and was probably designed as a comment upon this story.

'These dogs were given to Vulcan by his sister Diana, the goddess of hunting and of chastity, having bred them out of some of her hounds, in which she had observed this natural instinct and sagacity. It was thought she did it in spite of Venus, who, upon her return home, always found her husband in a good or bad humour, according to the reception which she met with from his dogs. They lived in the temple several years, but were such snappish curs, that they frighted away most of the votaries. The women of Sicily made a solemn deputation to the priest, by which they acquainted him, that they would not come up to the temple with their annual offerings unless he muzzled his mastiffs; and at last compromised the matter with him, that the offering should always be brought by a chorus of young girls, who were none of them above seven years old. It was wonderful, says the author, to see how different the treatment was which the dogs gave to these little misses, from that which they had shown to their mothers. It is said that the prince of Syracuse, having married a young lady, and being naturally of a jealous temper, made such an interest with the priests of this temple, that he procured a whelp from them of this famous breed. The young puppy was very troublesome to the fair lady at first, insomuch that she solicited her husband to send him away; but the good man cut her short with the old Sicilian proverb, "Love me, love my dog;" from which time she lived very peaceably with both of them. The ladies of Syracuse were very much annoyed with him, and several of very good reputation refused to come to court until he was discarded. There were indeed some of them that defied his sagacity; but it was observed, though he did not actually bite them, he would growl at them most confoundedly. To return to the dogs of the temple: after they had lived here in great repute for several years, it so happened, that as one of the priests, who had upon making a charitable visit to a widow who lived on the promontory of Lilybeum, returned home pretty late in the evening, the dogs flew at him with so much fury, that they would have worried him if his brethren had not come in to his assistance: upon which, says my author, the dogs were all of them hanged, as having lost their original instinct.'

I cannot conclude this paper without wishing that we had some of this breed of dogs in Great Britain, which would certainly do justice, I should say honour, to the ladies of our country, and show the world the difference between pagan women and those who are instructed in sounder principles of virtue and religion.

No. 580.] *Friday, August* 13, 1714.

> ——Si verbo audacia detur,
> Non metuam magni dixisse palatia cœli.
> *Ovid*, Met. Lib. i. 175.

> This place, the brightest mansion of the sky
> I'll call the palace of the Deity.—*Dryden*.

'SIR,—I considered in my two last letters that awful and tremendous subject, the ubiquity or omnipresence of the Divine Being. I have shown that he is equally present in all places throughout the whole extent of infinite space. This doctrine is so agreeable to reason, that we meet with it in the writings of the enlightened heathens, as I might show at large, were it not already done by other hands. But though the Deity be thus essentially present through all the immensity of space, there is one part of it in which he discovers himself in a most transcendent and visible glory; this is that place which is marked out in scripture under the different appellations of "Paradise, the third heaven, the throne of God, and the habitation of his glory." It is here where the glorified body of our Saviour resides, and where all the celestial hierarchies, and the innumerable hosts of angels, are represented as perpetually surrounding the seat of God with hallelujahs and hymns of praise. This is that presence of God which some of the divines call his glorious, and others his majestic, presence. He is indeed as essentially present in all other places as in this; but it is here where he resides in a sensible magnificence, and in the midst of all those splendours which can effect the imagination of created beings.

'It is very remarkable that this opinion of God Almighty's presence in heaven, whether discovered by the light of nature, or by a general tradition from our first parents, prevails among all the nations of the world, whatsoever different notions they entertain of the Godhead. If you look into Homer, the most ancient of the Greek writers, you see the supreme power seated in the heavens, and encompassed with inferior deities, among whom the Muses are represented as singing incessantly about his throne. Who does not here see the main strokes and outlines of this great truth we are speaking of? The same doctrine is shadowed out in many other heathen authors, though at the same time, like several other revealed truths, dashed and adulterated with a mixture of fables and human inventions. But to pass over the notions of the Greeks and Romans, those more enlightened parts of the pagan world, we find there is scarce a people among the late discovered nations who are not trained up in an opinion that heaven is the habitation of the divinity whom they worship.

'As in Solomon's temple there was the *Sanctum Sanctorum*, in which a visible glory appeared among the figures of the cherubims, and into which none but the high priest himself was permitted to enter, after having made an atonement for the sins of the people; so, if we consider the whole creation as one great temple, there is in it this Holy of holies, into which the High priest of our salvation entered, and took his place among angels and arch-angels, after having made a propitiation for the sins of mankind.

'With how much skill must the throne of God be erected! With what glorious designs is that habitation beautified, which is contrived and built by him who inspired Hiram with wisdom! How great must be the majesty of that place, where the whole art of creation has been employed, and where God has chosen to show himself in the most magnificent manner? What must be the architecture of infinite power under the direction of infinite wisdom? A spirit cannot but be transported, after an ineffable manner, with the sight of those objects, which were made to effect him by that Being who knows the inward frame of a soul, and how to please and ravish it in all its most secret powers and faculties. It is to this majestic presence of God we may apply those beautiful expressions in holy writ: 'Behold even to the moon and it shineth not; yea the stars are not pure in his sight.' The light of the sun, and all the glories of the world in which we live, are but as weak and sickly glimmerings, or rather darkness itself, in comparison of those splendours which encompass the throne of God.

'As the glory of this place is transcendent beyond imagination, so probably is the extent of it. There is light behind light, and glory within glory. How far that space may reach, in which God appears in per fect majesty, we cannot possibly conceive. Though it is not infinite, it may be indefinite; and, though not immeasurable in itself, it may be so with regard to any created eye or imagination. If he has made these lower regions of matter so inconceivably wide and magnificent for the habitation of mortal and perishable beings, how great may we suppose the courts of his house to be where he makes his residence in a more especial manner, and displays himself in the fulness of his glory, among an innumerable company of angels and spirits of just men made perfect?

'This is certain, that our imaginations cannot be raised too high, when we think on a place where omnipotence and omniscience have so signally exerted themselves, because that they are able to produce a scene infinitely more great and glorious than what we are able to imagine. It is not impossible but at the consummation of all things, these outward apartments of nature, which are now suited to those beings who inhabit them, may be taken in and added to that glorious place of which I am here speaking, and by that means made a proper habitation for beings who are exempt from mortality, and cleared of their imperfections: for so the scripture seems to intimate when it speaks of "new heavens and of a new earth, wherein dwelleth righteousness."

'I have only considered this glorious place with regard to the sight and imagination, though it is highly probable that our other senses may here likewise enjoy their highest gratifications. There is nothing which more ravishes and transports the soul than harmony; and we have great reason to believe, from the descriptions of this place in holy scripture, that this is one of the entertainments of it. And if the soul of man can be so wonderfully affected with those strains of music which human art is capable of producing, how much more will it be raised and elevated by those in which is exerted the whole power of harmony! The senses are faculties of the human soul, though they cannot be employed, during this our vital union, without proper instruments in the body. Why therefore should we exclude the satisfaction of these faculties, which we find by experience are inlets of great pleasure to the soul, from among those entertainments which are to make up our happiness hereafter! Why should we suppose that our hearing and seeing will not be gratified with those objects which are most agreeable to them, and which they cannot meet with in these lower regions of nature; objects, "which neither eye hath seen, nor ear heard, nor can it enter into the heart of man to conceive? I knew a man in Christ (says Saint Paul, speaking of himself) above fourteen years ago, (whether in the body I cannot tell, or whether out of the body I cannot tell: God knoweth) such a one caught up to the third heaven. And I knew such a man (whether in the body or out of the body, I cannot tell: God knoweth) how that he was caught up into Paradise, and heard unspeakable words, which it is not possible for a man to utter." By this is meant that what he heard was so infinitely different from any thing which he had heard in this world, that it was impossible to express it in such words, as might convey a notion of it to his hearers.

'It is very natural for us to take delight in inquiries concerning any foreign country, where we are some time or other to make our abode; and as we all hope to be admitted into this glorious place, it is both a laudable and useful curiosity to get what informations we can of it, whilst we make use of revelation for our guide. When these everlasting doors shall be open to us, we may be sure that the pleasures and beauties of this place will infinitely transcend our present hopes and expectations, and that the glorious appearance of the throne of God will rise infinitely beyond whatever we are able to conceive of it. We might here entertain ourselves with many other speculations on this subject, from those several hints which we find of it in the holy scriptures; as, whether there may not be different mansions and apartments of glory to beings of different natures; whether, as they excel one another in perfection, they are not admitted nearer to the throne of the Almighty, and enjoy greater manifestations of his presence; whether there are not solemn times and occasions, when all the multitude of heaven celebrate the presence of their Maker in more extraordinary forms of praise and adoration; as Adam, though he had continued in a state of innocence, would, in the opinion of our divines, have kept holy the Sabbath-day in a more particular manner than any other of the seven. These, and the like speculations we may very innocently indulge, so long as we make use of them to inspire us with a desire of becoming inhabitants of this delightful place.

'I have in this, and in two foregoing letters, treated on the most serious subject that can employ the mind of man—the omnipresence of the Deity; a subject which, if possible, should never depart from our meditations. We have considered the Divine Being as he inhabits infinitude, as he dwells among his works, as he is present to the mind of man, and as he discovers himself in a more glorious manner among the regions of the blest. Such a consideration should be kept awake in us at all times, and in all places, and possess our minds with a perpetual awe and reverence. It should be interwoven with all our thoughts and perceptions, and become one with the consciousness of our own being. It is not to be reflected on in the coldness of philosophy, but ought to sink us into the lowest prostration before him, who is so astonishingly great, wonderful, and holy.'

No. 581.] *Monday, August* 16, 1714.

Sunt bona, sunt quædam mediocria, sunt mala plura
Quæ legis—— *Mart.* Epig. xvii. Lib. I.

Some good, more bad, some neither one nor t'other.

'I AM at present sitting with a heap of letters before me, which I have received under the character of Spectator. I have complaints from lovers, schemes from projectors, scandal from ladies, congratulations, compliments, and advice in abundance.

I have not been thus long an author, to be insensible of the natural fondness every person must have for their own productions; and I begin to think I have treated my correspondents a little too uncivilly in stringing them altogether on a file, and letting them lie so long unregarded. I shall therefore, for the future, think myself at least obliged to take some notice of such letters as I receive, and may possibly do it at the end of every month.

In the mean time I intend my present paper as a short answer to most of those which have been already sent me.

The public, however, is not to expect I should let them into all my secrets; and, though I appear abstruse to most people, it is sufficient if I am understood by my particular correspondents.

My well-wisher Van Nath is very arch, but not quite enough so to appear in print.

Philadelphus will, in a little time, see his query fully answered by a treatise which is now in the press.

It was very improper at that time to comply with Mr. G.

Miss Kitty must excuse me.

The gentleman who sent me a copy of verses on his mistress's dancing is, I believe, too thoroughly in love to compose correctly.

I have too great a respect for both the universities to praise one at the expense of the other.

Tom Nimble is a very honest fellow, and I desire him to present my humble service to his cousin Fill Bumper.

I am obliged for the letter upon prejudice.

I may in due time animadvert on the case of Grace Grumble.

The petition of P. S. granted.

That of Sarah Loveit refused.

The papers of A. S. are returned.

I thank Aristippus for his kind invitation.

My friend at Woodstock is a bold man to undertake for all within ten miles of him.

I am afraid the entertainment of Tom Turnover will hardly be relished by the good cities of London and Westminster.

I must consider farther of it before I indulge W. F. in those freedoms he takes with the ladies' stockings.

I am obliged to the ingenious gentleman who sent me an ode on the subject of the late Spectator, and shall take particular notice of his last letter.

When the lady who wrote me a letter, dated July the 20th, in relation to some passages in a lover, will be more particular in her directions, I shall be so in my answer.

The poor gentleman who fancies my writings could reclaim a husband who can abuse such a wife as he describes, has, I am afraid, too great an opinion of my skill.

Philanthropos is, I dare say, a very well-meaning man, but a little too prolix in his compositions.

Constantius himself must be the best judge in the affair he mentions.

The letter dated from Lincoln is received.

Arethusa and her friend may hear farther from me.

Celia is a little too hasty.

Harriot is a good girl, but must not courtesy to folks she does not know.

I must ingenuously confess my friend Samson Benstaff has quite puzzled me, and writ me a long letter which I cannot comprehend one word of.

Collidan must also explain what he means by his 'drigelling.'

I think it beneath my spectatorial dignity to concern myself in the affair of the boiled dumpling.

I shall consult some literati on the project sent me for the discovery of the longitude.

I know not how to conclude this paper better than by inserting a couple of letters which are really genuine, and which I look upon to be two of the smartest pieces I have received from my correspondents of either sex:

'Brother Spec,—While you are surveying every object that falls in your way, I am wholly taken up with one. Had that sage who demanded what beauty was, lived to see the dear angel I love, he would not have asked such a question. Had another seen her, he would himself have loved the person in whom heaven has made virtue visible; and, were you yourself to be in her company, you could never, with all your loquacity, say enough of her good-humour and sense. I send you the outlines of a picture, which I can no more finish, than I can sufficiently admire the dear original. I am your most affectionate brother,

'CONSTANTIO SPEC.'

'Good Mr. Pert,—I will allow you nothing until you resolve me the following question. Pray what is the reason, that, while you only talk now upon Wednesdays, Fridays, and Mondays, you pretend to be a greater tattler than when you spoke every day, as you formerly used to do? If this be your plunging out of your taciturnity, pray let the length of your speeches compensate for the scarceness of them. I am, good Mr. Pert, your admirer, if you will be long enough for me,

'AMANDA LOVELENGTH.'

No. 582.] *Wednesday, August* 18, 1714.

——Tenet insanibile multos
Scribendi cacoethes—— *Juv.* Sat. vii. 51.

The curse of writing ⅰ an endless itch.
Ch. Dryden.

There is a certain distemper, which is mentione³ neither by Galen nor Hippocrates, nor to be met with in the London Dispensary. Juvenal in the motto of my paper, terms it a cacoethes; which is a hard word for a disease called in plain English, 'The itch of writing.' This cacoethes is as epidemical as the smallpox, there being very few who are not seized with it some time or other in their lives. There is, however, this difference in these two distempers, that the first, after having indisposed you for a time, never returns again; whereas, this I am speaking of, when it is once got into the blood, seldom comes out of it. The British nation is very much afflicted with this malady, and though very many remedies have been applied to persons infected with it, few of them have ever proved successful. Some have been cauterized with satires and lampoons, but have received little or no benefit from them; others have had their heads fastened for an hour together between a cleft board, which is made use of as a cure for the disease when it appears in its greatest malignity.* There is indeed, one kind of this malady which has been sometimes removed, like the biting of a tarantula, with the sound of a musical instrument, which is commonly known by the name of a cat-call.† But if you have a patient of this kind under your care, you may assure yourself there is no other way of recovering him effectually, but by forbidding him the use of pen, ink, and paper.

But, to drop the allegory before I have tired it out, there is no species of scribblers more offensive, and more incurable, than your periodical writers, whose works return upon the public on certain days, and at stated times. We have not the consolation in the perusal of these authors which we find at the reading of all others, namely, that we are sure if we have but patience, we may come to the end of their labours. I have often admired a humorous saying of Diogenes, who, reading a dull author to several of his friends, when every one began to be tired, finding he was almost come to a blank leaf at the end of it, cried, 'Courage, lads, I see land.' On the contrary, our progress through that kind of writers I am now speaking of is never at an end. One day makes work for another—we do not know when to promise ourselves rest.

It is a melancholy thing to consider that the art of printing, which might be the greatest blessing to mankind, should prove detrimental to us, and that it should be made use of to scatter prejudice and ignorance through a people, instead of conveying to them truth and knowledge.

I was lately reading a very whimsical treatise, entitled William Ramsay's‡ Vindication of Astrology. This profound author, among many mystical passages, has the following one: 'The absence of the sun is not the cause of night, forasmuch as his light is so great that it may illuminate the earth all over at once as clear as broad day; but there are tenebrificous and dark stars, by whose influence night is brought on, and which do ray out darkness and obscurity upon the earth as the sun does light.'

I consider writers in the same view this sage astrologer does the heavenly bodies. Some of them are stars that scatter light as others do darkness. I could mention several authors who are tenebrificous stars of the first magnitude, and point out a knot of gentlemen, who have been dull in concert, and may be looked upon as a dark constellation. The nation has been a great while benighted with several of these antiluminaries. I suffered them to ray out their darkness as long as I was able to endure it, till at length I came to a resolution of rising upon them, and hope in a little time to drive them quite out of the British hemisphere.

* Put in the pillory.

† Alluding to the noise made in the Theatres at the condemnation of a play.

‡ Ramsay (or more properly Ramesey,) contended that this absurdity of his was even supported by Scripture, where he read of "darkness over the land of Egypt that may be felt."

No. 583.] *Friday, August* 20, 1714.

Ipse thymum pinosque ferens de montibus altis,
Tecta serat late circum, cui talia curæ:
Ipse labore manum duro terat; ipse feraces
Figat humo plantas et amicos irriget imbres.
Virg. Georg. iv. 112.

With his own hand, the guardian of the bees
For slips of pines may search the mountain trees,
And with wild thyme and sav'ry plant the plain,
Till his hard horny fingers ache with pain;
And deck with fruitful trees the fields around,
And with refreshing waters drench the ground.
Dryden.

Every station of life has duties which are proper to it. Those who are determined by choice to any particular kind of business, are indeed more happy than those who are determined by necessity; but both are under an equal obligation of fixing on employments, which may be either useful to themselves or beneficial to others: no one of the sons of Adam ought to think himself exempt from that labour and industry which were denounced to our first parent, and in him to all his posterity. Those to whom birth or fortune may seem to make such an application unnecessary, ought to find out some calling or profession for themselves, that they may not lie as a burden on the species, and be the only useless parts of the creation.

Many of our country gentlemen in their busy hours apply themselves wholly to the chase, or to some other diversion which they find in the fields and woods. This gave occasion to one of our most eminent English writers to represent every one of them as lying under a kind of curse, pronounced to them in the words of Goliah, 'I will give thee to the fowls of the air and to the beasts of the field.'

Though exercises of this kind, when indulged with moderation, may have a good influence both on the mind and body, the country affords many other amusements of a more noble kind.

Among these, I know none more delightful in itself, and beneficial to the public, than that of planting. I could mention a nobleman whose fortune has placed him in several parts of England, and who has always left these visible marks behind him, which show he has been there: he never hired a house in his life, without leaving all about it the seeds of wealth, and bestowing legacies on the posterity of the owner. Had all the gentlemen of England made the same improvements upon their estates, our whole country would have been at this time as one great garden. Nor ought such an employment to be looked upon as too inglorious for men of the highest rank. There have been heroes in this art, as well as in others. We are told in particular of Cyrus the Great, that he planted all the Lesser Asia. There is indeed something truly magnificent in this kind of amusement: it gives a nobler air to several parts of nature; it fills the earth with a variety of beautiful scenes, and has something in it like creation. For this reason the pleasure of one who plants is something like that of a poet, who, as Aristotle observes, is more delighted with his productions than any other writer or artist whatsoever.

Plantations have one advantage in them which is not to be found in most other works, as they give a pleasure of a more lasting date, and continually improve in the eye of the planter. When you have finished a building, or any other undertaking of the like nature, it immediately decays upon your hands: you see it brought to the utmost point of perfection, and from that time hastening to its ruin. On the contrary, when you have finished your plantations, they are still arriving at greater degrees of perfection as long as you live, and appear more delightful in every succeeding year than they did in the foregoing.

But I do not only recommend this art to men of estates as a pleasing amusement, but as it is a kind of virtuous employment, and may therefore be inculcated by moral motives; particularly from the love which we ought to have for our country, and the regard which we ought to bear to our posterity. As for the first I need only mention what is frequently observed by others, that the increase of forest trees does by no means bear a proportion to the destruction of them, insomuch, that in a few ages the nation may be at a loss to supply itself with timber sufficient for the fleets of England. I know when a man talks of posterity in matters of this nature, he is looked upon with an eye of ridicule by the cunning and selfish part of mankind. Most people are of the humour of an old fellow of a college, who, when he was pressed by the society to come into something that might redound to the good of their successors, grew very peevish: 'We are always doing,' says he, 'something for posterity, but I would fain see posterity do something for us.'

But I think men are inexcusable, who fail in a duty of this nature, since it is so easily discharged. When a man considers that the putting a few twigs into the ground is doing good to one who will make his appearance in the world about fifty years hence, or that he is perhaps making one of his own descendants easy or rich, by so inconsiderable an expense, if he finds himself averse to it, he must conclude that he has a poor and base heart, void of all generous principles and love to mankind.

There is one consideration which may very much enforce what I have here said. Many honest minds, that are naturally disposed to do good in the world, and become beneficial to mankind, complain within themselves that they have not talents for it. This therefore is a good office, which is suited to the meanest capacities, and which may be performed by multitudes who have not abilities sufficient to deserve well of their country, and to recommend themselves to their posterity, by any other method. It is the phrase of a friend of mine, when any useful country neighbour dies, that 'you may trace him;' which I look upon as a good funeral oration, at the death of an honest husbandman who had left the impressions of his industry behind him in the place where he has lived.

Upon the foregoing considerations, I can scarcely forbear representing the subject of this paper as a kind of moral virtue; which, as I have already shown, recommends itself likewise by the pleasure that attends it. It must be confessed that this is none of those turbulent pleasures which are apt to gratify a man in the heats of youth; but, if it be not so tumultuous, it is more lasting. Nothing can be more delightful than to entertain ourselves with prospects of our own making, and to walk under those shades which our own industry has raised. Amusements of this nature compose the mind, and lay at rest all those passions which are uneasy to the soul of man, besides that they naturally engender good thoughts, and dispose us to laudable contemplations. Many of the old philosophers passed away the greatest parts of their lives among their gardens. Epicurus himself could not think sensual pleasure attainable in any other scene. Every reader, who is acquainted with Homer, Virgil, and Horace, the greatest geniuses of all antiquity, knows very well with how much rapture they have spoken on this subject; and that Virgil in particular has written a whole book on the art of planting.

This art seems to have been more especially adapted to the nature of man in his primæval state, when he had life enough to see his productions flourish in their utmost beauty, and gradually decay with him. One who lived before the flood might have seen a wood of the tallest oaks in the acorn. But I only mention this particular, in order to introduce, in my next paper, a history which I have found among the accounts of China, and which may be looked upon as an antediluvian novel.

No. 584.] *Monday, August* 23, 1714.

Hic gelidi fontes hic mollia prata, Lycori,
Hic nemus, hic toto tecum consumerer ævo.
Virg. Ecl. x. 42.

Come, see what pleasures in our plains abound:
The woods, the fountains, and the flow'ry ground;
Here I could live, and love, and die with only you.
Dryden.

HILPA was one of the hundred and fifty daughters of Zilpa, of the race of Cohu, by whom some of the learned think is meant Cain. She was exceedingly beautiful; and, when she was but a girl of threescore and ten years of age, received the addresses of several who made love to her. Among these were two brothers, Harpath and Shalum. Harpath being the first-born, was master of that fruitful region which lies at the foot of mount Tirzah, in the southern parts of China. Shalum (which is to say the planter in the Chinese language) possessed all the neighbouring hills, and that great range of mountains which goes under the name of Tirzah. Harpath was of a haughty contemptuous spirit; Shalum was of a gentle disposition, beloved both by God and man.

It is said that among the antediluvian women, the daughters of Cohu had their minds wholly set upon riches; for which reason the beautiful Hilpa preferred Harpath to Shalum, because of his numerous flocks and herds, that covered all the low country which runs along the foot of mount Tirzah, and is watered by several fountains and streams breaking out of the sides of that mountain.

Harpath made so quick a despatch of his courtship, that he married Hilpa in the hundredth year of her age; and, being of an insolent temper, laughed to scorn his brother Shalum for having pretended to the beautiful Hilpa, when he was master of nothing but a long chain of rocks and mountains. This so much provoked Shalum, that he is said to have cursed his brother in the bitterness of his heart, and to have prayed that one of his mountains might fall upon his head if ever he came within the shadow of it.

From this time forward Harpath would never venture out of the valleys, but came to an untimely end in the two hundred and fiftieth year of his age, being drowned in a river as he attempted to cross it. This river is called to this day, from his name who perished in it, the river Harpath; and, what is very remarkable, issues out of one of those mountains which Shalum wished might fall upon his brother, when he cursed him in the bitterness of his heart.

Hilpa was in the hundredth and sixtieth year of her age at the death of her husband, having brought him but fifty children before he was snatched away, as has been already related. Many of the antediluvians made love to the young widow; though no one was thought so likely to succeed in her affections as her first lover Shalum, who renewed his court to her about ten years after the death of Harpath; for it was not thought decent in those days that a widow should be seen by a man within ten years after the decease of her husband.

Shalum, falling into a deep melancholy, and resolving to take away that objection which had been raised against him when he made his first addresses to Hilpa, began immediately after her marriage with Harpath, to plant all that mountainous region which fell to his lot in the division of this country. He knew how to adapt every plant to its proper soil, and is thought to have inherited many traditional secrets of that art from the first man. This employment turned at length to his profit as well as to his amusement; his mountains were in a few years shaded with young trees, that gradually shot up into groves, woods, and forests, intermixed with walks, and lawns, and gardens; insomuch that the whole region, from a naked and desolate prospect, began now to look like a second Paradise. The pleasantness of the place, and the agreeable disposition of Shalum, who was reckoned one of the mildest and wisest of all who lived before the flood, drew into it multitudes of people, who were perpetually employed in the sinking of wells, the digging of trenches, and the hollowing of trees, for the better distribution of water through every part of this spacious plantation.

The habitations of Shalum looked every year more beautiful in the eyes of Hilpa, who, after the space of seventy autumns, was wonderfully pleased with the distant prospect of Shalum's hills, which were then covered with innumerable tufts of trees and gloomy scenes that gave a magnificence to the place, and converted it into one of the finest landscapes the eye of man could behold.

The Chinese record a letter which Shalum is said to have written to Hilpa in the eleventh year of her widowhood. I shall here translate it, without departing from that noble simplicity of sentiments and plainness of manners which appear in the original.

Shalum was at this time one hundred and eighty years old, and Hilpa one hundred and seventy.

'*I Shalum, Master of Mount Tirzah, to Hilpa, Mistress of the Valleys.*

'In the 788th year of the creation.

'What have I not suffered, O thou

daughter of Zilpa, since thou gavest thyself away in marriage to my rival? I grew weary of the light of the sun, and have been ever since covering myself with woods and forests. These threescore and ten years have I bewailed the loss of thee on the top of mount Tirzah, and soothed my melancholy among a thousand gloomy shades of my own raising. My dwellings are at present as the garden of God; every part of them is filled with fruits, and flowers, and fountains. The whole mountain is perfumed for thy reception. Come up into it, O my beloved, and let us people this spot of the new world with a beautiful race of mortals: let us multiply exceedingly among these delightful shades, and fill every quarter of them with sons and daughters. Remember, Oh thou daughter of Zilpa, that the age of man is but a thousand years; that beauty is the admiration but of a few centuries. It flourishes as a mountain oak, or as a cedar on the top of Tirzah, which in three or four hundred years will fade away, and never be thought of by posterity, unless a young wood springs from its roots. Think well on this, and remember thy neighbour in the mountains.'

Having here inserted this letter, which I look upon as the only antediluvian billet-doux now extant, I shall in my next paper give the answer to it, and the sequel of this story.

No. 585.] *Wednesday, August 25*, 1714.

Ipsi lætitia voces ad sidera jactant
Intonsi montes: ipsæ jam carmina rupes,
Ipsa sonant arbusta—— *Virg.* Ecl. v. 63.

The mountain-tops unshorn, the rocks rejoice;
The lowly shrubs partake of human voice.—*Dryden.*

THE SEQUEL OF THE STORY OF SHALUM AND HILPA.

The letter inserted in my last had so good an effect upon Hilpa, that she answered it in less than twelve months, after the following manner:

Hilpa, Mistress of the Valleys, to Shalum, Master of Mount Tirzah.

'In the 789th year of the creation.

'What have I to do with thee, O Shalum? Thou praiseth Hilpa's beauty, but art thou not secretly enamoured with the verdure of her meadows? Art thou not more affected with the prospect of her green valleys than thou wouldest be with the sight of her person? The lowings of my herds, and the bleatings of my flocks, make a pleasant echo in thy mountains, and sound sweetly in thy ears. What though I am delighted with the wavings of thy forests, and those breezes of perfumes which flow from the top of Tirzah, are these like the riches of the valley?

'I know thee, O Shalum; thou art more wise and happy than any of the sons of men. Thy dwellings are among the cedars, thou searchest out the diversity of soils, thou understandest the influences of the stars, and markest the change of seasons. Can a woman appear lovely in the eyes of such a one? Disquiet me not, O Shalum; let me alone, that I may enjoy those goodly possessions which are fallen to my lot. Win me not by thy enticing words. May thy trees increase and multiply; mayest thou add wood to wood, and shade to shade: but tempt not Hilpa to destroy thy solitude, and make thy retirement populous.'

The Chinese say, that a little time afterwards she accepted of a treat in one of the neighbouring hills to which Shalum had invited her. This treat lasted for two years, and is said to have cost Shalum five hundred antelopes, two thousand ostriches, and a thousand tons of milk; but what most of all recommended it, was that variety of delicious fruits and potherbs, in which no person then living could any way equal Shalum.

He treated her in the bower which he had planted amidst the wood of nightingales.—This wood was made up of such fruit-trees and plants as are most agreeable to the several kinds of singing birds; so that it had drawn into it all the music of the country, and was filled from one end of the year to the other with the most agreeable concert in season.

He showed her every day some beautiful and surprising scene in this new region of woodlands; and, as by this means he had all the opportunities he could wish for of opening his mind to her, he succeeded so well, that upon her departure she made him a kind of promise, and gave him her word to return him a positive answer in less than fifty years.

She had not been long among her own people in the valleys, when she received new overtures, and at the same time a most splendid visit from Mishpach, who was a mighty man of old, and had built a great city which he called after his own name. Every house was made for at least a thousand years; nay, there were some that were leased out for three lives; so that the quantity of stone and timber consumed in this building is scarce to be imagined by those who live in the present age of the world. This great man entertained her with the voice of musical instruments which had been lately invented, and danced before her to the sound of the timbrel. He also presented her with several domestic utensils wrought in brass and iron, which had been newly found out for the convenience of life. In the mean time Shalum grew very uneasy with himself, and was sorely displeased at Hilpa for the reception which she had given to Mishpach, insomuch that he never wrote to her or spoke of her during a whole revolution of Saturn; but, finding that this intercourse went no farther than a visit, he again renewed his addresses to her; who, during his long silence, is said very often to have cast a wishing eye upon mount Tirzah.

Her mind continued wavering about twenty years longer between Shalum and Mishpach: for though her inclinations favoured the former, her interest pleaded very powerfully for the other. While her heart was in this unsettled condition, the following accident happened, which determined her choice. A high tower of wood that stood in the city of Mishpach having caught fire by a flash of lightning, in a few days reduced the whole town to ashes. Mishpach resolved to rebuild the place whatever it should cost him; and having already destroyed all the timber of the country, he was forced to have recourse to Shalum, whose forests were now two hundred years old. He purchased these woods with so many herds of cattle and flocks of sheep, and with such a vast extent of fields and pastures, that Shalum was now grown more wealthy than Mishpach; and therefore appeared so charming in the eyes of Zilpah's daughter, that she no longer refused him in marriage. On the day in which he brought her up into the mountains, he raised a most prodigious pile of cedar, and of every sweet-smelling wood, which reached above three hundred cubits in height: he also cast into the pile bundles of myrrh, and sheaves of spikenard, enriching it with every spicy shrub, and making it fat with the gums of his plantations. This was the burnt offering which Shalum offered in the day of his espousals: the smoke of it ascended up to heaven, and filled the whole country with incense and perfume.

No. 586.] *Friday, August 27, 1714.*

—Quæ in vita usurpant homines, cogitant, curant, vident quæque agunt vigilantes, agitantquæ, ea cuique in somno accidunt. *Cic. de Div.*

The things which employ men's waking thoughts and actions recur to their imaginations in sleep.

By the last post, I received the following letter which is built upon a thought that is new, and very well carried on; for which reason I shall give it to the public without alteration, addition, or amendment.

'Sir,—It was a good piece of advice which Pythagoras gave to his scholars—that every night before they slept they should examine what they had been doing that day, and so discover what actions were worthy of pursuit to-morrow, and what little vices were to be prevented from slipping unawares into a habit. If I might second the philosopher's advice, it should be mine, that, in a morning, before my scholar rose, he should consider what he had been about that night, and with the same strictness, as if the condition he has believed himself to be in was real. Such a scrutiny into the actions of his fancy, must be of considerable advantage: for this reason, because the circumstances which a man imagines himself in during sleep are generally such as entirely favour his inclinations, good or bad, and give him imaginary opportunities of pursuing them to the utmost; so that his temper will lie fairly open to his view, while he considers how it is moved when free from those constraints which the accidents of real life put it under. Dreams are certainly the result of our waking thoughts, and our daily hopes and fears, are what give the mind such nimble relishes of pleasure, and such severe touches of pain in its midnight rambles. A man that murders his enemy, or deserts his friend, in a dream, had need to guard his temper against revenge and ingratitude, and take heed that he be not tempted to do a vile thing in the pursuit of false, or the neglect of true honour. For my part, I seldom receive a benefit, but in a night or two's time I make most noble returns for it; which, though my benefactor is not a whit the better for, yet it pleases me to think that it was from a principle of gratitude in me that my mind was susceptible of such generous transport, while I thought myself repaying the kindness of my friend: and I have often been ready to beg pardon, instead of returning an injury, after considering that, when the offender was in my power, I had carried my resentments much too far.

'I think it has been observed in the course of your papers, how much one's happiness or misery may depend upon the imagination: of which truth those strange workings of fancy in sleep are no inconsiderable instances; so that not only the advantage a man has of making discoveries of himself, but a regard to his own ease or disquiet, may induce him to accept of my advice. Such as are willing to comply with it, I shall put into a way of doing it with pleasure, by observing only one maxim which I shall give them, viz. "To go to bed with a mind entirely free from passion, and a body clear of the least intemperance."

'They, indeed, who can sink into sleep with their thoughts less calm or innocent than they should be, do but plunge themselves into scenes of guilt and misery; or they who are willing to purchase any midnight disquietudes for the satisfaction of a full meal, or a skin full of wine; these I have nothing to say to, as not knowing how to invite them to reflections full of shame and horror; but those that will observe this rule, I promise them they shall awake into health and cheerfulness, and be capable of recounting, with delight, those glorious moments, wherein the mind has been indulging itself in such luxury of thought, such noble hurry of imagination. Suppose a man's going supperless to bed should introduce him to the table of some great prince or other, where he shall be entertained with the noolest marks of honour and plenty, and do so much business after, that he shall rise with as good a stomach for his breakfast as if he had fasted all night long: or, suppose he should see his dearest friends remain all night in great distresses, which he could instantly have disengaged them from, could he have been content to have gone to bed without the other bottle; believe me these effects of fancy are no contemptible consequences of commanding or indulging one's appetite.

'I forbear recommending my advice upon many other accounts, until I hear how you and your readers relish what I have already said; among whom, if there be any that may pretend it is useless to them because they never dream at all, there may be others perhaps who do little else all day long. Were every one as sensible as I am what happens to him in his sleep, it would be no dispute whether we pass so considerable a portion of our time in the condition of stocks and stones, or whether the soul were not perpetually at work upon the principle of thought. However, it is an honest endeavour of mine to persuade my countrymen to reap some advantage from so many unregarded hours, and as such you will encourage it.

'I shall conclude with giving you a sketch or two of my way of proceeding.

'If I have any business of consequence to do to-morrow, I am scarce dropt asleep to-night but I am in the midst of it; and when awake, I consider the whole procession of the affair, and get the advantage of the next day's experience before the sun has risen upon it.

'There is scarcely a great post but what I have some time or other been in; but my behaviour while I was master of a college pleases me so well, that whenever there is a province of that nature vacant, I intend to step in as soon as I can.

'I have done many things that would not pass examination, when I have had the art of flying or being invisible; for which reason I am glad I am not possessed of those extraordinary qualities.

'Lastly, Mr. Spectator, I have been a great correspondent of yours, and have read many of my letters in your paper which I never wrote you. If you have a mind I should really be so, I have got a parcel of visions and other miscellanies in my noctuary, which I shall send you to enrich your paper on proper occasions. I am, &c.

'JOHN SHADOW.

'Oxford, Aug. 20.'

No. 587.] *Monday, August* 30, 1714.

Intus, et in cute novi. *Pers.* Sat. iii. 30.

I know thee to thy bottom; from within
Thy shallow centre to the utmost skin.—*Dryden.*

THOUGH the author of the following vision is unknown to me, I am apt to think it may be the work of that ingenious gentleman, who promised me, in the last paper, some extracts out of his noctuary.

'SIR,—I was the other day reading the life of Mahomet. Among many other extravagancies, I find it recorded of that impostor, that, in the fourth year of his age, the angel Gabriel caught him up whilst he was amongst his play-fellows; and carrying him aside, cut open his breast, plucked out his heart, and wrung out of it that black drop of blood, in which, say the Turkish divines, is contained the *fomes peccati*, so that he was free from sin ever after. I immediately said to myself, Though this story be a fiction, a very good moral may be drawn from it, would every man but apply it to himself, and endeavour to squeeze out of his heart whatever sins or ill qualities he finds in it.

'While my mind was wholly taken up with this contemplation, I insensibly fell into a most pleasing slumber, when methought two porters entered my chamber carrying a large chest between them. After having set it down in the middle of the room, they departed. I immediately endeavoured to open what was sent me, when a shape, like that in which we paint our angels, appeared before me, and forbade me. "Enclosed," said he, "are the hearts of several of your friends and acquaintance; but, before you can be qualified to see and animadvert on the failings of others, you must be pure yourself;" whereupon he drew out his incision knife, cut me open, took out my heart, and began to squeeze it. I was in a great confusion to see how many things, which I had always cherished as virtues, issued out of my heart on this occasion. In short, after it had been thoroughly squeezed, it looked like an empty bladder; when the phantom breathing a fresh particle of divine air into it, restored it safe to its former repository; and having sewed me up, we began to examine the chest.

'The hearts were all enclosed in transparent phials, and preserved in liquor which looked like spirits of wine. The first which I cast my eye upon, I was afraid would have broke the glass which contained it. It shot up and down, with incredible swiftness, through the liquor in which it swam, and very frequently bounced against the side of the phial. The *fomes*, or spot in the middle of it, was not large, but of a red fiery colour, and seemed to be the cause of these violent agitations. "That," says my instructor, "is the heart of Tom Dreadnought, who behaved himself well in the late wars, but has for these ten years last past been aiming at some post of honour to no purpose. He is lately retired into the country, where, quite choked up with spleen and choler, he rails at better men than himself, and will be for ever uneasy, because it is impossible he should think his merits sufficiently rewarded." The next heart that I examined was remarkable for its smallness; it lay still at the bottom of the phial, and I could hardly perceive that it beat at all. The *fomes* was quite black, and had almost diffused itself over the whole heart. "This," says my interpreter, "is the heart of Dick Gloomy, who never thirsted after any thing but money. Notwithstanding all his endeavours, he is still poor. This has flung him into a most deplorable state of melancholy and despair. He is a composition of envy and idleness; hates mankind, but gives them their revenge by being more uneasy to himself than to any one else."

'The phial I looked upon next contained a large fair heart, which beat very strongly. The *fomes* or spot in it was exceedingly small; but I could not help observing that, which way soever I turned the phial, it always appeared uppermost, and in the strongest point of light. "The heart you are examining," says my companion, "belongs to Will Worthy. He has, indeed, a most noble soul, and is possessed of a thousand good qualities. The speck which you discover is vanity."

'"Here," says the angel, "is the heart of Freelove, your intimate friend." Freelove and I," said I, "are at present very cold to one another, and I do not care for looking on the heart of a man which I fear is overcast with rancour." My teacher commanded me to look upon it; I did so, and, to my unspeakable surprise, found that a small swelling spot, which I at first took to be ill-will towards me, was only passion; and that upon my nearer inspection it wholly disappeared; upon which the phantom told me Freelove was one of the best-natured men alive.

'"This," says my teacher, "is a female heart of your acquaintance." I found the *fomes* in it of the largest size, and of a hundred different colours, which were still varying every moment. Upon my asking to whom it belonged, I was informed that it was the heart of Coquetilla.

'I set it down, and drew out another, in which I took the *fomes* at first sight to be very small, but was amazed to find that, as I looked steadfastly upon it, it grew still larger. It was the heart of Melissa, a noted prude, who lives the next door to me.

'"I show you this," said the phantom, "because it is indeed a rarity, and you have the happiness to know the person to whom it belongs." He then put into my hand a large chrystal glass, that enclosed a heart, in which, though I examined it with the utmost nicety, I could not perceive any blemish. I made no scruple to affirm that it must be the heart of Seraphina; and was glad, but not surprised, to find that it was so. "She is indeed," continued my guide, "the ornament, as well as the envy, of her sex." At these last words he pointed to the hearts of several of her female acquaintance which lay in different phials, and had very large spots in them, all of a deep blue. "You are not to wonder," says he, "that you see no spot in a heart whose innocence has been proof against all the corruptions of a depraved age. If it has any blemish, it is too small to be discovered by human eyes.

'I laid it down, and took up the hearts of other females, in all of which the *fomes* ran in several veins, which were twisted together, and made a very perplexed figure. I asked the meaning of it, and was told it represented deceit.

'I should have been glad to have examined the hearts of several of my acquaintance, whom I knew to be particularly addicted to drinking, gaming, intriguing, &c. but my interpreter told me, I must let that alone until another opportunity, and flung down the cover of the chest with so much violence as immediately awoke me.'

No. 588.] *Wednesday, September* 1, 1714.

Dicitis, omnis in imbecilitate est et gratia, et caritas.
Cicero.

You pretend that all kindness and benevolence is founded in weakness.

MAN may be considered in two views, as a reasonable and as a social being; capable of becoming himself either happy or miserable, and of contributing to the happiness or misery of his fellow-creatures. Suitably to this double capacity, the Contriver of human nature hath wisely furnished it with two principles of action, self-love and benevolence; designed one of them to render man wakeful to his own personal interest, the other to dispose him for giving his utmost assistance to all engaged in the same pursuit. This is such an account of our frame, so agreeable to reason, so much for the honour of our Maker, and the credit of our species, that it may appear somewhat unaccountable what should induce men to represent human nature as they do, under characters of disadvantage; or having drawn it with a little sordid aspect, what pleasure they can possibly take in such a picture. Do they reflect that it is their own; and if we would believe themselves, is not more odious than the original? One of the first that talked in this lofty strain of our nature was Epicurus. Beneficence, would his followers say, is all founded in weakness; and, whatever he pretended, the kindness that passeth between men and men is by every man directed to himself. This, it must be confessed, is of a piece with the rest of that hopeful philosophy, which having patched man up out of the four elements, attributes his being to chance, and derives all his actions from an unintelligible declination of atoms. And for these glorious discoveries, the poet is beyond measure transported in the praises of his hero, as if he must needs be something more than man, only for an endeavour to prove that man is in nothing superior to beasts. In this school was Mr. Hobbes instructed to speak after the same manner, if he did not rather draw his knowledge from an observation of his own temper; for he somewhere unluckily lays down this as a rule, 'that from the similitudes of thoughts and passions of one man to the thoughts and passions of another, whosoever looks into himself, and considers what he doth when he thinks, hopes, fears, &c. and upon what grounds, he shall hereby read and know what are the thoughts and passions of all other men upon the like occasions.' Now we will allow Mr. Hobbes to know best how he was inclined; but, in earnest, I should be heartily out of conceit with myself, if I thought myself of this unamiable temper, as he affirms, and should have as little kindness for myself as for any body in the world. Hitherto I always imagined that kind and benevolent propensions were the original growth of the heart of man, and, however checked and overtopped by counter inclinations, that have since sprung up within us, have still some force in the worst of tempers, and a considerable influence on the best. And, methinks, it is a fair step towards the proof of this, that the most beneficent of all beings is he who hath an absolute fulness of perfection in himself; who gave existence to the universe, and so cannot be supposed to want that which he communicated, without diminishing from the plenitude of his own power and happiness. The philosophers before mentioned have indeed done all that in them lay to invalidate this argument; for, placing the gods in a state of the most elevated blessedness, they describe them as selfish as we poor miserable mortals can be, and shut them out from all concern for mankind, upon the score of their having no need of us. But if He that sitteth in the heavens wants not us, we stand in continual need of him; and surely, next to the survey of the immense treasures of his own mind, the most exalted pleasures he receives is from beholding millions of creatures, lately drawn out of the gulf of non-existence, rejoicing in the various degrees of being and happiness imparted to them. And as this is the true, the glorious character of the Deity, so in forming a reasonable creature he would not, if possible, suffer his image to pass out of his hands unadorned with a resemblance of himself in this most lovely part of his nature. For what complacency could a mind, whose love is as unbounded as his knowledge, have in a work so unlike himself; a creature that should be capable of knowing and conversing with a vast circle of objects, and love none but himself? What proportion would there be between the head and the heart of such a creature, its affections and its understanding? Or could a society of such creatures, with no other bottom but self-love on which to maintain a commerce, ever flourish? Reason, it is certain, would oblige every man to pursue the general happiness as the means to procure and establish his own; and yet, if besides this consideration, there were not a natural instinct prompting men to desire the welfare and satisfaction of others, self-love, in defiance of the admonitions of reason, would quickly run all things into a state of war and confusion. As nearly interested as the soul is in the fate of the body, our provident Creator saw it necessary, by the constant returns of hunger and thirst, those importunate appetites, to put it in mind of its charge: knowing that if we should eat and drink no oftener than cold abstracted speculation should put us upon these exercises, and then leave it to reason to prescribe the quantity, we should soon refine ourselves out of this bodily life. And, indeed, it is obvious to remark, that we follow nothing heartily unless carried to it by inclinations which anticipate our reason, and, like a bias, draw the mind strongly towards it. In order, therefore, to establish a perpetual intercourse of benefits amongst mankind, their Maker would not fail to give them this generous prepossession of benevolence, if, as I have said, it were possible. And from whence can we go about to argue its impossibility? Is it inconsistent with self-love? Are their motions contrary? No more than the diurnal rotation of the earth is opposed to its annual, or, its motion round its own centre, which might be improved as an illustration of self-love, to that which whirls it about the common centre of the world, answering to universal benevolence. Is the force of self-love abated, or its interest prejudiced, by benevolence? So far from it, that benevolence, though a distinct principle, is extremely serviceable to self-love, and then doth most service when it is least designed.

But to descend from reason to matter of fact; the pity which arises on sight of persons in distress, and the satisfaction of mind which is the consequence of having removed them into a happier state, are instead of a thousand arguments to prove such a thing as a disinterested benevolence. Did pity proceed from a reflection we make upon our liableness to the same ill accidents we see befall others, it were nothing to the present purpose; but this is assigning an artificial cause of a natural passion, and can by no means be admitted as a tolerable account of it, because children and persons most thoughtless about their own condition, and incapable of entering into the prospects of futurity, feel the most violent touches of compassion. And then, as to that charming delight which immediately follows the giving joy to another, or relieving his sorrow, and is, when the objects are numerous, and the kindness of importance, really inexpressible, what can this be owing to but consciousness of a man's having done something praise-worthy, and expressive of a great soul? Whereas, if in all this he only sacrificed to vanity and self-love, as there would be nothing brave in actions that make the most shining appearance, so nature would not have rewarded them with this divine pleasure; nor could the commendations, which a person receives for benefits done upon selfish views, be at all more satisfactory than when he is applauded for what he doth without design; because, in both cases, the ends of self-love are equally answered. The conscience of approving ones self a benefactor to mankind is the noblest recompence for being so; doubtless it is, and the most interested cannot propose any thing so much to their own advantage; notwithstanding which, the inclination is nevertheless unselfish. The pleasure which attends the gratification of our hunger and thirst, is not the cause of these appetites; they are previous to any such prospect; and so likewise is the desire of doing good; with this difference, that, being seated in the intellectual part, this last, though antecedent to reason, may yet be improved and regulated by it; and, I will add, is no otherwise a virtue than as it is so. Thus have I contended for the dignity of that nature I have the honour to partake of; and, after all the evidence produced, I think I have a right to conclude, against the motto of this paper, that there is such a thing as generosity in the world. Though, if I were under a mistake in this, I should say as Cicero, in relation to the immortality of the soul, I willingly err, and should believe it very much for the interest of mankind to lie under the same delusion. For the contrary notion naturally tends to dispirit the mind, and sinks it into a meanness fatal to the god-like zeal of doing good: as, on the other hand, it teaches people to be ungrateful, by possessing them with a persuasion concerning their benefactors, that they have no regard to them in the benefits they bestow. Now he that banishes gratitude from among men, by so doing stops up the stream of beneficence: for though in conferring kindnesses, a truly generous man doth not aim at a return, yet he looks to the qualities of the person obliged; and as nothing renders a person more unworthy of a benefit than his being without all resentment of it, he will not be extremely forward to oblige such a man.

No. 589.] *Friday, September* 3, 1714.

Persequitur scelus ille suum; labefactaque tandem
Ictibus innumeris, adductaque funibus arbor
Corruit——— *Ovid*, Met. Lib. 8. 774.

The impious axe he plies, loud strokes resound:
Till dragg'd with ropes, and fell'd with many a wound,
The loosen'd tree comes rushing to the ground.

'Sir,—I am so great an admirer of rees, that the spot of ground I have chosen to build a smal. seat upon in the country is almost in the midst of a large wood. I was obliged, much against my will, to cut down several trees, that I might have any such thing as a walk in my gardens; but then I have taken care to leave the space, between every walk, as much a wood as I found it. The moment you turn either to the right or left, you are in a forest, where nature presents you with a much more beautiful scene than could have been raised by art.

'Instead of tulips or carnations, I can show you oaks in my garden of four hundred years standing, and a knot of elms that might shelter a troop of horse from the rain.

'It is not without the utmost indignation that I observe several prodigal young heirs in the neighbourhood felling down the most glorious monuments of their ancestors' industry, and ruining, in a day, the product of ages.

'I am mightily pleased with your discourse upon planting, which put me upon looking into my books, to give you some account of the veneration the ancients had for trees. There is an old tradition, that Abraham planted a cypress, a pine, and a cedar; and that these three incorporated into one tree, which was cut down for the building of the temple of Solomon.

'Isidorus, who lived in the reign of Constantius, assures us, that he saw, even in his time, that famous oak in the plains of Mamre, under which Abraham is reported to have dwelt; and adds, that the people looked upon it with a great veneration, and preserved it as a sacred tree.

'The heathens still went farther, and regarded it as the highest piece of sacrilege to injure certain trees which they took to be protected by some deity. The story of Erisicthon, the grove at Dodona, and that at Delphi, are all instances of this kind.

'If we consider the machine in Virgil, so much blamed by several critics, in this light, we shall hardly think it too violent.

'Æneas, when he built his fleet in order to sail for Italy, was obliged to cut down the grove on mount Ida, which however he durst not do until he had obtained leave from Cybele, to whom it was dedicated. The goddess could not but think herself obliged to protect these ships, which were made of consecrated timber, after a very extraordinary manner, and therefore desired Jupiter that they might not be obnoxious to the power of waves or winds. Jupiter would not grant this, but promised her that as many as came safe to Italy should be transformed into goddesses of the sea; which the poet tells us was accordingly executed.

"And now at length the numbered hours were come,
Prefix'd by Fate's irrevocable doom,
When the great mother of the gods was free
To save her ships, and finish Jove's decree.

First, from the quarter of the morn there sprung
A light that sing'd the heavens, and shot along:
Then from a cloud, fring'd round with golden fires,
Were timbrels heard, and Berecynthian quires:
And last a voice with more than mortal sounds,
Both hosts in arms oppos'd with equal horror wounds.
'O Trojan race, your needless aid forbear;
And know my ships are my peculiar care.
With greater ease the bold Rutulian may,
With hissing brands, attempt to burn the sea,
Than singe my sacred pines. But you, my charge,
Loos'd from your crooked anchors, launch at large,
Exalted each a nymph: forsake the sand,
And swim the seas, at Cybele's command.'
No sooner had the goddess ceas'd to speak,
When, lo, th' obedient ships their hawsers break,
And, strange to tell, like dolphins, in the main,
They plunge their prows, and dive and spring again:
As many beauteous maids the billows sweep,
As rode before tall vessels on the deep."

Dryden's Virg.

'The common opinion concerning the nymphs, whom the ancients called Hamadryads, is more to the honour of trees than any thing yet mentioned. It was thought the fate of these nymphs had so near a dependance on some trees, more especially oaks, that they lived and died together. For this reason they were extremely grateful to such persons who preserved those trees with which their being subsisted. Apollonius tells us a very remarkable story to this purpose, with which I shall conclude my letter.

'A certain man, called Rhæcus, observing an old oak ready to fall, and being moved with a sort of compassion towards the tree, ordered his servants to pour in fresh earth at the roots of it, and set it upright. The Hamadryad, or nymph, who must necessarily have perished with the tree, appeared to him the next day, and, after having returned him her thanks, told him she was ready to grant whatever he should ask. As she was extremely beautiful, Rhæcus desired he might be entertained as her lover. The Hamadryad, not much displeased with the request, promised to give him a meeting, but commanded him for some days to abstain from the embraces of all other women, adding that she would send a bee to him, to let him know when he was to be happy. Rhæcus was, it seems, too much addicted to gaming, and happened to be in a run of ill-luck when the faithful bee came buzzing about him; so that, instead of minding his kind invitation, he had like to have killed him for his pains. The Hamadryad was so provoked at her own disappointment, and the ill usage of her messenger, that she deprived Rhæcus of the use of his limbs. However, says the story, he was not so much a cripple, but he made a shift to cut down the tree, and consequently to fell his mistress.'

No. 590.] *Monday, September* 6, 1714.

———Assiduo labuntur tempora motu
Non secus ac flumen. Neque enim consistere flumen,
Nec levis hora potest: sed ut unda impellitur unda,
Urgeturque prior venienti, urgetque priorem,
Tempora sic fugiunt pariter, pariturque sequuntur;
Et nova sunt semper. Nam quod fuit ante, relictum est
Fitque quod haud fuerat: momentaque cuncta novantur.

Ovid, Met. Lib. xv. 179.

E'en times are in perpetual flux, and run,
Like rivers from their fountains, rolling on.
For time, no more than streams, is at a stay,
The flying hour is ever on her way;
And as the fountains still supply their store
The wave behind impels the wave before;
Thus in successive course the minutes run,
And urge their predecessor minutes on.
Still moving, ever new: for former things
Are laid aside, like abdicated kings:
And every moment alters what is done,
And innovates some act, till then unknown.

Dryden.

The following discourse comes from the same hand with the essays upon infinitude.

'We consider infinite space as an expansion without a circumference; we consider eternity, or infinite duration, as a line that has neither a beginning nor an end. In our speculations of infinite space, we consider that particular place in which we exist as a kind of centre to the whole expansion. In our speculatious of eternity, we consider the time which is present to us as the middle, which divides the whole line into two equal parts. For this reason, many witty authors compare the present time to an isthmus, or narrow neck of land, that rises in the midst of an ocean, immeasurably diffused on either side of it.

'Philosophy, and indeed common sense, naturally throws eternity under two divisions, which we may call in English that eternity which is past, and that eternity which is to come. The learned terms of *Æternitas a parte ante*, and *Æternitas a parte post*, may be more amusing to the reader, but can have no other idea affixed to them than what is conveyed to us by those words, an eternity that is past, and an eternity that is to come. Each of these eternities is bounded at the one extreme, or, in other words, the former has an end, and the latter a beginning.

'Let us first of all consider that eternity which is past, reserving that which is to come for the subject of another paper. The nature of this eternity is utterly inconceivable by the mind of man: our reason demonstrates to us that it has been, but at the same time can frame no idea of it, but what is big with absurdity and contradiction. We can have no other conception of any duration which is past, than that all of it was once present: and whatever was once present is at some certain distance from us, and whatever is at any certain distance from us, be the distance never so remote, cannot be eternity. The very notion of any duration being past implies that it was once present, for the idea of being once present is actually included in the idea of its being past. This therefore is a depth not to be sounded by human understanding. We are sure that there has been an eternity, and yet contradict ourselves when we measure this eternity by any notion which we can frame of it.

'If we go to the bottom of this matter, we shall find that the difficulties we meet with in our conceptions of eternity proceed from this single reason, that we can have no other idea of any kind of duration, than that by which we ourselves, and all other created beings, do exist; which is, a successive duration made up of past, present, and to come. There is nothing which exists after this manner, all the parts of whose existence were not once actually present, and consequently may be reached by a certain number of years applied to it. We may ascend as high as we please, and employ our being to that eternity which is to come, in adding millions of years to millions of years, and we can never come up to any fountain-head of duration, to any beginning in eternity: but at the same time we are sure, that whatever was once present does lie within the reach of numbers, though perhaps we can never be able to put enough of them together for that purpose. We may as well say, that any thing may be actually present in any part of infinite space, which does not lie at a certain distance from us, as that any part of infinite duration was once actually present, and does not also lie at some determined distance from us. The distance in both cases may be immeasurable and indefinite as to our faculties, but our reason tells us that it cannot be so in itself. Here therefore is that difficulty which human understanding is not capable of surmounting. We are sure that something must have existed from eternity, and are at the same time unable to conceive, that any thing which exists, according to our notion of existence, can have existed from eternity.

'It is hard for a reader, who has not rolled this thought in his own mind, to follow in such an abstracted speculation; but I have been the longer on it, because I think it is a demonstrative argument of the being and eternity of God: and, though there are many other demonstrations which lead us to this great truth, I do not think we ought to lay aside any proofs in this matter, which the light of reason has suggested to us, especially when it is such a one as has been urged by men famous for their penetration and force of understanding, and which appears altogether conclusive to those who will be at the pains to examine it.

'Having thus considered that eternity which is past, according to the best idea we can frame of it, I shall now draw up those several articles on this subject, which are dictated to us by the light of reason, and which may be looked upon as the creed of a philosopher in this great point.

'First, it is certain that no being could have made itself; for, if so, it must have acted before it was, which is a contradiction.

'Secondly, That therefore some being must have existed from all eternity.

'Thirdly, That whatever exists after the manner of created beings, or according to any notions which we have of existence, could not have existed from eternity.

'Fourthly, That this Eternal Being must therefore be the great Author of nature, "the Ancient of Days," who, being at an infinite distance in his perfections from all finite and created beings, exists in a quite different manner from them, and in a manner of which they can have no idea.

'I know that several of the schoolmen, who would not be thought ignorant of any thing, have pretended to explain the manner of God's existence, by telling us that he comprehends infinite duration in every moment: that eternity is with him a *punctum stans*, a fixed point; or, which is as good sense, an infinite instant; that nothing, with reference to his existence, is either past or to come: to which the ingenious Mr. Cowley alludes in his description of heaven:

> "Nothing is there to come, and nothing past,
> But an eternal *now* does always last."

'For my own part, I look upon these propositions as words that have no ideas annexed to them; and think men had better own their ignorance than advance doctrines by which they mean nothing, and which, indeed, are self-contradictory. We cannot be too modest in our disquisitions when we meditate on Him, who is environed with so much glory and perfection, who is the source of being, the fountain of all that existence which we and his whole creation derive from him. Let us therefore, with the utmost humility, acknowledge, that, as some being must necessarily have existed from eternity, so this being does exist after an incomprehensible manner, since it is impossible for a being to have existed from eternity after our manner or notions of existence. Revelation confirms these natural dictates of reason in the accounts which it gives us of the divine existence, where it tells us, that he is the same yesterday, to-day, and for ever; that he is the Alpha and Omega, the beginning and the ending; that a thousand years are with him as one day, and one day as a thousand years: by which, and the like expressions, we are taught that his existence, with relation to time or duration, is infinitely different from the existence of any of his creatures, and consequently that it is impossible for us to frame any adequate conceptions of it.

'In the first revelation which he makes of his own being, he entitles himself, "I Am that I Am;" and when Moses desires to know what name he shall give him in his embassy to Pharaoh, he bids him say that "I Am hath sent you." Our great Creator, by this revelation of himself, does in a manner exclude every thing else from a real existence, and distinguishes himself from his creatures as the only being which truly and really exists. The ancient Platonic notion, which was drawn from speculations of eternity wonderfully agrees with this revelation which God has made of himself. There is nothing, say they, which in reality exists, whose existence, as we call it, is pieced up of past, present, and to come. Such a flitting and successive existence is rather a shadow of existence, and something which is like it, than existence itself. He only properly exists whose existence is entirely present; that is, in other words, who exists in the most perfect manner, and in such a manner as we have no idea of.

'I shall conclude this speculation with one useful inference. How can we sufficiently prostrate ourselves and fall down before our Maker, when we consider that ineffable goodness and wisdom which contrived this existence for finite natures? What must be the overflowings of that good-will, which prompted our Creator to adapt existence to beings in whom it is not necessary? especially when we consider that he himself was before in the complete possession of existence and of happiness, and in the full enjoyment of eternity. What man can think of himself as called out and separated from nothing, of his being made a conscious, a reasonable, and a happy creature; in short, in being taken in as a sharer of existence, and a kind of partner in eternity, without being swallowed up in wonder, in praise, in adoration! It is indeed a thought too big for the mind of man, and rather to be entertained in the secresy of devotion, and in the silence of his soul, than to be expressed by words. The Supreme Being has not given us powers or faculties sufficient to extol and magnify such unutterable goodness.

'It is however some comfort to us, that we shall be always doing what we shall be never able to do, and that a work which cannot be finished, will however be the work of an eternity.'

No. 591.] *Wednesday, September* 8, 1714.

—Tenerorum lusor amorum.
Ovid, Trist. 3. El. iii. Lib. 3. 73.

Love, the soft subject of his sportive muse.

I HAVE just received a letter from a gentleman, who tells me he has observed with no small concern, that my papers have of late been very barren in relation to love; a subject which, when agreeably handled, can scarcely fail of being well received by both sexes.

If my invention therefore should be almost exhausted on this head, he offers to serve under me in the quality of a love-casuist; for which place he conceives himself to be thoroughly qualified, having made this passion his principal study, and observed it in all its different shapes and appearances, from the fifteenth to the forty-fifth year of his age.

He assures me, with an air of confidence, which I hope proceeds from his real abilities, that he does not doubt of giving judgment to the satisfaction of the parties concerned on the most nice and intricate cases which can happen in an amour; as,

How great the contraction of the fingers must be before it amounts to a squeeze by the hand.

What can be properly termed an absolute denial from a maid, and what from a widow.

What advances a lover may presume to make, after having received a pat upon his shoulder from his mistress's fan.

Whether a lady, at the first interview, may allow an humble servant to kiss her hand.

How far it may be permitted to caress the maid in order to succeed with the mistress.

What constructions a man may put upon a smile, and in what cases a frown goes for nothing.

On what occasions a sheepish look may do service, &c.

As a farther proof of his skill, he also sent me several maxims in love, which he assures me are the result of a long and profound reflection, some of which I think myself obliged to communicate to the public, not remembering to have seen them before in any author.

'There are more calamities in the world arising from love than from hatred.

'Love is the daughter of idleness, but the mother of disquietude.

'Men of grave natures, says Sir Francis Bacon, are the most constant; for the same reason men should be more constant than women.

'The gay part of mankind is most amorous, the serious most loving.

'A coquette often loses her reputation while she preserves her virtue.

'A prude often preserves her reputation when she has lost her virtue.

'Love refines a man's behaviour, but makes a woman's ridiculous.

'Love is generally accompanied with good-will in the young, interest in the middle-aged, and a passion too gross to name in the old.

'The endeavours to revive a decaying passion generally extinguish the remains of it.

'A woman who from being a slattern becomes over-neat, or from being over-neat becomes a slattern, is most certainly in love.'

I shall make use of this gentleman's skill as I see occasion; and since I am got upon the subject of love, shall conclude this paper with a copy of verses which were lately sent me by an unknown hand, as I look upon them to be above the ordinary run of sonnetteers.

The author tells me they were written in one of his despairing fits; and I find entertains some hope that his mistress may pity such a passion as he has described, before she knows that she herself is Corinna.

'Conceal, fond man, conceal thy mighty smart,
Nor tell Corinna she has fir'd thy heart.
In vain would'st thou complain, in vain pretend
To ask a pity which she must not lend.
She's too much thy superior to comply,
And too, too fair to let thy passion die.
Languish in secret, and with dumb surprise
Drink the resistless glances of her eyes.
At awful distance entertain thy grief,
Be still in pain, but never ask relief.
Ne'er tempt her scorn of thy consuming state,
Be any way undone, but fly her hate.
Thou must submit to see thy charmer bless
Some happier youth that shall admire her less;
Who in that lovely form, that heavenly mind,
Shall miss ten thousand beauties thou could'st find.
Who with low fancy shall approach her charms,
While, half enjoy'd, she sinks into his arms.
She knows not, must not know, thy nobler fire,
Whom she, and whom the muses do inspire;
Her image only shall thy breast employ,
And fill thy captive soul with shades of joy;
Direct thy dreams by night, thy thoughts by day;
And never, never from thy bosom stray.'*

No. 592.] *Friday, September* 10, 1714.

——Studium sine divite vena.
Hor. Ars Poet. 409.

Art without a vein.—*Roscommon.*

I LOOK upon the playhouse as a world within itself. They have lately furnished the middle region of it with a new set of meteors in order to give the sublime to many modern tragedies. I was there last winter at the first rehearsal of the new thunder,† which is much more deep and sonorous than any hitherto made use of. They have a Salmoneus behind the scenes who plays it off with great success. Their lightnings are made to flash more briskly than heretofore, their clouds are also better furbelowed, and more voluminous; not to mention a violent storm locked up in a great chest, that is designed for the Tempest. They are also provided with above a dozen showers of snow, which, as I am informed, are the plays of many unsuccessful poets artificially cut and shredded for that use. Mr. Ryner's Edgar is to fall in snow at the next acting of King Lear, in order to heighten, or rather to alleviate, the distress of that unfortunate prince; and to serve by way of decoration to a piece which that great critic has written against.

I do not indeed wonder that the actors should be such professed enemies to those among our nation who are commonly known by the name of critics, since it is a rule among these gentlemen to fall upon a play, not because it is ill written, but because it takes. Several of them lay it down as a maxim, that whatever dramatic performance has a long run, must of necessity be good for nothing; as though the first precept in poetry were 'not to please.' Whether this rule holds good or not, I shall leave to the determination of those who are better judges than myself: if it does, I am sure it tends very much to the honour of those gentlemen who have established it; few of their pieces have been disgraced by a run of three days, and most of them being so exquisitely written, that the town would never give them more than one night's hearing.

I have a great esteem for a true critic, such as Aristotle and Longinus among the Greeks: Horace and Quintilian among the Romans; Boileau and Dacier among the French. But it is our misfortune that some, who set up for professed critics among us, are so stupid that they do not know how to put ten words together with elegance or common propriety; and withal so illiterate, that they have no taste of the learned languages, and therefore criticise upon old authors only at second-hand. They judge of them by what others have written, and not by any notions they have of the authors themselves. The words unity, action, sentiment, and diction, pronounced with an air of authority, give them a figure among unlearned readers, who are apt to believe they are very deep, because they are unintelligible. The ancient critics are full of the praises of their contemporaries; they discover beauties which escaped the observation of the vulgar, and very often find out reasons palliating and excusing such little slips and oversights as were committed in the writings of eminent authors. On the contrary, most of the smatterers in criticism, who appear among us, make it their business to vilify and depreciate every new production that gains applause, to decry imaginary blemishes, and to prove, by far-fetched arguments, that what pass for beauties in any celebrated piece are faults and errors. In short, the writings of these critics, compared with those of the ancients, are like the works of the sophists compared with those of the old philosophers.

Envy and cavil are the natural fruits of laziness and ignorance: which was probably the reason that in the heathen mythology Momus is said to be the son of Nox and Somnus, of darkness and sleep. Idle men, who have not been at the pains to accomplish or distinguish themselves, are very apt to detract from others; as ignorant men are very subject to decry those beauties in a celebrated work which they

---

* These verses were written by Gilbert, the second brother of Eustace Budgel, esq.

† This is an allusion to Mr. Dennis's new and improved method of making thunder. Dennis had contrived this thunder for the advantage of his tragedy of Appius and Virginia; the players highly approved of it, and it is the same that is used at the present day. Notwithstanding the effect of this thunder, however, the play was coldly received, and laid aside. Some nights after, Dennis being in the pit at the representation of Macbeth, and hearing the thunder made use of, arose from his seat in a violent passion, exclaiming with an oath, that that was his thunder. 'See (said he) how these rascals use me: they will not let my pla run, and yet they steal my thunder.'

have not eyes to discover. Many of our sons of Momus, who dignify themselves by the name of critics, are the genuine descendants of these two illustrious ancestors. They are often led into those numerous absurdities, in which they daily instruct the people, by not considering that, first, there is sometimes a greater judgment shown in deviating from the rules of art than in adhering to them; and, secondly, that there is more beauty in the works of a great genius, who is ignorant of all the rules of art, than in the works of a little genius, who not only knows but scrupulously observes them.

First, We may often take notice of men who are perfectly acquainted with all the rules of good writing, and, notwithstanding, choose to depart from them on extraordinary occasions. I could give instances out of all the tragic writers of antiquity who have shown their judgment in this particular; and purposely receded from an established rule of the drama, when it has made way for a much higher beauty than the observation of such a rule would have been. Those who have surveyed the noblest pieces of architecture and statuary, both ancient and modern, know very well that there are frequent deviations from art in the works of the greatest masters, which have produced a much nobler effect than a more accurate and exact way of proceeding could have done. This often arises from what the Italians call the *gusto grande* in these arts, which is what we call the sublime in writing.

In the next place, our critics do not seem sensible that there is more beauty in the works of a great genius, who is ignorant of the rules of art, than in those of a little genius who knows and observes them. It is of these men of genius that Terence speaks, in opposition to the little artificial cavillers of his time:

> 'Quorum æmulari exoptat negligentiam
> Potius quam istorum obscuram diligentiam.'

'Whose negligence he would rather imitate than these men's obscure diligence.'

A critic may have the same consolation in the ill success of his play as Dr. South tells us a physician has at the death of a patient, that he was killed *secundum artem.* Our inimitable Shakspeare is a stumbling-block to the whole tribe of these rigid critics. Who would not rather read one of his plays, where there is not a single rule of the stage observed, than any production of a modern critic, where there is not one of them violated! Shakspeare was indeed born with all the seeds of poetry, and may be compared to the stone in Pyrrhus's ring, which, as Pliny tells us, had the figure of Apollo and the nine muses in the veins of it, produced by the spontaneous hand of nature, without any help from art.

No. 593.] *Monday, September* 13, 1714.

> Quale per incertam lunam sub luce maligna
> Est iter in sylvis—— *Virg. Æn.* vi. 270.
>
> Thus wander travellers in woods by night,
> By the moon's doubtful and malignant light.
> *Dryden.*

My dreaming correspondent, Mr. Shadow, has sent me a second letter, with several curious observations on dreams in general, and the method to render sleep improving: an extract of his letter will not, I presume, be disagreeable to my readers.

'Since we have so little time to spare, that none of it may be lost, I see no reason why we should neglect to examine those imaginary scenes we are presented with in sleep, only because they have less reality in them than our waking meditations. A traveller would bring his judgment in question, who would despise the directions of his map for want of real roads in it, because here stands a dot instead of a town, or a cypher instead of a city; and it must be a long day's journey to travel through two or three inches. Fancy in dreams gives us much such another landscape of life as that does of countries: and, though its appearance may seem strangely jumbled together, we may often observe such traces and footsteps of noble thoughts, as, if carefully pursued, might lead us into a proper path of action. There is so much rapture and ecstacy in our fancied bliss, and something so dismal and shocking in our fancied misery, that, though the inactivity of the body has given occasion for calling sleep the image of death, the briskness of the fancy affords us a strong intimation of something within us that can never die.

'I have wondered that Alexander the Great, who came into the world sufficiently dreamed of by his parents, and had himself a tolerable knack of dreaming, should often say, that sleep was one thing which made him sensible he was mortal. I, who have not such fields of action in the daytime to divert my attention from this matter, plainly perceive that in those operations of the mind, while the body is at rest, there is a certain vastness of conception very suitable to the capacity, and demonstrative of the force of that divine part in our composition which will last for ever. Neither do I much doubt but, had we a true account of the wonders the hero last-mentioned performed in his sleep, his conquering this little globe would hardly be worth mentioning. I may affirm, without vanity, that, when I compare several actions in Quintus Curtius with some others in my own noctuary, I appear the greater hero of the two.'

I shall close this subject with observing, that while we are awake we are at liberty to fix our thoughts on what we please, but in sleep we have not the command of them.

The ideas which strike the fancy arise in us without our choice, either from the occurrences of the day past, the temper we lie down in, or it may be the direction of some superior being.

It is certain the imagination may be so differently affected in sleep, that our actions of the day might be either rewarded or punished with a little age of happiness or misery. Saint Austin was of opinion that, if in Paradise there was the same vicissitude of sleeping and waking, as in the present world, the dreams of its inhabitants would be very happy.

And so far at present are our dreams in our power, that they are generally conformable to our waking thoughts, so that it is not impossible to convey ourselves to a concert of music, the conversation of distant friends, or any other entertainment which has been before lodged in the mind.

My readers, by applying these hints, will find the necessity of making a good day of it, if they heartily wish themselves a good night.

I have often considered Marcia's prayer, and Lucia's account of Cato, in this light.

'*Marc.* O ye mortal powers, that guard the just,
Watch round his couch, and soften his repose,
Banish his sorrows, and becalm his soul
With easy dreams; remember all his virtues,
And show mankind that goodness is your care.
Luc. Sweet are the slumbers of the virtuous man!
O Marcia, I have seen thy god-like father;
Some power invisible supports his soul,
And bears it up in all its wonted greatness.
A kind refreshing sleep has fallen upon him:
I saw him stretch'd at ease, his fancy lost
In pleasing dreams. As I drew near his couch
He smil'd, and cry'd, Cæsar, thou canst not hurt me.'

Mr. Shadow acquaints me in a postscript, that he has no manner of title to the vision which succeeded his first letter; but adds, that, as the gentleman who wrote it dreams very sensibly, he shall be glad to meet him some night or other under the great elm-tree, by which Virgil has given us a fine metaphorical image of sleep, in order to turn over a few of the leaves together, and oblige the public with an account of the dreams that lie under them.

No. 594.] *Wednesday, September* 15, 1714.

————Absentem qui rodit amicum;
Qui non defendit alio culpante; solutos
Qui captat risus hominum, famamque dicacis;
Fingere qui non visa potest; commissa tacere
Qui nequit; hic niger est: hunc tu, Romane, caveto.
Hor. Sat. iv. Lib. 1. 81.

He that shall rail against his absent friends,
Or hears them scandaliz'd, and not defends;
Sports with their fame, and speaks whate'er he can,
And only to be thought a witty man;
Tells tales, and brings his friends in disesteem;
That man's a knave;—be sure beware of him.
Creech.

Were all the vexations of life put together, we should find that a great part of them proceeds from those calumnies and reproaches which we spread abroad concerning one another.

There is scarce a man living, who is not, in some degree, guilty of this offence; though at the same time, however, we treat one another, it must be confessed, that we all consent in speaking ill of the persons who are notorious for this practice. It generally takes its rise either from an ill-will to mankind, a private inclination to make ourselves esteemed, an ostentation of wit, a vanity of being thought in the secrets of the world, or from a desire of gratifying any of these dispositions of mind in those persons with whom we converse.

The publisher of scandal is more or less odious to mankind, and criminal in himself, as he is influenced by any one or more of the foregoing motives. But, whatever may be the occasion of spreading these false reports, he ought to consider that the effect of them is equally prejudicial and pernicious to the person at whom they are aimed. The injury is the same, though the principle from which it proceeds may be different.

As every one looks upon himself with too much indulgence, when he passes a judgment on his own thoughts or actions, and as very few would be thought guilty of this abominable proceeding, which is so universally practised, and at the same time so universally blamed, I shall lay down three rules, by which I would have a man examine and search into his own heart before he stands acquitted to himself of that evil disposition of mind which I am here mentioning.

First of all, Let him consider whether he does not take delight in hearing the faults of others.

Secondly, Whether he is not too apt to believe such little blackening accounts, and more inclined to be credulous on the uncharitable than on the good-natured side.

Thirdly, Whether he is not ready to spread and propagate such reports as tend to the disreputation of another.

These are the several steps by which this vice proceeds and grows up into slander and defamation.

In the first place, a man who takes delight in hearing the faults of others, shows sufficiently that he has a true relish of scandal, and consequently the seeds of this vice within him. If his mind is gratified with hearing the reproaches which are cast on others, he will find the same pleasure in relating them, and be the more apt to do it, as he will naturally imagine every one he converses with is delighted in the same manner with himself. A man should endeavour, therefore, to wear out of his mind this criminal curiosity, which is perpetually heightened and inflamed by listening to such stories as tend to the disreputation of others.

In the second place, a man should consult his own heart, whether he be not apt to believe such little blackening accounts, and more inclined to be credulous on the uncharitable than on the good-natured side.

Such a credulity is very vicious in itself, and generally arises from a man's consciousness of his own secret corruptions. It is a pretty saying of Thales, 'Falsehood is just as far distant from truth as the ears are from the eyes.'* By which he would intimate, that a wise man should not easily give credit to the report of actions which he has not seen. I shall, under this head, mention two or three remarkable rules to be observed by the members of the celebrated Abbey de la Trappe, as they are published in a little French book.†

The fathers are there ordered never to give an ear to any accounts of base or criminal actions; to turn off all such discourse if possible; but, in case they hear any thing of this nature so well attested that they cannot disbelieve it, they are then to suppose that the criminal action may have proceeded from a good intention in him who is guilty of it. This is, perhaps, carrying charity to an extravagance; but it is certainly much more laudable than to suppose, as the ill-natured part of the world does, that indifferent and even good actions proceed from bad principles and wrong intentions.

In the third place, a man should examine his heart, whether he does not find in it a secret inclination to propagate such reports as tend to the disreputation of another.

When the disease of the mind, which I have hitherto been speaking of, arises to this degree of malignity, it discovers itself in its worst symptom, and is in danger of becoming incurable. I need not therefore insist upon the guilt in this last particular, which every one cannot but disapprove, who is not void of humanity, or even common discretion. I shall only add, that, whatever pleasure any man may take in spreading whispers of this nature, he will find an infinitely greater satisfaction in conquering the temptation he is under, by letting the secret die within his own breast.

No. 595.] *Friday, September* 17, 1714.

———Non ut placidis coeant immitia, non ut
Serpentes avibus geminentur, tigribus agni.
Hor. Ars Poet. ver. 12.

———Nature, and the common laws of sense,
Forbid to reconcile antipathies;
Or make a snake engender with a dove,
And hungry tigers court the tender lambs.
Roscommon.

If ordinary authors would condescend to write as they think, they would at least be allowed the praise of being intelligible. But they really take pains to be ridiculous: and, by the studied ornaments of style, perfectly disguise the little sense they aim at. There is a grievance of this sort in the commonwealth of letters, which I have for some time resolved to redress, and accordingly I have set this day apart for justice. What I mean is the mixture of inconsistent metaphors, which is a fault but too often found in learned writers, but in all the unlearned without exception.

In order to set this matter in a clear light to every reader, I shall in the first place observe, that a metaphor is a simile in one word, which serves to convey the thoughts of the mind under resemblances and images which affect the senses. There is not any thing in the world, which may not be compared to several things if considered in several distinct lights; or, in other words, the same thing may be expressed by different metaphors. But the mischief is, that an unskilful author shall run these metaphors so absurdly into one another, that there shall be no simile, no agreeable picture, no apt resemblance, but confusion, obscurity, and noise. Thus I have known a hero compared to a thunderbolt, a lion, and the sea; all and each of them proper metaphors for impetuosity, courage, or force. But by bad management it hath so happened, that the thunderbolt hath overflowed its banks, the lion hath been darted through the skies, and the billows have rolled out of the Libyan desert.

The absurdity, in this instance, is obvious. And yet every time that clashing metaphors are put together, this fault is committed more or less. It hath already been said, that metaphors are images of things which affect the senses. An image, therefore, taken from what acts upon the sight, cannot, without violence, be applied to the hearing; and so of the rest. It is no less an impropriety to make any being in nature or art to do things in its metaphorical state, which it could not do in its original. I shall illustrate what I have said by an instance which I have read more than once in controversial writers. 'The heavy lashes,' saith a celebrated author, 'that have dropped from your pen, &c.' I suppose this gentleman, having frequently heard of 'gall dropping from a pen, and being lashed in a satire,' he was resolved to have them both at any rate, and so uttered this complete piece of nonsense. It will most effectually discover the absurdity of these monstrous unions, if we will suppose these metaphors or images actually painted. Imagine then a hand holding a pen, and several lashes of whipcord falling from it, and you have the true representation of this sort of eloquence. I believe, by this very rule, a reader may be able to judge of the union of all metaphors whatsoever, and determine which are homogeneous, and which heterogeneous; or, to speak more plainly, which are consistent and which inconsistent.

There is yet one evil more which I must take notice of, and that is the running of metaphors into tedious allegories; which, though an error on the better hand, causes confusion as much as the other. This becomes abominable, when the lustre of one

* Stobæi Serm. 61.

† Felibien, Description de l'Abbaye de la Trappe, Paris, 1671; reprinted in 1682. It is a letter of M. Felibien to the dutchess of Liancourt.

word leads a writer out of his road, and makes him wander from his subject for a page together. I remember a young fellow of this turn, who, having said by chance that his mistress had a world of charms, thereupon took occasion to consider her as one possessed of frigid and torrid zones, and pursued her from one pole to the other.

I shall conclude this paper with a letter written in that enormous style, which I hope my reader hath by this time set his heart against. The epistle hath heretofore received great applause; but after what hath been said, let any man commend it if he dare.

'SIR,—After the many heavy lashes that have fallen from your pen, you may justly expect in return all the load that my ink can lay upon your shoulders. You have quartered all the foul language upon me that could be raked out of the air of Billingsgate, without knowing who I am, or whether I deserved to be cupped and sacrificed at this rate. I tell you, once for all, turn your eyes where you please, you shall never smell me out. Do you think that the panicks, which you sow about the parish, will ever build a monument to your glory? No, sir, you may fight these battles as long as you will, but when you come to balance the account you will find that you have been fishing in troubled waters, and that an *ignis fatuus* hath bewildered you, and that indeed you have built upon a sandy foundation, and brought your hogs to a fair market. I am, sir, yours, &c.'

No. 596.] *Monday, September* 20, 1714.

Molle meum levibus cor est violabile telis.
Ovid, Ep. xv. 79.

Cupid's light darts my tender bosom move.—*Pope.*

THE case of my correspondent, who sends me the following letter, has somewhat in it so very whimsical, that I know not how to entertain my readers better than by laying it before them.

'Middle-Temple, Sept. 18.

'SIR,—I am fully convinced that there is not upon earth a more impertinent creature than an importunate lover. We are daily complaining of the severity of our fate to people who are wholly unconcerned in it: and hourly improving a passion, which we would persuade the world is the torment of our lives. Notwithstanding this reflection, sir, I cannot forbear acquainting you with my own case. You must know, then, sir, that even from my childhood, the most prevailing inclination I could perceive in myself was a strong desire to be in favour with the fair-sex. I am at present in the one-and-twentieth year of my age; and should have made choice of a she-bedfellow many years since, had not my father, who has a pretty good estate of his own getting, and passes in the world for a prudent man, been pleased to lay it down as a maxim, that nothing spoils a young fellow's fortune so much as marrying early; and that no man ought to think of wedlock until six-and-twenty. Knowing his sentiments upon this head, I thought it in vain to apply myself to women of condition, who expect settlements; so that all my amours have hitherto been with ladies who had no fortunes: but I know not how to give you so good an idea of me, as by laying before you the history of my life.

'I can very well remember, that at my school-mistress's, whenever we broke up, I was always for joining myself with the miss who lay-in, and was constantly one of the first to make a party in the play of Husband and Wife. This passion for being well with the females still increased as I advanced in years. At the dancing-school I contracted so many quarrels by struggling with my fellow-scholars for the partner I liked best, that upon a ball-night, before our mothers made their appearance, I was usually up to the nose in blood. My father, like a discreet man, soon removed me from this stage of softness to a school of discipline, where I learnt Latin and Greek. I underwent several severities in this place, until it was thought convenient to send me to the university: though to confess the truth, I should not have arrived so early at that seat of learning, but from the discovery of an intrigue between me and my master's housekeeper; upon whom I had employed my rhetoric so effectually, that, though she was a very elderly lady, I had almost brought her to consent to marry me. Upon my arrival at Oxford, I found logic so dry, that, instead of giving attention to the dead, I soon fell to addressing the living. My first amour was with a pretty girl whom I shall call Parthenope: her mother sold ale by the town-wall.

'Being often caught there by the proctor, I was forced at last, that my mistress's reputation might receive no blemish, to confess my addresses were honourable. Upon this I was immediately sent home; but Parthenope soon after marrying a shoe-maker, I was again suffered to return. My next affair was with my tailor's daughter, who deserted me for the sake of a young barber. Upon my complaining to one of my particular friends of this misfortune, the cruel wag made a mere jest of my calamity, and asked me, with a smile, where the needle should turn but to the pole?* After this I was deeply in love with a milliner, and at last with my bed-maker; upon which I was sent away, or, in the university phrase, rusticated for ever.

'Upon my coming home, I settled to my studies so heartily, and contracted so great a reservedness by being kept from the company I most affected, that my father

---

* A pole was the common sign of a barber's shop. It is now seldom seen in the metropolis.

thought he might venture me at the Temple.

'Within a week after my arrival I began to shine again, and became enamoured with a mighty pretty creature, who had every thing but money to recommend her. Having frequent opportunities of uttering all the soft things which a heart formed for love could inspire me with, I soon gained her consent to treat of marriage; but, unfortunately for us all, in the absence of my charmer I usually talked the same language to her eldest sister, who is also very pretty. Now I assure you, Mr. Spectator, this did not proceed from any real affection I had conceived for her: but, being a perfect stranger to the conversation of men, and strongly addicted to associate with the women, I knew no other language but that of love. I should, however, be very much obliged to you, if you could free me from the perplexity I am at present in. I have sent word to my old gentleman in the country, that I am desperately in love with the younger sister; and her father, who knew no better, poor man, acquainted him by the same post, that I had for some time made my addresses to the elder. Upon this old Testy sends me up word, that he has heard so much of my exploits, that he intends immediately to order me to the South-sea. Sir, I have occasionally talked so much of dying, that I begin to think there is not much in it; and if the old 'squire persists in his design, I do hereby give him notice that I am providing myself with proper instruments for the destruction of despairing lovers: let him therefore look to it, and consider that by his obstinacy he may himself lose the son of his strength, the world a hopeful lawyer, my mistress a passionate lover, and you, Mr. Spectator, your constant admirer,

'JEREMIAH LOVEMORE.'

No. 597.] *Wednesday, September* 22, 1714.

——Mens sine pondere ludit.—*Petr.*

The mind uncumber'd plays.

Since I received my friend Shadow's letter, several of my correspondents have been pleased to send me an account how they have been employed in sleep, and what notable adventures they have been engaged in during that moonshine in the brain. I shall lay before my readers an abridgment of some few of their extravagances, in hopes that they will in time accustom themselves to dream a little more to the purpose.

One, who styles himself Gladio, complains heavily that his fair one charges him with inconstancy, and does not use him with half the kindness which the sincerity of his passion may demand; the said Gladio having, by valour and stratagem, put to death tyrants, enchanters, monsters, knights, &c. without number, and exposed himself to all manner of dangers for her sake and safety. He desires in his postscript to know whether, from a constant success in them, he may not promise himself to succeed in her esteem at last.

Another, who is very prolix in his narrative, writes me word, that having sent a venture beyond sea, he took occasion one night to fancy himself gone along with it, and grown on a sudden the richest man in all the Indies. Having been there about a year or two, a gust of wind that forced open his casement, blew him over to his native country again, where, awaking at six o'clock, and the change of the air not agreeing with him, he turned to his left side in order to a second voyage; but before he could get on ship-board was unfortunately apprehended for stealing a horse, tried and condemned for the fact, and in a fair way of being executed, if somebody stepping hastily into his chamber had not brought him a reprieve. This fellow too wants Mr. Shadow's advice; who, I dare say, would bid him be content to rise after his first nap, and learn to be satisfied as soon as nature is.

The next is a public-spirited gentleman, who tells me, that on the second of September, at night, the whole city was on fire, and would certainly have been reduced to ashes again by this time, if he had not flown over it with the New River on his back, and happily extinguished the flames before they had prevailed too far. He would be informed whether he has not a right to petition the lord mayor and aldermen for a reward.

A letter, dated September the ninth, acquaints me, that the writer, being resolved to try his fortune, had fasted all that day; and, that he might be sure of dreaming upon something at night, procured a handsome slice of bride-cake, which he placed very conveniently under his pillow. In the morning his memory happened to fail him, and he could recollect nothing but an odd fancy that he had eaten his cake; which being found upon search reduced to a few crumbs, he is resolved to remember more of his dreams another time, believing from this that there may possibly be somewhat of truth in them.

I have received numerous complaints from several delicious dreamers, desiring me to invent some method of silencing those noisy slaves, whose occupations lead them to take their early rounds about the city in a morning, doing a deal of mischief, and working strange confusion in the affairs of its inhabitants. Several monarchs have done me the honour to acquaint me how often they have been shook from their respective thrones by the rattling of a coach, or the rumbling of a wheelbarrow. And many private gentlemen, I find, have been bawled out of vast estates by fellows not worth three pence. A fair lady was just on the point of being married to a young, handsome, rich, ingenious nobleman, when an impertinent tinker passing by forbid the bans; and a hopeful youth who had been newly advanced to great honour and preferment, was forced by a neighbouring cobbler to resign all for an old song. It has been represented to me, that those inconsiderable rascals do nothing but go about dissolving of marriages, and spoiling of fortunes, impoverishing rich, and ruining great people, interrupting beauties in the midst of their conquests, and generals in the course of their victories. A boisterous peripatetic hardly goes through a street without waking half a dozen kings and princes, to open their shops or clean shoes, frequently transforming sceptres into paring-shovels, and proclamations into bills. I have by me a letter from a young statesman, who in five or six hours came to be emperor of Europe, after which he made war upon the Great Turk, routed him horse and foot, and was crowned lord of the universe in Constantinople: the conclusion of all his successes is, that on the 12th instant, about seven in the morning, his Imperial Majesty was deposed by a chimney-sweeper.

On the other hand, I have epistolary testimonies of gratitude from many miserable people, who owe to this clamorous tribe frequent deliverances from great misfortunes. A small-coal-man, by waking one of these distressed gentlemen, saved him from ten years' imprisonment. An honest watchman, bidding aloud good-morrow to another, freed him from the malice of many potent enemies, and brought all their designs against him to nothing. A certain valetudinarian confesses he has often been cured of a sore-throat by the hoarseness of a carman, and relieved from a fit of the gout by the sound of old shoes. A noisy puppy, that plagued a sober gentleman all night long with his impertinence, was silenced by a cinder-wench with a word speaking.

Instead, therefore, of suppressing this order of mortals, I would propose it to my readers to make the best advantage of their morning salutations. A famous Macedonian prince, for fear of forgetting himself in the midst of his good fortune, had a youth to wait on him every morning, and bid him remember that he was a man. A citizen, who is waked by one of these criers, may regard him as a kind of remembrancer, come to admonish him that it is time to return to the circumstances he has overlooked all the night time, to leave off fancying himself what he is not, and prepare to act suitably to the condition he is really placed in.

People may dream on as long as they please, but I shall take no notice of any imaginary adventures that do not happen while the sun is on this side the horizon. For which reason I stifle Fritilla's dream at church last Sunday, who, while the rest of the audience were enjoying the benefit of an excellent discourse, was losing her money and jewels to a gentleman at play, until after a strange run of ill-luck she was reduced to pawn three lovely pretty children for her last stake. When she had thrown them away, her companion went off, discovering himself by his usual tokens, a cloven foot and a strong smell of brimstone, which last proved a bottle of spirits, which a good old lady applied to her nose, to put her in a condition of hearing the preacher's third head concerning time.

If a man has no mind to pass abruptly from his imagined to his real circumstances, he may employ himself a while in that new kind of observation which my oneirocritical correspondent has directed him to make of himself. Pursuing the imagination through all its extravagances, whether in sleeping or waking, is no improper method of correcting and bringing it to act in subordination to reason, so as to be delighted only with such objects as will affect it with pleasure when it is never so cool and sedate.

No. 598.] *Friday, September* 24, 1714.

Jamne igitur laudas, quod de sapientibus alter
Ridebat, quoties a limine moverat unum
Protuleratque pedem: flebat contrarius alter?

Juv. Sat. x. 28.

Will ye not now the pair of sages praise,
Who the same end pursu'd by several ways?
One pity'd, one condemn'd, the woful times,
One laugh'd at follies, one lamented crimes.

Dryden.

Mankind may be divided into the merry and the serious, who both of them make a very good figure in the species so long as they keep their respective humours from degenerating into the neighbouring extreme: there being a natural tendency in the one to a melancholy moroseness, and in the other to a fantastic levity.

The merry part of the world are very amiable, while they diffuse a cheerfulness through conversation at proper seasons and on proper occasions; but, on the contrary, a great grievance to society when they infect every discourse with insipid mirth, and turn into ridicule such subjects as are not suited to it. For though laughter is looked upon by the philosophers as the property of reason, the excess of it has been always considered as the mark of folly.

On the other side, seriousness has its beauty whilst it is attended with cheerfulness and humanity, and does not come in unseasonably to pall the good humour of those with whom we converse.

These two sets of men, notwithstanding they each of them shine in their respective characters, are apt to bear a natural aversion and antipathy to one another.

What is more usual than to hear men of serious tempers, and austere morals, enlarging upon the vanities and follies of the young and gay part of the species, while they look with a kind of horror upon such pomps and diversions as are innocent in themselves, and only culpable when they draw the mind too much?

I could not but smile upon reading a passage in the account which Mr. Baxter gives of his own life, wherein he represents it as a great blessing that in his youth he very narrowly escaped getting a place at court.

It must indeed be confessed that levity of temper takes a man off his guard, and opens a pass to his soul for any temptation that assaults it. It favours all the approaches of vice, and weakens all the resistance of virtue: for which reason a renowned statesman in queen Elizabeth's days, after having retired from court and public business, in order to give himself up to the duties of religion, when any of his old friends used to visit him, had still this word of advice in his mouth, 'be serious.'

An eminent Italian author of this cast of mind, speaking of the great advantage of a serious and composed temper, wishes very gravely, that for the benefit of mankind he had Trophonius's cave in his possession; which, says he, would contribute more to the reformation of manners than all the workhouses and bridewells in Europe.

We have a very particular description of this cave in Pausanias, who tells us that it was made in the form of a huge oven, and had many particular circumstances, which disposed the person who was in it to be more pensive and thoughtful than ordinary; insomuch, that no man was ever observed to laugh all his life after, who had once made his entry into this cave. It was usual in those times, when any one carried a more than ordinary gloominess in his features, to tell him that he looked like one just come out of Trophonius's cave.

On the other hand, writers of a more merry complexion have been no less severe on the opposite party; and have had one advantage above them, that they have attacked them with more turns of wit and humour.

After all, if a man's temper were at his own disposal, I think he would not choose to be of either of these parties; since the most perfect character is that which is formed out of both of them. A man would neither choose to be a hermit nor a buffoon; human nature is not so miserable, as that we should be always melancholy; nor so happy, as that we should be always merry. In a word, a man should not live as if there was no God in the world, nor, at the same time, as if there were no men in it.

No. 599.] *Monday, September* 27, 1714.

——Ubique——
Luctus, ubique pavor.—*Virg. Æn.* ii. 369.

All parts resound with tumults, plaints, and fears.
Dryden.

It has been my custom, as I grow old, to allow myself some little indulgences, which I never took in my youth. Among others is that of an afternoon's nap, which I fell into in the fifty-fifth year of my age, and have continued for the three last years past. By this means I enjoy a double morning, and rise twice a day fresh to my speculations. It happens very luckily for me, that some of my dreams have proved instructive to my countrymen, so that I may be said to sleep, as well as to wake, for the good of the public. I was yesterday meditating on the account with which I have already entertained my readers concerning the cave of Trophonius. I was no sooner fallen into my usual slumber, but I dreamed that this cave was put into my possession, and that I gave public notice of its virtue, inviting every one to it who had a mind to be a serious man for the remaining part of his life. Great multitudes immediately resorted to me. The first who made the experiment was a Merry-andrew, who was put into my hand by a neighbouring justice of peace, in order to reclaim him from that profligate kind of life. Poor Pickle-herring had not taken above one turn in it, when he came out of the cave, like a hermit from his cell, with a penitential look and a most rueful countenance. I then put in a young laughing fop, and, watching for his return, asked him, with a smile, how he liked the place? He replied, 'Pr'ythee, friend, be not impertinent;' and stalked by me as grave as a judge. A citizen then desired me to give free ingress and egress to his wife who was dressed in the gayest coloured ribands I had ever seen. She went in with a flirt of her fan and a smirking countenance, but came out with the severity of a vestal; and throwing from her several female gewgaws, told me, with a sigh, that she resolved to go into deep mourning, and to wear black all the rest of her life. As I had many coquettes recommended to me by their parents, their husbands, and their lovers, I let them in all at once, desiring them to divert themselves together, as well as they could. Upon their emerging again into day-light, you would have fancied my cave to have been a nunnery, and that you had seen a solemn procession of religious marching out, one behind another, in the most profound silence and the most exemplary decency. As I was very much delighted with so edifying a sight, there came towards me a great company of males and females, laughing, singing, and dancing, in such a manner, that I could hear them a great while before I saw them. Upon my asking their leader what brought them thither? they told me all at once that they were French Protestants lately arrived in Great Britain, and that finding themselves of too gay a humour for my country, they applied themselves to me in order to compose them for British conversation. I told them that, to oblige them, I would soon spoil their mirth; upon which I admitted a whole shoal of them, who after having taken a survey of the place, came out in very good order, and with looks entirely English. I afterwards put in a Dutchman, who had a great fancy to see the kelder, as he called it; but I could not observe that I had made any alteration in him.

A comedian, who had gained great reputation in parts of humour, told me that he had a mighty mind to act Alexander the Great, and fancied that he should succeed very well in it if he could strike two or three laughing features out of his face. He tried the experiment, but contracted so very solid a look by it, that I am afraid he will be fit for no part hereafter but a Timon of Athens, or a Mute in The Funeral.

I then clapped up an empty fantastic citizen, in order to qualify him for an alderman. He was succeeded by a young rake of the Middle Temple, who was brought to me by his grandmother; but, to her great sorrow and surprise, he came out a quaker. Seeing myself surrounded with a body of freethinkers and scoffers at religion, who were making themselves merry at the sober looks and thoughtful brows of those who had been in the cave, I thrust them all in, one after another, and locked the door upon them. Upon my opening it, they all looked as if they had been frightened out of their wits, and were marching away with ropes in their hands to a wood that was within sight of the place. I found they were not able to bear themselves in their first serious thoughts; but, knowing these would quickly bring them to a better frame of mind, I gave them into the custody of their friends until that happy change was wrought in them.

The last that was brought to me was a young woman, who at the first sight of my short face fell into an immoderate fit of laughter, and was forced to hold her sides all the while her mother was speaking to me. Upon this, I interrupted the old lady, and taking her daughter by the hand, 'Madam,' said I, 'be pleased to retire into my closet while your mother tells me your case.' I then put her into the mouth of the cave; when the mother, after having begged pardon for the girl's rudeness, told me that she had often treated her father and the gravest of her relations in the same manner; that she would sit giggling and laughing with her companions from one end of a tragedy to the other; nay, that she would sometimes burst out in the middle of a sermon, and set the whole congregation a staring at her. The mother was going on, when the young lady came out of the cave to us with a composed countenance and a low courtesy. She was a girl of such exuberant mirth that her visit to Trophonius only reduced her to a more than ordinary decency of behaviour, and made a very pretty prude of her. After having performed innumerable cures, I looked about me with great satisfaction, and saw all my patients walking by themselves in a very pensive and musing posture, so that the whole space seemed covered with philosophers. I was at length resolved to go into the cave myself, and see what it was that had produced such wonderful effects upon the company; but as I was stooping at the entrance, the door being somewhat low, I gave such a nod in my chair that I awaked. After having recovered myself from my first startle, I was very well pleased at the accident which had befallen me, as not knowing but a little stay in the place might have spoiled my Spectators.

No. 600.] *Wednesday, September* 29, 1714.

Solemque suum, sua sidera norunt.

Virg. Æn. vi. 641.

Stars of their own, and their own suns they know.

Dryden.

I HAVE always taken a particular pleasure in examining the opinions which men of different religions, different ages, and different countries, have entertained concerning the immortality of the soul, and the state of happiness which they promise themselves in another world. For, whatever prejudices and errors human nature lies under, we find that either reason, or tradition from our first parents, has discovered to all people something in these great points which bears analogy to truth, and to the doctrines opened to us by divine revelation. I was lately discoursing on this subject with a learned person who has been very much conversant among the inhabitants of the more western parts of Africa.* Upon his conversing with several in that country, he tells me that their notion of heaven or of a future state of happiness is this, that every thing we there wish for will immediately present itself to us. We find, say they, our souls are of such a nature that they require variety, and are not capable of being always delighted with the same objects. The Supreme Being, therefore, in compliance with this taste of happiness which he has planted in the soul of man, will raise up from time to time, say they, every gratification which it is in the humour to be pleased with. If we wish to be in groves or bowers, among running streams, or falls of water, we shall immediately find ourselves in the midst of such a scene as we desire. If we would be entertained with music and the melody of sounds, the concert arises upon our wish, and the whole region about us is filled with harmony. In short, every desire will be followed by fruition; and whatever a man's inclination directs him to will be present with him. Nor is it material whether the Supreme Power creates in conformity to our wishes, or whether he only produces

* Addison's father, dean Launcelot Addison, who published an account of West Barbary, &c. He died in 1703, aged 71.

such a change in our imagination as makes us believe ourselves conversant among those scenes which delight us. Our happiness will be the same, whether it proceed from external objects, or from the impressions of the Deity upon our own private fancies. This is the account which I have received from my learned friend. Notwithstanding this system of belief be in general very chimerical and visionary, there is something sublime in its manner of considering the influence of a Divine Being on a human soul. It has also, like most other opinions of the heathen world upon these important points; it has, I say, its foundation in truth, as it supposes the souls of good men after this life to be in a state of perfect happiness; that in this state there will be no barren hopes, nor fruitless wishes, and that we shall enjoy every thing we can desire. But the particular circumstance which I am most pleased with in this scheme, and which arises from a just reflection upon human nature, is that variety of pleasures which it supposes the souls of good men will be possessed of in another world. This I think highly probable, from the dictates both of reason and revelation. The soul consists of many faculties, as the understanding, and the will, with all the senses, both outward and inward; or, to speak more philosophically, the soul can exert herself in many different ways of action. She can understand, will, imagine, see, and hear; love, and discourse, and apply herself to many other the like exercises of different kinds and natures; but, what is more to be considered, the soul is capable of receiving a most exquisite pleasure and satisfaction from the exercise of any of these its powers, when they are gratified with their proper objects; she can be entirely happy by the satisfaction of the memory, the sight, the hearing, or any other mode of perception. Every faculty is a distinct taste in the mind, and hath objects accommodated to its proper relish. Doctor Tillotson somewhere says, that he will not presume to determine in what consists the happiness of the blessed, because God Almighty is capable of making the soul happy by ten thousand different ways. Besides those several avenues to pleasure, which the soul is endowed with in this life, it is not impossible, according to the opinions of many eminent divines, but there may be new faculties in the souls of good men made perfect, as well as new senses, in their glorified bodies. This we are sure of, that there will be new objects offered to all those faculties which are essential to us.

We are likewise to take notice that every particular faculty is capable of being employed on a very great variety of objects. The understanding, for example, may be happy in the contemplation of moral, natural, mathematical, and other kinds of truth. The memory likewise may turn itself to an infinite multitude of objects, especially when the soul shall have passed through the space of many millions of years, and shall reflect with pleasure on the days of eternity. Every other faculty may be considered in the same extent.

We cannot question but that the happiness of a soul will be adequate to its nature; and that it is not endowed with any faculties which are to lie useless and unemployed. The happiness is to be the happiness of the whole man; and we may easily conceive to ourselves the happiness of the soul, while any one of its faculties is in the fruition of its chief good. The happiness may be of a more exalted nature in proportion as the faculty employed is so: but, as the whole soul acts in the exertion of any of its particular powers, the whole soul is happy in the pleasure which arises from any of its particular acts. For, notwithstanding, as has been before hinted, and as it has been taken notice of by one of the greatest modern philosophers,* we divide the soul into several powers and faculties, there is no such division in the soul itself, since it is the whole soul that remembers, understands, wills, or imagines. Our manner of considering the memory, understanding, will, imagination, and the like faculties, is for the better enabling us to express ourselves in such abstracted subjects of speculation, not that there is any such division in the soul itself.

Seeing then that the soul has many different faculties, or, in other words, many different ways of acting; that it can be intensely pleased or made happy by all these different faculties, or ways of acting; that it may be endowed with several latent faculties, which it is not at present in a condition to exert; that we cannot believe the soul is endowed with any faculty which is of no use to it; that, whenever any one of these faculties is transcendently pleased, the soul is in a state of happiness: and, in the last place, considering that the happiness of another world is to be the happiness of the whole man, who can question but that there is an infinite variety in those pleasures we are speaking of? and that this fulness of joy will be made up of all those pleasures which the nature of the soul is capable of receiving?

We shall be the more confirmed in this doctrine, if we observe the nature of variety with regard to the mind of man. The soul does not care to be always in the same bent. The faculties relieve one another by turns, and receive an additional pleasure from the novelty of those objects about which they are conversant.

Revelation likewise very much confirms this notion, under the different views which it gives us of our future happiness. In the description of the throne of God, it represents to us all those objects which are able

* Locke.

to gratify the senses and imagination: in very many places it intimates to us all the happiness which the understanding can possibly receive in that state, where all things shall be revealed to us, and we shall know even as we are known; the raptures of devotion, of divine love, the pleasure of conversing with our blessed Saviour, with an innumerable host of angels, and with the spirits of just men made perfect, are likewise revealed to us in several parts of the holy writings. There are also mentioned those hierarchies or governments in which the blessed shall be ranged one above another, and in which we may be sure a great part of our happiness will likewise consist: for it will not be there as in this world, where every one is aiming at power and superiority; but, on the contrary, every one will find that station the most proper for him in which he is placed, and will probably think that he could not have been so happy in any other station. These, and many other particulars, are marked in divine revelation, as the several ingredients of our happiness in heaven, which all imply such a variety of joys, and such a gratification of the soul in all its different faculties, as I have been here mentioning.

Some of the rabbins tell us, that the cherubims are a set of angels who know most, and the seraphims a set of angels who love most. Whether this distinction be not altogether imaginary, I shall not here examine; but it is highly probable that, among the spirits of good men, there may be some who will be more pleased with the employment of one faculty than of another; and this perhaps according to those innocent and virtuous habits or inclinations which have here taken the deepest root.

I might here apply this consideration to the spirits of wicked men, with relation to the pain which they shall suffer in every one of their faculties, and the respective miseries which shall be appropriated to each faculty in particular. But, leaving this to the reflection of my readers, I shall conclude with observing how we ought to be thankful to our great Creator, and rejoice in the being which he has bestowed upon us, for having made the soul susceptible of pleasure by so many different ways. We see by what a variety of passages joy and gladness may enter into the thoughts of man; how wonderfully a human spirit is framed, to imbibe its proper satisfactions, and taste the goodness of its Creator. We may therefore look into ourselves with rapture and amazement, and cannot sufficiently express our gratitude to Him who has encompassed us with such a profusion of blessings, and opened in us so many capacities of enjoying them.

There cannot be a stronger argument that God has designed us for a state of future happiness, and for that heaven which he has revealed to us, than that he has thus naturally qualified the soul for it, and made it a being capable of receiving so much bliss. He would never have made such faculties in vain, and have endowed us with powers that were not to be exerted on such objects as are suited to them. It is very manifest, by the inward frame and constitution of our minds, that he has adapted them to an infinite variety of pleasures and gratifications which are not to be met with in this life. We should therefore at all times take care that we do not disappoint this his gracious purpose and intention towards us, and make those faculties, which he formed as so many qualifications for happiness and rewards, to be the instruments of pain and punishment.

No. 601.] *Friday, October* 1, 1714.

'Ο ανθρωπος ευεργετος πεφυκως.

Antonin. Lib. ix.

Man is naturally a beneficent creature.

THE following essay comes from a hand which has entertained my readers once before.

'Notwithstanding a narrow contracted temper be that which obtains most in the world, we must not therefore conclude this to be the genuine characteristic of mankind; because there are some who delight in nothing so much as in doing good, and receive more of their happiness at second hand, or by rebound from others, than by direct and immediate sensation. Now, though these heroic souls are but few, and to appearance so far advanced above the grovelling multitude as if they were of another order of beings, yet in reality their nature is the same; moved by the same springs, and endowed with all the same essential qualities, only cleared, refined, and cultivated. Water is the same fluid body in winter and in summer; when it stands stiffened in ice as when it flows along in gentle streams, gladdening a thousand fields in its progress. It is a property of the heart of man to be diffusive: its kind wishes spread abroad over the face of the creation; and if there be those, as we may observe too many of them, who are all wrapped up in their own dear selves, without any visible concern for their species, let us suppose that their good nature is frozen, and by the prevailing force of some contrary quality, restrained in its operation. I shall therefore endeavour to assign some of the principal checks upon this generous propension of the human soul, which will enable us to judge whether, and by what method, this most useful principle may be unfettered, and restored to its native freedom of exercise.

'The first and leading cause is an unhappy complexion of body. The heathens, ignorant of the true source of moral evil, generally charged it on the obliquity of matter, which, being eternal and independent, was incapable of change in any of its properties, even by the Almighty Mind, who, when he came to fashion it into a world of beings, must take it as he found it. This notion, as most others of theirs, is a composition of truth and error. That matter is eternal, that, from the first union of a soul to it, it perverted its inclinations, and that the ill influence it hath upon the mind is not to be corrected by God himself, are all very great errors, occasioned by a truth as evident, that the capacities and dispositions of the soul depend, to a great degree, on the bodily temper. As there are some fools, others are knaves by constitution; and particularly it may be said of many, that they are born with an illiberal cast of mind; the matter that composes them is tenacious as birdlime; and a kind of cramp draws their hands and their hearts together, that they never care to open them, unless to grasp at more. It is a melancholy lot this; but attended with one advantage above theirs, to whom it would be as painful to forbear good offices as it is to these men to perform them; that whereas persons naturally beneficent often mistake instinct for virtue, by reason of the difficulty of distinguishing when one rules them and when the other, men of the opposite character may be more certain of the motive that predominates in every action. If they cannot confer a benefit with that ease and frankness which are necessary to give it a grace in the eye of the world, in requital, the real merit of what they do is enhanced by the opposition they surmount in doing it. The strength of their virtue is seen in rising against the weight of nature; and every time they have the resolution to discharge their duty, they make a sacrifice of inclination to conscience, which is always too grateful to let its followers go without suitable marks of its approbation. Perhaps the entire cure of this ill quality is no more possible than of some distempers that descend by inheritance. However, a great deal may be done by a course of beneficence obstinately persisted in; this, if any thing, being a likely way of establishing a moral habit, which shall be somewhat of a counterpoise to the force of mechanism. Only it must be remembered that we do not intermit, upon any pretence whatsoever, the custom of doing good, in regard, if there be the least cessation, nature will watch the opportunity to return, and in a short time to recover the ground it was so long in quitting: for there is this difference between mental habits and such as have their foundation in the body; that these last are in their nature more forcible and violent; and, to gain upon us, need only not to be opposed; whereas the former must be continually reinforced with fresh supplies, or they will languish and die away. And this suggests the reason why good habits in general require longer time for their settlement than bad, and yet are sooner displaced; the reason is, that vicious habits, as drunkenness for instance, produce a change in the body, which the others not doing, must be maintained the same way they are acquired, by the mere dint of industry, resolution, and vigilance.

'Another thing which suspends the operations of benevolence, is the love of the world; proceeding from a false notion men have taken up, that an abundance of the world is an essential ingredient in the happiness of life. Worldly things are of such a quality as to lessen upon dividing, so that the more partners there are the less must fall to every man's private share. The consequence of this is, that they look upon one another with an evil eye, each imagining all the rest to be embarked in an interest that cannot take place but to his prejudice. Hence are those eager competitions for wealth or power; hence one man's success becomes another's disappointment; and, like pretenders to the same mistress, they can seldom have common charity for their rivals. Not that they are naturally disposed to quarrel and fall out; but it is natural for a man to prefer himself to all others, and to secure his own interest first. If that which men esteem their happiness were, like the light, the same sufficient and unconfined good, whether ten thousand enjoy the benefit of it or but one, we should see men's good-will and kind endeavours would be as universal.

> "Homo qui erranti comiter monstrat viam,
> Quasi lumen de suo lumine accendat, facit,
> Nihilominus ipsi luceat, cum illi accenderit."

> "To direct a wanderer in the right way, is to light another man's candle by one's own, which loses none of its light by what the other gains."

'But, unluckily, mankind agree in making choice of objects which inevitably engage them in perpetual differences. Learn, therefore, like a wise man, the true estimate of things. Desire not more of the world than is necessary to accommodate you in passing through it; look upon every thing beyond, not as useless only, but burdensome. Place not your quiet in things which you cannot have without putting others beside them, and thereby making them your enemies; and which, when attained, will give you more trouble to keep than satisfaction in the enjoyment. Virtue is a good of a nobler kind; it grows by communication; and so little resembles earthly riches, that the more hands it is lodged in, the greater is every man's particular stock. So, by propagating and mingling their fires, not only all the lights of a branch together cast a more extensive brightness, but each single light burns with a stronger flame. And lastly, take this along with you, that if wealth be an instrument of pleasure, the greatest pleasure it can put into your power is that of doing good. It is worth considering, that the organs of sense act within a narrow compass, and the appetites will soon say they have enough. Which of the two therefore is the happier man—he who, confining all his regard to the gratification of his appetites, is capable but of short fits of pleasure—or the man who, reckoning himself a sharer in the satisfactions of others, especially those which come to them by his means, enlarges the sphere of his happiness?

'The last enemy to benevolence I shall mention is uneasiness of any kind. A guilty or a discontented mind, a mind ruffled by ill-fortune, disconcerted by its own passions, soured by neglect, or fretting at disappointments, hath not leisure to attend to the necessity or unreasonableness of a kindness desired, nor a taste for those pleasures which wait on beneficence, which demand a calm and unpolluted heart to relish them. The most miserable of all beings is the most envious; as, on the other hand, the most communicative is the happiest. And if you are in search of the seat of perfect love and friendship, you will not find it until you come to the region of the blessed, where happiness, like a refreshing stream, flows from heart to heart in an endless circulation, and is preserved sweet and untainted by the motion. It is old advice, if you have a favour to request of any one, to observe the softest times of address, when the soul, in a flash of good humour, takes a pleasure to show itself pleased. Persons conscious of their own integrity, satisfied with themselves and their condition, and full of confidence in a Supreme Being, and the hope of immortality, survey all about them with a flow of good-will; as trees which, like their soil, shoot out in expressions of kindness, and bend beneath their own precious load, to the hand of the gatherer. Now, if the mind be not thus easy, it is an infallible sign that it is not in its natural state: place the mind in its right posture, it will immediately discover its innate propension to beneficence.'

No. 602.] *Monday, October* 4, 1714.

Facit hoc illos hyacinthos
Juv. Sat. vi. ver. 110.

This makes them hyacinths.

THE following letter comes from a gentleman who I find is very diligent in making his observations, which I think too material not to be communicated to the public.

'SIR,—In order to execute the office of the love casuist of Great Britain, with which I take myself to be invested by your paper of September 8, I shall make some farther observations upon the two sexes in general, beginning with that which always ought to have the upper hand. After having observed, with much curiosity, the accomplishments which are apt to captivate female hearts, I find that there is no person so irresistible as one who is a man of importance, provided it be in matters of no consequence. One who makes himself talked of, though it be for the particular cock of his hat, or for prating aloud in the boxes at a play, is in a fair way of being a favourite. I have known a young fellow make his fortune by knocking down a constable; and may venture to say, though it may seem a paradox, that many a fair one has died by a duel in which both the combatants have survived.

'About three winters ago, I took notice of a young lady at the theatre, who conceived a passion for a notorious rake that headed a party of catcalls; and am credibly informed that the emperor of the Mohocks married a rich widow within three weeks after having rendered himself formidable in the cities of London and Westminster. Scouring and breaking of windows have done frequent execution upon the sex. But there is no set of these male charmers who make their way more successfully than those who have gained themselves a name for intrigue, and have ruined the greatest number of reputations. There is a strange curiosity in the female world to be acquainted with the dear man who has been loved by others, and to know what it is that makes him so agreeable. His reputation does more than half his business. Every one that is ambitious of being a woman of fashion, looks out for opportunities of being in his company; so that, to use the old proverb, "When his name is up he may lie a-bed."

'I was very sensible of the great advantage of being a man of importance upon these occasions on the day of the king's entry, when I was seated in a balcony behind a cluster of very pretty country ladies, who had one of these showy gentlemen in the midst of them. The first trick I caught him at was bowing to several persons of quality whom he did not know; nay, he had the impudence to hem at a blue garter who had a finer equipage than ordinary; and seemed a little concerned at the impertinent huzzas of the mob, that hindered his friend from taking notice of him. There was indeed one who pulled off his hat to him; and, upon the ladies asking who it was, he told them it was a foreign minister that he had been very merry with the night before; whereas in truth it was the city common hunt.

'He was never at a loss when he was asked any person's name, though he seldom knew any one under a peer. He found dukes and earls among the aldermen, very good-natured fellows among the privy-counsellors, with two or three agreeable old rakes among the bishops and judges.

'In short, I collected from his whole discourse, that he was acquainted with every body, and knew nobody. At the same time, I am mistaken if he did not that day make more advances in the affections of his mistress, who sat near him, than he could have done in half a year's courtship.

'Ovid has finely touched this method of

making love, which I shall here give my reader in Mr. Dryden's translation.

'Page the eleventh.

" Thus love in theatres did first improve,
And theatres are still the scene of love;
Nor shun the chariots, and the courser's race;
The Circus is no inconvenient place.
Nor need is there of talking on the hand,
Nor nods, nor signs, which lovers understand;
But boldly next the fair your seat provide,
Close as you can to hers, and side by side;
Pleas'd or unpleas'd, no matter, crowding sit;
For so the laws of public shows permit.
Then find occasion to begin discourse,
Inquire whose chariot this, and whose that horse;
To whatsoever side she is inclin'd,
Suit all your inclinations to her mind.
Like what she likes, from thence your court begin,
And, whom she favours, wish that he may win."

'Again, page the sixteenth,

" O when will come the day by heaven design'd,
When thou, the best and fairest of mankind,
Drawn by white horses, shall in triumph ride,
With conquer'd slaves attending on thy side;
Slaves that no longer can be safe in flight,
O glorious object! O surprising sight!
O day of public joy, too good to end in night!
On such a day, if thou, and next to thee
Some beauty sits, the spectacle to see;
If she inquires the names of conquer'd kings,
Of mountains, rivers, and their hidden springs;
Answer to all thou know'st; and if need be,
Of things unknown seem to speak knowingly:
This is Euphrates, crown'd with reeds; and there
Flows the swift Tigris, with his sea-green hair.
Invent new names of things unknown before;
Call this Armenia, that the Caspian shore;
Call this a Mede, and that the Parthian youth;
Talk probably: no matter for the truth."

No. 603.] *Wednesday, October* 6, 1714.

Ducite ab urbe domum, mea carmina, ducite Daphnim.
Virg. Ecl. viii. 68.

——————Restore my charms,
My lingering Daphnis, to my longing arms.—*Dryden*.

The following copy of verses comes from one of my correspondents,* and has something in it so original, that I do not much doubt but it will divert my readers.†

I.

'My time, O ye Muses, was happily spent,
When Phœbe went with me wherever I went;‡
Ten thousand sweet pleasures I felt in my breast.
Sure never fond shepherd like Colin was blest!
But now she has gone, and has left me behind,
What a marvellous change on a sudden I find!
When things were as fine as could possibly be,
I thought 'twas the spring; but, alas! it was she.

II.

'With such a companion to tend a few sheep,
To rise up and play, or to lie down and sleep:
I was so good-humour'd, so cheerful and gay,
My heart was as light as a feather all day.
But now I so cross and so peevish am grown;
So strangely uneasy as never was known.
My fair one is gone, and my joys are all drown'd,
And my heart—I am sure it weighs more than a pound.

III.

'The fountain that wont to run swiftly along,
And dance to soft murmurs the pebbles among;
Thou know'st little Cupid, if Phœbe was there,
'Twas pleasure to look at, 'twas music to hear:
But now she is absent, I walk by its side,
And still as it murmurs do nothing but chide.
Must you be so cheerful, when I go in pain?
Peace there with your bubbling, and hear me complain.

IV.

'When my lambkins around me would oftentimes play,
And when Phœbe and I were as joyful as they,
How pleasant their sporting, how happy their time,
When spring, love, and beauty, were all in their prime
But now in their frolics when by me they pass,
I fling at their fleeces a handful of grass;
Be still, then I cry, for it makes me quite mad
To see you so merry while I am so sad.

V.

'My dog I was ever well pleased to see
Come wagging his tail to my fair-one and me;
And Phœbe was pleas'd too, and to my dog said,
Come hither, poor fellow; and patted his head.
But now, when he's fawning, I with a sour look
Cry, Sirrah! and give him a blow with my crook.
And I'll give him another; for why should not Tray
Be as dull as his master, when Phœbe's away?

VI.

'When walking with Phœbe, what sights have I seen!
How fair was the flower, how fresh was the green!
What a lovely appearance the trees and the shade,
The corn-fields and hedges, and every thing made!
But now she has left me, though all are still there,
They none of them now so delightful appear:
'Twas nought but the magic, I find, of her eyes,
Made so many beautiful prospects arise.

VII.

'Sweet music went with us both all the wood through,
The lark, linnet, throstle, and nightingale too;
Winds over us whisper'd, flocks by us did bleat,
And chirp went the grasshopper under our feet.
But now she is absent, though still they sing on,
The woods are but lonely, the melody's gone:
Her voice in the concert, as now I have found,
Gave every thing else its agreeable sound.

VIII.

'Rose, what is become of thy delicate hue?
And where is the violet's beautiful blue?
Does aught of its sweetness the blossom beguile?
That meadow, those daisies, why do they not smile?
Ah! rivals, I see what it was that you dress'd
And made yourselves fine for; a place in her breast:
You put on your colours to pleasure her eye,
To be pluck'd by her hand, on her bosom to die.

IX.

'How slowly time creeps, till my Phœbe return!
While amidst the soft zephyr's cool breezes I burn!
Methinks if I knew whereabout he would tread,
I could breathe on his wings, and 'twould melt down the lead.
Fly swifter ye minutes, bring hither my dear,
And rest so much longer for't when she is here.
Ah, Colin! old Time is full of delay,
Nor will budge one foot faster for all thou canst say

X.

'Will no pitying power that hears me complain,
Or cure my disquiet, or soften my pain?
To be cur'd, thou must, Colin, thy passion remove:
But what swain is so silly to live without love.
No, deity, bid the dear nymph to return,
For ne'er was poor shepherd so sadly forlorn,
Ah! what shall I do? I shall die with despair!—
Take heed all ye swains, how ye love one so fair.'

* Mr. John Byron, author of the two papers on dreaming, No. 586 and 593.

† " It has been said, on good authority, that the Phœbe of this pastoral was Joanna, the daughter of Dr. Bentley, and that it was written, not so much from affection to the daughter, as with the aim of securing the interest of the doctor, in promoting the author's views with regard to the fellowship for which, at the period of its composition, he was a candidate."
Drake's Essays, vol. iii. p. 216.

‡ Ansty made a most happy parody of these two lines in his Bath Guide.

" My time, my dear mother's, been wretchedly spent,
With a gripe or a hickup wherever I went."

No. 604.] *Friday, October* 8, 1714.

Tu ne quæsieris (scire nefas) quem mihi, quem tibi,
Finem Dii dederint, Leuconoe; nec Babylonios
Tentaris numeros———— *Hor*. Od. xi. Lib. 1. 1

Ah do not strive too much to know,
My dear Leuconoe,
What the kind gods design to do
With me and thee.—*Creech*.

The desire of knowing future events, is one of the strongest inclinations in the mind of man. Indeed, an ability of foreseeing probable accidents is what, in the language of men, is called wisdom and prudence: but, not satisfied with the light that reason holds out, mankind hath endeavoured to penetrate more compendiously into futurity. Magic, oracles, omens, lucky hours, and the various arts of superstition, owe their rise to this powerful cause. As this principle is founded in self-love, every man is sure to be solicitous in the first place about his own fortune, the course of his life, and the time and manner of his death.

If we consider that we are free agents, we shall discover the absurdity of such inquiries. One of our actions, which we might have performed or neglected, is the cause of another that succeeds it, and so the whole chain of life is linked together. Pain, poverty, or infamy, are the natural product of vicious and imprudent acts; as the contrary blessings are of good ones; so that we cannot suppose our lot to be determined without impiety. A great enhancement of pleasure arises from its being unexpected; and pain is doubled by being foreseen. Upon all these, and several other accounts, we ought to rest satisfied in this portion bestowed on us; to adore the hand that hath fitted every thing to our nature, and hath not more displayed his goodness in our knowledge than in our ignorance.

It is not unworthy observation, that superstitious inquiries into future events prevail more or less, in proportion to the improvement of liberal arts and useful knowledge in the several parts of the world. Accordingly, we find that magical incantations remain in Lapland; in the more remote parts of Scotland they have their second sight; and several of our own countrymen have seen abundance of fairies. In Asia this credulity is strong; and the greatest part of refined learning there consists in the knowledge of amulets, talismans, occult numbers, and the like.

When I was at Grand Cairo, I fell into the acquaintance of a good-natured mussulman, who promised me many good offices which he designed to do me when he became the prime minister, which was a fortune bestowed on his imagination by a doctor very deep in the curious sciences. At his repeated solicitations I went to learn my destiny of this wonderful sage. For a small sum I had his promise, but was desired to wait in a dark apartment until he had run through the preparatory ceremonies. Having a strong propensity, even then, to dreaming, I took a nap upon the sofa where I was placed, and had the following vision, the particulars whereof I picked up the other day among my papers.

I found myself in an unbounded plain, where methought the whole world, in several habits and with different tongues, was assembled. The multitude glided swiftly along, and I found in myself a strong inclination to mingle in the train. My eyes quickly singled out some of the most splendid figures. Several in rich caftans and glittering turbans bustled through the throng, and trampled over the bodies of those they threw down; until, to my great surprise, I found that the great pace they went only hastened them to a scaffold or a bow-string. Many beautiful damsels on the other side moved forward with great gayety; some danced until they fell all along; and others painted their faces until they lost their noses. A tribe of creatures with busy looks falling into a fit of laughter at the misfortunes of the unhappy ladies, I turned my eyes upon them. They were each of them filling his pockets with gold and jewels, and when there was no room left for more, these wretches, looking round with fear and horror, pined away before my face with famine and discontent.

The prospect of human misery struck me dumb for some miles. Then it was, that to disburden my mind, I took pen and ink, and did every thing that has since happened under my office as Spectator. While I was employing myself for the good of mankind, I was surprised to meet with very unsuitable returns from my fellow-creatures. Never was poor author so beset by pamphleteers, who sometimes marched directly against me, but oftener shot at me from strong bulwarks, or rose up suddenly in ambush. They were of all characters and capacities, some with ensigns of dignity, and others in liveries;* but what most surprised me was to see two or three in black gowns among my enemies. It was no small trouble to me, sometimes to have a man come up to me with an angry face, and reproach me for having lampooned him, when I had never seen or heard of him in my life. With the ladies it was otherwise: many became my enemies for not being particularly pointed out; as there were others who resented the satire which they imagined I had directed against them. My great comfort was in the company of half a dozen friends, who, I found since, were the club which I have so often mentioned in my papers. I laughed often at Sir Roger in my sleep, and was the more diverted with Will Honeycomb's gallantries, (when we afterwards became acquainted,) because I had foreseen his marriage with a farmer's daughter. The regret which arose in my mind upon the death of my companions, my anxieties for the public, and the many calamities still fleeting before my eyes, made me repent my curiosity; when the magician entered the room, and awakened me, by telling me (when it was too late,) that he was just going to begin.

---

* This is pointed at the hirelings employed by the ministry in the last years of the queen's reign; Dr. Swift, Prior, Atterbury, Dr. Friend, Dr. King, Mr. Oldsworth, Mrs. Manley, &c

N. B. I have only delivered the prophecy of that part of my life which is past, it being inconvenient to divulge the second part until a more proper opportunity.

No. 605.] *Monday, October* 11, 1714.

Exuerint sylvestrem animum; cultuque frequenti,
In quascunque voces artes, haud tarda sequentur.
Virg. Georg. ii. 51.

———They change their savage mind,
Their wildness lose, and, quitting nature's part,
Obey the rules and discipline of art.—*Dryden.*

Having perused the following letter, and finding it to run upon the subject of love, I referred it to the learned casuist, whom I have retained in my service for speculations of that kind. He returned it to me the next morning with his report annexed to it, with both of which I shall here present my reader.

'Mr. Spectator,—Finding that you have entertained a useful person in your service in quality of love-casuist, I apply myself to you under a very great difficulty, that hath for some months perplexed me. I have a couple of humble servants, one of which I have no aversion to; the other I think of very kindly. The first hath the reputation of a man of good sense, and is one of those people that your sex are apt to value. My spark is reckoned a coxcomb among the men, but is a favourite of the ladies. If I marry the man of worth, as they call him, I shall oblige my parents, and improve my fortune; but with my dear beau I promise myself happiness, although not a jointure. Now I would ask you, whether I should consent to lead my life with a man that I have only no objection to, or with him against whom all objections to me appear frivolous. I am determined to follow the casuist's advice, and I dare say he will not put me upon so serious a thing as matrimony contrary to my inclination. I am, &c. FANNY FICKLE.

'P. S. I forgot to tell you, that the pretty gentleman is the most complaisant creature in the world, and is always of my mind; but the other, forsooth, fancies he has as much wit as myself, slights my lap-dog, and hath the insolence to contradict me when he thinks I am not in the right. About half an hour ago, he maintained to my face that a patch always implies a pimple.'

As I look upon it to be my duty rather to side with the parents than the daughter, I shall propose some considerations to my gentle querist, which may incline her to comply with those under whose direction she is; and at the same time convince her that it is not impossible but she may in time, have a true affection for him who is at present indifferent to her; or, to use the old family maxim, that, 'if she marries first, love will come after.'

The only objection that she seems to insinuate against the gentleman proposed to her, is his want of complaisance, which I perceive she is very willing to return. Now I can discover, from this very circumstance, that she and her lover, whatever they may think of it, are very good friends in their hearts. It is difficult to determine whether love delights more in giving pleasure or pain. Let Miss Fickle ask her own heart, if she doth not take a secret pride in making this man of good sense look very silly. Hath she ever been better pleased than when her behaviour hath made her lover ready to hang himself; or doth she ever rejoice more than when she thinks she hath driven him to the very brink of a purling stream? Let her consider, at the same time, that it is not impossible but her lover may have discovered her tricks, and hath a mind to give her as good as she brings. I remember a handsome young baggage that treated a hopeful Greek of my acquaintance, just come from Oxford, as if he had been a barbarian. The first week after she had fixed him, she took a pinch of snuff out of his rival's box, and apparently touched the enemy's little finger. She became a professed enemy to the arts and sciences, and scarce ever wrote a letter to him without wilfully misspelling his name. The young scholar, to be even with her, railed at coquettes as soon as he had got the word; and did not want parts to turn into ridicule her men of wit and pleasure of the town. After having irritated one another for the space of five months, she made an assignation with him fourscore miles from London. But, as he was very well acquainted with her pranks, he took a journey the quite contrary way. Accordingly they met, quarrelled, and in a few days were married. Their former hostilities are now the subject of their mirth, being content at present with that part of love only which bestows pleasure.

Women who have been married some time, not having it in their heads to draw after them a numerous train of followers, find their satisfaction in the possession of one man's heart. I know very well that ladies in their bloom desire to be excused in this particular. But, when time hath worn out their natural vanity, and taught them discretion, their fondness settles on its proper object. And it is probably for this reason that, among husbands, you will find more that are fond of women beyond their prime, than of those who are actually in the insolence of beauty. My reader will apply the same observation to the other sex.

I need not insist upon the necessity of their pursuing one common interest, and their united care for their children; but shall only observe, by the way, that married persons are both more warm in their love, and more hearty in their hatred than any others whatsoever. Mutual favours and obligations, which may be supposed to be greater here than in any other state, naturally beget an intense affection in generous minds. As, on the contrary, persons who have bestowed such favours have a particular bitterness in their resentments, when they think themselves ill-treated by those of whom they have deserved so much.

Besides, Miss Fickle may consider, that as there are often many faults concealed before marriage, so there are sometimes many virtues unobserved.

To this we may add the great efficacy of custom and constant conversation to produce a mutual friendship and benevolence in two persons. It is a nice reflection, which I have heard a friend of mine make, that you may be sure a woman loves a man, when she uses his expressions, tell his stories, or imitates his manner. This gives a secret delight; for imitation is a kind of artless flattery, and mightily favours the powerful principle of self-love. It is certain that married persons, who are possessed with a mutual esteem, not only catch the air and way of talk from one another, but fall into the same traces of thinking and liking. Nay, some have carried the remark so far as to assert, that the features of man and wife grow, in time, to resemble one another. Let my fair correspondent, therefore, consider, that the gentleman recommended will have a good deal of her own face in two or three years; which she must not expect from the beau, who is too full of his dear self to copy after another. And I dare appeal to her own judgment, if that person will not be the handsomest that is the most like herself.

We have a remarkable instance to our present purpose in the history of king Edgar, which I shall here relate, and leave it with my fair correspondent to be applied to herself.

This great monarch, who is so famous in British story, fell in love, as he made his progress through his kingdom, with a certain duke's daughter, who lived near Winchester, and was the most celebrated beauty of the age. His importunities and the violence of his passion were so great, that the mother of the young lady promised him to bring her daughter to his bed the next night, though in her heart she abhorred so infamous an office. It was no sooner dark than she conveyed into his room, a young maid of no disagreeable figure, who was one of her attendants, and did not want address to improve the opportunity for the advancement of her fortune. She made so good use of her time, that when she offered to rise a little before day, the king could by no means think of parting with her; so that, finding herself under a necessity of discovering who she was, she did it in so handsome a manner, that his majesty was exceeding gracious to her, and took her ever after under his protection: insomuch, that our chronicles tell us, he carried her along with him, made her his first minister of state, and continued true to her alone, until his marriage with the beautiful Elfrida.

No. 606.] *Wednesday, October* 13, 1714.

——longum cantu solata laborem
Arguto conjux percurrit pectine telas.
Virg. Georg. i. 294.

——mean time at home
The good wife singing plies the various loom.

'MR. SPECTATOR,—I have a couple of nieces under my direction, who so often run gadding abroad, that I do not know where to have them. Their dress, their tea, and their visits, take up all their time, and they go to bed as tired with doing nothing as I am after quilting a whole under-petticoat. The only time they are not idle is while they read your Spectators; which being dedicated to the interest of virtue, I desire you to recommend the long neglected art of needle-work. Those hours which in this age are thrown away on dress, play, visits, and the like, were employed, in my time, in writing out receipts, or working beds, chairs, and hangings, for the family. For my part, I have plied my needle these fifty years, and by my good will would never have it out of my hand. It grieves my heart to see a couple of proud idle flirts sipping their tea, for a whole afternoon, in a room hung round with the industry of their great grandmother. Pray, sir, take the laudable mystery of embroidery into your serious consideration, and, as you have a great deal of the virtue of the last age in you, continue your endeavours to reform the present. I am, &c.'

In obedience to the commands of my venerable correspondent, I have duly weighed this important subject, and promise myself, from the arguments here laid down, that all the fine ladies of England will be ready, as soon as their mourning is over,* to appear covered with the work of their own hands.

What a delightful entertainment must it be to the fair-sex, whom their native modesty and the tenderness of men towards them, exempt from public business, to pass their hours in imitating fruits and flowers and transplanting all the beauties of nature into their own dress, or raising a new creation in their closets and apartments! How pleasing is the amusement of walking among the shades and groves planted by themselves, in surveying heroes slain by their needle, or little cupids which they have brought into the world without pain!

This is, methinks, the most proper way wherein a lady can show a fine genius; and I cannot forbear wishing that several writers of that sex had chosen to apply themselves rather to tapestry than rhyme. Your pastoral poetesses may vent their fancy in rural landscapes, and place des-

* The general mourning on the death of queen Anne

pairing shepherds under silken willows, or drown them in a stream of mohair. The heroic writers may work up battles as successfully, and inflame them with gold or stain them with crimson. Even those who have only a turn to a song, or an epigram, may put many valuable stitches into a purse, and crowd a thousand graces into a pair of garters.

If I may, without breach of good manners, imagine that any pretty creature is void of genius, and would perform her part herein but very awkwardly, I must nevertheless insist upon her working, if it be only to keep her out of harm's way.

Another argument for busying good women in works of fancy is, because it takes them off from scandal, the usual attendant of tea-tables, and all other inactive scenes of life. While they are forming their birds and beasts, their neighbours will be allowed to be the fathers of their own children; and whig and tory will be but seldom mentioned where the great dispute is, whether blue or red is the more proper colour. How much greater glory would Sophronia do the general, if she would choose rather to work the battle of Blenheim in tapestry, than signalize herself with so much vehemence against those who are Frenchmen in their hearts!

A third reason that I shall mention, is the profit that is brought to the family where these pretty arts are encouraged. It is manifest that this way of life not only keeps fair ladies from running out into expenses, but is at the same time an actual improvement. How memorable would that matron be, who shall have it subscribed upon her monument, 'That she wrought out the whole Bible in tapestry, and died in a good old age, after having covered three hundred yards of wall in the mansion-house!'

The premises being considered, I humbly submit the following proposals to all mothers in Great Britain:

1. That no young virgin whatsoever be allowed to receive the addresses of her first lover, but in a suit of her own embroidering.

2. That before every fresh humble servant, she be obliged to appear with a new stomacher at the least.

3. That no one be actually married until she hath the child-bed pillows, &c. ready stitched, as likewise the mantle for the boy quite finished.

These laws, if I mistake not, would effectually restore the decayed art of needlework, and make the virgins of Great Britain exceedingly nimble-fingered in their business.

There is a memorable custom of the Grecian ladies, in this particular, preserved in Homer, which I hope will have a very good effect with my country-women. A widow, in ancient times, could not, without indecency, receive a second husband, until she had woven a shroud for her deceased lord, or the next of kin to him. Accordingly, the chaste Penelope having, as she thought, lost Ulysses at sea, she employed her time in preparing a winding-sheet for Laertes, the father of her husband. The story of her web being very famous, and yet not sufficiently known in its several circumstances, I shall give it to my reader, as Homer makes one of her wooers relate it.

'Sweet hope she gave to every youth apart,
With well-taught looks, and a deceitful heart:
A web she wove of many a slender twine,
Of curious texture, and perplext design;
My youths, she cried, my lord but newly dead,
Forbear a while to court my widow'd bed,
Till I have wove, as solemn vows require,
This web, a shroud for poor Ulysses' sire.
His limbs, when fate the hero's soul demands,
Shall claim this labour of his daughter's hands:
Lest all the dames of Greece my name despise,
While the great king without a covering lies.
'Thus she. Nor did my friends mistrust the guile:
All day she sped the long laborious toil:
But when the burning lamps supply'd the sun,
Each night unravell'd what the day begun.
Three live-long summers did the fraud prevail;
The fourth her maidens told th' amazing tale.
These eyes beheld, as close I took my stand,
The backward labours of her faithless hand:
Till watch'd at length, and press'd on every side,
Her task she ended, and commenc'd a bride.'

No. 607.] *Friday, October* 15, 1714.

Dicite Io Pæan, et Io bis dicite Pæan:
Decidit in casses præda petita meos.
Ovid Ars Amor. Lib. 1. 1.

Now Io Pæan sing, now wreaths prepare,
And with repeated Ios fill the air:
The prey is fallen in my successful toils.—*Anon.*

'Mr. Spectator,—Having in your paper of Monday last published my report on the case of Mrs. Fanny Fickle, wherein I have taken notice, that love comes after marriage; I hope your readers are satisfied of this truth, that as love generally produces matrimony, so it often happens that matrimony produces love.

'It perhaps requires more virtue to make a good husband or wife than what go to the finishing any the most shining character whatsoever.

'Discretion seems absolutely necessary; and accordingly we find that the best husbands have been most famous for their wisdom. Homer, who hath drawn a perfect pattern of a prudent man, to make it the more complete, hath celebrated him for the just returns of fidelity and truth to his Penelope; insomuch that he refused the caresses of a goddess for her sake; and, to use the expression of the best of Pagan authors, "*Vetulam suam prætulit immortalitati,*" his old woman was dearer to him than immortality.

'Virtue is the next necessary qualification for this domestic character, as it naturally produces constancy and mutual esteem. Thus Brutus and Porcia were more remarkable for virtue and affection than any others of the age in which they lived.

'Good-nature is a third necessary ingredient in the marriage state, without which it would inevitably sour upon a thousand occasions. When greatness of mind is joined with this amiable quality it attracts the admiration and esteem of all who behold it. Thus Cæsar, not more remarkable for his fortune and valour than for his humanity, stole into the hearts of the Roman people, when, breaking through the custom, he pronounced an oration at the funeral of his first and best-beloved wife.

'Good-nature is insufficient, unless it be steady and uniform, and accompanied with an evenness of temper, which is above all things to be preserved in this friendship contracted for life. A man must be easy within himself before he can be so to his other self. Socrates and Marcus Aurelius are instances of men, who, by the strength of philosophy, having entirely composed their minds, and subdued their passions, are celebrated for good husbands, notwithstanding the first was yoked with Xantippe, and the other with Faustina. If the wedded pair would but habituate themselves for the first year to bear with one another's faults, the difficulty would be pretty well conquered. This mutual sweetness of temper and complacency was finely recommended in the nuptial ceremonies among the heathens, who, when they sacrificed to Juno at that solemnity, always tore out the gall from the entrails of the victim, and cast it behind the altar.

'I shall conclude this letter with a passage out of Dr. Plot's Natural History of Staffordshire, not only as it will serve to fill up your present paper, but, if I find myself in the humour, may give rise to another; I having by me an old register belonging to the place here under-mentioned.

"Sir Philip de Somervile held the manors of Whichenovre, Scirescot, Ridware, Netherton, and Cowlee, all in the county of Stafford, of the earls of Lancaster, by this memorable service. The said Sir Philip shall find, maintain, and sustain, one baconflitch, hanging in his hall at Whichenovre, ready arrayed all times of the year but in Lent, to be given to every man or woman married, after the day and the year of their marriage be past, in form following.*

"Whensoever that any one such before named will come to inquire for the bacon, in their own person, they shall come to the bailiff, or to the porter of the lordship of Whichenovre, and shall say to them in the manner as ensueth:

'Bailiff, or porter, I do you to know, that I am come for myself to demand one baconflyke hanging in the hall of the lord of Whichenovre, after the form thereunto belonging.'

"After which relation, the bailiff or porter shall assign a day to him, upon promise by his faith to return, and with him to bring twain of his neighbours. And in the mean time, the said bailiff shall take with him twain of the freeholders of the lordship of Whichenovre, and they three shall go to the manor of Rudlow, belonging to Robert Knightleye, and there shall summon the aforesaid Knightleye, or his bailiff, commanding him to be ready at Whichenovre the day appointed, at prime of day, with his carriage, that is to say, a horse and a saddle, a sack and a pryke, for to convey the said bacon and corn a journey out of the county of Stafford, at his costages. And then the said bailiff shall, with the said freeholders, summon all the tenants of the said manor, to be ready at the day appointed at Whichenovre, for to do and perform the services which they owe to the bacon. And at the day assigned, all such as owe services to the bacon shall be ready at the gate of the manor of Whichenovre, from the sunrising to noon, attending and awaiting for the coming of him who fetcheth the bacon. And when he is come, there shall be delivered to him and his fellows, chapelets, and to all those which shall be there to do their services due to the bacon. And they shall lead the said demandant with trumps and tabors, and other manner of minstrelsy, to the hall door, where he shall find the lord of Whichenovre, or his steward, ready to deliver the bacon in this manner:

"He shall inquire of him which demandeth the bacon, if he have brought twain of his neighbours with him: which must answer, 'they be here ready.' And then the steward shall cause these two neighbours to swear, if the said demandant be a wedded man, or have been a man wedded; and if since his marriage one year and a day be past; and if he be a freeman or a villain.† And if his said neighbours make oath that he hath for him all these three points rehearsed, then shall the bacon be taken down and brought to the hall door, and shall there be laid upon one half-quarter of wheat, and upon one other of rye. And he that demandeth the bacon shall kneel upon his knee, and shall hold his right hand upon a book, which book shall be laid upon the bacon and the corn, and shall make oath in this manner:

'Hear ye, Sir Philip de Somervile, lord of Whichenovre, mayntener and gyver of this baconne; that I A sithe I wedded B my wife, and sithe I had hyr in my kepying, and at my wylle, by a year and a day after our marriage, I would not have chaunged for none other; farer ne fowler; richer ne pourer; ne for none other descended of greater lynage; slepying ne waking, at noo tyme.—And if the seyd B were sole, and I sole, I would take her to be my wife before all the wymen of the world, of what condiciones soever they be, good or evylle; as help me God and his seyntes, and this flesh and all fleshes.

* There was a similar institution at Dunmow in Essex, for an account of which see Leland's Itinerary.

† Villain, in the language of the time, signified a servant or bondman.

"And his neighbours shall make oath, that they trust verily he hath said truly. And if it be found by his neighbours before-named, that he be a freeman, there shall be delivered to him half a quarter of wheat and a cheese; and if he be a villain, he shall have half a quarter of rye without cheese. And then shall Knightleye, the lord of Rudlow, be called for, to carry all these things tofore rehearsed; and the said corn shall be laid on one horse, and the bacon above it: and he to whom the bacon appertaineth shall ascend upon his horse, and shall take the cheese before him, if he have a horse. And if he have none, the lord of Whichenovre shall cause him to have one horse and saddle, to such time as he be passed his lordship: and so shall they depart the manor of Whichenovre with the corn and the bacon, tofore him that hath won it, with trumpets, taborets, and other manner of minstrelsy. And all the free tenants of Whichenovre shall conduct him to be passed the lordship of Whichenovre. And then shall they all return except him to whom appertaineth to make the carriage and journey without the county of Stafford, at the costs of his lord of Whichenovre."

No. 608.] *Monday, October* 18, 1714.

——Perjuria ridet amantum.
Ovid Ars Amor. Lib. i. 633.

——Forgiving with a smile
The perjuries that easy maids beguile.—*Dryden.*

'Mr. Spectator,—According to my promise I herewith transmit to you a list of several persons, who from time to time demanded the flitch of bacon of Sir Philip de Somervile, and his descendants; as it is preserved in an ancient manuscript, under the title of "The Register of Whichenovre-hall, and of the bacon-flitch there maintained."

'In the beginning of this record is recited the law or institution in form, as it is already printed in your last paper: to which are added two bye-laws, as a comment upon the general law, the substance whereof is, that the wife shall take the same oath as the husband, *mutatis mutandis;* and that the judges shall, as they think meet, interrogate or cross-examine the witnesses. After this proceeds the register in manner following:

"Aubry de Falstaff, son of Sir John Falstaff, knight, with dame Maude his wife, were the first that demanded the bacon, he having bribed twain of his father's companions to swear falsely in his behoof, whereby he gained the flitch: but he and his said wife falling immediately into a dispute how the said bacon should be dressed, it was, by order of the judges, taken from him, and hung up again in the hall.

"Alison, the wife of Stephen Freckle, brought her said husband along with her, and set forth the good conditions and behaviour of her consort, adding withal that she doubted not but he was ready to attest the like of her, his wife; whereupon he, the said Stephen, shaking his head, she turned short upon him, and gave him a box on the ear.

"Philip de Waverland, having laid his hand upon the book, when the clause, 'were I sole and she sole,' was rehearsed, found a secret compunction rising in his mind, and stole it off again.

"Richard de Loveless, who was a courtier, and a very well-bred man, being observed to hesitate after the words, 'after our marriage,' was thereupon required to explain himself. He replied, by talking very largely of his exact complaisance while he was a lover; and alleged that he had not in the least disobliged his wife for a year and a day before marriage, which he hoped was the same thing.

"Rejected.

"Joceline Jolley, esq. making it appear, by unquestionable testimony, that he and his wife had preserved full and entire affection for the space of the first month, commonly called the honey-moon, he had, in consideration thereof, one rasher bestowed upon him."

'After this, says the record, many years passed over before any demandant appeared at Whichenovre-hall; insomuch that one would have thought that the whole country were turned Jews, so little was their affection to the flitch of bacon.

'The next couple enrolled had like to have carried it, if one of the witnesses had not deposed, that, dining on a Sunday with the demandant, whose wife had sat below the squire's lady at church, she, the said wife, dropped some expressions, as if she thought her husband deserved to be knighted; to which he returned a passionate pish! The judges, taking the premises into consideration, declared the aforesaid behaviour to imply an unwarrantable ambition in the wife, and anger in the husband.

'It is recorded as a sufficient disqualification of a certain wife, that, speaking of her husband, she said, "God forgive him."

'It is likewise remarked, that a couple were rejected upon the deposition of one of their neighbours, that the lady had once told her husband, that "it was her duty to obey;" to which he replied, "O my dear! you are never in the wrong!"

'The violent passion of one lady for her lap-dog; the turning away of the old house maid by another; a tavern bill torn by the wife, and a tailor's by the husband; a quarrel about the kissing-crust; spoiling of dinners, and coming in late of nights; are so many several articles which occasioned the reprobation of some scores of demandants, whose names are recorded in the aforesaid register.

'Without enumerating other particular persons, I shall content myself with observing that the sentence pronounced against one Gervase Poacher is, that "he might have had bacon to his eggs, if he had not hitherto scolded his wife when they were overboiled." And the deposition against Dorothy Dolittle runs in these words, "that she had so far usurped the dominion of the coal fire (the stirring whereof her husband claimed to himself,) that by her good-will she never would suffer the poker out of her hand."

'I find but two couples in this first century that were successful; the first was a sea-captain and his wife, who since the day of their marriage had not seen one another until the day of the claim. The second was an honest pair in the neighbourhood; the husband was a man of plain good sense, and a peaceable temper; the woman was dumb.'

No. 609.] *Wednesday, October* 20, 1714.

——Farrago libelli.—*Juv.* Sat. i. 86.

The miscellaneous subjects of my book.

'MR. SPECTATOR,—I have for some time desired to appear in your paper, and have therefore chosen a day* to steal into the Spectator, when I take it for granted you will not have many spare minutes for speculations of your own. As I was the other day walking with an honest country gentleman, he very often was expressing his astonishment to see the town so mightily crowded with doctors of divinity; upon which I told him he was very much mistaken if he took all those gentlemen he saw in scarfs to be persons of that dignity; for that a young divine, after his first degree in the university, usually comes hither only to show himself; and, on that occasion, is apt to think he is but half equipped with a gown and cassock for his public appearance, if he hath not the additional ornament of a scarf of the first magnitude to entitle him to the appellation of Doctor from his landlady, and the boy at Child's. Now, since I know that this piece of garniture is looked upon as a mark of vanity or affectation, as it is made use of among some of the little spruce adventurers of the town, I should be glad if you would give it a place among those extravagances you have justly exposed in several of your papers: being very well assured that the main body of the clergy, both in the country and the universities, who are almost to a man untainted with it, would be very well pleased to see this venerable foppery well exposed. When my patron did me the honour to take me into his family (for I must own myself of this order,) he was pleased to say he took me as a friend and companion; and whether he looked upon the scarf like the lace and shoulder-knot of a footman, as a badge of servitude and dependence, I do not know, but he was so kind as to leave my wearing of it to my own discretion; and, not having any just title to it from my degrees, I am content to be without the ornament. The privileges of our nobility to keep a certain number of chaplains are undisputed, though perhaps not one in ten of those reverend gentlemen have any relation to the noble families their scarfs belong to; the right generally of creating all chaplains, except the domestic (where there is one,) being nothing more than the perquisite of a steward's place, who, if he happens to outlive any considerable number of his noble masters, shall probably, at one and the same time, nave fifty chaplains, all in their proper accoutrements, of his own creation; though perhaps there hath been neither grace nor prayer said in the family since the introduction of the first coronet. I am, &c.'

'MR. SPECTATOR,—I wish you would write a philosophical paper about natural antipathies, with a word or two concerning the strength of imagination. I can give you a list upon the first notice, of a rational china cup, of an egg that walks upon two legs, and a quart-pot that sings like a nightingale. There is in my neighbourhood a very pretty prattling shoulder of veal, that squalls out at the sight of a knife. Then, as for natural antipathies, I know a general officer who was never conquered but by a smothered rabbit; and a wife that domineers over her husband by the help of a breast of mutton. A story that relates to myself on this subject may be thought not unentertaining, especially when I assure you that it is literally true. I had long made love to a lady, in the possession of whom I am now the happiest of mankind, whose hand I should have gained with much difficulty without the assistance of a cat. You must know then that my most dangerous rival had so strong an aversion to this species, that he infallibly swooned away at the sight of that harmless creature. My friend, Mrs. Lucy, her maid, having a greater respect for me and my purse than she had for my rival, always took care to pin the tail of a cat under the gown of her mistress, whenever she knew of his coming; which had such an effect, that every time he entered the room, he looked more like one of the figures in Mrs. Salmon's wax-work,† than a desirable lover In short, he grew sick of her company; which the young lady taking notice of (who no more knew why than he did,) she sent me a challenge to meet her in Lincoln's-inn chapel, which I joyfully accepted; and have, amongst other pleasures, the satisfaction of being praised by her for my stratagem. I am, &c.

'From the Hoop. TOM NIMBLE.'

* The 20th of October, 1714, was the day of the coronation of king George I.

† An exhibition then to be seen near St. Dunstan's church, Fleet-Street, but which, about fifteen years ago, was moved to the opposite side of the street.

'MR. SPECTATOR,—The virgins of Great Britain are very much obliged to you for putting them upon such tedious drudgeries in needle-work as were fit only for the Hilpas and the Nilpas that lived before the flood. Here is a stir indeed, with your histories in embroidery, your groves with shades of silk and streams of mohair! I would have you to know, that I hope to kill a hundred lovers before the best housewife in England can stitch out a battle; and do not fear but to provide boys and girls much faster than your disciples can embroider them. I love birds and beasts as well as you, but am content to fancy them when they are really made. What do you think of gilt leather for furniture? There is your pretty hangings for your chamber!* and, what is more, our own country is the only place in Europe where work of that kind is tolerably done. Without minding your musty lessons, I am this minute going to St. Paul's church-yard to bespeak a screen and a set of hangings; and am resolved to encourage the manufacture of my country. Yours, CLEORA.'

No. 610.] *Friday, October* 22, 1714.

Sic, cum transierint mei
Nullo cum strepitu dies,
Plebeius moriar senex,
Illi mors gravis incubat,
Qui, notus nimis omnibus,
Ignotus moritur sibi.—*Seneca.*

Thus, when my fleeting days at last,
Unheeded, silently are past,
Calmly I shall resign my breath,
In life unknown, forgot in death;
While he, o'ertaken unprepar'd,
Finds death an evil to be fear'd,
Who dies, to others too much known,
A stranger to himself alone.

I HAVE often wondered that the Jews should contrive such worthless greatness for the Deliverer whom they expected, as to dress him up in external pomp and pageantry, and represent him to their imaginations as making havoc among his creatures, and actuated with the poor ambition of a Cæsar or an Alexander. How much more illustrious does he appear in his real character, when considered as the author of universal benevolence among men, as refining our passions, exalting our nature, giving us vast ideas of immortality, and teaching us a contempt of that little showy grandeur wherein the Jews made the glory of their Messiah to consist!

'Nothing,' says Longinus, 'can be great, the contempt of which is great.' The possession of wealth and riches cannot give a man a title to greatness, because it is looked upon as a greatness of mind to contemn these gifts of fortune, and to be above the desire of them. I have therefore been inclined to think that there are greater men who lie concealed among the species, than those who come out and draw upon themselves the eyes and admiration of mankind. Virgil would never have been heard of, had not his domestic misfortunes driven him out of his obscurity, and brought him to Rome.

If we suppose that there are spirits, or angels, who look into the ways of men, as it is highly probable there are, both from reason and revelation, how different are the notions which they entertain of us, from those which we are apt to form of one another! Were they to give us in their catalogue of such worthies as are now living, how different would it be from that which any of our own species would draw up!

We are dazzled with the splendour of titles, the ostentation of learning, the noise of victories: they, on the contrary, see the philosopher in the cottage, who possesses his soul in patience and thankfulness, under the pressures of what little minds call poverty and distress. They do not look for great men at the head of armies, or among the pomps of a court, but often find them out in shades and solitudes, in the private walks and by-paths of life. The evening's walk of a wise man is more illustrious in their sight than the march of a general at the head of a hundred thousand men. A contemplation of God's works; a voluntary act of justice to our own detriment: a generous concern for the good of mankind; tears that are shed in silence for the misery of others; a private desire or resentment broken and subdued; in short, an unfeigned exercise of humility, or any other virtue, are such actions as are glorious in their sight, and denominate men great and reputable. The most famous among us are often looked upon with pity, with contempt, or with indignation; whilst those who are most obscure among their own species are regarded with love, with approbation, and esteem.

The moral of the present speculation amounts to this; that we should not be led away by the censures and applauses of men, but consider the figure that every person will make at that time, when 'Wisdom shall be justified of her children,' and nothing pass for great or illustrious, which is not an ornament and perfection to human nature.

The story of Gyges, the rich Lydian monarch, is a memorable instance to our present purpose. The oracle being asked by Gyges, who was the happiest man, replied, Aglaus. Gyges, who expected to have heard himself named on this occasion, was much surprised, and very curious to know who this Aglaus should be. After much inquiry, he was found to be an obscure countryman, who employed all his time in cultivating a garden, and a few acres of land about his house.

Cowley's agreeable relation of this story shall close this day's speculation.

* There was about this time a celebrated manufactory of tapestry at Chelsea.

'Thus Aglaus (a man unknown to men,
But the gods knew, and therefore lov'd him then)
Thus liv'd obscurely then without a name,
Aglaus, now consign'd t' eternal fame.
For Gyges, the rich king, wicked and great,
Presum'd at wise Apollo's Delphic seat,
Presum'd to ask, O thou, the whole world's eye,
Seest thou a man that happier is than I?
The god, who scorn'd to flatter man, reply'd,
Aglaus happier is. But Gyges cry'd,
In a proud rage, Who can that Aglaus be?
We've heard as yet of no such king as he.
And true it was, through the whole earth around,
No king of such a name was to be found.
Is some old hero of that name alive,
Who his high race does from the gods derive?
Is it some mighty gen'ral that has done
Wonders in fight, and godlike honours won?
Is it some man of endless wealth? said he.
None, none of these. Who can this Aglaus be?
After long search, and vain inquiries past,
In an obscure Arcadian vale at last,
(Th' Arcadian life has always shady been)
Near Sopho's town, which, he but once had seen,
This Aglaus, who monarchs' envy drew,
Whose happiness the gods stood witness to,
This mighty Aglaus was lab'ring found,
With his own hands, in his own little ground.
'So, gracious God, if it may lawful be
Among those foolish gods to mention thee,
So let me act, on such a private stage,
The last dull scenes of my declining age;
After long toils and voyages in vain,
This quiet port let my toss'd vessel gain;
Of heavn'ly rest this earnest to me lend,
Let my life sleep, and learn to love her end.'

No. 611.] *Monday, October 25, 1714.*

Perfide! sed duris genuit te cautibus horrens
Caucasus, Hyrcanæque admorunt ubera tigres.
Virg. Æn. iv. 366.

Perfidious man! thy parent was a rock,
And fierce Hyrcanian tigers gave thee suck.

I AM willing to postpone every thing, to do any the least service for the deserving and unfortunate. Accordingly I have caused the following letter to be inserted in my paper the moment that it came to my hands, without altering one tittle in an account which the lady relates so handsomely herself.

'MR. SPECTATOR,—I flatter myself you will not only pity, but, if possible, redress a misfortune myself and several others of my sex lie under. I hope you will not be offended, nor think I mean by this to justify my own imprudent conduct, or expect you should. No: I am sensible how severely, in some of your former papers, you have reproved persons guilty of the like mismanagement. I was scarce sixteen, and I may say, without vanity, handsome, when courted by a false perjured man; who, upon promise of marriage, rendered me the most unhappy of women. After he had deluded me from my parents, who were people of very good fashion, in less than three months he left me. My parents would not see nor hear from me; and, had it not been for a servant who had lived in our family, I must certainly have perished for want of bread. However, it pleased Providence, in a very short time, to alter my miserable condition. A gentleman saw me, liked me, and married me. My parents were reconciled; and I might be as happy in the change of my condition, as I was before miserable, but for some things, that you shall know, which are insupportable to me; and I am sure you have so much honour and compassion as to let those persons know, in some of your papers, how much they are in the wrong. I have been married near five years, and do not know that in all that time I ever went abroad without my husband's leave and approbation. I am obliged, through the importunities of several of my relations, to go abroad oftener than suits my temper. Then it is I labour under insupportable agonies. That man, or rather monster, haunts every place I go to. Base villain! by reason I will not admit his nauseous wicked visits and appointments, he strives all the ways he can to ruin me. He left me destitute of friend or money, nor ever thought me worth inquiring after, until he unfortunately happened to see me in a front-box sparkling with jewels. Then his passion returned. Then the hypocrite pretended to be a penitent. Then he practised all those arts that helped before to undo me. I am not to be deceived a second time by him. I hate and abhor his odious passion; and as he plainly perceives it, either out of spite or diversion he makes it his business to expose me. I never fail seeing him in all public company, where he is always most industriously spiteful. He hath, in short, told all his acquaintance of our unhappy affair; they tell theirs; so that it is no secret among his companions, which are numerous. They to whom he tells it, think they have a title to be very familiar. If they bow to me, and I out of good manners return it, then I am pestered with freedoms that are no ways agreeable to myself or company. If I turn my eyes from them, or seem displeased, they sour upon it, and whisper the next person; he his next; until I have at last the eyes of the whole company upon me. Nay they report abominable falsehoods, under that mistaken notion, "She that will grant favours to one man will to a hundred." I beg you will let those who are guilty know how ungenerous this way of proceeding is. I am sure he will know himself the person aimed at, and perhaps put a stop to the insolence of others. Cursed is the fate of unhappy women! that men may boast and glory in those things that we must think of with shame and horror! You have the art of making such odious customs appear detestable. For my sake, and, I am sure, for the sake of several others who dare not own it, but, like me, lie under the same misfortunes, make it as infamous for a man to boast of favours, or expose our sex, as it is to take the lie, or a box on the ear, and not resent it. Your constant reader and admirer, LESBIA.

'P. S. I am the more impatient under this misfortune, having received fresh provocation, last Wednesday, in the Abbey.'

I entirely agree with the amiable and unfortunate Lesbia, that an insult upon a woman in her circumstances is as infamous in a man, as a tame behaviour when the lie or a buffet is given: which truth I shall beg leave of her to illustrate by the following observation.

It is a mark of cowardice passively to forbear resenting an affront, the resenting of which would lead a man into danger; it is no less a sign of cowardice to affront a creature that hath not power to avenge itself. Whatever name therefore this ungenerous man may bestow on the helpless lady he hath injured, I shall not scruple to give him, in return for it, the appellation of coward.

A man that can so far descend from his dignity, as to strike a lady, can never recover his reputation with either sex, because no provocation is thought strong enough to justify such treatment from the powerful towards the weak. In the circumstances in which poor Lesbia is situated, she can appeal to no man whatsoever to avenge an insult more grievous than a blow. If she could open her mouth, the base man knows that a husband, a brother, a generous friend, would die to see her righted.

A generous mind, however enraged against an enemy, feels its resentments sink and vanish away when the object of its wrath falls into its power. An estranged friend, filled with jealousy and discontent towards a bosom acquaintance, is apt to overflow with tenderness and remorse, when a creature that was once dear to him undergoes any misfortune. What name then shall we give to his ingratitude, (who forgetting the favours he solicited with eagerness, and received with rapture) can insult the miseries that he himself caused, and make sport with the pain to which he owes his greatest pleasure? There is but one being in the creation whose province it is to practise upon the imbecilities of frail creatures, and triumph in the woes which his own artifices brought about; and we well know those who follow his example will receive his reward.

Leaving my fair correspondent to the direction of her own wisdom and modesty; and her enemy, and his mean accomplices, to the compunction of their own hearts; I shall conclude this paper with a memorable instance of revenge, taken by a Spanish lady upon a guilty lover, which may serve to show what violent effects are wrought by the most tender passion, when soured into hatred; and may deter the young and unwary from unlawful love. The story, however romantic it may appear, I have heard affirmed for a truth.

Not many years ago an English gentleman, who, in a rencounter by night in the streets of Madrid, had the misfortune to kill his man, fled into a church-porch for sanctuary. Leaning against the door, he was surprised to find it open, and a glimmering light in the church. He had the courage to advance towards the light; but was terribly startled at the sight of a woman in white, who ascended from a grave with a bloody knife in her hand. The phantom marched up to him, and asked him what he did there. He told her the truth, without reserve, believing that he had met a ghost; upon which she spoke to him in the following manner: 'Stranger, thou art in my power: I am a murderer as thou art. Know then that I am a nun of a noble family. A base perjured man undid me, and boasted of it. I soon had him despatched; but not content with the murder, I have bribed the sexton to let me enter his grave, and have now plucked out his false heart from his body; and thus I use a traitor's heart.' At these words she tore it in pieces and trampled it under her feet.

No. 612.] *Wednesday, October 27, 1714.*

Murranum hic, atavos et avorum antiqua sonantem
Nomina, per regesque actum genus omne Latinos,
Præcipitem scopulo, atque ingentis turbine saxi
Excutit effunditque solo— *Virg. Æn.* xii. 529.

Murranus, boasting of his blood, that springs
From a long royal race of Latin kings,
Is by the Trojan from his chariot thrown,
Crush'd with the weight of an unwieldy stone.
Dryden.

It is highly laudable to pay respect to men who are descended from worthy ancestors, not only out of gratitude to those who have done good to mankind, but as it is an encouragement to others to follow their example. But this is an honour to be received, not demanded, by the descendants of great men; and they who are apt to remind us of their ancestors only put us upon making comparisons to their own disadvantage. There is some pretence for boasting of wit, beauty, strength, or wealth, because the communication of them may give pleasure or profit to others; but we can have no merit, nor ought we to claim any respect, because our fathers acted well, whether we would or no.

The following letter ridicules the folly I have mentioned in a new, and I think, not disagreeable light.

'Mr. Spectator,—Were the genealogy of every family preserved, there would probably be no man valued or despised on account of his birth. There is scarce a beggar in the streets, who would not find himself lineally descended from some great man; nor any one of the highest title, who would not discover several base and indigent persons among his ancestors. It would be a pleasant entertainment to see one pedigree of men appear together, under the same characters they bore when they acted their respective parts among the living. Suppose, therefore, a gentleman, full of his illustrious family, should in the same manner Virgil makes Æneas look over his descendants, see the whole line of his progenitors pass in review before his eyes—with how many varying passions would he behold shepherds and soldiers, statesmen and artificers, princes and beggars, walk in the procession of five thousand years! How would his heart sink or flutter at the several sports of fortune, in a scene so diversified with rags and purple, handicraft tools and sceptres, ensigns of dignity, and emblems of disgrace! And how would his fears and apprehensions, his transports and mortifications, succeed one another, as the line of his genealogy appeared bright or obscure!

'In most of the pedigrees hung up in old mansion-houses, you are sure to find the first in the catalogue a great statesman, or a soldier with an honourable commission. The honest artificer that begot him, and all his frugal ancestors before him, are torn off from the top of the register; and you are not left to imagine that the noble founder of the family ever had a father. Were we to trace many boasted lines farther backwards, we should lose them in a mob of tradesmen, or a crowd of rustics, without hope of seeing them emerge again: not unlike the old Appian way, which, after having run many miles in length, loses itself in a bog.

'I lately made a visit to an old country gentleman, who is very far gone in this sort of family madness. I found him in his study perusing an old register of his family, which he had just then discovered as it was branched out in the form of a tree, upon a skin of parchment. Having the honour to have some of his blood in my veins, he permitted me to cast my eyes over the boughs of this venerable plant; and asked my advice in the reforming of some of the superfluous branches.

'We passed slightly over three or four of our immediate forefathers, whom we knew by tradition, but were soon stopped by an alderman of London, who I perceived made my kinsman's heart go pit-a-pat. His confusion increased when he found the alderman's father to be a grazier; but he recovered his fright upon seeing justice of the quorum at the end of his titles. Things went on pretty well as we threw our eyes occasionally over the tree, when unfortunately he perceived a merchant-tailor perched on a bough, who was said greatly to have increased the estate; he was just going to cut him off if he had not seen *gent.* after the name of his son; who was recorded to have mortgaged one of the manors his honest father had purchased. A weaver, who was burnt for his religion in the reign of queen Mary, was pruned away without mercy; as was likewise a yeoman, who died of a fall from his own cart. But great was our triumph in one of the blood who was beheaded for high treason: which nevertheless was not a little allayed by another of our ancestors who was hanged for stealing sheep. The expectations of my good cousin were wonderfully raised by a match into the family of a knight; but unfortunately for us this branch proved barren: on the other hand, Margery the milk-maid, being twined round a bough, it flourished out into so many shoots, and bent with so much fruit, that the old gentleman was quite out of countenance. To comfort me under this disgrace, he singled out a branch ten times more fruitful than the other, which he told me he valued more than any in the tree, and bade me be of good comfort. This enormous bough was a graft out of a Welsh heiress, with so many Ap's upon it, that it might have made a little grove by itself. From the trunk of the pedigree, which was chiefly composed of labourers and shepherds, arose a huge sprout of farmers: this was branched out into yeoman, and ended in a sheriff of the county, who was knighted for his good service to the crown in bringing up an address. Several of the names that seemed to disparage the family, being looked upon as mistakes, were lopped off as rotten or withered; as, on the contrary, no small number appearing without any titles, my cousin, to supply the defects of the manuscript, added *esq.* at the end of each of them.

'This tree, so pruned, dressed and cultivated, was, within a few days, transplanted into a large sheet of vellum, and placed in the great hall, where it attracts the veneration of his tenants every Sunday morning, while they wait until his worship is ready to go to church; wondering that a man who had so many fathers before him should not be made a knight, or at least a justice of the peace.'

No. 613.] *Friday, October* 29, 1714.

——Studiis florentem ignobilis oti.
Virg. Georg. iv. 564.

Affecting studies of less noisy praise.—*Dryden.*

It is reckoned a piece of ill-breeding for one man to engross the whole talk to himself. For this reason, since I keep three visiting-days in the week, I am content now and then to let my friends put in a word. There are several advantages hereby accruing both to my readers and myself. As first, young and modest writers have an opportunity of getting into print; again, the town enjoys the pleasures of variety; and posterity will see the humour of the present age, by the help of these lights into private and domestic life. The benefits I receive from thence are such as these: I gain more time for future speculations: pick up hints which I improve for the public good; give advice; redress grievances; and, by leaving commodious spaces between the several letters that I print, furnish out a Spectator, with little labour and great ostentation.

'Mr. Spectator---I was mightily pleased with your speculation of Friday. Your sentiments are noble, and the whole worked up in such a manner as cannot but strike upon every reader. But give me leave to make this remark; that while you write so pathetically on contentment, and a retired life, you sooth the passion of melancholy, and depress the mind from actions truly glorious. Titles and honours are the reward of virtue; we therefore ought to be affected with them; and though light minds are too much puffed up with exterior pomp, yet I cannot see why it is not as truly philosophical to admire the glowing ruby, or the sparkling green of an emerald, as the fainter and less permanent beauties of a rose or a myrtle. If there are men of extraordinary capacities, who lie concealed from the world, I should impute it to them as a blot in their characters, did not I believe it owing to the meanness of their fortune rather than of their spirit. Cowley, who tells the story of Aglaus with so much pleasure, was no stranger to courts, nor insensible of praise.

"What shall I do to be for ever known,
And make the age to come my own?"

was the result of a laudable ambition. It was not until after frequent disappointments that he termed himself the melancholy Cowley; and he praised solitude when he despaired of shining in a court. The soul of man is an active principle. He, therefore, who withdraws himself from the scene before he has played his part, ought to be hissed off the stage, and cannot be deemed virtuous, because he refuses to answer his end. I must own I am fired with an honest ambition to imitate every illustrious example. The battles of Blenheim and Ramilies have more than once made me wish myself a soldier. And, when I have seen those actions so nobly celebrated by our poets, I have secretly aspired to be one of that distinguished class. But in vain I wish, in vain I pant with the desire of action. I am chained down in obscurity, and the only pleasure I can take is in seeing so many brighter geniuses join their friendly lights to add to the splendour of the throne. Farewell, then, dear Spec, and believe me to be with great emulation, and no envy, your professed admirer,

'WILL HOPELESS.'

'Middle-Temple, Oct. 26, 1714.

'SIR,—Though you have formerly made eloquence the subject of one or more of your papers, I do not remember that you ever considered it as possessed by a set of people, who are so far from making Quintilian's rules their practice, that, I dare say for them, they never heard of such an author, and yet are no less masters of it than Tully or Demosthenes among the ancients, or whom you please among the moderns. The persons I am speaking of are our common beggars about this town; and, that what I say is true, I appeal to any man who has a heart one degree softer than a stone. As for my part, who do not pretend to more humanity than my neighbours, I have oftentimes gone from my chambers with money in my pocket, and returned to them not only pennyless, but destitute of a farthing, without bestowing of it any other way than on these seeming objects of pity. In short, I have seen more eloquence in a look from one of these despicable creatures than in the eye of the fairest she I ever saw, yet no one a greater admirer of that sex than myself. What I have to desire of you is, to lay down some directions in order to guard against these powerful orators, or else I know nothing to the contrary but I must myself be forced to leave the profession of the law, and endeavour to get the qualifications necessary to that more profitable one of begging. But, in whichsoever of these two capacities I shine, I shall always desire to be your constant reader, and ever will be your most humble servant,

'J. B.'

'SIR,—Upon reading a Spectator last week, where Mrs. Fanny Fickle submitted the choice of a lover for life to your decisive determination, and imagining I might claim the favour of your advice in an affair of the like, but much more difficult nature, I called for pen and ink, in order to draw the characters of seven humble servants, whom I have equally encouraged for some time. But, alas! while I was reflecting on the agreeable subject, and contriving an advantageous description of the dear person I was most inclined to favour, I happened to look into my glass. The sight of the small-pox, out of which I am just recovered, tormented me at once with the loss of my captivating arts and my captives. The confusion I was in, on this unhappy, unseasonable discovery, is inexpressible. Believe me, sir, I was so taken up with the thoughts of your fair correspondent's case, and so intent on my own design, that I fancied myself as triumphant in my conquests as ever.

'Now, sir, finding I was incapacitated to amuse myself on that pleasing subject, I resolved to apply myself to you, or your casuistical agent, for advice in my present circumstances. I am sensible the tincture of my skin, and the regularity of my features, which the malice of my late illness has altered, are irrecoverable; yet do not despair but that that loss by your assistance, may, in some measure, be repairable, if you will please to propose a way for the recovery of one only of my fugitives.

'One of them is in a more particular manner beholden to me than the rest; he, for some private reasons, being desirous to be a lover incognito, always addressed me with a billet-doux, which I was so careful of in my sickness, that I secured the key of my love magazine under my head, and, hearing a noise of opening a lock in my chamber, endangered my life by getting out of bed, to prevent, if it had been attempted, the discovery of that amour.

'I have formerly made use of all those artifices which our sex daily practise over yours, to draw, as it were, undesignedly, the eyes of a whole congregation to my pew; I have taken a pride in the number of admirers at my afternoon levee; but am now quite another creature. I think, could I regain the attractive influence I once had, if I had a legion of suitors, I should never be ambitious of entertaining more than one. I have almost contracted an antipathy to the trifling discourses of impertinent lovers; though I must needs own I have thought it very odd of late to hear gentlemen, instead of their usual complaisances, fall into disputes before me of politics, or else weary me with the tedious repetition of how thankful I ought to be, and satisfied with my recovery out of so dangerous a distemper: this, though I am very sensible of the blessing, yet I cannot but dislike, because such advice from them rather seems to insult than comfort me, and reminds me too much of what I was: which melancholy consideration I cannot yet perfectly surmount, but hope your sentiments on this head will make it supportable.

'To show you what a value I have for your dictates, these are to certify the persons concerned, that unless one of them returns to his colours, if I may so call them now, before the winter is over, I will voluntarily confine myself to a retirement, where I will punish them all with my needle. I will be revenged on them by decyphering them on a carpet, humbly begging admittance, myself scornfully refusing it. If you disapprove of this, as savouring too much of malice, be pleased to acquaint me with a draught you like better, and it shall be faithfully performed, by the unfortunate

'MONIMIA.'

No. 614.] *Monday, November* 1, 1714.

Si mihi non animo fixum immotumque sederet,
Ne cui me vinclo vellem sociare jugali,
Postquam primus amor deceptam morte fefellit;
Si non pertæsum thalami, tædæque fuisset;
Huic uni forsan potui succumbere culpæ.

Virg. Æn. iv. 15.

——Were I not resolved against the yoke
Of hapless marriage; never to be curs'd
With second love, so fatal was the first,
To this one error I might yield again.—*Dryden.*

The following account hath been transmitted to me by the love casuist.

'Mr. Spectator,—Having in some former papers taken care of the two states of virginity and marriage, and being willing that all people should be served in their turn, I this day draw out my drawer of widows, where I met with several cases, to each whereof I have returned satisfactory answers by the post. The cases are as follow:

'*Q.* Whether Amoret be bound by a promise of marriage to Philander, made during her husband's life?

'*Q.* Whether Sempronia, having faithfully given a promise to two several persons during the last sickness of her husband, is not thereby left at liberty to choose which of them she pleases, or to reject them both for the sake of a new lover?

'Cleora asks me, whether she be obliged to continue single according to a vow made to her husband at the time of his presenting her with a diamond necklace; she being informed by a very pretty young fellow, of a good conscience, that such vows are in their nature sinful?

'Another inquires, whether she hath not the right of widowhood, to dispose of herself to a gentleman of great merit, who presses very hard; her husband being irrecoverably gone in a consumption?

'An unreasonable creature hath the confidence to ask, whether it be proper for her to marry a man who is younger than her eldest son?

'A scrupulous well-spoken matron, who gives me a great many good words, only doubts whether she is not obliged, in conscience, to shut up her two marriageable daughters, until such time as she hath comfortably disposed of herself?

'Sophronia, who seems by her phrase and spelling to be a person of condition, sets forth, that whereas she hath a great estate, and is but a woman, she desires to be informed whether she would not do prudently to marry Camillus, a very idle tall young fellow, who hath no fortune of his own, and consequently hath nothing else to do but to manage hers?'

Before I speak of widows, I cannot but observe one thing, which I do not know how to account for; a widow is always more sought after than an old maid of the same age. It is common enough among ordinary people, for a stale virgin to set up a shop in a place where she is not known; where the large thumb-ring, supposed to be given by her husband, quickly recommends her to some wealthy neighbour, who takes a liking to the jolly widow, that would have overlooked the venerable spinster.

The truth of it is, if we look into this set of women, we find, according to the different characters or circumstances wherein they are left, that widows may be divided into those who raise love and those who raise compassion.

But, not to ramble from this subject, there are two things in which consists chiefly the glory of a widow—the love of her deceased husband, and the care of her children; to which may be added a third, arising out of the former, such a prudent conduct as may do honour to both.

A widow possessed of all these three qualities makes not only a virtuous but a sublime character.

There is something so great and so generous in this state of life, when it is accom panied with all its virtues, that it is the subject of one of the finest among our modern tragedies in the person of Andromache, and has met with a universal and deserved applause, when introduced upon our English stage by Mr. Philips.*

The most memorable widow in history is queen Artemisia, who not only erected the famous mausoleum, but drank up the ashes of her dead lord; thereby enclosing them in a nobler monument than that which she had built, though deservedly esteemed one of the wonders of architecture.

This last lady seems to have had a better title to a second husband than any I have read of, since not one dust of her first was remaining. Our modern heroines might think a husband a very bitter draught, and would have good reason to complain, if they might not accept of a second partner until they had taken such a troublesome method of losing the memory of the first.

I shall add to these illustrious examples out of ancient story, a remarkable instance of the delicacy of our ancestors in relation to the state of widowhood, as I find it recorded in Cowell's Interpreter. 'At East and West Enborne, in the county of Berks, if a customary tenant die, the widow shall have what the law calls her free-bench in all his copyhold lands, *dum sola et casta fuerit*, that is, while she lives single and chaste; but if she commits incontinency she forfeits her estate; yet if she will come into the court riding backward upon a black ram, with his tail in her hand, and say the words following, the steward is bound by the custom to re-admit her to her free-bench.†

'Here I am
Riding upon a black ram,
Like a whore as I am;
And for my *crincum crancum*,
Have lost my *bincum bancum*,
And for my tail's game,
Have done this worldly shame;
Therefore I pray you, Mr. Steward, let me have my land again.'

The like custom there is in the manor of Torre, in Devonshire, and other parts of the west.

It is not impossible but I may in a little time present you with a register of Berkshire ladies, and other western dames, who rode publicly upon this occasion; and I hope the town will be entertained with a cavalcade of widows.‡

* See Nos. 290 and 335.

† See Jacob's Law Dictionary, art. Free-bench.—Frank Bank, or Free-bench, [*Sedes Libera*, or, in Law-Latin, *Francus Bancus*] is that estate in copyhold lands, which the wife, being married, a virgin hath after the decease of her husband for a dower. Fitzherbert calls this a custom by which, in some cities, the wife shall have all the lands of her husband for dower.—*Les Termes de la Ley*, edit. 1667, p. 575.

‡ See No. 623. The custom in the manors of East and West Enborne, of Torre, and other parts in the West of England, is a kind of penance among jocular tenures to purge the offence, and has there, it seems, the force and validity of statute law. Jacob's Dict. *ut supra*, edit. 1736, in folio.

No. 615.] *Wednesday, November 3, 1714.*

——Qui Deorum——
Muneribus sapienter uti,
Duramque callet pauperiem pati,
Pejusque letho flagitium timet;
Non ille pro caris amicis
Aut patria timidus perire.
Hor. Od. ix. Lib. 4. 47.

Who spend their treasure freely as 'twas giv'n
By the large bounty of indulgent heav'n
Who in a fix'd unalterable state
Smile at the doubtful tide of fate,
And scorn alike her friendship and her hate:
Who poison less than falsehood fear,
Loath to purchase life so dear;
But kindly for their friend embrace cold death,
And seal their country's love with their departing breath.—*Stepney.*

It must be owned that fear is a very powerful passion, since it is esteemed one of the greatest virtues to subdue it. It being implanted in us for our preservation, it is no wonder that it sticks close to us as long as we have any thing we are willing to preserve. But as life, and all its enjoyments, would be scarce worth the keeping if we were under a perpetual dread of losing them, it is the business of religion and philosophy to free us from all unnecessary anxieties, and direct our fear to its proper object.

If we consider the painfulness of this passion, and the violent effects it produces, we shall see how dangerous it is to give way to it upon slight occasions. Some have frightened themselves into madness, others have given up their lives to these apprehensions. The story of a man who grew gray in the space of one night's anxiety is very famous.

'O nox, quam longa es, quæ facis una senem!'

'A tedious night indeed, that makes a young man old!'

These apprehensions if they proceed from a consciousness of guilt, are the sad warnings of reason; and may excite our pity, but admit of no remedy. When the hand of the Almighty is visibly lifted against the impious, the heart of mortal man cannot withstand him. We have this passion sublimely represented in the punishment of the Egyptians, tormented with the plague of darkness in the apocryphal book of Wisdom ascribed to Solomon.

'For when unrighteous men thought to oppress the holy nation; they being shut up in their houses, the prisoners of darkness, and fettered with the bonds of a long night, lay there exiled from the eternal Providence. For while they supposed to lie hid in their secret sins, they were scattered under a dark veil of forgetfulness, being horribly astonished and troubled with strange apparitions—For wickedness, condemned by her own witness, is very timorous, and, being oppressed with conscience, always forecasteth grievous things. For fear is nothing else but a betraying of the succours which reason offereth—For the whole world shined with clear light, and none were hindered in their labour. Over them only was spread a heavy night, an image of that darkness which should afterwards receive them; but yet were they unto themselves, more grievous than the darkness.'*

To fear, so justly grounded, no remedy can be proposed; but a man (who hath no great guilt hanging upon his mind, who walks in the plain path of justice and integrity, and yet, either by natural complexion, or confirmed prejudices, or neglect of serious reflection, suffers himself to be moved by this abject and unmanly passion) would do well to consider, that there is nothing which deserves his fear, but that beneficent Being who is his friend, his protector, his father. Were this one thought strongly fixed in the mind, what calamity would be dreadful? What load can infamy lay upon us when we are sure of the approbation of him who will repay the disgrace of a moment with the glory of eternity? What sharpness is there in pain and diseases, when they only hasten us on to the pleasures that will never fade? What sting is in death, when we are assured that it is only the beginning of life? A man who lives so as not to fear to die, is inconsistent with himself, if he delivers himself up to any incidental anxiety.

The intrepidity of a just good man is so nobly set forth by Horace, that it cannot be too often repeated:

> 'The man resolv'd and steady to his trust,
> Inflexible to ill, and obstinately just,
> May the rude rabble's insolence despise,
> Their senseless clamours, and tumultuous cries:
> The tyrant's fierceness he beguiles,
> And the stern brow, and the harsh voice defies,
> And with superior greatness smiles.
> 'Not the rough whirlwind, that deforms
> Adria's black gulf, and vexes it with storms,
> The stubborn virtue of his soul remove:
> Not the red arm of angry Jove,
> That flings the thunder from the sky,
> And gives it rage to roar, and strength to fly.
> 'Should the whole frame of nature round him break,
> In ruin and confusion hurl'd,
> He, unconcern'd, would hear this mighty crack,
> And stand secure amidst a falling world.'

The vanity of fear may be yet farther illustrated if we reflect,

First, what we fear may not come to pass. No human scheme can be so accurately projected, but some little circumstance intervening may spoil it. He who directs the heart of man at his pleasure, and understands the thoughts long before, may, by ten thousand accidents, or an immediate change in the inclinations of men, disconcert the most subtle project, and turn it to the benefit of his own servants.

In the next place we should consider, though the evil we imagine should come to pass, it may be much more supportable than it appeared to be. As there is no prosperous state of life without its calamities, so there is no adversity without its benefits. Ask the great and powerful, if they do not feel the pangs of envy and ambition. Inquire of the poor and needy, if they have not tasted the sweets of quiet and contentment. Even under the pains of body, the infidelity of friends, or the mis constructions put upon our laudable actions; our minds, when for some time accus tomed to these pressures, are sensible of secret flowings of comfort, the present reward of a pious resignation. The evils of this life appear like rocks and precipices, rugged and barren at a distance; but at our nearer approach we find little fruitful spots, and refreshing springs, mixed with the harshness and deformities of nature.

In the last place, we may comfort ourselves with this consideration, that, as the thing feared may not reach us, so we may not reach what we fear. Our lives may not extend to that dreadful point which we have in view. He who knows all our failings, and will not suffer us to be tempted beyond our strength, is often pleased, in his tender severity, to separate the soul from its body and miseries together.

If we look forward to him for help, we shall never be in danger of falling down those precipices which our imagination is apt to create. Like those who walk upon a line, if we keep our eye fixed upon one point, we may step forward securely; whereas an imprudent or cowardly glance on either side will infallibly destroy us.

* Wisd. xvii. *passim.*

No. 616.] *Friday, November 5, 1714*

> Qui bellus homo est, Cotta, pusillus homo est.
> *Mart.* Epig. [illegible].

A pretty fellow is but half a man.

CICERO hath observed, that a jest is never uttered with a better grace than when it is accompanied with a serious countenance. When a pleasant thought plays in the features before it discovers itself in words, it raises too great an expectation, and loses the advantage of giving surprise. Wit and humour are no less poorly recommended by a levity of phrase, and that kind of language which may be distinguished by the name of cant. Ridicule is never more strong than when it is concealed in gravity. True humour lies in the thought, and arises from the representation of images in odd circumstances and uncommon lights. A pleasant thought strikes us by the force of its natural beauty; and the mirth of it is generally rather palled than heightened, by that ridiculous phraseology which is so much in fashion among the pretenders to humour and pleasantry. This tribe of men are like our mountebanks; they make a man a wit by putting him in a fantastic habit.

Our little burlesque authors, who are the delight of ordinary readers, generally abound in these pert phrases, which have in them more vivacity than wit.

I lately saw an instance of this kind of writing, which gave me so lively an idea of it, that I could not forbear begging a copy of the letter from the gentleman who showed it to me. It is written by a country wit, upon the occasion of the rejoicings on the day of the king's coronation.

'Past two o'clock, and a frosty morning.

'DEAR JACK,—I have just left the right worshipful and his myrmidons about a sneaker of five gallons. The whole magistracy was pretty well disguised before I gave them the slip. Our friend the alderman was half-seas over before the bonfire was out. We had with us the attorney, and two or three other bright fellows. The doctor plays least in sight.

'At nine o'clock in the evening we set fire to the whore of Babylon. The devil acted his part to a miracle. He has made his fortune by it. We equipped the young dog with a tester a piece. Honest old Brown of England was very drunk, and showed his loyalty to the tune of a hundred rockets. The mob drank the king's health, on their marrow bones, in mother Day's double. They whipped us half a dozen hogsheads. Poor Tom Tyler had like to have been demolished with the end of a sky-rocket, that fell upon the bridge of his nose as he was drinking the king's health, and spoiled his tip. The mob was very loyal till about midnight, when they grew a little mutinous for more liquor. They had like to have dumbfounded the justice; but his clerk came in to his assistance, and took them all down in black and white.

'When I had been huzzaed out of my seven senses, I made a visit to the women, who were guzzling very comfortably. Mrs. Mayoress clipped the king's English. Clack was the word.

'I forgot to tell thee, that every one of the posse had his hat cocked with a distich; the senators sent us down a cargo of riband and metre for the occasion.

'Sir Richard, to show his zeal for the Protestant religion, is at the expense of a tar-barrel and a ball. I peeped into the knight's great hall, and saw a very pretty bevy of spinsters. My dear relict was amongst them, and ambled in a country dance as notably as the best of them.

'May all his majesty's liege subjects love him as well as his good people of this his ancient borough! Adieu.'

No. 617.] *Monday, November* 8, 1714.

Torva Mimalloneis implerunt cornua bombis,
Et raptum vitulo caput ablatura superbo
Bassaris, et lyncem Mænas flexura corymbis,
Evion ingeminat: reparabilis adsonat echo.
Pers. Sat. i. 99.

Their crooked horns the Mimallonian crew
With blasts inspir'd; and Bassaris, who slew
The scornful calf, with sword advanc'd on high,
Made from his neck his haughty head to fly.
And Mænas, when, with ivy-bridles bound,
She led the spotted lynx, then Evion rung around,
Evion, from woods and floods repairing echo's sound.
Dryden.

THERE are two extremes in the style of humour, one of which consists in the use of that little pert phraseology which I took notice of in my last paper; the other in the affectation of strained and pompous expressions, fetched from the learned languages. The first savours too much of the town; the other of the college.

As nothing illustrates better than example, I shall here present my reader with a letter of pedantic humour, which was written by a young gentleman of the university to his friend, on the same occasion, and from the same place, as the lively epistle published in my last Spectator:

'DEAR CHUM,—It is now the third watch of the night, the greatest part of which I have spent round a capacious bowl of China, filled with the choicest products of both the Indies. I was placed at a quadrangular table, diametrically opposite to the mace-bearer. The visage of that venerable herald was, according to custom, most gloriously illuminated on this joyful occasion. The mayor and aldermen, those pillars of our constitution, began to totter; and if any one at the board could have so far articulated, as to have demanded intelligibly a re-inforcement of liquor, the whole assembly had been by this time extended under the table.

'The celebration of this night's solemnity was opened by the obstreperous joy of drummers, who, with their parchment thunder, gave a signal for the appearance of the mob under their several classes and denominations. They were quickly joined by the melodious clank of marrow-bones and cleavers, while a chorus of bells filled up the concert. A pyramid of stack-fagots cheered the hearts of the populace with the promise of a blaze: the guns had no sooner uttered the prologue, but the heavens were brightened with artificial meteors and stars of our own making: and all the High-street lighted up from one end to another with a galaxy of candles. We collected a largess for the multitude, who tippled eleemosynary until they grew exceeding vociferous. There was a pasteboard pontiff, with a little swarthy demon at his elbow, who, by his diabolical whispers and insinuations, tempted his holiness into the fire, and then left him to shift for himself. The mobile were very sarcastic with their clubs, and gave the old gentleman several thumps upon his triple head-piece.* Tom Tyler's phiz is something damaged by the fall of a rocket, which hath almost spoiled the gnomon of his countenance. The mirth of the commons grew so very outrageous, that it found work for our friend of the quorum, who, by the help of his amanuensis, took down all their names and their crimes, with a design to produce his manuscript at the next quarter sessions, &c. &c.'

I shall subjoin to the foregoing piece of a letter the following copy of verses translated from an Italian poet, who was the

* The Pope's tiara, or triple mitre.

Cleveland of his age, and had multitudes of admirers. The subject is an accident that happened under the reign of Pope Leo, when a fire-work, that had been prepared upon the castle of St. Angelo, began to play before its time, being kindled by a flash of lightning. The author has written a poem in the same kind of style as that I have already exemplified in prose. Every line in it is a riddle, and the reader must be forced to consider twice or thrice, before he will know that the Cynic's tenement is a tub, and Bacchus's cast-coat a hogshead, &c.

* ''Twas night, and heaven, a Cyclops all the day,
An Argus now, did countless eyes display;
In every window Rome her joy declares,
All bright and studded with terrestrial stars.
A blazing chain of lights her roof entwines,
And round her neck the mingled lustre shines:
The Cynic's rolling tenement conspires
With Bacchus his cast-coat to feed the fires.

'The pile, still big with undiscover'd shows,
The Tuscan pile did last its freight disclose,
Where the proud tops of Rome's new Ætna rise,
Whence giants sally and invade the skies.

'Whilst now the multitude expect the time,
And their tir'd eyes the lofty mountain climb,
As thousand iron mouths their voices try,
And thunder out a dreadful harmony;
In treble notes the small artillery plays,
The deep-mouth'd cannon bellows in the bass;
The lab'ring pile now heaves, and having given
Proofs of its travail, sighs in flames to heaven.

'The clouds envelop'd heaven from human sight;
Quench'd ev'ry star, and put out ev'ry light;
Now real thunder grumbles in the skies,
And in disdainful murmurs Rome defies;
Nor doth its answered challenge Rome decline;
But, whilst both parties in full concert join,
While heav'n and earth in rival peals resound,
The doubtful cracks the hearers sense confound;
Whether the claps of thunderbolts they hear,
Or else the burst of cannon wounds their ear:
Whether clouds rag'd by struggling metals rent,
Or struggling clouds in Roman metals spent:
But, O my Muse, the whole adventure tell,
As ev'ry accident in order fell.

'Tall groves of trees the Hadrian tower surround,
Fictitious trees with paper garlands crown'd.
These know no spring, but when their bodies sprout
In fire, and shoot their gilded blossoms out;
When blazing leaves appear above their head,
And into branching flames their bodies spread.
Whilst real thunder splits the firmament,
And heav'n's whole roof in one vast cleft is rent,
The three-fork'd tongue amidst the rupture lolls,
Then drops, and on the airy turret falls.
The trees now kindle, and the garland burns,
And thousand thunderbolts for one returns:
Brigades of burning archers upward fly,
Bright spears and shining spearmen mount on high,
Flash in the clouds, and glitter in the sky.
A seven-fold shield of spheres doth heav'n defend,
And back again the blunted weapons send;
Unwillingly they fall, and, dropping down,
Pour out their souls, their sulph'rous souls, and groan.

'With joy, great sir, we view'd this pompous show,
While Heav'n, that sat spectator still till now,
Itself turn'd actor, proud to pleasure you:
And so, 'tis fit, when Leo's fires appear,
That Heav'n itself should turn an engineer;
That Heav'n itself should all its wonder's show,
And orbs above consent with orbs below.'

* These verses are translated from the Latin in Strada's Prolusiones Academicæ, &c. and are an imitation originally of the style and manner of Camello Querno, surnamed the Arch-poet. His character and his writings were equally singular; he was poet and buffoon to Leo X. and the common butt of that facetious pontiff and his courtiers. See Stradæ Prolusiones, Oxon. 1745, Bayle's Dictionary, art. Leo X. and Seward's Anecdotes, vol. iii.

No. 618.] *Wednesday, November* 10, 1714.

——Neque enim concludere versum
Dixeris esse satis: neque si quis scribat, uti nos,
Sermoni propriora, putes hunc esse poetam.
Hor. Sat. iv. Lib. 1. 40.

'Tis not enough the measur'd feet to close;
Nor will you give a poet's name to those
Whose humble verse, like mine, approaches prose.

'Mr. Spectator,—You have in your two last Spectators given the town a couple of remarkable letters in different styles: I take this opportunity to offer to you some remarks upon the epistolary way of writing in verse. This is a species of poetry by itself; and has not so much as been hinted at in any of the Arts of Poetry that have ever fallen into my hands: neither has it in any age, or in any nation, been so much cultivated as the other several kinds of poesy. A man of genius may, if he pleases, write letters in verse upon all manner of subjects that are capable of being embellished with wit and language, and may render them new and agreeable by giving the proper turn to them. But in speaking at present of epistolary poetry, I would be understood to mean only such writings in this kind as have been in use among the ancients, and have been copied from them by some moderns. These may be reduced into two classes: in the one I shall range love-letters, letters of friendship, and letters upon mournful occasions; in the other I shall place such epistles in verse as may properly be called familiar, critical, and moral; to which may be added letters of mirth and humour. Ovid for the first, and Horace for the latter, are the best originals we have left.

'He that is ambitious of succeeding in the Ovidian way, should first examine his heart well, and feel whether his passions (especially those of the gentle kind,) play easy; since it is not his wit, but the delicacy and tenderness of his sentiments, that will affect his readers. His versification likewise should be soft, and all his numbers flowing and querulous.

'The qualifications requisite for writing epistles, after the model given us by Horace, are of a quite different nature. He that would excel in this kind must have a good fund of strong masculine sense: to this there must be joined a thorough knowledge of mankind, together with an insight into the business and the prevailing humours of the age. Our author must have his mind well seasoned with the finest precepts of morality, and be filled with nice reflections upon the bright and dark sides of human life; he must be a master of refined raillery, and understand the delicacies as well as the absurdities of conversation. He must have a lively turn of wit, with an easy and concise manner of expression: every thing he says must be in a free and disengaged manner. He must be guilty of nothing that betrays the air of a recluse, but appear a man of the world throughout. His illustrations, his comparisons, and the greatest part of his images, must be drawn from common life. Strokes of satire and criticism, as well as panegyric, judiciously thrown in, (and as it were by the by,) give a wonderful life and ornament to compositions of this kind. But let our poet, while he writes epistles, though never so familiar, still remember that he writes in verse, and must for that reason have a more than ordinary care not to fall into prose, and a vulgar diction, excepting where the nature and humour of the thing does necessarily require it. In this point, Horace has been thought by some critics to be sometimes careless, as well as too negligent of his versification; of which he seems to have been sensible himself.

'All I have to add is, that both these manners of writing may be made as entertaining, in their way, as any other species of poetry, if undertaken by persons duly qualified; and the latter sort may be managed so as to become in a peculiar manner instructive. I am, &c.'

I shall add an observation or two to the remarks of my ingenious correspondent; and, in the first place, take notice, that subjects of the most sublime nature are often treated in the epistolary way with advantage, as in the famous epistle of Horace to Augustus. The poet surprises us with his pomp, and seems rather betrayed into his subject than to have aimed at it by design. He appears like the visit of a king incognito, with a mixture of familiarity and grandeur. In works of this kind, when the dignity of the subject hurries the poet into descriptions and sentiments, seemingly unpremeditated, by a sort of inspiration, it is usual for him to recollect himself, and fall back gracefully into the natural style of a letter.

I might here mention an epistolary poem, just published by Mr. Eusden,* on the king's accession to the throne; wherein, among many other noble and beautiful strokes of poetry, his reader may see this rule very happily observed.

No. 619.] *Friday, November* 12, 1714.

———————————dura
Exerce imperia, et ramos compesce fluentes.
Virg. Georg. ii. 369.

————Exert a rigorous sway,
And lop the two luxuriant boughs away.

I HAVE often thought that if the several letters which are written to me under the character of Spectator, and which I have not made use of, were published in a volume, they would not be an unentertaining collection.† The variety of the subjects, styles, sentiments, and informations, which are transmitted to me, would lead a very curious, or very idle reader, insensibly along through a great many pages.

I know some authors who would pick up a secret history out of such materials, and make a bookseller an alderman by the copy. I shall therefore carefully preserve the original papers in a room set apart for that purpose, to the end that they may be of service to posterity; but shall at present content myself with owning the receipt of several letters, lately come to my hands, the authors whereof are impatient for an answer.

Charissa, whose letter is dated from Cornhill, desires to be eased in some scruples relating to the skill of astrologers.—Referred to the dumb man for an answer.

J. C. who proposes a love case, as he calls it, to the love casuist, is hereby desired to speak of it to the minister of the parish; it being a case of conscience.

The poor young lady, whose letter is dated October 26, who complains of a harsh guardian and an unkind brother, can only have my good wishes, unless she pleases to be more particular.

The petition of a certain gentleman, whose name I have forgot, famous for renewing the curls of decayed periwigs, is referred to the censor of small wares.

The remonstrance of T. C. against the profanation of the sabbath by barbers, shoe-cleaners, &c. had better be offered to the society of reformers.

A learned and laborious treatise upon the art of fencing, returned to the author.

To the gentleman of Oxford, who desires me to insert a copy of Latin verses, which were denied a place in the university books. Answer: *Nonum prematur in annum.*

To my learned correspondent, who writes against master's gowns, and poke sleeves, with a word in defence of large scarfs. Answer: I resolve not to raise animosities amongst the clergy.

To the lady who writes with rage against one of her own sex, upon the account of party warmth. Answer: Is not the lady she writes against reckoned handsome?

I desire Tom Truelove (who sends me a sonnet upon his mistress, with a desire to print it immediately,) to consider, that it is long since I was in love

I shall answer a very profound letter from my old friend the upholsterer, who is still inquisitive whether the king of Sweden be living or dead, by whispering him in the ear, that I believe he is alive.

Let Mr. Dapperwit consider, What is that long story of the cuckoldom to me?

At the earnest desire of Monimia's lover, who declares himself very penitent, he is recorded in my paper by the name of the faithful Castalio.

The petition of Charles Cocksure, which the petitioner styles 'very reasonable,' rejected.

* A letter to Mr. Addison on the king's accession to the throne.

† They were published in 1725, by Charles Lillie, in 2 vols. 8vo.

The memorial of Philander, which he desires may be despatched out of hand, postponed.

I desire S. R. not to repeat the expression 'under the sun,' so often in his next letter.

The letter of P. S. who desires either to have it printed entire, or committed to the flames. Not to be printed entire.

No. 620.] *Monday, November* 15, 1714.

Hic vir, hic est, tibi quem promitti sæpius audis.
Virg. Æn. vi. 791.

Behold the promis'd chief!

HAVING lately presented my reader with a copy of verses full of the false sublime, I shall here communicate to him an excellent specimen of the true: though it hath not been yet published, the judicious reader will readily discern it to be the work of a master; and if he hath read that noble poem on the prospect of peace, he will not be at a loss to guess at the author.

THE ROYAL PROGRESS.

'When Brunswick first appear'd, each honest heart,
Intent on verse, disdain'd the rules of art;
For him the songsters, in unmeasur'd odes,
Debas'd Alcides, and dethron'd the gods;
In golden chains the kings of India led,
Or rent the turban from the sultan's head.
One, in old fables, and the pagan strain,
With nymphs and tritons, wafts him o'er the main;
Another draws fierce Lucifer in arms,
And fills th' infernal region with alarms:
A third awakes some druid, to foretell
Each future triumph from his dreary cell.
Exploded fancies! that in vain deceive,
While the mind nauseates what she can't believe.
My muse th' expected hero shall pursue
From clime to clime, and keep him still in view:
His shining march describe in faithful lays,
Content to paint him, nor presume to praise:
Their charms, if charms they have, the truth supplies,
And from the theme unlabour'd beauties rise.

'By longing nations for the throne design'd,
And call'd to guard the rights of human-kind;
With secret grief his godlike soul repines,
And Britain's crown with joyless lustre shines,
While pray'rs and tears his destin'd progress stay,
And crowds of mourners choak their sovereign's way.
Not so he march'd when hostile squadrons stood
In scenes of death, and fir'd his generous blood;
When his hot courser paw'd th' Hungarian plain,
And adverse legions stood the shock in vain.
His frontiers past, the Belgian bounds he views,
And cross the level fields his march pursues.
Here pleas'd the land of freedom to survey,
He greatly scorns the thirst of boundless sway.
O'er the thin soil, with silent joy, he spies
Transplanted woods and borrow'd verdure rise;
Where ev'ry meadow, won with toil and blood
From haughty tyrants and the raging flood,
With fruits and flowers the careful hind supplies,
And clothes the marshes in a rich disguise.
Such wealth for frugal hands doth Heaven decree,
And such thy gifts, celestial Liberty!

'Through stately towns, and many a fertile plain,
The pomp advances to the neighbouring main.
Whole nations crowd around with joyful cries,
And view the hero with insatiate eyes.

'In Haga's towers he waits till eastern gales
Propitious rise to swell the British sails.
Hither the fame of England's monarch brings
The vows and friendships of the neighb'ring kings;
Mature in wisdom, his extensive mind
Takes in the blended interests of mankind,
The world's great patriot. Calm thy anxious breast,
Secure in him, O Europe, take thy rest,
Henceforth thy kingdoms shall remain confin'd
By rocks and streams, the mounds which Heav'n design'd;
The Alps their new-made monarch shall restrain,
Nor shall thy hills, Pyrene, rise in vain.

'But see, to Britain's isle the squadron stand,
And leave the sinking towers and less'ning land.
The royal bark bounds o'er the floating plain,
Breaks through the billows, and divides the main.
O'er the vast deep, great monarch, dart thine eyes
A wat'ry prospect bounded by the skies;
Ten thousand vessels, from ten thousand shores,
Bring gums and gold, and either India's stores,
Behold the tributes hast'ning to thy throne,
And see the wide horizon all thy own.

'Still is it thine; though now the cheerful crew
Hail Albion's cliffs just whitening to the view,
Before the wind with swelling sails they ride,
Till Thames receives them in his opening tide.
The monarch hears the thund'ring peals around
From trembling woods and echoing hills rebound.
Nor misses yet, amid the deaf'ning train,
The roarings of the hoarse resounding main.

'As in the flood he sails, from either side
He views his kingdom in its rural pride;
A various scene the wide-spread landscape yields,
O'er rich inclosures and luxuriant fields:
A lowing herd each fertile pasture fills,
And distant flocks stray o'er a thousand hills.
Fair Greenwich hid in woods, with new delight,
(Shade above shade) now rises to the sight;
His woods ordain'd to visit every shore,
And guard the island which they grac'd before.

'The sun now rolling down the western way,
A blaze of fires, renews the fading day;
Unnumber'd barks the regal barge enfold,
Bright'ning the twilight with its beamy gold;
Less thick the finny shoals, a countless fry,
Before the whale or kingly dolphin fly;
In one vast shout he seeks the crowded strand,
And in a peal of thunder gains the land.

'Welcome, great stranger! to our longing eyes,
Oh! king desir'd, adopted Albion cries.
For thee the East breath'd out a prosp'rous breeze,
Bright were the suns, and gently swell'd the seas.
Thy presence did each doubtful heart compose,
And factions wonder'd that they once were foes;
That joyful day they lost each hostile name,
The same their aspect, and their voice the same.

'So two fair twins, whose features were design'd
At one soft moment in the mother's mind,
Show each the other with reflected grace,
And the same beauties bloom in either face;
The puzzled strangers which is which inquire
Delusion grateful to the smiling sire.

'From that fair hill,* where hoary sages boast
To name the stars, and count the heavenly host,
By the next dawn doth great Augusta rise,
Proud town! the noblest scene beneath the skies.
O'er Thames her thousand spires their lustre shed
And a vast navy hides his ample bed—
A floating forest! From the distant strand
A line of golden cars strikes o'er the land;
Britannia's peers in pomp and rich array,
Before their king, triumphant, led the way.
Far as the eye can reach, the gaudy train,
A bright procession, shines along the plain.

'So haply thro' the heav'n's wide pathless ways
A comet draws a long-extended blaze;
From east to west burns through th' ethereal frame,
And half heav'n's convex glitters with the flame.

'Now to the regal towers securely brought,
He plans Britannia's glories in his thought,
Resumes the delegated power he gave,
Rewards the faithful, and restores the brave.
Whom shall the Muse from out the shining throng
Select, to heighten and adorn her song?
Thee, Halifax! To thy capacious mind,
O man approv'd, is Britain's wealth consign'd.
Her coin (while Nassau fought) debas'd and rude,
By thee in beauty and in truth renew'd,
An arduous work! again thy charge we see,
And thy own care once more returns to thee.
O! form'd in every scene to awe and please,
Mix wit with pomp, and dignity with ease:

---

* Flamstead House

Though call'd to shine aloft, thou wilt not scorn
To smile on arts thyself did once adorn;
For this thy name succeeding time shall praise,
And envy less thy garter than thy bays.

'The Muse, if fir'd with thy enliv'ning beams,
Perhaps shall aim at more exalted themes;
Record our monarch in a nobler strain,
And sing the op'ning wonders of his reign;
Bright Carolina's heavenly beauties trace,
Her valiant consort, and his blooming race.
A train of kings their fruitful love supplies,
A glorious scene to Albion's ravish'd eyes:
Who sees by Brunswick's hand her sceptre sway'd,
And through his line from age to age convey'd.'

No. 621.] *Wednesday, November* 17, 1714.

——Postquam se lumine puro
Implevit, stellasque vagas miratur, et astra
Fixa polis, vidit quanta sub nocte jaceret
Nostra dies, risitque sui ludibria——
Lucan. Lib. 9. 11.

Now to the blest abode, with wonder fill'd,
The sun and moving planets he beheld;
Then, looking down on the sun's feeble ray,
Survey'd our dusky, faint, imperfect day,
And under what a cloud of night we lay.—*Rowe*.

THE following letter having in it some observations out of the common road, I shall make it the entertainment of this day.

'MR. SPECTATOR,—The common topics against the pride of man, which are laboured by florid and declamatory writers, are taken from the baseness of his original, the imperfections of his nature, or the short duration of those goods in which he makes his boast. Though it be true that we can have nothing in us that ought to raise our vanity, yet a consciousness of our own merit may be sometimes laudable. The folly therefore lies here: we are apt to pride ourselves in worthless, or, perhaps, shameful things; and on the other hand count that disgraceful which is our truest glory.

'Hence it is, that the lovers of praise take wrong measures to attain it. Would a vain man consult his own heart, he would find that if others knew his weakness as well as he himself doth, he could not have the impudence to expect the public esteem. Pride therefore flows from want of reflection, and ignorance of ourselves. Knowledge and humility come upon us together.

'The proper way to make an estimate of ourselves is to consider seriously what it is we value or despise in others. A man who boasts of the goods of fortune, a gay dress, or a new title, is generally the mark of ridicule. We ought therefore not to admire in ourselves what we are so ready to laugh at in other men.

'Much less can we with reason pride ourselves in those things, which at some time of our life we shall certainly despise. And yet, if we will give ourselves the trouble of looking backward and forward on the several changes which we have already undergone, and hereafter must try, we shall find that the greater degrees of our knowledge and wisdom serve only to show us our own imperfections.

'As we rise from childhood to youth, we look with contempt on the toys and trifles which our hearts have hitherto been set upon. When we advance to manhood, we are held wise, in proportion to our shame and regret for the rashness and extravagance of youth. Old age fills us with mortifying reflections upon a life mis-spent in the pursuit of anxious wealth, or uncertain honour. Agreeable to this gradation of thought in this life, it may be reasonably supposed that, in a future state, the wisdom, the experience, and the maxims of old age, will be looked upon by a separate spirit in much the same light as an ancient man now sees the little follies and toyings of infants. The pomps, the honours, the policies, and arts of mortal men, will be thought as trifling as hobby-horses, mock-battles, or any other sports that now employ all the cunning and strength, and ambition of rational beings, from four years old to nine or ten.

'If the notion of a gradual rise in beings, from the meanest to the Most High, be not a vain imagination, it is not improbable that an angel looks down upon a man as a man doth upon a creature which approaches nearest to the rational nature. By the same rule, if I may indulge my fancy in this particular, a superior brute looks with a kind of pride on one of an inferior species. If they could reflect, we might imagine, from the gestures of some of them, that they think themselves the sovereigns of the world, and that all things were made for them. Such a thought would not be more absurd in brute creatures than one which men are apt to entertain, namely, that all the stars in the firmament were created only to please their eyes and amuse their imaginations. Mr. Dryden, in his fable of the Cock and the Fox, makes a speech for his hero the cock, which is a pretty instance for this purpose.

"Then turning, said to Partlet, 'See, my dear,
How lavish nature hath adorn'd the year;
How the pale primrose and the violets spring,
And birds essay their throats, disus'd to sing:
All these are ours, and I with pleasure see
Man strutting on two legs, and aping me."

'What I would observe from the whole is this, that we ought to value ourselves upon those things only which superior beings think valuable, since that is the only way for us not to sink in our own esteem hereafter.'

No. 622.] *Friday, November* 19, 1714.

——Fallentis semita vitæ.—*Hor. Ep.* xviii. Lib. 1. 103.

——A safe private quiet, which betrays
Itself to ease, and cheats away the days.—*Pooley*.

'MR. SPECTATOR,—In a former speculation you have observed that true greatness doth not consist in that pomp and noise wherein the generality of mankind are apt to place it. You have there taken notice that virtue in obscurity often appears more illustrious in the eye of superior beings, than all that passes for grandeur and magnificence among men.

'When we look back upon the history of those who have borne the parts of kings, statesmen, or commanders, they appear to us stripped of those outside ornaments that dazzle their contemporaries; and we regard their persons as great or little, in proportion to the eminence of their virtues or vices. The wise sayings, generous sentiments, or disinterested conduct of a philosopher under mean circumstances of life, set him higher in our esteem than the mighty potentates of the earth, when we view them both through the long prospect of many ages. Were the memoirs of an obscure man, who lived up to the dignity of his nature, and according to the rules of virtue, to be laid before us, we should find nothing in such a character which might not set him on a level with men of the highest stations. The following extract out of the private papers of an honest country gentleman, will set this matter in a clear light. Your reader will, perhaps, conceive a greater idea of him from these actions done in secret, and without a witness, than of those which have drawn upon them the admiration of multitudes.

MEMOIRS.

"In my twenty-second year I found a violent affection for my cousin Charles's wife growing upon me, wherein I was in danger of succeeding, if I had not upon that account begun my travels into foreign countries.

"A little after my return to England, at a private meeting with my uncle Francis, I refused the offer of his estate, and prevailed upon him not to disinherit his son Ned.

"Mem. Never to tell this to Ned, lest he should think hardly of his deceased father; though he continues to speak ill of me for this very reason.

"Prevented a scandalous lawsuit betwixt my nephew Harry and his mother, by allowing her under-hand, out of my own pocket, so much money yearly as the dispute was about.

"Procured a benefice for a young divine, who is sister's son to the good man who was my tutor, and hath been dead twenty years.

"Gave ten pounds to poor Mrs. ——, my friend H——'s widow.

"Mem. To retrench one dish at my table, until I have fetched it up again.

"Mem. To repair my house and finish my gardens, in order to employ poor people after harvest-time.

"Ordered John to let out goodman D—'s sheep that were pounded, by night; but not to let his fellow-servants know it.

"Prevailed upon M. T. esq. not to take the law of the farmer's son for shooting a partridge, and to give him his gun again.

"Paid the apothecary for curing an old woman that confessed herself a witch.

"Gave away my favourite dog for biting a beggar.

"Made the minister of the parish and a whig justice of one mind, by putting them to explain their notions to one another.

"Mem. To turn off Peter for shooting a doe while she was eating acorns out of his hand.

"When my neighbour John, who hath often injured me, comes to make his request to-morrow:

"Mem. I have forgiven him.

"Laid up my chariot, and sold my horses, to relieve the poor in a scarcity of corn.

"In the same year remitted to my tenants a fifth part of their rents.

"As I was airing to-day I fell into a thought that warmed my heart, and shall, I hope, be the better for it as long as I live.

"Mem. To charge my son in private to erect no monument for me; but not to put this in my last will."

No. 623.] *Monday, November 22, 1714.*

Sed mihi vel tellus optem prius ima dehiscat,
Vel pater omnipotens adigat me fulmine ad umbras,
Pallentes umbras Erebi noctemque profundam,
Ante, pudor, quam te violem, aut tua jura resolvam,
Ille meos, primus qui me sibi junxit, amores
Abstulit: ille habeat secum servetque sepulchro.
Virg. Æn. iv. 24.

But first let yawning earth a passage rend,
And let me through the dark abyss descend;
First let avenging Jove, with flames from high,
Drive down this body to the nether sky,
Condemn'd with ghosts in endless night to lie;
Before I break the plighted faith I gave:
No: he who had my vows, shall ever have;
For whom I lov'd on earth, I worship in the grave.
Dryden.

I AM obliged to my friend, the love casuist, for the following curious piece of antiquity, which I shall communicate to the public in his own words.

'MR. SPECTATOR,—You may remember, that I lately transmitted to you an account of an ancient custom in the manors of East and West Enborne, in the county of Berks, and elsewhere. "If a customary tenant die, the widow shall have what the law calls her free-bench, in all his copyhold lands, *dum sola et casta fuerit*; that is, while she lives single and chaste; but if she commits incontinency, she forfeits her estate; yet if she will come into the court riding backward upon a black ram, with his tail in her hand, and say the words following, the steward is bound by the custom to re-admit her to her free-bench.

'Here I am
Riding on a black ram,
Like a whore as I am;
And for my *crincum crancum*,
Have lost my *bincum bancum*,
And for my tail's game,
Have done this worldly shame
Therefore I pray you, Mr. Steward, let me have
my land again.'

After having informed you that my lord Coke observes, that this is the most frail and slippery tenure in England, I shall tell you, since the writing of that letter, I have, according to my promise, been at great pains in searching out the records of the black ram; and have at last met with the proceedings of the court-baron, held in that behalf, for the space of a whole day. The record saith, that a strict inquisition having been made into the right of the tenants to their several estates, by the crafty old steward, he found that many of the lands of the manor were, by default of the several widows, forfeited to the lord, and accordingly would have entered on the premises: upon which the good women demanded the "benefit of the ram." The steward, after having perused their several pleas, adjourned the court to Barnaby-bright,* that they might have day enough before them.

'The court being set, and filled with a great concourse of people, who came from all parts to see the solemnity; the first who entered was the widow Frontly, who had made her appearance in the last year's cavalcade. The register observes, that finding it an easy pad-ram, and foreseeing she might have farther occasion for it, she purchased it of the steward.

'Mrs. Sarah Dainty, relict of Mr. John Dainty, who was the greatest prude of the parish, came next in the procession. She at first made some difficulty of taking the tail in her hand; and was observed, in pronouncing the form of penance, to soften the two most emphatical words into *clincum clancum:* but the steward took care to make her speak plain English before he would let her have her land again.

'The third widow that was brought to this worldly shame, being mounted upon a vicious ram, had the misfortune to be thrown by him: upon which she hoped to be excused from going through the rest of the ceremony; but the steward, being well versed in the law, observed very wisely upon this occasion, that breaking of the rope does not hinder the execution of the criminal.

'The fourth lady upon record was the widow Ogle, a famous coquette, who had kept half a score of young fellows off and on for the space of two years; but having been more kind to her carter John, she was introduced with the huzzas of all her lovers about her.

'Mrs. Sable appearing in her weeds, which were very new and fresh, and of the same colour with her whimsical palfrey, made a very decent figure in the solemnity.

'Another, who had been summoned to make her appearance, was excused by the steward, as well knowing in his heart that the good squire himself had qualified her for the ram.

'Mrs. Quick, having nothing to object against the indictment, pleaded her belly. But it was remembered that she made the same excuse the year before. Upon which the steward observed, that she might so contrive it, as never to do the service of the manor.

'The widow Fidget being cited into court, insisted that she had done no more since the death of her husband than what she used to do in his life time; and withal desired Mr. Steward to consider his own wife's case if he should chance to die before her.

'The next in order was a dowager of a very corpulent make, who would have been excused, as not finding any ram that was able to carry her: upon which the steward commuted her punishment, and ordered her to make her entry upon a black ox.

'The widow Maskwell, a woman who had long lived with a most unblemished character, having turned off her old chamber-maid in a pet, was by that revengeful creature brought in upon the black ram nine times the same day.

'Several widows of the neighbourhood, being brought upon their trial, showed that they did not hold of the manor, and were discharged accordingly.

'A pretty young creature, who closed the procession, came ambling in with so bewitching an air, that the steward was observed to cast a sheep's eye upon her, and married her within a month after the death of his wife.

'N. B. Mrs. Touchwood appeared according to summons, but had nothing laid to her charge; having lived irreproachably since the decease of her husband, who left her a widow in the sixty-ninth year of her age. I am, sir, &c.'

* Then the eleventh, now the twenty-second of June, being the longest day in the year.

No. 624.] *Wednesday, November* 24, 171–.

Audire, atque togam jubeo componere, quisquis
Ambitione mala, aut argenti pallet amore,
Quisquis luxuria——

Hor. Sat. iii. Lib. 2. 77.

Sit still, and hear, those whom proud thoughts do swell,
Those that look pale by loving coin too well;
Whom luxury corrupts.—*Creech.*

MANKIND is divided into two parts, the busy and the idle. The busy world may be divided into the virtuous and the vicious. The vicious again into the covetous, the ambitious, and the sensual. The idle part of mankind are in a state inferior to any one of these. All the other are engaged in the pursuit of happiness, though often misplaced, and are therefore more likely to be attentive to such means as shall be proposed to them for that end. The idle, who are neither wise for this world nor the next, are emphatically called by Dr. Tillotson, 'fools at large.' They propose to themselves no end, but run adrift with every wind. Advice, therefore, would be but thrown away upon them, since they would scarce take the pains to read it. I shall not fatigue any of this worthless tribe with a long harangue; but will leave them with this short saying of Plato, that 'labour is preferable to idleness, as brightness to rust.'

The pursuits of the active part of mankind are either in the paths of religion and virtue; or, on the other hand, in the roads to wealth, honours, or pleasure. I shall, therefore, compare the pursuits of avarice, ambition, and sensual delight with their opposite virtues; and shall consider which of these principles engages men in a course of the greatest labour, suffering, and assiduity. Most men, in their cool reasonings, are willing to allow that a course of virtue will in the end be rewarded the most amply; but represent the way to it as rugged and narrow. If, therefore, it can be made appear, that men struggle through as many troubles to be miserable, as they do to be happy, my readers may, perhaps, be persuaded to be good, when they find they shall lose nothing by it.

First, for avarice. The miser is more industrious than the saint: the pains of getting, the fears of losing, and the inability of enjoying his wealth, have been the mark of satire in all ages. Were his repentance upon his neglect of a good bargain, his sorrow for being over-reached, his hope of improving a sum, and his fear of falling into want, directed to their proper objects, they would make so many different Christian graces and virtue. He may apply to himself a great part of saint Paul's catalogue of sufferings. 'In journeying often: in perils of waters, in perils of robbers, in perils among false brethren. In weariness and painfulness, in watchings often, in hunger and thirst, in fastings often.'---At how much less expense might he 'lay up to himself treasures in heaven!' Or, if I may in this place be allowed to add the saying of a great philosopher, he may 'provide such possessions as fear neither arms, nor men, nor Jove himself.'

In the second place, if we look upon the toils of ambition in the same light as we have considered those of avarice, we shall readily own that far less trouble is requisite to gain lasting glory, than the power and reputation of a few years; or, in other words, we may with more ease deserve honour than obtain it. The ambitious man should remember cardinal Wolsey's complaint, 'Had I served God with the same application wherewith I served my king, he would not have forsaken me in my old age.' The cardinal here softens his ambition by the specious pretence of 'serving his king;' whereas his words, in the proper construction, imply, that, if instead of being acted* by ambition, he had been acted by religion, he should now have felt the comforts of it, when the whole world turned its back upon him.

Thirdly, let us compare the pains of the sensual with those of the virtuous, and see which are heavier in the balance. It may seem strange, at the first view, that the men of pleasure should be advised to change their course, because they lead a painful life. Yet when we see them so active and vigilant in quest of delight; under so many disquiets, and the sport of such various passions; let them answer, as they can, if the pains they undergo do not outweigh their enjoyments. The infidelities on the one part between the two sexes, and the caprices on the other, the debasement of reason, the pangs of expectation, the disappointments in possession, the stings of remorse, the vanities and vexations attending even the most refined delights that make up this business of life, render it so silly and uncomfortable, that no man is thought wise until he hath got over it, or happy, but in proportion as he hath cleared himself from it.

The sum of all is this. Man is made an active being. Whether he walks in the paths of virtue or vice, he is sure to meet with many difficulties to prove his patience and excite his industry. The same, if not greater labour, is required in the service of vice and folly as of virtue and wisdom: and he hath this easy choice left him—whether, with the strength he is master of, he will purchase happiness or repentance.

* Actuated.

No. 625.] *Friday, November 26, 1714.*

————amores
De tenero meditatur ungui.
Hor. Od. vi. Lib. 3. 23.

Love, from her tender years, her thoughts employ'd.

THE love casuist hath referred to me the following letter of queries with his answer to each question, for my approbation. I have accordingly considered the several matters therein contained, and hereby confirm and ratify his answers, and require the gentle querist to conform herself thereunto.

'SIR,---I was thirteen the 9th of November last, and must now begin to think of settling myself in the world; and so I would humbly beg your advice, what I must do with Mr. Fondle, who makes his addresses to me. He is a very pretty man, and hath the blackest eyes and whitest teeth you ever saw. Though he is but a younger brother, he dresses like a man of quality, and nobody comes into a room like him. I know he hath refused great offers, and if he cannot marry me, he will never have any body else. But my father hath forbid him the house, because he sent me a copy of verses; for he is one of the greatest wits in town. My eldest sister, who, with her good will, would call me miss as long as I live, must be married before me, they say. She tells them that Mr. Fondle makes a fool of me, and will spoil the child, as she calls me, like a confident thing as she is. In short, I am resolved to marry Mr. Fondle, if it be but to spite her. But because I would do nothing that is imprudent I beg of you to give me your answers to some questions I will write down, and desire you to get them printed in the Spectator, and I do not doubt but you will give such advice as, I am sure, I shall follow.

'When Mr. Fondle looks upon me for half an hour together, and calls me Angel, is he not in love?'

Answer. No.

'May not I be certain he will be a kind husband, that has promised me half my portion in pin-money, and to keep me a coach and six in the bargain.'

No.

'Whether I, who have been acquainted with him this whole year almost, am not a better judge of his merit than my father and mother, who never heard him talk but at table?'

No.

'Whether I am not old enough to choose for myself?'

No.

'Whether it would not have been rude in me to refuse a lock of his hair?'

No.

'Should not I be a very barbarous creature, if I did not pity a man who is always sighing for my sake?'

No.

'Whether you would not advise me to run away with the poor man?'

No.

'Whether you do not think, that if I will not have him, he will drown himself?'

No.

'What shall I say to him the next time he asks me if I will marry him?'

No.

The following letter requires neither introduction nor answer.

'Mr. Spectator,—I wonder that, in the present situation of affairs, you can take pleasure in writing any thing but news; for, in a word, who minds any thing else? The pleasure of increasing in knowledge, and learning something new every hour of life, is the noblest entertainment of a rational creature. I have a very good ear for a secret, and am naturally of a communicative temper; by which means I am capable of doing you great services in this way. In order to make myself useful, I am early in the anti-chamber, where I thrust my head into the thick of the press, and catch the news at the opening of the door, while it is warm. Sometimes I stand by the beef-eaters, and take the buz as it passes by me. At other times I lay my ear close to the wall, and suck in many a valuable whisper, as it runs in a straight line from corner to corner. When I am weary with standing, I repair to one of the neighbouring coffee-houses, where I sit sometimes for a whole day, and have the news as it comes from court fresh and fresh. In short, sir, I spare no pains to know how the world goes. A piece of news loses its flavour when it hath been an hour in the air. I love, if I may so speak, to have it fresh from the tree; and to convey it to my friends before it is faded. Accordingly my expenses in coach-hire make no small article: which you may believe when I assure you, that I post away from coffee-house to coffee-house, and fore-stall the Evening Post by two hours. There is a certain gentleman, who hath given me the slip twice or thrice, and hath been beforehand with me at Child's. But I have played him a trick. I have purchased a pair of the best coach-horses I could buy for money, and now let him out-strip me if he can. Once more, Mr. Spectator, let me advise you to deal in news. You may depend upon my assistance. But I must break off abruptly, for I have twenty letters to write. Your's in haste,

'THO. QUID NUNC.'

No. 626.] *Monday, November* 29, 1714.

——Dulcique animos novitate tenebo.
Ovid, Met. Lib. 4. 284.

With sweet novelty your taste I'll please.—*Eusden.*

I have seen a little work of a learned man, consisting of extemporary speculations, which owed their birth to the most trifling occurrences of life. His usual method, was to write down any sudden start of thought which arose in his mind upon the sight of any odd gesticulation in a man, any whimsical mimickry of reason in a beast, or whatever appeared remarkable in any object of the visible creation. He was able to moralize upon a snuff-box, would flourish eloquently upon a tucker or a pair of ruffles, and draw practical inferences from a full-bottomed perriwig. This I thought fit to mention, by way of excuse, for my ingenious correspondent, who hath introduced the following letter by an image which, I will beg leave to tell him, is too ridiculous in so serious and noble a speculation.

'Mr. Spectator,—When I have seen young puss playing her wanton gambols, and with a thousand antic shapes express her own gayety at the same time that she moved mine, while the old grannum hath sat by with the most exemplary gravity, unmoved at all that passed; it hath made me reflect what should be the occasion of humours so opposite in two creatures, between whom there was no visible difference but that of age; and I have been able to resolve it into nothing else but the force of novelty.

'In every species of creatures, those who have been least time in the world appear best pleased with their condition; for, besides that to a new comer the world hath a freshness on it that strikes the sense after a most agreeable manner, being itself unattended with any great variety of enjoyments, excites a sensation of pleasure: but, as age advances, every thing seems to wither, the senses are disgusted with their old en tertainments, and existence turns flat and insipid. We may see this exemplified in mankind. The child, let him be free from pain, and gratified in his change of toys, is diverted with the smallest trifle. Nothing disturbs the mirth of the boy but a little punishment or confinement. The youth must have more violent pleasures to employ his time. The man loves the hurry of an active life, devoted to the pursuits of wealth or ambition. And, lastly, old age, having lost its capacity for these avocations, becomes its own unsupportable burden. This variety may in part be accounted for by the vivacity and decay of the faculties; but I believe is chiefly owing to this, that the longer we have been in possession of being, the less sensible is the gust we have of it; and the more it requires of adventitious amusements to relieve us from the satiety and weariness it brings along with it.

'And as novelty is of a very powerful, so it is of a most extensive influence. Moralists have long since observed it to be the source of admiration, which lessens in proportion to our familiarity with objects, and upon a thorough acquaintance is utterly extinguished. But I think it hath not been so commonly remarked, that all the other passions depend considerably on the same circumstance. What is it but novelty that awakens desire, enhances delight, kindles anger, provokes envy, inspires horror? To this cause we must ascribe it, that love languishes with fruition, and friendship itself is recommended by intervals of absence: hence, monsters, by use, are beheld without loathing, and the most enchanting beauty without rapture. That emotion of the spirits, in which passion consists, is usually the effect of surprise, and, as long as it continues, heightens the agreeable or disagreeable qualities of its object; but as this emotion ceases, (and it ceases with the novelty) things appear in another light, and affect us even less than might be expected from their proper energy, for having moved us too much before.

'It may not be a useless inquiry, how far the love of novelty is the unavoidable growth of nature, and in what respects it is peculiarly adapted to the present state. To me it seems impossible, that a reasonable creature should rest absolutely satisfied in any acquisitions whatever, without endeavouring farther; for, after its highest improvements, the mind hath an idea of an infinity of things still behind, worth knowing, to the knowledge of which therefore it cannot be indifferent; as by climbing up a hill in the midst of a wide plain, a man hath his prospect enlarged, and together with that, the bounds of his desires. Upon this account, I cannot think he detracts from the state of the blessed, who conceives them to be perpetually employed in fresh searches into nature, and to eternity advancing into the fathomless depths of the divine perfections. In this thought there is nothing but what doth honour to these glorified spirits; provided still it be remembered, that their desire of more proceeds not from their disrelishing what they possess; and the pleasure of a new enjoyment is not with them measured by its novelty, (which is a thing merely foreign and accidental) but by its real intrinsic value. After an acquaintance of many thousand years with the works of God, the beauty and magnificence of the creation fills them with the same pleasing wonder and profound awe, which Adam felt himself seized with as he first opened his eyes upon this glorious scene. Truth captivates with unborrowed charms, and whatever hath once given satisfaction will always do it. In all which they have manifestly the advantage of us, who are so much governed by sickly and changeable appetites, that we can with the greatest coldness behold the stupendous displays of Omnipotence, and be in transports at the puny essays of human skill; throw aside speculations of the sublimest nature and vastest importance into some obscure corner of the mind, to make room for new notions of no consequence at all; are even tired of health, because not enlivened with alternate pain; and prefer the first reading of an indifferent author to the second or third perusal of one whose merit and reputation are established.

'Our being thus formed serves many useful purposes in the present state. It contributes not a little to the advancement of learning; for, as Cicero takes notice, that which makes men willing to undergo the fatigues of philosophical disquisitions, is not so much the greatness of objects as their novelty. It is not enough that there is field and game for the chase, and that the understanding is prompted with a restless thirst of knowledge, effectually to rouse the soul, sunk into a state of sloth and indolence; it is also necessary that there be an uncommon pleasure annexed to the first appearance of truth in the mind. This pleasure being exquisite for the time it lasts, but transient, it hereby comes to pass that the mind grows into an indifference to its former notions, and passes on after new discoveries, in hope of repeating the delight. It is with knowledge as with wealth, the pleasure of which lies more in making endless additions than in taking a review of our old store. There are some inconveniences that follow this temper, if not guarded against, particularly this, that through too great an eagerness of something new, we are many times impatient of staying long enough upon a question that requires some time to resolve it; or, which is worse, persuade ourselves that we are masters of the subject before we are so, only to be at the liberty of going upon a fresh scent: in Mr. Locke's words, "We see a little, presume a great deal, and so jump to the conclusion."

'A farther advantage of our inclination for novelty, as at present circumstantiated, is, that it annihilates all the boasted distinctions among mankind. Look not up with envy to those above thee! Sounding titles, stately buildings, fine gardens, gilded chariots, rich equipages, what are they? They dazzle every one but the possessor: to him that is accustomed to them they are cheap and regardless things; they supply him not with brighter images, or more sublime satisfactions, than the plain man may have, whose small estate will just enable him to support the charge of a simple unencumbered life. He enters heedless into his rooms of state, as you or I do under our poor sheds. The noble paintings and costly furniture are lost on him; he sees them not; as how can it be otherwise, when by custom a fabric infinitely more grand and finished, that of the universe, stands unobserved by the inhabitants, and the everlasting lamps of heaven are lighted up in vain, for any notice that mortals take of them? Thanks to indulgent nature, which not only placed her children originally upon a level, but still, by the strength of this principle, in a great measure preserves it, in spite of all the care of man to introduce artificial distinctions.

'To add no more—is not this fondness for novelty, which makes us out of conceit with all we already have, a convincing proof of a future state? Either man was made in vain, or this is not the only world he was made for: for there cannot be a greater instance of vanity than that to which man is liable, to be deluded from the cradle to the grave with fleeting shadows of happiness. His pleasures, and those not considerable neither, die in the possession, and fresh enjoyments do not rise fast enough to fill up half his life with satisfaction. When I see persons sick of themselves any longer than they are called away by something that is of force to chain down the present thought; when I see them hurry from country to town, and then from the town back again into the country, continually shifting postures, and placing life in all the different lights they can think of; "Surely," say I to myself, "life is vain, and the man beyond expression stupid, or prejudiced, who from the vanity of life cannot gather that he is designed for immortality."'

No. 627.] *Wednesday, December* 1, 1714.

Tantum inter densas umbrosa cacumina fagos
Assidue veniebat; ibi hæc incondita solus
Montibus et sylvis studio jactabat inani.
Virg. Ecl. ii. 3.

He, underneath the beaten shade, alone,
Thus to the woods and mountains made his moan.
Dryden.

THE following account, which came to my hands some time ago, may be no disagreeable entertainment to such of my readers as have tender hearts, and nothing to do.

'MR. SPECTATOR,—A friend of mine died of a fever last week, which he caught by walking too late in a dewy evening amongst his reapers. I must inform you that his greatest pleasure was in husbandry and gardening. He had some humours which seemed inconsistent with that good sense he was otherwise master of. His uneasiness in the company of women was very remarkable in a man of such perfect good-breeding; and his avoiding one particular walk in his garden, where he had used to pass the greatest part of his time, raised abundance of idle conjectures in the village where he lived. Upon looking over his papers we found out the reason, which he never intimated to his nearest friends. He was, it seems, a passionate lover in his youth, of which a large parcel of letters he left behind him are a witness. I send you a copy of the last he ever wrote upon that subject, by which you will find that he concealed the true name of his mistress under that of Zelinda.

"A long month's absence would be insupportable to me, if the business I am employed in were not for the service of my Zelinda, and of such a nature as to place her every moment in my mind. I have furnished the house exactly according to your fancy, or, if you please, my own; for I have long since learned to like nothing but what you do. The apartment designed for your use is so exact a copy of that which you live in, that I often think myself in your house when I step into it, but sigh when I find it without its proper inhabitant. You will have the most delicious prospect from your closet window that England affords: I am sure I should think it so, if the landscape that shows such variety did not at the same time suggest to me the greatness of the space that lies between us.

"The gardens are laid out very beautifully; I have dressed up every hedge in woodbines, sprinkled bowers and arbours in every corner, and made a little paradise around me: yet I am still like the first man in his solitude, but half blessed without a partner in my happiness. I have directed one walk to be made for two persons, where I promise ten thousand satisfactions to myself in your conversation. I already take my evening's turn in it, and have worn a path upon the edge of this little alley, while I soothed myself with the thought of your walking by my side. I have held many imaginary discourses with you in this retirement; and when I have been weary, have sat down with you in the midst of a row of jessamines. The many expressions of joy and rapture I use in these silent conversations have made me, for some time, the talk of the parish; but a neighbouring young fellow, who makes love to the farmer's daughter, hath found me out, and made my case known to the whole neighbourhood.

"In planting of the fruit trees, I have not forgot the peach you are so fond of. I have made a walk of elms along the river side, and intend to sow all the place about with cowslips, which I hope you will like as well as that I have heard you talk of by your father's house in the country.

"Oh! Zelinda, what a scheme of delight have I drawn up in my imagination! What day-dreams do I indulge myself in! When will the six weeks be at an end, that lie between me and my promised happiness!

"How could you break off so abruptly in your last, and tell me you must go and dress for the play? If you loved as I do, you would find no more company in a crowd than I have in my solitude. I am, &c."

'On the back of this letter is written, in the hand of the deceased, the following piece of history:

"Mem. Having waited a whole week for an answer to this letter, I hurried to town, where I found the perfidious creature married to my rival. I will bear it as becomes a man, and endeavour to find out happiness for myself in that retirement which I had prepared in vain for a false, ungrateful woman." I am, &c.'

No. 628.] *Friday, December* 3, 1714.

Labitur et labetur in omne volubilis ævum.
Hor. Ep. ii. Lib. 1. 43.

It rolls, and rolls, and will for ever roll.

'Mr. Spectator,—There are none of your speculations which please me more than those upon infinitude and eternity. You have already considered that part of eternity which is past, and I wish you would give us your thoughts upon that which is to come.

'Your readers will perhaps receive greater pleasure from this view of eternity than the former, since we have every one of us a concern in that which is to come: whereas a speculation on that which is past is rather curious than useful.

'Besides, we can easily conceive it possible for successive duration never to have an end; though, as you have justly observed, that eternity which never had a beginning is altogether incomprehensible; that is, we can conceive an eternal duration which may be, though we cannot an eternal duration which hath been; or, if I may use the the philosophical terms, we may apprehend a potential though not an actual eternity.

'This notion of a future eternity, which is natural to the mind of man, is an unanswerable argument that he is a being designed for it; especially if we consider that he is capable of being virtuous or vicious here; that he hath faculties improvable to all eternity; and, by a proper or wrong employment of them, may be happy or miserable throughout that infinite duration. Our idea indeed of this eternity is not of an adequate or fixed nature, but is perpetually growing and enlarging itself toward the object, which is too big for human comprehension. As we are now in the beginning of existence, so shall we always appear to ourselves as if we were for ever entering upon it. After a million or two of centuries, some considerable things, already past, may slip out of our memory, which if it be not strengthened in a wonderful manner, may possibly forget that ever there was a sun or planets; and yet, notwithstanding the long race we shall then have run, we shall still imagine ourselves just starting from the goal, and find no proportion between that space which we know had a beginning, and what we are sure will never have an end.

'But I shall leave this subject to your management, and question not but you will throw it into such lights as shall at once improve and entertain your reader.

'I have, enclosed, sent you a translation* of the speech of Cato on this occasion, which hath accidentally fallen into my hands, and which, for conciseness, purity, and elegance of phrase, cannot be sufficiently admired.

ACT V. SCEN. I.

CATO solus, &c.

'Sic, sic se habere rem necesse prorsus est,
Ratione vincis, do lubens manos, Plato.
Quid enim dedisset, quæ dedit frustra nihil,
Æternitatis insitam cupidinem
Natura? Quorsum hæc dulcis expectatio;
Vitæque non explenda melioris sitis?
Quid vult sibi aliud iste redeundi in nihil
Horror, sub imis quemque agens præcordiis?
Cur territa in se refugit anima, cur tremit
Attonita, quoties, morte ne pereat, timet?
Particula nempe est cuique nascenti indita
Divinior; quæ corpus incolens agit;
Hominique succinit, tua est æternitas.
Æternitas! O lubricum nimis aspici,
Mixtumque dulci gaudium formidine!

'Quæ demigrabitur alia hinc in corpora?
Quæ terra mox incognita? Quis orbis novus
Manet incolendus? Quanta erit mutatio?
Hæc intuenti spatia mihi quaqua patent
Immensa: sed caliginosa nox premit;
Nec luce clara vult videri singula.
Figendus hic pes; certa sunt hæc hactenus:
Si quod gubernet numen humanum genus,
(At, quod gubernet, esse clamant omnia)
Virtute non gaudere certe non potest;
Nec esse non beata, quà gaudet, potest.
Sed qua beata sede? Quove in tempore?
Hæc quanta terra, tota est Cæsaris.
Quid dubius hæret animus usque adeo? Brevi
Hic nodum hic omnem expediet Arma en induor.
[*Ensi manum admovens.*
In utramque partem facta; quæque vim inferant,
Et quæ propulsent! Dextera intentat necem;
Vitam sinistra: vulnus hæc dabit manus;
Altera medelam vulneris: hic ad exitum
Deducet, ictu simplici; hæc vetant mori.
Secura ridet anima mucronis minas,
Ensesque strictos, interire nescia.
Extinguet ætas sidera diuturnoir:
Ætate languens ipse sol obscurius
Emittet orbi consenescenti jubar:
Natura et ipsa sentiet quondam vices
Ætatis; annis ipsa deficiet gravis:
At tibi juventus, at tibi immortalitas:
Tibi parta divum est vita. Periment mutuis
Elementa sese et interibunt ictibus.
Tu permanebis sola semper integra,
Tu cuncta rerum quassa, cuncta naufraga,
Jam portu in ipso tuta, contemplabere.
Compage rupta, corruent in se invicem,
Orbesque fractis ingerentur orbibus;
Illæsa tu sedebis extra fragmina.'

---

* This translation was by Mr. (afterwards Dr.) Bland, once schoolmaster, then provost of Eton, and dean of Durham.

ACT V. SCENE I.

CATO alone, &c.

'It must be so——Plato, thou reason'st well—
Else whence this pleasing hope, this fond desire,
This longing after immortality?
Or whence this secret dread, and inward horror,
Of falling into nought? Why shrinks the soul
Back on herself, and startles at destruction?
'Tis the divinity that stirs within us;
'Tis Heaven itself that points out an hereafter,
And intimates an eternity to man.
Eternity! thou pleasing, dreadful thought!

'Through what variety of untry'd being,
Through what new scenes and changes must we pass!
The wide, th' unbounded prospect lies before me;
But shadows, clouds, and darkness, rest upon it.
Here will I hold. If there's a Power above us,
(And that there is all Nature cries aloud
Through all her works,) he must delight in virtue;
And that which he delights in must be happy.
But when, or where? This world was made for Cæsar,
I'm weary of conjectures—This must end them.
[*Laying his hand on his sword.*
Thus am I doubly arm'd; my death and life,
My bane and antidote, are both before me.
This in a moment brings me to an end;
But this informs me I shall never die.
The soul, secur'd in her existence, smiles
At the drawn dagger, and defies its point.
The stars shall fade away, the sun himself
Grow dim with age, and nature sink in years;
But thou shalt flourish in immortal youth,
Unhurt amidst the war of elements,
The wrecks of matter and the crush of worlds.'

No. 629.] *Monday, December* 6, 1714.

——Experiar quid consedatur in illos,
Quorum Flaminia tegitur cinis, atque Latina.
Juv. Sat. i. 170.

——Since none the living dare implead
Arraign them in the persons of the dead.—*Dryden.*

NEXT to the people who want a place, there are none to be pitied more than those who are solicited for one. A plain answer with a denial in it is looked upon as pride, and a civil answer as a promise.

Nothing is more ridiculous than the pretensions of people upon these occasions. Every thing a man hath suffered, whilst his enemies were in play, was certainly brought about by the malice of the opposite party. A bad cause would not have been lost, if such a one had not been upon the bench; nor a profligate youth disinherited, if he had not got drunk every night by toasting an outed ministry. I remember a tory, who, having been fined in a court of justice for a prank that deserved the pillory, desired upon the merit of it to be made a justice of the peace when his friends came into power; and shall never forget a whig criminal, who, upon being indicted for a rape, told his friends 'You see what a man suffers for sticking to his principles.'

The truth of it is, the sufferings of a man in a party are of a very doubtful nature. When they are such as have promoted a good cause, and fallen upon a man undeservedly, they have a right to be heard and recompensed beyond any other pretensions. But when they rise out of rashness or indiscretion, and the pursuit of such measures as have rather ruined than promoted the interest they aim at, which hath always been the case of many great sufferers, they only serve to recommend them to the children of violence or folly.

I have by me a bundle of memorials presented by several cavaliers upon the restoration of king Charles II. which may serve as so many instances to our present purpose.

Among several persons and pretensions recorded by my author, he mentions one of a very great estate, who, for having roasted an ox whole, and distributed a hogshead upon king Charles's birth-day, desired to be provided for as his majesty in his great wisdom should think fit.

Another put in to be prince Henry's governor, for having dared to drink his health in the worst of times.

A third petitioned for a colonel's commission, for having cursed Oliver Cromwell, the day before his death, on a public bowling-green.

But the most whimsical petition I have met with is that of B. B., esq. who desired the honour of knighthood, for having cuck oled Sir T. W. a notorious roundhead.

There is likewise the petition of one who, having let his beard grow from the martyrdom of king Charles the first, until the restoration of king Charles the second, desired in consideration thereupon to be made a privy-counsellor.

I must not omit a memorial setting forth that the memorialist had, with great despatch, carried a letter from a certain lord to a certain lord, wherein, as it afterwards appeared, measures were concerted for the restoration, and without which he verily believes that happy revolution had never been effected; who thereupon humbly prays to be made postmaster-general.

A certain gentleman, who seems to write with a great deal of spirit, and uses the words gallantry and gentleman-like very often in his petition, begs that (in consideration of his having worn his hat for ten years past in the royal cavalier-cock, to his great danger and detriment) he may be made a captain of the guards.

I shall close my account of this collection of memorials with the copy of one petition at length, which I recommend to my reader as a very valuable piece.

'*The Petition of E. H. Esq.*

'HUMBLY SHOWETH,

'That your petitioner's father's brother's uncle, colonel W. H. lost the third finger of his left hand at Edgehill fight.

'That your petitioner, notwithstanding the smallness of his fortune (he being a younger brother,) always kept hospitality, and drank confusion to the roundheads in half a score bumpers every Sunday in the year, as several honest gentlemen (whose names are underwritten) are ready to testify.

'That your petitioner is remarkable in his country, for having dared to treat Sir

P. P. a cursed sequestrator, and three members of the assembly of divines, with brawn and minced pies upon new-year's day.

'That your said humble petitioner hath been five times imprisoned in five several county-gaols, for having been a ringleader in five different riots; into which his zeal for the royal cause hurried him, when men of greater estates had not the courage to rise.

'That he, the said E. H. hath had six duels and four-and-twenty boxing matches in defence of his majesty's title; and that he received such a blow upon the head at a bonfire in Stratford-upon-Avon, as he hath been never the better for from that day to this.

'That your petitioner hath been so far from improving his fortune, in the late damnable times, that he verily believes, and hath good reason to imagine, that if he had been master of an estate, he had infallibly been plundered and sequestered.

'Your petitioner, in consideration of his said merits and sufferings, humbly requests that he may have the place of receiver of the taxes, collector of the customs, clerk of the peace, deputy lieutenant, or whatsoever else he shall be thought qualified for. And your petitioner shall ever pray, &c.'

No. 630.] *Wednesday, December* 8, 1714.

Favete linguis—— *Hor.* Od. i. Lib. 3. 2.

With mute attention wait.

HAVING no spare time to write any thing of my own, or to correct what is sent me by others, I have thought fit to publish the following letters:

'Oxford, Nov. 22.

'SIR,—If you would be so kind to me, as to suspend that satisfaction which the learned world must receive in reading one of your speculations, by publishing this endeavour, you will very much oblige and improve one, who has the boldness to hope that he may be admitted into the number of your correspondents.

'I have often wondered to hear men of good sense and good nature profess a dislike to music, when at the same time they do not scruple to own that it has the most agreeable and improving influences over their minds: it seems to me an unhappy contradiction, that those persons should have an indifference for an art which raises in them such a variety of sublime pleasures.

'However, though some few, by their own or the unreasonable prejudices of others, may be led into a distaste for those musical societies which are erected merely for entertainment, yet sure I may venture to say, that no one can have the least reason for disaffection to that solemn kind of melody which consists of the praises of our Creator.

'You have, I presume, already prevented me in an argument upon this occasion, which some divines have successfully advanced upon a much greater, that musical sacrifice and adoration has claimed a place in the laws and customs of the most different nations; as the Grecians and Romans of the profane, the Jews and Christians of the sacred world, did as unanimously agree in this as they disagreed in all other parts of their economy.

'I know there are not wanting some who are of opinion that the pompous kind of music which is in use in foreign churches, is the most excellent, as it most affects our senses. But I am swayed by my judgment to the modesty which is observed in the musical part of our devotions. Methinks there is something very laudable in the custom of a voluntary before the first lesson; by this we are supposed to be prepared for the admission of those divine truths which we are shortly to receive. We are then to cast all worldly regards from off our hearts, all tumults within are then becalmed, and there should be nothing near the soul but peace and tranquillity. So that in this short office of praise the man is raised above himself, and is almost lost already amidst the joys of futurity.

'I have heard some nice observers frequently commend the policy of our church in this particular, that it leads us on by such easy and regular methods that we are perfectly deceived into piety. When the spirits begin to languish, (as they too often do with a constant series of petitions,) she takes care to allow them a pious respite, and relieves them with the raptures of an anthem. Nor can we doubt that the sublimest poetry, softened in the most moving strains of music, can never fail of humbling or exalting the soul to any pitch of devotion. Who can hear the terrors of the Lord of Hosts described in the most expressive melody, without being awed into a veneration? Or who can hear the kind and endearing attributes of a merciful father, and not be softened into love towards him?

'As the rising and sinking of the passions, the casting soft or noble hints into the soul, is the natural privilege of music in general, so more particularly of that kind which is employed at the altar. Those impressions which it leaves upon the spirits are more deep and lasting, as the grounds from which it receives its authority are founded more upon reason. It diffuses a calmness all around us, it makes us drop all those vain or immodest thoughts which would be a hinderance to us in the performance of that great duty of thanksgiving, which, as we are informed by our Almighty Benefactor, is the most acceptable return which can be made for those infinite stores of blessings which he daily condescends to pour down upon his creatures. When we make use of this pathetical method of addressing ourselves to him, we can scarce contain from raptures! The heart is warmed with a sublimity of goodness! We are all piety and all love!

'How do the blessed spirits rejoice and wonder to behold unthinking man prostrating his soul to his dread Sovereign in such a warmth of piety as they themselves might not be ashamed of.

'I shall close these reflections with a passage taken out of the third book of Milton's Paradise Lost, where those harmonious beings are thus nobly described:

> "Then crown'd again, their golden harps they took,
> Harps ever tun'd, that, glitt'ring by their side,
> Like quivers hung, and with preamble sweet
> Of charming symphony they introduce
> The sacred song, and waken raptures high:
> No one exempt, no voice but well could join
> Melodious part—such concord is in heaven!"

'MR. SPECTATOR,—The town cannot be unacquainted that in divers parts of it there are vociferous sets of men who are called Rattling Clubs; but what shocks me most is, they have now the front to invade the church and institute these societies, there, as a clan of them have in late times done, to such a degree of insolence as has given the partition where they reside, in a church near one of the city gates, the denomination of the rattling pew. These gay fellows, from humble lay professions, set up for critics, without any tincture of letters or reading, and have the vanity to think they can lay hold of something from the parson which may be formed into ridicule.

'It is needless to observe that the gentlemen, who every Sunday have the hard province of instructing these wretches in a way they are in no present disposition to take, have a fixed character for learning and eloquence, not to be tainted by the weak efforts of this contemptible part of their audiences. Whether the pulpit is taken by these gentlemen, or any strangers their friends, the way of the club is this: if any sentiments are delivered too sublime for their conception; if any uncommon topic is entered on, or one in use new modified with the finest judgment and dexterity; or, any controverted point be never so elegantly handled; in short, whatever surpasses the narrow limits of their theology, or is not suited to their taste, they are all immediately upon the watch, fixing their eyes upon each other with as much warmth as our gladiators of Hockley-in-the-Hole, and waiting like them for a hit: if one touches, all take fire, and their noddles instantly meet in the centre of the pew: then, as by beat of drum, with exact discipline, they rear up into a full length of stature, and with odd looks and gesticulations confer together in so loud and clamorous a manner, continued to the close of the discourse, and during the after-psalm, as is not to be silenced but by the bells. Nor does this suffice them, without aiming to propagate their noise through all the church, by signals given to the adjoining seats, where others designed for this fraternity are sometimes placed upon trial to receive them.

'The folly as well as rudeness of this practice is in nothing more conspicuous than this, that all that follows in the sermon is lost; for, whenever our sparks take alarm, they blaze out and grow so tumultuous that no after-explanation can avail, it being impossible for themselves or any near them to give an account thereof. If any thing really novel is advanced, how averse soever it may be to their way of thinking, to say nothing of duty, men of less levity than these would be led by a natural curiosity to hear the whole.

'Laughter, where things sacred are transacted, is far less pardonable than whining at a conventicle; the last has at least a semblance of grace, and where the affectation is unseen, may possibly imprint wholesome lessons on the sincere; but the first has no excuse, breaking through all the rules of order and decency, and manifesting a remissness of mind in those important matters which require the strictest composure and steadiness of thought: a proof of the greatest folly in the world.

'I shall not here enter upon the veneration due to the sanctity of the place, the reverence owing the minister, or the respect that so great an assembly as a whole parish may justly claim. I shall only tell them, that, as the Spanish cobbler, to reclaim a profligate son, bid him have some regard to the dignity of his family, so they as gentlemen (for we who are citizens assume to be such one day in a week) are bound for the future to repent of, and abstain from, the gross abuses here mentioned, whereof they have been guilty in contempt of heaven and earth, and contrary to the laws in this case made and provided. I am, sir, your very humble servant, R. M.'

No. 631.] *Friday, December* 10, 1714.

> Simplex munditiis——
> *Hor.* Od. v. Lib. 1. 5.
>
> Elegant by cleanliness.——

I HAD occasion to go a few miles out of town, some days since, in a stage-coach, where I had for my fellow travellers a dirty beau, and a pretty young quaker woman. Having no inclination to talk much at that time, I placed myself backward, with a design to survey them, and pick a speculation out of my two companions. Their different figures were sufficient of themselves to draw my attention. The gentleman was dressed in a suit, the ground whereof had been black, as I perceived from some few spaces that had escaped the powder, which was incorporated with the greatest part of his coat: his periwig, which cost no small sum, was after so slovenly a manner cast over his shoulders, that it seemed not to have been combed since the year 1712; his linen, which was not much concealed, was daubed with plain Spanish from the chin to the lowest button; and the diamond upon his finger (which naturally dreaded the water) put me in mind how it sparkled amidst the rubbish of the mine where it was first discovered. On the other hand, the pretty quaker appeared in all the elegance of cleanliness. Not a speck was to be found upon her. A clear, clean, oval face, just edged about with little thin plaits of the purest cambric, received great advantages from the shade of her black hood; as did the whiteness of her arms from that sober-coloured stuff in which she had clothed herself. The plainness of her dress was very well suited to the simplicity of her phrases; all which, put together, though they could not give me a great opinion of her religion, they did of her innocence.

This adventure occasioned my throwing together a few hints upon cleanliness, which I shall consider as one of the half-virtues, as Aristotle calls them, and shall recommend it under the three following heads: as it is a mark of politeness; as it produces love; and as it bears analogy to purity of mind.

First, It is a mark of politeness. It is universally agreed upon, that no one unadorned with this virtue can go into company without giving a manifest offence. The easier or higher any one's fortune is, this duty arises proportionably. The different nations of the world are as much distinguished by their cleanliness as by their arts and sciences. The more any country is civilized, the more they consult this part of politeness. We need but compare our ideas of a female Hottentot and an English beauty, to be satisfied of the truth of what hath been advanced.

In the next place, cleanliness may be said to be the foster-mother of love. Beauty indeed most commonly produces the passion in the mind, but cleanliness preserves it. An indifferent face and person, kept in perpetual neatness, hath won many a heart from a pretty slattern. Age itself is not unamiable, while it is preserved clean and unsullied: like a piece of metal constantly kept smooth and bright, we look on it with more pleasure than on a new vessel that is cankered with rust.

I might observe farther, that as cleanliness renders us agreeable to others, so it makes us easy to ourselves: that it is an excellent preservative of health; and that several vices, destructive both to mind and body, are inconsistent with the habit of it. But these reflections I shall leave to the leisure of my readers, and shall observe, in the third place, that it bears a great analogy with purity of mind, and naturally inspires refined sentiments and passions.

We find from experience that, through the prevalence of custom, the most vicious actions lose their horror by being made familiar to us. On the contrary, those who live in the neighbourhood of good examples, fly from the first appearances of what is shocking. It fares with us much after the same manner as our ideas. Our senses, which are the inlets to all the images conveyed to the mind, can only transmit the impression of such things as usually surround them. So that pure and unsullied thoughts are naturally suggested to the mind, by those objects that perpetually encompass us when they are beautiful and elegant in their kind.

In the east, where the warmth of the climate makes cleanliness more immediately necessary than in colder countries, it is made one part of their religion; the Jewish law, and the Mahometan, which in some things copies after it, is filled with bathings, purifications, and other rites of the like nature. Though there is the above-named convenient reason to be assigned for these ceremonies, the chief intention undoubtedly was to typify inward purity and cleanliness of heart by those outward washings. We read several injunctions of this kind in the book of Deuteronomy, which confirm this truth; and which are but ill accounted for by saying, as some do, that they were only instituted for convenience in the desert, which otherwise could not have been habitable for so many years.

I shall conclude this essay with a story which I have somewhere read in an account of Mahometan superstitions.

A dervise of great sanctity one morning had the misfortune, as he took up a crystal cup which was consecrated to the prophet, to let it fall upon the ground and dash it in pieces. His son coming in some time after, he stretched out his hand to bless him, as his manner was every morning: but the youth going out stumbled over the threshold and broke his arm. As the old man wondered at these events, a caravan passed by in its way from Mecca; the dervise approached it to beg a blessing; but as he stroked one of the holy camels, he received a kick from the beast that sorely bruised him. His sorrow and amazement increased upon him, until he recollected that, through hurry and inadvertency, he had that morning come abroad without washing his hands.

No. 632.] *Monday, December* 13, 1714.

——Explebo numerum, reddarque tenebris.
Virg. Æn. vi. 145

——————the number I'll complete,
Then to obscurity well pleas'd retreat.

The love of symmetry and order, which is natural to the mind of man, betrays him sometimes into very whimsical fancies. 'This noble principle,' says a French author, 'loves to amuse itself on the most trifling occasions. You may see a profound philosopher,' says he, 'walk for an hour together in his chamber, and industriously treading, at every step, upon every other board in the flooring.' Every reader will recollect several instances of this nature without my assistance. I think it was Gregorio Leti, who had published as many books as he was years old;* which was a rule he had laid down and punctually observed to the year of his death. It was, perhaps, a thought of the like nature which determined Homer himself to divide each of his poems into as many books as there are letters in the Greek alphabet. Herodotus has in the same manner adapted his books to the number of the muses, for which reason many a learned man hath wished there had been more than nine of that sisterhood.

Several epic poets have religiously followed Virgil as to the number of his books: and even Milton is thought by many to have changed the number of his books from ten to twelve for no other reason; as Cowley tells us, it was his design, had he finished his Davideis, to have also imitated the Æneid in this particular. I believe every one will agree with me that a perfection of this nature hath no foundation in reason; and, with due respect to these great names, may be looked upon as something whimsical.

I mention these great examples in defence of my bookseller, who occasioned this eighth volume of Spectators, because, as he said, he thought seven a very odd number. On the other side, several grave reasons were urged on this important subject; as in particular, that seven was the precise number of the wise men, and that the most beautiful constellation in the heavens was composed of seven stars. This he allowed to be true, but still insisted that seven was an odd number: suggesting at the same time, that if he were provided with a sufficient stock of leading papers, he should find friends ready enough to carry on the work. Having by this means got his vessel launched and set afloat, he hath committed the steerage of it, from time to time, to such as he thought capable of conducting it.

The close of this volume, which the town may now expect in a little time, may possibly ascribe each sheet to its proper author.

It were no hard task to continue this paper a considerable time longer by the help of large contributions sent from unknown hands.

I cannot give the town a better opinion of the Spectator's correspondents than by publishing the following letter, with a very fine copy of verses upon a subject perfectly new.

* This voluminous writer boasted that he had been the author of a book and the father of a child for twenty years successively. Swift counted the number of steps he had made from London to Chelsea. And it is said and demonstrated in the Parentalia, that bishop Wren walked round the earth while a prisoner in the tower of London.

'Dublin, Nov. 30, 1714.

'MR. SPECTATOR,—You lately recommended to your female readers the good old custom of their grandmothers, who used to lay out a great part of their time in needle-work. I entirely agree with you in your sentiments, and think it would not be of less advantage to themselves and their posterity, than to the reputation of many of their good neighbours, if they passed many of those hours in this innocent entertainment which are lost at the tea-table. I would, however, humbly offer to your consideration the case of the poetical ladies, who, though they may be willing to take any advice given them by the Spectator, yet cannot so easily quit their pen and ink as you may imagine. Pray allow them, at least now and then, to indulge themselves in other amusements of fancy when they are tired with stooping to their tapestry. There is a very particular kind of work, which of late several ladies here in our kingdom are very fond of, which seems very well adapted to a poetical genius: it is the making of grottos. I know a lady who has a very beautiful one, composed by herself; nor is there one shell in it not stuck up by her own hands. I here send you a poem to the fair architect, which I would not offer to herself until I knew whether this method of a lady's passing her time were approved of by the British Spectator; which, with the poem, I submit to your censure, who am your constant reader, and humble servant,

A. B.'

TO MRS. ———, ON HER GROTTO.

" A grotto so complete, with such design,
What hands, Calypso, could have form'd but thine?
Each chequer'd pebble, and each shining shell,
So well proportion'd, and dispos'd so well,
Surprising lustre from thy thought receive,
Assuming beauties more than nature give.
To her their various shapes and glossy hue,
Their curious symmetry they owe to you.
Not fam'd Amphion's lute, whose powerful call
Made willing stones dance to the Theban wall,
In more harmonious ranks could make them fall
Not evening cloud a brighter arch can show,
Nor richer colours paint the heavenly bow

" Where can unpolish'd nature boast a piece
In all her mossy cells exact as this?
At the gay party-colour'd scene we start,
For chance too regular, too rude for art.

" Charm'd with the sight, my ravish'd breast is fir'd
With hints like those which ancient bards inspir'd;
All the feign'd tales by superstition told,
All the bright train of fabled nymphs of old,
Th' enthusiastic muse believes are true,
Thinks the spot sacred, and its genius you.
Lost in wild rapture would she fain disclose
How by degrees the pleasing wonder rose;
Industrious in a faithful verse to trace
The various beauties of the lovely place;
And, while she keeps the glowing work in view
Through every maze thy artful hand pursue.

" O, were I equal to the bold design,
Or could I boast such happy art as thine,
That could rude shells in such sweet order place,
Give common objects such uncommon grace!
Like them, my well-chose words in every line
As sweetly temper'd should as sweetly shine.
So just a fancy should my numbers warm,
Like the gay piece should the description charm.
Then with superior strength my voice I'd raise,
The echoing grotto should approve my lays,
Pleas'd to reflect the well-sung founder's praise "

No. 633.] *Wednesday, December 15, 1714.*

Omnia profecto, cum se a cœlestibus rebus referet ad humanas, excelsius magnificentiusque et dicet et sentiet. *Cicero.*

The contemplation of celestial things will make a man both speak and think more sublimely and magnificently when he descends to human affairs.

THE following discourse is printed, as it came to my hands, without variation.

'Cambridge, Dec. 11.

'IT was a very common inquiry among the ancients, why the number of excellent orators, under all the encouragements the most flourishing states could give them, fell so far short of the number of those who excelled in all other sciences. A friend of mine used merrily to apply to this case an observation of Herodotus, who says, that the most useful animals are the most fruitful in their generation; whereas the species of those beasts that are fierce and mischievous to mankind are but scarcely continued. The historian instances in a hare, which always either breeds or brings forth; and a lioness, which brings forth but once, and then loses all power of conception. But leaving my friend to his mirth, I am of opinion that in these latter ages we have greater cause of complaint than the ancients had. And since that solemn festival is approaching,* which calls for all the power of oratory, and which affords as noble a subject for the pulpit as any revelation has taught us, the design of this paper shall be to show, that our moderns have greater advantages towards true and solid eloquence than any which the celebrated speakers of antiquity enjoyed.

'The first great and substantial difference is, that their common-places, in which almost the whole force of amplification consists, were drawn from the profit or honesty of the action, as they regarded only this present state of duration. But Christianity, as it exalts morality to a greater perfection, as it brings the consideration of another life into the question, as it proposes rewards and punishments of a higher nature, and a longer continuance, is more adapted to affect the minds of the audience, naturally inclined to pursue what it imagines its greatest interest and concern. If Pericles, as historians report, could shake the firmest resolution of his hearers, and set the passions of all Greece in a ferment, when the present welfare of his country, or the fear of hostile invasions, was the subject; what may be expected from that orator who warns his audience against those evils which have no remedy, when once undergone, either from prudence or time? As much greater as the evils in a future state are than these at present, so much are the motives to persuasion under Christianity greater than those which mere moral considerations could supply us with. But what I now mention relates only to the power of moving the affections. There is another part of eloquence which is, indeed, its master-piece; I mean the marvellous or sublime. In this the Christian orator has the advantage beyond contradiction. Our ideas are so infinitely enlarged by revelation, the eye of reason has so wide a prospect into eternity, the notions of a Deity are so worthy and refined, and the accounts we have of a state of happiness or misery so clear and evident, that the contemplation of such objects will give our discourse a noble vigour, an invincible force, beyond the power of any human consideration. Tully requires in his perfect orator some skill in the nature of heavenly bodies; because, says he, his mind will become more extensive and unconfined; and when he descends to treat of human affairs, he will both think and write in a more exalted and magnificent manner. For the same reason, that excellent master would have recommended the study of those great and glorious mysteries which revelation has discovered to us; to which the noblest parts of this system of the world are as much inferior as the creature is less excellent than its Creator. The wisest and most knowing among the heathens had very poor and imperfect notions of a future state. They had indeed some uncertain hopes, either received by tradition, or gathered by reason, that the existence of virtuous men would not be determined by the separation of soul and body; but they either disbelieved a future state of punishment and misery; or, upon the same account that Appelles painted Antigonous with one side only towards the spectator, that the loss of his eye might not cast a blemish upon the whole piece: so these represented the condition of man in its fairest view, and endeavoured to conceal what they thought was a deformity to human nature. I have often observed, that whenever the above mentioned orator in his philosophical discourses is led by his argument to the mention of immortality, he seems like one awakened out of sleep: roused and alarmed with the dignity of the subject, he stretches his imagination to conceive something uncommon, and, with the greatness of his thoughts, casts, as it were, a glory round the sentence. Uncertain and unsettled as he was, he seems fired with the contemplation of it. And nothing but such a glorious prospect could have forced so great a lover of truth as he was, to declare his resolution never to part with his persuasion of immortality, though it should be proved to be an erroneous one. But had he lived to see all that Christianity has brought to light, how would he have lavished out all the force of eloquence in those noblest contemplations which human nature is capable of, the resurrection and the judgment that follows it! How had his breast glowed with pleasure, when the whole compass of futurity lay open and

* Christmas.

exposed to his view! How would his imagination have hurried him on in the pursuit of the mysteries of the incarnation! How would he have entered with the force of lightning, into the affections of his hearers, and fixed their attention, in spite of all the opposition of corrupt nature, upon those glorious themes which his eloquence hath painted in such lively and lasting colours!

'This advantage Christians have; and it was with no small pleasure I lately met with a fragment of Longinus, which is preserved as a testimony of that critic's judgment, at the beginning of a manuscript of the New Testament in the Vatican library. After that author has numbered up the most celebrated orators among the Grecians, he says, "add to these Paul of Tarsus, the patron of an opinion not yet fully proved." As a heathen, he condemns the Christian religion; and, as an impartial critic, he judges in favour of the promoter and preacher of it. To me it seems that the latter part of his judgment adds great weight to his opinion of St. Paul's abilities, since, under all the prejudice of opinions directly opposite, he is constrained to acknowledge the merit of that apostle. And no doubt, such as Longinus describes St. Paul, such he appeared to the inhabitants of those countries which he visited and blessed with those doctrines he was divinely commissioned to preach. Sacred story gives us, in one circumstance, a convincing proof of his eloquence, when the men of Lystra called him Mercury, "because he was the chief speaker;" and would have paid divine worship to him, as to the god who invented and presided over eloquence. This one account of our apostle sets his character, considered as an orator only, above all the celebrated relations of the skill and influence of Demosthenes and his contemporaries. Their power in speaking was admired, but still it was thought human: their eloquence warmed and ravished the hearers, but still it was thought the voice of man, not the voice of God. What advantage then had St. Paul above those of Greece or Rome? I confess I can ascribe this excellence to nothing but the power of the doctrines he delivered, which may have still the same influence on the hearers; which have still the power, when preached by a skilful orator, to make us break out in the same expressions as the disciples who met our Saviour in their way to Emmaus made use of; "Did not our hearts burn within us when he talked to us by the way, and while he opened to us the scriptures?" I may be thought bold in my judgment, by some, but I must affirm, that no one orator has left us so visible marks and footsteps of his eloquence as our apostle. It may perhaps be wondered at, that in his reasonings upon idolatry at Athens, where eloquence was born and flourished, he confines himself to strict argument only; but my reader may remember what many authors of the best credit have assured us, that all attempts upon the affections, and strokes of oratory, were expressly forbidden, by the laws of that country, in courts of judicature. His want of eloquence therefore here was the effect of his exact conformity to the laws; but his discourse on the resurrection to the Corinthians, his harangue before Agrippa upon his own conversion, and the necessity of that of others, are truly great, and may serve as full examples to those excellent rules for the sublime, which the best of critics has left us. The sum of all this discourse is, that our clergy have no farther to look for an example of the perfection they may arrive at, than to St. Paul's harangues; that when he, under the want of several advantages of nature, as he himself tells us, was heard, admired, and made a standard to succeeding ages by the best judges of a different persuasion in religion; I say, our clergy may learn that, however instructive their sermons are, they are capable of receiving a great addition: which St. Paul has given them a noble example of, and the Christian religion has furnished them with certain means of attaining to.'

No. 634.] *Friday, December* 17, 1714.

'Ο ελαχιστων δεομενος εγγιστα Θεων.
Socrates apud Xen.

The fewer our wants, the nearer we resemble the gods.

It was the common boast of the heathen philosophers, that by the efficacy of their several doctrines, they made human nature resemble the divine. How much mistaken soever they might be in the several means they proposed for this end, it must be owned that the design was great and glorious. The finest works of invention and imagination are of very little weight when put in the balance with what refines and exalts the rational mind. Longinus excuses Homer very handsomely, when he says the poet made his gods like men, that he might make his men appear like the gods. But it must be allowed that several of the ancient philosophers acted as Cicero wishes Homer had done: they endeavoured rather to make men like gods, than gods like men.

According to this general maxim in philosophy, some of them have endeavoured to place men in such a state of pleasure, or indolence at least, as they vainly imagined the happiness of the Supreme Being to consist in. On the other hand, the most virtuous sect of philosophers have created a chimerical wise man, whom they made exempt from passion and pain, and thought it enough to pronounce him all-sufficient.

This last character, when divested of the glare of human philosophy that surrounds it, signifies no more than that a good and wise man should so arm himself with patience, as not to yield tamely to the violence of passion and pain; that he should learn so to suppress and contract his desires as to nave few wants; and that he should cherish so many virtues in his soul as to have a perpetual source of pleasure in himself.

The Christian religion requires that, after having framed the best idea we are able of the divine nature, it should be our next care to conform ourselves to it as far as our imperfections will permit. I might mention several passages in the sacred writings on this head, to which I might add many maxims and wise sayings of moral authors among the Greeks and Romans.

I shall only instance a remarkable passage, to this purpose, out of Julian's Cæsars.* That emperor having represented all the Roman emperors, with Alexander the Great, as passing in review before the gods, and striving for the superiority, lets them all drop, excepting Alexander, Julius Cæsar, Augustus Cæsar, Trajan, Marcus Aurelius, and Constantine. Each of these great heroes of antiquity lays in his claim for the upper place; and, in order to it, sets forth his actions after the most advantageous manner. But the gods, instead of being dazzled with the lustre of their actions, inquire by Mercury into the proper motive and governing principle that influenced them throughout the whole series of their lives and exploits. Alexander tells them, that his aim was to conquer; Julius Cæsar, that his was to gain the highest post in his country; Augustus, to govern well; Trajan, that his was the same as that of Alexander, namely, to conquer. The question, at length, was put to Marcus Aurelius, who replied, with great modesty, that it had always been his care to imitate the gods. This conduct seems to have gained him the most votes and best place in the whole assembly. Marcus Aurelius, being afterwards asked to explain himself, declares that, by imitating the gods, he endeavoured to imitate them in the use of his understanding, and of all other faculties; and in particular, that it was always his study to have as few wants as possible in himself, and to do all the good he could to others.

Among the many methods by which revealed religion has advanced morality, this is one, that it has given us a more just and perfect idea of that Being whom every reasonable creature ought to imitate. The young man, in a heathen comedy, might justify his lewdness by the example of Jupiter; as, indeed, there was scarce any crime that might not be countenanced by those notions of the deity which prevailed among the common people in the heathen world. Revealed religion sets forth a proper object for imitation, in that Being who is the pattern, as well as the source, of all spiritual perfection.

While we remain in this life, we are subject to innumerable temptations, which, if listened to, will make us deviate from reason and goodness, the only things wherein we can imitate the Supreme Being. In the next life we meet with nothing to excite our inclinations that doth not deserve them. I shall therefore dismiss my reader with this maxim, viz. 'Our happiness in this world proceeds from the suppression of our desires, but in the next world from the gratification of them.'

* Spanheim, Les Cesars de l'Empereur Julien, 4to, 1728

No. 635.] *Monday, December* 20, 1714.

Sentio te sedem hominum ac domum contemplari; quæ si tibi parva (ut est) ita videtur, hæc cœlestia semper spectato; illa humana contemnito.

Cicero Somn. Scip.

I perceive you contemplate the seat and habitation of men; which if it appears as little to you as it really is, fix your eyes perpetually upon heavenly objects, and despise earthly.

THE following essay comes from the ingenious author of the letter upon novelty, printed in a late Spectator:† the notions are drawn from the Platonic way of thinking; but, as they contribute to raise the mind, and may inspire noble sentiments of our own future grandeur and happiness, I think it well deserves to be presented to the public.

If the universe be the creature of an intelligent mind, this mind could have no immediate regard to himself in producing it. He needed not to make trial of his omnipotence to be informed what effects were within its reach; the world, as existing in his eternal idea, was then as beautiful as now it is drawn forth into being; and in the immense abyss of his essence are contained far brighter scenes than will be ever set forth to view; it being impossible that the great Author of nature should bound his own power by giving existence to a system of creatures so perfect that he cannot improve upon it by any other exertions of his almighty will. Between finite and infinite there is an unmeasured interval, not to be filled up in endless ages; for which reason, the most excellent of all God's works must be equally short of what his power is able to produce as the most imperfect, and may be exceeded with the same ease.

This thought hath made some imagine (what it must be confessed is not impossible,) that the unfathomed space is ever teeming with new births, the younger still inheriting greater perfection than the elder. But as this doth not fall within my present view, I shall content myself with taking notice, that the consideration now mentioned proves undeniably, that the ideal worlds in the divine understanding yield a prospect incomparably more ample, various, and delightful, than any created world can do: and that, therefore, as it is not to be supposed that God should make a world merely of inanimate matter, however diversified, or inhabited only by creatures of no

† No. 626.

higher an order than brutes, so the end for which he designed his reasonable offspring in the contemplation of his works, the enjoyment of himself, and in both to be happy; having, to this purpose, endowed them with correspondent faculties and desires. He can have no greater pleasure from a bare review of his works than from a survey of his own ideas; but we may be assured that he is well pleased in the satisfaction derived to beings capable of it, and for whose entertainment he hath erected this immense theatre. Is not this more than an intimation of our immortality? Man, who, when considered as on his probation for a happy existence hereafter, is the most remarkable instance of divine wisdom, if we cut him off from all relation to eternity, is the most wonderful and unaccountable composition in the whole creation. He hath capacities to lodge a much greater variety of knowledge than he will be ever master of, and an unsatisfied curiosity to tread the secret paths of nature and providence: but, with this, his organs, in their present structure, are rather fitted to serve the necessities of a vile body, than to minister to his understanding; and, from the little spot to which he is chained, he can frame but wandering guesses concerning the innumerable worlds of light that encompass him; which, though in themselves of a prodigious bigness, do but just glimmer in the remote spaces of the heavens: and when, with a great deal of time and pains, he hath laboured a little way up the steep ascent of truth, and beholds with pity the grovelling multitude beneath, in a moment his foot slides, and he tumbles down headlong into the grave.

Thinking on this, I am obliged to believe, in justice to the Creator of the world, that there is another state when man shall be better situated for contemplation, or rather have it in his power to remove from object to object, and from world to world; and be accommodated with senses, and other helps, for making the quickest and most amazing discoveries. How does such a genius as Sir Isaac Newton, from amidst the darkness that involves human understanding, break forth, and appear like one of another species! The vast machine we inhabit lies open to him; he seems not unacquainted with the general laws that govern it, and while with the transport of a philosopher he beholds and admires the glorious work, he is capable of paying at once a more devout and more rational homage to his Maker. But, alas! how narrow is the prospect even of such a mind! And how obscure to the compass that is taken in by the ken of an angel, or of a soul but newly escaped from its imprisonment in the body! For my part, I freely indulge my soul in the confidence of its future grandeur; it pleases me to think that I, who know so small a portion of the works of the Creator, and with slow and painful steps creep up and down on the surface of this globe, shall ere long shoot away with the swiftness of imagination, trace out the hidden springs of nature's operations, be able to keep pace with the heavenly bodies in the rapidity of their career, be a spectator of the long chain of events in the natural and moral worlds, visit the several apartments of the creation, know how they are furnished and how inhabited, comprehend the order, and measure the magnitudes and distances of those orbs, which to us seem disposed without any regular design, and set all in the same circle; observe the dependence of the parts of each system, and (if our minds are big enough to grasp the theory) of the several systems upon one another, from whence results the harmony of the universe. In eternity, a great deal may be done of this kind. I find it of use to cherish this generous ambition; for, besides the secret refreshment it diffuses through my soul, it engages me in an endeavour to improve my faculties, as well as to exercise them conformably to the rank I now hold among reasonable beings, and the hope I have of being once advanced to a more exalted station.

The other, and that the ultimate end of man, is the enjoyment of God, beyond which he cannot form a wish. Dim at best are the conceptions we have of the Supreme Being, who, as it were, keeps his creatures in suspense, neither discovering nor hiding himself; by which means, the libertine hath a handle to dispute his existence, while the most are content to speak him fair, but in their hearts prefer every trifling satisfaction to the favour of their Maker, and ridicule the good man for the singularity of his choice. Will there not a time come, when the free-thinker shall see his impious schemes overturned, and be made a convert to the truths he hates? when deluded mortals shall be convinced of the folly of their pursuits; and the few wise who followed the guidance of Heaven, and, scorning the blandishments of sense, and the sordid bribery of the world, aspired to a celestial abode, shall stand possessed of their utmost wish in the vision of the Creator? Here the mind heaves a thought now and then towards him, and hath some transient glances of his presence: when in the instant it thinks itself to have the fastest hold, the object eludes its expectations, and it falls back tired and baffled to the ground. Doubtless there is some more perfect way of conversing with heavenly beings. Are not spirits capable of mutual intelligence, unless immersed in bodies, or by their intervention? Must superior natures depend on inferior for the main privilege of social beings, that of conversing with and knowing each other? What would they have done had matter never been created? I suppose, not have lived in eternal solitude. As incorporeal substances are of a nobler order, so, be sure, their manner of intercourse is answerably more expedite and intimate. This method of communication we call intellectual vision, as something analogous to the sense of seeing, which is the medium of our acquaintance with this visible world. And in some such way can God make himself the object of immediate intuition to the blessed; and as he can, it is not improbable that he will, always condescending, in the circumstances of doing it, to the weakness and proportion of finite minds. His works but faintly reflect the image of his perfections: it is a second-hand knowledge: to have a just idea of him, it may be necessary to see him as he is. But what is that? It s something that never entered into the heart of man to conceive; yet, what we can easily conceive, will be a fountain of unspeakable and everlasting rapture. All created glories will fade and die away in his presence. Perhaps it will be my happiness to compare the world with the fair exemplar of it in the Divine Mind; perhaps, to view the original plan of those wise designs that have been executing in a long succession of ages. Thus employed in finding out his works, and contemplating their Author, how shall I fall prostrate and adoring, my body swallowed up in the immensity of matter, my mind in the infinitude of his perfections!

THE END.

INDEX.

www.ingramcontent.com/pod-product-compliance
Lightning Source LLC
LaVergne TN
LVHW020935110826
845150LV00004B/868

* 9 7 8 1 4 2 5 5 5 2 1 1 4 *